D1462039

THE
POETICAL WORKS OF
GEORGE CRABBE

Edited by
A. J. CARLYLE and
R. M. CARLYLE

London
OXFORD UNIVERSITY PRESS
HUMPHREY MILFORD
1932
Republished 1977
SCHOLARLY PRESS, INC.
19722 E. Nine Mile Rd., St. Clair Shores, Michigan 48080

LC 33-27214
ISBN 0-403-00908-1

PREFACE

In this edition of Crabbe's works, we have reproduced the text of the author's own edition, adding only the posthumous volume of Tales, practically left ready for publication by the poet, and the few poems gathered together under the titles 'Juvenilia' and 'Occasional Poems', which are reprinted from his son's edition of 1834. It is true that some of these were condemned by Crabbe himself as unworthy to live, but they are already known to many readers, and could hardly be left out.

The only notes are those made by Crabbe himself.

The arrangement of the poems is chronological. For the biographical matter we are indebted to the Life by his son, prefixed to the edition of 1834, and to Mr. Ainger's *Life of Crabbe* in the English Men of Letters edition.

INTRODUCTION

IT is not so much to be wondered at that Crabbe has been almost forgotten as that he should still be remembered; for he wrote in the first years of the splendours and glories of the Romantic Movement, and it is not strange that his sober, uninspired voice should almost have been forgotten. Had his poetry appeared a few years earlier, it would have marked a great and almost revolutionary crisis in literature, but it was just a little too late, and his ' ineffectual fires ' paled before the dawn of the new day.

And yet there was a new light in Crabbe; his earlier work marks the appearance of a poet who, more than a decade before Wordsworth, looked out on human life with the same serious and faithful scrutiny, who had not, indeed, the power of interpreting what he saw in all its profounder significance, who had not learned like Wordsworth to see the glory which lies behind the grey day of human life, but who was at least sincere, sympathetic and real.

The literary movement of the eighteenth century had indeed advanced quickly, so quickly that it has often been found difficult to follow it, and people have continued to speak of the characteristic note of eighteenth-century literature under terms which apply only to the first quarter of the century. The Augustan manner in literature had indeed very rapidly given way to other influences. Pope is the last as well as the first of his school, with its cheerful optimism, its antithetical cleverness, its lucid but shallow conception of life. The place of the Augustan method in literature was taken by a movement which was at first simply realistic in a very bare literal sense, and described the external conditions and circumstances of life with an almost photographic minuteness and precision. Defoe, who is the first great writer of this manner, had turned from the conventional subjects of the Augustan literature to set forth the habits of life, and the manner of thought and feeling of his own time, in a fashion, bare, dry, uninspired, but sincere and veracious; and had brought to this new work artistic qualities and capacities of so high an order that he has made the life of the time real to us in literature much as Hogarth has done in painting. The method which Defoe had translated into English from the Spanish Picaresque novel, was carried on by Fielding, not more faithfully, but with a larger outlook and a greater sense of the picturesque variety and contrast of life, so that while the earlier chapters of *Captain Jack* are more realistic, more literally true, than the adventures of Tom Jones or of Captain Booth, the world of Fielding has a greater variety of life and colour.

We can trace in the work of Fielding the beginning of yet another movement; it may seem paradoxical to say it, but it is obviously true that Fielding, who began to write *Joseph Andrews* as a parody, is himself strongly influenced by the sentimental movement. The creator of Parson Adams, the author of the scenes in the house of the widow in *Tom Jones*, is himself a sentimentalist; that is, he has added to the external realism of Defoe something of the more intimate reality of the emotional and sentimental aspect of human life.

The revolt against the Augustan temper begins with the return to the bare, harsh, crude facts of external life, but very soon the artists of the eighteenth century were carried on to the appreciation of the artistic importance and significance of the sentiment and pathos of human life. In England just as in France, in Richardson just as in Marivaux and Prévost, the sentimental mood grew out of the realistic.

It is this sentimental movement which determines the interest and the manner of a great part of the English and European literature of the second half of the eighteenth century ; in poetry, the work of Young, Blair, Macpherson, Goldsmith, and, in some measure, Cowper, and in prose. Richardson, Sterne, Goldsmith, and Mackenzie, all represent the movement, while on the continent Rousseau raised it to the level of a creed of humanity, and Goethe transfigured it in *Werther* till it almost touched the highest level of artistic achievement. The greatest artists of the Revolution, like Goethe himself, like Wordsworth and Coleridge, passed beyond it, but the influence of the movement can be traced far on in the nineteenth century in England, and even more in France. This sentimental movement has many aspects, and deserves a much more careful study than is often given to it, for it is under the terms of the literature of emotion and sensibility that most progress was made towards that emancipation of the artist from the conventional and trivial, from the domination of the rational temper of good taste, which was finally completed in the Revolutionary or Romantic movement.

For the moment we have to consider rather its weakness than its strength ; for it had its very obvious weaknesses. The revulsion from the conventions and insincerities of the town led to a treatment of country life which was often graceful and charming, but was also often unreal and misleading because it was merely sentimental. We can find an excellent example of these merits and defects in Goldsmith's *Deserted Village*. Every one must feel how different is the gracious human feeling of this poem from the frigid banalities of the occasional pictures of human life in *The Seasons* ; but, at the same time, the humane temper, the kindly and gracious spirit of the poem, cannot hide from us the fact that Goldsmith is writing about the village and its life, not as it actually existed, but, partly at least, under the terms of a sentimental convention.

Sweet Auburn ! loveliest village of the plain,
Where health and plenty cheer'd the labouring swain,

Where smiling spring its earliest visit paid,
And parting summer's lingering blooms delay'd :
Dear lovely bowers of innocence and ease,
Seats of my youth, where every sport could please.

Such lines may pass ; we all have felt the emotion, we all know
the sentiment ; but what are we to say to these ?

A time there was, ere England's grief began,
When every rood of ground maintain'd its man ;
For him light labour spread the wholesome store,
Just gave what life required, but gave no more :
His best companions, innocence and health,
And his best riches, ignorance of wealth.

This is mere sentimentality, wanton and almost heartless.
The amiable and gentle artist has lost himself and his sense
of veracity, while he has given the reins to an emotionalism
which is not sincere.   The truth is, of course, that the ' return
to nature ' led to the revival of that idyllic sentiment which has
haunted all literature, the Alexandrian, the Mediaeval, the Neo-
classical, and even the Elizabethan, and the idyllic sentiment,
with all its grace, has a perilous tendency to the sugary sentiment
of a modern Christmas card.   In the eighteenth century, men
and women thought they were tired of the town, and imagined
a country life which had never existed, and this fell in very
naturally with their delight in the newly recovered sense of the
artistic value of their emotions.

Crabbe is not, indeed, untouched by this movement and these
sentiments, but his work, in great measure, represents a revolt
against certain aspects of it and a reversion to something more
like the earlier realistic movement.

Crabbe learned early that he had facility in the composition
of verse, and in his youthful days produced a great deal
which was moulded on the fashion of the Augustan poetry,
but it is hardly necessary to say anything about his early verse,
for it has no value.   It was not until the year 1783 that Crabbe
published any work which represents his own individual point

of view and his independence as an artist. The transition
from the conventional insipidity of his early work is indeed
very sudden, nothing has survived which enables us to trace
the development of his new temper, and to explain the origin
of his new work. He has suddenly moved from the banal
platitudes of his Augustan imitations to the strong, sincere manner
of his mature work. For in *The Village*, the first work of his
maturer style, Crabbe reached his highest level ; indeed, his
later work may be looked upon as little more than an expansion
of what he did there.

The Village was written in a mood, half scornful, half indignant,
and was clearly intended to be contrasted with Goldsmith's
Deserted Village. Here and there he quotes phrases from Gold-
smith, only to heighten the effect of his very different picture,
and we must allow something for the exaggeration which is
produced by the half-controversial intention. The picture is
too sombre, the shadows are too dark, the poem is so harsh
as to be unpleasing, and, as we judge, it is not wholly
true.

And yet there is this thing worth noticing. We have returned
to the sombre grey tones of Defoe's picture of the life of the
little beggar-boys in London, but there is a new note, a note
of passion, of protest, of indignation. What is it that has
happened ?

> The Village Life and every care that reigns
> O'er youthful peasants and declining swains ;
> What labour yields, and what, that labour past,
> Age, in its hours of languor, finds at last ;
> What form the real picture of the poor,
> Demand a song—the Muse can give no more.
>
> .   .   .   .
>
> Yes, thus the Muses sing of happy swains,
> Because the Muses never knew their pains.
>
> .   .   .   .
>
> I grant indeed that fields and flocks have charms
> For him that grazes or for him that farms ;

> But when amid such pleasing scenes I trace
> The poor laborious native of the place,
> And see the mid-day sun with fervid ray,
> On their bare heads and dewy temples play;
> While some with feebler heads and fainter hearts
> Deplore their fortune, yet sustain their parts;
> Then shall I dare those real ills to hide
> In tinsel trappings of poetic pride?

It is thus that Crabbe opens the new literature of the life of the labouring poor in town or country. He throws aside the traditional pastoral, the idyllic mood, the gracious temper, and he sets out to write the real life of the labourer. He has at least the desire to set out the truth.

He begins, therefore, with a description of a landscape, not idyllic, not beautiful, but hard and grim, a landscape not drawn from fancy, but literally sketched from the sandy flats of the eastern coast.

> Lo! where the heath with withering brake grown o'er,
> Lends the light turf that warms the neighb'ring poor;
> From thence a length of burning sand appears
> Where the thin harvest waves its wither'd ears.

Crabbe knows that there are other places where Nature is fairer and kinder, but the beauty of Nature is of no avail to make the life of the peasant easier.

> But yet in other scenes, more fair in view,
> Where Plenty smiles—alas! she smiles for few—
> And those who taste not, yet behold her store,
> Are as the slaves that dig the golden ore,
> The wealth around them makes them doubly poor.

The true character of the life of the peasant is better reflected in the harsh, unlovely aspect of Nature than in its more gracious and beautiful scenes, and he draws a picture, in vivid strokes, of the hard life, the want and hunger, the inevitable and rapid growth of physical infirmity.

> Or will you deem them amply paid in health,
> Labour's fair child, that languishes with wealth?

Go, then ! and see them rising with the sun,
Through a long course of daily toil to run ;
See them beneath the dogstar's raging heat,
When the knees tremble, and the temples beat ;
Behold them, leaning on their scythes, look o'er
The labour past, and toils to come explore ;
See them alternate suns and showers engage,
And hoard up aches and anguish for their age ;

.   .   .   .

Yet grant them health, 'tis not for us to tell,
Though the head droops not, that the heart is well ;
Or will you praise that homely, healthy fare,
Plenteous and plain that happy peasants share ?
Oh ! trifle not with wants you cannot feel,
Nor mock the misery of a stinted meal—
Homely, not wholesome, plain, not plenteous ; such
As you, who praise, would never deign to touch.

The picture is gloomy and almost unrelieved, and the second
part of the poem, which deals with the ' pleasures of the village ',
is gloomier still, for the pleasures of the poor, as Crabbe sees
them, are drunken revels, sordid vices ; the poor repeat only
too faithfully the lessons of debauch and riotousness which they
learn from the more prosperous classes.

It may be said that all this represents a morbid and extrava-
gant observation of social conditions in England, and it must
be admitted that the picture deals with only one side of things ;
but there is an unmistakable accent of sincerity in the work.
The truth is that Crabbe, the most respectable, the most con-
servative of artists, is yet the creature and child of the great
movements of Europe. Behind the prosaic and unimaginative
verses, there is a certain passion, a glow of indignation and
resentment which anticipates the mood of the Revolution ; and
it is just this which gives a new quality to what would otherwise
be rather poor poetry.

It is unnecessary to speak of his later work : where this is good
it carries on the quality of *The Village*, but while the range
of treatment is larger, it can hardly be said anywhere to reach

a higher level, and frequently enough it falls far below that of the earlier work.

Speaking broadly, Crabbe's poetry has always the same qualities, both good and bad. The verse is easy, but not musical; the method antithetical, the language frigid and often conventional; but, on the other hand, the observation of Nature and life is keen, shrewd, sincere, the poet's sympathy with human faults and distresses is real, and every now and then the poor verse glows with a passionate resentment which almost takes the place of imagination. A great poet Crabbe assuredly was not; he cannot be placed in the great society of Burns and Wordsworth and Shelley, but he belongs to the new world, he has shaken off the conventional blindness of the Augustan artists, has even risen above the gracious sentimentalism of Goldsmith, and he sees the world as it is, not, indeed, completely, or profoundly as Wordsworth does, but still sincerely, and he has the compelling force to make his readers feel the truth of his description.

A short account of Crabbe's life may help us to understand more clearly both the merits and limitations of his poetry. Aldeburgh, where he was born on Christmas Eve, 1754, is a small seaport on the coast of Suffolk. At one time fairly prosperous, the little town had suffered from the constant encroachments of the sea, and at the time of the poet's birth was a poor and squalid sort of place, with but ' two parallel, unpaved streets, running between mean and scrambling houses '. Nor was the country round much less depressing, being flat, treeless and marshy.

> " Rank weeds, that every art and care defy,
> Reign o'er the land and rot the blighted rye."

The poet's father, after trying to be a schoolmaster, settled down in his native town as collector of the salt-duties, a post which his father had filled before him. He had six children, of whom George was the eldest. He seems very early in life to have

shown a strong love for books, and some considerable capacity
for learning. Seeing this, his father determined to give him
as good an education as possible, and sent him first to a small
boarding-school at Bungay, and afterwards to a rather better
school at Stowmarket, where he seems to have made the most
of his opportunities. For he left the school before he was four-
teen, and yet he seems to have brought away with him a very fair
knowledge of many of the great classical authors as well as of
the best English poets. Wherever he came across books he read
them, and what he read he remembered. His father having
decided that he should become a doctor, he left school and
was apprenticed to a surgeon in a small village near Bury
St. Edmunds. Here he had also to help with the work of a farm,
and to sleep with the plough-boy : the life was rough and un-
congenial, and he was not making much progress in his proper
work, so after three years he left and went to Woodbridge,
where he worked under a Mr. Page for some four years,
but he never cared for the profession of medicine. The
time spent at Woodbridge, however, was a very happy one,
and was of very great service to him in the general develop-
ment of his mind. For there he found a little society of
young men who met together in the evening for the dis-
cussion of questions of mutual interest, and it is easy to
understand how helpful and quickening this must have been
to the young man, sore and sensitive as he was after the
rough farm-life and the unresponsive companionship of farm-
servants.

At Woodbridge, too, he met and loved the ' Mira ' of his poems.
This was a Miss Sarah Elmy, who lived with her uncle and aunt
at Parham, a village of great beauty and charm, very different
indeed from the dreary country to which Crabbe was accus-
tomed. Miss Elmy was of better position than he, and her
people were none too eager to welcome him as a suitor, but
they were courteous and kindly always, and the lady herself
never wavered. He had begun to write verses, some of which

found their way to magazines, and when he had been about
three years at Woodbridge he published, in the form of a
pamphlet, a longer and more ambitious poem, called *Inebriety*,
a didactic satire, showing the phases of intemperance as
observed by himself among various classes of society. He had
no doubt opportunities for observation of the vice, but his
treatment of the subject is dead, and too obviously imitative,
and it is not surprising that the poem attracted practically no
attention. In 1775 he returned to Aldeburgh, and for a little
while helped his father in his work at the quay, every now and
again getting some little occasion for practising his own pro-
fession. But he was increasingly conscious of his ignorance of
medicine and surgery, and after a short time at home he went
up to London to study further. His money did not last very
long, and soon he was back in Aldeburgh, taking over the practice
of an apothecary who had left the place in despair of making
a decent living. His patients were all of the poorest, and
there seemed little prospect of ever making enough to marry.
Gradually he was convinced that he was not made for the life
of an apothecary, and at last, towards the close of the year
1779, he made up his mind to cast everything aside, to go
to London and venture all. It was indeed a risk—his father
could not help him if he would, and indeed he was not greatly
inclined, for it was rather a bitter disappointment to him that
his son, for whom he had made considerable sacrifices, should,
after all, give up his profession and start afresh on new lines.
The Crabbes were all poor, and it seemed doubtful if money could
be raised for the journey to London. However, a Mr. Dudley
North was persuaded to advance £5, and Crabbe, having paid
his debts, set out for London with £3 in his pocket, and little
else beside. This was in April, 1780.

Then followed a period of poverty, of selling or pawning
what little belongings he possessed, of borrowing from friends,
of besieging possible patrons, of efforts to launch on the public
poems like *The Candidate*.

Poor Crabbe was very near despair : ' want stared him in
the face, and a gaol seemed the only immediate refuge for his
head.' As a last resort he resolved to make one more appeal
for help, and ' impelled ', as he says, ' by some propitious in-
fluence,' he fixed on Edmund Burke, and having written an
urgent letter of appeal, took it himself to Burke's house and
spent the whole night walking up and down Westminster Bridge
in an agony of suspense.

Along with the letter Crabbe had sent some specimens of his
verse. Whether it was that these impressed Burke with a sense of
their value, or that the letter was different from the usual run of
appeals, at any rate he replied by an immediate gift of money
and a promise of help in making Crabbe's poems known. In-
spired with fresh hope and energy Crabbe set to work to com-
plete and revise various of his poems, which he then submitted
to Burke for criticism. The great man was more than kind.
The poet ' was encouraged to lay open his views, past and present,
and to display whatever reading and acquirements he possessed,
to explain his causes for disappointment, and the cloudiness of his
prospects.' As a result, Burke helped him to publish *The Library*
(1781), commending him to the very publisher who had already
refused the poem, discussed the question of his future, and asked
him down to Beaconsfield, where he was treated as an honoured
guest.

Here he first met Charles James Fox and Sir Joshua Reynolds,
and through them came to know Samuel Johnson, who criticized
and offered emendations of his poems. And here Crabbe's
future was decided. Burke talked much with him and became
convinced he should turn to the Church : his gifts were much
more in that direction, he knew Latin fairly well, he had read very
widely, his piety was undoubted ; altogether Burke thought him
fitted for Orders and commended him to the Bishop of Norwich,
by whom he was ordained to the curacy of his native town on
December 31, 1781. Later on he was appointed Chaplain to
the Duke of Rutland in his Castle of Belvoir : the story of

'The Patron' was in all probability prompted by his experience in this dependent, and not altogether satisfactory, position.

The Village appeared in May, 1783, and in the same year Thurlow gave him two small livings in Devonshire, of no great value, but enough to allow him to marry : it was not thought necessary to reside in Devonshire, and Crabbe and his wife settled down in rooms assigned them in Belvoir Castle. But the position was not satisfactory, and, after a short trial of it, Crabbe found it advisable to accept a curacy in Leicestershire, and moved to the parsonage.

In 1785 he published *The Newspaper*, but it did not greatly add to his fame, being a return to the style of *The Library*, and lacking the life and realism of *The Village*. For twenty-two years he published nothing more : he continued to write, and wrote much, but most of it he burned. In 1789 the Chancellor allowed Crabbe to exchange his Devonshire livings for two in the Vale of Belvoir, and he then moved into the Rectory House at Muston, near Grantham. But he did not remain there very long. His wife's uncle died in 1792, and a great part of his estate came to Mrs. Elmy and eventually to Mrs. Crabbe. The old house at Parham became vacant, and the Crabbes moved thither. Here he again met Mr. Fox, who expressed his regret that he had ceased to write, and offered his help in revising any future poems.

His outward circumstances were now much more easy and comfortable, but he had grave anxieties in his home life. Of seven children only two survived, and this preyed on his wife's mind : for long she had wretched health and eventually her mind gave way. Crabbe nursed her devotedly till her death in 1813. No doubt this great trouble in his home helped to accentuate his inclination to look at the more gloomy side of life. The education of his two sons, and the care of his invalid wife, occupied the greater part of his time, but he continued to read largely and to write steadily.

After thirteen years' absence he returned to his rectory, urged thereto by his bishop, who had become alive to the evils of absenteeism. Crabbe did not very much care about going back to Muston, and found the life there rather irksome and not altogether easy. He had been too long away, and the changes which had taken place did not please him. No doubt the people were somewhat indifferent towards a clergyman who was content to remain so long away from them, and he did not improve his position by preaching violently against dissent.

It was now twenty-two years since he had published anything. In 1807 he brought out a volume of poems, old and new. The chief among them was *The Parish Register*, a series of narratives of the lives of the village poor, related by the clergyman of the parish. The book at once gained the public ear and established Crabbe's position as a poet of distinction. The reviews were unanimous in praise, and within eighteen months four editions were called for.

One great pleasure came to the poet from this publication. He sent a copy to Sir Walter Scott, who wrote acknowledging the gift and telling the poet how much he had been impressed by his earlier poems, some of which he had come across casually when only a lad of eighteen. This was the beginning of a friendship which lasted throughout the lives of both poets.

The success of *The Parish Register* encouraged Crabbe to go on with a long poem, *The Borough*, which had been in hand for some time. It was brought out in 1810, and was at once a success. The 'Borough' is his native place, Aldeburgh, the characters are the people he has known; the atmosphere is grey and depressing, the conditions of life narrow and uninspiring, but the whole picture is extraordinarily real and life-like. The critics warned the poet against ' his frequent lapses into disgusting representations ', and it was even suggested that the ' function of Poetry is not to present any truth if it is unpleasant '.

Crabbe was greatly exercised about these criticisms, and in

the preface to his next production, *The Tales* (1812), he strove to answer the objections raised. In this book he no longer dealt with the very poor ; many of the stories were based on incidents in the life of his own family or of his friends and acquaintance. The volume was well received by the public, and favourably reviewed by Jeffery, who, indeed, showed a remarkable appreciation of Crabbe's poems throughout.

In September, 1813, Mrs. Crabbe died. Her husband found life at Muston intolerably dreary, and gladly accepted the offer of the Rectory of Trowbridge. Here he found himself in the midst of a number of sympathetic, appreciative people, for Trowbridge is not very far from Bath, and Bath and its neighbourhood in those days was a favourite resort of the more intellectual world. Among others he made the acquaintance of the poet Rogers, by whose advice he went up to London for a time and mixed with the literary society of the day, working steadily all the while at his new poems. The *Tales of the Hall* were published in June, 1819, by John Murray, who two years previously had made an offer of £3000 for the new poems along with the copyright of Crabbe's earlier works. The new volume had much of the quality of the old, with here and there an increase of poetry, more careful writing, more eloquent descriptive passages.

The last thirteen years of his life were spent at Trowbridge, with an occasional visit to friends in the neighbourhood or in London, and one noteworthy visit to Scott in the autumn of 1822.

He still continued to write copiously. A large number of manuscript volumes were left at his death, among them another volume of *Tales* all but ready for the press. A selection from these were published as *Posthumous Tales* in the edition brought out by his son in 1834. In 1832 he died after a few days' illness.

CONTENTS

CONTENTS

CONTENTS

PAGE

POEMS

JUVENILIA

CONCLUDING LINES OF PRIZE POEM ON HOPE

[1772]

BUT, above all, the POET owns thy powers—
Hope leads him on, and every fear devours ;
He writes, and, unsuccessful, writes again,
Nor thinks the last laborious work in vain ;
New schemes he forms, and various plots he
    tries,
To win the laurel, and possess the PRIZE.

PARODY ON 'MY TIME, O YE MUSES'

[1772]

MY days, oh ye lovers, were happily sped,
Ere you or your whimsies got into my head ;
I could laugh, I could sing, I could trifle and
    jest,
And my heart play'd a regular tune in my
    breast.
But now, lack-a-day ! what a change for the
    worse,
'Tis as heavy as lead, yet as wild as a horse.

My fingers, ere love had tormented my mind,
Could guide my pen gently to what I design'd.
I could make an enigma, a rebus, or riddle,
Or tell a short tale of a dog and a fiddle ;
But since this vile Cupid has got in my brain,
I beg of the gods to assist in my strain.
And whatever my subject, the fancy still
    roves,
And sings of hearts, raptures, flames, sorrows,
    and loves.

THE WISH

[1772–4]

MY Mira, shepherds, is as fair
  As sylvan nymphs who haunt the vale,
As sylphs who dwell in purest air,
  As fays who skim the dusky dale,
As Venus was when Venus fled
From watery Triton's oozy bed.

My Mira, shepherds, has a voice
  As soft as Syrinx in her grove,
As sweet as echo makes her choice,
    As mild as whispering virgin-love ;
As gentle as the winding stream,
Or fancy's song when poets dream.

ON THE DEATH OF WILLIAM SPRINGALL LEVETT

[1774]

WHAT ! though no trophies peer above his
    dust,
Nor sculptured conquests deck his sober bust ;
What ! though no earthly thunders sound his
    name,
Death gives him conquest, and our sorrows
    fame ;
One sigh reflection heaves, but shuns excess—
More should we mourn him, did we love him
    less.

INEBRIETY ; A POEM[1]

[1775]

PREFACE

Presumption or meanness are but too often the only articles to be discovered in a preface. Whilst one author haughtily affects to despise the public attention, another timidly courts it. I would no more beg for than disdain applause, and therefore should advance nothing in favour of the following little Poem, did it not appear a cruelty and disregard to send a first production naked into the world.

The WORLD ! — how presumptuous, and yet how trifling the sound. Every man, gentle reader, has a world of his own, and whether it consists of half a score or half a thousand friends, 'tis his, and he loves to

[1] The following is given as in the edition of 1834.

CR.   B

boast of it. Into my world, therefore, I commit this, my Muse's earliest labour, nothing doubting the clemency of the climate, nor fearing the partiality of the censorious.

Something by way of apology for this trifle is, perhaps, necessary; especially for those parts wherein I have taken such great liberties with Mr. Pope. That gentleman, secure in immortal fame, would forgive me: forgive me, too, my friendly critic; I promise thee, thou wilt find the extracts from the Swan of Thames the best part of the performance.

INEBRIETY

THE mighty spirit, and its power, which stains [1]
The bloodless cheek, and vivifies the brains,
I sing. Say, ye, its fiery vot'ries true,
The jovial curate, and the shrill-tongued shrew;
Ye, in the floods of limpid poison nurst,
Where bowl the second charms like bowl the first;
Say how, and why, the sparkling ill is shed,
The heart which hardens, and which rules the head.

When winter stern his gloomy front uprears,
A sable void the barren earth appears;
The meads no more their former verdure boast,
Fast bound their streams, and all their beauty lost;
The herds, the flocks, in icy garments mourn,
And wildly murmur for the spring's return;
From snow-topp'd hills the whirlwinds keenly blow,
Howl through the woods, and pierce the vales below;
Through the sharp air a flaky torrent flies,
Mocks the slow sight, and hides the gloomy skies;
The fleecy clouds their chilly bosoms bare,
And shed their substance on the floating air;
The floating air their downy substance glides
Through springing waters, and prevents their tides;

Seizes the rolling waves, and, as a god,
Charms their swift race, and stops the refluent flood;
The opening valves, which fill the venal road,
Then scarcely urge along the sanguine flood;
The labouring pulse, a slower motion rules,
The tendons stiffen, and the spirit cools;
Each asks the aid of Nature's sister, Art,
To cheer the senses, and to warm the heart.

The gentle fair on nervous tea relies,
Whilst gay good-nature sparkles in her eyes;
An inoffensive scandal fluttering round,
Too rough to tickle, and too light to wound;
Champagne the courtier drinks, the spleen to chase,
The colonel burgundy, and port his grace;
Turtle and 'rrac the city rulers charm,
Ale and content the labouring peasants warm:
O'er the dull embers, happy Colin sits,
Colin, the prince of joke, and rural wits;
Whilst the wind whistles through the hollow panes,
He drinks, nor of the rude assault complains;
And tells the tale, from sire to son retold,
Of spirits vanishing near hidden gold;
Of moon-clad imps that tremble by the dew,
Who skim the air, or glide o'er waters blue:
The throng invisible that, doubtless, float
By mouldering tombs, and o'er the stagnant moat;
Fays dimly glancing on the russet plain,
And all the dreadful nothing of the green.

. . . . .

Peace be to such, the happiest and the best,
Who with the forms of fancy urge their jest;
Who wage no war with an avenger's rod,
Nor in the pride of reason curse their God.

When in the vaulted arch Lucina gleams,
And gaily dances o'er the azure streams;

. . . . .

On silent ether when a trembling sound
Reverberates, and wildly floats around,
Breaking through trackless space upon the ear,
Conclude the Bacchanalian rustic near:
O'er hills and vales the jovial savage reels,
Fire in his head and frenzy at his heels;
From paths direct the bending hero swerves,
And shapes his way in ill-proportioned curves.
Now safe arrived, his sleeping rib he calls,
And madly thunders on the muddy walls;

[1] 'The mighty Mother, and her son, who brings
The Smithfield muses to the ear of kings,'
&c.—POPE's *Dunciad*.

The well-known sounds an equal fury move,
For rage meets rage, as love enkindles love :

. . . . .

In vain the 'waken'd infant's accents shrill,
The humble regions of the cottage fill ;
In vain the cricket chirps the mansion through,
'Tis war, and blood, and battle must ensue.
As when, on humble stage, him Satan hight
Defies the brazen hero to the fight :
From twanging strokes what dire misfortunes
rise,
What fate to maple arms and glassen eyes !
Here lies a leg of elm, and there a stroke
From ashen neck has whirl'd a head of oak.
So drops from either power, with vengeance
big,
A remnant night-cap and an old cut wig ;
Titles unmusical retorted round,
On either ear with leaden vengeance sound ;
Till equal valour, equal wounds create,
And drowsy peace concludes the fell debate ;
Sleep in her woollen mantle wraps the pair,
And sheds her poppies on the ambient air ;
Intoxication flies, as fury fled,
On rooky pinions quits the aching head ;
Returning reason cools the fiery blood,
And drives from memory's seat the rosy god.
Yet still he holds o'er some his maddening
rule,
Still sways his sceptre, and still knows his
fool ;
Witness the livid lip, and fiery front,
With many a smarting trophy placed upon't ;
The hollow eye, which plays in misty springs,
And the hoarse voice, which rough and broken
rings :
These are his triumphs, and o'er these he
reigns,
The blinking deity of reeling brains.
See Inebriety ! her wand she waves,
And lo ! her pale, and lo ! her purple slaves !
Sots in embroidery, and sots in crape,
Of every order, station, rank, and shape :
The king, who nods upon his rattle throne ;
The staggering peer, to midnight revel prone ;
The slow-tongued bishop, and the deacon
sly,
The humble pensioner, and gownsman dry ;
The proud, the mean, the selfish, and the
great,
Swell the dull throng, and stagger into state.
Lo ! proud Flaminius at the splendid board,
The easy chaplain of an atheist lord,

Quaffs the bright juice, with all the gust of
sense,
And clouds his brain in torpid elegance ;
In china vases, see ! the sparkling ill,
From gay decanters view the rosy rill ;
The neat-carved pipes in silver settle laid,
The screw by mathematic cunning made :

. . . . .

Oh, happy priest ! whose God, like Egypt's,
lies,
At once the deity and sacrifice.
But is Flaminius then the man alone
To whom the joys of swimming brains are
known ?
Lo ! the poor toper whose untutor'd sense,
Sees bliss in ale, and can with wine dispense ; [1]
Whose head proud fancy never taught to steer,
Beyond the muddy ecstasies of beer ;
But simple nature can her longing quench,
Behind the settle's curve, or humbler bench :
Some kitchen fire diffusing warmth around,
The semi-globe by hieroglyphics crown'd ;
Where canvass purse displays the brass en-
roll'd,
Nor waiters rave, nor landlords thirst for gold;
Ale and content his fancy's bounds confine,
He asks no limpid punch, no rosy wine ;
But sees, admitted to an equal share,
Each faithful swain the heady potion bear :
Go wiser thou ! and in thy scale of taste,
Weigh gout and gravel against ale and
rest ;
Call vulgar palates what thou judgest so ;
Say beer is heavy, windy, cold, and slow ;
Laugh at poor sots with insolent pretence,
Yet cry, when tortured, where is Providence ?

. . . . .

In various forms the madd'ning spirit
moves,
This drinks and fights, another drinks and
loves.
A bastard zeal, of different kinds it shows,
And now with rage, and now religion glows :
The frantic soul bright reason's path defies,
Now creeps on earth, now triumphs in the
skies ;
Swims in the seas of error, and explores,
Through midnight mists, the fluctuating
shores ;

[1] 'Lo the poor Indian ! whose untutor'd
mind,
Sees God in clouds, and hears him in the
wind,' &c.—POPE's *Essay on Man*.

From wave to wave in rocky channel glides,
And sinks in woe, or on presumption slides ;
In pride exalted, or by shame deprest,
An angel-devil, or a human-beast.

      .   .   .   .

  Some rage in all the strength of folly mad ;
Some love stupidity, in silence clad,
Are never quarrelsome, are never gay,
But sleep, and groan, and drink the night
    away ;
Old Torpio nods, and as the laugh goes round,
Grunts through the nasal duct, and joins the
    sound,
Then sleeps again, and, as the liquors pass,
Wakes at the friendly jog, and takes his
    glass :
Alike to him who stands, or reels, or moves,
The elbow chair, good wine, and sleep he loves ;
Nor cares of state disturb his easy head,
By grosser fumes, and calmer follies fed ;
Nor thoughts of when, or where, or how to
    come,
The canvass general, or the general doom :
Extremes ne'er reach'd one passion of his
    soul,
A villain tame, and an unmettled fool,
To half his vices he has but pretence,
For they usurp the place of common sense ;
To half his little merits has no claim,
For very indolence has raised his name ;
Happy in this, that, under Satan's sway,
His passions tremble, but will not obey.
  The vicar at the table's front presides,
Whose presence a monastic life derides ;
The reverend wig, in sideway order placed,
The reverend band, by rubric stains disgraced,
The leering eye, in wayward circles roll'd,
Mark him the pastor of a jovial fold,
Whose various texts excite a loud applause,
Favouring the bottle, and the good old cause.
See ! the dull smile which fearfully appears,
When gross indecency her front uprears,
The joy conceal'd, the fiercer burns within,
As masks afford the keenest gust to sin ;
Imagination helps the reverend sire,
And spreads the sails of sub-divine desire ;
But when the gay immoral joke goes round,
When shame and all her blushing train are
    drown'd,
Rather than hear his God blasphemed, he
    takes
The last loved glass, and then the board for-
    sakes.

Not that religion prompts the sober thought,
But slavish custom has the practice taught ;
Besides, this zealous son of warm devotion
Has a true Levite bias for promotion.
Vicars must with discretion go astray,
Whilst bishops may be damn'd the nearest
    way :
So puny robbers individuals kill,
When hector-heroes murder as they will.
  Good honest Curio elbows the divine,
And strives a social sinner how to shine ;
The dull quaint tale is his, the lengthen'd tale,
That Wilton farmers give you with their ale,
How midnight ghosts o'er vaults terrific pass,
Dance o'er the grave, and slide along the grass;

      .   .   .   .

Or how pale Cicely within the wood
Call'd Satan forth, and bargain'd with her
    blood :
These, honest Curio, are thine, and these
Are the dull treasures of a brain at peace ;
No wit intoxicates thy gentle skull,
Of heavy, native, unwrought folly full :
Bowl upon bowl in vain exert their force,
The breathing spirit takes a downward course,
Or vainly soaring upwards to the head,
Meets an impenetrable fence of lead.
  Hast thou, oh reader ! search'd o'er gentle
    Gay,
Where various animals their powers display?
In one strange group a chattering race are
    hurl'd,
Led by the monkey who had seen the world.

      .   .   .   .

Like him Fabricio steals from guardian's side,
Swims not in pleasure's stream, but sips the
    tide :
He hates the bottle, yet but thinks it right
To boast next day the honours of the night ;
None like your coward can describe a fight.
See him as down the sparkling potion goes,
Labour to grin away the horrid dose ;
In joy-feign'd gaze his misty eyeballs float,
Th' uncivil spirit gurgling at his throat ;
So looks dim Titan through a wintry scene,
And faintly cheers the woe foreboding swain.

      .   .   .   .

  Timon, long practised in the school of art,
Has lost each finer feeling of the heart ;
Triumphs o'er shame, and, with delusive wiles,
Laughs at the idiot he himself beguiles :
So matrons past the awe of censure's tongue,
Deride the blushes of the fair and young.

Few with more fire on every subject spoke,
But chief he loved the gay immoral joke;
The words most sacred, stole from holy writ,
He gave a newer form, and call'd them wit.

. . . . . .

Vice never had a more sincere ally,
So bold no sinner, yet no saint so sly ;

. . . . . .

Learn'd, but not wise, and without virtue
brave,
A gay, deluding, philosophic knave.
When Bacchus' joys his airy fancy fire,
They stir a new, but still a false desire ;

. . . . . .

And to the comfort of each untaught fool,
Horace in English vindicates the bowl.
'The man,' says Timon, 'who is drunk is
blest,[1]
No fears disturb, no cares destroy his rest ;
In thoughtless joy he reels away his life,
Nor dreads that worst of ills, a noisy wife.'

. . . . . .

'Oh! place me, Jove, where none but women
come,
And thunders worse than thine afflict the
room,
Where one eternal nothing flutters round,
And senseless titt'ring sense of mirth con-
found ;
Or lead me bound to garret, Babel-high,
Where frantic poet rolls his crazy eye,
Tiring the ear with oft-repeated chimes,
And smiling at the never-ending rhymes :
E'en here, or there, I'll be as blest as Jove,
Give me tobacco, and the wine I love.'
Applause from hands the dying accents break,
Of stagg'ring sots who vainly try to speak ;
From Milo, him who hangs upon each word,
And in loud praises splits the tortured board,
Collects each sentence, ere it's better known,
And makes the mutilated joke his own,
At weekly club to flourish, where he rules,
The glorious president of grosser fools.
    But cease, my Muse! of those, or these
enough,
The fools who listen, and the knaves who
scoff ;
The jest profane, that mocks th' offended
God,
Defies his power, and sets at nought his rod ;

The empty laugh, discretion's vainest foe,
From fool to fool re-echoed to and fro ;
The sly indecency, that slowly springs
From barren wit, and halts on trembling
wings :
Enough of these, and all the charms of wine,
Be sober joys, and social evenings mine ;
Where peace and reason, unsoil'd mirth im-
prove
The powers of friendship and the joys of love ;
Where thought meets thought ere words its
form array,
And all is sacred, elegant, and gay :
Such pleasure leaves no sorrow on the mind,
Too great to pall, to sicken too refined ;
Too soft for noise, and too sublime for art,
The social solace of the feeling heart,
For sloth too rapid, and for wit too high,
'Tis VIRTUE'S pleasure, and can never die !

. . . . . .

THE LEARNING OF LOVE

[1776 ?]

AH! blest be the days when with Mira I took
The learning of Love . . .
When we pluck'd the wild blossoms that
blush'd in the grass,
And I taught my dear maid of their species
and class ;
For Conway, the friend of mankind, had de-
creed
That Hudson should show us the wealth of
the mead.

YE GENTLE GALES

Woodbridge, 1776.

YE gentle Gales, that softly move,
Go whisper to the Fair I love ;
Tell her I languish and adore,
And pity in return implore.

But if she's cold to my request,
Ye louder Winds, proclaim the rest—
My sighs, my tears, my griefs proclaim,
And speak in strongest notes my flame.

Still if she rests in mute disdain,
And thinks I feel a common pain—
Wing'd with my woes, ye Tempests, fly,
And tell the haughty Fair I die.

---

[1] 'Integer vitae, scelerisque purus,
    Non eget,' &c., &c.—HORACE.

MIRA

Aldborough, 1777.

A WANTON chaos in my breast raged high,
A wanton transport darted in mine eye ;
False pleasure urged, and ev'ry eager care,
That swell the soul to guilt and to despair.
My Mira came ! be ever blest the hour,
That drew my thoughts half way from folly's
    power ;
She first my soul with loftier notions fired ;
I saw their truth, and as I saw admired ;
With greater force returning reason moved,
And as returning reason urged, I loved ;
Till pain, reflection, hope, and love allied
My bliss precarious to a surer guide—
To Him who gives pain, reason, hope, and love,
Each for that end that angels must approve.
One beam of light He gave my mind to see,
And gave that light, my heavenly fair, by
    thee ;
That beam shall raise my thoughts, and mend
    my strain,
Nor shall my vows, nor prayers, nor verse be
    vain.

HYMN

Beccles, 1778.

OH, Thou ! who taught my infant eye
To pierce the air, and view the sky,
To see my God in earth and seas,
To hear him in the vernal breeze,
To know him midnight thoughts among,
O guide my soul, and aid my song.

Spirit of Light ! do thou impart
Majestic truths, and teach my heart ;
Teach me to know how weak I am ;
How vain my powers, how poor my frame ;
Teach me celestial paths untrod—
The ways of glory and of God.

No more let me, in vain surprise,
To heathen art give up my eyes—
To piles laborious science rear'd
For heroes brave, or tyrants fear'd ;
But quit Philosophy, and see
The Fountain of her works in Thee.

Fond man ! yon glassy mirror eye—
Go, pierce the flood, and there descry
The miracles that float between
The rainy leaves of wat'ry green ;
Old Ocean's hoary treasures scan ;
See nations swimming round a span.

Then wilt thou say—and rear no more
Thy monuments in mystic lore—
My God ! I quit my vain design,
And drop my work to gaze on Thine :
Henceforth I'll frame myself to be,
Oh, Lord ! a monument of Thee.

THE WISH

Aldborough, 1778.

GIVE me, ye Powers that rule in gentle hearts !
The full design, complete in all its parts,
Th' enthusiastic glow, that swells the soul—
When swell'd too much, the judgment to
    control—
The happy ear that feels the flowing force
Of the smooth line's uninterrupted course ;
Give me, oh give ! if not in vain the prayer,
That sacred wealth, poetic worth to share—
Be it my boast to please and to improve,
To warm the soul to virtue and to love ;
To paint the passions, and to teach mankind
Our greatest pleasures are the most refined ;
The cheerful tale with fancy to rehearse,
And gild the moral with the charm of verse.

THE COMPARISON

Parham, 1778.

FRIENDSHIP is like the gold refined,
    And all may weigh its worth ;
Love like the ore, brought undesign'd
    In virgin beauty forth.

Friendship may pass from age to age,
    And yet remain the same ;
Love must in many a toil engage,
    And melt in lambent flame.

GOLDSMITH TO THE AUTHOR

' Felix quem faciunt aliena pericula cautum.'

Aldborough, 1778.

YOU'RE in love with the Muses ! Well, grant
    it be true,
When, good Sir, were the Muses enamour'd of
    you ?
Read first,—if my lectures your fancy de-
    light,—
Your taste is diseased :—can your cure be
    to *write* ?

You suppose you're a genius, that ought to
   engage
The attention of wits, and the smiles of the
   age :
Would the wits of the age their opinion make
   known,
Why—every man thinks just the same of his
   own.

You imagine that Pope—but yourself you
   beguile—
Would have wrote the same things, had he
   chose the same style.
Delude not yourself with so fruitless a hope,—
Had he chose the same style, he had never
   been Pope.

You think of *my* muse with a friendly regard,
And rejoice in her author's esteem and re-
   ward :
But let not his glory your spirits elate,
When pleased with his honours, remember
   his fate.

FRAGMENT

' Lord, what is man, that thou art mindful
of him ? '

Aldborough, 1778.

PROUD, little Man, opinion's slave,
   Error's fond child, too duteous to be free,
Say, from the cradle to the grave,
   Is not the earth thou tread'st too grand for
     thee ?
This globe that turns thee, on her agile wheel
Moves by deep springs, which thou canst never
   feel :
Her day and night, her centre and her sun,
Untraced by thee, their annual courses run.
A busy fly, thou sharest the march divine,
And flattering fancy calls the motion thine ;
Untaught how soon some hanging grave may
   burst,
And join thy flimsy substance to the dust.

THE RESURRECTION

Aldborough, 1778.

THE wintry winds have ceased to blow,
   And trembling leaves appear ;
And fairest flowers succeed the snow,
   And hail the infant year.

So, when the world and all its woes
   Are vanish'd far away,
Fair scenes and wonderful repose
   Shall bless the new-born day,—

When, from the confines of the grave,
   The body too shall rise ;
No more precarious passion's slave,
   Nor error's sacrifice.

'Tis but a sleep—and Sion's king
   Will call the many dead :
'Tis but a sleep—and then we sing,
   O'er dreams of sorrow fled.

Yes !—wintry winds have ceased to blow,
   And trembling leaves appear,
And Nature has her types to show
   Throughout the varying year.

MY BIRTH-DAY

Aldborough, Dec. 24, 1778.

THROUGH a dull tract of woe, of dread,
The toiling year has pass'd and fled :
And, lo ! in sad and pensive strain,
I sing my birth-day date again.

Trembling and poor, I saw the light,
New waking from unconscious night :
Trembling and poor I still remain
To meet unconscious night again.

Time in my pathway strews few flowers,
To cheer or cheat the weary hours ;
And those few strangers, dear indeed,
Are choked, are check'd, by many a weed.

TO ELIZA

Beccles, 1779.

THE Hebrew king, with spleen possest,
By David's harp was soothed to rest ;
Yet, when the magic song was o'er,
The soft delusion charm'd no more :
The former fury fired the brain,
And every care return'd again.

But, had he known Eliza's skill
To bless the sense and bind the will,
To bid the gloom of care retire,
And fan the flame of fond desire,
Remembrance then had kept the strain,
And not a care return'd again.

LIFE

Aldborough, 1779.

THINK ye the joys that fill our early day,
  Are the poor prelude to some full repast?
Think you they *promise*?—ah! believe they
      pay;
  The purest ever, they are oft the last.
The jovial swain that yokes the morning team,
  And all the verdure of the field enjoys,
See him, how languid! when the noontide
      beam
  Plays on his brow, and all his force destroys.
So 'tis with us, when, love and pleasure fled,
  We at the summit of our hill arrive:
Lo! the gay lights of Youth are past—are
      dead,
  But what still deepening clouds of Care
      survive!

THE SACRAMENT

Aldborough, 1779.

O! SACRED gift of God to man,
  A faith that looks above,
And sees the deep amazing plan
  Of sanctifying love.

Thou dear and yet tremendous God,
  Whose glory pride reviles;
How did'st thou change thy awful rod
  To pard'ning grace and smiles!

Shut up with sin, with shame, below,
  I trust, this bondage past,
A great, a glorious change to know,
  And to be bless'd at last.

I *do* believe, that, God of light!
  Thou didst to earth descend,
With Satan and with Sin to fight—
  Our great, our only friend.

I *know* thou did'st ordain for me,
  Thy creature, bread and wine;
The depth of grace I cannot see,
  But worship the design.

NIGHT

Aldborough, 1779.

THE sober stillness of the night
  That fills the silent air,
And all that breathes along the shore
  Invite to solemn prayer.

Vouchsafe to me that spirit, Lord!
  Which points the sacred way,
And let thy creatures here below
  Instruct me how to pray.

FRAGMENT WRITTEN AT MIDNIGHT

Aldborough, 1779.

OH, great Apollo! by whose equal aid
The verse is written, and the med'cine made;
Shall thus a boaster, with his fourfold powers,
In triumph scorn this sacred art of ours?
Insulting quack! on thy sad business go,
And land the stranger on this world of woe.
Still I pass on, and now before me find
The restless ocean, emblem of my mind;
There wave on wave, here thought on thought
      succeeds,
Their produce idle works, and idle weeds:
Dark is the prospect o'er the rolling sea,
But not more dark than my sad views to me;
Yet from the rising moon the light beams
      dance
In troubled splendour o'er the wide expanse;
So on my soul, whom cares and troubles fright,
The Muse pours comfort in a flood of light.—
Shine out, fair flood! until the day-star flings
His brighter rays on all sublunar things.
  'Why in such haste? by all the powers of
      wit,
I have against thee neither bond nor writ;
If thou'rt a poet, now indulge the flight
Of thy fine fancy in this dubious light;
Cold, gloom, and silence shall assist thy
      rhyme,
And all things meet to form the true sub-
      lime.'—
  'Shall I, preserver deem'd around the place,
With abject rhymes a doctor's name disgrace?
Nor doctor solely, in the healing art
I'm all in all, and all in every part;
Wise Scotland's boast let that diploma be
Which gave me right to claim the golden fee:
Praise, then, I claim, to skilful surgeon due,
For mine th' advice and operation too;
And, fearing all the vile compounding tribe,
I make myself the med'cines I prescribe;
Mine, too, the chemic art; and not a drop
Goes to my patients from a vulgar shop.
But chief my fame and fortune I command,
From the rare skill of this obstetric hand:

This our chaste dames and prudent wives
allow,
With her who calls me from thy wonder now.'

A FAREWELL

[1779]

The hour arrived ! I sigh'd and said,
How soon the happiest hours are fled !
On wings of down they lately flew,
But then their moments pass'd with you ;
And still with you could I but be,
On downy wings they'd always flee.

Say, did you not, the way you went,
Feel the soft balm of gay content ?
Say, did you not all pleasures find,
Of which you left so few behind ?
I think you did : for well I know
My parting prayer would make it so !

May she, I said, life's choicest goods partake ;
Those, late in life, for nobler still forsake—
The bliss of one, th' esteem'd of many live,
With all that Friendship would, and all that
        Love can give !

TIME

[1780]

' The clock struck one ! we take no thought
        of Time,'
Wrapt up in night, and meditating rhyme :
All big with vision, we despise the powers
That vulgar beings link to days and hours ;
Those vile, mechanic things, that rule our
        hearts,
And cut our lives in momentary parts.
' That speech of Time was Wisdom's gift,'
        said Young :
Ah, Doctor ! better Time would hold his
        tongue :
What serves the clock ?   ' To warn the care-
        less crew
How much in little space they have to do ;
To bid the busy world resign their breath,
And beat each moment a soft call for death—
To give it, then, a tongue, was wise in man.'
Support the assertion, Doctor, if you can :
It tells the ruffian when his comrades wait ;
It calls the duns to crowd my hapless gate ;
It tells my heart the paralysing tale,
Of hours to come, when Misery must prevail.

THE CHOICE

[1780]

What vulgar title thus salutes the eye,
The schoolboy's first attempt at poesy ?
The long-worn theme of every humbler Muse,
For wits to scorn and nurses to peruse ;
The dull description of a scribbler's brain,
And sigh'd-for-wealth, for which he sighs in
        vain ;
A glowing chart of fairy-land estate,
Romantic scenes, and visions out of date,
Clear skies, clear streams, soft banks, and
        sober bowers,
Deer, whimpering brooks, and wind-perfum-
        ing flowers ?

Not thus ! too long have I in fancy wove
My slender webs of wealth, and peace, and
        love ;
Have dream'd of plenty, in the midst of want,
And sought, by Hope, what Hope can never
        grant,
Been fool'd by wishes, and still wish'd again,
And loved the flattery, while I knew it vain !
' Gain by the Muse ! '—alas ! thou might'st
        as soon
Pluck gain (as Percy honour) from the moon ;
As soon grow rich by ministerial nods,
As soon divine by dreaming of the gods,
As soon succeed by telling ladies truth,
Or preaching moral documents to youth :
To as much purpose, mortal ! thy desires,
As Tully's flourishes to country squires ;
As simple truth within St. James's state,
Or the soft lute in shrill-tongued Billingsgate.
' Gain by the Muse ! ' alas, preposterous hope !
Who ever gain'd by poetry—but Pope ?
And what art thou ?   No St. John taker thy
        part ;
No potent Dean commends thy head or heart !
What gain'st thou but the praises of the poor ?
They bribe no milkman to thy lofty door,
They wipe no scrawl from thy increasing score.
What did the Muse, or Fame, for Dryden,
        say ?
What for poor Butler ?   what for honest Gay ?
For Thomson, what ? or what to Savage give ?
Or how did Johnson—how did Otway live ?
Like thee ! dependent on to-morrow's good,
Their thin revenue never understood ;
Like thee, elate at what thou canst not know ;
Like thee, repining at each puny blow ;

Like thee they lived, each dream of Hope to
  mock,
Upon their wits—but with a larger stock.
  No, if for food thy unambitious pray'r,
With supple acts to supple minds repair ;
Learn of the base, in soft grimace to deal,
And deck thee with the livery genteel ;
Or trim the wherry, or the flail invite,
Draw teeth, or any viler thing but write.
Writers, whom once th' astonish'd vulgar saw,
Give nations language, and great cities law ;
Whom gods, they said—and surely gods—
  inspired,
Whom emp'rors honour'd, and the world
  admired—
Now common grown, they awe mankind no
  more,
But vassals are, who judges were before ;
Blockheads on wits their little talents waste,
As files gnaw metal that they cannot taste :
Though still some good, the trial may produce,
To shape the useful to a nobler use.
Some few of these, a statue and a stone
Has Fame decreed—but deals out bread to none.
Unhappy art ! decreed thine owner's curse,
Vile diagnostic of consumptive purse :
Members by bribes, and ministers by lies,
Gamesters by luck, by courage soldiers rise :
Beaux by the outside of their heads may win,
And wily sergeants by the craft within :
Who but the race, by Fancy's demon led,
Starve by the means they use to gain their
  bread ?
  Oft have I read, and, reading, mourn'd the
    fate
Of garret-bard, and his unpitied mate ;
Of children stinted in their daily meal !—
The joke of wealthier wits, who could not feel ;
Portentous spoke that pity in my breast !
And pleaded self—who ever pleads the best :
No ! thank my stars, my misery's all my
  own,—
To friends—to family—to foes unknown :
Who hates my verse, and damns the mean
  design,
Shall wound no peace—shall grieve no heart
  but mine.
  One trial past, let sober Reason speak :
Here shall we rest, or shall we further seek ?
Rest here, if our relenting stars ordain
A placid harbour from the stormy main :
Or, that denied, the fond remembrance weep,
And sink, forgotten, in the mighty deep.

A HUMBLE INVOCATION

[1780]

WHEN summer's tribe, her rosy tribe, are fled,
And drooping beauty mourns her blossoms
  shed,
Some humbler sweet may cheer the pensive
  swain,
And simpler beauties deck the withering plain.
And thus when Verse her wint'ry prospect
  weeps,
When Pope is gone, and mighty Milton sleeps,
When Gray in lofty lines has ceased to soar,
And gentle Goldsmith charms the town no
  more,
An humbler Bard the widow'd Muse invites,
Who led by hope and inclination writes :
With half their art, he tries the soul to move,
And swell the softer strain with themes of love.

FROM AN EPISTLE TO MIRA

[1780]

OF substance I've thought, and the varied
  disputes
On the nature of man and the notions of
  brutes ;
Of systems confuted, and systems explain'd,
Of science disputed, and tenets maintain'd . . .
These, and such speculations on these kind of
  things,
Have robb'd my poor Muse of her plume and
  her wings ;
Consumed the phlogiston you used to admire,
The spirit extracted, extinguish'd the fire ;
Let out all the ether, so pure and refined,
And left but a mere *caput mortuum* behind.

EPISTLE TO PRINCE WILLIAM
HENRY

[1780]

WHO thus aspiring sings ? would'st thou ex-
  plore ;
A Bard replies, who ne'er assumed before,—
One taught in hard affliction's school to bear
Life's ills, where every lesson costs a tear,
Who sees from thence, the proper point of
  view,
What the wise heed not, and the weak pursue.
  .   .   .   .

And now farewell, the drooping Muse ex-
   claims.
She lothly leaves thee to the shock of war,
And, fondly dwelling on her princely tar,
Wishes the noblest good her Harry's share,
Without her misery and without her care.
For, ah! unknown to thee, a rueful train,
Her hapless children, sigh, and sigh in vain ;
A numerous band, denied the boon to die,
Half-starved, half-fed by fits of charity.
Unknown to thee ! and yet, perhaps, thy ear
Has chanced each sad, amusing tale to hear,
How some, like Budgell, madly sank for ease,
How some, like Savage, sicken'd by degrees ;
How a pale crew, like helpless Otway, shed
The proud big tear on song-extorted bread ;
Or knew, like Goldsmith, some would stoop
   to choose
Contempt, and for the mortar quit the Muse.
   One of this train—and of these wretches
      one—
Slaves to the Muses, and to Misery son—
Now prays the Father of all Fates to shed,
On Henry, laurels ; on his poet, bread !
   Unhappy art ! decreed thine owner's
      curse ;
Vile diagnostic of consumptive purse ;
Still shall thy fatal force my soul perplex,
And every friend, and every brother vex !
Each fond companion !——No, I thank my
   God !
There rests my torment—there is hung the
   rod.
To friend, to fame, to family unknown,
Sour disappointments frown on me alone.
Who hates my song, and damns the poor de-
   sign,
Shall wound no peace—shall grieve no heart
   but mine !
   Pardon, sweet Prince ! the thoughts that
      will intrude,
For want is absent, and dejection rude.
Methinks I hear, amid the shouts of Fame,
Each jolly victor hail my Henry's name ;
And, Heaven forbid that, in that jovial day,
One British bard should grieve when all are
   gay.
No ! let him find his country has redress,
And bid adieu to every fond distress ;
Or, touch'd too near, from joyful scenes
   retire,
Scorn to complain, and with one sigh expire !

DRIFTING

[1780]

LIKE some poor bark on the rough ocean tost,
My rudder broken, and my compass lost,
My sails the coarsest, and too thin to last,
Pelted by rains, and bare to many a blast,
My anchor, Hope, scarce fix'd enough to stay
Where the strong current Grief sweeps all
   away,
I sail along, unknowing how to steer,
Where quicksands lie and frowning rocks
   appear.
Life's ocean teems with foes to my frail bark,
The rapid sword-fish, and the rav'ning shark,
Where torpid things crawl forth in splendid
   shell,
And knaves and fools and sycophants live well.
What have I left in such tempestuous sea ?
No Tritons shield, no Naiads shelter me !
A gloomy Muse, in Mira's absence, hears
My plaintive prayer, and sheds consoling
   tears—
Some fairer prospect, though at distance,
   brings,
Soothes me with song, and flatters as she sings.

TO THE RIGHT HON. THE EARL OF SHELBURNE

[1780]

AH ! SHELBURNE, blest with all that 's good
   or great,
T' adorn a rich, or save a sinking state,
If public Ills engross not all thy care,
Let private Woe assail a patriot's ear,
Pity confined, but not less warm, impart,
And unresisted win thy noble heart :
Nor deem I rob thy soul of Britain's share,
Because I hope to have some interest there ;
Still wilt thou shine on all a fostering sun,
Though with more fav'ring beams enlight'n-
   ing one,—
As Heaven will oft make some more amply
   blest,
Yet still in general bounty feeds the rest.
Oh hear the Virtue thou reverest plead ;
She'll swell thy breast, and there applaud the
   deed.
She bids thy thoughts one hour from greatness
   stray,
And leads thee on to fame a shorter way ;

Where, if no withering laurel 's thy reward,
There 's shouting Conscience, and a grateful
    Bard ;
A bard untrained in all but misery's school,
Who never bribed a knave or praised a fool ;—
'Tis Glory prompts, and as thou read'st
    attend,
She dictates pity, and becomes my friend ;
She bids each cold and dull reflection flee,
And yields her Shelburne to distress and
    me !—

AN EPISTLE TO A FRIEND

[1780]

Why, true, thou say'st the fools at Court
    denied,
Growl vengeance,—and then take the other
    side :
The unfed flatterer borrows satire's power,
As sweets unshelter'd run to vapid sour.
But thou, the counsel to my closest thought,
Beheld'st it ne'er in fulsome stanzas wrought.
The Muse I court ne'er fawn'd on venal souls,
Whom suppliants angle, and poor praise con-
    trols ;
She, yet unskill'd in all but fancy's dream,
Sang to the woods, and Mira was her theme.
But when she sees a titled nothing stand
The ready cipher of a trembling land,—
Not of that simple kind that placed alone
Are useless, harmless things, and threaten
    none,—
But those which, join'd to figures, well express
A strengthen'd tribe that amplify distress,
Grow in proportion to their number great,
And help each other in the ranks of state ;—
When this and more the pensive Muses see,
They leave the vales and willing nymphs to
    thee ;
To Court on wings of agile anger speed,
And paint to freedom's sons each guileful
    deed.
Hence rascals teach the virtues they detest,
And fright base action from sin's wavering
    breast ;
For though the knave may scorn the Muse's
    arts,
Her sting may haply pierce more timid hearts.
Some, though they wish it, are not steel'd
    enough,
Nor is each would-be villain conscience-proof.

And what, my friend, is left my song besides ?
No school-day wealth that roll'd in silver
    tides,
No dreams of hope that won my early will,
Nor love, that pain'd in temporary thrill ;
No gold to deck my pleasure-scorn'd abode,
No friend to whisper peace,—to give me
    food ;—
Poor to the World I'd yet not live in vain,
But show its lords their hearts, and my dis-
    dain.
Yet shall not Satire all my song engage
In indiscriminate and idle rage ;
True praise, where Virtue prompts, shall gild
    each line,
And long—if Vanity deceives not—shine.
For though in harsher strains, the strains of
    woe,
And unadorn'd, my heart-felt murmurs flow,
Yet time shall be when this thine humbled
    friend
Shall to more lofty heights his notes extend.
A Man—for other title were too poor—
Such as 'twere almost virtue to adore,
He shall the ill that loads my heart exhale,
As the sun vapours from the dew-press'd vale ;
Himself uninjuring shall new warmth infuse,
And call to blossom every want-nipp'd Muse.
Then shall my grateful strains his ear rejoice,
His name harmonious thrill'd on Mira's voice ;
Round the reviving bays new sweets shall
    spring,
And Shelburne's fame through laughing
    valleys ring.

THE CANDIDATE

A POETICAL EPISTLE TO THE AUTHORS OF THE 'MONTHLY REVIEW'

Multa quidem nobis facimus mala saepe
    poetae
(Ut vineta egomet caedam mea) cum tibi
    librum
Sollicito damus, aut fesso, &c.
            Hor. *Epist.* ii. 1.

AN INTRODUCTORY ADDRESS OF THE AUTHOR TO HIS POEMS.

Ye idler things, that soothed my hours of
    care,
Where would ye wander, triflers, tell me
    where ?

As maids neglected, do ye fondly dote,
On the fair type, or the embroider'd coat ;
Detest my modest shelf, and long to fly,
Where princely POPES, and mighty MILTONS
   lie ?
Taught but to sing, and that in simple style,
Of Lycia's lip, and Musidora's smile ;—
Go then ! and taste a yet unfelt distress,
The fear that guards the captivating press ;
Whose maddening region should ye once
   explore,
No refuge yields my tongueless mansion more.
But thus ye'll grieve, Ambition's plumage
   stript,
' Ah, would to Heaven, we'd died in manu-
   script ! '
Your unsoil'd page each yawning wit shall
   flee,
—For few will read, and none admire like
   me.—
Its place, where spiders silent bards enrobe,
Squeezed betwixt Cibber's Odes and Black-
   more's Job ;
Where froth and mud, that varnish and de-
   form,
Feed the lean critic and the fattening worm ;
Then sent disgraced—the unpaid printer's
   bane—
To mad Moorfields, or sober Chancery Lane,
On dirty stalls I see your hopes expire,
Vex'd by the grin of your unheeded sire,
Who half reluctant has his care resign'd,
Like a teased parent, and is rashly kind.
   Yet rush not all, but let some scout go forth,
View the strange land, and tell us of its worth ;
And should he there barbarian usage meet,
The patriot scrap shall warn us to retreat.
   And thou, the first of thy eccentric race,
A forward imp, go, search the dangerous place,
Where Fame's eternal blossoms tempt each
   bard,
Though dragon-wits there keep eternal guard ;
Hope not unhurt the golden spoil to seize,
The Muses yield, as the Hesperides ;
Who bribes the guardian, all his labour 's
   done,
For every maid is willing to be won.
   Before the lords of verse a suppliant stand,
And beg our passage through the fairy land :
Beg more—to search for sweets each blooming
   field,
And crop the blossoms, woods and valleys
   yield ;

To snatch the tints that beam on Fancy's
   bow ;
And feel the fires on Genius' wings that glow ;
Praise without meanness, without flattery
   stoop,
Soothe without fear, and without trembling
   hope.

TO THE READER

THE following Poem being itself of an
introductory nature, its author supposes it
can require but little preface.

It is published with a view of obtaining
the opinion of the candid and judicious
reader, on the merits of the writer, as a poet ;
very few, he apprehends, being in such cases
sufficiently impartial to decide for themselves.

It is addressed to the Authors of the
Monthly Review, as to critics of acknowledged
merit ; an acquaintance with whose labours
has afforded the writer of the Epistle a reason
for directing it to them in particular, and,
he presumes, will yield to others a just and
sufficient plea for the preference.

Familiar with disappointment, he shall not
be much surprised to find he has mistaken his
talent. However, if not egregiously the dupe
of his vanity, he promises to his readers some
entertainment, and is assured, that however
little in the ensuing Poem is worthy of ap-
plause, there is yet less that merits contempt.

TO THE AUTHORS OF THE
'MONTHLY REVIEW'

THE pious pilot, whom the Gods provide,
Through the rough seas the shatter'd bark to
   guide,
Trusts not alone his knowledge of the deep,
Its rocks that threaten, and its sands that
   sleep ;
But, whilst with nicest skill he steers his way,
The guardian Tritons hear their favourite
   pray.
Hence borne his vows to Neptune's coral
   dome,
The God relents, and shuts each gulfy tomb.
   I dread the storm, that ever rattles here,
Nor think enough, that long my yielding soul
Has felt the Muse's soft, but strong control,

Nor think enough that manly strength and
  ease,
Such as have pleased a friend, will strangers
  please,
But, suppliant, to the critic's throne I bow,
Here burn my incense, and here pay my vow ;
That censure hush'd, may every blast give
  o'er,
And the lash'd coxcomb hiss contempt no
  more.
And ye, whom authors dread or dare in vain,
Affecting modest hopes, or poor disdain,
Receive a bard, who, neither mad nor mean,
Despises each extreme, and sails between ;
Who fears ; but has, amid his fears confess'd,
The conscious virtue of a Muse oppress'd ;
A Muse in changing times and stations nursed,
By nature honour'd, and by fortune cursed.
  No servile strain of abject hope she brings,
Nor soars presumptuous, with unwearied
  wings,
But, pruned for flight—the future all her
  care—
Would know her strength, and, if not strong,
  forbear.
  The supple slave to regal pomp bows down,
Prostrate to power, and cringing to a crown ;
The bolder villain spurns a decent awe,
Tramples on rule, and breaks through every
  law ;
But he whose soul on honest truth relies,
Nor meanly flatters power, nor madly flies.
Thus timid authors bear an abject mind,
And plead for mercy they but seldom find.
Some, as the desperate, to the halter run,
Boldly deride the fate they cannot shun ;
But such there are, whose minds, not taught
  to stoop,
Yet hope for fame, and dare avow their hope,
Who neither brave the judges of their cause,
Nor beg in soothing strains a brief applause.
And such I'd be ;—and ere my fate is past,
Ere clear'd with honour, or with culprits cast,
Humbly at Learning's bar I'll state my case,
And welcome then, distinction or disgrace !
  When in the man the flights of fancy reign,
Rule in the heart, or revel in the brain,
As busy Thought her wild creation apes,
And hangs delighted o'er her varying shapes,
It asks a judgment, weighty and discreet,
To know where wisdom prompts, and where
  conceit ;
Alike their draughts to every scribbler's mind

(Blind to their faults as to their danger
  blind) ;—
We write enraptured, and we write in haste,
Dream idle dreams, and call them things of
  taste,
Improvement trace in every paltry line,
And see, transported, every dull design ;
Are seldom cautious, all advice detest,
And ever think our own opinions best ;
Nor shows my Muse a muse-like spirit here,
Who bids me pause, before I persevere.
  But she—who shrinks while meditating
  flight
In the wide way, whose bounds delude her
  sight,
Yet tired in her own mazes still to roam,
And cull poor banquets for the soul at home,
Would, ere she ventures, ponder on the
  way,   .
Lest dangers yet unthought-of flight betray ;
Lest her Icarian wing, by wits unplumed,
Be robb'd of all the honours she assumed ;
And Dulness swell,—a black and dismal sea,
Gaping her grave ; while censures madden me.
Such was his fate, who flew too near the sun,
Shot far beyond his strength, and was undone;
Such is his fate, who creeping at the shore
The billow sweeps him, and he 's found no
  more.
Oh ! for some God, to bear my fortunes fair
Midway betwixt presumption and despair !
  ' Has then some friendly critic's former
  blow
Taught thee a prudence authors seldom
  know ? '
  Not so ! their anger and their love untried,
A wo-taught prudence deigns to tend my
  side :
Life's hopes ill-sped, the Muse's hopes grow
  poor,
And though they flatter, yet they charm no
  more ;
Experience points where lurking dangers lay,
And as I run, throws caution in my way.
  There was a night, when wintry winds did
  rage,
Hard by a ruin'd pile, I met a sage ;
Resembling him the time-struck place ap-
  pear'd,
Hollow its voice, and moss its spreading
  beard ;
Whose fate-lopp'd brow, the bat's and
  beetle's dome,

Shook, as the hunted owl flew hooting home.
His breast was bronzed by many an eastern
     blast,
And fourscore winters seem'd he to have past,
His thread-bare coat the supple osier bound,
And with slow feet he press'd the sodden
     ground,
Where, as he heard the wild-wing'd Eurus
     blow,
He shook, from locks as white, December's
     snow ;
Inured to storm, his soul ne'er bid it cease,
But lock'd within him meditated peace.
     Father, I said—for silver hairs inspire,
And oft I call the bending peasant Sire—
Tell me, as here beneath this ivy bower,
That works fantastic round its trembling
     tower,
We hear Heaven's guilt-alarming thunders
     roar,
Tell me the pains and pleasures of the poor ;
For Hope, just spent, requires a sad adieu,
And Fear acquaints me I shall live with you.
     There was a time when, by Delusion led,
A scene of sacred bliss around me spread,
On Hope's, as Pisgah's lofty top, I stood,
And saw my Canaan there, my promised good;
A thousand scenes of joy the clime bestow'd,
And wine and oil through vision's valley
     flow'd ;
As Moses his, I call'd my prospect bless'd,
And gazed upon the good I ne'er possess'd :
On this side Jordan doom'd by fate to stand,
Whilst happier Joshuas win the promised land.
' Son,' said the Sage—' be this thy care sup-
     press'd ;
The state the Gods shall choose thee is the
     best :
Rich if thou art, they ask thy praises more,
And would thy patience when they make thee
     poor ;
But other thoughts within thy bosom reign,
And other subjects vex thy busy brain,
Poetic wreaths thy vainer dreams excite,
And thy sad stars have destined thee to write :
Then since that task the ruthless fates decree,
Take a few precepts from the Gods and me !
     ' Be not too eager in the arduous chace ;
Who pants for triumph seldom wins the race :
Venture not all, but wisely hoard thy worth,
And let thy labours one by one go forth :
Some happier scrap capricious wits may find
On a fair day, and be profusely kind ;

Which, buried in the rubbish of a throng,
Had pleased as little as a new-year's song,
Or lover's verse, that cloy'd with nauseous
     sweet,
Or birthday ode, that ran on ill-pair'd feet.
Merit not always—Fortune feeds the bard,
And as the whim inclines bestows reward :
None without wit, nor with it numbers gain;
To please is hard, but none shall please in
     vain :
As a coy mistress is the humour'd town,
Loth every lover with success to crown ;
He who would win must every effort try,
Sail in the mode, and to the fashion fly ;
Must gay or grave to every humour dress,
And watch the lucky Moment of Success ;
That caught, no more his eager hopes are
     crost ;
But vain are Wit and Love, when that is lost.'
     Thus said the God ; for now a God he grew,
His white locks changing to a golden hue,
And from his shoulders hung a mantle azure-
     blue.
His softening eyes the winning charm dis-
     closed
Of dove-like Delia when her doubts reposed ;
Mira's alone a softer lustre bear,
When wo beguiles them of an angel's tear ;
Beauteous and young the smiling phantom
     stood,
Then sought on airy wing his blest abode.
     Ah ! truth, distasteful in poetic theme,
Why is the Muse compell'd to own her dream ?
Whilst forward wits had sworn to every line,
I only wish to make its moral mine.
Say then, O ye who tell how authors speed,
May Hope indulge her flight, and I succeed ?
Say, shall my name, to future song prefix'd,
Be with the meanest of the tuneful mix'd ?
Shall my soft strains the modest maid engage,
My graver numbers move the silver'd sage,
My tender themes delight the lover's heart,
And comfort to the poor my solemn songs
     impart ?
     For Oh ! thou Hope's, thou Thought's
     eternal King,
Who gav'st them power to charm, and me to
     sing—
Chief to thy praise my willing numbers soar,
And in my happier transports I adore ;
Mercy ! thy softest attribute proclaim,
Thyself in abstract, thy more lovely name ;
That flings o'er all my grief a cheering ray,

As the full moon-beam gilds the watery way.
And then too, Love, my soul's resistless lord,
Shall many a gentle, generous strain afford,
To all the soil of sooty passions blind,
Pure as embracing angels, and as kind ;
Our Mira's name in future times shall shine,
And—though the harshest—Shepherds envy
    mine.
    Then ' let me, (pleasing task !) however
    hard,
Join, as of old, the prophet and the bard ;
If not, ah ! shield me from the dire disgrace,
That haunts the wild and visionary race ;
Let me not draw my lengthen'd lines along,
And tire in untamed infamy of song,
Lest, in some dismal Dunciad's future page,
I stand the CIBBER of this tuneless age ;
Lest, if another POPE th' indulgent skies
Should give, inspired by all their deities,
My luckless name, in his immortal strain,
Should, blasted, brand me as a second Cain ;
Doom'd in that song to live against my will,
Whom all must scorn, and yet whom none
    could kill.
    The youth, resisted by the maiden's art,
Persists, and time subdues her kindling heart ;
To strong entreaty yields the widow's vow,
As mighty walls to bold besiegers bow ;
Repeated prayers draw bounty from the sky,
And heaven is won by importunity ;
Ours, a projecting tribe, pursue in vain,
In tedious trials, an uncertain gain ;
Madly plunge on through every hope's defeat,
And with our ruin only, find the cheat.
    And why then seek that luckless doom to
    share ? '
Who, I ?—To shun it is my only care.
    I grant it true, that others better tell
Of mighty WOLFE, who conquer'd as he fell ; [1]
Of heroes born, their threaten'd realms to
    save,
Whom Fame anoints, and Envy tends whose
    grave ;
Of crimson'd fields, where Fate, in dire array,
Gives to the breathless the short-breathing
    clay ;
Ours, a young train, by humbler fountains
    dream,

[1] 'Scriberis Vario fortis, et hostium
    Victor, Maeonii carminis alite,
    Quam rem cumque ferox navibus, aut equis
    Miles, te duce, gesserit,' &c., &c.
                  HOR. Od. Lib. i. 6.

Nor taste presumptuous the Pierian stream ;
When Rodney's triumph comes on eagle-wing,
We hail the victor, whom we fear to sing ;
Nor tell we how each hostile chief goes on,
The luckless Lee, or wary Washington ;
How Spanish bombast blusters—they were
    beat,
And French politeness dulcifies—defeat.
My modest Muse forbears to speak of kings,
Lest fainting stanzas blast the name she sings ;
For who—the tenant of the beechen shade,
Dares the big thought in regal breasts per-
    vade ?
Or search his soul, whom each too-favouring
    God
Gives to delight in plunder, pomp, and blood ?
No ; let me, free from Cupid's frolic round,
Rejoice, or more rejoice by Cupid bound ;
Of laughing girls in smiling couplets tell,
And paint the dark-brow'd grove, where
    wood-nymphs dwell ;
Who bid invading youths their vengeance feel,
And pierce the votive hearts they mean to
    heal.
Such were the themes I knew in school-day
    ease,
When first the moral magic learn'd to please,
Ere Judgment told how transports warm'd
    the breast,
Transported Fancy there her stores imprest ;
The soul in varied raptures learn'd to fly,
Felt all their force, and never question'd
    why ;
No idle doubts could then her peace molest,
She found delight, and left to heaven the rest ;
Soft joys in Evening's placid shades were
    born ;
And where sweet fragrance wing'd the balmy
    morn,
When the wild thought roved vision's circuit
    o'er,
And caught the raptures, caught, alas ! no
    more :
No care did then a dull attention ask,
For study pleased, and that was every task ;
No guilty dreams stalk'd that heaven-favour'd
    round,
Heaven-guarded too, no Envy entrance found ;
Nor numerous wants, that vex advancing age,
Nor Flattery's silver'd tale, nor Sorrow's sage ;
T' o'erwhelm in future days the bleeding heart
No sceptic art veil'd Pride in Truth's disguise,

But prayer unsoil'd of doubt besieged the
skies ;
Ambition, avarice, care to man retired,
Nor came desires more quick, than joys de-
sired.
A summer morn there was, and passing fair,
Still was the breeze, and health perfumed the
air ;
The glowing east in crimson'd splendour shone,
What time the eye just marks the pallid moon,
Vi'let-wing'd Zephyr fann'd each opening
flower,
And brush'd from fragrant cups the limpid
shower ;
A distant huntsman fill'd his cheerful horn,
The vivid dew hung trembling on the thorn,
And mists, like creeping rocks, arose to meet
the morn.
Huge giant shadows spread along the plain,
Or shot from towering rocks o'er half the main,
There to the slumbering bark the gentle tide
Stole soft, and faintly beat against its side ;
Such is that sound, which fond designs convey,
When, true to love, the damsel speeds away ;
The sails unshaken, hung aloft unfurl'd,
And simpering nigh, the languid current
curl'd ;
A crumbling ruin, once a city's pride,
The well-pleased eye through withering oaks
descried,
Where Sadness, gazing on time's ravage,
hung,
And Silence to Destruction's trophy clung—
Save that as morning songsters swell'd their
lays,
Awaken'd Echo humm'd repeated praise :
The lark on quavering pinion woo'd the day,
Less towering linnets fill'd the vocal spray,
And song-invited pilgrims rose to pray.
Here at a pine-prest hill's embroider'd base
I stood, and hail'd the Genius of the place.
Then was it doom'd by fate, my idle heart,
Soften'd by Nature, gave access to Art ;
The Muse approach'd, her syren-song I heard,
Her magic felt, and all her charms revered :
E'er since she rules in absolute control,
And Mira only dearer to my soul.
Ah ! tell me not these empty joys to fly,
If they deceive, I would deluded die ;
To the fond themes my heart so early wed,
So soon in life to blooming visions led,
So prone to run the vague uncertain course,
'Tis more than death to think of a divorce.

What wills the poet of the favouring gods,
Led to their shrine, and blest in their abodes ?[1]
What when he fills the glass, and to each youth
Names his loved maid, and glories in his truth ?
Not India's spoils, the splendid nabob's pride,
Not the full trade of Hermes' own Cheapside,
Nor gold itself, nor all the Ganges laves,
Or shrouds, well shrouded in his sacred waves ;
Nor gorgeous vessels deck'd in trim array,
Which the more noble Thames bears far away;
Let those whose nod makes sooty subjects flee,
Hack with blunt steel the savory callipee ;
Let those whose ill-used wealth their country
fly,
Virtue-scorn'd wines from hostile France to
buy ;
Favour'd by fate, let such in joy appear,
Their smuggled cargoes landed thrice a year ;
Disdaining these, for simpler food I'll look,
And crop my beverage at the mantled brook.
O Virtue ! brighter than the noon-tide ray,
My humble prayers with sacred joys repay!
Health to my limbs may the kind Gods impart,
And thy fair form delight my yielding heart!
Grant me to shun each vile inglorious road,
To see thy way, and trace each moral good :
If more—let Wisdom's sons my page peruse,
And decent credit deck my modest Muse.
Nor deem it pride that prophesies, my song
Shall please the sons of taste, and please them
long.
Say ye ! to whom my Muse submissive brings
Her first-fruit offering, and on trembling wings,
May she not hope in future days to soar,
Where fancy's sons have led the way before ?
Where genius strives in each ambrosial bower
To snatch with agile hand the opening flower ?
To cull what sweets adorn the mountain's
brow,
What humbler blossoms crown the vales be-
low ?
To blend with these the stores by art refined,
And give the moral Flora to the mind ?
Far other scenes my timid hour admits,
Relentless critics, and avenging wits ;
E'en coxcombs take a licence from their pen,
And to each ' let-him-perish ' cry Amen !
And thus, with wits or fools my heart shall cry,
For if they please not, let the trifles die :

[1] Quid dedicatum poscit Apollinem
Vates ? quid orat, de patera novum
Fundens liquorem ? &c., &c.
HOR. *Carm.* Lib. i. xxxi.

Die, and be lost in dark oblivion's shore,
And never rise to vex their author more.
　　I would not dream o'er some soft liquid line,
Amid a thousand blunders form'd to shine ;
Yet rather this, than that dull scribbler be,
From every fault, and every beauty free,
Curst with tame thoughts and mediocrity.
Some have I found so thick beset with spots,
'Twas hard to trace their beauties through
　　　　their blots ;
And these, as tapers round a sick-man's room,
Or passing chimes, but warn'd me of the tomb !
　　O ! if you blast, at once consume my bays,
And damn me not with mutilated praise.

With candour judge ; and, a young bard in
　　　　view,
Allow for that, and judge with kindness too ;
Faults he must own, though hard for him to
　　　　find,
Not to some happier merits quite so blind ;
These if mistaken Fancy only sees,
Or Hope, that takes Deformity for these:
If Dunce, the crowd-befitting title, falls,
His lot, and Dulness her new subject calls,—
To the poor bard alone your censures give—
Let his fame die, but let his honour live ;
Laugh if you must—be candid as you can,
And when you lash the Poet, spare the Man.

DEDICATION AND PREFACE TO THE EDITION OF 1807

TO THE RIGHT HONOURABLE HENRY-RICHARD FOX, LORD HOLLAND,

OF HOLLAND, IN LINCOLNSHIRE; LORD HOLLAND, OF FOXLEY; AND FELLOW OF THE SOCIETY OF ANTIQUARIES.

My Lord,—That the longest poem in this collection was honoured by the notice of your Lordship's right honourable and ever-valued relation, Mr. Fox ; that it should be the last which engaged his attention ; and that some parts of it were marked with his approbation ; are circumstances productive of better hopes of ultimate success than I had dared to entertain before I was gratified with a knowledge of them : and the hope thus raised leads me to ask permission that I may dedicate this book to your Lordship, to whom that truly great and greatly lamented personage was so nearly allied in family, so closely bound in affection, and in whose mind presides the same critical taste which he exerted to the delight of all who heard him. He doubtless united with his unequalled abilities a fund of good-nature ; and this possibly led him to speak favourably of, and give satisfaction to writers, with whose productions he might not be entirely satisfied : nor must I allow myself to suppose his desire of obliging was withholden, when he honoured any effort of mine with his approbation : but, my Lord, as there was discrimination in the opinion he gave; as he did not veil indifference for insipid mediocrity of composition under any general expression of cool approval ; I allow myself to draw a favourable conclusion from the verdict of one who had the superiority of intellect few would dispute, which he made manifest by a force of eloquence peculiar to himself ; whose excellent judgment no one of his friends found cause to distrust, and whose acknowledged candour no enemy had the temerity to deny.

With such encouragement, I present my book to your Lordship : the Account of the *Life and Writings of Lopez de Vega* has taught me what I am to expect ; I there perceive how your Lordship can write, and am there taught how you can judge of writers : my faults, however numerous, I know will none of them escape through inattention, nor will any merit be lost for want of discernment : my verses are before him who has written elegantly, who has judged with accuracy, and who has given unequivocal proof of abilities in a work of difficulty ;—a translation of poetry, which few persons in this kingdom are able to read, and in the estimation of talents not hitherto justly appreciated. In this view, I cannot but feel some apprehension : but I know also, that your Lordship is apprised of the great difficulty of writing well ; that you will make much allowance for failures, if not too frequently repeated ; and, as you can accurately discern, so you will readily approve, all the better and more happy efforts of one, who places the highest value upon your Lordship's approbation, and who has the honour to be,

My Lord,

Your Lordship's most faithful

and obliged humble servant,

GEO. CRABBE.

PREFACE

ABOUT twenty-five years since was published a poem called *The Library* ; which, in no long time, was followed by two others, *The Village*, and *The Newspaper* : these, with a few alterations and additions, are here reprinted ; and are accompanied by a poem of greater length, and several shorter attempts, now, for the first time, before the public ; whose reception of them creates in their author something more than common solicitude, because he conceives that, with the judgment to be formed of these latter productions, upon whatever may be found intrinsically meritorious or defective, there will be united an inquiry into the relative degree of praise or blame which they may be thought to deserve, when compared with the more early attempts of the same writer.

And certainly, were it the principal employment of a man's life to compose verses, it might seem reasonable to expect that he would continue to improve as long as he continued to live ; though, even then, there is some doubt whether such improvement would follow, and perhaps proof might be adduced to show it would not : but when, to this ' idle trade,' is added some ' calling,' with superior claims upon his time and attention, his progress in the art of versification will probably be in proportion neither to the years he has lived, nor even to the attempts he has made.

While composing the first-published of these poems, the author was honoured with the notice and assisted by the advice of the Right Honourable Edmund Burke : part of it was written in his presence, and the whole submitted to his judgment ; receiving, in its progress, the benefit of his correction : I hope, therefore, to obtain pardon of the reader, if I eagerly seize the occasion, and, after so long a silence, endeavour to express a grateful sense of the benefits I have received from this gentleman, who was solicitous for my more essential interests, as well as benevolently anxious for my credit as a writer.

I will not enter upon the subject of his extraordinary abilities ; it would be vanity, it would be weakness in me to believe that I could make them better known or more admired than they now are : but of his private worth, of his wishes to do good, of his affability and condescension ; his readiness to lend assistance when he knew it was wanted, and his delight to give praise where he thought it was deserved ; of these I may write with some propriety. All know that his powers were vast, his acquirements various : and I take leave to add, that he applied them with unremitted attention to those objects which he believed tended to the honour and welfare of his country. But it may not be so generally understood that he was ever assiduous in the more private duties of a benevolent nature, that he delighted to give encouragement to any promise of ability, and assistance to any appearance of desert : to what purposes he employed his pen, and with what eloquence he spake in the senate, will be told by many, who yet may be ignorant of the solid instruction, as well as the fascinating pleasantry, found in his common conversation, amongst his friends, and his affectionate manners, amiable disposition, and zeal for their happiness, which he manifested in the hours of retirement with his family.

To this gentleman I was indebted for my knowledge of Sir Joshua Reynolds, who was as well known to his friends for his perpetual fund of good-humour and his unceasing wishes to oblige, as he was to the public for the extraordinary productions of his pencil and his pen. By him I was favoured with an introduction to Doctor Johnson, who honoured me with his notice, and assisted me, as Mr. Boswell has told, with remarks and emendations for a poem I was about to publish.[1] The doctor had been often wearied by applications, and did not readily comply with requests for his opinion ; not from any unwillingness to oblige, but from a painful

[1] See the *Life of S. Johnson*, by Boswell, vol. iv. p. 185, octavo edition.

intention in his mind, between a desire of giving pleasure and a determination to speak truth. No man can, I think, publish a work without some expectation of satisfying those who are to judge of its merit: but I can, with the utmost regard to veracity, speak my fears, as predominating over every pre-indulged thought of a more favourable nature, when I was told that a judge so discerning had consented to read and give his opinion of *The Village*, the poem I had prepared for publication. The time of suspense was not long protracted; I was soon favoured with a few words from Sir Joshua, who observed,—'If I knew how cautious Doctor Johnson was in giving commendation, I should be well satisfied with the portion dealt to me in his letter.'—Of that letter the following is a copy

' SIR,

' I have sent you back Mr. Crabbe's poem; which I read with great delight. It is original, vigorous, and elegant. The alterations which I have made, I do not require him to adopt; for my lines are, perhaps, not often better [than] his own: but he may take mine and his own together, and perhaps, between them, produce something better than either.—He is not to think his copy wantonly defaced: a wet sponge will wash all the red lines away, and leave the pages clean.—His Dedication [1] will be least liked: it were better to contract it into a short sprightly address.—I do not doubt of Mr. Crabbe's success.

' I am, Sir, your most humble servant,

' SAM: JOHNSON.'

' *March* 4, 1783.'

That I was fully satisfied, my readers will do me the justice to believe; and I hope they will pardon me, if there should appear to them any impropriety in publishing the favourable opinion expressed in a private

letter: they will judge, and truly, that by so doing, I wish to bespeak their good opinion, but have no design of extorting their applause. I would not hazard an appearance so ostentatious to gratify my vanity, but I venture to do it in compliance with my fears.

After these was published *The Newspaper*: it had not the advantage of such previous criticism from any friends, nor perhaps so much of my own attention as I ought to have given to it; but the impression was disposed of, and I will not pay so little respect to the judgment of my readers as now to suppress what they then approved.

Since the publication of this poem more than twenty years have elapsed, and I am not without apprehension, lest so long a silence should be construed into a blamable neglect of my own interest, which those excellent friends were desirous of promoting; or, what is yet worse, into a want of gratitude for their assistance; since it becomes me to suppose, they considered these first attempts as promises of better things, and their favours as stimulants to future exertion. And here, be the construction put upon my apparent negligence what it *may*, let me not suppress my testimony to the liberality of those who are looked up to, as patrons and encouragers of literary merit, or indeed of merit of any kind: their patronage has never been refused, I conceive, when it has been reasonably expected or modestly required; and it would be difficult, probably, to instance, in these times and in this country, any one who merited or was supposed to merit assistance, but who nevertheless languished in obscurity or necessity for want of it; unless in those cases where it was prevented by the resolution of impatient pride, or wearied by the solicitations of determined profligacy. And while the subject is before me, I am unwilling to pass silently over the debt of gratitude which I owe to the memory of two deceased noblemen, His Grace the late Duke of Rutland, and the Right Honourable the Lord Thurlow: sensible of the honour done me by their notice, and the benefits received from them, I trust this acknowledgment will be imputed to its only motive, a grateful sense of their favours.

Upon this subject I could dwell with much pleasure; but, to give a reason for that

---

[1] Neither of these were adopted; the author had written, about that time, some verses to the memory of Lord Robert Manners, brother to the late Duke of Rutland; and these, by a junction, it is presumed, not forced or unnatural, form the concluding part of *The Village*.

appearance of neglect, as it is more difficult, so, happily, it is less required. In truth, I have, for many years, intended a republication of these poems, as soon as I should be able to join with them such other of later date as might not deprive me of the little credit the former had obtained. Long indeed has this purpose been procrastinated : and if the duties of a profession, not before pressing upon me ; if the claims of a situation, at that time untried ; if diffidence of my own judgment, and the loss of my earliest friends, will not sufficiently account for my delay, I must rely upon the good-nature of my reader, that he will let them avail as far as he can, and find an additional apology in my fears of his censure.

These fears being so prevalent with me, I determined not to publish any thing more, unless I could first obtain the sanction of such an opinion as I might with some confidence rely upon. I looked for a friend who, having the discerning taste of Mr. Burke, and the critical sagacity of Doctor Johnson, would bestow upon my MS. the attention requisite to form his opinion, and would then favour me with the result of his observations : and it was my singular good fortune to gain such assistance ; the opinion of a critic so qualified, and a friend so disposed to favour me. I had been honoured by an introduction to the Right Honourable Charles-James Fox some years before, at the seat of Mr. Burke ; and being again with him, I received a promise that he would peruse any work I might send to him previous to its publication, and would give me his opinion ; at that time, I did not think myself sufficiently prepared ; and when, afterwards, I had collected some poems for his inspection, I found my right honourable friend engaged by the affairs of a great empire, and struggling with the inveteracy of a fatal disease ; as such time, upon such mind, ever disposed to oblige as that mind was, I could not obtrude the petty business of criticising verses : but he remembered the promise he had kindly given, and repeated an offer, which, though I had not presumed to expect, I was happy to receive. A copy of the poems, now first published, was immediately sent to him, and (as I have the information from Lord Holland, and his Lordship's permission to inform my readers) the poem which I have named *The Parish Register* was heard by Mr. Fox, and it excited interest enough, by some of its parts, to gain for me the benefit of his judgment upon the whole. Whatever he approved, the reader will readily believe, I have carefully retained ; the parts he disliked are totally expunged, and others are substituted, which I hope resemble those, more conformable to the taste of so admirable a judge. Nor can I deny myself the melancholy satisfaction of adding, that these poems (and more especially the storys of Phœbe Dawson, with some parts of the second book) were the last compositions of their kind that engaged and amused the capacious, the candid, the benevolent mind of this great man.

The above information I owe to the favour of the Right Honourable Lord Holland ; nor this only, but to his Lordship I am indebted for some excellent remarks upon the other parts of my MS. It was not indeed my good fortune then to know that my verses were in the hands of a nobleman who had given proof of his accurate judgment as a critic, and his elegance as a writer, by favouring the public with an easy and spirited translation of some interesting scenes of a dramatic poet, not often read in thi kingdom. The *Life of Lopez de Vega* was then unknown to me ; I had, in common with many English readers, heard of him, but could not judge whether his far-extended reputation was caused by the sublime efforts of a mighty genius, or the unequalled facility of a rapid composer, aided by peculiar and fortunate circumstances. That any part of my MS. was honoured by the remarks of Lord Holland yields me a high degree of satisfaction, and his Lordship will perceive the use I have made of them ; but I must feel some regret when I know to what small portion they were limited ; and discerning, as I do, the taste and judgment bestowed upon the verses of Lopez de Vega, I must perceive how much my own needed the assistance afforded to one, who cannot be sensible of the benefit he has received.

But how much soever I may lament the advantages lost, let me remember with gratitude the helps I have obtained. With a single exception, every poem in the ensuing collection has been submitted to the critical sagacity of a gentleman, upon whose skill and candour their author could rely. To publish by advice of friends has been severely ridiculed, and that too by a poet, who probably, without such advice, never made public any verses of his own : in fact, it may not be easily determined who acts with less discretion, the writer who is encouraged to publish his works, merely by the advice of friends whom he consulted, or he who, against advice, publishes from the sole encouragement of his own opinion. These are deceptions to be carefully avoided, and I was happy to escape the latter, by the friendly attentions of the Reverend Richard Turner, minister of Great Yarmouth. To this gentleman I am indebted more than I am able to describe, or than he is willing to allow, for the time he has bestowed upon the attempts I have made. He is, indeed, the kind of critic for whom every poet should devoutly wish, and the friend whom every man would be happy to acquire ; he has taste to discern all that is meritorious, and sagacity to detect whatsoever should be discarded ; he gives just the opinion an author's wisdom should covet, however his vanity might prompt him to reject it ; what altogether to expunge and what to improve he has repeatedly taught me, and, could I have obeyed him in the latter direction, as I invariably have in the former, the public would have found this collection more worthy its attention, and I should have sought the opinion of the critic more void of apprehension.

But whatever I may hope or fear, whatever assistance I have had or have needed, it becomes me to leave my verses to the judgment of the reader, without my endeavour to point out their merit, or an apology for their defects : yet as, among the poetical attempts of one who has been for many years a priest, it may seem a want of respect for the legitimate objects of his study, that nothing occurs, unless it be incidentally, of the great subjects of religion ; so it may appear a kind of ingratitude of a beneficed clergyman, that he has not employed his talent (be it estimated as it may) to some patriotic purpose ; as in celebrating the unsubdued spirit of his countrymen in their glorious resistance of those enemies, who would have no peace throughout the world,

except that which is dictated to the drooping spirit of suffering humanity by the triumphant insolence of military success.

Credit will be given to me, I hope, when I affirm that subjects so interesting have the due weight with me, which the sacred nature of the one, and the national importance of the other, must impress upon every mind not seduced into carelessness for religion by the lethargic influence of a perverted philosophy, nor into indifference for the cause of our country by hyperbolical or hypocritical professions of universal philanthropy : but, after many efforts to satisfy myself by various trials on these subjects, I declined all further attempt, from a conviction that I should not be able to give satisfaction to my readers. Poetry of religious nature must indeed ever be clogged with almost insuperable difficulty : but there are doubtless to be found poets who are well qualified to celebrate the unanimous and heroic spirit of our countrymen, and to describe in appropriate colours some of those extraordinary scenes, which have been and are shifting in the face of Europe, with such dreadful celerity ; and to such I relinquish the duty.

It remains for me to give the reader a brief view of those articles in the following collection, which for the first time solicit his attention.

In the *Parish Register*, he will find an endeavour once more to describe village-manners, not by adopting the notion of pastoral simplicity or assuming ideas of rustic barbarity, but by more natural views of the peasantry, considered as a mixed body of persons, sober or profligate, and hence, in a great measure, contented or miserable. To this more general description are added the various characters which occur in the three parts of a Register; Baptisms, Marriages, and Burials.

If the *Birth of Flattery* offer no moral, as an appendage to the fable, it is hoped that nothing of an immoral, nothing of improper tendency will be imputed to a piece of poetical playfulness ; in fact, genuine praise, like all other species of truth, is known by its bearing full investigation : it is what the giver is happy that he can justly bestow, and the receiver conscious that he may boldly accept ; but adulation must ever be afraid of inquiry, and must, in proportion to their degrees of moral sensibility,

Be shame ' to him that gives and him that takes.'

The verses in page 87 want a title; nor does the motto, although it gave occasion to them, altogether express the sense of the writer, who meant to observe that some of our best acquisitions, and some of our nobler conquests, are rendered ineffectual, by the passing away of opportunity, and the changes made by time; an argument that such acquirements and moral habits are reserved for a state of being in which they have the uses here denied them.

In the story of *Sir Eustace Grey*, an attempt is made to describe the wanderings of a mind first irritated by the consequences of error and misfortune, and afterwards soothed by a species of enthusiastic conversion, still keeping him insane; a task very difficult and, if the presumption of the attempt may find pardon, it will not be refused to the failure of the poet. It is said of our Shakspeare, respecting madness,

' In that circle none dare walk but he : '—

yet be it granted to one, who dares not to pass the boundary fixed for common minds, at least to step near to the tremendous verge, and form some idea of the terrors that are stalking in the interdicted space.

When first I had written *Aaron, or The Gipsy*, I had no unfavourable opinion of it; and had I been collecting my verses at that time for publication, I should certainly have included this tale. Nine years have since elapsed, and I continue to judge the same of it, thus literally obeying one of the directions given by the prudence of criticism to the eagerness of the poet: but how far I may have conformed to rules of more importance must be left to the less partial judgment of the readers.

The concluding poem, entitled *Woman!* was written at the time when the quotation from Mr. Ledyard was first made public; the expression has since become hackneyed; but the sentiment is congenial with our feelings, and though somewhat amplified in these verses, it is hoped they are not so far extended as to become tedious.

After this brief account of his subjects, the author leaves them to their fate, not presuming to make any remarks upon the kinds of versification he has chosen, or the merit of the execution : he has indeed brought forward the favourable opinion of his friends, and for that he earnestly hopes his motives will be rightly understood ; it was a step of which he felt the advantage while he foresaw the danger : he was aware of the benefit, if his readers would consider him as one who puts on a defensive armour against hasty and determined severity ; but he feels also the hazard, lest they should suppose he looks upon himself to be guarded by his friends, and so secure in the defence, that he may defy the fair judgment of legal criticism. It will probably be said, ' he has brought with him his testimonials to the bar of the public ; ' and he must admit the truth of the remark : but he begs leave to observe in reply, that, of those who bear testimonials of any kind, the greater numbers feel apprehension, and not security ; they are indeed so far from the enjoyment of victory, of the exultation of triumph, that with all they can do for themselves, with all their friends have done for them, they are, like him, in dread of examination, and in fear of disappointment.

Muston, Leicestershire,
September, 1807.

THE LIBRARY

[1781]

Books afford Consolation to the troubled Mind, by substituting a lighter Kind of Distress for its own—They are productive of other Advantages:—An Author's Hope of being known in distant Times—Arrangement of the Library—Size and Form of the Volumes—The ancient Folio, clasped and chained—Fashion prevalent even in this Place—The Mode of publishing in Numbers, Pamphlets, &c.—Subjects of the different Classes—Divinity—Controversy—The Friends of Religion often more dangerous than her Foes—Sceptical Authors—Reason too much rejected by the former Converts; exclusively relied upon by the latter—Philosophy ascending through the Scale of Being to moral Subjects—Books of Medicine: their Variety, Variance, and Proneness to System: the Evil of this and the Difficulty it causes—Farewell to this Study —Law: the increasing Number of its Volumes—Supposed happy State of Man without Laws—Progress of Society—Historians: their Subjects — Dramatic Authors, Tragic and Comic—Ancient Romances—The Captive Heroine—Happiness in the Perusal of such Books: why—Criticism—Apprehensions of the Author removed by the Appearance of the Genius of the Place; whose Reasoning and Admonition conclude the Subject.

When the sad soul, by care and grief oppress'd,
Looks round the world, but looks in vain for rest;
When every object that appears in view,
Partakes her gloom and seems dejected too;
Where shall affliction from itself retire?
Where fade away and placidly expire?
Alas! we fly to silent scenes in vain;
Care blasts the honours of the flow'ry plain:
Care veils in clouds the sun's meridian beam,
Sighs through the grove and murmurs in the stream;

For when the soul is labouring in despair,
In vain the body breathes a purer air:
No storm-toss'd sailor sighs for slumbering seas,—
He dreads the tempest, but invokes the breeze;
On the smooth mirror of the deep resides
Reflected wo, and o'er unruffled tides
The ghost of every former danger glides.
Thus, in the calms of life, we only see
A steadier image of our misery;
But lively gales and gently-clouded skies
Disperse the sad reflections as they rise;
And busy thoughts and little cares avail
To ease the mind, when rest and reason fail.
When the dull thought, by no designs employ'd,
Dwells on the past, or suffer'd or enjoy'd,
We bleed anew in every former grief,
And joys departed furnish no relief.

Not Hope herself, with all her flattering art,
Can cure this stubborn sickness of the heart:
The soul disdains each comfort she prepares,
And anxious searches for congenial cares;
Those lenient cares, which, with our own combined,
By mix'd sensations ease th' afflicted mind,
And steal our grief away and leave their own behind;
A lighter grief! which feeling hearts endure
Without regret, nor e'en demand a cure.

But what strange art, what magic can dispose
The troubled mind to change its native woes?
Or lead us willing from ourselves, to see
Others more wretched, more undone than we?
This, books can do;—nor this alone; they give
New views to life, and teach us how to live;
They soothe the grieved, the stubborn they chastise,
Fools they admonish, and confirm the wise:

Their aid they yield to all : they never shun
The man of sorrow, nor the wretch undone :
Unlike the hard, the selfish, and the proud,
They fly not sullen from the suppliant crowd ;
Nor tell to various people various things,
But show to subjects, what they show to
    kings.
  Come, Child of Care! to make thy soul
    serene,
Approach the treasures of this tranquil scene ;
Survey the dome, and, as the doors unfold,
The soul's best cure, in all her cares, behold !
Where mental wealth the poor in thought may
    find,
And mental physic the diseased in mind ;
See here the balms that passion's wounds as-
    suage ;
See coolers here, that damp the fire of rage ;
Here alt'ratives, by slow degrees control
The chronic habits of the sickly soul ;
And round the heart and o'er the aching head,
Mild opiates here their sober influence shed.
Now bid thy soul man's busy scenes exclude,
And view composed this silent multitude :—
Silent they are, but, though deprived of sound,
Here all the living languages abound ;
Here all that live no more ; preserved they lie,
In tombs that open to the curious eye.
  Bless'd be the gracious Power, who taught
    mankind
To stamp a lasting image of the mind !—
Beasts may convey,and tuneful birds may sing,
Their mutual feelings, in the opening spring ;
But man alone has skill and power to send
The heart's warm dictates to the distant
    friend :
'Tis his alone to please, instruct, advise
Ages remote, and nations yet to rise.
  In sweet repose, when labour's children
    sleep,
When joy forgets to smile and care to weep,
When passion slumbers in the lover's breast,
And fear and guilt partake the balm of rest,
Why then denies the studious man to share
Man's common good, who feels his common
    care ?
  Because the hope is his, that bids him fly
Night's soft repose, and sleep's mild power
    defy ;
That after-ages may repeat his praise,
And fame's fair meed be his, for length of days.
Delightful prospect ! when we leave behind
A worthy offspring of the fruitful mind !

Which, born and nursed through many an
    anxious day,
Shall all our labour, all our care repay.
  Yet all are not these births of noble kind,
Not all the children of a vigorous mind ;
But where the wisest should alone preside,
The weak would rule us, and the blind would
    guide ;
Nay, man's best efforts taste of man, and show
The poor and troubled source from which they
    flow :
Where most he triumphs, we his wants per-
    ceive,
And for his weakness in his wisdom grieve.
  But though imperfect all ; yet wisdom loves
This seat serene, and virtue's self approves :—
Here come the grieved, a change of thought to
    find ;
The curious here, to feed a craving mind ;
Here the devout their peaceful temple choose ;
And here the poet meets his favouring muse.
  With awe, around these silent walks I tread;
These are the lasting mansions of the dead :—
' The dead,' methinks a thousand tongues
    reply ;
' These are the tombs of such as cannot die !
Crown'd with eternal fame, they sit sublime,
And laugh at all the little strife of time.'
  Hail, then, immortals ! ye who shine above,
Each, in his sphere, the literary Jove ;
And ye the common people of these skies,
A humbler crowd of nameless deities ;
Whether 'tis yours to lead the willing mind
Through history's mazes, and the turnings
    find ;
Or whether, led by science, ye retire,
Lost and bewilder'd in the vast desire ;
Whether the Muse invites you to her bowers,
And crowns your placid brows with living
    flowers ;
Or godlike wisdom teaches you to show
The noblest road to happiness below ;
Or men and manners prompt the easy page
To mark the flying follies of the age :
Whatever good ye boast, that good impart ;
Inform the head and rectify the heart.
  Lo ! all in silence, all in order stand
And mighty folios first, a lordly band ;
Then quartos their well-order'd ranks main-
    tain,
And light octavos fill a spacious plain :
See yonder, ranged in more frequented rows,
A humbler band of duodecimos ;

While undistinguish'd trifles swell the scene,
The last new play and fritter'd magazine.
Thus 'tis in life, where first the proud, the
    great,
In leagued assembly keep their cumbrous
    state ;
Heavy and huge, they fill the world with
    dread,
Are much admired, and are but little read :
The commons next, a middle rank, are found ;
Professions fruitful pour their offspring round:
Reasoners and wits are next their place allow'd,
And last, of vulgar tribes a countless crowd.

First, let us view the form, the size, the
    dress ;
For these the manners, nay the mind express ;
That weight of wood, with leathern coat o'er-
    laid ;
Those ample clasps, of solid metal made ;
The close-press'd leaves, unclosed for many
    an age ;
The dull red edging of the well-fill'd page ;
On the broad back the stubborn ridges roll'd,
Where yet the title stands in tarnish'd gold ;
These all a sage and labour'd work proclaim,
A painful candidate for lasting fame :
No idle wit, no trifling verse can lurk
In the deep bosom of that weighty work ;
No playful thoughts degrade the solemn style,
Nor one light sentence claims a transient
    smile.

Hence, in these times, untouch'd the pages
    lie,
And slumber out their immortality :
They *had* their day, when, after all his toil,
His morning study, and his midnight oil,
At length an author's ONE great work ap-
    pear'd,
By patient hope, and length of days, en-
    dear'd :
Expecting nations hail'd it from the press ;
Poetic friends prefix'd each kind address ;
Princes and kings received the pond'rous
    gift,
And ladies read the work they could not lift.
Fashion, though Folly's child, and guide of
    fools,
Rules e'en the wisest, and in learning rules ;
From crowds and courts to Wisdom's seat she
    goes,
And reigns triumphant o'er her mother's foes.

For lo ! these fav'rites of the ancient mode
Lie all neglected like the Birth-day Ode ;

Ah ! needless now this 'veight of massy
    chain [1] ;
Safe in themselves, the once-loved works
    remain ;
No readers now invade their still retreat,
None try to steal them from their parent-
    seat ;
Like ancient beauties, they may now discard
Chains, bolts, and locks, and lie without a
    guard.
Our patient fathers trifling themes laid by,
And roll'd o'er labour'd works th' attentive
    eye ;
Page after page, the much-enduring men
Explored, the deeps and shallows of the pen ;
Till, every former note and comment known,
They mark'd the spacious margin with their
    own :
Minute corrections proved their studious care,
The little index, pointing, told us where ;
And many an emendation show'd the age
Look'd far beyond the rubric title-page.

Our nicer palates lighter labours seek,
Cloy'd with a folio-*Number* once a week ;
Bibles, with cuts and comments, thus go down:
E'en light Voltaire is *number'd* through the
    town :
Thus physic flies abroad, and thus the law,
From men of study, and from men of straw ;
Abstracts, abridgments, please the fickle
    times,
Pamphlets and plays, and politics and
    rhymes :
But though to write be now a task of ease,
The task is hard by manly arts to please,
When all our weakness is exposed to view,
And half our judges are our rivals too.

Amid these works, on which the eager eye
Delights to fix, or glides reluctant by,
When all combined, their decent pomp dis-
    play,
Where shall we first our early offering pay ?—

To thee, DIVINITY ! to thee, the light
And guide of mortals, through their mental
    night ;
By whom we learn our hopes and fears to
    guide ;
To bear with pain, and to contend with pride ;

[1] In the more ancient libraries, works of value
and importance were fastened to their places by
a length of chain ; and might so be perused, but
not taken away.

When grieved, to pray ; when injured, to for-
    give ;
And with the world in charity to live.
    Not truths like these inspired that numerous
    race,
Whose pious labours fill this ample space ;
But questions nice, where doubt on doubt
    arose,
Awaked to war the long-contending foes.
For dubious meanings, learn'd polemics
    strove,
And wars on faith prevented works of love ;
The brands of discord far around were
    hurl'd,
And holy wrath inflamed a sinful world :—
Dull though impatient, peevish though de-
    vout,
With wit disgusting and despised without ;
Saints in design, in execution men,
Peace in their looks, and vengeance in their
    pen.
    Methinks I see, and sicken at the sight,
Spirits of spleen from yonder pile alight ;
Spirits who prompted every damning page,
With pontiff pride and still-increasing rage :
Lo ! how they stretch their gloomy wings
    around,
And lash with furious strokes the trembling
    ground !
They pray, they fight, they murder, and they
    weep,—
Wolves in their vengeance, in their manners
    sheep ;
Too well they act the prophet's fatal part,
Denouncing evil with a zealous heart ;
And each, like Jonas, is displeased if God
Repent his anger, or withhold his rod.
    But here the dormant fury rests unsought,
And Zeal sleeps soundly by the foes she
    fought ;
Here all the rage of controversy ends,
And rival zealots rest like bosom-friends :
An Athanasian here, in deep repose,
Sleeps with the fiercest of his Arian foes ;
Socinians here with Calvinists abide,
And thin partitions angry chiefs divide ;
Here wily Jesuits simple Quakers meet,
And Bellarmine has rest at Luther's feet.
Great authors, for the church's glory fired,
Are, for the church's peace, to rest retired ;
And close beside, a mystic, maudlin race,
Lie, ' Crums of Comfort for the Babes of
    Grace.'

Against her foes Religion well defends
Her sacred truths, but often fears her friends ;
If learn'd, their pride, if weak, their zeal she
    dreads,
And their hearts' weakness, who have soundest
    heads :
But most she fears the controversial pen,
The holy strife of disputatious men ;
Who the bless'd Gospel's peaceful page explore,
Only to fight against its precepts more.
    Near to these seats, behold yon slender
    frames,
All closely fill'd and mark'd with modern
    names ;
Where no fair science ever shows her face,
Few sparks of genius, and no spark of grace ;
There sceptics rest, a still-increasing throng,
And stretch their widening wings ten thousand
    strong :
Some in close fight their dubious claims main-
    tain ;
Some skirmish lightly, fly and fight again ;
Coldly profane, and impiously gay,
Their end the same, though various in their
    way.
    When first Religion came to bless the land,
Her friends were then a firm believing band ;
To doubt was, then, to plunge in guilt ex-
    treme,
And all was gospel that a monk could dream ;
Insulted Reason fled the grov'ling soul,
For Fear to guide, and visions to control :
But now, when Reason has assumed her
    throne,
She, in her turn, demands to reign alone ;
Rejecting all that lies beyond her view,
And, being judge, will be a witness too :
Insulted Faith then leaves the doubtful mind,
To seek for truth, without a power to find :
Ah ! when will both in friendly beams unite,
And pour on erring man resistless light ?

    Next to the seats, well stored with works
    divine,
An ample space, PHILOSOPHY ! is thine ;
Our reason's guide, by whose assisting ligh
We trace the moral bounds of wrong and
    right ;
Our guide through nature, from the sterile clay,
To the bright orbs of yon celestial way !
'Tis thine, the great, the golden chain to trace,
Which runs through all, connecting race with
    race ;

Save where those puzzling, stubborn links re-
main,
Which thy inferior light pursues in vain :—
　How vice and virtue in the soul contend ;
How widely differ, yet how nearly blend !
What various passions war on either part,
And now confirm, now melt the yielding
　heart :
How Fancy loves around the world to stray,
While Judgment slowly picks his sober
　way ;
The stores of memory, and the flights sub-
lime
Of genius, bound by neither space nor
　time ;—
All these divine Philosophy explores,
Till, lost in awe, she wonders and adores.
From these, descending to the earth, she turns,
And matter, in its various form, discerns ;
She parts the beamy light with skill profound,
Metes the thin air, and weighs the flying
　sound ;
'Tis hers, the lightning from the clouds to call,
And teach the fiery mischief where to fall.
　Yet more her volumes teach,—on these we
look
As abstracts drawn from Nature's larger book:
Here, first described, the torpid earth appears,
And next, the vegetable robe it wears ;
Where flow'ry tribes, in valleys, fields and
　groves,
Nurse the still flame, and feed the silent loves ;
Loves, where no grief, nor joy, nor bliss, nor
　pain,
Warm the glad heart or vex the labouring
　brain ;
But as the green blood moves along the blade,
The bed of Flora on the branch is made ;
Where, without passion, love instinctive lives,
And gives new life, unconscious that it gives.
Advancing still in Nature's maze, we trace,
In dens and burning plains, her savage race ;
With those tame tribes who on their lord
　attend,
And find, in man, a master and a friend :
Man crowns the scene, a world of wonders new,
A moral world, that well demands our view.
　This world is here ; for, of more lofty kind,
These neighbouring volumes reason on the
　mind ;
They paint the state of man ere yet endued
With knowledge ;—man, poor, ignorant, and
　rude ;

Then, as his state improves, their pages swell,
And all its cares, and all its comforts, tell :
Here we behold how inexperience buys,
At little price, the wisdom of the wise ;
Without the troubles of an active state,
Without the cares and dangers of the great,
Without the miseries of the poor, we know
What wisdom, wealth, and poverty bestow ;
We see how reason calms the raging mind,
And how contending passions urge mankind :
Some, won by virtue, glow with sacred fire ;
Some, lured by vice, indulge the low desire ;
Whilst others, won by either, now pursue
The guilty chase, now keep the good in view ;
For ever wretched, with themselves at strife,
They lead a puzzled, vex'd, uncertain life ;
For transient vice bequeaths a lingering pain
Which transient virtue seeks to cure in vain.

　Whilst thus engaged, high views enlarge the
　soul,
New interests draw, new principles control :
Nor thus the soul alone resigns her grief,
But here the tortured body finds relief ;
For see where yonder sage Arachnè shapes
Her subtile gin, that not a fly escapes !
There Physic fills the space, and far around,
Pile above pile, her learned works abound :
Glorious their aim—to ease the labouring
　heart ;
To war with death, and stop his flying
　dart ;
To trace the source whence the fierce contest
　grew,
And life's short lease on easier terms renew ;
To calm the frenzy of the burning brain ;
To heal the tortures of imploring pain ;
Or, when more powerful ills all efforts brave,
To ease the victim no device can save,
And smooth the stormy passage to the grave.
　But man, who knows no good unmix'd and
　pure,
Oft finds a poison where he sought a cure ;
For grave deceivers lodge their labours here,
And cloud the science they pretend to clear :
Scourges for sin, the solemn tribe are sent ;
Like fire and storms, they call us to repent ;
But storms subside, and fires forget to rage,
These are eternal scourges of the age :
'Tis not enough that each terrific hand
Spreads desolation round a guilty land ;
But, train'd to ill, and harden'd by its crimes,
Their pen relentless kills through future times.

Say ye, who search these records of the
    dead,
Who read huge works, to boast what ye have
    read ;
Can all the real knowledge ye possess,
Or those (if such there are) who more than
    guess,
Atone for each impostor's wild mistakes,
And mend the blunders pride or folly makes ?
    What thought so wild, what airy dream so
        light,
That will not prompt a theorist to write ?
What art so prevalent, what proof so strong,
That will convince him his attempt is wrong ?
One in the solids finds each lurking ill,
Nor grants the passive fluids power to kill ;
A learned friend some subtler reason brings,
Absolves the channels, but condemns their
    springs ;
The subtile nerves, that shun the doctor's eye,
Escape no more his subtler theory ;
The vital heat, that warms the labouring
    heart,
Lends a fair system to these sons of art ;
The vital air, a pure and subtile stream,
Serves a foundation for an airy scheme,
Assists the doctor, and supports his dream.
Some have their favourite ills, and each
    disease
Is but a younger branch that kills from these :
One to the gout contracts all human pain,
He views it raging in the frantic brain ;
Finds it in fevers all his efforts mar,
And sees it lurking in the cold catarrh :
Bilious by some, by others nervous seen,
Rage the fantastic demons of the spleen ;
And every symptom of the strange disease
With every system of the sage agrees.
    Ye frigid tribe, on whom I wasted long
The tedious hours, and ne'er indulged in song ;
Ye first seducers of my easy heart,
Who promised knowledge ye could not im-
    part ;
Ye dull deluders, truth's destructive foes ;
Ye sons of fiction, clad in stupid prose ;
Ye treacherous leaders, who, yourselves in
    doubt,
Light up false fires, and send us far about ;—
Still may yon spider round your pages spin,
Subtile and slow, her emblematic gin !
Buried in dust and lost in silence, dwell,
Most potent, grave, and reverend friends—
    farewell !

Near these, and where the setting sun dis-
    plays,
Through the dim window, his departing rays,
And gilds yon columns, there, on either side,
The huge abridgments of the LAW abide ;
Fruitful as vice the dread correctors stand,
And spread their guardian terrors round the
    land ;
Yet, as the best that human care can do,
Is mix'd with error, oft with evil too,
Skill'd in deceit, and practised to evade,
Knaves stand secure, for whom these laws
    were made ;
And justice vainly each expedient tries,
While art eludes it, or while power defies.
' Ah ! happy age,' the youthful poet sings,
    When the free nations knew not laws nor
        kings ;
When all were bless'd to share a common
    store,
And none were proud of wealth, for none were
    poor ;
No wars nor tumults vex'd each still domain,
No thirst for empire, no desire of gain ;
No proud great man, nor one who would be
    great,
Drove modest merit from its proper state ;
Nor into distant climes would avarice roam,
To fetch delights for luxury at home :
Bound by no ties which kept the soul in
    awe,
They dwelt at liberty, and love was law ! '
    ' Mistaken youth ! each nation first was
        rude,
Each man a cheerless son of solitude,
To whom no joys of social life were known,
None felt a care that was not all his own ;
Or in some languid clime his abject soul
Bow'd to a little tyrant's stern control ;
A slave, with slaves his monarch's throne he
    raised,
And in rude song his ruder idol praised ;
The meaner cares of life were all he knew ;
Bounded his pleasures, and his wishes few :
But when by slow degrees the Arts arose,
And Science waken'd from her long repose ;
When Commerce, rising from the bed of ease,
Ran round the land, and pointed to the seas ;
When Emulation, born with jealous eye,
And Avarice, lent their spurs to industry ;
Then one by one the numerous laws were
    made,
Those to control, and these to succour trade ;

To curb the insolence of rude command,
To snatch the victim from the usurer's hand ;
To awe the bold, to yield the wrong'd redress,
And feed the poor with Luxury's excess.'
  Like some vast flood, unbounded, fierce,
      and strong,
His nature leads ungovern'd man along ;
Like mighty bulwarks made to stem that tide,
The laws are form'd and placed on ev'ry side :
Whene'er it breaks the bounds by these de-
      creed,
New statutes rise, and stronger laws succeed ;
More and more gentle grows the dying stream,
More and more strong the rising bulwarks
      seem ;
Till, like a miner working sure and slow,
Luxury creeps on, and ruins all below ;
The basis sinks, the ample piles decay ;
The stately fabric shakes and falls away ;
Primeval want and ignorance come on,
But freedom, that exalts the savage state, is
      gone.

  Next, HISTORY ranks ;—there full in front
      she lies,
And every nation her dread tale supplies ;
Yet History has her doubts, and every age
With sceptic queries marks the passing page ;
Records of old nor later date are clear,
Too distant those, and these are placed too
      near ;
There time conceals the objects from our view,
Here our own passions and a writer's too :
Yet, in these volumes, see how states arose !
Guarded by virtue from surrounding foes ;
Their virtue lost, and of their triumphs vain,
Lo ! how they sunk to slavery again !
Satiate with power, of fame and wealth
      possess'd,
A nation grows too glorious to be bless'd ;
Conspicuous made, she stands the mark of all,
And foes join foes to triumph in her fall.
  Thus speaks the page that paints ambition's
      race,
The monarch's pride, his glory, his disgrace ;
The headlong course, that madd'ning heroes
      run,
How soon triumphant, and how soon undone ;
How slaves, turn'd tyrants, offer crowns to sale,
And each fall'n nation's melancholy tale.

  Lo ! where of late the Book of Martyrs
      stood,
Old pious tracts, and Bibles bound in wood ;

There, such the taste of our degenerate age,
Stand the profane delusions of the STAGE :
Yet virtue owns the TRAGIC MUSE a friend,
Fable her means, morality her end ;
For this she rules all passions in their turns;
And now the bosom bleeds, and now it burns,
Pity with weeping eye surveys her bowl,
Her anger swells, her terror chills the soul ;
She makes the vile to virtue yield applause,
And own her sceptre while they break her laws;
For vice in others is abhorr'd of all,
And villains triumph when the worthless fall.

  Not thus her sister COMEDY prevails,
Who shoots at folly, for her arrow fails ;
Folly, by dulness arm'd, eludes the wound,
And harmless sees the feather'd shafts re-
      bound ;
Unhurt she stands, applauds the archer's skill,
Laughs at her malice, and is folly still.
Yet well the Muse portrays in fancied scenes,
What pride will stoop to, what profession
      means ;
How formal fools the farce of state applaud,
How caution watches at the lips of fraud ;
The wordy variance of domestic life ;
The tyrant husband, the retorting wife ;
The snares for innocence, the lie of trade,
And the smooth tongue's habitual masquerade.
  With her the virtues too obtain a place,
Each gentle passion, each becoming grace ;
The social joy in life's securer road,
Its easy pleasure, its substantial good ;
The happy thought that conscious virtue
      gives,
And all that ought to live, and all that lives.

  But who are these ? Methinks a noble
      mien
And awful grandeur in their form are seen,
Now in disgrace : what though by time is
      spread
Polluting dust o'er every reverend head ;
What though beneath yon gilded tribe they
      lie,
And dull observers pass insulting by :
Forbid it shame, forbid it decent awe,
What seems so grave, should no attention
      draw !
Come, let us then with reverend step advance,
And greet—the ancient worthies of ROMANCE.

  Hence, ye profane ! I feel a former dread,
A thousand visions float around my head :

Hark! hollow blasts through empty courts
    resound,
And shadowy forms with staring eyes stalk
    round ;
See! moats and bridges, walls and castles rise,
Ghosts, fairies, demons, dance before our eyes;
Lo ! magic verse inscribed on golden gate,
And bloody hand that beckons on to fate :—
' And who art thou, thou little page, unfold ?
Say, doth thy lord my Claribel withhold ?
Go tell him straight, Sir Knight, thou must
    resign
The captive queen ;—for Claribel is mine.'
Away he flies ; and now for bloody deeds,
Black suits of armour, masks, and foaming
    steeds ;
The giant falls ; his recreant throat I seize,
And from his corslet take the massy keys :—
Dukes, lords, and knights in long procession
    move,
Released from bondage with my virgin love:—
She comes ! she comes ! in all the charms of
    youth,
Unequall'd love and unsuspected truth!

Ah ! happy he who thus, in magic themes,
O'er worlds bewitch'd, in early rapture dreams,
Where wild Enchantment waves her potent
    wand,
And Fancy's beauties fill her fairy land ;
Where doubtful objects strange desires excite,
And Fear and Ignorance afford delight.

But lost, for ever lost, to me these joys,
Which Reason scatters, and which Time de-
    stroys ;
Too dearly bought : maturer judgment calls
My busied mind from tales and madrigals ;
My doughty giants all are slain or fled,
And all my knights, blue, green, and yellow,
    dead !
No more the midnight fairy tribe I view,
All in the merry moonshine tippling dew ;
E'en the last lingering fiction of the brain,
The church-yard ghost, is now at rest again ;
And all these wayward wanderings of my
    youth
Fly Reason's power and shun the light of
    truth.

With fiction then does real joy reside,
And is our reason the delusive guide ?
Is it then right to dream the syrens sing ?
Or mount enraptured on the dragon's wing ?
No, 'tis the infant mind, to care unknown,
That makes th' imagined paradise its own ;

Soon as reflections in the bosom rise,
Light slumbers vanish from the clouded eyes :
The tear and smile, that once together rose,
Are then divorced; the head and heart are foes:
Enchantment bows to Wisdom's serious plan,
And Pain and Prudence make and mar the
    man.

While thus, of power and fancied empire vain,
With various thoughts my mind I entertain ;
While books my slaves, with tyrant hand I
    seize,
Pleased with the pride that will not let them
    please ;
Sudden I find terrific thoughts arise,
And sympathetic sorrow fills my eyes ;
For, lo! while yet my heart admits the wound,
I see the CRITIC army ranged around.

Foes to our race ! if ever ye have known
A father's fears for offspring of your own ;—
If ever, smiling o'er a lucky line,
Ye thought the sudden sentiment divine,
Then paused and doubted, and then, tired of
    doubt,
With rage as sudden dash'd the stanza out ;—
If, after fearing much and pausing long,
Ye ventured on the world your labour'd song,
And from the crusty critics of those days
Implored the feeble tribute of their praise ;
Remember now the fears that moved you then,
And, spite of truth, let mercy guide your pen.

What vent'rous race are ours! what mighty
    foes
Lie waiting all around them to oppose
What treacherous friends betray them to the
    fight !
What dangers threaten them !—yet still they
    write :
A hapless tribe ! to every evil born,
Whom villains hate, and fools affect to scorn :
Strangers they come, amid a world of wo,
And taste the largest portion ere they go.

Pensive I spoke, and cast mine eyes around;
The roof, methought, return'd a solemn
    sound ;
Each column seem'd to shake, and clouds,
    like smoke,
From dusty piles and ancient volumes broke ;
Gathering above, like mists condensed they
    seem,
Exhaled in summer from the rushy stream ;
Like flowing robes they now appear, and twine
Round the large members of a form divine ;

His silver beard, that swept his aged breast,
His piercing eye, that inward light express'd,
Were seen,—but clouds and darkness veil'd
   the rest.
Fear chill'd my heart: to one of mortal race,
How awful seem'd the Genius of the place !
So in Cimmerian shores, Ulysses saw
His parent-shade, and shrunk in pious awe;
Like him I stood, and wrapt in thought pro-
   found,
When from the pitying power broke forth a
   solemn sound :—
   ' Care lives with all ; no rules, no precepts
      save
The wise from wo, no fortitude the brave ;
Grief is to man as certain as the grave :
Tempests and storms in life's whole progress
   rise,
And hope shines dimly through o'erclouded
   skies ;
Some drops of comfort on the favour'd fall,
But showers of sorrow are the lot of *all* :
Partial to talents, then, shall Heav'n with-
   draw
Th' afflicting rod, or break the general law ?
Shall he who soars, inspired by loftier views,
Life's little cares and little pains refuse ?
Shall he not rather feel a double share
Of mortal wo, when doubly arm'd to bear ?
   'Hard is his fate who builds his peace of
      mind
On the precarious mercy of mankind ;
Who hopes for wild and visionary things,
And mounts o'er unknown seas with vent'rous
   wings :
But as, of various evils that befal
The human race, some portion goes to all ;
To him perhaps the milder lot 's assign'd,
Who feels his consolation in his mind ;

And, lock'd within his bosom, bears about
A mental charm for every care without.
E'en in the pangs of each domestic grief,
Or health or vigorous hope affords relief ;
And every wound the tortured bosom feels,
Or virtue bears, or some preserver heals ;
Some generous friend, of ample power
   possess'd ;
Some feeling heart, that bleeds for the dis-
   tress'd ;
Some breast that glows with virtues all divine;
Some noble RUTLAND, Misery's friend and
   thine.
   ' Nor say, the Muse's song, the Poet's pen,
Merit the scorn they meet from little men.
With cautious freedom if the numbers flow,
Not wildly high, nor pitifully low ;
If vice alone their honest aims oppose,
Why so ashamed their friends, so loud their
   foes ?
Happy for men in every age and clime,
If all the sons of vision dealt in rhyme.
Go on then, Son of Vision ! still pursue
Thy airy dreams ; the world is dreaming too.
Ambition's lofty views, the pomp of state,
The pride of wealth, the splendour of the
   great,
Stripp'd of their mask, their cares and troubles
   known,
Are visions far less happy than thy own :
Go on ! and, while the sons of care complain,
Be wisely gay and innocently vain ;
While serious souls are by their fears undone,
Blow sportive bladders in the beamy sun,
And call them worlds ! and bid the greatest
   show
More radiant colours in their worlds below :
Then, as they break, the slaves of care reprove,
And tell them, Such are all the toys they love.'

THE VILLAGE

[1783]

IN TWO BOOKS

BOOK I

THE Village Life, and every care that reigns
O'er youthful peasants and declining swains;
What labour yields, and what, that labour
    past,
Age, in its hour of languor, finds at last;
What form the real picture of the poor,
Demand a song—the Muse can give no more.
  Fled are those times, when, in harmonious
    strains,
The rustic poet praised his native plains:
No shepherds now, in smooth alternate verse,
Their country's beauty or their nymphs'
    rehearse;
Yet still for these we frame the tender strain,
Still in our lays find Corydons complain,
And shepherds' boys their amorous pains
    reveal,
The only pains, alas! they never feel.
  On Mincio's banks, in Caesar's bounteous
    reign,
If Tityrus found the Golden Age again,
Must sleepy bards the flattering dream pro-
    long,
Mechanic echoes of the Mantuan song?
From Truth and Nature shall we widely stray,
Where Virgil, not where Fancy, leads the
    way?

  Yes, thus the Muses sing of happy swains,
Because the Muses never knew their pains:
They boast their peasants' pipes; but pea-
    sants now
Resign their pipes and plod behind the plough;
And few, amid the rural-tribe, have time
To number syllables, and play with rhyme;
Save honest Duck, what son of verse could
    share
The poet's rapture, and the peasant's care?
Or the great labours of the field degrade,
With the new peril of a poorer trade?
  From this chief cause these idle praises
    spring,
That themes so easy few forbear to sing;
For no deep thought the trifling subjects ask;
To sing of shepherds is an easy task ·
The happy youth assumes the common strain,
A nymph his mistress, and himself a swain;
With no sad scenes he clouds his tuneful
    prayer,
But all, to look like her, is painted fair.
  I grant indeed that fields and flocks have
    charms
For him that grazes or for him that farms;
But when amid such pleasing scenes I trace
The poor laborious natives of the place,
And see the mid-day sun, with fervid ray,
On their bare heads and dewy temples play;
While some, with feebler heads and fainter
    hearts,
Deplore their fortune, yet sustain their parts:
Then shall I dare these real ills to hide
In tinsel trappings of poetic pride?
  No; cast by Fortune on a frowning coast,
Which neither groves nor happy valleys boast;
Where other cares than those the Muse relates,
And other shepherds dwell with other
    mates;

By such examples taught, I paint the Cot,
As Truth will paint it, and as Bards will not:
Nor you, ye poor, of letter'd scorn complain,
To you the smoothest song is smooth in vain;
O'ercome by labour, and bow'd down by time,
Feel you the barren flattery of a rhyme?
Can poets soothe you, when you pine for
    bread,
By winding myrtles round your ruin'd shed?
Can their light tales your weighty griefs o'er-
    power,
Or glad with airy mirth the toilsome hour?
    Lo! where the heath, with withering brake
        grown o'er,
Lends the light turf that warms the neigh-
    bouring poor;
From thence a length of burning sand appears,
Where the thin harvest waves its wither'd ears;
Rank weeds, that every art and care defy,
Reign o'er the land, and rob the blighted rye:
There thistles stretch their prickly arms afar,
And to the ragged infant threaten war;
There poppies nodding, mock the hope of toil;
There the blue bugloss paints the sterile soil;
Hardy and high, above the slender sheaf,
The slimy mallow waves her silky leaf;
O'er the young shoot the charlock throws a
    shade,
And clasping tares cling round the sickly
    blade;
With mingled tints the rocky coasts abound,
And a sad splendour vainly shines around.
So looks the nymph whom wretched arts adorn,
Betray'd by man, then left for man to scorn;
Whose cheek in vain assumes the mimic rose,
While her sad eyes the troubled breast dis-
    close;
Whose outward splendour is but folly's dress,
Exposing most, when most it gilds distress.
Here joyless roam a wild amphibious race,
With sullen wo display'd in every face;
Who, far from civil arts and social fly,
And scowl at strangers with suspicious eye.
    Here too the lawless merchant of the main
Draws from his plough th' intoxicated swain;
Want only claim'd the labour of the day,
But vice now steals his nightly rest away.
    Where are the swains, who, daily labour
        done,
With rural games play'd down the setting sun;
Who struck with matchless force the bounding
    ball,
Or made the pond'rous quoit obliquely fall;

While some huge Ajax, terrible and strong,
Engaged some artful stripling of the throng,
And fell beneath him, foil'd, while far around
Hoarse triumph rose, and rocks return'd the
    sound?
Where now are these?—Beneath yon cliff
    they stand,
To show the freighted pinnace where to land;
To load the ready steed with guilty haste,
To fly in terror o'er the pathless waste,
Or, when detected, in their straggling course,
To foil their foes by cunning or by force;
Or, yielding part (which equal knaves de-
    mand),
To gain a lawless passport through the land.
    Here, wand'ring long, amid these frowning
        fields,
I sought the simple life that Nature yields;
Rapine and Wrong and Fear usurp'd her place,
And a bold, artful, surly, savage race;
Who, only skill'd to take the finny tribe,
The yearly dinner, or septennial bribe,
Wait on the shore, and, as the waves run high,
On the tost vessel bend their eager eye,
Which to their coast directs its vent'rous way;
Theirs, or the ocean's, miserable prey.
    As on their neighbouring beach yon swallows
        stand,
And wait for favouring winds to leave the
    land;
While still for flight the ready wing is spread:
So waited I the favouring hour, and fled;
Fled from these shores where guilt and famine
    reign,
And cried, Ah! hapless they who still remain;
Who still remain to hear the ocean roar,
Whose greedy waves devour the lessening
    shore;
Till some fierce tide, with more imperious
    sway,
Sweeps the low hut and all it holds away;
When the sad tenant weeps from door to door,
And begs a poor protection from the poor!
    But these are scenes where Nature's niggard
        hand
Gave a spare portion to the famish'd land;
Hers is the fault, if here mankind complain
Of fruitless toil and labour spent in vain;
But yet in other scenes more fair in view,
Where Plenty smiles—alas! she smiles for
    few—
And those who taste not, yet behold her store,
Are as the slaves that dig the golden ore,—

The wealth around them makes them doubly
    poor.
Or will you deem them amply paid in
    health,
Labour's fair child, that languishes with
    wealth ?
Go then ! and see them rising with the sun,
Through a long course of daily toil to run ;
See them beneath the dog-star's raging heat,
When the knees tremble and the temples beat;
Behold them, leaning on their scythes,look o'er
The labour past, and toils to come explore;
See them alternate suns and showers engage,
And hoard up aches and anguish for their age;
Through fens and marshy moors their steps
    pursue,
When their warm pores imbibe the evening
    dew ;
Then own that labour may as fatal be
To these thy slaves, as thine excess to thee.
    Amid this tribe too oft a manly pride
Strives in strong toil the fainting heart to hide;
There may you see the youth of slender frame
Contend with weakness, weariness, and shame;
Yet, urged along, and proudly loth to yield,
He strives to join his fellows of the field.
Till long-contending nature droops at last,
Declining health rejects his poor repast,
His cheerless spouse the coming danger sees,
And mutual murmurs urge the slow disease.
    Yet grant them health, 'tis not for us to tell,
Though the head droops not, that the heart
    is well ;
Or will you praise that homely, healthy fare,
Plenteous and plain, that happy peasants
    share !
Oh ! trifle not with wants you cannot feel,
Nor mock the misery of a stinted meal ;
Homely, not wholesome, plain, not plenteous,
    such
As you who praise would never deign to
    touch.
    Ye gentle souls, who dream of rural ease,
Whom the smooth stream and smoother son-
    net please ;
Go ! if the peaceful cot your praises share,
Go look within, and ask if peace be there ;
If peace be his—that drooping weary sire,
Or theirs, that offspring round their feeble fire;
Or hers, that matron pale, whose trembling
    hand
Turns on the wretched hearth th' expiring
    brand !

Nor yet can Time itself obtain for these
Life's latest comforts, due respect and ease;
For yonder see that hoary swain, whose age
Can with no cares except his own engage ;
Who, propp'd on that rude staff, looks up to
    see
The bare arms broken from the withering tree,
On which, a boy, he climb'd the loftiest bough,
Then his first joy, but his sad emblem now.
    He once was chief in all the rustic trade ;
His steady hand the straightest furrow made;
Full many a prize he won, and still is proud
To find the triumphs of his youth allow'd ;
A transient pleasure sparkles in his eyes,
He hears and smiles, then thinks again and
    sighs :
For now he journeys to his grave in pain ;
The rich disdain him ; nay, the poor dis-
    dain :
Alternate masters now their slave command,
Urge the weak efforts of his feeble hand,
And, when his age attempts its task in vain,
With ruthless taunts, of lazy poor complain.[1]
    Oft may you see him, when he tends the
    sheep,
His winter-charge, beneath the hillock weep;
Oft hear him murmur to the winds that blow
O'er his white locks and bury them in snow,
When, roused by rage and muttering in the
    morn,
He mends the broken hedge with icy thorn:—
    ' Why do I live, when I desire to be
At once from life and life's long labour free?
Like leaves in spring, the young are blown
    away,
Without the sorrows of a slow decay ;
I, like yon wither'd leaf, remain behind,
Nipp'd by the frost, and shivering in the
    wind ;
There it abides till younger buds come on,
As I, now all my fellow-swains are gone ;
Then, from the rising generation thrust,
It falls, like me, unnoticed to the dust.
    'These fruitful fields, these numerous flocks
    I see,
Are others' gain, but killing cares to me ;
To me the children of my youth are lords,
Cool in their looks, but hasty in their words :
Wants of their own demand their care; and
    who
Feels his own want and succours others too?
A lonely, wretched man, in pain I go,
None need my help, and none relieve my wo;

gained from them; since, the more of these Instructors a man reads, the less he will infallibly understand: nor would it have been very consistent in me, at the same time to censure their temerity and ignorance, and to adopt their rage.

I should have been glad to have made some discrimination in my remarks on these productions. There is, indeed, some difference; and I have observed, that one editor will sometimes convey his abuse with more decency, and colour his falsehood with more appearance of probability, than another: but until I see that paper, wherein no great character is wantonly abused, nor groundless insinuation wilfully disseminated, I shall not make any distinction in my remarks upon them.

It must, however, be confessed, that these things have their use; and are, besides, vehicles of much amusement: but this does not outweigh the evil they do to society, and the irreparable injury they bring upon the characters of individuals. In the following poem I have given those good properties their due weight: they have changed indignation into mirth, and turned, what would otherwise have been abhorrence, into derision.

February, 1785.

THE NEWSPAPER

E quibus hi vacuas implent sermonibus aures:
Hi narrata ferunt alio: mensuraque ficti
Crescit, et auditis aliquid novus adiicit auctor:
Illic Credulitas, illic temerarius Error,
Vanaque Laetitia est, consternatique Timores,
Seditioque recens, dubioque auctore Susurri.
OVID, *Metamorph.* lib. xii. 56–61.

This not a Time favourable to poetical Composition: and why—Newspapers Enemies to Literature, and their general Influence—Their Numbers—The Sunday Monitor—Their general Character—Their Effect upon Individuals—upon Society—in the Country—The Village Freeholder—What Kind of Composition a Newspaper is; and the Amusement it affords—Of what Parts it is chiefly composed—Articles of Intelligence: Advertisements: The Stage: Quacks: Puffing—The Correspondents to a Newspaper, political and poetical—Advice to the latter—Conclusion.

A TIME like this, a busy, bustling time,
Suits ill with writers, very ill with rhyme:
Unheard we sing, when party-rage runs strong,
And mightier madness checks the flowing song:
Or, should we force the peaceful Muse to wield
Her feeble arms amid the furious field,
Where party-pens a wordy war maintain,
Poor is her anger, and her friendship vain;
And oft the foes who feel her sting, combine,
Till serious vengeance pays an idle line;

For party-poets are like wasps, who dart
Death to themselves, and to their foes but smart.
　Hard then our fate: if general themes we choose,
Neglect awaits the song, and chills the Muse;
Or should we sing the subject of the day,
To-morrow's wonder puffs our praise away.
More bless'd the bards of that poetic time,
When all found readers who could find a rhyme;
Green grew the bays on every teeming head,
And Cibber was enthroned, and Settle read.
Sing, drooping Muse, the cause of thy decline;
Why reign no more the once-triumphant Nine?
Alas! new charms the wavering many gain,
And rival sheets the reader's eye detain;
A daily swarm, that banish every Muse,
Come flying forth, and mortals call them NEWS:
For these, unread, the noblest volumes lie;
For these, in sheets unsoil'd, the Muses die;
Unbought, unbless'd, the virgin copies wait
In vain for fame, and sink, unseen, to fate.
　Since, then, the town forsakes us for our foes,
The smoothest numbers for the harshest prose;
Let us, with generous scorn, the taste deride,
And sing our rivals with a rival's pride.
　Ye gentle poets, who so oft complain
That foul neglect is all your labours gain;

That pity only checks your growing spite
To erring man, and prompts you still to write;
That your choice works on humble stalls are
laid,
Or vainly grace the windows of the trade ;
Be ye my friends, if friendship e'er can warm
Those rival bosoms whom the Muses charm:
Think of the common cause wherein we go,
Like gallant Greeks against the Trojan foe;
Nor let one peevish chief his leader blame,
Till, crown'd with conquest, we regain our
fame ;
And let us join our forces to subdue
This bold assuming but successful crew.
I sing of NEWS, and all those vapid sheets
The rattling hawker vends through gaping
streets ;
Whate'er their name, whate'er the time they
fly,
Damp from the press, to charm the reader's
eye :
For, soon as morning dawns with roseate hue,
The Herald of the morn arises too ;
Post after Post succeeds, and, all day long,
Gazettes and Ledgers swarm, a noisy throng.
When evening comes, she comes with all her
train
Of Ledgers, Chronicles, and Posts again,
Like bats, appearing, when the sun goes down,
From holes obscure and corners of the town.
Of all these triflers, all like these, I write;
Oh ! like my subject could my song delight,
The crowd at Lloyd's one poet's name should
raise,
And all the Alley echo to his praise.
In shoals the hours their constant number
bring,
Like insects waking to th' advancing spring;
Which take their rise from grubs obscene
that lie
In shallow pools, or thence ascend the sky;
Such are these base ephemeras, so born
To die before the next revolving morn.
Yet thus they differ : insect-tribes are lost
In the first visit of a winter's frost ;
While these remain, a base but constant
breed,
Whose swarming sons their short-lived sires
succeed ;
No changing season makes their number less,
Nor Sunday shines a sabbath on the press!
Then lo ! the sainted Monitor is born,
Whose pious face some sacred texts adorn :

As artful sinners cloak the secret sin,
To veil with seeming grace the guile within;
So Moral Essays on his front appear,
But all is carnal business in the rear ;
The fresh-coin'd lie, the secret whisper'd last,
And all the gleanings of the six days past.
With these retired, through half the Sab-
bath-day,
The London-lounger yawns his hours away:
Not so, my little flock ! your preacher fly,
Nor waste the time no worldly wealth can buy;
But let the decent maid and sober clown
Pray for these idlers of the sinful town :
This day, at least, on nobler themes bestow,
Nor give to Woodfall, or the world below.
But, Sunday pass'd, what numbers flourish
then,
What wond'rous labours of the press and pen !
Diurnal most, some thrice each week affords,
Some only once,—O avarice of words !
When thousand starving minds such manna
seek,[1]
To drop the precious food but once a week.
Endless it were to sing the powers of all,
Their names, their numbers ; how they rise
and fall :
Like baneful herbs the gazer's eye they seize,
Rush to the head, and poison where they
please :
Like idle flies, a busy, buzzing train,
They drop their maggots in the trifler's brain:
That genial soil receives the fruitful store,
And there they grow, and breed a thousand
more.
Now be their arts display'd, how first they
choose
A cause and party, as the bard his muse;
Inspired by these, with clamorous zeal they
cry,
And through the town their dreams and omens
fly :
So the Sibylline leaves were blown about,[2]
Disjointed scraps of fate involved in doubt;
So idle dreams, the journals of the night,
Are right and wrong by turns, and mingle
wrong with right.—
Some champions for the rights that prop the
crown,
Some sturdy patriots, sworn to pull them
down ;
Some neutral powers, with secret forces
fraught,
Wishing for war, but willing to be bought :

While some to every side and party go,
Shift every friend, and join with every foe ;
Like sturdy rogues in privateers, they strike
This side and that, the foes of both alike ;
A traitor-crew, who thrive in troubled times,
Fear'd for their force, and courted for their
    crimes.

Chief to the prosperous side the numbers
    sail,
Fickle and false, they veer with every gale;
As birds that migrate from a freezing shore,
In search of warmer climes, come skimming
    o'er,
Some bold adventurers first prepare to try
The doubtful sunshine of the distant sky ;
But soon the growing Summer's certain sun
Wins more and more, till all at last are won :
So, on the early prospect of disgrace,
Fly in vast troops this apprehensive race ;
Instinctive tribes ! their failing food they
    dread,
And buy, with timely change, their future
    bread.

Such are our guides; how many a peaceful
    head,
Born to be still, have they to wrangling led !
How many an honest zealot, stol'n from trade,
And factious tools of pious pastors made !
With clews like these they tread the maze of
    state,
These oracles explore, to learn our fate ;
Pleased with the guides who can so well
    deceive,
Who cannot lie so fast as they believe.
Oft lend I, loth, to some sage friend an
    ear,
(For we who will not speak are doom'd to
    hear) ;
While he, bewilder'd, tells his anxious thought,
Infectious fear from tainted scribblers caught,
Or idiot hope ; for each his mind assails,
As Lloyd's court-light or Stockdale's gloom
    prevails.
Yet stand I patient while but one declaims,
Or gives dull comments on the speech he
    maims :
But oh ! ye Muses, keep your votary's feet
From tavern-haunts where politicians meet;
Where rector, doctor, and attorney pause,
First on each parish, then each public cause:
Indited roads and rates that still increase;
The murmuring poor, who will not fast in
    peace ;

Election-zeal and friendship, since declined;
A tax commuted, or a tithe in kind ;
The Dutch and Germans kindling into strife;
Dull port and poachers vile ! the serious ills
    of life.
Here comes the neighbouring justice,
    pleased to guide
His little club, and in the chair preside.
In private business his commands prevail,
On public themes his reasoning turns the
    scale ;
Assenting silence soothes his happy ear,
And, in or out, his party triumphs here.
Nor here th' infectious rage for party stops,
But flits along from palaces to shops ;
Our weekly journals o'er the land abound,
And spread their plague and influenzas round;
The village, too, the peaceful, pleasant plain,
Breeds the Whig-farmer and the Tory-swain ;
Brookes' and St. Alban's boasts not, but,
    instead,
Stares the Red Ram, and swings the Rodney's
    Head :—
Hither, with all a patriot's care, comes he
Who owns the little hut that makes him free;
Whose yearly forty shillings buy the smile
Of mightier men, and never waste the while ;
Who feels his freehold's worth, and looks
    elate,
A little prop and pillar of the state.
Here he delights the weekly news to con,
And mingle comments as he blunders on ;
To swallow all their varying authors teach,
To spell a title, and confound a speech :
Till with a muddled mind he quits the news,
And claims his nation's licence to abuse ;
Then joins the cry, ' That all the courtly
    race
Are venal candidates for power and place ; '
Yet feels some joy, amid the general vice,
That his own vote will bring its wonted price.
These are the ills the teeming press supplies,
The pois'nous springs from learning's foun-
    tain rise ;
Not there the wise alone their entrance find,
Imparting useful light to mortals blind ;
But, blind themselves, these erring guides
    hold out
Alluring lights, to lead us far about ;
Screen'd by such means, here Scandal whets
    her quill,
Here Slander shoots unseen, whene'er she
    will ;

Here Fraud and Falsehood labour to deceive,
And Folly aids them both, impatient to be-
    lieve.
  Such, sons of Britain! are the guides ye
    trust ;
So wise their counsel, their reports so just:—
Yet, though we cannot call their morals pure,
Their judgment nice, or their decisions sure;
Merit they have to mightier works unknown,
A style, a manner, and a fate their own.
  We, who for longer fame with labour strive,
Are pain'd to keep our sickly works alive ;
Studious we toil, with patient care refine,
Nor let our love protect one languid line.
Severe ourselves, at last our works appear,
When, ah! we find our readers more severe ;
For after all our care and pains, how few
Acquire applause, or keep it if they do !—
  Not so these sheets, ordain'd to happier
    fate,
Praised through their day, and but that day
    their date ;
Their careless authors only strive to join
As many words, as make an even line ; ³
As many lines, as fill a row complete ;
As many rows, as furnish up a sheet :
From side to side, with ready types they run,
The measure 's ended, and the work is done ;
Oh, born with ease, how envied and how
    blest !
Your fate to-day and your to-morrow's rest.
To you all readers turn, and they can look
Pleased on a paper, who abhor a book ;
Those, who ne'er deign'd their Bible to peruse,
Would think it hard to be denied their news;
Sinners and saints, the wisest with the weak,
Here mingle tastes, and one amusement seek ;
This, like the public inn, provides a treat,
Where each promiscuous guest sits down to
    eat ;
And such this mental food, as we may call
Something to all men, and to some men all.
  Next, in what rare production shall we trace
Such various subjects in so small a space ?
As the first ship upon the waters bore
Incongruous kinds who never met before ;
Or as some curious virtuoso joins,
In one small room, moths, minerals, and coins,
Birds, beasts, and fishes ; nor refuses place
To serpents, toads, and all the reptile race;
So here, compress'd within a single sheet,
Great things and small, the mean and mighty
    meet :

'Tis this which makes all Europe's business
    known,
Yet here a private man may place his own ;
And, where he reads of Lords and Commons, he
May tell their honours that he sells rappee.
  Add next th' amusement which the motley
    page
Affords to either sex and every age :
Lo! where it comes before the cheerful fire,—
Damps from the press in smoky curls aspire
(As from the earth the sun exhales the dew),
Ere we can read the wonders that ensue :
Then eager every eye surveys the part,
That brings its favourite subject to the heart;
Grave politicians look for facts alone,
And gravely add conjectures of their own :
The sprightly nymph, who never broke her
    rest
For tottering crowns, or mighty lands op-
    press'd,
Finds broils and battles, but neglects them all
For songs and suits, a birth-day, or a ball:
The keen warm man o'erlooks each idle tale
For 'Money's wanted,' and ' Estates on Sale ;'
While some with equal minds to all attend,
Pleased with each part, and grieved to find
    an end.
  So charm the News ; but we, who, far
    from town,
Wait till the postman brings the packet down,
Once in the week, a vacant day behold,
And stay for tidings, till they're three days
    old :
That day arrives ; no welcome post appears,
But the dull morn a sullen aspect wears ;
We meet, but ah! without our wonted smile,
To talk of headaches, and complain of bile ;
Sullen we ponder o'er a dull repast,
Nor feast the body while the mind must fast.
  A master-passion is the love of news,
Not music so commands, nor so the Muse :
Give poets claret, they grow idle soon ;
Feed the musician, and he 's out of tune ;
But the sick mind, of this disease possess'd,
Flies from all cure, and sickens when at rest.
  Now sing, my Muse, what various parts
    compose
These rival sheets of politics and prose.
  First, from each brother's hoard a part they
    draw,
A·mutual theft that never fear'd a law ;
Whate'er they gain, to each man's portion fall,
And read it once, you read it through them all:

For this their runners ramble day and night,
To drag each lurking deed to open light ;
For daily bread the dirty trade they ply,
Coin their fresh tales, and live upon the lie :
Like bees for honey, forth for news they
    spring,—
Industrious creatures ! ever on the wing ;
Home to their several cells they bear the
    store,
Cull'd of all kinds, then roam abroad for more.
  No anxious virgin flies to ' fair Tweed-
    side ; '
No injured husband mourns his faithless
    bride ;
No duel dooms the fiery youth to bleed ;
But through the town transpires each
    vent'rous deed.
  Should some fair frail-one drive her pranc-
    ing pair,
Where rival peers contend to please the fair ;
When, with new force, she aids her conquering
    eyes,
And beauty decks, with all that beauty buys ;
Quickly we learn whose heart her influence
    feels,
Whose acres melt before her glowing wheels.
  To these a thousand idle themes succeed,
Deeds of all kinds, and comments to each deed.
Here stocks, the state-barometers, we view,
That rise or fall, by causes known to few ;
Promotion's ladder who goes up or down ;
Who wed, or who seduced, amuse the town ;
What new-born heir has made his father blest ;
What heir exults, his father now at rest ;
That ample list the Tyburn-herald gives,
And each known knave, who still for Tyburn
    lives.
  So grows the work, and now the printer tries
His powers no more, but leans on his allies.
  When lo ! the advertising tribe succeed,
Pay to be read, yet find but few will read ;
And chief th' illustrious race, whose drops
    and pills
Have patent powers to vanquish human ills :
These, with their cures, a constant aid re-
    main,
To bless the pale composer's fertile brain ;
Fertile it is, but still the noblest soil
Requires some pause, some intervals from
    toil ;
And they at least a certain ease obtain
From Katterfelto's skill, and Graham's
    glowing strain.

  I too must aid, and pay to see my name
Hung in these dirty avenues to fame ;
Nor pay in vain, if aught the Muse has seen,
And sung, could make those avenues more
    clean ;
Could stop one slander ere it found its way,
And gave to public scorn its helpless prey.
By the same aid, the Stage invites her friends,
And kindly tells the banquet she intends ;
Thither from real life the many run,
With Siddons weep, or laugh with Abingdon ;
Pleased in fictitious joy or grief, to see
The mimic passion with their own agree ;
To steal a few enchanted hours away
From care, and drop the curtain on the day,
  But who can steal from self that wretched
    wight,
Whose darling work is tried, some fatal
    night ?
Most wretched man ! when, bane to every
    bliss,
He hears the serpent-critic's rising hiss ;
Then groans succeed : not traitors on the
    wheel
Can feel like him, or have such pangs to feel.
Nor end they here : next day he reads his fall
In every paper ; critics are they all ;
He sees his branded name, with wild affright,
And hears again the cat-calls of the night.
  Such help the STAGE affords : a larger
    space
Is fill'd by PUFFS and all the puffing race.
Physic had once alone the lofty style,
The well-known boast, that ceased to raise a
    smile :
Now all the province of that tribe invade,
And we abound in quacks of every trade.
  The simple barber, once an honest name,
Cervantes founded, Fielding raised his fame :
Barber no more—a gay perfumer comes,
On whose soft cheek his own cosmetic blooms ;
Here he appears, each simple mind to move,
And advertises beauty, grace, and love.
—' Come, faded belles, who would your youth
    renew,
And learn the wonders of Olympian dew ;
Restore the roses that begin to faint,
Nor think celestial washes vulgar paint ;
Your former features, airs, and arts assume,
Circassian virtues, with Circassian bloom.
—Come, batter'd beaux, whose locks are
    turn'd to grey,
And crop Discretion's lying badge away ;

Read where they vend these smart engaging
    things,
These flaxen frontlets with elastic springs ;
No female eye the fair deception sees,
Not Nature's self so natural as these.'
    Such are their arts, but not confined to them,
The Muse impartial must her sons condemn :
For they, degenerate ! join the venal throng.
And puff a lazy Pegasus along :
More guilty these, by Nature less design'd
For little arts that suit the vulgar-kind ;—
That barbers' boys, who would to trade
    advance,
Wish us to call them, smart Friseurs from
    France ;
That he who builds a chop-house, on his door
Paints ' The true old original Blue Boar ! '
    These are the arts by which a thousand live,
Where Truth may smile, and Justice may
    forgive :
But when, amid this rabble-rout, we find
A puffing poet to his honour blind ;
Who slily drops quotations all about,
Packet or Post, and points their merit out ;
Who advertises what reviewers say,
With sham editions every second day ;
Who dares not trust his praises out of sight,
But hurries into fame with all his might ;
Although the verse some transient praise
    obtains,
Contempt is all the anxious poet gains.
    Now puffs exhausted, advertisements past,
Their correspondents stand exposed at last ;
These are a numerous tribe, to fame unknown,
Who for the public good forego their own ;
Who volunteers in paper-war engage,
With double portion of their party's rage :
Such are the Bruti, Decii, who appear
Wooing the printer for admission here ;
Whose generous souls can condescend to pray
For leave to throw their precious time away.
    Oh ! cruel Woodfall ! when a patriot
        draws
His grey-goose quill in his dear country's
    cause,
To vex and maul a ministerial race,
Can thy stern soul refuse the champion
    place ?
Alas ! thou know'st not with what anxious
    heart
He longs his best-loved labours to impart ;
How he has sent them to thy brethren round,
And still the same unkind reception found :

At length indignant will he damn the state,
Turn to his trade, and leave us to our fate.
    These Roman souls, like Rome's great sons,
        are known
To live in cells on labours of their own.
Thus Milo, could we see the noble chief,
Feeds, for his country's good, on legs of beef :
Camillus copies deeds for sordid pay,
Yet fights the public battles twice a day :
E'en now the godlike Brutus views his score
Scroll'd on the bar-board, swinging with the
    door ;
Where, tippling punch, grave Cato's self you'll
    see,
And *Amor Patriae* vending smuggled tea.
    Last in these ranks, and least, their art's dis-
        grace,
Neglected stand the Muses' meanest race ;
Scribblers who court contempt, whose verse
    the eye
Disdainful views, and glances swiftly by :
This Poet's Corner is the place they choose,
A fatal nursery for an infant Muse ;
Unlike that corner where true poets lie,
These cannot live, and they shall never die ;
Hapless the lad whose mind such dreams in-
    vade,
And win to verse the talents due to trade
    Curb then, O youth ! these raptures as they
        rise,
Keep down the evil spirit and be wise ;
Follow your calling, think the Muses foes,
Nor lean upon the pestle and compose.
    I know your day-dreams, and I know the
        snare
Hid in your flow'ry path, and cry ' Beware.'
    Thoughtless of ill, and to the future
        blind,
A sudden couplet rushes on your mind ;
Here you may nameless print your idle
    rhymes,
And read your first-born work a thousand
    times ;
Th' infection spreads, your couplet grows
    apace,
Stanzas to Delia's dog or Celia's face :
You take a name ; Philander's odes are seen,
Printed, and praised, in every magazine :
Diarian sages greet their brother sage,
And your dark pages please th' enlighten'd
    age.—
Alas ! what years you thus consume in vain,
Ruled by this wretched bias of the brain !

Go! to your desks and counters all return;
Your sonnets scatter, your acrostics burn;
Trade, and be rich ; or, should your careful
    sires
Bequeath you wealth! indulge the nobler
    fires :
Should love of fame your youthful heart
    betray,
Pursue fair fame, but in a glorious way,
Nor in the idle scenes of Fancy's painting
    stray.
Of all the good that mortal men pursue,
The Muse has least to give, and gives to few;
Like some coquettish fair, she leads us on,
With smiles and hopes, till youth and peace
    are gone ;
Then, wed for life, the restless wrangling pair
Forget how constant one, and one how fair:

Meanwhile, Ambition, like a blooming bride,
Brings power and wealth to grace her lover's
    side ;
And though she smiles not with such flattering
    charms,
The brave will sooner win her to their arms.
    Then wed to her, if Virtue tie the bands,
Go spread your country's fame in hostile
    lands ;
Her court, her senate, or her arms adorn,
And let her foes lament that you were born:
Or weigh her laws, their ancient rights de-
    fend,
Though hosts oppose, be theirs and Reason's
    friend ;
Arm'd with strong powers, in their defence
    engage,
And rise the Thurlow of the future age.

NOTES TO 'THE NEWSPAPER'

Note 1, page 44, line 61.
*When thousand starving minds such manna
seek.*
    The Manna of Day.—Green's *Spleen.*

Note 2, page 44, line 75.
So the Sibylline leaves were blown about.
. . . in foliis descripsit carmina Virgo ;—
. . . et teneras turbavit ianua frondes.
    VIRG. *Aeneid*, lib. iii. 445, 449.

Note 3, page 46, lines 20, 21, and 22.
As many words, as make an even line ;
As many lines, as fill a row complete ;
As many rows, as furnish up a sheet.

How many hours bring about the day,
How many days will furnish up the year,
How many years a mortal man may live, &c.
    Shakspeare's *Henry VI*, Part III, Act II.
    Sc. 5.

THE PARISH REGISTER

IN THREE PARTS

[1807]

INTRODUCTION.

The Village Register considered, as containing principally the Annals of the Poor—State of the Peasantry as meliorated by Frugality and Industry—The Cottage of an industrious Peasant ; its Ornaments—Prints an Books—The Garden ; its Satisfactions —The State of the Poor, when improvident and vicious—The Row or Street, and its Inhabitants—The Dwelling of one of these—A Public House—Garden and its Append- ages—Gamesters ; rustic Sharpers, &c.—Conclusion of Introductory Part.

PART I.   BAPTISMS

Tum porro puer (ut saevis projectus ab undis,
Navita) nudus humi jacet infans, indigus omni
Vitali auxilio,—— . . . . .
Vagituque locum lugubri complet, ut aequum
    est,
Cui tantum in vitâ restet transire malorum..

    Lucret. *de Nat. Rerum*, lib. 5, vv. 223–5
    and 227–8. [1]

The Child of the Miller's Daughter, and Relation of her Misfortune—A frugal Couple : their Kind of Frugality—Plea of the Mother of a natural Child : her Churching—Large Family of Gerard Ablett: his Apprehensions : Comparison between his State and that of the wealthy Farmer his Master : his Consolation—An old Man's Anxiety for an Heir : the Jealousy of another on having many—Characters of the Grocer Dawkins and his Friend : their different Kinds of Disappointment—Three Infants named—An Orphan Girl and Village Schoolmistress—Gardener's Child : Pedantry and Conceit of the Father : his Botanical Discourse : Method of fixing the Embryo-fruit of Cucumbers—Absurd Effects of Rustic Vanity : observed in the Names of their Children—Relation of the Vestry Debate on a Foundling : Sir Richard Monday—Children of various Inhabitants— The poor Farmer—Children of a Profligate : his Character and Fate—Conclusion.

THE year revolves, and I again explore
The simple annals of my parish poor ;

What infant-members in my flock appear,
What pairs I bless'd in the departed year ;
And who, of old or young, or nymphs or swains,
Are lost to life, its pleasures and its pains.
  No Muse I ask, before my view to bring
The humble actions of the swains I sing.—
How pass'd the youthful, how the old their days ;
Who sank in sloth, and who aspired to praise;
Their tempers, manners, morals, customs, arts,
What parts they had, and how they 'mploy'd their parts ;
By what elated, soothed, seduced, depress'd,
Full well I know—these records give the rest.
  Is there a place, save one the poet sees,
A land of love, of liberty and ease ;
Where labour wearies not, nor cares suppress
Th' eternal flow of rustic happiness ;
Where no proud mansion frowns in awful state,
Or keeps the sunshine from the cottage-gate:
Where young and old, intent on pleasure, throng,
And half man's life is holiday and song ?
Vain search for scenes like these ! no view appears,
By sighs unruffled or unstain'd by tears ;
Since vice the world subdued and waters drown'd,
Auburn and Eden can no more be found.

---

[1] For the identification of many of the quotations prefixed to the various parts of *The Parish Register* and *The Borough* we are indebted to the valuable edition of Dr. A. W. Ward.

Hence good and evil mix'd, but man has
skill
And power to part them, when he feels the
will !
Toil, care, and patience bless th' abstemious
few,
Fear, shame, and want the thoughtless herd
pursue.
   Behold the cot ! where thrives-th' indus-
trious swain,
Source of his pride, his pleasure, and his
gain ;
Screen'd from the winter's wind, the sun's
last ray
Smiles on the window and prolongs the day ;
Projecting thatch the woodbine's branches
stop,
And turn their blossoms to the casement's top :
All need requires is in that cot contain'd,
And much that taste untaught and unre-
strain'd
Surveys delighted ; there she loves to trace,
In one gay picture, all the royal race ;
Around the walls are heroes, lovers, kings ;
The print that shows them and the verse that
sings.
   Here the last Lewis on his throne is seen,
And there he stands imprison'd, and his
queen ;
To these the mother takes her child, and shows
What grateful duty to his God he owes ;
Who gives to him a happy home, where he
Lives and enjoys his freedom with the free ;
When kings and queens, dethroned, insulted,
tried,
Are all these blessings of the poor denied.
   There is King Charles, and all his Golden
Rules,
Who proved Misfortune's was the best of
schools :
And there his son, who, tried by years of pain,
Proved that misfortunes may be sent in vain.
   The magic-mill that grinds the gran'nams
young,
Close at the side of kind Godiva hung ;
She, of her favourite place the pride and joy,
Of charms at once most lavish and most coy,
By wanton act, the purest fame could raise,
And give the boldest deed the chastest praise.
   There stands the stoutest Ox in England
fed ;
There fights the boldest Jew, Whitechapel
bred ;

And here Saint Monday's worthy votaries
live,
In all the joys that ale and skittles give.
   Now lo ! in Egypt's coast that hostile fleet,
By nations dreaded and by Nelson beat ;
And here shall soon another triumph come,
A deed of glory in a day of gloom ;
Distressing glory ! grievous boon of fate !
The proudest conquest, at the dearest rate.
   On shelf of deal beside the cuckoo-clock,
Of cottage-reading rests the chosen stock ;
Learning we lack, not books, but have a kind
For all our wants, a meat for every mind :
The tale for wonder and the joke for whim,
The half-sung sermon and the half-groan'd
hymn.
   No need of classing ; each within its place,
The feeling finger in the dark can trace ;
' First from the corner, farthest from the wall,'
Such all the rules, and they suffice for all.
   There pious works for Sunday's use are
found ;
Companions for that Bible newly bound ;
That Bible, bought by sixpence weekly saved,
Has choicest prints by famous hands en-
graved ;
Has choicest notes by many a famous head,
Such as to doubt have rustic readers led ;
Have made them stop to reason *why* ? and
how ?
And, where they once agreed, to cavil now.
Oh ! rather give me commentators plain,
Who with no deep researches vex the
brain ;
Who from the dark and doubtful love to
run,
And hold their glimmering tapers to the
sun ;
Who simple truth with nine-fold reason
back,
And guard the point no enemies attack.
   Bunyan's famed Pilgrim rests that shelf
upon ;
A genius rare but rude was honest John :
Not one who, early by the Muse beguiled,
Drank from her well the waters undefiled ;
Not one who slowly gain'd the hill sublime,
Then often sipp'd and little at a time ;
But one who dabbled in the sacred springs,
And drank them muddy, mix'd with baser
things.
   Here to interpret dreams we read the rules,
Science our own ! and never taught in schools ;

In moles and specks we Fortune's gifts discern,
And Fate's fix'd will from Nature's wander-
   ings learn.
Of Hermit Quarle we read, in island rare,
Far from mankind and seeming far from care;
Safe from all want, and sound in every limb;
Yes ! there was he, and there was care with
   him.
  Unbound and heap'd, these valued works
   beside,
Lay humbler works, the pedler's pack sup-
   plied ;
Yet these, long since, have all acquired a
   name ;
The Wandering Jew has found his way to
   fame ;
And fame, denied to many a labour'd song,
Crowns Thumb the great, and Hickerthrift
   the strong.
  There too is he, by wizard-power upheld,
Jack, by whose arm the giant-brood were
   quell'd :
His shoes of swiftness on his feet he placed ;
His coat of darkness on his loins he braced ;
His sword of sharpness in his hand he took,
And off the heads of doughty giants stroke :
Their glaring eyes beheld no mortal near ;
No sound of feet alarm'd the drowsy ear ;
No English blood their pagan sense could
   smell,
But heads dropp'd headlong, wondering why
   they fell.
  These are the peasant's joy, when, placed
   at ease,
Half his delighted offspring mount his knees.
  To every cot the lord's indulgent mind
Has a small space for garden-ground assign'd;
Here—till return of morn dismiss'd the farm—
The careful peasant plies the sinewy arm,
Warm'd as he works, and casts his look around
On every foot of that improving ground :
It is his own he sees ; his master's eye
Peers not about, some secret fault to spy ;
Nor voice severe is there, nor censure
   known ;—
Hope, profit, pleasure,—they are all his own.
Here grow the humble cives, and, hard by
   them,
The leek with crown globose and reedy
   stem ;
High climb his pulse in many an even row,
Deep strike the ponderous roots in soil
   below ;

And herbs of potent smell and pungent
   taste
Give a warm relish to the night's repast.
Apples and cherries grafted by his hand,
And cluster'd nuts for neighbouring market
   stand.
  Nor thus concludes his labour ; near the
   cot,
The reed-fence rises round some fav'rite spot;
Where rich carnations, pinks with purple eyes,
Proud hyacinths, the least some florist's prize,
Tulips tall-stemm'd and pounced auriculas
   rise.
  Here on a Sunday-eve, when service ends,
Meet and rejoice a family of friends ;
All speak aloud, are happy and are free,
And glad they seem, and gaily they agree.
  What, though fastidious ears may shun the
   speech,
Where all are talkers and where none can
   teach ;
Where still the welcome and the words are old,
And the same stories are for ever told ;
Yet theirs is joy that, bursting from the heart,
Prompts the glad tongue these nothings to
   impart ;
That forms these tones of gladness we despise,
That lifts their steps, that sparkles in their
   eyes ;
That talks or laughs or runs or shouts or plays,
And speaks in all their looks and all their
   ways.
  Fair scenes of peace ! ye might detain us
   long,
But vice and misery now demand the song;
And turn our view from dwellings simply
   neat,
To this infected row, we term our street.
  Here, in cabal, a disputatious crew
Each evening meet ; the sot, the cheat, the
   shrew :
Riots are nightly heard :—the curse, the cries
Of beaten wife, perverse in her replies ;
While shrieking children hold each threat'ning
   hand,
And sometimes life, and sometimes food de-
   mand :
Boys, in their first-stol'n rags, to swear begin,
And girls, who heed not dress, are skill'd in gin:
Snarers and smugglers here their gains divide;
Ensnaring females here their victims hide ;
And here is one, the sibyl of the row,
Who knows all secrets, or affects to know.

Seeking their fate, to her the simple run,
To her the guilty, theirs awhile to shun ;
Mistress of worthless arts, depraved in will,
Her care unbless'd and unrepaid her skill,
Slave to the tribe, to whose command she
    stoops,
And poorer than the poorest maid she dupes.
  Between the road-way and the walls, offence
Invades all eyes and strikes on every sense :
There lie, obscene, at every open door,
Heaps from the hearth and sweepings from
    the floor,
And day by day the mingled masses grow,
As sinks are disembogued and kennels flow.
  There hungry dogs from hungry children
    steal,
There pigs and chickens quarrel for a meal;
There dropsied infants wail without redress,
And all is want and wo and wretchedness :
Yet should these boys, with bodies bronzed
    and bare,
High-swoln and hard, outlive that lack of
    care—
Forced on some farm, the unexerted strength,
Though loth to action, is compell'd at length,
When warm'd by health, as serpents in the
    spring,
Aside their slough of indolence they fling.
  Yet, ere they go, a greater evil comes—
See ! crowded beds in those contiguous
    rooms ;
Beds but ill parted, by a paltry screen
Of paper'd lath or curtain dropp'd between;
Daughters and sons to yon compartments
    creep,
And parents here beside their children sleep:
Ye who have power, these thoughtless people
    part,
Nor let the ear be first to taint the heart.
  Come ! search within, nor sight nor smell
    regard ;
The true physician walks the foulest ward.
See ! on the floor what frouzy patches rest!
What nauseous fragments on yon fractured
    chest !
What downy dust beneath yon window-seat!
And round these posts that serve this bed for
    feet ;
This bed where all those tatter'd garments lie,
Worn by each sex, and now perforce thrown
    by !
See ! as we gaze, an infant lifts its head,
Left by neglect and burrow'd in that bed ;

The mother-gossip has the love suppress'd
An infant's cry once waken'd in her breast;
And daily prattles, as her round she takes,
(With strong resentment) of the want she
    makes.
  Whence all these woes ?—From want of
    virtuous will,
Of honest shame, of time-improving skill;
From want of care t' employ the vacant hour,
And want of ev'ry kind but want of power.
  Here are no wheels for either wool or flax,
But packs of cards—made up of sundry packs;
Here is no clock, nor will they turn the glass,
And see how swift th' important moments
    pass ;
Here are no books, but ballads on the wall,
Are some abusive, and indecent all ;
Pistols are here, unpair'd; with nets and
    hooks,
Of every kind, for rivers, ponds, and brooks;
An ample flask, that nightly rovers fill
With recent poison from the Dutchman's
    still ;
A box of tools, with wires of various size,
Frocks, wigs, and hats, for night or day dis-
    guise,
And bludgeons stout to gain or guard a prize.
  To every house belongs a space of ground,
Of equal size, once fenced with paling round ;
That paling now by slothful waste destroy'd,
Dead gorse and stumps of elder fill the void;
Save in the centre-spot, whose walls of clay
Hide sots and striplings at their drink or play:
Within, a board, beneath a tiled retreat,
Allures the bubble and maintains the cheat;
Where heavy ale in spots like varnish shows,
Where chalky tallies yet remain in rows ;
Black pipes and broken jugs the seats defile,
The walls and windows, rhymes and reck'nings
    vile ;
Prints of the meanest kind disgrace the door,
And cards, in curses torn, lie fragments on
    the floor.
  Here his poor bird th' inhuman cocker
    brings,
Arms his hard heel and clips his golden wings;
With spicy food th' impatient spirit feeds,
And shouts and curses as the battle bleeds.
Struck through the brain, deprived of both
    his eyes,
The vanquish'd bird must combat till he dies ;
Must faintly peck at his victorious foe,
And reel and stagger at each feeble blow :

When fall'n, the savage grasps his dabbled
            plumes,
His blood-stain'd arms, for other deaths as-
            sumes ;
And damns the craven fowl, that lost his stake,
And only bled and perish'd for his sake.
     Such are our peasants, those to whom we
            yield
Praise with relief, the fathers of the field ;
And these who take from our reluctant hands,
What Burn advises or the Bench commands.
     Our farmers round, well pleased with con-
            stant gain,
Like other farmers, flourish and complain.—
These are our groups; our portraits next
            appear,
And close our exhibition for the year.

     WITH evil omen we that year begin :
A Child of Shame,—stern Justice adds, of Sin,
Is first recorded ;—I would hide the deed,
But vain the wish ; I sigh and I proceed :
And could I well th' instructive truth convey,
'Twould warn the giddy and awake the gay.
     Of all the nymphs who gave our village
            grace,
The Miller's daughter had the fairest face :
Proud was the Miller; money was his pride;
He rode to market, as our farmers ride,
And 'twas his boast, inspired by spirits, there,
His favourite Lucy should be rich as fair ;
But she must meek and still obedient prove,
And not presume, without his leave, to love.
     A youthful Sailor heard him ;—' Ha !'
            quoth he,
' This Miller's maiden is a prize for me ;
Her charms I love, his riches I desire,
And all his threats but fan the kindling fire;
My ebbing purse no more the foe shall fill,
But Love's kind act and Lucy at the mill.'
     Thus thought the youth, and soon the
            chase began,
Stretch'd all his sail, nor thought of pause or
            plan :
His trusty staff in his bold hand he took,
Like him and like his frigate, heart of oak ;
Fresh were his features, his attire was new ;
Clean was his linen, and his jacket blue :
Of finest jean, his trowsers, tight and trim,
Brush'd the large buckle at the silver rim.
     He soon arrived, he traced the village-green,
There saw the maid, and was with pleasure
            seen ;

Then talk'd of love, till Lucy's yielding heart
Confess'd 'twas painful, though 'twas right to
            part.
     ' For ah ! my father has a haughty soul;
Whom best he loves, he loves but to control;
Me to some churl in bargain he'll consign,
And make some tyrant of the parish mine :
Cold is his heart, and he with looks severe
Has often forced but never shed the tear ;
Save, when my mother died, some drops
            express'd
A kind of sorrow for a wife at rest :—
To me a master's stern regard is shown,
I'm like his steed, prized highly as his own ;
Stroked but corrected, threaten'd when
            supplied,
His slave and boast, his victim and his pride.'
     ' Cheer up, my lass ! I'll to thy father go,
The Miller cannot be the Sailor's foe ;
Both live by Heaven's free gale, that plays
            aloud
In the stretch'd canvas and the piping shroud;
The rush of winds, the flapping sails above,
And rattling planks within, are sounds we love;
Calms are our dread; when tempests plough
            the deep,
We take a reef, and to the rocking sleep.'
     ' Ha !' quoth the Miller, moved at speech
            so rash,
' Art thou like me? then where thy notes and
            cash ?
Away to Wapping and a wife command,
With all thy wealth, a guinea, in thine hand;
There with thy messmates quaff the muddy
            cheer,
And leave my Lucy for thy betters here.'
     ' Revenge !   revenge !' the angry lover
            cried,
Then sought the nymph, and ' Be thou now
            my bride.'
Bride had she been, but they no priest could
            move
To bind in law, the couple bound by love.
     What sought these lovers then by day, by
            night ?
But stolen moments of disturb'd delight ;
Soft trembling tumults, terrors dearly prized,
Transports that pain'd, and joys that agonized:
Till the fond damsel, pleased with lad so trim,
Awed by her parent, and enticed by him,
Her lovely form from savage power to save,
Gave—not her hand—but ALL she could,
            she gave.

Then came the day of shame, the grievous
night,
The varying look, the wandering appetite;
The joy assumed, while sorrow dimm'd the
eyes,
The forced sad smiles that follow'd sudden
sighs ;
And every art, long used, but used in vain,
To hide thy progress, Nature, and thy pain.
    Too eager caution shows some danger 's
near,
The bully's bluster proves the coward's fear ;
His sober step the drunkard vainly tries,
And nymphs expose the failings they disguise.
    First, whispering gossips were in parties
seen ;
Then louder Scandal walk'd the village-green ;
Next babbling Folly told the growing ill,
And busy Malice dropp'd it at the mill.
    ' Go ! to thy curse and mine,' the Father
said,
' Strife and confusion stalk around thy bed ;
Want and a wailing brat thy portion be,
Plague to thy fondness, as thy fault to me ;—
Where skulks the villain ? '——
               ——' On the ocean wide
My William seeks a portion for his bride.'—
    ' Vain be his search ! but, till the traitor
come,
The higgler's cottage be thy future home ;
There with his ancient shrew and care abide,
And hide thy head,—thy shame thou canst
not hide.'
    Day after day was pass'd in pains and
grief ;
Week follow'd week,—and still was no relief :
Her boy was born—no lads nor lasses came
To grace the rite or give the child a name ;
Nor grave conceited nurse, of office proud,
Bore the young Christian roaring through
the crowd :
In a small chamber was my office done,
Where blinks through paper'd panes the
setting sun ;
Where noisy sparrows, perch'd on penthouse
near,
Chirp tuneless joy, and mock the frequent
tear ;
Bats on their webby wings in darkness move,
And feebly shriek their melancholy love.
    No Sailor came ; the months in terror fled !
Then news arrived—He fought, and he was
DEAD !

    At the lone cottage Lucy lives, and still
Walks for her weekly pittance to the mill ;
A mean seraglio there her father keeps,
Whose mirth insults her, as she stands and
weeps ;
And sees the plenty, while compell'd to stay,
Her father's pride, become his harlot's prey.
    Throughout the lanes she glides, at evening's
close,
And softly lulls her infant to repose ;
Then sits and gazes, but with viewless look,
As gilds the moon the rippling of the brook ;
And sings her vespers, but in voice so low,
She hears their murmurs as the waters flow :
And she too murmurs, and begins to find
The solemn wanderings of a wounded mind :
Visions of terror, views of wo succeed,
The mind's impatience, to the body's need ;
By turns to that, by turns to this a prey,
She knows what reason yields, and dreads
what madness may.
    Next, with their boy, a decent couple came,
And call'd him Robert, 'twas his father's
name ;
Three girls preceded, all by time endear'd,
And future births were neither hoped nor
fear'd :
Bless'd in each other, but to no excess ;
Health, quiet, comfort, form'd their happi-
ness ;
Love all made up of torture and delight,
Was but mere madness in this couple's sight :
Susan could think, though not without a sigh,
If she were gone, who should her place supply ;
And Robert, half in earnest, half in jest,
Talk of her spouse when he should be at rest :
Yet strange would either think it to be told,
Their love was cooling or their hearts were
cold.
Few were their acres,—but, with these con-
tent,
They were, each pay-day, ready with their
rent :
And few their wishes—what their farm
denied,
The neighbouring town at trifling cost sup-
plied.
If at the draper's window Susan cast
A longing look, as with her goods she pass'd,
And, with the produce of the wheel and churn,
Bought her a Sunday-robe on her return ;
True to her maxim, she would take no rest,
Till care repaid that portion to the chest :

Or if, when loitering at the Whitsun-fair,
Her Robert spent some idle shillings there ;
Up at the barn, before the break of day,
He made his labour for th' indulgence pay:
Thus both—that waste itself might work in
　　vain—
Wrought double tides, and all was well again.
　Yet, though so prudent, there were times
　　of joy,
(The day they wed, the christening of the
　　boy),
When to the wealthier farmers there was
　　shown
Welcome unfeign'd, and plenty like their own;
For Susan served the great, and had some
　　pride
Among our topmost people to preside :
Yet in that plenty, in that welcome free,
There was the guiding nice frugality,
That, in the festal as the frugal day,
Has, in a different mode, a sovereign sway;
As tides the same attractive influence know,
In the last ebb and in their proudest flow ;
The wise frugality, that does not give
A life to saving, but that saves to live ;
Sparing, not pinching, mindful though not
　　mean,
O'er all presiding, yet in nothing seen.
　Recorded next a babe of love I trace !
Of many loves, the mother's fresh disgrace.—
　' Again, thou harlot ! could not all thy pain,
All my reproof, thy wanton thoughts re-
　　strain ? '
　' Alas ! your reverence, wanton thoughts,
　　I grant,
Were once my motive, now the thoughts of
　　want ;
Women, like me, as ducks in a decoy,
Swim down a stream, and seem to swim in
　　joy ;
Your sex pursue us, and our own disdain ;
Return is dreadful, and escape is vain.
Would men forsake us, and would women
　　strive
To help the fall'n, their virtue might revive.'
　For rite of churching soon she made her
　　way,
In dread of scandal, should she miss the day :—
Two matrons came ! with them she humbly
　　knelt,
Their action copied and their comforts felt,
From that great pain and peril to be free,
Though still in peril of that pain to be ;

Alas ! what numbers, like this amorous dame
Are quick to censure, but are dead to shame!
　Twin-infants then appear ; a girl, a boy,
Th' o'erflowing cup of Gerard Ablett's joy :
One had I named in every year that pass'd
Since Gerard wed ! and twins behold at last!
Well pleased, the bridegroom smiled to hear—
　' A vine
Fruitful and spreading round the walls be
　　thine,
And branch-like be thine offspring !'—
　　Gerard then
Look'd joyful love, and softly said, ' Amen.'
Now of that vine he'd have no more increase,
Those playful branches now disturb his peace:
Them he beholds around his table spread,
But finds, the more the branch, the less the
　　bread ;
And while they run his humble walls about,
They keep the sunshine of good-humour out.
　Cease, man, to grieve ! thy master's lot
　　survey,
Whom wife and children, thou and thine
　　obey ;
A farmer proud, beyond a farmer's pride,
Of all around the envy or the guide ;
Who trots to market on a steed so fine,
That when I meet him, I'm ashamed of mine;
Whose board is high up-heap'd with generous
　　fare,
Which five stout sons and three tall daughters
　　share :
Cease, man, to grieve, and listen to his care.
　A few years fled, and all thy boys shall be
Lords of a cot, and labourers like thee :
Thy girls unportion'd neighb'ring youths
　　shall lead
Brides from my church, and thenceforth thou
　　art freed :
But then thy master shall of cares complain,
Care after care, a long connected train ;
His sons for farms shall ask a large supply,
For farmers' sons each gentle miss shall sigh;
Thy mistress, reasoning well of life's decay,
Shall ask a chaise, and hardly brook delay;
The smart young cornet who, with so much
　　grace,
Rode in the ranks and betted at the race,
While the vex'd parent rails at deed so rash,
Shall d—n his luck, and stretch his hand for
　　cash.
Sad troubles, Gerard ! now pertain to thee,
When thy rich master seems from trouble free;

But 'tis one fate at different times assign'd,
And thou shalt lose the cares that he must
  find.
    ' Ah ! ' quoth our village Grocer, rich and
      old,
' Would I might one such cause for care
    behold ! '
To whom his Friend, ' Mine greater bliss
    would be,
Would Heav'n take those my spouse assigns
    to me.'
    Aged were both, that Dawkins, Ditchem
      this,
Who much of marriage thought, and much
    amiss ;
Both would delay, the one, till—riches gain'd,
The son he wish'd might be to honour train'd ;
His Friend—lest fierce intruding heirs should
    come,
To waste his hoard and vex his quiet home.
    Dawkins, a dealer once, on burthen'd back
Bore his whole substance in a pedler's pack ;
To dames discreet, the duties yet unpaid,
His stores of lace and hyson he convey'd :
When thus enrich'd, he chose at home to stop,
And fleece his neighbours in a new-built shop ;
Then woo'd a spinster blithe, and hoped,
    when wed,
For love's fair favours and a fruitful bed.
    Not so his Friend ; — on widow fair and
      staid
He fix'd his eye, but he was much afraid ;
Yet woo'd ; while she his hair of silver hue
Demurely noticed, and her eye withdrew :
Doubtful he paused—' Ah ! were I sure,' he
    cried,
' No craving children would my gains divide ;
Fair as she is, I would my widow take,
And live more largely for my partner's sake.'
    With such their views some thoughtful
    years they pass'd,
And hoping, dreading, they were bound at
    last.
And what their fate ?   Observe them as they
    go,
Comparing fear with fear and wo with wo.
    ' Humphrey ! ' said Dawkins, ' envy in my
    breast
Sickens to see thee in thy children bless'd ;
They are thy joys, while I go grieving home
To a sad spouse, and our eternal gloom :
We look despondency ; no infant near,
To bless the eye or win the parent's ear ;

Our sudden heats and quarrels to allay,
And soothe the petty sufferings of the day :
Alike our want, yet both the want reprove ;
Where are, I cry, these pledges of our love ?
When she, like Jacob's wife, makes fierce reply,
Yet fond—Oh ! give me children, or I die :
And I return—still childless doom'd to live,
Like the vex'd patriarch—Are they mine to
    give ?
Ah ! much I envy thee thy boys, who ride
On poplar branch, and canter at thy side ;
And girls, whose cheeks thy chin's fierce
    fondness know,
And with fresh beauty at the contact glow.'
    ' Oh !   simple friend,' said Ditchem,
    ' would'st thou gain
A father's pleasure by a husband's pain ?
Alas ! what pleasure—when some vig'rous
    boy
Should swell thy pride, some rosy girl thy
    joy ;
Is it to doubt who grafted this sweet flower,
Or whence arose that spirit and that power ?
    Four years I've wed ; not one has pass'd in
    vain :
Behold the fifth ! behold, a babe again !
My wife's gay friends th' unwelcome imp
    admire,
And fill the room with gratulation dire :
While I in silence sate, revolving all
That influence ancient men, or that befall ;
A gay pert guest—Heav'n knows his business
    —came ;
A glorious boy, he cried, and what the name ?
Angry I growl'd,—My spirit cease to tease,
Name it yourselves,—Cain, Judas, if you
    please ;
His father's give him, — should you that
    explore,
The devil's or yours :—I said, and sought the
    door.
My tender partner not a word or sigh
Gives to my wrath, nor to my speech reply ;
But takes her comforts, triumphs in my pain,
And looks undaunted for a birth again.'
    Heirs thus denied afflict the pining heart,
And thus afforded, jealous pangs impart ;
Let, therefore, none avoid, and none demand
These arrows number'd for the giant's hand.
    Then with their infants three, the parents
    came,
And each assign'd—'twas all they had—a
    name ;

Names of no mark or price; of them not one
Shall court our view on the sepulchral stone,
Or stop the clerk, th' engraven scrolls to spell,
Or keep the sexton from the sermon bell.
  An orphan-girl succeeds: ere she was born
Her father died, her mother on that morn:
The pious mistress of the school sustains
Her parents' part, nor their affection feigns,
But pitying feels: with due respect and joy,
I trace the matron at her loved employ;
What time the striplings, wearied e'en with
    play,
Part at the closing of the summer's day,
And each by different path returns the well-
    known way—
Then I behold her at her cottage-door,
Frugal of light;—her Bible laid before,
When on her double duty she proceeds,
Of time as frugal—knitting as she reads:
Her idle neighbours, who approach to tell
Some trifling tale, her serious looks compel
To hear reluctant,—while the lads who pass,
In pure respect, walk silent on the grass:
Then sinks the day, but not to rest she goes,
Till solemn prayers the daily duties close.
  But I digress, and lo! an infant train
Appear, and call me to my task again.
  'Why Lonicera wilt thou name thy child?'
I ask'd the Gardener's wife, in accents mild:
  'We have a right,' replied the sturdy
    dame,—
And Lonicera was the infant's name.
If next a son shall yield our Gardener joy,
Then Hyacinthus shall be that fair boy;
And if a girl, they will at length agree,
That Belladonna that fair maid shall be.
  High-sounding words our worthy Gardener
    gets,
And at his club to wondering swains repeats;
He then of Rhus and Rododendron speaks,
And Allium calls his onions and his leeks;
Nor weeds are now, for whence arose the
    weed,
Scarce plants, fair herbs, and curious flowers
    proceed;
Where Cuckoo-pints and Dandelions sprung,
(Gross names had they our plainer sires
    among,)
There Arums, there Leontodons we view,
And Artemisia grows, where Wormwood grew.
  But though no weed exists his garden round,
From Rumex strong our Gardener frees his
    ground,

Takes soft Senicio from the yielding land,
And grasps the arm'd Urtica in his hand.
  Not Darwin's self had more delight to sing
Of floral courtship, in th' awaken'd Spring,
Than Peter Pratt, who simpering loves to tell
How rise the Stamens, as the Pistils swell;
How bend and curl the moist-top to the spouse,
And give and take the vegetable vows;
How those esteem'd of old but tips and
    chives,
Are tender husbands and obedient wives;
Who live and love within the sacred bower,—
That bridal bed, the vulgar term a flower.
  Hear Peter proudly, to some humble friend,
A wondrous secret, in his science, lend:—
'Would you advance the nuptial hour, and
    bring
The fruit of Autumn with the flowers of
    Spring;
View that light frame where Cucumis lies
    spread,
And trace the husbands in their golden bed,
Three powder'd Anthers;—then no more
    delay,
But to the Stigma's tip their dust convey;
Then by thyself, from prying glance secure,
Twirl the full tip and make your purpose sure;
A long-abiding race the deed shall pay,
Nor one unbless'd abortion pine away.'
  T' admire their friend's discourse our swains
    agree,
And call it science and philosophy.
  'Tis good, 'tis pleasant, through th'
    advancing year,
To see unnumber'd growing forms appear;
What leafy-life from Earth's broad bosom
    rise!
What insect-myriads seek the summer skies!
What scaly tribes in every streamlet move!
What plumy people sing in every grove!
All with the year awaked to life, delight, and
    love.
Then names are good; for how, without their
    aid,
Is knowledge, gain'd by man, to man con-
    vey'd?
But from that source shall all our pleasures
    flow?
Shall all our knowledge be those names to
    know?
Then he, with memory bless'd, shall bear away
The palm from Grew, and Middleton, and
    Ray:

No ! let us rather seek, in grove and field,
What food for wonder, what for use they
    yield ;
Some just remark from Nature's people bring,
And some new source of homage for her King.
    Pride lives with all ; strange names our
    rustics give
To helpless infants, that their own may live;
Pleased to be known, they'll some attention
    claim,
And find some by-way to the house of fame.
    The straightest furrow lifts the ploughman's
    art,
The hat he gain'd has warmth for head and
    heart ;
The bowl that beats the greater number down
Of tottering nine-pins, gives to fame the
    clown ;
Or, foil'd in these, he opes his ample jaws,
And lets a frog leap down, to gain applause ;
Or grins for hours, or tipples for a week,
Or challenges a well-pinch'd pig to squeak :
Some idle deed, some child's preposterous
    name,
Shall make him known, and give his folly
    fame.
    To name an infant meet our village-sires,
Assembled all, as such event requires ;
Frequent and full, the rural sages sate,
And speakers many urged the long debate,—
Some harden'd knaves, who roved the country
    round,
Had left a babe within the parish-bound.—
First, of the fact they question'd—' Was it
    true ? '
The child was brought—' What then remain'd
    to do ?
Was't dead or living ? ' This was fairly
    proved,—
'Twas pinch'd, it roar'd, and every doubt
    removed.
Then by what name th' unwelcome guest to
    call
Was long a question, and it posed them all ;
For he who lent it to a babe unknown,
Censorious men might take it for his own :
They look'd about, they gravely spoke to all
And not one Richard answe.'d to the call.
Next they inquired the day, when, passing by,
Th' unlucky peasant heard the stranger's cry;
This known,—how food and raiment they
    might give,
Was next debated—for the rogue would live;

At last, with all their words and work content,
Back to their homes the prudent vestry went,
And Richard Monday to the workhouse sent.
There was he pinch'd and pitied, thump'd and
    fed,
And duly took his beatings and his bread ;
Patient in all control, in all abuse,
He found contempt and kicking have their
    use :
Sad, silent, supple ; bending to the blow,
A slave of slaves, the lowest of the low ;
His pliant soul gave way to all things base,
He knew no shame, he dreaded no disgrace.
It seem'd, so well his passions he suppress'd,
No feeling stirr'd his ever-torpid breast ;
Him might the meanest pauper bruise and
    cheat,
He was a footstool for the beggar's feet ;
His were the legs that ran at all commands;
They used on all occasion Richard's hands :
His very soul was not his own ; he stole
As others order'd, and without a dole ;
In all disputes, on either part he lied,
And freely pledged his oath on either side ;
In all rebellions Richard join'd the rest,
In all detections Richard first confess'd :
Yet, though disgraced, he watch'd his time so
    well,
He rose in favour, when in fame he fell ;
Base was his usage, vile his whole employ,
And all despised and fed the pliant boy.
At length, ''tis time he should abroad be sent,'
Was whisper'd near him,—and abroad he
    went ;
One morn they call'd him, Richard answer'd
    not ;
They deem'd him hanging, and in time
    forgot,—
Yet miss'd him long, as each, throughout the
    clan,
Found he ' had better spared a better man.'
    Now Richard's talents for the world were
    fit,
He'd no small cunning, and had some small
    wit ;
Had that calm look which seem'd to all assent,
And that complacent speech which nothing
    meant :
He'd but one care, and that he strove to hide,
How best for Richard Monday to provide.
Steel, through opposing plates, the magnet
    draws,
And steely atoms culls from dust and straws;

And thus our hero, to his interest true,
Gold through all bars and from each trifle
    drew ;
But still more surely round the world to go,
This fortune's child had neither friend nor
    foe.

  Long lost to us, at last our man we trace,—
Sir Richard Monday died at Monday-place :
His lady's worth, his daughter's we peruse,
And find his grandsons all as rich as Jews :
He gave reforming charities a sum,
And bought the blessings of the blind and
    dumb ;
Bequeathed to missions money from the
    stocks,
And Bibles issued from his private box ;
But to his native place severely just,
He left a pittance bound in rigid trust ;—
Two paltry pounds, on every quarter's-day,
(At church produced) for forty loaves should
    pay ;
A stinted gift, that to the parish shows
He kept in mind their bounty and their blows !

  To farmers three, the year has given a son,
Finch on the Moor, and French, and Middle-
    ton.
Twice in this year a female Giles I see,
A Spalding once, and once a Barnaby :—
A humble man is he, and, when they meet,
Our farmers find him on a distant seat ;
There for their wit he serves a constant
    theme,—
' They praise his dairy, they extol his team,
They ask the price of each unrivall'd steed,
And whence his sheep, that admirable breed ?
His thriving arts they beg he would explain,
And where he puts the money he must gain.
They have their daughters, but they fear
    their friend
Would think his sons too much would con-
    descend ;—
They have their sons who would their fortunes
    try,
But fear his daughters will their suit deny.'
So runs the joke, while James, with sigh pro-
    found,
And face of care, looks moveless on the
    ground ;
His cares, his sighs, provoke the insult more,
And point the jest—for Barnaby is poor.

  Last in my list, five untaught lads appear;
Their father dead, compassion sent them
    here,—

For still that rustic infidel denied
To have their names with solemn rite applied:
His, a lone house, by Deadman's Dyke-way
    stood ;
And his, a nightly haunt, in Lonely-wood :
Each village inn has heard the ruffian boast,
That he believed ' in neither God nor ghost;
That, when the sod upon the sinner press'd,
He, like the saint, had everlasting rest ;
That never priest believed his doctrines true,
But would, for profit, own himself a Jew,
Or worship wood and stone, as honest heathen
    do ;
That fools alone on future worlds rely,
And all who die for faith, deserve to die.'
  These maxims,—part th' attorney's clerk
    profess'd,
His own transcendent genius found the rest.
Our pious matrons heard, and, much amazed,
Gazed on the man, and trembled as they
    gazed ;
And now his face explored, and now his feet,
Man's dreaded foe, in this bad man, to meet:
But him our drunkards as their champion
    raised,
Their bishop call'd, and as their hero praised;
Though most, when sober, and the rest, when
    sick,
Had little question whence his bishopric.
  But he, triumphant spirit ! all things
    dared,
He poach'd the wood, and on the warren
    snared ;
'Twas his, at cards, each novice to trepan,
And call the wants of rogues the rights of
    man ;
Wild as the winds, he let his offspring rove,
And deem'd the marriage-bond the bane of
    love.

  What age and sickness, for a man so bold,
Had done, we know not ;—none beheld him
    old :
By night, as business urged, he sought the
    wood,—
The ditch was deep,—the rain had caused a
    flood,—
The foot-bridge fail'd,—he plunged beneath
    the deep,
And slept, if truth were his, th' eternal sleep.
  These have we named ; on life's rough sea
    they sail,
With many a prosperous, many an adverse
    gale !

Where passion soon, like powerful winds, will rage,
And prudence, wearied, with their strength engage :
Then each, in aid, shall some companion ask,
For help or comfort in the tedious task ;
And what that help—what joys from union flow,

What good or ill, we next prepare to show ;
And row, meantime, our weary bark ashore,
As Spenser his—but not with Spenser's oar.[1]

[1] Allusions of this kind are to be found in the *Fairy Queen.* See the end of the first book, and other places.

PART II.   MARRIAGES

Nubere si quà voles, quamvis properabitis ambo,
Differ ;   habent parvae commoda magna morae.
Ovid, Fast. lib. iii. vv. 393, 4.

Previous Consideration necessary: yet not too long Delay—Imprudent Marriage of old Kirk and his Servant—Comparison between an ancient and youthful Partner to a young Man—Prudence of Donald the Gardener—Parish Wedding: the compelled Bridegroom: Day of Marriage, how spent—Relation of the Accomplishments of Phœbe Dawson, a rustic Beauty : her Lover: his Courtship: their Marriage—Misery of Precipitation—The wealthy Couple: Reluctance in the Husband ; why ?—Unusually fair Signatures in the Register: the common Kind—Seduction of Lucy Collins by Footman Daniel : her rustic Lover : her Return to him—An ancient Couple : Comparisons on the Occasion—More pleasant View of Village Matrimony : Farmers celebrating the Day of Marriage : their Wives—Reuben and Rachel, a happy Pair : an Example of prudent Delay—Reflections on their State who were not so prudent, and its Improvement towards the Termination of Life : an old Man so circumstanced—Attempt to seduce a Village Beauty : Persuasion and Reply : the Event.

DISPOSED to wed, e'en while you hasten, stay ;
There 's great advantage in a small delay:—
Thus Ovid sang, and much the wise approve
This prudent maxim of the priest of Love :
If poor, delay for future want prepares,
And eases humble life of half its cares ;
If rich, delay shall brace the thoughtful mind,
T' endure the ills that e'en the happiest find :
Delay shall knowledge yield on either part,
And show the value of the vanquish'd heart;

The humours, passions, merits, failings prove,
And gently raise the veil that 's worn by Love ;
Love, that impatient guide !—too proud to think
Of vulgar wants, of clothing, meat and drink,
Urges our amorous swains their joys to seize,
And then, at rags and hunger frighten'd, flees :—
Yet not too long in cold debate remain ;
Till age refrain not—but if old, refrain.
  By no such rule would Gaffer Kirk be tried;
First in the year he led a blooming bride,
And stood a wither'd elder at her side.
Oh ! Nathan ! Nathan ! at thy years trepann'd,
To take a wanton harlot by the hand !
Thou, who wert used so tartly to express
Thy sense of matrimonial happiness,
Till every youth, whose bans at church were read,
Strove not to meet, or meeting, hung his head ;
And every lass forbore at thee to look,
A sly old fish, too cunning for the hook ;—
And now at sixty, that pert dame to see,
Of all thy savings mistress, and of thee ;
Now will the lads, rememb'ring insults past,
Cry, ' What, the wise-one in the trap at last ! '
Fie ! Nathan ! fie ! to let an artful jade
The close recesses of thine heart invade ;
What grievous pangs ! what suffering she'll impart,
And fill with anguish that rebellious heart ;
For thou wilt strive incessantly, in vain,
By threatening speech, thy freedom to regain :
But she for conquest married, nor will prove
A dupe to thee, thine anger, or thy love ;
Clamorous her tongue will be ;—of either sex,
She'll gather friends around thee and perplex

Thy doubtful soul;—thy money she will
  waste,
In the vain ramblings of a vulgar taste;
And will be happy to exert her power,
In every eye, in thine, at every hour.
  Then wilt thou bluster—'No! I will not
    rest,
And see consumed each shilling of my chest:'
Thou wilt be valiant,—'When thy cousins
    call,
I will abuse and shut my door on all:'
Thou wilt be cruel!—'What the law allows,
That be thy portion, my ungrateful spouse!
Nor other shillings shalt thou then receive,
And when I die'——'What! may I this
    believe?
Are these true tender tears? and does my
    Kitty grieve?
Ah! crafty vixen, thine old man has fears;
But weep no more! I'm melted by thy tears;
Spare but my money; thou shalt rule ME
    still,
And see thy cousins—there! I burn the
    will.'—
  Thus with example sad, our year began,
A wanton vixen and a weary man;
'But had this tale in other guise been told,'
Young let the lover be, the lady old,
And that disparity of years shall prove
No bane of peace, although some bar to love:
'Tis not the worst, our nuptial ties among,
That joins the ancient bride and bridegroom
    young;—
Young wives, like changing winds, their
    power display,
By shifting points and varying day by day;
Now zephyrs mild, now whirlwinds in their
    force,
They sometimes speed, but often thwart our
    course;
And much experienced should that pilot be,
Who sails with them on life's tempestuous sea.
But like a trade-wind is the ancient dame,
Mild to your wish, and every day the same;
Steady as time, no sudden squalls you fear,
But set full sail and with assurance steer;
Till every danger in your way be pass'd,
And then she gently, mildly breathes her last;
Rich you arrive, in port awhile remain,
And for a second venture sail again.
  For this, blithe Donald southward made his
    way,
And left the lasses on the banks of Tay;

Him to a neighbouring garden fortune sent,
Whom we beheld, aspiringly content:
Patient and mild, he sought the dame to
    please,
Who ruled the kitchen and who bore the keys.
Fair Lucy first, the laundry's grace and pride,
With smiles and gracious looks, her fortune
    tried;
But all in vain she praised his 'pawky eyne,'
Where never fondness was for Lucy seen:
Him the mild Susan, boast of dairies, loved,
And found him civil, cautious, and unmoved:
From many a fragrant simple, Catharine's
    skill
Drew oil and essence from the boiling still;
But not her warmth, nor all her winning ways,
From his cool phlegm could Donald's spirit
    raise:
Of beauty heedless, with the merry mute,
To Mistress Dobson he preferr'd his suit;
There proved his service, there address'd his
    vows,
And saw her mistress,—friend,—protectress,
    —spouse;
A butler now, he thanks his powerful bride,
And, like her keys, keeps constant at her side.
  Next at our altar stood a luckless pair,
Brought by strong passions and a warrant
    there;
By long rent cloak, hung loosely, strove the
    bride,
From ev'ry eye, what all perceived, to hide.
While the boy-bridegroom, shuffling in his
    pace,
Now hid awhile and then exposed his face;
As shame alternately with anger strove,
The brain confused with muddy ale to move:
In haste and stammering he perform'd his
    part,
And look'd the rage that rankled in his heart;
(So will each lover inly curse his fate,
Too soon made happy and made wise too late:)
I saw his features take a savage gloom,
And deeply threaten for the days to come.
Low spake the lass, and lisp'd and minced the
    while,
Look'd on the lad, and faintly tried to smile;
With soften'd speech and humbled tone she
    strove
To stir the embers of departed love:
While he, a tyrant, frowning walk'd before,
Felt the poor purse and sought the public
    door,

She sadly following in submission went,
And saw the final shilling foully spent ; –
Then to her father's hut the pair withdrew,
And bade to love and comfort long adieu !
Ah ! fly temptation, youth, refrain ! refrain !
I preach for ever ; but I preach in vain !

Two summers since, I saw, at Lammas Fair,
The sweetest flower that ever blossom'd there,
When Phœbe Dawson gaily cross'd the Green,
In haste to see and happy to be seen :
Her air, her manners, all who saw, admired ;
Courteous though coy, and gentle though
    retired ;
The joy of youth and health her eyes dis-
    play'd,
And ease of heart her every look convey'd ;
A native skill her simple robes express'd,
As with untutor'd elegance she dress'd :
The lads around admired so fair a sight,
And Phœbe felt, and felt she gave, delight.
Admirers soon of every age she gain'd,
Her beauty won them and her worth retain'd ;
Envy itself could no contempt display,
They wish'd her well, whom yet they wish'd
    away.
Correct in thought, she judged a servant's
    place
Preserved a rustic beauty from disgrace ;
But yet on Sunday-eve, in freedom's hour,
With secret joy she felt that beauty's power,
When some proud bliss upon the heart would
    steal,
That, poor or rich, a beauty still must feel.—
At length, the youth, ordain'd to move her
    breast,
Before the swains with bolder spirit press'd ;
With looks less timid made his passion known,
And pleased by manners most unlike her own ;
Loud though in love, and confident though
    young ;
Fierce in his air, and voluble of tongue ;
By trade a tailor, though, in scorn of trade,
He served the 'Squire, and brush'd the coat
    he made :
Yet now, would Phœbe her consent afford,
Her slave alone, again he'd mount the board ;
With her should years of growing love be
    spent,
And growing wealth :—she sigh'd and look'd
    consent.
Now, through the lane, up hill, and 'cross
    the green,
(Seen by but few, and blushing to be seen—

Dejected, thoughtful, anxious, and afraid,)
Led by the lover, walk'd the silent maid :
Slow through the meadow roved they, many
    a mile
Toy'd by each bank and trifled at each stile ;
Where, as he painted every blissful view,
And highly colour'd what he strongly drew,
The pensive damsel, prone to tender fears,
Dimm'd the false prospect with prophetic
    tears.—
Thus pass'd th' allotted hours, till lingering
    late,
The lover loiter'd at the master's gate ;
There he pronounced adieu ! and yet would
    stay,
Till chidden — soothed — entreated — forced
    away ;
He would of coldness, though indulged, com-
    plain,
And oft retire and oft return again ;
When, if his teasing vex'd her gentle mind,
The grief assumed, compell'd her to be kind !
For he would proof of plighted kindness crave,
That she resented first and then forgave,
And to his grief and penance yielded more
Than his presumption had required before.—
Ah ! fly temptation, youth, refrain ! re-
    frain !
Each yielding maid and each presuming
    swain !

Lo ! now with red rent cloak and bonnet
    black,
And torn green gown loose hanging at her
    back,
One who an infant in her arms sustains,
And seems in patience striving with her pains ;
Pinch'd are her looks, as one who pines for
    bread,
Whose cares are growing and whose hopes are
    fled ;
Pale her parch'd lips, her heavy eyes sunk
    low,
And tears unnoticed from their channels flow ;
Serene her manner, till some sudden pain
Frets the meek soul, and then she 's calm
    again ;—
Her broken pitcher to the pool she takes,
And every step with cautious terror makes ;
For not alone that infant in her arms,
But nearer cause, her anxious soul alarms.
With water burthen'd, then she picks her
    way,
Slowly and cautious, in the clinging clay ;

Till, in mid-green, she trusts a place unsound,
And deeply plunges in th' adhesive ground;
Thence, but with pain, her slender foot she
    takes,
While hope the mind as strength the frame
    forsakes :
For when so full the cup of sorrow grows,
Add but a drop, it instantly o'erflows.
And now her path, but not her peace, she
    gains,
Safe from her task, but shivering with her
    pains ;
Her home she reaches, open leaves the door,
And placing first her infant on the floor,
She bares her bosom to the wind, and sits,
And sobbing struggles with the rising fits :
In vain, they come, she feels th' inflating
    grief,
That shuts the swelling bosom from relief ;
That speaks in feeble cries a soul distress'd,
Or the sad laugh that cannot be repress'd.
The neighbour-matron leaves her wheel and
    flies
With all the aid her poverty supplies ;
Unfee'd, the calls of Nature she obeys,
Not led by profit, nor allured by praise ;
And waiting long, till these contentions cease,
She speaks of comfort, and departs in peace.
    Friend of distress! the mourner feels thy aid,
She cannot pay thee, but thou wilt be paid.
    But who this child of weakness, want, and
    care ?
'Tis Phœbe Dawson, pride of Lammas Fair;
Who took her lover for his sparkling eyes,
Expressions warm, and love-inspiring lies :
Compassion first assail'd her gentle heart,
For all his suffering, all his bosom's smart :
' And then his prayers! they would a savage
    move,
And win the coldest of the sex to love : '—
But ah ! too soon his looks success declared,
Too late her loss the marriage-rite repaired;
The faithless flatterer then his vows forgot,
A captious tyrant or a noisy sot :
If present, railing, till he saw her pain'd ;
If absent, spending what their labours gain'd ;
Till that fair form in want and sickness pined,
And hope and comfort fled that gentle mind.
Then fly temptation, youth; resist, refrain!
Nor let me preach for ever and in vain !
    Next came a well-dress'd pair, who left
    their coach,
And made, in long procession, slow approach:

For this gay bride had many a female friend,
And youths were there, this favour'd youth
    t' attend :
Silent, nor wanting due respect, the crowd
Stood humbly round, and gratulation bow'd;
But not that silent crowd, in wonder fix'd,
Not numerous friends, who praise and envy
    mix'd,
Nor nymphs attending near to swell the pride
Of one more fair, the ever-smiling bride;
Nor that gay bride, adorn'd with every grace,
Nor love nor joy triumphant in her face,
Could from the youth's, sad signs of sorrow
    chase :
Why didst thou grieve ? wealth, pleasure,
    freedom thine ;
Vex'd it thy soul, that freedom to resign ?
Spake Scandal truth? 'Thou didst not then
    intend
So soon to bring thy wooing to an end ? '
Or, was it, as our prating rustics say,
To end as soon, but in a different way ?
'Tis told thy Phillis is a skilful dame,
Who play'd uninjured with the dangerous
    flame :
That, while, like Lovelace, thou thy coat dis-
    play'd,
And hid the snare for her affection laid,
Thee, with her net, she found the means to
    catch,
And at the amorous see-saw, won the match: [1]
Yet others tell, the Captain fix'd thy doubt,
He'd call thee brother, or he'd call thee out :—
But rest the motive—all retreat too late,
Joy like thy bride's should on thy brow have
    sate ;
The deed had then appear'd thine own intent,
A glorious day, by gracious fortune sent,
In each revolving year to be in triumph spent.
Then in few weeks that cloudy brow had been
Without a wonder or a whisper seen ;
And none had been so weak as to inquire,
' Why pouts my Lady ? ' or ' why frowns the
    Squire ? '
    How fair these names, how much unlike
    they look
To all the blurr'd subscriptions in my book:
The bridegroom's letters stand in row above,
Tapering yet stout, like pine-trees in his grove;
While free and fine the bride's appear below,
As light and slender as her jasmines grow.

---

[1] *Clarissa*, vol. vii, Lovelace's Letter.

Mark now in what confusion, stoop or stand,
The crooked scrawls of many a clownish hand;
Now out, now in, they droop, they fall, they
    rise,
Like raw recruits drawn forth for exercise ;
Ere yet reform'd and modell'd by the drill,
The free-born legs stand striding as they will.
    Much have I tried to guide the fist along,
But still the blunderers placed their blottings
    wrong :
Behold these marks uncouth ! how strange
    that men,
Who guide the plough, should fail to guide the
    pen :
For half a mile, the furrows even lie ;
For half an inch the letters stand awry ;—
Our peasants, strong and sturdy in the field,
Cannot these arms of idle students wield :
Like them, in feudal days, their valiant lords
Resign'd the pen and grasp'd their conqu'ring
    swords ;
They to robed clerks and poor dependent men
Left the light duties of the peaceful pen ;
Nor to their ladies wrote, but sought to prove,
By deeds of death, their hearts were fill'd with
    love.
    But yet, small arts have charms for female
    eyes ;
Our rustic nymphs the beau and scholar prize;
Unletter'd swains and ploughmen coarse they
    slight,
For those who dress, and amorous scrolls in-
    dite.
    For Lucy Collins happier days had been,
Had Footman Daniel scorn'd his native green;
Or when he came an idle coxcomb down,
Had he his love reserved for lass in town;
To Stephen Hill she then had pledged her
    truth,—
A sturdy, sober, kind, unpolish'd youth ;
But from that day, that fatal day she spied
The pride of Daniel, Daniel was her pride.
In all concerns was Stephen just and true ;
But coarse his doublet was and patch'd in
    view,
And felt his stockings were, and blacker than
    his shoe ;
While Daniel's linen all was fine and fair,—
His master wore it, and he deign'd to wear :
(To wear his livery, some respect might prove ;
To wear his linen, must be sign of love :)
Blue was his coat, unsoil'd by spot or stain ;
His hose were silk, his shoes of Spanish-grain ;

A silver knot his breadth of shoulder bore ;
A diamond buckle blazed his breast before—
Diamond he swore it was ! and show'd it as he
    swore ;
Rings on his fingers shone ; his milk-white
    hand
Could pick-tooth case and box for snuff
    command :
And thus, with clouded cane, a fop complete,
He stalk'd, the jest and glory of the street.
Join'd with these powers, he could so sweetly
    sing,
Talk with such toss, and saunter with such
    swing ;
Laugh with such glee, and trifle with such art,
That Lucy's promise fail'd to shield her heart.
    Stephen, meantime, to ease his amorous
    cares,
Fix'd his full mind upon his farm's affairs ;
Two pigs, a cow, and wethers half a score,
Increased his stock, and still he look'd for
    more.
He, for his acres few, so duly paid,
That yet more acres to his lot were laid ;
Till our chaste nymphs no longer felt disdain,
And prudent matrons praised the frugal swain;
Who thriving well, through many a fruitful
    year,
Now clothed himself anew, and acted overseer.
    Just then poor Lucy, from her friend in
    town,
Fled in pure fear, and came a beggar down;
Trembling, at Stephen's door she knock'd
    for bread,—
Was chidden first, next pitied, and then fed ;
Then sat at Stephen's board, then shared in
    Stephen's bed :
All hope of marriage lost in her disgrace,
He mourns a flame revived, and she a love of
    lace.
    Now to be wed a well-match'd couple came;
Twice had old Lodge been tied, and twice the
    dame ;
Tottering they came and toying, (odious
    scene !)
And fond and simple, as they'd always been.
Children from wedlock we by laws restrain;
Why not prevent them, when they're such
    again ?
Why not forbid the doting souls, to prove
Th' indecent fondling of preposterous love ?
In spite of prudence, uncontroll'd by shame,
The amorous senior woos the toothless dame,

CR.

Relating idly, at the closing eve,
The youthful follies he disdains to leave ;
Till youthful follies wake a transient fire,
When arm in arm they totter and retire.

So a fond pair of solemn birds, all day,
Blink in their seat and doze the hours away;
Then by the moon awaken'd, forth they move,
And fright the songsters with their cheerless love.

So two sear trees, dry, stunted, and un-
sound,
Each other catch, when dropping to the
ground ;
Entwine their wither'd arms 'gainst wind and
weather,
And shake their leafless heads and drop
together.

So two cold limbs, touch'd by Galvani's
wire,
Move with new life, and feel awaken'd fire;
Quivering awhile, their flaccid forms remain,
Then turn to cold torpidity again.

' But ever frowns your Hymen ? man and
maid,
Are all repenting, suffering, or betray'd ? '
Forbid it, Love ! we have our couples here
Who hail the day in each revolving year :
These are with us, as in the world around ;
They are not frequent, but they may be
found.

Our farmers too, what though they fail to
prove,
In Hymen's bonds, the tenderest slaves of
love,
(Nor, like those pairs whom sentiment unites,
Feel they the fervour of the mind's delights;)
Yet coarsely kind and comfortably gay,
They heap the board and hail the happy day:
And though the bride, now freed from school,
admits,
Of pride implanted there, some transient fits,
Yet soon she casts her girlish flights aside,
And in substantial blessings rests her pride.
No more she moves in measured steps, no
more
Runs, with bewilder'd ear, her music o'er ;
No more recites her French the hinds among,
But chides her maidens in her mother-tongue;
Her tambour-frame she leaves and diet spare,
Plain work and plenty with her house to
share ;
Till, all her varnish lost, in few short years,
In all her worth, the farmer's wife appears.

Yet not the ancient kind ; nor she who
gave
Her soul to gain—a mistress and a slave :
Who not to sleep allow'd the needful time ;
To whom repose was loss, and sport a crime ;
Who, in her meanest room (and all were
mean),
A noisy drudge, from morn till night was
seen ;—
But she, the daughter, boasts a decent room,
Adorn'd with carpet, form'd in Wilton's
loom ;
Fair prints along the paper'd wall are spread;
There, Werter sees the sportive children fed,
And Charlotte, here, bewails her lover dead.
'Tis here, assembled, while in space apart
Their husbands, drinking, warm the opening
heart,
Our neighbouring dames, on festal days,
unite
With tongues more fluent and with hearts as
light ;
Theirs is that art, which English wives alone
Profess—a boast and privilege their own ;
An art it is, where each at once attends
To all, and claims attention from her friends,
When they engage the tongue, the eye, the
ear,
Reply when list'ning, and when speaking
hear :
The ready converse knows no dull delays,
' But double are the pains, and double be the
praise [1].'
Yet not to those alone who bear command
Heaven gives a heart to hail the marriage
band ;
Among their servants, we the pairs can show,
Who much to love and more to prudence owe:
Reuben and Rachel, though as fond as doves,
Were yet discreet and cautious in their
loves ;
Nor would attend to Cupid's wild commands,
Till cool reflection bade them join their hands:
When both were poor, they thought it argued
ill
Of hasty love to make them poorer still ;
Year after year, with savings long laid by,
They bought the future dwelling's full supply;
Her frugal fancy cull'd the smaller ware,
The weightier purchase ask'd her Reuben's
care ;

[1] Spenser.

Together then their last year's gain they
    threw,
And lo ! an auction'd bed, with curtains neat
    and new.
Thus both, as prudence counsell'd, wisely
    stay'd,
And cheerful then the calls of Love obey'd :
What if, when Rachel gave her hand, 'twas
    one
Embrown'd by Winter's ice and Summer's
    sun ?
What if, in Reuben's hair, the female eye
Usurping grey among he black could spy ?
What if, in both, life's bloomy flush was lost,
And their full autumn felt the mellowing frost ?
Yet time, who blow'd the rose of youth away,
Had left the vigorous stem without decay ;
Like those tall elms, in Farmer Frankford's
    ground,
They'll grow no more,—but all their growth is
    sound ;
By time confirm'd and rooted in the land,
The storms they've stood, still promise they
    shall stand.
    These are the happier pairs, their life has
    rest,
Their hopes are strong, their humble portion
    bless'd ;
While those more rash to hasty marriage led,
Lament th' impatience which now stints their
    bread :
When such their union, years their cares in-
    crease,
Their love grows colder, and their pleasures
    cease ;
In health just fed, in sickness just relieved ;
By hardships harass'd and by children
    grieved ;
In petty quarrels and in peevish strife,
The once fond couple waste the spring of life :
But when to age mature those children grown,
Find hopes and homes and hardships of their
    own,
The harass'd couple feel their lingering woes
Receding slowly, till they find repose.
Complaints and murmurs then are laid aside,
(By reason these subdued, and those by
    pride ;)
And, taught by care, the patient man and wife
Agree to share the bitter-sweet of life ;
(Life that has sorrow much and sorrow's cure,
Where they who most enjoy shall much en-
    dure :)

Their rest, their labours, duties, sufferings,
    prayers,
Compose the soul, and fit it for its cares ;
Their graves before them and their griefs
    behind,
Have each a med'cine for the rustic mind ;
Nor shall he care to whom his wealth shall go,
Or who shall labour with his spade and hoe ;
But as he lends the strength that yet remains,
And some dead neighbour on his bier sustains,
(One with whom oft he whirl'd the bounding
    flail,
Toss'd the broad coit, or took th' inspiring
    ale,)
' For me,' (he meditates), ' shall soon be done
This friendly duty, when my race be run ;
'Twas first in trouble as in error pass'd,
Dark clouds and stormy cares whole years
    o'ercast,
But calm my setting day, and sunshine smiles
    at last :
My vices punish'd and my follies spent,
Not loth to die, but yet to live content,
I rest :'—then casting on the grave his eye,
His friend compels a tear, and his own griefs
    a sigh.
    Last on my list appears a match of love,
And one of virtue ;—happy may it prove !—
Sir Edward Archer is an amorous knight,
And maidens chaste and lovely shun his
    sight ;
His bailiff's daughter suited much his taste,
For Fanny Price was lovely and was chaste ;
To her the Knight with gentle looks drew
    near,
And timid voice assumed, to banish fear.—
    ' Hope of my life, dear sovereign of my
    breast,
Which, since I knew thee, knows not joy nor
    rest ;
Know, thou art all that my delighted eyes,
My fondest thoughts, my proudest wishes
    prize ;
And is that bosom—(what on earth so fair !)
To cradle some coarse peasant's sprawling
    heir ?
To be that pillow which some surly swain
May treat with scorn and agonize with pain ?
Art thou, sweet maid, a ploughman's wants
    to share,
To dread his insult, to support his care ;
To hear his follies, his contempt to prove,
And (oh ! the torment !) to endure his love ;

Till want and deep regret those charms de-
stroy,
That time would spare, if time were pass'd in
joy ?
With him, in varied pains, from morn till
night,
Your hours shall pass ; yourself a ruffian's
right ;
Your softest bed shall be the knotted wool ;
Your purest drink the waters of the pool ;
Your sweetest food will but your life sustain,
And your best pleasure be a rest from pain ;
While, through each year, as health and
strength abate,
You'll weep your woes and wonder at your
fate ;
And cry, " Behold," as life's last cares come
on,
" My burthens growing when my strength is
gone."
' Now turn with me, and all the young desire,
That taste can form, that fancy can require ;
All that excites enjoyment, or procures
Wealth, health, respect, delight, and love, are
yours :
Sparkling, in cups of gold, your wines shall
flow,
Grace that fair hand, in that dear bosom
glow ;
Fruits of each clime, and flowers, through all
the year,
Shall on your walls and in your walks appear ;
Where all beholding, shall your praise repeat,
No fruit so tempting and no flower so sweet :
The softest carpets in your rooms shall lie,
Pictures of happiest loves shall meet your
eye,
And tallest mirrors, reaching to the floor,
Shall show you all the object I adore ;

Who, by the hands of wealth and fashion
dress'd,
By slaves attended and by friends caress'd,
Shall move, a wonder, through the public
ways,
And hear the whispers of adoring praise.
Your female friends, though gayest of the gay,
Shall see you happy, and shall, sighing, say,
While smother'd envy rises in the breast,—
" Oh ! that we lived so beauteous and so
bless'd ! "
' Come then, my mistress, and my wife ;
for she
Who trusts my honour is the wife for me ;
Your slave, your husband, and your friend
employ,
In search of pleasures we may both enjoy.'
To this the damsel, meekly firm, replied :
' My mother loved, was married, toil'd, and
died ;
With joys, she'd griefs, had troubles in her
course,
But not one grief was pointed by remorse ;
My mind is fix'd, to Heaven I resign,
And be her love, her life, her comforts mine.'
Tyrants have wept ; and those with hearts
of steel,
Unused the anguish of the heart to heal,
Have yet the transient power of virtue known,
And felt th' imparted joy promote their own.
Our Knight relenting, now befriends a
youth,
Who to the yielding maid had vow'd his
truth ;
And finds in that fair deed a sacred joy,
That will not perish, and that cannot cloy ;—
A living joy, that shall its spirit keep,
When every beauty fades, and all the passions
sleep.

PART III. BURIALS

Qui vultus Acherontis atri,
Qui Styga tristem, non tristis, videt,—
. . . .
Par ille Regi, par Superis erit.
SENECA, *in Agamem.* vv. 607–8 and 610.

True Christian Resignation not frequently to be seen—The Register a melancholy Record—A dying Man, who at length sends for a Priest: for what Purpose? answered—Old Collet of the Inn, an Instance of Dr. Young's slow-sudden Death: his Character and Conduct—The Manners and Management of the Widow Goe: her successful Attention to Business: her Decease unexpected—The Infant-Boy of Gerard Ablett dies: Reflections on his Death, and the Survivor his Sister Twin—The Funeral of the deceased Lady of the Manor described: her neglected Mansion: Undertaker and Train: the Character which her Monument will hereafter display—Burial of an ancient Maiden: some former Drawback on her Virgin-fame: Description of her House and Household: Her Manners, Apprehensions, Death—Isaac Ashford, a virtuous Peasant, dies: his manly Character: Reluctance to enter the Poor-House: and why—Misfortune and Derangement of Intellect in Robin Dingley: whence they proceeded: he is not restrained by Misery from a wandering Life: his various Returns to his Parish: his final Return—Wife of Farmer Frankford dies in Prime of Life: Affliction in Consequence of such Death: melancholy View of her House, &c. on her Family's Return from her Funeral: Address to Sorrow—Leah Cousins, a Midwife: her Character; and successful Practice: at length opposed by Doctor Glibb: Opposition in the Parish: Argument of the Doctor; of Leah: her Failure and Decease—Burial of Roger Cuff, a Sailor: his Enmity to his Family; how it originated: his Experiment and its Consequence—The Register terminates—A Bell heard: Inquiry for whom? The Sexton—Character of old Dibble, and the five Rectors whom he served—Reflections—Conclusion.

THERE was, 'tis said, and I believe, a time,
When humble Christians died with views
  sublime;

When all were ready for their faith to bleed,
But few to write or wrangle for their creed;
When lively Faith upheld the sinking heart,
And friends, assured to meet, prepared to
  part;
When Love felt hope, when Sorrow grew
  serene,
And all was comfort in the death-bed scene.
  Alas! when now the gloomy king they
  wait,
'Tis weakness yielding to resistless fate;
Like wretched men upon the ocean cast,
They labour hard and struggle to the last;
' Hope against hope,' and wildly gaze around,
In search of help that never shall be found:
Nor, till the last strong billow stops the breath,
Will they believe them in the jaws of Death!
  When these my records I reflecting read,
And find what ills these numerous births
  succeed;
What powerful griefs these nuptial ties attend,
With what regret these painful journeys end;
When from the cradle to the grave I look,
Mine I conceive a melancholy book.
  Where now is perfect resignation seen?
Alas! it is not on the village-green:—
I've seldom known, though I have often read
Of happy peasants on their dying-bed;
Whose looks proclaim'd that sunshine of the
  breast,
That more than hope, that Heaven itself
  express'd.
  What I behold are feverish fits of strife,
'Twixt fears of dying and desire of life:
Those earthly hopes, that to the last endure;
Those fears, that hopes superior fail to cure;
At best a sad submission to the doom,
Which, turning from the danger, lets it come.
Sick lies the man, bewilder'd, lost, afraid,
His spirits vanquish'd and his strength de-
  cay'd;
No hope the friend, the nurse, the doctor
  lend—
' Call then a priest, and fit him for his end.'
A priest is call'd; 'tis now, alas! too late,
Death enters with him at the cottage-gate;
Or time allow'd—he goes, assured to find
The self-commending, all-confiding mind;

And sighs to hear, what we may justly call
Death's common-place, the train of thought in
    all.
  ' True, I'm a sinner,' feebly he begins,
' But trust in Mercy to forgive my sins : '
(Such cool confession no past crimes excite!
Such claim on Mercy seems the sinner's right!)
' I know, mankind are frail, that God is just,
And pardons those who in his mercy trust ;
We're sorely tempted in a world like this,
All men have done, and I like all, amiss ;
But now, if spared, it is my full intent
On all the past to ponder and repent :
Wrongs against me I pardon great and small,
And if I die, I die in peace with all.'
  His merits thus and not his sins confess'd,
He speaks his hopes, and leaves to Heaven
    the rest.
Alas ! are these the prospects, dull and cold,
That dying Christians to their priests unfold ?
Or mends the prospect when th' enthusiast
    cries,
' I die assured ! ' and in a rapture dies ?
  Ah, where that humble, self-abasing
    mind,
With that confiding spirit, shall we find ;
The mind that, feeling what repentance
    brings,
Dejection's terrors and Contrition's stings,
Feels then the hope, that mounts all care
    above,
And the pure joy that flows from pardoning
    love ?
  Such have I seen in death, and much
    deplore,
So many dying—that I see no more :
Lo ! now my records, where I grieve to trace,
How Death has triumph'd in so short a space;
Who are the dead, how died they, I relate,
And snatch some portion of their acts from
    fate.
  With Andrew Collett we the year begin,
The blind, fat landlord of the Old Crown
    Inn,—
Big as his butt, and, for the self-same use,
To take in stores of strong fermenting juice.
On his huge chair beside the fire he sate,
In revel chief, and umpire in debate ;
Each night his string of vulgar tales he told;
When ale was cheap and bachelors were bold:
His heroes all were famous in their days,
Cheats were his boast and drunkards had his
    praise ;

' One, in three draughts, three mugs of ale
    took down,
As mugs were then—the champion of the
    Crown ;
For thrice three days another lived on ale,
And knew no change but that of mild and stale;
Two thirsty soakers watch'd a vessel's side,
When he the tap, with dexterous hand,
    applied ;
Nor from their seats departed, till they found
That butt was out and heard the mournful
    sound.
  He praised a poacher, precious child of fun!
Who shot the keeper with his own spring-gun;
Nor less the smuggler who the exciseman tied,
And left him hanging at the birch-wood side,
There to expire ;—but one who saw him hang
Cut the good cord—a traitor of the gang.
  His own exploits with boastful glee he told,
What ponds he emptied and what pikes he
    sold ;
And how, when bless'd with sight alert and
    gay,
The night's amusements kept him through the
    day.
  He sang the praises of those times, when all
' For cards and dice, as for their drink, might
    call ;
When justice wink'd on every jovial crew,
And ten-pins tumbled in the parson's view.'
  He told, when angry wives, provoked to rail,
Or drive a third-day drunkard from his ale,
What were his triumphs, and how great the
    skill
That won the vex'd virago to his will ;
Who raving came ;—then talk'd in milder
    strain,—
Then wept, then drank, and pledged her
    spouse again.
  Such were his themes : how knaves o'er
    laws prevail,
Or, when made captives, how they fly from
    jail ;
The young how brave, how subtle were the
    old :
And oaths attested all that Folly told.
  On death like his what name shall we
    bestow,
So very sudden ! yet so very slow ?
'Twas slow : — Disease, augmenting year by
    year,
Show'd the grim king by gradual steps
    brought near :

'Twas not less sudden; in the night he
    died,
He drank, he swore, he jested, and he lied;
Thus aiding folly with departing breath :—
' Beware, Lorenzo, the slow-sudden death.'
    Next died the Widow Goe, an active dame,
Famed ten miles round, and worthy all her
    fame ;
She lost her husband when their loves were
    young,
But kept her farm, her credit, and her tongue:
Full thirty years she ruled, with matchless
    skill,
With guiding judgment and resistless will ;
Advice she scorn'd, rebellions she suppress'd,
And sons and servants bow'd at her behest.
Like that great man's, who to his Saviour
    came,
Were the strong words of this commanding
    dame ;—
' Come,' if she said, they came ; if ' go,' were
    gone ;
And if ' do this,'—that instant it was done:
Her maidens told she was all eye and ear,
In darkness saw and could at distance hear;—
No parish-business in the place could stir,
Without direction or assent from her ;
In turn she took each office as it fell,
Knew all their duties, and discharged them
    well ;
The lazy vagrants in her presence shook,
And pregnant damsels fear'd her stern
    rebuke ;
She look'd on want with judgment clear and
    cool,
And felt with reason and bestow'd by rule;
She match'd both sons and daughters to her
    mind,
And lent them eyes, for Love, she heard, was
    blind ;
Yet ceaseless still she throve, alert, alive,
The working bee, in full or empty hive ;
Busy and careful, like that working bee,
No time for love nor tender cares had she ;
But when our farmers made their amorous
    vows,
She talk'd of market-steeds and patent-
    ploughs.
Not unemploy'd her evenings pass'd away,
Amusement closed, as business waked the
    day ;
When to her toilet's brief concern she ran,
And conversation with her friends began,

Who all were welcome, what they saw, to
    share ;
And joyous neighbours praised her Christmas
    fare,
That none around might, in their scorn, com-
    plain
Of Gossip Goe as greedy in her gain.
    Thus long she reign'd, admired, if not ap-
    proved ;
Praised, if not honour'd ; fear'd, if not
    beloved ;—
When, as the busy days of Spring drew
    near,
That call'd for all the forecast of the year ;
When lively hope the rising crops survey'd,
And April promised what September paid ;
When stray'd her lambs where gorse and
    greenweed grow ;
When rose her grass in richer vales below ;
When pleased she look'd on all the smiling
    land,
And viewed the hinds, who wrought at her
    command ;
(Poultry in groups still follow'd where she
    went ;)
Then dread o'ercame her,—that her days
    were spent.
    ' Bless me! I die, and not a warning giv'n,—
With *much* to do on Earth, and ALL for
    Heav'n !—
No reparation for my soul's affairs,
No leave petition'd for the barn's repairs ;
Accounts perplex'd, my interest yet unpaid,
My mind unsettled, and my will unmade ;—
A lawyer haste, and in your way, a priest ;
And let me die in one good work at least. '
She spake, and, trembling, dropp'd upon her
    knees,
Heaven in her eye and in her hand her keys;
And still the more she found her life decay,
With greater force she grasp'd those signs of
    sway :
Then fell and died !—In haste her sons drew
    near,
And dropp'd, in haste, the tributary tear,
Then from th' adhering clasp the keys un-
    bound,
And consolation for their sorrow found.
    Death has his infant-train; his bony arm
Stri_es from the baby-cheek the rosy charm;
The brightest eye his glazing film makes
    dim,
And his cold touch sets fast the lithest limb:

He seized the sick'ning boy to Gerard lent,[1]
When three days' life, in feeble cries, were
    spent ;
In pain brought forth, those painful hours to
    stay,
To breathe in pain and sigh its soul away !
  ' But why thus lent, if thus recall'd again,
To cause and feel, to live and die in, pain ? '
Or rather say, Why grievous these appear,
If all it pays for Heaven's eternal year ;
If these sad sobs and piteous sighs secure
Delights that live, when worlds no more
    endure ?
  The sister-spirit long may lodge below,
And pains from nature, pains from reason,
    know ;
Through all the common ills of life may run,
By hope perverted and by love undone ;
A wife's distress, a mother's pangs, may
    dread,
And widow-tears, in bitter anguish, shed ;
May at old age arrive through numerous
    harms,
With children's children in those feeble arms :
Nor till by years of want and grief oppress'd,
Shall the sad spirit flee and be at rest !
  Yet happier therefore shall we deem the
    boy,
Secured from anxious care and dangerous
    joy ?
  Not so ! for then would Love Divine in
    vain
Send all the burthens weary men sustain ;
All that now curb the passions when they
    rage,
The checks of youth and the regrets of
    age ;
All that now bid us hope, believe, endure,
Our sorrow's comfort and our vice's cure ;
All that for Heaven's high joys the spirits
    train,
And charity, the crown of all, were vain.
  Say, will you call the breathless infant
    bless'd,
Because no cares the silent grave molest ?
So would you deem the nursling from the
    wing
Untimely thrust and never train'd to sing ;
But far more bless'd the bird whose grateful
    voice
Sings its own joy and makes the woods rejoice,

1 See p. 56.

Though, while untaught, ere yet he charm'd
    the ear,
Hard were his trials and his pains severe !
  Next died the Lady who yon Hall possess'd ;
And here they brought her noble bones to rest.
In Town she dwelt ;—forsaken stood the Hall :
Worms ate the floors, the tap'stry fled the
    wall :
No fire the kitchen's cheerless grate display'd ;
No cheerful light the long-closed sash con-
    vey'd ;
The crawling worm, that turns a summer-fly,
Here spun his shroud and laid him up to die
The winter-death :—upon the bed of state,
The bat shrill-shrieking woo'd his flickering
    mate ;
To empty rooms the curious came no more,
From empty cellars turn'd the angry poor,
And surly beggars cursed the ever-bolted
    door.
To one small room the steward found his way,
Where tenants follow'd to complain and pay ;
Yet no complaint before the Lady came,
The feeling servant spared the feeble dame ;
Who saw her farms with his observing eyes,
And answer'd all requests with his replies :—
She came not down, her falling groves to view ;
Why should she know, what one so faithful
    knew ?
Why come, from many clamorous tongues to
    hear,
What one so just might whisper in her ear ?
Her oaks or acres, why with care explore ;
Why learn the wants, the sufferings of the
    poor ;
When one so knowing all their worth could
    trace,
And one so piteous govern'd in her place ?
  Lo ! now, what dismal sons of Darkness
    come,
To bear this daughter of Indulgence home ;
Tragedians all, and well arranged in black !
Who nature, feeling, force, expression lack ;
Who cause no tear, but gloomily pass by,
And shake their sables in the wearied eye,
That turns disgusted from the pompous scene,
Proud without grandeur, with profusion,
    mean !
The tear of kindness past affection owes ;
For worth deceased the sigh from reason
    flows ;
E'en well-feign'd passion for our sorrows call,
And real tears for mimic miseries fall :

But this poor farce has neither truth nor art,
To please the fancy or to touch the heart ;
Unlike the darkness of the sky, that pours
On the dry ground its fertilizing showers ;
Unlike to that which strikes the soul with
    dread,
When thunders roar and forky fires are shed ;
Dark but not awful, dismal but yet mean,
With anxious bustle moves the cumbrous
    scene ;
Presents no objects tender or profound,
But spreads its cold unmeaning gloom around.
    When woes are feign'd, how ill such forms
        appear ;
And oh ! how needless, when the wo 's sincere.
    Slow to the vault they come, with heavy
        tread,
Bending beneath the Lady and her lead ;
A case of elm surrounds that ponderous chest,
Close on that case the crimson velvet's press'd ;
Ungenerous this, that to the worm denies,
With niggard-caution, his appointed prize ;
For now, ere yet he works his tedious way,
Through cloth and wood and metal to his prey,
That prey dissolving shall a mass remain,
That fancy loathes and worms themselves
    disdain.
    But see ! the master-mourner makes his way,
To end his office for the coffin'd clay ;
Pleased that our rustic men and maids behold
His plate like silver, and his studs like gold,
As they approach to spell the age, the name,
And all the titles of th' illustrious dame.—
This as (my duty done) some scholar read,
A village-father look'd disdain and said :
' Away, my friends ! why take such pains to
    know
What some brave marble soon in church shall
    show ?
Where not alone her gracious name shall stand,
But how she lived—the blessing of the land ;
How much we all deplored the noble dead,
What groans we utter'd and what tears we
    shed ;
Tears, true as those, which in the sleepy eyes
Of weeping cherubs on the stone shall rise ;
Tears, true as those, which, ere she found her
    grave,
The noble Lady to our sorrows gave.'
    Down by the church-way walk and where
        the brook
Winds round the chancel like a shepherd's
    crook ;

In that small house, with those green pales
    before,
Where jasmine trails on either side the door ;
Where those dark shrubs that now grow wild
    at will,
Were clipp'd in form and tantalized with
    skill ;
Where cockles blanch'd and pebbles neatly
    spread,
Form'd shining borders for the larkspurs'
    bed ;—
There lived a Lady, wise, austere, and nice,
Who show'd her virtue by her scorn of vice ;
In the dear fashions of her youth she dress'd,
A pea-green Joseph was her favourite vest ;
Erect she stood, she walk'd with stately mien,
Tight was her length of stays, and she was
    tall and lean.
    There long she lived in maiden-state im-
        mured,
From looks of love and treacherous man
    secured ;
Though evil fame—(but that was long before)
Had blown her dubious blast at Catherine's
    door :
A Captain thither, rich from India came,
And though a cousin call'd, it touch'd her
    fame :
Her annual stipend rose from his behest,
And all the long-prized treasures she pos-
    sess'd :—
If aught like joy awhile appear'd to stay
In that stern face, and chase those frowns
    away ;
'Twas when her treasures she disposed, for
    view,
And heard the praises to their splendour due ;
Silks beyond price, so rich, they'd stand
    alone,
And diamonds blazing on the buckled zone ;
Rows of rare pearls by curious workmen set,
And bracelets fair in box of glossy jet ;
Bright polish'd amber precious from its size,
Of forms the fairest fancy could devise :
Her drawers of cedar, shut with secret springs,
Conceal'd the watch of gold and rubied rings ;
Letters, long proofs of love, and verses fine
Round the pink'd rims of crisped Valentine.
Her china-closet, cause of daily care,
For woman's wonder held her pencill'd ware ;
That pictured wealth of China and Japan,
Like its cold mistress, shunn'd the eye of
    man.

Her neat small room, adorn'd with maiden-
taste,
A clipp'd French puppy, first of favourites,
graced :
A parrot next, but dead and stuff'd with art;
(For Poll, when living, lost the Lady's heart,
And then his life ; for he was heard to speak
Such frightful words as tinged his Lady's
cheek :)
Unhappy bird ! who had no power to prove,
Save by such speech, his gratitude and love.
A grey old cat his whiskers lick'd beside ;
A type of sadness in the house of pride.
The polish'd surface of an India chest,
A glassy globe, in frame of ivory, press'd ;
Where swam two finny creatures ; one of
gold,
Of silver one ; both beauteous to behold:—
All these were form'd the guiding taste to suit;
The beasts well-manner'd and the fishes mute.
A widow'd Aunt was there, compell'd by need
The nymph to flatter and her tribe to feed ;
Who, veiling well her scorn, endured the clog,
Mute as the fish and fawning as the dog.
As years increased, these treasures, her
delight,
Arose in value in their owner's sight :
A miser knows that, view it as he will,
A guinea kept is but a guinea still ;
And so he puts it to its proper use,
That something more this guinea may pro-
duce :
But silks and rings, in the possessor's eyes,
The oft'ner seen, the more in value rise,
And thus are wisely hoarded to bestow
The kind of pleasure that with years will grow.
But what avail'd their worth—if worth had
they,—
In the sad summer of her slow decay ?
Then we beheld her turn an anxious look
From trunks and chests, and fix it on her
book,—
A rich-bound Book of Prayer the Captain
gave,
(Some Princess had it, or was said to have;)
And then once more, on all her stores, look
round,
And draw a sigh so piteous and profound,
That told, 'Alas ! how hard from these to
part,
And for new hopes and habits form the heart!
What shall I do, (she cried) my peace of mind
To gain in dying, and to die resign'd ? '

' Hear,' we return'd;—' these baubles cast
aside,
Nor give thy God a rival in thy pride ;
Thy closets shut, and ope thy kitchen's door;
There own thy failings, *here* invite the poor;
A friend of Mammon let thy bounty make;
For widows' prayers, thy vanities forsake ;
And let the hungry, of thy pride, partake :
Then shall thy inward eye with joy survey
The angel Mercy tempering Death's delay !'
Alas ! 'twas hard; the treasures still had
charms,
Hope still its flattery, sickness its alarms ;
Still was the same unsettled, clouded view,
And the same plaintive cry, 'What shall I do?'
Nor change appear'd: for when her race
was run,
Doubtful we all exclaim'd, 'What has been
done ? '
Apart she lived, and still she lies alone ;
Yon earthly heap awaits the flattering stone,
On which invention shall be long employ'd,
To show the various worth of Catherine Lloyd.

Next to these ladies, but in nought allied,
A noble Peasant, Isaac Ashford, died.
Noble he was, contemning all things mean,
His truth unquestion'd and his soul serene :
Of no man's presence Isaac felt afraid ;
At no man's question Isaac look'd dismay'd :
Sh me knew him not, he dreaded no disgrace;
Truth, simple truth, was written in his face;
Yet while the serious thought his soul ap-
proved,
Cheerful he seem'd, and gentleness he loved:
To bliss domestic he his heart resign'd,
And, with the firmest, had the fondest mind:
Were others joyful, he look'd smiling on,
And gave allowance where he needed none;
Good he refused with future ill to buy,
Nor knew a joy that caused reflection's sigh;
A friend to virtue, his unclouded breast
No envy stung, no jealousy distress'd ;
(Bane of the poor ! it wounds their weaker
mind,
To miss one favour which their neighbours
find :)
Yet far was he from stoic pride removed ;
He felt humanely, and he warmly loved :
I mark'd his action, when his infant died,
And his old neighbour for offence was tried;
The still tears, stealing down that furrow'd
cheek,
Spoke pity, plainer than the tongue can speak.

If pride were his, 'twas not their vulgar pride,
Who, in their base contempt, the great deride;
Nor pride in learning,—though my clerk
    agreed,
If fate should call him, Ashford might succeed;
Nor pride in rustic skill, although we knew
None his superior, and his equals few :—
But if that spirit in his soul had place,
It was the jealous pride that shuns disgrace;
A pride in honest fame, by virtue gain'd,
In sturdy boys to virtuous labours train'd ;
Pride, in the power that guards his country's
    coast,
And all that Englishmen enjoy and boast ;
Pride, in a life that slander's tongue defied,—
In fact, a noble passion, misnamed pride.

   He had no party's rage, no sect'ry's whim ;
Christian and countryman was all with him :
True to his church he came ; no Sunday-
    shower
Kept him at home in that important hour ;
Nor his firm feet could one persuading sect,
By the strong glare of their new light, direct;—
' On hope, in mine own sober light, I gaze,
But should be blind and lose it, in your blaze.'

   In times severe, when many a sturdy swain
Felt it his pride, his comfort, to complain ;
Isaac their wants would soothe, his own would
    hide,
And feel in that his comfort and his pride.

   At length he found, when seventy years
    were run,
His strength departed, and his labour done ;
When he, save honest fame, retain'd no more,
But lost his wife and saw his children poor :
'Twas then, a spark of—say not discontent—
Struck on his mind, and thus he gave it vent :
   ' Kind are your laws, ('tis not to be denied,)
That in yon house, for ruin'd age, provide,
And they are just ;—when young, we give
    you all,
And for assistance in our weakness call.—
Why then this proud reluctance to be fed,
To join your poor, and eat the parish-bread?
But yet I linger, loth with him to feed,
Who gains his plenty by the sons of need ;
He who, by contract, all your paupers took,
And gauges stomachs with an anxious look :
On some old master I could well depend ;
See him with joy and thank him as a friend ;
But ill on him, who doles the day's supply,
And counts our chances, who at night may
    die :

Yet help me, Heav'n ! and let me not com-
    plain
Of what I suffer, but my fate sustain.'
   Such were his thoughts, and so resign'd he
    grew ;
Daily he placed the workhouse in his view !
But came not there, for sudden was his fate,
He dropp'd, expiring, at his cottage-gate.

   I feel his absence in the hours of prayer,
And view his seat and sigh for Isaac there :
I see no more those white locks thinly spread
Round the bald polish of that honour'd head;
No more that awful glance on playful wight,
Compell'd to kneel and tremble at the sight,
To fold his fingers, all in dread the while,
Till Mister Ashford soften'd to a smile ;
No more that meek and suppliant look in
    prayer,
Nor the pure faith (to give it force), are
    there :—
But he is bless'd, and I lament no more
A wise good man contented to be poor.

   Then died a Rambler ; not the one who
    sails
And trucks, for female favours, beads and
    nails ;
Not one, who posts from place to place—of
    men
And manners treating with a flying pen ;
Not he, who climbs, for prospects, Snowden's
    height,
And chides the clouds that intercept the sight;
No curious shell, rare plant, or brilliant spar,
Enticed our traveller from his home so far;
But all the reason, by himself assign'd
For so much rambling, was, a restless mind;
As on, from place to place, without intent,
Without reflection, Robin Dingley went.
   Not thus by nature ;—never man was found
Less prone to wander from his parish-bound :
Claudian's old Man, to whom all scenes were
    new,
Save those where he and where his apples
    grew,
Resembled Robin, who around would look,
And his horizon, for the earth's, mistook.
   To this poor swain a keen Attorney came ;—
' I give thee joy, good fellow ! on thy name;
The rich old Dingley's dead ;—no child has he,
Nor wife, nor will ; his ALL is left for thee :
To be his fortune's heir thy claim is good ;
Thou hast the name, and we will prove the
    blood.'

The claim was made; 'twas tried,—it would
not stand ;
They proved the blood, but were refused the
land.
    Assured of wealth, this man of simple heart,
To every friend had predisposed a part :
His wife had hopes indulged of various kind;
The three Miss Dingleys had their school
assign'd,
Masters were sought for what they each
required,
And books were bought and harpsichords were
hired :
So high was hope :—the failure touch'd his
brain,
And Robin never was himself again ;
Yet he no wrath, no angry wish express'd,
But tried, in vain, to labour or to rest ;
Then cast his bundle on his back, and went
He knew not whither, not for what intent.
    Years fled ;—of Robin all remembrance
past,
When home he wander'd in his rags at last:
A sailor's jacket on his limbs was thrown,
A sailor's story he had made his own ;
Had suffer'd battles, prisons, tempests,
storms,
Encountering death in all his ugliest forms:
His cheeks were haggard, hollow was his eye,
Where madness lurk'd, conceal'd in misery;
Want, and th' ungentle world, had taught a
part,
And prompted cunning to that simple heart:
' He now bethought him, he would roam no
more,
But live at home and labour as before.'
    Here clothed and fed, no sooner he began
To round and redden, than away he ran ;
His wife was dead, their children past his aid :
So, unmolested, from his home he stray'd :
Six years elapsed, when, worn with want and
pain,
Came Robin, wrapt in all his rags, again:—
We chide, we pity ;—placed among our poor,
He fed again, and was a man once more.
    As when a gaunt and hungry fox is found,
Entrapp'd alive in some rich hunter's ground;
Fed for the field, although each day 's a feast,
Fatten you may, but never *tame* the beast ;
A house protects him, savoury viands sustain;
But loose his neck and off he goes again :
So stole our vagrant from his warm retreat,
To rove a prowler and be deemed a cheat.

Hard was his fare ; for, him at length we
saw,
In cart convey'd and laid supine on straw.
His feeble voice now spoke a sinking heart;
His groans now told the motions of the cart ;
And when it stopp'd, he tried in vain to
stand ;
Closed was his eye, and clench'd his clammy
hand ;
Life ebb'd apace, and our best aid no more
Could his weak sense or dying heart restore :
But now he fell, a victim to the snare,
That vile attorneys for the weak prepare ;—
They who, when profit or resentment call,
Heed not the groaning victim they enthrall.
    Then died lamented, in the strength of life,
A valued Mother and a faithful Wife ;
Call'd not away, when time had loosed each
hold
On the fond heart, and each desire grew cold ;
But when, to all that knit us to our kind,
She felt fast-bound, as charity can bind ;—
Not when the ills of age, its pain, its care,
The drooping spirit for its fate prepare ;
And, each affection failing, leaves the heart
Loosed from life's charm and willing to de-
part;—
But all her ties the strong invader broke,
In all their strength, by one tremendous
stroke !
Sudden and swift the eager pest came on,
And terror grew, till every hope was gone:
Still those around appear'd for hope to seek !
But view'd the sick and were afraid to speak.—
    Slowly they bore, with solemn step, the
dead ;
When grief grew loud and bitter tears were
shed :
My part began ; a crowd drew near the place,
Awe in each eye, alarm in every face :
So swift the ill, and of so fierce a kind,
That fear with pity mingled in each mind ;
Friends with the husband came their griefs
to blend ;
For good-man Frankford was to all a friend.
The last-born boy they held above the bier,
He knew not grief, but cries express'd his fear;
Each different age and sex reveal'd its pain,
In now a louder, now a lower strain ;
While the meek father, listening to their tones,
Swell'd the full cadence of the grief by groans.
    The elder sister strove her pangs to hide,
And soothing words to younger minds applied:

' Be still, be patient,' oft she strove to say ;
But fail'd as oft, and weeping turn'd away.
  Curious and sad, upon the fresh-dug hill,
The village-lads stood melancholy still ;
And idle children, wandering to-and-fro,
As Nature guided, took the tone of wo.
  Arrived at home, how then they gazed
      around,
In every place,—where she—no more was
      found ;—
The seat at table she was wont to fill ;
The fire-side chair, still set, but vacant still ;
The garden-walks, a labour all her own ;
The latticed bower, with trailing shrubs o'er-
      grown ;
The Sunday-pew she fill'd with all her race,—
Each place of hers, was now a sacred place,
That, while it call'd up sorrows in the eyes,
Pierced the full heart and forced them still to
      rise.
  Oh sacred sorrow ! by whom souls are tried,
Sent not to punish mortals, but to guide ;
If thou art mine, (and who shall proudly dare
To tell his Maker, he has had his share ?)
Still let me feel for what thy pangs are sent,
And be my guide and not my punishment !
  Of Leah Cousins next the name appears,
With honours crown'd and bless'd with length
      of years,
Save that she lived to feel, in life's decay,
The pleasure die, the honours drop away ;
A matron she, whom every village-wife
View'd as the help and guardian of her life ;
Fathers and sons, indebted to her aid,
Respect to her and her profession paid ;
Who in the house of plenty largely fed,
Yet took her station at the pauper's bed ;
Nor from that duty could be bribed again,
While fear or danger urged her to remain :
In her experience all her friends relied,
Heaven was her help and nature was her
      guide.
  Thus Leah lived ; long trusted, much
      caress'd,
Till a Town-Dame a youthful Farmer bless'd ;
A gay vain bride, who would example give
To that poor village where she deign'd to live ;
Some few months past, she sent, in hour of
      need,
For Doctor Glibb, who came with wond'rous
      speed :
Two days he waited, all his art applied,
To save the mother when her infant died :—

  ' 'Twas well I came,' at last he deign'd to
      say ;
'Twas wond'rous well ; '—and proudly rode
      away.
The news ran round ;—' How vast the Doc-
      tor's pow'r !
He saved the Lady in the trying hour ;
Saved her from death, when she was dead to
      hope,
And her fond husband had resign'd her up :
So all, like her, may evil fate defy,
If Doctor Glibb, with saving hand, be nigh.'
  Fame (now his friend), fear, novelty, and
      whim,
And fashion, sent the varying sex to him :
From this, contention in the village rose ;
And *these* the Dame espoused ; the Doctor
      those :
The wealthier part, to him and science went ;
With luck and her the poor remain'd content.
  The matron sigh'd ; for she was vex'd at
      heart,
With so much profit, so much fame, to part :
' So long successful in my art,' she cried,
' And this proud man, so young and so un-
      tried ! '
   ' Nay,' said the Doctor, ' dare you trust
      your wives,
The joy, the pride, the solace of your lives,
To one who acts and knows no reason why,
But trusts, poor hag ! to luck for an ally ?—
Who, on experience, can her claims advance,
And own the powers of accident and chance ?
A whining dame, who prays in danger's view,
(A proof she knows not what beside to do ;)
What 's her experience ? In the time that 's
      gone,
Blundering she wrought and still she blunders
      on :—
And what is Nature ? One who acts in aid
Of gossips half asleep, and half afraid :
With such allies I scorn my fame to blend,
Skill is my luck and courage is my friend :
No slave to Nature, 'tis my chief delight
To win my way and act in her despite :—
Trust then my art, that, in itself complete,
Needs no assistance and fears no defeat.'
  Warm'd by her well-spiced ale and aiding
      pipe,
The angry matron grew for contest ripe.
  ' Can you,' she said, ' ungrateful and un-
      just,
Before experience, ostentation trust !

What is your hazard, foolish daughters, tell?
If safe, you're certain ; if secure, you're well :
That I have luck must friend and foe confess,
And what's good judgment but a lucky guess?
He boasts but what he *can* do :—will you run
From me, your friend ! who, all *he* boasts,
      have done ?
By proud and learned words his powers are
      known ;
By healthy boys and handsome girls my own :
Wives ! fathers ! children ! by my help you
      live ;
Has this pale Doctor more than life to give ?
No stunted cripple hops the village round ;
Your hands are active and your heads are
      sound :
My lads are all your fields and flocks require ;
My lasses all those sturdy lads admire.
Can this proud leech, with all his boasted skill,
Amend the soul or body, wit or will ?
Does he for courts the sons of farmers frame,
Or make the daughter differ from the dame ?
Or, whom he brings into this world of wo,
Prepares he them their part to undergo ?
If not, this stranger from your doors repel,
And be content to *be* and to be *well*.'
    She spake ; but, ah ! with words too strong
      and plain ;
Her warmth offended, and her truth was vain :
The *many* left her, and the friendly *few*,
If never colder, yet they older grew ;
Till, unemploy'd, she felt her spirits droop,
And took, insidious aid ! th' inspiring cup ;
Grew poor and peevish as her powers decay'd,
And propp'd the tottering frame with stronger
      aid,—
Then died !—I saw our careful swains convey,
From this our changeful world, the matron's
      clay,
Who to this world, at least, with equal care,
Brought them its changes, good and ill to
      share.
    Now to his grave was Roger Cuff convey'd,
And strong resentment's lingering spirit laid.
Shipwreck'd in youth, he home return'd, and
      found
His brethren three—and thrice they wish'd
      him drown'd.
' Is this a landman's love ? Be certain then,
We part for ever ! '—and they cried, ' Amen !'
    His words were truth's :—Some forty sum-
      mers fled ;
His brethren died ; his kin supposed him dead :

Three nephews these, one sprightly niece, and
      one,
Less near in blood—they call'd him *surly
      John* ;
He worked in woods apart from all his kind,
Fierce were his looks and moody was his
      mind.
    For home the Sailor now began to sigh :—
' The dogs are dead, and I'll return and die;
When all I have, my gains, in years of care,
The younger Cuffs with kinder souls shall
      share :—
Yet hold ! I'm rich ;—with one consent they'll
      say,
" You're welcome, Uncle, as the flowers in
      May."
No ; I'll disguise me, be in tatters dress'd,
And best befriend the lads who treat me
      best.'
    Now all his kindred,—neither rich nor
      poor,—
Kept the wolf want some distance from the
      door.
In piteous plight he knock'd at George's
      gate,
And begg'd for aid, as he described his
      state :—
But stern was George ;—' Let them who had
      thee strong,
Help thee to drag thy weaken'd frame along ;
To us a stranger, while your limbs would
      move,
From us depart and try a stranger's love :—
Ha ! dost thou murmur ? '—for, in Roger's
      throat,
Was ' Rascal ! ' rising with disdainful note.
    To pious James he then his prayer ad-
      dress'd ;—
' Good lack,' quoth James, ' thy sorrows
      pierce my breast ;
And, had I wealth, as have my brethren
      twain,
One board should feed us and one roof con-
      tain :
But plead I will thy cause and I will pray :
And so farewell ! Heaven help thee on thy
      way ! '
    ' Scoundrel ! ' said Roger, (but apart ;)—
      and told
His case to Peter ;—Peter too was cold :—
' The rates are high ; we have a-many poor ;
But I will think,'—he said, and shut the
      door.

Then the gay Niece the seeming pauper
    press'd :—
' Turn, Nancy, turn, and view this form dis-
    tress'd :
Akin to thine is this declining frame,
And this poor beggar claims an Uncle's
    name.'
    'Avaunt ! begone ! ' the courteous maiden
    said,
Thou vile impostor ! Uncle Roger's dead :
I hate thee, beast ; thy look my spirit shocks !
Oh ! that I saw thee starving in the stocks ! '
    ' My gentle niece ! ' he said—and sought the
    wood.—
' I hunger, fellow ; prithee, give me food ! '
    ' Give ! am I rich ? This hatchet take, and
    try
Thy proper strength, nor give those limbs the
    lie ;
Work, feed thyself, to thine own powers
    appeal,
Nor whine out woes, thine own right-hand
    can heal :
And while that hand is thine and thine a leg,
Scorn of the proud or of the base to beg.'
    ' Come, surly John, thy wealthy kinsman
    view,'
Old Roger said :—' thy words are brave and
    true ;
Come, live with me : we'll vex those scoundrel
    boys,
And that prim shrew shall, envying, hear our
    joys.—
Tobacco's glorious fume all day we'll share,
With beef and brandy kill all kinds of care ;
We'll beer and biscuit on our table heap,
And rail at rascals, till we fall asleep.'
    Such was their life : but when the wood-
    man died,
His grieving kin for Roger's smiles applied—
In vain ; he shut, with stern rebuke, the
    door,
And dying, built a refuge for the poor ;
With this restriction, That no Cuff should
    share
One meal, or shelter for one moment there.
    My record ends :—But hark ! e'en now
    I hear
The bell of death, and know not whose to
    fear :
Our farmers all, and all our hinds were well ;
In no man's cottage danger seem'd to
    dwell ;—

Yet death of man proclaim these heavy chimes,
For thrice they sound, with pausing space,
    three times.
' Go ; of my sexton seek, Whose days are
    sped ?—
What ! he, himself ! —and is old Dibble
    dead ? '
His eightieth year he reach'd, still undecay'd,
And rectors five to one close vault con-
    vey'd :—
But he is gone ; his care and skill I lose,
And gain a mournful subject for my Muse :
His masters lost, he'd oft in turn deplore,
And kindly add,—' Heaven grant, I lose no
    more ! '
Yet, while he spake, a sly and pleasant glance
Appear'd at variance with his complaisance :
For, as he told their fate and varying worth,
He archly look'd,—' I yet may bear thee
    forth.'
' When first '—(he so began)—' my trade I
    plied,
Good master Addle was the parish-guide ;
His clerk and sexton, I beheld with fear
His stride majestic, and his frown severe ;
A noble pillar of the church he stood,
Adorn'd with college-gown and parish-hood :
Then as he paced the hallow'd aisles about,
He fill'd the sevenfold surplice fairly out !
But in his pulpit, wearied down with prayer,
He sat and seem'd as in his study's chair ;
For while the anthem swell'd, and when it
    ceased,
Th' expecting people view'd their slumbering
    priest :
Who, dozing, died.—Our Parson Peele was
    next ;
" I will not spare you," was his favourite
    text ;
Nor did he spare, but raised them many a
    pound ;
Ev'n me he mulct for my poor rood of ground ;
Yet cared he nought, but with a gibing
    speech,
" What should I do," quoth he, " but what
    I preach ? "
His piercing jokes (and he'd a plenteous store)
Were daily offer'd both to rich and poor ;
His scorn, his love, in playful words he spoke ;
His pity, praise, and promise, were a joke :
But though so young and bless'd with spirits
    high,
He died as grave as any judge could die :

The strong attack subdued his lively powers,—
His was the grave, and Doctor Grandspear
    ours.
  ' Then were there golden times the village
    round ;
In his abundance all appear'd t' abound ;
Liberal and rich, a plenteous board he spread,
E'en cool Dissenters at his table fed ;
Who wish'd, and hoped,—and thought a man
    so kind
A way to Heaven, though not their own,
    might find ;
To them, to all, he was polite and free,
Kind to the poor, and, ah ! most kind to me :
" Ralph," would he say, " Ralph Dibble, thou
    art old ;
" That doublet fit, 'twill keep thee from the
    cold :
How does my Sexton ?—What ! the times
    are hard ;
Drive that stout pig, and pen him in thy
    yard."
But most, his rev'rence loved a mirthful
    jest :—
" Thy coat is thin ; why, man, thou'rt *barely*
    dress'd ;
It 's worn to th' thread : but I have nappy
    beer ;
Clap that within, and see how they will
    wear ! "
  'Gay days were these ; but they were
    quickly past :
When first he came, we found he cou'dn't
    last :
A whoreson cough (and at the fall of leaf)
Upset him quite :—but what 's the gain of
    grief ?
  'Then came the Author-Rector: his delight
Was all in books ; to read them, or to write :
Women and men he strove alike to shun,
And hurried homeward when his tasks were
    done :
Courteous enough, but careless what he said,
For points of learning he reserved his head ;
And when addressing either poor or rich,
He knew no better than his cassock which :
He, like an osier, was of pliant kind,
Erect by nature, but to bend inclined ;
Not like a creeper falling to the ground,
Or meanly catching on the neighbours
    round :—
Careless was he of surplice, hood, and band,—
And kindly took them as they came to hand :

Nor, like the doctor, wore a world of hat,
As if he sought for diginity in that :
He talk'd, he gave, but not with cautious
    rules :—
Nor turn'd from gipsies, vagabonds, or fools ;
It was his nature, but they thought it whim,
And so our beaux and beauties turn'd from
    him :
Of questions, much he wrote, profound and
    dark,—
How spake the serpent, and where stopp'd
    the ark ;
From what far land the Queen of Sheba came ;
Who Salem's priest, and what his father's
    name ;
He made the Song of Songs its mysteries
    yield,
And Revelations, to the world, reveal'd.
He sleeps i' the aisle,—but not a stone records
His name or fame, his actions or his words :
And truth, your reverence, when I look
    around,
And mark the tombs in our sepulchral
    ground,
(Though dare I not of one man's hope to
    doubt),
I'd join the party who repose without.
  ' Next came a youth from Cambridge, and,
    in truth,
He was a sober and a comely youth ;
He blush'd in meekness as a modest man,
And gain'd attention ere his task began ;
When preaching, seldom ventured on reproof,
But touch'd his neighbours tenderly enough.
Him, in his youth, a clamorous sect assail'd,
Advised and censured, flatter'd,—and pre-
    vail'd.—
Then did he much his sober hearers vex,
Confound the simple, and the sad perplex ;
To a new style his reverence rashly took ;
Loud grew his voice, to threat'ning swell'd his
    look ;
Above, below, on either side, he gazed,
Amazing all, and most himself amazed :
No more he read his preachments pure and
    plain,
But launch'd outright, and rose and sank
    again :
At times he smiled in scorn, at times he
    wept,
And such sad coil with words of vengeance
    kept,
That our best sleepers started as they slept.

" Conviction comes like lightning," he would
    cry ;
" In vain you seek it, and in vain you fly ;
'Tis like the rushing of the mighty wind,
Unseen its progress, but its power you find ;
It strikes the child ere yet its reason wakes ;
His reason fled, the ancient sire it shakes ;
The proud, learn'd man, and him who loves
    to know
How and from whence these gusts of grace
    will blow,
It shuns,—but sinners in their way impedes,
And sots and harlots visits in their deeds :
Of faith and penance it supplies the place ;
Assures the vilest that they live by grace,
And, without running, makes them win the
    race."
   'Such was the doctrine our young prophet
    taught ;
And here conviction, there confusion
    wrought;
When his thin cheek assumed a deadly hue,
And all the rose to one small spot withdrew :
They call'd it hectic ; 'twas a fiery flush,
More fix'd and deeper than the maiden blush ;
His paler lips the pearly teeth disclosed,
And lab'ring lungs the length'ning speech
    opposed.
No more his span-girth shanks and quiv'ring
    thighs
Upheld a body of the smaller size ;
But down he sank upon his dying bed,
And gloomy crotchets fill'd his wandering
    head.—
   ' " Spite of my faith, all-saving faith," he
    cried,
" I fear of worldly works the wicked pride ;
Poor as I am, degraded, abject, blind,
The good I've wrought still rankles in my
    mind ;

My alms-deeds all, and every deed I've
    done,
My moral-rags defile me every one ;
It should not be :—what say'st thou ? tell
    me, Ralph."
Quoth I, " Your reverence, I believe, you're
    safe ;
Your faith's your prop, nor have you pass'd
    such time
In life's good-works as swell them to a crime.
If I of pardon for my sins were sure,
About my goodness I would rest secure."
   'Such was his end ; and mine approaches
    fast ;
I've seen my best of preachers,—and my
    last.'—
   He bow'd, and archly smiled at what he
    said,
Civil but sly :—' And is old Dibble dead ? '
   Yes ! he is gone : and WE are going all ;
Like flowers we wither, and like leaves we
    fall ;—
Here, with an infant, joyful sponsors come,
Then bear the new-made Christian to its
    home ;
A few short years and we behold him
    stand,
To ask a blessing, with his bride in hand :
A few, still seeming shorter, and we hear
His widow weeping at her husband's bier :—
Thus, as the months succeed, shall infants
    take
Their names ; thus parents shall the child
    forsake ;
Thus brides again and bridegrooms blithe
    shall kneel,
By love or law compell'd their vows to
    seal,
Ere I again, or one like me, explore
These simple annals of the VILLAGE POOR.

THE BIRTH OF FLATTERY

[1807]

Omnia habeo, neque quicquam habeo ;
. . . . . .
Quidquid dicunt, laudo ; id rursum si negant,
    laudo id quoque :
Negat quis, nego ; ait, aio :
Postremo imperavi egomet mihi
Omnia assentari.
    TERENT. *in Eunuch.* Act II, Sc. 2, v. 12, . . .
      20, 21.

    It has been held in ancient rules,
    That flattery is the food of fools ;
    Yet now and then your men of wit
    Will condescend to taste a bit.
      SWIFT, *Cadenus and Vanessa*, l. 758.

———

The Subject—Poverty and Cunning described
—When united, a jarring Couple—Mutual
Reproof—The Wife consoled by a Dream
—Birth of a Daughter—Description and
Prediction of Envy—How to be rendered
ineffectual, explained in a Vision—Simula-
tion foretells the future Success and
Triumphs of Flattery—Her Power over
various Characters and different Minds ;
over certain Classes of Men ; over Envy
himself—Her successful Art of softening
the Evils of Life ; of changing Characters;
of meliorating Prospects, and affixing Value
to Possessions, Pictures, &c.—Conclusion.

———

MUSE of my Spenser, who so well could sing
    The passions all, their bearings and their
      ties ;
Who could in view those shadowy beings
    bring,
    And with bold hand remove each dark
      disguise,
    Wherein love, hatred, scorn, or anger lies :
Guide him to Fairy-land, who now intends
    That way his flight ; assist him as he flies,
To mark those passions, Virtue's foes and
    friends,
By whom when led she droops, when leading
    she ascends.

Yes ! they appear, I see the fairy-train !
    And who that modest nymph of meek
      address ?
Not Vanity, though loved by all the vain ;
    Not Hope, though promising to all success ;
    Nor Mirth, nor Joy, though foe to all dis-
      tress ;
Thee, sprightly syren, from this train I choose,
    Thy birth relate, thy soothing arts confess;
'Tis not in thy mild nature to refuse,
When poets ask thine aid, so oft their meed
    and muse.

———

    In Fairy-land, on wide and cheerless plain,
Dwelt, in the house of Care, a sturdy swain ;
A hireling he, who, when he till'd the soil,
Look'd to the pittance that repaid his toil ;
And to a master left the mingled joy
And anxious care that follow'd his employ :
Sullen and patient he at once appear'd,
As one who murmur'd, yet as one who fear'd ;
Th' attire was coarse that clothed his sinewy
    frame,
Rude his address, and Poverty his name.
    In that same plain a nymph, of curious
      taste,
A cottage (plann'd with all her skill) had
    placed ;
Strange the materials, and for what design'd
The various parts, no simple man might find ;
What seem'd the door, each entering guest
    withstood,
What seem'd a window was but painted wood;
But by a secret spring the wall would move,
And daylight drop through glassy door above :
'Twas all her pride, new traps for praise to
    lay,
And all her wisdom was to hide her way ;
In small attempts incessant were her pains,
And Cunning was her name among the swains.

Now, whether fate decreed this pair should
    wed,
And blindly drove them to the marriage-bed ;
Or whether love in some soft hour inclined
The damsel's heart, and won her to be kind,
Is yet unsung : they were an ill-match'd
    pair,
But both diposed to wed—and wed they
    were.
    Yet, though united in their fortune, still
Their ways were diverse ; varying was their
    will ;
Nor long the maid had bless'd the simple man,
Before dissensions rose, and she began :—
    ' Wretch that I am ! since to thy fortune
    bound,
What plan, what project, with success is
    crown'd ?
I, who a thousand secret arts possess,
Who every rank approach with right address ;
Who've loosed a guinea from a miser's chest,
And worm'd his secret from a traitor's breast ;
Thence gifts and gains collecting, great and
    small,
Have brought to thee, and thou consum'st
    them all :
For want like thine—a bog without a base—
Ingulfs all gains I gather for the place ;
Feeding, unfill'd ; destroying, undestroy'd ;
It craves for ever, and is ever void :—
Wretch that I am ! what misery have I found,
Since my sure craft was to thy calling
    bound ! '
    ' Oh ! vaunt of worthless art,' the swain
    replied,
Scowling contempt, ' how pitiful this pride !
What are these specious gifts, these paltry
    gains,
But base rewards for ignominious pains ?
With all thy tricking, still for bread we strive,
Thine is, proud wretch ! the care that cannot
    thrive ;
By all thy boasted skill and baffled hooks,
Thou gain'st no more than students by their
    books ;
No more than I for my poor deeds am paid,
Whom none can blame, will help, or dare up-
    braid.
    ' Call this our need, a bog that all devours,—
Then what thy petty arts, but summer-
    flowers,
Gaudy and mean, and serving to betray
The place they make unprofitably gay ?

Who know it not, some useless beauties
    see,—
But ah ! to prove it, was reserved for me.'
    Unhappy state ! that, in decay of love,
Permits harsh truth his errors to disprove ;
While he remains, to wrangle and to jar,
Is friendly tournament, not fatal war ;
Love in his play will borrow arms of hate,
Anger and rage, upbraiding and debate ;
And by his power the desperate weapons
    thrown,
Become as safe and pleasant as his own ;
But left by him, their natures they assume,
And fatal, in their poisoning force, become.
    Time fled, and now the swain compell'd to
    see
New cause for fear—' Is this thy thrift ? '
    quoth he :
To whom the wife with cheerful voice
    replied :—
' Thou moody man, lay all thy fears aside,
I've seen a vision ;—they, from whom I came,
A daughter promise, promise wealth and
    fame ;
Born with my features, with my arts, yet she
Shall patient, pliant, persevering be,
And in thy better ways resemble thee.
The fairies round shall at her birth attend,
The friend of all in all shall find a friend,
And save that one sad star that hour must
    gleam
On our fair child, how glorious were my
    dream ! '
    This heard the husband, and, in surly
    smile,
Aim'd at contempt, but yet he hoped the
    while :
For as, when sinking, wretched men are found
To catch at rushes rather than be drown'd ;
So on a dream our peasant placed his
    hope,
And found that rush as valid as a rope.
    Swift fled the days, for now in hope they
    fled,
When a fair daughter bless'd the nuptial bed ;
Her infant-face the mother's pains beguiled,
She look'd so pleasing, and so softly smiled ;
Those smiles, those looks, with sweet sensa-
    tions moved
The gazer's soul, and, as he look'd, he loved.
    And now the fairies came, with gifts, to
    grace
So mild a nature and so fair a face.

They gave, with beauty, that bewitching art,
That holds in easy chains the human heart;
They gave her skill to win the stubborn mind,
To make the suffering to their sorrows blind,
To bring on pensive looks the pleasing smile,
And Care's stern brow of every frown beguile.
 These magic favours graced the infant-maid,
Whose more enlivening smile the charming
  gifts repaid.
 Now Fortune changed, who, were she con-
  stant long,
Would leave us few adventures for our song.
 A wicked elfin roved this land around,
 Whose joys proceeded from the griefs he
  found;
Envy his name:—his fascinating eye
From the light bosom drew the sudden sigh;
Unsocial he, but with malignant mind,
He dwelt with man, that he might curse man-
  kind;
Like the first foe, he sought th' abode of Joy,
Grieved to behold, but eager to destroy;
Round blooming beauty, like the wasp, he
  flew,
Soil'd the fresh sweet, and changed the rosy
  hue;
The wise, the good, with anxious heart he
  saw,
And here a failing found, and there a flaw;
Discord in families 'twas his to move,
Distrust in friendship, jealousy in love;
He told the poor, what joys the great pos-
  sess'd,
The great—what calm content the cottage
  bless'd;
To part the learned and the rich he tried,
Till their slow friendship perish'd in their
  pride.
Such was the fiend, and so secure of prey,
That only Misery pass'd unstung away.
 Soon as he heard the fairy-babe was born,
Scornful he smiled, but felt no more than
  scorn;
For why, when Fortune placed her state so
  low,
In useless spite his lofty malice show?
Why, in a mischief of the meaner kind,
Exhaust the vigour of a ranc'rous mind?
But, soon as Fame the fairy-gifts proclaim'd,
Quick-rising wrath his ready soul inflamed,
To swear, by vows that e'en the wicked tie,
The nymph should weep her varied destiny;

That every gift, that now appear'd to shine
In her fair face, and make her smiles divine,
Should all the poison of his magic prove,
And they should scorn her, whom she sought
  for love.
 His spell prepared, in form an ancient dame,
A fiend in spirit, to the cot he came;
There gain'd admittance, and the infant
  press'd
(Muttering his wicked magic) to his breast;
And thus he said:—' Of all the powers who
  wait
On Jove's decrees, and do the work of fate,
Was I alone, despised or worthless, found,
Weak to protect, or impotent to wound?
See then thy foe, regret the friendship lost,
And learn my skill, but learn it at your cost.
 ' Know then, O child! devote to fates severe,
The good shall hate thy name, the wise shall
  fear;
Wit shall deride, and no protecting friend
Thy shame shall cover, or thy name defend.
Thy gentle sex, who, more than ours, should
  spare
A humble foe, will greater scorn declare;
The base alone thy advocates shall be,
Or boast alliance with a wretch like thee.'
 He spake and vanish'd, other prey to find,
And waste in slow disease the conquer'd mind.
 Awed by the elfin's threats, and fill'd with
  dread,
The parents wept, and sought their infant's
  bed:
Despair alone the father's soul possess'd;
But hope rose gently in the mother's breast;
For well she knew that neither grief nor joy
Pain'd without hope, or pleased without alloy;
And while these hopes and fears her heart
  divide,
A cheerful vision bade the fears subside.
 She saw descending to the world below
An ancient form, with solemn pace and slow.
' Daughter, no more be sad,' (the phantom
  cried),
' Success is seldom to the wise denied;
In idle wishes fools supinely stay,
Be there a will and wisdom finds a way:
Why art thou grieved? Be rather glad, that
  he
Who hates the happy, aims his darts at thee;
But aims in vain; thy favour'd daughter
  lies,
Serenely blest, and shall to joy arise.

For, grant that curses on her name shall wait,
(So envy wills and such the voice of fate,)
Yet if that name be prudently suppress'd,
She shall be courted, favoured, and caress'd.
  'For what are names? and where agree
    mankind,
In those to persons or to acts assign'd?
Brave, learn'd, or wise, if some their favour-
    ites call,
Have they the titles or the praise from all?
Not so, but others will the brave disdain
As rash, and deem the sons of wisdom vain;
The self-same mind shall scorn or kindness
    move,
And the same deed attract contempt and love.
  'So all the powers who move the human
    soul,
With all the passions who the will control,
Have various names—One giv'n by Truth
    Divine,
(As Simulation thus was fix'd for mine,)
The rest by man, who now, as wisdom's, prize
My secret counsels, now as art despise;
One hour, as just, those counsels they em-
    brace,
And spurn, the next, as pitiful and base.
  'Thee, too, my child, those fools as Cunning
    fly,
Who on thy counsel and thy craft rely;
That worthy craft in others they condemn,
But 'tis their prudence, while conducting
    them.
  'Be FLATTERY, then, thy happy infant's
    name,
Let Honour scorn her and let Wit defame;
Let all be true that Envy dooms, yet all,
Not on herself, but on her name, shall fall;
While she thy fortune and her own shall raise,
And decent Truth be call'd, and loved, as
    modest Praise.
  'O happy child! the glorious day shall
    shine,
When every ear shall to thy speech incline,
Thy words alluring and thy voice divine:
The sullen pedant and the sprightly wit,
To hear thy soothing eloquence, shall sit;
And both, abjuring Flattery, will agree
That truth inspires, and they must honour
    thee.
  'Envy himself shall to thy accents bend,
Force a faint smile and sullenly attend,
When thou shalt call him Virtue's jealous
    friend,

Whose bosom glows with generous rage to
    find
How fools and knaves are flatter'd by man-
    kind.
  'The sage retired, who spends alone his days,
And flies th' obstreperous voice of public
    praise;—
The vain, the vulgar cry,—shall gladly meet,
And bid thee welcome to his still retreat;
Much will he wonder, how thou cam'st to find
A man to glory dead, to peace consign'd.
O Fame! he'll cry, (for he will call thee
    Fame,)
From thee I fly, from thee conceal my name;
But thou shalt say, Though Genius takes his
    flight,
He leaves behind a glorious train of light,
And hides in vain:—yet prudent he that flies
The flatterer's art, and for himself is wise.
  'Yes, happy child! I mark th' approaching
    day,
When warring natures will confess thy sway;
When thou shalt Saturn's golden reign
    restore,
And vice and folly shall be known no more.
  'Pride shall not then in human-kind have
    place,
Changed by thy skill, to Dignity and Grace;
While Shame, who now betrays the inward
    sense
Of secret ill, shall be thy Diffidence;
Avarice shall thenceforth prudent Forecast be,
And bloody Vengeance, Magnanimity;
The lavish tongue shall honest truths impart,
The lavish hand shall show the generous heart,
And Indiscretion be, contempt of art:
Folly and Vice shall then, no longer known,
Be, this as Virtue, that as Wisdom, shown.
  'Then shall the Robber, as the Hero, rise
To seize the good that churlish law denies;
Throughout the world shall rove the generous
    band,
And deal the gifts of Heaven from hand to
    hand.
  'In thy blest days no tyrant shall be seen,
Thy gracious king shall rule contented men;
In thy blest days shall not a rebel be,
But patriots all and well approved of thee.
  'Such powers are thine, that man, by thee
    shall wrest
The gainful secret from the cautious breast;
Nor then, with all his care, the good retain,
But yield to thee the secret and the gain.

In vain shall much experience guard the heart
Against the charm of thy prevailing art ;
Admitted once, so soothing is thy strain,
It comes the sweeter, when it comes again ;
And when confess'd as thine, what mind so
    strong
Forbears the pleasure it indulged so long ?
'Soft'ner of every ill ! of all our woes
The balmy solace ! friend of fiercest foes !
Begin thy reign, and like the morning rise !
Bring joy, bring beauty, to our eager eyes ;
Break on the drowsy world like opening day,
While grace and gladness join thy flow'ry way;
While every voice is praise, while every heart
    is gay.
   'From thee all prospects shall new beauties
    take,
'Tis thine to seek them and 'tis thine to make;
On the cold fen I see thee turn thine eyes,
Its mists recede, its chilling vapour flies ;
Th' enraptured lord th' improving ground
    surveys,
And for his Eden asks the traveller's praise,
Which yet, unview'd of thee, a bog had been,
Where spungy rushes hide the plashy green.
   'I see thee breathing on the barren moor,
That seems to bloom although so bleak
    before ;
There, if beneath the gorse the primrose
    spring,
Or the pied daisy smile below the ling,
They shall new charms, at thy command,
    disclose,
And none shall miss the myrtle or the rose.
The wiry moss, that whitens all the hill,
Shall live a beauty by thy matchless skill ;
Gale[1] from the bog shall yield Arabian balm,
And the grey willow wave a golden palm.
   'I see thee smiling in the pictured room,
Now breathing beauty, now reviving bloom ;
There, each immortal name 'tis thine to give,
To graceless forms, and bid the lumber live.
Should'st thou coarse boors or gloomy martyrs
    see,
These shall thy Guidos, those thy Teniers be ;

[1] *Myrica Gale*, a shrub growing in boggy and
fenny grounds.

There shalt thou Raphael's saints and angels
    trace,
There make for Rubens and for Reynolds
    place,
And all the pride of art shall find, in her,
    disgrace.
   'Delight of either sex ! thy reign commence;
With balmy sweetness soothe the weary sense,
And to the sickening soul thy cheering aid
    dispense.
Queen of the mind ! thy golden age begin ;
In mortal bosoms varnish shame and sin,
Let all be fair without, let all be calm within.'
   The Vision fled, the happy mother rose,
Kiss'd the fair infant, smiled at all her foes,
And FLATTERY made her name :—her reign
    began,
Her own dear sex she ruled, then vanquish'd
    man ;
A smiling friend, to every class, she spoke,
Assumed their manners, and their habits
    took ;
Her, for her humble mien, the modest loved ;
Her cheerful looks the light and gay ap-
    proved ;
The just beheld her, firm ; the valiant, brave ;
Her mirth the free, her silence pleased the
    grave ;
Zeal heard her voice, and, as he preach'd
    aloud,
Well-pleased he caught her whispers from the
    crowd,
(Those whispers, soothing-sweet to every ear,
Which some refuse to pay, but none to hear) :
Shame fled her presence ; at her gentle strain,
Care softly smiled, and guilt forgot its pain ;
The wretched thought, the happy found her
    true,
The learn'd confess'd that she their merits
    knew ;
The rich—could they a constant friend con-
    demn ?
The poor believed—for who should flatter
    them ?
   Thus on her name though all disgrace
    attend,
In every creature she beholds a friend.

REFLECTIONS

[1807]

Quid juvat errores, mersâ iam puppe, fateri ?
Quid lacrymae delicta iuvant commissa se-
    cutae ?
    CLAUDIAN, *in Eutropium*, lib. ii. line 7.

What avails it, when shipwreck'd, that error
    appears ?
Are the crimes we commit wash'd away by
    our tears ?

WHEN all the fiercer passions cease,
  (The glory and disgrace of youth) ;
When the deluded soul, in peace,
  Can listen to the voice of truth ;
When we are taught in whom to trust,
  And how to spare, to spend, to give ;
(Our prudence kind, our pity just,)
  'Tis then we rightly learn to live.

Its weakness when the body feels,
  Nor danger in contempt defies ;
To reason, when desire appeals,
  When, on experience, hope relies ;
When every passing hour we prize,
  Nor rashly on our follies spend ;
But use it, as it quickly flies,
  With sober aim to serious end ;
When prudence bounds our utmost views,
  And bids us wrath and wrong forgive ;
When we can calmly gain or lose,—
  'Tis then we rightly learn to live.

Yet thus, when we our way discern,
  And can upon our care depend,
To travel safely, when we learn,
  Behold ! we're near our journey's end.
We've trod the maze of error round,
  Long wand'ring in the winding glade ;
And now the torch of truth is found,
  It only shows us where we stray'd :
Light for ourselves, what is it worth,
  When we no more our way can choose ?
For others, when we hold it forth,
  They, in their pride, the boon refuse.

By long experience taught, we now
  Can rightly judge of friends and foes,
Can all the worth of these allow,
  And all their faults discern in those
Relentless hatred, erring love,
  We can for sacred truth forego ;
We can the warmest friend reprove,
  And bear to praise the fiercest foe :
To what effect ? Our friends are gone,
  Beyond reproof, regard, or care ;
And of our foes remains there one,
  The mild relenting thoughts to share ?

Now 'tis our boast that we can quell
  The wildest passions in their rage ;
Can their destructive force repel,
  And their impetuous wrath assuage :
Ah ! Virtue, dost thou arm, when now
  This bold rebellious race are fled ;
When all these tyrants rest, and thou
  Art warring with the mighty dead ?
Revenge, ambition, scorn, and pride,
  And strong desire and fierce disdain,
The giant-brood, by thee defied,
  Lo ! Time's resistless strokes have slain.

Yet Time, who could that race subdue,
  (O'erpow'ring strength, appeasing rage,)
Leaves yet a persevering crew,
  To try the failing powers of age.
Vex'd by the constant call of these,
  Virtue awhile for conquest tries,
But weary grown and fond of ease,
  She makes with them a compromise :
Av'rice himself she gives to rest,
  But rules him with her strict commands ;
Bids Pity touch his torpid breast,
  And Justice hold his eager hands.

Yet is there nothing men can do,
  When chilling Age comes creeping on ?
Cannot we yet some good pursue ?
  Are talents buried ? genius gone ?

If passions slumber in the breast,
  If follies from the heart be fled ;
Of laurels let us go in quest,
  And place them on the poet's head.

Yes, we'll redeem the wasted time,
  And to neglected studies flee ;
We'll build again the lofty rhyme,
  Or live, Philosophy, with thee ;
For reasoning clear, for flight sublime,
  Eternal fame reward shall be ;
And to what glorious heights we'll climb,
  Th' admiring crowd shall envying see.

Begin the song ! begin the theme !—
  Alas ! and is Invention dead ?
Dream we no more the golden dream ?
  Is Mem'ry with her treasures fled ?
Yes, 'tis too late,—now Reason guides
  The mind, sole judge in all debate ;

And thus th' important point decides,
  For laurels, 'tis, alas ! too late.
    What is possess'd we may retain,
    But for new conquests strive in vain.

Beware then, Age, that what was won,
  In life's past labours, studies, views,
Be lost not, now the labour's done,
  When all thy part is,—not to lose :
    When thou canst toil or gain no more,
    Destroy not what was gain'd before.

For, all that's gain'd of all that's good,
  When time shall his weak frame destroy,
(Their use then rightly understood,)
  Shall man, in happier state, enjoy.
Oh ! argument for truth divine,
  For study's cares, for virtue's strife ;
To know th' enjoyment will be thine,
  In that renew'd, that endless life !

SIR EUSTACE GREY

[1807]

SCENE—A MAD-HOUSE

PERSONS—VISITOR, PHYSICIAN, AND PATIENT

Veris miscens falsa.—
  SENECA, *in Herc. furente*, v. 1070.

VISITOR

I'LL know no more ;—the heart is torn
  By views of wo, we cannot heal ;
Long shall I see these things forlorn,
  And oft again their griefs shall feel,
As each upon the mind shall steal ;
  That wan projector's mystic style,
  That lumpish idiot leering by,
That peevish idler's ceaseless wile,
  And that poor maiden's half-form'd smile,
    While struggling for the full-drawn sigh !
I'll know no more.

PHYSICIAN
        —Yes, turn again ;
Then speed to happier scenes thy way,
  When thou hast view'd, what yet remain,
The ruins of Sir Eustace Grey,
  The sport of madness, misery's prey :
But he will no historian need,
  His cares, his crimes, will he display,
And show (as one from frenzy freed)
  The proud-lost mind, the rash-done deed.
That cell to him is Greyling Hall :—
  Approach ; he'll bid thee welcome there ;
Will sometimes for his servant call,
  And sometimes point the vacant chair :

Yes, Aaron had each manly charm,
  All in the May of youthful pride,
He scarcely fear'd his father's arm,
  And every other arm defied.—

Oft, when they grew in anger warm,
  (Whom will not love and power divide ?)
I rose, their wrathful souls to calm,
  Not yet in sinful combat tried.

His father was our party's chief,
  And dark and dreadful was his look ;
His presence fill'd my heart with grief,
  Although to me he kindly spoke.

With Aaron I delighted went,
  His favour was my bliss and pride ;
In growing hope our days we spent,
  Love growing charms in either spied,
It saw them, all which Nature lent,
  It lent them, all which she denied.

Could I the father's kindness prize,
  Or grateful looks on him bestow,
Whom I beheld in wrath arise,
  When Aaron sunk beneath his blow ?

He drove him down with wicked hand,
  It was a dreadful sight to see ;
Then vex'd him, till he left the land,

And told his cruel love to me ;—
The clan were all at his command,
  Whatever his command might be.

The night was dark, the lanes were deep,
  And one by one they took their way ;
He bade me lay me down and sleep,
  I only wept and wish'd for day.

Accursed be the love he bore,
  Accursed was the force he used,
So let him of his God implore
  For mercy, and be so refused !

You frown again,—to show my wrong,
  Can I in gentle language speak ?
My woes are deep, my words are strong,—
  And hear me, or my heart will break.

MAGISTRATE

I hear thy words, I feel thy pain ;
  Forbear awhile to speak thy woes ;
Receive our aid, and then again
  The story of thy life disclose.

For, though seduced and led astray,
  Thou'st travell'd far and wander'd long ;
Thy God hath seen thee all the way,
  And all the turns that led thee wrong.

PART II

Quondam ridentes oculi, nunc fonte perenni
Deplorant poenas nocte dieque suas.
  Corn. Galli Eleg.

MAGISTRATE

COME, now again thy woes impart,
  Tell all thy sorrows, all thy sin ;
We cannot heal the throbbing heart
  Till we discern the wounds within.

Compunction weeps our guilt away,
  The sinner's safety is his pain ;
Such pangs for our offences pay,
  And these severer griefs are gain.

VAGRANT

The son came back—he found us wed,
  Then dreadful was the oath he swore ;—
His way through Blackburn Forest led,—
  His father we beheld no more.

Of all our daring clan not one
  Would on the doubtful subject dwell :
For all esteem'd the injured son,
  And fear'd the tale which he could tell.

But I had mightier cause for fear
  For slow and mournful round my bed
I saw a dreadful form appear,—
  It came when I and Aaron wed.

(Yes ! we were wed, I know my crime,—
  We slept beneath the elmin tree ;
But I was grieving all the time,
  And Aaron frown'd my tears to see.

For he not yet had felt the pain
  That rankles in a wounded breast ;
He waked to sin, then slept again,
  Forsook his God, yet took his rest.—

But I was forced to feign delight,
  And joy in mirth and music sought,—
And mem'ry now recalls the night,
  With such surprise and horror fraught,
That reason felt a moment's flight,
  And left a mind to madness wrought.)

When waking, on my heaving breast
  I felt a hand as cold as death ;
A sudden fear my voice suppress'd,
  A chilling terror stopp'd my breath.—

I seem'd—no words can utter how !
  For there my father-husband stood,—
And thus he said :—' Will God allow,
  ' The great avenger, just and good,
A wife to break her marriage vow ?
  A son to shed his father's blood ? '

I trembled at the dismal sounds,
  But vainly strove a word to say ;
So, pointing to his bleeding wounds,
  The threat'ning spectre stalk'd away.[1]

I brought a lovely daughter forth,
  His father's child, in Aaron's bed ;
He took her from me in his wrath,
  ' Where is my child ? '—' Thy child is dead.'

'Twas false—we wander'd far and wide,
  Through town and country, field and fen,
Till Aaron, fighting, fell and died,
  And I became a wife again.

I then was young :—my husband sold
  My fancied charms for wicked price ;
He gave me oft, for sinful gold,
  The slave, but not the friend of vice :—
Behold me, Heaven ! my pains behold,
  And let them for my sins suffice !

The wretch who lent me thus for gain,
  Despised me when my youth was fled ;
Then came disease, and brought me pain :—
  Come, death, and bear me to the dead !
For though I grieve, my grief is vain,
  And fruitless all the tears I shed.

True, I was not to virtue train'd,
  Yet well I knew my deeds were ill ;
By each offence my heart was pain'd,
  I wept, but I offended still ;
My better thoughts my life disdain'd,
  But yet the viler led my will.

[1] The state of mind here described will account for a vision of this nature, without having recourse to any supernatural appearance.

My husband died, and now no more
  My smile was sought, or ask'd my hand,
A widow'd vagrant, vile and poor,
  Beneath a vagrant's vile command.

Ceaseless I roved the country round,
  To win my bread by fraudful arts,
And long a poor subsistence found,
  By spreading nets for simple hearts.

Though poor, and abject, and despised,
  Their fortunes to the crowd I told ;
I gave the young the love they prized,
  And promised wealth to bless the old ;
Schemes for the doubtful I devised,
  And charms for the forsaken sold.

At length for arts like these confined
  In prison with a lawless crew,
I soon perceived a kindred mind,
  And there my long-lost daughter knew :

His father's child, whom Aaron gave
  To wander with a distant clan,
The miseries of the world to brave,
  And be the slave of vice and man.

She knew my name—we met in pain,
  Our parting pangs can I express ?
She sail'd a convict o'er the main,
  And left an heir to her distress.

This is that heir to shame and pain,
  For whom I only could descry
A world of trouble and disdain :
  Yet, could I bear to see her die,
Or stretch her feeble hands in vain,
  And, weeping, beg of me supply ?

No ! though the fate thy mother knew
  Was shameful ! shameful though thy
    race
Have wander'd all, a lawless crew,
  Outcasts, despised in every place ;

Yet as the dark and muddy tide,
  When far from its polluted source,
Becomes more pure, and, purified,
  Flows in a clear and happy course ;—

In thee, dear infant ! so may end
  Our shame, in thee our sorrows cease !
And thy pure course will then extend,
  In floods of joy, o'er vales of peace.

Oh ! by the GOD who loves to spare,
  Deny me not the boon I crave ;
Let this loved child your mercy share,
  And let me find a peaceful grave ;
Make her yet spotless soul your care,
  And let my sins their portion have ;
Her for a better fate prepare,
  And punish whom 'twere sin to save !

MAGISTRATE

Recall the word, renounce the thought,
  Command thy heart and bend thy knee.
There is to all a pardon brought,
  A ransom rich, assured and free ;
'Tis full when found, 'tis found if sought,
  Oh ! seek it, till 'tis seal'd to thee.

VAGRANT

But how my pardon shall I know ?

MAGISTRATE

By feeling dread that 'tis not sent,
By tears for sin that freely flow,
  By grief, that all thy tears are spent,
By thoughts on that great debt we
    owe,
With all the mercy GOD has lent,
By suffering what thou canst not show,
  Yet showing how thine heart is rent,
Till thou canst feel thy bosom glow,
  And say, 'My SAVIOUR, I REPENT ! '

WOMAN !

[1807]

MR. LEDYARD, AS QUOTED BY M. PARKE IN
HIS TRAVELS INTO AFRIC.

' To a Woman I never addressed myself in the
language of decency and friendship, without
receiving a decent and friendly answer. If
I was hungry or thirsty, wet or sick, they
did not hesitate, like Men, to perform a
generous action : in so free and kind a
manner did they contribute to my relief,
that if I was dry, I drank the sweetest
draught ; and if hungry, I ate the coarsest
morsel with a double relish.'

PLACE the white man on Afric's coast,
  Whose swarthy sons in blood delight,
Who of their scorn to Europe boast,
  And paint their very demons white :
There, while the sterner sex disdains
  To soothe the woes they cannot feel,
Woman will strive to heal his pains,
  And weep for those she cannot heal :
Hers is warm pity's sacred glow ;
  From all her stores, she bears a part,
And bids the spring of hope re-flow,
  That languish'd in the fainting heart.

' What though so pale his haggard face,
  So sunk and sad his looks,'—she cries ;
' And far unlike our nobler race,
  With crisped locks and rolling eyes ;
    Yet misery marks him of our kind ;
    We see him lost, alone, afraid ;
  And pangs of body, griefs in mind,
    Pronounce him man, and ask our
      aid.

' Perhaps in some far-distant shore,
  There are who in these forms delight ;
Whose milky features please them more,
  Than ours of jet thus burnish'd bright ;
    Of such may be his weeping wife,
      Such children for their sire may call,
    And if we spare his ebbing life,
      Our kindness may preserve them
        all.'

Thus her compassion Woman shows,
  Beneath the line her acts are these ;
Nor the wide waste of Lapland-snows
  Can her warm flow of pity freeze :—

CR.   E

'From some sad land the stranger
  comes,
  Where joys, like ours, are never found;
Let's soothe him in our happy homes,
  Where freedom sits, with plenty
  crown'd.

''Tis good the fainting soul to cheer,
  To see the famish'd stranger fed ;
To milk for him the mother-deer,
  To smooth for him the furry bed.
    The powers above our Lapland bless
    With good no other people know ;
    T' enlarge the joys that we possess,
    By feeling those that we bestow !'

Thus in extremes of cold and heat,
  Where wandering man may trace his
  kind ;

Wherever grief and want retreat,
  In Woman they compassion find ;
She makes the female breast her seat,
  And dictates mercy to the mind.

Man may the sterner virtues know,
  Determined justice, truth severe :
But female hearts with pity glow,
  And Woman holds affliction dear ;
For guiltless woes her sorrows flow,
  And suffering vice compels her tear ;
'Tis hers to soothe the ills below,
  And bid life's fairer views appear :
To Woman's gentle kind we owe
  What comforts and delights us here ;
They its gay hopes on youth bestow,
  And care they soothe and age they
  cheer.

THE BOROUGH

[1810]

PAULO MAJORA CANAMUS.—VIRGIL, *Ecl.* iv. 1.

TO HIS GRACE
THE DUKE OF RUTLAND, MARQUIS OF GRANBY;

RECORDER OF CAMBRIDGE AND SCARBOROUGH; LORD-LIEUTENANT AND CUSTOS-
ROTULORUM OF THE COUNTY OF LEICESTER; K.G. AND LL.D.

MY LORD,

THE poem, for which I have ventured to solicit your Grace's attention, was composed in a situation so near to Belvoir Castle, that the author had all the advantage to be derived from prospects extensive and beautiful, and from works of grandeur and sublimity : and though nothing of the influence arising from such situation should be discernible in these verses, either from want of adequate powers in the writer, or because his subjects do not assimilate with such views, yet would it be natural for him to indulge a wish, that he might inscribe his labours to the lord of a scene which perpetually excited his admiration, and he would plead the propriety of placing the titles of the House of Rutland at the entrance of a volume written in the Vale of Belvoir.

But, my Lord, a motive much more powerful than a sense of propriety, a grateful remembrance of benefits conferred by the noble family in which you preside, has been the great inducement for me to wish that I might be permitted to inscribe this work to your Grace : the honours of that time were to me unexpected, they were unmerited, and they were transitory : but since I am thus allowed to make public my gratitude, I am in some degree restored to the honour of that period ; I have again the happiness to find myself favoured, and my exertions stimulated, by the condescension of the Duke of Rutland.

It was my fortune, in a poem which yet circulates, to write of the virtues, talents, and heroic death of Lord Robert Manners, and to bear witness to the affection of a brother whose grief was poignant, and to be soothed only by remembrance of his worth whom he so deeply deplored. In a patron thus favourably predisposed, my Lord, I might look for much lenity, and could not fear the severity of critical examination : from your Grace, who, happily, have no such impediment to justice, I must not look for the same kind of indulgence. I am assured, by those whose situation gave them opportunity for knowledge, and whose abilities and attention guarded them from error, that I must not expect my failings will escape detection from want of discernment, neither am I to fear that any merit will be undistinguished through deficiency of taste. It is from this information, my Lord, and a consciousness of much which needs forgiveness, that I entreat your Grace to read my verses, with a wish, I had almost added, with a purpose to be pleased, and to make every possible allowance for subjects not always pleasing, for manners sometimes gross, and for language too frequently incorrect.

With the fullest confidence in your Grace's ability and favour, in the accuracy of your judgment, and the lenity of your decision ; with grateful remembrance of benefits received, and due consciousness of the little I could merit ; with prayers that your Grace may long enjoy the dignities of the House of Rutland, and continue to dictate improvement for the surrounding country ;—I terminate an address, in which a fear of offending your Grace has made me so cautious in my expressions, that I may justly fear to offend many of my readers, who will think that something more of animation should have been excited by the objects I view, the benevolence I honour, and the gratitude I profess.

I have the honour to be, my Lord,
Your Grace's most obliged
and obedient, humble servant,
GEORGE CRABBE.

PREFACE

WHETHER, if I had not been encouraged by some proofs of public favour, I should have written the Poem now before the reader, is a question which I cannot positively determine; but I will venture to assert, that I should not, in that case, have committed the work to the press ; I should not have allowed my own opinion of it to have led me into further disappointment, against the voice of judges impartial and indifferent, from whose sentence it had been fruitless to appeal : the success of a late publication, therefore, may be fairly assigned as the principal cause for the appearance of this.

When the ensuing Letters were so far written, that I could form an opinion of them, and when I began to conceive that they might not be unacceptable to the public, I felt myself prompted by duty, as well as interest, to put them to the press ; I considered myself bound by gratitude for the favourable treatment I had already received, to show that I was not unmindful of it ; and, however this might be mixed with other motives, it operated with considerable force upon my mind, acting as a stimulus to exertions naturally tardy, and to expectations easily checked.

It must nevertheless be acknowledged, that although such favourable opinion had been formed, I was not able, with the requisite impartiality, to determine the comparative value of an unpublished manuscript, and a work sent into the world. Books, like children, when established, have doubtless our parental affection and good wishes; we rejoice to hear that they are doing well, and are received and respected in good company : but it is to manuscripts in the study, as to children in the nursery, that our care, our anxiety, and our tenderness are principally directed : they are fondled as our endearing companions ; their faults are corrected with the lenity of partial love, and their good parts are exaggerated by the strength of parental imagination ; nor is it easy even for the more cool and reasonable among parents, thus circumstanced, to decide upon the comparative merits of their offspring, whether they be children of the bed or issue of the brain.

But, however favourable my own opinion may have been, or may still be, I could not venture to commit so long a Poem to the press without some endeavour to obtain the more valuable opinion of less partial judges : at the same time, I am willing to confess that I have lost some portion of the timidity once so painful, and that I am encouraged to take upon myself the decision of various points, which heretofore I entreated my friends to decide. Those friends were then my council, whose opinion I was implicitly to follow; they are now advisers, whose ideas I am at liberty to reject. This will not, I hope, seem like arrogance : it would be more safe, it would be more pleasant, still to have that reliance on the judgment of others ; but it cannot always be obtained ; nor are they, however friendly disposed, ever ready to lend a helping hand to him whom they consider as one who ought by this time to have cast away the timidity of inexperience, and to have acquired the courage that would enable him to decide for himself.

When it is confessed that I have less assistance from my friends, and that the appearance of this work is, in a great measure, occasioned by the success of a former ; some readers will, I fear, entertain the opinion that the book before them was written in haste, and published without due examination and revisal : should this opinion be formed, there will doubtless occur many faults which may appear as originating in neglect : Now, readers are, I believe, disposed to treat with more than common severity those writers who have been led into presumption by the approbation bestowed on their diffidence, and into idleness and unconcern, by the praises given to their attention. I am therefore even anxious it should be generally known that sufficient time and application were bestowed upon this work, and by this I mean that no material alteration would be effected by delay : it is true that this confession removes one plea for the errors of the book, want of time ; but, in my opinion, there is not much consolation to be drawn by reasonable minds from this resource : if a work fails, it appears to be poor satisfaction when it is observed, that if the author had taken more care, the event had been less disgraceful.

When the reader enters into the Poem, he will find the author retired from view, and an imaginary personage brought forward to describe his Borough for him : to him it seemed convenient to speak in the first person : but the inhabitant of a village, in the centre of the kingdom, could not appear in the character of a residing burgess in a large sea-port ; and when, with this point, was considered what relations were to be given, what manners delineated, and what situations described, no method appeared to be so convenient as that of borrowing the assistance of an ideal friend : by this means the reader is in some degree kept from view of any particular place, nor will he perhaps be so likely to determine where those persons reside, and what their connexions, who are so intimately known to this man of straw.

From the title of this Poem, some persons will, I fear, expect a political satire,—an attack upon corrupt principles in a general view, or upon the customs and manners of some particular place ; of these they will find nothing satirized, nothing related. It may be that graver readers would have preferred a more historical account of so considerable a Borough—its charter, privileges, trade, public structures, and subjects of this kind ; but I have an apology for the omission

of these things, in the difficulty of describing them, and in the utter repugnancy which subsists between the studies and objects of topography and poetry. What I thought I could best describe, that I attempted :—the sea, and the country in the immediate vicinity ; the dwellings, and the inhabitants ; some incidents and characters, with an exhibition of morals and manners, offensive perhaps to those of extremely delicate feelings, but sometimes, I hope, neither unamiable nor unaffecting : an Election indeed forms a part of one Letter, but the evil there described is one not greatly nor generally deplored, and there are probably many places of this kind where it is not felt.

From the variety of relations, characters, and descriptions which a Borough affords, several were rejected which a reader might reasonably expect to have met with : in this case he is entreated to believe that these, if they occurred to the author, were considered by him as beyond his ability, as subjects which he could not treat in a manner satisfactory to himself. Possibly the admission of some will be thought to require more apology than the rejection of others : in such variety, it is to be apprehended, that almost every reader will find something not according with his ideas of propriety, or something repulsive to the tone of his feelings ; nor could this be avoided but by the sacrifice of every event, opinion, and even expression, which could be thought liable to produce such effect ; and this casting away so largely of our cargo, through fears of danger, though it might help us to clear it, would render our vessel of little worth when she came into port. I may likewise entertain a hope, that this very variety, which gives scope to objection and censure, will also afford a better chance for approval and satisfaction.

Of these objectionable parts many must be to me unknown ; of others some opinion may be formed, and for their admission some plea may be stated.

In the first Letter is nothing which particularly calls for remark, except possibly the last line—giving a promise to the reader that he should both smile and sigh in the perusal of the following Letters. This may appear vain, and more than an author ought to promise ; but let it be considered that the character assumed is that of a friend, who gives an account of objects, persons, and events to his correspondent, and who was therefore at liberty, without any imputation of this kind, to suppose in what manner he would be affected by such descriptions.

Nothing, I trust, in the second Letter, which relates to the imitation of what are called weather-stains on buildings, will seem to any invidious or offensive. I wished to make a comparison between those minute and curious bodies which cover the surface of some edifices, and those kinds of stain which are formed of boles and ochres, and laid on with a brush. Now, as the work of time cannot be anticipated in such cases, it may be very judicious to have recourse to such expedients as will give to a recent structure the venerable appearance of antiquity; and in this case, though I might still observe the vast difference between the living varieties of nature, and the distant imitation of the artist, yet I would not forbear to make use of his dexterity, because he could not clothe my freestone with *mucor, lichen,* and *byssus.*

The wants and mortifications of a poor Clergyman are the subjects of one portion of the third Letter; and he being represented as a stranger in the Borough, it may be necessary to make some apology for his appearance in the Poem. Previous to a late meeting of a literary society, whose benevolent purpose is well known to the public, I was induced by a friend to compose a few verses, in which, with the general commendation of the design, should be introduced a hint that the bounty might be farther extended; these verses a gentleman did me the honour to recite at the meeting, and they were printed as an extract from the Poem, to which in fact they may be called an appendage.

I am now arrived at that part of my work, which I may expect will bring upon me some animadversion. Religion is a subject deeply interesting to the minds of many, and when these minds are weak, they are often led by a warmth of feeling into the violence of causeless resentment: I am therefore anxious that my purpose should be understood; and I wish to point out what things they are which an author may hold up to ridicule

and be blameless. In referring to the two principal divisions of enthusiastical teachers, I have denominated them, as I conceive they are generally called, *Calvinistic* and *Arminian* Methodists. The *Arminians,* though divided and perhaps subdivided, are still, when particular accuracy is not intended, considered as one body, having had, for many years, one head, who is yet held in high respect by the varying members of the present day: but the Calvinistic societies are to be looked upon rather as separate and independent congregations; and it is to one of these (unconnected, as is supposed, with any other) I more particularly allude. But while I am making use of this division, I must entreat that I may not be considered as one who takes upon him to censure the religious opinions of any society or individual: the reader will find that the spirit of the enthusiast, and not his opinions, his manners and not his creed, have engaged my attention. I have nothing to observe of the Calvinist and Arminian, considered as such; but my remarks are pointed at the enthusiast and the bigot, at their folly and their craft.

To those readers who have seen the journals of the first Methodists, or the extracts quoted from them by their opposers * in the early times of this spiritual influenza, are sufficiently known all their leading notions and peculiarities; so that I have no need to enter into such unpleasant inquiries in this place: I have only to observe that their tenets remain the same, and have still the former effect on the minds of the converted: There is yet that imagined contention with the powers of darkness, that is at once so lamentable and so ludicrous: there is the same offensive familiarity with the Deity, with a full trust and confidence both in the immediate efficacy of their miserably delivered supplications, and in the reality of numberless small miracles wrought at their request and for their convenience: there still exists that delusion, by which some of the most common diseases of the body are regarded as proofs of the malignity of Satan contending for dominion over the soul: and there still remains the same wretched jargon, composed of scriptural language, debased by vulgar

* *Methodists and Papists compared; Treatise on Grace,* by Bishop Warburton, &c.

expressions, which has a kind of mystic influence on the minds of the ignorant. It will be recollected that it is the abuse of those scriptural terms which I conceive to be improper: they are doubtless most significant and efficacious when used with propriety; but it is painful to the mind of a soberly devout person, when he hears every rise and fall of the animal spirits, every whim and notion of enthusiastic ignorance, expressed in the venerable language of the Apostles and Evangelists.

The success of these people is great, but not surprising: as the powers they claim are given, and come not of education, many may, and therefore do, fancy they are endowed with them; so that they who do not venture to become preachers, yet exert the minor gifts, and gain reputation for the faculty of prayer, as soon as they can address the Creator in daring flights of unpremeditated absurdity. The less indigent gain the praise of hospitality, and the more harmonious become distinguished in their choirs: curiosity is kept alive by succession of ministers, and self-love is flattered by the consideration that they are the persons at whom the world wonders; add to this, that, in many of them, pride is gratified by their consequence as new members of a sect whom their conversion pleases, and by the liberty, which as seceders they take, of speaking contemptuously of the Church and ministers, whom they have relinquished.

Of those denominated *Calvinistic Methodists*, I had principally one sect in view, or, to adopt the term of its founder, *a church*. This *church* consists of several ongregations in town and country, unknown perhaps in many parts of the kingdom, but, where known, the cause of much curiosity and some amusement. To such of my readers as may judge an enthusiastic teacher and his peculiarities to be unworthy any serious attention, I would observe that there is something unusually daring in the boast of this man, who claims the authority of a messenger sent from God, and declares without hesitation that his call was immediate; that he is assisted by the sensible influence of the Spirit, and that miracles are perpetually wrought in his favour and for his convenience.

As it was and continues to be my desire

to give proof that I had advanced nothing respecting this extraordinary person, his operations or assertions, which might not be readily justified by quotations from his own writings, I had collected several of these and disposed them under certain heads; but I found that by this means a very disproportioned share of attention must be given to the subject, and after some consideration, I have determined to relinquish the design; and, should any have curiosity to search whether my representation of the temper and disposition, the spirit an manners, the knowledge and capacity, of a very popular teacher be correct, he is referred to about fourscore pamphlets, whose titles will be found on the covers of the late editions of the *Bank of Faith*, itself a wonderful performance, which (according to the turn of mind in the reader) will either highly excite, or totally extinguish, curiosity. In these works will be abundantly seen, abuse and contempt of the Church of England and its ministers; vengeance and virulent denunciation against all offenders; scorn for morality and heathen virtue, with that kind of learning which the author possesses, and his peculiar style of composition. A few of the titles placed below will give some information to the reader respecting the merit and design of those performances.*

As many of the preacher's subjects are controverted and nice questions in divinity, he has sometimes allowed himself relaxation from the severity of study, and favoured his admirers with the effects of an humbler kind of inspiration, viz. that of the Muse. It must be confessed that these flights of fancy are very humble, and have nothing of that daring and mysterious nature which the prose of the author leads us to expect. *The Dimensions of eternal* LOVE is a title of one of his more learned productions, with which might have been expected (as a fit companion), *The Bounds of infinite Grace*; but no such work appears, and possibly the

* Barbar, in two parts; Bond-Child; Cry of Little Faith; Satan's Lawsuit; Forty Stripes for Satan; Myrrh and Odour of Saints; the Naked Bow of God; Rule and Riddle; Way and Fare for Wayfaring Men; Utility of the Books and Excellency of the Parchments; Correspondence between *Noctau, Aurita*, (the words so separated) and *Philomela*, &c.

author considered one attempt of this kind was sufficient to prove the extent and direction of his abilities.

Of the whole of this mass of inquiry and decision, of denunciation and instruction (could we suppose it read by intelligent persons), different opinions would probably be formed ; the more indignant and severe would condemn the whole as the produce of craft and hypocrisy, while the more lenient would allow that such things might originate in the wandering imagination of a dreaming enthusiast.

None of my readers will, I trust, do me so much injustice as to suppose I have here any other motive than a vindication of what I have advanced in the verses which describe this kind of character, or that I had there any other purpose than to express (what I conceive to be) justifiable indignation against the assurance, the malignity, and (what is of more importance) the pernicious influence of such sentiments on the minds of the simple and ignorant, who, if they give credit to his relations, m ist be no more than tools and instruments under the control and management of one *called to be their Apostle.*

Nothing would be more easy for me, as I have observed, than to bring forward quotations such as would justify all I have advanced ; but even had I room, I cannot tell whether there be not something degrading in such kind of attack : the reader might smile at those miraculous accounts, but he would consider them and the language of the author as beneath his further attention : I therefore once more refer him to those pamphlets, which will afford matter for pity and for contempt, by which some would be amused and others astonished—not without sorrow, when they reflect that thousands look up to the writer as a man literally inspired, to whose wants they administer with their substance, and to whose guidance they prostrate their spirit and understanding.

Having been so long detained by this Letter, I must not permit my desire of elucidating what may seem obscure, or of defending what is liable to misconstruction, any further to prevail over a wish for brevity, and the fear of giving an air of importance to subjects which have perhaps little in themselves.

The circumstance recorded in the fifth

Letter is a fact ; although it may appear to many almost incredible, that, in this country, and but few years since, a close and successful man should be a stranger to the method of increasing money by the loan of it. The Minister of the place where the honest Fisherman resided has related to me the apprehension and suspicion he witnessed : With trembling hand and dubious look, the careful man received and surveyed the bond given to him ; and, after a sigh or two of lingering mistrust, he placed it in the coffer whence he had just before taken his cash ; for which, and for whose increase, he now indulged a belief, that it was indeed both promise and security.

If the Letter which treats of Inns should be found to contain nothing interesting or uncommon ; if it describe things which we behold every day, and some which we do not wish to behold at any time ; let it be considered that this Letter is one of the shortest, and that from a Poem whose subject was a Borough, populous and wealthy, these places of public accommodation could not, without some impropriety, be excluded.

I entertain the strongest, because the most reasonable hope, that no liberal practitioner in the Law will be offended by the notice taken of dishonourable and crafty attorneys. The increased difficulty of entering into the profession will in time render it much more free than it now is, from those who disgrace it ; at present such persons remain ; and it would not be difficult to give instances of neglect, ignorance, cruelty, oppression, and chicanery ; nor are they by any means confined to one part of the country : quacks and impostors are indeed in every profession, as well with a licence as without one. The character and actions of *Swallow* might doubtless be contrasted by the delineation of an able and upright Solicitor ; but this Letter is of sufficient length, and such persons, without question, are already known to my readers.

When I observe, under the article Physic, that the young and less experienced physician will write rather with a view of making himself known, than to investigate and publish some useful fact, I would not be thought to extend this remark to all the publications of such men. I could point out a work, containing experiments the most judicious, and conclusions the most interesting, made by a gentleman, then young, which would have given just celebrity to a man after long practice. The observation is nevertheless generally true : many opinions have been adopted and many books written, not that the theory might be well defended, but that a young physician might be better known.

If I have in one Letter praised the good-humour of a man confessedly too inattentive to business, and, in another, if I have written somewhat sarcastically of ' the brick-floored parlour which the butcher lets ; ' be credit given to me, that in the one case I had no intention to apologize for idleness, nor any design in the other to treat with contempt the resources of the poor. The good-humour is considered as the consolation of disap-pointment, and the room is so mentioned because the lodger is vain. Most of my readers will perceive this ; but I shall be sorry if by any I am supposed to make pleas for the vices of men, or treat their wants and infirmities with derision or with disdain.

It is probable, that really polite people, with cultivated minds and harmonious tem-pers, may judge my description of a Card-club conversation to be highly exaggerated, if not totally fictitious ; and I acknowledge that the club must admit a particular kind of members to afford such specimens of acrimony and objurgation : yet that such language is spoken, and such manners exhibited, is most certain, chiefly among those who, being successful in life, without previous education, not very nice in their feelings, or very attentive to improprieties, sit down to game with no other view than that of adding the gain of the evening to the profits of the day ; whom therefore dis-appointment itself makes angry, and, when caused by another, resentful and vindictive.

The Letter on Itinerant Players will to some appear too harshly written, their profligacy exaggerated, and their distresses magnified ; but though the respectability of a part of these people may give us a more favourable view of the whole body ; though some actors be sober, and some managers prudent ; still there is vice and misery left, more than sufficient to justify my description. But if I could find only one woman who

(passing forty years on many stages, and sustaining many principal characters) laments in her unrespected old age, that there was no workhouse to which she could legally sue for admission ; if I could produce only one female, seduced upon the boards, and starved in her lodging, compelled by her poverty to sing, and by her sufferings to weep, without any prospect but misery, or any consolation but death ; if I could exhibit only one youth who sought refuge from parental authority in the licentious freedom of a wandering company ; yet, with three such examples, I should feel myself justified in the account I have given :—but such characters and sufferings are common, and there are few of these societies which could not show members of this description. To some, indeed, the life has its satisfactions : they never expected to be free from labour, and their present kind they think is light : they have no delicate ideas of shame, and there-fore duns and hisses give them no other pain than what arises from the fear of not being trusted, joined with the apprehension that they may have nothing to subsist upon except their credit.

For the Alms-House itself, its Governors and Inhabitants, I have not much to offer, in favour of the subject or of the characters. One of these, *Sir Denys Brand*, may be con-sidered as too highly placed for an author (who seldom ventures above middle-life) to delineate ; and indeed I had some idea of reserving him for another occasion, where he might have appeared with those in his own rank ; but then it is most uncertain whether he would ever appear, and he has been so many years prepared for the public whenever opportunity might offer, that I have at length given him place, and though with his inferiors, yet as a ruler over them. Of these, one (*Benbow*) may be thought too low and despicable to be admitted here ; but he is a Borough-character, and, however disgusting in some respects a picture may be, it will please some, and be tolerated by many, if it can boast that one merit of being a faithful likeness.

Blaney and *Clelia*, a male and female in-habitant of this mansion, are drawn at some length ; and I may be thought to have given them attention which they do not merit.

I plead not for the originality, but for the truth of the character; and though it may not be very pleasing, it may be useful to delineate (for certain minds) these mixtures of levity and vice; people who are thus incurably vain and determinately worldly; thus devoted to enjoyment and insensible of shame, and so miserably fond of their pleasures, that they court even the remembrance with eager solicitation, by conjuring up the ghosts of departed indulgences with all the aid that memory can afford them. These characters demand some attention, because they hold out a warning to that numerous class of young people who are too lively to be discreet; to whom the purpose of life is amusement, and who are always in danger of falling into vicious habits, because they have too much activity to be quiet, and too little strength to be steady.

The characters of the Hospital-Directors were written many years since, and, so far as I was capable of judging, are drawn with *fidelity*. I mention this circumstance, that, if any reader should find a difference in the versification or expression, he will be thus enabled to account for it.

The Poor are here almost of necessity introduced, for they must be considered, in every place, as a large and interesting portion of its inhabitants. I am aware of the great difficulty of acquiring just notions on the maintenance and management of this class of our fellow-subjects, and I forbear to express any opinion of the various modes which have been discussed or adopted: of one method only I venture to give my sentiments, that of collecting the poor of a hundred into one building. This admission of a vast number of persons, of all ages and both sexes, of very different inclinations, habits, and capacities, into a society, must at a first view, I conceive, be looked upon as a cause of both vice and misery; nor does any thing which I have heard or read invalidate the opinion; happily, it is not a prevailing one, as these houses are, I believe, still confined to that part of the kingdom where they originated.

To this subject follow several Letters describing the follies and crimes of persons in lower life, with one relation of a happier and more consolatory kind. It has been a

subject of greater vexation to me than such trifle ought to be, that I could not, without destroying all appearance of arrangement, separate these melancholy narratives, and place the fallen Clerk in Office at a greater distance from the Clerk of the Parish, especially as they resembled each other in several particulars; both being tempted, seduced, and wretched. Yet are there, I conceive, considerable marks of distinction: their guilt is of different kind; nor would either have committed the offence of the other. The Clerk of the Parish could break the commandment, but he could not have been induced to have disowned an article of that creed for which he had so bravely contended, and on which he fully relied; and the upright mind of the Clerk in Office would have secured him from being guilty of wrong and robbery, though his weak and vacillating intellect could not preserve him from infidelity and profaneness. Their melancholy is nearly alike, but not its consequences. *Jachin* retained his belief, and though he hated life, he could never be induced to quit it voluntarily; but *Abel* was driven to terminate his misery in a way which the unfixedness of his religious opinions rather accelerated than retarded. I am therefore not without hope that the more observant of my readers will perceive many marks of discrimination in these characters.

The Life of *Ellen Orford*, though sufficiently burthened with error and misfortune, has in it little besides, which resembles those of the above unhappy men, and is still more unlike that of *Grimes*, in a subsequent Letter. There is in this character cheerfulness and resignation, a more uniform piety, and an immovable trust in the aid of religion: this, with the light texture of the introductory part, will, I hope, take off from that idea of sameness which the repetition of crimes and distresses is likely to create. The character of *Grimes*, his obduracy and apparent want of feeling, his gloomy kind of misanthropy, the progress of his madness, and the horrors of his imagination, I must leave to the judgment and observation of my readers. The mind here exhibited is one untouched by pity, unstung by remorse, and uncorrected by shame: yet is this hardihood of temper and spirit broken by want, disease, solitude, and disappoint-

ment ; and he becomes the victim of a dis-
tempered and horror-stricken fancy. It is
evident, therefore, that no feeble vision, no
half-visible ghost, not the momentary glance
of an unbodied being, nor the half-audible
voice of an invisible one, would be created
by the continual workings of distress on
a mind so depraved and flinty. The ruffian
of Mr. Scott * has a mind of this nature :
he has no shame or remorse : but the
corrosion of hopeless want, the wasting of
unabating disease, and the gloom of unvaried
solitude, will have their effect on every
nature ; and the harder that nature is, and
the longer time required to work upon it, so
much the more strong and indelible is the
impression. This is all the reason I am able
to give, why a man of feeling so dull should
yet become insane, should be of so horrible
a nature.

That a Letter on Prisons should follow
those narratives is unfortunate, but not to be
easily avoided. I confess it is not pleasant
to be detained so long by subjects so repulsive
to the feelings of many, as the sufferings of
mankind : but though I assuredly would
have altered this arrangement, had I been
able to have done it by substituting a better,
yet am I not of opinion that my verses, or
indeed the verses of any other person, can so
represent the evils and distresses of life as to
make any material impression on the mind,
and much less any of injurious nature. Alas!
sufferings real, evident, continually before us,
have not effects very serious or lasting, even
in the minds of the more reflecting and com-
passionate ; nor indeed does it seem right
that the pain caused by sympathy should
serve for more than a stimulus to benevo-
lence. If then the strength and solidity of
truth placed before our eyes have effect so
feeble and transitory, I need not be very
apprehensive that my representations of
Poor-houses and Prisons, of wants and suffer-
ings, however faithfully taken, will excite
any feelings which can be seriously lamented.
It has always been held as a salutary exercise
of the mind, to contemplate the evils and
miseries of our nature : I am not therefore
without hope, that even this gloomy subject
of Imprisonment, and more especially the
Dream of the condemned Highwayman, will

* Marmion.

excite in some minds that mingled pity and
abhorrence, which, while it is not unpleasant
to the feelings, is useful in its operation : it
ties and binds us to all mankind by sensations
common to us all, and in some degree con-
nects us, without degradation, even to the
most miserable and guilty of our fellow-
men.

Our concluding subject is Education ; and
some attempt is made to describe its various
seminaries, from that of the Poor Widow,
who pronounces the alphabet for infants, to
seats whence the light of learning is shed
abroad on the world. If, in this Letter,
I describe the lives of literary men as embit-
tered by much evil ; if they be often disap-
pointed, and sometimes unfitted for the world
they improve ; let it be considered that they
are described as men who possess that great
pleasure, the exercise of their own talents,
and the delight which flows from their own
exertions : they have joy in their pursuits,
and glory in their acquirements of knowledge.
Their victory over difficulties affords the most
rational cause of triumph, and the attainment
of new ideas leads to incalculable riches, such
as gratify the glorious avarice of aspiring and
comprehensive minds. Here then I place the
reward of learning.—Our Universities pro-
duce men of the first scholastic attainments,
who are heirs to large possessions, or de-
scendants from noble families. Now, to
those so favoured, talents and acquirements
are, unquestionably, means of arriving at
the most elevated and important situations ;
but these must be the lot of a few : in general,
the diligence, acuteness, and perseverance
of a youth at the University, have no other
reward than some College honours and emolu-
ments, which they desire to exchange, many
of them for very moderate incomes in the
obscurity of some distant village : so that,
in stating the reward of an ardent and power-
ful mind to consist principally (I might have
said entirely) in its own views, efforts, and
excursions, I place it upon a sure foundation,
though not one so elevated as the more
ambitious aspire to. It is surely some en-
couragement to a studious man to reflect,
that if he be disappointed, he cannot be
without gratification ; and that if he gets
but a very humble portion of what the world
can give, he has a continual fruition of un-

wearying enjoyment, of which it has not power to deprive him.

Long as I have detained the reader, I take leave to add a few words on the subject of imitation, or, more plainly speaking, borrowing. In the course of a long Poem, and more especially of two long ones, it is very difficult to avoid a recurrence of the same thoughts, and of similar expressions ; and, however careful I have been myself in detecting and removing these kinds of repetitions, my readers, I question not, would, if disposed to seek them, find many remaining. For these I can only plead that common excuse —they are the offences of a bad memory, and not of voluntary inattention ; to which I must add the difficulty (I have already mentioned) of avoiding the error : this kind of plagiarism will therefore, I conceive, be treated with lenity : and of the more criminal kind, borrowing from others, I plead, with much confidence, ' not guilty.' But while I claim exemption from guilt, I do not affirm that much of sentiment and much of expression may not be detected in the vast collection of English poetry : it is sufficient for an author, that he uses not the words or ideas of another without acknowledgment, and this, and no more than this, I mean, by disclaiming debts of the kind ; yet resemblances are sometimes so very striking, that it requires faith in a reader to admit they were undesigned. A line in the second Letter,

'And monuments themselves memorials need,'

was written long before the author, in an accidental recourse to Juvenal, read—

Quandoquidem data sunt ipsis quoque fata sepulchris.

Sat. x. l. 146.

and for this I believe the reader will readily give me credit. But there is another apparent imitation in the life of *Blaney* (Letter xiv), a simile of so particular a kind, that its occurrence to two writers at the same time must appear as an extraordinary event ; for this reason I once determined to exclude it from the relation ; but, as it was truly unborrowed, and suited the place in which it stood, this seemed, on after-consideration, to be an act of cowardice, and the lines are therefore printed as they were written about two months before the very same thought (prosaically drest) appeared in a periodical work of the last summer. It is highly probable, in these cases, that both may derive the idea from a forgotten but common source ; and in this way I must entreat the reader to do me justice, by accounting for other such resemblances, should any be detected.

I know not whether to some readers the placing two or three Latin quotations to a Letter may not appear pedantic and ostentatious, while both they and the English ones may be thought unnecessary. For the necessity I have not much to advance ; but if they be allowable (and certainly the best writers have adopted them), then, when two or three different subjects occur, so many of these mottoes seem to be required : nor will a charge of pedantry remain, when it is considered that these things are generally taken from some books familiar to the school-boy, and the selecting them is facilitated by the use of a book of common-place : yet, with this help, the task of motto-hunting has been so unpleasant to me, that I have in various instances given up the quotation I was in pursuit of, and substituted such English verse or prose as I could find or invent for my purpose.

THE BOROUGH

[1810]

LETTER I. GENERAL DESCRIPTION

These did the ruler of the deep ordain,
To build proud navies, and to rule the main.
POPE'S Homer's Iliad, book vi, ll. 45, 46.

Such place hath Deptford, navy-building
town,
  Woolwich and Wapping, smelling strong of
    pitch ;
Such Lambeth, envy of each band and gown,
  And Twick'nam such, which fairer scenes
    enrich.
POPE'S Imitation of Spenser, vi. 1-4.

    . . . Et cum coelestibus undis
Aequoreae miscentur aquae : caret ignibus
   aether,
Caecaque nox premitur tenebris hiemisque
   suisque ;
Discutiunt tamen has, praebentque micantia
   lumen
Fulmina : fulmineis ardescunt ignibus undae.
OVID, Metamorph. lib. xi, ll. 519-23.

The Difficulty of describing Town Scenery—
A Comparison with certain Views in the
Country—The River and Quay—The
Shipping and Business—Ship-Building—
Sea-Boys and Port-Views—Village and
Town Scenery again compared—Walks
from Town—Cottage and adjoining Heath,
&c.—House of Sunday Entertainment—
The Sea : a Summer and Winter View—
A Shipwreck at Night, and its Effects
on Shore—Evening Amusements in the
Borough—An Apology for the imperfect
View which can be given of these Subjects.

' DESCRIBE the Borough '—though our idle
  tribe
May love description, can we so describe,
That you shall fairly streets and buildings
  trace,
And all that gives distinction to a place ?
This cannot be ; yet, moved by your request,
A part I paint—let fancy form the rest.
  Cities and towns, the various haunts of
   men,
Require the pencil ; they defy the pen :
Could he, who sang so well the Grecian fleet,
So well have sung of alley, lane, or street ?

Can measured lines these various buildings
  show,
The Town-Hall Turning, or the Prospect
  Row ?
Can I the seats of wealth and want explore,
And lengthen out my lays from door to door ?
  Then let thy fancy aid me—I repair
From this tall mansion of our last-year's
  mayor,
Till we the outskirts of the Borough reach,
And these half-buried buildings next the
  beach ;
Where hang at open doors the net and cork,
While squalid sea-dames mend the meshy
  work ;
Till comes the hour, when fishing through the
  tide,
The weary husband throws his freight aside ;
A living mass, which now demands the wife,
Th' alternate labours of their humble life.
  Can scenes like these withdraw thee from
   thy wood,
Thy upland forest or thy valley's flood ?
Seek then thy garden's shrubby bound, and
  look,
As it steals by, upon the bordering brook ;
That winding streamlet, limpid, lingering,
  slow,
Where the reeds whisper when the zephyrs
  blow ;
Where in the midst, upon her throne of green,
Sits the large lily [1] as the water's queen ;
And makes the current, forced awhile to stay,
Murmur and bubble as it shoots away ;
Draw then the strongest contrast to that
  stream,
And our broad river will before thee seem.
  With ceaseless motion comes and goes the
   tide,
Flowing, it fills the channel vast and wide ;
Then back to sea, with strong majestic sweep
It rolls, in ebb yet terrible and deep ;
Here sampire-banks [2] and salt-wort [3] bound
  the flood,
There stakes and sea-weeds withering on the
  mud ;

And higher up, a ridge of all things base,
Which some strong tide has roll'd upon the
place.
　Thy gentle river boasts its pigmy boat,
Urged on by pains, half grounded, half afloat ;
While at her stern an angler takes his stand,
And marks the fish he purposes to land ;
From that clear space, where, in the cheerful
ray
Of the warm sun, the scaly people play.
　Far other craft our prouder river shows,
Hoys, pinks and sloops ; brigs, brigantines
and snows :
Nor angler we on our wide stream descry,
But one poor dredger where his oysters lie :
He, cold and wet, and driving with the
tide,
Beats his weak arms against his tarry side,
Then drains the remnant of diluted gin,
To aid the warmth that languishes within ;
Renewing oft his poor attempts to beat
His tingling fingers into gathering heat.
　He shall again be seen when evening comes,
And social parties crowd their favourite
rooms :
Where on the table pipes and papers lie,
The steaming bowl or foaming tankard by ;
'Tis then, with all these comforts spread
around,
They hear the painful dredger's welcome
sound ;
And few themselves the savoury boon deny,
The food that feeds, the living luxury.
　Yon is our quay ! those smaller hoys from
town,
Its various wares, for country-use, bring
down ;
Those laden waggons, in return, impart
The country-produce to the city mart ;
Hark ! to the clamour in that miry road,
Bounded and narrow'd by yon vessels' load ;
The lumbering wealth she empties round the
place,
Package, and parcel, hogshead, chest, and
case :
While the loud seaman and the angry hind,
Mingling in business, bellow to the wind.
　Near these a crew amphibious, in the docks,
Rear, for the sea, those castles on the stocks ;
See ! the long keel, which soon the waves
must hide ;
See ! the strong ribs which form the roomy
side ;

Bolts yielding slowly to the sturdiest stroke,
And planks [4] which curve and crackle in the
smoke.
Around the whole rise cloudy wreaths, and far
Bear the warm pungence of o'er-boiling tar.
　Dabbling on shore half-naked sea-boys
crowd,
Swim round a ship, or swing upon the shroud ;
Or in a boat purloin'd, with paddles play,
And grow familiar with the watery way :
Young though they be, they feel whose sons
they are,
They know what British seamen do and dare ;
Proud of that fame, they raise and they enjoy
The rustic wonder of the village-boy.
　Before you bid these busy scenes adieu,
Behold the wealth that lies in public view,
Those far-extended heaps of coal and coke,
Where fresh-fill'd lime-kilns breathe their
stifling smoke.
This shall pass off, and you behold, instead,
The night-fire gleaming on its chalky bed ;
When from the light-house brighter beams
will rise,
To show the shipman where the shallow lies.
　Thy walks are ever pleasant ; every scene
Is rich in beauty, lively, or serene——
Rich—is that varied view with woods around,
Seen from thy seat, within the shrubb'ry
bound ;
Where shines the distant lake, and where
appear
From ruins bolting, unmolested deer ;
Lively—the village-green, the inn, the place,
Where the good widow schools her infant
race.
Shops, whence are heard the hammer and the
saw,
And village-pleasures unreproved by law ;
Then how serene ! when in your favourite
room,
Gales from your jasmines soothe the evening
gloom ;
When from your upland paddock you look
down,
And just perceive the smoke which hides the
town ;
When weary peasants at the close of day
Walk to their cots, and part upon the
way ;
When cattle slowly cross the shallow brook,
And shepherds pen their folds, and rest upon
their crook.

We prune our hedges, prime our slender
    trees,
And nothing looks untutor'd and at ease ;
On the wide heath, or in the flow'ry vale,
We scent the vapours of the sea-born gale ;
Broad-beaten paths lead on from stile to stile,
And sewers from streets, the road-side banks
    defile ;
Our guarded fields a sense of danger show,
Where garden-crops with corn and clover
    grow ;
Fences are form'd of wreck and placed around,
(With tenters tipp'd) a strong repulsive
    bound ;
Wide and deep ditches by the gardens run,
And there in ambush lie the trap and gun ;
Or yon broad board, which guards each
    tempting prize,
' Like a tall bully, lifts its head and lies.'
    There stands a cottage with an open door,
Its garden undefended blooms before :
Her wheel is still, and overturn'd her stool,
While the lone widow seeks the neighb'ring
    pool :
This gives us hope, all views of town to shun—
No ! here are tokens of the sailor-son ;
That old blue jacket, and that shirt of check,
And silken kerchief for the seaman's neck ;
Sea-spoils and shells from many a distant
    shore,
And furry robe from frozen Labrador.
    Our busy streets and sylvan-walks between,
Fen, marshes, bog and heath all intervene ;
Here pits of crag, with spongy, plashy base,
To some enrich th' uncultivated space :
For there are blossoms rare, and curious
    rush,
The gale's rich balm, and sun-dew's crimson
    blush,
Whose velvet leaf with radiant beauty dress'd,
Forms a gay pillow for the plover's breast.
    Not distant far, a house commodious made,
(Lonely yet public stands) for Sunday-trade ;
Thither, for this day free, gay parties go,
Their tea-house walk, their tippling rendez-
    vous ;
There humble couples sit in corner-bowers,
Or gaily ramble for th' allotted hours ;
Sailors and lasses from the town attend,
The servant-lover, the apprentice-friend ;
With all the idle social tribes who seek,
And find their humble pleasures once a
    week.

Turn to the watery world !—but who to
    thee
(A wonder yet unview'd) shall paint—the
    sea ?
Various and vast, sublime in all its forms,
When lull'd by zephyrs, or when roused by
    storms,
Its colours changing, when from clouds and
    sun
Shades after shades upon the surface run ;
Embrown'd and horrid now, and now serene,
In limpid blue, and evanescent green ;
And oft the foggy banks on ocean lie,
Lift the fair sail, and cheat th' experienced
    eye.[5]
    Be it the summer-noon : a sandy space
The ebbing tide has left upon its place ;
Then just the hot and stony beach above,
Light twinkling streams in bright confusion
    move ;
(For heated thus, the warmer air ascends,
And with the cooler in its fall contends)—
Then the broad bosom of the ocean keeps
An equal motion ; swelling as it sleeps,
Then slowly sinking ; curling to the strand,
Faint, lazy waves o'ercreep the ridgy sand,
Or tap the tarry boat with gentle blow,
And back return in silence, smooth and
    slow.
Ships in the calm seem anchor'd ; for they
    glide
On the still sea, urged solely by the tide ;
Art thou not present, this calm scene before,
Where all beside is pebbly length of shore,
And far as eye can reach, it can discern no
    more ?
    Yet sometimes comes a ruffling cloud to
    make
The quiet surface of the ocean shake ;
As an awaken'd giant with a frown
Might show his wrath, and then to sleep sink
    down.
    View now the winter-storm ! above, one
    cloud,
Black and unbroken, all the skies o'ershroud ;
Th' unwieldy porpoise through the day before
Had roll'd in view of boding men on shore ;
And sometimes hid and sometimes show'd his
    form,
Dark as the cloud, and furious as the storm.
    All where the eye delights, yet dreads to
    roam,
The breaking billows cast the flying foam

Upon the billows rising—all the deep
Is restless change ; the waves so swell'd and
    steep,
Breaking and sinking, and the sunken swells,
Nor one, one moment, in its station dwells :
But nearer land you may the billows trace,
As if contending in their watery chase ;
May watch the mightiest till the shoal they
    reach,
Then break and hurry to their utmost stretch ;
Curl'd as they come, they strike with furious
    force,
And then re-flowing, take their grating course,
Raking the rounded flints, which ages past
Roll'd by their rage, and shall to ages last.
    Far off the petrel in the troubled way
Swims with her brood, or flutters in the spray;
She rises often, often drops again,
And sports at ease on the tempestuous main.
    High o'er the restless deep, above the reach
Of gunner's hope, vast flights of wild-ducks
    stretch ;
Far as the eye can glance on either side,
In a broad space and level line they glide ;
All in their wedge-like figures from the north,
Day after day, flight after flight, go forth.
    In-shore their passage tribes of sea-gulls
    urge,
And drop for prey within the sweeping surge ;
Oft in the rough opposing blast they fly
Far back, then turn, and all their force apply,
While to the storm they give their weak com-
    plaining cry ;
Or clap the sleek white pinion to the breast,
And in the restless ocean dip for rest.
    Darkness begins to reign ; the louder wind
Appals the weak and awes the firmer mind ;
But frights not him, whom evening and the
    spray
In part conceal—yon prowler on his way :
Lo ! he has something seen ; he runs apace,
As if he fear'd companion in the chase ;
He sees his prize, and now he turns again,
Slowly and sorrowing—' Was your search in
    vain ? '
Gruffly he answers, ' 'Tis a sorry sight !
A seaman's body: there'll be more to-night ! '
    Hark ! to those sounds ! they're from
    distress at sea :
How quick they come ! What terrors may
    there be !
Yes, 'tis a driven vessel : I discern
Lights, signs of terror, gleaming from the stern;

Others behold them too, and from the town
In various parties seamen hurry down ;
Their wives pursue, and damsels urged by
    dread,
Lest men so dear be into danger led ;
Their head the gown has hooded, and their
    call
In this sad night is piercing like the squall ;
They feel their kinds of power, and when they
    meet,
Chide, fondle, weep, dare, threaten, or entreat.
    See one poor girl, all terror and alarm,
Has fondly seized upon her lover's arm ;
' Thou shalt not venture ; ' and he answers
    ' No !
I will not '—still she cries, ' Thou shalt not go.'
    No need of this ; not here the stoutest boat
Can through such breakers, o'er such billows
    float ;
Yet may they view these lights upon the beach,
Which yield them hope, whom help can never
    reach.
    From parted clouds the moon her radiance
    throws
On the wild waves, and all the danger shows ;
But shows them beaming in her shining vest,
Terrific splendour ! gloom in glory dress'd !
This for a moment, and then clouds again
Hide every beam, and fear and darkness reign.
    But hear we now those sounds ? Do lights
    appear ?
I see them not ! the storm alone I hear :
And lo ! the sailors homeward take their way;
Man must endure—let us submit and pray.
    Such are our winter-views ; but night
    comes on—
Now business sleeps, and daily cares are gone;
Now parties form, and some their friends assist
To waste the idle hours at sober whist ;
The tavern's pleasure or the concert's charm
Unnumber'd moments of their sting disarm ;
Play-bills and open doors a crowd invite,
To pass off one dread portion of the night ;
And show and song and luxury combined,
Lift off from man this burthen of mankind.
    Others advent'rous walk abroad and meet
Returning parties pacing through the street ;
When various voices, in the dying day,
Hum in our walks, and greet us in our way;
When tavern-lights flit on from room to room,
And guide the tippling sailor staggering home:
There as we pass, the jingling bells betray
How business rises with the closing day :

Now walking silent, by the river's side,
The ear perceives the rippling of the tide ;
Or measured cadence of the lads who tow
Some enter'd hoy, to fix her in her row ;
Or hollow sound, which from the parish-bell
To some departed spirit bids farewell !
  Thus shall you something of our BOROUGH
     know,
Far as a verse, with Fancy's aid, can show ;

Of sea or river, of a quay or street,
The best description must be incomplete ;
But when a happier theme succeeds, and
    when
Men are our subjects and the deeds of men ;
Then may we find the Muse in happier
    style,
And we may sometimes sigh and sometimes
    smile.

LETTER II. THE CHURCH

. . . Festinat enim decurrere velox
Flosculus angustae miseraeque brevissima
  vitae
Portio ; dum bibimus, dum serta, unguenta,
  puellas
Poscimus, obrepit non intellecta senectus.
      JUVENAL, *Sat.* ix. ll. 126-9.

And when at last thy love shall die,
  Wilt thou receive his parting breath ?
Wilt thou repress each struggling sigh,
  And cheer with smiles the bed of death ?
           PERCY.

Several Meanings of the word *Church*—The
Building so called, here intended—Its
Antiquity and Grandeur—Columns and
Ailes—The Tower : the Stains made by
Time compared with the mock Antiquity
of the Artist—Progress of Vegetation on
such Buildings—Bells—Tombs : one in
decay—Mural Monuments, and the Nature
of their Inscriptions—An Instance in a
departed Burgess—Churchyard Graves—
Mourners for the Dead—A Story of a
betrothed Pair in humble Life, and Effects
of Grief in the Survivor.

'WHAT is a Church ? '—Let Truth and
  Reason speak,
They would reply, ' The faithful, pure, and
  meek ;
From Christian folds, the one selected race,
Of all professions, and in every place.'
' What is a Church ? '—' A flock,' our vicar
  cries,
' Whom bishops govern and whom priests
  advise ;
Wherein are various states and due degrees,
The bench for honour, and the stall for
  ease ;
That ease be mine, which, after all his cares,
The pious, peaceful prebendary shares.'

' What is a Church ? '—Our honest sexton
  tells,
' 'Tis a tall building, with a tower and bells;
Where priest and clerk with joint exertion
  strive
To keep the ardour of their flock alive ;
That, by his periods eloquent and grave ;
This, by responses, and a well-set stave :
These for the living ; but when life be fled,
I toll myself the requiem for the dead.'
  'Tis to this Church I call thee, and that
    place
Where slept our fathers when they'd run their
    race :
We too shall rest, and then our children keep
Their road in life, and then, forgotten, sleep ;
Meanwhile the building slowly falls away,
And, like the builders, will in time decay.
  The old foundation—but it is not clear
When it was laid—you care not for the year ;
On this, as parts decay'd by time and storms,
Arose these various disproportion'd forms ;
Yet Gothic, all the learn'd who visit us
(And small wonders) have decided thus :
' Yon noble Gothic arch,' ' That Gothic door;'
So have they said ; of proof you'll need no
  more.
  Here large plain columns rise in solemn style,
You'd love the gloom they make in either aile;
When the sun's rays, enfeebled as they pass
(And shorn of splendour) through the storied
    glass,
Faintly displays the figures on the floor,
Which pleased distinctly in their place before.
  But ere you enter, yon bold tower survey,
Tall and entire, and venerably gray,
For time has soften'd what was harsh when
    new,
And now the stains are all of sober hue ;

The living stains which Nature's hand alone,
Profuse of life, pours forth upon the stone ;
For ever growing ; where the common eye
Can but the bare and rocky bed descry :
There Science loves to trace her tribes minute,
The juiceless foliage, and the tasteless fruit;
There she perceives them round the surface
    creep,
And while they meet, their due distinction
    keep ;
Mix'd but not blended; each its name retains,
And these are Nature's ever-during stains.
  And wouldst thou, artist ! with thy tints
    and brush,
Form shades like these ? Pretender, where
    thy blush ?
In three short hours shall thy presuming hand
Th' effect of three slow centuries command ? [1]
Thou may'st thy various greens and grays
    contrive,
They are not lichens, nor like aught alive ;—
But yet proceed, and when thy tints are lost,
Fled in the shower, or crumbled by the frost ;
When all thy work is done away as clean
As if thou never spread'st thy gray and green ;
Then may'st thou see how Nature's work is
    done,
How slowly true she lays her colours on ;
When her least speck upon the hardest flint
Has mark and form and is a living tint ;
And so embodied with the rock, that few
Can the small germ upon the substance view.[2]
  Seeds, to our eye invisible, will find
On the rude rock the bed that fits their kind ;
There, in the rugged soil, they safely dwell,
Till showers and snows the subtle atoms swell,
And spread th' enduring foliage ;—then we
    trace
The freckled flower upon the flinty base ;
These all increase, till in unnoticed years
The stony tower as gray with age appears ;
With coats of vegetation, thinly spread,
Coat above coat, the living on the dead :
These then dissolve to dust, and make a way
For bolder foliage, nursed by their decay :
The long-enduring ferns in time will all
Die and depose their dust upon the wall ;
Where the wing'd seed may rest, till many
    a flower
Show Flora's triumph o'er the falling tower.
  But ours yet stands, and has its bells
    renown'd
For size magnificent and solemn sound ;

Each has its motto : some contrived to tell,
In monkish rhyme, the uses of a bell [3] ;
Such wond'rous good, as few conceive could
    spring
From ten loud coppers when their clappers
    swing.
Enter'd the Church ; we to a tomb proceed,
Whose names and titles few attempt to read ;
Old English letters, and those half pick'd out,
Leave us, unskilful readers, much in doubt ;
Our sons shall see its more degraded state ;
The tomb of grandeur hastens to its fate ;
That marble arch, our sexton's favourite
    show,
With all those ruff'd and painted pairs below ;
The noble lady and the lord who rest
Supine, as courtly dame and warrior dress'd ;
All are departed from their state sublime,
Mangled and wounded in their war with time
Colleagued with mischief ; here a leg is fled,
And lo ! the baron with but half a head ;
Midway is cleft the arch ; the very base
Is batter'd round and shifted from its place.
  Wonder not, mortal, at thy quick decay—
See ! men of marble piece-meal melt away ;
When whose the image we no longer read,
But monuments themselves memorials need.[4]
  With few such stately proofs of grief or
    pride
By wealth erected, is our Church supplied ;
But we have mural tablets, every size,
That wo could wish, or vanity devise.
  Death levels man,—the wicked and the just,
The wise, the weak, lie blended in the dust ;
And by the honours dealt to every name,
The king of terrors seems to level fame.
  —See ! here lamented wives, and every wife
The pride and comfort of her husband's life ;
Here, to her spouse, with every virtue graced,
His mournful widow has a trophy placed ;
And here 'tis doubtful if the duteous son,
Or the good father, be in praise outdone.
  This may be nature ; when our friends we
    lose,
Our alter'd feelings alter too our views ;
What in their tempers teased us or distress'd,
Is, with our anger and the dead, at rest ;
And much we grieve, no longer trial made,
For that impatience which we then display'd ;
Now to their love and worth of every kind
A soft compunction turns th' afflicted mind ;
Virtues neglected then, adored become,
And graces slighted, blossom on the tomb.

'Tis well ; but let not love nor grief believe
That we assent (who neither loved nor grieve)
To all that praise which on the tomb is read,
To all that passion dictates for the dead ;
But more indignant, we the tomb deride,
Whose bold inscription flattery sells to pride.

Read of this Burgess—on the stone appear
How worthy he ! how virtuous ! and how
    dear !
What wailing was there when his spirit fled,
How mourn'd his lady for her lord when dead,
And tears abundant through the town were
    shed ;
See ! he was liberal, kind, religious, wise,
And free from all disgrace and all disguise ;
His sterling worth, which words cannot ex-
    press,
Lives with his friends, their pride and their
    distress.

All this of Jacob Holmes ? for his the name;
He thus kind, liberal, just, religious ?—shame!
What is the truth ? Old Jacob married thrice ;
He dealt in coals, and av'rice was his vice ;
He ruled the Borough when his year came on,
And some forget, and some are glad he's gone ;
For never yet with shilling could he part,
But when it left his hand, it struck his heart.

Yet, here will love its last attentions pay,
And place memorials on these beds of clay.
Large level stones lie flat upon the grave,
And half a century's sun and tempest brave ;
But many an honest tear and heartfelt sigh
Have follow'd those who now unnoticed lie ;
Of these what numbers rest on every side !
Without one token left by grief or pride ;
Their graves soon levell'd to the earth, and
    then
Will other hillocks rise o'er other men ;
Daily the dead on the decay'd are thrust,
And generations follow, ' dust to dust.'

Yes ! there are real mourners—I have seen
A fair, sad girl, mild, suffering, and serene ;
Attention (through the day) her duties claim'd,
And to be useful as resign'd she aim'd :
Neatly she dress'd, nor vainly seem'd t' expect
Pity for grief, or pardon for neglect ;
But when her wearied parents sunk to sleep,
She sought her place to meditate and weep :
Then to her mind was all the past display'd,
That faithful memory brings to sorrow's aid :
For then she thought on óne regretted
    youth,
Her tender trust, and his unquestion'd truth ;

In ev'ry place she wander'd, where they'd
    been,
And sadly-sacred held the parting-scene ;
Where last for sea he took his leave—that
    place
With double interest would she nightly trace ;
For long the courtship was, and he would
    say,
Each time he sail'd,—' This once, and then
    the day : '
Yet prudence tarried, but when last he went,
He drew from pitying love a full consent.

Happy he sail'd, and great the care she
    took,
That he should softly sleep, and smartly look ;
White was his better linen, and his check
Was made more trim than any on the deck ;
And every comfort men at sea can know
Was hers to buy, to make, and to bestow :
For he to Greenland sail'd, and much she told,
How he should guard against the climate's
    cold ;
Yet saw not danger ; dangers he'd withstood,
Nor could she trace the fever in his blood :
His messmates smiled at flushings in his
    cheek,
And he too smiled, but seldom would he
    speak ;
For now he found the danger, felt the pain,
With grievous symptoms he could not ex-
    plain ;
Hope was awaken'd, as for home he sail'd,
But quickly sank, and never more prevail'd.

He call'd his friend, and prefaced with
    a sigh
A lover's message—' Thomas, I must die :
Would I could see my Sally, and could rest
My throbbing temples on her faithful breast,
And gazing go !—if not, this trifle take,
And say, till death I wore it for her sake ;
Yes ! I must die—blow on, sweet breeze,
    blow on !
Give me one look, before my life be gone,
Oh ! give me that, and let me not despair,
One last fond look—and now repeat the
    prayer.'
He had his wish, had more ; I will not
    paint
The lovers' meeting : she beheld him faint,—
With tender fears, she took a nearer view,
Her terrors doubling as her hopes withdrew ;
He tried to smile, and, half succeeding, said,
' Yes ! I must die ; ' and hope for ever fled.

Still long she nursed him : tender thoughts
    meantime
Were interchanged, and hopes and views
    sublime.
To her he came to die, and every day
She took some portion of the dread away ;
With him she pray'd, to him his Bible read,
Soothed the faint heart, and held the aching
    head :
She came with smiles the hour of pain to
    cheer ;
Apart she sigh'd ; alone, she shed the tear ;
Then, as if breaking from a cloud, she gave
Fresh light, and gilt the prospect of the grave.
    One day he lighter seem'd, and they forgot
The care, the dread, the anguish of their lot ;
They spoke with cheerfulness, and seem'd to
    think,
Yet said not so—' Perhaps he will not sink : '
A sudden brightness in his look appear'd,
A sudden vigour in his voice was heard ;—
She had been reading in the Book of Prayer,
And led him forth, and placed him in his chair;
Lively he seem'd, and spoke of all he knew,
The friendly many, and the favourite few ;
Nor one that day did he to mind recall
But she has treasured, and she loves them all ;
When in her way she meets them, they appear
Peculiar people—death has made them dear.
He named his friend, but then his hand she
    press'd,
And fondly whisper'd, ' Thou must go to
    rest ; '

' I go,' he said ; but as he spoke, she found
His hand more cold, and fluttering was the
    sound !
Then gazed affrighten'd ; but she caught
    a last,
A dying look of love,—and all was past !
    She placed a decent stone his grave above,
Neatly engraved—an offering of her love ;
For that she wrought, for that forsook her
    bed,
Awake alike to duty and the dead ;
She would have grieved, had friends presumed
    to spare
The least assistance—'twas her proper care.
    Here will she come, and on the grave will
    sit,
Folding her arms, in long abstracted fit ;
But if observer pass, will take her round,
And careless seem, for she would not be
    found ;
Then go again, and thus her hour employ,
While visions please her, and while woes
    destroy.
    Forbear, sweet maid ! nor be by fancy led,
To hold mysterious converse with the dead ;
For sure at length thy thoughts, thy spirits
    pain,
In this sad conflict will disturb thy brain ;
All have their tasks and trials ; thine are
    hard,
But short the time and glorious the reward ;
Thy patient spirit to thy duties give,
Regard the dead, but to the living live.[5]

LETTER III. THE VICAR—THE CURATE, ETC.

And telling me the sov'reign'st thing on earth
Was parmacity for an inward bruise.
    SHAKSPEARE, *Henry IV*, Part I., Act i,
        Scene 3.

So gentle, yet so brisk, so wond'rous sweet,
So fit to prattle at a lady's feet.
    CHURCHILL, *The Author*, 359, 360.

Much are the precious hours of youth mispent
In climbing learning's rugged, steep ascent :
When to the top the bold adventurer 's got,
He reigns vain monarch o'er a barren spot;
Whilst in the vale of ignorance below,
Folly and vice to rank luxuriance grow ;

Honours and wealth pour in on every side,
And proud preferment rolls her golden tide.
    CHURCHILL, *The Author*, 5-12.

VICAR

The late departed Minister of the Borough—
    His soothing and supplicatory Manners—
    His cool and timid Affections—No Praise
    due to such negative Virtue—Address to
    Characters of this Kind—The Vicar's Em-
    ployments—His Talents and moderate
    Ambition—His Dislike of Innovation—His
    mild but ineffectual Benevolence—A Sum-
    mary of his Character.

CURATE

Mode of paying the Borough-Minister—The
Curate has no such Resources—His Learn-
ing and Poverty—Erroneous Idea of his
Parent—His Feelings as a Husband and
Father—The dutiful Regard of his numerous
Family—His Pleasure as a Writer, how
interrupted—No Resource in the Press—
Vulgar Insult—His Account of a Literary
Society, and a Fund for the Relief of in-
digent Authors, &c.

THE VICAR

WHERE ends our chancel in a vaulted space,
Sleep the departed vicars of the place ;
Of most, all mention, memory, thought are
    past—
But like a slight memorial of the last.

To what famed college we our Vicar owe,
To what fair county, let historians show :
Few now remember when the mild young man,
Ruddy and fair, his Sunday-task began ;
Few live to speak of that soft soothing look
He cast around, as he prepared his book ;
It was a kind of supplicating smile,
But nothing hopeless of applause, the while ;
And when he finish'd, his corrected pride
Felt the desert, and yet the praise denied.
Thus he his race began, and to the end
His constant care was, no man to offend ;
No haughty virtues stirr'd his peaceful mind,
Nor urged the priest to leave the flock behind ;
He was his Master's soldier, but not one
To lead an army of his martyrs on :
Fear was his ruling passion ; yet was love,
Of timid kind, once known his heart to move ;
It led his patient spirit where it paid
Its languid offerings to a listening maid ;
She, with her widow'd mother, heard him
    speak,
And sought awhile to find what he would seek:
Smiling he came, he smiled when he withdrew,
And paid the same attention to the two ;
Meeting and parting without joy or pain,
He seem'd to come that he might go again.
The wondering girl, no prude, but something
    nice,
At length was chill'd by his unmelting ice ;
She found her tortoise held such sluggish pace,
That she must turn and meet him in the chase :
This not approving, she withdrew till one
Came who appear'd with livelier hope to run ;
Who sought a readier way the heart to move,
Than by faint dalliance of unfixing love.

Accuse me not that I approving paint
Impatient hope or love without restraint ;
Or think the passions, a tumultuous throng,
Strong as they are, ungovernably strong :
But is the laurel to the soldier due,
Who cautious comes not into danger's view ?
What worth has virtue by desire untried,
When Nature's self enlists on duty's side ?
The married dame in vain assail'd the truth
And guarded bosom of the Hebrew-youth ;
But with the daughter of the Priest of On
The love was lawful, and the guard was gone ;
But Joseph's fame had lessen'd in our view,
Had he, refusing, fled the maiden too.
Yet our good priest to Joseph's praise
    aspired,
As once rejecting what his heart desired ;
' I am escaped,' he said, when none pursued ;
When none attacked him, ' I am un-
    subdued ; '
' Oh pleasing pangs of love,' he sang again,
Cold to the joy, and stranger to the pain.
Ev'n in his age would he address the young,
' I too have felt these fires, and they are
    strong ; '
But from the time he left his favourite maid,
To ancient females his devoirs were paid ;
And still they miss him after morning prayer ;
Nor yet successor fills the Vicar's chair,
Where kindred spirits in his praise agree,
A happy few, as mild and cool as he ;
The easy followers in the female train,
Led without love, and captives without
    chain.

Ye lilies male ! think (as your tea you sip,
While the town small-talk flows from lip to
    lip ;
Intrigues half-gather'd, conversation-scraps,
Kitchen-cabals, and nursery-mishaps,)
If the vast world may not some scene produce,
Some state where your small talents might
    have use ;
Within seraglios you might harmless move,
'Mid ranks of beauty, and in haunts of love ;
There from too daring man the treasures
    guard,
An easy duty, and its own reward ;
Nature's soft substitutes, you there might
    save
From crime the tyrant, and from wrong the
    slave.

But let applause be dealt in all we may,
Our priest was cheerful, and in season gay ;

His frequent visits seldom fail'd to please ;
Easy himself, he sought his neighbour's ease :
To a small garden with delight he came,
And gave successive flowers a summer's fame ;
These he presented with a grace his own
To his fair friends, and made their beauties
    known,
Not without moral compliment ; how they
' Like flowers were sweet, and must like
    flowers decay.'
Simple he was, and loved the simple truth,
Yet had some useful cunning from his youth ;
A cunning never to dishonour lent,
And rather for defence than conquest meant ;
'Twas fear of power, with some desire to rise,
But not enough to make him enemies ;
He ever aim'd to please ; and to offend
Was ever cautious ; for he sought a friend ;
Yet for the friendship never much would pay,
Content to bow, be silent, and obey,
And by a soothing suff'rance find his way.

Fiddling and fishing were his arts : at times
He alter'd sermons, and he aim'd at rhymes ;
And his fair friends, not yet intent on cards,
Oft he amused with riddles and charades.

Mild were his doctrines, and not one dis-
    course
But gain'd in softness what it lost in force :
Kind his opinions ; he would not receive
An ill report, nor evil act believe ;
' If true, 'twas wrong ; but blemish great or
    small
Have all mankind ; yea, sinners are we all.'

If ever fretful thought disturb'd his breast,
If aught of gloom that cheerful mind op-
    press'd,
It sprang from innovation ; it was then
He spake of mischief made by restless men ;
Not by new doctrines : never in his life
Would he attend to controversial strife ;
For sects he cared not ; ' They are not of us,
Nor need we, brethren, their concerns discuss ;
But 'tis the change, the schism at home I feel ;
Ills few perceive, and none have skill to heal ;
Not at the altar our young brethren read
(Facing their flock) the decalogue and creed ;
But at their duty, in their desks they stand,
With naked surplice, lacking hood and band :
Churches are now of holy song bereft,
And half our ancient customs changed or
    left ;
Few sprigs of ivy are at Christmas seen,
Nor crimson berry tips the holly's green ;

Mistaken choirs refuse the solemn strain
Of ancient Sternhold, which from ours amain
Comes flying forth from aile to aile about,
Sweet links of harmony and long drawn out.'

These were to him essentials ; all things new
He deem'd superfluous, useless, or untrue ;
To all beside indifferent, easy, cold,
Here the fire kindled, and the wo was told.

Habit with him was all the test of truth,
' It must be right : I've done it from my
    youth.'
Questions he answer'd in as brief a way,
' It must be wrong—it was of yesterday.'

Though mild benevolence our priest
    possess'd,
'Twas but byw ishes or by words express'd :
Circles in water, as they wider flow,
The less conspicuous in their progress grow ;
And when at last they touch upon the shore,
Distinction ceases, and they're view'd no
    more.
His love, like that last circle, all embraced,
But with effect that never could be traced.

Now rests our Vicar. They who knew him
    best,
Proclaim his life t' have been entirely rest ;
Free from all evils which disturb his mind,
Whom studies vex and controversies blind.

The rich approved,—of them in awe he
    stood ;
The poor admired,—they all believed him
    good ;
The old and serious of his habits spoke ;
The frank and youthful loved his pleasant
    joke ;
Mothers approved a safe contented guest,
And daughters one who back'd each small
    request :
In him his flock found nothing to condemn ;
Him sectaries liked,—he never troubled them ;
No trifles fail'd his yielding mind to please,
And all his passions sunk in early ease ;
Nor one so old has left this world of sin,
More like the being that he enter'd in.

THE CURATE

ASK you what lands our pastor tithes ?—Alas !
But few our acres, and but short our grass :
In some fat pastures of the rich, indeed,
May roll the single cow or favourite steed ;
Who, stable-fed, is here for pleasure seen,
His sleek sides bathing in the dewy green :

But these, our hilly heath and common wide
Yield a slight portion for the parish-guide ;
No crops luxuriant in our borders stand,
For here we plough the ocean, not the land ;
Still reason wills that we our pastor pay,
And custom does it on a certain day :
Much is the duty, small the legal due,
And this with grateful minds we keep in view ;
Each makes his off'ring, some by habit led,
Some by the thought, that all men must be fed;
Duty and love, and piety and pride,
Have each their force, and for the priest
     provide.

Not thus our Curate, one whom all believe
Pious and just, and for whose fate they grieve;
All see him poor, but ev'n the vulgar know
He merits love, and their respect bestow.
A man so learn'd you shall but seldom see,
Nor one so honour'd, so aggrieved as he ;—
Not grieved by years alone; though his appear
Dark and more dark ; severer on severe :
Not in his need,—and yet we all must grant
How painful 'tis for feeling age to want :
Nor in his body's sufferings ; yet we know
Where time has plough'd, there misery loves
     to sow ;
But in the wearied mind, that all in vain
Wars with distress, and struggles with its pain.
His father saw his powers—' I'll give,'
     quoth he,
' My first-born learning ; 'twill a portion be : '
Unhappy gift ! a portion for a son !
But all he had :—he learn'd, and was undone !

Better, apprenticed to an humble trade,
Had he the cassock for the priesthood made,
Or thrown the shuttle, or the saddle shaped,
And all these pangs of feeling souls escaped.

He once had hope—hope ardent, lively, light;
His feelings pleasant, and his prospects bright:
Eager of fame, he read, he thought, he wrote,
Weigh'd the Greek page, and added note on
     note ;
At morn, at evening at his work was he,
And dream'd what his Euripides would be.
Then care began ;—he loved, he woo'd, he
     wed ;
Hope cheer'd him still, and Hymen bless'd
     his bed—
A Curate's bed ! then came the woful years ;
The husband's terrors, and the father's tears;
A wife grown feeble, mourning, pining, vex'd,
With wants and woes—by daily cares
     perplex'd ;

No more a help, a smiling, soothing aid,
But boding, drooping, sickly, and afraid.

A kind physician, and without a fee,
Gave his opinion—' Send her to the sea.'
' Alas ! ' the good man answer'd, ' can I send
A friendless woman ? Can I find a friend ?
No ; I must with her, in her need, repair
To that new place ; the poor lie everywhere;—
Some priest will pay me for my pious pains : '—
He said, he came, and here he yet remains.

Behold his dwelling ; this poor hut he hires,
Where he from view, though not from want,
     retires ;
Where four fair daughters, and five sorrowing
     sons,
Partake his sufferings, and dismiss his duns ;
All join their efforts, and in patience learn
To want the comforts they aspire to earn ;
For the sick mother something they'd obtain,
To soothe her grief and mitigate her pain ;
For the sad father something they'd procure,
To ease the burthen they themselves endure.

Virtues like these at once delight and press
On the fond father with a proud distress ;
On all around he looks with care and love,
Grieved to behold, but happy to approve.

Then from his care, his love, his grief he
     steals,
And by himself an author's pleasure feels ;
Each line detains him ; he omits not one,
And all the sorrows of his state are gone.—
Alas ! ev'n then, in that delicious hour,
He feels his fortune, and laments its power.
Some tradesman's bill his wandering eyes
     engage,
Some scrawl for payment thrust 'twixt page
     and page ;
Some bold, loud rapping at his humble
     door,
Some surly message he has heard before,
Awake, alarm, and tell him he is poor.
An angry dealer, vulgar, rich, and proud,
Thinks of his bill, and passing, raps aloud ;
The elder daughter meekly makes him way—
' I want my money, and I cannot stay—
My mill is stopp'd ; what, Miss ! I cannot
     grind ;
Go tell your father he must raise the wind : '
Still trembling, troubled, the dejected maid
Says, ' Sir, my father !—' and then stops
     afraid :
Ev'n his hard heart is soften'd, and he hears
Her voice with pity ; he respects her tears ;

His stubborn features half admit a smile,
And his tone softens—' Well ! I'll wait awhile.'
   Pity ! a man so good, so mild, so meek,
At such an age, should have his bread to seek ;
And all those rude and fierce attacks to dread,
That are more harrowing than the want of
     bread ;
Ah ! who shall whisper to that misery peace !
And say that want and insolence shall cease ?
   ' But why not publish ? '—those who know
     too well,
Dealers in Greek, are fearful 'twill not sell ;
Then he himself is timid, troubled, slow,
Nor likes his labours nor his griefs to show ;
The hope of fame may in his heart have
     place,
But he has dread and horror of disgrace ;
Nor has he that confiding, easy way,
That might his learning and himself display ;
But to his work he from the world retreats,
And frets and glories o'er the favourite sheets.
   But see ! the man himself ; and sure I trace
Signs of new joy exulting in that face
O'er care that sleeps—we err, or we discern
Life in thy looks—the reason may we learn ?
   ' Yes,' he replied, ' I'm happy, I confess,
To learn that some are pleased with happiness
Which others feel—there are who now com-
     bine
The worthiest natures in the best design,
To aid the letter'd poor, and soothe such ills
     as mine :
We who more keenly feel the world's con-
     tempt,
And from its miseries are the least exempt ;
Now hope shall whisper to the wounded breast,
And grief, in soothing expectation, rest.
   ' Yes, I am taught that men who think,
     who feel,
Unite the pains of thoughtful men to heal ;
Not with disdainful pride, whose bounties
     make
The needy curse the benefits they take ;
Not with the idle vanity that knows
Only a selfish joy when it bestows ;
Not with o'erbearing wealth, that, in disdain,
Hurls the superfluous bliss at groaning pain ;

But these are men who yield such bless'd
     relief,
That with the grievance they destroy the
     grief ;
Their timely aid the needy sufferers find,
Their generous manner soothes the suffering
     mind ;
Theirs is a gracious bounty, form'd to raise
Him whom it aids ; their charity is praise ;
A common bounty may relieve distress,
But whom the vulgar succour, they oppress
This though a favour, is an honour too,
Though mercy's duty, yet 'tis merit's due ;
When our relief from such resources rise,
All painful sense of obligation dies ;
And grateful feelings in the bosom wake,
For 'tis their offerings, not their alms, we
     take.
   ' Long may these founts of charity remain,
And never shrink, but to be fill'd again ;
True ! to the author they are now confined,
To him who gave the treasure of his mind,
His time, his health, and thankless found
     mankind :
But there is hope that from these founts may
     flow
A sideway stream, and equal good bestow ;
Good that may reach us, whom the day's
     distress
Keeps from the fame and perils of the press ;
Whom study beckons from the ills of life,
And they from study ; melancholy strife !
Who then can say, but bounty now so free,
And so diffused, may find its way to me ?
   ' Yes ! I may see my decent table yet
Cheer'd with the meal that adds not to my
     debt ;
May talk of those to whom so much we owe,
And guess their names whom yet we may not
     know ;
Bless'd we shall say are those who thus can
     give,
And next who thus upon the bounty live ;
Then shall I close with thanks my humble
     meal,
And feel so well—Oh ! God ! how I shall
     feel ! '

LETTER IV. SECTS AND PROFESSIONS IN RELIGION

... But cast your eyes again,
And view those errors which new sects main-
   tain,
Or which of old disturb'd the Church's peace-
   ful reign :
And we can point each period of the time
When they began and who begat the crime ;
Can calculate how long th' eclipse endured ;
Who interposed ; what digits were obscured ;
Of all which are already pass'd away,
We knew the rise, the progress, and decay.
          DRYDEN, *Hind and Panther*,
                    Part II, 1174–1182.
Oh ! said the Hind, how many sons have you
Who call you mother, whom you never knew ?
But most of them who that relation plead
Are such ungracious youths as wish you
   dead ;
They gape at rich revenues which you hold,
And fain would nibble at your grandame gold.
   Hind and Panther, Part III, 1438–1443.

Sects and Professions in Religion are nu-
   merous and successive—General Effect of
   false Zeal—Deists—Fanatical Idea of
   Church Reformers—The Church of Rome—
   Baptists — Swedenborgians— Universalists
   —Jews.
Methodists of two Kinds ; Calvinistic and
   Arminian.
The Preaching of a Calvinistic Enthusiast—
   His Contempt of Learning—Dislike to
   sound Morality : why—His Idea of Con-
   version—His Success and Pretensions to
   Humility.
The Arminian Teacher of the older Flock—
   Their Notions of the Operations and Power
   of Satan—Description of his Devices—
   Their Opinion of regular Ministers—Com-
   parison of these with the Preacher himself
   —A Rebuke to his Hearers ; introduces a
   Description of the powerful Effects of the
   Word in the early and awakening Days of
   Methodism.

' SECTS in Religion ? '—Yes, of every race
We nurse some portion in our favour'd place ;
Not one warm preacher of one growing sect
Can say our Borough treats him with neglect ;
Frequent as fashions, they with us appear,
And you might ask, ' how think we for the
   year ? '

They come to us as riders in a trade,
And with much art exhibit and persuade.
Minds are for sects of various kinds decreed,
As diff'rent soils are form'd for diff'rent seed ;
Some when converted sigh in sore amaze,
And some are wrapt in joy's ecstatic blaze ;
Others again will change to each extreme,
They know not why—as hurried in a dream ;
Unstable they, like water, take all forms,
Are quick and stagnant ; have their calms
   and storms ;
High on the hills, they in the sunbeams glow,
Then muddily they move debased and slow ;
Or cold and frozen rest, and neither rise nor
   flow.
Yet none the cool and prudent teacher prize,
On him they dote who wakes their ecstasies ;
With passions ready primed such guide they
   meet,
And warm and kindle with th' imparted heat ;
'Tis he who wakes the nameless strong desire,
The melting rapture, and the glowing fire ;
'Tis he who pierces deep the tortured breast,
And stirs the terrors, never more to rest.
Opposed to these we have a prouder kind,
Rash without heat, and without raptures
   blind ;
These our *Glad Tidings* unconcern'd peruse,
Search without awe, and without fear refuse :
The truths, the blessings found in Sacred Writ,
Call forth their spleen, and exercise their wit ;
Respect from these nor saints nor martyrs
   gain,
The zeal they scorn, and they deride the pain ;
And take their transient, cool, contemptuous
   view,
Of that which must be tried, and doubtless—
   may be true.
Friends of our faith we have, whom doubts
   like these,
And keen remarks, and bold objections please;
They grant such doubts have weaker minds
   oppress'd,
Till sound conviction gave the troubled rest.
' But still,' they cry, ' let none their cen-
   sures spare,
They but confirm the glorious hopes we share ;

From doubt, disdain, derision, scorn, and lies,
With five-fold triumph sacred truth shall rise.'
  Yes! I allow, so truth shall stand at last,
And gain fresh glory by the conflict past :—
As Solway-Moss (a barren mass and cold,
Death to the seed, and poison to the fold,)
The smiling plain and fertile vale o'erlaid,
Choked the green sod, and kill'd the springing
    blade ;
That, changed by culture, may in time be
    seen,
Enrich'd by golden grain, and pasture green ;
And these fair acres rented and enjoy'd,
May those excel by Solway-Moss destroy'd.[1]
  Still must have mourn'd the tenant of the
    day,
For hopes destroy'd, and harvests swept away;
To him the gain of future years unknown,
The instant grief and suffering were his own :
So must I grieve for many a wounded heart,
Chill'd by those doubts which bolder minds
    impart :
Truth in the end shall shine divinely clear,
But sad the darkness till those times appear ;
Contests for truth, as wars for freedom, yield
Glory and joy to those who gain the field :
But still the Christian must in pity sigh
For all who suffer, and uncertain die.
  Here are, who all the Church maintains
    approve,
But yet the Church herself they will not love ;
In angry speech, they blame the carnal tie,
Which pure Religion lost her spirit by ;
What time from prisons, flames, and tortures
    led,
She slumber'd careless in a royal bed ;
To make, they add, the Church's glory shine,
Should Diocletian reign, not Constantine.
  ' In pomp,' they cry, ' is England's Church
    array'd,
Her cool reformers wrought like men afraid,
We would have pull'd her gorgeous temples
    down,
And spurn'd her mitre, and defiled her gown ;
We would have trodden low both bench and
    stall,
Nor left a tithe remaining, great or small.'
  Let us be serious—Should such trials come,
Are they themselves prepared for martyrdom?
It seems to us that our reformers knew
Th' important work they undertook to do ;
An equal priesthood they were loth to try,
Lest zeal and care should with ambition die;

To them it seem'd that, take the tenth away,
Yet priests must eat, and you must feed or
    pay :
Would they indeed, who hold such pay in
    scorn,
Put on the muzzle when they tread the corn ?
Would they all, gratis, watch and tend the
    fold,
Nor take one fleece to keep them from the
    cold ?
  Men are not equal, and 'tis meet and right
That robes and titles our respect excite ;
Order requires it ; 'tis by vulgar pride
That such regard is censured and denied ;
Or by that false enthusiastic zeal,
That thinks the spirit will the priest reveal,
And show to all men, by their powerful speech,
Who are appointed and inspired to teach :
Alas ! could we the dangerous rule believe,
Whom for their teacher should the crowd
    receive ?
Since all the varying kinds demand respect,
All press you on to join their chosen sect,
Although but in this single point agreed,
' Desert your churches and adopt our creed.'
  We know full well how much our forms
    offend
The burthen'd papist and the simple friend ;
Him, who new robes for every service takes,
And who in drab and beaver sighs and shakes ;
He on the priest, whom hood and band adorn,
Looks with the sleepy eye of silent scorn ;
But him I would not for my friend and guide,
Who views such things with spleen, or wears
    with pride.
  See next our several sects,—but first behold
The Church of Rome, who here is poor and
    old :
Use not triumphant rail'ry, or at least,
Let not thy mother be a whore and beast ;
Great was her pride indeed in ancient times,
Yet shall we think of nothing but her crimes ?
Exalted high above all earthly things,
She placed her foot upon the neck of kings ;
But some have deeply since avenged the
    crown,
And thrown her glory and her honours down ;
Nor neck nor ear can she of kings command,
Nor place a foot upon her own fair land.
  Among her sons, with us a quiet few,
Obscure themselves, her ancient state review ;
And fond and melancholy glances cast
On power insulted, and on triumph pass'd :

They look, they can but look, with many
    a sigh,
On sacred buildings doom'd in dust to lie ;
' On seats,' they tell, ' where priests 'mid
    tapers dim
Breathed the warm prayer, or tuned the
    midnight hymn ;
Where trembling penitents their guilt con-
    fess'd,
Where want had succour, and contrition rest ;
There weary men from trouble found relief,
There men in sorrow found repose from grief :
To scenes like these the fainting soul retired ;
Revenge and anger in these cells expired ;
By pity soothed, remorse lost half her fears,
And soften'd pride dropp'd penitential tears.
  ' Then convent-walls and nunnery-spires
    arose,
In pleasant spots which monk or abbot chose ;
When counts and barons saints devoted fed,
And making cheap exchange, had pray'r for
    bread.
  ' Now all is lost, the earth where abbeys
    stood
Is layman's land, the glebe, the stream, the
    wood ;
His oxen low where monks retired to eat,
His cows repose upon the prior's seat ;
And wanton doves within the cloisters bill,
Where the chaste votary warr'd with wanton
    will.'
  Such is the change they mourn, but they
    restrain
The rage of grief, and passively complain.
  We've Baptists old and new ; forbear to
    ask
What the distinction—I decline the task ;
This I perceive, that when a sect grows old,
Converts are few, and the converted cold :
First comes the hot-bed heat, and while it
    glows
The plants spring up, and each with vigour
    grows ;
Then comes the cooler day, and though awhile
The verdure prospers and the blossoms smile,
Yet poor the fruit, and form'd by long delay,
Nor will the profits for the culture pay ;
The skilful gard'ner then no longer stops,
But turns to other beds for bearing crops.
  Some Swedenborgians in our streets are
    found,
Those wandering walkers on enchanted
    ground ;

Who in our world can other worlds survey,
And speak with spirits though confined in clay :
Of Bible-mysteries they the keys possess,
Assured themselves, where wiser men but
    guess :
'Tis theirs to see around, about, above,—
How spirits mingle thoughts, and angels move;
Those whom our grosser views from us exclude,
To them appear—a heavenly multitude ;
While the dark sayings, seal'd to men like us,
Their priests interpret, and their flocks dis-
    cuss.
  But while these gifted men, a favour'd fold,
New powers exhibit and new worlds behold ;
Is there not danger lest their minds confound
The pure above them with the gross around ?
May not these Phaetons, who thus contrive
'Twixt heaven above and earth beneath to
    drive,
When from their flaming chariots they descend,
The worlds they visit in their fancies blend ?
Alas ! too sure on both they bring disgrace,
Their earth is crazy, and their heav'n is base.
  We have, it seems, who treat, and doubtless
    well,
Of a chastising, not awarding hell ;
Who are assured that an offended God
Will cease to use the thunder and the rod ;
A soul on earth, by crime and folly stain'd,
When here corrected has improvement gain'd;
In other state still more improved to grow,
And nobler powers in happier world to know ;
New strength to use in each divine employ,
And, more enjoying, looking to more joy.
  A pleasing vision ! could we thus be sure
Polluted souls would be at length so pure ;
The view is happy, we may think it just,
It may be true—but who shall add it must ?
To the plain words and sense of sacred writ,
With all my heart I reverently submit ;
But where it leaves me doubtful, I'm afraid
To call conjecture to my reason's aid ;
Thy thoughts, thy ways, great God ! are not
    as mine,
And to thy mercy I my soul resign.
  Jews are with us, but far unlike to those,
Who, led by David, warr'd with Israel's foes;
Unlike to those whom his imperial son
Taught truths divine—the preacher Solomon :
Nor war nor wisdom yield our Jews delight ;
They will not study, and they dare not fight.[2]
  These are, with us, a slavish, knavish crew,
Shame and dishonour to the name of Jew ;

The poorest masters of the meanest arts,
With cunning heads, and cold and cautious
    hearts ;
They grope their dirty way to petty gains,
While poorly paid for their nefarious pains.
    Amazing race ! deprived of land and laws,
A general language, and a public cause ;
With a religion none can now obey,
With a reproach that none can take away :
A people still, whose common ties are gone ;
Who, mix'd with every race, are lost in none.
    What said their prophet ?—' Shouldst thou
        disobey,
The Lord shall take thee from thy land away ;
Thou shalt a by-word and a proverb be,
And all shall wonder at thy woes and thee ;
Daughter and son shalt thou, while captive,
    have,
And see them made the bond-maid and the
    slave ;
He, whom thou leav'st, the Lord thy God,
    shall bring
War to thy country on an eagle-wing :
A people strong and dreadful to behold,
Stern to the young, remorseless to the old ;
Masters whose speech thou canst not under-
    stand,
By cruel signs shall give the harsh command :
Doubtful of life shalt thou by night, by day,
For grief, and dread, and trouble pine away ;
Thy evening-wish,—Would God ! I saw the
    sun ;
Thy morning-sigh,—Would God ! the day
    were done.
Thus shalt thou suffer, and to distant times
Regret thy misery, and lament thy crimes.' [3]
    A part there are, whom doubtless man
        might trust,
Worthy as wealthy, pure, religious, just ;
They who with patience, yet with rapture look
On the strong promise of the sacred book :
As unfulfill'd th' endearing words they view,
And blind to truth, yet own their prophets
    true ;
Well pleased they look for Sion's coming state,
Nor think of Julian's boast and Julian's fate. [4]
    More might I add ; I might describe the
        flocks
Made by seceders from the ancient stocks ;
Those who will not to any guide submit,
Nor find one creed to their conceptions fit—
Each sect, they judge, in something goes astray,
And every church has lost the certain way ;

Then for themselves they carve out creeds and
    laws,
And weigh their atoms, and divide their
    straws.
    A sect remains, which though divided long
In hostile parties, both are fierce and strong,
And into each enlists a warm and zealous
    throng.
Soon as they rose in fame, the strife arose,
The Calvinistic these, th' Arminian those ;
With Wesley some remain'd, the remnant
    Whitfield chose.
Now various leaders both the parties take,
And the divided hosts their new divisions
    make.
    See yonder preacher ! to his people pass,
Borne up and swell'd by tabernacle-gas ;
Much he discourses, and of various points,
All unconnected, void of limbs and joints ;
He rails, persuades, explains, and moves the
    will,
By fierce, bold words, and strong mechanic
    skill.
    ' That Gospel, Paul with zeal and love
        maintain'd,
To others lost, to you is now explain'd ;
No worldly learning can these points discuss,
Books teach them not as they are taught to us;
Illiterate call us ! let their wisest man
Draw forth his thousands as your teacher can :
They give their moral precepts ; so, they say,
Did Epictetus once, and Seneca ;
One was a slave, and slaves we all must be,
Until the Spirit comes and sets us free.
Yet hear you nothing from such men but
    works ;
They make the Christian service like the
    Turks'.
    ' Hark to the churchman : day by day he
        cries,
" Children of men, be virtuous and be wise ;
Seek patience, justice, temp'rance, meekness,
    truth ;
In age be courteous, be sedate in youth."—
So they advise, and when such things be read,
How can we wonder that their flocks are dead ?
    ' The heathens wrote of virtue, they could
        dwell
On such light points : in them it might be well,
They might for virtue strive ; but I maintain,
Our strife for virtue would be proud and vain.
When Samson carried Gaza's gates so far,
Lack'd he a helping hand to bear the bar ?

Thus the most virtuous must in bondage
    groan :
Samson is grace, and carries all alone.[5]
   ' Hear you not priests their feeble spirits
    spend,
In bidding sinners turn to God, and mend ;
To check their passions and to walk aright,
To run the race, and fight the glorious fight ?
Nay more—to pray, to study, to improve,
To grow in goodness, to advance in love ?
   ' Oh ! babes and sucklings, dull of heart
    and slow,
Can grace be gradual ? Can conversion
    grow ?
The work is done by instantaneous call ;
Converts at once are made, or not at all ;
Nothing is left to grow, reform, amend ;
The first emotion is the movement's end :
If once forgiven, debt can be no more ;
If once adopted, will the heir be poor ?
The man who gains the twenty-thousand prize,
Does he by little and by little rise ?
There can no fortune for the soul be made,
By peddling cares and savings in her trade.
   ' Why are our sins forgiven?—Priests reply,
—" Because by faith on mercy we rely ;
Because, believing, we repent and pray."—
Is this their doctrine ?—then they go astray :
We're pardon'd neither for belief nor deed,
For faith nor practice, principle nor creed ;
Nor for our sorrow for our former sin,
Nor for our fears when better thoughts begin ;
Nor prayers nor penance in the cause avail,
All strong remorse, all soft contrition fail ;—
It is the *call* ! till that proclaims us free,
In darkness, doubt, and bondage we must be ;
Till that *assures* us, we've in vain endured,
And all is over when we're once assured.
   ' This is conversion :—First there comes
    a cry
Which utters, " Sinner, thou'rt condemn'd to
    die ; "
Then the struck soul to every aid repairs,
To church and altar, ministers and prayers ;
In vain she strives,—involv'd, ingulf'd in sin,
She looks for hell, and seems already in :
When in this travail, the new birth comes on,
And in an instant every pang is gone ;
The mighty work is done without our pains,—
Claim but a part, and not a part remains.
   ' All this experience tells the soul, and yet
These moral men their pence and farthings set
Against the terrors of the countless debt :

But such compounders, when they come to
    jail,
Will find that virtues never serve as bail.
   ' So much to duties : now to learning look,
And see their priesthood piling book on book ;
Yea, books of infidels, we're told, and plays,
Put out by heathens in the wink'd-on days ;
The very letters are of crooked kind,
And show the strange perverseness of their
    mind.
Have I this learning ? When the Lord would
    speak,
Think ye he needs the Latin or the Greek ?
And lo ! with all their learning, when they rise
To preach, in view the ready sermon lies ;
Some low-prized stuff they purchased at the
    stalls,
And more like Seneca's than mine or Paul's :
Children of bondage, how should they explain
The spirit's freedom, while they wear a chain ?
They study words, for meanings grow per-
    plex'd,
And slowly hunt for truth from text to text,
Through Greek and Hebrew :—we the mean-
    ing seek
Of that within, who every tongue can speak :
This all can witness ; yet the more I know,
The more a meek and humble mind I show.
   ' No ; let the pope, the high and mighty
    priest,
Lord to the poor, and servant to the beast;
Let bishops, deans, and prebendaries swell
With pride and fatness till their hearts rebel :
I'm meek and modest—If I could be proud,
This crowded meeting, lo ! th' amazing crowd!
Your mute attention, and your meek respect,
My spirit's fervour, and my words' effect,
Might stir th' unguarded soul ; and oft to me
The tempter speaks, whom I compel to flee ;
He goes in fear, for he my force has tried,—
Such is my power ! but can you call it pride ?
   ' No, fellow-pilgrims ! of the things I've
    shown
I might be proud, were they indeed my own !
But they are lent ; and well you know the
    source,
Of all that 's mine, and must confide of course ;
Mine ! no, I err ; 'tis but consign'd to me,
And I am nought but steward and trustee.'

FAR other doctrines yon Arminian speaks;
' Seek grace,' he cries, ' for he shall find who
    seeks.'

This is the ancient stock by Wesley led ;
They the pure body, he the reverend head :
All innovation they with dread decline,
Their John the elder, was the John divine.
Hence, still their moving prayer, the melting
    hymn,
The varied accent, and the active limb ;
Hence that implicit faith in Satan's might,
And their own matchless prowess in the fight.
In every act they see that lurking foe,
Let loose awhile, about the world to go ;
A dragon flying round the earth, to kill
The heavenly hope, and prompt the carnal
    will ;
Whom sainted knights attack in sinners' cause,
And force the wounded victim from his paws ;
Who but for them would man's whole race
    subdue,
For not a hireling will the foe pursue.
  ' Show me one churchman who will rise and
    pray
Through half the night, though lab'ring all
    the day,
Always abounding—show me him, I say : '—
Thus cries the preacher, and he adds, ' their
    sheep
Satan devours at leisure as they sleep.
Not so with us ; we drive him from the fold,
For ever barking and for ever bold :
While they securely slumber, all his schemes
Take full effect,—the devil never dreams :
Watchful and changeful through the world
    he goes,
And few can trace this deadliest of their foes ;
But I detect, and at his work surprise
The subtle serpent under all disguise
  ' Thus to man's soul the foe of souls will
    speak,
—" A saint elect, you can have nought to
    seek ;
Why all this labour in so plain a case,
Such care to run, when certain of the race ? "
All this he urges to the carnal will,
He knows you're slothful, and would have
    you still :
Be this your answer,—" Satan, I will keep
Still on the watch till you are laid asleep."
Thus too the Christian's progress he'll re-
    tard :—
" The gates of mercy are for ever barr'd ;
And that with bolts so driven and so stout,
Ten thousand workmen cannot wrench them
    out."

To this deceit you have but one reply,—
Give to the father of all lies, the lie.
  ' A sister's weakness he'll by fits surprise,
His her wild laughter, his her piteous cries ;
And should a pastor at her side attend,
He'll use her organs to abuse her friend :
These are possessions—unbelieving wits
Impute them all to nature : " They're her fits,
Caused by commotions in the nerves and
    brains ; "—
Vain talk ! but they'll be fitted for their pains.
  ' These are in part the ills the foe has
    wrought,
And these the churchman thinks not worth
    his thought ;
They bid the troubled try for peace and rest,
Compose their minds, and be no more dis-
    tress'd ;
As well might they command the passive shore
To keep secure, and be o'erflowed no more ;
To the wrong subject is their skill applied,—
To act like workmen, they should stem the tide.
  ' These are the church-physicians ; they
    are paid
With noble fees for their advice and aid ;
Yet know they not the inward pulse to feel,
To ease the anguish, or the wound to heal.
With the sick sinner, thus their work begins,
" Do you repent you of your former sins ?
Will you amend if you revive and live ?
And, pardon seeking, will you pardon give ?
Have you belief in what your Lord has done,
And are you thankful ?—all is well, my son."
  ' A way far different ours—we thus surprise
A soul with questions, and demand replies ;
  ' " How dropp'd you first," I ask, " the
    legal yoke ?
What the first word the living Witness spoke ?
Perceived you thunders roar and lightnings
    shine,
And tempests gathering ere the birth divine ?
Did fire, and storm, and earthquake all
    appear
Before that still small voice, *What dost thou
    here ?*
Hast thou by day and night, and soon and late,
Waited and watch'd before Admission-gate ;
And so a pilgrim and a soldier pass'd
To Sion's hill through battle and through
    blast ?
Then in thy way didst thou thy foe attack,
And mad'st thou proud Apollyon turn his
    back ? "

'Heart-searching things are these, and
    shake the mind,
Yea, like the rustling of a mighty wind.
  'Thus would I ask :—" Nay, let me ques-
    tion now,
How sink my sayings in your bosoms ? how ?
Feel you a quickening ? drops the subject
    deep ?
Stupid and stony, no ! you're all asleep ;
Listless and lazy, waiting for a close,
As if at church—Do I allow repose ?
Am I a legal minister ? do I
With form or rubrick, rule or rite comply ?
Then whence this quiet, tell me, I beseech ?
One might believe you heard your rector
    preach,
Or his assistant dreamer :—Oh ! return,
Ye times of burning, when the heart would burn,
Now hearts are ice, and you, my freezing fold,
Have spirits sunk and sad, and bosoms stony-
    cold."
  'Oh ! now again for those prevailing powers,
Which once began this mighty work of ours ;
When the wide field, God's temple, was the
    place,
And birds flew by to catch a breath of grace ;
When 'mid his timid friends and threat'ning
    foes,
Our zealous chief as Paul at Athens rose :
When with infernal spite and knotty clubs
The ill-one arm'd his scoundrels and his scrubs;
And there were flying all around the spot
Brands at the preacher, but they touch'd
    him not ;
Stakes brought to smite him, threaten'd in
    his cause,
And tongues, attuned to curses, roar'd
    applause ;
Louder and louder grew his awful tones,
Sobbing and sighs were heard, and rueful
    groans ;

Soft women fainted, prouder man express'd
Wonder and wo, and butchers smote the
    breast ;
Eyes wept, ears tingled ; stiff'ning on each
    head, ·
The hair drew back, and Satan howl'd and fled.
  'In that soft season when the gentle breeze
Rises all round, and swells by slow degrees ;
Till tempests gather, when through all the
    sky
The thunders rattle, and the lightnings fly ;
When rain in torrents wood and vale deform,
And all is horror, hurricane, and storm :
  'So, when the preacher in that glorious time,
Than clouds more melting, more than storm
    sublime,
Dropp'd the new word, there came a charm
    around ;
Tremors and terrors rose upon the sound ;
The stubborn spirits by his force he broke,
As the fork'd lightning rives the knotted oak :
Fear, hope, dismay, all signs of shame or grace,
Chain'd every foot, or featured every face ;
Then took his sacred trump a louder swell,
And now they groan'd, they sicken'd, and
    they fell ;
Again he sounded, and we heard the cry
Of the word-wounded, as about to die ;
Further and further spread the conquering
    word,
As loud he cried—" the battle of the Lord."
Ev'n those apart who were the sound denied,
Fell down instinctive, and in spirit died.
Nor staid he yet—his eye, his frown, his
    speech,
His very gesture had a power to teach ;
With outstretch'd arms, strong voice and
    piercing call,
He won the field, and made the Dagons fall ;
And thus in triumph took his glorious way,
Through scenes of horror, terror, and dismay.'

LETTER V.   ELECTIONS

Say then which class to greater folly stoop,
The great in promise, or the poor in hope ?
Be brave, then, for your captain is brave, and
  vows reformation ;   there shall be in
England seven halfpenny loaves sold for
a penny ;   the three-hooped pot shall have
ten hoops and I will make it felony to
drink small beer : all shall eat and drink
on my score, and I will apparel them all in
one livery, that they may agree like
brothers— . . . and worship me their lord.
          SHAKSPEARE, *Henry VI*, Part II,
                          Act iv, Sc. 2.

The Evils of the Contest, and how in part to
  be avoided—The Miseries endured by a
  Friend of the Candidate—The various
  Liberties taken with him, who has no
  personal Interest in the Success—The
  unreasonable Expectations of Voters—
  The Censures of the opposing Party—The
  Vices as well as Follies shown in such Time
  of Contest—Plans and Cunning of Electors
  —Evils which remain after the Decision,
  opposed in vain by the Efforts of the
  Friendly, and of the Successful ; among
  whom is the Mayor—Story of his Advance-
  ment till he was raised to the Government
  of the Borough—These Evils not to be
  placed in Balance with the Liberty of the
  People, but are yet Subjects of just Com-
  plaint.

YES, our Election's past, and we've been free,
Somewhat as madmen without keepers be ;
And such desire of freedom has been shown,
That both the parties wish'd her all their own:
All our free smiths and cobblers in the town
Were loth to lay such pleasant freedom down ;
To put the bludgeon and cockade aside,
And let us pass unhurt and undefied.
   True ! you might then your party's sign
      produce,
And so escape with only half th' abuse ;
With half the danger as you walk'd along,
With rage and threat'ning but from half the
      throng :
This you might do, and not your fortune mend,
For where you lost a foe, you gain'd a friend ;
And to distress you, vex you, and expose,
Election-friends are worse than any foes ;
The party-curse is with the canvass past,
But party-friendship, for your grief, will last.

Friends of all kinds, the civil and the rude,
Who humbly wish, or boldly dare t' intrude ;
These beg or take a liberty to come,
(Friends should be free,) and make your house
      their home ;
They know that warmly you their cause
      espouse,
And come to make their boastings and their
      bows :
You scorn their manners, you their words
      mistrust,
But you must hear them, and they know you
      must.
   One plainly sees a friendship firm and true,
Between the noble candidate and you ;
So humbly begs (and states at large the case),
' You'll think of Bobby and the little place.'
   Stifling his shame by drink, a wretch will
      come,
And prate your wife and daughter from the
      room :
In pain you hear him, and at heart despise,
Yet with heroic mind your pangs disguise ;
And still in patience to the sot attend,
To show what men can bear to serve a friend.
   One enters hungry—not to be denied,
And takes his place and jokes—' We're of
      a side.'
Yet worse, the proser who, upon the strength
Of his one vote, has tales of three hours' length;
This sorry rogue you bear, yet with surprise
Start at his oaths, and sicken at his lies.
   Then comes there one, and tells in friendly
      way,
What the opponents in their anger say ;
All that through life has vex'd you, all abuse,
Will this kind friend in pure regard produce ;
And having through your own offences run,
Adds (as appendage) what your friends have
      done.
   Has any female cousin made a trip
To Gretna-Green, or more vexatious slip ?
Has your wife's brother, or your uncle's son
Done aught amiss, or is he thought t' have
      done ?
Is there of all your kindred some who lack
Vision direct, or have a gibbous back ?
From your unlucky name may quips and puns
Be made by these upbraiding Goths and Huns?

To some great public character have you
Assign'd the fame to worth and talents due,
Proud of your praise ?—In this, in any case,
Where the brute-spirit may affix disgrace,
These friends will smiling bring it, and the while
You silent sit, and practise for a smile.

Vain of their power, and of their value sure,
They nearly guess the tortures you endure ;
Nor spare one pang—for they perceive your heart
Goes with the cause ; you'd die before you'd start ;
Do what they may, they're sure you'll not offend
Men who have pledged their honours to your friend.

Those friends indeed, who start as in a race,
May love the sport, and laugh at this disgrace ;
They have in view the glory and the prize,
Nor heed the dirty steps by which they rise :
But we their poor associates lose the fame,
Though more than partners in the toil and shame.

Were this the whole ; and did the time produce
But shame and toil, but riot and abuse ;
We might be then from serious griefs exempt,
And view the whole with pity and contempt.
Alas ! but here the vilest passions rule ;
It is Seduction's, is Temptation's school ;
Where vices mingle in the oddest ways,
The grossest slander and the dirtiest praise ;
Flattery enough to make the vainest sick,
And clumsy stratagem, and scoundrel trick ;
Nay more, your anger and contempt to cause,
These, while they fish for profit, claim applause ;
Bribed, bought and bound, they banish shame and fear ;
Tell you they're stanch, and have a soul sincere ;
Then talk of honour, and if doubt's express'd,
Show where it lies, and smite upon the breast.

Among these worthies, some at first declare
For whom they vote ; he then has most to spare ;
Others hang off—when coming to the post
Is spurring time, and then he'll spare the most :
While some demurring, wait, and find at last
The bidding languish, and the market pass'd ;

These will affect all bribery to condemn,
And be it Satan laughs, he laughs at them.
Some too are pious—One desired the Lord
To teach him where ' to drop his little word ;
To lend his vote, where it will profit best ;
Promotion came not from the east or west ;
But as their freedom had promoted some,
He should be glad to know which way 'twould come.
It was a naughty world, and where to sell
His precious charge, was more than he could tell.'
' But you succeeded ? '—true, at mighty cost,
And our good friend, I fear, will think he 's lost :
Inns, horses, chaises, dinners, balls and notes ;
What fill'd their purses, and what drench'd their throats ;
The private pension, and indulgent lease,—
Have all been granted to these friends who fleec ;
Friends who will hang like burs upon his coat,
And boundless judge the value of a vote.
And though the terrors of the time be pass'd,
There still remain the scatterings of the blast ;
The boughs are parted that entwined before,
And ancient harmony exists no more ;
The gusts of wrath our peaceful seats deform,
And sadly flows the sighing of the storm :
Those who have gain'd are sorry for the gloom,
But they who lost, unwilling peace should come ;
There open envy, here suppress'd delight,
Yet live till time shall better thoughts excite,
And so prepare us by a six-years' truce,
Again for riot, insult, and abuse.
Our worthy mayor, on the victorious part,
Cries out for peace, and cries with all his heart ;
He, civil creature ! ever does his best,
To banish wrath from every voter's breast ;
' For where,' says he, with reason strong and plain,
' Where is the profit ? what will anger gain ? '
His short stout person he is wont to brace
In good brown broad-cloth, edged with two-inch lace,

CR.   F

When in his seat; and still the coat seems
   new,
Preserved b. common use of seaman's blue
   He was a fisher from his earliest day,
And placed his nets within the Borough's bay;
Where by his skates, his herrings, and his
   soles,
He lived, nor dream'd of corporation-doles [1];
But toiling saved, and saving, never ceased
Till he had box'd up twelve score pounds at
   least:
He knew not money's power, but judged it best
Safe in his trunk to let his treasure rest;
Yet to a friend complain'd : ' Sad charge, to
   keep
So many pounds, and then I cannot sleep : '
' Then put it out,' replied the friend :—
      ' What, give
My money up ? why then I could not live : '
' Nay, but for interest place it in his hands,
Who'll give you mortgage on his house or
   lands.'
' Oh but,' said Daniel, ' that 's a dangerous
   plan ;
He may be robb'd like any other man : '
' Still he is bound, and you may be at rest,
More safe the money than within your chest ;
And you'll receive, from all deductions clear,
Five pounds for every hundred, every year.'
' What good in that ? ' quoth Daniel, ' for 'tis
   plain,
If part I take, there can but part remain : '
' What ! you, my friend, so skill'd in gainful
   things,
Have you to learn what interest money
   brings ? '
' Not so,' said Daniel, ' perfectly I know,
He 's the most interest who has most to
   show.'
' True ! and he'll show the more, the more he
   lends ;
Thus he his weight and consequence extends ;
For they who borrow must restore each sum,
And pay for use—What, Daniel, art thou
   dumb ? '
For much amazed was that good man—
      ' Indeed ! '
Said he with glad'ning eye, ' will money breed ?

How have I lived ? I grieve, with all my
   heart,
For my late knowledge in this precious art :—
Five pounds for every hundred will he give ?
And then the hundred ?——I begin to live.'—
So he began, and other means he found,
As he went on, to multiply a pound :
Though blind so long to interest, all allow
That no man better understands it now :
Him in our body-corporate we chose,
And once among us, he above us rose ;
Stepping from post to post, he reach'd the
   chair,
And there he now reposes—that 's the mayor.
   But 'tis not he, 'tis not the kinder few,
The mild, the good, who can our peace renew ;
A peevish humour swells in every eye,
The warm are angry, and the cool are shy ;
There is no more the social board at whist,
The good old partners are with scorn dis-
   miss'd ;
No more with dog and lantern comes the
   maid,
To guide the mistress when the rubber's
   play'd ;
Sad shifts are made lest ribbons blue and
   reen
Should at one table, at one time be seen :
On care and merit none will now rely,
'Tis party sells, what party-friends must
      buy:
The warmest burgess wears a bodger's coat,
And fashion gains less int'rest than a vote ;
Uncheck'd the vintner still his poison vends,
For he too votes, and can command his friends.
   But this admitted ; be it still agreed,
These ill effects from noble cause proceed ;
Though like some vile excrescences they be,
The tree they spring from is a sacred tree,
And its true produce, strength and liberty.
   Yet if we could th' attendant ills suppress,
If we could make the sum of mischief less ;
If we could warm and angry men persuade
No more man's common comforts to invade ;
And that old ease and harmony re-seat
In all our meetings, so in joy to meet ;
Much would of glory to the Muse ensue,
And our good vicar would have less to do.

LETTER VI. PROFESSIONS—LAW

Quid leges sine moribus
Vanae proficiunt ?
HORACE, *Carm.* lib. iii, od. 24. 35, 36.
Vae misero mihi! Mea nunc facinora
Aperiuntur, clam quae speravi fore.
PLAUT. *Trucul.* Act iv, Sc. 3, v. 20.

Trades and Professions of every Kind to be found in the Borough—Its Seamen and Soldiers—Law, the Danger of the Subject —Coddrington's Offence—Attorneys increased ; their Splendid Appearance, how supported—Some worthy Exceptions— Spirit of Litigation, how stirred up— A Boy articled as a Clerk ; his Ideas— How this Profession perverts the Judgment—Actions appear through this Medium in a false Light—Success from honest Application—Archer a worthy Character —Swallow a Character of different Kind —His Origin, Progress, Success, &c.

' TRADES and Professions '—these are themes
    the Muse,
Left to her freedom, would forbear to
    choose ;
But to our Borough they in truth belong,
And we, perforce, must take them in our song.
Be it then known that we can boast of these
In all denominations, ranks, degrees ;
All who our numerous wants through life
    supply,
Who soothe us sick, attend us when we die,
Or for the dead their various talents try.
Then have we those who live by secret arts,
By hunting fortunes, and by stealing hearts ;
Or who by nobler means themselves advance ;
Or who subsist by charity and chance.
    Say, of our native heroes shall I boast,
Born in our streets, to thunder on our coast,
Our Borough-seamen ? Could the timid Muse
More patriot-ardour in their breasts infuse ;
Or could she paint their merit or their skill,
She wants not love, alacrity, or will ;
But needless all, that ardour is their own,
And for their deeds, themselves have made
    them known.
    Soldiers in arms ! Defenders of our soil !
Who from destruction save us ; who from
    spoil
Protect the sons of peace, who traffic, or who
    toil ;

Would I could duly praise you ; that each
    deed
Your foes might honour, and your friends
    might read :
This too is needless ; you've imprinted well
Your powers, and told what I should feebly
    tell :
Beside, a Muse like mine, to satire prone,
Would fail in themes where there is praise
    alone.
    —Law shall I sing, or what to Law belongs ?
Alas ! there may be danger in such songs ;
A foolish rhyme, 'tis said, a trifling thing,
The law found treason, for it touch'd the
    king.
But kings have mercy, in these happy times,
Or surely *one* had suffer'd for his rhymes ;
Our glorious Edwards and our Henrys bold ;
So touch'd, had kept the reprobate in hold,
But he escaped,—nor fear, thank Heav'n,
    have I,
Who love my king, for such offence to die.
But I am taught the danger would be much,
If these poor lines should one attorney
    touch—
(One of those *limbs* of law who're always here ;
The *heads* come down to guide them twice a
    year.)
I might not swing indeed, but he in sport
Would whip a rhymer on from court to court ;
Stop him in each, and make him pay for all
The long proceedings in that dreaded Hall :—
Then let my numbers flow discreetly on,
Warn'd by the fate of luckless Coddrington,*
Lest some *attorney* (pardon me the name)
Should wound a poor *solicitor* for fame.
    One man of law in George the Second's
    reign
Was all our frugal fathers would maintain ;
He too was kept for forms ; a man of peace,
To frame a contract, or to draw a lease :
He had a clerk, with whom he used to write
All the day long, with whom he drank at
    night ;
Spare was his visage, moderate his bill,
And he so kind, men doubted of his skill.

---

    * The account of Coddrington occurs in *The Mirrour for Magistrates :* he suffered in the reign of Richard III.

Who thinks of this, with some amazement
sees,
For one so poor, three flourishing at ease ;
Nay, one in splendour !—see that mansion
tall,
That lofty door, the far-resounding hall ;
Well-furnish'd rooms, plate shining on the
board,
Gay liveried lads, and cellar proudly stored :
Then say how comes it that such fortunes
crown
These sons of strife, these terrors of the town ?
Lo! that small office! there th' incautious
guest
Goes blindfold in, and that maintains the
rest ;
There in his web, th' observant spider lies,
And peers about for fat intruding flies ;
Doubtful at first, he hears the distant hum,
And feels them flutt'ring as they nearer come ;
They buzz and blink, and doubtfully they
tread
On the strong birdlime of the utmost thread ;
But when they're once entangled by the gin,
With what an eager clasp he draws them in ;
Nor shall they 'scape, till after long delay,
And all that sweetens life is drawn away.
    ' Nay, this,' you cry, ' is common-place, the
tale
Of petty tradesmen o'er their evening-ale ;
There are who, living by the legal pen,
Are held in honour,—" honourable men." '
    Doubtless—there are who hold manorial
courts,
Or whom the trust of powerful friends sup-
ports ;
Or who, by labouring through a length of
time,
Have pick'd their way, unsullied by a crime.
These are the few—in this, in every place,
Fix the litigious rupture-stirring race ;
Who to contention as to trade are led,
To whom dispute and strife are bliss and
bread.
    There is a doubtful pauper, and we think
'Tis not with us to give him meat and
drink ;
There is a child, and 'tis not mighty clear
Whether the mother lived with us a year :
A road 's indicted, and our seniors doubt
If in our proper boundary or without :
But what says our attorney ? He our friend
Tells us 'tis just and manly to contend.

' What ! to a neighbouring parish yield
your cause,
While you have money, and the nation laws ?
What ! lose without a trial, that which tried,
May—nay it must—be given on our side ?
All men of spirit would contend ; such men
Than lose a pound would rather hazard
ten.
What, be imposed on ? No ! a British soul
Despises imposition, hates control ;
The law is open ; let them, if they dare,
Support their cause ; the Borough need not
spare :
All I advise is vigour and good-will :
Is it agreed then ?—Shall I file a bill ? '
    The trader, grazier, merchant, priest and
all,
Whose sons aspiring, to professions call,
Choose from their lads some bold and subtle
boy,
And judge him fitted for this grave employ :
Him a keen old practitioner admits,
To write five years and exercise his wits :
The youth has heard—it is in fact his creed—
Mankind dispute, that lawyers may be
fee'd :
Jails, bailiffs, writs, all terms and threats of
law,
Grow now familiar as once top and taw ;
Rage, hatred, fear, the mind's severer ills,
All bring employment, all augment his bills :
As feels the surgeon for the mangled limb,
The mangled mind is but a job for him ;
Thus taught to think, these legal reasoners
draw
Morals and maxims from their views of law ;
They cease to judge by precepts taught in
schools,
By man's plain sense, or by religious rules ;
No ! nor by law itself, in truth discern'd,
But as its statutes may be warp'd and turn'd :
How should they judge of man, his word and
deed,
They in their books and not their bosoms
read :
Of some good act you speak with just ap-
plause,
' No ! no ! ' says he, ' 'twould be a losing
cause : '
Blame you some tyrant's deed ?—he answers
' Nay,
He'll get a verdict ; heed you what you
say.'

LETTER VI   LAW

Thus to conclusions from examples led,
The heart resigns all judgment to the head ;
Law, law alone for ever kept in view,
His measures guides, and rules his conscience
    too ;
Of ten commandments, he confesses three
Are yet in force, and tells you which they be,
As law instructs him, thus : ' Your neigh-
    bour's wife
You must not take, his chattels, nor his life ;
Break these decrees, for damage you must
    pay ;
These you must reverence, and the rest—
    you may.'
    Law was design'd to keep a state in peace ;
To punish robbery, that wrong might cease ;
To be impregnable ; a constant fort,
To which the weak and injured might resort :
But these perverted minds its force employ,
Not to protect mankind, but to annoy ;
And long as ammunition can be found,
Its lightning flashes and its thunders sound.
    Or law with lawyers is an ample still,
Wrought by the passions' heat with chymic
    skill ;
While the fire burns, the gains are quickly
    made,
And freely flow the profits of the trade ;
Nay, when the fierceness fails, these artists
    blow
The dying fire, and make the embers glow,
As long as they can make the smaller profits
    flow ;
At length the process of itself will stop,
When they perceive they've drawn out every
    drop.
    Yet I repeat, there are, who nobly strive
To keep the sense of moral worth alive ;
Men who would starve, ere meanly deign to live
On what deception and chican'ry give ;
And these at length succeed ; they have their
    strife,
Their apprehensions, stops, and rubs in life ;
But honour, application, care, and skill,
Shall bend opposing fortune to their will.
    Of such is Archer, he who keeps in awe
Contending parties by his threats of law :
He, roughly honest, has been long a guide
In Borough-business, on the conquering side ;
And seen so much of both sides, and so long,
He thinks the bias of man's mind goes wrong :
Thus, though he 's friendly, he is still severe
Surly though kind, suspiciously sincere :

So much he 's seen of baseness in the mind,
That, while a friend to man, he scorns man-
    kind ;
He knows the human heart, and sees with
    dread,
By slight temptation, how the strong are led ;
He knows how interest can asunder rend
The bond of parent, master, guardian, friend,
To form a new and a degrading tie
'Twixt needy vice and tempting villany.
Sound in himself, yet when such flaws appear,
He doubts of all, and learns that self to fear :
For where so dark the moral view is grown,
A timid conscience trembles for her own ;
The pitchy taint of general vice is such
As daubs the fancy, and you dread the touch.
    Far unlike him was one in former times,
Famed for the spoil he gather'd by his crimes ;
Who, while his brethren nibbling held their
    prey,
He like an eagle seized and bore the whole
    away.
    Swallow, a poor attorney, brought his boy
Up at his desk, and gave him his employ ;
He would have bound him to an honest trade,
Could preparations have been duly made.
The clerkship ended, both the sire and son
Together did what business could be done ;
Sometimes they'd luck to stir up small dis-
    putes
Among their friends, and raise them into suits:
Though close and hard, the father was content
With this resource, now old and indolent :
But his young Swallow, gaping and alive
To fiercer feelings, was resolved to thrive :—
' Father,' he said, ' but little can they win,
Who hunt in couples where the game is thin ;
Let's part in peace, and each pursue his gain
Where it may start—our love may yet
    remain.'
The parent growl'd, he couldn't think that
    love
Made the young cockatrice his den remove ;
But, taught by habit, he the truth suppress'd,
Forced a frank look, and said he ' thought it
    best.'
Not long they'd parted ere dispute arose ;
The game they hunted quickly made them
    foes :
Some house, the father by his art had won,
Seem'd a fit cause of contest to the son,
Who raised a claimant, and then found a way
By a stanch witness to secure his prey.

The people cursed him, but in times of need
Trusted in one so certain to succeed :
By law's dark by-ways he had stored his mind
With wicked knowledge, how to cheat man-
    kind.
Few are the freeholds in our ancient town ;
A copy-right from heir to heir came down,
From whence some heat arose, when there
    was doubt
In point of heirship ; but the fire went out,
Till our attorney had the art to raise
The dying spark, and blow it to a blaze :
For this he now began his friends to treat ;
His way to starve them was to make them eat,
And drink oblivious draughts—to his ap-
    plause
It must be said, he never starved a cause ;
He'd roast and boil'd upon his board ; the
    boast
Of half his victims was his boil'd and roast ;
And these at every hour :—he seldom took
Aside his client, till he'd praised his cook ;
Nor to an office led him, there in pain
To give his story and go out again ;
But first, the brandy and the chine were seen,
And then the business came by starts be-
    tween.
'Well, if 'tis so, the house to you belongs ;
But have you money to redress these wrongs ?
Nay, look not sad, my friend ; if you're cor-
    rect,
You'll find the friendship that you'd not
    expect.'
    If right the man, the house was Swallow's
        own ;
If wrong, his kindness and good-will were
    shown ;
'Rogue !' 'Villain !' 'Scoundrel !' cried
    the losers all ;
He let them cry, for what would that recall ?
At length he left us, took a village seat,
And like a vulture look'd abroad for meat ;
The Borough-booty, give it all its praise,
Had only served the appetite to raise ;
But if from simple heirs he drew their land,
He might a noble feast at will command ;
Still he proceeded by his former rules,
His bait, their pleasures, when he fish'd for
    fools ;—
Flagons and haunches on his board were
    placed,
And subtle avarice look'd like thoughtless
    waste :

Most of his friends, though youth from him
    had fled,
Were young, were minors, of their sires in
    dread ;
Or those whom widow'd mothers kept in
    bounds,
And check'd their generous rage for steeds
    and hounds ;
Or such as travell'd 'cross the land to view
A Christian's conflict with a boxing Jew :
Some too had run upon Newmarket heath
With so much speed that they were out of
    breath ;
Others had tasted claret, till they now
To humbler port would turn, and knew not
    how.
All these for favours would to Swallow run,
Who never sought their thanks for all he'd
    done ;
He kindly took them by the hand, then bow'd
Politely low, and thus his love avow'd—
(For he'd a way that many judged polite,
A cunning dog—he'd fawn before he'd bite)—
    'Observe, my friends, the frailty of our
        race
When age unmans us—let me state a case :
There's our friend Rupert—we shall soon
    redress
His present evil—drink to our success—
I flatter not ; but did you ever see
Limbs better turn'd ? a prettier boy than he ?
His senses all acute, his passions such
As nature gave—she never does too much ;
His bold wish the cup of joy to drain,
And strength to bear it without qualm or pain.
    'Now view his father as he dozing lies,
Whose senses wake not when he opes his eyes;
Who slips and shuffles when he means to walk,
And lisps and gabbles if he tries to talk ;
Feeling he's none, he could as soon destroy
The earth itself, as aught it holds enjoy ;
A nurse attends him to lay straight his limbs,
Present his gruel, and respect his whims :
Now shall this dotard from our hero hold
His lands and lordships ?   Shall he hide his
    gold ?
That which he cannot use, and dare not show,
And will not give—why longer should he owe ?
Yet, 'twould be murder should we snap the
    locks,
And take the thing he worships from the box ;
So let him dote and dream : but, till he die,
Shall not our generous heir receive supply ?

For ever sitting on the river's brink,
And ever thirsty, shall he fear to drink ?
The means are simple, let him only wish,
Then say he 's willing, and I'll fill his dish.'
  They all applauded, and not least the boy,
Who now replied, ' It fill'd his heart with
      joy
To find he needed not deliv'rance crave
Of death, or wish the justice in the grave ;
Who, while he spent, would every art retain
Of luring home the scatter'd gold again ;
Just as a fountain gaily spirts and plays
With what returns in still and secret ways.'
  Short was the dream of bliss ; he quickly
      found,
His father's acres all were Swallow's ground.
Yet to those arts would other heroes lend
A willing ear, and Swallow was their friend ;
Ever successful, some began to think
That Satan help'd him to his pen and ink ;
And shrewd suspicions ran about the place,
' There was a compact '—I must leave the
      case.
But of the parties, had the fiend been one,
The business could not have been speedier
      done :
Still when a man has angled day and night,
The silliest gudgeons will refuse to bite :
So Swallow tried no more ; but if they came
To seek his friendship, that remain'd the
      same :
Thus he retired in peace, and some would
      say
He'd balk'd his partner, and had learn'd to
      pray.
To this some zealots lent an ear, and sought
How Swallow felt, then said ' a change is
      wrought : '
'Twas true there wanted all the signs of grace,
But there were strong professions in their
      place ;
Then too, the less that men from him expect,
The more the praise to the converting sect ;
He had not yet subscribed to all their creed,
Nor own'd a call, but he confess'd the need :
His acquiescent speech, his gracious look,
That pure attention, when the brethren spoke,
Was all contrition,—he had felt the wound,
And with confession would again be sound.

True, Swallow's board had still the sump-
      tuous treat ;
But could they blame ? the warmest zealots
      eat :
He drank—'twas needful his poor nerves to
      brace ;
He swore—'twas habit ; he was grieved—
      'twas grace :
What could they do a new-born zeal to nurse ?
' His wealth 's undoubted— let him hold our
      purse ;
He'll add his bounty, and the house we'll raise
Hard by the church, and gather all her
      strays ;
We'll watch her sinners as they home retire,
And pluck the brands from the devouring
      fire.'
  Alas ! such speech was but an empty
      boast ;
The good men reckon'd, but without their
      host ;
Swallow, delighted, took the trusted store,
And own'd the sum : they did not ask for
      more,
Till more was needed ; when they call'd for
      aid—
And had it ?—No, their agent was afraid ;
' Could he but know to whom he should
      refund,
He would most gladly—nay, he'd go beyond ;
But when such numbers claim'd, when some
      were gone,
And others going—he must hold it on ;
The Lord would help them '—Loud their
      anger grew,
And while they threat'ning from his door
      withdrew,
He bow'd politely low, and bade them all
      adieu.
  But lives the man by whom such deeds are
      done ?
Yes, many such—but Swallow's race is run ;
His name is lost,—for though his sons have
      name,
It is not his, they all escape the shame ;
Nor is there vestige now of all he had,
His means are wasted, for his heir was mad ;
Still we of Swallow as a monster speak,
A hard bad man, who prey'd upon the weak.

LETTER VII.   PROFESSIONS—PHYSIC

Iam mala finissem leto, sed credula vitam
Spes fovet, et fore cras semper ait melius.
        TIBULLUS, lib. ii. vi, vv. 20, 21.

He fell to juggle, cant, and cheat——
For as those fowls that live in water
Are never wet, he did but smatter ;
Whate'er he labour'd to appear,
His understanding still was clear.
.   .   .   .
A paltry wretch he had, half-starved,
That him in place of zany served.
        BUTLER'S *Hudibras*, Part II, Canto III,
        218–222, 323, 324.

The Worth and Excellence of the true Physi-
cian—Merit, not the sole Cause of Success
—Modes of advancing Reputation—Motives
of medical Men for publishing their Works
—The great Evil of Quackery—Present
State of advertising Quacks—Their Hazard
—Some fail, and why—Causes of Success
—How men of Understanding are prevailed
upon to have Recourse to Empirics, and
to permit their Names to be advertised—
Evils of Quackery : to nervous Females :
to Youth : to Infants—History of an
advertising Empiric, &c.

NEXT, to a graver tribe we turn our view,
And yield the praise to worth and science due;
But this with serious words and sober style,
For these are friends with whom we seldom
        smile :
Helpers of men * they're call'd, and we confess
Theirs the deep study, theirs the lucky guess ;
We own that numbers join with care and skill,
A temperate judgment, a devoted will ;
Men who suppress their feelings, but who feel
The painful symptoms they delight to heal ;
Patient in all their trials, they sustain
The starts of passion, the reproach of pain ;
With hearts affected, but with looks serene,
Intent they wait through all the solemn
        scene ;
Glad if a hope should rise from nature's strife,
To aid their skill and save the lingering life ;
But this must virtue's generous effort be,
And spring from nobler motives than a fee :
To the physicians of the soul, and these,
Turn the distress'd for safety, hope, and ease.

        * Opiferque per orbem dicor.

But as physicians of that nobler kind
Have their warm zealots, and their sectaries
        blind ;
So among these for knowledge most renown'd,
Are dreamers strange, and stubborn bigots
        found :
Some, too, admitted to this honour'd name,
Have, without learning, found a way to fame;
And some by learning—young physicians
        write,
To set their merit in the fairest light ;
With them a treatise is a bait that draws
Approving voices—'tis to gain applause,
And to exalt them in the public view,
More than a life of worthy toil could do.
When 'tis proposed to make the man re-
        nown'd,
In every age, convenient doubts abound ;
Convenient themes in every period start,
Which he may treat with all the pomp of art ;
Curious conjectures he may always make,
And either side of dubious questions take :
He may a system broach, or, if he please,
Start new opinions of an old disease ;
Or may some simple in the woodland trace,
And be its patron, till it runs its race ;
As rustic damsels from their woods are won,
And live in splendour till their race be run ;
It weighs not much on what their powers be
        shown,
When all his purpose is to make them known.
   To show the world what long experience
        gains,
Requires not courage, though it calls for pains;
But at life's outset to inform mankind,
Is a bold effort of a valiant mind.
   The great good man, for noblest cause,
        displays
What many labours taught, and many days ;
These sound instruction from experience
        give,
The others show us how they mean to live ;
That they have genius, and they hope man-
        kind
Will to its efforts be no longer blind.
   There are beside, whom powerful friends
        advance,
Whom fashion favours, person, patrons,
        chance :

And merit sighs to see a fortune made
By daring rashness or by dull parade.
  But these are trifling evils ; there is one
Which walks uncheck'd, and triumphs in the
    sun :
There was a time, when we beheld the quack,
On public stage, the licensed trade attack ;
He made his labour'd speech with poor
    parade ;
And then a laughing zany lent him aid :
Smiling we pass'd him, but we felt the while
Pity so much, that soon we ceased to smile ;
Assured that fluent speech and flow'ry vest
Disguised the troubles of a man distress'd.
  But now our quacks are gamesters, and they
    play
With craft and skill to ruin and betray ;
With monstrous promise they delude the
    mind,
And thrive on all that tortures human-kind.
Void of all honour, avaricious, rash,
The daring tribe compound their boasted
    trash—
Tincture or syrup, lotion, drop or pill ;
All tempt the sick to trust the lying bill ;
And twenty names of cobblers turn'd to
    squires,
Aid the bold language of these blushless liars.
There are among them those who cannot
    read,
And yet they'll buy a patent, and succeed ;
Will dare to promise dying sufferers aid,
For who, when dead, can threaten or up-
    braid ?
With cruel avarice still they recommend
More draughts, more syrup to the journey's
    end :
' I feel it not ; '—' Then take it every hour : '
' It makes me worse ; '—' Why then it shows
    its power : '
' I fear to die ; '—' Let not your spirits sink,
You're always safe, while you believe and
    drink.'
  How strange to add, in this nefarious trade,
That men of parts are dupes by dunces made :
That creatures, nature meant should clean our
    streets,
Have purchased lands and mansions, parks
    and seats ;
Wretches with conscience so obtuse, they leave
Their untaught sons their parents to deceive ;
And when they're laid upon their dying-bed,
No thought of murder comes into their head ;

Nor one revengeful ghost to them appears,
To fill the soul with penitential fears.
  Yet not the whole of this imposing train
Their gardens, seats, and carriages obtain ;
Chiefly, indeed, they to the robbers fall,
Who are most fitted to disgrace them all :
But there is hazard—patents must be bought,
Venders and puffers for the poison sought ;
And then in many a paper through the year,
Must cures and cases, oaths and proofs ap-
    pear ;
Men snatch'd from graves, as they were
    dropping in,
Their lungs cough'd up, their bones pierced
    through their skin ;
Their liver all one scirrhus, and the frame
Poison'd with evils which they dare not name;
Men who spent all upon physicians' fees,
Who never slept, nor had a moment's ease,
Are now as roaches sound, and all as brisk as
    bees.
  If the sick gudgeons to the bait attend,
And come in shoals, the angler gains his end ;
But should the advertising cash be spent,
Ere yet the town has due attention lent,
Then bursts the bubble, and the hungry cheat
Pines for the bread he ill deserves to eat ;
It is a lottery, and he shares perhaps
The rich man's feast, or begs the pauper's
    scraps.
  From powerful causes spring th' empiric's
    gains,
Man's love of life, his weakness, and his pains;
These first induce him the vile trash to try,
Then lend his name, that other men may
    buy :
This love of life, which in our nature rules,
To vile imposture makes us dupes and tools ;
Then pain compels th' impatient soul to seize
On promised hopes of instantaneous ease ;
And weakness too with every wish complies,
Worn out and won by importunities.
  Troubled with something in your bile or
    blood,
You think your doctor does you little good ;
And, grown impatient, you require in haste
The nervous cordial, nor dislike the taste ;
It comforts, heals, and strengthens ; nay,
    you think
It makes you better every time you drink ;
' Then lend your name '—you're loth, but
    yet confess
Its powers are great, and so you acquiesce :

Yet think a moment, ere your name you lend,
With whose 'tis placed, and what you recom-
    mend ;
Who tipples brandy will some comfort feel,
But will he to the med'cine set his seal ?
Wait, and you'll find the cordial you admire
Has added fuel to your fever's fire :
Say, should a robber chance your purse to
    spare,
Would you the honour of the man declare ?
Would you assist his purpose ? swell his
    crime ?
Besides, he might not spare a second time.
  Compassion sometimes sets the fatal sign ;
The man was poor, and humbly begg'd a
    line ;
Else how should noble names and titles back
The spreading praise of some advent'rous
    quack ?
But he the moment watches, and entreats
Your honour's name,—your honour joins the
    cheats ;
You judged the med'cine harmless, and you
    lent
What help you could, and with the best intent;
But can it please you, thus to league with all
Whom he can beg or bribe to swell the scrawl ?
Would you these wrappers with your name
    adorn,
Which hold the poison for the yet unborn ?
  No class escapes them—from the poor
    man's pay,
The nostrum takes no trifling part away ;
See ! those square patent bottles from the
    shop,
Now decoration to the cupboard's top ;
And there a favourite hoard you'll find within,
Companions meet ! the julep and the gin.
  Time too with cash is wasted ; 'tis the fate
Of real helpers to be call'd too late ;
This find the sick, when (time and patience
    gone)
Death with a tenfold terror hurries on.
  Suppose the case surpasses human skill,
There comes a quack to flatter weakness still ;
What greater evil can a flatterer do,
Than from himself to take the sufferer's view ?
To turn from sacred thoughts his reasoning
    powers,
And rob a sinner of his dying hours ?
Yet this they dare, and craving to the last,
In hope's strong bondage hold their victim
    fast :

For soul or body no concern have they,
All their inquiry, ' Can the patient pay ?
And will he swallow draughts until his dying
    day ? '
  Observe what ills to nervous females flow,
When the heart flutters, and the pulse is low ;
If once induced these cordial sips to try,
All feel the ease, and few the danger fly ;
For while obtain'd, of drams they've all the
    force,
And when denied, then drams are the resource.
  Nor these the only evils—there are those
Who for the troubled mind prepare repose ;
They write : the young are tenderly address'd,
Much danger hinted, much concern express'd ;
They dwell on freedom lads are prone to take,
Which makes the doctor tremble for their
    sake ;
Still if the youthful patient will but trust
In one so kind, so pitiful, and just ;
If he will take the tonic all the time,
And hold but moderate intercourse with
    crime ;
The sage will gravely give his honest word,
That strength and spirits shall be both re-
    stored ;
In plainer English—if you mean to sin,
Fly to the drops, and instantly begin.
  Who would not lend a sympathizing sigh,
To hear yon infant's pity-moving cry ?
That feeble sob, unlike the new-born note,
Which came with vigour from the op'ning
    throat ;
When air and light first rush'd on lungs and
    eyes,
And there was life and spirit in the cries ;
Now an abortive, faint attempt to weep
Is all we hear ; sensation is asleep :
The boy was healthy, and at first express'd
His feelings loudly, when he fail'd to rest ;
When cramm'd with food, and tighten'd
    every limb,
To cry aloud, was what pertain'd to him ;
Then the good nurse, (who, had she borne
    a brain,
Had sought the cause that made her babe
    complain,)
Has all her efforts, loving soul ! applied,
To set the cry, and not the cause, aside ;
She gave her powerful sweet without remorse,
The sleeping cordial—she had tried its force,
Repeating oft : the infant freed from pain,
Rejected food, but took the dose again,

Sinking to sleep ; while she her joy express'd,
That her dear charge could sweetly take his
  rest :
Soon may she spare her cordial ; not a doubt
Remains, but quickly he will rest without.
  This moves our grief and pity, and we sigh
To think what numbers from these causes
  die :
But what contempt and anger should we show,
Did we the lives of these impostors know !
  Ere for the world's I left the cares of school,
One I remember who assumed the fool :
A part well suited—when the idler boys
Would shout around him, and he loved the
  noise ;
They call'd him Neddy ;—Neddy had the art
To play with skill his ignominious part ;
When he his trifles would for sale display,
And act the mimic for a schoolboy's pay.
For many years he plied his humble trade,
And used his tricks and talents to persuade ;
The fellow barely read, but chanced to look
Among the fragments of a tatter'd book ;
Where after many efforts made to spell
One puzzling word, he found it *oxymel* ;
A potent thing, 'twas said, to cure the ills
Of ailing lungs—the *oxymel of squills* :
Squills he procured, but found the bitter
  strong,
And most unpleasant ; none would take it
  long ;
But the pure acid and the sweet would
  make
A med'cine numbers would for pleasure take.
  There was a fellow near, an artful knave,
Who knew the plan, and much assistance
  gave ;
He wrote the puffs, and every talent plied
To make it sell : it sold, and then he died.
  Now all the profit fell to Ned's control,
And Pride and Avarice quarrell'd for his
  soul ;
When mighty profits by the trash were made,
Pride built a palace, Avarice groan'd and
  paid ;
Pride placed the signs of grandeur all about,
And Avarice barr'd his friends and children
  out.
  Now see him doctor ! yes, the idle fool,
The butt, the robber of the lads at school ;

Who then knew nothing, nothing since ac-
  quired,
Became a doctor, honour'd and admired ;
His dress, his frown, his dignity were such,
Some who had known him thought his know-
  ledge much ;
Nay, men of skill, of apprehension quick,
Spite of their knowledge, trusted him when
  sick :
Though he could neither reason, write, nor
  spell,
They yet had hope his trash would make
  them well ;
And while they scorn'd his parts, they took
  his oxymel.
Oh ! when his nerves had once received a
  shock,
Sir Isaac Newton might have gone to Rock : *
Hence impositions of the grossest kind,
Hence thought is feeble, understanding blind ;
Hence sums enormous by those cheats are
  made,
And deaths unnumber'd by their dreadful
  trade.
  Alas ! in vain is my contempt express'd,
To stronger passions are their words address'd;
To pain, to fear, to terror their appeal,
To those who, weakly reasoning, strongly
  feel.
  What then our hopes ?—perhaps there
  may by law
Be method found, these pests to curb and
  awe ;
Yet in this land of freedom, law is slack
With any being to commence attack ;
Then let us trust to science—there are those
Who can their falsehoods and their frauds
  disclose,
All their vile trash detect, and their low
  tricks expose :
Perhaps their numbers may in time confound
Their arts—as scorpions give themselves the
  wound :
For when these curers dwell in every place,
While of the cured we not a man can trace,
Strong truth may then the public mind per-
  suade,
And spoil the fruits of this nefarious trade.

  * An empiric who *flourished* at the same time
with this great man.

LETTER VIII. TRADES

Non possidentem multa vocaveris
Recte beatum : rectius occupat
Nomen Beati, qui Deorum
Muneribus sapienter uti,
Duramque callet pauperiem pati.
    Hor. *Carm.* lib. iv, 9, vv. 45–49.

Non uxor salvum te vult, non filius : omnes
Vicini oderunt ; noti, pueri atque puellae.
Miraris, cum tu argento post omnia ponas,
Si nemo praestet, quem non merearis,
   amorem ?
    Hor. *Sat.* lib. i, Sat. i, vv. 84–7.

Non propter vitam faciunt patrimonia qui-
   dam,
Sed vitio caeci propter patrimonia vivunt.
    Juvenal, *Sat.* xii, vv. 50, 51.

No extensive Manufactories in the Borough :
yet considerable Fortunes made there—Ill
Judgment of Parents in disposing of their
Sons—The best educated not the most
likely to succeed—Instance—Want of
Success compensated by the lenient Power
of some Avocations—The Naturalist—
The Weaver an Entomologist, &c.—A
Prize-Flower—Story of Walter and William.

Of manufactures, trade, inventions rare,
Steam-towers and looms, you'd know our
   Borough's share—
'Tis small : we boast not these rich subjects
   here,
Who hazard thrice ten thousand pounds a
   year ;
We've no huge buildings, where incessant
   noise
Is made by springs and spindles, girls and
   boys ;
Where, 'mid such thundering sounds, the
   maiden's song
Is ' Harmony in Uproar ' [1] all day long.
   Still common minds with us in common
   trade,
Have gain'd more wealth than ever student
   made ;
And yet a merchant, when he gives his son
His college-learning, thinks his duty done ;
A way to wealth he leaves his boy to find,
Just when he 's made for the discovery blind.
   Jones and his wife perceived their elder
   boy
Took to his learning, and it gave them joy ;

This they encouraged, and were bless'd to see
Their son a fellow with a high degree ;
A living fell, he married, and his sire
Declared 'twas all a father could require ;
Children then bless'd them, and when letters
   came,
The parents proudly told each grandchild's
   name.
   Meantime the sons at home in trade were
   placed,
Money their object—just the father's taste ;
Saving he lived and long, and when he died,
He gave them all his fortune to divide :
' Martin,' said he, ' at vast expense was
   taught ;
He gain'd his wish, and has the ease he
   sought.'
   Thus the good priest (the Christian-
   scholar !) finds
What estimate is made by vulgar minds ;
He sees his brothers, who had every gift
Of thriving, now assisted in their thrift ;
While he whom learning, habits, all prevent,
Is largely mulct for each impediment.
   Yet let us own that trade has much of
   chance,
Not all the careful by their care advance ;
With the same parts and prospects, one a seat
Builds for himself ; one finds it in the Fleet.
Then to the wealthy you will see denied
Comforts and joys that with the poor abide :
There are who labour through the year, and
   yet
No more have gain'd than—not to be in
   debt ;
Who still maintain the same laborious course,
Yet pleasure hails them from some favourite
   source ;
And health, amusements, children, wife or
   friend,
With life's dull views their consolations blend.
   Nor these alone possess the lenient power
Of soothing life in the desponding hour ;
Some favourite studies, some delightful care,
The mind, with trouble and distresses, share ;
And by a coin, a flower, a verse, a boat,
The stagnant spirits have been set afloat ;
They pleased at first, and then the habit grew,
Till the fond heart no higher pleasure knew ;

Till, from all cares and other comforts freed,
Th' important nothing took in life the lead.
With all his phlegm, it broke a Dutchman's
    heart,
At a vast price, with one loved root to part ;
And toys like these fill many a British mind,
Although their hearts are found of firmer
    kind.
    Oft have I smiled the happy pride to see
Of humble tradesmen, in their evening glee ;
When of some pleasing, fancied good pos-
    sess'd,
Each grew alert, was busy, and was bless'd ;
Whether the call-bird yield the hour's delight,
Or, magnified in microscope, the mite ;
Or whether tumblers, croppers, carriers seize
The gentle mind, they rule it and they please.
    There is my friend the Weaver ; strong
    desires
Reign in his breast ; 'tis beauty he admires :
See ! to the shady grove he wings his way,
And feels in hope the raptures of the day—
Eager he looks ; and soon, to glad his eyes,
From the sweet bower, by nature form'd,
    arise
Bright troops of virgin moths and fresh-born
    butterflies ;
Who broke that morning from their half-
    year's sleep,
To fly o'er flow'rs where they were wont to
    creep.
    Above the sovereign oak, a sovereign skims,
The purple Emp'ror, strong in wing and
    limbs :
There fair Camilla takes her flight serene,
Adonis blue, and Paphia silver-queen ;
With every filmy fly from mead or bower,
And hungry Sphinx who threads the honey'd
    flower ;
She o'er the Larkspur's bed, where sweets
    abound,
Views ev'ry bell, and hums th' approving
    sound ;
Poised on her busy plumes, with feeling nice
She draws from every flower, nor tries a floret
    twice.
    He fears no bailiff's wrath, no baron's blame,
His is untax'd and undisputed game ;
Nor less the place of curious plant he knows ; [2]
He both his Flora and his Fauna shows ;
For him is blooming in its rich array
The glorious flower which bore the palm
    away ;

In vain a rival tried his utmost art,
His was the prize, and joy o'erflow'd his heart.
    ' This, this ! is beauty ; cast, I pray, your
    eyes
On this my glory ! see the grace ! the size !
Was ever stem so tall, so stout, so strong,
Exact in breadth, in just proportion, long !
These brilliant hues are all distinct and clean,
No kindred tint, no blending streaks between ;
This is no shaded, run-off,[3] pin-eyed [4] thing,
A king of flowers, a flower for England's
    king :
I own my pride, and thank the favouring star,
Which shed such beauty on my fair Bizarre.''[5]
    Thus may the poor the cheap indulgence
    seize,
While the most wealthy pine and pray for
    ease ;
Content not always waits upon success,
And more may he enjoy who profits less.
    Walter and William took (their father dead)
Jointly the trade to which they both were
    bred ;
When fix'd, they married, and they quickly
    found
With due success their honest labours crown'd:
Few were their losses, but although a few,
Walter was vex'd, and somewhat peevish
    grew :
' You put your trust in every pleading fool,'
Said he to William, and grew strange and cool.
' Brother, forbear,' he answer'd ; ' take our
    due,
Nor let my lack of caution injure you ; '
Half friends they parted,—better so to close,
Than longer wait to part entirely foes.
    Walter had knowledge, prudence, jealous
    care ;
He let no idle views his bosom share ;
He never thought nor felt for other men—
' Let one mind one, and all are minded then.'
Friends he respected, and believed them just,
But they were men, and he would no man
    trust ;
He tried and watch'd his people day and
    night,—
The good it harm'd not ; for the bad 'twas
    right :
He could their humours bear, nay disrespect,
But he could yield no pardon to neglect ;
That all about him were of him afraid,
' Was right,' he said—' so should we be
    obey'd.'

These merchant-maxims, much good-
fortune too,
And ever keeping one grand point in view,
To vast amount his once small portion drew.
William was kind and easy ; he complied
With all requests, or grieved when he denied ;
To please his wife he made a costly trip,
To please his child he let a bargain slip ;
Prone to compassion, mild with the distress'd,
He bore with all who poverty profess'd,
And some would he assist, nor one would he
arrest.
He had some loss at sea, bad debts at land,
His clerk absconded with some bills in hand,
And plans so often fail'd that he no longer
plann'd.
To a small house (his brother's) he withdrew,
At easy rent—the man was not a Jew ;
And there his losses and his cares he bore,
Nor found that want of wealth could make
him poor.
No, he in fact was rich ; nor could he move,
But he was follow'd by the looks of love ;
All he had suffer'd, every former grief,
Made those around more studious in relief ;
He saw a cheerful smile in every face,
And lost all thoughts of error and disgrace.
Pleasant it was to see them in their walk
Round their small garden, and to hear them
talk ;
Free are their children, but their love refrains
From all offence—none murmurs, none com-
plains ;
Whether a book amused them, speech or play,
Their looks were lively, and their hearts were
gay ;
There no forced efforts for delight were made,
Joy came with prudence, and without parade ;
Their common comforts they had all in view,
Light were their troubles, and their wishes few :
Thrift made them easy for the coming day,
Religion took the dread of death away ;
A cheerful spirit still insured content,
And love smiled round them wheresoe'er they
went.
Walter, meantime, with all his wealth's
increase,
Gain'd many points, but could not purchase
peace ;
When he withdrew from business for an hour,
Some fled his presence, all confess'd his power ;
He sought affection, but received instead
Fear undisguised, and love-repelling dread ;

He look'd around him—' Harriet, dost thou
love ? '
' I do my duty,' said the timid dove ;
' Good Heav'n, your duty ! prithee, tell me
now—
To love and honour—was not that your vow ?
Come, my good Harriet, I would gladly seek
Your inmost thought—Why can't the woman
speak ?
Have you not all things ? '—' Sir, do I com-
plain ? '—
' No, that 's my part, which I perform in vain ;
I want a simple answer, and direct—
But you evade ; yes ! 'tis as I suspect.
Come then, my children ! Watt ! upon your
knees
Vow that you love me.'—' Yes, sir, if you
please.'—
' Again ! by Heav'n, it mads me ; I require
Love, and they'll do whatever I desire :
Thus too my people shun me ; I would spend
A thousand pounds to get a single friend ;
I would be happy—I have means to pay
For love and friendship, and you run away ;
Ungrateful creatures ! why, you seem to dread
My very looks ; I know you wish me dead.
Come hither, Nancy ! you must hold me dear;
Hither, I say ; why ! what have you to fear ?
You see I'm gentle—Come, you trifler, come ;
My God ! she trembles ! Idiot, leave the room!
Madam ! your children hate me ; I suppose
They know their cue : you make them all my
foes ;
I've not a friend in all the world—not one :
I'd be a bankrupt sooner ; nay, 'tis done ;
In every better hope of life I fail,
You're all tormentors, and my house a jail ;
Out of my sight ! I'll sit and make my will—
What, glad to go ? stay, devils, and be still ;
'Tis to your uncle's cot you wish to run,
To learn to live at ease and be undone ;
Him you can love, who lost his whole estate,
And I, who gain you fortunes, have your hate ;
'Tis in my absence, you yourselves enjoy :
Tom ! are you glad to lose me ? tell me, boy :
Yes ! does he answer ? '—' Yes ! upon my
soul ; '
' No awe, no fear, no duty, no control !
Away ! away ! ten thousand devils seize
All I possess, and plunder where they please !
What 's wealth to me ?—yes, yes ! it gives
me sway,
And you shall feel it—Go ! begone, I say.'

LETTER IX. AMUSEMENTS

Interpone tuis interdum gaudia curis,
Ut possis animo quemvis sufferre laborem.
    CATULL. lib. iii.

     . . . Nostra fatescit
Laxaturque chelys, vires instigat alitque
Tempestiva quies, major post otia virtus.
    STATIUS, *Sylv.* lib. iv. 4, vv. 32–34.

Iamque mare et tellus nullum discrimen
  habebant ;
Omnia pontus erant : deerant quoque littora
  ponto.
    OVID, *Metamorph.* lib. i, vv. 291, 292.

Common Amusements of a Bathing-place
—Morning Rides, Walks, &c.—Company
resorting to the Town—Different Choice
of Lodgings—Cheap Indulgences—Sea-
side Walks—Wealthy Invalid—Summer-
Evening on the Sands—Sea Productions—
'Water parted from the Sea'—Winter
Views serene—In what Cases to be avoided
—Sailing upon the River—A small Islet
of Sand off the Coast—Visited by Company
—Covered by the Flowing of the Tide—
Adventure in that Place.

OF our amusements ask you ?—We amuse
Ourselves and friends with sea-side walks and
  views,
Or take a morning ride, a novel, or the news ;
Or, seeking nothing, glide about the street,
And so engaged, with various parties meet ;
Awhile we stop, discourse of wind and tide,
Bathing and books, the raffle, and the ride,
Thus, with the aid which shops and sailing
  give,
Life passes on ; 'tis labour, but we live.

 When evening comes, our invalids awake,
Nerves cease to tremble, heads forbear to ache;
Then cheerful meals the sunken spirits raise,
Cards or the dance, wine, visiting, or plays.

 Soon as the season comes, and crowds arrive,
To their superior rooms the wealthy drive ;
Others look round for lodging snug and small,
Such is their taste—they've hatred to a hall ;
Hence one his fav'rite habitation gets,
The brick-floor'd parlour which the butcher
  lets ;
Where, through his single light, he may regard
The various business of a common yard,
Bounded by backs of buildings form'd of clay,
By stable, sties, and coops, et-caetera.

 The needy-vain, themselves awhile to shun,
For dissipation to these dog-holes run ;
Where each (assuming petty pomp) appears,
And quite forgets the shopboard and the
  shears.
For them are cheap amusements : they
  may slip
Beyond the town and take a private dip ;
When they may urge that to be safe they
  mean,
They've heard there's danger in a light
  machine ;
They too can gratis move the quays about,
And gather kind replies to every doubt ;
There they a pacing, lounging tribe may view,
The stranger's guides, who've little else to do ;
The Borough's placemen, where no more they
  gain
Than keeps them idle, civil, poor, and vain.

Then may the poorest with the wealthy look
On ocean, glorious page of Nature's book !
May see its varying views in every hour,
All softness now, then rising with all power,
As sleeping to invite, or threat'ning to devour :
'Tis this which gives us all our choicest views ;
Its waters heal us, and its shores amuse.

 See ! those fair nymphs upon that rising
  strand,
Yon long salt lake has parted from the land ;
Well pleased to press that path, so clean, so
  pure,
To seem in danger, yet to feel secure ;
Trifling with terror, while they strive to shun
The curling billows ; laughing as they run ;
They know the neck that joins the shore and
  sea,
Or, ah ! how changed that fearless laugh
  would be.
 Observe how various parties take their way,
By sea-side walks, or make the sand-hills gay ;
There group'd are laughing maids and sighing
  swains,
And some apart who feel unpitied pains ;
Pains from diseases, pains which those who
  feel,
To the physician, not the fair, reveal :
For nymphs (propitious to the lover's sigh)
Leave these poor patients to complain and
  die.

Lo ! where on that huge anchor sadly leans
That sick tall figure, lost in other scenes ;
He late from India's clime impatient sail'd,
There, as his fortune grew, his spirits fail'd ;
For each delight, in search of wealth he went,
For ease alone, the wealth acquired is spent—
And spent in vain ; enrich'd, aggrieved, he
    sees
The envied poor possess'd of joy and ease :
And now he flies from place to place, to gain
Strength for enjoyment, and still flies in vain :
Mark ! with what sadness, of that pleasant
    crew,
Boist'rous in mirth, he takes a transient view ;
And fixing then his eye upon the sea,
Thinks what has been and what must shortly
    be :
Is it not strange that man should health
    destroy,
For joys that come when he is dead to joy ?
  Now is it pleasant in the summer-eve,
When a broad shore retiring waters leave,
Awhile to wait upon the firm fair sand,
When all is calm at sea, all still at land ;
And there the ocean's produce to explore,
As floating by, or rolling on the shore ;
Those living jellies [1] which the flesh inflame,
Fierce as a nettle, and from that its name ;
Some in huge masses, some that you may
    bring
In the small compass of a lady's ring ;
Figured by hand divine—there 's not a gem
Wrought by man's art to be compared to
    them ;
Soft, brilliant, tender, through the wave they
    glow,
And make the moonbeam brighter where they
    flow.
Involved in sea-wrack, here you find a race,
Which science doubting, knows not where to
    place ;
On shell or stone is dropp'd the embryo-
    seed,
And quickly vegetates a vital breed.[2]
  While thus with pleasing wonder you in-
    spect
Treasures the vulgar in their scorn reject,
See as they float along th' entangled weeds
Slowly approach, upborne on bladdery beads ;
Wait till they land, and you shall then behold
The fiery sparks those tangled frons' infold,
Myriads of living points [3] ; th' unaided eye
Can but the fire and not the form descry.

And now your view upon the ocean turn,
And there the splendour of the waves discern ;
Cast but a stone, or strike them with an oar,
And you shall flames within the deep explore ;
Or scoop the stream phosphoric as you stand,
And the cold flames shall flash along your
    hand ;
When, lost in wonder, you shall walk and
    gaze
On weeds that sparkle, and on waves that
    blaze.[4]
  The ocean too has winter-views serene,
When all you see through densest fog is seen ;
When you can hear the fishers near at hand
Distinctly speak, yet see not where they
    stand ;
Or sometimes them and not their boat discern,
Or half-conceal'd some figure at the stern ;
The view 's all bounded, and from side to
    side
Your utmost prospect but a few ells wide ;
Boys who, on shore, to sea the pebble cast,
Will hear it strike against the viewless mast;
While the stern boatman growls his fierce
    disdain,
At whom he knows not, whom he threats in
    vain.
  'Tis pleasant then to view the nets float
    past,
Net after net till you have seen the last ;
And as you wait till all beyond you slip,
A boat comes gliding from an anchor'd ship,
Breaking the silence with the dipping oar,
And their own tones, as labouring for the
    shore ;
Those measured tones which with the scene
    agree,
And give a sadness to serenity.
  All scenes like these the tender maid should
    shun,
Nor to a misty beach in autumn run ;
Much should she guard against the evening
    cold,
And her slight shape with fleecy warmth in-
    fold ;
This she admits, but not with so much ease
Gives up the night-walk when th' attendants
    please :
Her have I seen, pale, vapour'd through the
    day,
With crowded parties at the midnight play ;
Faint in the morn, no powers could she exert ;
At night with Pam delighted and alert ;

In a small shop she 's raffled with a crowd,
Breathed the thick air, and cough'd and
   laugh'd aloud ;
She who will tremble if her eye explore
' The smallest monstrous mouse that creeps
   on floor ; '
Whom the kind doctor charged with shaking
   head,
At early hour to quit the beaux for bed :
She has, contemning fear, gone down the
   dance,
Till she perceived the rosy morn advance ;
Then has she wonder'd, fainting o'er her tea,
Her drops and julep should so useless be :
Ah ! sure her joys must ravish every sense,
Who buys a portion at such vast expense.
   Among those joys, 'tis one at eve to sail
On the broad river with a favourite gale ;
When no rough waves upon the bosom ride,
But the keel cuts, nor rises on the tide ;
Safe from the stream the nearer gunwale
   stands,
Where playful children trail their idle hands :
Or strive to catch long grassy leaves that
   float
On either side of the impeded boat ;
What time the moon arising shows the mud,
A shining border to the silver flood :
When, by her dubious light, the meanest
   views,
Chalk, stones, and stakes, obtain the richest
   hues ;
And when the cattle, as they gazing stand,
Seem nobler objects than when view'd from
   land :
Then anchor'd vessels in the way appear,
And sea-boys greet them as they pass—
   ' What cheer ? '
The sleeping shell-ducks at the sound arise,
And utter loud their unharmonious cries ;
Fluttering they move their weedy beds
   among,
Or instant diving, hide their plumeless young.
   Along the wall, returning from the town,
The weary rustic homeward wanders down ;
Who stops and gazes at such joyous crew,
And feels his envy rising at the view ;
He the light speech and laugh indignant hears,
And feels more press'd by want, more vex'd
   by fears.
   Ah ! go in peace, good fellow, to thine
   home,
Nor fancy these escape the general doom ;

Gay as they seem, be sure with them are
   hearts
With sorrow tried ; there 's sadness in their
   parts :
If thou couldst see them when they think
   alone,
Mirth, music, friends, and these amusements
   gone ;
Couldst thou discover every secret ill
That pains their spirit, or resists their will ;
Couldst thou behold forsaken Love's distress,
Or Envy's pang at glory and success,
Or Beauty, conscious of the spoils of Time,
Or Guilt alarm'd when Memory shows the
   crime ;
All that gives sorrow, terror, grief and
   gloom ;
Content would cheer thee trudging to thine
   home.[5]
   There are, 'tis true, who lay their cares
   aside,
And bid some hours in calm enjoyment glide;
Perchance some fair-one to the sober night
Adds (by the sweetness of her song) delight ;
And, as the music on the water floats,
Some bolder shore returns the soften'd notes ;
Then, youth, beware, for all around conspire
To banish caution and to wake desire ;
The day's amusement, feasting, beauty, wine,
These accents sweet and this soft hour com-
   bine,
When most unguarded, then to win that heart
   of thine :
But see, they land ! the fond enchantment
   flies,
And in its place life's common views arise.
   Sometimes a party, row'd from town, will
   land
On a small islet form'd of shelly sand,
Left by the water when the tides are low,
But which the floods in their return o'erflow :
There will they anchor, pleased awhile to
   view
The watery waste, a prospect wild and new ;
The now receding billows give them space,
On either side the growing shores to pace ;
And then returning, they contract the scene,
Till small and smaller grows the walk between;
As sea to sea approaches, shore to shores,
Till the next ebb the sandy isle restores.
   Then what alarm ! what danger and dis-
   may,
If all their trust, their boat should drift away ;

And once it happen'd—gay the friends ad-
vanced,
They walk'd, they ran, they play'd, they sang,
they danced ;
The urns were boiling, and the cups went
round,
And not a grave or thoughtful face was found;
On the bright sand they trod with nimble
feet,
Dry shelly sand that made the summer-seat ;
The wondering mews flew fluttering o'er the
head,
And waves ran softly up their shining bed.

Some form'd a party from the rest to stray,
Pleased to collect the trifles in their way ;
These to behold they call their friends around,
No friends can hear, or hear another sound ;
Alarm'd, they hasten, yet perceive not why,
But catch the fear that quickens as they fly.

For lo ! a lady sage, who paced the sand
With her fair children, one in either hand,
Intent on home, had turn'd, and saw the boat
Slipp'd from her moorings, and now far
afloat ;
She gazed, she trembled, and though faint her
call,
It seem'd, like thunder, to confound them all.
Their sailor-guides, the boatman and his
mate,
Had drank, and slept regardless of their state ;
' Awake !' they cried aloud ; ' Alarm the
shore !
Shout all, or never shall we reach it more !'
Alas ! no shout the distant land can reach,
Nor eye behold them from the foggy beach :
Again they join in one loud powerful cry,
Then cease, and eager listen for reply ;
None came—the rising wind blew sadly by :
They shout once more, and then they turn
aside,
To see how quickly flow'd the coming tide ;
Between each cry they find the waters steal
On their strange prison, and new horrors feel ;
Foot after foot on the contracted ground
The billows fall, and dreadful is the sound ;
Less and yet less the sinking isle became,
And there was wailing, weeping, wrath, and
blame.

Had one been there, with spirit strong and
high,

Who could observe, as he prepared to die,
He might have seen of hearts the varying kind,
And traced the movement of each different
mind :
He might have seen, that not the gentle maid
Was more than stern and haughty man afraid;
Such, calmly grieving, will their fears sup-
press,
And silent prayers to Mercy's throne address ;
While fiercer minds, impatient, angry, loud,
Force their vain grief on the reluctant crowd :
The party's patron, sorely sighing, cried,
' Why would you urge me ? I at first denied.'
Fiercely they answer'd, ' Why will you com-
plain,
Who saw no danger, or was warn'd in vain ? '
A few essay'd the troubled soul to calm,
But dread prevail'd, and anguish and alarm.

Now rose the water through the lessening
sand,
And they seem'd sinking while they yet could
stand ;
The sun went down, they look'd from side to
side,
Nor aught except the gathering sea descried ;
Dark and more dark, more wet, more cold it
grew,
And the most lively bade to hope adieu ;
Children, by love then lifted from the seas,
Felt not the water at the parents' knees,
But wept aloud ; the wind increased the
sound,
And the cold billows as they broke around.
' Once more, yet once again, with all our
strength,
Cry to the land—we may be heard at length.'
Vain hope, if yet unseen ! but hark ! an oar,
That sound of bliss ! comes dashing to their
shore ;
Still, still the water rises, ' Haste!' they cry,
' Oh ! hurry, seamen ; in delay we die : '
(Seamen were these, who in their ship per-
ceived
The drifted boat, and thus her crew relieved.)
And now the keel just cuts the cover'd sand,
Now to the gunwale stretches every hand :
With trembling pleasure all confused embark,
And kiss the tackling of their welcome ark ;
While the most giddy, as they reach the shore,
Think of their danger, and their GOD adore.

LETTER X. CLUBS AND SOCIAL MEETINGS

Non inter lances mensasque nitentes,
Cum stupet insanis acies fulgoribus, et cum
Acclinis falsis animus meliora recusat ;
Verum hic impransi mecum disquirite.
HOR. *Sat.* ii, lib. 2, vv. 4–7.

O prodiga rerum
Luxuries, numquam parvo contenta paratis,
Et quaesitorum terra pelagoque ciborum
Ambitiosa fames et lautae gloria mensae.
LUCAN, lib. iv. 373–6.

Sed quae non prosunt singula, multa juvant.
OVID, *Rem. Amor.* v. 420.

Rusticus agricolam, miles fera bella gerentem,
Rectorem dubiae navita puppis amat.
OVID, *Pont.* lib. ii, vv. 61, 62.

Desire of Country Gentlemen for Town Associations—Book-clubs—Too much of literary Character expected from them—Literary Conversation prevented : by Feasting : by Cards—Good, notwithstanding, results—Card-club with Eagerness resorted to—Players—Umpires at the Whist Table—Petulances of Temper there discovered—Free-and-easy Club : not perfectly easy or free—Freedom, how interrupted—The superior Member—Termination of the Evening—Drinking and Smoking Clubs—The Midnight Conversation of the delaying Members—Society of the poorer Inhabitants : its Use : gives Pride and Consequence to the humble Character—Pleasant Habitation of the frugal Poor—Sailor returning to his Family—Freemasons' Club—The Mystery—What its Origin—Its professed Advantages—Griggs and Gregorians—A Kind of Masons—Reflections on these various Societies.

You say you envy in your calm retreat
Our social meetings ;—'tis with joy we meet:
In these our parties you are pleased to find
Good sense and wit, with intercourse of mind ;
Composed of men, who read, reflect, and write,
Who, when they meet, must yield and share delight :
To you our Book-club has peculiar charm,
For which you sicken in your quiet farm ;
Here you suppose us at our leisure placed,
Enjoying freedom, and displaying taste ;
With wisdom cheerful, temperately gay,
Pleased to enjoy, and willing to display.

If thus your envy gives your ease its gloom,
Give wings to fancy, and among us come.
We're now assembled ; you may soon attend—
I'll introduce you—' Gentlemen, my friend.'
' Now are you happy ? you have pass'd a night
In gay discourse, and rational delight.'
' Alas ! not so : for how can mortals think,
Or thoughts exchange, if thus they eat and drink ?
No ! I confess, when we had fairly dined,
That was no time for intercourse of mind ;
There was each dish prepared with skill t' invite,
And to detain the struggling appetite ;
On such occasions minds with one consent
Are to the comforts of the body lent ;
There was no pause—the wine went quickly round,
Till struggling Fancy was by Bacchus bound ;
Wine is to wit as water thrown on fire,
By duly sprinkling both are raised the higher ;
Thus largely dealt, the vivid blaze they choke,
And all the genial flame goes off in smoke.'
' But when no more your boards these loads contain,
When wine no more o'erwhelms the labouring brain,
But serves, a gentle stimulus ; we know
How wit must sparkle, and how fancy flow.'
It might be so, but no such club-days come :
We always find these dampers in the room ;
If to converse were all that brought us here,
A few odd members would in turn appear ;
Who dwelling nigh, would saunter in and out,
O'erlook the list, and toss the books about ;
Or yawning read them, walking up and down,
Just as the loungers in the shops in town ;
Till fancying nothing would their minds amuse,
They'd push them by, and go in search of news.
But our attractions are a stronger sort,
The earliest dainties and the oldest port ;
All enter then with glee in every look,
And not a member thinks about a book.
Still let me own, there are some vacant hours,
When minds might work, and men exert their powers :

Ere wine to folly spurs the giddy guest,
But gives to wit its vigour and its zest ;
Then might we reason, might in turn display
Our several talents, and be wisely gay ;
We might—but who a tame discourse regards,
When whist is named, and we behold the
    cards ?
    We from that time are neither grave nor
        gay ;
Our thought, our care, our business is to play :
Fix'd on these spots and figures, each attends
Much to his partners, nothing to his friends.
    Our public cares, the long, the warm debate,
That kept our patriots from their beds so late ;
War, peace, invasion, all we hope or dread,
Vanish like dreams when men forsake their
    bed ;
And groaning nations and contending kings
Are all forgotten for these painted things :
Paper and paste, vile figures and poor spots,
Level all minds, philosophers and sots ;
And give an equal spirit, pause, and force,
Join'd with peculiar diction, to discourse :
' Who deals ?—you led—we're three by cards
    —had you
Honour in hand ? '—' Upon my honour, two.'
Hour after hour, men thus contending sit,
Grave without sense, and pointed without wit.
    Thus it appears these envied clubs possess
No certain means of social happiness ;
Yet there 's a good that flows from scenes like
    these—
Man meets with man at leisure and at ease ;
We to our neighbours and our equals come,
And rub off pride that man contracts at
    home ;
For there, admitted master, he is prone
To claim attention and to talk alone :
But here he meets with neither son nor
    spouse ;
No humble cousin to his bidding bows ;
To his raised voice his neighbours' voices
    rise,
To his high look as lofty look replies ;
When much he speaks, he finds that ears are
    closed,
And certain signs inform him when he 's
    prosed ;
Here all the value of a listener know,
And claim, in turn, the favour they bestow.
    No pleasure gives the speech, when all
        would speak,
And all in vain a civil hearer seek.

To chance alone we owe the free discourse,
In vain you purpose what you cannot force ;
'Tis when the favourite themes unbidden
    spring,
That fancy soars with such unwearied wing ;
Then may you call in aid the moderate glass,
But let it slowly and unprompted pass ;
So shall there all things for the end unite,
And give that hour of rational delight.
    Men to their clubs repair, themselves to
        please,
To care for nothing, and to take their ease ;
In fact, for play, for wine, for news they
    come :
Discourse is shared with friends or found at
    home.

            _____

    But cards with books are incidental things:
We've nights devoted to these queens and
    kings :
Then if we choose the social game, we may ;
Now 'tis a duty, and we're bound to play ;
Nor ever meeting of the social kind
Was more engaging, yet had less of mind.
    Our eager parties, when the lunar light
Throws its full radiance on the festive night,
Of either sex, with punctual hurry come,
And fill, with one accord, an ample room ;
Pleased, the fresh packs on cloth of green they
    see,
And seizing, handle with preluding glee ;
They draw, they sit, they shuffle, cut and
    deal ;
Like friends assembled, but like foes to feel :
But yet not all,—a happier few have joys
Of mere amusement, and their cards are toys ;
No skill nor art, nor fretful hopes have they,
But while their friends are gaming, laugh and
    play.
    Others there are, the veterans of the game,
Who owe their pleasure to their envied fame ;
Through many a year, with hard-contested
    strife,
Have they attain'd this glory of their life :
Such is that ancient burgess, whom in vain
Would gout and fever on his couch detain ;
And that large lady, who resolves to come,
Though a first fit has warn'd her of her
    doom !
These are as oracles : in every cause
They settle doubts, and their decrees are laws;
But all are troubled, when, with dubious look,
Diana questions what Apollo spoke.

Here avarice first, the keen desire of gain,
Rules in each heart, and works in every
    brain ;
Alike the veteran-dames and virgins feel,
Nor care what gray-beards or what striplings
    deal ;
Sex, age, and station, vanish from their view,
And gold, their sov'reign good, the mingled
    crowd pursue.

Hence they are jealous, and as rivals, keep
A watchful eye on the beloved heap ;
Meantime discretion bids the tongue be still,
And mild good-humour strives with strong
    ill-will ;
Till prudence fails ; when, all impatient
    grown,
They make their grief, by their suspicions,
    known.

' Sir, I protest, were Job himself at play,
He'd rave to see you throw your cards away ;
Not that I care a button—not a pin
For what I lose ; but we had cards to win :
A saint in heaven would grieve to see such
    hand
Cut up by one who will not understand.'
' Complain of me ! and so you might indeed,
If I had ventured on that foolish lead,
That fatal heart—but I forgot your play—
Some folk have ever thrown their hearts
    away.'
' Yes, and their diamonds ; I have heard of
    one
Who made a beggar of an only son.'
' Better a beggar, than to see him tied
To art and spite, to insolence and pride.'
' Sir, were I you, I'd strive to be polite,
Against my nature, for a single night.'
' So did you strive, and, madam ! with
    success ;
I knew no being we could censure less ! '
Is this too much ? alas ! my peaceful muse
Cannot with half their virulence abuse.
And hark ! at other tables discord reigns,
With feign'd contempt for losses and for
    gains ;
Passions awhile are bridled ; then they rage,
In waspish youth, and in resentful age ;
With scraps of insult—' Sir, when next you
    play,
Reflect whose money 'tis you throw away
No one on earth can less such things regard,
But when one's partner doesn't know a
    card—— '

' I scorn suspicion, ma'am, but while you
    stand
Behind that lady, pray keep down your
    hand.'
' Good heav'n, revoke ! remember, if the
    set
Be lost, in honour you should pay the debt.'
' There, there 's your money ; but, while
    I have life,
I'll never more sit down with man and wife ;
They snap and snarl indeed, but in the heat
Of all their spleen, their understandings meet;
They are Freemasons, and have many a sign,
That we, poor devils ! never can divine :
May it be told, do ye divide th' amount,
Or goes it all to family account ? '

Next is the club, where to their friends in
    town
Our country neighbours once a month come
    down ;
We term it Free-and-easy, and yet we
Find it no easy matter to be free :
Ev'n in our small assembly, friends among,
Are minds perverse, there 's something will
    be wrong ;
Men are not equal ; some will claim a right
To be the kings and heroes of the night ;
Will their own favourite themes and notions
    start,
And you must hear, offend them, or depart.
There comes Sir Thomas from his village-
    seat,
Happy, he tells us, all his friends to meet ;
He brings the ruin'd brother of his wife,
Whom he supports, and makes him sick of
    life ;
A ready witness whom he can produce
Of all his deeds—a butt for his abuse ;
Soon as he enters, has the guests espied,
Drawn to the fire, and to the glass applied—
' Well, what 's the subject ?—what are you
    about ?
The news, I take it—come, I'll help you
    out ; '—
And then, without one answer, he bestows
Freely upon us all he hears and knows ;
Gives us opinions, tells us how he votes,
Recites the speeches, adds to them his notes,
And gives old ill-told tales for new-born
    anecdotes ;
Yet cares he nothing what we judge or think,
Our only duty 's to attend and drink :

At length, admonish'd by his gout, he ends
The various speech, and leaves at peace his
    friends ;
But now, alas ! we've lost the pleasant hour,
And wisdom flies from wine's superior power.
  Wine, like the rising sun, possession gains,
And drives the mist of dulness from the brains;
The gloomy vapour from the spirit flies,
And views of gaiety and gladness rise :
Still it proceeds ; till from the glowing heat,
The prudent calmly to their shades retreat;—
Then is the mind o'ercast—in wordy rage
And loud contention angry men engage ;
Then spleen and pique, like fire-works thrown
    in spite,
To mischief turn the pleasures of the night ;
Anger abuses, Malice loudly rails,
Revenge awakes, and Anarchy prevails :
Till wine, that raised the tempest, makes it
    cease,
And maudlin Love insists on instant peace ;
He noisy mirth and roaring song commands,
Gives idle toasts, and joins unfriendly hands ;
Till fuddled Friendship vows esteem and
    weeps,
And jovial Folly drinks and sings and sleeps.

  A club there is of Smokers—Dare you come
To that close, clouded, hot, narcotic room ?
When, midnight past, the very candles seem
Dying for air, and give a ghastly gleam ;
When curling fumes in lazy wreaths arise,
And prosing topers rub their winking eyes ;
When the long tale, renew'd when last they
    met,
Is spliced anew, and is unfinish'd yet ;
When but a few are left the house to tire,
And they half-sleeping by the sleepy fire ;
Ev'n the poor ventilating vane, that flew
Of late so fast, is now grown drowsy too ;
When sweet, cold, clammy punch its aid
    bestows,
Then thus the midnight conversation flows :—
' Then, as I said, and—mind me—as I say,
At our last meeting—you remember'—'Ay;'
' Well, very well—then freely as I drink
I spoke my thought—you take me—what I
    think :
And sir, said I, if I a freeman be,
It is my bounden duty to be free.'
  ' Ay, there you posed him : I respect the
    chair,
But man is man, although the man's a mayor:

If Muggins live—no, no !—if Muggins die,
He'll quit his office—neighbour, shall I try ? '
  ' I'll speak my mind, for here are none but
    friends :
They're all contending for their private ends ;
No public spirit—once a vote would bring,
I say a vote—was then a pretty thing ;
It made a man to serve his country and his
    king :
But for that place, that Muggins must resign,
You've my advice—'tis no affair of mine.'

  The poor man has his club ; he comes and
    spends
His hoarded pittance with his chosen friends ;
Nor this alone,—a monthly dole he pays,
To be assisted when his health decays ;
Some part his prudence, from the day's
    supply,
For cares and troubles in his age, lays by ;
The printed rules he guards with painted
    frame,
And shows his children where to read his
    name :
Those simple words his honest nature move,
That bond of union tied by laws of love ;
This is his pride, it gives to his employ
New value, to his home another joy ;
While a religious hope its balm applies
For all his fate inflicts and all his state denies.
  Much would it please you, sometimes to
    explore
The peaceful dwellings of our borough poor ;
To view a sailor just return'd from sea,
His wife beside ; a child on either knee,
And others crowding near, that none may lose
The smallest portion of the welcome news;
What dangers pass'd, ' when seas ran moun-
    tains high,
When tempests raved, and horrors veil'd the
    sky ;
When prudence fail'd, when courage grew
    dismay'd,
When the strong fainted, and the wicked
    pray'd,—
Then in the yawning gulf far down we drove,
And gazed upon the billowy mount above ;
Till up that mountain, swinging with the
    gale,
We view'd the horrors of the watery vale.'
  The trembling children look with stedfast
    eyes,
And panting, sob involuntary sighs :

Soft sleep awhile his torpid touch delays,
And all is joy and piety and praise.

Masons are ours, Freemasons—but, alas !
To their own bards I leave the mystic class ;
In vain shall one, and not a gifted man,
Attempt to sing of this enlighten'd clan :
I know no word, boast no directing sign,
And not one token of the race is mine ;
Whether with Hiram, that wise widow's son,
They came from Tyre to royal Solomon,
Two pillars raising by their skill profound,
Boaz and Jachin through the East renown'd :
Whether the sacred books their rise express,
Or books profane, 'tis vain for me to guess ;
It may be, lost in date remote and high,
They know not what their own antiquity:
It may be too, derived from cause so low,
They have no wish their origin to show :
If, as crusaders, they combined to wrest
From heathen lords the land they long pos-
  sess'd ;
Or were at first some harmless club, who made
Their idle meetings solemn by parade ;
Is but conjecture—for the task unfit,
Awe-struck and mute, the puzzling theme I
  quit :
Yet, if such blessings from their order flow,
We should be glad their moral code to know ;
Trowels of silver are but simple things,
And aprons worthless as their apron-strings ;
But if indeed you have the skill to teach
A social spirit, now beyond our reach ;
If man's warm passions you can guide and
  bind,
And plant the virtues in the wayward mind ;
If you can wake to christian-love the heart,—
In mercy, something of your powers impart.
But as it seems, we Masons must become
To know the secret, and must then be dumb ;
And as we venture for uncertain gains,
Perhaps the profit is not worth the pains.
  When Bruce, that dauntless traveller,
    thought he stood
On Nile's first rise ! the fountain of the flood,
And drank exulting in the sacred spring,
The critics told him it was no such thing ;
That springs unnumber'd round the country
  ran,
But none could show him where they first
  began :
So might we feel, should we our time bestow,
To gain these secrets and these signs to know ;

Might question still if all the truth we found,
And firmly stood upon the certain ground ;
We might our title to the mystery dread,
And fear we drank not at the river-head.

  Griggs and Gregorians here their meetings
    hold,
Convivial sects, and Bucks alert and bold;
A kind of Masons, but without their sign ;
The bonds of union—pleasure, song, and wine :
Man, a gregarious creature, loves to fly
Where he the trackings of the herd can spy ;
Still to be one with many he desires,
Although it leads him through the thorns and
  briers.
  A few ! but few there are, who in the mind
Perpetual source of consolation find ;
The weaker many to the world will come,
For comforts seldom to be found from home.
  When the faint hands no more a brimmer
    hold,
When flannel-wreaths the useless limbs infold,
The breath impeded, and the bosom cold ;
When half the pillow'd man the palsy chains,
And the blood falters in the bloated veins,—
Then, as our friends no further aid supply
Than hope's cold phrase and courtesy's soft
  sigh,
We should that comfort for ourselves ensure,
Which friends could not, if we could friends,
  procure.
  Early in life, when we can laugh aloud,
There 's something pleasant in a social crowd,
Who laugh with us—but will such joy remain,
When we lie struggling on the bed of pain ?
When our physician tells us with a sigh,
No more on hope and science to rely,
Life's staff is useless then ; with labouring
  breath
We pray for hope divine—the staff of death—
This is a scene which few companions grace,
And where the heart's first favourites yield
  their place.
Here all the aid of man to man must end,
Here mounts the soul to her eternal Friend ;
The tenderest love must here its tie resign,
And give th' aspiring heart to love divine.
  Men feel their weakness, and to numbers run,
Themselves to strengthen, or themselves to
  shun ;
But though to this our weakness may be
  prone,
Let 's learn to live, for we must die, alone.

LETTER XI. INNS

ALL the comforts of life in a tavern are known,
'Tis his home who possesses not one of his
own ;
And to him that has rather too much of that
one,
'Tis the house of a friend where he 's welcome
to run :
The instant you enter my door you're my
lord,
With whose taste and whose pleasure I'm
proud to accord ;
And the louder you call and the longer you
stay,
The more I am happy to serve and obey.

To the house of a friend if you're pleased to
retire,
You must all things admit, you must all things
admire ;
You must pay with observance the price of
your treat,
You must eat what is praised, and must praise
what you eat :
But here you may come, and no tax we require,
You may loudly condemn what you greatly
admire ;
You may growl at our wishes and pains to
excel,
And may snarl at the rascals who please you
so well.

At your wish we attend, and confess that your
speech
On the nation's affairs might the minister
teach ;
His views you may blame, and his measures
oppose,
There 's no tavern-treason—you're under the
Rose :
Should rebellions arise in your own little
state,
With me you may safely their consequence
wait ;
To recruit your lost spirits 'tis prudent to come
And to fly to a friend when the devil 's at home.

That I've faults is confess'd ; but it won't be
denied,
'Tis my interest the faults of my neighbours
to hide ;
If I've sometimes lent Scandal occasion to
prate,
I've often conceal'd what she'd love to relate ;
If to Justice's bar some have wander'd from
mine,
'Twas because the dull rogues wouldn't stay
by their wine ;

And for brawls at my house, well the poet
explains,
That men drink *shallow draughts,* and so
madden their brains.

A difficult Subject for Poetry—Invocation of
the Muse—Description of the principal Inn
and those of the first Class—The large
deserted Tavern—Those of a second Order
—Their Company—One of particular De-
scription—A lower Kind of Public-Houses :
yet distinguished among themselves—
Houses on the Quays for Sailors—The
Green-Man : its Landlord, and the Ad-
venture of his Marriage, &c.

MUCH do I need, and therefore will I ask,
A Muse to aid me in my present task ;
For then with special cause we beg for aid,
When of our subject we are most afraid:
Inns are this subject—'tis an ill-drawn lot,
So, thou who gravely triflest, fail me not.
Fail not, but haste, and to my memory bring
Scenes yet unsung, which few would choose
to sing :
Thou mad'st a Shilling splendid ; thou hast
thrown
On humble themes the graces all thine own;
By thee the Mistress of a village-school
Became a queen, enthroned upon her stool ;
And far beyond the rest thou gav'st to shine
Belinda's Lock—that deathless work was
thine.
Come, lend thy cheerful light, and give to
please,
These seats of revelry, these scenes of ease ;
Who sings of Inns much danger has to dread,
And needs assistance from the fountain-head.
High in the street, o'erlooking all the place,
The rampant Lion shows his kingly face ;
His ample jaws extend from side to side,
His eyes are glaring, and his nostrils wide ;
In silver shag the sovereign form is dress'd,
A mane horrific sweeps his ample chest ;
Elate with pride, he seems t' assert his reign,
And stands the glory of his wide domain.
Yet nothing dreadful to his friends the sight,
But sign and pledge of welcome and delight :
To him the noblest guest the town detains
Flies for repast, and in his court remains ;
Him too the crowd with longing looks admire,
Sighs for his joys, and modestly retire ;

Here not a comfort shall to them be lost
Who never ask or never feel the cost.
   The ample yards on either side contain
Buildings where order and distinction reign ;
The splendid carriage of the wealthier guest,
The ready chaise and driver smartly dress'd ;
Whiskeys and gigs and curricles are there,
And high-fed prancers many a raw-boned pair.
On all without a lordly host sustains
The care of empire, and observant reigns ;
The parting guest beholds him at his side,
With pomp obsequious, bending in his pride ;
Round all the place his eyes all objects meet,
Attentive, silent, civil, and discreet.
O'er all within the lady-hostess rules,
Her bar she governs, and her kitchen schools ;
To every guest th' appropriate speech is made,
And every duty with distinction paid ;
Respectful, easy, pleasant, or polite—
' Your honour's servant—Mister Smith, good-
   night.'
   Next, but not near, yet honour'd through
   the town,
There swing, incongruous pair ! the Bear and
   Crown ;
That Crown suspended gems and ribands deck,
A golden chain hangs o'er that furry neck :
Unlike the nobler beast, the Bear is bound,
And with the Crown so near him, scowls un-
   crown'd ;
Less his dominion, but alert are all
Without, within, and ready for the call ;
Smart lads and light run nimbly here and there,
Nor for neglected duties mourns the Bear.
   To his retreats, on the election-day,
The losing party found their silent way ;
There they partook of each consoling good,
Like him uncrown'd, like him in sullen mood—
Threat'ning, but bound.—Here meet a social
   kind,
Our various clubs for various cause combined ;
Nor has he pride, but thankful takes as gain
The dew-drops shaken from the Lion's mane :
A thriving couple here their skill display,
And share the profits of no vulgar sway.
   Third in our Borough's list appears the sign
Of a fair queen—the gracious Caroline ;
But in decay—each feature in the face
Has stain of Time, and token of disgrace.
The storm of winter, and the summer-sun,
Have on that form their equal mischief done ;
The features now are all disfigured seen,
And not one charm adorns th' insulted queen :

To this poor face was never paint applied,
Th' unseemly work of cruel Time to hide ;
Here we may rightly such neglect upbraid,
Paint on such faces is by prudence laid.
Large the domain, but all within combine
To correspond with the dishonour'd sign ;
And all around dilapidates ; you call—
But none replies—they're inattentive all :
At length a ruin'd stable holds your steed.
While you through large and dirty rooms
   proceed,
Spacious and cold ; a proof they once had been
In honour—now magnificently mean ;
Till in some small half-furnish'd room you rest,
Whose dying fire denotes it had a guest.
In those you pass'd where former splendour
   reign'd,
You saw the carpets torn, the paper stain'd ;
Squares of discordant glass in windows fix'd,
And paper oil'd in many a space betwixt ;
A soil'd and broken sconce, a mirror crack'd,
With table underpropp'd, and chairs new-
   back'd ;
A marble side-slab with ten thousand stains,
And all an ancient tavern's poor remains.
   With much entreaty, they your food pre-
   pare,
And acid wine afford, with meagre fare ;
Heartless you sup ; and when a dozen times
You've read the fractured window's senseless
   rhymes ;
Have been assured that Phœbe Green was
   fair,
And Peter Jackson took his supper there ;
You reach a chilling chamber, where you
   dread
Damps, hot or cold, from a tremendous bed ;
Late comes your sleep, and you are waken'd
   soon
By rustling tatters of the old festoon.
   O'er this large building, thus by time de-
   faced,
A servile couple has its owner placed,
Who not unmindful that its style is large,
To lost magnificence adapt their charge :
Thus an old beauty, who has long declined,
Keeps former dues and dignity in mind ;
And wills that all attention should be paid
For graces vanish'd and for charms decay'd.
   Few years have pass'd, since brightly 'cross
   the way,
Lights from each window shot the lengthen'd
   ray,

And busy looks in every face were seen,
Through the warm precincts of the reigning
   Queen :
There fires inviting blazed, and all around
Was heard the tinkling bells' seducing sound ;
The nimble waiters to that sound from far
Sprang to the call, then hasten'd to the bar ;
Where a glad priestess of the temple sway'd,
The most obedient, and the most obey'd ;
Rosy and round, adorn'd in crimson vest,
And flaming ribands at her ample breast :
She, skill'd like Circe, tried her guests to
   move,
With looks of welcome and with words of love ;
And such her potent charms, that men unwise
Were soon transform'd and fitted for the sties.
   Her port in bottles stood, a well-stain'd
   row,
Drawn for the evening from the pipe below ;
Three powerful spirits fill'd a parted case,
Some cordial-bottles stood in secret place ;
Fair acid fruits in nets above were seen,
Her plate was splendid, and her glasses clean ;
Basins and bowls were ready on the stand,
And measures clatter'd in her powerful hand.
   Inferior houses now our notice claim,
But who shall deal them their appropriate
   fame ?
Who shall the nice, yet known distinction,
   tell,
Between the peal complete and single bell ?
   Determine, ye, who on your shining nags
Wear oil-skin beavers and bear seal-skin bags;
Or ye, grave topers, who with coy delight
Snugly enjoy the sweetness of the night ;
Ye travellers all, superior inns denied
By moderate purse, the low by decent pride ;
Come and determine,—will ye take your place
At the *full* orb, or *half* the lunar face ?
With the Black-Boy or Angel will ye dine ?
Will ye approve the Fountain or the Vine ?
Horses the *white* or *black* will ye prefer ?
The Silver-Swan, or swan opposed to her—
Rare bird ! whose form the raven-plumage
   decks,
And graceful curve her three alluring necks ?
   All these a decent entertainment give,
And by their comforts comfortably live.
   Shall I pass by the Boar ?—there are who
   cry,
' Beware the Boar,' and pass determined by :
Those dreadful tusks, those little peering eyes
And churning chaps, are tokens to the wise.

There dwells a kind old aunt, and there you
   see
Some kind young nieces in her company ;
Poor village nieces, whom the tender dame
Invites to town, and gives their beauty fame ;
The grateful sisters feel th' important aid,
And the good aunt is flatter'd and repaid.
   What though it may some cool observers
   strike,
That such fair sisters should be so unlike ;
That still another and another comes,
And at the matron's table smiles and blooms ;
That all appear as if they meant to stay
Time undefined, nor name a parting day ;
And yet, though all are valued, all are dear,
Causeless, they go, and seldom more appear :
Yet let Suspicion hide her odious head,
And Scandal vengeance from a burgess dread :
A pious friend, who with the ancient dame
At sober cribbage takes an evening game ;
His cup beside him, through their play he
   quaffs,
And oft renews, and innocently laughs ;
Or growing serious, to the text resorts,
And from the Sunday-sermon makes reports ;
While all, with grateful glee, his wish attend,
A grave protector and a powerful friend :
But Slander says, who indistinctly sees,
Once he was caught with Silvia on his knees;—
A cautious burgess with a careful wife
To be so caught !—'tis false, upon my life.
   Next are a lower kind, yet not so low
But they, among them, their distinctions
   know ;
And when a thriving landlord aims so high
As to exchange the Chequer for the Pye,
Or from Duke William to the Dog repairs,
He takes a finer coat and fiercer airs.
   Pleased with his power, the poor man loves
   to say
What favourite inn shall share his evening's
   pay ;
Where he shall sit the social hour, and
   lose
His past day's labours and his next day's
   views.
Our seamen too have choice : one takes a
   trip
In the warm cabin of his favourite ship ;
And on the morrow in the humbler boat
He rows, till fancy feels herself afloat ;
Can he the sign—Three Jolly Sailors—pass,
Who hears a fiddle and who sees a lass ?

The Anchor too affords the seaman joys,
In small smoked room, all clamour, crowd,
    and noise ;
Where a curved settle half surrounds the fire,
Where fifty voices put l and punch require :
They come for pleasure in their leisure hour,
And they enjoy it to their utmost power ;
Standing they drink, they swearing smoke,
    while all
Call or make ready for a second call :
There is no time for trifling—' Do ye see ?
We drink and drub the French extempore.'
    See ! round the room, on every beam and
    balk,
Are mingled scrolls of hieroglyphic chalk ;
Yet nothing heeded—would one stroke suffice
To blot out all, here honour is too nice,—
' Let knavish landsmen think such dirty
    things,
We're British tars, and British tars are kings.'
    But the Green-Man shall I pass by unsung,
Which mine own James upon his sign-post
    hung ?
His sign, his image,—for he once was seen
A squire's attendant, clad in keeper's green ;
Ere yet with wages more, and honour less,
He stood behind me in a graver dress.
    James in an evil hour went forth to woo
Young Juliet Hart, and was her Romeo :
They'd seen the play, and thought it vastly
    sweet
For two young lovers by the moon to meet ;
The nymph was gentle, of her favours free,
Ev'n at a word—no Rosalind was she ;
Nor, like that other Juliet, tried his truth
With—' Be thy purpose marriage, gentle
    youth ? '
But him received, and heard his tender tale
When sang the lark, and when the nightingale :
So in few months the generous lass was seen
I' the way that all the Capulets had been.
    Then first repentance seized the amorous
    man,
And—shame on love—he reason'd and he ran ;
The thoughtful Romeo trembled for his purse,
And the sad sounds, ' for better and for worse.'
    Yet could the lover not so far withdraw,
But he was haunted both by love and law :
Now law dismay'd him as he view'd its fangs,
Now pity seized him for his Juliet's pangs ;
Then thoughts of justice and some dread of jail,
Where all would blame him and where none
    might bail ;

These drew him back, till Juliet's hut ap-
    pear'd,
Where love had drawn him when he should
    have fear'd.
There sat the father in his wicker throne,
Uttering his curses in tremendous tone :
With foulest names his daughter he reviled,
And look'd a very Herod at the child :
Nor was she patient, but with equal scorn,
Bade him remember when his Joe was born :
Then rose the mother, eager to begin
Her plea for frailty, when the swain came in.
    To him she turn'd, and other theme began,
Show'd him his boy, and bade him be a man ;
' An honest man, who, when he breaks the
    laws,
Will make a woman honest if there 's cause.'
With lengthen'd speech she proved what
    came to pass
Was no reflection on a loving lass :
' If she your love as wife and mother claim,
What can it matter which was first the name ?
But 'tis most base, 'tis perjury and theft,
When a lost girl is like a widow left ;
The rogue who ruins '—here the father found
His spouse was treading on forbidden ground.
    ' That 's not the point,' quoth he,—' I don't
    suppose
My good friend Fletcher to be one of those ;
What 's done amiss he'll mend in proper
    time—
I hate to hear of villany and crime :
'Twas my misfortune, in the days of youth,
To find two lasses pleading for my truth ;
The case was hard, I would with all my soul
Have wedded both, but law is our control ;
So one I took, and when we gain'd a home,
Her friend agreed—what could she more ?—
    to come ;
And when she found that I'd a widow'd bed,
Me she desired—what could I less ?—to wed.
An easier case is yours : you've not the smart
That two fond pleaders cause in one man's
    heart ;
You've not to wait from year to year dis-
    tress'd,
Before your conscience can be laid at rest ;
There smiles your bride, there sprawls your
    new-born son,
—A ring, a licence, and the thing is done.'
    ' My loving James,'—the lass began her
    plea,
' I'll make thy reason take a part with me :

Had I been froward, skittish, or unkind,
Or to thy person or thy passion blind ;
Had I refused, when 'twas thy part to pray,
Or put thee off with promise and delay ;
Thou might'st in justice and in conscience fly,
Denying her who taught thee to deny :
But, James, with me thou hadst an easier task,
Bonds and conditions I forbore to ask ;
I laid no traps for thee, no plots or plans,
Nor marriage named by licence or by banns ;
Nor would I now the parson's aid employ,
But for this cause,'—and up she held her boy.
Motives like these could heart of flesh resist?
James took the infant and in triumph kiss'd;

Then to his mother's arms the child re-
    stored,
Made his proud speech, and pledged his
    worthy word.
' Three times at church our banns shall
    publish'd be,
Thy health be drunk in bumpers three times
    three ;
And thou shalt grace (bedeck'd in garments
    gay)
The christening-dinner on the wedding day.'
    James at my door then made his parting
    bow,
Took the Green-Man, and is a master now.

LETTER XII.   PLAYERS

These are monarchs none respect,
    Heroes, yet an humbled crew,
Nobles, whom the crowd correct,
    Wealthy men, whom duns pursue ;
Beauties, shrinking from the view
    Of the day's detecting eye ;
Lovers, who with much ado
Long-forsaken damsels woo,
    And heave the ill-feign'd sigh.

These are misers, craving means
    Of existence through the day,
Famous scholars, conning scenes
    Of dull bewildering play ;
Ragged beaux and misses grey,
    Whom the rabble praise and blame ;
Proud and mean, and sad and gay, .
Toiling after ease, are they,
    Infamous *, and boasting fame.

Players arrive in the Borough—Welcomed by
their former Friends—Are better fitted for
Comic than Tragic Scenes : yet better
approved in the latter by one Part of their
Audience—Their general Character and
Pleasantry—Particular Distresses and
Labours—Their Fortitude and Patience—
A private Rehearsal—The Vanity of the
aged Actress—A Heroine from the Milliner's
Shop—A deluded Tradesman—Of what Per-
sons the Company is composed—Character
and Adventures of Frederick Thompson.

DRAWN by the annual call, we now behold
Our troop dramatic, heroes known of old,
And those, since last they march'd, inlisted
    and enroll'd :

* Strolling players are thus held in a legal
sense.

Mounted on hacks or borne in waggons some,
The rest on foot (the humbler brethren) come.
Three favour'd places, an unequal time,
Join to support this company sublime :
Ours for the longer period—see how light
Yon parties move, their former friends in sight,
Whose claims are all allow'd, and friendship
    glads the night.
Now public rooms shall sound with words
    divine,
And private lodgings hear how heroes shine ;
No talk of pay shall yet on pleasure steal,
But kindest welcome bless the friendly meal ;
While o'er the social jug and decent cheer,
Shall be described the fortunes of the year.
    Peruse these bills, and see what each can
        · do,—
Behold ! the prince, the slave, the monk, the
    Jew ;
Change but the garment, and they'll all engage
To take each part, and act in every age :
Cull'd from all houses, what a house are they !
Swept from all barns, our borough-critics say;
But with some portion of a critic's ire,
We all endure them ; there are some admire :
They might have praise, confined to farce
    alone ;
Full well they grin, they should not try to
    groan ;
But then our servants' and our seamen's wives
Love all that rant and rapture as their lives ;
He who 'Squire Richard's part could well
    sustain,
Finds as King Richard he must roar amain—

' My horse ! my horse ! '—Lo ! now to their
abodes,
Come lords and lovers, empresses and gods.
The master-mover of these scenes has made
No trifling gain in this adventurous trade ;
Trade we may term it, for he duly buys
Arms out of use and undirected eyes ;
These he instructs, and guides them as he can,
And vends each night the manufactured man :
Long as our custom lasts, they gladly stay,
Then strike their tents, like Tartars ! and
away !
The place grows bare where they too long
remain,
But grass will rise ere they return again.
   Children of Thespis, welcome ! knights and
queens !
Counts ! barons ! beauties ! when before
your scenes,
And mighty monarchs thund'ring from your
throne ;
Then step behind, and all your glory 's gone :
Of crown and palace, throne and guards
bereft,
The pomp is vanish'd, and the care is left.
Yet strong and lively is the joy they feel,
When the full house secures the plenteous
meal ;
Flatt'ring and flatter'd, each attempts to raise
A brother's merits for a brother's praise :
For never hero shows a prouder heart,
Than he who proudly acts a hero's part ;
Nor without cause ; the boards, we know,
can yield
Place for fierce contest, like the tented field.
   Graceful to tread the stage, to be in turn
The prince we honour, and the knave we
spurn ;
Bravely to bear the tumult of the crowd,
The hiss tremendous, and the censure loud :
These are their parts,—and he who these
sustains
Deserves some praise and profit for his pains.
Heroes at least of gentler kind are they,
Against whose swords no weeping widows
pray,
No blood their fury sheds, nor havoc marks
their way.
   Sad happy race ! soon raised and soon
depress'd,
Your days all pass'd in jeopardy and jest ;
Poor without prudence, with afflictions vain,
Not warn'd by misery, not enrich'd by gain ;

Whom justice pitying, chides from place to
place,
A wandering, careless, wretched, merry race,
Who cheerful looks assume, and play the parts
Of happy rovers with repining hearts ;
Then cast off care, and in the mimic pain
Of tragic wo, feel spirits light and vain,
Distress and hope—the mind's, the body's
wear,
The man's affliction, and the actor's tear :
Alternate times of fasting and excess
Are yours, ye smiling children of distress.
   Slaves though ye be, your wandering free-
dom seems,
And with your varying views and restless
schemes,
Your griefs are transient, as your joys are
dreams.
    Yet keen those griefs—ah ! what avail thy
charms,
Fair Juliet ! what that infant in thine arms ;
What those heroic lines thy patience learns,
What all the aid thy present Romeo earns,
Whilst thou art crowded in that lumbering
wain,
With all thy plaintive sisters to complain ?
   Nor is there lack of labour—To rehearse,
Day after day, poor scraps of prose and verse;
To bear each other's spirit, pride, and spite ;
To hide in rant the heart-ache of the night ;
To dress in gaudy patch-work, and to force
The mind to think on the appointed course ;—
This is laborious, and may be defined
The bootless labour of the thriftless mind.
   There is a veteran dame ; I see her stand
Intent and pensive with her book in hand ;
Awhile her thoughts she forces on her part,
Then dwells on objects nearer to the heart ;
Across the room she paces, gets her tone,
And fits her features for the Danish throne ;
To-night a queen—I mark her motion slow,
I hear her speech, and Hamlet's mother know.
   Methinks 'tis pitiful to see her try
For strength of arms and energy of eye ;
With vigour lost, and spirits worn away,
Her pomp and pride she labours to display;
And when awhile she 's tried her part to act,
To find her thoughts arrested by some fact ;
When struggles more and more severe are
seen
In the plain actress than the Danish queen,—
At length she feels her part, she finds delight,
And fancies all the plaudits of the night :

Old as she is, she smiles at every speech,
And thinks no youthful part beyond her reach;
But as the mist of vanity again
Is blown away, by press of present pain,
Sad and in doubt she to her purse applies
For cause of comfort, where no comfort lies;
Then to her task she sighing turns again,—
' Oh ! Hamlet, thou hast cleft my heart in
     twain ! '
    And who that poor, consumptive, wither'd
     thing,
Who strains her slender throat and strives to
     sing ?
Panting for breath, and forced her voice to
     drop,
And far unlike the inmate of the shop,
Where she, in youth and health, alert and gay,
Laugh'd off at night the labours of the day ;
With novels, verses, fancy's fertile powers,
And sister-converse pass'd the evening-hours;
But Cynthia's soul was soft, her wishes strong,
Her judgment weak, and her conclusions
     wrong :
The morning-call and counter were her dread,
And her contempt the needle and the thread :
But when she read a gentle damsel's part,
Her wo, her wish !—she had them all by heart.
    At length the hero of the boards drew nigh,
Who spake of love till sigh re-echo'd sigh ;
He told in honey'd words his deathless flame,
And she his own by tender vows became ;
Nor ring nor licence needed souls so fond,
Alphonso's passion was his Cynthia's bond :
And thus the simple girl, to shame betray'd,
Sinks to the grave forsaken and dismay'd.
    Sick without pity, sorrowing without hope,
See her ! the grief and scandal of the troop ;
A wretched martyr to a childish pride,
Her wo insulted, and her praise denied :
Her humble talents, though derided, used,
Her prospects lost, her confidence abused ;
All that remains—for she not long can brave
Increase of evils—is an early grave.
    Ye gentle Cynthias of the shop, take heed
What dreams ye cherish and what books ye
     read.
    A decent sum had Peter Nottage made,
By joining bricks—to him a thriving trade :
Of his employment master and his wife,
This humble tradesman led a lordly life ;
The house of kings and heroes lack'd repairs,
And Peter, though reluctant, served the
     players :

Connected thus, he heard in way polite,—
' Come, Master Nottage, see us play to-night.'
At first 'twas folly, nonsense, idle stuff,
But seen for nothing it grew well enough ;
And better now—now best, and every night,
In this fool's paradise he drank delight ;
And as he felt the bliss, he wish'd to know
Whence all this rapture and these joys could
     flow ;
For if the seeing could such pleasure bring,
What must the feeling ?—feeling like a king ?
    In vain his wife, his uncle, and his friend,
Cried—' Peter ! Peter ! let such follies end ;
'Tis well enough these vagabonds to see,
But would you partner with a showman be ? '
    ' Showman ! ' said Peter, ' did not Quin
     and Clive,
And Roscius-Garrick, by the science thrive ?
Showman !—'tis scandal ; I'm by genius led
To join a class who've Shakspeare at their
     head.'
    Poor Peter thus by easy steps became
A dreaming candidate for scenic fame,
And, after years consumed, infirm and poor,
He sits and takes the tickets at the door.
    Of various men these marching troops are
     made,—
Pen-spurning clerks, and lads contemning
     trade ;
Waiters and servants by confinement teased,
And youths of wealth by dissipation eased;
With feeling nymphs, who, such resource at
     hand,
Scorn to obey the rigour of command ;
Some, who from higher views by vice are won,
And some of either sex by love undone ;
The greater part lamenting as their fall,
What some an honour and advancement call.
    There are who names in shame or fear
     assume,
And hence our Bevilles and our Savilles come;
It honours him, from tailor's board kick'd
     down,
As Mister Dormer to amuse the town ;
Falling, he rises : but a kind there are
Who dwell on former prospects, and despair;
Justly but vainly they their fate deplore,
And mourn their fall who fell to rise no more.
    Our merchant Thompson, with his sons
     around,
Most mind and talent in his Frederick found :
He was so lively, that his mother knew,
If he were taught, that honour must ensue ;

The father's views were in a different line,
But if at college he were sure to shine,
Then should he go—to prosper who could
   doubt ?
When school-boy stigmas would be all wash'd
   out ;
For there were marks upon his youthful face,
'Twixt vice and error—a neglected case—
These would submit to skill ; a little time,
And none could trace the error or the crime;
Then let him go, and once at college, he
Might choose his station—what would
   Frederick be ?
   'Twas soon determined—He could not
      descend
To pedant-laws and lectures without end ;
And then the chapel—night and morn to pray,
Or mulct and threaten'd if he kept away ;
No ! not to be a bishop—so he swore,
And at his college he was seen no more.
   His debts all paid, the father, with a sigh,
Placed him in office—' Do, my Frederick, try;
Confine thyself a few short months, and
   then—— '
He tried a fortnight, and threw down the pen.
   Again demands were hush'd : ' My son,
      you're free,
But you're unsettled ; take your chance at
   sea : '
So in few days the midshipman equipp'd,
Received the mother's blessing and was
   shipp'd.
   Hard was her fortune ; soon compell'd to
      meet
The wretched stripling staggering through the
   street ;
For, rash, impetuous, insolent and vain,
The captain sent him to his friends again :
About the borough roved th' unhappy boy,
And ate the bread of every chance-employ ;
Of friends he borrow'd, and the parents yet
In secret fondness authorised the debt ;
The younger sister, still a child, was taught
To give with feign'd affright the pittance
   sought ;
For now the father cried—' It is too late
For trial more—I leave him to his fate,'—
Yet left him not ; and with a kind of joy
The mother heard of her desponding boy :
At length he sicken'd, and he found, when sick,
All aid was ready, all attendance quick ;
A fever seized him, and at once was lost
The thought of trespass, error, crime and cost;

Th' indulgent parents knelt beside the youth,
They heard his promise and believed his truth;
And when the danger lessen'd on their view,
They cast off doubt, and hope assurance
   grew ;—
Nursed by his sisters, cherish'd by his sire,
Begg'd to be glad, encouraged to aspire,
His life, they said, would now all care repay,
And he might date his prospects from that
   day ;
A son, a brother to his home received,
They hoped for all things, and in all believed.
   And now will pardon, comfort, kindness,
      draw
The youth from vice? will honour, duty, law?
Alas ! not all : the more the trials lent,
The less he seem'd to ponder and repent ;
Headstrong, determined in his own career,
He thought reproof unjust and truth severe ;
The soul's disease was to its crisis come,
He first abused and then abjured his home ;
And when he chose a vagabond to be,
He made his shame his glory—' I'll be free.'
   Friends, parents, relatives, hope, reason,
      love,
With anxious ardour for that empire strove ;
In vain their strife, in vain the means applied,
They had no comfort, but that all were tried;
One strong vain trial made, the mind to move,
Was the last effort of parental love.
   Ev'n then he watch'd his father from his
      home,
And to his mother would for pity come,
Where, as he made her tender terrors rise,
He talk'd of death, and threaten'd for supplies.
   Against a youth so vicious and undone,
All hearts were closed, and every door but one:
The players received him, they with open
   heart
Gave him his portion and assign'd his part ;
And ere three days were added to his life,
He found a home, a duty, and a wife.
   His present friends, though they were
      nothing nice,
Nor ask'd how vicious he, or what his vice,
Still they expected he should now attend
To the joint duty as an useful friend ;
The leader too declared, with frown severe,
That none should pawn a robe that kings
   might wear ;
And much it moved him, when he Hamlet
   play'd,
To see his Father's Ghost so drunken made :

Then too the temper, the unbending pride
Of this ally would no reproof abide :—
So leaving these, he march'd away and join'd
Another troop, and other goods purloin'd ;
And other characters, both gay and sage,
Sober and sad, made stagger on the stage ;
Then to rebuke, with arrogant disdain,
He gave abuse and sought a home again.

  Thus changing scenes, but with unchanging
    vice,
Engaged by many, but with no one twice :
Of this, a last and poor resource, bereft,
He to himself, unhappy guide : was left—
And who shall say where guided ? to what
    seats
Of starving villany ? of thieves and cheats ?

  In that sad time of many a dismal scene
Had he a witness (not inactive) been ;
Had leagued with petty pilferers, and had crept
Where of each sex degraded numbers slept :
With such associates he was long allied,
Where his capacity for ill was tried,
And that once lost, the wretch was cast aside :
For now, though willing with the worst to act,
He wanted powers for an important fact ;
And while he felt as lawless spirits feel,
His hand was palsied, and he couldn't steal.

  By these rejected, is there lot so strange,
So low ! that he could suffer by the change ?
Yes ! the new station as a fall we judge,—
He now became the harlots' humble drudge,
Their drudge in common : they combined to
    save
Awhile from starving their submissive slave ;
For now his spirit left him, and his pride,
His scorn, his rancour, and resentment died ;
Few were his feelings—but the keenest these,
The rage of hunger, and the sigh for ease ;
He who abused indulgence, now became
By want subservient and by misery tame ;
A slave, he begg'd forbearance ; bent with
    pain,
He shunn'd the blow,—'Ah ! strike me not
    again.'

  Thus was he found : the master of a hoy
Saw the sad wretch, whom he had known a
    boy ;
At first in doubt, but Frederick laid aside
All shame, and humbly for his aid applied :

He, tamed and smitten with the storms gone
    by,
Look'd for compassion through one living eye,
And stretch'd th' unpalsied hand : the sea-
    man felt
His honest heart with gentle pity melt,
And his small boon with cheerful frankness
    dealt ;
Then made inquiries of th' unhappy youth,
Who told, nor shame forbade him, all the
    truth.

  ' Young Frederick Thompson to a chand-
    ler's shop
By harlots order'd and afraid to stop !—
What ! our good merchant's favourite to be
    seen
In state so loathsome and in dress so mean?'—
  So thought the seaman as he bade adieu,
And, when in port, related all he knew.

  But time was lost, inquiry came too late,
Those whom he served knew nothing of his
    fate ;
No ! they had seized on what the sailor gave,
Nor bore resistance from their abject slave ;
The spoil obtain'd, they cast him from the
    door,
Robb'd, beaten, hungry, pain'd, diseased and
    poor.

  Then nature (pointing to the only spot
Which still had comfort for so dire a lot,)
Although so feeble, led him on the way,
And hope look'd forward to a happier day :
He thought, poor prodigal ! a father yet
His woes would pity and his crimes forget ;
Nor had he brother who with speech severe
Would check the pity or refrain the tear :
A lighter spirit in his bosom rose,
As near the road he sought an hour's repose.

  And there he found it: he had left the
    town,
But buildings yet were scatter'd up and down;
To one of these, half-ruin'd and half-built,
Was traced this child of wretchedness and
    guilt ;
There on the remnant of a beggar's vest,
Thrown by in scorn ! the sufferer sought for
    rest ;
There was this scene of vice and wo to close,
And there the wretched body found repose.

LETTER XIII.   THE ALMS-HOUSE AND TRUSTEES

Do good by stealth, and blush to find it fame.
    POPE, *Epilogue to Satires*, line 136.

There are a sort of men whose visages
Do cream and mantle like a standing pond,
And do a wilful stillness entertain,
With purpose to be dress'd in an opinion ;
          .   .   .   .
As who should say, ' I am Sir Oracle,
And when I ope my lips let no dog bark.'
                  Merchant of Venice, Act i, Sc. 1.

Sum felix ; quis enim neget ? felixque
    manebo ;
Hoc quoque quis dubitet ?   Tutum me copia
    fecit.

The frugal Merchant—Rivalship in Modes
of Frugality—Private Exceptions to the
general Manners—Alms-House built—Its
Description—Founder dies—Six Trustees
—Sir Denys Brand, a Principal—His
Eulogium in the Chronicles of the Day—
Truth reckoned invidious on these Occa-
sions—An Explanation of the Magnanimity
and Wisdom of Sir Denys—His Kinds of
Moderation and Humility—Laughton, his
Successor, a planning, ambitious, wealthy
Man—Advancement in Life his perpetual
Object, and all Things made the Means of
it—His Idea of Falsehood—His Resent-
ment dangerous : how removed—Success
produces Love of Flattery : his daily
Gratification—His Merits and Acts of
Kindness—His proper Choice of Alms-Men
—In this Respect meritorious—His Pre-
decessor not so cautious.

LEAVE now our streets, and in yon plain
    behold
Those pleasant seats for the reduced and old ;
A merchant's gift, whose wife and children
    died,
When he to saving all his powers applied ;
He wore his coat till bare was every thread,
And with the meanest fare his body fed.
He had a female cousin, who with care
Walk'd in his steps and learn'd of him to spare;
With emulation and success they strove,
Improving still, still seeking to improve,
As if that useful knowledge they would gain—
How little food would human life sustain :
No pauper came their table's crums to crave;
Scraping they lived, but not a scrap they gave :

When beggars saw the frugal merchant pass,
It moved their pity, and they said, ' Alas !
Hard is thy fate, my brother,' and they felt
A beggar's pride as they that pity dealt :
The dogs, who learn of man to scorn the poor,
Bark'd him away from ev'ry decent door ;
While they who saw him bare, but thought
    him rich,
To show respect or scorn, they knew not
    which.
  But while our merchant seem'd so base
    and mean,
He had his wanderings, sometimes, ' not
    unseen ; '
To give in secret was a favourite act,
Yet more than once they took him in the fact:
To scenes of various wo he nightly went,
And serious sums in healing misery spent ;
Oft has he cheer'd the wretched, at a rate
For which he daily might have dined on plate;
He has been seen—his hair all silver-white,
Shaking and shining—as he stole by night,
To feed unenvied on his still delight.
A two-fold taste he had ; to give and spare,
Both were his duties, and had equal care ;
It was his joy, to sit alone and fast,
Then send a widow and her boys repast :
Tears in his eyes would, spite of him, appear,
But he from other eyes has kept the tear :
All in a wint'ry night from far he came,
To soothe the sorrows of a suff'ring dame ;
Whose husband robb'd him, and to whom he
    meant
A ling'ring, but reforming punishment :
Home then he walk'd, and found his anger rise,
When fire and rush-light met his troubled
    eyes ;
But these extinguish'd, and his prayer ad-
    dress'd
To Heaven in hope, he calmly sank to rest.
  His seventieth year was pass'd, and then
    was seen
A building rising on the northern green ;
There was no blinding all his neighbours' eyes,
Or surely no one would have seen it rise :
Twelve rooms contiguous stood, and six were
    near,
There men were placed, and sober matrons
    here ;

CR.   G

There were behind small useful gardens made,
Benches before, and trees to give them shade;
In the first room were seen, above, below,
Some marks of taste, a few attempts at show;
The founder's picture and his arms were there,
(Not till he left us,) and an elbow'd chair ;
There, 'mid these signs of his superior place,
Sat the mild ruler of this humble race.

Within the row are men who strove in vain,
Through years of trouble, wealth and ease
        to gain ;
Less must they have than an appointed sum,
And freemen been, or hither must not come ;
They should be decent and command respect,
(Though needing fortune,) whom these doors
        protect,
And should for thirty dismal years have tried
For peace unfelt and competence denied.
    Strange ! that o'er men thus train'd in
        sorrow's school,
Power must be held, and they must live by
        rule ;
Infirm, corrected by misfortunes, old,
Their habits settled and their passions cold ;
Of health, wealth, power, and worldly cares,
        bereft,
Still must they not at liberty be left ;
There must be one to rule them, to restrain
And guide the movements of his erring train.
    If then control imperious, check severe,
Be needed where such reverend men appear ;
To what would youth, without such checks,
        aspire,
Free the wild wish, uncurb'd the strong desire?
And where (in college or in camp) they found
The heart ungovern'd and the hand unbound?
    His house endow'd, the generous man
        resign'd
All power to rule, nay power of choice declined;
He and the female saint survived to view
Their work complete, and bade the world
        adieu !
    Six are the guardians of this happy seat,
And one presides when they on business meet;
As each expires, the five a brother choose;
Nor would Sir Denys Brand the charge refuse;
True, 'twas beneath him, ' but to do men good
Was motive never by his heart withstood :'
He too is gone, and they again must strive
To find a man in whom his gifts survive.
    Now, in the various records of the dead,
Thy worth, Sir Denys, shall be weigh'd and
        read ;

There we the glory of thy house shall trace,
With each alliance of thy noble race.
    Yes ! here we have him !—' Came in
        William's reign,
The Norman-Brand ; the blood without a
        stain ;
From the fierce Dane and ruder Saxon clear,
Pict, Irish, Scot, or Cambrian mountaineer ;
But the pure Norman was the sacred spring,
And he, Sir Denys, was in heart a king :
Erect in person and so firm in soul,
Fortune he seem'd to govern and control ;
Generous as he who gives his all away,
Prudent as one who toils for weekly pay ;
In him all merits were decreed to meet,
Sincere though cautious, frank and yet dis-
        creet,
Just all his dealings, faithful every word,
His passions' master, and his temper's lord.'
    Yet more, kind dealers in decaying fame ?
His magnanimity you next proclaim ;
You give him learning, join'd with sound
        good sense,
And match his wealth with his benevolence ;
What hides the multitude of sins, you add,
Yet seem to doubt if sins he ever had.
    Poor honest Truth ! thou writ'st of living
        men,
And art a railer and detractor then ;
They die, again to be described, and now
A foe to merit and mankind art thou!
    Why banish truth? it injures not the dead,
It aids not them with flattery to be fed ;
And when mankind such perfect pictures
        view,
They copy less. the more they think them true.
Let us a mortal as he was behold,
And see the dross adhering to the gold ;
When we the errors of the virtuous state,
Then erring men their worth may emulate.
    View then this picture of a noble mind,
Let him be wise, magnanimous, and kind ;
What was the wisdom? Was it not the frown
That keeps all question, all inquiry down ?
His words were powerful and decisive all,
But his slow reasons came for no man's call.
"Tis thus,' he cried, no doubt with kind
        intent,
To give results and spare all argument :—
    ' Let it be spared—all men at least agree
Sir Denys Brand had magnanimity :
His were no vulgar charities ; none saw
Him like the merchant to the hut withdraw*

He left to meaner minds the simple deed,
By which the houseless rest, the hungry feed ;
His was a public bounty vast and grand,
'Twas not in him to work with viewless hand ;
He raised the room that towers above the
street,
A public room where grateful parties meet;
He first the life boat plann'd ; to him the
place
Is deep in debt—'twas he revived the race;
To every public act this hearty friend
Would give with freedom or with frankness
lend ;
His money built the jail, nor prisoner yet
Sits at his ease, but he must feel the debt;
To these let candour add his vast display,
Around his mansion all is grand and gay,
And this is bounty with the name of pay.'

I grant the whole, nor from one deed re-
tract,
But wish recorded too the private act ;
All these were great, but still our hearts
approve
Those simpler tokens of the christian love;
'Twould give me joy some gracious deed to
meet,
That has not call'd for glory through the
street :
Who felt for many, could not always shun,
In some soft moment, to be kind to one ;
And yet they tell us, when Sir Denys died,
That not a widow in the Borough sigh'd ;
Great were his gifts, his mighty heart I own,
But why describe what all the world has
known ?

The rest is petty pride, the useless art
Of a vain mind to hide a swelling heart :
Small was his private room; men found him
there
By a plain table, on a paltry chair ;
A wretched floor-cloth, and some prints
around,
The easy purchase of a single pound :
These humble trifles and that study small
Make a strong contrast with the servants'
hall ;
There barely comfort, here a proud excess,
The pompous seat of pamper'd idleness,
Where the sleek rogues with one consent
declare,
They would not live upon his honour's fare;
He daily took but one half-hour to dine,
On one poor dish and some three sips of wine;

Then he'd abuse them for their sumptuous
feasts,
And say, 'My friends! you make yourselves
like beasts ;
One dish suffices any man to dine,
But you are greedy as a herd of swine ;
Learn to be temperate.'—Had they dared
t' obey,
He would have praised and turn'd them all
away.

Friends met Sir Denys riding in his ground,
And there the meekness of his spirit found :
For that grey coat, not new for many a year,
Hides all that would like decent dress appear;
An old brown pony 'twas his will to ride,
Who shuffled onward, and from side to side;
A five-pound purchase, but so fat and sleek,
His very plenty made the creature weak.

'Sir Denys Brand ! and on so poor a steed !'
' Poor ! it may be—such things I never heed :'
And who that youth behind, of pleasant mien,
Equipp'd as one who wishes to be seen,
Upon a horse, twice victor for a plate,
A noble hunter, bought at dearest rate ?—
Him the lad fearing, yet resolved to guide,
He curbs his spirit, while he strokes his pride.
' A handsome youth, Sir Denys ; and a
horse
Of finer figure never trod the course,—
Yours, without question ? '—'Yes ! I think
a groom
Bought me the beast; I cannot say the sum:
I ride him not, it is a foolish pride
Men have in cattle—but my people ride ;
The boy is—hark ye, sirrah ! what 's your
name ?
Ay, Jacob, yes ! I recollect—the same ;
As I bethink me now, a tenant's son—
I think a tenant—is your father one ? '
There was an idle boy who ran about,
And found his master's humble spirit out ;
He would at awful distance snatch a look,
Then run away and hide him in some nook;
' For oh !' quoth he, 'I dare not fix my sight
On him, his grandeur puts me in a fright ;
Oh ! Mister Jacob, when you wait on him,
Do you not quake and tremble every limb?'
The steward soon had orders—' Summers,
see
That Sam be clothed, and let him wait on me.'

___

Sir Denys died, bequeathing all affairs
In trust to Laughton's long experienced cares;

Before a guardian, and Sir Denys dead,
All rule and power devolved upon his head:
Numbers are call'd to govern, but in fact
Only the powerful and assuming act.
Laughton, too wise to be a dupe to fame,
Cared not a whit of what descent he came,
Till he was rich; he then conceived the
thought
To fish for pedigree, but never caught:
All his desire, when he was young and poor,
Was to advance; he never cared for more:
'Let me buy, sell, be factor, take a wife,
Take any road to get along in life.'
Was he a miser then? a robber? foe
To those who trusted? a deceiver?—No!
He was ambitious; all his powers of mind
Were to one end controll'd, improved, com-
bined;
Wit, learning, judgment, were, by his account,
Steps for the ladder he design'd to mount:
Such step was money: wealth was but his
slave,
For power he gain'd it, and for power he gave;
Full well the Borough knows that he'd the art
Of bringing money to the surest mart;
Friends too were aids, they led to certain ends,
Increase of power and claim on other friends.
A favourite step was marriage: then he gain'd
Seat in our hall, and o'er his party reign'd;
Houses and lands he bought, and long'd to
buy,
But never drew the springs of purchase dry,
And thus at last they answer'd every call,
The failing found him ready for their fall:
He walks along the street, the mart, the quay,
And looks and mutters, 'This belongs to me.'
His passions all partook the general bent;
Interest inform'd him when he should resent,
How long resist, and on what terms relent:
In points where he determined to succeed,
In vain might reason or compassion plead;
But gain'd his point, he was the best of men,
'Twas loss of time to be vexatious then:
Hence he was mild to all men whom he led,
Of all who dared resist the scourge and dread.
Falsehood in him was not the useless lie
Of boasting pride or laughing vanity;
It was the gainful, the persuading art,
That made its way and won the doubting
heart
Which argued, soften'd, humbled, and pre-
vail'd;
Nor was it tried till ev'ry truth had fail'd;

No sage on earth could more than he despise
Degrading, poor, unprofitable lies.
Though fond of gain, and grieved by
wanton waste,
To social parties he had no distaste;
With one presiding purpose in his view,
He sometimes could descend to trifle too!
Yet, in these moments, he had still the art
To ope the looks and close the guarded heart;
And, like the public host, has sometimes made
A grand repast, for which the guests have paid.
At length, with power endued and wealthy
grown,
Frailties and passions, long suppress'd, were
shown;
Then to provoke him was a dangerous thing,
His pride would punish, and his temper sting;
His powerful hatred sought th' avenging
hour,
And his proud vengeance struck with all his
power,
Save when th' offender took a prudent way
The rising storm of fury to allay:
This might he do, and so in safety sleep,
By largely casting to the angry deep;
Or, better yet (its swelling force t' assuage,)
By pouring oil of flattery on its rage.
And now, of all the heart approved,
possess'd,
Fear'd, favour'd, follow'd, dreaded, and
caress'd,
He gently yields to one mellifluous joy,
The only sweet that is not found to cloy,
Bland adulation! other pleasures pall
On the sick taste, and transient are they all;
But this one sweet has such enchanting power,
The more we take, the faster we devour;
Nauseous to those who must the dose apply,
And most disgusting to the standers-by;
Yet in all companies will Laughton feed,
Nor care how grossly men perform the deed.
As gapes the nursling, or, what comes more
near,
Some Friendly-island chief, for hourly cheer;
When wives and slaves, attending round his
seat,
Prepare by turns the masticated meat:
So for this master, husband, parent, friend,
His ready slaves their various efforts blend,
And, to their lord still eagerly inclined,
Pour the crude trash of a dependent mind.
But let the muse assign the man his due;
Worth he possess'd, nor were his virtues few;—

He sometimes help'd the injured in their
  cause ;
His power and purse have back'd the failing
  laws;
He for religion has a due respect,
And all his serious notions are correct ;
Although he pray'd and languish'd for a son,
He grew resign'd when Heaven denied him
  one ;
He never to this quiet mansion sends
Subject unfit, in compliment to friends :
Not so Sir Denys, who would yet protest
He always chose the worthiest and the best;

Not men in trade by various loss brought down,
But those whose glory once amazed the town,
Who their last guinea in their pleasures spent,
Yet never fell so low as to repent ;
To these his pity he could largely deal,
Wealth they had known, and therefore want
  could feel.
  Three seats were vacant while Sir Denys
    reign'd,
And three such favourites their admission
  gain'd ;
These let us view, still more to understand
The moral feelings of Sir Denys Brand.

LETTER XIV. INHABITANTS OF THE ALMS-HOUSE

BLANEY

Sed quam caecus inest vitlis amor ! Omne
  futurum
Despicitur, suadentque brevem praesentia
  fructum,
Et ruit in vetitum damni secura libido.
  CLAUDIAN, *In Eutrop.* lib. ii. 50–2.

  Numquam parvo contenta paratu
Et quaesitorum terra pelagoque ciborum
Ambitiosa fames et lautae gloria mensae.
  LUCAN, *De Bell. Civ.* (or *Phars.*), lib. iv.
  374–6.

  . . . . . .
Et Luxus, populator opum, quem semper
  adhaerens,
Infelix humili gressu comitatur Egestas.
  CLAUDIAN, *In Rufinum,* lib. i. 35–6.

Behold what blessings wealth to life can lend !
  POPE, *Moral Essays,* Ep. iii. 297.

Blaney, a wealthy Heir, dissipated, and
reduced to Poverty—His Fortune restored
by Marriage : again consumed—His Man-
ner of living in the West Indies—Recalled
to a larger Inheritance—His more refined
and expensive Luxuries—His Method of
quieting Conscience—Death of his Wife—
Again become poor—His Method of sup-
porting Existence—His Ideas of Religion
—His Habits and Connexions when old—
Admitted into the Alms-House.

OBSERVE that tall pale veteran ! what a look
Of shame and guilt ! who cannot read that
  book ?
Misery and mirth are blended in his face,
Much innate vileness and some outward grace;

There wishes strong and stronger griefs are seen,
Looks ever changed, and never one serene:
Show not that manner, and these features all,
The serpent's cunning and the sinner's fall?
  Hark to that laughter!—'tis the way he takes
To force applause for each vile jest he makes;
Such is yon man, by partial favour sent
To these calm seats to ponder and repent.
  Blaney, a wealthy heir at twenty-one,
At twenty-five was ruin'd and undone—
These years with grievous crimes we need
    not load,
He found his ruin in the common road ;—
Gamed without skill, without inquiry bought,
Lent without love, and borrow'd without
    thought.
But, gay and handsome, he had soon the
    dower
Of a kind wealthy widow in his power :
Then he aspired to loftier flights of vice,
To singing harlots of enormous price :
He took a jockey in his gig to buy
A horse, so valued, that a duke was shy :
To gain the plaudits of the knowing few,
Gamblers and grooms, what would not
    Blaney do?
His dearest friend, at that improving age
Was Hounslow Dick, who drove the western
    stage.
  Cruel he was not—If he left his wife,
He left her to her own pursuits in life ;
Deaf to reports, to all expenses blind,
Profuse, not just, and careless, but not kind.
  Yet thus assisted, ten long winters pass'd
In wasting guineas ere he saw his last ;

Then he began to reason, and to feel
He could not dig, nor had he learn'd to steal;
And should he beg as long as he might live,
He justly fear'd that nobody would give :
But he could charge a pistol, and at will,
All that was mortal, by a bullet kill :
And he was taught, by those whom he would call
Man's surest guides—that he was mortal all.
   While thus he thought, still waiting for the
      day,
When he should dare to blow his brains away,
A place for him a kind relation found,
Where England's monarch ruled, but far
      from English ground ;
He gave employ that might for bread suffice,
Correct his habits and restrain his vice.
   Here Blaney tried (what such man's
      miseries teach)
To find what pleasures were within his reach;
These he enjoy'd, though not in just the style
He once possess'd them in his native isle ;
Congenial souls he found in every place,
Vice in all soils, and charms in every race :
His lady took the same amusing way,
And laugh'd at Time till he had turn'd them
      grey :
At length for England once again they steer'd,
By ancient views and new designs endear'd ;
His kindred died, and Blaney now became
An heir to one who never heard his name.
   What could he now?—The man had tried
      before
The joys of youth, and they were joys no
      more :
To vicious pleasure he was still inclined,
But vice must now be season'd and refined ;
Then as a swine he would on pleasure seize,
Now common pleasures had no power to
      please :
Beauty alone has for the vulgar charms,
He wanted beauty trembling with alarms :
His was no more a youthful dream of joy,
The wretch desired to ruin and destroy ;
He bought indulgence with a boundless price,
Most pleased when decency bow'd down to
      vice,
When a fair dame her husband's honour sold,
And a frail countess play'd for Blaney's gold.
   ' But did not conscience in her anger rise ? '
Yes ! and he learn'd her terrors to despise;
When stung by thought, to soothing books he
      fled,
And grew composed and harden'd as he read;

Tales of Voltaire, and essays gay and slight,
Pleased him and shone with their phosphoric
      light ;
Which, though it rose from objects vile and
      base,
Where'er it came threw splendour on the place,
And was that light which the deluded youth,
And this grey sinner, deem'd the light of truth.
   He different works for different cause
      admired,
Some fix'd his judgment, some his passions
      fired ;
To cheer the mind and raise a dormant flame,
He had the books, decreed to lasting shame,
Which those who read are careful not to name:
These won to vicious act the yielding heart,
And then the cooler reasoners soothed the
      smart.
   He heard of Blount, and Mandeville, and
      Chubb,
How they the doctors of their day would drub;
How Hume had dwelt on miracles so well,
That none would now believe a miracle ;
And though he cared not works so grave to
      read,
He caught their faith and sign'd the sinner's
      creed.
   Thus was he pleased to join the laughing side,
Nor ceased the laughter when his lady died;
Yet was he kind and careful of her fame,
And on her tomb inscribed a virtuous name;
' A tender wife, respected, and so forth,'—
The marble still bears witness to the worth.
   He has some children, but he knows not
      where ;
Something they cost, but neither love nor care;
A father's feelings he has never known,
His joys, his sorrows, have been all his own.
   He now would build—and lofty seat he
      built,
And sought, in various ways, relief from guilt.
Restless, for ever anxious to obtain
Ease for the heart by ramblings of the brain,
He would have pictures, and of course a taste,
And found a thousand means his wealth to
      waste.
Newmarket steeds he bought at mighty cost;
They sometimes won, but Blaney always lost.
   Quick came his ruin, came when he had still
For life a relish, and in pleasure skill :
By his own idle reckoning he supposed
His wealth would last him till his life **was**
      closed ;

But no! he found his final hoard was spent,
While he had years to suffer and repent.
Yet at the last, his noble mind to show,
And in his misery how he bore the blow,
He view'd his only guinea, then suppress'd,
For a short time, the tumults in his breast,
And, moved by pride, by habit and despair,
Gave it an opera-bird to hum an air.
Come ye! who live for pleasure, come,
  behold
A man of pleasure when he's poor and old;
When he looks back through life, and cannot
  find
A single action to relieve his mind;
When he looks forward, striving still to keep
A steady prospect of eternal sleep;
When not one friend is left, of all the train
Whom 'twas his pride and boast to entertain,—
Friends now employ'd from house to house
  to run
And say, 'Alas! poor Blaney is undone!'—
Those whom he shook with ardour by the hand,
By whom he stood as long as he could stand,
Who seem'd to him from all deception clear,
And who, more strange! might think them-
  selves sincere.
  Lo! now the hero shuffling through the
  town,
To hunt a dinner and to beg a crown;
To tell an idle tale, that boys may smile;
To bear a strumpet's billet-doux a mile;
To cull a wanton for a youth of wealth,
(With reverend view to both his taste and
  health):
To be a useful, needy thing between
Fear and desire—the pander and the screen;
To flatter pictures, houses, horses, dress,
The wildest fashion or the worst excess;
To be the grey seducer, and entice
Unbearded folly into acts of vice;
And then, to level every fence which law
And virtue fix to keep the mind in awe,
He first inveigles youth to walk astray,
Next prompts and soothes them in their
  fatal way,
Then vindicates the deed, and makes the
  mind his prey.
  Unhappy man! what pains he takes to
  state—
(Proof of his fear!) that all below is fate;
That all proceed in one appointed track,
Where none can stop, or take their journey
  back:

Then what is vice or virtue?—Yet he'll rail
At priests till memory and quotation fail;
He reads, to learn the various ills they've done,
And calls them vipers, every mother's son.
  He is the harlot's aid, who wheedling tries
To move her friend for vanity's supplies;
To weak indulgence he allures the mind,
Loth to be duped, but willing to be kind;
And if successful—what the labour pays?
He gets the friend's contempt and Chloe's
  praise,
Who, in her triumph, condescends to say,
'What a good creature Blaney was to-day!'
  Hear the poor daemon when the young
  attend,
And willing ear to vile experience lend;
When he relates (with laughing, leering eye)
The tale licentious, mix'd with blasphemy:
No genuine gladness his narrations cause,
The frailest heart denies sincere applause:
And many a youth has turn'd him half aside,
And laugh'd aloud, the sign of shame to hide.
  Blaney, no aid in his vile cause to lose,
Buys pictures, prints, and a licentious muse;
He borrows every help from every art,
To stir the passions and mislead the heart:
But from the subject let us soon escape,
Nor give this feature all its ugly shape:
Some to their crimes escape from satire owe;
Who shall describe what Blaney dares to
  show?
  While thus the man, to vice and passion
  slave,
Was, with his follies, moving to the grave,
The ancient ruler of this mansion died,
And Blaney boldly for the seat applied;
Sir Denys Brand, then guardian, join'd his
  suit:
'Tis true,' said he, 'the fellow's quite a
  brute—
A very beast; but yet, with all his sin,
He has a manner—let the devil in.'
  They half complied, they gave the wish'd
  retreat,
But raised a worthier to the vacant seat.
  Thus forced on ways unlike each former
  way,
Thus led to prayer without a heart to pray,
He quits the gay and rich, the young and
  free,
Among the badge-men with a badge to be:
He sees an humble tradesman raised to rule
The grey-beard pupils of this moral school;

Where he himself, an old licentious boy,
Will nothing learn, and nothing can enjoy ;
In temp'rate measures he must eat and drink,
And, pain of pains ! must live alone and think.
  In vain, by fortune's smiles, thrice affluent made,
Still has he debts of ancient date unpaid ;

Thrice into penury by error thrown,
Not one right maxim has he made his own ;
The old men shun hím,—some his vices hate,
And all abhor his principles and prate ;
Nor love nor care for him will mortal show,
Save a frail sister in the female row.

LETTER XV.   INHABITANTS OF THE ALMS-HOUSE

CLELIA

She early found herself mistress of herself.
All she did was right : all she said was admired. Early, very early, did she dismiss
blushes from her cheek : she could not blush,
because she could not doubt ; and silence,
whatever was the subject, was as much a
stranger to her as diffidence.
RICHARDSON.

Quo fugit Venus? heu! Quo ve color? decens
Quo motus ? Quid habes illius, illius,
  Quae spirabat amores,
    Quae me surpuerat mihi ?
HORATIUS, lib. iv. Od. 13, vv. 17–20.

Her lively and pleasant Manners—Her
Reading and Decision—Her Intercourse
with different Classes of Society—Her
Kind of Character—The favoured Lover
—Her Management of him : his of her—
After one Period, Clelia with an Attorney ;
her Manner and Situation there—Another
such Period, when her Fortune still declines—Mistress of an Inn—A Widow—
Another such Interval : she becomes poor
and infirm, but still vain and frivolous—
The fallen Vanity—Admitted into the
House : meets Blaney.

WE had a sprightly nymph—in every town
Are some such sprights, who wander up and down ;
She had her useful arts, and could contrive,
In time's despite, to stay at twenty-five ;—
' Here will I rest ; move on, thou lying year,
This is mine age, and I will rest me here.'
  Arch was her look, and she had pleasant ways
Your good opinion of her heart to raise ;
Her speech was lively, and with ease express'd,
And well she judged the tempers she address'd :

If some soft stripling had her keenness felt,
She knew the way to make his anger melt ;
Wit was allow'd her, though but few could bring
Direct example of a witty thing ;
'Twas that gay, pleasant, smart, engaging speech,
Her beaux admired, and just within their reach ;
Not indiscreet perhaps, but yet more free
Than prudish nymphs allow their wit to be.
  Novels and plays, with poems, old and new,
Were all the books our nymph attended to ;
Yet from the press no treatise issued forth,
But she would speak precisely of its worth.
  She with the London stage familiar grew,
And every actor's name and merit knew ;
She told how this or that their part mistook,
And of the rival Romeos gave the look ;
Of either house 'twas hers the strength to see,
Then judge with candour—' Drury-Lane for me.'
  What made this knowledge, what this skill complete ?
A fortnight's visit in Whitechapel-street.
  Her place in life was rich and poor between,
With those a favourite, and with these a queen ;
She could her parts assume, and condescend
To friends more humble while an humble friend ;
And thus a welcome, lively guest could pass,
Threading her pleasant way from class to class.
  ' Her reputation ? '—That was like her wit,
And seem'd her manner and her state to fit ;
Something there was, what, none presumed to say,
Clouds lightly passing on a smiling day.—
Whispers and hints which went from ear to ear,
And mix'd reports no judge on earth could clear.

But of each sex a friendly number press'd
To joyous banquets this alluring guest :
There, if indulging mirth, and freed from awe,
If pleasing all, and pleased with all she saw,
Her speech were free, and such as freely dwelt
On the same feelings all around her felt ;
Or if some fond presuming favourite tried
To come so near as once to be denied ;
Yet not with brow so stern or speech so nice,
But that he ventured on denial twice :—
If these have been, and so has scandal taught,
Yet malice never found the proof she sought.

But then came one, the Lovelace of his day,
Rich, proud, and crafty, handsome, brave,
    and gay;
Yet loved he not those labour'd plans and arts,
But left the business to the ladies' hearts,
And when he found them in a proper train,
He thought all else superfluous and vain :
But in that training he was deeply taught,
And rarely fail'd of gaining all he sought ;
He knew how far directly on to go,
How to recede and dally to and fro ;
How to make all the passions his allies,
And, when he saw them in contention rise,
To watch the wrought-up heart, and conquer
    by surprise.

Our heroine fear'd him not ; it was her part,
To make sure conquest of such gentle heart—
Of one so mild and humble ; for she saw
In Henry's eye a love chastised by awe.
Her thoughts of virtue were not all sublime,
Nor virtuous all her thoughts ; 'twas now her
    time
To bait each hook, in every way to please,
And the rich prize with dext'rous hand to seize.
She had no virgin-terrors ; she could stray
In all love's maze, nor fear to lose her way ;
Nay, could go near the precipice, nor dread
A failing caution or a giddy head ;
She'd fix her eyes upon the roaring flood,
And dance upon the brink where danger stood.
'Twas nature all, she judged, in one so
    young,
To drop the eye and falter in the tongue ;
To be about to take, and then command
His daring wish, and only view the hand :
Yes ! all was nature ; it became a maid
Of gentle soul t' encourage love afraid ;—
He, so unlike the confident and bold,
Would fly in mute despair to find her cold :
The young and tender germ requires the sun
To make it spread ; it must be smiled upon.

Thus the kind virgin gentle means devised,
To gain a heart so fond, a hand so prized ;
More gentle still she grew, to change her way,
Would cause confusion, danger and delay :
Thus (an increase of gentleness her mode),
She took a plain, unvaried, certain road,
And every hour believed success was near,
Till there was nothing left to hope or fear.

It must be own'd that in this strife of hearts,
Man has advantage—has superior arts :
The lover's aim is to the nymph unknown,
Nor is she always certain of her own ;
Or has her fears, nor these can so disguise,
But he who searches, reads them in her eyes,
In the avenging frown, in the regretting sighs:
These are his signals, and he learns to steer
The straighter course whenever they appear.

'Pass we ten years, and what was Clelia's
    fate ? '
At an attorney's board alert she sate,
Not legal mistress : he with other men
Once sought her hand, but other views were
    then ;
And when he knew he might the bliss command,
He other blessing sought, without the hand ;
For still he felt alive the lambent flame,
And offer'd her a home,—and home she came.

There, though her higher friendships lived
    no more,
She loved to speak of what she shared before—
' Of the dear Lucy, heiress of the hall,—
Of good Sir Peter,—of their annual ball,
And the fair countess !—Oh ! she loved them
    all ! '
The humbler clients of her friend would stare,
The knowing smile,—but neither caused her
    care ;
She brought her spirits to her humble state,
And soothed with idle dreams her frowning
    fate.

' Ten summers pass'd, and how was Clelia
    then ? '
Alas ! she suffer'd in this trying ten ;
The pair had parted : who to him attend,
Must judge the nymph unfaithful to her
    friend ;
But who on her would equal faith bestow,
Would think him rash,—and surely she must
    know.
Then as a matron Clelia taught a school,
But nature gave not talents fit for rule :

Yet now, though marks of wasting years
　　were seen,
Some touch of sorrow, some attack of spleen;
Still there was life, a spirit quick and gay,
And lively speech and elegant array.
　　The Griffin's landlord these allured so far,
He made her mistress of his heart and bar;
He had no idle retrospective whim,
Till she was his, her deeds concern'd not him:
So far was well,—but Clelia thought not fit
(In all the Griffin needed) to submit:
Gaily to dress and in the bar preside,
Soothed the poor spirit of degraded pride;
But cooking, waiting, welcoming a crew
Of noisy guests, were arts she never knew:
Hence daily wars, with temporary truce,
His vulgar insult, and her keen abuse;
And as their spirits wasted in the strife,
Both took the Griffin's ready aid of life;
But she with greater prudence—Harry tried
More powerful aid, and in the trial died;
Yet drew down vengeance: in no distant time,
Th' insolvent Griffin struck his wings sub-
　　lime;—
Forth from her palace walk'd th' ejected
　　queen,
And show'd to frowning fate a look serene;
Gay spite of time, though poor, yet well
　　attired,
Kind without love, and vain if not admired.

　　Another term is past; ten other years
In various trials, troubles, views, and fears:
Of these some pass'd in small attempts at
　　trade;
Houses she kept for widowers lately made;
For now she said, ' They'll miss th' endearing
　　friend,
And I'll be there the soften'd heart to bend: '
And true a part was done as Clelia plann'd—
The heart was soften'd, but she miss'd the
　　hand.
She wrote a novel, and Sir Denys said,
The dedication was the best he read;
But Edgeworths, Smiths, and Radcliffes so
　　engross'd
The public ear, that all her pains were lost.
To keep a toy-shop was attempt the last,
There too she fail'd, and schemes and hopes
　　were past.
　　Now friendless, sick and old, and wanting
　　bread,
The first-born tears of fallen pride were shed—

True, bitter tears; and yet that wounded
　　pride,
Among the poor, for poor distinctions sigh'd.
Though now her tales were to her audience
　　fit;
Though loud her tones, and vulgar grown her
　　wit;
Though now her dress—(but let me not explain
The piteous patch-work of the needy-vain,
The flirtish form to coarse materials lent,
And one poor robe through fifty fashions
　　sent);
Though all within was sad, without was
　　mean,—
Still 'twas her wish, her comfort to be seen:
She would to plays on lowest terms resort,
Where once her box was to the beaux a court;
And, strange delight! to that same house,
　　where she
Join'd in the dance, all gaiety and glee,
Now with the menials crowding to the wall,
She'd see, not share, the pleasures of the ball,
And with degraded vanity unfold,
How she too triumph'd in the years of old.
To her poor friends 'tis now her pride to tell
On what a height she stood before she fell;
At church she points to one tall seat, and
　　' There
We sat,' she cries, ' when my papa was mayor.'
Not quite correct in what she now relates,
She alters persons, and she forgets dates;
And finding memory's weaker help decay'd,
She boldly calls invention to her aid.
　　Touch'd by the pity he had felt before,
For her Sir Denys op'd the alms-house door:
' With all her faults,' he said, ' the woman
　　knew
How to distinguish—had a manner too;
And, as they say, she is allied to some
In decent station—let the creature come.'
　　Here she and Blaney meet, and take their
　　view
Of all the pleasures they would still pursue:
Hour after hour they sit, and nothing hide
Of vices past; their follies are their pride;
What to the sober and the cool are crimes,
They boast—exulting in those happy times;
The darkest deeds no indignation raise,
The purest virtue never wins their praise;
But still they on their ancient joys dilate,
Still with regret departed glories state,
And mourn their grievous fall, and curse their
　　rigorous fate.

LETTER XVI. INHABITANTS OF THE ALMS-HOUSE

BENBOW

Thou art the knight of the Burning Lamp
. . . if thou wert any way given to virtue, I
would swear by thy face ; my oath should be
by this fire. Oh ! thou art a perpetual
triumph, . . . thou hast saved me a thousand
marks in links and torches, walking with thee
in the night betwixt tavern and tavern.
SHAKSPEARE, *Henry IV*, Part I, Act iii, Sc. 3.

Ebrietas tibi fida comes, tibi Luxus, et atris
Circa te semper volitans Infamia pennis.
Silius Italicus.

———

Benbow, an improper Companion for the
Badgemen of the Alms-house—He re-
sembles Bardolph—Left in Trade by his
Father—Contracts useless Friendships—
His Friends drink with him, and employ
others—Called worthy and honest ! Why—
Effect of Wine on the Mind of Man—
Benbow's common Subject—the Praise of
departed Friends and Patrons—'Squire
Asgill, at the Grange : his Manners, Ser-
vants, Friends—True to his Church : ought
therefore to be spared—His Son's different
Conduct—Vexation of the Father's Spirit
if admitted to see the Alteration—Captain
Dowling, a boon Companion, ready to
drink at all Times, and with any Company :
famous in his Clubroom—His easy Depar-
ture—Dolly Murray, a Maiden advanced
in Years : abides by Ratafia and Cards—
Her free Manners—Her Skill in the Game
—Her Preparation and Death—Benbow,
how interrupted : his Submission.

SEE! yonder badgeman, with that glowing face,
A meteor shining in this sober place ;
Vast sums were paid, and many years were
past,
Ere gems so rich around their radiance cast !
Such was the fiery front that Bardolph wore,
Guiding his master to the tavern-door ;
There first that meteor rose, and there alone,
In its due place, the rich effulgence shone :
But this strange fire the seat of peace invades,
And shines portentous in these solemn shades.
Benbow, a boon companion, long approved
By jovial sets, and (as he thought) beloved,
Was judged as one to joy and friendship prone,
And deem'd injurious to himself alone ;

Gen'rous and free, he paid but small regard
To trade, and fail'd ; and some declared
  ' 'twas hard : '
These were his friends—his foes conceived
  the case
Of common kind ; he sought and found
  disgrace :
The reasoning few, who neither scorn'd nor
  loved,
His feelings pitied and his faults reproved.
Benbow, the father, left possessions fair,
A worthy name and business to his heir ;
Benbow, the son, those fair possessions sold,
And lost his credit, while he spent the gold :
He was a jovial trader : men enjoy'd
The night with him ; his day was unemploy'd ;
So when his credit and his cash were spent,
Here, by mistaken pity, he was sent ;
Of late he came, with passions unsubdued,
And shared and cursed the hated solitude,
Where gloomy thoughts arise, where grievous
  cares intrude.
Known but in drink—he found an easy
  friend,
Well pleased his worth and honour to com-
  mend ;
And thus inform'd, the guardian of the trust
Heard the applause and said the claim was
  just ;
A worthy soul ! unfitted for the strife,
Care and contention of a busy life ;—
Worthy, and why ?—that o'er the midnight
  bowl
He made his friend the partner of his soul,
And any man his friend :—then thus in glee,
' I speak my mind, I love the truth,' quoth he ;
Till 'twas his fate that useful truth to find,
'Tis sometimes prudent not to speak the mind.
With wine inflated, man is all upblown,
And feels a power which he believes his own ;
With fancy soaring to the skies, he thinks
His all the virtues all the while he drinks ;
But when the gas from the balloon is gone,
When sober thoughts and serious cares come
  on,
Where then the worth that in himself he
  found ?—
Vanish'd—and he sank grov'ling on the
  ground.

Still some conceit will Benbow's mind
    inflate,
Poor as he is,—'tis pleasant to relate
The joys he once possess'd—it soothes his
    present state.
Seated with some grey beadsman, he regrets
His former feasting, though it swell'd his
    debts ;
Topers once famed, his friends in earlier days,
Well he describes, and thinks description
    praise :
Each hero's worth with much delight he
    paints :
Martyrs they were, and he would make them
    saints.
   ' Alas ! alas !' Old England now may say,
' My glory withers ; it has had its day :
We're fallen on evil times ; men read and
    think ;
Our bold forefathers loved to fight and drink.
   ' Then lived the good 'Squire Asgill—what
    a change
Has death and fashion shown us at the
    Grange !
He bravely thought it best became his rank,
That all his tenants and his tradesmen drank ;
He was delighted from his favourite room
To see them 'cross the park go daily home,
Praising aloud the liquor and the host,
And striving who should venerate him most.
   ' No pride had he, and there was difference
    small
Between the master's and the servants' hall ;
And here or there the guests were welcome all.
Of Heaven's free gifts he took no special care,
He never quarrel'd for a simple hare ;
But sought, by giving sport, a sportsman's
    name,
Himself a poacher, though at other game :
He never planted nor inclosed—his trees
Grew like himself, untroubled and at ease :
Bounds of all kinds he hated, and had felt
Choked and imprison'd in a modern belt,
Which some rare genius now has twined about
The good old house, to keep old neighbours
    out :
Along his valleys, in the evening-hours,
The borough-damsels stray'd to gather
    flowers,
Or by the brakes and brushwood of the park,
To take their pleasant rambles in the dark.
   ' Some prudes, of rigid kind, forbore to call
On the kind females—favourites at the hall ;

But better natures saw, with much delight,
The different orders of mankind unite ;
'Twas schooling pride to see the footman wait,
Smile on his sister and receive her plate.
   ' His worship ever was a churchman true,
He held in scorn the methodistic crew ;
May God defend the Church,and save theKing,
He'd pray devoutly and divinely sing.
Admit that he the holy day would spend
As priests approved not, still he was a friend:
Much then I blame the preacher, as too nice,
To call such trifles by the name of vice ;
Hinting, though gently and with cautious
    speech,
Of good example—'tis their trade to preach:
But still 'twas pity, when the worthy 'squire
Stuck to the church ; what more could they
    require ?
'Twas almost joining that fanatic crew,
To throw such morals at his honour's pew ;
A weaker man, had he been so reviled,
Had left the place—he only swore and smiled.
   ' But think, ye rectors and ye curates, think,
Who are your friends, and at their frailties
    wink ;
Conceive not—mounted on your Sunday-
    throne,
Your fire-brands fall upon your foes alone ;
They strike your patrons—and, should all
    withdraw,
In whom your wisdoms may discern a flaw,
You would the flower of all your audience lose,
And spend your crackers on their empty pews.
   ' The father dead, the son has found a wife,
And lives a formal, proud, unsocial life ;—
The lands are now enclosed ; the tenants all,
Save at a rent-day, never see the hall :
No lass is suffer'd o'er the walks to come,
And if there's love, they have it all at home.
   ' Oh ! could the ghost of our good 'squire
    arise,
And see such change ; would it believe its
    eyes ?
Would it not glide about from place to place,
And mourn the manners of a feebler race ?
At that long table, where the servants found
Mirth and abundance while the year went
    round ;
Where a huge pollard on the winter-fire,
At a huge distance made them all retire ;
Where not a measure in the room was kept,
And but one rule—they tippled till they
    slept,—

There would it see a pale old hag preside,
A thing made up of stinginess and pride ;
Who carves the meat, as if the flesh could
feel,
Careless whose flesh must miss the plenteous
meal :
Here would the ghost a small coal-fire behold,
Not fit to keep one body from the cold ;
Then would it flit to higher rooms, and stay
To view a dull, dress'd company at play ;
All the old comfort, all the genial fare
For ever gone ! how sternly would it stare :
And though it might not to their view appear,
'Twould cause among them lassitude and fear ;
Then wait to see—where he delight has seen—
The dire effect of fretfulness and spleen.
  'Such were the worthies of these better days:
We had their blessings—they shall have our
praise.
  ' Of Captain Dowling would you hear me
speak?
I'd sit and sing his praises for a week :
He was a man, and man-like all his joy,—
I'm led to question was he ever boy ?
Beef was his breakfast;—if from sea and
salt,
It relish'd better with his wine of malt ;
Then, till he dined, if walking in or out,
Whether the gravel teased him or the gout,
Though short in wind and flannel'd every
limb,
He drank with all who had concerns with
him :
Whatever trader, agent, merchant, came,
They found him ready, every hour the same ;
Whatever liquors might between them pass,
He took them all, and never balk'd his glass :
Nay, with the seamen working in the ship,
At their request he'd share the grog and
flip :
But in the club-room was his chief delight,
And punch the favourite liquor of the night ;
Man after man they from the trial shrank,
And Dowling ever was the last who drank :
Arrived at home, he, ere he sought his bed,
With pipe and brandy would compose his
head ;
Then half an hour was o'er the news beguiled,
When he retired as harmless as a child.
Set but aside the gravel and the gout,
And breathing short—his sand ran fairly out.
  ' At fifty-five we lost him—after that
Life grows insipid and its pleasures flat ;

He had indulged in all that man can have,
He did not drop a dotard to his grave :
Still to the last, his feet upon the chair,
With rattling lungs now gone beyond repair ;
When on each feature death had fix'd his
stamp,
And not a doctor could the body vamp :
Still at the last, to his beloved bowl
He clung, and cheer'd the sadness of his soul;
For though a man may not have much to
fear,
Yet death looks ugly, when the view is near :
—" I go," he said, " but till my friends shall
say,
'Twas as a man—I did not sneak away ;
An honest life with worthy souls I've spent,—
Come, fill my glass ; "—he took it and he
went.
  ' Poor Dolly Murray !—I might live to see
My hundredth year, but no such lass as she.
Easy by nature, in her humour gay,
She chose her comforts, ratafia and play :
She loved the social game, the decent glass ;
And was a jovial, friendly, laughing lass ;
We sat not then at Whist demure and still,
But pass'd the pleasant hours at gay Quad-
rille :
Lame in her side, we placed her in her seat,
Her hands were free, she cared not for her
feet ;
As the game ended, came the glass around,
(So was the loser cheer'd, the winner crown'd.)
Mistress of secrets, both the young and old
In her confided—not a tale she told ;
Love never made impression on her mind,
She held him weak, and all his captives blind ;
She suffer'd no man her free soul to vex,
Free from the weakness of her gentle sex ;
One with whom ours unmoved conversing
sate,
In cool discussion or in free debate.
  'Once in her chair we'd placed the good old
lass,
Where first she took her preparation-glass ;
By lucky thought she'd been that day at
prayers,
And long before had fix'd her small affairs ;
So all was easy—on her cards she cast
A smiling look ; I saw the thought that pass'd:
" A king," she call'd—though conscious of
her skill,
" Do more," I answer'd—" More," she said,
" I will ; "

And more she did—cards answer'd to her call,
She saw the mighty to her mightier fall :
" A vole ! a vole ! " she cried, " 'tis fairly
        won,
My game is ended and my work is done ; "—
This said, she gently, with a single sigh,
Died as one taught and practised how to die.

' Such were the dead-departed ; I survive,
To breathe in pain among the dead-alive.'
    The bell then call'd these ancient men to
        pray,
' Again ! ' said Benbow, —' tolls it every day ?
Where is the life I led ? '—He sigh'd and
    walk'd his way.

LETTER XVII. THE HOSPITAL AND GOVERNORS

Blessed be the man who provideth for the
sick and needy : the Lord shall deliver him
in time of trouble.
        Psalm xli. 1, Prayer Book, Communion
        Service.

Quas dederis, solas semper habebis opes.
        MARTIAL, Lib. v, *Epig.* 42.

Nil negat, et sese vel non poscentibus offert.
        CLAUDIAN, *In Eutrop.*, Lib. i. v. 365.

Decipies alios verbis vultuque benigno ;
    Nam mihi iam notus dissimulator eris.
        MARTIAL, Lib. iv, *Epig.* 88.

———

Christian Charity anxious to provide for
future as well as present Miseries—Hence
the Hospital for the Diseased—Description
of a recovered Patient—The Building :
how erected—The Patrons and Governors
—Eusebius—The more active Manager of
Business a moral and correct Contributor
—One of different Description—Good, the
Result, however intermixed with imper-
fection.

———

AN ardent spirit dwells with christian love,
The eagle's vigour in the pitying dove ;
'Tis not enough that we with sorrow sigh,
That we the wants of pleading man supply ;
That we in sympathy with sufferers feel,
Nor hear a grief without a wish to heal ;
Not these suffice—to sickness, pain, and wo,
The christian spirit loves with aid to go;
Will not be sought, waits not for want to
        plead,
But seeks the duty—nay, prevents the need;
Her utmost aid to every ill applies,
And plans relief for coming miseries.
    Hence yonder building rose : on either side
Far stretch'd the wards, all airy, warm, and
    wide ;
And every ward has beds by comfort spread,
And smooth'd for him who suffers on the bed :

There have all kindness, most relief,—for some
Is cure complete,—it is the sufferer's home :
Fevers and chronic ills, corroding pains,
Each accidental mischief man sustains ;
Fractures and wounds, and wither'd limbs
        and lame,
With all that, slow or sudden, vex our frame,
Have here attendance—here the sufferers lie,
(Where love and science every aid apply),
And heal'd with rapture live, or soothed by
        comfort die.
    See ! one relieved from anguish, and to-day
Allow'd to walk and look an hour away ;
Two months confined by fever, frenzy, pain,
He comes abroad and is himself again :
'Twas in the spring, when carried to the place,
The snow fell down and melted in his face.
    'Tis summer now ; all objects gay and new,
Smiling alike the viewer and the view :
He stops as one unwilling to advance,
Without another and another glance ;
With what a pure and simple joy he sees
Those sheep and cattle browzing at their ease;
Easy himself, there 's nothing breathes or
        moves
But he would cherish—all that lives he loves :
Observing every ward as round he goes,
He thinks what pain, what danger they
        enclose ;
Warm in his wish for all who suffer there,
At every view he meditates a prayer :
No evil counsels in his breast abide,
There joy, and love, and gratitude reside.
    The wish that Roman necks in one were
        found,
That he who form'd the wish might deal the
        wound,
This man had never heard ; but of the kind,
Is that desire which rises in his mind ;
He'd have all English hands (for further he
Cannot conceive extends our charity),

All but his own, in one right-hand to grow,
And then what hearty shake would he bestow.
  ' How rose the building?'—Piety first laid
A strong foundation, but she wanted aid ;
To Wealth unwieldy was her prayer address'd,
Who largely gave, and she the donor bless'd :
Unwieldy Wealth then to his couch withdrew,
And took the sweetest sleep he ever knew.
  Then busy Vanity sustain'd her part,
' And much, she said, ' it moved her tender
          heart :
To her all kinds of man's distress were known,
And all her heart adopted as its own.'
  Then Science came—his talents he display'd,
And Charity with joy the dome survey'd ;
Skill, Wealth, and Vanity, obtain the fame,
And Piety, the joy that makes no claim.
  Patrons there are, and governors, from
          whom
The greater aid and guiding orders come ;
Who voluntary cares and labours take,
The sufferers' servants for the service' sake ;
Of these a part I give you—but a part,—
Some hearts are hidden, some have not a
          heart.
  First let me praise—for so I best shall paint
That pious moralist, that reasoning saint !
Can I of worth like thine, Eusebius, speak ?
The man is willing, but the muse is weak ;—
'Tis thine to wait on wo ! to soothe ! to heal !
With learning social, and polite with zeal :
In thy pure breast although the passions
          dwell,
They're train'd by virtue and no more rebel ;
But have so long been active on her side,
That passion now might be itself the guide.
  Law, conscience, honour, all obey'd ; all give
Th' approving voice, and make it bliss to live ;
While faith, when life can nothing more
          supply,
Shall strengthen hope, and make it bliss to die.
  He preaches, speaks and writes with manly
          sense,
No weak neglect, no labour'd eloquence ;
Goodness and wisdom are in all his ways,
The rude revere him and the wicked praise.
  Upon humility his virtues grow,
And tower so high because so fix'd below ;
As wider spreads the oak his boughs around,
When deeper with his roots he digs the solid
          ground.
  By him, from ward to ward, is every aid
The sufferer needs, with every care convey'd :

Like the good tree he brings his treasure forth,
And, like the tree, unconscious of his worth :
Meek as the poorest Publican is he,
And strict as lives the straitest Pharisee ;
Of both, in him unite the better part,
The blameless conduct and the humble heart.
  Yet he escapes not ; he, with some, is wise
In carnal things, and loves to moralize :
Others can doubt, if all that christian care
Has not its price—there 's something he may
          share :
But this and ill severer he sustains,
As gold the fire, and as unhurt remains ;
When most reviled, although he feels the
          smart,
It wakes to nobler deeds the wounded heart,
As the rich olive, beaten for its fruit,
Puts forth at every bruise a bearing shoot.
  A second friend we have, whose care and
          zeal
But few can equal—few indeed can feel ;
He lived a life obscure, and profits made
In the coarse habits of a vulgar trade.
His brother, master of a hoy, he loved
So well, that he the calling disapproved :
' Alas ! poor Tom ! ' the landman oft would
          sigh,
When the gale freshen'd and the waves ran
          high ;
And when they parted, with a tear he'd
          say,
' No more adventure !—here in safety stay.'
Nor did he feign ; with more than half he had,
He would have kept the seaman, and been
          glad.
  Alas ! how few resist, when strongly tried—
A rich relation's nearer kinsman died ;
He sicken'd, and to him the landman went,
And all his hours with cousin Ephraim spent.
This Thomas heard, and cared not : ' I,'
          quoth he,
' Have one in port upon the watch for me.'
So Ephraim died, and when the will was
          shown,
Isaac, the landman, had the whole his own :
Who to his brother sent a moderate purse,
Which he return'd in anger, with his curse,
Then went to sea, and made his grog so
          strong,
He died before he could forgive the wrong.
  The rich man built a house, both large and
          high,
He enter'd in and set him down to sigh ;

He planted ample woods and gardens fair,
And walk'd with anguish and compunction
    there :
The rich man's pines, to every friend a treat,
He saw with pain, and he refused to eat ;
His daintiest food, his richest wines, were all
Turn'd by remorse to vinegar and gall :
The softest down, by living body press'd,
The rich man bought, and tried to take his
    rest ;
But care had thorns upon his pillow spread,
And scatter'd sand and nettles in his bed :
Nervous he grew,—would often sigh and
    groan,
He talk'd but little, and he walk'd alone ;
Till by his priest convinced, that from one
    deed
Of genuine love would joy and health proceed;
He from that time with care and zeal began
To seek and soothe the grievous ills of man ;
And as his hands their aid to grief apply,
He learns to smile and he forgets to sigh.

  Now he can drink his wine and taste his
    food,
And feel the blessings, Heav'n has dealt, are
    good ;
And, since the suffering seek the rich man's
    door,
He sleeps as soundly as when young and poor.
  Here much he gives—is urgent more to gain;
He begs—rich beggars seldom sue in vain :
Preachers most famed he moves, the crowd
    to move,
And never wearies in the work of love :
He rules all business, settles all affairs,
He makes collections, he directs repairs ;
And if he wrong'd one brother,—Heav'n
    forgive
The man by whom so many brethren live !

  Then, 'mid our signatures, a name appears
Of one for wisdom famed above his years ;
And these were forty : he was from his youth
A patient searcher after useful truth :
To language little of his time he gave,
To science less, nor was the muse's slave ;
Sober and grave, his college sent him down,
A fair example for his native town.
  Slowly he speaks, and with such solemn air,
You'd think a Socrates or Solon there ;
For though a Christian, he 's disposed to draw
His rules from reason's and from nature's
    law.

' Know,' he exclaims, ' my fellow mortals,
    know,
Virtue alone is happiness below ;
And what is virtue ? prudence first to choose
Life's real good,—the evil to refuse ;
Add justice then, the eager hand to hold,
To curb the lust of power and thirst of gold ;
Join temp'rance next, that cheerful health
    insures,
And fortitude unmoved, that conquers or
    endures.'
  He speaks, and lo !—the very man you see,
Prudent and temperate, just and patient he,
By prudence taught his worldly wealth to
    keep.
No folly wastes, no avarice swells the heap :
He no man's debtor, no man's patron lives ;
Save sound advice, he neither asks nor gives ;
By no vain thoughts or erring fancy sway'd,
His words are weighty, or at least are weigh'd;
Temp'rate in every place—abroad, at home,
Thence will applause, and hence will profit
    come ;
And health from either he in time prepares
For sickness, age, and their attendant cares,
But not for fancy's ills ;—he never grieves
For love that wounds or friendship that
    deceives ;
His patient soul endures what Heav'n ordains,
But neither feels nor fears ideal pains.
  ' Is aught then wanted in a man so wise ?'—
Alas !—I think he wants infirmities ;
He wants the ties that knit us to our kind—
The cheerful, tender, soft, complacent mind,
That would the feelings, which he dreads,
    excite,
And make the virtues he approves delight ; ·
What dying martyrs, saints, and patriots
    feel,
The strength of action and the warmth of
    zeal.
  Again attend !—and see a man whose cares
Are nicely placed on either world's affairs,—
Merchant and saint ; 'tis doubtful if he knows
To which account he most regard bestows ;
Of both he keeps his ledger :—there he reads
Of gainful ventures and of godly deeds ;
There all he gets or loses find a place,
A lucky bargain and a lack of grace.
  The joys above this prudent man invite
To pay his tax—devotion !—day and night ;
The pains of hell his timid bosom awe,
And force obedience to the church's law ;

Hence that continual thought,—that solemn
    air,—
Those sad good works, and that laborious
    prayer.
    All these (when conscience, waken'd and
        afraid,
To think how avarice calls and is obey'd)
He in his journal finds, and for his grief
Obtains the transient opium of relief.
    ' Sink not, my soul!—my spirit, rise and
        look
O'er the fair entries of this precious book:
Here are the sins, our debts;—this fairer
    side
Has what to carnal wish our strength denied;
Has those religious duties every day
Paid,—which so few upon the sabbath pay;
Here too are conquests over frail desires,
Attendance due on all the church requires;
Then alms I give—for I believe the word
Of holy writ, and lend unto the Lord,
And if not all th' importunate demand,
The fear of want restrains my ready hand;
—Behold! what sums I to the poor resign,
Sums placed in Heaven's own book, as well as
    mine:
Rest then, my spirit!—fastings, prayers, and
    alms,
Will soon suppress these idly-raised alarms,
And weigh'd against our frailties, set in view
A noble balance in our favour due:
Add that I yearly here affix my name,
Pledge for large payment—not from love of
    fame,

But to make peace within;—that peace to
    make,
What sums I lavish! and what gains forsake!
Cheer up, my heart!—let's cast off every
    doubt,
Pray without dread, and place our money out.'
    Such the religion of a mind that steers
Its way to bliss, between its hopes and fears;
Whose passions in due bounds each other
    keep,
And thus subdued, they murmur till they
    sleep;
Whose virtues all their certain limits know,
Like well-dried herbs that neither fade nor
    grow;
Who for success and safety ever tries,
And with both worlds alternately complies.
    Such are the guardians of this bless'd estate,
Whate'er without, they're praised within the
    gate;
That they are men, and have their faults, is
    true,
But here their worth alone appears in view:
The Muse indeed, who reads the very breast,
Has something of the secrets there express'd,
But yet in charity;—and when she sees
Such means for joy or comfort, health or ease,
And knows how much united minds effect,
She almost dreads their failings to detect;
But truth commands:—in man's erroneous
    kind,
Virtues and frailties mingle in the mind;
Happy!—when fears to public spirit move,
And even vices to the work of love.

LETTER XVIII. THE POOR AND THEIR DWELLINGS

Bene paupertas
Humili tecto contenta latet.
SENECA, *Oct.*, Act v. 884–5.

Omnes quibus res sunt minus secundae, magis
      sunt, nescio quo modo,
Suspitiosi ; ad contumeliam omnia accipiunt
      magis ;
Propter suam impotentiam se semper credunt
      ludier.
TERENT., *in Adelph.*, Act iv, Sc. 3.

Show not to the poor thy pride,
   Let their home a cottage be ;
Nor the feeble body hide
   In a palace fit for thee ;
Let him not about him see
Lofty ceilings, ample halls,
   Or a gate his boundary be,
Where nor friend or kinsman calls.
Let him not one walk behold,
   That only one which he must tread,
Nor a chamber large and cold,
   Where the aged and sick are led ;
Better far his humble shed,
Humble sheds of neighbours by,
   And the old and tatter'd bed,
Where he sleeps and hopes to die.

To quit of torpid sluggishness the lair,
And from the pow'rful arms of sloth get free,
'Tis rising from the dead—Alas ! it cannot be.
THOMSON'S *Castle of Indolence*, Canto II, v. 61.

The Method of treating the Borough Paupers
—Many maintained at their own Dwellings
—Some Characters of the Poor—The
School-mistress, when aged—The Idiot—
The poor Sailor—The declined Tradesman
and his Companion—This contrasted with
the Maintenance of the Poor in a common
Mansion erected by the Hundred—The
Objections to this Method : not Want, nor
Cruelty, but the necessary Evils of this
Mode—What they are—Instances of the
Evil—A Return to the Borough Poor—
The Dwellings of these—The Lanes and
By-ways—No Attention here paid to
Convenience—The Pools in the Path-ways
—Amusements of Sea-port Children—The
Town-Flora—Herbs on Walls and vacant
Spaces—A female Inhabitant of an Alley
—A large Building let to several poor In-
habitants—Their Manners and Habits.

YES ! we've our Borough-vices, and I know
How far they spread, how rapidly they grow;

Yet think not virtue quits the busy place,
Nor charity, the virtues' crown and grace.
   ' Our poor, how feed we ?'—To the most
      we give
A weekly dole, and at their homes they live;—
Others together dwell,—but when they come
To the low roof, they see a kind of home,
A social people whom they've ever known,
With their own thoughts and manners like
      their own.
   At her old house, her dress, her air the same,
I see mine ancient letter-loving dame :
' Learning, my child,' said she, ' shall fame
      command ;
Learning is better worth than house or land—
For houses perish, lands are gone and spent ;
In learning then excel, for that 's most
      excellent.'
   ' And what her learning ?'—'Tis with awe
      to look
In every verse throughout one sacred book ;
From this her joy, her hope, her peace is
      sought :
This she has learn'd, and she is nobly taught.
   If aught of mine have gain'd the public ear ;
If RUTLAND deigns these humble Tales to
      hear ;
If critics pardon, what my friends approved ;
Can I mine ancient widow pass unmoved ?
Shall I not think what pains the matron took,
When first I trembled o'er the gilded book ?
How she, all patient, both at eve and morn,
Her needle pointed at the guarding horn ;
And how she soothed me, when, with study
      sad,
I labour'd on to reach the final zad ?
Shall I not grateful still the dame survey,
And ask the muse the poet's debt to pay ?
   Nor I alone, who hold a trifler's pen,
But half our bench of wealthy, weighty men,
Who rule our Borough, who enforce our laws ;
They own the matron as the leading cause,
And feel the pleasing debt, and pay the just
      applause :
To her own house is borne the week's supply ;
There she in credit lives, there hopes in peace
      to die.
   With her a harmless idiot we behold,
Who hoards up silver shells for shining gold ;

These he preserves, with unremitted care,
To buy a seat, and reign the Borough's mayor:
Alas!—who could th' ambitious changeling
   tell,
That what he sought our rulers dared to sell?

  Near these a sailor, in that hut of thatch
(A fish-boat's cabin is its nearest match),
Dwells, and the dungeon is to him a seat,
Large as he wishes—in his view complete:
A lockless coffer and a lidless hutch
That hold his stores, have room for twice as
   much:
His one spare shirt, long glass, and iron box,
Lie all in view; no need has he for locks:
Here he abides, and, as our strangers pass,
He shows the shipping, he presents the glass;
He makes (unask'd) their ports and business
   known,
And (kindly heard) turns quickly to his own,
Of noble captains, heroes every one,—
You might as soon have made the steeple run:
And then his messmates, if you're pleased to
   stay,
He'll one by one the gallant souls display,
And as the story verges to an end,
He'll wind from deed to deed, from friend to
   friend;
He'll speak of those long lost, the brave of old,
As princes gen'rous and as heroes bold;
Then will his feelings rise, till you may trace
Gloom, like a cloud, frown o'er his manly
   face,—
And then a tear or two, which sting his pride;
These he will dash indignantly aside,
And splice his tale;—now take him from
   his cot,
And for some cleaner birth exchange his lot,
How will he all that cruel aid deplore?
His heart will break, and he will fight no
   more.

  Here is the poor old merchant: he declined,
And, as they say, is not in perfect mind;
In his poor house, with one poor maiden
   friend,
Quiet he paces to his journey's end.
  Rich in his youth, he traded and he fail'd;
Again he tried, again his fate prevail'd;
His spirits low and his exertions small,
He fell perforce, he seem'd decreed to fall:
Like the gay knight, unapt to rise was he,
But downward sank with sad alacrity.
A borough-place we gain'd him—in disgrace
For gross neglect, he quickly lost the place;

But still he kept a kind of sullen pride,
Striving his wants to hinder or to hide:
At length, compell'd by very need, in grief
He wrote a proud petition for relief.

  ' He did suppose a fall, like his, would prove
Of force to wake their sympathy and love;
Would make them feel the changes all may
   know,
And stir them up a new regard to show.'

  His suit was granted;—to an ancient maid,
Relieved herself, relief for him was paid:
Here they together (meet companions) dwell,
And dismal tales of man's misfortunes tell:
' 'Twas not a world for them, God help them!
   they
Could not deceive, nor flatter, nor betray;
But there's a happy change, a scene to come,
And they, God help them! shall be soon at
   home.'

  If these no pleasures nor enjoyments gain,
Still none their spirits nor their speech re-
   strain;
They sigh at ease, 'mid comforts they com-
   plain.
The poor will grieve, the poor will weep and
   sigh,
Both when they know, and when they know
   not why;
But we our bounty with such care bestow,
That cause for grieving they shall seldom
   know.

  Your plan I love not;—with a number you
Have placed your poor, your pitiable few;
There, in one house, throughout their lives to
   be,
The pauper-palace which they hate to see:
That giant-building, that high-bounding wall,
Those bare-worn walks, that lofty thund'ring
   hall!
That large loud clock, which tolls each
   dreaded hour,
Those gates and locks, and all those signs of
   power:
It is a prison, with a milder name,
Which few inhabit without dread or shame.

  Be it agreed—the poor who hither come
Partake of plenty, seldom found at home;
That airy rooms and decent beds are meant
To give the poor by day, by night, content;
That none are frighten'd, once admitted here,
By the stern looks of lordly overseer:
Grant that the guardians of the place attend,
And ready ear to each petition lend;

That they desire the grieving poor to show
What ills they feel, what partial acts they
    know,
Not without promise, nay desire to heal
Each wrong they suffer and each wo they feel.
  Alas! their sorrows in their bosoms dwell;
They've much to suffer, but have nought to
    tell;
They have no evil in the place to state,
And dare not say, it is the house they hate:
They own there's granted all such place can
    give,
But live repining, for 'tis there they live.
  Grandsires are there, who now no more
    must see,
No more must nurse upon the trembling knee
The lost loved daughter's infant progeny:
Like death's dread mansion, this allows not
    place
For joyful meetings of a kindred race.
  Is not the matron there, to whom the son
Was wont at each declining day to run;
He (when his toil was over) gave delight,
By lifting up the latch, and one 'good night?'
Yes, she is here; but nightly to her door
The son, still lab'ring, can return no more.
Widows are here, who in their huts were left,
Of husbands, children, plenty, ease bereft;
Yet all that grief within the humble shed
Was soften'd, soften'd in the humble bed:
But here, in all its force, remains the grief,
And not one soft'ning object for relief.
  Who can, when here, the social neighbour
    meet?
Who learn the story current in the street?
Who to the long-known intimate impart
Facts they have learn'd or feelings of the
    heart?—
They talk indeed, but who can choose a friend,
Or seek companions at their journey's end?
  Here are not those whom they, when
    infants, knew;
Who, with like fortune, up to manhood grew
Who, with like troubles, at old age arrived;
Who, like themselves, the joy of life survived;
Whom time and custom so familiar made,
That looks the meaning in the mind convey'd:
But here to strangers, words nor looks impart
The various movements of the suffering heart;
Nor will that heart with those alliance own,
To whom its views and hopes are all unknown.
  What, if no grievous fears their lives annoy,
Is it not worse no prospects to enjoy?

'Tis cheerless living in such bounded view,
With nothing dreadful, but with nothing new;
Nothing to bring them joy, to make them
    weep,—
The day itself is, like the night, asleep:
Or on the sameness if a break be made,
'Tis by some pauper to his grave convey'd;
By smuggled news from neighb'ring village
    told,
News never true, or truth a twelvemonth old;
By some new inmate doom'd with them to
    dwell,
Or justice come to see that all goes well;
Or change of room, or hour of leave to crawl
On the black footway winding with the wall,
Till the stern bell forbids, or master's sterner
    call.
  Here too the mother sees her children
    train'd,
Her voice excluded and her feelings pain'd:
Who govern here, by general rules must move,
Where ruthless custom rends the bond of love.
Nations we know have nature's law trans-
    gress'd,
And snatch'd the infant from the parent's
    breast;
But still for public good the boy was train'd,
The mother suffer'd, but the matron gain'd:
Here nature's outrage serves no cause to aid;
The ill is felt, but not the Spartan made.
  Then too I own, it grieves me to behold
Those ever virtuous, helpless now and old,
By all for care and industry approved,
For truth respected, and for temper loved;
And who, by sickness and misfortune tried,
Gave want its worth and poverty its pride:
I own it grieves me to behold them sent
From their old home; 'tis pain, 'tis punish-
    ment,
To leave each scene familiar, every face,
For a new people and a stranger race;
For those who, sunk in sloth and dead to shame
From scenes of guilt with daring spirits came;
Men, just and guileless, at such manners start,
And bless their God that time has fenced
    their heart,
Confirm'd their virtue, and expell'd the fear
Of vice in minds so simple and sincere.
  Here the good pauper, losing all the praise
By worthy deeds acquired in better days,
Breathes a few months, then, to his chamber
    led,
Expires, while strangers prattle round his bed.

The grateful hunter, when his horse is old,
Wills not the useless favourite to be sold ;
He knows his former worth, and gives him
    place
In some fair pasture, till he runs his race :
But has the labourer, has the seaman done
Less worthy service, though not dealt to one ?
Shall we not then contribute to their ease,
In their old haunts, where ancient objects
    please ?
That, till their sight shall fail them, they
    may trace
The well-known prospect and the long-loved
    face.

The noble oak, in distant ages seen,
With far-stretch'd boughs and foliage fresh
    and green,
Though now its bare and forky branches show
How much it lacks the vital warmth below,
The stately ruin yet our wonder gains,
Nay, moves our pity, without thought of
    pains :
Much more shall real wants and cares of age
Our gentler passions in their cause engage ;—
Drooping and burthen'd with a weight of years,
What venerable ruin man appears !
How worthy pity, love, respect, and grief—
He claims protection—he compels relief ;—
And shall we send him from our view, to brave
The storms abroad, whom we at home might
    save,
And let a stranger dig our ancient brother's
    grave ?
No !—we will shield him from the storm he
    fears,
And when he falls, embalm him with our tears.

Farewell to these ; but all our poor to know,
Let's seek the winding lane, the narrow row,
Suburbian prospects, where the traveller stops
To see the sloping tenement on props,
With building yards immix'd, and humble
    sheds and shops ;
Where the Cross-Keys and Plumber's-Arms
    invite
Laborious men to taste their coarse delight ;
Where the low porches, stretching from the
    door,
Gave some distinction in the days of yore,
Yet now neglected, more offend the eye,
By gloom and ruin, than the cottage by :
Places like these the noblest town endures,
The gayest palace has its sinks and sewers.

Here is no pavement, no inviting shop,
To give us shelter when compell'd to stop ;
But plashy puddles stand along the way,
Fill'd by the rain of one tempestuous day ;
And these so closely to the buildings run,
That you must ford them, for you cannot
    shun ;
Though here and there convenient bricks are
    laid,
And door-side heaps afford their dubious aid.
Lo ! yonder shed ; observe its garden-
    ground,
With the low paling, form'd of wreck, around :
There dwells a fisher ; if you view his boat,
With bed and barrel—'tis his house afloat ;
Look at his house, where ropes, nets, blocks
    abound,
Tar, pitch, and oakum—'tis his boat aground :
That space enclosed, but little he regards,
Spread o'er with relics of masts, sails, and
    yards :
Fish by the wall, on spit of elder, rest,
Of all his food, the cheapest and the best,
By his own labour caught, for his own hunger
    dress'd.
Here our reformers come not ; none object
To paths polluted, or upbraid neglect ;
None care that ashy heaps at doors are cast,
That coal-dust flies along the blinding blast :
None heed the stagnant pools on either side,
Where new-launch'd ships of infant sailors
    ride :
Rodneys in rags here British valour boast,
And lisping Nelsons fright the Gallic coast.
They fix the rudder, set the swelling sail,
They point the bowsprit, and they blow the
    gale :
True to her port, the frigate scuds away,
And o'er that frowning ocean finds her bay :
Her owner rigg'd her, and he knows her worth,
And sees her, fearless, gunwale-deep go forth ;
Dreadless he views his sea, by breezes curl'd,
When inch-high billows vex the watery world.
There, fed by food they love, to rankest
    size,
Around the dwellings docks and wormwood
    rise ;
Here the strong mallow strikes her slimy
    root,
Here the dull night-shade hangs her deadly
    fruit ;
On hills of dust the henbane's faded green,
And pencil'd flower of sickly scent is seen :

At the wall's base the fiery nettle springs,
With fruit globose and fierce with poison'd
    stings ;
Above (the growth of many a year) is spread
The yellow level of the stone-crop's bed ;
In every chink delights the fern to grow,
With glossy leaf and tawny bloom below : [1]
These, with our sea-weeds, rolling up and
    down,
Form the contracted Flora [2] of the town.
    Say, wilt thou more of scenes so sordid
        know ?
Then will I lead thee down the dusty row ;
By the warm alley and the long close lane,—
There mark the fractured door and paper'd
    pane,
Where flags the noon-tide air, and, as we
    pass,
We fear to breathe the putrefying mass :
But fearless yonder matron ; she disdains
To sigh for zephyrs from ambrosial plains ;
But mends her meshes torn, and pours her lay
All in the stifling fervour of the day.
    Her naked children round the alley run,
And roll'd in dust, are bronzed beneath the
    sun ;
Or gambol round the dame, who, loosely
    dress'd,
Woos the coy breeze, to fan the open breast :
She, once a handmaid, strove by decent art
To charm her sailor's eye and touch his heart;
Her bosom then was veil'd in kerchief clean,
And fancy left to form the charms unseen.
    But when a wife, she lost her former care,
Nor thought on charms, nor time for dress
    could spare ;
Careless she found her friends who dwelt
    beside,
No rival beauty kept alive her pride :
Still in her bosom virtue keeps her place,
But decency is gone, the virtues' guard and
    grace.
    See that long boarded building !—By these
        stairs
Each humble tenant to that home repairs—
By one large window lighted—it was made
For some bold project, some design in trade:
This fail'd,—and one, a humorist in his way,
(Ill was the humour), bought it in decay;
Nor will he sell, repair, or take it down ;
'Tis his,—what cares he for the talk of town ?
' No! he will let it to the poor ;—a home
Where he delights to see the creatures come : '

' They may be thieves ; '—' Well, so are
    richer men ; '
' Or idlers, cheats, or prostitutes : '—' What
    then ? '
' Outcasts pursued by justice, vile and
    base ; '—
' They need the more his pity and the place : '
Convert to system his vain mind has built,
He gives asylum to deceit and guilt.
    In this vast room, each place by habit fix'd,
Are sexes, families, and ages mix'd,—
To union forced by crime, by fear, by need,
And all in morals and in modes agreed ;
Some ruin'd men, who from mankind remove;
Some ruin'd females, who yet talk of love ;
And some grown old in idleness—the prey
To vicious spleen, still railing through the day;
And need and misery, vice and danger bind
In sad alliance each degraded mind.
    That window view !—oil'd paper and old
        glass
Stain the strong rays, which, though im-
    peded, pass,
And give a dusty warmth to that huge room,
The conquer'd sunshine's melancholy gloom;
When all those western rays, without so bright,
Within become a ghastly glimmering light,
As pale and faint upon the floor they fall,
Or feebly gleam on the opposing wall :
That floor, once oak, now pieced with fir
    unplaned,
Or, where not pieced, in places bored and
    stain'd ;
That wall once whiten'd, now an odious sight,
Stain'd with all hues, except its ancient white;
The only door is fasten'd by a pin,
Or stubborn bar, that none may hurry in:
For this poor room, like rooms of greater pride,
At times contains what prudent men would
    hide.
    Where'er the floor allows an even space,
Chalking and marks of various games have
    place ;
Boys without foresight, pleased in halters
    swing ;
On a fix'd hook men cast a flying ring ;
While gin and snuff their female neighbours
    share,
And the black beverage in the fractured ware.
    On swinging shelf are things incongruous
        stored,—
Scraps of their food,—the cards and cribbage-
    board,—

With pipes and pouches; while on peg below,
Hang a lost member's fiddle and its bow:
That still reminds them how he'd dance and
    play,
Ere sent untimely to the convicts' bay.
  Here by a curtain, by a blanket there,
Are various beds conceal'd, but none with
    care ;
Where some by day and some by night, as best
Suit their employments, seek uncertain rest;
The drowsy children at their pleasure creep
To the known crib, and there securely sleep.
  Each end contains a grate, and these beside
Are hung utensils for their boil'd and fried—
All used at any hour, by night, by day,
As suit the purse, the person, or the prey.
  Above the fire, the mantel-shelf contains
Of china-ware some poor unmatch'd remains;
There many a tea-cup's gaudy fragment stands,
All placed by vanity's unwearied hands ;

For here she lives, e'en here she looks about,
To find some small consoling objects out :
Nor heed these Spartan dames their house,
    nor sit
'Mid cares domestic,—they nor sew nor
    knit;
But of their fate discourse, their ways, their
    wars,
With arm'd authorities, their 'scapes and
    scars :
These lead to present evils, and a cup,
If fortune grant it, winds description up.
  High hung at either end, and next the
    wall,
Two ancient mirrors show the forms of all,
In all their force ;—these aid them in their
    dress,
But with the good, the evils too express,
Doubling each look of care, each token of
    distress.

LETTER XIX.   THE POOR OF THE BOROUGH

THE PARISH-CLERK
Nam dives qui fieri vult,
Et citò vult fieri ; sed quae reverentia legum,
Quis metus, aut pudor est unquam pro-
  perantis avari ?
    JUVENAL, *Sat.* xiv, vv. 176–8.
Nocte brevem si fortè indulsit cura soporem,
Et toto versata toro iam membra quiescunt,
Continuò templum et violati Numinis aras,
Et quod praecipuis mentem sudoribus urget,
Te videt in somnis ; tua sacra et major imago
Humana turbat pavidum, cogitque fateri.
    JUVENAL, *Sat.* xiii, vv. 217–22.

The Parish-Clerk began his Duties with the
late Vicar, a grave and austere Man ; one
fully orthodox ; a Detecter and Opposer
of the Wiles of Satan—His Opinion of his
own Fortitude—The more frail offended
by these Professions—His good Advice
gives further Provocation—They invent
Stratagems to overcome his Virtue—His
Triumph—He is yet not invulnerable : is
assaulted by Fear of Want, and Avarice—
He gradually yields to the Seduction—He
reasons with himself and is persuaded—He
offends, but with Terror ; repeats his
Offence ; grows familiar with Crime ; is
detected—His Sufferings and Death.

WITH our late vicar, and his age the same,
His clerk, hight Jachin, to his office came :
The like slow speech was his, the like tall
    slender frame :
But Jachin was the gravest man on ground,
And heard his master's jokes with look pro-
    found ;
For worldly wealth this man of letters sigh'd,
And had a sprinkling of the spirit's pride :
But he was sober, chaste, devout, and just,
One whom his neighbours could believe and
    trust :
Of none suspected, neither man nor maid
By him were wrong'd, or were of him afraid.
  There was indeed a frown, a trick of state
In Jachin ;—formal was his air and gait ;
But if he seem'd more solemn and less kind
Than some light men to light affairs confined,
Still 'twas allow'd that he should so behave
As in high seat, and be severely grave.
  This book-taught man, to man's first foe
    profess'd
Defiance stern, and hate that knew not
    rest ;
He held that Satan, since the world began,
In every act, had strife with every man ;

That never evil deed on earth was done,
But of the acting parties he was one ;
The flattering guide to make ill prospects
　　clear ;
To smooth rough ways the constant pioneer ;
The ever-tempting, soothing, softening power,
Ready to cheat, seduce, deceive, devour.
　' Me has the sly seducer oft withstood,'
Said pious Jachin,—' but he gets no good ;
I pass the house where swings the tempting
　　sign,
And pointing, tell him, " Satan, that is thine :"
I pass the damsels pacing down the street,
And look more grave and solemn when we
　　meet ;
Nor doth it irk me to rebuke their smiles,
Their wanton ambling and their watchful
　　wiles :
Nay, like the good John Bunyan, when I view
Those forms, I'm angry at the ills they do ;
That I could pinch and spoil, in sin's despite,
Beauties ! which frail and evil thoughts
　　excite.*
　'At feasts and banquets seldom am I found,
And (save at church) abhor a tuneful sound ;
To plays and shows I run not to and fro,
And where my master goes forbear to go.'
　No wonder Satan took the thing amiss,
To be opposed by such a man as this—
A man so grave, important, cautious, wise,
Who dared not trust his feeling or his eyes ;
　No wonder he should lurk and lie in wait,
Should fit his hooks and ponder on his bait,
Should on his movements keep a watchful
　　eye ;
For he pursued a fish who led the fry.
　With his own peace our clerk was not
　　content,
He tried, good man ! to make his friends
　　repent.
　' Nay, nay, my friends, from inns and
　　taverns fly ;
You may suppress your thirst, but not supply :
A foolish proverb says, " the devil's at
　　home ; "
But he is there, and tempts in every room ;
Men feel, they know not why, such places
　　please ;
His are the spells—they're idleness and ease ;

* John Bunyan, in one of the many productions
of his zeal, has ventured to make public this ex-
traordinary sentiment, which the frigid piety of
our clerk so readily adopted.

Magic of fatal kind he throws around,
Where care is banish'd but the heart is bound.
　' Think not of beauty ; when a maid you
　　meet,
Turn from her view and step across the street ;
Dread all the sex : their looks create a charm,
A smile should fright you and a word alarm :
E'en I myself, with all my watchful care,
Have for an instant felt th' insidious snare,
And caught my sinful eyes at th' endangering
　　stare ;
Till I was forced to smite my bounding breast
With forceful blow and bid the bold-one rest.
　' Go not with crowds when they to pleasure
　　run,
But public joy in private safety shun :
When bells, diverted from their true intent,
Ring loud for some deluded mortal sent
To hear or make long speech in parliament ;
What time the many, that unruly beast,
Roars its rough joy and shares the final feast :
Then heed my counsel, shut thine ears and
　　eyes ;
A few will hear me—for the few are wise.'
　Not Satan's friends, nor Satan's self could
　　bear
The cautious man who took of souls such care ;
An interloper,—one who, out of place,
Had volunteer'd upon the side of grace :
There was his master ready once a week—
To give advice ; what further need he seek ?
' Amen, so be it : '—what had he to do
With more than this ?—'twas insolent and
　　new ;
And some determined on a way to see
How frail he was, that so it might not be.
　First they essay'd to tempt our saint to sin,
By points of doctrine argued at an inn ;
Where he might warmly reason, deeply drink,
Then lose all power to argue and to think.
　In vain they tried ; he took the question up,
Clear'd every doubt, and barely touch'd the
　　cup :
By many a text he proved his doctrine sound,
And look'd in triumph on the tempters round.
　Next 'twas their care an artful lass to find,
Who might consult him, as perplex'd in mind ;
She they conceived might put her case with
　　fears,
With tender tremblings and seducing tears ;
She might such charms of various kind dis-
　　play,
That he would feel their force and melt away :

For why of nymphs such caution and such
    dread,
Unless he felt and fear'd to be misled ?
  She came, she spake : he calmly heard her
    case,
And plainly told her 'twas a want of grace;
Bade her ' such fancies and affections check,
And wear a thicker muslin on her neck.'
Abased, his human foes the combat fled,
And the stern clerk yet higher held his head.
They were indeed a weak, impatient set,
But their shrewd prompter had his engines
    yet ;
Had various means to make a mortal trip,
Who shunn'd a flowing bowl and rosy lip;
And knew a thousand ways his heart to move,
Who flies from banquets and who laughs at
    love.
  Thus far the playful Muse has lent her aid,
But now departs, of graver theme afraid ;
Her may we seek in more appropriate time,—
There is no jesting with distress and crime.
  Our worthy clerk had now arrived at fame,
Such as but few in his degree might claim ;
But he was poor, and wanted not the sense
That lowly rates the praise without the pence :
He saw the common herd with reverence treat
The weakest burgess whom they chanced to
    meet ;
While few respected his exalted views,
And all beheld his doublet and his shoes :
None, when they meet, would to his parts allow
(Save his poor boys) a hearing or a bow :
To this false judgment of the vulgar mind,
He was not fully, as a saint, resign'd ;
He found it much his jealous soul affect,
To fear derision and to find neglect.
  The year was bad, the christening-fees were
    small,
The weddings few, the parties paupers all ;
Desire of gain with fear of want combined,
Raised sad commotion in his wounded mind;
Wealth was in all his thoughts, his views, his
    dreams,
And prompted base desires and baseless
    schemes.
  Alas ! how often erring mortals keep
The strongest watch against the foes who
    sleep ;
While the more wakeful, bold and artful foe
Is suffer'd guardless and unmark'd to go.
  Once in a month the sacramental bread
Our clerk with wine upon the table spread ;

The custom this, that, as the vicar reads,
He for our off'rings round the church pro-
    ceeds :
Tall spacious seats the wealthier people hid,
And none had view of what his neighbour did;
Laid on the box and mingled when they fell,
Who should the worth of each oblation tell ?
Now as poor Jachin took the usual round,
And saw the alms and heard the metal sound,
He had a thought ;—at first it was no more
Than—' these have cash and give it to the
    poor : '
A second thought from this to work began—
' And can they give it to a poorer man ? '
Proceeding thus,—' My merit could they
    know,
And knew my need, how freely they'd bestow;
But though they know not, these remain the
    same ;
And are a strong, although a secret claim :
To me, alas ! the want and worth are known,
Why then, in fact, 'tis but to take my
    own.'
  Thought after thought pour'd in, a tempting
    train,—
' Suppose it done,—who is it could complain?
How could the poor ? for they such trifles
    share,
As add no comfort, as suppress no care ;
But many a pittance makes a worthy heap,—
What says the law ? that silence puts to
    sleep :—
Nought then forbids, the danger could we
    shun,
And sure the business may be safely done.
  ' But am I earnest ?—earnest? No.—I say,
If such my mind, that I could plan a way ;
Let me reflect ;—I've not allow'd me time
To purse the pieces, and if dropp'd they'd
    chime : '
Fertile is evil in the soul of man,—
He paused,—said Jachin, ' They may drop on
    bran.
Why then 'tis safe and (all consider'd) just,
The poor receive it,—'tis no breach of trust
The old and widows may their trifles miss,
There must be evil in a good like this :
But I'll be kind—the sick I'll visit twice,
When now but once, and freely give advice.
Yet let me think again : '—Again he tried,
For stronger reasons on his passion's side,
And quickly these were found, yet slowly he
    complied.

The morning came : the common service
  done,—
Shut every door,—the solemn rite begun,—
And, as the priest the sacred sayings read,
The clerk went forward, trembling as he tread ;
O'er the tall pew he held the box, and heard
The offer'd piece, rejoicing as he fear'd :
Just by the pillar, as he cautious tripp'd,
And turn'd the aile, he then a portion slipp'd
From the full store, and to the pocket sent,
But held a moment—and then down it went.
  The priest read on, on walk'd the man
  afraid,
Till a gold offering in the plate was laid ;
Trembling he took it, for a moment stopp'd,
Then down it fell, and sounded as it dropp'd ;
Amazed he started, for th' affrighted man,
Lost and bewilder'd, thought not of the bran ;
But all were silent, all on things intent
Of high concern, none ear to money lent ;
So on he walk'd, more cautious than before,
And gain'd the purposed sum and one piece
  more.
  Practice makes perfect ;—when the month
  came round,
He dropp'd the cash, nor listen'd for a sound ;
But yet, when last of all th' assembled flock,
He ate and drank,—it gave th' electric shock :
Oft was he forced his reasons to repeat,
Ere he could kneel in quiet at his seat ;
But custom soothed him—ere a single year
All this was done without restraint or fear :
Cool and collected, easy and composed,
He was correct till all the service closed ;
Then to his home, without a groan or sigh,
Gravely he went, and laid his treasure by.
  Want will complain : some widows had
  express'd
A doubt if they were favour'd like the rest ;
The rest described with like regret their dole,
And thus from parts they reason'd to the
  whole ;
When all agreed some evil must be done,
Or rich men's hearts grew harder than a stone.
Our easy vicar cut the matter short ;
He would not listen to such vile report.
  All were not thus—there govern'd in that
  year
A stern stout churl, an angry overseer ;
A tyrant fond of power, loud, lewd, and most
  severe :
Him the mild vicar, him the graver clerk,
Advised, reproved, but nothing would he mark,

Save the disgrace, 'and that, my friends,'
  said he,
' Will I avenge, whenever time may be.'
And now, alas ! 'twas time ;—from man to
  man
Doubt and alarm and shrewd suspicions ran.
  With angry spirit and with sly intent,
This parish-ruler to the altar went ;
A private mark he fix'd on shillings three,
And but one mark could in the money see :
Besides, in peering round, he chanced to note
A sprinkling slight on Jachin's Sunday-coat :
All doubt was over :—when the flock were
  bless'd,
In wrath he rose, and thus his mind express'd.
  ' Foul deeds are here ! ' and saying this,
  he took
The clerk, whose conscience, in her cold-fit,
  shook :
His pocket then was emptied on the place ;
All saw his guilt ; all witness'd his disgrace :
He fell, he fainted, not a groan, a look,
Escaped the culprit ; 'twas a final stroke—
A death-wound never to be heal'd—a fall
That all had witness'd, and amazed were all.
  As he recover'd, to his mind it came,
' I owe to Satan this disgrace and shame : '
All the seduction now appear'd in view ;
' Let me withdraw,' he said, and he withdrew;
No one withheld him, all in union cried,
E'en the avenger,—' We are satisfied : '
For what has death in any form to give,
Equal to that man's terrors, if he live ?
  He lived in freedom, but he hourly saw
How much more fatal justice is than law ;
He saw another in his office reign,
And his mild master treat him with disdain ;
He saw that all men shunn'd him, some
  reviled,
The harsh pass'd frowning, and the simple
  smiled ;
The town maintain'd him, but with some
  reproof,
' And clerks and scholars proudly kept aloof.'
  In each lone place, dejected and dismay'd,
Shrinking from view, his wasting form he laid ;
Or to the restless sea and roaring wind
Gave the strong yearnings of a ruin'd mind :
On the broad beach, the silent summer-day,
Stretch'd on some wreck, he wore his life away;
Or where the river mingles with the sea,
Or on the mud-bank by the elder-tree,
Or by the bounding marsh-dyke, there was he:

And when unable to forsake the town,
In the blind courts he sate desponding down—
Always alone ; then feebly would he crawl
The church-way walk, and lean upon the
    wall :
Too ill for this, he lay beside the door,
Compell'd to hear the reasoning of the poor :
He look'd so pale, so weak, the pitying crowd
Their firm belief of his repentance vow'd ;
They saw him then so ghastly and so thin,
That they exclaim'd, ' Is this the work of
    sin ? '

' Yes,' in his better moments, he replied,
' Of sinful avarice and the spirit's pride ;—
While yet untempted, I was safe and well ;
Temptation came ; I reason'd, and I fell :
To be man's guide and glory I design'd,
A rare example for our sinful kind ;
But now my weakness and my guilt I see,
And am a warning—man, be warn'd by me ! '
    He said, and saw no more the human face;
To a lone loft he went, his dying place,
And, as the vicar of his state inquired,
Turn'd to the wall and silently expired !

LETTER XX. THE POOR OF THE BOROUGH

ELLEN ORFORD

    Patience and sorrow strove
Who should express her goodliest.
       SHAKSPEARE, *Lear*, Act iv, Sc. 3.

  No charms she now can boast,'—'tis true,
But other charmers wither too :
' And she is old,'—the fact I know,
And old will other heroines grow ;
But not like them has she been laid,
In ruin'd castle, sore dismay'd ;
Where naughty man and ghostly spright,
  Fill'd her pure mind with awe and dread,
Stalk'd round the room, put out the light,
  And shook the curtains round her bed.
No cruel uncle kept her land,
No tyrant father forced her hand ;
  She had no vixen virgin-aunt,
Without whose aid she could not eat,
And yet who poison'd all her meat,
  With gibe and sneer and taunt.
Yet of the heroine she'd a share,
She saved a lover from despair,
And granted all his wish, in spite
Of what she knew and felt was right :
  But heroine then no more,
She own'd the fault, and wept and pray'd,
And humbly took the parish aid,
  And dwelt among the poor.

The Widow's Cottage—Blind Ellen one—Hers
not the Sorrows or Adventures of Heroines
—What these are, first described—Deserted
Wives ; rash Lovers ; courageous Damsels :
in desolated Mansions ; in grievous Per-
plexity—These Evils, however severe, of
short Duration—Ellen's Story—Her Em-
ployment in Childhood—First Love ; first
Adventure ; its miserable Termination—
An idiot Daughter—A Husband—Care in

Business without Success—The Man's
Despondency and its Effect—Their Chil-
dren : how disposed of — One particularly
unfortunate—Fate of the Daughter—Ellen
keeps a School and is happy — Becomes
blind : loses her School—Her Consolations.

OBSERVE yon tenement, apart and small,
Where the wet pebbles shine upon the wall;
Where the low benches lean beside the door,
And the red paling bounds the space before ;
Where thrift and lavender, and lad's-love [1]
  bloom,—
That humble dwelling is the widow's home ;
There live a pair, for various fortunes known,
But the blind Ellen will relate her own ;—
Yet ere we hear the story she can tell,
On prouder sorrows let us briefly dwell.
  I've often marvel'd, when by night, by day,
I've mark'd the manners moving in my way,
And heard the language and beheld the lives
Of lass and lover, goddesses and wives,
That books, which promise much of life to give,
Should show so little how we truly live.
  To me it seems, their females and their men
Are but the creatures of the author's pen ;
Nay, creatures borrow'd and again convey'd
From book to book—the shadows of a shade :
Life, if they'd search, would show them many
  a change ;
The ruin sudden and the misery strange !
With more of grievous, base, and dreadful
  things,
Than novelists relate or poet sings :
But they, who ought to look the world around,
Spy out a single spot in fairy-ground ;

Where all, in turn, ideal forms behold,
And plots are laid and histories are told.
   Time have I lent—I would their debt were less—
To flow'ry pages of sublime distress ;
And to the heroine's soul-distracting fears
I early gave my sixpences and tears :
Oft have I travell'd in these tender tales,
To Darnley-Cottages and Maple-Vales,
And watch'd the fair-one from the first-born sigh,
When Henry pass'd and gazed in passing by ;
Till I beheld them pacing in the park,
Close by a coppice where 'twas cold and dark ;
When such affection with such fate appear'd,
Want and a father to be shunn'd and fear'd,
Without employment, prospect, cot, or cash,
That I have judged th' heroic souls were rash.
   Now shifts the scene,—the fair in tower confined,
In all things suffers but in change of mind ;
Now woo'd by greatness to a bed of state,
Now deeply threaten'd with a dungeon's grate ;
Till suffering much and being tried enough,
She shines, triumphant maid!—temptation-proof.
   Then was I led to vengeful monks, who mix
With nymphs and swains, and play unpriestly tricks ;
Then view'd banditti who in forest wide,
And cavern vast, indignant virgins hide ;
Who, hemm'd with bands of sturdiest rogues about,
Find some strange succour, and come virgins out.
   I've watch'd a wint'ry night on castle-walls,
I've stalked by moonlight through deserted halls,
And when the weary world was sunk to rest,
I've had such sights as—may not be ex-press'd.
   Lo ! that chateau, the western tower de-cay'd,
The peasants shun it,—they are all afraid ;
For there was done a deed !—could walls reveal,
Or timbers tell it, how the heart would feel !
Most horrid was it :—for, behold, the floor
Has stain of blood, and will be clean no more :
Hark to the winds ! which through the wide saloon
And the long passage send a dismal tune,—

Music that ghosts delight in ;—and now heed
Yon beauteous nymph, who must unmask the deed ;
See ! with majestic sweep she swims alone
Through rooms, all dreary, guided by a groan :
Though windows rattle, and though tap'stries shake,
And the feet falter every step they take,
'Mid moans and gibing sprights she silent goes,
To find a something, which will soon expose
The villanies and wiles of her determined foes :
And, having thus adventured, thus endured,
Fame, wealth, and lover, are for life secured.
   Much have I fear'd, but am no more afraid,
When some chaste beauty, by some wretch betray'd,
Is drawn away with such distracted speed,
That she anticipates a dreadful deed :
Not so do I—Let solid walls impound
The captive fair, and dig a moat around ;
Let there be brazen locks and bars of steel,
And keepers cruel, such as never feel ;
With not a single note the purse supply,
And when she begs, let men and maids deny :
Be windows those from which she dares not fall,
And help so distant, 'tis in vain to call ;
Still means of freedom will some power devise,
And from the baffled ruffian snatch his prize.
   To Northern Wales, in some sequester'd spot,
I've follow'd fair Louisa to her cot ;
Where, then a wretched and deserted bride,
The injured fair-one wish'd from man to hide ;
Till by her fond repenting Belville found,
By some kind chance—the straying of a hound,
He at her feet craved mercy, nor in vain,
For the relenting dove flew back again.
   There's something rapturous in distress or, oh !
Could Clementina bear her lot of wo ?
Or what she underwent could maiden un-dergo ?
The day was fix'd ; for so the lover sigh'd,
So knelt and craved, he couldn't be denied ;
When, tale most dreadful ! every hope adieu,—
For the fond lover is the brother too :
All other griefs abate ; this monstrous grief
Has no remission, comfort, or relief ;
Four ample volumes, through each page disclose,—
Good Heaven protect us ! only woes on woes ;

Till some strange means afford a sudden view
Of some vile plot, and every wo adieu ! [2]
  Now should we grant these beauties all
    endure
Severest pangs, they've still the speediest cure;
Before one charm be wither'd from the face,
Except the bloom, which shall again have
    place,
In wedlock ends each wish, in triumph all
    disgrace ;
And life to come, we fairly may suppose,
One light, bright contrast to these wild dark
    woes.
  These let us leave, and at her sorrows look,
Too often seen, but seldom in a book ;
Let her who felt, relate them :—on her chair
The heroine sits—in former years, the fair,
Now aged and poor; but Ellen Orford knows,
That we should humbly take what Heaven
    bestows.
  ' My father died—again my mother wed,
And found the comforts of her life were fled ;
Her angry husband, vex'd through half his
    years
By loss and troubles, fill'd her soul with fears:
Their children many, and 'twas my poor place
To nurse and wait on all the infant-race ;
Labour and hunger were indeed my part,
And should have strengthen'd an erroneous
    heart.
  ' Sore was the grief to see him angry come,
And, teased with business, make distress at
    home :
The father's fury and the children's cries
I soon could bear, but not my mother's sighs;
For she look'd back on comforts, and would
    say,
" I wrong'd thee, Ellen," and then turn away :
Thus for my age's good, my youth was tried,
And this my fortune till my mother died.
  ' So, amid sorrow much and little cheer—
A common case, I pass'd my twentieth year ;
For these are frequent evils; thousands share
An equal grief—the like domestic care.
  ' Then in my days of bloom, of health and
    youth,
One, much above me, vow'd his love and
    truth :
We often met, he dreading to be seen,
And much I question'd what such dread
    might mean ;
Yet I believed him true ; my simple heart
And undirected reason took his part.

' Can he who loves me, whom I love, deceive?
Can I such wrong of one so kind believe,
Who lives but in my smile, who trembles
    when I grieve ?
  ' He dared not marry, but we met to prove
What sad encroachments and deceits has love:
Weak that I was, when he, rebuked, withdrew,
I let him see that I was wretched too ;
When less my caution, I had still the pain
Of his or mine own weakness to complain.
  ' Happy the lovers class'd alike in life,
Or happier yet the rich endowing wife ;
But most aggrieved the fond believing maid,
Of her rich lover tenderly afraid :
You judge th' event ; for grievous was my
    fate,
Painful to feel, and shameful to relate :
Ah ! sad it was my burthen to sustain,
When the least misery was the dread of pain;
When I have grieving told him my disgrace,
And plainly mark'd indifference in his face.
  ' Hard ! with these fears and terrors to
    behold
The cause of all, the faithless lover cold ;
Impatient grown at every wish denied,
And barely civil, soothed and gratified ;
Peevish when urged to think of vows so
    strong,
And angry when I spake of crime and wrong.
  ' All this I felt, and still the sorrow grew,
Because I felt that I deserved it too,
And begg'd my infant stranger to forgive
The mother's shame, which in herself must
    live.
  ' When known that shame, I, soon expell'd
    from home,
With a frail sister shared a hovel's gloom ;
There barely fed—(what could I more
    request ?)
My infant slumberer sleeping at my breast,
I from my window saw his blooming bride,
And my seducer smiling at her side ;
Hope lived till then ; I sank upon the floor,
And grief and thought and feeling were no
    more :
Although revived, I judged that life would
    close,
And went to rest, to wonder that I rose :
My dreams were dismal, wheresoe'er I stray'd,
I seem'd ashamed, alarm'd, despised, be-
    tray'd ;
Always in grief, in guilt, disgraced, forlorn,
Mourning that one so weak, so vile, was born;

The earth a desert, tumult in the sea,
The birds affrighted fled from tree to tree,
Obscured the setting sun, and every thing
　　like me :
But Heav'n had mercy, and my need at length
Urged me to labour and renew'd my strength.

'I strove for patience as a sinner must,
Yet felt th' opinion of the world unjust :
There was my lover, in his joy, esteem'd,
And I in my distress, as guilty deem'd ;
Yet sure, not all the guilt and shame belong
To her who feels and suffers for the wrong:
The cheat at play may use the wealth he's won,
But is not honour'd for the mischief done ;
The cheat in love may use each villain-art,
And boast the deed that breaks the victim's
　　heart.

'Four years were past; I might again have
　　found
Some erring wish, but for another wound :
Lovely my daughter grew, her face was fair,
But no expression ever brighten'd there ;
I doubted long, and vainly strove to make
Some certain meaning of the words she spake;
But meaning there was none, and I survey'd
With dread the beauties of my idiot-maid.

'Still I submitted ;—Oh ! 'tis meet and fit
In all we feel to make the heart submit ;
Gloomy and calm my days, but I had then,
It seem'd, attractions for the eyes of men :
The sober master of a decent trade
O'erlook'd my errors, and his offer made;
Reason assented :—true, my heart denied,
" But thou," I said, " shalt be no more my
　　guide."

'When wed, our toil and trouble, pains and
　　care,
Of means to live procured us humble share ;
Five were our sons,—and we, though careful,
　　found
Our hopes declining as the year came round:
For I perceived, yet would not soon perceive,
My husband stealing from my view to grieve;
Silent he grew, and when he spoke he sigh'd,
And surly look'd and peevishly replied :
Pensive by nature, he had gone of late
To those who preach'd of destiny and fate,
Of things fore-doom'd, and of election-grace,
And how in vain we strive to run our race ;
That all by works and moral worth we gain
Is to perceive our care and labour vain ;
That still the more we pay,, our debts the
　　more remain :

That he who feels not the mysterious call,
Lies bound in sin, still grov'ling from the fall.
My husband felt not :—our persuasion, prayer,
And our best reason darken'd his despair;
His very nature changed ; he now reviled
My former conduct,—he reproached my child:
He talk'd of bastard slips, and cursed his bed,
And from our kindness to concealment fled ;
For ever to some evil change inclined,
To every gloomy thought he lent his mind,
Nor rest would give to us, nor rest himself
　　could find ;
His son suspended saw him, long bereft
Of life, nor prospect of revival left.

'With him died all our prospects, and once
　　more
I shared th' allotments of the parish poor ;
They took my children too, and this I know
Was just and lawful, but I felt the blow :
My idiot-maid and one unhealthy boy
Were left, a mother's misery and her joy.

'Three sons I follow'd to the grave, and
　　one—
Oh ! can I speak of that unhappy son ?
Would all the memory of that time were
　　fled,
And all those horrors, with my child, were
　　dead !
Before the world seduced him, what a grace
And smile of gladness shone upon his face!
Then he had knowledge ; finely would he
　　write ;
Study to him was pleasure and delight ;
Great was his courage, and but few could
　　stand
Against the sleight and vigour of his hand;
The maidens loved him;—when he came to
　　die,
No, not the coldest could suppress a sigh :
Here I must cease—how can I say, my child
Was by the bad of either sex beguiled ?
Worst of the bad—they taught him that the
　　laws
Made wrong and right ; there was no other
　　cause ;
That all religion was the trade of priests,
And men, when dead, must perish like the
　　beasts :—
And he, so lively and so gay before——
Ah ! spare a mother—I can tell no more.

'Int'rest was made that they should not
　　destroy
The comely form of my deluded boy—

But pardon came not; damp the place and deep
Where he was kept, as they'd a tiger keep;
For he, unhappy ! had before them all
Vow'd he'd escape, whatever might befall.
  'He'd means of dress, and dress'd beyond
        his means,
And so to see him in such dismal scenes,
I cannot speak it—cannot bear to tell
Of that sad hour—I heard the passing-bell !
  'Slowly they went; he smiled and look'd
        so smart,
Yet sure he shudder'd when he saw the cart,
And gave a look—until my dying-day,
That look will never from my mind away :
Oft as I sit, and ever in my dreams,
I see that look, and they have heard my
        screams.
  'Now let me speak no more—yet all declared
That one so young, in pity should be spared,
And one so manly ;—on his graceful neck,
That chain of jewels may be proud to deck,
To a small mole a mother's lips have press'd,—
And there the cord—my breath is sore
        oppress'd.
  'I now can speak again :—my elder boy
Was that year drown'd,—a seaman in a hoy:
He left a numerous race ; of these would some
In their young troubles to my cottage come,
And these I taught—an humble teacher I—
Upon their heavenly Parent to rely.
  'Alas ! I needed such reliance more :
My idiot-girl, so simply gay before,
Now wept in pain ; some wretch had found
        a time,
Depraved and wicked, for that coward-crime;

I had indeed my doubt, but I suppress'd
The thought that day and night disturb'd
        my rest ;
She and that sick-pale brother—but why
        strive
To keep the terrors of that time alive ?
  'The hour arrived, the new, th'undreaded
        pain,
That came with violence and yet came in
        vain.
I saw her die : her brother too is dead;
Nor own'd such crime—what is it that I
        dread ?
  'The parish-aid withdrawn, I look'd around.
And in my school a bless'd subsistence found—
My winter-calm of life ; to be of use
Would pleasant thoughts and heavenly hopes
        produce;
I loved them all ; it soothed me to presage
The various trials of their riper age,
Then dwell on mine, and bless the Power
        who gave
Pains to correct us, and remorse to save.
  'Yes ! these were days of peace, but they
        are past,—
A trial came, I will believe, a last ;
I lost my sight, and my employment gone,
Useless I live, but to the day live on ;
Those eyes, which long the light of heaven
        enjoy'd,
Were not by pain, by agony destroy'd :
My senses fail not all ; I speak, I pray;
By night my rest, my food I take by day ;
And as my mind looks cheerful to my end,
I love mankind and call my GOD my friend.'

LETTER XXI. THE POOR OF THE BOROUGH

ABEL KEENE

Coepisti melius quam desinis : ultima primis
  Cedunt. Dissimiles : hic vir et ille puer.
OVID, *Deianira Herculi.* (*Heroid.* ix. 23, 24.)

Now the Spirit speaketh expressly, that,
in the latter times, some shall depart from the
faith, giving heed to seducing spirits and
doctrines of devils.
            1st Epistle to Timothy, iv. I.

Abel, a poor Man, Teacher of a School of the
lower Order ; is placed in the Office of a
Merchant ; is alarmed by Discourses of
the Clerks ; unable to reply ; becomes a

Convert ; dresses, drinks, and ridicules
his former Conduct—The Remonstrance of
his Sister, a devout Maiden—Its Effect—
The Merchant dies—Abel returns to
Poverty unpitied ; but relieved—His abject
Condition—His Melancholy—He wanders
about : is found—His own Account of
himself, and the Revolutions in his Mind.

A QUIET simple man was Abel Keene,
He meant no harm, nor did he often mean:
He kept a school of loud rebellious boys,
And growing old, grew nervous with the
        noise ;

When a kind merchant hired his useful pen,
And made him happiest of accompting men,
With glee he rose to every easy day,
When half the labour brought him twice the
    pay.
  There were young clerks, and there the
    merchant's son,
Choice spirits all, who wish'd him to be one;
It must, no question, give them lively joy,
Hopes long indulged, to combat and destroy;
At these they level'd all their skill and
    strength,—
He fell not quickly, but he fell at length :
They quoted books, to him both bold and new,
And scorn'd as fables all he held as true;
'Such monkish stories and such nursery lies,'
That he was struck with terror and surprise.
  'What ! all his life had he the laws obey'd,
Which they broke through and were not once
    afraid ?
Had he so long his evil passions check'd,
And yet at last had nothing to expect ?
While they their lives in joy and pleasure led,
And then had nothing, at the end, to dread ?
Was all his priest with so much zeal convey'd,
A part ! a speech ! for which the man was
    paid ?
And were his pious books, his solemn prayers,
Not worth one tale of the admired Voltaire's?
Then was it time, while yet some years
    remain'd,
To drink untroubled and to think unchain'd,
And on all pleasures, which his purse could
    give,
Freely to seize, and while he lived, to live.'
  Much time he passed in this important
    strife,
The bliss or bane of his remaining life ;
For converts all are made with care and grief,
And pangs attend the birth of unbelief ;
Nor pass they soon ;—with awe and fear he
    took
The flow'ry way, and cast back many a look.
  The youths applauded much his wise
    design,
With weighty reasoning o'er their evening
    wine ;
And much in private 'twould their mirth
    improve,
To hear how Abel spake of life and love;
To hear him own what grievous pains it
    cost,
Ere the old saint was in the sinner lost,

Ere his poor mind with every deed alarm'd,
By wit was settled, and by vice was charm'd.
  For Abel enter'd in his bold career,
Like boys on ice, with pleasure and with fear;
Lingering, yet longing for the joy, he went,
Repenting now, now dreading to repent:
With awkward pace, and with himself at war,
Far gone, yet frighten'd that he went so far;
Oft for his efforts he'd solicit praise,
And then proceed with blunders and delays:
The young more aptly passion's calls pursue,
But age and weakness start at scenes so new,
And tremble when they've done, for all they
    dared to do.
  At length example Abel's dread removed,
With small concern he sought the joys he
    loved ;
Not resting here, he claim'd his share of fame,
And first their votary, then their wit became;
His jest was bitter and his satire bold,
When he his tales of formal brethren told:
What time with pious neighbours he discuss'd,
Their boasted treasure and their boundless
    trust :
'Such were our dreams,'the jovial elder cried;
'Awake and live,' his youthful friends replied.
  Now the gay clerk a modest drab despised,
And clad him smartly as his friends advised ;
So fine a coat upon his back he threw,
That not an alley-boy old Abel knew ;
Broad polish'd buttons blazed that coat upon,
And just beneath the watch's trinkets shone,—
A splendid watch, that pointed out the time,
To fly from business and make free with
    crime :
The crimson waistcoat and the silken hose
Rank'd the lean man among the Borough
    beaux :
His raven hair he cropp'd with fierce disdain,
And light elastic locks encased his brain:
More pliant pupil who could hope to find,
So deck'd in person and so changed in mind ?
  When Abel walk'd the streets, with pleasant
    mien
He met his friends, delighted to be seen ;
And when he rode along the public way,
No beau so gaudy and no youth so gay.
  His pious sister, now an ancient maid,
For Abel fearing, first in secret pray'd ;
Then thus in love and scorn her notions she
    convey'd :
  'Alas ! my brother ! can I see thee pace
Hoodwink'd to hell, and not lament thy case,

Nor stretch my feeble hand to stop thy head-
    long race ?
Lo ! thou art bound ; a slave in Satan's chain,
The righteous Abel turn'd the wretched Cain ;
His brother's blood against the murderer cried,
Against thee thine, unhappy suicide !
Are all our pious nights and peaceful days,
Our evening readings and our morning praise,
Our spirits' comfort in the trials sent,
Our hearts' rejoicings in the blessings lent,
All that o'er grief a cheering influence shed,
Are these for ever and for ever fled ?
    ' When in the years gone by, the trying years,
When faith and hope had strife with wants
    and fears,
Thy nerves have trembled till thou couldst
    not eat
(Dress'd by this hand) thy mess of simple
    meat ;
When, grieved by fastings, gall'd by fates
    severe,
Slow pass'd the days of the successless year ;
Still in these gloomy hours, my brother then
Had glorious views, unseen by prosperous
    men :
And when thy heart has felt its wish denied,
What gracious texts hast thou to grief applied ;
Till thou hast enter'd in thine humble bed,
By lofty hopes and heavenly musings fed ;
Then I have seen thy lively looks express
The spirit's comforts in the man's distress.
    ' Then didst thou cry, exulting, " Yes, 'tis fit,
'Tis meet and right, my heart ! that we
    submit : "
And wilt thou, Abel, thy new pleasures weigh
Against such triumphs ?—Oh ! repent and
    pray.
    ' What are thy pleasures ?—with the gay to
    sit,
And thy poor brain torment for awkward wit ;
All thy good thoughts (thou hat'st them) to
    restrain,
And give a wicked pleasure to the vain ;
Thy long lean frame by fashion to attire,
That lads may laugh and wantons may
    admire ;
To raise the mirth of boys, and not to see,
Unhappy maniac ! that they laugh at thee.
    ' These boyish follies, which alone the boy
Can idly act or gracefully enjoy,
Add new reproaches to thy fallen state,
And make men scorn what they would only
    hate.

    ' What pains, my brother, dost thou take
    to prove
A taste for follies which thou canst not love ?
Why do thy stiffening limbs the steed be-
    stride—
That lads may laugh to see thou canst not
    ride ?
And why (I feel the crimson tinge my cheek)
Dost thou by night in Diamond-Alley sneak ?
    ' Farewell ! the parish will thy sister keep,
Where she in peace shall pray and sing and
    sleep,
Save when for thee she mourns, thou wicked,
    wandering sheep !
When youth is fall'n, there's hope the young
    may rise,
But fallen age for ever hopeless lies :
Torn up by storms and placed in earth once
    more,
The younger tree may sun and soil restore ;
But when the old and sapless trunk lies low,
No care or soil can former life bestow ;
Reserved for burning is the worthless tree ,
And what, O Abel ! is reserved for thee ? '
    These angry words our hero deeply felt,
Though hard his heart, and indisposed to melt !
To gain relief he took a glass the more,
And then went on as careless as before ;
Thenceforth, uncheck'd, amusements he par-
    took,
And (save his ledger) saw no decent book :
Him found the merchant punctual at his task,
And that perform'd, he'd nothing more to ask ;
He cared not how old Abel played the fool,
No master he, beyond the hours of school :
Thus they proceeding, had their wine and joke
Till merchant Dixon felt a warning stroke,
And, after struggling half a gloomy week,
Left his poor clerk another friend to seek.
    Alas ! the son, who led the saint astray.
Forgot the man whose follies made him gay :
He cared no more for Abel in his need,
Than Abel cared about his hackney steed ;
He now, alas ! had all his earnings spent,
And thus was left to languish and repent ;
No school nor clerkship found he in the place,
Now lost to fortune, as before to grace.
    For town-relief the grieving man applied,
And begg'd with tears what some with scorn
    denied ;
Others look'd down upon the glowing vest,
And frowning, ask'd him at what price he
    dress'd ?

CR.   H

Happy for him his country's laws are mild,
They must support him, though they still
    reviled ;
Grieved, abject, scorn'd, insulted, and be-
    tray'd,
Of God unmindful, and of man afraid,—
No more he talk'd ; 'twas pain, 'twas shame
    to speak,
His heart was sinking and his frame was weak.
His sister died with such serene delight,
He once again began to think her right ;
Poor like himself, the happy spinster lay,
And sweet assurance bless'd her dying-day :
Poor like the spinster, he, when death was
    nigh,
Assured of nothing, felt afraid to die.
The cheerful clerks who sometimes pass'd the
    door,
Just mention'd ' Abel ! ' and then thought
    no more.
So Abel, pondering on his state forlorn,
Look'd round for comfort, and was chased by
    scorn.
And now we saw him on the beach reclined,
Or causeless walking in the wint'ry wind ;
And when it raised a loud and angry sea,
He stood and gazed, in wretched reverie :
He heeded not the frost, the rain, the
    snow ;
Close by the sea he walk'd alone and slow :
Sometimes his frame through many an hour
    he spread
Upon a tombstone, moveless as the dead ;
And was there found a sad and silent place,
There would he creep with slow and measured
    pace :
Then would he wander by the river's side,
And fix his eyes upon the falling tide ;
The deep dry ditch, the rushes in the fen,
And mossy crag-pits were his lodgings then :
There, to his discontented thoughts a prey,
The melancholy mortal pined away.
    The neighb'ring poor at length began to
    speak
Of Abel's ramblings—he'd been gone a week ;
They knew not where, and little care they
    took
For one so friendless and so poor to look ;
At last a stranger, in a pedler's shed,
Beheld him hanging—he had long been dead.
He left a paper, penn'd at sundry times,
Intitled thus—' My Groanings and my
    Crimes ! '

' I was a christian man, and none could lay
Aught to my charge ; I walk'd the narrow
    way :
All then was simple faith, serene and pure,
My hope was steadfast and my prospects sure;
Then was I tried by want and sickness sore,
But these I clapp'd my shield of faith before,
And cares and wants and man's rebukes I
    bore :
Alas ! new foes assail'd me ; I was vain,
They stung my pride and they confused my
    brain :
Oh ! these deluders! with what glee they saw
Their simple dupe transgress the righteous
    law ;
'Twas joy to them to view that dreadful strife,
When faith and frailty warr'd for more than
    life ;
So with their pleasures they beguiled the
    heart,
Then with their logic they allay'd the smart;
They proved (so thought I then) with reasons
    strong,
That no man's feelings ever led him wrong :
And thus I went, as on the varnish'd ice,
The smooth career of unbelief and vice.
Oft would the youths, with sprightly speech
    and bold,
Their witty tales of naughty priests unfold;
" 'Twas all a craft," they said, " a cunning
    trade,
Not she the priests, but priests religion
    made : "
So I believed : '—No, Abel ! to thy grief,
So thou relinquish'dst all that was belief :—
' I grew as very flint, and when the rest
Laugh'd at devotion, I enjoy'd the jest ;
But this all vanish'd like the morning-dew ;
When unemploy'd, and poor again I grew ;
Yea ! I was doubly poor, for I was wicked
    too.
'The mouse that trespass'd and the treasure
    stole,
Found his lean body fitted to the hole ;
Till having fatted, he was forced to stay,
And, fasting, starve his stolen bulk away :
Ah ! worse for me—grown poor, I yet re-
    main
In sinful bonds, and pray and fast in vain.
' At length I thought, although these friends
    of sin
Have spread their net and caught their prey
    therein ;

Though my hard heart could not for mercy
    call,
Because, though great my grief, my faith was
    small ;
Yet, as the sick on skilful men rely,
The soul diseased may to a doctor fly.
   ' A famous one there was, whose skill had
    wrought
Cures past belief, and him the sinners sought;
Numbers there were defiled by mire and filth,
Whom he recover'd by his goodly tilth :—
"Come then," I said, "let me the man behold,
And tell my case "—I saw him and I told.
   ' With trembling voice, " Oh ! reverend
    sir," I said,
" I once believed, and I was then misled ;
And now such doubts my sinful soul beset,
I dare not say that I'm a Christian yet ;
Canst thou, good sir, by thy superior skill,
Inform my judgment and direct my will ?
Ah ! give thy cordial ; let my soul have rest,
And be the outward man alone distress'd ;
For at my state I tremble."—"Tremble
    more,"
Said the good man, " and then rejoice there-
    fore ;
'Tis good to tremble ; prospects then are fair,
When the lost soul is plunged in deep despair:
Once thou wert simply honest, just and
    pure,
Whole, as thou thought'st, and never wish'd
    a cure :
Now thou hast plunged in folly, shame,
    disgrace ;
Now thou'rt an object meet for healing grace;
No merit thine, no virtue, hope, belief,
Nothing hast thou, but misery, sin, and grief,
The best, the only titles to relief."
   '" What must I do," I said, "my soul to
    free ? "
" —Do nothing, man ; it will be done for
    thee."
" But must I not, my reverend guide, be-
    lieve ? "
" —If thou art call'd, thou wilt the faith
    receive : "—

" But I repent not."—Angry he replied,
" If thou art call'd, thou needest nought
    beside :
Attend on us, and if 'tis Heaven's decree,
The call will come,—if not, ah ! wo for thee."
   'There then I waited, ever on the watch,
A spark of hope, a ray of light to catch ;
His words fell softly like the flakes of snow,
But I could never find my heart o'erflow :
He cried aloud, till in the flock began
The sigh, the tear, as caught from man to
    man ;
They wept and they rejoiced, and there was I,
Hard as a flint, and as the desert dry :
To me no tokens of the call would come,
I felt my sentence and received my doom :
But I complain'd—"Let thy repinings cease,
Oh ! man of sin, for they thy guilt increase;
It bloweth where it listeth ;—die in peace."
—" In peace, and perish ? " I replied;
    " impart
Some better comfort to a burthen'd heart."—
" Alas ! " the priest return'd, " can I direct
The heavenly call ?—Do I proclaim th' elect?
Raise not thy voice against th' Eternal will,
But take thy part with sinners and be still."[1]
   ' Alas ! for me, no more the times of peace
Are mine on earth—in death my pains may
    cease.
   'Foes to my soul! ye young seducers, know,
What serious ills from your amusements
    flow;
Opinions, you with so much ease profess,
O'erwhelm the simple and their minds op-
    press :
Let such be happy, nor with reasons strong,
That make them wretched, prove their
    notions wrong ;
Let them proceed in that they deem the
    way,
Fast when they will, and at their pleasure
    pray :
Yes, I have pity for my brethren's lot,
And so had Dives, but it help'd him not :
And is it thus ?—I'm full of doubts:—Adieu !
Perhaps his reverence is mistaken too.'

LETTER XXII. THE POOR OF THE BOROUGH

PETER GRIMES

————Was a sordid soul,
Such as does murder for a meed :
Who but for fear knows no control,
Because his conscience, sear'd and foul,
Feels not the import of the deed ;
One whose brute feeling ne'er aspires
Beyond his own more brute desires.
      SCOTT, *Marmion*, Canto II. 22.

Methought the souls of all that I had murder'd
Came to my tent, and every one did threat.
      SHAKSPEARE, *Richard III*, Act v, Sc. 3.

            The times have been,
That when the brains were out, the man
            would die,
And there an end ; but now they rise again,
With twenty mortal murders on their crowns,
And push us from our stools.
            Macbeth, Act iii, Sc. 4.

The Father of Peter a Fisherman—Peter's
early Conduct—His Grief for the old Man
—He takes an Apprentice—The Boy's
Suffering and Fate—A second Boy : how
he died—Peter acquitted—A third Ap-
prentice—A Voyage by Sea : the Boy does
not return—Evil Report on Peter : he is
tried and threatened—Lives alone—His
Melancholy and incipient Madness—Is
observed and visited—He escapes and is
taken : is lodged in a Parish-house :
Women attend and watch him—He speaks
in a Delirium : grows more collected—His
Account of his Feelings and visionary
Terrors previous to his Death.

OLD Peter Grimes made fishing his employ,
His wife he cabin'd with him and his boy,
And seem'd that life laborious to enjoy :
To town came quiet Peter with his fish,
And had of all a civil word and wish.
He left his trade upon the sabbath-day,
And took young Peter in his hand to pray :
But soon the stubborn boy from care broke
      loose,
At first refused, then added his abuse :
His father's love he scorn'd, his power de-
      fied,
But being drunk, wept sorely when he died.
   Yes ! then he wept, and to his mind there
      came
Much of his conduct, and he felt the shame,—

How he had oft the good old man reviled,
And never paid the duty of a child ;
How, when the father in his Bible read,
He in contempt and anger left the shed :
' It is the word of life,' the parent cried ;
—' This is the life itself,' the boy replied ;
And while old Peter in amazement stood,
Gave the hot spirit to his boiling blood :—
How he, with oath and furious speech, began
To prove his freedom and assert the man ;
And when the parent check'd his impious rage,
How he had cursed the tyranny of age,—
Nay, once had dealt the sacrilegious blow
On his bare head, and laid his parent low ;
The father groan'd—' If thou art old,' said he,
' And hast a son—thou wilt remember me :
Thy mother left me in a happy time,
Thou kill'dst not her—Heav'n spares the
      double crime.'
   On an inn-settle, in his maudlin grief,
This he revolved, and drank for his relief.
   Now lived the youth in freedom, but
      debarr'd
From constant pleasure, and he thought it
      hard ;
Hard that he could not every wish obey,
But must awhile relinquish ale and play ;
Hard ! that he could not to his cards attend,
But must acquire the money he would spend.
   With greedy eye he look'd on all he saw,
He knew not justice, and he laugh'd at law ;
On all he mark'd he stretch'd his ready hand ;
He fish'd by water, and he filch'd by land :
Oft in the night has Peter dropp'd his oar,
Fled from his boat and sought for prey on
      shore ;
Oft up the hedge-row glided, on his back
Bearing the orchard's produce in a sack,
Or farm-yard load, tugg'd fiercely from the
      stack ;
And as these wrongs to greater numbers rose,
The more he look'd on all men as his foes.
   He built a mud-wall'd hovel, where he kept
His various wealth, and there he oft-times
      slept ;
But no success could please his cruel soul,
He wish'd for one to trouble and control ;
He wanted some obedient boy to stand
And bear the blow of his outrageous hand ;

And hoped to find in some propitious hour
A feeling creature subject to his power.
   Peter had heard there were in London
then,—
Still have they being!—workhouse-clearing
men,
Who, undisturb'd by feelings just or kind,
Would parish-boys to needy tradesmen bind:
They in their want a trifling sum would take,
And toiling slaves of piteous orphans make.
   Such Peter sought, and when a lad was
found,
The sum was dealt him, and the slave was
bound.
Some few in town observed in Peter's trap
A boy, with jacket blue and woollen cap;
But none inquired how Peter used the rope,
Or what the bruise, that made the stripling
stoop;
None could the ridges on his back behold,
None sought him shiv'ring in the winter's
cold;
None put the question,—' Peter, dost thou
give
The boy his food ?—What, man ! the lad
must live :
Consider, Peter, let the child have bread,
He'll serve thee better if he's stroked and fed.'
None reason'd thus—and some, on hearing
cries,
Said calmly, ' Grimes is at his exercise.'
   Pinn'd, beaten, cold, pinch'd, threaten'd,
and abused—
His efforts punish'd and his food refused,—
Awake tormented,—soon aroused from
sleep,—
Struck if he wept, and yet compell'd to weep,
The trembling boy dropp'd down and strove
to pray,
Received a blow, and trembling turn'd away,
Or sobb'd and hid his piteous face;—while he,
The savage master, grinn'd in horrid glee:
He'd now the power he ever loved to show,
A feeling being subject to his blow.
   Thus lived the lad, in hunger, peril, pain,
His tears despised, his supplications vain :
Compell'd by fear to lie, by need to steal,
His bed uneasy and unbless'd his meal,
For three sad years the boy his tortures bore,
And then his pains and trials were no more.
   ' How died he, Peter ? ' when the people
said,
He growl'd—' I found him lifeless in his bed;

Then tried for softer tone, and sigh'd, ' Poor
Sam is dead.'
Yet murmurs were there, and some questions
ask'd,—
How he was fed, how punish'd, and how
task'd ?
Much they suspected, but they little proved,
And Peter pass'd untroubled and unmoved.
   Another boy with equal ease was found,
The money granted, and the victim bound;
And what his fate ?—One night it chanced
he fell
From the boat's mast and perish'd in her
well,
Where fish were living kept, and where the boy
(So reason'd men) could not himself
destroy :—
   ' Yes ! so it was,' said Peter, ' in his play,
(For he was idle both by night and day,)
He climb'd the main-mast and then fell
below ; '—
Then show'd his corpse and pointed to the
blow :
' What said the jury ? '—they were long in
doubt,
But sturdy Peter faced the matter out :
So they dismiss'd him, saying at the time,
' Keep fast your hatchway when you've boys
who climb.'
This hit the conscience, and he colour'd
more
Than for the closest questions put before.
   Thus all his fears the verdict set aside,
And at the slave-shop Peter still applied.
   Then came a boy, of manners soft and
mild,—
Our seamen's wives with grief beheld the
child ;
All thought (the poor themselves) that he was
one
Of gentle blood, some noble sinner's son,
Who had, belike, deceived some humble
maid,
Whom he had first seduced and then be-
tray'd :—
However this, he seem'd a gracious lad,
In grief submissive and with patience sad.
   Passive he labour'd, till his slender frame
Bent with his loads, and he at length was
lame :
Strange that a frame so weak could bear so
long
The grossest insult and the foulest wrong;

But there were causes—in the town they gave
Fire, food, and comfort, to the gentle slave;
And though stern Peter, with a cruel hand,
And knotted rope, enforced the rude com-
mand,
Yet he consider'd what he'd lately felt,
And his vile blows with selfish pity dealt.

One day such draughts the cruel fisher
made,
He could not vend them in his borough-trade,
But sail'd for London-mart: the boy was ill,
But ever humbled to his master's will;
And on the river, where they smoothly sail'd,
He strove with terror and awhile prevail'd;
But new to danger on the angry sea,
He clung affrighten'd to his master's knee:
The boat grew leaky and the wind was strong,
Rough was the passage and the time was
long;
His liquor fail'd, and Peter's wrath arose,—
No more is known—the rest we must suppose,
Or learn of Peter;—Peter says, he ' spied
The stripling's danger and for harbour tried;
Meantime the fish, and then th' apprentice
died.'
The pitying women raised a clamour round,
And weeping said, ' Thou hast thy 'prentice
drown'd.'

Now the stern man was summon'd to the
hall,
To tell his tale before the burghers all:
He gave th' account; profess'd the lad he
loved,
And kept his brazen features all unmoved.
The mayor himself with tone severe re-
plied,—
' Henceforth with thee shall never boy abide;
Hire thee a freeman, whom thou durst not
beat,
But who, in thy despite, will sleep and eat:
Free thou art now!—again shouldst thou
appear,
Thou'lt find thy sentence, like thy soul,
severe.'
Alas! for Peter not a helping hand,
So was he hated, could he now command;
Alone he row'd his boat, alone he cast
His nets beside, or made his anchor fast;
To hold a rope or hear a curse was none,—
He toil'd and rail'd; he groan'd and swore
alone.

Thus by himself compell'd to live each day,
To wait for certain hours the tide's delay;

At the same times the same dull views to see,
The bounding marsh-bank and the blighted
tree;
The water only, when the tides were high,
When low, the mud half-cover'd and half-dry;
The sun-burnt tar that blisters on the planks,
And bank-side stakes in their uneven ranks;
Heaps of entangled weeds that slowly float,
As the tide rolls by the impeded boat.

When tides were neap, and, in the sultry day,
Through the tall bounding mud-banks made
their way,
Which on each side rose swelling, and below
The dark warm flood ran silently and slow;
There anchoring, Peter chose from man to
hide,
There hang his head, and view the lazy tide
In its hot slimy channel slowly glide;
Where the small eels that left the deeper way
For the warm shore, within the shallows
play;
Where gaping muscles, left upon the mud,
Slope their slow passage to the fallen flood;—
Here dull and hopeless he'd lie down and trace
How sidelong crabs had scrawl'd their crooked
race;
Or sadly listen to the tuneless cry
Of fishing gull or clanging golden-eye;
What time the sea-birds to the marsh would
come,
And the loud bittern, from the bull-rush
home,
Gave from the salt-ditch side the bellowing
boom:
He nursed the feelings these dull scenes
produce,
And loved to stop beside the opening sluice;
Where the small stream, confined in narrow
bound,
Ran with a dull, unvaried, sadd'ning sound;
Where all, presented to the eye or ear,
Oppress'd the soul with misery, grief, and fear.
Besides these objects, there were places
three,
Which Peter seem'd with certain dread to see;
When he drew near them he would turn from
each,
And loudly whistle till he pass'd the reach.*

* The reaches in a river are those parts which
extend from point to point. Johnson has not the
word precisely in this sense; but it is very
common, and, I believe, used wheresoever a navi-
gable river can be found in this country.

A change of scene to him brought no relief;
In town, 'twas plain, men took him for a thief:
The sailors' wives would stop him in the
    street,
And say, ' Now, Peter, thou'st no boy to
    beat : '
Infants at play, when they perceived him, ran,
Warning each other—' That 's the wicked
    man : '
He growl'd an oath, and in an angry tone
Cursed the whole place and wish'd to be alone.
    Alone he was, the same dull scenes in view,
And still more gloomy in his sight they grew :
Though man he hated, yet employ'd alone
At bootless labour, he would swear and groan,
Cursing the shoals that glided by the spot,
And gulls that caught them when his arts
    could not.
    Cold nervous tremblings shook his sturdy
    frame,
And strange disease—he couldn't say the
    name ;
Wild were his dreams, and oft he rose in fright,
Waked by his view of horrors in the night,—
Horrors that would the sternest minds amaze,
Horrors that demons might be proud to raise:
And though he felt forsaken, grieved at heart,
To think he lived from all mankind apart;
Yet, if a man approach'd, in terrors he would
    start.
    A winter pass'd since Peter saw the town,
And summer-lodgers were again come down;
These, idly curious, with their glasses spied
The ships in bay as anchor'd for the tide,—
The river's craft,—the bustle of the quay,—
And sea-port views, which landmen love to see.
    One, up the river, had a man and boat
Seen day by day, now anchor'd, now afloat;
Fisher he seem'd, yet used no net nor hook;
Of sea-fowl swimming by no heed he took,
But on the gliding waves still fix'd his lazy
    look :
At certain stations he would view the stream,
As if he stood bewilder'd in a dream,
Or that some power had chain'd him for a
    time,
To feel a curse or meditate on crime.
    This known, some curious, some in pity
    went,
And others question'd—' Wretch, dost thou
    repent ? '
He heard, he trembled, and in fear resign'd
His boat : new terror fill'd his restless mind;

Furious he grew, and up the country ran,
And there they seized him—a distemper'd
    man :—
Him we received, and to a parish-bed,
Follow'd and cursed, the groaning man was
    led.
    Here when they saw him, whom they used
    to shun,
A lost, lone man, so harass'd and undone ;
Our gentle females, ever prompt to feel,
Perceived compassion on their anger steal ;
His crimes they could not from their memories
    blot,
But they were grieved, and trembled at his lot.
    A priest too came, to whom his words are
    told ;
And all the signs they shudder'd to behold.
    ' Look ! look ! ' they cried ; ' his limbs
    with horror shake.
And as he grinds his teeth, what noise they
    make!
How glare his angry eyes, and yet he 's not
    awake :
See ! what cold drops upon his forehead stand,
And how he clenches that broad bony hand.'
    The priest attending, found he spoke at
    times
As one alluding to his fears and crimes :
' It was the fall,' he mutter'd, ' I can show
The manner how—I never struck a blow : '—
And then aloud—' Unhand me, free my chain;
On oath, he fell—it struck him to the brain:—
Why ask my father ?—that old man will swear
Against my life ; besides, he wasn't there:—
What, all agreed ?—Am I to die to-day ?—
My Lord, in mercy, give me time to pray.'
    Then, as they watch'd him, calmer he
    became,
And grew so weak he couldn't move his frame,
But murmuring spake,—while they could see
    and hear
The start of terror and the groan of fear ;
See the large dew-beads on his forehead rise,
And the cold death-drop glaze his sunken
    eyes ;
Nor yet he died, but with unwonted force
Seem'd with some fancied being to discourse:
He knew not us, or with accustom'd art
He hid the knowledge, yet exposed his heart;
'Twas part confession and the rest defence,
A madman's tale, with gleams of waking sense.
    ' I'll tell you all,' he said, ' the very day
When the old man first placed them in my way:

My father's spirit—he who always tried
To give me trouble, when he lived and died—
When he was gone, he could not be content
To see my days in painful labour spent,
But would appoint his meetings, and he made
Me watch at these, and so neglect my trade.
    ' 'Twas one hot noon, all silent, still, serene,
No living being had I lately seen ;
I paddled up and down and dipp'd my net,
But (such his pleasure) I could nothing get,—
A father's pleasure, when his toil was done,
To plague and torture thus an only son !
And so I sat and look'd upon the stream,
How it ran on, and felt as in a dream :
But dream it was not ; no !—I fix'd my eyes
On the mid stream and saw the spirits rise ;
I saw my father on the water stand,
And hold a thin pale boy in either hand ;
And there they glided ghastly on the top
Of the salt flood, and never touch'd a drop :
I would have struck them, but they knew
    th' intent,
And smiled upon the oar, and down they went.
    ' Now, from that day, whenever I began
To dip my net, there stood the hard old man—
He and those boys : I humbled me and pray'd
They would be gone ;—they heeded not, but
    stay'd :
Nor could I turn, nor would the boat go by,
But gazing on the spirits, there was I :
They bade me leap to death, but I was loth
    to die :
And every day, as sure as day arose,
Would these three spirits meet me ere the
    close ;
To hear and mark them daily was my doom,
And " Come," they said, with weak, sad
    voices, " come."
To row away with all my strength I try'd,
But there were they, hard by me in the tide,
The three unbodied forms—and " Come,"
    still " come," they cried.
    'Fathers should pity—but this old man shook
His hoary locks, and froze me by a look :
Thrice, when I struck them, through the
    water came
A hollow groan, that weaken'd all my frame :
" Father ! " said I, " have mercy : "—He
    replied,
I know not what—the angry spirit lied,—
" Didst thou not draw thy knife ? " said
    he :—'Twas true,
But I had pity and my arm withdrew :

He cried for mercy which I kindly gave,
But he has no compassion in his grave.
    ' There were three places, where they ever
    rose,—
The whole long river has not such as those,—
Places accursed, where, if a man remain,
He'll see the things which strike him to the
    brain ;
And there they made me on my paddle lean,
And look at them for hours ;—accursed scene !
When they would glide to that smooth eddy-
    space,
Then bid me leap and join them in the place ;
And at my groans each little villain sprite
Enjoy'd my pains and vanish'd in delight.
    ' In one fierce summer-day, when my poor
    brain
Was burning hot and cruel was my pain,
Then came this father-foe, and there he stood
With his two boys again upon the flood ;
There was more mischief in their eyes, more
    glee
In their pale faces when they glared at me :
Still did they force me on the oar to rest,
And when they saw me fainting and oppress'd,
He, with his hand, the old man, scoop'd the
    flood,
And there came flame about him mix'd with
    blood ;
He bade me stoop and look upon the place,
Then flung the hot-red liquor in my face ;
Burning it blazed, and then I roar'd for pain,
I thought the demons would have turn'd my
    brain.
    ' Still there they stood, and forced me to
    behold
A place of horrors—they cannot be told—
Where the flood open'd, there I heard the
    shriek
Of tortured guilt—no earthly tongue can
    speak :
" All days alike ! for ever ! " did they say,
" And unremitted torments every day "—
Yes, so they said : '—But here he ceased and
    gazed
On all around, affrighten'd and amazed ;
And still he tried to speak, and look'd in dread
Of frighten'd females gathering round his
    bed ;
Then dropp'd exhausted and appear'd at rest,
Till the strong foe the vital powers possess'd :
Then with an inward, broken voice he cried,
' Again they come,' and mutter'd as he died.

LETTER XXIII. PRISONS

Poena autem vehemens ac multò saevior illis,
Quas et Caedicius gravis invenit et Rhada-
    manthus,
Nocte dieque suum gestare in pectore testem.
                        JUVENAL, *Sat.* 13. 196–8.

Learn, good soul,
To think our former state a happy dream,
From which awaked, the truth of what we are
Shows us but this,—I am sworn brother sweet
To grim Necessity, and he and I
Will keep a league till death.
                        Richard II, Act v, Sc. 1.

The Mind of Man accommodates itself to all
    Situations ; Prisons otherwise would be in-
    tolerable—Debtors: their different Kinds:
    three particularly described ; others more
    briefly—An arrested Prisoner : his Account
    of his Feelings and his Situation—The
    Alleviations of a Prison—Prisoners for
    Crimes—Two condemned : a vindictive
    Female : a Highwayman—The Interval
    between Condemnation and Execution—
    His Feelings as the Time approaches—His
    Dream.

'TIS well—that man to all the varying states
Of good and ill his mind accommodates ;
He not alone progressive grief sustains,
But soon submits to unexperienced pains :
Change after change, all climes his body bears;
His mind repeated shocks of changing cares :
Faith and fair virtue arm the nobler breast;
Hope and mere want of feeling aid the rest.
    Or who could bear to lose the balmy air
Of summer's breath, from all things fresh and
    fair,
With all that man admires or loves below ;
All earth and water, wood and vale bestow,
Where rosy pleasures smile, whence real
    blessings flow ;
With sight and sound of every kind that lives,
And crowning all with joy that freedom gives?
    Who could from these, in some unhappy
        day,
Bear to be drawn by ruthless arms away,
To the vile nuisance of a noisome room,
Where only insolence and misery come ?
(Save that the curious will by chance appear,
Or some in pity drop a fruitless tear ;)
To a damp prison, where the very sight
Of the warm sun is favour and not right ;

Where all we hear or see the feelings shock,
The oath and groan, the fetter and the lock ?
    Who could bear this and live ?—Oh !
        many a year
All this is borne, and miseries more severe ;
And some there are, familiar with the scene,
Who live in mirth, though few become serene.
    Far as I might the inward man perceive,
There was a constant effort—not to grieve;
Not to despair, for better days would come,
And the freed debtor smile again at home :
Subdued his habits, he may peace regain,
And bless the woes that were not sent in vain.
    Thus might we class the debtors here con-
        fined,
The more deceived, the more deceitful kind;
Here are the guilty race, who mean to live
On credit, that credulity will give ;
Who purchase, conscious they can never pay ;
Who know their fate, and traffic to betray ;
On whom no pity, fear, remorse, prevail,
Their aim a statute, their resource a jail;—
These as the public spoilers we regard,
No dun so harsh, no creditor so hard.
    A second kind are they, who truly strive
To keep their sinking credit long alive ;
Success,nay prudence,they may want,but yet
They would be solvent, and deplore a debt ;
All means they use, to all expedients run,
And are by slow, sad steps, at last undone :
Justly, perhaps,you blame their want of skill,
But mourn their feelings and absolve their will.
    There is a debtor, who his trifling *all*
Spreads in a shop ; it would not fill a stall:
There at one window his temptation lays,
And in new modes disposes and displays :
Above the door you shall his name behold,
And what he vends in ample letters told,
The words *repository*, *warehouse*, all
He uses to enlarge concerns so small :
He to his goods assigns some beauty's name,
Then in their reign, and hopes they'll share her
        fame ;
And talks of credit, commerce, traffic, trade,
As one important by their profit made ;
But who can paint the vacancy, the gloom,
And spare dimensions of one backward room ?
Wherein he dines, if so 'tis fit to speak,
Of one day's herring and the morrow's steak;

An anchorite in diet, all his care
Is to display his stock and vend his ware.
　Long waiting hopeless, then he tries to meet
A kinder fortune in a distant street ;
There again displays, increasing yet
Corroding sorrow and consuming debt :
Alas ! he wants the requisites to rise—
The true connexions, the availing ties ;
They who proceed on certainties advance,
These are not times when men prevail by
　　chance :
But still he tries, till, after years of pain,
He finds, with anguish, he has tried in vain.
Debtors are these on whom 'tis hard to press,
'Tis base, impolitic, and merciless.
　To these we add a miscellaneous kind,
By pleasure, pride, and indolence confined ;
Those whom no calls, no warnings could
　　divert,
The unexperienced and the inexpert ;
The builder, idler, schemer, gamester, sot,—
The follies different, but the same their lot ;
Victims of horses, lasses, drinking, dice,
Of every passion, humour, whim, and vice.
　See ! that sad merchant, who but yester-
　　day
Had a vast household in command and pay ;
He now entreats permission to employ
A boy he needs, and then entreats the boy.
　And there sits one, improvident but kind,
Bound for a friend, whom honour could not
　　bind ;
Sighing, he speaks to any who appear,
' A treach'rous friend—'twas that which sent
　　me here :
I was too kind,—I thought I could depend
On his bare word—he was a treach'rous
　　friend.'
　A female too !—it is to her a home,
She came before—and she again will come :
Her friends have pity ; when their anger
　　drops,
They take her home ;—she's tried her schools
　　and shops—
Plan after plan ;—but fortune would not
　　mend,
She to herself was still the treach'rous friend ;
And wheresoe'er began, all here was sure to
　　end :
And there she sits, as thoughtless and as gay,
As if she'd means, or not a debt to pay—
Or knew to-morrow she'd be call'd away—
Or felt a shilling and could dine to-day.

　While thus observing, I began to trace
The sober'd features of a well-known face—
Looks once familiar, manners form'd to please,
And all illumined by a heart at ease :
But fraud and flattery ever claim'd a part
(Still unresisted) of that easy heart ;
But he at length beholds me—' Ah ! my
　　friend !
And have thy pleasures this unlucky end ? '
　' Too sure,' he said, and smiling as he sigh'd ;
' I went astray, though prudence seem'd my
　　guide ;
All she proposed I in my heart approved,
And she was honour'd, but my pleasure
　　loved—
Pleasure, the mistress to whose arms I fled,
From wife-like lectures angry prudence read.
' Why speak the madness of a life like mine,
The powers of beauty, novelty, and wine ?
Why paint the wanton smile, the venal vow,
Or friends whose worth I can appreciate now ?
'Oft I perceived my fate, and then would say,
I'll think to-morrow, I must live to-day :
So am I here—I own the laws are just—
And here, where thought is painful, think I
　　must :
But speech is pleasant, this discourse with
　　thee
Brings to my mind the sweets of liberty,
Breaks on the sameness of the place, and
　　gives
The doubtful heart conviction that it lives.
　' Let me describe my anguish in the hour
When law detain'd me and I felt its power.
' When in that shipwreck, this I found my
　　shore,
And join'd the wretched, who were wreck'd
　　before ;
When I perceived each feature in the face,
Pinch'd through neglect or turbid by disgrace ;
When in these wasting forms affliction stood
In my afflicted view, it chill'd my blood ;—
And forth I rush'd, a quick retreat to make,
Till a loud laugh proclaim'd the dire mistake :
But when the groan had settled to a sigh,
When gloom became familiar to the eye,
When I perceive how others seem to rest,
With every evil rankling in my breast,—
Led by example, I put on the man,
Sing off my sighs, and trifle as I can.
　' Homer ! nay Pope ! (for never will I seek
Applause for learning—nought have I with
　　Greek)

Gives us the secrets of his pagan hell,
Where ghost with ghost in sad communion
    dwell ;
Where shade meets shade, and round the
    gloomy meads
They glide and speak of old heroic deeds,—
What fields they conquer'd, and what foes
    they slew
And sent to join the melancholy crew.

  'When a new spirit in that world was found,
A thousand shadowy forms came flitting
    round ;
Those who had known him, fond inquiries
    made,—
" Of all we left, inform us, gentle shade,
Now as we lead thee in our realms to dwell,
Our twilight groves, and meads of asphodel."

  'What paints the poet, is our station here,
Where we like ghosts and flitting shades
    appear :
This is the hell he sings, and here we meet,
And former deeds to new-made friends repeat;
Heroic deeds, which here obtain us fame,
And are in fact the causes why we came :
Yes ! this dim region is old Homer's hell,
Abate but groves and meads of asphodel.

  ' Here, when a stranger from your world
    we spy,
We gather round him and for news apply;
He hears unheeding, nor can speech endure,
But shivering gazes on the vast obscure :
We smiling pity, and by kindness show
We felt his feelings and his terrors know ;
Then speak of comfort—time will give him
    sight,
Where now 'tis dark ; where now 'tis wo—
    delight.

  ' " Have hope," we say, " and soon the
    place to thee
Shall not a prison but a castle be ;
When to the wretch whom care and guilt
    confound,
The world 's a prison, with a wider bound ;
Go where he may, he feels himself confined,
And wears the fetters of an abject mind."

  ' But now adieu ! those giant keys appear,
Thou art not worthy to be inmate here :
Go to thy world, and to the young declare
What we, our spirits and employments, are ;
Tell them how we the ills of life endure,
Our empire stable, and our state secure ;
Our dress, our diet, for their use describe,
And bid them haste to join the gen'rous tribe:

Go to thy world, and leave us here to dwell,
Who to its joys and comforts bid farewell.'

  Farewell to these; but other scenes I view,
And other griefs, and guilt of deeper hue ;
Where conscience gives to outward ills her
    pain,
Gloom to the night, and pressure to the chain:
Here separate cells awhile in misery keep
Two doom'd to suffer : there they strive for
    sleep ;
By day indulged, in larger space they range,
Their bondage certain, but their bounds have
    change.

  One was a female, who had grievous ill
Wrought in revenge, and she enjoy'd it still :
With death before her, and her fate in view,
Unsated vengeance in her bosom grew :
Sullen she was and threat'ning ; in her eye
Glared the stern triumph that she dared to
    die :
But first a being in the world must leave—
'Twas once reproach ; 'twas now a short
    reprieve.

  She was a pauper bound, who early gave
Her mind to vice, and doubly was a slave ;
Upbraided, beaten, held by rough control,
Revenge sustain'd, inspired, and fill'd her soul:
She fired a full-stored barn, confess'd the fact,
And laugh'd at law and justified the act :
Our gentle vicar tried his powers in vain,
She answer'd not, or answer'd with disdain :
Th'approaching fate she heard without a sigh,
And neither cared to live nor fear'd to die.

  Not so he felt, who with her was to pay
The forfeit, life—with dread he view'd the day,
And that short space which yet for him
    remain'd,
Till with his limbs his faculties were chain'd :
He paced his narrow bounds some ease to find,
But found it not,—no comfort reach'd his
    mind :
Each sense was palsied ; when he tasted food,
He sigh'd and said, ' Enough—'tis very good.'
Since his dread sentence, nothing seem'd to be
As once it was—he seeing could not see,
Nor hearing, hear aright ;—when first I came
Within his view, I fancied there was shame,
I judged resentment ; I mistook the air,—
These fainter passions live not with despair ;
Or but exist and die:—Hope, fear, and love,
Joy, doubt, and hate, may other spirits move,
But touch not his, who every waking hour
Has one fix'd dread, and always feels its power.

'But will not mercy?'—No! she cannot
    plead
For such an outrage ;—'twas a cruel deed :
He stopp'd a timid traveller;—to his breast,
With oaths and curses, was the danger
    press'd :—
No! he must suffer ; pity we may find
For one man's pangs, but must not wrong
    mankind.

Still I behold him, every thought employ'd
On one dire view!—all others are destroy'd ;
This makes his features ghastly, gives the tone
Of his few words resemblance to a groan :
He takes his tasteless food, and when 'tis done,
Counts up his meals, now lessen'd by that one ;
For expectation is on time intent,
Whether he brings us joy or punishment.

Yes! e'en in sleep the impressions all
    remain,
He hears the sentence and he feels the chain;
He sees the judge and jury, when he shakes,
And loudly cries, 'Not guilty,' and awakes :
Then chilling tremblings o'er his body creep,
Till worn-out nature is compell'd to sleep.

Now comes the dream again ; it shows
    each scene,
With each small circumstance that comes
    between—
The call to suffering and the very deed—
There crowds go with him, follow, and pre-
    cede ;
Some heartless shout, some pity, all condemn,
While he in fancied envy looks at them :
He seems the place for that sad act to see,
And dreams the very thirst which then will be :
A priest attends—it seems, the one he knew,
In his best days, beneath whose care he grew.

At this his terrors take a sudden flight,
He sees his native village with delight ;
The house, the chamber, where he once array'd
His youthful person ; where he knelt and
    pray'd :
Then too the comforts he enjoy'd at home,
The days of joy ; the joys themselves are
    come ;—
The hours of innocence ;—the timid look
Of his loved maid, when first her hand he took
And told his hope ; her trembling joy appears,
Her forced reserve and his retreating fears.

All now is present;—'tis a moment's gleam
Of former sunshine—stay, delightful dream !
Let him within his pleasant garden walk,
Give him her arm, of blessings let them talk.

Yes! all are with him now, and all the while
Life's early prospects and his Fanny's smile :
Then come his sister and his village-friend,
And he will now the sweetest moments spend
Life has to yield ;—No ! never will he find
Again on earth such pleasure in his mind :
He goes through shrubby walks these friends
    among :
Love in their looks and honour on the tongue:
Nay, there's a charm beyond what nature
    shows,
The bloom is softer and more sweetly glows;—
Pierced by no crime, and urged by no desire
For more than true and honest hearts require,
They feel the calm delight, and thus proceed
Through the green lane,—then linger in the
    mead,—
Stray o'er the heath in all its purple bloom,—
And pluck the blossom where the wild bees
    hum ;
Then through the broomy bound with ease
    they pass,
And press the sandy sheep-walk's slender grass,
Where dwarfish flowers among the gorse are
    spread,
And the lamb browses by the linnet's bed ;
Then 'cross the bounding brook they make
    their way
O'er its rough bridge—and there behold the
    bay !—
The ocean smiling to the fervid sun—
The waves that faintly fall and slowly run—
The ships at distance and the boats at hand ;
And now they walk upon the sea-side sand,
Counting the number and what kind they be,
Ships softly sinking in the sleepy sea :
Now arm in arm, now parted, they behold
The glitt'ring waters on the shingles roll'd :
The timid girls, half dreading their design,
Dip the small foot in the retarded brine,
And search for crimson weeds, which spread-
    ing flow,
Or lie like pictures on the sand below ;
With all those bright red pebbles that the sun
Through the small waves so softly shines upon;
And those live lucid jellies which the eye
Delights to trace as they swim glitt'ring by :
Pearl-shells and rubied star-fish they admire,
And will arrange above the parlour-fire,—
Tokens of bliss !—'Oh ! horrible ! a wave
Roars as it rises—save me, Edward ! save !'
She cries :—Alas ! the watchman on his way
Calls and lets in—truth, terror, and the day!

LETTER XXIV. SCHOOLS

Tu quoque ne metuas, quamvis schola verbere
    multo
Increpet et truculenta senex geret ora
    magister ;
Degeneres animos timor arguit ; at tibi
    consta
Intrepidus, nec te clamor plagaeque sonantes,
Nec matutinis agitet formido sub horis,
Quòd sceptrum vibrat ferulae, quòd multa
    supellex
Virgea quod molis scuticam praetexit aluta,
Quòd fervent trepido subsellia vestra tumultu,
Pompa loci, et vani fugiatur scena timoris.
    AUSONIUS *in Protreptico ad Nepotem.*

Be it a weakness, it deserves some praise,—
We love the play-place of our early days ;
The scene is touching, and the heart is stone
That feels not at that sight—and feels at none.
The wall on which we tried our graving skill ;
The very name we carved subsisting still ;
The bench on which we sat while deep em-
    ploy'd,
Though mangled, hack'd, and hew'd, yet not
    destroyed.
The little ones unbutton'd, glowing hot,
Playing our games, and on the very spot ;
As happy as we once to kneel and draw
The chalky ring and knuckle down at taw.
   .   .   .   .   .   .
This fond attachment to the well known place,
When first we started into life's long race,
Maintains its hold with such unfailing sway,
We feel it e'en in age and at our latest day.
    COWPER, *Tirocinium, a Review of Schools.*

Schools of every Kind to be found in the
Borough—The School for Infants—The
School Preparatory : the Sagacity of the
Mistress in foreseeing Character—Day-
Schools of the lower Kind—A Master with
Talents adapted to such Pupils : one of
superior Qualifications—Boarding-Schools :
that for young Ladies : one going first to
the Governess, one finally returning Home
—School for Youth : Master and Teacher ;
various Dispositions and Capacities—The
Miser-Boy — The Boy-Bully — Sons of
Farmers : how amused—What Study will
effect, examined—A College Life : one
sent from his College to a Benefice ; one
retained there in Dignity—The Advantages
in either Case not considerable—Where
then the Good of a literary Life ?—
Answered—Conclusion.

To every class we have a school assign'd,
Rules for all ranks and food for every mind :
Yet one there is, that small regard to rule
Or study pays, and still is deem'd a school ;
That, where a deaf, poor, patient widow sits,
And awes some thirty infants as she knits ;
Infants of humble, busy wives, who pay
Some trifling price for freedom through the
    day.
At this good matron's hut the children meet,
Who thus becomes the mother of the street :
Her room is small, they cannot widely stray,—
Her threshold high, they cannot run away :
Though deaf, she sees the rebel-heroes shout,—
Though lame, her white rod nimbly walks
    about ;
With band of yarn she keeps offenders in,
And to her gown the sturdiest rogue can pin :
Aided by these, and spells, and tell-tale birds,
Her power they dread and reverence her words.
  To learning's second seats we now proceed,
Where humming students gilded primers read ;
Or books with letters large and pictures gay,
To make their reading but a kind of play—
' Reading made Easy,' so the titles tell ;
But they who read must first begin to spell :
There may be profit in these arts, but still
Learning is labour, call it what you will ;
Upon the youthful mind a heavy load,
Nor must we hope to find the royal road.
Some will their easy steps to science show,
And some to heav'n itself their by-way know ;
Ah ! trust them not,—who fame or bliss
    would share,
Must learn by labour, and must live by care.
  Another matron of superior kind,
For higher schools prepares the rising mind ;
Preparatory she her learning calls,
The step first made to colleges and halls.
  She early sees to what the mind will grow,
Nor abler judge of infant-powers I know ;
She sees what soon the lively will impede,
And how the steadier will in turn succeed ;
Observes the dawn of wisdom, fancy, taste,
And knows what parts will wear and what
    will waste :
She marks the mind too lively, and at once
Sees the gay coxcomb and the rattling
    dunce.

Long has she lived, and much she loves to trace
Her former pupils, now a lordly race ;
Whom when she sees rich robes and furs bedeck,
She marks the pride which once she strove to check :
A burgess comes, and she remembers well
How hard her task to make his worship spell;
Cold, selfish, dull, inanimate, unkind,
'Twas but by anger he display'd a mind :
Now civil, smiling, complaisant, and gay,
The world has worn th' unsocial crust away;
That sullen spirit now a softness wears,
And, save by fits, e'en dulness disappears :
But still the matron can the man behold,
Dull, selfish, hard, inanimate, and cold.
A merchant passes,—' probity and truth,
Prudence and patience, mark'd thee from thy youth.'
Thus she observes, but oft retains her fears
For him, who now with name unstain'd appears ;
Nor hope relinquishes, for one who yet
Is lost in error and involved in debt ;
For latent evil in that heart she found,
More open here, but here the core was sound.

Various our day-schools : here behold we one
Empty and still:—the morning duties done,
Soil'd, tatter'd, worn, and thrown in various heaps,
Appear their books, and there confusion sleeps ;
The workmen all are from the Babel fled,
And lost their tools, till the return they dread :
Meantime the master, with his wig awry,
Prepares his books for business by-and-by :
Now all th' insignia of the monarch laid
Beside him rest, and none stand by afraid;
He, while his troop light-hearted leap and play,
Is all intent on duties of the day ;
No more the tyrant stern or judge severe,
He feels the father's and the husband's fear.
Ah ! little think the timid trembling crowd,
That one so wise, so powerful, and so proud,
Should feel himself, and dread the humble ills
Of rent-day charges and of coalman's bills ;
That while they mercy from their judge implore,
He fears himself—a knocking at the door ;

And feels the burthen as his neighbour states
His humble portion to the parish-rates.
They sit th' allotted hours, then eager run,
Rushing to pleasure when the duty 's done ;
His hour of leisure is of different kind,
Then cares domestic rush upon his mind,
And half the ease and comfort he enjoys,
Is when surrounded by slates, books, and boys.

Poor Reuben Dixon has the noisiest school
Of ragged lads, who ever bow'd to rule ; ⟵
Low in his price—the men who heave our coals,
And clean our causeways, send him boys in shoals :
To see poor Reuben, with his fry beside,—
Their half-check'd rudeness and his half-scorn'd pride,
Their room, the sty in which th' assembly meet,
In the close lane behind the Northgate-street;
T' observe his vain attempts to keep the peace,
Till tolls the bell, and strife and troubles cease,—
Calls for our praise; his labour praise deserves,
But not our pity ; Reuben has no nerves :
'Mid noise and dirt, and stench, and play, and prate,
He calmly cuts the pen or views the slate.

But Leonard !—yes, for Leonard's fate I grieve,
Who loathes the station which he dares not leave ;
He cannot dig, he will not beg his bread,
All his dependence rests upon his head ;
And deeply skill'd in sciences and arts,
On vulgar lads he wastes superior parts.
Alas ! what grief that feeling mind sustains,
In guiding hands and stirring torpid brains ;
He whose proud mind from pole to pole will move,
And view the wonders of the worlds above;
Who thinks and reasons strongly :—hard his fate,
Confined for ever to the pen and slate :
True, he submits, and when the long dull day
Has slowly pass'd, in weary tasks, away,
To other worlds with cheerful view he looks,
And parts the night between repose and books.
Amid his labours, he has sometimes tried
To turn a little from his cares aside ;
Pope, Milton, Dryden, with delight has seized,
His soul engaged and of his trouble eased :

When, with a heavy eye and ill-done sum,
No part conceived, a stupid boy will come;
Then Leonard first subdues the rising frown,
And bids the blockhead lay his blunders down;
O'er which disgusted he will turn his eye,
To his sad duty his sound mind apply,
And, vex'd in spirit, throw his pleasures by.

Turn we to schools which more than these
    afford—
The sound instruction and the wholesome
    board ;
And first our school for ladies :—pity calls
For one soft sigh, when we behold these walls,
Placed near the town, and where, from
    window high,
The fair, confined, may our free crowds espy,
With many a stranger gazing up and down,
And all the envied tumult of the town ;
May, in the smiling summer-eve, when they
Are sent to sleep the pleasant hours away,
Behold the poor (whom they conceive the
    bless'd)
Employ'd for hours, and grieved they cannot
    rest.

Here the fond girl, whose days are sad and
    few
Since dear mamma pronounced the last adieu,
Looks to the road, and fondly thinks she
    hears
The carriage-wheels, and struggles with her
    tears :
All yet is new, the misses great and small,
Madam herself, and teachers, odious all ;
From laughter, pity, nay command, she turns,
But melts in softness, or with anger burns ;
Nauseates her food, and wonders who can
    sleep
On such mean beds, where she can only weep;
She scorns condolence—but to all she hates
Slowly at length her mind accommodates ;
Then looks on bondage with the same concern
As others felt, and finds that she must learn
As others learn'd—the common lot to share,
To search for comfort and submit to care.

There are, 'tis said, who on these seats
    attend,
And to these ductile minds destruction vend ;
Wretches (to virtue, peace, and nature, foes)
To these soft minds, their wicked trash expose;
Seize on the soul, ere passions take the sway,
And lead the heart, ere yet it feels, astray :
Smugglers obscene!—and can there be who take
Infernal pains, the sleeping vice to wake ?

Can there be those, by whom the thought
    defiled
Enters the spotless bosom of a child ?
By whom the ill is to the heart convey'd,
Who lend the foe, not yet in arms, their aid,
And sap the city-walls before the siege be laid?
Oh ! rather skulking in the by-ways steal,
And rob the poorest traveller of his meal ;
Burst through the humblest trader's bolted
    door ;
Bear from the widow's hut her winter-store;
With stolen steed, on highways take your
    stand,
Your lips with curses arm'd, with death your
    hand ;—
Take all but life—the virtuous more would say,
Take life itself, dear as it is, away,
Rather than guilty thus the guileless soul
    betray.

Years pass away—let us suppose them past,
Th' accomplish'd nymph for freedom looks
    at last ;
All hardships over, which a school contains,
The spirit's bondage and the body's pains ;
Where teachers make the heartless, trembling
    set
Of pupils suffer for their own regret ;
Where winter's cold, attack'd by one poor fire,
Chills the fair child, commanded to retire ;
She felt it keenly in the morning air,
Keenly she felt it at the evening prayer.
More pleasant summer ; but then walks were
    made,
Not a sweet ramble, but a slow parade ;
They moved by pairs beside the hawthorn-
    hedge,
Only to set their feelings on an edge ;
And now at eve, when all their spirits rise,
Are sent to rest, and all their pleasure dies;
Where yet they all the town alert can see,
And distant plough-boys pacing o'er the lea.
These and the tasks successive masters
    brought—
The French they conn'd, the curious works
    they wrought :
The hours they made their taper fingers strike,
Note after note, all dull to them alike ;
Their drawings, dancings on appointed days,
Playing with globes, and getting parts of plays;
The tender friendships made 'twixt heart
    and heart,
When the dear friends had nothing to im-
    part :—

All ! all ! are over ;—now th' accomplish'd
          maid
Longs for the world, of nothing there afraid :
Dreams of delight invade her gentle breast,
And fancied lovers rob the heart of rest ;
At the paternal door a carriage stands,
Love knits their hearts and Hymen joins
          their hands.
    Ah !—world unknown ! how charming is
          thy view,
Thy pleasures many, and each pleasure new :
Ah !—world experienced ! what of thee is
          told ?
How few thy pleasures, and those few how old!
    Within a silent street, and far apart
From noise of business, from a quay or mart,
Stands an old spacious building, and the din
You hear without, explains the work within;
Unlike the whispering of the nymphs, this
          noise
Loudly proclaims a ' boarding-school for
          boys : '
The master heeds it not, for thirty years
Have render'd all familiar to his ears ;
He sits in comfort, 'mid the various sound
Of mingled tones for ever flowing round;
Day after day he to his task attends,—
Unvaried toil, and care that never ends :
Boys in their works proceed ; while his employ
Admits no change, or changes but the boy;
Yet time has made it easy ;—he beside
Has power supreme, and power is sweet to
          pride :
But grant him pleasure;—what can teachers
          feel,
Dependent helpers always at the wheel ?
Their power despised, their compensation
          small,
Their labour dull, their life laborious all ;
Set after set the lower lads to make
Fit for the class which their superiors take ;
The road of learning for a time to track
In roughest state, and then again go back :
Just the same way on other troops to wait,—
Attendants fix'd at learning's lower gate.
    The day-tasks now are over,—to their
          ground
Rush the gay crowd with joy-compelling
          sound ;
Glad to illude the burthens of the day,
The eager parties hurry to their play :
Then in these hours of liberty we find
The native bias of the opening mind ;

They yet possess not skill the mask to place,
And hide the passions glowing in the face;
Yet some are found—the close, the sly, the
          mean,
Who know already all must not be seen.
    Lo ! one who walks apart, although so
          young,
He lays restraint upon his eye and tongue ;
Nor will he into scrapes or dangers get,
And half the school are in the stripling's debt:
Suspicious, timid, he is much afraid
Of trick and plot :—he dreads to be betray'd:
He shuns all friendship, for he finds they lend,
When lads begin to call each other friend:
Yet self with self has war ; the tempting sight
Of fruit on sale provokes his appetite ;—
See ! how he walks the sweet seduction by;
That he is tempted, costs him first a sigh,—
'Tis dangerous to indulge, 'tis grievous to
          deny !
This he will choose, and whispering asks the
          price,
The purchase dreadful, but the portion nice ;
Within the pocket he explores the pence ;
Without, temptation strikes on either sense,
The sight, the smell;—but then he thinks again
Of money gone ! while fruit nor taste remain.
Meantime there comes an eager thoughtless
          boy,
Who gives the price and only feels the joy :
Example dire ! the youthful miser stops,
And slowly back the treasured coinage drops:
Heroic deed ! for should he now comply,
Can he to-morrow's appetite deny ?
Beside, these spendthrifts who so friendly live,
Cloy'd with their purchase, will a portion
          give :—
Here ends debate, he buttons up his store,
And feels the comfort that it burns no more.
    Unlike to him the tyrant-boy, whose sway
All hearts acknowledge; him the crowds obey:
At his command they break through every
          rule;
Whoever governs, he controls the school :
'Tis not the distant emperor moves their
          fear,
But the proud viceroy who is ever near.
    Verres could do that mischief in a day,
For which not Rome, in all its power, could
          pay;
And these boy-tyrants will their slaves
          distress,
And do the wrongs no master can redress :

The mind they load with fear: it feels disdain
For its own baseness ; yet it tries in vain
To shake th' admitted power;—the coward
     comes again :
'Tis more than present pain these tyrants give,
Long as we've life some strong impressions
     live ;
And these young ruffians in the soul will sow
Seeds of all vices that on weakness grow.

     Hark ! at his word the trembling young-
        lings flee,
Where he is walking none must walk but he ;
See ! from the winter-fire the weak retreat,
His the warm corner, his the favourite seat,
Save when he yields it to some slave to keep
Awhile, then back, at his return, to creep :
At his command his poor dependants fly,
And humbly bribe him as a proud ally ;
Flatter'd by all, the notice he bestows,
Is gross abuse, and bantering and blows ;
Yet he 's a dunce, and, spite of all his fame
Without the desk, within he feels his shame :
For there the weaker boy, who felt his scorn,
For him corrects the blunders of the morn ;
And he is taught, unpleasant truth ! to find
The trembling body has the prouder mind.

     Hark ! to that shout, that burst of empty
        noise,
From a rude set of bluff, obstreperous boys ;
They who, like colts let loose, with vigour
     bound,
And thoughtless spirit, o'er the beaten ground;
Fearless they leap, and every youngster feels
His Alma active in his hands and heels.

     These are the sons of farmers, and they
        come
With partial fondness for the joys of home ;
Their minds are coursing in their fathers'
     fields,
And e'en the dream a lively pleasure yields ;
They, much enduring, sit th' allotted hours,
And o'er a grammar waste their sprightly
     powers ;
They dance ; but them can measured steps
     delight,
Whom horse and hounds to daring deeds
     excite ?
Nor could they bear to wait from meal to
     meal,
Did they not slyly to the chamber steal,
And there the produce of the basket seize,
The mother's gift ! still studious of their
     ease.

Poor Alma, thus oppress'd, forbears to rise,
But rests or revels in the arms and thighs.*
     ' But is it sure that study will repay
The more attentive and forbearing ?'—Nay!
The farm, the ship, the humble shop have each
Gains which severest studies seldom reach.

     At college place a youth, who means to
        raise
His state by merit and his name by praise ;
Still much he hazards ; there is serious strife
In the contentions of a scholar's life :
Not all the mind's attention, care, distress,
Nor diligence itself, ensure success :
His jealous heart a rival's power may dread,
Till its strong feelings have confused his head,
And, after days and months, nay, years of
     pain,
He finds just lost the object he would gain.

     But grant him this and all such life can give,
For other prospects he begins to live ;
Begins to feel that man was form'd to look
And long for other objects than a book :
In his mind's eye his house and glebe he sees,
And farms and talks with farmers at his ease ;
And time is lost, till fortune sends him forth
To a rude world unconscious of his worth ;
There in some petty parish to reside,
The college-boast, then turn'd the village-
     guide ;
And though awhile his flock and dairy please,
He soon reverts to former joys and ease,
Glad when a friend shall come to break his
     rest,
And speak of all the pleasures they possess'd,
Of masters, fellows, tutors, all with whom
They shared those pleasures, never more to
     come ;
Till both conceive the times by bliss endear'd,
Which once so dismal and so dull appear'd.

     But fix our scholar, and suppose him
     crown'd
With all the glory gain'd on classic ground ;
Suppose the world without a sigh resign'd,
And to his college all his care confined ;
Give him all honours that such states allow,
The freshman's terror and the tradesman's
     bow ;
Let his apartments with his taste agree,
And all his views be those he loves to see ;

---

* Should any of my readers find themselves at
a loss in this place, I beg leave to refer them to
a poem of Prior, called *Alma, or the Progress of the
Mind.*

Let him each day behold the savoury treat,
For which he pays not, but is paid to eat;
These joys and glories soon delight no more,
Although withheld, the mind is vex'd and sore;
The honour too is to the place confined,
Abroad they know not each superior mind :
Strangers no *wranglers* in these figures see,
Nor give they worship to a high degree ;
Unlike the prophet's is the scholar's case,
His honour all is in his dwelling-place :
And there such honours are familiar things ;
What is a monarch in a crowd of kings ?
Like other sovereigns he's by forms address'd,
By statutes govern'd and with rules oppress'd.

When all these forms and duties die away,
And the day passes like the former day,
Then of exterior things at once bereft,
He's to himself and one attendant left ;
Nay, John too goes ; nor aught of service more
Remains for him ; he gladly quits the door,
And as he whistles to the college-gate,
He kindly pities his poor master's fate.

Books cannot always please, however good;
Minds are not ever craving for their food ;
But sleep will soon the weary soul prepare
For cares to-morrow that were this day's care :
For forms, for feasts, that sundry times have past,
And formal feasts that will for ever last.
' But then from study will no comforts rise ? '—

Yes ! such as studious minds alone can prize;
Comforts, yea !—joys ineffable they find,
Who seek the prouder pleasures of the mind :
The soul, collected in those happy hours,
Then makes her efforts, then enjoys her powers ;
And in those seasons feels herself repaid,
For labours past and honours long delay'd.

No ! 'tis not worldly gain, although by chance
The sons of learning may to wealth advance ;
Nor station high, though in some favouring hour
The sons of learning may arrive at power ;
Nor is it glory, though the public voice
Of honest praise will make the heart rejoice :
But 'tis the mind's own feelings give the joy,
Pleasures she gathers in her own employ—

Pleasures that gain or praise cannot bestow.
Yet can dilate and raise them when they flow.

For this the poet looks the world around,
Where form and life and reasoning man are found :
He loves the mind, in all its modes, to trace,
And all the manners of the changing race ;
Silent he walks the road of life along,
And views the aims of its tumultuous throng :
He finds what shapes the Proteus-passions take,
And what strange waste of life and joy they make,
And loves to show them in their varied ways,
With honest blame or with unflattering praise:
'Tis good to know, 'tis pleasant to impart,
These turns and movements of the human heart:
The stronger features of the soul to paint,
And make distinct the latent and the faint;
Man as he is, to place in all men's view,
Yet none with rancour, none with scorn pursue :
Nor be it ever of my portraits told—
' Here the strong lines of malice we behold.'—

This let me hope, that when in public view
I bring my pictures, men may feel them true ;
' This is a likeness,' may they all declare,
' And I have seen him, but I know not where:'
For I should mourn the mischief I had done,
If as the likeness all would fix on one.

Man's vice and crime I combat as I can,
But to his GOD and conscience leave the man;
I search (a Quixotte !) all the land about,
To find its giants and enchanters out,
(The giant-folly, the enchanter-vice,
Whom doubtless I shall vanquish in a trice ;)
But is there man whom I would injure ?—no !
I am to him a fellow, not a foe,—
A fellow-sinner, who must rather dread
The bolt, than hurl it at another's head.

No ! let the guiltless, if there such be found,
Launch forth the spear, and deal the deadly wound ;
How can I so the cause of virtue aid,
Who am myself attainted and afraid ?
Yet as I can, I point the powers of rhyme,
And, sparing criminals, attack the crime.—

NOTES TO 'THE BOROUGH'

LETTER I
Note 1, page 109, line 22.
Sits the large lily as the water's queen.
The white water-lily, *Nymphaea alba.*

Note 2, page 109, line 31.
Sampire-banks.

The jointed glasswort. *Salicornia* is here meant, not the true sampire, the *Crithmum maritimum.*

Note 3, page 109, line 31.
Salt-wort.
The *salsola* of botanists.

Note 4, page 110, line 42.
And planks which curve and crackle in the smoke.

The curvature of planks for the sides of a ship, &c., is, I am informed, now generally made by the power of steam. Fire is nevertheless still used for boats and vessels of the smaller kind.

Note 5, page 111, lines 51 and 52.
And oft the foggy banks on ocean lie,
Lift the fair sail, and cheat th' experienced eye.

Of the effect of these mists, known by the name of fog-banks, wonderful and indeed incredible relations are given ; but their property of appearing to elevate ships at sea, and to bring them in view, is, I believe, generally acknowledged.

LETTER II
Note 1, page 114, lines 13 and 14.
In three short hours shall thy presuming hand
Th' effect of three slow centuries command ?

If it should be objected, that centuries are not slower than hours, because the speed of time must be uniform, I would answer, that I understand so much, and mean that they are slower in no other sense, than because they are not finished so soon.

Note 2, page 114, line 26.
Can the small germ upon the substance view.

This kind of vegetation, as it begins upon siliceous stones, is very thin, and frequently not to be distinguished from the surface of the flint. The *byssus jolithus* of Linnaeus

(*lepraria jolithus* of the present system), an adhesive carmine crust on rocks and old buildings, was, even by scientific persons, taken for the substance on which it spread. A great variety of these minute vegetables are to be found in some parts of the coast, where the beach, formed of stones of various kinds, is undisturbed, and exposed to every change of weather ; in this situation, the different species of lichen, in their different stages of growth, have an appearance interesting and agreeable even to those who are ignorant of, and indifferent to the cause.

Note 3, page 114, lines 45 and 46.
Each has its motto : some contrived to tell,
In monkish rhyme, the uses of a bell.

The several purposes for which bells are used are expressed in two Latin verses of this kind.

Note 4, page 114, line 68.
But monuments themselves memorials need.
Quandoquidem data sunt ipsis quoque fata sepulchris.
JUVENAL, *Sat.* 10, l. 146.

Note 5, page 116, line 50.
Regard the dead, but to the living live.

It has been observed to me, that in the first part of the story I have represented this young woman as resigned and attentive to her duties ; from which it should appear that the concluding advice is unnecessary ; but if the reader will construe the expression ' to the living live,' into the sense—live entirely for them, attend to duties only which are real, and not those imposed by the imagination, I shall have no need to alter the line which terminates the story.

LETTER IV
Note 1, page 122, line 12.
May those excel by Solway-Moss destroy'd.
For an account of this extraordinary and interesting event, I refer my readers to the Journals of the year 1772.

Note 2, page 123, line 84.
They will not study, and they dare not fight.
Some may object to this assertion ; to whom I beg leave to answer, that I do not

use the word *fight* in the sense of the Jew Mendoza.

Note 3, page 124, line 28.
Regret thy misery, and lament thy crimes.

See the Book of Deuteronomy, chapter xxviii. and various other places.

Note 4, page 124, line 36.
Nor think of Julian's boast and Julian's fate.

His boast, that he would rebuild the Temple at Jerusalem ; his fate (whatever becomes of the miraculous part of the story), that he died before the foundation was laid.

Note 5, page 125, line 2.
Samson is grace, and carries all alone.

Whoever has attended to the books or preaching of these enthusiastic people, must have observed much of this kind of absurd and foolish application of scripture history ; it seems to them as reasoning.

LETTER V
Note 1, page 130, line 6.
He lived, nor dream'd of corporation-doles.

I am informed that some explanation is here necessary, though I am ignorant for what class of my readers it can be required. Some corporate bodies have actual property, as appears by their receiving rents ; and they obtain money on the admission of members into their society : this they may lawfully share perhaps. There are, moreover, other doles, of still greater value, of which it is not necessary for me to explain the nature, or to inquire into the legality.

LETTER VIII
Note 1, page 140, line 8.
Is ' Harmony in Uproar ' all day long.

The title of a short piece of humour by Arbuthnot.

Note 2, page 141, line 36
Nor less the place of curious plant he knows.

In botanical language ' *the habitat*,' the favourite soil or situation of the more scarce species.

Note 3, page 141, line 48.
This is no shaded, run-off, pin-eyed thing

This, it must be acknowledged, is contrary to the opinion of Thomson, and I believe of some other poets, who, in describing the varying hues of our most beautiful flowers, have considered them as lost and blended with each other ; whereas their beauty, in the eye of a florist (and I conceive in that of the uninitiated also), depends upon the distinctness of their colours: the stronger the bounding line, and the less they break into the neighbouring tint, so much the richer and more valuable is the flower esteemed.

Note 4, page 141, line 48.
Pin-eyed.

An auricula, or any other single flower, is so called when the *stigma* (the part which arises from the seed-vessel) is protruded beyond the tube of the flower, and becomes visible.

Note 5, page 141, line 51.
Which shed such beauty on my fair Bizarre.

This word, so far as it relates to flowers, means those variegated with three or more colours irregularly and indeterminately.

LETTER IX
Note 1, page 144, line 23.
Those living jellies which the flesh inflame.

Some of the smaller species of the *Medusa* (sea-nettle) are exquisitely beautiful : their form is nearly oval, varied with serrated longitudinal lines; they are extremely tender, and by no means which I am acquainted with can be preserved, for they soon dissolve in either spirit of wine or water, and lose every vestige of their shape, and indeed of their substance : the larger species are found in mis-shapen masses of many pounds weight ; these, when handled, have the effect of the nettle, and the stinging is often accompanied or succeeded by the more unpleasant feeling, perhaps in a slight degree resembling that caused by the torpedo.

Note 2, page 144, line 34.
And quickly vegetates a vital breed.

Various tribes and species of marine *vermes* are here meant : that which so nearly resembles a vegetable in its form, and perhaps, in some degree, manner of growth, is the coralline called by naturalists *Sertularia*, of which there are many species in almost every part of the coast. The animal protrudes its many claws (apparently in search of prey) from certain pellucid vesicles which proceed from a horny, tenacious, branchy stem.

Note 3, page 144, line 41.
Myriads of living points : th' unaided eye Can but the fire and not the form descry.

These are said to be a minute kind of

animal of the same class ; when it does not shine, it is invisible to the naked eye.

Note 4, page 144, line 50.
On weeds that sparkle, and on waves that blaze.

For the cause or causes of this phenomenon, which is sometimes, though rarely, observed on our coasts, I must refer the reader to the writers on natural philosophy and natural history.

Note 5, page 145, line 52.
Content would chee thee trudging to thine home.

This is not offered as a reasonable source of contentment, but as one motive for resignation : there would not be so much envy if there were more discernment.

LETTER XVIII
Note 1, page 182, line 6.
With glossy leaf and tawny bloom below.

This scenery is, I must acknowledge, in a certain degree like that heretofore described in the Village ; but that also was a maritime country :—if the objects be similar, the pictures must (in their principal features) be alike, or be bad pictures. I have varied them as much as I could, consistently with my wish to be accurate.

Note 2, page 182, line 8.
Form the contracted Flora of the town.

The reader unacquainted with the language of botany is informed, that the Flora of a place means the vegetable species it contains, and is the title of a book which describes them.

LETTER XX
Note 1, page 187, line 5.
Where thrift and lavender, and lad's-love bloom.

The lad's or boy's love of some counties is the plant southernwood, the *artemisia abrotanum* of botanists.

Note 2, page 189, line 2.
Of some vile plot, and every wo adieu!

As this incident points out the work alluded to, I wish it to be remembered, that the gloomy tenour, the querulous melancholy of the story, is all I censure. The language of the writer is often animated, and is, I believe, correct ; the characters well drawn, and the manners described from real life ; but the perpetual occurrence of sad events, the protracted list of teasing and perplexing mischances, joined with much waspish invective, unallayed by pleasantry or sprightliness, and these continued through many

hundred pages, render publications, intended for amusement and executed with ability, heavy and displeasing :—you find your favourite persons happy in the end ; but they have teased you so much with their perplexities by the way, that you were frequently disposed to quit them in their distresses.

LETTER XXI
Note 1, page 195, line 23.
But take thy part with sinners and be still.

In a periodical work for the month of June last, the preceding dialogue is pronounced to be a most abominable caricature, if meant to be applied to Calvinists in general, and greatly distorted, if designed for an individual : now the author in his preface has declared, that he takes not upon him the censure of any sect or society for their opinions ; and the lines themselves evidently point to an individual, whose sentiments they very fairly represent, without any distortion whatsoever. In a pamphlet intitled ' A Cordial for a Sin-despairing Soul,' originally written by a teacher of religion, and lately re-published by another teacher of greater notoriety, the reader is informed that after he had full assurance of his salvation, the Spirit entered particularly into the subject with him ; and, among many other matters of like nature, assured him that ' his sins were fully and freely forgiven, as if they had never been committed ; not for any act done by him, whether believing in Christ, or repenting of sin ; nor yet for the sorrows and miseries he endured, nor for any service he should be called upon in his militant state, but for his own name and for his glory's sake,' * &c. And the whole drift and tenour of the book is to the same purpose, viz. the uselessness of all religious duties, such as prayer, contrition, fasting, and good works : he shows the evil done by reading such books as the Whole Duty of Man, and the Practice of Piety ; and complains heavily of his relation, an Irish bishop, who wanted him to join with the household in family prayer : in fact, the whole work inculcates that sort of quietism which this dialogue alludes to, and that without any recommendation of attendance on the teachers of the Gospel, but rather holding forth encouragement to the supineness of man's nature ; by the information that he in vain looks for acceptance by the employment of his talents, and that his hopes of glory are rather extinguished than raised by any application to the means of grace.

* *Cordial*, &c., page 87.

TALES

[1812]

TO HER GRACE ISABELLA

DUCHESS DOWAGER OF RUTLAND

MADAM,

The dedication of works of literature to persons of superior worth and eminence appears to have been a measure early adopted, and continued to the present time ; so that whatever objections have been made to the language of dedicators, such addresses must be considered as perfectly consistent with reason and propriety ; in fact, superior rank and elevated situation in life naturally and justly claim such respect ; and it is the prerogative of greatness to give countenance and favour to all who appear to merit and to need them : it is likewise the prerogative of every kind of superiority and celebrity, of personal merit when peculiar or extraordinary, of dignity, elegance, wealth, and beauty ; certainly of superior intellect and intellectual acquirements : every such kind of eminence has its privilege, and being itself an object of distinguished approbation, it gains attention for whomsoever its possessor distinguishes and approves.

Yet the causes and motives for an address of this kind rest not entirely with the merit of the patron, the feelings of the author himself having their weight and consideration in the choice he makes : he may have gratitude for benefits received, or pride not illaudable in aspiring to the favour of those whose notice confers honour ; or he may entertain a secret but strong desire of seeing a name in the entrance of his work which he is accustomed to utter with peculiar satisfaction, and to hear mentioned with veneration and delight.

Such, madam, are the various kinds of eminence for which an author on these occasions would probably seek, and they meet in your grace ; such too are the feelings by which he would be actuated, and they centre in me : let me therefore entreat your grace to take this book into your favour and protection, and to receive it as an offering of the utmost respect and duty, from,

May it please Your Grace,

Your Grace's

Most obedient, humble,

And devoted servant,

GEORGE CRABBE.

MUSTON, *July* 31, 1812.

PREFACE

THAT the appearance of the present work before the public is occasioned by a favourable reception of the former two, I hesitate not to acknowledge ; because, while the confession may be regarded as some proof of gratitude, or at least of attention from an author to his readers, it ought not to be considered as an indication of vanity. It is unquestionably very pleasant to be assured that our labours are well received ; but, nevertheless, this must not be taken for a just and full criterion of their merit : publications of great intrinsic value have been met with so much coolness, that a writer who succeeds in obtaining some degree of notice should look upon himself rather as one favoured than meritorious, as gaining a prize from Fortune, and not a recompense for desert ; and, on the contrary, as it is well known that books of very inferior kind have been at once pushed into the strong current of popularity, and are there kept buoyant by the force of the stream, the writer who acquires not this adventitious help may be reckoned rather as unfortunate than undeserving; and from these opposite considerations it follows, that a man may speak of success without incurring justly the odium of conceit, and may likewise acknowledge a disappointment without an adequate cause for humiliation or self-reproach.

But were it true that something of the complacency of self-approbation would insinuate itself into an author's mind with the idea of success, the sensation would not be that of unalloyed pleasure ; it would perhaps assist him to bear, but it would not enable him to escape, the mortification he must encounter from censures, which, though he may be unwilling to admit, yet he finds himself unable to confute ; as well as from advice, which, at the same time that he cannot but approve, he is compelled to reject.

Reproof and advice, it is probable, every author will receive, if we except those who merit so much of the former, that the latter is contemptuously denied them; now of these, reproof, though it may cause more temporary uneasiness, will in many cases create less difficulty, since errors may be corrected when opportunity occurs: but advice, I repeat, may be of such nature, that it will be painful to reject, and yet impossible to follow it ; and in this predicament I conceive myself to be placed. There has been recommended to me, and from authority which neither inclination nor prudence leads me to resist, in any new work I might undertake, an unity of subject, and that arrangement of my materials which connects the whole and gives additional interest to every part ; in fact, if not an Epic Poem, strictly so denominated, yet such composition as would possess a regular succession of events, and a catastrophe to which every incident should be subservient, and which every character, in a greater or less degree, should conspire to accomplish.

In a Poem of this nature, the principal and inferior characters in some degree resemble a general and his army, where no one pursues his peculiar objects and adventures, or pursues them in unison with the movements and grand purposes of the whole body ; where there is a community of interests and a sub-

ordination of actors : and it was upon this view of the subject, and of the necessity for such distribution of persons and events, that I found myself obliged to relinquish an undertaking, for which the characters I could command, and the adventures I could describe, were altogether unfitted.

But if these characters which seemed to be at my disposal were not such as would coalesce into one body, nor were of a nature to be commanded by one mind, so neither on examination did they appear as an unconnected multitude, accidentally collected, to be suddenly dispersed ; but rather beings of whom might be formed groups and smaller societies, the relations of whose adventures and pursuits might bear that kind of similitude to an Heroic Poem, which these minor associations of men (as pilgrims on the way to their saint, or parties in search of amusement, travellers excited by curiosity, or adventurers in pursuit of gain) have in points of connexion and importance with a regular and disciplined army.

Allowing this comparison, it is manifest that while much is lost for want of unity of subject and grandeur of design, something is gained by greater variety of incident and more minute display of character, by accuracy of description and diversity of scene : in these narratives we pass from gay to grave, from lively to severe, not only without impropriety, but with manifest advantage. In one continued and connected Poem, the reader is, in general, highly gratified or severely disappointed ; by many independent narratives, he has the renovation of hope, although he has been dissatisfied, and a prospect of reiterated pleasure, should he find himself entertained.

I mean not, however, to compare these different modes of writing as if I were balancing their advantages and defects before I could give preference to either ; with me the way I take is not a matter of choice, but of necessity : I present not my Tales to the reader as if I had chosen the best method of ensuring his approbation, but as using the only means I possessed of engaging his attention.

It may probably be remarked that Tales, however dissimilar, might have been connected by some associating circumstance to which the whole number might bear equal affinity, and that examples of such union are to be found in Chaucer, in Boccace, and other collectors and inventors of Tales, which, considered in themselves, are altogether independent; and to this idea I gave so much consideration as convinced me that I could not avail myself of the benefit of such artificial mode of affinity. To imitate the English poet, characters must be found adapted to their several relations, and this is a point of great difficulty and hazard: much allowance seems to be required even for Chaucer himself, since it is difficult to conceive that on any occasion the devout and delicate Prioress, the courtly and valiant Knight, and ' the poure good Man the persone of a Towne,' would be the voluntary companions of the drunken Miller, the licentious Sompnour, and ' the Wanton Wife of Bath,' and enter into that colloquial and travelling intimacy which, if a common pilgrimage to the shrine of St. Thomas may be said to excuse, I know nothing beside (and certainly nothing in these times) that would produce such effect. Boccace, it is true, avoids all difficulty of this kind, by not assigning to the ten relators of his hundred Tales any marked or peculiar characters; nor though there are male and female in company, can the sex of the narrator be distinguished in the narration. To have followed the method of Chaucer might have been of use, but could scarcely be adopted, from its difficulty; and to have taken that of the Italian writer would have been perfectly easy, but could be of no service: the attempt at union therefore has been relinquished, and these relations are submitted to the public, connected by no other circumstance than their being the productions of the same author, and devoted to the same purpose, the entertainment of his readers.

It has been already acknowledged, that these compositions have no pretensions to be estimated with the more lofty and heroic kind of poems, but I feel great reluctance in admitting that they have not a fair and legitimate claim to the poetic character: in vulgar estimation, indeed, all that is not prose passes for poetry; but I have not ambition of so humble a kind as to be satisfied with a concession which requires nothing in the poet, except his ability for counting syllables; and I trust something more of the poetic character will be allowed to the succeeding pages than what the heroes of the Dunciad might share with the author: nor was I aware that by describing, as faithfully as I could, men, manners, and things, I was forfeiting a just title to a name which has been freely granted to many whom to equal, and even to excel, is but very stinted commendation.

In this case it appears that the usual comparison between poetry and painting entirely fails: the artist who takes an accurate likeness of individuals, or a faithful representation of scenery, may not rank so high in the public estimation as one who paints an historical event, or an heroic action; but he is nevertheless a painter, and his accuracy is so far from diminishing his reputation, that it procures for him in general both fame and emolument: nor is it perhaps with strict justice determined that the credit and reputation of those verses which strongly and faithfully delineate character and manners, should be lessened in the opinion of the public by the very accuracy which gives value and distinction to the productions of the pencil.

Nevertheless, it must be granted that the pretensions of any composition to be regarded as poetry will depend upon that definition of the poetic character which he who undertakes to determine the question has considered as decisive; and it is confessed also that one of great authority may be adopted, by which the verses now before the reader, and many others which have probably amused and delighted him, must be excluded: a definition like this will be found in the words which the greatest of poets, not divinely inspired, has given to the most noble and valiant Duke of Athens—

The poet's eye, in a fine frenzy rolling,
Doth glance from heaven to earth, from earth
    to heaven;
And as Imagination bodies forth
The forms of things unknown, the poet's pen
Turns them to shapes, and gives to airy
    nothing
A local habitation, and a name.*

* *Midsummer Night's Dream*, Act v, Scene 1.

Hence we observe the poet is one who, in the excursions of his fancy between heaven and earth, lights upon a kind of fairy-land, in which he places a creation of his own, where he embodies shapes, and gives action and adventure to his ideal offspring ; taking captive the imagination of his readers, he elevates them above the grossness of actual being, into the soothing and pleasant atmosphere of supra-mundane existence : there he obtains for his visionary inhabitants the interest that engages a reader's attention without ruffling his feelings, and excites that moderate kind of sympathy which the realities of nature oftentimes fail to produce, either because they are so familiar and insignificant that they excite no determinate emotion, or are so harsh and powerful that the feelings excited are grating and distasteful.

Be it then granted that (as Duke Theseus observes) ' such tricks hath strong Imagination,' and that such poets ' are of imagination all compact ; ' let it be further conceded, that theirs is a higher and more dignified kind of composition, nay, the only kind that has pretensions to inspiration ; still, that these poets should so entirely engross the title as to exclude those who address their productions to the plain sense and sober judgment of their readers, rather than to their fancy and imagination, I must repeat that I am unwilling to admit—because I conceive that, by granting such right of exclusion, a vast deal of what has been hitherto received as genuine poetry would no longer be entitled to that appellation.

All that kind of satire wherein character is skilfully delineated must (this criterion being allowed) no longer be esteemed as genuine poetry ; and for the same reason many affecting narratives which are founded on real events, and borrow no aid whatever from the imagination of the writer, must likewise be rejected : a considerable part of the poems, as they have hitherto been denominated, of Chaucer, are of this naked and unveiled character : and there are in his Tales many pages of coarse, accurate, and minute, but very striking description. Many small poems in a subsequent age, of most impressive kind, are adapted and addressed to the common sense of the reader, and

prevail by the strong language of truth and nature : they amused our ancestors, and they continue to engage our interest, and excite our feelings, by the same powerful appeals to the heart and affections. In times less remote, Dryden has given us much of this poetry, in which the force of expression and accuracy of description have neither needed nor obtained assistance from the fancy of the writer ; the characters in his Absalom and Achitophel are instances of this, and more especially those of Doeg and Og in the second part : these, with all their grossness, and almost offensive accuracy, are found to possess that strength and spirit which has preserved from utter annihilation the dead bodies of Tate, to whom they were inhumanly bound, happily with a fate the reverse of that caused by the cruelty of Mezentius ; for there the living perished in the putrefaction of the dead, and here the dead are preserved by the vitality of the living. And, to bring forward one other example, it will be found that Pope himself has no small portion of this actuality of relation, this nudity of description, and poetry without an atmosphere ; the lines beginning, ' In the worst inn's worst room,' are an example, and many others may be seen in his Satires, Imitations, and above all in his Dunciad : the frequent absence of those ' Sports of Fancy,' and ' Tricks of strong Imagination,' have been so much observed, that some have ventured to question whether even this writer were a poet ; and though, as Dr. Johnson has remarked, it would be difficult to form a definition of one in which Pope should not be admitted, yet they who doubted his claim, had, it is likely, provided for his exclusion by forming that kind of character for their poet, in which this elegant versifier, for so he must be then named, should not be comprehended.

These things considered, an author will find comfort in his expulsion from the rank and society of poets, by reflecting that men much his superiors were likewise shut out, and more especially when he finds also that men not much his superiors are entitled to admission.

But in whatever degree I may venture to differ from any others in my notions of the qualifications and character of the true poet, I most cordially assent to their opinion who assert that his principal exertions must be made to engage the attention of his readers; and further, I must allow that the effect of poetry should be to lift the mind from the painful realities of actual existence, from its every-day concerns, and its perpetually-occurring vexations, and to give it repose by substituting objects in their place which it may contemplate with some degree of interest and satisfaction : but what is there in all this, which may not be effected by a fair representation of existing character ? nay, by a faithful delineation of those painful realities, those every-day concerns, and those perpetually-occurring vexations themselves, provided they be not (which is hardly to be supposed) the very concerns and distresses of the reader ? for when it is admitted that they have no particular relation to him, but are the troubles and anxieties of other men, they excite and interest his feelings as the imaginary exploits, adventures, and perils of romance ;—they soothe his mind, and keep his curiosity pleasantly awake ; they appear to have enough of reality to engage his sympathy, but possess not interest sufficient to create painful sensations. Fiction itself, we know, and every work of fancy, must for a time have the effect of realities ; nay, the very enchanters, spirits, and monsters of Ariosto and Spenser must be present in the mind of the reader while he is engaged by their operations, or they would be as the objects and incidents of a nursery tale to a rational understanding, altogether despised and neglected : in truth, I can but consider this pleasant effect upon the mind of a reader, as depending neither upon the events related (whether they be actual or imaginary), nor upon the characters introduced (whether taken from life or fancy), but upon the manner in which the poem itself is conducted ; let that be judiciously managed, and the occurrences actually copied from life will have the same happy effect as the inventions of a creative fancy ;—while, on the other hand, the imaginary persons and incidents to which the poet has given ' a local habitation, and a name,' will make upon the concurring feelings of the reader the same impressions with those taken from truth and nature, because they will appear to be derived from that source, and therefore of necessity will have a similar effect.

Having thus far presumed to claim for the ensuing pages the rank and title of poetry, I attempt no more, nor venture to class or compare them with any other kinds of poetical composition ; their place will doubtless be found for them.

A principal view and wish of the poet must be to engage the mind of his readers, as, failing in that point, he will scarcely succeed in any other : I therefore willingly confess that much of my time and assiduity has been devoted to this purpose ; but, to the ambition of pleasing, no other sacrifices have, I trust, been made, than of my own labour and care. Nothing will be found that militates against the rules of propriety and good manners, nothing that offends against the more important precepts of morality and religion ; and with this negative kind of merit, I commit my book to the judgment and taste of the reader—not being willing to provoke his vigilance by professions of accuracy, nor to solicit his indulgence by apologies for mistakes.

TALE I. THE DUMB ORATORS; OR,
THE BENEFIT OF SOCIETY

In fair round belly with good capon lined,
With eyes severe—
Full of wise saws and modern instances.
As You Like It, Act ii, Scene 7.

Deep shame had struck me dumb.
King John, Act iv, Scene 2.

He gives the bastinado with his tongue,
Our ears are cudgell'd.
King John, Act ii, Scene 1.

Dick.   Let's kill all the lawyers ; . . .
Cade.   Now show yourselves men : 'tis for
   liberty :
We will not leave one lord or gentleman.
2 Henry VI, Act iv, Scene 2.

And thus the whirligig of time brings in his
   revenges.
Twelfth Night, Act v, Scene last.

THAT all men would be cowards if they dare,
Some men we know have courage to declare ;
And this the life of many an hero shows,
That like the tide, man's courage ebbs and
   flows :
With friends and gay companions round
   them, then
Men boldly speak and have the hearts of men;
Who, with opponents seated, miss the aid
Of kind applauding looks, and grow afraid ;
Like timid trav'llers in the night, they fear
Th' assault of foes, when not a friend is near.
   In contest mighty and of conquest proud
Was Justice Bolt, impetuous, warm, and loud ;
His fame, his prowess all the country knew,
And disputants, with one so fierce, were few :
He was a younger son, for law design'd,
With dauntless look and persevering mind ;
While yet a clerk, for disputation famed,
No efforts tired him, and no conflicts tamed.
   Scarcely he bade his master's desk adieu,
When both his brothers from the world
   withdrew.
An ample fortune he from them possess'd,
And was with saving care and prudence
   bless'd.
Now would he go and to the country give
Example how an English 'squire should live ;
How bounteous, yet how frugal man may be,
By a well-order'd hospitality ;

He would the rights of all so well maintain
That none should idle be, and none complain.
   All this and more he purposed—and what
      man
Could do, he did to realize his plan :
But time convinced him that we cannot keep
A breed of reasoners like a flock of sheep ;
For they, so far from following as we lead,
Make that a cause why they will not proceed.
Man will not follow where a rule is shown,
But loves to take a method of his own ;
Explain the way with all your care and skill,
This will he quit, if but to prove he will.—
Yet had our Justice honour—and the crowd,
Awed by his presence, their respect avowed.
   In later years he found his heart incline,
More than in youth, to gen'rous food and
      wine ;
But no indulgence check'd the powerful love
He felt to teach, to argue, and reprove.
   Meetings, or public calls, he never miss'd—
To dictate often, always to assist.
Oft he the clergy join'd, and not a cause
Pertain'd to them but he could quote the
      laws ;
He upon tithes and residence display'd
A fund of knowledge for the hearer's aid ;
And could on glebe and farming, wool and
      grain,
A long discourse, without a pause, maintain.
   To his experience and his native sense
He join'd a bold imperious eloquence ;
The grave, stern look of men inform'd and
      wise,
A full command of feature, heart, and eyes,
An awe-compelling frown, and fear-inspiring
      size.
When at the table, not a guest was seen
With appetite so ling'ring, or so keen ;
But when the outer man no more required,
The inner waked, and he was man inspired.
His subjects then were those, a subject true
Presents in fairest form to public view ;
Of Church and State, of Law, with mighty
      strength
Of words he spoke, in speech of mighty length.
And now, into the vale of years declined,
He hides too little of the monarch-mind :

He kindles anger by untimely jokes,
And opposition by contempt provokes ;
Mirth he suppresses by his awful frown,
And humble spirits, by disdain, keeps down ;
Blamed by the mild, approved by the severe,
The prudent fly him, and the valiant fear.

For overbearing is his proud discourse,
And overwhelming of his voice the force ;
And overpowering is he when he shows
What floats upon a mind that always over-
    flows.

This ready man at every meeting rose,
Something to hint, determine, or propose ;
And grew so fond of teaching, that he taught
Those who instruction needed not or sought :
Happy our hero, when he could excite
Some thoughtless talker to the wordy fight :
Let him a subject at his pleasure choose,
Physic or Law, Religion or the Muse ;
On all such themes he was prepared to shine,
Physician, poet, lawyer, and divine.
Hemm'd in by some tough argument, borne
    down
By press of language and the awful frown,
In vain for mercy shall the culprit plead ;
His crime is past, and sentence must proceed :
Ah ! suffering man, have patience, bear thy
    woes—
For lo ! the clock—at ten the Justice goes.

This powerful man, on business or to please
A curious taste, or weary grown of ease,
On a long journey travell'd many a mile
Westward, and halted midway in our isle ;
Content to view a city large and fair,
Though none had notice—what a man was
    there !

Silent two days, he then began to long
Again to try a voice so loud and strong ;
To give his favourite topics some new grace,
And gain some glory in such distant place ;
To reap some present pleasure, and to sow
Seeds of fair fame, in after-time to grow :
Here will men say, ' We heard, at such an hour,
The best of speakers—wonderful his power.'

Inquiry made, he found that day would
    meet
A learned club, and in the very street :
Knowledge to gain and give, was the design ;
To speak, to hearken, to debate, and dine :
This pleased our traveller, for he felt his force
In either way, to eat or to discourse.

Nothing more easy than to gain access
To men like these, with his polite address :

So he succeeded, and first look'd around,
To view his objects and to take his ground ;
And therefore silent chose awhile to sit,
Then enter boldly by some lucky hit ;
Some observation keen or stroke severe,
To cause some wonder or excite some fear.

Now, dinner past, no longer he suppress'd
His strong dislike to be a silent guest ;
Subjects and words were now at his com-
    mand—
When disappointment frown'd on all he
    plann'd ;
For, hark !—he heard amazed, on every side,
His church insulted and her priests belied ;
The laws reviled, the ruling power abused,
The land derided, and its foes excused :—
He heard and ponder'd,—What, to men so
    vile,
Should be his language ? For his threat'ning
    style
They were too many ;—if his speech were
    meek,
They would despise such poor attempts to
    speak :
At other times with every word at will,
He now sat lost, perplex'd, astonish'd,
    still.

Here were Socinians, Deists, and indeed
All who, as foes to England's church, agreed ;
But still with creeds unlike, and some without
    a creed :
Here, too, fierce friends of liberty he saw,
Who own'd no prince and who obey no law ;
There were Reformers of each different sort,
Foes to the laws, the priesthood, and the
    court ;
Some on their favourite plans alone intent,
Some purely angry and malevolent :
The rash were proud to blame their country's
    laws ;
The vain, to seem supporters of a cause ;
One call'd for change that he would dread to
    see ;
Another sigh'd for Gallic liberty !
And numbers joining with the forward crew,
For no one reason—but that numbers do.

' How,' said the Justice, ' can this trouble
    rise,
This shame and pain, from creatures I de-
    spise ? '
And conscience answer'd—' The prevailing
    cause
Is thy delight in listening to applause ;

Here, thou art seated with a tribe, who spurn
Thy favourite themes, and into laughter turn
Thy fears and wishes ; silent and obscure,
Thyself, shalt thou the long harangue endure ;
And learn, by feeling, what it is to force
On thy unwilling friends the long discourse :
What though thy thoughts be just, and these,
    it seems,
Are traitors' projects, idiots' empty schemes ;
Yet minds like bodies cramm'd, reject their
    food,
Nor will be forced and tortured for their good !
    At length, a sharp, shrewd, sallow man
    arose,
And begg'd he briefly might his mind disclose ;
' It was his duty, in these worst of times,
T' inform the govern'd of their rulers' crimes :'
This pleasant subject to attend, they each
Prepared to listen, and forbore to teach.
    Then voluble and fierce the wordy man
Through a long chain of favourite horrors
    ran :—
First, of the church, from whose enslaving
    power
He was deliver'd, and he bless'd the hour ;
' Bishops and deans, and prebendaries all,'
He said, ' were cattle fatt'ning in the stall ;
Slothful and pursy, insolent and mean,
Were every bishop, prebendary, dean,
And wealthy rector : curates, poorly paid,
Were only dull ;—he would not them up-
    braid.'
    From priests he turn'd to canons, creeds,
    and prayers,
Rubrics and rules, and all our church affairs ;
Churches themselves, desk, pulpit, altar, all
The Justice reverenced—and pronounced
    their fall.
    Then from religion Hammond turn'd his
    view,
To give our rulers the correction due ;
Not one wise action had these triflers plann'd ;
There was, it seem'd, no wisdom in the land ;
Save in this patriot tribe, who meet at times
To show the statesman's errors and his crimes.
    Now here was Justice Bolt compell'd to
    sit,
To hear the deist's scorn, the rebel's wit ;
The fact mis-stated, the envenom'd lie,
And staring, spell-bound, made not one reply.
    Then were our laws abused—and with the
    laws,
All who prepare, defend, or judge a cause :

' We have no lawyer whom a man can trust,'
Proceeded Hammond—' if the laws were just ;
But they are evil ; 'tis the savage state
Is only good, and ours sophisticate !
See ! the free creatures in their woods and
    plains,
Where without laws each happy monarch
    reigns,
King of himself—while we a number dread,
By slaves commanded and by dunces led ;
Oh, let the name with either state agree—
Savage our own we'll name, and civil theirs
    shall be.'
    The silent Justice still astonish'd sate,
And wonder'd much whom he was gazing at ;
Twice he essay'd to speak—but in a cough
The faint, indignant, dying speech went off :
' But who is this ? ' thought he—' a daemon
    vile,
With wicked meaning and a vulgar style :
Hammond they call him ; they can give the
    name
Of man to devils.—Why am I so tame ?
Why crush I not the viper ? '—Fear replied,
' Watch him awhile, and let his strength be
    tried ;
He will be foil'd, if man ; but if his aid
Be from beneath, 'tis well to be afraid.'
    ' We are call'd free ! ' said Hammond—
    ' doleful times
When rulers add their insult to their crimes ;
For should our scorn expose each powerful
    vice,
It would be libel, and we pay the price.'
    Thus with licentious words the man went
    on,
Proving that liberty of speech was gone ;
That all were slaves—nor had we better chance
For better times than as allies to France.
    Loud groan'd the stranger—Why, he must
    relate ;
And own'd, ' In sorrow for his country's fate ; '
' Nay, she were safe,' the ready man replied,
' Might patriots rule her, and could reasoners
    guide ;
When all to vote, to speak, to teach, are free,
Whate'er their creeds or their opinions be ;
When books of statutes are consumed in
    flames,
And courts and copyholds are empty names ;
Then will be times of joy—but ere they come,
Havock, and war, and blood must be our
    doom.'

The man here paused—then loudly for
　　reform
He call'd, and hail'd the prospect of the storm;
The wholesome blast, the fertilizing flood—
Peace gain'd by tumult, plenty bought with
　　blood :
Sharp means, he own'd ; but when the land's
　　disease
Asks cure complete, no med'cines are like
　　these.

　　Our Justice now, more led by fear than rage,
Saw it in vain with madness to engage ;
With imps of darkness no man seeks to fight,
Knaves to instruct, or set deceivers right :
Then as the daring speech denounced these
　　woes,
Sick at the soul, the grieving guest arose ;
Quick on the board his ready cash he threw,
And from the daemons to his closet flew :
There when secured, he pray'd with earnest
　　zeal,
That all they wish'd these patriot-souls might
　　feel ;
' Let them to France, their darling country,
　　haste,
And all the comforts of a Frenchman taste ;
Let them his safety, freedom, pleasure know,
Feel all their rulers on the land bestow ;
And be at length dismiss'd by one unerring
　　blow ;
Not hack'd and hew'd by one afraid to strike,
But shorn by that which shears all men alike ;
Nor, as in Britain, let them curse delay
Of law, but borne without a form away—
Suspected, tried, condemn'd, and carted in
　　a day ;
Oh ! let them taste what they so much
　　approve,
These strong fierce freedoms of the land they
　　love.' *

　　Home came our hero, to forget no more
The fear he felt and ever must deplore :
For though he quickly join'd his friends again,
And could with decent force his themes main-
　　tain,

* The reader will perceive in these and the
preceding verses allusions to the state of France,
as that country was circumstanced some years
since, rather than as it appears to be in the
present date ; several years elapsing between
the alarm of the loyal magistrate on the occasion
now related, and a subsequent event that farther
illustrates the remark with which the narrative
commences.

Still it occurr'd that, in a luckless time,
He fail'd to fight with heresy and crime ;
It was observed his words were not so strong,
His tones so powerful, his harangues so long,
As in old times—for he would often drop
The lofty look, and of a sudden stop ;
When conscience whisper'd, that he once was
　　still,
And let the wicked triumph at their will ;
And therefore now, when not a foe was near,
He had no right so valiant to appear.
　　Some years had pass'd, and he perceived
　　his fears
Yield to the spirit of his earlier years—
When at a meeting, with his friends beside,
He saw an object that awaked his pride ;
His shame, wrath, vengeance, indignation—
　　all
Man's harsher feelings did that sight recall.
　　For lo ! beneath him fix'd, our man of law
That lawless man the foe of order saw ;
Once fear'd, now scorn'd ; once dreaded,
　　now abhorr'd ;
A wordy man, and evil every word :
Again he gazed—' It is,' said he, ' the same ;
Caught and secure : his master owes him
　　shame : '
So thought our hero, who each instant found
His courage rising, from the numbers round.
　　As when a felon has escaped and fled,
So long, that law conceives the culprit dead ;
And back recall'd her myrmidons, intent
On some new game, and with a stronger scent;
Till she beholds him in a place, where none
Could have conceived the culprit would have
　　gone ;
There he sits upright in his seat, secure,
As one whose conscience is correct and pure ;
This rouses anger for the old offence,
And scorn for all such seeming and pretence ;
So on this Hammond look'd our hero bold,
Remated emb'ring well that vile offence of old ;
And now he saw the rebel dared t' intrude
Among the pure, the loyal, and the good ;
The crime provoked his wrath, the folly
　　stirr'd his blood :
Nor wonder was it if so strange a sight
Caused joy with vengeance, terror with
　　delight ;
Terror like this a tiger might create,
A joy like that to see his captive state,
At once to know his force and then decree
　　his fate.

Hammond, much praised by numerous
friends, was come
To read his lectures, so admired at home ;
Historic lectures, where he loved to mix
His free plain hints on modern politics :
Here, he had heard, that numbers had design,
Their business finish'd, to sit down and dine ;
This gave him pleasure, for he judged it right
To show by day, that he could speak at night.
Rash the design—for he perceived, too late,
Not one approving friend beside him sate ; '
The greater number, whom he traced around,
Were men in black, and he conceived they
frown'd.
' I will not speak,' he thought ; ' no pearls
of mine
Shall be presented to this herd of swine ; '
Not this avail'd him, when he cast his eye
On Justice Bolt ; he could not fight, nor fly :
He saw a man to whom he gave the pain,
Which now he felt must be return'd again ;
His conscience told him with what keen
delight
He, at that time, enjoy'd a stranger's fright ;
That stranger now befriended—he alone,
For all his insult, friendless, to atone ;
Now he could feel it cruel that a heart
Should be distress'd, and none to take its part;
' Though one by one,' said Pride, ' I would defy
Much greater men, yet meeting every eye,
I do confess a fear—but he will pass me by.'
   Vain hope ! the Justice saw the foe's
distress,
With exultation he could not suppress ;
He felt the fish was hook'd—and so forbore,
In playful spite, to draw it to the shore.
Hammond look'd round again ; but none
were near,
With friendly smile, to still his growing fear ;
But all above him seem'd a solemn row
Of priests and deacons, so they seem'd below ;
He wonder'd who his right-hand man might
be—
Vicar of Holt cum Uppingham was he ;
And who the man of that dark frown pos-
sess'd—
Rector of Bradley and of Barton-west ;
' A pluralist,' he growl'd—but check'd the
word,
That warfare might not, by his zeal, be stirr'd.
   But now began the man above to show
Fierce looks and threat'nings to the man
below :

Who had some thoughts his peace by flight
to seek—
But how then lecture, if he dared not speak !—
   Now as the Justice for the war prepared,
He seem'd just then to question if he dared ;
' He may resist, although his power be small,
And growing desperate may defy us all ;
One dog attack, and he prepares for flight—
Resist another, and he strives to bite ;
Nor can I say, if this rebellious cur
Will fly for safety, or will scorn to stir.'
Alarm'd by this, he lash'd his soul to rage,
Burn'd with strong shame, and hurried to
engage.
As a male turkey straggling on the green,
When by fierce harriers, terriers, mongrels
seen,
He feels the insult of the noisy train,
And skulks aside, though moved by much
disdain ;
But when that turkey, at his own barn-door,
Sees one poor straying puppy and no more,
(A foolish puppy who had left the pack,
Thoughtless what foe was threat'ning at his
back,)
He moves about, as ship prepared to sail,
He hoists his proud rotundity of tail,
The half-seal'd eyes and changeful neck he
shows,
Where, in its quick'ning colours, vengeance
glows ;
From red to blue the pendant wattles turn,
Blue mix'd with red, as matches when they
burn ;
And thus th' intruding snarler to oppose,
Urged by enkindling wrath, he gobbling
goes.
So look'd our hero in his wrath, his cheeks
Flush'd with fresh fires and glow'd in tingling
streaks ;
His breath by passion's force awhile restrain'd,
Like a stopp'd current, greater force regain'd;
So spoke, so look'd he, every eye and ear
Were fix'd to view him, or were turn'd to hear.
   ' My friends, you know me, you can witness
all,
How, urged by passion, I restrain my gall ;
And every motive to revenge withstand—
Save when I hear abused my native land.
   ' Is it not known, agreed, confirm'd, confess'd,
That of all people, we are govern'd best ?
We have the force of monarchies ; are free,
As the most proud republicans can be ;

And have those prudent counsels that arise
In grave and cautious aristocracies ;
And live there those, in such all-glorious state,
Traitors protected in the land they hate ?
Rebels, still warring with the laws that give
To them subsistence ?—Yes, such wretches
    live.
    ' Ours is a church reform'd, and now no
        more
Is aught for man to mend or to restore ;
'Tis pure in doctrines, 'tis correct in creeds,
Has nought redundant, and it nothing needs ;
No evil is therein—no wrinkle, spot,
Stain, blame, or blemish :—I affirm there 's
    not.
    ' All this you know—now mark what once
        befell,
With grief I bore it, and with shame I tell ;
I was entrapp'd—yes, so it came to pass,
Mid heathen rebels, a tumultuous class ;
Each to his country bore a hellish mind,
Each like his neighbour was of cursed kind ;
The land that nursed them they blasphemed ;
    the laws,
Their sovereign's glory, and their country's
    cause ;
And who their mouth, their master-fiend,
    and who
Rebellion's oracle ?——You, caitiff, you ! '
    He spoke, and standing stretch'd his
        mighty arm,
And fix'd the man of words, as by a charm.
    ' How raved that railer ! Sure some hellish
        power
Restrain'd my tongue in that delirious hour,
Or I had hurl'd the shame and vengeance due
On him, the guide of that infuriate crew ;
But to my eyes such dreadful looks appear'd,
Such mingled yell of lying words I heard,
That I conceived around were daemons all,
And till I fled the house, I fear'd its fall.
    ' Oh ! could our country from our coasts
        expel
Such foes ! to nourish those who wish her
    well :
This her mild laws forbid, but we may still
From us eject them by our sovereign will ;
This let us do.'—He said, and then began
A gentler feeling for the silent man ;

Ev'n in our hero's mighty soul arose
A touch of pity for experienced woes ;
But this was transient, and with angry eye
He sternly look'd, and paused for a reply.
    'Twas then the man of many words would
        speak—
But, in his trial, had them all to seek :
To find a friend he look'd the circle round,
But joy or scorn in every feature found ;
He sipp'd his wine, but in those times of dread
Wine only adds confusion to the head ;
In doubt he reason'd with himself—' And how
Harangue at night, if I be silent now ? '
From pride and praise received, he sought to
    draw
Courage to speak, but still remain'd the awe ;
One moment rose he with a forced disdain,
And then abash'd, sunk sadly down again ;
While in our hero's glance he seem'd to read,
' Slave and insurgent ! what hast thou to
    plead ? '—
    By desperation urged, he now began :
' I seek no favour—I—the Rights of Man !
Claim ; and I—nay !—but give me leave—
    and I
Insist—a man—that is—and in reply,
I speak.'——Alas ! each new attempt was
    vain :
Confused he stood, he sate, he rose again ;
At length he growl'd defiance, sought the door,
Cursed the whole synod, and was seen no
    more.
    ' Laud we,' said Justice Bolt, ' the Powers
        above ;
Thus could our speech the sturdiest foe
    remove.'
Exulting now he gain'd new strength of fame,
And lost all feelings of defeat and shame.
    ' He dared not strive, you witness'd—
        dared not lift
His voice, nor drive at his accursed drift :
So all shall tremble, wretches who oppose
Our church or state—thus be it to our foes.'
    He spoke, and, seated with his former air,
Look'd his full self, and fill'd his ample chair ;
Took one full bumper to each favourite cause,
And dwelt all night on politics and laws,
With high applauding voice, that gain'd him
    high applause.

TALE II.   THE PARTING HOUR

I did not take my leave of him, but had
Most pretty things to say : ere I could tell him
How I would think on him, at certain hours,
Such thoughts and such ; . . . or ere I could
Give him that parting kiss, which I had set
Betwixt two charming words—comes in my
    father—
       Cymbeline, Act i, Scene 3.

O, grief hath changed me since you saw me last,
And careful hours with Time's deformed hand
Have written strange defeatures in my face.
       Comedy of Errors, Act v, Scene 1.

Oh ! if thou be'st the same Aegeon, speak,
And speak unto the same Aemilia.
       Comedy of Errors, Act v, Scene 1.

I ran it through, ev'n from my boyish days
To the very moment that he bade me tell it,
Wherein I spake of most disastrous chances,
Of moving accidents, by flood, and field ; . . .
Of being taken by the insolent foe
And sold to slavery.
       Othello, Act i, Scene 3.

An old man, broken with the storms of state,
Is come to lay his weary bones among ye ;
Give him a little earth for charity.
       Henry VIII, Act iv, Scene 2.

MINUTELY trace man's life ; year after year,
Through all his days let all his deeds appear,
And then, though some may in that life be
    strange,
Yet there appears no vast nor sudden change:
The links that bind those various deeds are
    seen,
And no mysterious void is left between.

But let these binding links be all destroy'd,
All that through years he suffer'd or enjoy'd;
Let that vast gap be made, and then behold—
This was the youth, and he is thus when old ;
Then we at once the work of Time survey,
And in an instant see a life's decay ;
Pain mix'd with pity in our bosoms rise,
And sorrow takes new sadness from surprise.

Beneath yon tree, observe an ancient pair—
A sleeping man ; a woman in her chair,
Watching his looks with kind and pensive air;
No wife, nor sister she, nor is the name
Nor kindred of this friendly pair the same ;
Yet so allied are they, that few can feel
Her constant, warm, unwearied, anxious zeal ;

Their years and woes, although they long
    have loved,
Keep their good name and conduct unre-
    proved ;
Thus life's small comforts they together share,
And while life lingers for the grave prepare.

No other subjects on their spirits press,
Nor gain such int'rest as the past distress
Grievous events that from the mem'ry drive
Life's common cares, and those alone survive,
Mix with each thought, in every action share,
Darken each dream, and blend with every
    prayer.

To David Booth, his fourth and last-born
    boy,
Allen his name, was more than common joy ;
And as the child grew up, there seem'd in
    him
A more than common life in every limb ;
A strong and handsome stripling he became,
And the gay spirit answer'd to the frame ;
A lighter, happier lad was never seen,
For ever easy, cheerful, or serene ;
His early love he fix'd upon a fair
And gentle maid—they were a handsome pair.
They at an infant-school together play'd,
Where the foundation of their love was laid;
The boyish champion would his choice attend
In every sport, in every fray defend.
As prospects open'd and as life advanced,
They walk'd together, they together danced ;
On all occasions, from their early years,
They mix'd their joys and sorrows, hopes and
    fears ;
Each heart was anxious, till it could impart
Its daily feelings to its kindred heart ;
As years increased, unnumber'd petty wars
Broke out between them ; jealousies and jars,
Causeless indeed, and follow'd by a peace,
That gave to love—growth, vigour, and
    increase.
Whilst yet a boy, when other minds are void,
Domestic thoughts young Allen's hours
    employ'd ;
Judith in gaining hearts had no concern,
Rather intent the matron's part to learn ;
Thus early prudent and sedate they grew,
While lovers, thoughtful—and though chil-
    dren, true.

                I

To either parents not a day appear'd,
When with this love they might have inter-
    fered :
Childish at first, they cared not to restrain ;
And strong at last, they saw restriction vain ;
Nor knew they when that passion to reprove—
Now idle fondness, now resistless love.

So while the waters rise, the children tread
On the broad estuary's sandy bed ;
But soon the channel fills, from side to side
Comes danger rolling with the deep'ning tide ;
Yet none who saw the rapid current flow
Could the first instant of that danger know.

The lovers waited till the time should come
When they together could possess a home :
In either house were men and maids unwed,
Hopes to be soothed, and tempers to be led.
Then Allen's mother of his favourite maid
Spoke from the feelings of a mind afraid :
' Dress and amusements were her sole employ,'
She said—' entangling her deluded boy ; '
And yet, in truth, a mother's jealous love
Had much imagined and could little prove ;
Judith had beauty—and if vain, was kind,
Discreet, and mild, and had a serious mind.

Dull was their prospect—when the lovers
    met,
They said, we must not—dare not venture yet:
' Oh ! could I labour for thee,' Allen cried,
Why should our friends be thus dissatisfied ?
On my own arm I could depend, but they
Still urge obedience—must I yet obey ? '
Poor Judith felt the grief, but grieving begg'd
delay.

At length a prospect came that seem'd to
    smile,
And faintly woo them, from a Western Isle ;
A kinsman there a widow's hand had gain'd,
' Was old, was rich, and childless yet remain'd ;
Would some young Booth to his affairs attend,
And wait awhile, he might expect a friend.'
The elder brothers, who were not in love,
Fear'd the false seas, unwilling to remove ;
But the young Allen, an enamour'd boy,
Eager an independence to enjoy,
Would through all perils seek it,—by the
    sea,—
Through labour, danger, pain, or slavery.
The faithful Judith his design approved,
For both were sanguine, they were young
and loved.
The mother's slow consent was then obtain'd ;
The time arrived, to part alone remain'd :

All things prepared, on the expected day
Was seen the vessel anchor'd in the bay.
From her would seamen in the evening come,
To take th' advent'rous Allen from his home ;
With his own friends the final day he pass'd,
And every painful hour, except the last.
The grieving father urged the cheerful glass,
To make the moments with less sorrow pass ;
Intent the mother look'd upon her son,
And wish'd th' assent withdrawn, the deed
    undone ;
The younger sister, as he took his way,
Hung on his coat, and begg'd for more delay,
But his own Judith call'd him to the shore,
Whom he must meet, for they might meet no
    more ;—
And there he found her—faithful, mournful,
    true,
Weeping and waiting for a last adieu !
The ebbing tide had left the sand, and there
Moved with slow steps the melancholy pair :
Sweet were the painful moments—but how
    sweet,
And without pain, when they again should
    meet !
Now either spoke, as hope and fear impress'd
Each their alternate triumph in the breast.
    Distance alarm'd the maid—she cried,
        ' 'Tis far ! '
And danger too—' it is a time of war :
Then in those countries are diseases strange,
And women gay, and men are prone to
    change ;
What then may happen in a year, when things
Of vast importance every moment brings !
But hark ! an oar ! ' she cried, yet none
    appear'd—
'Twas love's mistake, who fancied what it
    fear'd ;
And she continued—' Do, my Allen, keep
Thy heart from evil, let thy passions sleep ;
Believe it good, nay glorious, to prevail,
And stand in safety where so many fail ;
And do not, Allen, or for shame, or pride,
Thy faith abjure, or thy profession hide ;
Can I believe *his* love will lasting prove,
Who has no rev'rence for the God I love ?
I know thee well ! how good thou art and
    kind ;
But strong the passions that invade thy
    mind.—
Now, what to me hath Allen to commend ? '—
' Upon my mother,' said the youth, ' attend ;

Forget her spleen, and in my place appear ;
Her love to me will make my Judith dear :
Oft I shall think, (such comfort lovers seek),
Who speaks of me, and fancy what they speak;
Then write on all occasions, always dwell
On hope's fair prospects, and be kind and well,
And ever choose the fondest, tenderest style.'
She answer'd, ' No,' but answer'd with a
    smile.

' And now, my Judith, at so sad a time,
Forgive my fear, and call it not my crime ;
When with our youthful neighbours 'tis thy
    chance
To meet in walks, the visit or the dance,
When every lad would on my lass attend,
Choose not a smooth designer for a friend ;
That fawning Philip !—nay, be not severe,
A rival's hope must cause a lover's fear.'

Displeased she felt, and might in her reply
Have mix'd some anger, but the boat was nigh,
Now truly heard !—it soon was full in sight ;—
Now the sad farewell, and the long good-night;
For, see !—his friends come hast'ning to the
    beach,
And now the gunwale is within the reach ;
' Adieu!—farewell!—remember !'—and what
    more
Affection taught, was utter'd from the shore !
But Judith left them with a heavy heart,
Took a last view, and went to weep apart !
And now his friends went slowly from the place,
Where she stood still, the dashing oar to trace,
Till all were silent!—for the youth she pray'd,
And softly then return'd the weeping maid.

They parted, thus by hope and fortune led,
And Judith's hours in pensive pleasure fled ;
But when return'd the youth ?—the youth no
    more
Return'd exulting to his native shore ;
But forty years were past, and then there
    came
A worn-out man with wither'd limbs and lame,
His mind oppress'd with woes, and bent with
    age his frame :
Yes ! old and grieved, and trembling with
    decay,
Was Allen landing in his native bay,
Willing his breathless form should blend with
    kindred clay.
In an autumnal eve he left the beach,
In such an eve he chanced the port to reach :
He was alone ; he press'd the very place
Of the sad parting, of the last embrace :

There stood his parents, there retired the
    maid,
So fond, so tender, and so much afraid ;
And on that spot, through many a year, his
    mind
Turn'd mournful back, half sinking, half
    resign'd.

No one was present ; of its crew bereft,
A single boat was in the billows left ;
Sent from some anchor'd vessel in the bay,
At the returning tide to sail away :
O'er the black stern the moonlight softly
    play'd,
The loosen'd foresail flapping in the shade ;
All silent else on shore ; but from the town
A drowsy peal of distant bells came down :
From the tall houses here and there, a light
Served some confused remembrance to excite:
' There,' he observed, and new emotions felt,
' Was my first home—and yonder Judith
    dwelt ;
Dead ! dead are all ! I long—I fear to know,'
He said, and walk'd impatient, and yet slow.

Sudden there broke upon his grief a noise
Of merry tumult and of vulgar joys :
Seamen returning to their ship, were come,
With idle numbers straying from their home ;
Allen among them mix'd, and in the old
Strove some familiar features to behold ;
While fancy aided memory :—' Man ! what
    cheer ? '
A sailor cried ; ' Art thou at anchor here ? '
Faintly he answer'd, and then tried to trace
Some youthful features in some aged face :
A swarthy matron he beheld, and thought
She might unfold the very truths he sought :
Confused and trembling, he the dame
    address'd :
' The Booths ! yet live they ? ' pausing and
    oppress'd ;
Then spake again :—' Is there no ancient man,
David his name ?—assist me, if you can.—
Flemmings there were—and Judith, doth she
    live ? '
The woman gazed, nor could an answer give
Yet wond'ring stood, and all were silent by,
Feeling a strange and solemn sympathy.
The woman musing said—' She knew full
    well
Where the old people came at last to dwell ;
They had a married daughter and a son,
But they were dead, and now remain'd not
    one.'

' Yes,' said an elder, who had paused intent
On days long past, ' there was a sad event ;—
One of these Booths—it was my mother's
    tale—
Here left his lass, I know not where to sail :
She saw their parting, and observed the pain ;
But never came th' unhappy man again :'
The ship was captured '—Allen meekly said,
' And what became of the forsaken maid ? '
The woman answer'd : ' I remember now,
She used to tell the lasses of her vow,
And of her lover's loss, and I have seen
The gayest hearts grow sad where she has
    been ;
Yet in her grief she married, and was made
Slave to a wretch, whom meekly she obey'd
And early buried—but I know no more.
And hark ! our friends are hast'ning to the
    shore.'
    Allen soon found a lodging in the town,
And walk'd a man unnoticed up and down.
This house, and this, he knew, and thought
    a face
He sometimes could among a number trace :
Of names remember'd there remain'd a few,
But of no favourites, and the rest were new ;
A merchant's wealth, when Allen went to sea,
Was reckon'd boundless.—Could he living be ?
Or lived his son ? for one he had, the heir
To a vast business, and a fortune fair.
No ! but that heir's poor widow, from her shed,
With crutches went to take her dole of bread :
There was a friend whom he had left a boy,
With hope to sail the master of a hoy ;
Him, after many a stormy day, he found
With his great wish, his life's whole purpose,
    crown'd.
This hoy's proud captain look'd in Allen's
    face,—
' Yours is, my friend,' said he ' a woful case ;
We cannot all succeed ; I now command
The Betsy sloop, and am not much at land ;
But when we meet, you shall your story tell
Of foreign parts—I bid you now farewell ! '
    Allen so long had left his native shore,
He saw but few whom he had seen before ;
The older people, as they met him, cast
A pitying look, oft speaking as they pass'd—
' The man is Allen Booth, and it appears
He dwelt among us in his early years ;
We see the name engraved upon the stones,
Where this poor wanderer means to lay his
    bones.'

Thus where he lived and loved—unhappy
    change !—
He seems a stranger, and finds all are strange.
    But now a widow, in a village near,
Chanced of the melancholy man to hear ;
Old as she was, to Judith's bosom came
Some strong emotions at the well-known
    name ;
He was her much-loved Allen, she had stay'd
Ten troubled years, a sad afflicted maid ;
Then was she wedded, of his death assured,
And much of mis'ry in her lot endured ;
Her husband died ; her children sought their
    bread
In various places, and to her were dead.
The once fond lovers met ; not grief nor age,
Sickness or pain, their hearts could disengage:
Each had immediate confidence ; a friend
Both now beheld, on whom they might depend:
' Now is there one to whom I can express
My nature's weakness and my soul's distress.'
Allen look'd up, and with impatient heart—
' Let me not lose thee—never let us part :
So Heaven this comfort to my sufferings give,
It is not all distress to think and live.'
Thus Allen spoke—for time had not removed
The charms attach'd to one so fondly loved ;
Who with more health, the mistress of their
    cot,
Labours to soothe the evils of his lot.
To her, to her alone, his various fate,
At various times, 'tis comfort to relate ;
And yet his sorrow—she too loves to hear
What wrings her bosom, and compels the
    tear.
    First he related how he left the shore,
Alarm'd with fears that they should meet no
    more :
Then, ere the ship had reach'd her purposed
    course,
They met and yielded to the Spanish force ;
Then 'cross th' Atlantic seas they bore their
    prey,
Who grieving landed from their sultry bay ;
And marching many a burning league, he
    found
Himself a slave upon a miner's ground :
There a good priest his native language spoke,
And gave some ease to his tormenting yoke ;
Kindly advanced him in his master's grace,
And he was station'd in an easier place :
There, hopeless ever to escape the land.
He to a Spanish maiden gave his hand ;

In cottage shelter'd from the blaze of day
He saw his happy infants round him play ;
Where summer shadows, made by lofty trees,
Waved o'er his seat, and soothed his reveries ;
E'en then he thought of England, nor could
    sigh,
But his fond Isabel demanded, ' Why ? '
Grieved by the story, she the sigh repaid,
And wept in pity for the English maid :
Thus twenty years were pass'd, and pass'd
    his views
Of further bliss, for he had wealth to lose :
His friend now dead, some foe had dared to
    paint
' His faith as tainted : he his spouse would
    taint ;
Make all his children infidels, and found
An English heresy on Christian ground.'
    ' Whilst I was poor,' said Allen, ' none
        would care
What my poor notions of religion were ;
None ask'd me whom I worshipp'd, how I
    pray'd,
If due obedience to the laws were paid :
My good adviser taught me to be still,
Nor to make converts had I power or will.
I preach'd no foreign doctrine to my wife,
And never mention'd Luther in my life ;
I, all they said, say what they would, allow'd,
And when the fathers bade me bow, I bow'd,
Their forms I follow'd, whether well or sick,
And was a most obedient Catholic.
But I had money, and these pastors found
My notions vague, heretical, unsound :
A wicked book they seized ; the very Turk
Could not have read a more pernicious work ;
To me pernicious, who if it were good
Or evil question'd not, nor understood :
Oh ! had I little but the book possess'd,
I might have read it, and enjoy'd my rest.'
    Alas ! poor Allen, through his wealth was
        seen
Crimes that by poverty conceal'd had been :
Faults that in dusty pictures rest unknown
Are in an instant through the varnish shown.
    He told their cruel mercy ; how at last,
In Christian kindness for the merits past,
They spared his forfeit life, but bade him fly,
Or for his crime and contumacy die ;
Fly from all scenes, all objects of delight :
His wife, his children, weeping in his sight,
All urging him to flee, he fled, and cursed his
    flight.

    He next related how he found a way,
Guideless and grieving, to Campeachy Bay :
There in the woods he wrought, and there,
    among
Some lab'ring seamen, heard his native tongue:
The sound, one moment, broke upon his pain
With joyful force ; he longed to hear again.
Again he heard ; he seized an offer'd hand,
' And when beheld you last our native land ?'
He cry'd, ' and in what county ? quickly
    say '—
The seamen answer'd—strangers all were they;
One only at his native port had been ;
He, landing once, the quay and church had
    seen,
For that esteem'd ; but nothing more he
    knew.
Still more to know, would Allen join the crew,
Sail where they sail'd, and, many a peril past,
They at his kinsman's isle their anchor cast ;
But him they found not, nor could one relate
Aught of his will, his wish, or his estate.
This grieved not Allen ; then again he sail'd
For England's coast, again his fate prevail'd :
War raged, and he, an active man and strong,
Was soon impress'd, and served his country
    long.
By various shores he pass'd, on various seas,
Never so happy as when void of ease.—
And then he told how in a calm distress'd,
Day after day his soul was sick of rest ;
When, as a log upon the deep they stood,
Then roved his spirit to the inland wood ;
Till, while awake, he dream'd, that on the
    seas
Were his loved home, the hill, the stream, the
    trees :
He gazed, he pointed to the scenes :—' There
    stand
My wife, my children, 'tis my lovely land ;
See ! there my dwelling—oh ! delicious scene
Of my best life—unhand me—are ye men ? '
    And thus the frenzy ruled him, till the wind
Brush'd the fond pictures from the stagnant
    mind.
    He told of bloody fights, and how at length
The rage of battle gave his spirits strength :
'Twas in the Indian seas his limb he lost,
And he was left half-dead upon the coast ;
But living gain'd, 'mid rich aspiring men,
A fair subsistence by his ready pen.
'Thus,' he continued, ' pass'd unvaried years,
Without events producing hopes or fears.'

Augmented pay procured him decent wealth,
But years advancing undermined his health ;
Then oft-times in delightful dream he flew
To England's shore, and scenes his childhood
knew :
He saw his parents, saw his fav'rite maid,
No feature wrinkled, not a charm decay'd ;
And thus excited, in his bosom rose
A wish so strong, it baffled his repose ;
Anxious he felt on English earth to lie ;
To view his native soil, and there to die.
    He then described the gloom, the dread he
found,
When first he landed on the chosen ground,
Where undefined was all he hoped and fear'd,
And how confused and troubled all appear'd ;
His thoughts in past and present scenes
employ'd,
All views in future blighted and destroy'd :
His were a medley of bewild'ring themes,
Sad as realities, and wild as dreams.
    Here his relation closes, but his mind
Flies back again some resting-place to find ;
Thus silent, musing through the day, he sees
His children sporting by those lofty trees,
Their mother singing in the shady scene,
Where the fresh springs burst o'er the lively
green ;—
So strong his eager fancy, he affrights
The faithful widow by its powerful flights ;
For what disturbs him he aloud will tell,
And cry—' 'Tis she, my wife ! my Isabel !
Where are my children ? '—Judith grieves to
hear
How the soul works in sorrows so severe ;

Assiduous all his wishes to attend,
Deprived of much, he yet may boast a friend ;
Watch'd by her care, in sleep, his spirit takes
Its flight, and watchful finds her when he
wakes.
'Tis now her office ; her attention see !
While her friend sleeps beneath that shading
tree,
Careful she guards him from the glowing heat,
And pensive muses at her Allen's feet.
    And where is he ?   Ah ! doubtless in those
scenes
Of his best days, amid the vivid greens,
Fresh with unnumber'd rills, where ev'ry gale
Breathes the rich fragrance of the neighb'ring
vale ;
Smiles not his wife, and listens as there comes
The night-bird's music from the thick'ning
glooms ?
And as he sits with all these treasures nigh,
Blaze not with fairy light the phosphor-fly,
When like a sparkling gem it wheels illumined
by ?
This is the joy that now so plainly speaks
In the warm transient flushing of his cheeks ;
For he is list'ning to the fancied noise
Of his own children, eager in their joys :
All this he feels, a dream's delusive bliss
Gives the expression, and the glow like this.
And now his Judith lays her knitting by,
These strong emotions in her friend to spy ;
For she can fully of their nature deem——
But see ! he breaks the long-protracted theme,
And wakes and cries—' My God ! 'twas but
a dream.'

TALE III.   THE GENTLEMAN FARMER

          Pause there, . . .
And weigh thy value with an even hand ;
If thou be'st rated by thy estimation,
Thou dost deserve enough.
       Merchant of Venice, Act ii, Scene 7.

    Because I will not do them the wrong to
mistrust any, I will do myself the right to
trust none ; and the fine is (for the which I
may go the finer), I will live a bachelor.
       Much Ado about Nothing, Act i, Scene 1.

    Throw physic to the dogs, I'll none of it.
       Macbeth, Act v, Scene 3.

His promises were, as he then was, mighty ;
But his performance, as he is now, nothing.
       Henry VIII, Act iv, Scene 2.

GWYN was a farmer, whom the farmers all,
Who dwelt around, the Gentleman would
call ;
Whether in pure humility or pride,
They only knew, and they would not decide.
    Far diff'rent he from that dull plodding
tribe,
Whom it was his amusement to describe ;

Creatures no more enliven'd than a clod,
But treading still as their dull fathers trod;
Who lived in times when not a man had seen
Corn sown by drill, or thresh'd by a machine:
He was of those whose skill assigns the prize
For creatures fed in pens, and stalls, and sties;
And who, in places where improvers meet,
To fill the land with fatness, had a seat;
Who in large mansions live like petty kings,
And speak of farms but as amusing things;
Who plans encourage, and who journals keep,
And talk with lords about a breed of sheep.

    Two are the species in this genus known;
One, who is rich in his profession grown,
Who yearly finds his ample stores increase,
From fortune's favours and a favouring lease;
Who rides his hunter, who his house adorns;
Who drinks his wine, and his disbursements
    scorns;
Who freely lives, and loves to show he can—
This is the farmer made the gentleman.

    The second species from the world is sent,
Tired with its strife, or with his wealth con-
    tent;
In books and men beyond the former read,
To farming solely by a passion led,
Or by a fashion; curious in his land;
Now planning much, now changing what ne
    plann'd;
Pleased by each trial, not by failures vex'd,
And ever certain to succeed the next;
Quick to resolve, and easy to persuade—
This is the gentleman, a farmer made.

    Gwyn was of these; he from the world
    withdrew
Early in life, his reasons known to few;
Some disappointment said, some pure good
    sense,
The love of land, the press of indolence;
His fortune known, and coming to retire,
If not a farmer, men had call'd him 'squire.

    Forty and five his years, no child or wife
Cross'd the still tenour of his chosen life;
Much land he purchased, planted far around,
And let some portions of superfluous ground
To farmers near him, not displeased to say,
'My tenants,' nor 'our worthy landlord,' they.

    Fix'd in his farm, he soon display'd his
    skill
In small-boned lambs, the horse-hoe, and the
    drill;
From these he rose to themes of nobler kind,
And show'd the riches of a fertile mind;

To all around their visits he repaid,
And thus his mansion and himself display'd,
His rooms were stately, rather fine than neat.
And guests politely call'd his house a seat;
At much expense was each apartment graced,
His taste was gorgeous, but it still was taste;
In full festoons the crimson curtains fell,
The sofas rose in bold elastic swell;
Mirrors in gilded frames display'd the tints
Of glowing carpets and of colour'd prints;
The weary eye saw every object shine,
And all was costly, fanciful, and fine.

    As with his friends he pass'd the social
    hours,
His generous spirit scorn'd to hide its powers;
Powers unexpected, for his eye and air
Gave no sure signs that eloquence was there;
Oft he began with sudden fire and force,
As loth to lose occasion for discourse;
Some, 'tis observed, who feel a wish to speak,
Will a due place for introduction seek;
On to their purpose step by step they steal,
And all their way, by certain signals, feel;
Others plunge in at once, and never heed
Whose turn they take, whose purpose they
    impede;
Resolved to shine, they hasten to begin,
Of ending thoughtless—and of these was
    Gwyn.
And thus he spake—
       ——'It grieves me to the soul
To see how man submits to man's control;
How overpower'd and shackled minds are led
In vulgar tracks, and to submission bred;
The coward never on himself relies,
But to an equal for assistance flies;
Man yields to custom as he bows to fate,
In all things ruled—mind, body, and estate;
In pain, in sickness, we for cure apply
To them we know not, and we know not why;
But that the creature has some jargon read,
And got some Scotchman's system in his head;
Some grave impostor, who will health insure,
Long as your patience or your wealth endure;
But mark them well, the pale and sickly crew,
They have not health, and can they give it
    you?
These solemn cheats their various methods
    choose;
A system fires them, as a bard his muse:
Hence wordy wars arise; the learn'd divide,
And groaning patients curse each erring
    guide.

Next, our affairs are govern'd, buy or sell,
Upon the deed the law must fix its spell ;
Whether we hire or let, we must have still
The dubious aid of an attorney's skill ;
They take a part in every man's affairs,
And in all business some concern is theirs ;
Because mankind in ways prescribed are
          found,
Like flocks that follow on a beaten ground,
Each abject nature in the way proceeds,
That now to shearing, now to slaughter leads.
   ' Should you offend, though meaning no
          offence,
You have no safety in your innocence ;
The statute broken then is placed in view,
And men must pay for crimes they never
          knew :
Who would by law regain his plunder'd store,
Would pick up fallen merc'ry from the floor ;
If he pursue it, here and there it slides ;
He would collect it, but it more divides ;
This part and this he stops, but still in vain,
It slips aside, and breaks in parts again ;
Till, after time and pains, and care and cost,
He finds his labour and his object lost.
   ' But most it grieves me, (friends alone are
          round),
To see a man in priestly fetters bound ;
Guides to the soul, these friends of Heaven
          contrive,
Long as man lives, to keep his fears alive ;
Soon as an infant breathes, their rites begin ;
Who knows not sinning, must be freed from
          sin ;
Who needs no bond, must yet engage in vows ;
Who has no judgment, must a creed espouse :
Advanced in life, our boys are bound by rules,
Are catechised in churches, cloisters, schools,
And train'd in thraldom to be fit for tools :
The youth grown up, he now a partner needs,
And lo ! a priest, as soon as he succeeds.
What man of sense can marriage-rites ap-
          prove ?
What man of spirit can be bound to love ?
Forced to be kind ! compell'd to be sincere !
Do chains and fetters make companions dear ?
Pris'ners indeed we bind ; but though the
          bond
May keep them safe, it does not make them
          fond :
The ring, the vow, the witness, licence,
          prayers,
All parties known ! made public all affairs !

Such forms men suffer, and from these they
          date
A deed of love begun with all they hate :
Absurd ! that none the beaten road should
          shun,
But love to do what other dupes have done.
   ' Well, now your priest has made you one of
          twain,
Look you for rest ? Alas ! you look in vain.
If sick, he comes ; you cannot die in peace,
Till he attends to witness your release ;
To vex your soul, and urge you to confess
The sins you feel, remember, or can guess :
Nay, when departed, to your grave he goes,
But there indeed he hurts not your repose.
   ' Such are our burthens ; part we must
          sustain,
But need not link new grievance to the chain ;
Yet men like idiots will their frames surround
With these vile shackles, nor confess they're
          bound :
In all that most confines them they confide,
Their slavery boast, and make their bonds
          their pride ;
E'en as the pressure galls them, they declare,
(Good souls !) how happy and how free they
          are !
As madmen, pointing round their wretched
          cells,
Cry, " Lo ! the palace where our honour
          dwells."
   ' Such is our state ; but I resolve to live
By rules my reason and my feelings give ;
No legal guards shall keep enthrall'd my mind,
No slaves command me, and no teachers
          blind.
   ' Tempted by sins, let me their strength defy,
But have no second in a surplice by ;
No bottle-holder, with officious aid,
To comfort conscience, weaken'd and afraid :
Then if I yield, my frailty is not known ;
And, if I stand, the glory is my own.
   ' When Truth and Reason are our friends,
          we seem
Alive ! awake !—the superstitious dream.
   ' Oh ! then, fair Truth, for thee alone I seek,
Friend to the wise, supporter of the weak ;
From thee we learn whate'er is right and just ;
Forms to despise, professions to distrust ;
Creeds to reject, pretensions to deride,
And, following thee, to follow none beside.'
   Such was the speech ; it struck upon the ear
Like sudden thunder, none expect to hear.

He saw men's wonder with a manly pride,
And gravely smiled at guest electrified ;
' A farmer this ! ' they said, ' Oh ! let him
    seek
That place where he may for his country speak;
On some great question to harangue for hours,
While speakers hearing, envy nobler powers!'
    Wisdom like this, as all things rich and rare,
Must be acquired with pains, and kept with
    care ;
In books he sought it, which his friends might
    view,
When their kind host the guarding curtain
    drew.
There were historic works for graver hours,
And lighter verse, to spur the languid powers;
There metaphysics, logic there had place ;
But of devotion not a single trace—
Save what is taught in Gibbon's florid page,
And other guides of this inquiring age ;
There Hume appear'd, and near, a splendid
    book
Composed by Gay's good Lord of Bolingbroke:
With these were mix'd the light, the free, the
    vain,
And from a corner peep'd the sage Tom Paine:
Here four neat volumes Chesterfield were
    named,
For manners much and easy morals famed ;
With chaste Memoirs of Females, to be read
When deeper studies had confused the head.
    Such his resources, treasures where he
    sought
For daily knowledge till his mind was fraught:
Then when his friends were present, for their
    use
He would the riches he had stored produce ;
He found his lamp burn clearer, when each day
He drew for all he purposed to display :
For these occasions, forth his knowledge
    sprung,
As mustard quickens on a bed of dung ;
All was prepared, and guests allow'd the
    praise,
For what they saw he could so quickly raise.
    Such this new friend ; and when the year
    came round,
The same impressive, reasoning sage was
    found :
Then, too, was seen the pleasant mansion
    graced
With a fair damsel—his no vulgar taste ;
The neat Rebecca—sly, observant, still ;

Watching his eye, and waiting on his will ;
Simple yet smart her dress, her manners meek,
Her smiles spoke for her, she would seldom
    speak :
But watch'd each look, each meaning to
    detect,
And (pleased with notice) felt for all neglect.
    With her lived Gwyn a sweet harmonious
    life,
Who, forms excepted, was a charming wife.
The wives indeed, so made by vulgar law,
Affected scorn, and censured what they saw ;
And what they saw not, fancied ; said 'twas
    sin,
And took no notice of the wife of Gwyn :
But he despised their rudeness, and would
    prove
Theirs was compulsion and distrust, not love;
' Fools as they were ! could they conceive
    that rings
And parsons' blessings were substantial
    things ? '
They answer'd ' Yes ; ' while he contemp-
    tuous spoke
Of the low notions held by simple folk ;
Yet, strange that anger in a man so wise
Should from the notions of these fools arise ;
Can they so vex us, whom we so despise ?
    Brave as he was, our hero felt a dread
Lest those who saw him kind should think
    him led ;
If to his bosom fear a visit paid,
It was, lest he should be supposed afraid :
Hence sprang his orders ; not that he desired
The things when done : obedience he re-
    quired ;
And thus, to prove his absolute command,
Ruled every heart, and moved each subject
    hand,
Assent he ask'd for every word and whim,
To prove that *he alone was king of him.*
    The still Rebecca, who her station knew,
With ease resign'd the honours not her due ;
Well pleased, she saw that men her board
    would grace,
And wish'd not there to see a female face ;
When by her lover she his spouse was styled,
Polite she thought it, and demurely smiled ;
But when he wanted wives and maidens round
So to regard her, she grew grave, and frown'd ;
And sometimes whisper'd—' Why should you
    respect
These people's notions, yet their forms reject ? '

I 3

Gwyn, though from marriage bond and
    fetter free,
Still felt abridgment in his liberty ;
Something of hesitation he betray'd,
And in her presence thought of what he said.
Thus fair Rebecca, though she walk'd astray,
His creed rejecting, judged it right to pray ;
To be at church, to sit with serious looks,
To read her Bible and her Sunday-books :
She hated all those new and daring themes,
And call'd his free conjectures, ' devil's
    dreams : '
She honour'd still the priesthood in her fall,
And claim'd respect and reverence for them
    all ;
Call'd them ' of sin's destructive power the
    foes,
And not such blockheads as he might suppose.'
Gwyn to his friends would smile, and some-
    times say,
' 'Tis a kind fool, why vex her in her way ? '
Her way she took, and still had more in view,
For she contrived that he should take it too.
The daring freedom of his soul, 'twas plain,
In part was lost in a divided reign ;
A king and queen, who yet in prudence sway'd
Their peaceful state, and were in turn obey'd.
    Yet such our fate, that when we plan the
    best,
Something arises to disturb our rest :
For though in spirits high, in body strong,
Gwyn something felt—he knew not what—
    was wrong ;
He wish'd to know, for he believed the thing,
If unremoved, would other evil bring :
' She must perceive of late he could not eat,
And when he walk'd, he trembled on his
    feet :
He had forebodings, and he seem'd as one
Stopp'd on the road, or threaten'd by a dun ;
He could not live, and yet, should he apply
To those physicians—he must sooner die.'
    The mild Rebecca heard with some disdain,
And some distress, her friend and lord com-
    plain :
His death she fear'd not, but had painful doubt
What his distemper'd nerves might bring
    about ;
With power like hers she dreaded an ally,
And yet there was a person in her eye ;—
She thought, debated, fix'd—' Alas ! ' she
    said,
' A case like yours must be no more delay'd :

You hate these doctors : well ! but were
    a friend
And doctor one, your fears would have an end :
My cousin Mollet—Scotland holds him now—
Is above all men skilful, all allow ;
Of late a doctor, and within a while
He means to settle in this favour'd isle ;
Should he attend you, with his skill profound,
You must be safe, and shortly would be sound.'
    When men in health against physicians rail,
They should consider that their nerves may
    fail ;
Who calls a lawyer rogue, may find, too late,
On one of these depends his whole estate :
Nay, when the world can nothing more
    produce,
The priest, th' insulted priest, may have his
    use ;
Ease, health, and comfort, lift a man so high,
These powers are dwarfs that he can scarcely
    spy ;
Pain, sickness, languor keep a man so low,
That these neglected dwarfs to giants grow.
Happy is he who through the medium sees
Of clear good sense—but Gwyn was not of
    these.
    He heard and he rejoiced : ' Ah ! let him
    come,
And till he fixes, make my house his home.'
Home came the doctor—he was much
    admired ;
He told the patient what his case required ;
His hours for sleep, his time to eat and drink ;
When he should ride, read, rest, compose, or
    think.
Thus join'd peculiar skill and art profound,
To make the fancy-sick no more than fancy-
    sound.
    With such attention, who could long be ill ?
Returning health proclaim'd the doctor's skill.
Presents and praises from a grateful heart
Were freely offer'd on the patient's part ;
In high repute the doctor seem'd to stand,
But still had got no footing in the land ;
And, as he saw the seat was rich and fair,
He felt disposed to fix his station there :
To gain his purpose he perform'd the part
Of a good actor, and prepared to start ;
Not like a traveller in a day serene,
When the sun shone and when the roads
    were clean ;
Not like the pilgrim, when the morning gray,
The ruddy eve succeeding, sends his way ;

But in a season when the sharp east wind
Had all its influence on a nervous mind ;
When past the parlour's front it fiercely blew,
And Gwyn sat pitying every bird that flew,
This strange physician said—' Adieu ! adieu !
Farewell !—Heaven bless you !—if you should
    —but no,
You need not fear—farewell ! 'tis time to go.'
    The doctor spoke ; and as the patient heard,
His old disorders (dreadful train !) appear'd ;
' He felt the tingling tremor, and the stress
Upon his nerves that he could not express ;
Should his good friend forsake him, he perhaps
Might meet his death, and surely a relapse.'
    So, as the doctor seem'd intent to part,
He cried in terror—' Oh ! be where thou art :
Come, thou art young, and unengaged ; oh !
    come,
Make me thy friend, give comfort to mine
    home ;
I have now symptoms that require thine aid,
Do, doctor, stay '—th' obliging doctor stay'd.
    Thus Gwyn was happy ; he had now a friend,
And a meek spouse on whom he could depend :
But now possess'd of male and female guide,
Divided power he thus must subdivide :
In earlier days he rode, or sat at ease
Reclined, and having but himself to please ;
Now if he would a fav'rite nag bestride
He sought permission—' Doctor, may I ride?'
(Rebecca's eye her sovereign pleasure told)—
' I think you may, but guarded from the cold,
Ride forty minutes.'—Free and happy soul !
He scorn'd submission, and a man's control ;
But where such friends in every care unite
All for his good, obedience is delight.
    Now Gwyn a sultan bade affairs adieu,
Led and assisted by the faithful two ;
The favourite fair, Rebecca, near him sat,
And whisper'd whom to love, assist, or hate ;
While the chief vizier eased his lord of cares,
And bore himself the burden of affairs :
No dangers could from such alliance flow,
But from that law, that changes all below.
    When wint'ry winds with leaves bestrew'd
    the ground,
And men were coughing all the village round ;
When public papers of invasion told,
Diseases, famines, perils new and old ;
When philosophic writers fail'd to clear
The mind of gloom, and lighter works to cheer ;
Then came fresh terrors on our hero's mind—
Fears unforeseen, and feelings undefined.

' In outward ills,' he cried, ' I rest assured
Of my friend's aid ; they will in time be cured :
But can his art subdue, resist, control
These inward griefs and troubles of the soul ?
Oh ! my Rebecca ! my disorder'd mind,
No help in study, none in thought can find ;
What must I do, Rebecca ? ' She proposed
The parish guide ; but what could be disclosed
To a proud priest ?—' No ! him have I defied,
Insulted, slighted—shall he be my guide ?
But one there is, and if report be just,
A wise good man, whom I may safely trust ;
Who goes from house to house, from ear to
    ear,
To make his truths, his Gospel truths, appear ;
True if indeed they be, 'tis time that I should
    hear :
Send for that man ; and if report be just,
I, like Cornelius, will the teacher trust ;
But if deceiver, I the vile deceit
Shall soon discover, and discharge the cheat.'
    To Doctor Mollet was the grief confess'd,
While Gwyn the freedom of his mind ex-
    press'd ;
Yet own'd it was to ills and errors prone,
And he for guilt and frailty must atone.
' My books, perhaps,' the wav'ring mortal
    cried,
' Like men deceive—I would be satisfied ;
And to my soul the pious man may bring
Comfort and light—do let me try the thing.'
    The cousins met, what pass'd with Gwyn
    was told :
' Alas ! ' the doctor said, ' how hard to hold
These easy minds, where all impressions made
At first sink deeply, and then quickly fade ;
For while so strong these new-born fancies
    reign,
We must divert them, to oppose is vain :
You see him valiant now, he scorns to heed
The bigot's threat'nings or the zealot's creed ;
Shook by a dream, he next for truth receives
What frenzy teaches, and what fear believes ;
And this will place him in the power of one
Whom we must seek, because we cannot shun.'
    Wisp had been ostler at a busy inn,
Where he beheld and grew in dread of sin ;
Then to a Baptists' meeting found his way,
Became a convert, and was taught to pray ;
Then preach'd ; and being earnest and sincere,
Brought other sinners to religious fear :
Together grew his influence and his fame,
Till our dejected hero heard his name :

His little failings were a grain of pride,
Raised by the numbers he presumed to guide :
A love of presents, and of lofty praise
For his meek spirit and his humble ways ;
But though this spirit would on flattery
feed,
No praise could blind him and no arts mis-
lead :—
To him the doctor made the wishes known
Of his good patron, but conceal'd his own ;
He of all teachers had distrust and doubt,
And was reserved in what he came about ;
Though on a plain and simple message sent,
He had a secret and a bold intent :
Their minds at first were deeply veil'd ;
disguise
Form'd the slow speech, and op'd the eager
eyes ;
Till by degrees sufficient light was thrown
On every view, and all the business shown.
Wisp, as a skilful guide who led the blind,
Had powers to rule and awe the vapourish
mind ;
But not the changeful will, the wavering fear
to bind :
And should his conscience give him leave to
dwell
With Gwyn, and every rival power expel
(A dubious point), yet he, with every care,
Might soon the lot of the rejected share ;
And other Wisps be found like him to reign,
And then be thrown upon the world again :
He thought it prudent then, and felt it
just,
The present guides of his new friend to trust ;
True, he conceived, to touch the harder heart
Of the cool doctor, was beyond his art ;
But mild Rebecca he could surely sway,
While Gwyn would follow where she led the
way :
So to do good, (and why a duty shun,
Because rewarded for the good when done ?)
He with his friends would join in all they
plann'd,
Save when his faith or feelings should with-
stand ;
There he must rest, sole judge of his affairs,
While they might rule exclusively in theirs.

When Gwyn his message to the teacher sent,
He fear'd his friends would show their dis-
content ;
And prudent seem'd it to th' attendant pair,
Not all at once to show an aspect fair :
On Wisp they seem'd to look with jealous eye,
And fair Rebecca was demure and shy ;
But by degrees the teacher's worth they knew,
And were so kind, they seem'd converted too.
Wisp took occasion to the nymph to say,
' You must be married : will you name the
day ? '
She smiled,—' 'Tis well ; but should he not
comply,
Is it quite safe th' experiment to try ? '—
' My child,' the teacher said, ' who feels
remorse,
(And feels not he ?) must wish relief of course ;
And can he find it, while he fears the crime ?—
You must be married ; will you name the
time ? '
Glad was the patron as a man could be,
Yet marvell'd too, to find his guides agree ;
' But what the cause ? ' he cried ; ' 'tis
genuine love for me.'
Each found his part, and let one act describe
The powers and honours of th' accordant
tribe :—
A man for favour to the mansion speeds,
And cons his threefold task as he proceeds ;
To teacher Wisp he bows with humble air,
And begs his interest for a barn's repair :
Then for the doctor he inquires, who loves
To hear applause for what his skill improves,
And gives for praise, assent,—and to the fair
He brings of pullets a delicious pair ;
Thus sees a peasant with discernment nice,
A love of power, conceit, and avarice.
Lo ! now the change complete : the convert
Gwyn
Has sold his books, and has renounced his
sin ;
Mollet his body orders, Wisp his soul,
And o'er his purse the lady takes control ;
No friends beside he needs, and none attend—
Soul, body, and estate, has each a friend ;
And fair Rebecca leads a virtuous life—
She rules a mistress, and she reigns a wife.

TALE IV. PROCRASTINATION

Heaven witness
I have been to you a true and humble wife.
Henry VIII, Act ii, Scene 4.

Gentle lady,
When I did first impart my love to you,
I freely told you all the wealth I had.
Merchant of Venice, Act iii, Scene 2.

The leisure and the fearful time
Cuts off the ceremonious vows of love,
And ample interchange of sweet discourse,
Which so long sunder'd friends should dwell
upon.   *Richard III*, Act v, Scene 3.

I know thee not, old man ; fall to thy prayers.
2 Henry IV, Act v, Scene 5.

Farewell,
Thou pure impiety, and impious purity,
For thee I'll lock up all the gates of love.
Much Ado about Nothing, Act iv, Scene 1.

LOVE will expire, the gay, the happy dream
Will turn to scorn, indiff'rence, or esteem :
Some favour'd pairs, in this exchange, are
bless'd,
Nor sigh for raptures in a state of rest ;
Others, ill match'd, with minds unpair'd,
repent
At once the deed, and know no more content ;
From joy to anguish they, in haste, decline,
And with their fondness, their esteem resign :
More luckless still their fate, who are the prey
Of long-protracted hope and dull delay ;
'Mid plans of bliss the heavy hours pass on,
Till love is wither'd, and till joy is gone.

This gentle flame two youthful hearts
possess'd,
The sweet disturber of unenvied rest :
The prudent Dinah was the maid beloved,
And the kind Rupert was the swain approved :
A wealthy aunt her gentle niece sustain'd,
He, with a father, at his desk remain'd ;
The youthful couple, to their vows sincere,
Thus loved expectant ; year succeeding year,
With pleasant views and hopes, but not a
prospect near.
Rupert some comfort in his station saw,
But the poor virgin lived in dread and awe ;
Upon her anxious looks the widow smiled,
And bade her wait, ' for she was yet a child.'
She for her neighbour had a due respect,
Nor would his son encourage or reject ;

And thus the pair, with expectations vain,
Beheld the seasons change and change again :
Meantime the nymph her tender tales perused,
Where cruel aunts impatient girls refused ;
While hers, though teasing, boasted to be kind,
And she, resenting, to be all resign'd.

The dame was sick, and when the youth
applied
For her consent, she groan'd, and cough'd,
and cried :
Talk'd of departing, and again her breath
Drew hard, and cough'd, and talk'd again of
death :
' Here you may live, my Dinah ! here the boy
And you together my estate enjoy ; '
Thus to the lovers was her mind express'd,
Till they forbore to urge the fond request.

Servant, and nurse, and comforter, and
friend,
Dinah had still some duty to attend ;
But yet their walk, when Rupert's evening call
Obtain'd an hour, made sweet amends for all ;
So long they now each other's thoughts had
known,
That nothing seem'd exclusively their own ;
But with the common wish, the mutual fear,
They now had travell'd to their thirtieth year.

At length a prospect open'd—but, alas !
Long time must yet, before the union, pass ;
Rupert was call'd in other clime, t' increase
Another's wealth, and toil for future peace ;
Loth were the lovers ; but the aunt declared
'Twas fortune's call, and they must be pre-
pared ;
' You now are young, and for this brief delay,
And Dinah's care, what I bequeath will pay ;
All will be yours ; nay, love, suppress that
sigh ;
The kind must suffer, and the best must die : '
Then came the cough, and strong the signs it
gave
Of holding long contention with the grave.

The lovers parted with a gloomy view,
And little comfort but that both were true ;
He for uncertain duties doom'd to steer,
While hers remain'd too certain and severe.

Letters arrived, and Rupert fairly told
' His cares were many, and his hopes were
cold ;

The view more clouded, that was never fair,
And love alone preserved him from despair : '
In other letters brighter hopes he drew,
' His friends were kind, and he believed them
        true.'
  ⌐ When the sage widow Dinah's grief descried,
She wonder'd much why one so happy sigh'd :
Then bade her see how her poor aunt sustain'd
The ills of life, nor murmur'd nor complain'd.
To vary pleasures, from the lady's chest
Were drawn the pearly string and tabby vest ;
Beads, jewels, laces, all their value shown,
With the kind notice—' They will be your
        own.'
    This hope, these comforts cherish'd day by
        day,
To Dinah's bosom made a gradual way ;
Till love of treasure had as large a part,
As love of Rupert, in the virgin's heart.
Whether it be that tender passions fail,
From their own nature, while the strong
        prevail ;
Or whether av'rice, like the poison-tree,*
Kills all beside it, and alone will be ;
Whatever cause prevail'd, the pleasure
        grew
In Dinah's soul,—she loved the hoards to
        view ;
With lively joy those comforts she survey'd,
And love grew languid in the careful maid.
    Now the grave niece partook the widow's
        cares,
Look'd to the great and ruled the small affairs ;
Saw clean'd the plate, arranged the china
        show,
And felt her passion for a shilling grow :
Th' indulgent aunt increased the maid's
        delight,
By placing tokens of her wealth in sight ;
She loved the value of her bonds to tell,
And spake of stocks, and how they ros and
        fell.
    This passion grew, and gain'd at length
        such sway,
That other passions shrank to make it way ;
Romantic notions now the heart forsook,
She read but seldom, and she changed her
        book ;

    * Allusion is here made, not to the well-known
species of *sumach*, called the poison oak, or
toxicodendron, but to the *upas*, or poison-tree of
Java : whether it be real or imaginary, this is no
proper place for inquiry.

And for the verses she was wont to send,
Short was her prose, and she was Rupert's
        friend.
Seldom she wrote, and then the widow's
        cough,
And constant call, excused her breaking off ;
Who, now oppress'd, no longer took the air,
But sate and dozed upon an easy chair.
The cautious doctor saw the case was clear,
But judged it best to have companions near ;
They came, they reason'd, they prescribed—
        at last,
Like honest men, they said their hopes were
        past ;
Then came a priest—'tis comfort to reflect,
When all is over, there was no neglect ;
And all was over—by her husband's bones,
The widow rests beneath the sculptured stones,
That yet record their fondness and their fame,
While all they left the virgin's care became ;
Stock, bonds, and buildings ;—it disturb'd
        her rest,
To think what load of troubles she possess'd :
Yet, if a trouble, she resolved to take
Th' important duty, for the donor's sake ;
She too was heiress to the widow's taste,
Her love of hoarding, and her dread of waste.
    Sometimes the past would on her mind
        intrude,
And then a conflict full of care ensued ;
The thoughts of Rupert on her mind would
        press,
His worth she knew, but doubted his success ;
Of old she saw him heedless ; what the boy
Forbore to save, the man would not enjoy ;
Oft had he lost the chance that care would
        seize,
Willing to live, but more to live at ease :
Yet could she not a broken vow defend,
And Heav'n, perhaps, might yet enrich her
        friend.
    Month after month was pass'd, and all were
        spent
In quiet comfort and in rich content :
Miseries there were, and woes the world
        around,
But these had not her pleasant dwelling found ;
She knew that mothers grieved, and widows
        wept,
And she was sorry, said her prayers, and
        slept :
Thus pass'd the seasons, and to Dinah's board
Gave what the seasons to the rich afford ;

For she indulged, nor was her heart so small,
That one strong passion should engross it all.

A love of splendour now with av'rice strove,
And oft appear'd to be the stronger love :
A secret pleasure fill'd the widow's breast,
When she reflected on the hoards possess'd ;
But livelier joy inspired th' ambitious maid,
When she the purchase of those hoards displ
play'd :
In small but splendid room she loved to see
That all was placed in view and harmony ;
There, as with eager glance she look'd around,
She much delight in every object found ;
While books devout were near her—to destroy,
Should it arise, an overflow of joy.

Within that fair apartment, guests might see
The comforts cull'd for wealth by vanity :
Around the room an Indian paper blazed,
With lively tint and figures boldly raised ;
Silky and soft upon the floor below,
Th' elastic carpet rose with crimson glow ;
All things around implied both cost and care,
What met the eye was elegant or rare :
Some curious trifles round the room were laid,
By hope presented to the wealthy maid :
Within a costly case of varnish'd wood,
In level rows, her polish'd volumes stood ;
Shown as a favour to a chosen few,
To prove what beauty for a book could do :
A silver urn with curious work was fraught ;
A silver lamp from Grecian pattern wrought :
Above her head, all gorgeous to behold,
A time-piece stood on feet of burnish'd gold ;
A stag's head crest adorned the pictured case,
Through the pure crystal shone th' enamell'd
face ;
And while on brilliants moved the hands of
steel,
It click'd from pray'r to pray'r, from meal to
meal.

Here as the lady sate, a friendly pair
Step in t' admire the view, and took their chair:
They then related how the young and gay
Were thoughtless wandering in the broad
highway ;
How tender damsels sail'd in tilted boats,
And laugh'd with wicked men in scarlet coats;
And how we live in such degen'rate times,
That men conceal their wants, and show
their crimes ;
While vicious deeds are screen'd by fashion's
name,
And what was once our pride is now our shame.

Dinah was musing, as her friends discoursed,
When these last words a sudden entrance
forced
Upon her mind, and what was once her pride
And now her shame, some painful views
supplied ;
Thoughts of the past within her bosom press'd,
And there a change was felt, and was confess'd :
While thus the virgin strove with secret pain,
Her mind was wandering o'er the troubled
main ;
Still she was silent, nothing seem'd to see,
But sate and sigh'd in pensive reverie.

The friends prepared new subjects to begin,
When tall Susannah, maiden starch, stalk'd
in ;
Not in her ancient mode, sedate and slow,
As when she came, the mind she knew, to
know ;
Nor as, when list'ning half an hour before,
She twice or thrice tapp'd gently at the door ;
But, all decorum cast in wrath aside,
' I think the devil's in the man ! ' she cried ;
' A huge tall sailor, with his tawny cheek,
And pitted face, will with my lady speak ;
He grinn'd an ugly smile, and said he knew,
Please you, my lady, 'twould be joy to you ;
What must I answer ? '—Trembling and
distress'd
Sank the pale Dinah by her fears oppress'd ;
When thus alarm'd, and brooking no delay,
Swift to her room the stranger made his way.
' Revive, my love ! ' said he, ' I've done
thee harm,
Give me thy pardon,' and he look'd alarm :
Meantime the prudent Dinah had contrived
Her soul to question, and she then revived.
' See ! my good friend,' and then she raised
her head,
' The bloom of life, the strength of youth is
fled ;
Living we die ; to us the world is dead ;
We parted bless'd with health, and I am now
Age-struck and feeble, so I find art thou ;
Thine eye is sunken, furrow'd is thy face,
And downward look'st thou—so we run our
race ;
And happier they, whose race is nearly run,
Their troubles over, and their duties done.'
' True, lady, true, we are not girl and boy ;
But time has left us something to enjoy.'

'What! thou hast learn'd my fortune?—
　　yes, I live
To feel how poor the comforts wealth can give;
Thou too perhaps art wealthy; but our fate
Still mocks our wishes, wealth is come too
　　late.'
　'To me nor late nor early; I am come
Poor as I left thee to my native home:
Nor yet,' said Rupert, 'will I grieve; 'tis mine
To share thy comforts, and the glory thine;
For thou wilt gladly take that generous part
That both exalts and gratifies the heart;
While mine rejoices.'—'Heavens!' return'd
　　the maid,
'This talk to one so wither'd and decay'd?
No! all my care is now to fit my mind
For other spousal, and to die resign'd:
As friend and neighbour, I shall hope to see
These noble views, this pious love in thee;
That we together may the change await,
Guides and spectators in each other's fate;
When fellow-pilgrims, we shall daily crave
The mutual prayer that arms us for the grave.'
　Half angry, half in doubt, the lover gazed
On the meek maiden, by her speech amazed;
'Dinah,' said he, 'dost thou respect thy vows?
What spousal mean'st thou?—thou art
　　Rupert's spouse;
The chance is mine to take, and thine to give;
But, trifling this, if we together live:
Can I believe, that, after all the past,
Our vows, our loves, thou wilt be false at last?
Something thou hast—I know not what—in
　　view;
I find thee pious—let me find thee true.'
　'Ah! cruel this; but do, my friend, depart;
And to its feelings leave my wounded heart.'
　'Nay, speak at once; and Dinah, let me
　　know,
Mean'st thou to take me, now I'm wreck'd,
　　in tow?
Be fair; nor longer keep me in the dark;
Am I forsaken for a trimmer spark?
Heav'n's spouse thou art not; nor can I
　　believe
That God accepts her who will man deceive:
True I am shatter'd, I have service seen,
And service done, and have in trouble been;
My cheek (it shames me not) has lost its red,
And the brown buff is o'er my features spread;
Perchance my speech is rude; for I among
Th' untamed have been, in temper and in
　　tongue;

Have been trepann'd, have lived in toil and
　　care,
And wrought for wealth I was not doom'd to
　　share;
It touch'd me deeply, for I felt a pride
In gaining riches for my destined bride:
Speak then my fate; for these my sorrows
　　past,
Time lost, youth fled, hope wearied, and at
　　last
This doubt of thee—a childish thing to tell,
But certain truth—my very throat they
　　swell;
They stop the breath, and but for shame
　　could I
Give way to weakness, and with passion cry;
These are unmanly struggles, but I feel
This hour must end them, and perhaps will
　　heal.'—
　Here Dinah sigh'd as if afraid to speak—
And then repeated—'They were frail and
　　weak;
His soul she loved, and hoped he had the grace
To fix his thoughts upon a better place.'
　She ceased;—with steady glance, as if to see
The very root of this hypocrisy,—
He her small fingers moulded in his hard
And bronzed broad hand; then told her his
　　regard,
His best respect were gone, but love had still
Hold in his heart, and govern'd yet the will—
Or he would curse her:—saying this, he threw
The hand in scorn away, and bade adieu
To every lingering hope, with every care in
　　view.
　Proud and indignant, suffering, sick, and
　　poor,
He grieved unseen; and spoke of love no
　　more—
Till all he felt in indignation died,
As hers had sunk in avarice and pride.
　In health declining, as in mind distress'd,
To some in power his troubles he confess'd,
And shares a parish-gift;—at prayers he sees
The pious Dinah dropped upon her knees;
Thence as she walks the street with stately air,
As chance directs, oft meet the parted pair:
When he, with thickset coat of badge-man's
　　blue,
Moves near her shaded silk of changeful hue;
When his thin locks of grey approach her
　　braid,
A costly purchase made in beauty's aid;

When his frank air, and his unstudied pace,
Are seen with her soft manner, air, and grace,
And his plain artless look with her sharp
    meaning face ;
It might some wonder in a stranger move,
How these together could have talk'd of love.
    Behold them now !—see there a tradesman
      stands,
And humbly hearkens to some fresh com-
    mands ;
He moves to speak, she interrupts him—
    ' Stay,'
Her air expresses—' Hark ! to what I say : '
Ten paces off, poor Rupert on a seat
Has taken refuge from the noon-day heat,
His eyes on her intent, as if to find
What were the movements of that subtle
    mind :
How still!—how earnest is he !—it appears
His thoughts are wand'ring through his
    earlier years ;
Through years of fruitless labour, to the day
When all his earthly prospects died away :

' Had I,' he thinks, ' been wealthier of the two,
Would she have found me so unkind, untrue ?
Or knows not man when poor, what man
    when rich will do ?
Yes, yes ! I feel that I had faithful proved,
And should have soothed and raised her,
    bless'd and loved.'
    But Dinah moves—she had observed before
The pensive Rupert at an humble door :
Some thoughts of pity raised by his distress,
Some feeling touch of ancient tenderness ;
Religion, duty urged the maid to speak
In terms of kindness to a man so weak :
But pride forbad, and to return would prove
She felt the shame of his neglected love ;
Nor wrapp'd in silence could she pass, afraid
Each eye should see her, and each heart
    upbraid ;
One way remain'd—the way the Levite took,
Who without mercy could on misery look ;
(A way perceived by craft, approved by pride),
She cross'd, and pass'd him on the other
    side.

TALE V. THE PATRON

               It were all one,
That I should love a bright particular star,
And think to wed it ; he is so above me :
In his bright radiance and collateral light
Must I be comforted, not in his sphere.
        All's Well that Ends Well, Act i, Scene 1.

        Poor wretches, that depend
On greatness' favour, dream as I have done,—
Wake and find nothing.
        Cymbeline, Act v, Scene 4.

        And since . . .
Th' affliction of my mind amends, with which
I fear a madness held me.
        The Tempest, Act v, Scene 1.

A BOROUGH-BAILIFF, who to law was train'd,
A wife and sons in decent state maintain'd ;
He had his way in life's rough ocean steer'd,
And many a rock and coast of danger clear'd :
He saw where others fail'd, and care had he
Others in him should not such failings see ;
His sons in various busy states were placed,
And all began the sweets of gain to taste,
Save John, the younger ; who, of sprightly
    parts,
Felt not a love for money-making arts :

In childhood feeble, he, for country air,
Had long resided with a rustic pair ;
All round whose room were doleful ballads,
    songs,
Of lovers' sufferings and of ladies' wrongs ;
Of peevish ghosts who came at dark mid-
    night,
For breach of promise, guilty men to fright ;
Love, marriage, murder, were the themes,
    with these,
All that on idle, ardent spirits seize ;
Robbers at land and pirates on the main,
Enchanters foil'd, spells broken, giants slain ;
Legends of love, with tales of halls and bowers,
Choice of rare songs, and garlands of choice
    flowers,
And all the hungry mind without a choice
    devours.

    From village-children kept apart by pride,
With such enjoyments, and without a guide,
Inspired by feelings all such works infused,
John snatch'd a pen, and wrote as he pe-
    rused :
With the like fancy he could make his knight
Slay half an host and put the rest to flight ;

With the like knowledge, he could make him
    ride
From isle to isle at Parthenissa's side ;
And with a heart yet free, no busy brain
Form'd wilder notions of delight and pain,
The raptures smiles create, the anguish of
    disdain.
    Such were the fruits of John's poetic toil,
Weeds, but still proofs of vigour in the soil :
He nothing purposed but with vast delight,
Let Fancy loose, and wonder'd at her flight :
His notions of poetic worth were high,
And of his own still-hoarded poetry ;—
These to his father's house he bore with pride,
A miser's treasure, in his room to hide ;
Till spurr'd by glory, to a reading friend
He kindly show'd the sonnets he had penn'd :
With erring judgment, though with heart
    sincere,
That friend exclaim'd, ' These beauties must
    appear.'
In Magazines they claim'd their share of fame,
Though undistinguish'd by their author's
    name ;
And with delight the young enthusiast found
The muse of Marcus with applauses crown'd.
This heard the father, and with some alarm :
' The boy,' said he, ' will neither trade nor
    farm ;
He for both law and physic is unfit ;
Wit he may have, but cannot live on wit :
Let him his talents then to learning give,
Where verse is honour'd, and where poets
    live.''
    John kept his terms at college unreproved,
Took his degree, and left the life he loved ;
Not yet ordain'd, his leisure he employ'd
In the light labours he so much enjoy'd ;
His favourite notions and his daring views
Were cherish'd still, and he adored the Muse.
    ' A little time, and he should burst to light,
And admiration of the world excite ;
And every friend, now cool and apt to blame
His fond pursuit, would wonder at his fame.'
When led by fancy, and from view retired,
He call'd before him all his heart desired ;
' Fame shall be mine, then wealth shall I
    possess,
And beauty next an ardent lover bless ;
For me the maid shall leave her nobler state,
Happy to raise and share her poet's fate.'
He saw each day his father's frugal board,
With simple fare by cautious prudence stored;

Where each indulgence was foreweigh'd with
    care,
And the grand maxims were to save and spare:
Yet in his walks, his closet, and his bed,
All frugal cares and prudent counsels fled ;
And bounteous Fancy, for his glowing mind,
Wrought various scenes, and all of glorious
    kind ;
Slaves of the *ring* and *lamp* ! what need of you
When Fancy's self such magic deeds can do ?
    Though rapt in visions of no vulgar kind,
To common subjects stoop'd our poet's mind ;
And oft,when wearied with more ardent flight,
He felt a spur satiric song to write ;
A rival burgess his bold muse attack'd,
And whipp'd severely for a well-known fact ;
For while he seem'd to all demure and shy,
Our poet gazed at what was passing by ;
And ev'n his father smiled when playful wit,
From his young bard, some haughty object
    hit.
    From ancient times the borough where they
    dwelt
Had mighty contest at elections felt :
Sir Godfrey Ball, 'tis true, had held in pay
Electors many for the trying day ;
But in such golden chains to bind them all
Required too much for e'en Sir Godfrey Ball.
A member died, and to supply his place,
Two heroes enter'd for th' important race ;
Sir Godfrey's friend and Earl Fitzdonnel's son,
Lord Frederick Damer, both prepared to run ;
And partial numbers saw with vast delight
Their good young lord oppose the proud old
    knight.
    Our poet's father, at a first request,
Gave the young lord his vote and interest ;
And what he could our poet, for he stung
The foe by verse satiric, said and sung.
Lord Frederick heard of all this youthful zeal,
And felt as lords upon a canvass feel ;
He read the satire, and he saw the use
That such cool insult, and such keen abuse,
Might on the wavering minds of voting men
    produce ;
Then too his praises were in contrast seen,
' A lord as noble as the knight was mean.'
    ' I much rejoice,' he cried, ' such worth to
    find ;
To this the world must be no longer blind :
His glory will descend from sire to son,
The Burns of English race, the happier
    Chatterton.'

Our poet's mind, now hurried and elate,
Alarm'd the anxious parent for his fate ;
Who saw with sorrow, should their friend
    succeed,
That much discretion would the poet need.
  Their friend succeeded, and repaid the zeal
The poet felt, and made opposers feel,
By praise (from lords how soothing and how
    sweet !)
And invitation to his noble seat.
The father ponder'd, doubtful if the brain
Of his proud boy such honour could sustain ;
Pleased with the favours offer'd to a son,
But seeing dangers few so ardent shun.
  Thus, when they parted, to the youthful
    breast
The father's fears were by his love impress'd :
'There will you find, my son, the courteous ease
That must subdue the soul it means to please ;
That soft attention which ev'n beauty pays
To wake our passions, or provoke our praise ;
There all the eye beholds will give delight,
Where every sense is flattered like the sight :
This is your peril ; can you from such scene
Of splendour part, and feel your mind serene,
And in the father's humble state resume
The frugal diet and the narrow room ? '
To this the youth with cheerful heart replied,
Pleased with the trial, but as yet untried ;
And while professing patience, should he fail,
He suffer'd hope o'er reason to prevail.
  Impatient, by the morning mail convey'd,
The happy guest his promised visit paid ;
And now arriving at the hall, he tried
For air composed, serene and satisfied ;
As he had practised in his room alone,
And there acquired a free and easy tone :
There he had said, ' Whatever the degree
\ man obtains, what more than man is he ? '
\d when arrived—' This room is but a room;
.1 aught we see the steady soul o'ercome ?
..t me in all a manly firmness show,
Upheld by talents, and their value know.'
  This reason urged; but it surpass'd his skill
To be in act as manly as in will :
When he his lordship and the lady saw,
Brave as he was, he felt oppress'd with awe ;
And spite of verse, that so much praise had
    won,
The poet found he was the bailiff's son.
  But dinner came, and the succeeding hours
Fix'd his weak nerves, and raised his failing
    powers ;

Praised and assured, he ventured once or
    twice
On some remark, and bravely broke the ice ;
So that at night, reflecting on his words,
He found, in time, he might converse with
    lords.
  Now was the sister of his patron seen—
A lovely creature, with majestic mien ;
Who, softly smiling while she look'd so fair,
Praised the young poet with such friendly air ;
Such winning frankness in her looks express'd,
And such attention to her brother's guest,
That so much beauty, join'd with speech so
    kind,
Raised strong emotions in the poet's mind ;
Till reason fail'd his bosom to defend
From the sweet power of this enchanting
    friend.—
Rash boy ! what hope thy frantic mind
    invades ?
What love confuses, and what pride per-
    suades ?
Awake to truth ! shouldst thou deluded feed
On hopes so groundless, thou art mad indeed.
  What say'st thou, wise-one ? ' that all-
    powerful love
' Can fortune's strong impediments remove ;
Nor is it strange that worth should wed to
    worth,
The pride of genius with the pride of birth.'
While thou art dreaming thus, the beauty
    spies
Love in thy tremor, passion in thine eyes ;
And with th' amusement pleased, of conquest
    vain,
She seeks her pleasure, careless of thy pain ;
She gives thee praise to humble and confound,
Smiles to ensnare, and flatters thee to wound.
  Why has she said that in the lowest state
The noble mind insures a noble fate ?
And why thy daring mind to glory call ?
That thou may'st dare and suffer, soar and
    fall.
Beauties are tyrants, and if they can reign,
They have no feeling for their subjects' pain ;
Their victim's anguish gives their charms
    applause,
And their chief glory is the woe they cause :
Something of this was felt, in spite of love,
Which hope, in spite of reason, would remove.
  Thus lived our youth, with conversation,
    books,
And Lady Emma's soul-subduing looks ;

Lost in delight, astonish'd at his lot,
All prudence banish'd, all advice forgot—
Hopes, fears, and every thought, were fix'd
    upon the spot.
   'Twas autumn yet, and many a day must
    frown
On Brandon-Hall, ere went my lord to town ;
Meantime the father, who had heard his boy
Lived in a round of luxury and joy,
And justly thinking that the youth was one
Who, meeting danger, was unskill'd to shun ;
Knowing his temper, virtue, spirit, zeal,
How prone to hope and trust, believe and feel;
These on the parent's soul their weight
    impress'd,
And thus he wrote the counsels of his breast.
   ' John, thou'rt a genius ; thou hast some
    pretence,
I think, to wit, but hast thou sterling sense ?
That which, like gold, may through the world
    go forth,
And always pass for what 'tis truly worth ?
Whereas this genius, like a bill, must take
Only the value our opinions make.
   'Men famed for wit, of dangerous talents vain,
Treat those of common parts with proud
    disdain ;
The powers that wisdom would, improving,
    hide,
They blaze abroad with inconsid'rate pride ;
While yet but mere probationers for fame,
They seize the honour they should then
    disclaim :
Honour so hurried to the light must fade,
The lasting laurels flourish in the shade.
   ' Genius is jealous ; I have heard of some
Who, if unnoticed, grew perversely dumb ;
Nay, different talents would their envy raise;
Poets have sicken'd at a dancer's praise ;
And one, the happiest writer of his time,
Grew pale at hearing Reynolds was sublime ;
That Rutland's duchess wore a heavenly
    smile—
And I, said he, neglected all the while !
   ' A waspish tribe are these, on gilded wings,
Humming their lays, and brandishing their
    stings ;
And thus they move their friends and foes
    among,
Prepared for soothing or satiric song.
   ' Hear me, my boy ; thou hast a virtuous
    mind—
But be thy virtues of the sober kind ;

Be not a Quixote, ever up in arms
To give the guilty and the great alarms :
If never heeded, thy attack is vain ;
And if they heed thee, they'll attack again ;
Then too in striking at that heedless rate,
Thou in an instant may'st decide thy fate.
   ' Leave admonition—let the vicar give
Rules how the nobles of his flock should live :
Nor take that simple fancy to thy brain,
That thou canst cure the wicked and the vain.
   ' Our Pope, they say, once entertain'd the
    whim,
Who fear'd not God should be afraid of him ;
But grant they fear'd him, was it further said,
That he reform'd the hearts he made afraid ?
Did Chartres mend ? Ward, Waters, and a
    score
Of flagrant felons, with his floggings sore ?
Was Cibber silenced ? No : with vigour
    bless'd,
And brazen front, half earnest, half in jest,
He dared the bard to battle, and was seen
In all his glory match'd with Pope and spleen;
Himself he stripp'd, the harder blow to hit,
Then boldly match'd his ribaldry with wit ;
The poet's conquest Truth and Time proclaim,
But yet the battle hurt his peace and fame.
   ' Strive not too much for favour ; seem at
    ease,
And rather pleased thyself, than bent to
    please :
Upon thy lord with decent care attend,
But not too near ; thou canst not be a friend;
And favourite be not, 'tis a dangerous post—
Is gain'd by labour, and by fortune lost :
Talents like thine may make a man approved,
But other talents trusted and beloved.
Look round, my son, and thou wilt early see
The kind of man thou art not form'd to be.
   ' The real favourites of the great are they
Who to their views and wants attention pay,
And pay it ever ; who, with all their skill,
Dive to the heart, and learn the secret will;
If that be vicious, soon can they provide
The favourite ill, and o'er the soul preside ;
For vice is weakness, and the artful know
Their power increases as the passions grow;
If indolent the pupil, hard their task :
Such minds will ever for amusement ask :
And great the labour : for a man to choose
Objects for one whom nothing can amuse ;
For ere those objects can the soul delight,
They must to joy the soul herself excite ;

Therefore it is, this patient, watchful kind
With gentle friction stir the drowsy mind :
Fix'd on their end, with caution they proceed,
And sometimes give, and sometimes take the
    lead ;
Will now a hint convey, and then retire,
And let the spark awake the lingering fire ;
Or seek new joys and livelier pleasures bring,
To give the jaded sense a quick'ning spring.
  'These arts, indeed, my son must not pursue ;
Nor must he quarrel with the tribe that do :
It is not safe another's crimes to know,
Nor is it wise our proper worth to show :—
" My lord," you say, " engaged me for that
    worth ; "—
True, and preserve it ready to come forth :
If question'd, fairly answer—and that done,
Shrink back, be silent, and thy father's son ;
For they who doubt thy talents scorn thy
    boast,
But they who grant them will dislike thee
    most :
Observe the prudent ; they in silence sit,
Display no learning, and affect no wit ;
They hazard nothing, nothing they assume,
But know the useful art of *acting dumb.*
Yet to their eyes each varying look appears,
And every word finds entrance at their ears.
  ' Thou art religion's advocate—take heed,
Hurt not the cause, thy pleasure 'tis to plead ;
With wine before thee, and with wits beside,
Do not in strength of reas'ning powers confide;
What seems to thee convincing, certain, plain,
They will deny, and dare thee to maintain ;
And thus will triumph o'er thy eager youth,
While thou wilt grieve for so disgracing truth.
  ' With pain I've seen, these wrangling wits
    among,
Faith's weak defenders, passionate and young;
Weak thou art not, yet not enough on guard,
Where wit and humour keep their watch and
    ward :
Men gay and noisy will o'erwhelm thy sense,
Then loudly laugh at Truth's and thy expense;
While the kind ladies will do all they can
To check their mirth, and cry, " *The good
    young man !* "
  ' Prudence, my boy, forbids thee to com-
    mend
The cause or party of thy noble friend ;
What are his praises worth, who must be
    known
To take a patron's maxims for his own ?

When ladies sing, or in thy presence play,
Do not, dear John, in rapture melt away ;
'Tis not thy part, there will be list'ners round,
To cry *divine !* and dote upon the sound ;
Remember too, that though the poor have
    ears,
They take not in the music of the spheres ;
They must not feel the warble and the thrill,
Or be dissolved in ecstacy at will ;
Beside, 'tis freedom in a youth like thee
To drop his awe, and deal in ecstacy !
  ' In silent ease, at least in silence, dine,
Nor one opinion start of food or wine :
Thou know'st that all the science thou canst
    boast
Is of thy father's simple boil'd and roast ;
Nor always these ; he sometimes saved his
    cash,
By interlinear days of frugal hash :
Wine hadst thou seldom ; wilt thou be so vain
As to decide on claret or champagne ?
Dost thou from me derive this taste sublime,
Who ordered port the dozen at a time ?
When (every glass held precious in our eyes)
We judged the value by the bottle's size :
Then never merit for thy praise assume,
Its worth well knows each servant in the room.
  ' Hard, boy, thy task, to steer thy way among
That servile, supple, shrewd, insidious throng;
Who look upon thee as of doubtful race,
An interloper, one who wants a place :
Freedom with these let thy free soul condemn,
Nor with thy heart's concerns associate them.
  ' Of all be cautious—but be most afraid
Of the pale charms that grace my lady's maid ;
Of those sweet dimples, of that fraudful eye,
The frequent glance design'd for thee to spy ;
The soft bewitching look, the fond bewailing
    sigh :
Let others frown and envy ; she the while
(Insidious syren !) will demurely smile ;
And for her gentle purpose, every day
Inquire thy wants, and meet thee in thy way ;
She has her blandishments, and though so
    weak,
Her person pleases, and her actions speak :
At first her folly may her aim defeat ;
But kindness shown at length will kindness
    meet :
Have some offended ? them will she disdain,
And, for thy sake, contempt and pity feign ;
She hates the vulgar, she admires to look
On woods and groves, and dotes upon a book ;

Let her once see thee on her features dwell,
And hear one sigh, then liberty farewell.
  ' But, John, remember we cannot maintain
A poor, proud girl, extravagant and vain.
    ' Doubt much of friendship : shouldst thou
    find a friend
Pleased to advise thee, anxious to commend ;
Should he the praises he had heard report,
And confidence (in thee confiding) court ;
Much of neglectful patrons should he say,
And then exclaim—" How long must merit
    stay ! "
Then show how high thy modest hopes may
    stretch,
And point to stations far beyond thy reach ;
Let such designer, by thy conduct, see
(Civil and cool) he makes no dupe of thee ;
And he will quit thee, as a man too wise
For him to ruin first, and then despise.
    ' Such are thy dangers ;—yet, if thou canst
    steer
Past all the perils, all the quicksands clear,
Then may'st thou profit ; but if storms pre-
    vail,
If foes beset thee, if thy spirits fail,—
No more of winds or waters be the sport,
But in thy father's mansion find a port.'
    Our poet read.—' It is in truth,' said he,
' Correct in part, but what is *this* to me ?
I love a foolish Abigail ! in base
And sordid office ! fear not such disgrace :
Am I so blind ? ' ' Or thou wouldst surely see
That lady's fall, if she should stoop to thee ! '
' The cases differ.' ' True ! for what sur-
    prise
Could from thy marriage with the maid arise ?
But through the island would the shame be
    spread,
Should the fair mistress deign with thee to
    wed.'
    John saw not this ; and many a week had
    pass'd,
While the vain beauty held her victim fast ;
The noble friend still condescension show'd,
And, as before, with praises overflow'd ;
But his grave lady took a silent view
Of all that pass'd, and smiling, pitied too.
    Cold grew the foggy morn, the day was
    brief,
Loose on the cherry hung the crimson leaf ;
The dew dwelt ever on the herb ; the woods
Roar'd with strong blasts, with mighty
    showers the floods :

All green was vanish'd, save ot pine and yew,
That still display'd their melancholy hue ;
Save the green holly with its berries red,
And the green moss that o'er the gravel spread.
    To public views my lord must soon attend ;
And soon the ladies—would they leave their
    friend ?
The time was fix'd—approach'd—was near—
    was come ;
The trying time that fill'd his soul with gloom:
Thoughtful our poet in the morning rose,
And cried, ' One hour my fortune will disclose ;
Terrific hour ! from thee have I to date
Life's loftier views, or my degraded state ;
For now to be what I have been before
Is so to fall, that I can rise no more.'
    The morning meal was past, and all around
The mansion rang with each discordant sound;
Haste was in every foot, and every look
The trav'ller's joy for London-journey spoke :
Not so our youth ; whose feelings, at the noise
Of preparation, had no touch of joys ;
He pensive stood, and saw each carriage
    drawn,
With lackeys mounted, ready on the lawn :
The ladies came ; and John in terror threw
One painful glance, and then his eyes with-
    drew ;
Not with such speed, but he in other eyes
With anguish read—' I pity but despise—
Unhappy boy ! presumptuous scribbler !—
    you
To dream such dreams !—be sober, and
    adieu ! '
    Then came the noble friend—' And will my
    lord
Vouchsafe no comfort ? drop no soothing
    word ?
Yes, he must speak : ' he speaks, ' My good
    young friend,
You know my views ; upon my care depend ;
My hearty thanks to your good father pay,
And be a student.—Harry, drive away.'
    Stillness reign'd all around ; of late so full
The busy scene, deserted now and dull :
Stern is his nature who forbears to feel
Gloom o'er his spirits on such trials steal ;
Most keenly felt our poet as he went
From room to room without a fix'd intent ;
' And here,' he thought, ' I was caress'd ;
    admired
Were here my songs ; she smiled, and I
    aspired :

The change how grievous ! ' As he mused,
   a dame
Busy and peevish to her duties came ;
Aside the tables and the chairs she drew,
And sang and mutter'd in the poet's view :—
' This was her fortune ; here they leave the
   poor ;
Enjoy themselves, and think of us no more ;
I had a promise '— here his pride and shame
Urged him to fly from this familiar dame ;
He gave one farewell look, and by a coach
Reach'd his own mansion at the night's
   approach.
  His father met him with an anxious air,
Heard his sad tale, and check'd what seem'd
   despair ;
Hope was in him corrected, but alive ;
My lord would something for a friend con-
   trive ;
His word was pledged ; our hero's feverish
   mind
Admitted this, and half his grief resign'd :
But when three months had fled, and every
   day
Drew from the sickening hopes their strength
   away,
The youth became abstracted, pensive, dull ;
He utter'd nothing, though his heart was full ;
Teased by inquiring words and anxious looks,
And all forgetful of his muse and books ;
Awake he mourn'd, but in his sleep perceived
A lovely vision that his pain relieved :
His soul transported, hail'd the happy seat,
Where once his pleasure was so pure and
   sweet ;
Where joys departed came in blissful view,
Till reason waked, and not a joy he knew.
  Questions now vex'd his spirit, most from
   those
Who are called friends, because they are not
   foes :
' John ! ' they would say ; he, starting,
   turn'd around ;
' John ! ' there was something shocking in
   the sound ;
Ill brook'd he then the pert familiar phrase,
The untaught freedom, and th' inquiring gaze :
Much was his temper touch'd, his spleen
   provoked,
When ask'd how ladies talk'd, or walk'd, or
   look'd ?
' What said my lord of politics ? how spent
He there his time ? and was he glad he went ? '

At length a letter came, both cool and brief,
But still it gave the burthen'd heart relief :
Though not inspired by lofty hopes, the youth
Placed much reliance on Lord Frederick's
   truth ;
Summon'd to town, he thought the visit one
Where something fair and friendly would be
   done ;
Although he judged not, as before his fall,
When all was love and promise at the hall.
  Arrived in town, he early sought to know
The fate such dubious friendship would
   bestow ;
At a tall building trembling he appear'd,
And his low rap was indistinctly heard ;
A well-known servant came—' A while,'
   said he,
' Be pleased to wait ; my lord has company.'
Alone our hero sate ; the news in hand,
Which though he read, he could not under-
   stand :
Cold was the day ; in days so cold as these
There needs a fire, where minds and bodies
   freeze ;
The vast and echoing room, the polish'd grate,
The crimson chairs, the sideboard with its
   plate ;
The splendid sofa, which, though made for
   rest,
He then had thought it freedom to have
   press'd ;
The shining tables, curiously inlaid,
Were all in comfortless proud style display'd ;
And to the troubled feelings terror gave,
That made the once-dear friend, the sick'ning
   slave.
  ' Was he forgotten ? ' Thrice upon his ear
Struck the loud clock, yet no relief was near ;
Each rattling carriage, and each thundering
   stroke
On the loud door, the dream of fancy broke ;
Oft as a servant chanced the way to come,
' Brings he a message ? ' no ! he pass'd the
   room :
At length 'tis certain ; ' Sir, you will attend
At twelve on Thursday ! ' Thus the day had
   end.
  Vex'd by these tedious hours of needless
   pain,
John left the noble mansion with disdain ;
For there was something in that still, cold
   place,
That seem'd to threaten and portend disgrace.

Punctual again the modest rap declared
The youth attended ; then was all prepared :
For the same servant, by his lord's command,
A paper offer'd to his trembling hand :
' No more ! ' he cried ; ' disdains he to afford
One kind expression, one consoling word ? '
  With troubled spirit he began to read
That ' In the church my lord could not
    succeed ; '
Who had ' to peers of either kind applied,
And was with dignity and grace denied ;
While his own livings were by men possess'd,
Not likely in their chancels yet to rest ;
And therefore, all things weigh'd (as he, my
    lord,
Had done maturely, and he pledged his
    word),
Wisdom it seem'd for John to turn his view
To busier scenes, and bid the church adieu ! '
  Here grieved the youth ; he felt his father's
    pride
Must with his own be shock'd and mortified ;
But when he found his future comforts placed
Where he, alas ! conceived himself disgraced —
In some appointment on the London quays,
He bade farewell to honour and to ease ;
His spirit fell, and, from that hour assured
How vain his dreams, he suffer'd and was
    cured.
  Our poet hurried on, with wish to fly
From all mankind, to be conceal'd, and die.
Alas ! what hopes, what high romantic views
Did that one visit to the soul infuse,
Which cherish'd with such love, 'twas worse
    than death to lose !
Still he would strive, though painful was the
    strife,
To walk in this appointed road of life ;
On these low duties duteous he would wait,
And patient bear the anguish of his fate.
Thanks to the patron, but of coldest kind,
Express'd the sadness of the poet's mind ;
Whose heavy hours were pass'd with busy
    men,
In the dull practice of th' official pen ;
Who to superiors must in time impart
(The custom this) his progress in their art :
But so had grief on his perception wrought,
That all unheeded were the duties taught ;
No answers gave he when his trial came,
Silent he stood, but suffering without shame ;
And they observed that words severe or kind
Made no impression on his wounded mind ;

For all perceived from whence his failure rose,
Some grief whose cause he deign'd not to
    disclose.
A soul averse from scenes and works so new,
Fear ever shrinking from the vulgar crew ;
Distaste for each mechanic law and rule,
Thoughts of past honour and a patron cool ;
A grieving parent, and a feeling mind,
Timid and ardent, tender and refined :
These all with mighty force the youth assail'd,
Till his soul fainted, and his reason fail'd :
When this was known, and some debate arose
How they who saw it should the fact disclose,
He found their purpose, and in terror fled
From unseen kindness, with mistaken dread.
  Meantime the parent was distress'd to find
His son no longer for a priest design'd ;
But still he gain'd some comfort by the news
Of John's promotion, though with humbler
    views :
For he conceived that in no distant time
The boy would learn to scramble and to
    climb ;
He little thought a son, his hope and pride,
His favour'd boy, was now a home denied :
Yes ! while the parent was intent to trace
How men in office climb from place to place,
By day, by night, o'er moor and heath and
    hill,
Roved the sad youth, with ever-changing will,
Of every aid bereft, exposed to every ill.
  Thus as he sate, absorb'd in all the care
And all the hope that anxious fathers share,
A friend abruptly to his presence brought,
With trembling hand, the subject of his
    thought ;
Whom he had found afflicted and subdued
By hunger, sorrow, cold, and solitude.
  Silent he enter'd the forgotten room,
As ghostly forms may be conceived to come ;
With sorrow-shrunken face and hair upright,
He look'd dismay, neglect, despair, affright ;
But, dead to comfort, and on misery thrown,
His parent's loss he felt not, nor his own.
  The good man, struck with horror, cried
    aloud,
And drew around him an astonish'd crowd ;
The sons and servants to the father ran,
To share the feelings of the grieved old man.
' Our brother, speak ! ' they all exclaim'd ;
    ' explain
Thy grief, thy suffering : '—but they ask'd
    in vain :

The friend told all he knew; and all was known,
Save the sad causes whence the ills had grown:
But, if obscure the cause, they all agreed
From rest and kindness must the cure proceed:
And he was cured; for quiet, love, and care,
Strove with the gloom, and broke on the despair;
Yet slow their progress, and, as vapours move
Dense and reluctant from the wintry grove;
All is confusion till the morning light
Gives the dim scene obscurely to the sight;
More and yet more defined the trunks appear,
Till the wild prospect stands distinct and clear;—
So the dark mind of our young poet grew
Clear and sedate; the dreadful mist withdrew;
And he resembled that bleak wintry scene,
Sad, though unclouded; dismal, though serene.
At times he utter'd, ' What a dream was mine!
And what a prospect! glorious and divine!
Oh! in that room, and on that night to see
Those looks, that sweetness beaming all on me;
That syren-flattery—and to send me then,
Hope-raised and soften'd, to those heartless men;
That dark-brow'd stern director, pleased to show
Knowledge of subjects, I disdain'd to know;
Cold and controlling—but 'tis gone, 'tis past;
I had my trial, and have peace at last.'
    Now grew the youth resign'd; he bade adieu
To all that hope, to all that fancy drew;
His frame was languid, and the hectic heat
Flush'd on his pallid face, and countless beat
The quick'ning pulse, and faint the limbs that bore
The slender form that soon would breathe no more.
    Then hope of holy kind the soul sustain'd,
And not a lingering thought of earth remain'd;
Now Heaven had all, and he could smile at love,
And the wild sallies of his youth reprove;
Then could he dwell upon the tempting days
The proud aspiring thought, the partial praise;

Victorious now, his worldly views were closed,
And on the bed of death the youth reposed.
    The father grieved—but as the poet's heart
Was all unfitted for his earthly part;
As, he conceived, some other haughty fair
Would, had he lived, have led him to despair,
As, with this fear, the silent grave shut out
All feverish hope, and all tormenting doubt,
While the strong faith the pious youth possess'd,
His hopes enlivening, gave his sorrows rest;
Soothed by these thoughts, he felt a mournful joy
For his aspiring and devoted boy.
    Meantime the news through various channels spread,
The youth, once favour'd with such praise, was dead:
' Emma,' the lady cried, ' my words attend,
Your syren-smiles have kill'd your humble friend;
The hope you raised can now delude no more,
Nor charms, that once inspired, can now restore.'
    Faint was the flush of anger and of shame,
That o'er the cheek of conscious beauty came:
' You censure not,' she said, ' the sun's bright rays,
When fools imprudent dare the dangerous gaze;
And should a stripling look till he were blind,
You would not justly call the light unkind:
But is he dead? and am I to suppose
The power of poison in such looks as those?'
She spoke, and, pointing to the mirror, cast
A pleased gay glance, and curtsied as she pass'd.
    My lord, to whom the poet's fate was told,
Was much affected, for a man so cold:
' Dead!' said his lordship, ' run distracted, mad!
Upon my soul I'm sorry for the lad;
And now, no doubt, th' obliging world will say
That my harsh usage help'd him on his way:
What! I suppose, I should have nursed his muse,
And with champagne have brighten'd up his views;
Then had he made me famed my whole life long,
And stunn'd my ears with gratitude and song.

Still should the father hear that I regret
Our joint misfortune—Yes! I'll not forget.'—
  Thus they :—The father to his grave con-
    vey'd
The son he loved, and his last duties paid.
  'There lies my boy,' he cried, ' of care
    bereft,
And, Heav'n be praised, I've not a genius
  left :

No one among ye, sons! is doom'd to live
On high-raised hopes of what the great may
    give ;
None, with exalted views and fortunes mean,
To die in anguish, or to live in spleen :
Your pious brother soon escaped the strife
Of such contention, but it cost his life ;
You then, my sons, upon yourselves depend,
And in your own exertions find the friend.'

TALE VI. THE FRANK COURTSHIP

  Yes, faith, it is my cousin's duty to make
curtsy, and say, ' Father, as it please you ' ;
but yet for all that, cousin, let him be a hand-
some fellow, or else make another curtsy,
and say, ' Father, as it please me.'
      Much Ado about Nothing, Act ii, Scene 1.

          He cannot flatter, he !
An honest mind and plain—he must speak
  truth.
                King Lear, Act ii, Scene 2.

God hath given you one face, and you
make yourselves another ; you jig, you
amble, and you lisp and you nick-name God's
creatures, and make your wantonness your
ignorance.
                Hamlet, Act iii, Scene 1.

What fire is in mine ears ? Can this be true ?
Stand I condemn'd for pride and scorn so
  much ?
      Much Ado about Nothing, Act iii, Scene 1.

GRAVE Jonas Kindred, Sybil Kindred's sire,
Was six feet high, and look'd six inches higher ;
Erect, morose, determined, solemn, slow,
Who knew the man, could never cease to
    know ;
His faithful spouse, when Jonas was not by,
Had a firm presence and a steady eye ;
But with her husband dropp'd her look and
    tone,
And Jonas ruled unquestion'd and alone.
  He read, and oft would quote the sacred
    words,
How pious husbands of their wives were
    lords ;
Sarah called Abraham lord ! and who could
    be,
So Jonas thought, a greater man than he ?
Himself he view'd with undisguised respect,
And never pardon'd freedom or neglect.

They had one daughter, and this favourite
    child
Had oft the father of his spleen beguiled ;
Soothed by attention from her early years,
She gain'd all wishes by her smiles or tears :
But Sybil then was in that playful time,
When contradiction is not held a crime ;
When parents yield their children idle praise
For faults corrected in their after days.
  Peace in the sober house of Jonas dwelt,
Where each his duty and his station felt :
Yet not that peace some favour'd mortals find,
In equal views and harmony of mind ;
Not the soft peace that blesses those who love,
Where all with one consent in union move ;
But it was that which one superior will
Commands, by making all inferiors still ;
Who bids all murmurs, all objections cease,
And with imperious voice announces—Peace !
  They were, to wit, a remnant of that crew,
Who, as their foes maintain, their sovereign
    slew ;
An independent race, precise, correct,
Who ever married in the kindred sect :
No son or daughter of their order wed
A friend to England's king who lost his head ;
Cromwell was still their saint, and when they
    met,
They mourn'd that saints* were not our rulers
    yet.
  Fix'd were their habits ; they arose betimes,
Then pray'd their hour, and sang their party-
    rhymes :
Their meals were plenteous, regular, and plain ;
The trade of Jonas brought him constant gain ;

  * This appellation is here not used ironically,
nor with malignity ; but it is taken merely to
designate a morosely devout people, with pecu-
liar austerity of manners.

Vender of hops and malt, of coals and corn—
And, like his father, he was merchant born :
Neat was their house ; each table, chair, and
stool,
Stood in its place, or moving moved by rule ;
No lively print or picture graced the room ;
A plain brown paper lent its decent gloom ;
But here the eye, in glancing round, survey'd
A small recess that seem'd for china made ;
Such pleasing pictures seem'd this pencill'd
ware,
That few would search for nobler objects
there—
Yet, turn'd by chosen friends, and there
appear'd
His stern, strong features, whom they all
revered ;
For there in lofty air was seen to stand
The bold protector of the conquer'd land ;
Drawn in that look with which he wept and
swore,
Turn'd out the members, and made fast the
door,
Ridding the house of every knave and drone,
Forced, though it grieved his soul, to rule
alone.
The stern still smile each friend approving
gave,
Then turn'd the view, and all again were
grave.
   There stood a clock, though small the
owner's need,
For habit told when all things should proceed ;
Few their amusements, but when friends
appear'd,
They with the world's distress their spirits
cheer'd ;
The nation's guilt, that would not long endure
The reign of men so modest and so pure :
Their town was large, and seldom pass'd a day
But some had fail'd, and others gone astray ;
Clerks had absconded, wives eloped, girls flown
To Gretna-Green, or sons rebellious grown ;
Quarrels and fires arose ;—and it was plain
The times were bad ; the saints had ceased
to reign !
A few yet lived to languish and to mourn
For good old manners never to return.
   Jonas had sisters, of these was one
Who lost a husband and an only son :
Twelve months her sables she in sorrow wore,
And mourn'd so long that she could mourn
no more.

Distant from Jonas, and from all her race,
She now resided in a lively place ;
There, by the sect unseen, at whist she play'd,
Nor was of churchmen or their church afraid :
If much of this the graver brother heard,
He something censured, but he little fear'd ;
He knew her rich and frugal ; for the rest,
He felt no care, or, if he felt, suppress'd :
Nor for companion when she ask'd her niece,
Had he suspicions that disturb'd his peace ;
Frugal and rich, these virtues as a charm
Preserved the thoughtful man from all alarm ;
An infant yet, she soon would home return,
Nor stay the manners of the world to learn ;
Meantime his boys would all his care engross,
And be his comforts if he felt the loss.
   The sprightly Sybil, pleased and unconfined,
Felt the pure pleasure of the op'ning mind :
All here was gay and cheerful—all at home
Unvaried quiet and unruffled gloom :
There were no changes, and amusements few ;
Here, all was varied, wonderful, and new ;
There were plain meals, plain dresses, and
grave looks—
Here, gay companions and amusing books ;
And the young beauty soon began to taste
The light vocations of the scene she graced.
   A man of business feels it as a crime
On calls domestic to consume his time ;
Yet this grave man had not so cold a heart,
But with his daughter he was grieved to part :
And he demanded that in every year
The aunt and niece should at his house appear.
   ' Yes ! we must go, my child, and by our
dress
A grave conformity of mind express ;
Must sing at meeting, and from cards refrain,
The more t' enjoy when we return again.'
   Thus spake the aunt, and the discerning
child
Was pleased to learn how fathers are beguiled.
Her artful part the young dissembler took,
And from the matron caught th' approving
look :
When thrice the friends had met, excuse was
sent
For more delay, and Jonas was content ;
Till a tall maiden by her sire was seen,
In all the bloom and beauty of sixteen ;
He gazed admiring ;—she, with visage prim,
Glanced an arch look of gravity on him ;
For she was gay at heart, but wore disguise,
And stood a vestal in her father's eyes :

Pure, pensive, simple, sad ; the damsel's
  heart,
When Jonas praised, reproved her for the
  part ;
For Sybil, fond of pleasure, gay and light,
Had still a secret bias to the right ;
Vain as she was—and flattery made her
  vain—
Her simulation gave her bosom pain.

Again return'd, the matron and the niece
Found the late quiet gave their joy increase;
The aunt infirm, no more her visits paid,
But still with her sojourn'd the favourite
  maid.
Letters were sent when franks could be
  procured,
And when they could not, silence was endured;
All were in health, and if they older grew,
It seem'd a fact that none among them knew ;
The aunt and niece still led a pleasant life,
And quiet days had Jonas and his wife.

Near him a widow dwelt of worthy fame,
Like his her manners, and her creed the same;
The wealth her husband left, her care retain'd
For one tall youth, and widow she remain'd ;
His love respectful, all her care repaid,
Her wishes watch'd, and her commands
  obey'd.

Sober he was and grave from early youth,
Mindful of forms, but more intent on truth;
In a light drab he uniformly dress'd,
And look serene th' unruffled mind express'd;
A hat with ample verge his brows o'erspread,
And his brown locks curl'd graceful on his
  head ;
Yet might observers in his speaking eye
Some observation, some acuteness spy ;
The friendly thought it keen, the treacherous
  deem'd it sly ;
Yet not a crime could foe or friend detect,
His actions all were, like his speech, correct;
And they who jested on a mind so sound,
Upon his virtues must their laughter found ;
Chaste, sober, solemn, and devout they named
Him who was thus, and not of *this* ashamed.

Such were the virtues Jonas found in one
In whom he warmly wish'd to find a son :
Three years had pass'd since he had Sybil
  seen ;
But she was doubtless what she once had been,
Lovely and mild, obedient and discreet ;
The pair must love whenever they should
  meet ;

Then ere the widow or her son should choose
Some happier maid, he would explain his
  views ;
Now she, like him, was politic and shrewd,
With strong desire of lawful gain embued ;
To all he said, she bow'd with much respect,
Pleased to comply, yet seeming to reject ;
Cool and yet eager, each admired the strength
Of the opponent, and agreed at length :
As a drawn battle shows to each a force,
Powerful as his, he honours it of course ;
So in these neighbours, each the power
  discern'd,
And gave the praise that was to each return'd.
Jonas now ask'd his daughter—and the aunt,
Though loth to lose her, was obliged to
  grant :—
But would not Sybil to the matron cling,
And fear to leave the shelter of her wing ?
No ! in the young there lives a love of change,
And to the easy they prefer the strange !
Then too the joys she once pursued with zeal,
From whist and visits sprung, she ceased to
  feel ;
When with the matrons Sybil first sat down,
To cut for partners and to stake her crown,
This to the youthful maid preferment seem'd,
Who thought what woman she was then
  esteem'd ;
But in few years, when she perceived, indeed,
The real woman to the girl succeed,
No longer tricks and honours fill'd her mind,
But other feelings, not so well defined ;
She then reluctant grew, and thought it hard,
To sit and ponder o'er an ugly card ;
Rather the nut-tree shade the nymph
  preferr'd,
Pleased with the pensive gloom and evening
  bird ;
Thither, from company retired, she took
The silent walk, or read the fav'rite book.

The father's letter, sudden, short, and kind,
Awaked her wonder, and disturb'd her mind ;
She found new dreams upon her fancy seize,
Wild roving thoughts and endless reveries :
The parting came ;—and when the aunt
  perceived
The tears of Sybil, and how much she
  grieved—
To love for her that tender grief she laid,
That various, soft, contending passions made.
When Sybil rested in her father's arms,
His pride exulted in a daughter's charms ;

A maid accomplish'd he was pleased to find,
Nor seem'd the form more lovely than the
     mind :
But when the fit of pride and fondness fled,
He saw his judgment by his hopes misled ;
High were the lady's spirits, far more free
Her mode of speaking than a maid's should be ;
Too much, as Jonas thought, she seem'd to
     know,
And all her knowledge was disposed to show ;
' Too gay her dress, like theirs who idly dote
On a young coxcomb, or a coxcomb's coat ;
In foolish spirits when our friends appear,
And vainly grave when not a man is near.'

     Thus Jonas, adding to his sorrow blame,
And terms disdainful to his sister's name :—
' The sinful wretch has by her arts defiled
The ductile spirit of my darling child.'
     'The maid is virtuous,' said the dame—
          Quoth he,
' Let her give proof, by acting virtuously :
Is it in gaping when the elders pray ?
In reading nonsense half a summer's day ?
In those mock forms that she delights to trace,
Or her loud laughs in Hezekiah's face ?
She—O Susannah !—to the world belongs ;
She loves the follies of its idle throngs,
And reads soft tales of love, and sings love's
     soft'ning songs.
But, as our friend is yet delay'd in town,
We must prepare her till the youth comes
     down ;
You shall advise the maiden ; I will threat ;
Her fears and hopes may yield us comfort
     yet.'
     Now the grave father took the lass aside,
Demanding sternly, 'Wilt thou be a bride ? '
She answer'd, calling up an air sedate,
' I have not vow'd against the holy state.'
     ' No folly, Sybil,' said the parent ; ' know
What to their parents virtuous maidens owe :
A worthy, wealthy youth, whom I approve,
Must thou prepare to honour and to love.
Formal to thee his air and dress may seem,
But the good youth is worthy of esteem ;
Shouldst thou with rudeness treat him ; of
     disdain
Should he with justice or of slight complain,
Or of one taunting speech give certain proof,
Girl ! I reject thee from my sober roof.'
     ' My aunt,' said Sybil, ' will with pride
          protect
One whom a father can for this reject ;

Nor shall a formal, rigid, soul-less boy
My manners alter, or my views destroy ! '
     Jonas then lifted up his hands on high,
And utt'ring something 'twixt a groan and
     sigh,
Left the determined maid, her doubtful
     mother by.
     ' Hear me,' she said ; ' incline thy heart,
And fix thy fancy on a man so mild :
Thy father, Sybil, never could be moved
By one who loved him, or by one he loved.
Union like ours is but a bargain made
By slave and tyrant—he will be obey'd ;
Then calls the quiet, comfort—but thy youth
Is mild by nature, and as frank as truth.'
     ' But will he love ? ' said Sybil ; ' I am told
That these mild creatures are by nature cold.'
     ' Alas ! ' the matron answer'd, ' much I dread
That dangerous love by which the young are
     led !
That love is earthy ; you the creature prize,
And trust your feelings and believe your eyes :
Can eyes and feelings inward worth descry ?
No ! my fair daughter, on our choice rely !
Your love, like that display'd upon the stage,
Indulged is folly, and opposed is rage ;—
More prudent love our sober couples show,
All that to mortal beings, mortals owe ;
All flesh is grass—before you give a heart,
Remember, Sybil, that in death you part ;
And should your husband die before your love,
What needless anguish must a widow prove !
No ! my fair child, let all such visions cease ;
Yield but esteem, and only try for peace.'
     ' I must be loved,' said Sybil ; ' I must see
The man in terrors who aspires to me ;
At my forbidding frown, his heart must ache,
His tongue must falter, and his frame must
     shake :
And if I grant him at my feet to kneel,
What trembling, fearful pleasure must he feel ;
Nay, such the raptures that my smiles inspire,
That reason's self must for a time retire.'
     ' Alas ! for good Josiah,' said the dame,
' These wicked thoughts would fill his soul with
     shame ;
He kneel and tremble at a thing of dust !
He cannot, child : '—the child replied, 'He
     must.'
     They ceased : the matron left her with a
          frown ;
So Jonas met her when the youth came down :

'Behold,' said he, 'thy future spouse attends;
Receive him, daughter, as the best of friends;
Observe, respect him—humble be each word,
That welcomes home thy husband and thy
　　lord.'
　Forewarn'd, thought Sybil, with a bitter
　　smile,
I shall prepare my manner and my style.
　Ere yet Josiah enter'd on his task,
The father met him—' Deign to wear a mask
A few dull days, Josiah—but a few—
It is our duty, and the sex's due;
I wore it once, and every grateful wife
Repays it with obedience through her life:
Have no regard to Sybil's dress, have none
To her pert language, to her flippant tone:
Henceforward thou shalt rule unquestioned
　　and alone;
And she thy pleasure in thy looks shall seek—
How she shall dress, and whether she may
　　speak.'
　A sober smile return'd the youth, and said,
' Can I cause fear, who am myself afraid ? '
　Sybil, meantime, sat thoughtful in her room,
And often wonder'd—' Will the creature
　　come ?
Nothing shall tempt, shall force me to bestow
My hand upon him—yet I wish to know.'
　The door unclosed, and she beheld her sire
Lead in the youth, then hasten to retire;
' Daughter, my friend—my daughter, friend '
　　—he cried,
And gave a meaning look, and stepp'd aside;
That look contain'd a mingled threat and
　　prayer,
' Do take him, child—offend him, if you dare.'
　The couple gazed—were silent, and the maid
Look'd in his face, to make the man afraid;
The man, unmoved, upon the maiden cast
A steady view—so salutation pass'd:
But in this instant Sybil's eye had seen
The tall fair person, and the still staid mien;
The glow that temp'rance o'er the cheek had
　　spread,
Where the soft down half veil'd the purest
　　red;
And the serene deportment that proclaim'd
A heart unspotted, and a life unblamed:
But then with these she saw attire too plain,
The pale brown coat, though worn without
　　a stain;
The formal air, and something of the pride
That indicates the wealth it seems to hide;

And looks that were not, she conceived,
　　exempt
From a proud pity, or a sly contempt.
　Josiah's eyes had their employment too,
Engaged and soften'd by so bright a view;
A fair and meaning face, an eye of fire,
That check'd the bold, and made the free
　　retire:
But then with these he mark'd the studied
　　dress
And lofty air, that scorn or pride express;
With that insidious look, that seem'd to hide
In an affected smile the scorn and pride;
And if his mind the virgin's meaning caught,
He saw a foe with treacherous purpose
　　fraught—
Captive the heart to take, and to reject it
　　caught.
　Silent they sate—thought Sybil, that he
　　seeks
Something, no doubt; I wonder if he speaks:
Scarcely she wonder'd, when these accents fell
Slow in her ear—'Fair maiden, art thou well ?
' Art thou physician ? ' she replied; ' my
　　hand,
My pulse, at least, shall be at thy command.'
　She said—and saw, surprised, Josiah kneel,
And gave his lips the offer'd pulse to feel;
The rosy colour rising in her cheek,
Seem'd that surprise unmix'd with wrath to
　　speak;
Then sternness she assumed, and—' Doctor,
　　tell,
Thy words cannot alarm me—am I well ? '
　' Thou art,' said he; ' and yet thy dress
　　so light,
I do conceive, some danger must excite : '
' In whom ? ' said Sybil, with a look demure:
' In more,' said he, ' than I expect to cure.
I, in thy light luxuriant robe, behold
Want and excess, abounding and yet cold;
Here needed, there display'd, in many a
　　wanton fold:
Both health and beauty, learned authors
　　show,
From a just medium in our clothing flow.'
　' Proceed, good doctor; if so great my need,
What is thy fee ?　Good doctor ! pray pro-
　　ceed.'
　' Large is my fee, fair lady, but I take
None till some progress in my cure I make:
Thou hast disease, fair maiden; thou art vain;
Within that face sit insult and disdain;

Thou art enamour'd of thyself ; my art
Can see the naughty malice of thy heart :
With a strong pleasure would thy bosom
    move,
Were I to own thy power, and ask thy love ;
And such thy beauty, damsel, that I might,
But for thy pride, feel danger in thy sight,
And lose my present peace in dreams of vain
    delight.'
    ' And can thy patients,' said the nymph,
        ' endure
Physic like this ? and will it work a cure ? '
    ' Such is my hope, fair damsel ; thou, I find,
Hast the true tokens of a noble mind ;
But the world wins thee, Sybil, and thy joys
Are placed in trifles, fashions, follies, toys ;
Thou hast sought pleasure in the world around,
That in thine own pure bosom should be found :
Did all that world admire thee, praise and
    love,
Could it the least of nature's pains remove ?
Could it for errors, follies, sins atone,
Or give thee comfort, thoughtful and alone ?
It has, believe me, maid, no power to charm
Thy soul from sorrow, or thy flesh from harm :
Turn then, fair creature, from a world of
    sin,
And seek the jewel happiness within.'
    'Speak'st thou at meeting ? ' said the
        nymph ; ' thy speech
Is that of mortal very prone to teach ;
But wouldst thou, doctor, from the patient
    learn
Thine own disease ?—The cure is thy con-
    cern.'
    ' Yea, with good will.'—'Then know, 'tis thy
        complaint,
That, for a sinner, thou'rt too much a saint ;
Hast too much show of the sedate and pure,
And without cause art formal and demure :
This makes a man unsocial, unpolite ;
Odious when wrong, and insolent if right.
Thou may'st be good, but why should good-
    ness be
Wrapt in a garb of such formality ?
Thy person well might please a damsel's eye,
In decent habit with a scarlet dye ;
But, jest apart—what virtue canst thou trace
In that broad brim that hides thy sober face ?
Does that long-skirted drab, that over-nice
And formal clothing, prove a scorn of vice ?
Then for thine accent—what in sound can be
So void of grace as dull monotony ?

Love has a thousand varied notes to move
The human heart ;—thou may'st not speak
    of love
Till thou hast cast thy formal ways aside,
And those becoming youth and nature tried
Not till exterior freedom, spirit, ease,
Prove it thy study and delight to please ;
Not till these follies meet thy just disdain,
While yet thy virtues and thy worth remain.'
    ' This is severe !—Oh ! maiden, wilt not
        thou
Something for habits, manners, modes,
    allow ? '—
    ' Yes ! but allowing much, I much require,
In my behalf, for manners, modes, attire ! '
    ' True, lovely Sybil ; and, this point agreed,
Let me to those of greater weight proceed :
Thy father ! '—'Nay,' she quickly interposed,
' Good doctor, here our conference is closed! '
    Then left the youth, who, lost in his retreat,
Pass'd the good matron on her garden-seat ;
His looks were troubled, and his air, once mild
And calm, was hurried :—' My audacious
        child ! '
Exclaim'd the dame, ' I read what she has
        done
In thy displeasure—Ah! the thoughtless one ;
But yet, Josiah, to my stern good man
Speak of the maid as mildly as you can :
Can you not seem to woo a little while
The daughter's will, the father to beguile ?
So that his wrath in time may wear away ;
Will you preserve our peace, Josiah ? say.'
    ' Yes ! my good neighbour,' said the gentle
        youth,
' Rely securely on my care and truth ;
And should thy comfort with my efforts cease,
And only then—perpetual is thy peace.'
    The dame had doubts : she well his virtues
        knew,
His deeds were friendly, and his words were
        true ;
' But to address this vixen is a task
He is ashamed to take, and I to ask.'
Soon as the father from Josiah learn'd
What pass'd with Sybil, he the truth discern'd.
' He loves,' the man exclaim'd, ' he loves, 'tis
        plain,
The thoughtless girl, and shall he love in vain ?
She may be stubborn, but she shall be tried,
Born as she is of wilfulness and pride.'
    With anger fraught, but willing to persuade,
The wrathful father met the smiling maid :

' Sybil,' said he, ' I long, and yet I dread
To know thy conduct—hath Josiah fled ?
And, grieved and fretted by thy scornful air,
For his lost peace betaken him to prayer ?
Couldst thou his pure and modest mind
   distress,
By vile remarks upon his speech, address,
Attire, and voice ? '—' All this I must con-
   fess.'—
' Unhappy child ! what labour will it cost
To win him back !'—'I do not think him lost.'
'Courts he then, trifler! insult and disdain?'—
' No : but from these he courts me to refrain.'

' Then hear me, Sybil—should Josiah leave
Thy father's house ? '—' My father's child
   would grieve : '
' That is of grace, and if he come again
To speak of love ? '—' I might from grief
   refrain.'—
' Then wilt thou, daughter, our design
   embrace ? '—
' Can I resist it, if it be of grace ? '
' Dear child ! in three plain words thy mind
   express—
Wilt thou have this good youth ? ' ' Dear
   father ! yes.'

TALE VII. THE WIDOW'S TALE

Ah me! for aught that I could ever read,
Could ever hear by tale or history,
The course of true love never did run smooth ;
But either it was different in blood, . . .
Or else misgraffed in respect of years, . . .
Or else it stood upon the choice of friends; . . .
Or if there were a sympathy in choice,
War, death, or sickness did lay siege to it.
   Midsummer Night's Dream, Act i, Scene 1.

Oh! thou didst then ne'er love so heartily
If thou remember'st not the slightest folly
That ever love did make thee run into.
   As You Like It, Act ii, Scene 4.

Cry the man mercy ; love him, take his offer.
   As You Like It, Act iii, Scene 5.

To farmer Moss, in Langar Vale, came down
His only daughter, from her school in town ;
A tender, timid maid ! who knew not how
To pass a pig-sty, or to face a cow :
Smiling she came, with petty talents graced,
A fair complexion, and a slender waist.

   Used to spare meals, disposed in manner
      pure,
Her father's kitchen she could ill endure ;
Where by the steaming beef he hungry sat,
And laid at once a pound upon his plate ;
Hot from the field, her eager brother seized
An equal part, and hunger's rage appeased ;
The air, surcharged with moisture, flagg'd
   around,
And the offended damsel sigh'd and frown'd ;
The swelling fat in lumps conglomerate laid,
And fancy's sickness seized the loathing
   maid :

But when the men beside their station took,
The maidens with them, and with these the
   cook ;
When one huge wooden bowl before them
   stood,
Fill'd with huge balls of farinaceous food ;
With bacon, mass saline, where never lean
Beneath the brown and bristly rind was seen ;
When from a single horn the party drew
Their copious draughts of heavy ale and new ;
When the coarse cloth she saw, with many
   a stain,
Soil'd by rude hinds who cut and came again—
She could not breathe ; but,with a heavy sigh,
Rein'd the fair neck, and shut th' offended
   eye ;
She minced the sanguine flesh in frustums fine,
And wonder'd much to see the creatures dine :
When she resolved her father's heart to move,
If hearts of farmers were alive to love.

   She now entreated by herself to sit
In the small parlour, if papa thought fit,
And there to dine, to read, to work alone :—
' No ! ' said the farmer, in an angry tone ;
' These are your school-taught airs ; your
   mother's pride
Would send you there ; but I am now your
   guide.—
Arise betimes, our early meal prepare,
And this despatch'd, let business be your care;
Look to the lasses, let there not be one
Who lacks attention, till her tasks be done ;
In every household work your portion take,
And what you make not, see that others make:

At leisure times attend the wheel, and see
The whit'ning web be sprinkled on the Lea ;
When thus employ'd, should our young
    neighbour view
An useful lass, you may have more to do.'
    Dreadful were these commands; but worse
        than these
The parting hint—a farmer could not please:
'Tis true she had without abhorrence seen
Young Harry Carr, when he was smart and
    clean ;
But to be married—be a farmer's wife—
A slave ! a drudge !—she could not, for her
    life.
    With swimming eyes the fretful nymph
        withdrew,
And, deeply sighing, to her chamber flew ;
There on her knees, to Heav'n she grieving
    pray'd
For change of prospect to a tortured maid.
    Harry, a youth whose late-departed sire
Had left him all industrious men require,
Saw the pale beauty—and her shape and air
Engaged him much, and yet he must forbear :
' For my small farm what can the damsel
    do ? '
He said—then stopp'd to take another view :
' Pity so sweet a lass will nothing learn
Of household cares—for what can beauty earn
By those small arts which they at school
    attain,
That keep them useless, and yet make them
    vain ? '
    This luckless damsel look'd the village
        round,
To find a friend, and one was quickly found ;
A pensive widow—whose mild air and dress
Pleased the sad nymph, who wish'd her soul's
    distress
To one so seeming kind, confiding, to con-
    fess.—
    ' What lady that ? ' the anxious lass
        inquired,
Who then beheld the one she most admired :
' Here,' said the brother, ' are no ladies seen—
That is a widow dwelling on the green ;
A dainty dame, who can but barely live
On her poor pittance, yet contrives to give ;
She happier days has known, but seems at
    ease,
And you may call her lady, if you please :
But if you wish, good sister, to improve,
You shall see twenty better worth your love.

These Nancy met ; but, spite of all they
    taught,
This useless widow was the one she sought :
The father growl'd ; but said he knew no harm
In such connexion that could give alarm ;
' And if we thwart the trifler in her course,
'Tis odds against us she will take a worse.'
    Then met the friends ; the widow heard the
        sigh
That ask'd at once compassion and reply :—
' Would you, my child, converse with one so
    poor,
Yours were the kindness—yonder is my door ;
And, save the time that we in public pray,
From that poor cottage I but rarely stray.'
    There went the nymph, and made her
        strong complaints,
Painting her wo as injured feeling paints.
    ' Oh, dearest friend ! do think how one
        must feel,
Shock'd all day long, and sicken'd every meal ;
Could you behold our kitchen (and to you
A scene so shocking must indeed be new),
A mind like yours, with true refinement
    graced,
Would let no vulgar scenes pollute your taste ;
And yet, in truth, from such a polish'd mind
All base ideas must resistance find,
And sordid pictures from the fancy pass,
As the breath startles from the polish'd glass.
    ' Here you enjoy a sweet romantic scene,
Without so pleasant, and within so clean ;
These twining jess'mines, what delicious
    gloom
And soothing fragrance yield they to the
    room !
What lovely garden ! there you oft retire,
And tales of wo and tenderness admire :
In that neat case your books, in order placed,
Soothe the full soul, and charm the cultured
    taste ;
And thus, while all about you wears a charm,
How must you scorn the farmer and the
    farm ! '
    The widow smiled, and ' Know you not,'
        said she,
' How much these farmers scorn or pity me ;
Who see what you admire, and laugh at all
    they see ?
True, their opinion alters not my fate,
By falsely judging of an humble state :
This garden, you with such delight behold,
Tempts not a feeble dame who dreads the cold ;

These plants, which please so well your
    livelier sense,
To mine but little of their sweets dispense ;
Books soon are painful to my failing sight,
And oftener read from duty than delight ;
(Yet let me own, that I can sometimes find
Both joy and duty in the act combined ;)
But view me rightly, you will see no more
Than a poor female, willing to be poor ;
Happy indeed, but not in books nor flowers
Not in fair dreams, indulged in earlier hours,
Of never-tasted joys ;—such visions shun,
My youthful friend, nor scorn the farmers'
    son.'
  ' Nay,' said the damsel, nothing pleased to
    see
A friend's advice could like a father's be,
' Bless'd in your cottage, you must surely
    smile
At those who live in our detested style :
To my Lucinda's sympathizing heart
Could I my prospects and my griefs impart,
She would console me ; but I dare not show
Ills that would wound her tender soul to
    know :
And I confess, it shocks my pride to tell
The secrets of the prison where I dwell ;
For that dear maiden would be shock'd to feel
The secrets I should shudder to reveal ;
When told her friend was by a parent ask'd,
Fed you the swine ?—Good heav'n ! how I
    am task'd !
What ! can you smile ? Ah ! smile not at
    the grief
That woos your pity and demands relief.'
  ' Trifles, my love ; you take a false alarm;
Think, I beseech you, better of the farm :
Duties in every state demand your care,
And light are those that will require it there :
Fix on the youth a favouring eye, and these,
To him pertaining, or as his, will please.'
  ' What words,' the lass replied, ' offend my
    ear !
Try you my patience ? Can you be sincere ?
And am I told a willing hand to give
To a rude farmer, and with rustic live ?
Far other fate was yours :—some gentle youth
Admired your beauty, and avow'd his truth ;
The power of love prevail'd, and freely both
Gave the fond heart, and pledged the binding
    oath ;
And then the rival's plot, the parent's power,
And jealous fears, drew on the happy hour :

Ah ! let not memory lose the blissful view,
But fairly show what love has done for you.'
  ' Agreed, my daughter ; what my heart
    has known
Of love's strange power shall be with frank-
    ness shown :
But let me warn you, that experience finds
Few of the scenes that lively hope designs.'—
  ' Mysterious all,' said Nancy ; ' you, I
    know,
Have suffer'd much ; now deign the grief to
    show ;—
I am your friend, and so prepare my heart
In all your sorrows to receive a part.'
  The widow answer'd : ' I had once, like you,
Such thoughts of love ; no dream is more
    untrue :
You judge it fated and decreed to dwell
In youthful hearts, which nothing can expel,
A passion doom'd to reign, and irresistible.
The struggling mind, when once subdued, in
    vain
Rejects the fury or defies the pain ;
The strongest reason fails the flame t' allay,
And resolution droops and faints away :
Hence, when the destined lovers meet, they
    prove
At once the force of this all-powerful love ;
Each from that period feels the mutual smart,
Nor seeks to cure it—heart is changed for
    heart ;
Nor is there peace till they delighted stand,
And, at the altar—hand is join'd to hand.
  'Alas! my child, there are who, dreaming so,
Waste their fresh youth, and waking feel the
    wo ;
There is no spirit sent the heart to move
With such prevailing and alarming love ;
Passion to reason will submit—or why
Should wealthy maids the poorest swains
    deny ?
Or how could classes and degrees create
The slightest bar to such resistless fate ?
Yet high and low, you see, forbear to mix ;
No beggars' eyes the heart of kings transfix ;
And who but am'rous peers or nobles sigh
When titled beauties pass triumphant by ?
For reason wakes, proud wishes to reprove :
You cannot hope, and therefore dare not
    love :
All would be safe, did we at first inquire—
" Does reason sanction what our hearts
    desire ? "

But quitting precept, let example show
What joys from love uncheck'd by prudence
    flow.
   ' A youth my father in his office placed,
Of humble fortune, but with sense and taste ;
But he was thin and pale, had downcast looks;
He studied much, and pored upon his books :
Confused he was when seen, and, when he saw
Me or my sisters, would in haste withdraw ;
And had this youth departed with the year,
His loss had cost us neither sigh nor tear.
   ' But with my father still the youth remain'd,
And more reward and kinder notice gain'd :
He often, reading, to the garden stray'd,
Where I by books or musing was delay'd ;
This to discourse in summer evenings led,
Of these same evenings, or of what we read :
On such occasions we were much alone ;
But, save the look, the manner, and the tone,
(These might have meaning,) all that we
    discuss'd
We could with pleasure to a parent trust.
   ' At length 'twas friendship—and my friend
    and I
Said we were happy, and began to sigh :
My sisters first, and then my father, found
That we were wandering o'er enchanted
    ground ;
But he had troubles in his own affairs,
And would not bear addition to his cares :
With pity moved, yet angry, "Child," said
    he,
"Will you embrace contempt and beggary ?
Can you endure to see each other cursed
By want, of every human wo the worst ?
Warring for ever with distress, in dread
Either of begging or of wanting bread ;
While poverty, with unrelenting force,
Will your own offspring from your love
    divorce ;
They, through your folly, must be doom'd to
    pine,
And you deplore your passion, or resign ;
For, if it die, what good will then remain ?
And if it live, it doubles every pain." '
   ' But you were true,' exclaim'd the lass,
    ' and fled
The tyrant's power who fill'd your soul with
    dread ? '
   ' But,' said the smiling friend, ' he fill'd my
    mouth with bread :
And in what other place that bread to gain
We long consider'd, and we sought in vain :

This was my twentieth year—at thirty-five
Our hope was fainter, yet our love alive ;
So many years in anxious doubt had pass'd.'
   ' Then,' said the damsel, ' you were bless'd
    at last ? '
A smile again adorn'd the widow's face,
But soon a starting tear usurp'd its place.
   ' Slow pass'd the heavy years, and each
    had more
Pains and vexations than the years before.
My father fail'd ; his family was rent,
And to new states his grieving daughters sent;
Each to more thriving kindred found a way,
Guests without welcome—servants without
    pay ;
Our parting hour was grievous ; still I feel
The sad, sweet converse at our final meal ;
Our father then reveal'd his former fears,
Cause of his sternness, and then join'd our
    tears ;
Kindly he strove our feelings to repress,
But died, and left us heirs to his distress.
The rich, as humble friends, my sisters chose,
I with a wealthy widow sought repose ;
Who with a chilling frown her friend received,
Bade me rejoice, and wonder'd that I grieved:
In vain my anxious lover tried his skill
To rise in life, he was dependent still ;
We met in grief, nor can I paint the fears
Of these unhappy, troubled, trying years ;
Our dying hopes and stronger fears between,
We felt no season peaceful or serene ;
Our fleeting joys, like meteors in the night,
Shone on our gloom with inauspicious light ;
And then domestic sorrows, till the mind,
Worn with distresses, to despair inclined ;
Add too the ill that from the passion flows,
When its contemptuous frown the world
    bestows,
The peevish spirit caused by long delay,
When, being gloomy, we contemn the gay,
When, being wretched, we incline to hate
And censure others in a happier state ;
Yet loving still, and still compell'd to move
In the sad labyrinth of ling'ring love :
While you, exempt from want, despair, alarm,
May wed—oh ! take the farmer and the farm.'
   ' Nay,' said the nymph, ' joy smiled on you
    at last ? '
' Smiled for a moment,' she replied, ' and
    pass'd :
My lover still the same dull means pursued,
Assistant call'd, but kept in servitude ;

His spirits wearied in the prime of life,
By fears and wishes in eternal strife ;
At length he urged impatient—" Now consent;
With thee united, fortune may relent."
I paused, consenting ; but a friend arose,
Pleased a fair view, though distant, to dis-
    close ;
From the rough ocean we beheld a gleam
Of joy, as transient as the joys we dream ;
By lying hopes deceived, my friend retired,
And sail'd—was wounded—reach'd us—and
    expired !
You shall behold his grave, and when I die,
There—but 'tis folly—I request to lie.'
   ' Thus,' said the lass, ' to joy you bade
    adieu !
But how a widow ?—that cannot be true :
Or was it force, in some unhappy hour,
That placed you, grieving, in a tyrant's
    power ? '
   ' Force, my young friend, when forty years
   are fled,
Is what a woman seldom has to dread ;
She needs no brazen locks nor guarding walls;
And seldom comes a lover though she calls ;
Yet moved by fancy, one approved my face,
Though time and tears had wrought it much
    disgrace.
   ' The man I married was sedate and meek,
And spoke of love as men in earnest speak ;
Poor as I was, he ceaseless sought, for years,
A heart in sorrow and a face in tears ;
That heart I gave not ; and 'twas long before
I gave attention, and then nothing more ;
But in my breast some grateful feeling rose
For one whose love so sad a subject chose ;
Till long delaying, fearing to repent,
But grateful still, I gave a cold assent.
   ' Thus we were wed ; no fault had I to find,
And he but one ; my heart could not be kind :
Alas ! of every early hope bereft,
There was no fondness in my bosom left ;
So had I told him, but had told in vain,
He lived but to indulge me and complain :
His was this cottage, he inclosed this ground,
And planted all these blooming shrubs around;
He to my room these curious trifles brought,
And with assiduous love my pleasure sought ;
He lived to please me, and I ofttimes strove,
Smiling, to thank his unrequited love :
" Teach me," he cried, " that pensive mind
   to ease,
For all my pleasure is the hope to please."

' Serene, though heavy, were the days we
   spent,
Yet kind each word, and gen'rous each intent;
But his dejection lessen'd every day,
And to a placid kindness died away :
In tranquil ease we pass'd our latter years,
By griefs untroubled, unassail'd by fears.
   ' Let not romantic views your bosom sway,
Yield to your duties, and their call obey :
Fly not a youth, frank, honest, and sincere ;
Observe his merits, and his passion hear !
'Tis true, no hero, but a farmer sues—
Slow in his speech, but worthy in his views ;
With him you cannot that affliction prove,
That rends the bosom of the poor in love :
Health, comfort, competence, and cheerful
   days,
Your friends' approval, and your father's
   praise,
Will crown the deed, and you escape *their* fate
Who plan so wildly, and are wise too late.'
   The damsel heard ; at first th' advice was
   strange,
Yet wrought a happy, nay, a speedy change :
' I have no care,' she said, when next they met,
' But one may wonder he is silent yet ;
He looks around him with his usual stare,
And utters nothing—not that I shall care.'
   This pettish humour pleased th' experienced
   friend—
None need despair, whose silence can offend ;
' Should I,' resumed the thoughtful lass,
   ' consent
To hear the man, the man may now repent :
Think you my sighs shall call him from the
   plough,
Or give one hint, that " You may woo me
   now ? " '
   ' Persist, my love,' replied the friend, ' and
   gain
A parent's praise, *that* cannot be in vain.'
   The father saw the change, but not the
   cause,
And gave the alter'd maid his fond applause :
The coarser manners she in part removed,
In part endured, improving and improved ;
She spoke of household works, she rose be-
   times,
And said neglect and indolence were crimes ;
The various duties of their life she weigh'd,
And strict attention to her dairy paid ;
The names of servants now familiar grew,
And fair Lucinda's from her mind withdrew :

As prudent travellers for their ease assume
Their modes and language to whose lands
   they come :
So to the farmer this fair lass inclined,
Gave to the business of the farm her mind ;
To useful arts she turn'd her hand and eye ;
And by her manners told him—' You may try.'
  Th' observing lover more attention paid,
With growing pleasure, to the alter'd maid ;
He fear'd to lose her, and began to see
That a slim beauty might a helpmate be :
'Twixt hope and fear he now the lass address'd,
And in his Sunday robe his love express'd :
She felt no chilling dread, no thrilling joy,
Nor was too quickly kind, too slowly coy ;
But still she lent an unreluctant ear
To all the rural business of the year ;
Till love's strong hopes endured no more delay,
And Harry ask'd, and Nancy named the day.
  ' A happy change ! my boy,' the father
   cried :
' How lost your sister all her school-day
   pride ? '
The youth replied, ' It is the widow's deed :
The cure is perfect, and was wrought with
   speed.'—

And comes there, boy, this benefit of books,
Of that smart dress, and of those dainty looks?
We must be kind—some offerings from the
   farm
To the white cot will speak our feelings warm;
Will show that people, when they know the
   fact,
Where they have judged severely, can retract.
Oft have I smiled, when I beheld her pass
With cautious step, as if she hurt the grass ;
Where if a snail's retreat she chanced to storm,
She look'd as begging pardon of the worm ;
And what, said I, still laughing at the view,
Have these weak creatures in the world to do?
But some are made for action, some to speak;
And, while she looks so pitiful and meek,
Her words are weighty, though her nerves
   are weak.'
  Soon told the village-bells the rite was done,
That join'd the school-bred miss and farmer's
   son ;
Her former habits some slight scandal raised,
But real worth was soon perceived and
   praised ;
She, her neat taste imparted to the farm,
And he, th' improving skill and vigorous arm.

TALE VIII. THE MOTHER

    What though you have no beauty, . . .
Must you be therefore proud and pitiless ?
    As You Like It, Act iii, Scene 5.

I would not marry her, though she were
endowed with all that Adam had left him
before he transgressed.
    Much Ado about Nothing, Act ii, Scene 1.

Wilt thou love such a woman ? What ! to
make thee an instrument, and play false
strains upon thee !—Not to be endured.
    As You Like It, Act iv, Scene 3.

       Your son,
As mad in folly, lack'd the sense to know
Her estimation home.
    All's Well that Ends Well, Act v, Scene 3.

    Be this sweet Helen's knell ; . . .
He a wife lost whose words all ears took
   captive, . . .
Whose dear perfection, hearts that scorn'd to
   serve
Humbly call'd mistress.
    All's Well that Ends Well, Act v, Scene 3.

There was a worthy, but a simple pair,
Who nursed a daughter, fairest of the fair :
Sons they had lost, and she alone remain'd,
Heir to the kindness they had all obtain'd ;
Heir to the fortune they design'd for all,
Nor had th' allotted portion then been small ;
But now, by fate enrich'd with beauty rare,
They watch'd their treasure with peculiar
   care :
The fairest features they could early trace,
And, blind with love, saw merit in her face—
Saw virtue, wisdom, dignity, and grace ;
And Dorothea, from her infant years,
Gain'd all her wishes from their pride or fears
She wrote a billet, and a novel read,
And with her fame her vanity was fed ;
Each word, each look, each action was a cause
For flattering wonder, and for fond applause ;
She rode or danced, and ever glanced around,
Seeking for praise, and smiling when she found.
The yielding pair to her petitions gave
An humble friend to be a civil slave ;

Who for a poor support herself resign'd
To the base toil of a dependent mind :
By nature cold, our heiress stoop'd to art,
To gain the credit of a tender heart.
Hence at her door must suppliant paupers
      stand,
To bless the bounty of her beauteous hand :
And now, her education all complete,
She talk'd of virtuous love and union sweet ;
She was indeed by no soft passion moved,
But wish'd, with all her soul, to be be-
      loved.
Here on the favour'd beauty fortune smiled ;
Her chosen husband was a man so mild,
So humbly temper'd, so intent to please,
It quite distress'd her to remain at ease,
Without a cause to sigh, without pretence to
      tease :
She tried his patience in a thousand modes,
And tired it not upon the roughest roads.
Pleasure she sought, and, disappointed, sigh'd
For joys, she said, ' to her alone denied ; '
And she was ' sure her parents, if alive,
Would many comforts for their child con-
      trive : '
The gentle husband bade her name him one ;
' No—that,' she answer'd, ' should for her be
      done ;
How could she say what pleasures were
      around ?
But she was certain many might be found.'—
' Would she some sea-port, Weymouth,
      Scarborough, grace ? '—
' He knew she hated every watering-place : '—
' The town ? '—' What ! now 'twas empty,
      joyless, dull ? '
—' In winter ? '—' No ; she liked it worse
      when full.'
She talk'd of building—' Would she plan
      a room ? '—
' No ! she could live, as he desired, in gloom : '
' Call then our friends and neighbours : '—
      ' He might call,
And they might come and fill his ugly hall ;
A noisy vulgar set, he knew she scorn'd them
      all : '—
' Then might their two dear girls the time
      employ,
And their improvement yield a solid joy.'—
' Solid indeed ! and heavy—oh ! the bliss
Of teaching letters to a lisping Miss ! '—
' My dear, my gentle Dorothea, say,
Can I oblige you ? '—' You may go away.'

Twelve heavy years this patient soul
      sustain'd
This wasp's attacks, and then her praise
      obtain'd,
Graved on a marble tomb, where he at peace
      remain'd.
   Two daughters wept their loss ; the one
      a child
With a plain face, strong sense, and temper
      mild,
Who keenly felt the mother's angry taunt,
' Thou art the image of thy pious aunt : '
Long time had Lucy wept her slighted face,
And then began to smile at her disgrace.
   Her father's sister, who the world had seen
Near sixty years when Lucy saw sixteen,
Begg'd the plain girl : the gracious mother
      smiled,
And freely gave her grieved but passive child ;
And with her elder-born, the beauty bless'd,
This parent rested, if such minds can rest :
No miss her waxen babe could so admire,
Nurse with such care, or with such pride
      attire ;
They were companions meet, with equal mind,
Bless'd with one love, and to one point in-
      clined ;
Beauty to keep, adorn, increase, and guard,
Was their sole care, and had its full reward :
In rising splendor with the one it reign'd,
And in the other was by care sustain'd,
The daughter's charms increased, the parent's
      yet remain'd.
   Leave we these ladies to their daily care,
To see how meekness and discretion fare :—
A village maid, unvex'd by want or love,
Could not with more delight than Lucy
      move ;
The village-lark, high mounted in the spring,
Could not with purer joy than Lucy sing ;
Her cares all light, her pleasures all sincere,
Her duty joy, and her companion dear ;
In tender friendship and in true respect
Lived aunt and niece, no flattery, no neglect—
They read, walk'd, visited—together pray'd,
Together slept the matron and the maid :
There was such goodness, such pure nature
      seen
In Lucy's looks, a manner so serene ;
Such harmony in motion, speech, and air,
That without fairness she was more than fair :
Had more than beauty in each speaking grace,
That lent their cloudless glory to the face ;

Where mild good sense in placid looks were
   shown,
And felt in every bosom but her own.
The one presiding feature in her mind,
Was the pure meekness of a will resign'd ;
A tender spirit, freed from all pretence
Of wit, and pleased in mild benevolence ;
Bless'd in protecting fondness she reposed,
With every wish indulged though undisclosed;
But love, like zephyr on the limpid lake,
Was now the bosom of the maid to shake,
And in that gentle mind a gentle strife to
   make.
   Among their chosen friends a favour'd few,
The aunt and niece a youthful rector knew ;
Who, though a younger brother, might address
A younger sister, fearless of success :
His friends, a lofty race, their native pride
At first display'd, and their assent denied ;
But, pleased such virtues and such love to
   trace,
They own'd she would adorn the loftiest race.
The aunt, a mother's caution to supply,
Had watch'd the youthful priest with jealous
   eye ;
And, anxious for her charge, had view'd
   unseen
The cautious life that keeps the conscience
   clean :
In all she found him all she wish'd to find,
With slight exception of a lofty mind :
A certain manner that express'd desire,
To be received as brother to the 'squire.
Lucy's meek eye had beam'd with many a tear,
Lucy's soft heart had beat with many a fear,
Before he told (although his looks, she thought,
Had oft confess'd) that he her favour sought :
But when he kneel'd, (she wish'd him not to
   kneel,)
And spoke the fears and hopes that lovers
   feel ;
When too the prudent aunt herself confess'd,
Her wishes on the gentle youth would rest ;
The maiden's eye with tender passion beam'd,
She dwelt with fondness on the life she
   schemed ;
The household cares, the soft and lasting ties
Of love, with all his binding charities ;
Their village taught, consoled, assisted, fed,
Till the young zealot tears of pleasure shed.
   But would her mother ? Ah ! she fear'd
   it wrong
To have indulged these forward hopes so long;

Her mother loved, but was not used to grant
Favours so freely as her gentle aunt.—
Her gentle aunt, with smiles that angels wear,
Dispell'd her Lucy's apprehensive tear :
Her prudent foresight the request had made
To one whom none could govern, few per-
   suade ;
She doubted much if one in earnest woo'd
A girl with not a single charm endued ;
The sister's nobler views she then declared,
And what small sum for Lucy could be spared;
' If more than this the foolish priest requires,
Tell him,' she wrote, ' to check his vain
   desires.'
At length, with many a cold expression mix'd,
With many a sneer on girls so fondly fix'd,
There came a promise—should they not
   repent,
But take with grateful minds the portion
   meant,
And wait the sister's day—the mother might
   consent.
   And here, might pitying hope o'er truth
   prevail,
Or love o'er fortune, we would end our tale :
For who more bless'd than youthful pair
   removed
From fear of want—by mutual friends
   approved—
Short time to wait, and in that time to live
With all the pleasures hope and fancy give ;
Their equal passion raised on just esteem,
When reason sanctions all that love can
   dream ?
   Yes ! reason sanctions what stern fate
   denies :
The early prospect in the glory dies,
As the soft smiles on dying infants play
In their mild features, and then pass away.
   The beauty died, ere she could yield her
   hand
In the high marriage by the mother plann'd:
Who grieved indeed, but found a vast relief
In a cold heart, that ever warr'd with grief.
   Lucy was present when her sister died,
Heiress to duties that she ill supplied :
There were no mutual feelings, sister arts,
No kindred taste, nor intercourse of hearts
When in the mirror play'd the matron's smile,
The maiden's thoughts were trav'lling all the
   while ;
And when desired to speak, she sigh'd to find
Her pause offended ; ' Envy made her blind :

Tasteless she was, nor had a claim in life
Above the station of a rector's wife ;
Yet as an heiress, she must shun disgrace,
Although no heiress to her mother's face :
It is your duty,' said th' imperious dame,
'(Advanced your fortune) to advance your
    name,
And with superior rank, superior offers claim:
Your sister's lover, when his sorrows die,
May look upon you, and for favour sigh ;
Nor can you offer a reluctant hand ;
His birth is noble, and his seat is grand.'
  Alarm'd was Lucy, was in tears—' A fool !
Was she a child in love ?—a miss at school ?
Doubts any mortal, if a change of state
Dissolves all claims and ties of earlier date ? '
  The rector doubted, for he came to mourn
A sister dead, and with a wife return :
Lucy with heart unchanged received the
    youth,
True in herself, confiding in his truth ;
But own'd her mother's change : the haughty
    dame
Pour'd strong contempt upon the youthful
    flame ;
She firmly vow'd her purpose to pursue,
Judged her own cause, and bade the youth
    adieu !
The lover begg'd, insisted, urged his pain
His brother wrote to threaten and complain,
Her sister reasoning proved the promise made,
Lucy appealing to a parent pray'd ;
But all opposed th' event that she design'd,
And all in vain—she never changed her mind ;
But coldly answer'd in her wonted way,
That she ' would rule, and Lucy must obey.'
  With peevish fear, she saw her health
    decline,
And cried, ' Oh ! monstrous, for a man to
    pine ;
But if your foolish heart must yield to love,
Let him possess it whom I now approve;
This is my pleasure : '—Still the rector came
With larger offers and with bolder claim ;
But the stern lady would attend no more—
She frown'd, and rudely pointed to the door ;
Whate'er he wrote, he saw unread return'd,
And he, indignant, the dishonour spurn'd ;
Nay, fix'd suspicion where he might confide,
And sacrificed his passion to his pride.
  Lucy, meantime, though threaten'd and
    distress'd,
Against her marriage made a strong protest :

All was domestic war : the aunt rebell'd
Against the sovereign will, and was expell'd ;
And every power was tried and every art,
To bend to falsehood one determined heart ;
Assail'd, in patience it received the shock,
Soft as the wave, unshaken as the rock :
But while th' unconquer'd soul endures the
    storm
Of angry fate, it preys upon the form ;
With conscious virtue she resisted still,
And conscious love gave vigour to her will :
But Lucy's trial was at hand ; with joy
The mother cried—' Behold your constant
    boy—
Thursday—was married :—take the paper,
    sweet,
And read the conduct of your reverend cheat ;
See with what pomp of coaches, in what crowd
The creature married—of his falsehood proud!
False, did I say ?—at least no whining fool ;
And thus will hopeless passions ever cool :
But shall his bride your single state reproach ?
No ! give him crowd for crowd, and coach
    for coach.
Oh ! you retire ; reflect then, gentle miss,
And gain some spirit in a cause like this.'
  Some spirit Lucy gain'd ; a steady soul,
Defying all persuasion, all control :
In vain reproach, derision, threats were tried ;
The constant mind all outward force defied,
By vengeance vainly urged, in vain assail'd
    by pride :
Fix'd in her purpose, perfect in her part,
She felt the courage of a wounded heart ;
The world receded from her rising view,
When Heaven approach'd as earthly things
    withdrew ;
Not strange before, for in the days of love,
Joy, hope, and pleasure, she had thoughts
    above ;
Pious when most of worldly prospects fond,
When they best pleased her she could look
    beyond :
Had the young priest a faithful lover died,
Something had been her bosom to divide :
Now Heaven had all, for in her holiest views
She saw the matron whom she fear'd to lose;
While from her parent, the dejected maid
Forced the unpleasant thought, or thinking
    pray'd.
  Surprised, the mother saw the languid
    frame,
And felt indignant, yet forbore to blame :

Once with a frown she cried, ' And do you
    mean
To die of love—the folly of fifteen ? '
But as her anger met with no reply,
She let the gentle girl in quiet die ;
And to her sister wrote, impell'd by pain,
' Come quickly, Martha, or you come in vain.'
Lucy meantime profess'd with joy sincere,
That nothing held, employ'd, engaged her
    here.
   ' I am an humble actor, doom'd to play
A part obscure, and then to glide away ;
Incurious how the great or happy shine,
Or who have parts obscure and sad as mine ;
In its best prospect I but wish'd, for life,
To be th' assiduous, gentle, useful wife ;
That lost, with wearied mind, and spirit poor,
I drop my efforts, and can act no more ;
With growing joy I feel my spirits tend
To that last scene where all my duties end.'
  Hope, ease, delight, the thoughts of dying
    gave,
Till Lucy spoke with fondness of the grave ;
She smiled with wasted form, but spirit firm,
And said, ' She left but little for the worm : '
As toll'd the bell, ' There 's one,' she said,
   ' hath press'd
Awhile before me to the bed of rest ; '
And she beside her with attention spread
The decorations of the maiden dead.
  While quickly thus the mortal part de-
    clined,
The happiest visions fill'd the active mind ;
A soft, religious melancholy gain'd
Entire possession, and for ever reign'd :
On holy writ her mind reposing dwelt,
She saw the wonders, she the mercies felt ;
Till in a bless'd and glorious reverie,
She seem'd the Saviour as on earth to see,
And, fill'd with love divine, th' attending
    friend to be ;
Or she who trembling, yet confiding, stole
Near to the garment, touch'd it, and was
    whole ;
When, such th' intenseness of the working
    thought,
On her it seem'd the very deed was wrought ;
She the glad patient's fear and rapture found,
The holy transport, and the healing wound ;
This was so fix'd, so grafted in the heart,
That she adopted, nay became the part :

But one chief scene was present to her sight,
Her Saviour resting in the tomb by night ;
Her fever rose, and still her wedded mind
Was to that scene, that hallow'd cave, con-
    fined—
Where in the shade of death the body laid,
There watch'd the spirit of the wandering
    maid ;
Her looks were fix'd, entranced, illumed,
    serene,
In the still glory of the midnight scene :
There at her Saviour's feet, in visions bless'd,
Th' enraptured maid a sacred joy possess'd ;
In patience waiting for the first-born ray
Of that all-glorious and triumphant day :
To this idea all her soul she gave,
Her mind reposing by the sacred grave ;
Then sleep would seal the eye, the vision close,
And steep the solemn thoughts in brief repose.
  Then grew the soul serene, and all its powers
Again restored illumed the dying hours ;
But reason dwelt where fancy stray'd before,
And the mind wander'd from its views no
    more ;
Till death approach'd, when every look
    express'd
A sense of bliss, till every sense had rest.
  The mother lives, and has enough to buy
Th' attentive ear and the submissive eye
Of abject natures—these are daily told,
How triumph'd beauty in the days of old ;
How, by her window seated, crowds have
    cast
Admiring glances, wondering as they pass'd ;
How from her carriage as she stepp'd to pray,
Divided ranks would humbly make her way ;
And how each voice in the astonish'd throng
Pronounced her peerless as she moved along.
  Her picture then the greedy dame displays ;
Touch'd by no shame, she now demands its
    praise ;
In her tall mirror then she shows a face,
Still coldly fair with unaffecting grace ;
These she compares, ' It has the form,' she
    cries,
' But wants the air, the spirit, and the eyes ;
This, as a likeness, is correct and true,
But there alone the living grace we view.'
This said, th' applauding voice the dame
    required,
And, gazing, slowly from the glass retired.

TALE IX. ARABELLA

Thrice blessed they that master so their blood—

. . . . .

But earthlier happy is the rose distill'd,
Than that which, withering on the virgin thorn,
Grows, lives, and dies in single blessedness.
Midsummer Night's Dream, Act i, Scene 1.

I something do excuse the thing I hate,
For his advantage whom I dearly love.
Measure for Measure, Act ii, Scene 4.

Contempt, farewell! and maiden pride, adieu!
Much Ado about Nothing, Act iii, Scene 1.

———

Of a fair town where Doctor Rack was guide,
His only daughter was the boast and pride;
Wise Arabella, yet not wise alone,
She like a bright and polish'd brilliant shone;
Her father own'd her for his prop and stay,
Able to guide, yet willing to obey;
Pleased with her learning while discourse could please,
And with her love in languor and disease:
To every mother were her virtues known,
And to their daughters as a pattern shown;
Who in her youth had all that age requires,
And with her prudence, all that youth admires:
These odious praises made the damsels try
Not to obtain such merits, but deny;
For, whatsoever wise mammas might say,
To guide a daughter, this was not the way;
From such applause disdain and anger rise,
And envy lives where emulation dies.
In all his strength, contends the noble horse,
With one who just precedes him on the course;
But when the rival flies too far before,
His spirit fails, and he attempts no more.

This reasoning maid, above her sex's dread,
Had dared to read, and dared to say she read;
Not the last novel, not the new-born play;
Not the mere trash and scandal of the day;
But (though her young companions felt the shock)
She studied Berkeley, Bacon, Hobbes, and Locke:
Her mind within the maze of history dwelt,
And of the moral muse the beauty felt;
The merits of the Roman page she knew,
And could converse with Moore and Montagu:

Thus she became the wonder of the town,
From that she reap'd, to that she gave renown,
And strangers coming, all were taught t' admire
The learned lady, and the lofty spire.

Thus fame in public fix'd the maid, where all
Might throw their darts, and see the idol fall;
A hundred arrows came with vengeance keen,
From tongues envenom'd, and from arms unseen;
A thousand eyes were fix'd upon the place,
That, if she fell, she might not fly disgrace:
But malice vainly throws the poison'd dart,
Unless our frailty shows the peccant part;
And Arabella still preserved her name
Untouch'd, and shone with undisputed fame;
Her very notice some respect would cause,
And her esteem was honour and applause.

Men she avoided; not in childish fear,
As if she thought some savage foe was near;
Not as a prude, who hides that man should seek,
Or who by silence hints that they should speak;
But with discretion all the sex she view'd,
Ere yet engaged, pursuing, or pursued;
Ere love had made her to his vices blind,
Or hid the favourite's failings from her mind,
Thus was the picture of the man portray'd,
By merit destined for so rare a maid;
At whose request she might exchange her state,
Or still be happy in a virgin's fate.

He must be one with manners like her own,
His life unquestion'd, his opinions known;
His stainless virtue must all tests endure,
His honour spotless, and his bosom pure;
She no allowance made for sex or times,
Of lax opinion—crimes were ever crimes;
No wretch forsaken must his frailty curse,
No spurious offspring drain his private purse:
He at all times his passions must command,
And yet possess—or be refused her hand.

All this without reserve the maiden told,
And some began to weigh the rector's gold;
To ask what sum a prudent man might gain,
Who had such store of virtues to maintain?

A Doctor Campbell, north of Tweed, came
      forth,
Declared his passion, and proclaim'd his
      worth :
Not unapproved, for he had much to say
On every cause, and in a pleasant way ;
Not all his trust was in a pliant tongue,
His form was good, and ruddy he, and young :
But though the Doctor was a man of parts,
He read not deeply male or female hearts ;
But judged that all whom he esteem'd as wise
Must think alike, though some assumed
      disguise ;
That every reasoning Bramin, Christian, Jew,
Of all religions took their liberal view ;
And of her own, no doubt, this learned maid
Denied the substance, and the forms obey'd ;
And thus persuaded, he his thoughts express'd
Of her opinions, and his own profess'd :
' All states demand this aid, the vulgar need
Their priests and pray'rs, their sermons and
      their creed ;
And those of stronger minds should never
      speak
(In his opinion) what might hurt the weak :
A man may smile, but still he should attend
His hour at church, and be the church's friend,
What there he thinks conceal, and what he
      hears commend.'
Frank was the speech, but heard with high
      disdain,
Nor had the Doctor leave to speak again ;
A man who own'd, nay gloried in deceit,
' He might despise her, but he should not
      cheat.'
      Then Vicar Holmes appear'd ; he heard it
      said
That ancient men best pleased the prudent
      maid ;
And true it was her ancient friends she loved,
Servants when old she favour'd and approved;
Age in her pious parents she revered,
And neighbours were by length of days
      endear'd ;
But, if her husband too must ancient be,
The good old Vicar found it was not he.
      On Captain Bligh her mind in balance
      hung—
Though valiant, modest ; and reserved,
      though young :
Against these merits must defects be set—
Though poor, imprudent ; and though proud,
      in debt

In vain the Captain close attention paid ;
She found him wanting, whom she fairly
      weigh'd.
      Then came a youth, and all their friends
      agreed,
That Edward Huntly was the man indeed ;
Respectful duty he had paid awhile,
Then ask'd her hand, and had a gracious
      smile :
A lover now declared, he led the fair
To woods and fields, to visits and to pray'r;
Then whisper'd softly—' Will you name the
      day ? '
She softly whisper'd—' If you love me, stay : '
' Oh ! try me not beyond my strength,' he
      cried :
' Oh ! be not weak,' the prudent maid replied ;
' But by some trial your affection prove—
Respect and not impatience argues love :
And love no more is by impatience known,
Than Ocean's depth is by its tempests shown :
He whom a weak and fond impatience sways,
But for himself with all his fervour prays,
And not the maid he woos, but his own will
      obeys ;
And will she love the being who prefers,
With so much ardour, his desire to hers ? '
      Young Edward grieved, but let not grief
      be seen :
He knew obedience pleased his fancy's queen :
Awhile he waited, and then cried—' Behold !
The year advancing, be no longer cold ! '
For she had promised—' Let the flowers
      appear,
And I will pass with thee the smiling year :
Then pressing grew the youth ; the more he
      press'd,
The less inclined the maid to his request :
' Let June arrive.'—Alas ! when April came,
It brought a stranger, and the stranger,
      shame ;
Nor could the lover from his house persuade
A stubborn lass whom he had mournful made;
Angry and weak, by thoughtless vengeance
      moved,
She told her story to the fair beloved ;
In strongest words th' unwelcome truth was
      shown,
To blight his prospects, careless of her own.
      Our heroine grieved, but had too firm a heart
For him to soften, when she swore to part ;
In vain his seeming penitence and pray'r,
His vows, his tears ; she left him in despair:

His mother fondly laid her grief aside,
And to the reason of the nymph applied—
   ' It well becomes thee, lady, to appear,
But not to be, in very truth, severe ;
Although the crime be odious in thy sight,
That daring sex is taught such things to slight:
His heart is thine, although it once was frail ;
Think of his grief, and let his love prevail !— '
   ' Plead thou no more,' the lofty lass
      return'd ;
' Forgiving woman is deceived and spurn'd :
Say that the crime is common—shall I take
A common man my wedded lord to make ?
See ! a weak woman by his arts betray'd,
An infant born his father to upbraid ;
Shall I forgive his vileness, take his name,
Sanction his error, and partake his shame ?
No ! this assent would kindred frailty prove,
A love for him would be a vicious love :
Can a chaste maiden secret counsel hold
With one whose crime by every mouth is told?
Forbid it spirit, prudence, virtuous pride ;
He must despise me, were he not denied :
The way from vice the erring mind to win
Is with presuming sinners to begin,
And show, by scorning them, a just contempt
      for sin.'
   The youth repulsed, to one more mild
      convey'd
His heart, and smiled on the remorseless maid;
The maid, remorseless in her pride, the while
Despised the insult, and return'd the smile.
   First to admire, to praise her, and defend,
Was (now in years advanced) a virgin friend :
Much she preferr'd, she cried, a single state,
' It was her choice '—it surely was her fate ;
And much it pleased her in the train to view
A maiden vot'ress, wise and lovely too.
   Time to the yielding mind his change im-
      parts,
He varies notions, and he alters hearts ;
'Tis right, 'tis just to feel contempt for vice,
But he that shows it may be over-nice :
There are who feel, when young, the false
      sublime.
And proudly love to show disdain for crime ;
To whom the future will new thoughts supply,
The pride will soften, and the scorn will die ;
Nay, where they still the vice itself condemn,
They bear the vicious, and consort with them:
Young Captain Grove, when one had changed
      his side,
Despised the venal turn-coat, and defied ;

Old Colonel Grove now shakes him by the
      hand,
Though he who bribes may still his vote
      command :
Why would not Ellen to Belinda speak,
When she had flown to London for a week ;
And then return'd, to every friend's surprise,
With twice the spirit, and with half the size ?
She spoke not then—but after years had
      flown,
A better friend had Ellen never known :
Was it the lady her mistake had seen ?
Or had she also such a journey been ?
No : 'twas the gradual change in human
      hearts,
That time, in commerce with the world,
      imparts ;
That on the roughest temper throws disguise,
And steals from virtue her asperities.
The young and ardent, who with glowing zeal
Felt wrath for trifles, and were proud to feel,
Now find those trifles all the mind engage,
To soothe dull hours, and cheat the cares of
      age ;
As young Zelinda, in her quaker-dress,
Disdain'd each varying fashion's vile excess,
And now her friends on old Zelinda gaze,
Pleased in rich silks and orient gems to blaze :
Changes like these tis' folly to condemn,
So virtue yields not, nor is changed with them.
   Let us proceed :—Twelve brilliant years
      were past,
Yet each with less of glory than the last ;
Whether these years to this fair virgin gave
A softer mind—effect they often have ;
Whether the virgin-state was not so bless'd
As that good maiden in her zeal profess'd ;
Or whether lovers falling from her train,
Gave greater price to those she could retain,
Is all unknown ;—but Arabella now
Was kindly listening to a merchant's vow ;
Who offer'd terms so fair, against his love
To strive was folly, so she never strove.—
Man in his earlier days we often find
With a too easy and unguarded mind ;
But by increasing years and prudence taught,
He grows reserved, and locks up every
      thought :
Not thus the maiden, for in blooming youth
She hides her thought, and guards the tender
      truth :
This, when no longer young, no more she hides,
But frankly in the favour'd swain confides :

TALE XI. EDWARD SHORE

Seem they grave and learned ?
Why, so didst thou. . . Seem they religious ?
Why, so didst thou ; or are they spare in diet,
Free from gross passion, or of mirth or anger,
Constant in spirit, not swerving with the
blood,
Garnish'd and deck'd in modest complement,
Not working with the eye without the ear,
And but in purged judgment trusting neither
Such and so finely bolted didst thou seem.
Henry V, Act ii, Scene 2.

Better I were distract,
So should my thoughts be sever'd from my
griefs,
And woes by wrong imaginations lose
The knowledge of themselves.
King Lear, Act iv, Scene 6.

Genius ! thou gift of Heav'n ! thou light
divine !
Amid what dangers art thou doom'd to shine !
Oft will the body's weakness check thy force,
Oft damp thy vigour, and impede thy course ;
And trembling nerves compel thee to restrain
Thy nobler efforts, to contend with pain ;
Or Want (sad guest !) will in thy presence
come,
And breathe around her melancholy gloom ;
To life's low cares will thy proud thought
confine,
And make her sufferings, her impatience,
thine.
Evil and strong, seducing passions prey
On soaring minds, and win them from their
way ;
Who then to vice the subject spirits give,
And in the service of the conqu'ror live ;
Like captive Samson making sport for all,
Who fear'd their strength, and glory in their
fall.
Genius, with virtue, still may lack the aid
Implored by humbler minds and hearts
afraid ;
May leave to timid souls the shield and sword
Of the tried faith, and the resistless word ;
Amid a world of dangers venturing forth,
Frail, but yet fearless, proud in conscious
worth,
Till strong temptation, in some fatal time,
Assails the heart, and wins the soul to crime ;

When left by honour, and by sorrow spent,
Unused to pray, unable to repent,
The nobler powers that once exalted high
Th' aspiring man, shall then degraded lie :
Reason, through anguish, shall her throne
forsake,
And strength of mind but stronger madness
make.
When Edward Shore had reach'd his
twentieth year,
He felt his bosom light, his conscience clear ;
Applause at school the youthful hero gain'd,
And trials there with manly strength sus-
tain'd :
With prospects bright upon the world he
came,
Pure love of virtue, strong desire of fame :
Men watch'd the way his lofty mind would
take,
And all foretold the progress he would make.
Boast of these friends, to older men a guide,
Proud of his parts, but gracious in his pride ;
He bore a gay good-nature in his face,
And in his air were dignity and grace ;
Dress that became his state and years he wore,
And sense and spirit shone in Edward Shore.
Thus while admiring friends the youth
beheld,
His own disgust their forward hopes repell'd ;
For he unfix'd, unfixing, look'd around,
And no employment but in seeking found ;
He gave his restless thoughts to views refined,
And shrank from worldly cares with wounded
mind.
Rejecting trade, awhile he dwelt on laws,
' But who could plead, if unapproved the
cause ? '
A doubting, dismal tribe physicians seem'd ;
Divines o'er texts and disputations dream'd ;
War and its glory he perhaps could love,
But there again he must the cause approve.
Our hero thought no deed should gain
applause,
Where timid virtue found support in laws ;
He to all good would soar, would fly all sin,
By the pure prompting of the will within ;
' Who needs a law that binds him not to
steal,'
Ask'd the young teacher, ' can he rightly feel ?

To curb the will, or arm in honour's cause,
Or aid the weak—are these enforced by laws ?
Should we a foul, ungenerous action dread,
Because a law condemns th' adulterous bed ?
Or fly pollution, not for fear of stain,
But that some statute tells us to refrain ?
The grosser herd in ties like these we bind,
In virtue's freedom moves th' enlighten'd
        mind.'
    ' Man's heart deceives him,' said a friend :
    ' Of course,'
Replied the youth, ' but, has it power to force?
Unless it forces, call it as you will,
It is but wish, and proneness to the ill.'
    ' Art thou not tempted ? ' ' Do I fall ? '
        said Shore :
' The pure have fallen.'—' Then are pure no
    more :
While reason guides me, I shall walk aright,
Nor need a steadier hand, or stronger light ;
Nor this in dread of awful threats, design'd
For the weak spirit and the grov'ling mind ;
But that, engaged by thoughts and views
        sublime,
I wage free war with grossness and with
        crime.'
Thus look'd he proudly on the vulgar crew,
Whom statutes govern, and whom fears sub-
    due.
    Faith, with his virtue, he indeed profess'd,
But doubts deprived his ardent mind of
    rest ;
Reason, his sovereign mistress, failed to show
Light through the mazes of the world below ;
Questions arose, and they surpass'd the skill
Of his sole aid, and would be dubious still ;
These to discuss he sought no common guide,
But to the doubters in his doubts applied ;
When all together might in freedom speak,
And their loved truth with mutual ardour
    seek.
Alas ! though men who feel their eyes decay
Take more than common pains to find their
        way,
Yet, when for this they ask each other's aid,
Their mutual purpose is the more delay'd :
Of all their doubts, their reasoning clear'd not
    one,
Still the same spots were present in the sun ;
Still the same scruples haunted Edward's
    mind,
Who found no rest, nor took the means to
    find.

    But though with shaken faith, and slave
        to fame,
Vain and aspiring on the world he came ;
Yet was he studious, serious, moral, grave,
No passion's victim, and no system's slave ;
Vice he opposed, indulgence he disdained,
And o'er each sense in conscious triumph
        reign'd.
    Who often reads, will sometimes wish to
        write,
And Shore would yield instruction and
        delight :
A serious drama he design'd, but found
'Twas tedious travelling in that gloomy
        ground ;
A deep and solemn story he would try,
But grew ashamed of ghosts, and laid it by ;
Sermons he wrote, but they who knew his
        creed,
Or knew it not, were ill disposed to read ;
And he would lastly be the nation's guide,
But, studying, fail'd to fix upon a side ;
Fame he desired, and talents he possess'd,
But loved not labour, though he could not
        rest,
Nor firmly fix the vacillating mind,
That, ever working, could no centre find.
    'Tis thus a sanguine reader loves to trace
The Nile forth rushing on his glorious race ;
Calm and secure the fancied traveller goes
Through sterile deserts and by threat'ning
        foes ;
He thinks not then of Afric's scorching sands,
Th' Arabian sea, the Abyssinian bands ;
Fasils * and Michaels, and the robbers all,
Whom we politely chiefs and heroes call :
He of success alone delights to think,
He views that fount, he stands upon the
        brink,
And drinks a fancied draught, exulting so to
        drink.
    In his own room, and with his books around,
His lively mind its chief employment found ;
Then idly busy, quietly employ'd,
And, lost to life, his visions were enjoy'd :

    * Fasil was a rebel chief, and Michael the
general of the royal army in Abyssinia, when
Mr. Bruce visited that country. In all other re-
spects their characters were nearly similar. They
are both represented as cruel and treacherous ;
and even the apparently strong distinction of
loyal and rebellious is in a great measure set
aside, when we are informed that Fasil was an
open enemy, and Michael an insolent and am-
bitious controller of the royal person and family.

Yet still he took a keen inquiring view
Of all that crowds neglect, desire, pursue ;
And thus abstracted, curious, still, serene,
He, unemploy'd, beheld life's shifting scene ;
Still more averse from vulgar joys and cares,
Still more unfitted for the world's affairs.

There was a house where Edward ofttimes
    went,
And social hours in pleasant trifling spent ;
He read, conversed and reason'd, sang and
    play'd,
And all were happy while the idler stay'd ;
Too happy one, for thence arose the pain,
Till this engaging trifler came again.

But did he love ?   We answer, day by day,
The loving feet would take th' accustom'd
    way,
The amorous eye would rove as if in quest
Of something rare, and on the mansion rest ;
The same soft passion touch'd the gentle
    tongue,
And Anna's charms in tender notes were
    sung ;
The ear too seem'd to feel the common flame,
Sooth'd and delighted with the fair one's
    name ;
And thus as love each other part possess'd,
The heart, no doubt, its sovereign power
    confessed.

Pleased in her sight, the youth required no
    more ;
Not rich himself, he saw the damsel poor ;
And he too wisely, nay, too kindly loved,
To pain the being whom his soul approved.

A serious friend our cautious youth pos-
    sess'd,
And at his table sat a welcome guest ;
Both unemploy'd, it was their chief delight
To read what free and daring authors write ;
Authors who loved from common views to soar,
And seek the fountains never traced before ;
Truth they profess'd, yet often left the true
And beaten prospect, for the wild and new.
His chosen friend his fiftieth year had seen,
His fortune easy, and his air serene ;
Deist and atheist call'd ; for few agreed
What were his notions, principles, or creed ;
His mind reposed not, for he hated rest,
But all things made a query or a jest ;
Perplex'd himself, he ever sought to prove
That man is doom'd in endless doubt to rove ;
Himself in darkness he profess'd to be,
And would maintain that not a man could see.

The youthful friend, dissentient, reason'd
    still
Of the soul's prowess, and the subject will ;
Of virtue's beauty, and of honour's force,
And a warm zeal gave life to his discourse :
Since from his feelings all his fire arose
And he had interest in the themes he chose.

The friend, indulging a sarcastic smile,
Said—' Dear enthusiast ! thou wilt change
    thy style,
When man's delusions, errors, crimes, deceit,
No more distress thee, and no longer cheat.

Yet lo ! this cautious man, so coolly wise,
On a young beauty fix'd unguarded eyes ;
And her he married : Edward at the view
Bade to his cheerful visits long adieu ;
But haply err'd, for this engaging bride
No mirth suppress'd, but other cause sup-
    plied :
And when she saw the friends, by reasoning
    long,
Confused if right, and positive if wrong.
With playful speech and smile, that spoke
    delight,
She made them careless both of wrong and
    right.

This gentle damsel gave consent to wed,
With school and school-day dinners in her
    head :
She now was promised choice of daintiest
    food,
And costly dress, that made her sovereign
    good ;
With walks on hilly heath to banish spleen,
And summer-visits when the roads were lean.
All these she loved, to these she gave consent,
And she was married to her heart's content.

Their manner this—the friends together
    read,
Till books a cause for disputation bred ;
Debate then follow'd, and the vapour'd child
Declared they argued till her head was wild ;
And strange to her it was that mortal brain
Could seek the trial, or endure the pain.

Then as the friend reposed, the younger
    pair
Sat down to cards, and play'd beside his chair
Till he awaking, to his books applied,
Or heard the music of th' obedient bride :
If mild the evening, in the fields they stray'd,
And their own flock with partial eye survey'd ;
But oft the husband, to indulgence prone,
Resumed his book, and bade them walk alone.

' Do, my kind Edward ! I must take mine ease,
Name the dear girl the planets and the trees ;
Tell her what warblers pour their evening song,
What insects flutter, as you walk along ;
Teach her to fix the roving thoughts, to bind
The wandering sense, and methodize the mind.'
    This was obey'd ; and oft when this was done,
They calmly gazed on the declining sun ;
In silence saw the glowing landscape fade,
Or, sitting, sang beneath the arbour's shade :
Till rose the moon, and on each youthful face
Shed a soft beauty, and a dangerous grace.
    When the young wife beheld in long debate
The friends, all careless as she seeming sate ;
It soon appear'd, there was in one combined
The nobler person and the richer mind :
He wore no wig, no grisly beard was seen,
And none beheld him careless or unclean ;
Or watch'd him sleeping :—we indeed have heard
Of sleeping beauty, and it has appear'd ;
'Tis seen in infants—there indeed we find
The features soften'd by the slumbering mind ;
But other beauties, when disposed to sleep,
Should from the eye of keen inspector keep :
The lovely nymph who would her swain surprise,
May close her mouth, but not conceal her eyes ;
Sleep from the fairest face some beauty takes,
And all the homely features homelier makes ;
So thought our wife, beholding with a sigh
Her sleeping spouse, and Edward smiling by.
    A sick relation for the husband sent,
Without delay the friendly sceptic went ;
Nor fear'd the youthful pair, for he had seen
The wife untroubled, and the friend serene :
No selfish purpose in his roving eyes,
No vile deception in her fond replies :
So judged the husband, and with judgment true,
For neither yet the guilt or danger knew.
    What now remain'd ? but they again should play
Th' accustom'd game, and walk th' accustom'd way ;

With careless freedom should converse or read,
And the friend's absence neither fear nor heed :
But rather now they seem'd confused, constrain'd ;
Within their room still restless they remain'd,
And painfully they felt, and knew each other pain'd.—
Ah ! foolish men ! how could ye thus depend,
One on himself, the other on his friend ?
    The youth with troubled eye the lady saw,
Yet felt too brave, too daring to withdraw ;
While she, with tuneless hand the jarring keys
Touching, was not one moment at her ease :
Now would she walk, and call her friendly guide,
Now speak of rain and cast her cloak aside ;
Seize on a book, unconscious what she read,
And restless still, to new resources fled ;
Then laugh'd aloud, then tried to look serene,
And ever changed, and every change was seen.
    Painful it is to dwell on deeds of shame—
The trying day was past, another came ;
The third was all remorse, confusion, dread,
And (all too late !) the fallen hero fled.
    Then felt the youth, in that seducing time,
How feebly honour guards the heart from crime :
Small is his native strength ; man needs the stay,
The strength imparted in the trying day ;
For all that honour brings against the force
Of headlong passion, aids its rapid course ;
Its slight resistance but provokes the fire,
As wood-work stops the flame, and then conveys it higher.
    The husband came ; a wife by guilt made bold
Had, meeting, sooth'd him, as in days of old ;
But soon this fact transpired ; her strong distress,
And his friend's absence, left him nought to guess.
    Still cool, though grieved, thus prudence bade him write—
' I cannot pardon, and I will not fight ;
Thou art too poor a culprit for the laws,
And I too faulty to support my cause :
All must be punish'd ; I must sigh alone,
At home thy victim for her guilt atone ;

And thou, unhappy! virtuous now no more,
Must loss of fame, peace, purity deplore;
Sinners with praise will pierce thee to the
    heart,
And saints deriding, tell thee what thou art.'
    Such was his fall; and Edward, from that
        time,
Felt in full force the censure and the crime—
Despised, ashamed; his noble views before,
And his proud thoughts, degraded him the
    more:
Should he repent—would that conceal his
    shame?
Could peace be his? It perish'd with his
    fame:
Himself he scorn'd, nor could his crime for-
    give;
He fear'd to die, yet felt ashamed to live:
Grieved, but not contrite was his heart;
    oppress'd,
Not broken; not converted, but distress'd;
He wanted will to bend the stubborn knee,
He wanted light the cause of ill to see,
To learn how frail is man, how humble then
    should be;
For faith he had not, or a faith too weak
To gain the help that humbled sinners seek;
Else had he pray'd—to an offended God
His tears had flown a penitential flood
Though far astray, he would have heard the
    call
Of mercy—' Come! return, thou prodigal;'
Then, though confused, distress'd, ashamed,
    afraid,
Still had the trembling penitent obey'd;
Though faith had fainted, when assail'd by
    fear,
Hope to the soul had whisper'd, ' Persevere!'
Till in his Father's house an humbled guest,
He would have found forgiveness, comfort,
    rest.
    But all this joy was to our youth denied
By his fierce passions and his daring pride;
And shame and doubt impell'd him in a
    course,
Once so abhorr'd, with unresisted force.
Proud minds and guilty, whom their crimes
    oppress,
Fly to new crimes for comfort and redress;
So found our fallen youth a short relief
In wine, the opiate guilt applies to grief,—
From fleeting mirth that o'er the bottle lives,
From the false joy its inspiration gives;

And from associates pleased to find a friend,
With powers to lead them, gladden, and
    defend,
In all those scenes where transient ease is
    found,
For minds whom sins oppress, and sorrows
    wound.
    Wine is like anger; for it makes us strong,
Blind and impatient, and it leads us wrong;
The strength is quickly lost, we feel the error
    long:
Thus led, thus strengthen'd in an evil cause,
For folly pleading, sought the youth ap-
    plause;
Sad for a time, then eloquently wild,
He gaily spoke as his companions smiled;
Lightly he rose, and with his former grace
Proposed some doubt, and argued on the case;
Fate and fore-knowledge were his favourite
    themes—
How vain man's purpose, how absurd his
    schemes:
' Whatever is, was ere our birth decreed;
We think our actions from ourselves proceed,
And idly we lament th' inevitable deed;
It seems our own, but there's a power above
Directs the motion, nay, that makes us move;
Nor good nor evil can you beings name,
Who are but rooks and castles in the game;
Superior natures with their puppets play,
Till, bagg'd or buried, all are swept away.'
    Such were the notions of a mind to ill
Now prone, but ardent, and determined still:
Of joy now eager, as before of fame,
And screen'd by folly when assail'd by shame,
Deeply he sank; obey'd each passion's call,
And used his reason to defend them all.
    Shall I proceed, and step by step relate
The odious progress of a sinner's fate?
No—let me rather hasten to the time
(Sure to arrive) when misery waits on crime.
    With virtue, prudence fled; what Shore
        possess'd
Was sold, was spent, and he was now dis-
    tress'd:
And Want, unwelcome stranger pale and
    wan,
Met with her haggard looks the hurried man;
His pride felt keenly what he must expect
From useless pity and from cold neglect.
    Struck by new terrors, from his friends he
        fled,
And wept his woes upon a restless bed;

Retiring late, at early hour to rise,
With shrunken features, and with bloodshot
　　eyes :
If sleep one moment closed the dismal view,
Fancy her terrors built upon the true ;
And night and day had their alternate
　　woes,
That baffled pleasure, and that mock'd re-
　　pose ;
Till to despair and anguish was consign'd
The wreck and ruin of a noble mind.

　Now seized for debt, and lodged within a jail,
He tried his friendships, and he found them
　　fail ;
Then fail'd his spirits, and his thoughts were
　　all
Fix'd on his sins, his sufferings, and his fall :
His ruffled mind was pictured in his face,
Once the fair seat of dignity and grace :
Great was the danger of a man so prone
To think of madness, and to think alone ;
Yet pride still lived, and struggled to sustain
The drooping spirit and the roving brain ;
But this too fail'd : a friend his freedom
　　gave,
And sent him help the threat'ning world to
　　brave ;
Gave solid counsel what to seek or flee,
But still would stranger to his person be :
In vain ! the truth determined to explore,
He traced the friend whom he had wrong'd
　　before.

　This was too much ; both aided and advised
By one who shunn'd him, pitied, and de-
　　spised ;
He bore it not ; 'twas a deciding stroke,
And on his reason like a torrent broke :
In dreadful stillness he appear'd awhile,
With vacant horror and a ghastly smile ;
Then rose at once into the frantic rage,
That force controll'd not, nor could love
　　assuage.

　Friends now appear'd, but in the man was
　　seen
The angry maniac, with vindictive mien ;
Too late their pity gave to care and skill
The hurried mind and ever-wandering will ;
Unnoticed pass'd all time, and not a ray
Of reason broke on his benighted way ;
But now he spurn'd the straw in pure disdain,
And now laughed loudly at the clinking chain.

　Then as its wrath subsided, by degrees
The mind sank slowly to infantine ease ;

To playful folly, and to causeless joy,
Speech without aim, and without end, em-
　　ploy ;
He drew fantastic figures on the wall,
And gave some wild relation of them all ;
With brutal shape he join'd the human face,
And idiot smiles approved the motley race.

　Harmless at length th' unhappy man was
　　found,
The spirit settled, but the reason drown'd ;
And all the dreadful tempest died away,
To the dull stillness of the misty day.

　And now his freedom he attain'd—if free,
The lost to reason, truth, and hope, can be ;
His friends, or wearied with the charge, or
　　sure
The harmless wretch was now beyond a cure,
Gave him to wander where he pleased, and
　　find
His own resources for the eager mind ;
The playful children of the place he meets,
Playful with them he rambles through the
　　streets ;
In all they need, his stronger arm he lends,
And his lost mind to these approving friends.

　That gentle maid, whom once the youth
　　had loved,
Is now with mild religious pity moved ;
Kindly she chides his boyish flights, while he
Will for a moment fix'd and pensive be ;
And as she trembling speaks, his lively eyes
Explore her looks, he listens to her sighs ;
Charm'd by her voice, th' harmonious sounds
　　invade
His clouded mind, and for a time persuade :
Like a pleased infant, who has newly caught
From the maternal glance a gleam of thought,
He stands enrapt, the half-known voice to
　　hear,
And starts, half-conscious, at the falling tear.

　Rarely from town, nor then unwatch'd, he
　　goes,
In darker mood, as if to hide his woes ;
Returning soon, he with impatience seeks
His youthful friends, and shouts, and sings,
　　and speaks ;
Speaks a wild speech with action all as wild—
The children's leader, and himself a child ;
He spins their top, or, at their bidding, bends
His back, while o'er it leap his laughing
　　friends ;
Simple and weak, he acts the boy once more,
And heedless children call him Silly Shore.

TALE XII. 'SQUIRE THOMAS; OR,
THE PRECIPITATE CHOICE

Such smiling rogues as these,
Like rats, oft bite the holy cords a-twain,
Which are too intrinse t' unloose—
              King Lear, Act ii, Scene 2.

My other self, my counsel's consistory,
My oracle, my prophet, . . .
I as a child will go by thy direction.
              Richard III, Act ii, Scene 2.

If I do not take pity of her, I am a villain ;
if I do not love her, I am a Jew.
  Much Ado about Nothing, Act ii, Scene 3.

Women are soft, mild, pitiful and flexible ;
Thou stern, obdurate, flinty, rough, remorse-
less.
          3 Henry VI, Act i, Scene 4.

He must be told on't, and he shall ; the office
Becomes a woman best; I'll take it upon
me ;
If I prove honey-mouth'd, let my tongue
blister.
          Winter's Tale, Act ii, Scene 2.

Disguise—I see thou art a wickedness.
          Twelfth Night, Act ii, Scene 2.

'SQUIRE THOMAS flatter'd long a wealthy aunt,
Who left him all that she could give or grant :
Ten years he tried, with all his craft and skill,
To fix the sovereign lady's varying will ;
Ten years enduring at her board to sit,
He meekly listen'd to her tales and wit ;
He took the meanest office man can take,
And his aunt's vices for her money's sake :
By many a threat'ning hint she waked his
fear,
And he was pain'd to see a rival near ;
Yet all the taunts of her contemptuous pride
He bore, nor found his grov'ling spirit tried :
Nay, when she wish'd his parents to traduce,
Fawning he smiled, and justice call'd
th' abuse ;
' They taught you nothing ; are you not, at
best,'
Said the proud dame, ' a trifler, and a jest ?
Confess you are a fool ! '—he bow'd and he
confess'd.
  This vex'd him much, but could not always
last :
The dame is buried, and the trial past.

There was a female, who had courted long
Her cousin's gifts, and deeply felt the wrong ;
By a vain boy forbidden to attend
The private counsels of her wealthy friend,
She vow'd revenge, nor should that crafty boy
In triumph undisturb'd his spoils enjoy ;
He heard, he smiled, and when the will was
read,
Kindly dismiss'd the kindred of the dead ;
' The dear deceased,' he call'd her, and the
crowd
Moved off with curses deep and threat'nings
loud.
  The youth retired, and, with a mind at ease,
Found he was rich, and fancied he must
please :
He might have pleased, and to his comfort
found
The wife he wish'd, if he had sought around ;
For there were lasses of his own degree,
With no more hatred to the state than he :
But he had courted spleen and age so long,
His heart refused to woo the fair and young ;
So long attended on caprice and whim,
He thought attention now was due to him ;
And as his flattery pleased the wealthy dame,
Heir to the wealth, he might the flattery
claim ;
But this the fair, with one accord, denied,
Nor waved for man's caprice the sex's pride :
There is a season when to them is due
Worship and awe, and they will claim it too :
' Fathers,' they cry, ' long hold us in their
chain,
Nay, tyrant brothers claim a right to reign ;
Uncles and guardians we in turn obey,
And husbands rule with ever-during sway ;
Short is the time when lovers at the feet
Of beauty kneel, and own the slavery sweet ;
And shall we this our triumph, this the aim
And boast of female power, forbear to claim ?
No ! we demand that homage, that respect,
Or the proud rebel punish and reject.'
  Our hero, still too indolent, too nice
To pay for beauty the accustom'd price,
No less forbore t' address the humbler maid,
Who might have yielded with the price unpaid;

But lived, himself to humour and to please,
To count his money, and enjoy his ease.
　It pleased a neighbouring 'squire to re-
　　commend
A faithful youth, as servant to his friend ;
Nay, more than servant, whom he praised
　　for parts
Ductile yet strong, and for the best of hearts ;
One who might ease him in his small affairs,
With tenants, tradesmen, taxes, and repairs ;
Answer his letters, look to all his dues,
And entertain him with discourse and news.
　The 'squire believed, and found the trusted
　　youth
A very pattern for his care and truth ;
Not for his virtues to be praised alone,
But for a modest mien and humble tone ;
Assenting always, but as if he meant
Only to strength of reasons to assent :
For was he stubborn, and retain'd his doubt,
Till the more subtle 'squire had forced it out;
' Nay, still was right, but he perceived that
　　strong
And powerful minds could make the right the
　　wrong.'
　When the 'squire's thoughts on some fair
　　damsel dwelt,
The faithful friend his apprehensions felt ;
It would rejoice his faithful heart to find
A lady suited to his master's mind ;
But who deserved that master ?　who would
　　prove
That hers was pure, uninterested love ?
Although a servant, he would scorn to take
A countess, till she suffer'd for his sake ;
Some tender spirit, humble, faithful, true,
Such, my dear master! must be sought for you.
　Six months had pass'd, and not a lady seen,
With just this love, 'twixt fifty and fifteen ;
All seem'd his doctrine or his pride to shun,
All would be woo'd before they would be won ;
When the chance naming of a race and fair,
Our 'squire disposed to take his pleasure there:
The friend profess'd, ' although he first began
To hint the thing, it seem'd a thoughtless plan:
The roads, he fear'd, were foul, the days were
　　short,
The village far, and yet there might be sport.'
　' What !　you of roads and starless nights
　　afraid ?
You think to govern !　you to be obey'd ! '
Smiling he spoke, the humble friend declared
His soul's obedience, and to go prepared.

The place was distant, but with great delight
They saw a race, and hail'd the glorious sight :
The 'squire exulted, and declared the ride
Had amply paid, and he was satisfied.
They gazed, they feasted, and, in happy mood,
Homeward return'd, and hastening as they
　　rode ;
For short the day, and sudden was the change
From light to darkness, and the way was
　　strange ;
Our hero soon grew peevish, then distress'd ;
He dreaded darkness, and he sigh'd for rest :
Going, they pass'd a village ; but, alas !
Returning saw no village to repass ;
The 'squire remember'd too a noble hall,
Large as a church, and whiter than its wall :
This he had noticed as they rode along,
And justly reason'd that their road was wrong.
George, full of awe, was modest in reply—
' The fault was his, 'twas folly to deny ;
And of his master's safety were he sure,
There was no grievance he would not endure.'
This made his peace with the relenting 'squire,
Whose thoughts yet dwelt on supper and
　　a fire ;
When, as they reach'd a long and pleasant
　　green,
Dwellings of men, and next a man, were seen.
　' My friend,' said George, ' to travellers
　　astray
Point out an inn, and guide us on the way.'
　The man look'd up ; ' Surprising !　can it be
My master's son ? as I'm alive, 'tis he.'
　' How !　Robin,' George replied, ' and are
　　we near
My father's house ? how strangely things
　　appear !—
Dear sir, though wanderers, we at last are
　　right :
Let us proceed, and glad my father's sight ;
We shall at least be fairly lodged and fed,
I can ensure a supper and a bed ;
Let us this night, as one of pleasure date,
And of surprise : it is an act of fate.'
　' Go on,' the 'squire in happy temper cried ;
' I like such blunder !　I approve such guide.'
　They ride, they halt, the farmer comes in
　　haste,
Then tells his wife how much their house is
　　graced ;
They bless the chance, they praise the lucky
　　son,
That caused the error—Nay !　it was not one ;

But their good fortune—Cheerful grew the
   'squire,
Who found dependants, flattery, wine, and
   fire ;
He heard the jack turn round ; the busy dame
Produced her damask ; and with supper came
The daughter, dress'd with care, and full of
   maiden-shame.
   Surprised, our hero saw the air and dress,
And strove his admiration to express ;
Nay ! felt it too—for Harriot was, in truth,
A tall fair beauty in the bloom of youth ;
And from the pleasure and surprise, a grace
Adorn'd the blooming damsel's form and face;
Then too, such high respect and duty paid
By all—such silent reverence in the maid ;
Vent'ring with caution, yet with haste, a
   glance ;
Loth to retire, yet trembling to advance,
Appear'd the nymph, and in her gentle guest
Stirr'd soft emotions till the hour of rest :
Sweet was his sleep, and in the morn again
He felt a mixture of delight and pain :
' How fair, how gentle,' said the 'squire, ' how
   meek,
And yet how sprightly, when disposed to
   speak !
Nature has bless'd her form, and Heaven her
   mind,
But in her favours Fortune is unkind ;
Poor is the maid—nay, poor she cannot prove
Who is enrich'd with beauty, worth, and love.'
   The 'squire arose, with no precise intent
To go or stay—uncertain what he meant :
He moved to part—they begg'd him first to
   dine ;
And who could then escape from love and
   wine ?
As came the night, more charming grew the
   fair,
And seem'd to watch him with a two-fold
   care :
On the third morn, resolving not to stay,
Though urged by love, he bravely rode away.
   Arrived at home, three pensive days he gave
To feelings fond and meditations grave ;
Lovely she was, and, if he did not err,
As fond of him as his fond heart of her ;
Still he delay'd, unable to decide
Which was the master-passion, love or pride :
He sometimes wonder'd how his friend could
   make,
And then exulted in, the night's mistake ;

Had she but fortune,' doubtless then,' he cried,
' Some happier man had won the wealthy
   bride.'
   While thus he hung in balance, now inclined
To change his state, and then to change his
   mind—
That careless George dropp'd idly on the
   ground
A letter, which his crafty master found ;
The stupid youth confess'd his fault, and
   pray'd
The generous 'squire to spare a gentle maid ;
Of whom her tender mother, full of fears,
Had written much—' She caught her oft in
   tears,
For ever thinking on a youth above
Her humble fortune—still she own'd not love ;
Nor can define, dear girl ! the cherish'd pain,
But would rejoice to see the cause again :
That neighbouring youth, whom she endured
   before,
She now rejects, and will behold no more :
Raised by her passion, she no longer stoops
To her own equals, but she pines and droops,
Like to a lily, on whose sweets the sun
Has withering gazed—she saw and was un-
   done :
His wealth allured her not—nor was she moved
By his superior state, himself she loved ;
So mild, so good, so gracious, so genteel—
But spare your sister, and her love conceal ;
We must the fault forgive, since she the pain
   must feel.'
   ' Fault !' said the 'squire, ' there 's coarse-
   ness in the mind
That thus conceives of feelings so refined ;
Here end my doubts, nor blame yourself, my
   friend,
Fate made you careless—here my doubts
   have end.'
   The way is plain before us—there is now
The lover's visit first, and then the vow
Mutual and fond, the marriage-rite, the bride
Brought to her home with all a husband's
   pride ;
The 'squire receives the prize his merits won,
And the glad parents leave the patron-son.
   But in short time he saw with much sur-
   prise,
First gloom, then grief, and then resentment
   rise,
From proud, commanding frowns and anger-
   darting eyes :

'Is there in Harriot's humble mind this fire,
This fierce impatience?' ask'd the puzzled
   'squire:
'Has marriage changed her? or the mask
   she wore
Has she thrown by, and is herself once more?'
  Hour after hour, when clouds on clouds
   appear,
Dark and more dark, we know the tempest
   near;
And thus the frowning brow, the restless form,
And threat'ning glance, forerun domestic
   storm:
So read the husband, and, with troubled mind,
Reveal'd his fears—'My love, I hope you find
All here is pleasant—but I must confess
You seem offended, or in some distress;
Explain the grief you feel, and leave me to
   redress.'
  'Leave it to you?' replied the nymph—
   'indeed!
What—to the cause from whence the ills
   proceed?
Good Heaven! to take me from a place, where I
Had every comfort underneath the sky;
And then immure me in a gloomy place,
With the grim monsters of your ugly race,
That from their canvas staring, make me
   dread
Through the dark chambers where they hang
   to tread!
No friend nor neighbour comes to give that
   joy,
Which all things here must banish or destroy:
Where is the promised coach? the pleasant
   ride?
Oh! what a fortune has a farmer's bride!
Your sordid pride has placed mè just above
Your hired domestics—and what pays me?
   love!
A selfish fondness I endure each hour,
And share unwitness'd pomp, unenvied power;
I hear your folly, smile at your parade,
And see your favourite dishes duly made;
Then am I richly dress'd for you t' admire,
Such is my duty and my lord's desire;
Is this a life for youth, for health, for joy?
Are these my duties—this my base employ?
No! to my father's house will I repair,
And make your idle wealth support me there;
Was it your wish to have an humble bride
For bondage thankful? Curse upon your pride!

Was it a slave you wanted? You shall see
That if not happy, I at least am free;
Well, sir, your answer:'—silent stood the
   'squire,
As looks a miser at his house on fire;
Where all he deems is vanish'd in that flame,
Swept from the earth his substance and his
   name;
So, lost to every promised joy of life,
Our 'squire stood gaping at his angry wife;—
His fate, his ruin, where he saw it vain
To hope for peace, pray, threaten, or com-
   plain;
And thus, betwixt his wonder at the ill
And his despair—there stood he gaping still.
  'Your answer, sir—shall I depart a spot
I thus detest?'—'Oh, miserable lot!'
Exclaim'd the man. 'Go, serpent! nor remain
To sharpen wo by insult and disdain:
A nest of harpies was I doom'd to meet;
What plots, what combinations of deceit!
I see it now—all plann'd, design'd, contrived;
Served by that villain—by this fury wived—
What fate is mine! What wisdom, virtue,
   truth,
Can stand, if dæmons set their traps for
   youth?
He lose his way! vile dog! he cannot lose
The way a villain through his life pursues;
And thou, deceiver! thou afraid to move,
And hiding close the serpent in the dove!
I saw—but, fated to endure disgrace—
Unheeding saw, the fury in thy face;
And call'd it spirit—Oh! I might have found
Fraud and imposture—all the kindred round!
A nest of vipers'——
      ——'Sir, I'll not admit
These wild effusions of your angry wit:
Have you that value, that we all should use
Such mighty arts for such important views?
Are you such prize—and is my state so fair,
That they should sell their souls to get me
   there?
Think you that we alone our thoughts dis-
   guise?
When in pursuit of some contended prize,
Mask we alone the heart, and soothe whom
   we despise!
Speak you of craft and subtle schemes, who
   know
That all your wealth you to deception owe;
Who play'd for ten dull years a scoundrel-part,
To worm yourself into a widow's heart?

Now, when you guarded, with superior skill,
That lady's closet, and preserved her will,
Blind in your craft, you saw not one of those
Opposed by you might you in turn oppose ;
Or watch your motions, and by art obtain
Share of that wealth you gave your peace to
      gain ?
Did conscience never '——
      ——' Cease, Tormentor, cease—
Or reach me poison——-let me rest in peace ! '
  ' Agreed—but hear me—let the truth
      appear ; '
' Then state your purpose—I'll be calm and
      hear.'—
' Know then, this wealth, sole object of your
      care,
I had some right, without your hand, to share;
My mother's claim was just—but soon she saw
Your power, compell'd, insulted, to withdraw:
'Twas then my father, in his anger, swore
You should divide the fortune, or restore ;
Long we debated—and you find me now
Heroic victim to a father's vow ;
Like Jephtha's daughter, but in different
      state,
And both decreed to mourn our early fate ;
Hence was my brother servant to your pride,
Vengeance made him your slave—and me
      your bride !
Now all is known—a dreadful price I pay
For our revenge—but still we have our day ;
All that you love you must with others share,
Or all you dread from their resentment dare !
Yet terms I offer—let contention cease :
Divide the spoil, and let us part in peace.'

Our hero trembling heard—he saw —he
      rose —
Nor could his motions nor his mind compose ;
He paced the room—and, stalking to her side,
Gazed on the face of his undaunted bride ;
And nothing there but scorn and calm
      aversion spied.
He would have vengeance, yet he fear'd the
      law :
Her friends would threaten, and their power
      he saw ;
' Then let her go : '—but oh ! a mighty sum
Would that demand, since he had let her come;
Nor from his sorrows could he find redress,
Save that which led him to a like distress,
And all his ease was in his wife to see
A wretch as anxious and distress'd as he :
Her strongest wish the fortune to divide
And part in peace, his avarice denied ;
And thus it happen'd, as in all deceit,
The cheater found the evil of the cheat ;
The husband grieved—nor was the wife at
      rest ;
Him she could vex, and he could her molest ;
She could his passion into frenzy raise,
But when the fire was kindled, fear'd the
      blaze :
As much they studied, so in time they found
The easiest way to give the deepest wound ;
But then, like fencers, they were equal still,
Both lost in danger what they gain'd in skill ;
Each heart a keener kind of rancour gain'd,
And paining more, was more severely pain'd ;
And thus by both were equal vengeance dealt,
And both the anguish they inflicted felt.

TALE XIII. JESSE AND COLIN

Then she plots, then she ruminates, then
she devises, and what they think in their hearts
they may effect, they will break their hearts
but they will effect.
  Merry Wives of Windsor, Act ii, Scene 2.
She has spoke what she should not, I am
sure of that ; Heaven knows what she hath
known.
              Macbeth, Act v, Scene 1.
Our house is hell, and thou a merry devil.
  Merchant of Venice, Act ii, Scene 3.
And yet, for aught I see, they are as sick
that surfeit with too much, as they that starve

with nothing ; it is no mean happiness, there-
fore, to be seated in the mean.
          Merchant of Venice, Act i, Scene 2.

A VICAR died, and left his daughter poor—
It hurt her not, she was not rich before :
Her humble share of worldly goods she
      sold,
Paid every debt, and then her fortune told ;
And found, with youth and beauty, hope and
      health,
Two hundred guineas was her worldly wealth ;

It then remain'd to choose her path in life,
And first, said Jesse, ' Shall I be a wife ?—
Colin is mild and civil, kind and just,
I know his love, his temper I can trust ;
But small his farm, it asks perpetual care,
And we must toil as well as trouble share :
True, he was taught in all the gentle arts
That raise the soul, and soften human hearts ;
And boasts a parent, who deserves to shine
In higher class, and I could wish her mine ;
Nor wants he will his station to improve,
A just ambition waked by faithful love ;—
Still is he poor—and here my father's friend
Deigns for his daughter, as her own, to send ;
A worthy lady, who it seems has known
A world of griefs and troubles of her own :
I was an infant, when she came, a guest
Beneath my father's humble roof to rest ;
Her kindred all unfeeling, vast her woes,
Such her complaint, and there she found
        repose ;
Enrich'd by fortune, now she nobly lives,
And nobly, from the blest abundance, gives ;
The grief, the want of human life, she knows,
And comfort there and here relief bestows ;
But are they not dependants?—Foolish pride!
Am I not honour'd by such friend and guide ?
Have I a home,' (here Jesse dropp'd a tear),
' Or friend beside ? '—A faithful friend was
        near.
    Now Colin came, at length resolved to lay
His heart before her and to urge her stay ;
True, his own plough the gentle Colin drove,
An humble farmer with aspiring love :
Who, urged by passion, never dared till now,
Thus urged by fears, his trembling hopes
        avow :
Her father's glebe he managed ; every year
The grateful vicar held the youth more dear ;
He saw indeed the prize in Colin's view,
And wish'd his Jesse with a man so true ;
Timid as true, he urged with anxious air
His tender hope, and made the trembling
        prayer ;
When Jesse saw, nor could with coldness see,
Such fond respect, such tried sincerity :
Grateful for favours to her father dealt,
She more than grateful for his passion felt ;
Nor could she frown on one so good and kind,
Yet fear'd to smile, and was unfix'd in mind ;
But prudence placed the female friend in
        view—
What might not one so rich and grateful do ?

So lately, too, the good old vicar died,
His faithful daughter must not cast aside
The signs of filial grief, and be a ready bride :
Thus, led by prudence, to the lady's seat
The village-beauty purposed to retreat ;
But, as in hard-fought fields the victor knows
What to the vanquish'd he, in honour, owes,
So in this conquest over powerful love,
Prudence resolved a generous foe to prove ;
And Jesse felt a mingled fear and pain
In her dismission of a faithful swain,
Gave her kind thanks, and when she saw
        his wo,
Kindly betray'd that she was loth to go ;
' But would she promise, if abroad she met
A frowning world, she would remember yet
Where dwelt a friend ? '—' That could she
        not forget.'
And thus they parted; but each faithful heart
Felt the compulsion, and refused to part.
    Now by the morning mail the timid maid
Was to that kind and wealthy dame convey'd;
Whose invitation, when her father died,
Jesse as comfort to her heart applied ;
She knew the days her generous friend' had
        seen—
As wife and widow, evil days had been ;
She married early, and for half her life
Was an insulted and forsaken wife ;
Widow'd and poor, her angry father gave,
Mix'd with reproach, the pittance of a slave ;
Forgetful brothers pass'd her, but she knew
Her humbler friends, and to their home
        withdrew ;
The good old vicar to her sire applied
For help, and help'd her when her sire denied ;
When in few years death stalk'd through
        bower and hall,
Sires, sons, and sons of sons, were buried all :
She then abounded, and had wealth to spare
For softening grief she once was doom'd to
        share ;
Thus train'd in misery's school, and taught
        to feel,
She would rejoice an orphan's woes to heal :
So Jesse thought, who look'd within her
        breast,
And thence conceived how bounteous minds
        are bless'd.
    From her vast mansion look'd the lady down
On humbler buildings of a busy town ;
Thence came her friends of either sex, and all,
With whom she lived on terms reciprocal :

They pass'd the hours with their accustom'd
    ease,
As guests inclined, but not compelled to
    please ;
But there were others in the mansion found,
For office chosen, and by duties bound ;
Three female rivals, each of power possess'd,
Th' attendant-maid, poor friend, and kindred-
    guest.

To these came Jesse, as a seaman thrown
By the rude storm upon a coast unknown :
The view was flattering, civil seem'd the race,
But all unknown the dangers of the place.

Few hours had pass'd, when, from attend-
    ants freed,
The lady utter'd—' This is kind indeed ;
Believe me, love ! that I for one like you
Have daily pray'd, a friend discreet and true ;
Oh ! wonder not that I on you depend,
You are mine own hereditary friend :
Hearken, my Jesse, never can I trust
Beings ungrateful, selfish, and unjust ;
But you are present, and my load of care
Your love will serve to lighten and to share :
Come near me, Jesse—let not those below
Of my reliance on your friendship know ;
Look as they look, be in their freedoms free—
But all they say do you convey to me.'

Here Jesse's thoughts to Colin's cottage
    flew,
And with such speed she scarce their absence
    knew.

' Jane loves her mistress, and should she
    depart,
I lose her service, and she breaks her heart ;
My ways and wishes, looks and thoughts she
    knows,
And duteous care by close attention shows :
But is she faithful ? in temptation strong ?
Will she not wrong me ? ah ! I fear the wrong :
Your father loved me ; now, in time of need,
Watch for my good, and to his place succeed.

' Blood doesn't bind—that girl, who every
    day
Eats of my bread, would wish my life away ;
I am her *dear relation*, and she thinks
To make her fortune, an ambitious minx !
She only courts me for the prospect's sake,
Because she knows I have a will to make ;
Yes, love ! my will delay'd, I know not how—
But you are here, and I will make it now.

' That idle creature, keep her in your view,
See what she does, what she desires to do ;

On her young mind may artful villains prey,
And to my plate and jewels find a way ;
A pleasant humour has the girl : her smile
And cheerful manner tedious hours beguile :
But well observe her, ever near her be,
Close in your thoughts, in your professions
    free.

' Again, my Jesse, hear what I advise,
And watch a woman ever in disguise ;
Issop, that widow, serious, subtle, sly—
But what of this ?—I must have company :
She markets for me, and although she makes
Profit, no doubt, of all she undertakes,
Yet she is one I can to all produce,
And all her talents are in daily use ;
Deprived of her, I may another find
As sly and selfish, with a weaker mind :
But never trust her, she is full of art,
And worms herself into the closest heart ;
Seem then, I pray you, careless in her sight,
Nor let her know, my love, how we unite.

' Do, my good Jesse, cast a view around,
And let no wrong within my house be found ;
That girl associates with——I know not who
Are her companions, nor what ill they do ;
'Tis then the widow plans, 'tis then she tries
Her various arts and schemes for fresh
    supplies ;
Tis then, if ever, Jane her duty quits,
And, whom I know not, favours and admits :
Oh ! watch their movements all ; for me 'tis
    hard,
Indeed is vain, but you may keep a guard ;
And I, when none your watchful glance
    deceive,
May make my will, and think what I shall
    leave.'

Jesse, with fear, disgust, alarm, surprise,
Heard of these duties for her ears and eyes ;
Heard by what service she must gain her
    bread,
And went with scorn and sorrow to her bed.

Jane was a servant fitted for her place,
Experienced, cunning, fraudful, selfish, base ;
Skill'd in those mean humiliating arts
That make their way to proud and selfish
    hearts ;
By instinct taught, she felt an awe, a fear,
For Jesse's upright, simple character ;
Whom with gross flattery she awhile assail'd,
And then beheld with hatred when it fail'd ;
Yet trying still upon her mind for hold,
She all the secrets of the mansion told ;

And to invite an equal trust, she drew
Of every mind a bold and rapid view ;
But on the widow'd friend with deep disdain,
And rancorous envy, dwelt the treacherous
    Jane :—
In vain such arts ; without deceit or pride,
With a just taste and feeling for her guide,
From all contagion Jesse kept apart,
Free in her manners, guarded in her heart.
    Jesse one morn was thoughtful, and her
      sigh
The widow heard as she was passing by ;
And—' Well ! ' she said, ' is that some
    distant swain,
Or aught with us, that gives your bosom pain?
Come, we are fellow-sufferers, slaves in thrall,
And tasks and griefs are common to us all ;
Think not my frankness strange : they love
    to paint
Their state with freedom, who endure
    restraint ;
And there is something in that speaking eye
And sober mien, that prove I may rely :
You came a stranger ; to my words attend,
Accept my offer, and you find a friend ;
It is a labyrinth in which you stray,
Come, hold my clue, and I will lead the way.
    ' Good Heav'n! that one so jealous, envious,
      base,
Should be the mistress of so sweet a place ;
She, who so long herself was low and poor,
Now broods suspicious on her useless store ;
She loves to see us abject, loves to deal
Her insult round, and then pretends to feel ;
Prepare to cast all dignity aside,
For know your talents will be quickly tried ;
Nor think, from favours past, a friend to gain,
'Tis but by duties we our posts maintain :
I read her novels, gossip through the town,
And daily go, for idle stories, down ;
I cheapen all she buys, and bear the curse
Of honest tradesmen for my niggard-purse ;
And, when for her this meanness I display,
She cries, "I heed not what I throw away ; "
Of secret bargains I endure the shame,
And stake my credit for our fish and game ;
Oft has she smiled to hear " her generous soul
Would gladly give, but stoops to my control : "
Nay ! I have heard her, when she chanced to
    come
Where I contended for a petty sum,
Affirm 'twas painful to behold such care,
" But Issop's nature is to pinch and spare : "

Thus all the meanness of the house is mine,
And my reward—to scorn her, and to dine.
    ' See next that giddy thing with neither pride
To keep her safe, nor principle to guide :
Poor, idle, simple flirt ! as sure as fate
Her maiden-fame will have an early date :
Of her beware ; for all who live below
Have faults they wish not all the world to
    know ;
And she is fond of listening, full of doubt,
And stoops to guilt to find an error out.
    ' And now once more observe the artful
      maid,
A lying, prying, jilting, thievish jade ;
I think, my love, you would not condescend
To call a low, illiterate girl your friend :
But in our troubles we are apt, you know,
To lean on all who some compassion show ;
And she has flexile features, acting eyes,
And seems with every look to sympathise ;
No mirror can a mortal's grief express
With more precision, or can feel it less ;
That proud, mean spirit, she by fawning
    courts,
By vulgar flattery, and by vile reports ;
And by that proof she every instant gives
To one so mean, that yet a meaner lives.—
    ' Come, I have drawn the curtain, and you
      see
Your fellow-actors, all our company ;
Should you incline to throw reserve aside,
And in my judgment and my love confide,
I could some prospects open to your view,
That ask attention—and, till then, adieu.'
    ' Farewell ! ' said Jesse, hastening to her
      room,
Where all she saw within, without, was gloom:
Confused, perplex'd, she pass'd a dreary hour,
Before her reason could exert its power ;
To her all seem'd mysterious, all allied
To avarice, meanness, folly, craft, and pride ;
Wearied with thought, she breathed the
    garden's air,
Then came the laughing lass, and join'd her
    there.
    ' My sweetest friend has dwelt with us a
      week,
And does she love us ? be sincere and speak ;
My aunt you cannot—Lord ! how I should
    hate
To be like her, all misery and state !
Proud, and yet envious, she disgusted sees
All who are happy, and who look at ease.

Let friendship bind us, I will quickly show
Some favourites near us, you'll be bless'd to
    know;
My aunt forbids it—but, can she expect
To soothe her spleen, we shall ourselves
    neglect?
Jane and the widow were to watch and stay
My free-born feet; I watch'd as well as they;
Lo! what is this? this simple key explores
The dark recess that holds the spinster's
    stores;
And led by her ill star, I chanced to see
Where Issop keeps her stock of ratafie;
Used in the hours of anger and alarm,
It makes her civil, and it keeps her warm;
Thus bless'd with secrets, both would choose
    to hide,
Their fears now grant me what their scorn
    denied.
    'My freedom thus by their assent secured,
Bad as it is, the place may be endured;
And bad it is, but her estates, you know,
And her beloved hoards, she must bestow;
So we can slyly our amusements take,
And friends of dæmons, if they help us, make.'
    'Strange creatures these,' thought Jesse,
    half inclined
To smile at one malicious and yet kind;
Frank and yet cunning, with a heart to
    love
And malice prompt—the serpent and the
    dove;
Here could she dwell? or could she yet
    depart?
Could she be artful? could she bear with
    art?—
This splendid mansion gave the cottage grace,
She thought a dungeon was a happier place;
And Colin pleading, when he pleaded best,
Wrought not such sudden change in Jesse's
    breast.
    The wondering maiden, who had only read
Of such vile beings, saw them now with dread;
Safe in themselves—for nature has design'd
The creature's poison harmless to the kind;
But all beside who in the haunts are found
Must dread the poison, and must feel the
    wound.
    Days full of care, slow weary weeks pass'd
    on,
Eager to go, still Jesse was not gone;
Her time in trifling or in tears she spent,
She never gave, she never felt content:

The lady wonder'd that her humble guest
Strove not to please, would neither lie nor jest;
She sought no news, no scandal would convey,
But walk'd for health, and was at church to
    pray;
All this displeased, and soon the widow cried:
' Let me be frank—I am not satisfied;
You know my wishes, I your judgment trust;
You can be useful, Jesse, and you must;
Let me be plainer, child—I want an ear,
When I am deaf, instead of mine to hear,
When mine is sleeping, let your eye awake;
When I observe not, observation take;
Alas! I rest not on my pillow laid,
Then threat'ning whispers make my soul
    afraid;
The tread of strangers to my ear ascends,
Fed at my cost, the minions of my friends;
While you, without a care, a wish to please,
Eat the vile bread of idleness and ease.'
    Th' indignant girl astonish'd answer'd—
    ' Nay!
This instant, madam, let me haste away;
Thus speaks my father's, thus an orphan's
    friend?
This instant, lady, let your bounty end.'
    The lady frown'd indignant—' What!' she
    cried,
' A vicar's daughter with a princess' pride!
And pauper's lot! but pitying I forgive;
How, simple Jesse, do you think to live?
Have I not power to help you, foolish maid?
To my concerns be your attention paid;
With cheerful mind th' allotted duties take,
And recollect I have a will to make.'
    Jesse, who felt as liberal natures feel,
When thus the baser their designs reveal,
Replied—' Those duties were to her unfit,
Nor would her spirit to her tasks submit.'
    In silent scorn the lady sate awhile,
And then replied with stern contemptuous
    smile—
    ' Think you, fair madam, that you came
    to share
Fortunes like mine without a thought or care?
A guest, indeed! from every trouble free,
Dress'd by my help, with not a care for me;
When I a visit to your father made,
I for the poor assistance largely paid;
To his domestics I their tasks assign'd,
I fix'd the portion for his hungry hind;
And had your father (simple man!) obey'd
My good advice, and watch'd as well as pray'd,

He might have left you something with his
prayers,
And lent some colour for these lofty airs.—
    ' In tears ! my love ! Oh, then my soften'd
heart
Cannot resist—we never more will part ;
I need your friendship—I will be your friend,
And thus determined, to my will attend.'
    Jesse went forth, but with determined soul
To fly such love, to break from such control ;
' I hear enough,' the trembling damsel cried ;
'Flight be my care, and Providence my guide:
Ere yet a prisoner, I escape will make ;
Will, thus display'd, th' insidious arts forsake,
And, as the rattle sounds, will fly the fatal
snake.'
    Jesse her thanks upon the morrow paid,
Prepared to go, determined though afraid.
    ' Ungrateful creature,' said the lady, ' this
Could I imagine ?—are you frantic, miss ?
What ! leave your friend, your prospects—
is it true ? '
This Jesse answer'd by a mild ' Adieu ! '
    The dame replied, ' Then houseless may
you rove,
The starving victim to a guilty love ;
Branded with shame, in sickness doom'd to
nurse
An ill-form'd cub, your scandal and your
curse ;
Spurn'd by its scoundrel father, and ill fed
By surly rustics with the parish-bread !—
Relent you not ?—speak—yet I can forgive ;
Still live with me '—' With you,' said Jesse,
' live ?
No ! I would first endure what you describe,
Rather than breathe with your detested tribe ;
Who long have feign'd, till now their very
hearts
Are firmly fix'd in their accursed parts ;
Who all profess esteem, and feel disdain,
And all, with justice, of deceit complain ;
Whom I could pity, but that, while I stay,
My terror drives all kinder thoughts away ;
Grateful for this, that when I think of you,
I little fear what poverty can do.'
    The angry matron her attendant Jane
Summon'd in haste to soothe the fierce dis-
dain :
    ' A vile detested wretch ! ' the lady cried,
' Yet shall she be, by many an effort, tried,
And, clogg'd with debt and fear, against her
will abide ;

And once secured, she never shall depart
Till I have proved the firmness of her heart ;
Then when she dares not, would not, cannot
go,
I'll make her feel what 'tis to use me so.'
    The pensive Colin in his garden stray'd,
But felt not then the beauties it display'd ;
There many a pleasant object met his view,
A rising wood of oaks behind it grew ;
A stream ran by it, and the village-green
And public road were from the gardens seen ;
Save where the pine and larch the bound'ry
made,
And on the rose-beds threw a softening shade.
    The mother sat beside the garden-door,
Dress'd as in times ere she and hers were poor;
The broad-laced cap was known in ancient
days,
When madam's dress compell'd the village
praise ;
And still she look'd as in the times of old,
Ere his last farm the erring husband sold ;
While yet the mansion stood in decent state,
And paupers waited at the well-known gate.
    'Alas! my son!' the mother cried, ' and why
That silent grief and oft-repeated sigh ?
True we are poor, but thou hast never felt
Pangs to thy father for his error dealt ;
Pangs from strong hopes of visionary gain,
For ever raised, and ever found in vain.
He rose unhappy ! from his fruitless schemes,
As guilty wretches from their blissful dreams;
But thou wert then, my son, a playful child,
Wondering at grief, gay, innocent, and wild ;
Listening at times to thy poor mother's sighs,
With curious looks and innocent surprise ;
Thy father dying, thou, my virtuous boy,
My comfort always, waked my soul to joy ;
With the poor remnant of our fortune left,
Thou hast our station of its gloom bereft :
Thy lively temper, and thy cheerful air,
Have cast a smile on sadness and despair ;
Thy active hand has dealt to this poor space
The bliss of plenty and the charm of grace ;
And all around us wonder when they find
Such taste and strength, such skill and power
combined ;
There is no mother, Colin, no not one,
But envies me so kind, so good a son ;
By thee supported on this failing side,
Weakness itself awakes a parent's pride :
I bless the stroke that was my grief before,
And feel such joy that 'tis disease no more ;

Shielded by thee, my want becomes my
    wealth—
And soothed by Colin, sickness smiles at
    health ;
The old men love thee, they repeat thy praise,
And say, like thee were youth in earlier days ;
While every village-maiden cries, " How gay,
How smart, how brave, how good is Colin
    Grey ! "
    ' Yet art thou sad ; alas ! my son, I know
Thy heart is wounded, and the cure is slow ;
Fain would I think that Jesse still may come
To share the comforts of our rustic home :
She surely loved thee ; I have seen the maid,
When thou hast kindly brought the vicar
    aid—
When thou hast eased his bosom of its pain,
Oh ! I have seen her—she will come again.'
    The matron ceased ; and Colin stood the
    while
Silent, but striving for a grateful smile ;
He then replied—' Ah ! sure, had Jesse stay'd,
And shared the comforts of our sylvan shade,
The tenderest duty and the fondest love
Would not have fail'd that generous heart to
    move ;
A grateful pity would have ruled her breast,
And my distresses would have made me blest.
    ' But she is gone, and ever has in view
Grandeur and taste—and what will then
    ensue ?
Surprise and then delight in scenes so fair and
    new ;
For many a day, perhaps for many a week,
Home will have charms, and to her bosom
    speak ;
But thoughtless ease, and affluence, and pride,
Seen day by day, will draw her heart aside :
And she at length, though gentle and sincere,
Will think no more of our enjoyments here.'
    Sighing he spake—but hark ! he hears
    th' approach
Of rattling wheels ! and lo ! the evening-
    coach ;

Once more the movement of the horses' feet
Makes the fond heart with strong emotion
    beat ;
Faint were his hopes, but ever had the sight
Drawn him to gaze beside his gate at night ;
And when with rapid wheels it hurried by,
He grieved his parent with a hopeless sigh ;
And could the blessing have been bought—
    what sum
Had he not offer'd, to have Jesse come !
She came—he saw her bending from the door,
Her face, her smile, and he beheld no more ;
Lost in his joy—the mother lent her aid
T' assist and to detain the willing maid ;
Who thought her late, her present home to
    make,
Sure of a welcome for the vicar's sake :
But the good parent was so pleased, so kind,
So pressing Colin, she so much inclined,
That night advanced ; and then so long
    detain'd,
No wishes to depart she felt, or feign'd ;
Yet long in doubt she stood, and then per-
    force remain'd.
    Here was a lover fond, a friend sincere ;
Here was content and joy, for she was here :
In the mild evening, in the scene around,
The maid, now free, peculiar beauties found ;
Blended with village-tones, the evening-gale
Gave the sweet night-bird's warblings to the
    vale ;
The youth embolden'd, yet abash'd, now
    told
His fondest wish, nor found the maiden
    cold ;
The mother smiling whisper'd—' Let him go
And seek the licence ! ' Jesse answer'd, ' No : '
But Colin went. I know not if they live
With all the comforts wealth and plenty
    give ;
But with pure joy to envious souls denied,
To suppliant meanness and suspicious pride ;
And village-maids of happy couples say,
' They live like Jesse Bourn and Colin Grey.'

TALE XIV. THE STRUGGLES OF CONSCIENCE

I am a villain ; yet I lie, I am not ;
Fool ! of thyself speak well :—Fool ! do not
    flatter.
My Conscience hath a thousand several
    tongues,
And every tongue brings in a several tale.
          Richard III, Act v, Scene 3.

  My Conscience is but a kind of hard Con-
science. . . . The fiend gives the more friendly
counsel.
        Merchant of Venice, Act ii, Scene 2.

  Thou hast it now . . . and I fear
Thou play'dst most foully for't.
          Macbeth, Act iii, Scene 1.

Canst thou not minister to a mind diseased,
Pluck from the memory a rooted sorrow,
Rase out the written troubles of the brain,
And with some sweet oblivious antidote
Cleanse the stuff'd bosom of that perilous
    stuff
Which weighs upon the heart ?
          Macbeth, Act v, Scene 3.

. . . Soft ! I did but dream—
Oh ! coward Conscience, how dost thou afflict
  me !
          Richard III, Act v, Scene 3.

A SERIOUS toyman in the city dwelt,
Who much concern for his religion felt ;
Reading, he changed his tenets, read again,
And various questions could with skill main-
    tain ;
Papist and quaker if we set aside,
He had the road of every traveller tried ;
There walk'd awhile, and on a sudden turn'd
Into some by-way he had just discern'd :
He had a nephew, Fulham—Fulham went
His uncle's way, with every turn content ;
He saw his pious kinsman's watchful care,
And thought such anxious pains his own
    might spare,
And he, the truth obtain'd, without the toil,
    might share.
In fact, young Fulham, though he little read,
Perceived his uncle was by fancy led ;
And smiled to see the constant care he took,
Collating creed with creed, and book with book.
  At length the senior fix'd ; I pass the sect
He call'd a church, 'twas precious and elect ;
Yet the seed fell not in the richest soil,
For few disciples paid the preacher's toil ;

All in an attic-room were wont to meet,
These few disciples at their pastor's feet
With these went Fulham, who, discreet and
    grave,
Follow'd the light his worthy uncle gave ;
Till a warm preacher found a way t' impart
Awakening feelings to his torpid heart :
Some weighty truths, and of unpleasant kind,
Sank, though resisted, in his struggling mind ;
He wish'd to fly them, but compell'd to stay,
Truth to the waking Conscience found her
    way ;
For though the youth was call'd a prudent lad,
And prudent was, yet serious faults he had ;
Who now reflected—' Much am I surprised,
I find these notions cannot be despised ;
No ! there is something I perceive at last,
Although my uncle cannot hold it fast ;
Though I the strictness of these men reject,
Yet I determine to be circumspect :
This man alarms me, and I must begin
To look more closely to the things within ;
These sons of zeal have I derided long,
But now begin to think the laughers wrong ;
Nay, my good uncle, by all teachers moved,
Will be preferr'd to him who none approved ;
Better to love amiss than nothing to have
    loved.'
  Such were his thoughts, when Conscience
    first began
To hold close converse with th' awaken'd
    man :
He from that time reserved and cautious
    grew,
And for his duties felt obedience due ;
Pious he was not, but he fear'd the pain
Of sins committed, nor would sin again.
Whene'er he stray'd, he found his Conscience
    rose,
Like one determined what was ill t' oppose,
What wrong t' accuse, what secret to disclose:
To drag forth every latent act to light,
And fix them fully in the actor's sight :
This gave him trouble, but he still confess'd
The labour useful, for it brought him rest.
  The uncle died, and when the nephew read
The will, and saw the substance of the dead—
Five hundred guineas, with a stock in trade—
He much rejoiced, and thought his fortune
    made ;

Yet felt aspiring pleasure at the sight,
And for increase, ncreasing appetite :
Desire of profit, idle habits check'd,
(For Fulham's virtue was to be correct);
He and his Conscience had their compact
   made—
' Urge me with truth, and you will soon
   persuade ;
But not,' he cried, ' for mere ideal things
Give me to feel those terror-breeding stings.'
   ' Let not such thoughts,' she said, ' your
   mind confound ;
Trifles may wake me, but they never wound ;
In them indeed there is a wrong and right,
But you will find me pliant and polite,
Not like a Conscience of the dotard kind,
Awake to dreams, to dire offences blind :
Let all within be pure, in all beside
Be your own master, governor, and guide ;
Alive to danger, in temptation strong,
And I shall sleep our whole existence long.'
   Sweet be thy sleep,' said Fulham ; ' strong
   must be
The tempting ill that gains access to me :
Never will I to evil deed consent,
Or, if surprised, oh ! how will I repent !
Should gain be doubtful, soon would I re-
   store
The dangerous good, or give it to the poor ;
Repose for them my growing wealth shall
   buy—
Or build—who knows ?—an hospital like
   Guy ?—
Yet why such means to soothe the smart
   within,
While firmly purposed to renounce the sin ? '
   Thus our young Trader and his Conscience
   dwelt
In mutual love, and great the joy they felt ;
But yet in small concerns, in trivial things,
'She was,' he said,' too ready with the stings;'
And he too apt, in search of growing gains,
To lose the fear of penalties and pains :
Yet these were trifling bickerings, petty jars,
Domestic strifes, preliminary wars ;
He ventured little, little she express'd
Of indignation, and they both had rest.
   Thus was he fix'd to walk the worthy way,
When profit urged him to a bold essay :—
A time was that when all at pleasure gamed
In lottery-chances, yet of law unblamed ;
This Fulham tried, who would to him advance
A pound or crown, he gave in turn a chance

For weighty prize—and should they nothing
   share,
They had their crown or pound in Fulham's
   ware ;
Thus the old stores within the shop were sold
For that which none refuses, new or old.
   Was this unjust ? yet Conscience could not
   rest,
But made a mighty struggle in the breast ;
And gave th' aspiring man an early proof,
That should they war he would have work
   enough :
' Suppose,' said she, ' your vended numbers
   rise
The same with those which gain each real
   prize,
(Such your proposal,) can you ruin shun ? '
' A hundred thousand,' he replied, ' to one.'
' Still it may happen: ' ' I the sum must pay.'
' You know you cannot : ' ' I can run away.'
' That is dishonest : '—' Nay, but you must
   wink
At a chance-hit ; it cannot be, I think :
Upon my conduct as a whole decide,
Such trifling errors let my virtues hide ;
Fail I at meeting ? am I sleepy there ?
My purse refuse I with the priest to share ?
Do I deny the poor a helping hand ?
Or stop the wicked women in the Strand ?
Or drink at club beyond a certain pitch ?
Which are your charges ? Conscience, tell
   me which ? '
   ' 'Tis well,' said she, ' but— ' ' Nay, I pray,
   have done :
Trust me, I will not into danger run.'
   The lottery drawn, not one demand was
   made ;
Fulham gain'd profit and increase of trade.
' See now,' said he—for Conscience yet
   arose—
' How foolish 'tis such measures to oppose :
Have I not blameless thus my state ad-
   vanced ? '—
' Still,' mutter'd Conscience, ' still it might
   have chanced.'
' Might ! ' said our hero, ' who is so exact
As to inquire what might have been a fact ? '
   Now Fulham's shop contain'd a curious
   view
Of costly trifles elegant and new :
The papers told where kind mammas might
   buy
The gayest toys to charm an infant's eye ;

Where generous beaux might gentle damsels
    please,
And travellers call who cross the land or seas,
And find the curious art, the neat device
Of precious value and of trifling price.
    Here Conscience rested, she was pleased to
    find
No less an active than an honest mind ;
But when he named his price, and when he
    swore,
His Conscience check'd him, that he ask'd no
    more,
When half he sought had been a large increase
On fair demand, she could not rest in peace :
(Beside th' affront to call th' adviser in,
Who would prevent, to justify the sin ?)
She therefore told him, that ' he vainly tried
To soothe her anger, conscious that he lied ;
If thus he grasp'd at such usurious gains,
He must deserve, and should expect her pains.'
    The charge was strong ; he would in part
    confess
Offence there was—But, who offended less ?
' What ! is a mere assertion call'd a lie ?
And if it be, are men compell'd to buy ?
'Twas strange that Conscience on such points
    should dwell,
While he was acting (he would call it) well ;
He bought as others buy, he sold as others sell ;
There was no fraud, and he demanded cause
Why he was troubled, when he kept the
    laws ? '
    ' My laws ? ' said Conscience : ' What,'
    said he, ' are thine ?
Oral or written, human or divine ?
Show me the chapter, let me see the text ;
By laws uncertain subjects are perplex'd :
Let me my finger on the statute lay,
And I shall feel it duty to obey.'
    ' Reflect,' said Conscience, ' 'twas your own
    desire
That I should warn you—does the compact
    tire ?
Repent you this ? then bid me not advise,
And rather hear your passions as they rise ;
So you may counsel and remonstrance shun,
But then remember it is war begun ;
And you may judge from some attacks, my
    friend,
What serious conflicts will on war attend.'
    ' Nay, but,' at length the thoughtful man
    replied,
' I say not that ; I wish you for my guide ;

Wish for your checks and your reproofs—but
    then
Be like a Conscience of my fellow-men ;
Worthy I mean, and men of good report,
And not the wretches who with Conscience
    sport :
There 's Bice, my friend, who passes off his
    grease
Of pigs for bears', in pots a crown apiece ;
His Conscience never checks him when he
    swears
The fat he sells is honest fat of bears ;
And so it is, for he contrives to give
A drachm to each—'tis thus that tradesmen
    live :
Now why should you and I be over-nice ;
What man is held in more repute than Bice ? '
    Here ended the dispute ; but yet 'twas plain
The parties both expected strife again :
Their friendship cool'd, he look'd about and
    saw
Numbers who seem'd unshackled by his awe ;
While like a school-boy he was threaten'd still,
Now for the deed, now only for the will ;
Here Conscience answer'd, ' To thy neigh-
    bour's guide
Thy neighbour leave, and in thine own
    confide.'
    Such were each day the charges and replies,
When a new object caught the trader's eyes ;
A vestry-patriot, could he gain the name,
Would famous make him, and would pay the
    fame :
He knew full well the sums bequeath'd in
    charge
For schools, for alms-men, for the poor, were
    large ;
Report had told, and he could feel it true,
That most unfairly dealt the trusted few ;
No partners would they in their office take,
Nor clear accounts at annual meetings make ;
Aloud our hero in the vestry spoke
Of hidden deeds, and vow'd to draw the cloak ;
It was the poor man's cause, and he for one
Was quite determined to see justice done :
His foes affected laughter, then disdain,
They too were loud and threat'ning, but in
    vain ;
The pauper's friend, their foe, arose and
    spoke again :
Fiercely he cried, ' Your garbled statements
    show
That you determine we shall nothing know ;

But we shall bring your hidden crimes to
    light,
Give you to shame, and to the poor their
    right.'
   Virtue like this might some approval ask—
But Conscience sternly said, 'You wear a
    mask!'
'At least,' said Fulham, 'if I have a view
To serve myself, I serve the public too.'
   Fulham, though check'd, retain'd his former
    zeal,
And this the cautious rogues began to feel:
'Thus will he ever bark,' in peevish tone,
An elder cried—' the cur must have a bone:'
They then began to hint, and to begin
Was all they needed—it was felt within;
In terms less veil'd an offer then was made,
Though distant still, it fail'd not to persuade:
More plainly then was every point proposed,
Approved, accepted, and the bargain closed.
'Th' exulting paupers hail'd their friend's
    success,
And bade adieu to murmurs and distress.'
   Alas! their friend had now superior light,
And, view'd by that, he found that all was
    right;
'There were no errors, the disbursements
    small;
This was the truth, and truth was due to all.'
   And rested Conscience? No! she would
    not rest,
Yet was content with making a protest:
Some acts she now with less resistance bore,
Nor took alarm so quickly as before:
Like those in towns besieged, who every ball
At first with terror view, and dread them all,
But, grown familiar with the scenes, they fear
The danger less, as it approaches near;
So Conscience, more familiar with the view
Of growing evils, less attentive grew:
Yet he who felt some pain, and dreaded more,
Gave a peace-offering to the angry poor.
   Thus had he quiet—but the time was brief;
From his new triumph sprang a cause of grief;
In office join'd, and acting with the rest,
He must admit the sacramental test:
Now, as a sectary, who had all his life,
As he supposed, been with the church at strife,
(No rules of hers, no laws had he perused,
Nor knew the tenets he by rote abused);
Yet Conscience here arose more fierce and
    strong
Than when she told of robbery and wrong;

'Change his religion! No! he must be sure
That was a blow no Conscience could endure.'
   Though friend to virtue, yet she oft abides
In early notions, fix'd by erring guides;
And is more startled by a call from those,
Than when the foulest crimes her rest oppose;
By error taught, by prejudice misled,
She yields her rights, and fancy rules instead;
When Conscience all her stings and terror
    deals,
Not as truth dictates, but as fancy feels:
And thus within our hero's troubled breast,
Crime was less torture than the odious test.
New forms, new measures, he must now
    embrace,
With sad conviction that they warr'd with
    grace;
To his new church no former friend would
    come,
They scarce preferr'd her to the church of
    Rome:
But thinking much, and weighing guilt and
    gain,
Conscience and he commuted for her pain;
Then promised Fulham to retain his creed,
And their peculiar paupers still to feed;
Their attic-room (in secret) to attend,
And not forget he was the preacher's friend;
Thus he proposed, and Conscience, troubled,
    tried,
And wanting peace, reluctantly complied.
   Now care subdued, and apprehensions gone,
In peace our hero went aspiring on;
But short the period—soon a quarrel rose,
Fierce in the birth, and fatal in the close;
With times of truce between, which rather
    proved
That both were weary, than that either loved.
   Fulham ev'n now disliked the heavy thrall,
And for her death would in his anguish call,
As Rome's mistaken friend exclaim'd, *Let
    Carthage fall!*
So felt our hero, so his wish express'd,
Against this powerful sprite—*delenda est:*
Rome in her conquest saw not danger near,
Freed from her rival, and without a fear;
So, Conscience conquer'd, men perceive how
    free,
But not how fatal such a state must be.
Fatal not free our hero's; foe or friend,
Conscience on him was destined to attend:
She dosed indeed, grew dull, nor seem'd to sp̄
Crime following crime, and each of deeper dye;

But all were noticed, and the reckoning time
With her account came on—crime following
        crime.
   This, once a foe, now brother in the trust,
Whom Fulham late described as fair and just,
Was the sole guardian of a wealthy maid,
Placed in his power, and of his frown afraid :
Not quite an idiot, for her busy brain
Sought, by poor cunning, trifling points to
        gain ;
Success in childish projects her delight,
She took no heed of each important right.
   The friendly parties met—the guardian
        cried,
' I am too old ; my sons have each a bride :
Marth , my ward, would make an easy wife ;
On easy terms I'll make her yours for life ;
And then the creature is so weak and mild,
She may be soothed and threaten'd as a
        child ; '—
' Yet not obey,' said Fulham, ' for your fools,
Female and male, are obstinate as mules.'
   Some points adjusted, these new friends
        agreed,
Proposed the day, and hurried on the deed,
   ' 'Tis a vile act,' said Conscience :—' It will
        prove,'
Replied the bolder man, ' an act of love ;
Her wicked guardian might the girl have
        sold
To endless misery for a tyrant's gold ;
Now may her life be happy—for I mean
To keep my temper even and serene.'
' I cannot thus compound,' the spirit cried,
' Nor have my laws thus broken and defied :
This is a fraud, a bargain for a wife ;
Expect my vengeance, or amend your life.'
   The wife was pretty, trifling, childish, weak ;
She could not think, but would not cease to
        speak :
This he forbad—she took the caution ill,
And boldly rose against his sovereign will ;
With idiot-cunning she would watch the hour,
When friends were present, to dispute his
        power :
With tyrant-craft, he then was still and calm,
But raised in private terror and alarm :
By many trials, she perceived how far
To vex and tease, without an open war ;
And he discover'd that so weak a mind
No art could lead, and no compulsion bind ;
The rudest force would fail such mind to tame,
And she was callous to rebuke and shame ;

Proud of her wealth, the power of law she
        knew,
And would assist him in the spending too :
His threat'ning words with insult she defied,
To all his reasoning with a stare replied ;
And when he begg'd her to attend, would
        say,
' Attend I will—but let me have my way.'
   Nor rest had Conscience : ' While you
        merit pain
From me,' she cried, ' you seek redress in
        vain.'
His thoughts were grievous : ' All that I
        possess
From this vile bargain adds to my distress ;
To pass a life with one who will not mend,
Who cannot love, nor save, nor wisely spend,
Is a vile prospect, and I see no end ;
For if we part, I must of course restore
Much of her money, and must wed no more.
' Is there no way ? '—here Conscience rose
        in power,
' Oh ! fly the danger of this fatal hour ;
I am thy Conscience faithful, fond, and true,
Ah, fly this thought, or evil must ensue ;
Fall on thy knees, and pray with all thy soul,
Thy purpose banish, thy design control ;
Let every hope of such advantage cease,
Or never more expect a moment's peace.'
   Th' affrighten'd man a due attention paid,
Felt the rebuke, and the command obey'd.
   Again the wife rebell'd, again express'd
A love for pleasure—a contempt of rest ;
' She, whom she pleased, would visit, would
        receive
Those who pleased her, nor deign to ask for
        leave.'
   ' One way there is,' said he ; ' I might
        contrive
Into a trap this foolish thing to drive :
Who pleased her, said she ?—I'll be certain
        who— '
' Take heed,' said Conscience, ' what thou
        mean'st to do :
Ensnare thy wife ? '—' Why yes,' he must
        confess,
' It might be wrong—but there was no re-
        dress ;
Beside, to think,' said he, ' is not to sin.'
' Mistaken man ! ' replied the power within.
No guest unnoticed to the lady came,
He judged th' event with mingled joy and
        shame ;

'Should her Eliza—no ! she was too just,
Too good and kind—but ah ! too young to
    trust.'
Anna return'd, her former place resumed,
And faded beauty with new grace re-bloom'd ;
And if some whispers of the past were heard,
They died innoxious, as no cause appear'd ;
But other cares on Anna's bosom press'd,
She saw her father gloomy and distress'd ;
He died o'erwhelm'd with debt, and soon was
    shed
The filial sorrow o'er a mother dead :
She sought Eliza's arms, that faithful friend
    was wed ;
Then was compassion by the countess shown,
And all th' adventures of her life are known.
    And now beyond her hopes—no longer tried
By slavish awe—she lived a yeoman's bride ;
Then bless'd her lot, and with a grateful mind
Was careful, cheerful, vigilant, and kind :
The gentle husband felt supreme delight,
Bless'd by her joy, and happy in her sight ;
He saw with pride in every friend and guest
High admiration and regard express'd :
With greater pride, and with superior joy,
He look'd exulting on his first-born boy ;
To her fond breast the wife her infant strain'd,
Some feelings utter'd, some were not explain'd ;
And she enraptured with her treasure grew,
The sight familiar, but the pleasure new.
    Yet there appear'd within that tranquil
        state
Some threat'ning prospect of uncertain fate ;
Between the married when a secret lies,
It wakes suspicion from enforced disguise :
Still thought the wife upon her absent friend,
With all that must upon her truth depend ;
' There is no being in the world beside,
Who can discover what that friend will hide ;
Who knew the fact, knew not my name or
    state,
Who these can tell cannot the fact relate ;
But thou, Eliza, canst the whole impart,
And all my safety is thy generous heart.'
    Mix'd with these fears—but light and
        transient these—
Fled years of peace, prosperity, and ease ;
So tranquil all that scarce a gloomy day
For days of gloom unmix'd prepared the way :
One eve, the wife, still happy in her state,
Sang gaily, thoughtless of approaching fate ;
Then came a letter, that (received in dread
Not unobserved) she in confusion read ;

The substance this—' Her friend rejoiced to
    find
That she had riches with a grateful mind ;
While poor Eliza had from place to place
Been lured by hope to labour for disgrace ;
That every scheme her wandering husband
    tried,
Pain'd while he lived, and perish'd when he
    died.'
She then of want in angry style complain'd,
Her child a burthen to her life remain'd,
Her kindred shunn'd her prayers, no friend
    her soul sustain'd.
    ' Yet why neglected ?   Dearest Anna knew
Her worth once tried, her friendship ever true ;
She hoped, she trusted, though by wants
    oppress'd,
To lock the treasured secret in her breast ;
Yet, vex'd by trouble, must apply to one,
For kindness due to her for kindness done.'
    In Anna's mind was tumult, in her face
Flushings of dread had momentary place :
' I must,' she judged, ' these cruel lines expose,
Or fears, or worse than fears, my crime
    disclose.'
    The letter shown, he said, with sober smile—
' Anna, your friend has not a friendly style :
Say, where could you with this fair lady dwell,
Who boasts of secrets that she scorns to tell ? '
' At school,' she answer'd : he ' at school ! '
    replied ;
' Nay, then I know the secrets you would hide :
Some longings these, without dispute,
Some youthful gaspings for forbidden fruit :
Why so disorder'd, love? are such the crimes,
That give us sorrow in our graver times ?
Come, take a present for your friend, and rest
In perfect peace—you find you are confess'd.'
    This cloud, though past, alarm'd the con-
        scious wife,
Presaging gloom and sorrow for her life ;
Who to her answer join'd a fervent prayer,
That her Eliza would a sister spare :
If she again—but was there cause ?—should
    send,
Let her direct—and then she named a friend :
A sad expedient untried friends to trust,
And still to fear the tried may be unjust :
Such is his pain, who, by his debt oppress'd,
Seeks by new bonds a temporary rest.
    Few were her peaceful days till Anna read
The words she dreaded, and had cause to
    dread :—

' Did she believe, did she, unkind, suppose
That thus Eliza's friendship was to close ?
No ! though she tried, and her desire was
    plain,
To break the friendly bond, she strove in vain :
Ask'd she for silence ? why so loud the call,
And yet the token of her love so small ?
By means like these will you attempt to bind
And check the movements of an injured mind ?
Poor as I am, I shall be proud to show
What dangerous secrets I may safely know :
Secrets to men of jealous minds convey'd,
Have many a noble house in ruins laid :
Anna, I trust, although with wrongs beset,
And urged by want, I shall be faithful yet ;
But what temptation may from these arise,
To take a slighted woman by surprise,
Becomes a subject for your serious care—
For who offends, must for offence prepare.'
  Perplex'd, dismay'd, the wife foresaw her
    doom ;
A day deferr'd was yet a day to come ;
But still, though painful her suspended state,
She dreaded more the crisis of her fate ;
Better to die than Stafford's scorn to meet,
And her strange friend perhaps would be
    discreet :
Presents she sent, and made a strong appeal
To woman's feelings, begging her to feel ;
With too much force she wrote of jealous men,
And her tears falling spoke beyond the pen ;
Eliza's silence she again implored,
And promised all that prudence could afford.
  For looks composed and careless Anna tried ;
She seem'd in trouble, and unconscious sigh'd :
The faithful husband, who devoutly loved
His silent partner, with concern reproved :
' What secret sorrows on my Anna press,
That love may not partake, nor care redress ?'
' None, none,' she answer'd, with a look so
    kind,
That the fond man determined to be blind.
  A few succeeding weeks of brief repose
In Anna's cheek revived the faded rose ;
A hue like this the western sky displays,
That glows awhile, and withers as we gaze.
  Again the friend's tormenting letter came—
' The wants she suffer'd were affection's
    shame ;
She with her child a life of terrors led,
Unhappy fruit ! but of a lawful bed :
Her friend was tasting every bliss in life,
The joyful mother, and the wealthy wife ;

While she was placed in doubt, in fear, in want,
To starve on trifles that the happy grant ;
Poorly for all her faithful silence paid,
And tantalized by ineffectual aid :
She could not thus a beggar's lot endure ;
She wanted something permanent and sure :
If they were friends, then equal be their lot,
And she was free to speak if they were not.'
  Despair and terror seized the wife, to find
The artful workings of a vulgar mind :
Money she had not, but the hint of dress
Taught her new bribes, new terrors to redress :
She with such feeling then described her woes,
That envy's self might on the view repose ;
Then to a mother's pains she made appeal,
And painted grief like one compell'd to feel.
  Yes ! so she felt, that in her air, her face,
In every purpose, and in every place ;
In her slow motion, in her languid mien,
The grief, the sickness of her soul were seen
Of some mysterious ill the husband sure,
Desired to trace it, for he hoped to cure ;
Something he knew obscurely, and had seen
His wife attend a cottage on the green ;
Love, loth to wound, endured conjecture long,
Till fear would speak, and spoke in language
    strong.
  ' All I must know, my Anna—truly know
Whence these emotions, terrors, troubles flow ;
Give me thy grief, and I will fairly prove
Mine is no selfish, no ungenerous love.'
  Now Anna's soul the seat of strife became,
Fear with respect contended, love with shame ;
But fear prevailing was the ruling guide,
Prescribing what to show and what to hide.
  ' It is my friend,' she said—' but why
    disclose
A woman's weakness struggling with her woes ?
Yes, she has grieved me by her fond com-
    plaints,
The wrongs she suffers, the distress she paints :
Something we do—but she afflicts me still,
And says, with power to help, I want the will ;
This plaintive style I pity and excuse,
Help when I can, and grieve when I refuse ;
But here my useless sorrows I resign,
And will be happy in a love like thine.'
  The husband doubted ; he was kind but
    cool :—
' 'Tis a strong friendship to arise at school ;
Once more then, love, once more the sufferer
    aid, —
I too can pity, but I must upbraid ;

Of these vain feelings then thy bosom free,
Nor be o'erwhelm'd by useless sympathy.'
　The wife again despatch'd the useless bribe,
Again essay'd her terrors to describe ;
Again with kindest words entreated peace,
And begg'd her offerings for a time might
　　cease.
A calm succeeded, but too like the one
That causes terror ere the storm comes on :
A secret sorrow lived in Anna's heart,
In Stafford's mind a secret fear of art ;
Not long they lasted—this determined foe
Knew all her claims, and nothing would
　forego ;
Again her letter came, where Anna read,
' My child, one cause of my distress, is dead :
Heav'n has my infant : ' ' Heartless wretch ! '
　she cried,
' Is this thy joy ? ' ' I am no longer tied :
Now will I, hast'ning to my friend, partake
Her cares and comforts, and no more forsake;
Now shall we both in equal station move,
Save that my friend enjoys a husband's love.'
　Complaint and threats so strong the wife
　　amazed,
Who wildly on her cottage-neighbour gazed;
Her tones, her trembling, first betray'd her
　grief ;
When floods of tears gave anguish its relief.
She fear'd that Stafford would refuse assent,
And knew her selfish friend would not relent ;
She must petition, yet delay'd the task,
Ashamed, afraid, and yet compell'd to ask ;
Unknown to him some object fill'd her mind,
And, once suspicious, he became unkind :
They sate one evening, each absorb'd in gloom,
When, hark ! a noise and rushing to the room,
The friend tripp'd lightly in, and laughing
　said, ' I come.'
Anna received her with an anxious mind,
And meeting whisper'd, ' Is Eliza kind ? '
Reserved and cool, the husband sought to
　prove
The depth and force of this mysterious love.
To nought that pass'd between the stranger-
　friend
And his meek partner seem'd he to attend ;
But, anxious, listen'd to the lightest word
That might some knowledge of his guest
　afford ;
And learn the reason one to him so dear
Should feel such fondness, yet betray such
　fear.

　Soon he perceived this uninvited guest,
Unwelcome too, a sovereign power possess'd;
Lofty she was and careless, while the meek
And humbled Anna was afraid to speak :
As mute she listen'd with a painful smile,
Her friend sate laughing and at ease the while,
Telling her idle tales with all the glee
Of careless and unfeeling levity.
With calm good sense he knew his wife endued,
And now with wounded pride her conduct
　view'd ;
Her speech was low,her every look convey'd—
' I am a slave, subservient and afraid.'
All trace of comfort vanish'd if she spoke,
The noisy friend upon her purpose broke ;
To her remarks with insolence replied,
And her assertions doubted or denied ;
While the meek Anna like an infant shook,
Wo-struck and trembling at the serpent's look.
　' There is,' said Stafford, ' yes, there is a
　　cause—
This creature frights her,overpowers and awes.'
Six weeks had pass'd—' In truth, my love,
　this friend
Has liberal notions ; what does she intend ?
Without a hint she came, and will she stay
Till she receives the hint to go away ? '
　Confused the wife replied, in spite of truth,
' I love the dear companion of my youth.'
' 'Tis well,' said Stafford ; ' then your loves
　renew ;
Trust me, your rivals, Anna, will be few.'
　Though playful this, she felt too much
　　distress'd
T' admit the consolation of a jest :
Ill she reposed, and in her dreams would sigh,
And murmuring forth her anguish beg to die ;
With sunken eye, slow pace, and pallid cheek,
She look'd confusion, and she fear'd to speak.
　All this the friend beheld, for, quick of sight,
She knew the husband eager for her flight ;
And that by force alone she could retain
The lasting comforts she had hope to gain :
She now perceived, to win her post for life,
She must infuse fresh terrors in the wife ;
Must bid to friendship's feebler ties adieu,
And boldly claim the object in her view :
She saw the husband's love, and knew the
　power
Her friend might use in some propitious hour.
　Meantime the anxious wife, from pure
　　distress
Assuming courage, said, ' I will confess ; '

But with her children felt a parent's pride,
And sought once more the hated truth to hide.

Offended, grieved, impatient, Stafford bore
The odious change till he could bear no more ;
A friend to truth, in speech and action plain,
He held all fraud and cunning in disdain ;
But fraud to find, and falsehood to detect,
For once he fled to measures indirect.

One day the friends were seated in that
room
The guest with care adorn'd, and named her
home :
To please the eye, there curious prints were
placed,
And some light volumes to amuse the taste ;
Letters and music, on a table laid,
The favourite studies of the fair betray'd ;
Beneath the window was the toilet spread,
And the fire gleam'd upon a crimson bed.

In Anna's looks and falling tears were seen
How interesting had their subjects been :
' Oh ! then,' resumed the friend, ' I plainly
find
That you and Stafford know each other's
mind ;
I must depart, must on the world be thrown,
Like one discarded, worthless and unknown ;
But shall I carry, and to please a foe,
A painful secret in my bosom ? No !
Think not your friend a reptile you may tread
Beneath your feet, and say, the worm is dead ;
I have some feeling, and will not be made
The scorn of her whom love cannot persuade :
Would not your word, your slightest wish,
effect
All that I hope, petition, or expect ?
The power you have, but you the use de-
cline—
Proof that you feel not, or you fear not
mine.
There was a time, when I, a tender maid,
Flew at a call, and your desires obey'd ;
A very mother to the child became,
Consoled your sorrow, and conceal'd your
shame ;
But now, grown rich and happy, from the door
You thrust a bosom-friend, despised and poor ;
That child alive, its mother might have known
The hard, ungrateful spirit she has shown.'

Here paused the guest, and Anna cried at
length—
' You try me, cruel friend ! beyond my
strength ;

Would I had been beside my infant laid,
Where none would vex me, threaten, or
upbraid.'

In Anna's looks the friend beheld despair ;
Her speech she soften'd, and composed her air;
Yet, while professing love, she answered still—
' You can befriend me, but you want the will.'
They parted thus, and Anna went her way,
To shed her secret sorrows, and to pray.

Stafford, amused with books, and fond of
home,
By reading oft dispell'd the evening gloom ;
History or tale—all heard him with delight,
And thus was pass'd this memorable night.

The listening friend bestow'd a flattering
smile ;
A sleeping boy the mother held the while ;
And ere she fondly bore him to his bed,
On his fair face the tear of anguish shed.

And now his task resumed, ' My tale,'
said he,
' Is short and sad, short may our sadness
be ! '—

The Caliph Harun *, as historians tell,
Ruled, for a tyrant, admirably well ;
Where his own pleasures were not touch'd,
to men
He was humane, and sometimes even then ;
Harun was fond of fruits, and gardens fair,
And wo to all whom he found poaching there :
Among his pages was a lively boy,
Eager in search of every trifling joy ;
His feelings vivid, and his fancy strong,
He sigh'd for pleasure while he shrank from
wrong ;
When by the caliph in the garden placed
He saw the treasures which he long'd to taste ;
And oft alone he ventured to behold
Rich hanging fruits with rind of glowing gold ;
Too long he staid forbidden bliss to view,
His virtue failing, as his longings grew ;
Athirst and wearied with the noon-tide heat,
Fate to the garden led his luckless feet ;
With eager eyes and open mouth he stood,
Smelt the sweet breath, and touch'd the
fragrant food ;
The tempting beauty sparkling in the sun
Charm'd his young sense—he ate, and was
undone :

* The sovereign here meant is the Haroun
Alraschid, or Harun al Raschid, who died early
in the ninth century: he is often the hearer,
and sometimes the hero, of a tale in the Arabian
Nights' Entertainments.

When the fond glutton paused, his eyes around
He turn'd, and eyes upon him turning found ;
Pleased he beheld the spy, a brother-page,
A friend allied in office and in age ;
Who promised much that secret he would be,
But high the price he fix'd on secrecy.
' "Were you suspected, my unhappy friend,"
Began the boy, " where would your sorrows
     end ?
In all the palace there is not a page
The caliph would not torture in his rage :
I think I see thee now impaled alive,
Writhing in pangs—but come, my friend !
     revive ;
Had some beheld you, all your purse contains
Could not have saved you from terrific pains ;
I scorn such meanness ; and, if not in debt,
Would not an asper on your folly set."
     ' The hint was strong ; young Osmyn
     search'd his store
For bribes, and found he soon could bribe no
     more ;
That time arrived, for Osmyn's stock was
     small,
And the young tyrant now possess'd it all ;
The cruel youth, with his companions near,
Gave the broad hint that raised the sudden
     fear ;
Th' ungenerous insult now was daily shown,
And Osmyn's peace and honest pride were
     flown ;
Then came augmenting woes, and fancy strong
Drew forms of suffering, a tormenting throng ;
He felt degraded, and the struggling mind
Dared not be free, and could not be resign'd ;
And all his pains and fervent prayers obtain'd
Was truce from insult, while the fears re-
     main'd.
     ' One day it chanced that this degraded boy
And tyrant-friend were fix'd at their employ ;
Who now had thrown restraint and form
     aside,
And for his bribe in plainer speech applied :
" Long have I waited, and the last supply
Was but a pittance, yet how patient I !
But give me now what thy first terrors gave,
My speech shall praise thee, and my silence
     save."
     Osmyn had found, in many a dreadful
     day,
The tyrant fiercer when he seem'd in play :
He begg'd forbearance ; " I have not to give ;
Spare me awhile, although 'tis pain to live :

Oh ! had that stolen fruit the power possess'd
To war with life, I now had been at rest."
     ' "So fond of death," replied the boy, "'tis
     plain
Thou hast no certain notion of the pain ;
But to the caliph were a secret shown,
Death has no pain that would be then
     unknown."
     ' Now,' says the story, ' in a closet near,
The monarch seated, chanced the boys to hear ;
There oft he came, when wearied on his
     throne,
To read, sleep, listen, pray, or be alone.
     ' The tale proceeds, when first the caliph
     found
That he was robb'd, although alone, he
     frown'd ;
And swore in wrath, that he would send the
     boy
Far from his notice, favour, or employ ;
But gentler movements soothed his ruffled
     mind,
And his own failings taught him to be kind.
     ' Relenting thoughts then painted Osmyn
     young,
His passion urgent, and temptation strong ;
And that he suffer'd from that villain-spy
Pains worse than death till he desired to die ;
Then if his morals had received a stain,
His bitter sorrows made him pure again :
To Reason, Pity lent her generous aid,
For one so tempted, troubled, and betray'd ;
And a free pardon the glad boy restored
To the kind presence of a gentle lord ;
Who from his office and his country drove
That traitor-friend, whom pains nor pray'rs
     could move ;
Who raised the fears no mortal could endure,
And then with cruel av'rice sold the cure.
     ' My tale is ended ; but, to be applied,
I must describe the place where caliphs hide.'
     Here both the females look'd alarm'd,
     distress'd,
With hurried passions hard to be express'd.
     ' It was a closet by a chamber placed,
Where slept a lady of no vulgar taste ;
Her friend attended in that chosen room
That she had honour'd and proclaim'd her
     home ;
To please the eye were chosen pictures placed,
And some light volumes to amuse the taste ;
Letters and music on a table laid,
For much the lady wrote, and often play'd ;

Beneath the window was a toilet spread,
And a fire gleam'd upon a crimson bed.'
　He paused, he rose ; with troubled joy the wife
Felt the new era of her changeful life ;
Frankness and love appear'd in Stafford's face,
And all her trouble to delight gave place.

Twice made the guest an effort to sustain
Her feelings, twice resumed her seat in vain,
Nor could suppress her shame, nor could support her pain :
Quick she retired, and all the dismal night
Thought of her guilt, her folly, and her flight;
Then sought unseen her miserable home,
To think of comforts lost, and brood on wants to come.

TALE XVII.　RESENTMENT

He hath a tear for pity, and a hand
Open as day for melting charity ;
Yet, notwithstanding, being incensed, he 's flint . . .
His temper, therefore, must be well observed.
　　　　　　　　2 *Henry IV*, Act iv, Scene 4.

Three or four wenches where I stood cried—
' Alas ! good soul !' and forgave him with all their hearts : but there 's no heed to be taken of them ; if Caesar had stabb'd their mothers, they would have done no less.
　　　　　　　　Julius Caesar, Act i, Scene 2.

How dost ? . . . Art cold ?
I'm cold myself—Where is this straw, my fellow ?
The art of our necessities is strange,
That can make vile things precious.
　　　　　　　　King Lear, Act iii, Scene 2.

FEMALES there are of unsuspicious mind,
Easy and soft, and credulous and kind ;
Who, when offended for the twentieth time,
Will hear th' offender and forgive the crime :
And there are others whom, like these to cheat,
Asks but the humblest effort of deceit ;
But they, once injured, feel a strong disdain,
And, seldom pardoning, never trust again ;
Urged by religion, they forgive—but yet
Guard the warm heart, and never more forget:
Those are like wax—apply them to the fire,
Melting, they take th' impressions you desire ;
Easy to mould, and fashion as you please,
And again moulded with an equal ease :
Like smelted iron these the forms retain,
But once impress'd will never melt again.

A busy port a serious merchant made
His chosen place to recommence his trade ;
And brought his lady, who, their children dead,
Their native seat of recent sorrow fled :

The husband duly on the quay was seen,
The wife at home became at length serene ;
There in short time the social couple grew
With all acquainted, friendly with a few ;
When the good lady, by disease assail'd,
In vain resisted—hope and science fail'd :
Then spake the female friends, by pity led,
' Poor merchant Paul ! what think ye ? will he wed ?
A quiet, easy, kind, religious man,
Thus can he rest ?—I wonder if he can.'
　He too, as grief subsided in his mind,
Gave place to notions of congenial kind ;
Grave was the man, as we have told before ;
His years were forty—he might pass for more;
Composed his features were, his stature low,
His air important, and his motion slow ;
His dress became him, it was neat and plain,
The colour purple, and without a stain ;
His words were few, and special was his care
In simplest terms his purpose to declare ;
No man more civil, sober, and discreet,
More grave and courteous, you could seldom meet :
Though frugal he, yet sumptuous was his board,
As if to prove how much he could afford ;
For though reserved himself, he loved to see
His table plenteous, and his neighbours free :
Among these friends he sat in solemn style,
And rarely soften'd to a sober smile ;
For this observant friends their reasons gave—
' Concerns so vast would make the idlest grave;
And for such man to be of language free,
Would seem incongruous as a singing tree :
Trees have their music, but the birds they shield
The pleasing tribute for protection yield ;

Each ample tree the tuneful choir defends,
As this rich merchant cheers his happy
    friends ! '
    In the same town it was his chance to meet
A gentle lady, with a mind discreet ;
Neither in life's decline, nor bloom of youth,
One fam'd for maiden modesty and truth :
By nature cool, in pious habits bred,
She look'd on lovers with a virgin's dread :
Deceivers, rakes, and libertines were they,
And harmless beauty their pursuit and prey ;
As bad as giants in the ancient times
Were modern lovers, and the same their
    crimes :
Soon as she heard of her all-conquering
    charms,
At once she fled to her defensive arms ;
Conn'd o'er the tales her maiden aunt had told,
And, statue-like, was motionless and cold ;
From prayer of love, like that Pygmalion
    pray'd,
Ere the hard stone became the yielding
    maid—
A different change in this chaste nymph
    ensued,
And turn'd to stone the breathing flesh and
    blood :
Whatever youth described his wounded heart,
' He came to rob her, and she scorn'd his art ;
And who of raptures once presumed to speak,
Told listening maids he thought them fond
    and weak ;
But should a worthy man his hopes display
In few plain words, and beg a *yes* or *nay*,
He would deserve an answer just and plain,
Since adulation only moved disdain—
Sir, if my friends object not, come again.'
    Hence, our grave lover, though he liked the
    face,
Praised not a feature—dwelt not on a grace ;
But in the simplest terms declared his state,
' A widow'd man, who wish'd a virtuous mate;
Who fear'd neglect, and was compell'd to
    trust
Dependents wasteful, idle, or unjust ;
Or should they not the trusted stores destroy,
At best, they could not help him to enjoy ;
But with her person and her prudence blest,
His acts would prosper, and his soul have
    rest:
Would she be his ? '—' Why, that was much
    to say ;
She would consider : he awhile might stay ;

She liked his manners, and believed his word ;
He did not flatter, flattery she abhorr'd :
It was her happy lot in peace to dwell—
Would change make better what was now so
    well ?
But she would ponder.'—' This,' he said,
    ' was kind,'
And begg'd to know ' when she had fix'd her
    mind.'
    Romantic maidens would have scorn'd the
    air,
And the cool prudence of a mind so fair ;
But well it pleased this wiser maid to find
Her own mild virtues in her lover's mind.
    His worldly wealth she sought, and quickly
    grew
Pleased with her search, and happy in the
    view
Of vessels freighted with abundant stores,
Of rooms whose treasures press'd the groan-
    ing floors ;
And he of clerks and servants could display
A little army, on a public day :
Was this a man like needy bard to speak
Of balmy lip, bright eye, or rosy cheek ?
    The sum appointed for her widow'd state,
Fix'd by her friend, excited no debate ;
Then the kind lady gave her hand and heart,
And, never finding, never dealt with art :
In his engagements she had no concern ;
He taught her not, nor had she wish to learn :
On him in all occasions she relied,
His word her surety, and his worth her
    pride.
    When ship was launch'd, and merchant
    Paul had share,
A bounteous feast became the lady's care ;
Who then her entry to the dinner made,
In costly raiment, and with kind parade.
    Call'd by this duty on a certain day,
And robed to grace it in a rich array,
Forth from her room with measured step she
    came,
Proud of th' event, and stately look'd the
    dame :
The husband met her at his study-door—
' This way, my love—one moment and no
    more :
A trifling business—you will understand,
The law requires that you affix your hand ;
But first attend, and you shall learn the cause
Why forms like these have been prescribed
    by laws : '

Then from his chair a man in black arose,
And with much quickness hurried off his
    prose :
That ' Ellen Paul the wife, and so forth, freed
From all control, her own the act and deed,
And forasmuch '——said she, ' I've no
    distrust,
For he that asks it is discreet and just ;
Our friends are waiting—where am I to
    sign ?—
There !——Now be ready when we meet to
    dine.'
    This said, she hurried off in great delight,
The ship was launch'd, and joyful was the
    night.
    Now, says the reader, and in much disdain,
This serious merchant was a rogue in grain ;
A treacherous wretch, an artful, sober knave,
And ten times worse for manners cool and
    grave ;
And she devoid of sense, to set her hand
To scoundrel deeds she could not understand.
    Alas ! 'tis true ; and I in vain had tried
To soften crime, that cannot be denied ;
And might have labour'd many a tedious
    verse
The latent cause of mischief to rehearse :
Be it confess'd, that long, with troubled look,
This trader view'd a huge accompting book
(His former marriage for a time delay'd
The dreaded hour, the present lent its aid) ;
But he too clearly saw the evil day,
And put the terror, by deceit, away ;
Thus by connecting with his sorrows crime,
He gain'd a portion of uneasy time.—
All this too late the injured lady saw ;
What law had given, again she gave to law ;
His guilt, her folly—these at once impress'd
Their lasting feelings on her guileless breast.
    ' Shame I can bear,' she cried, ' and want
    sustain,
But will not see this guilty wretch again : '
For all was lost, and he, with many a tear,
Confess'd the fault—she turning scorn'd to
    hear.
To legal claims he yielded all his worth,
But small the portion, and the wrong'd were
    wroth,
Nor to their debtor would a part allow ;
And where to live he knew not—knew not
    how.
    The wife a cottage found, and thither went
The suppliant man, but she would not relent :

Thenceforth she utter'd with indignant tone,
' I feel the misery, and will feel alone : '—
He would turn servant for her sake, would
    keep
The poorest school ; the very streets would
    sweep,
To show his love—' It was already shown :
And her affliction should be all her own.
His wants and weakness might have touch'd
    her heart,
But from his meanness she resolved to part.'
    In a small alley was she lodged, beside
Its humblest poor, and at the view she cried :
' Welcome—yes ! let me welcome, if I can,
The fortune dealt me by this cruel man ;
Welcome this low thatch'd roof, this shatter'd
    door,
These walls of clay, this miserable floor ;
Welcome my envied neighbours ; this, to you,
Is all familiar—all to me is new :
You have no hatred to the loathsome meal ;
Your firmer nerves no trembling terrors feel,
Nor, what you must expose, desire you to
    conceal ;
What your coarse feelings bear without
    offence,
Disgusts my taste, and poisons every sense :
Daily shall I your sad relations hear,
Of wanton women, and of men severe ;
There will dire curses, dreadful oaths abound,
And vile expressions shock me and confound ;
Noise of dull wheels, and songs with horrid
    words,
Will be the music that this lane affords ;
Mirth that disgusts, and quarrels that degrade
The human mind, must my retreat invade :
Hard is my fate ! yet easier to sustain,
Than to abide with guilt and fraud again ;
A grave impostor ! who expects to meet,
In such grey locks and gravity, deceit ?
Where the sea rages, and the billows roar,
Men know the danger, and they quit the
    shore ;
But, be there nothing in the way descried,
When o'er the rocks smooth runs the wicked
    tide—
Sinking unwarn'd, they execrate the shock,
And the dread peril of the sunken rock.'
    A frowning world had now the man to
    dread,
Taught in no arts, to no profession bred ;
Pining in grief, beset with constant care,
Wandering he went, to rest he knew not where.

Meantime the wife—but she abjured the
     name—
Endured her lot, and struggled with the
     shame ;
When lo ! an uncle on the mother's side,
In nature something, as in blood allied,
Admired her firmness, his protection gave,
And show'd a kindness she disdain'd to crave.

Frugal and rich the man, and frugal grew
The sister-mind, without a selfish view ;
And further still—the temp'rate pair agreed
With what they saved the patient poor to
     feed :
His whole estate, when to the grave consign'd,
Left the good kinsman to the kindred mind ;
Assured that law, with spell secure and tight,
Had fix'd it as her own peculiar right.

Now to her ancient residence removed,
She lived as widow, well endow'd and loved ;
Decent her table was, and to her door
Came daily welcomed the neglected poor :
The absent sick were soothed by her relief,
As her free bounty sought the haunts of grief;
A plain and homely charity had she,
And loved the objects of her alms to see ;
With her own hands she dress'd the savoury
     meat,
With her own fingers wrote the choice receipt ;
She heard all tales that injured wives relate,
And took a double interest in their fate ;
But of all husbands not a wretch was known
So vile, so mean, so cruel, as her own.

This bounteous lady kept an active spy,
To search th' abodes of want, and to supply ;
The gentle Susan served the liberal dame—
Unlike their notions, yet their deeds the same:
No practised villain could a victim find,
Than this stern lady more completely blind ;
Nor (if detected in his fraud) could meet
One less disposed to pardon a deceit ;
The wrong she treasured, and on no pretence
Received th' offender, or forgot th' offence :
But the kind servant, to the thrice-proved
     knave
A fourth time listen'd, and the past forgave.

First in her youth, when she was blithe and
     gay,
Came a smooth rogue, and stole her love away;
Then to another and another flew,
To boast the wanton mischief he could do :
Yet she forgave him, though so great her
     pain,
That she was never blithe or gay again.

Then came a spoiler, who, with villain-art,
Implored her hand, and agonized her heart ;
He seized her purse, in idle waste to spend
With a vile woman, whom she call'd her
     friend ;
Five years she suffer'd—he had revell'd five—
Then came to show her he was just alive ;
Alone he came, his vile companion dead ;
And he, a wand'ring pauper, wanting bread ;
His body wasted, wither'd life and limb,
When this kind soul became a slave to him ;
Nay, she was sure that, should he now survive,
No better husband would be left alive ;
For him she mourn'd, and then, alone and
     poor,
Sought and found comfort at her lady's door :
Ten years she served, and, mercy her employ,
Her tasks were pleasure, and her duty joy.

Thus lived the mistress and the maid,
     design'd
Each other's aid—one cautious, and both
     kind :
Oft at their window, working, they would sigh
To see the aged and the sick go by ;
Like wounded bees, that at their home arrive,
Slowly and weak, but labouring for the hive.

The busy people of a mason's yard
The curious lady view'd with much regard ;
With steady motion she perceived them
     draw
Through blocks of stone the slowly-working
     saw ;
It gave her pleasure and surprise to see
Among these men the signs of revelry :
Cold was the season, and confined their view,
Tedious their tasks, but merry were the crew :
There she beheld an aged pauper wait,
Patient and still, to take an humble freight ;
Within the panniers on an ass he laid
The ponderous grit, and for the portion paid ;
This he re-sold, and, with each trifling gift,
Made shift to live, and wretched was the shift.

Now will it be by every reader told
Who was this humble trader, poor and old.—
In vain an author would a name suppress,
From the least hint a reader learns to guess ;
Of children lost, our novels sometimes treat,
We never care—assured again to meet :
In vain the writer for concealment tries,
We trace his purpose under all disguise ;
Nay, though he tells us they are dead and
     gone,
Of whom we wot—they will appear anon ;

Our favourites fight, are wounded, hopeless lie,
Survive they cannot—nay, they cannot die ;
Now, as these tricks and stratagems are known,
'Tis best, at once, the simple truth to own.
　　This was the husband—in an humble shed
He nightly slept, and daily sought his bread :
Once for relief the weary man applied ;
' Your wife is rich,' the angry vestry cried :
Alas ! he dared not to his wife complain,
Feeling her wrongs, and fearing her disdain :
By various methods he had tried to live,
But not one effort would subsistence give :
He was an usher in a school, till noise
Made him less able than the weaker boys ;
On messages he went, till he in vain
Strove names, or words, or meanings to retain;
Each small employment in each neighbouring
　　town
By turn he took, to lay as quickly down :
For, such his fate, he fail'd in all he plann'd,
And nothing prosper'd in his luckless hand.
　　At his old home, his motive half suppress'd,
He sought no more for riches, but for rest :
There lived the bounteous wife, and at her gate
He saw in cheerful groups the needy wait ;
' Had he a right with bolder hope t' apply ? '
He ask'd—was answer'd, and went groaning
　　by :
For some remains of spirit, temper, pride,
Forbade a prayer he knew would be denied.
　　Thus was the grieving man, with burthen'd
　　ass,
Seen day by day along the street to pass :
' Who is he, Susan ? who the poor old man ?
He never calls—do make him, if you can.'—
The conscious damsel still delay'd to speak,
She stopp'd confused, and had her words to
　　seek ;
From Susan's fears the fact her mistress knew,
And cried—' The wretch ! what scheme has
　　he in view ?
Is this his lot ?—but let him, let him feel—
Who wants the courage, not the will to steal.'
　　A dreadful winter came, each day severe,
Misty when mild, and icy cold when clear ;
And still the humble dealer took his load,
Returning slow, and shivering on the road :
The lady, still relentless, saw him come,
And said—' I wonder, has the wretch a
　　home ? '
' A hut ! a hovel ! '—' Then his fate appears
To suit his crime ; '—' Yes lady, not his
　　years ;—

No ! nor his sufferings—nor that form
　　decay'd.'
' Well, let the parish give its paupers aid :
You must the vileness of his acts allow ; '
' And you, dear lady, that he feels it now.'
' When such dissemblers on their deeds reflect,
Can they the pity they refused expect ?
He that doth evil, evil shall he dread.'—
' The snow,' quoth Susan, ' falls upon his
　　bed—
It blows beside the thatch—it melts upon his
　　head.'—
' 'Tis weakness, child, for grieving guilt to
　　feel : '
' Yes, but he never sees a wholesome meal ;
Through his bare dress appears his shrivell'd
　　skin,
And ill he fares without, and worse within :
With that weak body, lame, diseased, and
　　slow,
What cold, pain, peril, must the sufferer
　　know ! '
' Think on his crime.'—' Yes, sure 'twas very
　　wrong ;
But look, (God bless him !) how he gropes
　　along.'—
' Brought me to shame.'—' Oh ! yes, I know
　　it all—
What cutting blast ! and he can scarcely
　　crawl ;
He freezes as he moves—he dies ! if he should
　　fall :
With cruel fierceness drives this icy sleet—
And must a Christian perish in the street,
In sight of Christians ?—There ! at last, he
　　lies ;—
Nor unsupported can he ever rise ;
He cannot live.'—' But is he fit to die ? '—
Here Susan softly mutter'd a reply,
Look'd round the room—said something of
　　its state,
Dives the rich, and Lazarus at his gate ;
And then aloud—' In pity do behold
The man affrighten'd, weeping, trembling,
　　cold :
Oh ! how those flakes of snow their entrance
　　win
Through the poor rags, and keep the frost
　　within ;
His very heart seems frozen as he goes,
Leading that starved companion of his woes :
He tried to pray—his lips, I saw them move,
And he so turn'd his piteous looks above ;

But the fierce wind the willing heart opposed,
And, ere he spoke, the lips in misery closed :
Poor suffering object ! yes, for ease you
    pray'd,
And God will hear—he only, I'm afraid.'
  ' Peace ! Susan, peace ! Pain ever follows
    sin.'—
' Ah ! then,' thought Susan, ' when will ours
    begin ?
' When reach'd his home, to what a cheerless
    fire
And chilling bed will those cold limbs retire !
Yet ragged, wretched as it is, that bed
Takes half the space of his contracted shed ;
I saw the thorns beside the narrow grate,
With straw collected in a putrid state :
There will he, kneeling, strive the fire to
    raise,
And that will warm him, rather than the blaze;
The sullen, smoky blaze, that cannot last
One moment after his attempt is past :
And I so warmly and so purely laid,
To sink to rest—indeed, I am afraid.'—
' Know you his conduct ? '—' Yes, indeed,
    I know—
And how he wanders in the wind and snow :
Safe in our rooms the threat'ning storm we
    hear,
But he feels strongly what we faintly fear.'
' Wilful was rich, and he the storm defied ;
Wilful is poor, and must the storm abide ; '
Said the stern lady—' 'Tis in vain to feel ;
Go and prepare the chicken for our meal.'
  Susan her task reluctantly began,
And utter'd as she went—' The poor old
    man ! '—
But while her soft and ever-yielding heart
Made strong protest against her lady's part,
The lady's self began to think it wrong,
To feel so wrathful and resent so long.
  No more the wretch would she receive
    again,
No more behold him—but she would sus-
    tain ;
Great his offence, and evil was his mind—
But he had suffer'd, and she would be kind :
She spurn'd such baseness, and she found
    within
A fair acquittal from so foul a sin ;
Yet she too err'd, and must of Heaven expect
To be rejected, him should she reject.'
  Susan was summon'd—' I'm about to do
A foolish act, in part seduced by you ;

Go to the creature—say that I intend,
Foe to his sins, to be his sorrow's friend ;
Take, for his present comforts, food and
    wine,
And mark his feelings at this act of mine :
Observe if shame be o'er his features spread,
By his own victim to be soothed and fed ;
But, this inform him, that it is not love
That prompts my heart, that duties only
    move :
Say, that no merits in his favour plead,
But miseries only, and his abject need ;
Nor bring me grov'ling thanks, nor high-
    flown praise ;
I would his spirits, not his fancy raise :
Give him no hope that I shall ever more
A man so vile to my esteem restore ;
But warn him rather, that, in time of rest,
His crimes be all remember'd and con-
    fess'd :
I know not all that form the sinner's debt,
But there is one that he must not forget.'
  The mind of Susan prompted her with speed
To act her part in every courteous deed :
All that was kind she was prepared to say,
And keep the lecture for a future day ;
When he had all life's comforts by his side,
Pity might sleep, and good advice be tried.
  This done, the mistress felt disposed to look,
As self-approving, on a pious book :
Yet, to her native bias still inclined,
She felt her act too merciful and kind ;
But when, long musing on the chilling
    scene
So lately past—the frost and sleet so keen—
The man's whole misery in a single view—
Yes ! she could think some pity was his
    due.
  Thus fix'd, she heard not her attendant
    glide
With soft slow step—till, standing by her
    side,
The trembling servant gasp'd for breath, and
    shed
Relieving tears, then utter'd—' He is dead ! '
  ' Dead !' said the startled lady ; ' Yes, he
    fell
Close at the door where he was wont to dwell ;
There his sole friend, the ass, was standing by,
Half dead himself, to see his master die.'
  ' Expired he then, good Heaven ! for want
    of food ? '
  ' No ! crusts and water in a corner stood ;—

To have this plenty, and to wait so
　　long,
And to be right too late, is doubly wrong :
Then, every day to see him totter by,
And to forbear—Oh ! what a heart had I ! '
　' Blame me not, child ; I tremble at the
　　news.'
' 'Tis my own heart,' said Susan, ' I accuse :

To have this money in my purse—to know
What grief was his, and what to grief we owe ;
To see him often, always to conceive
How he must pine and languish, groan and
　　grieve ;
And every day in ease and peace to dine,
And rest in comfort !—what a heart is
　　mine ! '—

TALE XVIII.　THE WAGER

'Tis thought your deer does hold you at a bay.
　　　Taming of the Shrew, Act v, Scene 2.

I choose her for myself :
If she and I are pleased, what 's that to you ?
　　　Ibid., Act v, Scene 2.

Let's each one send unto his wife,
And he whose wife is most obedient . . .
. . . Shall win the wager.
　　　Ibid., Act v, Scene 2.

Now by the world it is a lusty wench,
I love her ten times more than e'er I did.
　　　Ibid., Act ii, Scene 1.

COUNTER and CLUBB were men in trade, whose
　　pains,
Credit, and prudence, brought them constant
　　gains ;
Partners and punctual, every friend agreed
Counter and Clubb were men who must
　　succeed.
When they had fix'd some little time in life,
Each thought of taking to himself a wife :
As men in trade alike, as men in love
They seem'd with no according views to move ;
As certain ores in outward view the same,
They show'd their difference when the magnet
　　came.
Counter was vain : with spirit strong and high,
'Twas not in him like suppliant swain to sigh :
' His wife might o'er his men and maids
　　preside,
And in her province be a judge and guide ;
But what he thought, or did, or wish'd to do,
She must not know, or censure if she knew ;
At home, abroad, by day, by night, if he
On aught determined, so it was to be :
How is a man,' he ask'd, ' for business fit,
Who to a female can his will submit ?
Absent awhile, let no inquiring eye
Or plainer speech presume to question why :

But all be silent ; and, when seen again,
Let all be cheerful—shall a wife complain ?
Friends I invite, and who shall dare t' object,
Or look on them with coolness or neglect ?
No ! I must ever of my house be head,
And, thus obey'd, I condescend to wed.'
　Clubb heard the speech—' My friend is
　　nice,' said he ;
' A wife with less respect will do for me :
How is he certain such a prize to gain ?
What he approves, a lass may learn to feign,
And so affect t' obey till she begins to reign ;
Awhile complying, she may vary then,
And be as wives of more unwary men ;
Beside, to him who plays such lordly part,
How shall a tender creature yield her heart ?
Should he the promised confidence refuse,
She may another more confiding choose ;
May show her anger, yet her purpose hide,
And wake his jealousy, and wound his pride.
In one so humbled, who can trace the friend ?
I on an equal, not a slave, depend ;
If true, my confidence is wisely placed,
And being false, she only is disgraced.'
　Clubb, with these notions, cast his eye
　　around,
And one so easy soon a partner found.
The lady chosen was of good repute ;
Meekness she had not, and was seldom mute ;
Though quick to anger, still she loved to
　　smile ;
And would be calm if men would wait awhile :
She knew her duty, and she loved her way,
More pleased in truth to govern than obey ;
She heard her priest with reverence, and her
　　spouse
As one who felt the pressure of her vows :
Useful and civil, all her friends confess'd—
Give her her way, and she would choose the
　　best ;

Though some indeed a sly remark would make—
Give it her not, and she would choose to take.
All this, when Clubb some cheerful months had spent,
He saw, confess'd, and said he was content.
Counter meantime selected, doubted, weigh'd,
And then brought home a young complying maid ;—
A tender creature, full of fears as charms,
A beauteous nursling from its mother's arms ;
A soft, sweet blossom, such as men must love,
But to preserve must keep it in the stove :
She had a mild, subdued, expiring look—
Raise but the voice, and this fair creature shook ;
Leave her alone, she felt a thousand fears—
Chide, and she melted into floods of tears ;
Fondly she pleaded and would gently sigh,
For very pity, or she knew not why ;
One whom to govern none could be afraid—
Hold up the finger, this meek thing obey'd ;
Her happy husband had the easiest task—
Say but his will, no question would she ask ;
She sought no reasons, no affairs she knew,
Of business spoke not, and had nought to do.
Oft he exclaim'd, ' How meek ! how mild ! how kind !
With her 'twere cruel but to seem unkind ;
Though ever silent when I take my leave,
It pains my heart to think how hers will grieve ;
'Tis heaven on earth with such a wife to dwell,
I am in raptures to have sped so well ;
But let me not, my friend, your envy raise,
No ! on my life, your patience has my praise.'
His friend, though silent, felt the scorn implied—
' What need of patience ? ' to himself he cried :
' Better a woman o'er her house to rule,
Than a poor child just hurried from her school ;
Who has no care, yet never lives at ease ;
Unfit to rule, and indisposed to please ;
What if he govern, there his boast should end,
No husband's power can make a slave his friend.'
It was the custom of these friends to meet
With a few neighbours in a neighbouring street ;

Where Counter ofttimes would occasion seize,
To move his silent friend by words like these :
' A man,' said he, ' if govern'd by his wife,
Gives up his rank and dignity in life ;
Now better fate befalls my friend and me '—
He spoke, and look'd th' approving smile to see.
The quiet partner, when he chose to speak,
Desired his friend, ' another theme to seek ;
When thus they met, he judged that state-affairs
And such important subjects should be theirs :'
But still the partner, in his lighter vein,
Would cause in Clubb affliction or disdain ;
It made him anxious to detect the cause
Of all that boasting—' Wants my friend applause ?
This plainly proves him not at perfect ease,
For, felt he pleasure, he would wish to please.—
These triumphs here for some regrets atone—
Men who are blest let other men alone.'
Thus made suspicious, he observed and saw
His friend each night at early hour withdraw ;
He sometimes mention'd Juliet's tender nerves,
And what attention such a wife deserves :
' In this,' thought Clubb, ' full sure some mystery lies—
He laughs at me, yet he with much complies,
And all his vaunts of bliss are proud apologies.'
With such ideas treasured in his breast,
He grew composed, and let his anger rest ;
Till Counter once (when wine so long went round
That friendship and discretion both were drown'd)
Began in teasing and triumphant mood
His evening banter—' Of all earthly good,
The best,' he said, ' was an obedient spouse,
Such as my friend's—that every one allows :
What if she wishes his designs to know ?
It is because she would her praise bestow ;
What if she wills that he remains at home ?
She knows that mischief may from travel come.
I, who am free to venture where I please,
Have no such kind preventing checks as these ;
But mine is double duty, first to guide
Myself aright, then rule a house beside ;
While this our friend, more happy than the free,
Resigns all power, and laughs at liberty.'

' By Heaven,' said Clubb, ' excuse me if I swear,
I'll bet a hundred guineas, if he dare,
That uncontroll'd I will such freedoms take,'
That he will fear to equal—there's my stake.'
  ' A match ! ' said Counter, much by wine inflamed ;
' But we are friends—let smaller stake be named :
Wine for our future meeting, that will I
Take and no more—what peril shall we try ? '
' Let's to Newmarket,' Clubb replied ; ' or choose
Yourself the place, and what you like to lose ;
And he who first returns, or fears to go,
Forfeits his cash— ' Said Counter, ' Be it so.'
  The friends around them saw with much delight
The social war, and hail'd the pleasant night ;
Nor would they further hear the cause discuss'd,
Afraid the recreant heart of Clubb to trust.
  Now sober thoughts return'd as each withdrew,
And of the subject took a serious view ;
' 'Twas wrong,' thought Counter, ' and will grieve my love ; '
' 'Twas wrong,' thought Clubb, ' my wife will not approve ;
But friends were present ; I must try the thing,
Or with my folly half the town will ring.'
  He sought his lady—'Madam, I'm to blame,
But was reproach'd, and could not bear the shame ;
Here in my folly—for 'tis best to say
The very truth—I've sworn to have my way :
To that Newmarket—(though I hate the place,
And have no taste or talents for a race,
Yet so it is—well, now prepare to chide)—
I laid a wager that I dared to ride ;
And I must go : by Heaven, if you resist
I shall be scorn'd, and ridiculed, and hiss'd ;
Let me with grace before my friends appear,
You know the truth, and must not be severe ;
He too must go, but that he will of course ;
Do you consent ?—I never think of force.'
  ' You never need,' the worthy dame replied;
' The husband's honour is the woman's pride ;
If I in trifles be the wilful wife,
Still for your credit I would lose my life ;
Go ! and when fix'd the day of your return,
Stay longer yet, and let the blockheads learn,

That though a wife may sometimes wish to rule,
She would not make th' indulgent man a fool ;
I would at times advise—but idle they
Who think th' assenting husband *must* obey.'
  The happy man, who thought his lady right
In other cases, was assured to-night ;
Then for the day with proud delight prepared,
To show his doubting friends how much he dared.
  Counter—who grieving sought his bed, his rest
Broken by pictures of his love distress'd—
With soft and winning speech the fair prepared ;
' She all his councils, comforts, pleasures shared :
She was assured he loved her from his soul,
She never knew and need not fear control ;
But so it happen'd—he was grieved at heart,
It happen'd so, that they awhile must part—
A little time—the distance was but short,
And business call'd him—he despised the sport ;
But to Newmarket he engaged to ride,
With his friend Clubb,' and there he stopp'd and sigh'd.
  Awhile the tender creature look'd dismay'd,
Then floods of tears the call of grief obey'd :—
' She an objection ! No ! ' she sobb'd, ' not one ;
Her work was finish'd, and her race was run ;
For die she must, indeed she would not live
A week alone, for all the world could give ;
He too must die in that same wicked place ;
It always happen'd—was a common case ;
Among those horrid horses, jockeys, crowds,
'Twas certain death—they might bespeak their shrouds ;
He would attempt a race, be sure to fall—
And she expire with terror—that was all ;
With love like hers she was indeed unfit
To bear such horrors, but she must submit.'
  ' But for three days, my love ! three days at most— '
' Enough for me ; I then shall be a ghost— '
' My honour 's pledged ! '—' Oh ! yes, my dearest life,
I know your honour must outweigh your wife ;
But ere this absence, have you sought a friend ?
I shall be dead—on whom can you depend ?
Let me one favour of your kindness crave—
Grant me the stone I mention'd for my grave.— '

'Nay, love, attend—why, bless my soul—
    I say
I will return—there—weep no longer—
    nay !—'
'Well ! I obey, and to the last am true,
But spirits fail me ; I must die ; adieu ! '
    'What, madam ! must ?—'tis wrong—I'm
    angry—zounds !
Can I remain and lose a thousand pounds ? '
    ' Go then, my love ! it is a monstrous sum,
Worth twenty wives—go, love ! and I am
    dumb—
Nor be displeased—had I the power to live,
You might be angry, now you must forgive ;
Alas ! I faint—ah ! cruel—there's no need
Of wounds or fevers—this has done the deed.'
    The lady fainted, and the husband sent
For every aid, for every comfort went ;
Strong terror seized him ; ' Oh ! she loved
    so well,
And who th' effect of tenderness could tell ? '
    She now recover'd, and again began
With accent querulous—' Ah ! cruel man—'
Till the sad husband, conscience-struck,
    confess'd,
'Twas very wicked with his friend to jest ;
For now he saw that those who were obey'd,
Could like the most subservient feel afraid ;
And though a wife might not dispute the will
Of her liege lord, she could prevent it still.
    The morning came, and Clubb prepared to
    ride
With a smart boy, his servant and his guide ;
When, ere he mounted on the ready steed,
Arrived a letter, and he stopp'd to read.
    ' My friend,' he read—' our journey I
    decline,
A heart too tender for such strife is mine ;
Yours is the triumph, be you so inclined ;
But you are too considerate and kind :
In tender pity to my Juliet's fears
I thus relent, o'ercome by love and tears ;
She knows your kindness ; I have heard her
    say,
A man like you 'tis pleasure to obey :

Each faithful wife, like ours, must disapprove
Such dangerous trifling with connubial love ;
What has the idle world, my friend, to do
With our affairs ? they envy me and you :
What if I could my gentle spouse command—
Is that a cause I should her tears withstand ?
And what if you, a friend of peace, submit
To one you love—is that a theme for wit ?
'Twas wrong, and I shall henceforth judge it
    weak
Both of submission and control to speak :
Be it agreed that all contention cease,
And no such follies vex our future peace ;
Let each keep guard against domestic strife,
And find nor slave nor tyrant in his wife.'
    ' Agreed,' said Clubb, ' with all my soul
    agreed '—
And to the boy, delighted, gave his steed ;
' I think my friend has well his mind express'd,
And I assent ; such things are not a jest.'
    ' True,' said the wife, ' no longer he can hide
The truth that pains him by his wounded
    pride :
Your friend has found it not an easy thing,
Beneath his yoke, this yielding soul to bring ;
These weeping willows, though they seem
    inclined
By every breeze, yet not the strongest wind
Can from their bent divert this weak but
    stubborn kind ;
Drooping they seek your pity to excite,
But 'tis at once their nature and delight ;
Such women feel not ; while they sigh and
    weep,
'Tis but their habit—their affections sleep ;
They are like ice that in the hand we hold,
So very melting, yet so very cold ;
On such affection let not man rely,
The husbands suffer, and the ladies sigh :
But your friend's offer let us kindly take,
And spare his pride for his vexation's sake ;
For he has found, and through his life will find,
'Tis easiest dealing with the firmest mind—
More just when it resists, and, when it yields,
    more kind.'

TALE XIX.   THE CONVERT

A tapster is a good trade, an old cloak
makes a new jerkin ; a wither'd serving-man,
a fresh tapster.
Merry Wives of Windsor, Act i, Scene 3.

A fellow, sir, that I have known go about with
troll-my-dames.
Winter's Tale, Act iv, Scene 2.

I myself, sometimes leaving the fear of
God on the left hand, and hiding mine honour
in my necessity, am fain to shuffle, to hedge,
and to lurch.
Merry Wives of Windsor, Act ii, Scene 2.

Yea, at that very moment,
Consideration like an angel came,
And whipp'd the offending Adam out of him.
Henry V, Act i, Scene 1.

I have liv'd long enough : My May of life
Is fall'n into the sear, the yellow leaf ;
And that which should accompany old age,
As honour, love, obedience, troops of friends,
I must not look to have.
Macbeth, Act v, Scene 3.

SOME to our hero have a hero's name
Denied, because no father's he could claim ;
Nor could his mother with precision state
A full fair claim to her certificate ;
On her own word the marriage must depend—
A point she was not eager to defend :
But who, without a father's name, can raise
His own so high, deserves the greater praise :
The less advantage to the strife he brought,
The greater wonders has his prowess wrought ;
He who depends upon his wind and limbs,
Needs neither cork or bladder when he swims ;
Nor will by empty breath be puff'd along,
As not himself—but in his helpers—strong.
  Suffice it then, our hero's name was clear,
For, call John Dighton, and he answer'd,
    ' Here ! '
But who that name in early life assign'd
He never found, he never tried to find ;
Whether his kindred were to John disgrace,
Or John to them, is a disputed case :
His infant-state owed nothing to their care—
His mind neglected, and his body bare ;
All his success must on himself depend,
He had no money, counsel, guide, or friend ;
But in a market-town an active boy
Appear'd, and sought in various ways employ;

Who soon, thus cast upon the world, began
To show the talents of a thriving man.
  With spirit high John learn'd the world to
    brave,
And in both senses was a ready knave ;
Knave as of old, obedient, keen, and quick,
Knave as at present, skill'd to shift and trick ;
Some humble part of many trades he caught,
He for the builder and the painter wrought ;
For serving-maids on secret errands ran,
The waiter's helper, and the hostler's man ;
And when he chanced (oft chanced he) place
    to lose,
His varying genius shone in blacking shoes :
A midnight fisher by the pond he stood,
Assistant poacher, he o'erlook'd the wood ;
At an election John's impartial mind
Was to no cause nor candidate confined ;
To all in turn he full allegiance swore,
And in his hat the various b⸻ bore :
His liberal soul with ever⸻ ⸻eed,
Unheard their reasons, he ⸻ ⸻ their creed;
At church he deign'd the ⸻ s to fill,
And at the meeting sang bot⸻ ⸻ ill :
But the full purse these different m⸻ ⸻ 'd,
By strong demands his lively passions d⸻ 'd;
Liquors he loved of each inflaming kind,
To midnight revels flew with ardent mind ;
Too warm at cards, a losing game he play'd,
To fleecing beauty his attention paid ;
His boiling passions were by oaths express'd,
And lies he made his profit and his jest.
  Such was the boy, and such the man had
    been,
But fate or happier fortune changed the scene;
A fever seized him, ' He should surely die— '
He fear'd, and lo ! a friend was praying by ;
With terror moved, this teacher he address'd,
And all the errors of his youth confess'd :
The good man kindly clear'd the sinner's
    way
To lively hope, and counsell'd him to pray ;
Who then resolved, should he from sickness
    rise,
To quit cards, liquors, poaching, oaths, and
    lies :
His health restored, he yet resolved, and grew
True to his masters, to their meeting true ;
His old companions at his sober face
Laugh'd loud, while he, attesting it was grace,

With tears besought them all his calling to
    embrace :
To his new friends such convert gave applause,
Life to their zeal, and glory to their cause :
Though terror wrought the mighty change,
    yet strong
Was the impression, and it lasted long ;
John at the lectures due attendance paid,
A convert meek, obedient, and afraid.
His manners strict, though form'd on fear
    alone,
Pleased the grave friends, nor less his solemn
    tone,
The lengthen'd face of care, the low and
    inward groan :
The stern good men exulted, when they saw
Those timid looks of penitence and awe ;
Nor thought that one so passive, humble,
    meek,
Had yet a creed and principles to seek.
    The faith that reason finds, confirms, avows,
The hopes, the views, the comforts he allows—
These were not his, who by his feelings found,
And by them only, that his faith was sound ;
Feelings of terror these, for evil past,
Feelings of hope, to be received at last ;
Now weak, now lively, changing with the
    day,
These were his feelings, and he felt his way.
    Sprung from such sources, will this faith
    remain
While these supporters can their strength
    retain :
As heaviest weights the deepest rivers pass,
While icy chains fast bind the solid mass ;
So, born of feelings, faith remains secure,
Long as their firmness and their strength
    endure :
But when the waters in their channel glide,
A bridge must bear us o'er the threat'ning
    tide ;
Such bridge is reason, and there faith relies,
Whether the varying spirits fall or rise.
    His patrons, still disposed their aid to lend,
Behind a counter placed their humble friend ;
Where pens and paper were on shelves
    display'd,
And pious pamphlets on the windows laid :
By nature active, and from vice restrain'd,
Increasing trade his bolder views sustain'd ;
His friends and teachers, finding so much zeal
In that young convert whom they taught to
    feel,

His trade encouraged, and were pleased to find
A hand so ready, with such humble mind.
    And now, his health restored, his spirits
    eased,
He wish'd to marry, if the teachers pleased.
They, not unwilling, from the virgin-class
Took him a comely and a courteous lass ;
Simple and civil, loving and beloved,
She long a fond and faithful partner proved ;
In every year the elders and the priest
Were duly summon'd to a christening feast ;
Nor came a babe, but by his growing trade,
John had provision for the coming made ;
For friends and strangers all were pleased to
    deal
With one whose care was equal to his zeal.
    In human friendships, it compels a sigh,
To think what trifles will dissolve the tie.
John, now become a master of his trade,
Perceived how much improvement might be
    made ;
And as this prospect open'd to his view,
A certain portion of his zeal withdrew ;
His fear abated—' What had he to fear—
His profits certain, and his conscience clear ? '
Above his door a board was placed by John,
And ' Dighton, stationer,' was gilt thereon ;
His window next, enlarged to twice the size,
Shone with such trinkets as the simple prize ;
While in the shop with pious works were seen
The last new play, review, or magazine :
In orders punctual, he observed—' The books
He never read, and could he judge their looks ?
Readers and critics should their merits try,
He had no office but to sell and buy ;
Like other traders, profit was his care ;
Of what they print, the authors must beware.'
He held his patrons and his teachers dear,
But with his trade—they must not interfere.
    'Twas certain now that John had lost the
    dread
And pious thoughts that once such terrors
    bred ;
His habits varied, and he more inclined
To the vain world, which he had half resign'd :
He had moreover in his brethren seen,
Or he imagined, craft, conceit, and spleen ;
' They are but men,' said John, ' and shall
    I then
Fear man's control, or stand in awe of men ?
'Tis their advice (their convert's rule and
    law),
And good it is—I will not stand in awe.'

Moreover Dighton, though he thought of
    books
As one who chiefly on the title looks,
Yet sometimes ponder'd o'er a page to find,
When vex'd with cares, amusement for his
    mind ;
And by degrees that mind had treasured much
From works his teachers were afraid to touch :
Satiric novels, poets bold and free,
And what their writers term philosophy ;
All these were read, and he began to feel
Some self-approval on his bosom steal.
Wisdom creates humility, but he
Who thus collects it, will not humble be :
No longer John was fill'd with pure delight
And humble reverence in a pastor's sight ;
Who, like a grateful zealot, listening stood,
To hear a man so friendly and so good ;
But felt the dignity of one who made
Himself important by a thriving trade ;
And growing pride in Dighton's mind was bred
By the strange food on which it coarsely fed.
    Their brother's fall the grieving brethren
    heard,
The pride indeed to all around appear'd ;
The world his friends agreed had won the soul
From its best hopes, the man from their
    control :
To make him humble, and confine his views
Within their bounds, and books which they
    peruse ;
A deputation from these friends select,
Might reason with him to some good effect ;
Arm'd with authority, and led by love,
They might those follies from his mind re-
    move ;
Deciding thus, and with this kind intent,
A chosen body with its speaker went.
    ' John,' said the teacher, ' John,' with
    great concern,
' We see thy frailty, and thy fate discern—
Satan with toils thy simple soul beset,
And thou art careless, slumbering in the net ;
Unmindful art thou of thy early vow ;
Who at the morning-meeting sees thee now ?
Who at the evening ? where is brother John ?
We ask—are answer'd, To the tavern gone :
Thee on the sabbath seldom we behold ;
Thou canst not sing, thou'rt nursing for a
    cold:
This from the churchmen thou hast learn'd,
    for they
Have colds and fevers on the sabbath-day ;

When in some snug warm room they sit, and
    pen
Bills from their ledgers, (world-entangled
    men !)
' See with what pride thou hast enlarged thy
    shop ;
To view thy tempting stores the heedless
    stop ;
By what strange names dost thou these
    baubles know,
Which wantons wear, to make a sinful show ?
Hast thou in view these idle volumes placed
To be the pander of a vicious taste ?
What's here ? a book of dances !—you
    advance
In goodly knowledge—John, wilt learn to
    dance ?
How ! " Go— " it says, and " to the devil go !
And shake thyself ! " I tremble—but 'tis
    so——
Wretch as thou art, what answer canst thou
    make ?
Oh ! without question, thou wilt go and shake.
What's here ? the " School for Scandal "—
    pretty schools !
Well, and art thou proficient in the rules ?
Art thou a pupil, is it thy design
To make our names contemptible as thine ?
" Old Nick, a Novel ! " oh ! 'tis mighty well—
A fool has courage when he laughs at hell ;
" Frolic and Fun," the humours of " Tim
    Grin ; "
Why, John, thou grow'st facetious in thy sin ;
And what ? " The Archdeacon's Charge "—
    'tis mighty well—
If Satan publish'd, thou wouldst doubtless
    sell ;
Jests, novels, dances, and this precious stuff,
To crown thy folly we have seen enough ;
We find thee fitted for each evil work—
Do print the Koran, and become a Turk.
    ' John, thou art lost ; success and worldly
    pride
O'er all thy thoughts and purposes preside,
Have bound thee fast, and drawn thee far
    aside :
Yet turn ; these sin-traps from thy shop expel,
Repent and pray, and all may yet be well.
    ' And here thy wife, thy Dorothy, behold,
How fashion's wanton robes her form infold !
Can grace, can goodness with such trappings
    dwell ?
John, thou hast made thy wife a Jezebel :

See ! on her bosom rests the sign of sin,
The glaring proof of naughty thoughts within;
What ? 'tis a cross ; come hither—as a friend,
Thus from thy neck the shameful badge I rend.'
   ' Rend, if you dare,' said Dighton ; ' you
      shall find
A man of spirit, though to peace inclined ;
Call me ungrateful ! have I not my pay
At all times ready for the expected day ?—
To share my plenteous board you deign to
      come,
Myself your pupil, and my house your home ;
And shall the persons who my meat enjoy
Talk of my faults, and treat me as a boy ?
Have you not told how Rome's insulting
      priests
Led their meek laymen like a herd of beasts ;
And by their fleecing and their forgery made
Their holy calling an accursed trade ?
Can you such acts and insolence condemn,
Who to your utmost power resemble them ?
   ' Concerns it you what books I set for sale ?
The tale perchance may be a virtuous tale ;
And for the rest, 'tis neither wise nor just,
In you, who read not, to condemn on trust ;
Why should th' Archdeacon's Charge your
      spleen excite ?
He, or perchance th' archbishop, may be right.
   ' That from your meetings I refrain, is true;
I meet with nothing pleasant—nothing new ;
But the same proofs, that not one text explain,
And the same lights, where all things dark
      remain ;
I thought you saints on earth—but I have
      found
Some sins among you, and the best unsound ;
You have your failings, like the crowds below,
And at your pleasure hot and cold can blow :
When I at first your grave deportment saw,
(I own my folly,) I was fill'd with awe ;
You spoke so warmly, and it seems so well,
I should have thought it treason to rebel ;
Is it a wonder that a man like me
Should such perfection in such teachers see ;
Nay, should conceive you sent from Heav'n
      to brave
The host of sin, and sinful souls to save ?
But as our reason wakes, our prospects clear,
And failings, flaws, and blemishes appear.
   ' When you were mounted in your rostrum
      high,
We shrank beneath your tone, your frown,
      your eye ;

Then you beheld us abject, fallen, low,
And felt your glory from our baseness grow ;
Touch'd by your words, I trembled like the
      rest,
And my own vileness and your power con-
      fess'd :
These, I exclaim'd, are men divine, and gazed
On him who taught, delighted and amazed ;
Glad when he finish'd, if by chance he cast
One look on such a sinner, as he pass'd.
   ' But when I view'd you in a clearer light,
And saw the frail and carnal appetite ;
When, at his humble pray'r, you deign'd to
      eat,
Saints as you are, a civil sinner's meat ;
When as you sat contented and at ease,
Nibbling at leisure on the ducks and peas,
And, pleased some comforts in such place to
      find,
You could descend to be a little kind ;
And gave us hope, in Heaven there might
      be room
For a few souls beside your own to come ;
While this world's good engaged your carnal
      view,
And like a sinner you enjoy'd it too ;
All this perceiving, can you think it strange
That change in you should work an equal
      change ? '
   ' Wretch that thou art,' an elder cried,
      ' and gone
For everlasting.'——' Go thyself,' said John;
' Depart this instant, let me hear no more ;
My house my castle is, and that my door.'
   The hint they took, and from the door
      withdrew,
And John to meeting bade a long adieu ;
Attach'd to business, he in time became
A wealthy man of no inferior name.
It seem'd, alas ! in John's deluded sight,
That all was wrong because not all was right ;
And when he found his teachers had their
      stains,
Resentment and not reason broke his chains :
Thus on his feelings he again relied,
And never look'd to reason for his guide :
Could he have wisely view'd the frailty shown,
And rightly weigh'd their wanderings and his
      own,
He might have known that men may be
      sincere,
Though gay and feasting on the savoury
      cheer;

That doctrines sound and sober they may
　　teach,
Who love to eat with all the glee they preach ;
Nay, who believe the duck, the grape, the
　　pine,
Were not intended for the dog and swine :
But Dighton's hasty mind on every theme
Ran from the truth, and rested in th' extreme :
Flaws in his friends he found, and then with-
　　drew
(Vain of his knowledge) from their virtues too.
Best of his books he loved the liberal kind,
That, if they improve not, still enlarge the
　　mind ;
And found himself, with such advisers, free
From a fix'd creed, as mind enlarged could be.
His humble wife at these opinions sigh'd,
But her he never heeded till she died ;
He then assented to a last request,
And by the meeting-window let her rest ;
And on her stone the sacred text was seen,
Which had her comfort in departing been.

　　Dighton with joy beheld his trade advance,
Yet seldom published, loth to trust to chance ;
Then wed a doctor's sister—poor indeed,
But skill'd in works her husband could not
　　read ;
Who, if he wish'd new ways of wealth to seek,
Could make her half-crown pamphlet in a
　　week :
This he rejected, though without disdain,
And chose the old and certain way to gain.
　　Thus he proceeded ; trade increased the
　　while,
And fortune woo'd him with perpetual smile :
On early scenes he sometimes cast a thought,
When on his heart the mighty change was
　　wrought ;
And all the ease and comfort converts find
Was magnified in his reflecting mind :
Then on the teacher's priestly pride he dwelt,
That caused his freedom, but with this he
　　felt
The danger of the free—for since that day,
No guide had shown, no brethren join'd his
　　way ;
Forsaking one, he found no second creed,
But reading doubted, doubting what to read.
　　Still, though reproof had brought some
　　present pain,
The gain he made was fair and honest gain ;
He laid his wares indeed in public view,
But that all traders claim a right to do :

By means like these, he saw his wealth
　　increase,
And felt his consequence, and dwelt in peace.
　　Our hero's age was threescore years and five,
When he exclaim'd, ' Why longer should I
　　strive ?
Why more amass, who never must behold
A young John Dighton to make glad the old?'
(The sons he had to early graves were gone,
And girls were burdens to the mind of John.)
' Had I a boy, he would our name sustain,
That now to nothing must return again ;
But what are all my profits, credit, trade,
And parish-honours ?—folly and parade.'
　　Thus Dighton thought, and in his looks
　　appear'd
Sadness increased by much he saw and heard :
The brethren often at the shop would stay,
And make their comments ere they walk'd
　　away :
They mark'd the window, fill'd in every pane
With lawless prints of reputations slain ;
Distorted forms of men with honours graced,
And our chief rulers in derision placed :
Amazed they stood, remembering well the
　　days,
When to be humble was their brother's praise;
When at the dwelling of their friend they
　　stopp'd
To drop a word, or to receive it dropp'd ;
Where they beheld the prints of men renown'd,
And far-famed preachers pasted all around ;
(Such mouths ! eyes ! hair ! so prim ! so
　　fierce ! so sleek !
They look'd as speaking what is wo to speak):
On these the passing brethren loved to dwell—
How long they spake ! how strongly !
　　warmly ! well !
What power had each to dive in mysteries
　　deep,
To warm the cold, to make the harden'd weep;
To lure, to fright, to soothe, to awe the soul,
And list'ning flocks to lead and to control !
　　But now discoursing, as they linger'd near,
They tempted John (whom they accused) to
　　hear
Their weighty charge—' And can the lost-one
　　feel,
As in the time of duty, love, and zeal ;
When all were summon'd at the rising sun,
And he was ready with his friends to run ;
When he, partaking with a chosen few,
Felt the great change, sensation rich and new ?

No ! all is lost, her favours Fortune shower'd
Upon the man, and he is overpower'd ;
The world has won him with its tempting store
Of needless wealth, and that has made him
    poor :
Success undoes him ; he has risen to fall,
Has gain'd a fortune, and has lost his all ;
Gone back from Sion, he will find his age
Loth to commence a second pilgrimage ;
He has retreated from the chosen track ;
And now must ever bear the burden on his
    back.'
    Hurt by such censure, John began to find
Fresh revolutions working in his mind ;
He sought for comfort in his books, but read
Without a plan or method in his head ;
What once amused, now rather made him sad,
What should inform, increased the doubts he
    had ;
Shame would not let him seek at church a
    guide,
And from his meeting he was held by pride ;
His wife derided fears she never felt,
And passing brethren daily censures dealt ;
Hope for a son was now for ever past,
He was the first John Dighton, and the last ;
His stomach fail'd, his case the doctor knew,
But said, ' he still might hold a year or two : '
' No more ! ' he said, ' but why should I com-
    plain ?
A life of doubt must be a life of pain :
Could I be sure—but why should I despair ?
I'm sure my conduct has been just and fair ;

In youth indeed I had a wicked will,
But I repented, and have sorrow still :
I had my comforts, and a growing trade
Gave greater pleasure than a fortune made ;
And as I more possess'd and reason'd more,
I lost those comforts I enjoy'd before,
When reverend guides I saw my table round,
And in my guardian guest my safety found :
Now sick and sad, no appetite, no ease,
Nor pleasure have I, nor a wish to please ;
Nor views, nor hopes, nor plans, nor taste
    have I,
Yet sick of life, have no desire to die.'
    He said, and died ; his trade, his name is
    gone,
And all that once gave consequence to John.
    Unhappy Dighton ! had he found a friend,
When conscience told him it was time to
    mend !
A friend discreet, considerate, kind, sincere,
Who would have shown the grounds of hope
    and fear ;
And proved that spirits, whether high or low,
No certain tokens of man's safety show ;
Had reason ruled him in her proper place,
And virtue led him while he lean'd on grace ;
Had he while zealous been discreet and pure,
His knowledge humble, and his hope secure ;—
These guides had placed him on the solid rock,
Where faith had rested, nor received a shock ;
But his, alas ! was placed upon the sand,
Where long it stood not, and where none can
    stand.

TALE XX. THE BROTHERS

              A brother noble,
Whose nature is so far from doing harms,
That he suspects none ; on whose foolish
    honesty
My practices ride easy.
              King Lear, Act i, Scene 2.
    He lets me feed with his hinds,
Bars me the place of a brother.
         As You Like It, Act i, Scene 1.
    'Twas I, but 'tis not I ; I do not shame
To tell you what I was, . . . being the thing
I am.
         As You Like It, Act iv, Scene 3.

    THAN old George Fletcher, on the British coast,
Dwelt not a seaman who had more to boast ;

Kind, simple, and sincere—he seldom spoke,
But sometimes sang and chorus'd—' *Hearts
    of Oak* ; '
In dangers steady, with his lot content,
His days in labour and in love were spent.
    He left a son so like him, that the old
With joy exclaim'd, ' 'Tis Fletcher we be-
    hold ; '
But to his brother when the kinsmen came,
And view'd his form, they grudged the
    father's name.
    George was a bold, intrepid, careless lad,
With just the failings that his father had ;
Isaac was weak, attentive, slow, exact,
With just the virtues that his father lack'd.

George lived at sea: upon the land a guest—
He sought for recreation, not for rest—
While, far unlike, his brother's feebler form
Shrank from the cold, and shudder'd at the
storm ;
Still with the seaman's to connect his trade,
The boy was bound where blocks and ropes
were made.
George, strong and sturdy, had a tender
mind,
And was to Isaac pitiful and kind ;
A very father, till his art was gain'd,
And then a friend unwearied he remain'd :
He saw his brother was of spirit low,
His temper peevish, and his motions slow ;
Not fit to bustle in a world, or make
Friends to his fortune for his merit's sake :
But the kind sailor could not boast the art
Of looking deeply in the human heart ;
Else had he seen that this weak brother knew
What men to court—what objects to pursue ;
That he to distant gain the way discern'd,
And none so crooked but his genius learn'd.
Isaac was poor, and this the brother felt ;
He hired a house, and there the landman
dwelt ;
Wrought at his trade, and had an easy home,
For there would George with cash and com-
forts come ;
And when they parted, Isaac look'd around,
Where other friends and helpers might be
found.
He wish'd for some port-place, and one
might fall,
He wisely thought, if he should try for all ;
He had a vote—and, were it well applied,
Might have its worth—and he had views
beside ;
Old Burgess Steel was able to promote
An humble man who served him with a
vote ;
For Isaac felt not what some tempers feel,
But bow'd and bent the neck to Burgess Steel;
And great attention to a lady gave,
His ancient friend, a maiden spare and grave :
One whom the visage long and look demure
Of Isaac pleased—he seem'd sedate and pure ;
And his soft heart conceived a gentle flame
For her who waited on this virtuous dame :
Not an outrageous love, a scorching fire,
But friendly liking and chastised desire ;
And thus he waited, patient in delay,
In present favour and in fortune's way.

George then was coasting—war was yet
delay'd,
And what he gain'd was to his brother paid ;
Nor ask'd the seaman what he saved or spent :
But took his grog, wrought hard, and was
content ;
Till war awaked the land, and George began
To think what part became a useful man :
' Press'd, I must go ; why, then, 'tis better far
At once to enter like a British tar,
Than a brave captain and the foe to shun,
As if I fear'd the music of a gun.'
' Go not ! ' said Isaac—' You shall wear
disguise.'
' What ! ' said the seaman, ' clothe myself
with lies ? '—
' Oh ! but there's danger.'—' Danger in the
fleet ?
You cannot mean, good brother, of defeat ;
And other dangers I at land must share—
So now adieu ! and trust a brother's care.'
Isaac awhile demurr'd—but, in his heart,
So might he share, he was disposed to part :
The better mind will sometimes feel the pain
Of benefactions—favour is a chain ;
But they the feeling scorn, and what they
wish, disdain ;—
While beings form'd in coarser mould will hate
The helping hand they ought to venerate ;
No wonder George should in this cause prevail,
With one contending who was glad to fail :
' Isaac, farewell ! do wipe that doleful eye ;
Crying we came, and groaning we may die.
Let us do something 'twixt the groan and cry :
And hear me, brother, whether pay or prize,
One half to thee I give and I devise ;
For thou hast oft occasion for the aid
Of learn'd physicians, and they will be paid :
Their wives and children men support, at sea,
And thou, my lad, art wife and child to me :
Farewell !—I go where hope and honour call,
Nor does it follow that who fights must fall.'
Isaac here made a poor attempt to speak,
And a huge tear moved slowly down his cheek ;
Like Pluto's iron drop, hard sign of grace,
It slowly roll'd upon the rueful face,
Forced by the striving will alone its way to
trace.
Years fled—war lasted—George at sea
remain'd,
While the slow landman still his profits gain'd :
A humble place was vacant—he besought
His patron's interest, and the office caught ;

For still the virgin was his faithful friend,
And one so sober could with truth commend,
Who of his own defects most humbly thought,
And their advice with zeal and reverence
　　sought :
Whom thus the mistress praised, the maid
　　approved,
And her he wedded whom he wisely loved.
　　No more he needs assistance—but, alas !
He fears the money will for liquor pass ;
Or that the seaman might to flatterers lend,
Or give support to some pretended friend :
Still he must write—he wrote, and he confess'd
That, till absolved, he should be sore dis-
　　tress'd ;
But one so friendly would, he thought, forgive
The hasty deed—Heav'n knew how he should
　　live ;
' But you,' he added, ' as a man of sense,
Have well consider'd danger and expense :
I ran, alas ! into the fatal snare,
And now for trouble must my mind prepare ;
And how, with children, I shall pick my way,
Through a hard world, is more than I can say :
Then change not, brother, your more happy
　　state,
Or on the hazard long deliberate.'
　　George answer'd gravely, ' It is right and fit,
In all our crosses, humbly to submit :
Your apprehensions are unwise, unjust ;
Forbear repining, and expel distrust.'—
He added, ' Marriage was the joy of life,'
And gave his service to his brother's wife ;
Then vow'd to bear in all expense a part,
And thus concluded, ' Have a cheerful heart.'
Had the glad Isaac been his brother's guide,
In these same terms the seaman had replied ;
At such reproofs the crafty landman smiled,
And softly said—' This creature is a child.'
　　Twice had the gallant ship a capture made—
And when in port the happy crew were paid,
Home went the sailor, with his pocket stored,
Ease to enjoy, and pleasure to afford ;
His time was short, joy shone in every face,
Isaac half fainted in the fond embrace :
The wife resolved her honour'd guest to please,
The children clung upon their uncle's knees ;
The grog went round, the neighbours drank
　　his health,
And George exclaim'd—' Ah ! what to this
　　is wealth ?
Better,' said he, ' to bear a loving heart,
Than roll in riches——but we now must part ! '

All yet is still—but hark ! the winds
　　o'ersweep
The rising waves, and howl upon the deep ;
Ships late becalm'd on mountain-billows
　　ride—
So life is threaten'd, and so man is tried.
　　Ill were the tidings that arrived from sea,
The worthy George must now a cripple be ;
His leg was lopp'd ; and though his heart
　　was sound,
Though his brave captain was with glory
　　crown'd—
Yet much it vex'd him to repose on shore,
An idle log, and be of use no more :
True, he was sure that Isaac would receive
All of his brother that the foe might leave ;
To whom the seaman his design had sent,
Ere from the port the wounded hero went :
His wealth and expectations told, he ' knew
Wherein they fail'd, what Isaac's love would
　　do ;
That he the grog and cabin would supply,
Where George at anchor during life would lie.'
　　The landman read—and, reading, grew
　　distress'd :—
' Could he resolve t' admit so poor a guest ?
Better at Greenwich might the sailor stay,
Unless his purse could for his comforts pay ;'
So Isaac judged, and to his wife appeal'd,
But yet acknowledged it was best to yield :
' Perhaps his pension, with what sums remain
Due or unsquander'd, may the man main-
　　tain ;
Refuse we must not.'—With a heavy sigh
The lady heard, and made her kind reply :—
' Nor would I wish it, Isaac, were we sure
How long his crazy building will endure ;
Like an old house, that every day appears
About to fall—he may be propp'd for years ;
For a few months, indeed, we might comply,
But these old batter'd fellows never die.'
　　The hand of Isaac, George on entering took,
With love and resignation in his look ;
Declared his comfort in the fortune past,
And joy to find his anchor safely cast ;
' Call then my nephews, let the grog be
　　brought,
And I will tell them how the ship was fought.'
　　Alas ! our simple seaman should have
　　known,
That all the care, the kindness, he had shown,
Were from his brother's heart, if not his
　　memory, flown :

All swept away to be perceived no more,
Like idle structures on the sandy shore;
The chance amusement of the playful boy,
That the rude billows in their rage destroy.
  Poor George confess'd, though loth the truth to find,
Slight was his knowledge of a brother's mind:
The vulgar pipe was to the wife offence,
The frequent grog to Isaac an expense;
Would friends like hers, she question'd,
  'choose to come,
Where clouds of poison'd fume defiled a room?
This could their lady-friend, and Burgess Steel.
(Teased with his worship's asthma,) bear to feel?
Could they associate or converse with him—
A loud rough sailor with a timber limb?'
  Cold as he grew, still Isaac strove to show,
By well-feign'd care, that cold he could not grow;
And when he saw his brother look distress'd,
He strove some petty comforts to suggest;
On his wife solely their neglect to lay,
And then t' excuse it, as a woman's way;
He too was chidden when her rules he broke,
And then she sicken'd at the scent of smoke.
  George, though in doubt, was still consoled to find
His brother wishing to be reckon'd kind:
That Isaac seem'd concern'd by his distress,
Gave to his injured feelings some redress;
But none he found disposed to lend an ear
To stories, all were once intent to hear:
Except his nephew, seated on his knee,
He found no creature cared about the sea;
But George indeed—for George they call'd the boy,
When his good uncle was their boast and joy—
Would listen long, and would contend with sleep,
To hear the woes and wonders of the deep;
Till the fond mother cried—' That man will teach
The foolish boy his loud and boisterous speech.'
So judged the father—and the boy was taught
To shun the uncle, whom his love had sought.
  The mask of kindness now but seldom worn,
George felt each evil harder to be borne;
And cried (vexation growing day by day),
'Ah! brother Isaac!—What! I'm in the way! ²²

'No! on my credit, look ye, No! but I
Am fond of peace, and my repose would buy
On any terms—in short, we must comply:
My spouse had money—she must have her will—
Ah! brother—marriage is a bitter pill.'—
  George tried the lady—' Sister, I offend.'
' Me?' she replied—' Oh no!—you may depend
On my regard—but watch your brother's way,
Whom I, like you, must study and obey.'
  ' Ah!' thought the seaman, ' what a head was mine,
That easy berth at Greenwich to resign!
I'll to the parish '——but a little pride,
And some affection, put the thought aside.
  Now gross neglect and open scorn he bore
In silent sorrow—but he felt the more:
The odious pipe he to the kitchen took,
Or strove to profit by some pious book.
  When the mind stoops to this degraded state,
New griefs will darken the dependent's fate;
' Brother!' said Isaac, ' you will sure excuse
The little freedom I'm compell'd to use:
My wife's relations—(curse the haughty crew)—
Affect such niceness, and such dread of you:
You speak so loud—and they have natures soft—
Brother——I wish——do go upon the loft!'
  Poor George obey'd, and to the garret fled,
Where not a being saw the tears he shed:
But more was yet required, for guests were come,
Who could not dine if he disgraced the room.
It shock'd his spirit to be esteem'd unfit
With an own brother and his wife to sit;
He grew rebellious—at the vestry spoke
For weekly aid——they heard it as a joke:
' So kind a brother, and so wealthy——you
Apply to us?——No! this will never do:
Good neighbour Fletcher,' said the overseer,
' We are engaged—you can have nothing here!'
  George mutter'd something in despairing tone,
Then sought his loft, to think and grieve alone;
Neglected, slighted, restless on his bed,
With heart half broken, and with scraps ill fed;
Yet was he pleased, that hours for play design'd
Were given to ease his ever-troubled mind;

The child still listen'd with increasing joy,
And he was soothed by the attentive boy.

At length he sicken'd, and this duteous child
Watch'd o'er his sickness, and his pains
    beguiled ;
The mother bade him from the loft refrain,
But, though with caution, yet he went again ;
And now his tales the sailor feebly told,
His heart was heavy, and his limbs were cold :
The tender boy came often to entreat
His good kind friend would of his presents
    eat ;
Purloin'd or purchased, for he saw, with
    shame,
The food untouch'd that to his uncle came ;
Who, sick in body and in mind, received
The boy's indulgence, gratified and grieved.

'Uncle will die !' said George—the piteous
    wife
Exclaim'd, ' she saw no value in his life ;
But sick or well, to my commands attend,
And go no more to your complaining friend.'
The boy was vex'd, he felt his heart reprove
The stern decree.—What ! punish'd for his
    love !
No ! he would go, but softly to the room,
Stealing in silence—for he knew his doom.

Once in a week the father came to say,
' George, are you ill ? '—and hurried him
    away ;
Yet to his wife would on their duties dwell,
And often cry, ' Do use my brother well : '
And something kind, no question, Isaac
    meant,
Who took vast credit for the vague intent.

But truly kind, the gentle boy essay'd
To cheer his uncle, firm, although afraid ;
But now the father caught him at the door,
And, swearing—yes, the man in office swore,
And cried, ' Away ! How ! Brother, I'm
    surprised,
That one so old can be so ill advised :
Let him not dare to visit you again,
Your cursed stories will disturb his brain ;
Is it not vile to court a foolish boy,
Your own absurd narrations to enjoy ?
What ! sullen !—ha ! George Fletcher ! you
    shall see,
Proud as you are, your bread depends on
    me !'

He spoke, and, frowning, to his dinner went,
Then cool'd and felt some qualms of discon-
    tent ;

And thought on times when he compell'd his
    son
To hear these stories, nay, to beg for one :
But the wife's wrath o'ercame the brother's
    pain,
And shame was felt, and conscience rose in
    vain.

George yet stole up, he saw his uncle lie
Sick on the bed, and heard his heavy sigh :
So he resolved, before he went to rest,
To comfort one so dear and so distress'd ;
Then watch'd his time, but with a child-like
    art,
Betray'd a something treasured at his heart :
Th' observant wife remark'd, ' the boy is
    grown
So like your brother, that he seems his own ;
So close and sullen ! and I still suspect
They often meet—do watch them and detect.'
George now remark'd that all was still as
    night,
And hasten'd up with terror and delight ;
' Uncle !' he cried, and softly tapp'd the door;
' Do let me in '—but he could add no more ;
The careful father caught him in the fact,
And cried,—' You serpent ! is it thus you act?
Back to your mother ! '—and with hasty
    blow,
He sent th' indignant boy to grieve below ;
Then at the door an angry speech began—
' Is this your conduct ?—is it thus you plan ?
Seduce my child, and make my house a scene
Of vile dispute——What is it that you
    mean ?—
George, are you dumb ? do learn to know
    your friends,
And think awhile on whom your bread
    depends :
What ! not a word ? be thankful I am cool—
But, sir, beware, nor longer play the fool ;
Come ! brother, come ! what is it that you seek
By this rebellion ?—Speak, you villain,
    speak !—
Weeping ! I warrant—sorrow makes you
    dumb :
I'll ope your mouth, impostor ! if I come :
Let me approach—I'll shake you from the bed,
You stubborn dog——Oh God ! my brother's
    dead !—'

Timid was Isaac, and in all the past
He felt a purpose to be kind at last ;
Nor did he mean his brother to depart,
Till he had shown this kindness of his heart :

But day by day he put the cause aside,
Induced by av'rice, peevishness, or pride.

But now awaken'd, from this fatal time
His conscience Isaac felt, and found his crime:
He raised to George a monumental stone,
And there retired to sigh and think alone;
An ague seized him, he grew pale, and shook—
' So,' said his son, ' would my poor uncle look.'
' And so, my child, shall I like him expire.'
' No ! you have physic and a cheerful fire.'
' Unhappy sinner ! yes, I'm well supplied
With every comfort my cold heart denied.'
He view'd his brother now, but not as one
Who vex'd his wife by fondness for her son;
Not as with wooden limb, and seaman's tale,
The odious pipe, vile grog, or humbler ale :
He now the worth and grief alone can view
Of one so mild, so generous, and so true ;
' The frank, kind brother, with such open
     heart,
And I to break it——'twas a daemon's part !'

So Isaac now, as led by conscience, feels,
Nor his unkindness palliates or conceals ;
' This is your folly,' said his heartless wife :
' Alas ! my folly cost my brother's life ;
It suffer'd him to languish and decay,
My gentle brother, whom I could not pay,
And therefore left to pine, and fret his life
     away.'

He takes his son, and bids the boy unfold
All the good uncle of his feelings told,
All he lamented—and the ready tear
Falls as he listens, soothed, and grieved to
     hear.
' Did he not curse me, child ? '—' He never
     cursed,
But could not breathe, and said his heart
     would burst : '
' And so will mine : '—' Then, father, you
     must pray ;
My uncle said it took his pains away.'

Repeating thus his sorrows, Isaac shows
That he, repenting, feels the debt he owes,
And from this source alone his every comfort
     flows.

He takes no joy in office, honours, gain ;
They make him humble, nay, they give him
     pain ;
' These from my heart,' he cries, ' all feeling
     drove ;
They made me cold to nature, dead to love : '
He takes no joy in home, but sighing, sees
A son in sorrow, and a wife at ease :
He takes no joy in office—see him now,
And Burgess Steel has but a passing bow ;
Of one sad train of gloomy thoughts possess'd,
He takes no joy in friends, in food, in rest—
Dark are the evil days, and void of peace the
     best.
And thus he lives, if living be to sigh,
And from all comforts of the world to fly,
Without a hope in life—without a wish to die.

TALE XXI.   THE LEARNED BOY

        Like one well studied in a sad ostent,
To please his grandam.
          Merchant of Venice, Act ii, Scene 2.

   And then the whining school-boy, with his
          satchel
And shining morning face, creeping like snail,
Unwillingly to school.
          As You Like It, Act ii, Scene 7.

He is a better scholar than I thought he
     was——
He is a good sprag memory.
   Merry Wives of Windsor, Act iv, Scene 1.

               One that feeds
On objects, orts, and imitations,
Which out of use, and stal'd by other men,
Begin his fashion.
          Julius Caesar, Act iv, Scene 1.

Oh ! torture me no more—I will confess.
          2 *Henry VI*, Act iii, Scene 3.

———

An honest man was Farmer Jones, and true,
He did by all as all by him should do ;
Grave, cautious, careful, fond of gain was he,
Yet famed for rustic hospitality :
Left with his children in a widow'd state,
The quiet man submitted to his fate ;
Though prudent matrons waited for his call,
With cool forbearance he avoided all ;
Though each profess'd a pure maternal joy,
By kind attention to his feeble boy :
And though a friendly widow knew no rest,
Whilst neighbour Jones was lonely and
     distress'd ;

Nay, though the maidens spoke in tender tone
Their hearts' concern to see him left alone—
Jones still persisted in that cheerless life,
As if 'twere sin to take a second wife.

Oh! 'tis a precious thing, when wives are
     dead,
To find such numbers who will serve instead :
And in whatever state a man be thrown,
'Tis that precisely they would wish their own ;
Left the departed infants—then their joy
Is to sustain each lovely girl and boy :
Whatever calling his, whatever trade,
To that their chief attention has been paid ;
His happy taste in all things they approve,
His friends they honour, and his food they
     love ;
His wish for order, prudence in affairs,
And equal temper, (thank their stars!) are
     theirs ;
In fact, it seem'd to be a thing decreed,
And fix'd as fate, that marriage must succeed;
Yet some like Jones, with stubborn hearts
     and hard,
Can hear such claims, and show them no regard.

Soon as our farmer, like a general, found
By what strong foes he was encompass'd
     round—
Engage he dared not, and he could not fly,
But saw his hope in gentle parley lie ;
With looks of kindness then, and trembling
     heart,
He met the foe, and art opposed to art.

Now spoke that foe insidious—gentle tones,
And gentle looks, assumed for Farmer Jones :
' Three girls,' the widow cried, ' a lively three
To govern well—indeed it cannot be.'
' Yes,' he replied, ' it calls for pains and care ;
But I must bear it : '—' Sir, you cannot bear ;
Your son is weak, and asks a mother's eye : '
' That, my kind friend, a father's may supply :'
' Such growing griefs your very soul will
     tease : '
' To grieve another would not give me ease—
I have a mother '—' She, poor ancient soul !
Can she the spirits of the young control ?
Can she thy peace promote, partake thy care,
Procure thy comforts, and thy sorrows share ?
Age is itself impatient, uncontroll'd : '
' But wives like mothers must at length be
     old.'
' Thou hast shrewd servants—they are evils
     sore : '
' Yet a shrewd mistress might afflict me more.'

' Wilt thou not be a weary wailing man ? '
' Alas ! and I must bear it as I can.'
Resisted thus, the widow soon withdrew,
That in his pride the hero might pursue ;
And off his wonted guard, in some retreat,
Find from a foe prepared entire defeat :
But he was prudent, for he knew in flight
These Parthian warriors turn again and fight :
He but at freedom, not at glory aim'd,
And only safety by his caution claim'd.

Thus, when a great and powerful state
     decrees,
Upon a small one, in its love, to seize—
It vows in kindness to protect, defend,
And be the fond ally, the faithful friend ;
It therefore wills that humbler state to place
Its hopes of safety in a fond embrace ;
Then must that humbler state its wisdom
     prove,
By kind rejection of such pressing love ;
Must dread such dangerous friendship to
     commence,
And stand collected in its own defence :—
Our farmer thus the proffer'd kindness fled,
And shunn'd the love that into bondage led.

The widow failing, fresh besiegers came,
To share the fate of this retiring dame :
And each foresaw a thousand ills attend
The man, that fled from so discreet a friend ;
And pray'd, kind soul ! that no event might
     make
The harden'd heart of Farmer Jones to ache.

But he still govern'd with resistless hand,
And where he could not guide he would com-
     mand :
With steady view in course direct he steer'd,
And his fair daughters loved him, though
     they fear'd ;
Each had her school, and as his wealth was
     known,
Each had in time a household of her own.

The boy indeed was, at the grandam's side,
Humour'd and train'd, her trouble and her
     pride :
Companions dear, with speech and spirits
     mild,
The childish widow and the vapourish child ;
This nature prompts ; minds uninform'd and
     weak
In such alliance ease and comfort seek ;
Push'd by the levity of youth aside,
The cares of man, his humour, or his pride,
They feel, in their defenceless state, allied :

The child is pleased to meet regard from age,
The old are pleased ev'n children to engage ;
And all their wisdom, scorn'd by proud man-
     kind,
They love to pour into the ductile mind ;
By its own weakness into error led,
And by fond age with prejudices fed.

  The father, thankful for the good he had,
Yet saw with pain a whining timid lad ;
Whom he instructing led through cultured
     fields,
To show what man performs, what nature
     yields :
But Stephen, listless, wander'd from the view,
From beasts he fled, for butterflies he flew,
And idly gazed about, in search of something
     new.
The lambs indeed he loved, and wish'd to play
With things so mild, so harmless, and so gay ;
Best pleased the weakest of the flock to see,
With whom he felt a sickly sympathy.

  Meantime, the dame was anxious, day and
     night,
To guide the notions of her babe aright,
And on the favourite mind to throw her
     glimmering light ;
Her Bible-stories she impress'd betimes,
And fill'd his head with hymns and holy
     rhymes ;
On powers unseen, the good and ill, she dwelt,
And the poor boy mysterious terrors felt ;
From frightful dreams, he waking sobb'd in
     dread,
Till the good lady came to guard his bed.

  The father wish'd such errors to correct,
But let them pass in duty and respect :
But more it grieved his worthy mind to see
That Stephen never would a farmer be ;
In vain he tried the shiftless lad to guide,
And yet 'twas time that something should be
     tried :
He at the village-school perchance might gain
All that such mind could gather and retain ;
Yet the good dame affirm'd her favourite child
Was apt and studious, though sedate and
     mild ;
'That he on many a learned point could speak,
And that his body, not his mind, was weak.'

  The father doubted—but to school was sent
The timid Stephen, weeping as he went :
There the rude lads compell'd the child to
     fight,
And sent him bleeding to his home at night ;

At this the grandam more indulgent grew,
And bade her darling ' shun the beastly crew ;
Whom Satan ruled, and who were sure to lie,
Howling in torments, when they came to die ; '
This was such comfort, that in high disdain
He told their fate, and felt their blows again :
Yet if the boy had not a hero's heart,
Within the school he play'd a better part ;
He wrote a clean fine hand, and at his slate,
With more success than many a hero, sate ;
He thought not much indeed—but what
     depends
On pains and care, was at his fingers' ends.

  This had his father's praise, who now espied
A spark of merit, with a blaze of pride :
And though a farmer he would never make,
He might a pen with some advantage take ;
And as a clerk that instrument employ,
So well adapted to a timid boy.

  A London cousin soon a place obtain'd,
Easy but humble—little could be gain'd :
The time arrived when youth and age must
     part,
Tears in each eye, and sorrow in each heart ;
The careful father bade his son attend
To all his duties, and obey his friend ;
To keep his church and there behave aright,
As one existing in his Maker's sight,
Till acts to habits led, and duty to delight :
' Then try, my boy, as quickly as you can,
T' assume the looks and spirit of a man ;
I say, be honest, faithful, civil, true,
And this you may, and yet have courage too :
Heroic men, their country's boast and pride,
Have fear'd their God, and nothing fear'd
     beside ;
While others daring, yet imbecile, fly
The power of man, and that of God defy :
Be manly then, though mild, for sure as fate,
Thou art, my Stephen, too effeminate ;
Here, take my purse, and make a worthy use
('Tis fairly stock'd) of what it will produce :
And now my blessing, not as any charm
Or conjuration ; but 'twill do no harm.'

  Stephen, whose thoughts were wandering
     up and down,
Now charm'd with promised sights in London-
     town,
Now loth to leave his grandam—lost the force,
The drift and tenor of this grave discourse ;
But, in a general way, he understood
'Twas good advice, and meant, ' My son, be
     good ; '

And Stephen knew that all such precepts mean,
That lads should read their Bible, and be clean.
 The good old lady, though in some distress,
Begg'd her dear Stephen would his grief suppress ;
' Nay, dry those eyes, my child—and, first of all,
Hold fast thy faith, whatever may befall :
Hear the best preacher, and preserve the text
For meditation, till you hear the next ;
Within your Bible night and morning look—
There is your duty, read no other book ;
Be not in crowds, in broils, in riots seen,
And keep your conscience and your linen clean :
Be you a Joseph, and the time may be,
When kings and rulers will be ruled by thee.'
 ' Nay,' said the father——' Hush, my son,' replied
The dame——' The Scriptures must not be denied.'
 The lad, still weeping, heard the wheels approach,
And took his place within the evening coach,
With heart quite rent asunder : On one side
Was love, and grief, and fear, for scenes untried ;
Wild-beasts and wax-work fill'd the happier part
Of Stephen's varying and divided heart :
This he betray'd by sighs and questions strange,
Of famous shows, the Tower, and the Exchange.
 Soon at his desk was placed the curious boy,
Demure and silent at his new employ :
Yet as he could, he much attention paid
To all around him, cautious and afraid ;
On older clerks his eager eyes were fix'd,
But Stephen never in their council mix'd :
Much their contempt he fear'd, for if like them,
He felt assured he should himself contemn ;
 Oh ! they were all so eloquent, so free,
No ! he was nothing—nothing could he be :
They dress so smartly, and so boldly look,
And talk as if they read it from a book ;
But I,' said Stephen, ' will forbear to speak,
And they will think me prudent and not weak.
They talk, the instant they have dropp'd the pen,
Of singing-women and of acting-men ;

Of plays and places where at night they walk
Beneath the lamps, and with the ladies talk ;
While other ladies for their pleasure sing,
Oh ! 'tis a glorious and a happy thing :
They would despise me, did they understand
I dare not look upon a scene so grand ;
Or see the plays when critics rise and roar,
And hiss and groan, and cry—Encore ! encore !—
There 's one among them looks a little kind ;
If more encouraged, I would ope my mind.'
 Alas ! poor Stephen, happier had he kept
His purpose secret, while his envy slept ;
Virtue, perhaps, had conquer'd, or his shame
At least preserved him simple as he came.
A year elapsed before this clerk began
To treat the rustic something like a man ;
He then in trifling points the youth advised,
Talk'd of his coat, and had it modernized ;
Or with the lad a Sunday-walk would take,
And kindly strive his passions to awake ;
Meanwhile explaining all they heard and saw,
Till Stephen stood in wonderment and awe :
To a neat garden near the town they stray'd,
Where the lad felt delighted and afraid ;
There all he saw was smart, and fine, and fair—
He could but marvel how he ventured there :
Soon he observed, with terror and alarm,
His friend enlock'd within a lady's arm,
And freely talking—' But it is,' said he,
' A near relation, and that makes him free ;'
And much amazed was Stephen, when he knew
This was the first and only interview :
Nay, had that lovely arm by him been seized,
The lovely owner had been highly pleased :
'Alas ! ' he sigh'd, ' I never can contrive,
At such bold, blessed freedoms to arrive ;
Never shall I such happy courage boast,
I dare as soon encounter with a ghost.'
 Now to a play the friendly couple went,
But the boy murmur'd at the money spent ;
' He loved,' he said, ' to buy, but not to spend —
They only talk awhile, and there 's an end.'
 ' Come, you shall purchase books,' the friend replied ;
' You are bewilder'd, and you want a guide ;
To me refer the choice, and you shall find
The light break in upon your stagnant mind !'
 The cooler clerks exclaim'd, ' In vain your art
T' improve a cub without a head or heart ;

Rustics though coarse, and savages though
    wild,
Our cares may render liberal and mild ;
But what, my friend, can flow from all these
    pains ?
There is no dealing with a lack of brains.'—
  'True I am hopeless to behold him man,
But let me make the booby what I can :
Though the rude stone no polish will display,
Yet you may strip the rugged coat away.'
  Stephen beheld his books—' I love to know
How money goes—now here is that to show :
And now,' he cried, ' I shall be pleased to get
Beyond the Bible—there I puzzle yet.'
  He spoke abash'd—' Nay, nay !' the
    friend replied,
' You need not lay the good old book aside ;
Antique and curious, I myself indeed
Read it at times, but as a man should read ;
A fine old work it is, and I protest
I hate to hear it treated as a jest ;
The book has wisdom in it, if you look
Wisely upon it, as another book :
For superstition (as our priests of sin
Are pleased to tell us) makes us blind within :
Of this hereafter—we will now select
Some works to please you, others to direct :
Tales and romances shall your fancy feed,
And reasoners form your morals and your
    creed.'
  The books were view'd, the price was fairly
    paid,
And Stephen read undaunted, undismay'd :
But not till first he paper'd all the row,
And placed in order, to enjoy the show ;
Next letter'd all the backs with care and speed,
Set them in ranks, and then began to read.
  The love of order—I the thing receive
From reverend men, and I in part believe—
Shows a clear mind and clean, and whoso
    needs
This love, but seldom in the world succeeds ;
And yet with this some other love must be,
Ere I can fully to the fact agree :
Valour and study may by order gain,
By order sovereigns hold more steady reign ;
Through all the tribes of nature order runs,
And rules around in systems and in suns :
Still has the love of order found a place,
With all that's low, degrading, mean, and
    base,
With all that merits scorn, and all that meets
    disgrace :

In the cold miser, of all change afraid,
In pompous men in public seats obey'd :
In humble placemen, heralds, solemn drones,
Fanciers of flowers, and lads like Stephen
    Jones ;
Order to these is armour and defence,
And love of method serves in lack of sense.
  For rustic youth could I a list produce
Of Stephen's books, how great might be the
    use ;
But evil fate was theirs—survey'd, enjoy'd
Some happy months, and then by force
    destroy'd :
So will'd the fates—but these with patience,
    read,
Had vast effect on Stephen's heart and head.
  This soon appear'd—within a single week
He oped his lips, and made attempt to speak ;
He fail'd indeed—but still his friend confess'd
The best have fail'd, and he had done his
    best :
The first of swimmers, when at first he swims,
Has little use or freedom in his limbs ;
Nay, when at length he strikes with manly
    force,
The cramp may seize him, and impede his
    course.
  Encouraged thus, our clerk again essay'd
The daring act, though daunted and afraid ;
Succeeding now, though partial his success,
And pertness mark'd his manner and address,
Yet such improvement issued from his books,
That all discern'd it in his speech and looks ;
He ventured then on every theme to speak,
And felt no feverish tingling in his cheek ;
His friend approving, hail'd the happy change,
The clerks exclaim'd—' 'Tis famous, and 'tis
    strange.'
  Two years had pass'd ; the youth attended
    still,
(Though thus accomplish'd) with a ready
    quill ;
He sat th' allotted hours, though hard the
    case,
While timid prudence ruled in virtue's place ;
By promise bound, the son his letters penn'd
To his good parent, at the quarter's end.
At first he sent those lines, the state to tell
Of his own health, and hoped his friends were
    well ;
He kept their virtuous precepts in his mind,
And needed nothing—then his name was
    sign'd :

But now he wrote of Sunday walks and views,
Of actors' names, choice novels, and strange
   news ;
How coats were cut, and of his urgent need
For fresh supply, which he desired with speed.
The father doubted, when these letters came,
To what they tended, yet was loth to blame :
' Stephen was once *my duteous son*, and now
My most obedient—this can I allow ?
Can I with pleasure or with patience see
A boy at once so heartless, and so free ? '
   But soon the kinsman heavy tidings told,
That love and prudence could no more with-
   hold :
' Stephen, though steady at his desk, was
   grown
A rake and coxcomb—this he grieved to own ;
His cousin left his church, and spent the day
Lounging about in quite a heathen way ;
Sometimes he swore, but had indeed the grace
To show the shame imprinted on his face :
I search'd his room, and in his absence read
Books that I knew would turn a stronger
   head ;
The works of atheists half the number made,
The rest were lives of harlots leaving trade ;
Which neither man nor boy would deign to
   read,
If from the scandal and pollution freed :
I sometimes threaten'd, and would fairly state
My sense of things so vile and profligate ;
But I'm a cit, such works are lost on me—
They're knowledge, and (good Lord !)
   philosophy.'
   ' Oh, send him down,' the father soon
   replied ;
' Let me behold him, and my skill be tried :
If care and kindness lose their wonted use,
Some rougher medicine will the end produce.'
   Stephen with grief and anger heard his
   doom—
' Go to the farmer ? to the rustic's home ?
Curse the base threat'ning— ' ' Nay, child,
   never curse ;
Corrupted long, your case is growing worse.'—
' I ! ' quoth the youth, ' I challenge all man-
   kind
To find a fault ; what fault have you to find ?
Improve I not in manner, speech, and grace ?
Inquire—my friends will tell it to your face ;
Have I been taught to guard his kine and
   sheep ?
A man like me has other things to keep ;

This let him know.'—' It would his wrath
   excite :
But come, prepare, you must away to-night.'
' What ! leave my studies, my improvements
   leave,
My faithful friends and intimates to grieve !'—
' Go to your father, Stephen, let him see
All these improvements ; they are lost on me.'
   The youth, though loth, obey'd, and soon
   he saw
The farmer-father, with some signs of awe ;
Who kind, yet silent, waited to behold
How one would act, so daring, yet so cold :
And soon he found, between the friendly pair
That secrets pass'd which he was not to share;
But he resolved those secrets to obtain,
And quash rebellion in his lawful reign.
   Stephen, though vain, was with his father
   mute ;
He fear'd a crisis, and he shunn'd dispute ;
And yet he long'd with youthful pride to show
He knew such things as farmers could not
   know ;
These to the grandam he with freedom spoke,
Saw her amazement, and enjoy'd the joke :
But on the father when he cast his eye,
Something he found that made his valour shy ;
And thus there seem'd to be a hollow truce,
Still threat'ning something dismal to produce.
   Ere this the father at his leisure read
The son's choice volumes, and his wonder fled ;
He saw how wrought the works of either kind
On so presuming, yet so weak a mind ;
These in a chosen hour he made his prey,
Condemn'd, and bore with vengeful thoughts
   away ;
Then in a close recess the couple near,
He sat unseen to see, unheard to hear.
   There soon a trial for his patience came ;
Beneath were placed the youth and ancient
   dame,
Each on a purpose fix'd—but neither thought
How near a foe, with power and vengeance
   fraught.
   And now the matron told, as tidings sad,
What she had heard of her beloved lad ;
How he to graceless, wicked men gave heed,
And wicked books would night and morning
   read ;
Some former lectures she again began,
And begg'd attention of her little man ;
She brought, with many a pious boast, in view
His former studies, and condemn'd the new :

Once he the names of saints and patriarchs old,
Judges and kings, and chiefs and prophets, told ;
Then he in winter-nights the Bible took,
To count how often in the sacred book
The sacred name appear'd, and could rehearse
Which were the middle chapter, word, and verse,
The very letter in the middle placed,
And so employ'd the hours that others waste.
    ' Such wert thou once ; and now, my child, they say
Thy faith like water runneth fast away ;
The prince of devils hath, I fear, beguiled
The ready wit of my backsliding child.'
    On this, with lofty looks, our clerk began
His grave rebuke, as he assumed the man—
    ' There is no devil,' said the hopeful youth,
' Nor prince of devils ; that I know for truth :
Have I not told you how my books describe
The arts of priests and all the canting tribe ?
Your Bible mentions Egypt, where it seems
Was Joseph found when Pharaoh dream'd his dreams :
Now in that place, in some bewilder'd head,
(The learned write,) religious dreams were bred;
Whence through the earth, with various forms combined,
They came to frighten and afflict mankind,
Prone (so I read) to let a priest invade
Their souls with awe, and by his craft be made
Slave to his will, and profit to his trade :
So say my books, and how the rogues agreed
To blind the victims, to defraud and lead ;
When joys above to ready dupes were sold,
And hell was threaten'd to the shy and cold.
    ' Why so amazed, and so prepared to pray ?
As if a Being heard a word we say :
This may surprise you ; I myself began
To feel disturb'd, and to my Bible ran ;
I now am wiser—yet agree in this,
The book has things that are not much amiss ;
It is a fine old work, and I protest
I hate to hear it treated as a jest :
The book has wisdom in it, if you look
Wisely upon it as another book.'—
    ' Oh ! wicked ! wicked ! my unhappy child,
How hast thou been by evil men beguiled ! '
    ' How ! wicked, say you ? you can little guess
The gain of that which you call wickedness :

Why, sins you think it sinful but to name
Have gain'd both wives and widows wealth and fame ;
And this because such people never dread
Those threaten'd pains ; hell comes not in their head :
Love is our nature, wealth we all desire,
And what we wish 'tis lawful to acquire ;
So say my books—and what beside they show
'Tis time to let this honest farmer know.
Nay, look not grave ; am I commanded down
To feed his cattle and become his clown ?
Is such his purpose ? then he shall be told
The vulgar insult—— '
       ——' Hold, in mercy hold— '
    ' Father, oh ! father ! throw the whip away ;
I was but jesting, on my knees I pray—
There, hold his arm—oh ! leave us not alone :
In pity cease, and I will yet atone
For all my sin— ' In vain ; stroke after stroke,
On side and shoulder, quick as mill-wheels broke ;
Quick as the patient's pulse, who trembling cried,
And still the parent with a stroke replied ;
Till all the medicine he prepared was dealt,
And every bone the precious influence felt ;
Till all the panting flesh was red and raw,
And every thought was turn'd to fear and awe;
Till every doubt to due respect gave place—
Such cures are done when doctors know the case.
    ' Oh ! I shall die—my father ! do receive
My dying words ; indeed I do believe ;
The books are lying books, I know it well,
There is a devil, oh ! there is a hell ;
And I'm a sinner : spare me, I am young,
My sinful words were only on my tongue ;
My heart consented not ; 'tis all a lie :
Oh ! spare me then, I'm not prepared to die.'
    ' Vain, worthless, stupid wretch ! ' the father cried,
' Dost thou presume to teach ? art thou a guide ?
Driveller and dog, it gave the mind distress
To hear thy thoughts in their religious dress ;
Thy pious folly moved my strong disdain,
Yet I forgave thee for thy want of brain :
But Job in patience must the man exceed
Who could endure thee in thy present creed ;
Is it for thee, thou idiot, to pretend
The wicked cause a helping hand to lend ?

Canst thou a judge in any question be ?
Atheists themselves would scorn a friend like
    thee.—
  'Lo ! yonder blaze thy worthies ; in one
    heap
Thy scoundrel-favourites must for ever sleep :
Each yields its poison to the flame in turn,
Where whores and infidels are doom'd to burn ;
Two noble faggots made the flame you see,
Reserving only two fair twigs for thee ;
That in thy view the instruments may stand,
And be in future ready for my hand :
The just mementos that, though silent, show
Whence thy correction and improvements
    flow ;

Beholding these, thou wilt confess their power,
And feel the shame of this important hour.
  'Hadst thou been humble, I had first
    design'd
By care from folly to have freed thy mind ;
And when a clean foundation had been laid,
Our priest, more able, would have lent his
    aid :
But thou art weak, and force must folly guide,
And thou art vain, and pain must humble
    pride :
Teachers men honour, learners they allure ;
But learners teaching, of contempt are sure ;
Scorn is their certain meed, and smart their
    only Cure ! '

TALES OF THE HALL

[1819]

TO HER GRACE THE DUCHESS OF RUTLAND

MADAM,

It is the privilege of those who are placed in that elevated situation to which your Grace is an ornament, that they give honour to the person upon whom they confer a favour. When I dedicate to your Grace the fruits of many years, and speak of my debt to the House of Rutland, I feel that I am not without pride in the confession nor insensible to the honour which such gratitude implies. Forty years have elapsed since this debt commenced. On my entrance into the cares of life, and while contending with its difficulties, a Duke and Duchess of Rutland observed and protected me—in my progress a Duke and Duchess of Rutland favoured and assisted me—and, when I am retiring from the world, a Duke and Duchess of Rutland receive my thanks, and accept my offering. All, even in this world of mutability, is not change: I have experienced unvaried favour—I have felt undiminished respect.

With the most grateful remembrance of what I owe, and the most sincere conviction of the little I can return, I present these pages to your Grace's acceptance, and beg leave to subscribe myself,

May it please your Grace,
With respect and gratitude,
Your Grace's
Most obedient and devoted Servant,
GEORGE CRABBE.

Trowbridge,
June, 1819.

PREFACE

If I did not fear that it would appear to my readers like arrogancy, or if it did not seem to myself indecorous to send two volumes of considerable magnitude from the press without preface or apology, without one petition for the reader's attention, or one plea for the writer's defects, I would most willingly spare myself an address of this kind, and more especially for these reasons; first, because a preface is a part of a book seldom honoured by a reader's perusal; secondly, because it is both difficult and distressing to write that which we think will be disregarded, and thirdly, because I do not conceive that I am called upon for such introductory matter by any of the motives which usually influence an author when he composes his prefatory address.

When a writer, whether of poetry or prose, first addresses the public, he has generally something to offer which relates to himself or to his work, and which he considers as a necessary prelude to the work itself, to prepare his readers for the entertainment or the instruction they may expect to receive, for one of these every man who publishes must suppose he affords—this the act itself implies; and in proportion to his conviction of this fact must be his feeling of the difficulty in which he has placed himself: the difficulty consists in reconciling the implied presumption of the undertaking, whether to please or to instruct mankind, with the diffidence and modesty of an untried candidate for fame or favour. Hence originate the many reasons an author assigns for his appearance in that character, whether they actually exist, or are merely offered to hide the motives which cannot be openly avowed ; namely, the want or the vanity of the man, as his wishes for profit or reputation may most prevail with him.

Now, reasons of this kind, whatever they may be, cannot be availing beyond their first appearance. An author, it is true, may again feel his former apprehensions, may again be elevated or depressed by the suggestions of vanity and diffidence, and may be again subject to the cold and hot fit of aguish expectation ; but he is no more a stranger to the press, nor has the motives or privileges of one who is. With respect to myself, it is certain they belong not to me. Many years have elapsed since I became a candidate for indulgence as an inexperienced writer ; and to assume the language of such writer now, and to plead for his indulgences, would be proof of my ignorance of the place assigned to me, and the degree of favour which I have experienced ; but of that place I am not uninformed, and with that degree of favour I have no reason to be dissatisfied.

It was the remark of the pious, but on some occasions the querulous, author of the *Night Thoughts*, that he had ' been so long remembered, he was forgotten ; ' an expression in which there is more appearance of discontent than of submission : if he had patience, it was not the patience that *smiles at grief*. It is not therefore entirely in the sense of the good Doctor that I apply these words to myself, or to my more early publications. So many years indeed have passed since their first appearance, that I have no reason to complain, on that account, if they be now slumbering with other poems of decent reputation in their day—not dead indeed, nor entirely forgotten, but certainly not the subjects of discussion or conversation as when first introduced to the notice of the public, by those whom the public will not forget, whose protection was credit to their author, and whose approbation was fame to them. Still these early publications had so long preceded any other, that, if not altogether

unknown, I was, when I came again before the public, in a situation which excused, and perhaps rendered necessary some explanation ; but this also has passed away, and none of my readers will now take the trouble of making any inquiries respecting my motives for writing or for publishing these Tales or verses of any description : known to each other as readers and authors are known, they will require no preface to bespeak their good will, nor shall I be under the necessity of soliciting the kindness which experience has taught me, endeavouring to merit, I shall not fail to receive.

There is one motive—and it is a powerful one—which sometimes induces an author, and more particularly a poet, to ask the attention of his readers to his prefatory address. This is when he has some favourite and peculiar style or manner which he would explain and defend, and chiefly if he should have adopted a mode of versification of which an uninitiated reader was not likely to perceive either the merit or the beauty. In such case it is natural, and surely pardonable, to assert and to prove, as far as reason will bear us on, that such method of writing has both ; to show in what the beauty consists, and what peculiar difficulty there is, which, when conquered, creates the merit. How far any particular poet has or has not succeeded in such attempt is not my business nor my purpose to inquire : I have no peculiar notion to defend, no poetical heterodoxy to support, nor theory of any kind to vindicate or oppose —that which I have used is probably the most common measure in our language ; and therefore, whatever be its advantages or defects, they are too well known to require from me a description of the one, or an apology for the other.

Perhaps still more frequent than any explanation of the work is an account of the author himself, the situation in which he is placed, or some circumstances of peculiar kind in his life, education, or employment. How often has youth been pleaded for deficiencies or redundancies, for the existence of which youth may be an excuse, and yet be none for their exposure ! Age too has been pleaded for the errors and failings in a work which the octogenarian had the discernment to perceive, and yet had not the fortitude to suppress. Many other circumstances are made apologies for a writer's infirmities; his much employment, and many avocations, adversity, necessity, and the good of mankind. These, or any of them, however availing in themselves, avail not me. I am neither so young nor so old, so much engaged by one pursuit, or by many,—I am not so urged by want, or so stimulated by a desire of public benefit,—that I can borrow one apology from the many which I have named. How far they prevail with our readers, or with our judges, I cannot tell; and it is unnecessary for me to inquire into the validity of arguments which I have not to produce.

If there be any combination of circumstances which may be supposed to affect the mind of a reader, and in some degree to influence his judgment, the junction of youth, beauty, and merit in a female writer may be allowed to do this; and yet one of the most forbidding of titles is ' Poems by a very young Lady,' and this although beauty and merit were largely insinuated. Ladies, it is true, have of late little need of any indulgence as authors, and names may readily be found which rather excite the envy of man than plead for his lenity. Our estimation of title also in a writer has materially varied from that of our predecessors; ' Poems by a Nobleman' would create a very different sensation in our minds from that which was formerly excited when they were so announced. A noble author had then no pretensions to a seat so secure on the ' sacred hill,' that authors not noble, and critics not gentle, dared not attack; and they delighted to take revenge by their contempt and derision of the poet, for the pain which their submission and respect to the man had cost them. But in our times we find that a nobleman writes, not merely as well, but better than other men; insomuch that readers in general begin to fancy that the Muses have relinquished their old partiality for rags and a garret, and are become altogether aristocratical in their choice. A conceit so well supported by fact would be readily admitted, did it not appear at the same time, that there were in the higher ranks of society men, who could write as tamely, or as absurdly, as they had ever been accused of doing. We may, therefore,

regard the works of any noble author as extraordinary productions; but must not found any theory upon them; and, notwithstanding their appearance, must look on genius and talent as we are wont to do on time and chance, that happen indifferently to all mankind.

But whatever influence any peculiar situation of a writer might have, it cannot be a benefit to me, who have no such peculiarity. I must rely upon the willingness of my readers to be pleased with that which was designed to give them pleasure, and upon the cordiality which naturally springs from a remembrance of our having before parted without any feelings of disgust on the one side, or of mortification on the other.

With this hope I would conclude the present subject; but I am called upon by duty to acknowledge my obligations, and more especially for two of the following Tales:— the Story of Lady Barbara in Book XVI and that of Ellen in Book XVIII. The first of these I owe to the kindness of a fair friend, who will, I hope, accept the thanks which I very gratefully pay, and pardon me if I have not given to her relation the advantages which she had so much reason to expect. The other story, that of Ellen, could I give it in the language of him who related it to me, would please and affect my readers. It is by no means my only debt, though the one I now more particularly acknowledge; for who shall describe all that he gains in the social, the unrestrained, and the frequent conversations with a friend, who is at once communicative and judicious?—whose opinions, on all subjects of literary kind, are founded on good taste, and exquisite feeling? It is one of the greatest ' pleasures of my memory' to recall in absence those conversations; and if I do not in direct terms mention with whom I conversed, it is both because I have no permission, and my readers will have no doubt.

The first intention of the poet must be to please; for, if he means to instruct, he must render the instruction which he hopes to convey palatable and pleasant. I will not assume the tone of a moralist, nor promise that my relations shall be beneficial to mankind; but I have endeavoured, not unsuccessfully I trust, that, in whatsoever I have

Yet past twelve years before her son was told,
To his surprise, ' your father you behold.'
But he beheld not with his mother's eye
The new relation, and would not comply ;
But all obedience, all connexion spurn'd,
And fled their home, where he no more
        return'd.
His father's brother was a man whose mind
Was to his business and his bank confined ;
His guardian care the captious nephew sought,
And was received, caress'd, advised, and
        taught.
' That Irish beggar, whom your mother
        took,
Does you this good, he sends you to your book;
Yet love not books, beyond their proper worth,
But when they fit you for the world, go forth:
They are like beauties, and may blessings
        prove,
When we with caution study them, or love ;
But when to either we our souls devote,
We grow unfitted for that world, and dote '
    George to a school of higher class was sent,
But he was ever grieving that he went :
A still, retiring, musing, dreaming boy,
He relish'd not their sudden bursts of joy ;
Nor the tumultuous pleasures of a rude,
A noisy, careless, fearless multitude :
He had his own delights, as one who flies
From every pleasure that a crowd supplies :
Thrice he return'd, but then was weary grown,
And was indulged with studies of his own.
    Still could the rector and his friend relate
The small adventures of that distant date ;
And Richard listen'd as they spake of time
Past in that world of misery and crime.
    Freed from his school, a priest of gentle kind
The uncle found to guide the nephew's mind ;
Pleased with his teacher, George so long
        remain'd,
The mind was weaken'd by the store it gain'd.
    His guardian uncle, then on foreign ground,
No time to think of his improvements found ;
Nor had the nephew, now to manhood grown,
Talents or taste for trade or commerce shown,
But shunn'd a world of which he little knew,
Nor of that little did he like the view.
    His mother chose, nor I the choice upbraid,
An Irish soldier of an house decay'd,
And passing poor, but precious in her eyes
As she in his ; they both obtain'd a prize.
To do the captain justice, she might share
What of her jointure his affairs could spare :

Irish he was in his profusion—true,
But he was Irish in affection too ;
And though he spent her wealth and made
        her grieve,
He always said ' my dear,' and ' with your
        leave.'
Him she survived : she saw his boy possess'd
Of manly spirit, and then sank to rest.
    Her sons thus left, some legal cause required
That they should meet, but neither this
        desired :
George, a recluse, with mind engaged, was one
Who did no business, with whom none was
        done ;
Whose heart, engross'd by its peculiar care,
Shared no one's counsel—no one his might
        share.
    Richard, a boy, a lively boy, was told
Of his half-brother, haughty, stern, and cold ;
And his boy folly, or his manly pride,
Made him on measures cool and harsh decide :
So, when they met, a distant cold salute
Was of a long-expected day the fruit ;
The rest by proxies managed, each with-
        drew,
Vex'd by the business and the brother too ;
But now they met when time had calm'd the
        mind,
Both wish'd for kindness, and it made them
        kind :
George had no wife or child, and was disposed
To love the man on whom his hope reposed :
Richard had both ; and those so well beloved,
Husband and father were to kindness moved ;
And thus th' affections check'd, subdued,
        restrain'd,
Rose in their force, and in their fulness reign'd.
    The bell now bids to dine : the friendly
        priest,
Social and shrewd, the day's delight increased :
Brief and abrupt their speeches while they
        dined,
Nor were their themes of intellectual kind ;
Nor, dinner past, did they to these advance,
But left the subjects they discuss'd to chance.
    Richard, whose boyhood in the place was
        spent,
Profound attention to the speakers lent,
Who spake of men ; and, as he heard a name,
Actors and actions to his memory came :
Then, too, the scenes he could distinctly trace,
Here he had fought, and there had gain'd
        a race ;

In that church-walk he had affrighted been,
In that old tower he had a something seen ;
What time, dismiss'd from school, he upward
     cast
A fearful look, and trembled as he past.

     No private tutor Richard's parents sought,
Made keen by hardship, and by trouble taught;
They might have sent him—some the counsel
     gave—
Seven gloomy winters of the North to brave,
Where a few pounds would pay for board and
     bed,
While the poor frozen boy was taught and fed ;
When, say he lives, fair, freckled, lank and lean,
The lad returns shrewd, subtle, close and keen;
With all the northern virtues, and the rules
Taught to the thrifty in these thriving schools:
There had he gone, and borne this trying part,
But Richard's mother had a mother's heart.

     Now squire and rector were return'd to
     school,
And spoke of him who there had sovereign
     rule :
He was, it seem'd, a tyrant of the sort
Who make the cries of tortured boys his sport;
One of a race, if not extinguish'd, tamed,
The flogger now is of the act ashamed ;
But this great mind all mercy's calls with-
     stood,
This Holofernes was a man of blood.

     ' Students,' he said, ' like horses on the road,
Must well be lash'd before they take the load ;
They may be willing for a time to run,
But you must whip them ere the work be done:
To tell a boy, that, if he will improve,
His friends will praise him, and his parents love,

Is doing nothing—he has not a doubt
But they will love him, nay, applaud, with-
     out:
Let no fond sire a boy's ambition trust,
To make him study, let him see he must.'
     Such his opinion ; and to prove it true,
At least sincere, it was his practice too :
Pluto they call'd him, and they named him
     well,
'Twas not an heaven where he was pleased
     to dwell :
From him a smile was like the Greenland sun,
Surprising, nay portentous, when it shone ;
Or like the lightning, for the sudden flash
Prepared the children for the thunder's crash.
     O ! had Narcissa, when she fondly kiss'd
The weeping boy whom she to school dis-
     miss'd,
Had she beheld him shrinking from the arm
Uplifted high to do the greater harm,
Then seen her darling stript, and that pure
     white,
And—O ! her soul had fainted at the sight;
And with those looks that love could not
     withstand,
She would have cried, ' Barbarian, hold thy
     hand ! '
In vain ! no grief to this stern soul could
     speak,
No iron-tear roll down this Pluto's cheek.
     Thus far they went, half earnest, half in
     jest,
Then turn'd to themes of deeper interest ;
While Richard's mind, that for awhile had
     stray'd,
Call'd home its powers, and due attention paid.

BOOK III. BOYS AT SCHOOL

The School—School-Boys—The Boy-Tyrant
—Sir Hector Blane—School-Boys in after
Life how changed—how the same—The
patronized Boy, his Life and Death—Re-
flections—Story of Harry Bland.

     WE name the world a school, for day by
     day
We something learn, till we are call'd away ;
The school we name a world,—for vice and
     pain,
Fraud and contention, there begin to reign ;

And much, in fact, this lesser world can
     show
Of grief and crime that in the greater grow.
' You saw,' said George, ' in that still-hated
     school,
How the meek suffer, how the haughty rule ;
There soft, ingenuous, gentle minds endure
Ills that ease, time, and friendship fail to
     cure :
There the best hearts, and those, who shrink
     from sin,
Find some seducing imp to draw them in ;

Who takes infernal pleasure to impart
The strongest poison to the purest heart.
Call to your mind this scene—Yon boy
    behold :
How hot the vengeance of a heart so cold !
See how he beats, whom he had just reviled
And made rebellious—that imploring child :
How fierce his eye, how merciless his blows,
And how his anger on his insult grows ;
You saw this Hector and his patient slave,
Th' insulting speech, the cruel blows he gave.
  Mix'd with mankind, his interest in his
    sight,
We found this Nimrod civil and polite ;
There was no triumph in his manner seen,
He was so humble you might think him mean :
Those angry passions slept till he attain'd
His purposed wealth, and waked when that
    was gain'd ;
He then resumed the native wrath and pride,
The more indulged, as longer laid aside ;
Wife, children, servants, all obedience pay,
The slaves at school no greater slaves than
    they.
No more dependant, he resumes the rein,
And shows the school-boy turbulence again.
  Were I a poet, I would say, he brings
To recollection some impetuous springs ;
See ! one that issues from its humble source,
To gain new powers, and run its noisy course ;
Frothy and fierce among the rocks it goes,
And threatens all that bound it or oppose :
Till wider grown, and finding large increase,
Though bounded still, it moves along in peace ;
And as its waters to the ocean glide,
They bear a busy people on its tide ;
But there arrived, and from its channel free,
Those swelling waters meet the mighty sea ;
With threat'ning force the new-form'd billows
    swell,
And now affright the crowd they bore so well.'
  Yet,' said the rector, ' all these early signs
Of vice are lost, and vice itself declines ;
Religion counsels, troubles, sorrows rise,
And the vile spirit in the conflict dies.
  Sir Hector Blane, the champion of the
    school,
Was very blockhead, but was form'd for rule :
Learn he could not ; he said he could not
    learn,
But he profess'd it gave him no concern :
Books were his horror, dinner his delight,
And his amusement to shake hands and fight ;

Argue he could not, but in case of doubt,
Or disputation, fairly box'd it out :
This was his logic, and his arm so strong,
His cause prevail'd, and he was never wrong ;
But so obtuse—you must have seen his look,
Desponding, angry, puzzled o'er his book.
  ' Can you not see him on the morn that
    proved
His skill in figures ? Pluto's self was moved—
" Come, six times five ? " th' impatient
    teacher cried ;
In vain, the pupil shut his eyes, and sigh'd.
" Try, six times count your fingers ; how he
    stands !—
Your fingers, idiot ! "—" What, of both my
    hands ? "
  ' With parts like these his father felt as-
    sured,
In busy times, a ship might be procured ;
He too was pleased to be so early freed,
He now could fight, and he in time might read.
So he has fought, and in his country's cause
Has gain'd him glory, and our hearts'
    applause.
No more the blustering boy a school defies,
We see the hero from the tyrant rise,
And in the captain's worth the student's
    dulness dies.'
  ' Be all allow'd ; ' replied the squire, ' I give
Praise to his actions ; may their glory live !
Nay, I will hear him in his riper age
Fight his good ship, and with the foe engage ;
Nor will I quit him when the cowards fly,
Although, like them, I dread his energy.
  ' But still, my friend, that ancient spirit
    reigns,
His powers support the credit of his brains,
Insisting ever that he must be right,
And for his reasons still prepared to fight.
Let him a judge of England's prowess be,
And all her floating terrors on the sea ;
But this contents not, this is not denied,
He claims a right on all things to decide ;
A kind of patent-wisdom, and he cries,
" 'Tis so ! " and bold the hero that denies.
Thus the boy-spirit still the bosom rules,
And the world's maxims were at first the
    school's.'
  ' No doubt,' said Jacques, ' there are in
    minds the seeds
Of good and ill, the virtues and the weeds ;
But is it not of study the intent
This growth of evil nature to prevent ?

To check the progress of each idle shoot
That might retard the ripening of the fruit?
Our purpose certain! and we much effect,
We something cure, and something we correct;
But do your utmost, when the man you see,
You find him what you saw the boy would be,
Disguised a little; but we still behold
What pleased and what offended us of old.
Years from the mind no native stain remove,
But lay the varnish of the world above.
Still, when he can, he loves to step aside
And be the boy, without a check or guide;
In the old wanderings he with pleasure strays,
And reassumes the bliss of earlier days.
　'I left at school the boy with pensive look,
Whom some great patron order'd to his book,
Who from his mother's cot reluctant came,
And gave *my lord*, for this compassion, fame;
Who, told of all his patron's merit, sigh'd,
I know not why, in sorrow or in pride;
And would, with vex'd and troubled spirit,
　　cry,
"I am not happy; let your envy die."
Him left I with you; who, perhaps, can tell
If fortune bless'd him, or what fate befell:
I yet remember how the idlers ran
To see the carriage of the godlike man,
When pride restrain'd me; yet I thought the
　　deed
Was noble, too,—and how did it succeed?'
　Jacques answer'd not till he had backward
　　cast
His view, and dwelt upon the evil past;
Then, as he sigh'd, he smiled;—from folly rise
Such smiles, and misery will create such sighs.
And Richard now from his abstraction broke,
Listening attentive as the rector spoke.

———————

　'This noble lord was one disposed to try
And weigh the worth of each new luxury;
Now, at a certain time, in pleasant mood,
He tried the luxury of doing good;
For this he chose a widow's handsome boy,
Whom he would first improve, and then
　　employ.
The boy was gentle, modest, civil, kind,
But not for bustling through the world
　　design'd;
Reserved in manner, with a little gloom,
Apt to retire, but never to assume;
Possess'd of pride that he could not subdue,
Although he kept his origin in view.

Him sent my lord to school, and this became
A theme for praise, and gave his lordship
　　fame;
But when the boy was told how great his debt,
He proudly ask'd, " is it contracted yet?"
　'With care he studied, and with some
　　success;
His patience great, but his acquirements less:
Yet when he heard that Charles would not
　　excel,
His lordship answer'd, with a smile, "'tis well;
Let him proceed, and do the best he can,
I want no pedant, but a useful man."
　'The speech was heard, and praise was
　　amply dealt,
His lordship felt it, and he said he felt—
"It is delightful," he observed, "to raise
And foster merit,—it is more than praise."
　'Five years at school th' industrious boy
　　had past,
"And what," was whisper'd, "will be done
　　at last?"
My lord was troubled, for he did not mean
To have his bounty watch'd and overseen;
Bounty that sleeps when men applaud no
　　more,
The generous act that waked their praise
　　before;
The deed was pleasant while the praise was
　　new,
But none the progress would with wonder
　　view:
It was a debt contracted; he who pays
A debt is just, but must not look for praise:
The deed that once had fame must still
　　proceed,
Though fame no more proclaims "how great
　　the deed!"
The boy is taken from his mother's side,
And he who took him must be now his guide.
But this, alas! instead of bringing fame,
A tax, a trouble, to my lord became.
　'"The boy is dull, you say,—why then by
　　trade,
By law, by physic, nothing can be made;
If a small living—mine are both too large,
And then the college is a cursed charge:
The sea is open; should he there display
Signs of dislike, he cannot run away."
　'Now Charles, who acted no heroic part,
And felt no seaman's glory warm his heart,
Refused the offer—anger touch'd my lord.—
"He does not like it—Good, upon my word—

If I at college place him, he will need
Supplies for ever, and will not succeed ;—
Doubtless in me 'tis duty to provide
Not for his comfort only, but his pride—
Let him to sea ! ''—He heard the words again,
With promise join'd—with threat'ning ; all
    in vain :
Charles had his own pursuits ; for aid to these
He had been thankful, and had tried to please;
But urged again, as meekly as a saint,
He humbly begg'd to stay at home, and
    paint.
    Yes, pay some dauber, that this stubborn
    fool
May grind his colours, and may boast his
    school.''
        As both persisted, '' Choose, good sir,
        youɪ way,''
The peer exclaim'd, '' I have no more to say.
I seek your good, but I have no command
Upon your will, nor your desire withstand.''
    ' Resolved and firm, yet dreading to offend,
Charles pleaded *genius* with his noble friend :
Genius ! '' he cried, '' the name that triflers
    give
To their strong wishes without pains to live;
Genius ! the plea of all who feel desire
Of fame, yet grudge the labours that acquire :
But say 'tis true ; how poor, how late the
    gain,
And certain ruin if the hope be vain ! ''
Then to the world appeal'd my lord, and cried,
    Whatever happens, I am justified.''
Nay, it was trouble to his soul to find
There was such hardness in the human mind :
He wash'd his hands before the world, and
    swore
That he '' such minds would patronize no
    more.''
        Now Charles his bread by daily labours
        sought,
And this his solace, '' so Corregio wrought.''
Alas, poor youth ! however great his name,
And humble thine, thy fortune was the same :
' harles drew and painted, and some praise
    obtain'd
For care and pains; but little more was gain' '
Fame was his hope, and he contempt display'd
for approbation, when 'twas coolly paid :
His daily tasks he call'd a waste of mind,
Vex'd at his fate, and angry with mankind :
'' Thus have the blind to merit ever done,
And Genius mourn'd for each neglected son.''

' Charles murmur'd thus, and angry and
    alone
Half breathed the curse, and half suppress'd
    the groan ;
Then still more sullen grew, and still more
    proud,
Fame so refused he to himself allow'd,
Crowds in contempt he held, and all to him
    was crowd.
    ' If aught on earth, the youth his mother
    loved,
And, at her death, to distant scenes removed.
    ' Years past away, and where he lived, and
    how,
Was then unknown—indeed we know not
    now ;
But once at twilight walking up and down,
In a poor alley of the mighty town,
Where, in her narrow courts and garrets, hide
The grieving sons of genius, want, and pride,
I met him musing : sadness I could trace,
And conquer'd hope's meek anguish, in his face.
See him I must : but I with ease address'd,
And neither pity nor surprise express'd ;
I strove both grief and pleasure to restrain,
But yet I saw that I was giving pain.
He said, with quick'ning pace, as loth to hold
A longer converse, that '' the day was cold,
That he was well, that I had scarcely light
To aid my steps,'' and bade me then good
    night !
    ' I saw him next where he had lately come,
A silent pauper in a crowded room ;
I heard his name, but he conceal'd his face,
To his sad mind his misery was disgrace :
In vain I strove to combat his disdain
Of my compassion——'' Sir, I pray refrain ; ''
For I had left my friends and stepp'd aside,
Because I fear'd his unrelenting pride.
    ' He then was sitting on a workhouse-bed,
And on the naked boards reclined his head,
Around were children with incessant cry,
And near was one, like him, about to die ;
A broken chair's deal bottom held the store
That he required—he soon would need no
    more ;
A yellow tea-pot, standing at his side,
From its half spout the cold black tea sup-
    plied.
    ' Hither, it seem'd, the fainting man was
    brought,
Found without food,—it was no longer
    sought :

For his employers knew not whom they paid,
Nor where to seek him whom they wish'd to
　　aid :
Here brought, some kind attendant he
　　address'd,
And sought some trifles which he yet pos-
　　sess'd ;
Then named a lightless closet, in a room
Hired at small rate, a garret's deepest gloom.
They sought the region, and they brought
　　him all
That he his own, his proper wealth could call :
A better coat, less pieced ; some linen neat,
Not whole ; and papers many a valued sheet ;
Designs and drawings ; these, at his desire,
Were placed before him at the chamber fire,
And while th' admiring people stood to gaze,
He, one by one, committed to the blaze,
Smiling in spleen ; but one he held awhile,
And gave it to the flames, and could not smile.
　　' The sickening man—for such appear'd
　　　　the fact—
Just in his need, would not a debt contract ;
But left his poor apartment for the bed
That earth might yield him, or some way-
　　side shed ;
Here he was found, and to this place convey'd,
Where he might rest, and his last debt be paid :
Fame his wish, but he so far from fame,
That no one knew his kindred, or his name,
Or by what means he lived, or from what
　　place he came.
　　' Poor Charles ! unnoticed by thy titled
　　　　friend,
Thy days had calmly past, in peace thine end :
Led by thy patron's vanity astray,
Thy own misled thee in thy trackless way,
Urging thee on by hope absurd and vain,
Where never peace or comfort smiled again !
　　' Once more I saw him, when his spirits fail'd,
And my desire to aid him then prevail'd ;
He show'd a softer feeling in his eye,
And watch'd my looks, and own'd the
　　sympathy :
'Twas now the calm of wearied pride ; so long
As he had strength was his resentment strong,
But in such place, with strangers all around,
And they such strangers, to have something
　　found
Allied to his own heart, an early friend,
One, only one, who would on him attend,
To give and take a look ! at this his journey's
　　end ;

One link, however slender, of the chain
That held him where he could not long
　　remain ;
The one sole interest !—No, he could not now
Retain his anger ; Nature knew not how ;
And so there came a softness to his mind,
And he forgave the usage of mankind.
His cold long fingers now were press'd to mine,
And his faint smile of kinder thoughts gave
　　sign ;
His lips moved often as he tried to lend
His words their sound, and softly whisper'd
　　" friend ! "
Not without comfort in the thought express'd
By that calm look with which he sank to rest.'

　　' The man,' said George, ' you see, through
　　　　life retain'd
The boy's defects ; his virtues too remain'd.
　　' But where are now those minds so light
　　　　and gay,
So forced on study, so intent on play,
Swept, by the world's rude blasts, from hope's
　　dear views away ?
Some grieved for long neglect in earlier times,
Some sad from frailties, some lamenting
　　crimes ;
Thinking, with sorrow, on the season lent
For noble purpose, and in trifling spent ;
And now, at last, when they in earnest view
The nothings done—what work they find to
　　do !
Where is that virtue that the generous boy
Felt, and resolved that nothing should de-
　　stroy ?
He who with noble indignation glow'd
When vice had triumph ? who his tear
　　bestow'd
On injured merit ? he who would possess
Power, but to aid the children of distress !
Who has such joy in generous actions shown,
And so sincere, they might be call'd his own ;
Knight, hero, patriot, martyr ! on whose
　　tongue,
And potent arm, a nation's welfare hung ;
He who to public misery brought relief,
And soothed the anguish of domestic grief.
Where now this virtue's fervour, spirit, zeal ?
Who felt so warmly, has he ceased to feel ?
The boy's emotions of that noble kind,
Ah ! sure th' experienced man has not
　　resign'd ;

Or are these feelings varied ? has the knight,
Virtue's own champion, now refused to fight ?
Is the deliverer turn'd th' oppressor now ?
Has the reformer dropt the dangerous vow ?
Or has the patriot's bosom lost its heat,
And forced him, shivering, to a snug retreat ?
Is such the grievous lapse of human pride ?
Is such the victory of the worth untried ?
    ' Here will I pause, and then review the shame
Of Harry Bland, to hear his parent's name ;
That mild, that modest boy, whom well we knew,
In him long time the secret sorrow grew ;
He wept alone ; then to his friend confess'd
The grievous fears that his pure mind oppress'd ;
And thus, when terror o'er his shame obtain'd
A painful conquest, he his case explain'd :
And first his favourite question'd—" Willie, tell,
Do all the wicked people go to hell ? "
    ' Willie with caution answer'd, " Yes, they do,
Or else repent ; but what is this to you ? "
' O ! yes, dear friend : " he then his tale began—
He fear'd his father was a wicked man,
Nor had repented of his naughty life ;
The wife he had indeed was not a wife,
Not as my mother was ; the servants all
Call her a name—I'll whisper what they call.
She saw me weep, and ask'd, in high disdain,
If tears could bring my mother back again ?
This I could bear, but not when she pretends
Such fond regard, and what I speak commends ;
Talks of my learning, fawning wretch ! and tries
To make me love her,—love ! when I despise.
Indeed I had it in my heart to say
Words of reproach, before I came away ;
And then my father's look is not the same,
He puts his anger on to hide his shame.
    ' With all these feelings delicate and nice,
This dread of infamy, this scorn of vice,
He left the school, accepting, though with pride,
His father's aid—but there would not reside ;
He married then a lovely maid, approved
Of every heart as worthy to be loved ;

Mild as the morn in summer, firm as truth,
And graced with wisdom in the bloom of youth.
    ' How is it, men, when they in judgment sit
On the same fault, now censure, now acquit ?
Is it not thus, that *here* we view the sin,
And *there* the powerful cause that drew us in ?
'Tis not that men are to the evil blind,
But that a different object fills the mind.
In judging others we can see too well
Their grievous fall, but not how grieved they fell ;
Judging ourselves, we to our minds recall,
Not how we fell, but how we grieved to fall.
    ' Or could this man, so vex'd in early time,
By this strong feeling for his father's crime,
Who to the parent's sin was barely just,
And mix'd with filial fear the man's disgust ;
Could he, without some strong delusion, quit
The path of duty, and to shame submit ?
Cast off the virtue he so highly prized,
" And be the very creature he despised ? "
    ' A tenant's wife, half forward, half afraid,
Features, it seem'd, of powerful cast display'd,
That bore down faith and duty ; common fame
Speaks of a contract that augments the shame.
    ' There goes he, not unseen, so strong the will,
And blind the wish, that bear him to the mill ;
There he degraded sits, and strives to please
The miller's children, laughing at his knees ;
And little Dorcas, now familiar grown,
Talks of her rich papa, and of her own.
He woos the mother's now precarious smile
By costly gifts, that tempers reconcile ;
While the rough husband, yielding to the pay
That buys his absence, growling stalks away.
'Tis said th' offending man will sometimes sigh,
And say, " My God, in what a dream am I ?
I will awake : " but, as the day proceeds,
The weaken'd mind the day's indulgence needs ;
Hating himself at every step he takes,
His mind approves the virtue he forsakes,
And yet forsakes her. O ! how sharp the pain,
Our vice, ourselves, our habits to disdain ;
To go where never yet in peace we went,
To feel our hearts can bleed, yet not relent ;
To sigh, yet not recede ; to grieve, yet not repent ! '

BOOK IV. ADVENTURES OF RICHARD

Meeting of the Brothers in the Morning—
Pictures, Music, Books—The Autumnal
Walk—The Farm—The Flock—Effect of
Retirement upon the Mind—Dinner—
Richard's Adventure at Sea—George in-
quires into the Education of his Brother—
Richard's account of his Occupations in his
early Life ; his Pursuits, Associations, Par-
tialities, Affections, and Feelings—His Love
of Freedom—The Society he chose—The
Friendships he engaged in—and the Habits
he contracted.

  EIGHT days had past ; the Brothers now
    could meet
With ease, and take the customary seat.
' These,' said the host, for he perceived
    where stray'd
His brother's eye, and what he now survey'd ;
' These are the costly trifles that we buy,
Urged by the strong demands of vanity,
The thirst and hunger of a mind diseased,
That must with purchased flattery be
    appeased ;
But yet, 'tis true, the things that you behold
Serve to amuse us as we're getting old :
These pictures, as I heard our artists say,
Are genuine all, and I believe they may ;
They cost the genuine sums, and I should
    grieve
If, being willing, I could not believe.
And there is music ; when the ladies come,
With their keen looks they scrutinize the room
To see what pleases, and I must expect
To yield them pleasure, or to find neglect :
For, as attractions from our person fly,
Our purses, Richard, must the want supply ;
Yet would it vex me could the triflers know
That they can shut out comfort or bestow.
  ' But see this room : here, Richard, you will
    find
Books for all palates, food for every mind ;
This readers term the ever-new delight,
And so it is, if minds have appetite :
Mine once was craving ; great my joy, in-
    deed,
Had I possess'd such food when I could feed ;
When at the call of every new-born wish
I could have keenly relish'd every dish—

Now, Richard, now, I stalk around and look
Upon the dress and title of a book,
Try half a page, and then can taste no more,
But the dull volume to its place restore ;
Begin a second slowly to peruse,
Then cast it by, and look about for news
The news itself grows dull in long debates,—
I skip, and see what the conclusion states,—
And many a speech, with zeal and study made
Cold and resisting spirits to persuade,
Is lost on mine ; alone, we cease to feel
What crowds admire, and wonder at their
    zeal.
  ' But how the day ?   No fairer will it be ?
Walk you ? Alas ! 'tis requisite for me—
Nay, let me not prescribe—my friends and
    guests are free.'

  It was a fair and mild autumnal sky,
And earth's ripe treasures met th' admiring
    eye,
As a rich beauty, when her bloom is lost,
Appears with more magnificence and cost :
The wet and heavy grass, where feet had
    stray'd,
Not yet erect, the wanderer's way betray'd ;
Showers of the night had swell'd the deep'ning
    rill,
The morning breeze had urged the quick'ning
    mill ;
Assembled rooks had wing'd their sea-ward
    flight,
By the same passage to return at night,
While proudly o'er them hung the steady kite,
Then turn'd him back, and left the noisy
    throng,
Nor deign'd to know them as he sail'd along.
Long yellow leaves, from oziers, strew'd
    around,
Choked the small stream, and hush'd the
    feeble sound ;
While the dead foliage dropt from loftier trees
Our squire beheld not with his wonted ease,
But to his own reflections made reply,
And said aloud, ' Yes ! doubtless we must
    die.'
  ' We must ; ' said Richard, ' and we would
    not live
To feel what dotage and decay will give ;

But we yet taste whatever we behold,
The morn is lovely, though the air is cold :
There is delicious quiet in this scene,
At once so rich, so varied, so serene ;
Sounds too delight us,—each discordant tone
Thus mingled please, that fail to please alone;
This hollow wind, this rustling of the brook,
The farm-yard noise, the woodman at yon
    oak—
See, the axe falls !—now listen to the stroke !
That gun itself, that murders all this peace,
Adds to the charm, because it soon must
    cease.'
  ' No doubt,' said George, ' the country has
    its charms !
My farm behold ! the model for all farms !
Look at that land—you find not there a weed,
We grub the roots, and suffer none to seed.
  ' To land like this no botanist will come,
To seek the precious ware he hides at home ;
Pressing the leaves and flowers with effort
    nice,
As if they came from herbs in Paradise ;
Let them their favourites with my neighbours
    see,
They have no—what ?—no *habitat* with me.
  ' Now see my flock, and hear its glory ;—
    none
Have that vast body and that slender bone ;
They are the village boast, the dealer's theme,
Fleece of such staple ! flesh in such esteem ! '
  ' Brother,' said Richard, ' do I hear aright ?
Does the land truly give so much delight ? '
  'So says my bailiff: sometimes I have tried
To catch the joy, but nature has denied ;
It will not be—the mind has had a store
Laid up for life, and will admit no more :
Worn out in trials, and about to die,
In vain to these we for amusement fly ;
We farm, we garden, we our poor employ,
And much command, though little we enjoy ;
Or, if ambitious, we employ our pen,
We plant a desert, or we drain a fen ;
And—here, behold my medal !—this will show
What men may merit when they nothing
    know.'
  ' Yet reason here,' said Richard, ' joins
    with pride :— '
  ' I did not ask th' alliance,' George replied—
  ' I grant it true, such trifle may induce
A dull, proud man to wake and be of use ;
And there are purer pleasures, that a mind
Calm and uninjured may in villas find ;

But where th' affections have been deeply
    tried,
With other food that mind must be supplied :
'Tis not in trees or medals to impart
The powerful medicine for an aching heart ;
The agitation dies, but there is still
The backward spirit, the resisting will.
Man takes his body to a country seat,
But minds, dear Richard, have their own
    retreat ;
Oft when the feet are pacing o'er the green
The mind is gone where never grass was seen,
And never thinks of hill, or vale, or plain,
Till want of rest creates a sense of pain,
That calls that wandering mind, and brings
    it home again.
No more of farms : but here I boast of minds
That make a friend the richer when he finds ;
These shalt thou see;—but, Richard, be it
    known,
Who thinks to see must in his turn be
    shown :—
But now farewell ! to thee will I resign
Woods, walks, and valleys ! take them till
    we dine.'

    The Brothers dined, and with that plenteous
    fare
That seldom fails to dissipate our care,
At least the lighter kind ; and oft prevails
When reason, duty, nay, when kindness fails.
Yet food and wine, and all that mortals bless,
Lead them to think of peril and distress ;
Cold, hunger, danger, solitude, and pain,
That men in life's adventurous ways sustain.
  ' Thou hast sail'd far, dear brother,' said
    the 'squire—
' Permit me of these unknown lands t' inquire,
Lands never till'd, where thou hast wondering
    been,
And all the marvels thou hast heard and seen :
Do tell me something of the miseries felt
In climes where travellers freeze, and where
    they melt ;
And be not nice,—we know 'tis not in men,
Who travel far, to hold a steady pen :
Some will, 'tis true, a bolder freedom take,
And keep our wonder always wide awake ;
We know of those whose dangers far exceed
Our frail belief, that trembles as we read ;
Such as in deserts burn, and thirst, and die,
Save a last gasp that they recover by :

Then, too, their hazard from a tyrant's arms,
A tiger's fury, or a lady's charms ;
Beside th' accumulated evils borne
From the bold outset to the safe return.
These men abuse ; but thou hast fair pretence
To modest dealing, and to mild good sense ;
Then let me hear thy struggles and escapes
In the far lands of crocodiles and apes :
Say, hast thou, Bruce-like, knelt upon the bed
Where the young Nile uplifts his branchy head?
Or been partaker of th' unhallow'd feast,
Where beast-like man devours his fellow
　　beast,
And churn'd the bleeding life ? while each
　　great dame
And sovereign beauty bade adieu to shame ?
Or did the storm, that thy wreck'd pinnace
　　bore,
Impel thee gasping on some unknown shore ;
Where, when thy beard and nails were savage
　　grown,
Some swarthy princess took thee for her own,
Some danger-dreading Yarico, who, kind,
Sent thee away, and, prudent, staid behind ?
　　' Come—I am ready wonders to receive,
Prone to assent, and willing to believe.'
　　Richard replied : ' It must be known, to you,
That tales improbable may yet be true ;
And yet it is a foolish thing to tell
A tale that shall be judged improbable ;
While some impossibilities appear
So like the truth, that we assenting hear :
Yet, with your leave, I venture to relate
A chance-affair, and fact alone will state ;
Though, I confess, it may suspicion breed,
And you may cry, " Improbable, indeed ! "

　　' When first I tried the sea, I took a trip,
But duty none, in a relation's ship ;
Thus, unengaged, I felt my spirits light,
Kept care at distance, and put fear to flight ;
Oft this same spirit in my friends prevail'd,
Buoyant in dangers, rising when assail'd ;
When, as the gale at evening died away,
And die it will with the retiring day,
Impatient then, and sick of very ease,
We loudly whistled for the slumbering breeze.
　　' One eve it came ; and, frantic in my joy,
I rose and danced, as idle as a boy :
The cabin-lights were down, that we might
　　learn
A trifling something from the ship astern ;

The stiffening gale bore up the growing wave,
And wilder motion to my madness gave :
Oft have I since, when thoughtful and at rest,
Believed some maddening power my mind
　　possess'd ;
For, in an instant, as the stern sank low,
(How moved I knew not—What can madness
　　know ?)
Chance that direction to my motion gave,
And plunged me headlong in the roaring wave :
Swift flew the parting ship,—the fainter light
Withdrew,—or horror took them from my
　　sight.
　　' All was confused above, beneath, around ;
All sounds of terror ; no distinguish'd sound
Could reach me, now on sweeping surges tost,
And then between the rising billows lost ;
An undefined sensation stopp'd my breath ;
Disorder'd views and threat'ning signs of death
Met in one moment, and a terror gave—
I cannot paint it—to the moving grave.
My thoughts were all distressing, hurried,
　　mix'd,
On all things fixing, not a moment fix'd :
Vague thoughts of instant danger brought
　　their pain,
New hopes of safety banish'd them again ;
Then the swoln billow all these hopes
　　destroy'd,
And left me sinking in the mighty void :
Weaker I grew, and grew the more dismay'd,
Of aid all hopeless, yet in search of aid ;
Struggling awhile upon the wave to keep,
Then, languid, sinking in the yawning deep ·
So tost, so lost, so sinking in despair,
I pray'd in heart an indirected prayer,
And then once more I gave my eyes to view
The ship now lost, and bade the light adieu !
From my chill'd frame th' enfeebled spirit fled,
Rose the tall billows round my deep'ning bed,
Cold seized my heart, thought ceased, and
　　I was dead.
　　' Brother, I have not,—man has not the
　　power
To paint the horrors of that life-long hour ;
Hour !—but of time I knew not—when I
　　found
Hope, youth, life, love, and all they pro-
　　mised, drown'd ;
When all so indistinct, so undefined,
So dark and dreadful, overcame the mind ;
When such confusion on the spirit dwelt,
That, feeling much, it knew not what it felt.

' Can I, my brother—ought I to forget
That night of terror ? No ! it threatens yet.
Shall I days, months—nay, years, indeed,
    neglect,
Who then could feel what moments must effect,
Were aught effected ? who, in that wild
    storm,
Found there was nothing I could well per-
    form ;
For what to us are moments, what are hours,
If lost our judgment, and confused our
    powers ?
  ' Oft in the times when passion strives to
    reign,
When duty feebly holds the slacken'd chain,
When reason slumbers, then remembrance
    draws
This view of death, and folly makes a pause—
The view o'ercomes the vice, the fear the
    frenzy awes.
  ' I know there wants not this to make it
    true,
What danger bids be done, in safety do ;
Yet such escapes may make our purpose sure,
Who slights such warning may be too secure.'
  ' But the escape ! '—' Whate'er they judged
    might save
Their sinking friend they cast upon the wave ;
Something of these my heaven-directed arm
Unconscious seized, and held as by a charm :
The crew astern beheld me as I swam,
And I am saved—O ! let me say I am.'

  ' Brother,' said George, ' I have neglected
    long
To think of all thy perils :—it was wrong ;
But do forgive me ; for I could not be
Than of myself more negligent of thee.
Now tell me, Richard, from the boyish years
Of thy young mind, that now so rich appears,
How was it stored ? 'twas told me, thou wert
    wild,
A truant urchin,—a neglected child.
I heard of this escape, and sat supine
Amid the danger that exceeded thine ;
Thou couldst but die—the waves could but
    infold
Thy warm gay heart, and make that bosom
    cold—
While I——but no ! Proceed, and give me
    truth ;
How past the years of thy unguided youth ?

Thy father left thee to the care of one
Who could not teach, could ill support a son ;
Yet time and trouble feeble minds have
    stay'd,
And fit for long-neglected duties made :
I see thee struggling in the world, as late
Within the waves, and with an equal fate,
By Heaven preserved—but tell me, whence
    and how
Thy gleaning came ?—a dexterous gleaner
    thou ! '
  ' Left by that father, who was known to
    few,
And to that mother, who has not her due
Of honest fame,' said Richard, ' our retreat
Was a small cottage, for our station meet,
On Barford Downs : that mother, fond and
    poor,
There taught some truths, and bade me seek
    for more,
Such as our village-school and books a few
Supplied ; but such I cared not to pursue ;
I sought the town, and to the ocean gave
My mind and thoughts, as restless as the wave :
Where crowds assembled, I was sure to run,
Hear what was said, and mused on what was
    done ;
Attentive listening in the moving scene,
And often wondering what the men could
    mean.
When ships at sea made signals of their need,
I watch'd on shore the sailors, and their speed :
Mix'd in their act, nor rested till I knew
Why they were call'd, and what they were
    to do.
  ' Whatever business in the port was done,
I, without call, was with the busy one ;
Not daring question, but with open ear
And greedy spirit, ever bent to hear.
  ' To me the wives of seamen loved to tell
What storms endanger'd men esteem'd so
    well ;
What wond'rous things in foreign parts they
    saw,
Lands without bounds, and people without
    law.
  ' No ships were wreck'd upon that fatal
    beach,
But I could give the luckless tale of each ;
Eager I look'd, till I beheld a face
Of one disposed to paint their dismal case ;
Who gave the sad survivors' doleful tale,
From the first brushing of the mighty gale

Until they struck ; and, suffering in their fate,
I long'd the more they should its horrors state;
While some, the fond of pity, would enjoy
The earnest sorrows of the feeling boy.
I sought the men return'd from regions cold,
The frozen straits, where icy mountains roll'd ;
Some I could win to tell me serious tales
Of boats uplifted by enormous whales,
Or, when harpoon'd, how swiftly through the sea
The wounded monsters with the cordage flee ;
Yet some uneasy thoughts assail'd me then,
The monsters warr'd not with, nor wounded men :
The smaller fry we take, with scales and fins,
Who gasp and die—this adds not to our sins ;
But so much blood ! warm life, and frames so large
To strike, to murder—seem'd an heavy charge.
　' They told of days, where many goes to one—
Such days as ours ; and how a larger sun,
Red, but not flaming, roll'd, with motion slow,
On the world's edge, and never dropt below.
　' There were fond girls, who took me to their side
To tell the story how their lovers died ;
They praised my tender heart, and bade me prove
Both kind and constant when I came to love.
In fact, I lived for many an idle year
In fond pursuit of agitations dear ;
For ever seeking, ever pleased to find,
The food I loved, I thought not of its kind ;
It gave affliction while it brought delight,
And joy and anguish could at once excite.
　' One gusty day, now stormy and now still,
I stood apart upon the western hill,
And saw a race at sea : a gun was heard,
And two contending boats in sail appear'd :
Equal awhile ; then one was left behind,
And for a moment had her chance resign'd,
When, in that moment, up a sail they drew—
Not used before—their rivals to pursue.
Strong was the gale ! in hurry now there came
Men from the town, their thoughts, their fears the same ;
And women too ! affrighted maids and wives,
All deeply feeling for their sailors' lives.
　' The strife continued ; in a glass we saw
The desperate efforts, and we stood in awe,

When the last boat shot suddenly before,
Then fill'd, and sank—and could be seen no more !
　' Then were those piercing shrieks, that frantic flight,
All hurried ! all in tumult and affright !
A gathering crowd from different streets drew near,
All ask, all answer—none attend, none hear !
　' One boat is safe ; and see ! she backs her sail
To save the sinking—Will her care avail ?
　' O ! how impatient on the sands we tread,
And the winds roaring, and the women led,
As up and down they pace with frantic air,
And scorn a comforter, and will despair ;
They know not who in either boat is gone,
But think the father, husband, lover, one.
　' And who is she apart ? She dares not come
To join the crowd, yet cannot rest at home :
With what strong interest looks she at the waves,
Meeting and clashing o'er the seamen's graves:
'Tis a poor girl betroth'd—a few hours more,
And he will lie a corpse upon the shore.
　'Strange, that a boy could love these scenes, and cry
In very pity—but that boy was I.
With pain my mother would my tales receive,
And say, " my Richard, do not learn to grieve."
One wretched hour had past before we knew
Whom they had saved ! Alas ! they were but two,
An orphan'd lad and widow'd man—no more !
And they unnoticed stood upon the shore,
With scarce a friend to greet them—widows view'd
This man and boy, and then their cries renew'd :—
'Twas long before the signs of wo gave place
To joy again ; grief sat on every face.
　' Sure of my mother's kindness, and the joy
She felt in meeting her rebellious boy,
I at my pleasure our new seat forsook,
And, undirected, these excursions took :
I often rambled to the noisy quay,
Strange sounds to hear, and business strange to me ;
Seamen and carmen, and I know not who,
A lewd, amphibious, rude, contentious crew—
Confused as bees appear about their hive,
Yet all alert to keep their work alive.

' Here, unobserved as weed upon the wave,
My whole attention to the scene I gave ;
I saw their tasks, their toil, their care, their
    skill,
Led by their own and by a master-will ;
And though contending, toiling, tugging on,
The purposed business of the day was done.
  ' The open shops of craftsmen caught my
    eye,
And there my questions met the kind reply :
Men, when alone, will teach ; but, in a crowd,
The child is silent, or the man is proud ;
But, by themselves, there is attention paid
To a mild boy, so forward, yet afraid.
  ' I made me interest at the inn's fire-side,
Amid the scenes to bolder boys denied ;
For I had patrons there, and I was one,
They judged, who noticed nothing that was
    done.
" A quiet lad ! " would my protector say ;
" To him, now, this is better than his play :
Boys are as men ; some active, shrewd, and
    keen,
They look about if aught is to be seen ;
And some, like Richard here, have not a mind
That takes a notice—but the lad is kind."
  ' I loved in summer on the heath to walk,
And seek the shepherd—shepherds love to
    talk :
His superstition was of ranker kind,
And he with tales of wonder stored my mind ;
  ' Wonders that he in many a lonely eve
Had seen, himself, and therefore must believe.
His boy, his Joe, he said, from duty ran,
Took to the sea, and grew a fearless man :
" On yonder knoll—the sheep were in the
    fold—
His spirit past me, shivering-like and cold !
I felt a fluttering, but I knew not how,
And heard him utter, like a whisper, ' now ! '
Soon came a letter from a friend—to tell
That he had fallen, and the time he fell."
  ' Even to the smugglers' hut the rocks
    between,
I have, adventurous in my wandering, been :
Poor, pious Martha served the lawless tribe,
And could their merits and their faults
    describe ;
Adding her thoughts; "I talk, my child, to you,
Who little think of what such wretches do."
  ' I loved to walk where none had walk'd
    before,
About the rocks that ran along the shore ;

Or far beyond the sight of men to stray,
And take my pleasure when I lost my
    way ;
For then 'twas mine to trace the hilly heath,
And all the mossy moor that lies beneath :
Here had I favourite stations, where I stood
And heard the murmurs of the ocean-flood,
With not a sound beside, except when flew
Aloft the lapwing, or the gray curlew,
Who with wild notes my fancied power defied,
And mock'd the dreams of solitary pride.
  ' I loved to stop at every creek and bay
Made by the river in its winding way,
And call to memory—not by marks they bare,
But by the thoughts that were created there.
  ' Pleasant it was to view the sea-gulls strive
Against the storm, or in the ocean dive,
With eager scream, or when they dropping
    gave
Their closing wings to sail upon the wave :
Then as the winds and waters raged around,
And breaking billows mix'd their deafening
    sound,
They on the rolling deep securely hung,
And calmly rode the restless waves among.
Nor pleased it less around me to behold,
Far up the beach, the yesty sea-foam roll'd ;
Or from the shore upborn, to see on high,
Its frothy flakes in wild confusion fly :
While the salt spray that clashing billows
    form,
Gave to the taste a feeling of the storm.
  ' Thus, with my favourite views, for many
    an hour
Have I indulged the dreams of princely
    power ;
When the mind, wearied by excursions bold,
The fancy jaded, and the bosom cold,
Or when those wants, that will on kings
    intrude,
Or evening-fears, broke in on solitude ;
When I no more my fancy could employ,
I left in haste what I could not enjoy,
And was my gentle mother's welcome boy.
  ' But now thy walk,—this soft autumnal
    gloom
Bids no delay—at night I will resume
My subject, showing, not how I improved
In my strange school, but what the things
    I loved,
My first-born friendships, ties by forms
    uncheck'd,
And all that boys acquire whom men neglect.'

BOOK V. RUTH

Richard resumes his Narrative—Visits a
Family in a Seaport—The Man and his
Wife—Their Dwelling—Books, Number
and Kind—The Friendship contracted—
Employment there—Hannah, the Wife, her
Manner ; open Mirth and latent Grief—She
gives the Story of Ruth, her Daughter—Of
Thomas, a Sailor—Their Affection—A
Press-gang—Reflections—Ruth disturbed
in Mind—A Teacher sent to comfort her—
His Fondness—Her Reception of him—Her
Supplication—Is refused—She deliberates
—Is decided.

RICHARD would wait till George the tale
    should ask,
Nor waited long—He then resumed the task.
' South in the port, and eastward in the
    street,
Rose a small dwelling, my beloved retreat,
Where lived a pair, then old ; the sons had
    fled
The home they fill'd : a part of them were
    dead ;
Married a part ; while some at sea remain'd,
And stillness in the seaman's mansion reign'd ;
Lord of some petty craft, by night and day,
The man had fish'd each fathom of the bay.
' My friend the matron woo'd me, quickly
    won,
To fill the station of an absent son ;
(Him whom at school I knew, and Peter
    known,
I took his home and mother for my own) :
I read, and doubly was I paid to hear
Events that fell upon no listless ear :
She grieved to say her parents could neglect
Her education !—'twas a sore defect ;
She, who had ever such a vast delight
To learn, and now could neither read nor
    write :
But hear she could, and from our stores I took,
Librarian meet ! at her desire, our book.
Full twenty volumes—I would not exceed
The modest truth—were there for me to read ;
These a long shelf contain'd, and they were
    found
Books truly speaking, volumes fairly bound ;
The rest,—for some of other kinds remain'd,
And these a board beneath the shelf con-
    tain'd.—

Had their deficiencies in part ; they lack'd
One side or both, or were no longer back'd ;
But now became degraded from their place,
And were but pamphlets of a bulkier race.
Yet had we pamphlets, an inviting store,
From sixpence downwards—nay, a part were
    more ;
Learning abundance, and the various kinds
For relaxation—food for different minds ;
A piece of Wingate—thanks for all we have—
What we of figures needed, fully gave ;
Culpepper, new in numbers, cost but thrice
The ancient volume's unassuming price,
But told what planet o'er each herb had
    power.
And how to take it in the lucky hour.
' History we had—wars, treasons, treaties,
    crimes,
From Julius Caesar to the present times ;
Questions and answers, teaching what to ask
And what reply,—a kind, laborious task ;
A scholar's book it was, who, giving, swore
It held the whole he wish'd to know, and more.
' And we had poets, hymns and songs
    divine ;
The most we read not, but allow'd them fine.
' Our tracts were many, on the boldest
    themes—
We had our metaphysics, spirits, dreams,
Visions and warnings, and portentous sights
Seen, though but dimly, in the doleful nights,
When the good wife her wintry vigil keeps,
And thinks alone of him at sea, and weeps.
' Add to all these our works in single sheets,
That our Cassandras sing about the streets ;
These, as I read, the grave good man would
    say,
" Nay, Hannah ! " and she answer'd " What
    is Nay ?
What is there, pray, so hurtful in a song ?
It is our fancy only makes it wrong ;
His purer mind no evil thoughts alarm,
And innocence protects him like a charm."
Then would the matron, when the song had
    past,
And her laugh over, ask an hymn at last ;
To the coarse jest she would attention lend,
And to the pious psalm in reverence bend :
She gave her every power and all her mind ·
As chance directed, or as taste inclined.

' More of our learning I will now omit,
We had our Cyclopaedias of Wit,
And all our works, rare fate, were to our
     genius fit.
   ' When I had read, and we were weary
     grown
Of other minds, the dame disclosed her own ;
And long have I in pleasing terror stay'd
To hear of boys trepann'd, and girls betray'd ;
Ashamed so long to stay, and yet to go afraid.
   ' I could perceive, though Hannah bore full
     well
The ills of life, that few with her would dwell,
But pass away, like shadows o'er the plain
From flying clouds, and leave it fair again ;
Still every evil, be it great or small,
Would one past sorrow to the mind recall,
The grand disease of life, to which she turns,
And common cares and lighter suffering
     spurns.
" O ! these are nothing,—they will never heed
Such idle contests who have fought indeed,
And have the wounds unclosed."—I under-
     stood
My hint to speak, and my design pursued,
Curious the secret of that heart to find,
To mirth, to song, to laughter loud inclined,
And yet to bear and feel a weight of grief
     behind :
How does she thus her little sunshine throw
Always before her ?—I should like to know.
My friend perceived, and would no longer hide
The bosom's sorrow—Could she not confide,
In one who wept, unhurt—in one who felt,
     untried ?
   ' " Dear child, I show you sins and suffer-
     ings strange,
But you, like Adam, must for knowledge
     change
That blissful ignorance : remember, then,
What now you feel should be a check on men ;
For then your passions no debate allow,
And therefore lay up resolution now.
'Tis not enough, that when you can persuade
A maid to love, you know there 's promise
     made ;
'Tis not enough, that you design to keep
That promise made, nor leave your lass to
     weep :
But you must guard yourself against the sin,
And think it such to draw the party in ;
Nay, the more weak and easy to be won,
The viler you who have the mischief done.

   ' " I am not angry, love ; but men should
     know
They cannot always pay the debt they owe
Their plighted honour; they may cause the ill
They cannot lessen, though they feel a will ;
For *he* had truth with love, but love in youth
Does wrong, that cannot be repair'd by truth.
   ' " Ruth—I may tell, too oft had she been
     told—
Was tall and fair, and comely to behold ;
Gentle and simple, in her native place
Not one compared with her in form or face ;
She was not merry, but she gave our hearth
A cheerful spirit that was more than mirth.
   ' " There was a sailor boy, and people said
He was, as man, a likeness of the maid ;
But not in this—for he was ever glad,
While Ruth was apprehensive, mild, and sad ;
A quiet spirit hers, and peace would seek
In meditation : tender, mild, and meek !
Her loved the lad most truly : and, in truth,
She took an early liking to the youth :
To her alone were his attentions paid,
And they became the bachelor and maid.
He wish'd to marry, but so prudent we
And worldly wise, we said it could not be :
They took the counsel,—may be they
     approved,—
But still they grieved and waited, hoped and
     loved.
   ' " Now, my young friend, when of such
     state I speak
As one of danger, you will be to seek ;
You know not, Richard, where the danger lies
In loving hearts, kind words, and speaking
     eyes ;
For lovers speak their wishes with their looks
As plainly, love, as you can read your books.
Then, too, the meetings and the partings,
     all
The playful quarrels in which lovers fall,
Serve to one end—each lover is a child,
Quick to resent and to be reconciled ;
And then their peace brings kindness that
     remains,
And so the lover from the quarrel gains :
When he has faults that she reproves, his
     fear
And grief assure her she was too severe,
And that brings kindness—when he bears
     an ill,
Or disappointment, and is calm and still,
She feels his own obedient to her will,

And that brings kindness—and what kindness
brings
I cannot tell you :—these were trying things.
They were as children, and they fell at length ;
The trial, doubtless, is beyond their strength
Whom grace supports not ; and will grace
support
The too confiding, who their danger court ?
Then they would marry,—but were now too
late,—
All could their fault in sport or malice state ;
And though the day was fix'd, and now drew
on,
I could perceive my daughter's peace was
gone ;
She could not bear the bold and laughing eye
That gazed on her—reproach she could not
fly ;
Her grief she would not show, her shame
could not deny :
For some with many virtues come to shame,
And some that lose them all preserve their
name.
   ' " Fix'd was the day ; but ere that day
appear'd,
A frightful rumour through the place was
heard ;
War, who had slept awhile, awaked once more,
And gangs came pressing till they swept the
shore :
Our youth was seized and quickly sent away,
Nor would the wretches for his marriage stay,
But bore him off, in barbarous triumph bore,
And left us all our miseries to deplore :
There were wives, maids, and mothers on the
beach,
And some sad story appertain'd to each ;
Most sad to Ruth—to neither could she go !
But sat apart, and suffer'd matchless wo !
On the vile ship they turn'd their earnest view,
Not one last look allow'd,—not one adieu !
They saw the men on deck, but none dis-
tinctly knew.
And there she staid, regardless of each eye,
With but one hope, a fervent hope to die :
Nor cared she now for kindness—all beheld
Her, who invited none, and none repell'd ;
For there are griefs, my child, that sufferers
hide,
And there are griefs that men display with
pride ;
But there are other griefs that, so we feel,
We care not to display them nor conceal :

Such were our sorrows on that fatal day,
More than our lives the spoilers tore away ;
Nor did we heed their insult—some distress
No form or manner can make more or less,
And this is of that kind—this misery of a
press !
They say such things must be—perhaps they
must ;
But, sure, they need not fright us and disgust ;
They need not soul-less crews of ruffians send
At once the ties of humble love to rend :
A single day had Thomas stay'd on shore,
He might have wedded, and we ask'd no
more ;
And that stern man, who forced the lad away,
Might have attended, and have graced the
day ;
His pride and honour might have been at rest,
It is no stain to humble a couple blest !
Blest !—no, alas ! it was to ease the heart
Of one sore pang, and then to weep and part !
But this he would not,—English seamen fight
For England's gain and glory—it is right :
But will that public spirit be so strong,
Fill'd, as it must be, with their private wrong?
Forbid it, honour ! one in all the fleet
Should hide in war, or from the foe retreat ;
But is it just, that he who so defends
His country's cause, should hide him from
her friends ?
Sure, if they must upon our children seize,
They might prevent such injuries as these ;
Might hours—nay, days—in many a case
allow,
And soften all the griefs we suffer now.
Some laws, some orders might in part redress
The licensed insults of a British press,
That keeps the honest and the brave in awe,
Where might is right, and violence is law.
   ' " Be not alarm'd, my child ; there 's none
regard
What you and I conceive so cruel-hard :
There is compassion, I believe ; but still
One wants the power to help, and one the will,
And so from war to war the wrongs remain,
While Reason pleads, and Misery sighs in
vain.
   ' " Thus my poor Ruth was wretched and
undone,
Nor had an husband for her only son,
Nor had he father ; hope she did awhile,
And would not weep, although she could not
smile ;

Till news was brought us that the youth was
    slain,
And then, I think, she never smiled again ;
Or if she did, it was but to express
A feeling far, indeed, from happiness !
Something that her bewilder'd mind con-
    ceived :
When she inform'd us that she never grieved,
But was right merry, then her head was wild,
And grief had gain'd possession of my child ;
Yet, though bewilder'd for a time, and prone
To ramble much and speak aloud, alone ;
Yet did she all that duty ever ask'd,
And more, her will self-govern'd and untask'd :
With meekness bearing all reproach, all joy
To her was lost ; she wept upon her boy,
Wish'd for his death, in fear that he might live
New sorrow to a burden'd heart to give.
  ' " There was a teacher, where my husband
    went—
Sent, as he told the people—what he meant
You cannot understand, but—he was sent :
This man from meeting came, and strove to
    win
Her mind to peace by drawing off the sin,
Or what it was, that, working in her breast,
Robb'd it of comfort, confidence, and rest :
He came and reason'd, and she seem'd to feel
The pains he took—her griefs began to heal ;
She ever answer'd kindly when he spoke,
And always thank'd him for the pains he took ;
So, after three long years, and all the while
Wrapt up in grief, she blest us with a smile,
And spoke in comfort ; but she mix'd no more
With younger persons, as she did before.
  ' " Still Ruth was pretty ; in her person
    neat ;
So thought the teacher, when they chanced
    to meet :
He was a weaver by his worldly trade,
But powerful work in the assemblies made ;
People came leagues to town to hear him
    sift
The holy text,—he had the grace and gift ;
Widows and maidens flock'd to hear his voice ;
Of either kind he might have had his choice ;—
But he had chosen—we had seen how shy
The girl was getting, my good man and I ;
That when the weaver came, she kept with us,
Where he his points and doctrines might
    discuss ;
But in our bit of garden, or the room
We call our parlour, there he must not come.

She loved him not, and though she could
    attend
To his discourses, as her guide and friend,
Yet now to these she gave a listless ear,
As if a friend she would no longer hear ;
This might he take for woman's art, and cried,
'Spouse of my heart, I must not be denied !'—
Fearless he spoke, and I had hope to see
My girl a wife—but this was not to be.
  " My husband, thinking of his worldly store,
And not, frail man, enduring to be poor,
Seeing his friend would for his child provide
And hers, he grieved to have the man denied ;
For Ruth, when press'd, rejected him, and
    grew
To her old sorrow, as if that were new.
' Who shall support her ? ' said her father,
    ' how
Can I, infirm and weak as I am now ?
And here a loving fool '——this gave her pain,
Severe, indeed, but she would not complain ;
Nor would consent, although the weaver grew
More fond, and would the frighten'd girl
    pursue.
  ' " O ! much she begg'd him to forbear, to
    stand
Her soul's kind friend, and not to ask her
    hand :
She could not love him.—' Love me ! ' he
    replied,
' The love you mean is love unsanctified,
An earthly, wicked, sensual, sinful kind,
A creature-love, the passion of the blind.'
He did not court her, he would have her know,
For that poor love that will on beauty grow ;
No ! he would take her as the prophet took
One of the harlots in the holy book ;
And then he look'd so ugly and severe !
And yet so fond—she could not hide her fear.
  ' " This fondness grew her torment ; she
    would fly,
In woman's terror, if he came but nigh ;
Nor could I wonder he should odious prove,
So like a ghost that left a grave for love.
  ' " But still her father lent his cruel aid
To the man's hope, and she was more afraid :
He said, no more she should his table share,
But be the parish or the teacher's care.
' Three days I give you : see that all be right
On Monday-morning—this is Thursday-
    night—
Fulfil my wishes, girl ! or else forsake my
    sight ! '

' " I see her now; and, she that was so meek,
It was a chance that she had power to speak,
Now spoke in earnest—' Father ! I obey,
And will remember the appointed day ! '
' " Then came the man : she talk'd with him apart,
And, I believe, laid open all her heart ;
But all in vain—she said to me, in tears,
' Mother ! that man is not what he appears :
He talks of heaven, and let him, if he will,
But he has earthly purpose to fulfil ;
Upon my knees I begg'd him to resign
The hand he asks—he said, it shall be mine :
What ! did the holy men of Scripture deign,
To hear a woman when she said ' refrain ? '
Of whom they chose they took them wives, and these
Made it their study and their wish to please ;
The women then were faithful and afraid,
As Sarah Abraham, they their lords obey'd,
And so she styled him ; 'tis in later days
Of foolish love that we our women praise,
Fall on the knee, and raise the suppliant hand,
And court the favour that we might command.
' " O! my dear mother, when this man has power,
How will he treat me—first may beasts devour !
Or death in every form that I could prove,
Except this selfish being's hateful love.'
' " I gently blamed her, for I knew how hard
It is to force affection and regard.
' " Ah ! my dear lad, I talk to you as one
Who knew the misery of an heart undone ;
You know it not; but, dearest boy, when man,
Do not an ill because you find you can :
Where is the triumph ? when such things men seek
They only drive to wickedness the weak.
' " Weak was poor Ruth, and this good man so hard,
That to her weakness he had no regard :
But we had two days' peace; he came, and then
My daughter whisper'd, ' Would there were no men !
None to admire or scorn us, none to vex
A simple, trusting, fond, believing sex ;
Who truly love the worth that men profess,
And think too kindly for their happiness.' "

' Poor Ruth ! few heroines in the tragic page
Felt more than thee in thy contracted stage ;
Fair, fond, and virtuous, they our pity move,
Impell'd by duty, agonized by love ;
But no Mandane, who in dread has knelt
On the bare boards, has greater terrors felt,
Nor been by warring passions more subdued
Than thou, by this man's grovelling wish pursued ;
Doom'd to a parent's judgment, all unjust,
Doom'd the chance mercy of the world to trust,
Or to wed grossness and conceal disgust.
' " If Ruth was frail, she had a mind too nice
To wed with that which she beheld as vice ;
To take a reptile, who, beneath a show
Of peevish zeal, let carnal wishes grow ;
Proud and yet mean, forbidding and yet full
Of eager appetites, devout and dull,
Waiting a legal right that he might seize
His own, and his impatient spirit ease,
Who would at once his pride and love indulge,
His temper humour, and his spite divulge.
' " This the poor victim saw—a second time,
Sighing, she said, ' Shall I commit the crime,
And now untempted ? Can the form or rite
Make me a wife in my Creator's sight ?
Can I the words without a meaning say ?
Can I pronounce love, honour, or obey ?
And if I cannot, shall I dare to wed,
And go an harlot to a loathed bed ?
Never, dear mother ! my poor boy and I
Will at the mercy of a parish lie ;
Reproved for wants that vices would remove,
Reproach'd for vice that I could never love,
Mix'd with a crew long wedded to disgrace,
A vulgar, forward, equalizing race,—
And am I doom'd to beg a dwelling in that place ? '
' " Such was her reasoning : many times she weigh'd
The evils all, and was of each afraid ;
She loath'd the common board, the vulgar seat,
Where shame, and want, and vice, and sorrow meet,
Where frailty finds allies, where guilt insures retreat.
But peace again is fled : the teacher comes,
And new importance, haughtier air assumes.
' " No hapless victim of a tyrant's love
More keenly felt, or more resisting strove

Against her fate; she look'd on every side,
But there were none to help her, none to
    guide;—
And he, the man who should have taught the
    soul,
Wish'd but the body in his base control.
  ' " She left her infant on the Sunday morn,
A creature doom'd to shame! in sorrow born;
A thing that languish'd, nor arrived at age
When the man's thoughts with sin and pain
    engage—
She came not home to share our humble meal,
Her father thinking what his child would feel
From his hard sentence—still she came not
    home.
The night grew dark, and yet she was not
    come;
The east-wind roar'd, the sea return'd the
    sound,
And the rain fell as if the world were drown'd:
There were no lights without, and my good man,
To kindness frighten'd, with a groan began
To talk of Ruth, and pray; and then he took
The Bible down, and read the holy book;
For he had learning: and when that was done
We sat in silence—whither could we run?
We said, and then rush'd frighten'd from the
    door,
For we could bear our own conceit no more:
We call'd on neighbours—there she had not
    been;
We met some wanderers—ours they had not
    seen:
We hurried o'er the beach, both north and
    south,
Then join'd, and wander'd to our haven's
    mouth:

Where rush'd the falling waters wildly out,
I scarcely heard the good man's fearful shout,
Who saw a something on the billow ride,
And—Heaven have mercy on our sins! he
    cried,
It is my child!—and to the present hour
So he believes—and spirits have the power.
  ' " And she was gone! the waters wide and
    deep
Roll'd o'er her body as she lay asleep.
She heard no more the angry waves and wind,
She heard no more the threat'ning of man-
    kind;
Wrapt in dark weeds, the refuse of the storm,
To the hard rock was borne her comely form!
  ' " But O! what storm was in that mind?
    what strife,
That could compel her to lay down her life?
For she was seen within the sea to wade,
By one at distance, when she first had pray'd;
Then to a rock within the hither shoal
Softly and with a fearful step she stole;
Then, when she gain'd it, on the top she stood
A moment still—and dropt into the flood!
The man cried loudly, but he cried in vain,—
She heard not then—she never heard again!
She had—pray, Heav'n!—she had that world
    in sight,
Where frailty mercy finds, and wrong has
    right;
But, sure, in this her portion such has been,
Well had it still remain'd a world unseen! "
  ' Thus far the dame: the passions will dis-
    pense
To such a wild and rapid eloquence—
Will to the weakest mind their strength impart,
And give the tongue the language of the heart.'

BOOK VI.   ADVENTURES OF RICHARD CONCLUDED

Richard relates his Illness and Retirement—
A Village Priest and his two Daughters—
His peculiar Studies—His Simplicity of
Character—Arrival of a third Daughter—
Her Zeal in his Conversion—Their Friend-
ship—How terminated—An happy Day—
Its Commencement and Progress—A
Journey along the Coast—Arrival as a
Guest—Company—A Lover's Jealousy—
it increases—dies away—An Evening Walk
—Suspense—Apprehension—Resolution—
Certainty.

  ' This then, dear Richard, was the way
    you took
To gain instruction—thine a curious book,
Containing much of both the false and
    true;
But thou hast read it, and with profit too;
  ' Come, then, my Brother, now thy tale
    complete—
I know thy first embarking in the fleet,
Thy entrance in the army, and thy gain
Of plenteous laurels in the wars in Spain,

And what then follow'd ; but I wish to know
When thou that heart hadst courage to
　　bestow,
When to declare it gain'd, and when to stand
Before the priest, and give the plighted hand ;
So shall I boldness from thy frankness gain
To paint the frenzy that possess'd my brain ;
For rather there than in my heart I found
Was my disease ; a poison, not a wound,
A madness, Richard—but, I pray thee, tell
Whom hast thou loved so dearly and so well ? '
　　The younger man his gentle host obey'd,
For some respect, though not required, was
　　paid,
Perhaps with all that independent pride
Their different states would to the memory
　　glide ;
Yet was his manner unconstrain'd and free,
And nothing in it like servility.
　　Then he began :—' When first I reach'd
　　the land,
I was so ill that death appeared at hand ;
And though the fever left me, yet I grew
So weak 'twas judged that life would leave
　　me too.
I sought a village-priest, my mother's friend,
And I believed with him my days would end :
The man was kind, intelligent, and mild,
Careless and shrewd, yet simple as the child ;
For of the wisdom of the world his share
And mine were equal—neither had to spare ;
Else—with his daughters, beautiful and
　　poor—
He would have kept a sailor from his door :
Two then were present, who adorn'd his
　　home,
But ever speaking of a third to come ;
Cheerful they were, not too reserved or free,
I loved them both, and never wish'd them
　　three.
　　' The vicar's self, still further to describe,
Was of a simple, but a studious tribe ;
He from the world was distant, not retired,
Nor of it much possess'd, nor much desired :
Grave in his purpose, cheerful in his eye,
And with a look of frank benignity.
He lost his wife when they together past
Years of calm love, that triumph'd to the last.
He much of nature, not of man had seen,
Yet his remarks were often shrewd and keen ;
Taught not by books t' approve or to con-
　　demn,
He gain'd but little that he knew from them ;

He read with reverence and respect the few,
Whence he his rules and consolations drew ;
But men and beasts, and all that lived or
　　moved,
Were books to him ; he studied them and
　　loved.
　　' He knew the plants in mountain, wood,
　　or mead ;
He knew the worms that on the foliage feed ;
Knew the small tribes that 'scape the careless
　　eye,
The plant's disease that breeds the embryo-
　　fly ;
And the small creatures who on bark or bough
Enjoy their changes, changed we know not
　　how ;
But now th' imperfect being scarcely moves,
And now takes wing and seeks the sky it loves.
　　' He had no system, and forbore to read
The learned labours of th' immortal Swede ;
But smiled to hear the creatures he had known
So long, were now in class and order shown,
Genus and species—" is it meet," said he,
" This creature's name should one so sounding
　　be ?
'Tis but a fly, though first-born of the spring—
Bombylius majus, dost thou call the thing ?
Majus, indeed ! and yet, in fact, 'tis true,
We all are majors, all are minors too,
Except the first and last,—th' immensely
　　distant two.
And here again,—what call the learned this ?
Both Hippobosca and Hirundinis ?
Methinks the creature should be proud to find
That he employs the talents of mankind ;
And that his sovereign master shrewdly looks,
Counts all his parts, and puts them in his
　　books.
Well ! go thy way, for I do feel it shame
To stay a being with so proud a name."
　　' Such were his daughters, such my quiet
　　friend,
And pleasant was it thus my days to spend ;
But when Matilda at her home I saw,
Whom I beheld with anxiousness and awe,
The ease and quiet that I found before
At once departed, and return'd no more.
No more their music soothed me as they
　　play'd,
But soon her words a strong impression made ;
The sweet enthusiast, so I deem'd her, took
My mind, and fix'd it to her speech and
　　look ;

My soul, dear girl! she made her constant
    care,
But never whisper'd to my heart " beware! "
In love no dangers rise till we are in the snare.
Her father sometimes question'd of my creed,
And seem'd to think it might amendment
    need ;
But great the difference when the pious maid
To the same errors her attention paid ;
Her sole design that I should think aright,
And my conversion her supreme delight :
Pure was her mind, and simple her intent,
Good all she sought, and kindness all she
    meant.
Next to religion friendship was our theme,
Related souls and their refined esteem :
We talk'd of scenes where this is real found,
And love subsists without a dart or wound ;
But there intruded thoughts not all serene,
And wishes not so calm would intervene.'
  ' Saw not her father ? '
            ' Yes ; but saw no more
Than he had seen without a fear before :
He had subsisted by the church and plough,
And saw no cause for apprehension now.
We, too, could live : he thought not passion
    wrong,
But only wonder'd we delay'd so long.
More had he wonder'd had he known esteem
Was all we mention'd, friendship was our
    theme.—
Laugh, if you please, I must my tale pursue—
This sacred friendship thus in secret grew
An intellectual love, most tender, chaste, and
    true :
Unstain'd, we said, nor knew we how it
    chanced
To gain some earthly soil as it advanced ;
But yet my friend, and she alone, could prove
How much it differ'd from romantic love—
But this and more I pass—No doubt, at
    length,
We could perceive the weakness of our
    strength.
  ' O! days remember'd well! remember'd
    all!
The bitter-sweet, the honey and the gall ;
Those garden rambles in the silent night,
Those trees so shady, and that moon so
    bright ;
That thickset alley by the arbour closed,
That woodbine seat where we at last re-
    posed ;

And then the hopes that came and then were
    gone,
Quick as the clouds beneath the moon past
    on ;
Now, in this instant, shall my love be shown,
I said—O ! no, the happy time is flown !
  ' You smile ; remember, I was weak and
    low,
And fear'd the passion as I felt it grow :
Will she, I said, to one so poor attend,
Without a prospect, and without a friend ?
I dared not ask her—till a rival came,
But hid the secret, slow-consuming flame.
  ' I once had seen him ; then familiar, free,
More than became a common guest to be ;
And sure, I said, he has a look of pride
And inward joy—a lover satisfied.
  ' Can you not, Brother, on adventures past
A thought, as on a lively prospect, cast ?
On days of dear remembrance ! days that
    seem,
When past—nay, even when present, like
    a dream—
These white and blessed days, that softly
    shine
On few, nor oft on them—have they been
    thine ? '
  George answer'd, ' Yes ! dear Richard,
    through the years
Long past, a day so white and mark'd appears :
As in the storm that pours destruction round,
Is here and there a ship in safety found ;
So in the storms of life some days appear
More blest and bright for the preceding fear ;
These times of pleasure that in life arise,
Like spots in deserts, that delight, surprise,
And to our wearied senses give the more,
For all the waste behind us and before ;
And thou, dear Richard, hast then had thy
    share
Of those enchanting times that baffle care ? '
  ' Yes, I have felt this life-refreshing gale
That bears us onward when our spirits fail ;
That gives those spirits vigour and delight—
I would describe it, could I do it right.
  ' Such days have been—a day of days was
    one
When, rising gaily with the rising sun,
I took my way to join a happy few,
Known not to me, but whom Matilda knew,
To whom she went a guest, and message
    sent,
" Come thou to us," and as a guest I went.

' There are two ways to Brandon—by the
      heath
Above the cliff, or on the sand beneath,
Where the small pebbles, wetted by the wave,
To the new day reflected lustre gave :
At first above the rocks I made my way,
Delighted looking at the spacious bay,
And the large fleet that to the northward
      steer'd
Full sail, that glorious in my view appear'd ;
For where does man evince his full control
O'er subject matter, where displays the soul
Its mighty energies with more effect
Than when her powers that moving mass
      direct ?
Than when man guides the ship man's art
      has made,
And makes the winds and waters yield him
      aid ?
   ' Much as I longed to see the maid I loved,
Through scenes so glorious I at leisure moved ;
For there are times when we do not obey
The master-passion—when we yet delay—
When absence, soon to end, we yet prolong,
And dally with our wish although so strong.
   ' High were my joys, but they were sober
      too,
Nor reason spoil'd the pictures fancy drew ;
I felt—rare feeling in a world like this—
The sober certainty of waking bliss ;
Add too the smaller aids to happy men,
Convenient helps—these too were present
      then.
   ' But what are spirits ? light indeed and
      gay
They are, like winter flowers, nor last a day ;
Comes a rude icy wind,—they feel, and fade
      away.
   ' High beat my heart when to the house
      I came,
And when the ready servant gave my name ;
But when I enter'd that pernicious room,
Gloomy it look'd, and painful was the gloom ;
And jealous was the pain, and deep the sigh
Caused by this gloom, and pain, and jealousy,
For there Matilda sat, and her beside
That rival soldier, with a soldier's pride ;
With self-approval in his laughing face,
His seem'd the leading spirit of the place :
She was all coldness—yet I thought a look,
But that corrected, tender welcome spoke :
It was as lightning which you think you see,
But doubt, and ask if lightning it could be.

   ' Confused and quick my introduction
      pass'd,
When I, a stranger and on strangers cast,
Beheld the gallant man as he display'd
Uncheck'd attention to the guilty maid :
O ! how it grieved me that she dared t' excite
Those looks in him that show'd so much
      delight ;
Egregious coxcomb ! there—he smiled again,
As if he thought to aggravate my pain :
Still she attends—I must approach—and find,
Or make, a quarrel, to relieve my mind.
   ' In vain I try—politeness as a shield
The angry strokes of my contempt repell'd ;
Nor must I violate the social law
That keeps the rash and insolent in awe.
Once I observed, on hearing my replies,
The woman's terror fix'd on me the eyes
That look'd entreaty ; but the guideless rage
Of jealous minds no softness can assuage.
But, lo ! they rise, and all prepare to take
The promised pleasure on the neighbouring
      lake.
   ' Good heaven ! they whisper ! Is it come
      to this ?
Already !—then may I my doubt dismiss :
Could he so soon a timid girl persuade ?
What rapid progress has the coxcomb made ;
And yet how cool her looks, and how demure !
The falling snow nor lily's flower so pure :
What can I do ? I must the pair attend,
And watch this horrid business to its end.
   ' There, forth they go ! He leads her to
      the shore—
Nay, I must follow,—I can bear no more :
What can the handsome gipsy have in view
In trifling thus, as she appears to do ?
I, who for months have labour'd to succeed,
Have only lived her vanity to feed.
   ' O ! you will make me room—'tis very
      kind,
And meant for him—it tells him he must
      mind ;
Must not be careless :—I can serve to draw
The soldier on, and keep the man in awe.
O ! I did think she had a guileless heart,
Without deceit, capriciousness, or art ;
And yet a stranger, with a coat of red,
Has, by an hour's attention, turn'd her head.
   ' Ah ! how delicious was the morning-drive,
The soul awaken'd, and its hopes alive :
How dull this scene by trifling minds enjoy'd,
The heart in trouble and its hope destroy'd.

' Well, now we land—And will he yet sup-
   port
This part ? What favour has he now to court ?
Favour ! O, no ! He means to quit the fair ;
How strange ! how cruel ! Will she not de-
   spair ?
   ' Well ! take her hand—no further if you
   please,
I cannot suffer fooleries like these :—
How ? " Love to Julia ! " to his wife ?—
   O ! dear
And injured creature, how must I appear,
Thus haughty in my looks, and in my words
   severe ?
Her love to Julia, to the school-day friend
To whom those letters she has lately penn'd !
Can she forgive ? And now I think again,
The man was neither insolent nor vain ;
Good humour chiefly would a stranger trace,
Were he impartial, in the air or face ;
And I so splenetic the whole way long,
And she so patient—it was very wrong.
   ' The boat had landed in a shady scene ;
The grove was in its glory, fresh and green ;
The showers of late had swell'd the branch
   and bough,
And the sun's fervour made them pleasant
   now.
Hard by an oak arose in all its pride,
And threw its arms along the water's side ;
Its leafy limbs, that on the glassy lake
Stretch far, and all those dancing shadows
   make.
   ' And now we walk—now smaller parties
   seek
Or sun or shade as pleases—Shall I speak ?
Shall I forgiveness ask, and then apply
For——O ! that vile and intercepting cry.
Alas ! what mighty ills can trifles make,—
An hat ! the idiot's—fallen in the lake !
What serious mischief can such idlers do ?
I almost wish the head had fallen too.
   ' No more they leave us, but will hover
   round,
As if amusement at our cost they found ;
Vex'd and unhappy I indeed had been,
Had I not something in my charmer seen
Like discontent, that, though corrected, dwelt
On that dear face, and told me what she
   felt.
   ' Now must we cross the lake, and as we
   cross'd
Was my whole soul in sweet emotion lost ;

Clouds in white volumes roll'd beneath the
   moon,
Softening her light that on the waters shone :
This was such bliss ! even then it seem'd
   relief
To veil the gladness in a show of grief :
We sighed as we conversed, and said, how
   deep
This lake on which those broad dark shadows
   sleep ;
There is between us and a watery grave
But a thin plank, and yet our fate we brave.
" What if it burst ? " Matilda, then my care
Would be for thee : all danger I would dare,
And, should my efforts fail, thy fortune would
   I share.
" The love of life," she said, " would powerful
   prove ! "
O ! not so powerful as the strength of love :—
A look of kindness gave the grateful maid,
That had the real effort more than paid.
   ' But here we land, and haply now may
   choose
Companions home—our way, too, we may
   lose :
In these drear, dark, inosculating lanes,
The very native of his doubt complains ;
No wonder then that in such lonely ways
A stranger, heedless of the country, strays ;
A stranger, too, whose many thoughts all
   meet
In one design, and none regard his feet.
   ' " Is this the path ? " the cautious fair
   one cries ;
I answer, Yes !—" We shall our friends sur-
   prise,"
She added, sighing—I return the sighs.
   ' " Will they not wonder ? " O ! they
   would, indeed,
Could they the secrets of this bosom read,
These chilling doubts, these trembling hopes
   I feel !
The faint, fond hopes I can no more conceal—
I love thee, dear Matilda !—to confess
The fact is dangerous, fatal to suppress.
   ' And now in terror I approach the home
Where I may wretched but not doubtful come,
Where I must be all ecstasy, or all,—
O ! what will you a wretch rejected call ?
Not man, for I shall lose myself, and be
A creature lost to reason, losing thee.
   ' Speak, my Matilda ! on the rack of fear
Suspend me not—I would my sentence hear,

Would learn my fate——Good Heaven! and
　　what portend
These tears?—and fall they for thy wretched
　　friend?
Or——but I cease; I cannot.paint the bliss,
From a confession soft and kind as this;
Nor where we walk'd, nor how our friends
　　we met,
Or what their wonder—I am wondering yet;
For he who nothing heeds has nothing to
　　forget.
　' All thought, yet thinking nothing—all
　　delight
In every thing, but nothing in my sight!
Nothing I mark or learn, but am possess'd
Of joys I cannot paint, and I am bless'd
In all that I conceive—whatever is, is best.
Ready to aid all beings, I would go
The world around to succour human wo;
Yet am so largely happy, that it seems
There are no woes, and sorrows are but
　　dreams.
　' There is a college joy, to scholars known,
When the first honours are proclaim'd their
　　own;
There is ambition's joy, when in their race
A man surpassing rivals gains his place;

There is a beauty's joy, amid a crowd
To have that beauty her first fame allow'd;
And there's the conqueror's joy, when,
　　dubious held
And long the fight, he sees the foe repell'd:
　' But what are these, or what are other joys,
That charm kings, conquerors, beauteous
　　nymphs and boys,
Or greater yet, if greater yet be found,
To that delight when love's dear hope is
　　crown'd?
To the first beating of a lover's heart,
When the loved maid endeavours to impart,
Frankly yet faintly, fondly yet in fear,
The kind confession that he holds so dear.
Now in the morn of our return how strange
Was this new feeling, this delicious change;
That sweet delirium, when I gazed in fear,
That all would yet be lost and disappear.
　' Such was the blessing that I sought for
　　pain,
In some degree to be myself again;
And when we met a shepherd old and lame,
Cold and diseased, it seem'd my blood to
　　tame;
And I was thankful for the moral sight,
That soberized the vast and wild delight.'

BOOK VII.　THE ELDER BROTHER

Conversation—Story of the elder Brother—
His romantic Views and Habits—The Scene
of his Meditations—Their Nature—Inter-
rupted by an Adventure—The Conse-
quences of it—A strong and permanent
Passion—Search of its Object—Long inef-
fectual—How found—The first Interview
—The second—End of the Adventure—
Retirement.

　' THANKS, my dear Richard; and, I pray
　　thee, deign
To speak the truth—does all this love remain,
And all this joy? for views and flights sub-
　　lime,
Ardent and tender, are subdued by time.
Speaks't thou of her to whom thou mad'st thy
　　vows,
Of my fair sister, of thy lawful spouse?
Or art thou talking some frail love about,
The rambling fit, before th' abiding gout?'

　' Nay, spare me, Brother, an adorer spare:
Love and the gout! thou wouldst not these
　　compare?'
　' Yea, and correctly; teasing ere they
　　come,
They then confine their victim to his home:
In both are previous feints and false attacks,
Both place the grieving patient on their
　　racks:
They both are ours, with all they bring, for
　　life,
'Tis not in us t' expel or gout or wife;
On man a kind of dignity they shed,
A sort of gloomy pomp about his bed:
Then if he leaves them, go where'er he
　　will,
They have a claim upon his body still;
Nay, when they quit him, as they sometimes
　　do,
What is there left t' enjoy or to pursue?—

But dost thou love this woman ? '
                ' O ! beyond
What I can tell thee of the true and fond :
Hath she not soothed me, sick, enrich'd me,
    poor,
And banish'd death and misery from my
    door ?
Has she not cherish'd every moment's bliss,
And made an Eden of a world like this ?
When Care would strive with us his watch
    to keep,
Has she not sung the snarling fiend to sleep ?
And when Distress has look'd us in the face,
Has she not told him, " thou art not Dis-
    grace ? " ' '
    ' I must behold her, Richard ; I must see
This patient spouse who sweetens misery—
But didst thou need, and wouldst thou not
    apply ?—
Nay, thou wert right—but then how wrong
    was I ! '
    ' My indiscretion was—— '
                ' No more repeat ;
Would I were nothing worse than indis-
    creet ;—
But still there is a plea that I could bring,
Had I the courage to describe the thing.'
    ' Then thou too, Brother, couldst of weak-
    ness tell ;
Thou, too, hast found the wishes that rebel
Against the sovereign reason ; at some time
Thou hast been fond, heroic, and sublime ;
Wrote verse, it may be, and for one dear maid
The sober purposes of life delay'd ;
From year to year the fruitless chase pursued,
And hung enamour'd o'er the flying good :
Then be thy weakness to a Brother shown,
And give him comfort who displays his own.'
    ' Ungenerous youth ! dost thou presuming
    ask
A man so grave his failings to unmask ?
What if I tell thee of a waste of time,
That on my spirit presses as a crime,
Wilt thou despise me ?—I, who, soaring, fell
So late to rise—Hear then the tale I tell ;
Who tells what thou shalt hear, esteems his
    hearer well.

    ' Yes, my dear Richard, thou shalt hear
    me own
Follies and frailties thou hast never known ;
Thine was a frailty,—folly, if you please,—
But mine a flight, a madness, a disease.

    ' Turn with me to my twentieth year, for
    then
The lover's frenzy ruled the poet's pen ;
When virgin reams were soil'd with lays of
    love,
The flinty hearts of fancied nymphs to move :
Then was I pleased in lonely ways to tread,
And muse on tragic tales of lovers dead ;
For all the merit I could then descry
In man or woman was for love to die.
    ' I mused on charmers chaste, who pledged
    their truth,
And left no more the once-accepted youth ;
Though he disloyal, lost, diseased, became,
The widow'd turtle's was a deathless flame :
This faith, this feeling, gave my soul delight,
Truth in the lady, ardour in the knight.
    ' I built me castles wondrous rich and rare,
Few castle-builders could with me compare ;
The hall, the palace, rose at my command,
And these I fill'd with objects great and
    grand.
Virtues sublime, that nowhere else would live,
Glory and pomp, that I alone could give ;
Trophies and thrones by matchless valour
    gain'd,
Faith unreproved, and chastity unstain'd ;
With all that soothes the sense and charms
    the soul,
Came at my call, and were in my control.
    ' And who was I ? a slender youth and tall,
In manner awkward, and with fortune small ;
With visage pale, my motions quick and slow,
That fall and rising in the spirits show ;
For none could more by outward signs express
What wise men lock within the mind's recess ;
Had I a mirror set before my view,
I might have seen what such a form could do ;
Had I within the mirror truth beheld,
I should have such presuming thoughts re-
    pell'd ;
But awkward as I was, without the grace
That gives new beauty to a form or face ;
Still I expected friends most true to prove,
And grateful, tender, warm, assiduous love.
    ' Assured of this, that love's delicious bond
Would hold me ever faithful, ever fond ;
It seem'd but just that I in love should find
A kindred heart as constant and as kind.
Give me, I cried, a beauty ; none on earth
Of higher rank or nobler in her birth ;
Pride of her race, her father's hope and care,
Yet meek as children of the cottage are ;

Nursed in the court, and there by love pursued,
But fond of peace, and blest in solitude ;
By rivals honour'd, and by beauties praised,
Yet all unconscious of the envy raised ;
Suppose her this, and from attendants freed,
To want my prowess in a time of need,
When safe and grateful she desires to show
She feels the debt that she delights to owe,
And loves the man who saved her in distress—
So fancy will'd, nor would compound for less.
   ' This was my dream.—In some auspicious hour,
In some sweet solitude, in some green bower,
Whither my fate should lead me, there, unseen,
I should behold my fancy's gracious queen,
Singing sweet song! that I should hear awhile,
Then catch the transient glory of a smile ;
Then at her feet with trembling hope should kneel,
Such as rapt saints and raptured lovers feel ;
To watch the chaste unfoldings of her heart,
In joy to meet, in agony to part,
And then in tender song to soothe my grief,
And hail, in glorious rhyme, my *Lady of the Leaf.*
   ' To dream these dreams I chose a woody scene,
My guardian-shade, the world and me between ;
A green inclosure, where beside its bound
A thorny fence beset its beauties round,
Save where some creature's force had made a way
For me to pass, and in my kingdom stray :
Here then I stray'd, then sat me down to call,
Just as I will'd, my shadowy subjects all !
Fruits of all minds conceived on every coast,
Fay, witch, enchanter, devil, demon, ghost ;
And thus with knights and nymphs, in halls and bowers,
In war and love, I pass'd unnumber'd hours :
Gross and substantial beings all forgot,
Ideal glories beam'd around the spot,
And all that was, with me, of this poor world was not.
   ' Yet in this world there was a single scene,
That I allow'd with mine to intervene ;
This house, where never yet my feet had stray'd,
I with respect and timid awe survey'd ;
With pleasing wonder I have oft-times stood,
To view these turrets rising o'er the wood ;

When fancy to the halls and chambers flew,
Large, solemn, silent, that I must not view ;
The moat was then, and then o'er all the ground
Tall elms and ancient oaks stretch'd far around ;
And where the soil forbad the nobler race,
Dwarf trees and humbler shrubs had found their place,
Forbidding man in their close hold to go,
Haw, gatter, holm, the service and the sloe ;
With tangling weeds that at the bottom grew,
And climbers all above their feathery branches threw.
Nor path of man or beast was there espied,
But there the birds of darkness loved to hide,
The loathed toad to lodge, and speckled snake to glide.
   ' To me this hall, thus view'd in part, appear'd
A mansion vast. I wonder'd, and I fear'd ;
There as I wander'd, fancy's forming eye
Could gloomy cells and dungeons dark espy ;
Winding through these, I caught th' appalling sound
Of troubled souls, that guilty minds confound,
Where murder made its way, and mischief stalk'd around.
Above the roof were raised the midnight storms,
And the wild lights betray'd the shadowy forms.
   ' With all these flights and fancies, then so dear,
I reach'd the birth-day of my twentieth year :
And in the evening of a day in June
Was singing—as I sang—some heavenly tune;
My native tone, indeed, was harsh and hoarse,
But he who feels such powers can sing of course—
Is there a good on earth, or gift divine,
That fancy cannot say, behold ! 'tis mine ?
   ' So was I singing, when I saw descend
From this old seat a lady and her friend ;
Downward they came with steady pace and slow,
Arm link'd in arm, to bless my world below.
I knew not yet if they escaped, or chose
Their own free way,—if they had friends or foes,—
But near to my dominion drew the pair,
Link'd arm in arm, and walk'd, conversing, there.

' I saw them ere they came, myself unseen,
My lofty fence and thorny bound between—
And one alone, one matchless face I saw,
And, though at distance, felt delight and awe :
Fancy and truth adorn'd her ; fancy gave
Much, but not all ; truth help'd to make
    their slave ;
For she was lovely, all was not the vain
Or sickly homage of a fever'd brain ;
No ! she had beauty, such as they admire
Whose hope is earthly, and whose love desire ;
Imagination might her aid bestow,
But she had charms that only truth could show.
  ' Their dress was such as well became the
    place,
But one superior ; hers the air, the grace,
The condescending looks, that spoke the
    nobler race.
Slender she was and tall : her fairy-feet
Bore her right onward to my shady seat ;
And O ! I sigh'd that she would nobly dare
To come, nor let her friend th' adventure
    share ;
But see how I in my dominion reign,
And never wish to view the world again.
  ' Thus was I musing, seeing with my eyes
These objects, with my mind her fantasies,
And chiefly thinking—is this maid, divine
As she appears, to be this queen of mine ?
Have I from henceforth beauty in my view,
Not airy all, but tangible and true ?
Here then I fix, here bound my vagrant views,
And here devote my heart, my time, my muse.
  ' She saw not this, though ladies early trace
Their beauty's power, the glories of their face;
Yet knew not this fair creature—could not
    know—
That new-born love ! that I too soon must
    show :
And I was musing—how shall I begin ?
How make approach my unknown way to win,
And to that heart, as yet untouch'd, make
    known
The wound, the wish, the weakness of my
    own ?
Such is my part, but——Mercy ! what alarm?
Dare aught on earth that sovereign beauty
    harm ?
Again—the shrieking charmers—how they
    rend
The gentle air——The shriekers lack a friend—
They are my princess and th' attendant maid
In so much danger, and so much afraid !—

But whence the terror ?—Let me haste and see
What has befallen them who cannot flee—
Whence can the peril rise ? What can the
    peril be ?
  ' It soon appear'd, that while this nymph
    divine
Moved on, there met her rude uncivil kine,
Who knew her not—the damsel was not there
Who kept them—all obedient—in her care ;
Strangers they thus defied and held in scorn,
And stood in threat'ning posture, hoof and
    horn ;
While Susan—pail in hand—could stand the
    while
And prate with Daniel at a distant stile.
  ' As feeling prompted, to the place I ran,
Resolved to save the maids and show the
    man :
Was each a cow like that which challenged
    Guy,
I had resolved t' attack it, and defy
In mortal combat ! to repel or die.
That was no time to parley—or to say,
I will protect you—fly in peace away !
Lo ! yonder stile—but with an air of grace,
As I supposed, I pointed to the place.
  ' The fair ones took me at my sign, and flew,
Each like a dove, and to the stile withdrew ;
Where safe, at distance, and from terrors free,
They turn'd to view my beastly foes and me.
  ' I now had time my business to behold,
And did not like it—let the truth be told :
The cows, though cowards, yet in numbers
    strong,
Like other mobs, by might defended wrong ;
In man's own pathway fix'd, they seem'd
    disposed
For hostile measure, and in order closed,
Then halted near me, as I judged, to treat,
Before we came to triumph or defeat.
  ' I was in doubt : 'twas sore disgrace, I
    knew,
To turn my back, and let the cows pursue ;
And should I rashly mortal strife begin,
'Twas all unknown who might the battle win ;
And yet to wait, and neither fight nor fly,
Would mirth create,—I could not that deny ;
It look'd as if for safety I would treat,
Nay, sue for peace—No ! rather come defeat !
" Look to me, loveliest of thy sex ! and give
One cheering glance, and not a cow shall live ;
For lo ! this iron bar, this strenuous arm,
And those dear eyes to aid me as a charm."

'Say, goddess! Victory! say, on man or cow
Meanest thou now to perch?—On neither
  now—
For, as I ponder'd, on their way appear'd
The Amazonian milker of the herd;
These, at the wonted signals, made a stand,
And woo'd the nymph of the relieving hand;
Nor heeded now the man, who felt relief
Of other kind, and not unmix'd with grief;
For now he neither should his courage prove,
Nor in his dying moments boast his love.
  ' My sovereign beauty with amazement
  saw—
So she declared—the horrid things in awe;
Well pleased, she witness'd what respect was
  paid
By such brute natures—Every cow afraid,
And kept at distance by the powers of one,
Who had to her a dangerous service done,
That prudence had declined, that valour's
  self might shun.
  ' So thought the maid, who now, beyond
  the stile,
Received her champion with a gracious smile;
Who now had leisure on those charms to dwell,
That he could never from his thought expel;
There are, I know, to whom a lover seems,
Praising his mistress, to relate his dreams;
But, Richard, looks like those, that angel-face
Could I no more in sister-angel trace;
O! it was more than fancy! it was more
Than in my darling views I saw before,
When I my idol made, and my allegiance
  swore.
  ' Henceforth 'twas bliss upon that face to
  dwell,
Till every trace became indelible;
I bless'd the cause of that alarm, her fright,
And all that gave me favour in her sight,
Who then was kind and grateful, till my mind,
Pleased and exulting, awe awhile resign'd.
For in the moment when she feels afraid,
How kindly speaks the condescending maid;
She sees her danger near, she wants her
  lover's aid;
As fire electric, when discharged, will strike
All who receive it, and they feel alike,
So in the shock of danger and surprise
Our minds are struck, and mix, and sym-
  pathise.
  ' But danger dies, and distance comes
  between
My state and that of my all glorious queen;

Yet much was done—upon my mind a chain
Was strongly fix'd, and likely to remain;
Listening, I grew enamour'd of the sound,
And felt to her my very being bound;
I bless'd the scene, nor felt a power to move,
Lost in the ecstacies of infant-love.
  ' She saw and smiled; the smile delight
  convey'd,
My love encouraged, and my act repaid:
In that same smile I read the charmer meant
To give her hero chaste encouragement; '
It spoke, as plainly as a smile can speak,
" Seek whom you love, love freely whom you
  seek."
  ' Thus, when the lovely witch had wrought
  her charm,
She took th' attendant maiden by the arm,
And left me fondly gazing, till no more
I could the shade of that dear form explore;
Then to my secret haunt I turn'd again,
Fire in my heart, and fever in my brain;
That face of her for ever in my view,
Whom I was henceforth fated to pursue,
To hope I knew not what, small hope in what
  I knew.
  ' O! my dear Richard, what a waste of time
Gave I not thus to lunacy sublime;
What days, months, years (to useful purpose
  lost),
Has not this dire infatuation cost?
To this fair vision I, a bounded slave,
Time, duty, credit, honour, comfort, gave;
Gave all—and waited for the glorious things
That hope expects, but fortune never brings.
Yet let me own, while I my fault reprove,
There is one blessing still affix'd to love—
To love like mine—for, as my soul it drew
From reason's path, it shunn'd dishonour's
  too;
It made my taste refined, my feelings nice,
And placed an angel in the way of vice.
  ' This angel now, whom I no longer view'd,
Far from this scene her destined way pursued;
No more that mansion held a form so fair,
She was away, and beauty was not there.
  ' Such, my dear Richard, was my early
  flame,
My youthful frenzy—give it either name;
It was the withering bane of many a year,
That past away in causeless hope and fear;
The hopes, the fears, that every dream could
  kill,
Or make alive, and lead my passive will.

' At length I learnt one name my angel bore,
And Rosabella I must now adore :
Yet knew but this—and not the favour'd
    place
That held the angel or th' angelic race ;
Nor where, admired, the sweet enchantress
    dwelt.
But I had lost her—that, indeed, I felt.
   ' Yet, would I say, she will at length be
    mine !
Did ever hero hope or love resign ?
Though men oppose, and fortune bids despair,
She will in time her mischief well repair,
And I, at last, shall wed this fairest of the
    fair !
   ' My thrifty uncle, now return'd, began
To stir within me what remained of man ;
My powerful frenzy painted to the life,
And ask'd me if I took a dream to wife ?
Debate ensued, and though not well content,
Upon a visit to his house I went :
He, the most saving of mankind, had still
Some kindred feeling ; he would guide my
    will,
And teach me wisdom—so affection wrought,
That he to save me from destruction sought :
To him destruction, the most awful curse
Of misery's children, was—an empty purse !
He his own books approved, and thought the
    pen
An useful instrument for trading men ;
But judged a quill was never to be slit
Except to make it for a merchant fit :
He, when informed how men of taste could
    write,
Look'd on his ledger with supreme delight ;
Then would he laugh, and, with insulting
    joy,
Tell me aloud, " that 's poetry, my boy ;
These are your golden numbers—them repeat,
The more you have, the more you'll find them
    sweet—
Their numbers move all hearts—no matter
    for their feet.
Sir, when a man composes in this style,
What is to him a critic's frown or smile ?
What is the puppy's censure or applause
To the good man who on his banker draws,
Buys an estate, and writes upon the grounds,
' Pay to A. B. an hundred thousand pounds ? '
Thus, my dear nephew, thus your talents
    prove ;
Leave verse to poets, and the poor to love."

' Some months I suffered thus, compell'd
    to sit
And hear a wealthy kinsman aim at wit ;
Yet there was something in his nature good,
And he had feeling for the tie of blood :
So while I languish'd for my absent maid
I some observance to my uncle paid.'
   ' Had you inquired ? ' said Richard.
                      ' I had placed
Inquirers round, but nothing could be traced ;
Of every reasoning creature at this Hall,
And tenant near it, I applied to all——
Tell me if she—and I described her well—
Dwelt long a guest, or where retired to dwell ?
But no ! such lady they remember'd not—
They saw that face, strange beings ! and for-
    got.
Nor was inquiry all ; but I pursued
My soul's first wish, with hope's vast strength
    endued :
I cross'd the seas, I went where strangers go,
And gazed on crowds as one who dreads a foe,
Or seeks a friend ; and, when I sought in vain,
Fled to fresh crowds, and hoped, and gazed
    again.'
   ' It was a strong possession '—' Strong and
    strange,
I felt the evil, yet desired not change :
Years now had flown, nor was the passion
    cured,
But hope had life, and so was life endured ;
The mind's disease, with all its strength,
    stole on,
Till youth, and health, and all but love were
    gone.
And there were seasons, Richard, horrid hours
Of mental suffering ! they o'erthrew my
    powers,
And made my mind unsteady—I have still,
At times, a feeling of that nameless ill,
That is not madness—I could always tell
My mind was wandering—knew it was not
    well ;
Felt all my loss of time, the shameful waste
Of talents perish'd, and of parts disgraced :
But though my mind was sane, there was
    a void—
My understanding seem'd in part destroy'd ;
I thought I was not of my species one,
But unconnected ! injured and undone.
   ' While in this state, once more my uncle
    pray'd
That I would hear—I heard, and I obey'd ;

For I was thankful that a being broke
On this my sadness, or an interest took
In my poor life—but, at his mansion, rest
Came with its halcyon stillness to my breast :
Slowly there enter'd in my mind concern
For things about me—I would something
    learn,
And to my uncle listen ; who, with joy,
Found that ev'n yet I could my powers
    employ,
Till I could feel new hopes my mind possess,
Of ease at least, if not of happiness :
Till, not contented, not in discontent,
As my good uncle counsell'd, on I went ;
Conscious of youth's great error—nay, the
    crime
Of manhood now—a dreary waste of time !
Conscious of that account which I must give
How life had past with me—I strove to live.
    ' Had I, like others, my first hope attain'd,
I must, at least, a certainty have gain'd ;
Had I, like others, lost the hope of youth,
Another hope had promised greater truth ;
But I in baseless hopes, and groundless views,
Was fated time, and peace, and health to lose,
Impell'd to seek, for ever doom'd to fail,
Is——I distress you—let me end my tale.
    ' Something one day occurr'd about a bill
That was not drawn with true mercantile skill,
And I was ask'd and authorized to go
To seek the firm of Clutterbuck and Co. ;
Their hour was past—but when I urged the
    case,
There was a youth who named a second place,
Where, on occasions of important kind,
I might the man of occupation find
In his retirement, where he found repose
From the vexations that in business rose.
I found, though not with ease, this private
    seat
Of soothing quiet, wisdom's still retreat.
    ' The house was good, but not so pure and
    clean
As I had houses of retirement seen ;
Yet men, I knew, of meditation deep,
Love not their maidens should their studies
    sweep ;
His room I saw, and must acknowledge, there
Were not the signs of cleanliness or care :
A female servant, void of female grace,
Loose in attire, proceeded to the place ;
She stared intrusive on my slender frame,
And boldly ask'd my business and my name.

' I gave them both ; and, left to be amused,
Well as I might, the parlour I perused.
The shutters half unclosed, the curtains fell
Half down, and rested on the window-sill,
And thus, confusedly, made the room half
    visible :
Late as it was, the little parlour bore
Some tell-tale tokens of the night before ;
There were strange sights and scents about
    the room,
Of food high season'd, and of strong perfume ;
Two unmatch'd sofas ample rents display'd,
Carpet and curtains were alike decay'd ;
A large old mirror, with once-gilded frame,
Reflected prints that I forbear to name,
Such as a youth might purchase—but, in truth,
Not a sedate or sober-minded youth :
The cinders yet were sleeping in the grate,
Warm from the fire, continued large and late,
As left by careless folk, in their neglected
    state ;
The chairs in haste seem'd whirl'd about the
    room,
As when the sons of riot hurry home,
And leave the troubled place to solitude and
    gloom.
    ' All this, for I had ample time, I saw,
And prudence question'd—should we not
    withdraw ?
For he who makes me thus on business wait,
Is not for business in a proper state ;
But man there was not, was not he for whom
To this convenient lodging I was come ;
No ! but a lady's voice was heard to call
On my attention—and she had it all ;
For lo ! she enters, speaking ere in sight,
" Monsieur ! I shall not want the chair to-
    night—
Where shall I see him ? "—This dear hour
    atones
For all affection's hopeless sighs and groans—
Then turning to me—" Art thou come at last ?
A thousand welcomes—be forgot the past ;
Forgotten all the grief that absence brings,
Fear that torments, and jealousy that stings—
All that is cold, injurious, and unkind,
Be it for ever banish'd from the mind ;
And in that mind, and in that heart be now
The soft endearment, and the binding vow."
    ' She spoke—and o'er the practised features
    threw
The looks that reason charm, and strength
    subdue.

' Will you not ask, how I beheld that face,
Or read that mind, and read it in that place ?
I have tried, Richard, oft-times, and in vain,
To trace my thoughts, and to review their
    train—
If train there were—that meadow, grove, and
    stile,
The fright, th' escape, her sweetness and her
    smile ;
Years since elapsed, and hope, from year to
    year,
To find her free—and then to find her here !
' But is it she ?—O ! yes ; the rose is dead,
All beauty, fragrance, freshness, glory fled :
But yet 'tis she—the same and not the same—
Who to my bower an heavenly being came ;
Who waked my soul's first thought of real
    bliss,
Whom long I sought, and now I find her—
    this.
   ' I cannot paint her—something I had seen
So pale and slim, and tawdry and unclean ;
With haggard looks, of vice and wo the prey,
Laughing in langour, miserably gay :
Her face, where face appear'd, was amply
    spread,
By art's coarse pencil, with ill-chosen red,
The flower's fictitious bloom, the blushing of
    the dead :
But still the features were the same, and
    strange
My view of both—the sameness and the
    change,
That fix'd me gazing and my eye enchain'd,
Although so little of herself remain'd ;
It is the creature whom I loved, and yet
Is far unlike her—Would I could forget
The angel or her fall ! the once adored
Or now despised ! the worshipp'd or deplored!
   ' " O ! Rosabella ! " I prepared to say,
" Whom I have loved," but prudence
    whisper'd nay,
And folly grew ashamed—discretion had her
    day.
She gave her hand ; which, as I lightly
    press'd,
The cold but ardent grasp my soul oppress'd ;
The ruin'd girl disturb'd me, and my eyes
Look'd, I conceive, both sorrow and surprise.
   ' I spoke my business—" He," she answer'd,
    " comes
And lodges here—he has the backward
    rooms—

He now is absent, and I chanced to hear
Will not before to-morrow eve appear,
And may be longer absent——O ! the night
When you preserved me in that horrid fright ;
A thousand, thousand times, asleep, awake,
I thought of what you ventured for my sake—
Now have you thought—yet tell me so—
    deceive
Your Rosabella, willing to believe ?
O ! there is something in love's first-born pain
Sweeter than bliss—it never comes again—
But has your heart been faithful ? "—Here
    my pride
To anger rising, her attempt defied—
" My faith must childish in your sight appear,
Who have been faithful—to how many,
    dear ? "
   ' If words had fail'd, a look explain'd their
    style,
She could not blush assent, but she could
    smile :
Good heaven ! I thought, have I rejected
    fame,
Credit and wealth, for one who smiles at
    shame ?
   ' She saw me thoughtful—saw it, as I
    guess'd,
With some concern, though nothing she ex-
    press'd.
   ' " Come, my dear friend, discard that look
    of care,
All things were made to be, as all things are ;
All to seek pleasure as the end design'd,
The only good in matter or in mind ;
So was I taught by one, who gave me all
That my experienced heart can wisdom call.
   ' " I saw thee young, love's soft obedient
    slave,
And many a sigh to my young lover gave ;
And I had, spite of cowardice or cow,
Return'd thy passion, and exchanged my vow;
But while I thought to bait the amorous hook,
One set for me my eager fancy took ;
There was a crafty eye, that far could see,
And through my failings fascinated me :
Mine was a childish wish, to please my boy ;
His a design, his wishes to enjoy.
O ! we have both about the world been tost,
Thy gain I know not—I, they cry, am lost ;
So let the wise ones talk ; they talk in vain,
And are mistaken both in loss and gain ;
'Tis gain to get whatever life affords,
'Tis loss to spend our time in empty words.

' " I was a girl, and thou a boy wert then,
Nor ought of women knew, nor I of men;
But I have traffick'd in the world, and thou,
Doubtless, canst boast of thy experience now;
Let us the knowledge we have gain'd produce,
And kindly turn it to our common use."
' Thus spoke the siren in voluptuous style,
While I stood gazing and perplex'd the while,
Chain'd by that voice, confounded by that
    smile.
And then she sang, and changed from grave
    to gay,
Till all reproach and anger died away.

' " My Damon was the first to wake
    The gentle flame that cannot die;
My Damon is the last to take
    The faithful bosom's softest sigh:
The life between is nothing worth,
    O! cast it from thy thought away;
Think of the day that gave it birth,
    And this its sweet returning day.

' " Buried be all that has been done,
    Or say that naught is done amiss;
For who the dangerous path can shun
    In such bewildering world as this?
But love can every fault forgive,
    Or with a tender look reprove;
And now let naught in memory live,
    But that we meet, and that we love."

' And then she moved my pity; for she
    wept,
And told her miseries till resentment slept;
For when she saw she could not reason blind,
She pour'd her heart's whole sorrows on my
    mind,
With features graven on my soul, with sighs
Seen but not heard, with soft imploring eyes,
And voice that needed not, but had the aid
Of powerful words to soften and persuade.
' " O! I repent me of the past; and sure
Grief and repentance make the bosom pure;
Yet meet thee not with clean and single heart,
As on the day we met!—and but to part,
Ere I had drank the cup that to my lip
Was held, and press'd till I was forced to sip:
I drank indeed, but never ceased to hate,—
It poison'd, but could not intoxicate:
T' excuse my fall I plead not love's excess,
But a weak orphan's need and loneliness.
I had no parent upon earth—no door
Was oped to me—young, innocent, and poor,

Vain, tender and resentful—and my friend
Jealous of one who must on her depend,
Making life misery—You could witness then
That I was precious in the eyes of men;
So, made by them a goddess, and denied
Respect and notice by the women's pride;
Here scorn'd, there worshipp'd—will it
    strange appear,
Allured and driven, that I settled here?
Yet loved it not; and never have I pass'd
One day, and wish'd another like the last.
There was a fallen angel, I have read,
For whom their tears the sister-angels shed,
Because, although she ventured to rebel,
She was not minded like a child of hell.—
Such is my lot! and will it not be given
To grief like mine, that I may think of
    heaven?
Behold how there the glorious creatures shine,
And all my soul to grief and hope resign?"
' I wonder'd, doubting—and is this a fact,
I thought; or part thou art disposed to act?
' " Is it not written, He, who came to save
Sinners, the sins of deepest dye forgave?
That he his mercy to the sufferers dealt,
And pardon'd error when the ill was felt?
Yes! I would hope, there is an eye that reads
What is within, and sees the heart that
    bleeds——
But who on earth will one so lost deplore,
And who will help that lost one to restore?
Who will on trust the sigh of grief receive;
And—all things warring with belief—
    believe?"
' Soften'd, I said—" Be mine the hand and
    heart,
If with your world you will consent to part."
She would—she tried——Alas! she did not
    know
How deeply rooted evil habits grow:
She felt the truth upon her spirits press,
But wanted ease, indulgence, show, excess,
Voluptuous banquets, pleasures—not refined,
But such as soothe to sleep th' opposing
    mind—
She look'd for idle vice, the time to kill,
And subtle, strong apologies for ill;
And thus her yielding, unresisting soul
Sank, and let sin confuse her and control:
Pleasures that brought disgust yet brought
    relief,
And minds she hated help'd to war with
    grief.'

' Thus then she perish'd ? '—
      ' Nay—but thus she proved
Slave to the vices that she never loved :
But while she thus her better thoughts
    opposed,
And woo'd the world, the world's deceptions
    closed :—
I had long lost her ; but I sought in vain
To banish pity :—still she gave me pain,
Still I desired to aid her—to direct,
And wish'd the world, that won her, to reject :
Nor wish'd in vain—there came, at length,
    request
That I would see a wretch with grief oppress'd,
By guilt affrighted—and I went to trace
Once more the vice-worn features of that face,
That sin-wreck'd being ! and I saw her laid
Where never worldly joy a visit paid :
That world receding fast ! the world to come
Conceal'd in terror, ignorance, and gloom ;
Sins, sorrow, and neglect : with not a spark
Of vital hope,—all horrible and dark—
It frighten'd me !—I thought, and shall not I
Thus feel ? thus fear ?—this danger can I fly ?
Do I so wisely live that I can calmly die ?
'The wants I saw I could supply with ease,
But there were wants of other kind than
    these ;
Th' awakening thought, the hope-inspiring
    view—
The doctrines awful, grand, alarming, true—
Most painful to the soul, and yet most healing
    too :
Still I could something offer, and could send
For other aid—a more important friend,
Whose duty call'd him, and his love no less,
To help the grieving spirit in distress ;
To save in that sad hour the drooping prey,
And from its victim drive despair away.
All decent comfort round the sick was seen ;
The female helpers quiet, sober, clean ;
Her kind physician with a smile appear'd,
And zealous love the pious friend endear'd :
While I, with mix'd sensations, could inquire,
Hast thou one wish, one unfulfill'd desire ?
Speak every thought, nor unindulged depart,
If I can make thee happier than thou art !
'Yes ! there was yet a female friend, an old
And grieving nurse ! to whom it should be
    told—
If I would tell—that she, her child, had fail'd,
And turn'd from truth ! yet truth at length
    prevail'd.

' 'Twas in that chamber, Richard, I began
To think more deeply of the end of man :
Was it to jostle all his fellows by,
To run before them, and say, " here am I,
Fall down and worship ? "—Was it, life
    throughout,
With circumspection keen to hunt about
As spaniels for their game, where might be
    found
Abundance more for coffers that abound ?
Or was it life's enjoyments to prefer,
Like this poor girl, and then to die like her ?
No ! He, who gave the faculties, design'd
Another use for the immortal mind :
There is a state in which it will appear
With all the good and ill contracted here ;
With gain and loss, improvement and defect ;
And then, my soul ! what hast thou to expect
For talents laid aside, life's waste, and time's
    neglect ?
' Still as I went came other change—the
    frame
And features wasted, and yet slowly came
The end ; and so inaudible the breath,
And still the breathing, we exclaim'd—'tis
    death !
But death it was not : when, indeed, she died,
I sat and his last gentle stroke espied :
When—as it came—or did my fancy trace
That lively, lovely flushing o'er the face ?
Bringing back all that my young heart im-
    press'd !
It came—and went !—She sigh'd, and was at
    rest !
' Adieu, I said, fair Frailty ! dearly cost
The love I bore thee—time and treasure lost ;
And I have suffer'd many years in vain ;
Now let me something in my sorrows gain :
Heaven would not all this wo for man in-
    tend
If man's existence with his wo should end ;
Heaven would not pain, and grief, and anguish
    give,
If man was not by discipline to live ;
And for that brighter, better world prepare,
That souls with souls, when purified, shall
    share,
Those stains all done away that must not
    enter there.
' Home I return'd, with spirits in that state
Of vacant wo, I strive not to relate,
Nor how, deprived of all her hope and strength,
My soul turn'd feebly to the world at length.

I travell'd then till health again resumed
Its former seat—I must not say re-bloom'd ;
And then I fill'd, not loth, that favourite place
That has enrich'd some seniors of our race ;
Patient and dull I grew ; my uncle's praise
Was largely dealt me on my better days ;
A love of money—other love at rest—
Came creeping on, and settled in my breast ;
The force of habit held me to the oar,
Till I could relish what I scorn'd before :
I now could talk and scheme with *men of sense*,
Who deal for millions, and who sigh for pence,
And grew so like them, that I heard with joy
Old Blueskin said I was a pretty boy ;
For I possess'd the caution with the zeal,
That all true lovers of their interest feel :
Exalted praise ! and to the creature due,
Who loves that interest solely to pursue.
   ' But I was sick, and sickness brought
      disgust ;
My peace I could not to my profits trust :

Again some views of brighter kind appear'd,
My heart was humbled, and my mind was
    clear'd ;
I felt those helps that souls diseased restore,
And that cold frenzy, avarice, raged no more.
From dreams of boundless wealth I then
    arose ;
This place, the scene of infant bliss, I chose,
And here I find relief, and here I seek repose.
   ' Yet much is lost, and not yet much is
      found,
But what remains, I would believe, is sound ;
That first wild passion, that last mean desire,
Are felt no more ; but holier hopes require
A mind prepared and steady—my reform
Has fears like his, who, suffering in a storm,
Is on a rich but unknown country cast,
The future fearing, while he feels the past ;
But whose more cheerful mind, with hope
    imbued,
Sees through receding clouds the rising good.'

BOOK VIII. THE SISTERS

Morning Walk and Conversation—Visit at
a Cottage—Characters of the Sisters—Lucy
and Jane—Their Lovers—Their Friend the
Banker and his Lady—Their Intimacy—
Its Consequence—Different Conduct of the
Lovers—The Effect upon the Sisters—
Their present State—The Influence of their
Fortune upon the Minds of either.

THE morning shone in cloudless beauty
    bright ;
Richard his letters read with much delight ;
George from his pillow rose in happy tone,
His bosom's lord sat lightly on his throne :
They read the morning news—they saw the sky
Inviting call'd them, and the earth was dry.
   ' The day invites us, brother,' said the
    'squire ;
' Come, and I'll show thee something to
    admire :
We still may beauty in our prospects trace ;
If not, we have them in both mind and face.
   ' 'Tis but two miles—to let such women live
Unseen of him, what reason can I give ?
Why should not Richard to the girls be
    known ?
Would I have all their friendship for my own ?

Brother, there dwell, yon northern hill below,
Two favourite maidens, whom 'tis good to
    know ;
Young, but experienced ; dwellers in a
    cot,
Where they sustain and dignify their lot,
The best good girls in all our world below—
O ! you must know them—Come ! and you
    shall know.
   ' But lo ! the morning wastes—here, Jacob,
    stir—
If Phoebe comes, do you attend to her ;
And let not Mary get a chattering press
Of idle girls to hear of her distress :
Ask her to wait till my return—and hide
From her meek mind your plenty and your
    pride ;
Nor vex a creature, humble, sad, and still,
By your coarse bounty, and your rude good-
    will.'
   This said, the brothers hasten'd on their
    way,
With all the foretaste of a pleasant day.
The morning purpose in the mind had fix'd
The leading thought, and that with others
    mix'd.

' How well it is,' said George, ' when we
    possess
The strength that bears us up in our distress ;
And need not the resources of our pride,
Our fall from greatness and our wants to hide ;
But have the spirit and the wish to show,
We know our wants as well as others know.
'Tis true, the rapid turns of fortune's wheel
Make even the virtuous and the humble feel :
They for a time must suffer, and but few
Can bear their sorrows and our pity too.
    ' Hence all these small expedients, day by
    day,
Are used to hide the evils they betray :
When, if our pity chances to be seen,
The wounded pride retorts, with anger keen,
And man's insulted grief takes refuge in
    his spleen.
'When Timon's board contains a single dish,
Timon talks much of market-men and fish,
Forgetful servants, and th' infernal cook,
Who always spoil'd whate'er she undertook.
    ' But say, it tries us from our height to fall,
Yet is not life itself a trial all ?
And not a virtue in the bosom lives,
That gives such ready pay as patience gives ;
That pure submission to the ruling mind,
Fix'd, but not forced ; obedient, but not
    · blind ;
The will of heaven to make her own she tries,
Or makes her own to heaven a sacrifice.
    ' And is there aught on earth so rich or rare,
Whose pleasures may with virtue's pains
    compare ?
This fruit of patience, this the pure delight,
That 'tis a trial in her Judge's sight ;
Her part still striving duty to sustain,
Not spurning pleasure, not defying pain ;
Never in triumph till her race be won,
And never fainting till her work be done.'
    With thoughts like these they reach'd the
    village brook,
And saw a lady sitting with her book ;
And so engaged she heard not, till the men
Were at her side, nor was she frighten'd then ;
But to her friend, the 'squire, his smile
    return'd,
Through which the latent sadness he dis-
    cern'd.
The stranger-brother at the cottage door
Was now admitted, and was strange no more :
Then of an absent sister he was told,
Whom they were not at present to behold ;

Something was said of nerves, and that disease,
Whose varying powers on mind and body
    seize,
Enfeebling both !—Here chose they to remain
One hour in peace, and then return'd again.
    ' I know not why,' said Richard, ' but I feel
The warmest pity on my bosom steal
For that dear maid ! How well her looks
    express
For this world's good a cherish'd hopeless-
    ness !
A resignation that is so entire,
It feels not now the stirrings of desire ;
What now to her is all the world esteems ?
She is awake, and cares not for its dreams ;
But moves while yet on earth, as one above
Its hopes and fears—its loathing and its love.
    ' But shall I learn,' said he, ' these sisters'
    fate ? '—
And found his brother willing to relate.

    ' The girls were orphans early ; yet I saw,
When young, their father—his profession law ;
He left them but a competence, a store
That made his daughters neither rich nor
    poor ;
Not rich, compared with some who dwelt
    around ;
Not poor, for want they neither fear'd nor
    found ;
Their guardian uncle was both kind and just,
One whom a parent might in dying trust ;
Who, in their youth, the trusted store im-
    proved,
And, when he ceased to guide them, fondly
    loved.
    ' These sister beauties were in fact the grace
Of yon small town,—it was their native place ;
Like Saul's famed daughters were the lovely
    twain,
As Micah, Lucy, and as Merab, Jane :
For this was tall, with free commanding air,
And that was mild, and delicate, and fair.
    ' Jane had an arch delusive smile, that
    charm'd
And threaten'd too ; alluring, it alarm'd ;
The smile of Lucy her approval told,
Cheerful, not changing ; neither kind nor
    cold.
    ' When children, Lucy love alone possess'd,
Jane was more punish'd and was more
    caress'd ;

If told the childish wishes, one bespoke
A lamb, a bird, a garden, and a brook ;
The other wish'd a joy unknown, a rout
Or crowded ball, and to be first led out.
  'Lucy loved all that grew upon the ground,
And loveliness in all things living found ;
The gilded fly, the fern upon the wall,
Were nature's works, and admirable all ;
Pleased with indulgence of so cheap a kind,
Its cheapness never discomposed her mind.
  ' Jane had no liking for such things as these,
Things pleasing her must her superiors please ;
The costly flower was precious in her eyes,
That skill can vary, or that money buys ;
Her taste was good, but she was still afraid,
Till fashion sanction'd the remarks she made.
   ' The sisters read, and Jane with some
     delight,
The satires keen that fear or rage excite,
That men in power attack, and ladies high,
And give broad hints that we may know
    them by.
She was amused when sent to haunted rooms,
Or some dark passage where the spirit comes
Of one once murder'd ! then she laughing
    read,
And felt at once the folly and the dread :
As rustic girls to crafty gipsies fly,
And trust the liar though they fear the lie,
Or as a patient, urged by grievous pains,
Will fee the daring quack whom he disdains,
So Jane was pleased to see the beckoning
    hand,
And trust the magic of the Ratcliffe-wand.
  'In her religion—for her mind, though light,
Was not disposed our better views to slight—
Her favourite authors were a solemn kind,
Who fill with dark mysterious thoughts the
    mind ;
And who with such conceits her fancy plied,
Became her friend, philosopher, and guide.
  ' She made the Progress of the Pilgrim one
To build a thousand pleasant views upon ;
All that connects us with a world above
She loved to fancy, and she long'd to prove ;
Well would the poet please her, who could
    lead
Her fancy forth, yet keep untouch'd her
    creed.
Led by an early custom, Lucy spied,
When she awaked, the Bible at her side ;
That, ere she ventured on a world of care,
She might for trials, joys or pains prepare,

For every dart a shield, a guard for every
    snare.
  ' She read not much of high heroic deeds,
Where man the measure of man's power
    exceeds ;
But gave to luckless love and fate severe
Her tenderest pity and her softest tear.
  ' She mix'd not faith with fable, but she
    trod
Right onward, cautious in the ways of God ;
Nor did she dare to launch on seas unknown,
In search of truths by some adventurers
    shown,
But her own compass used, and kept a course
    her own.
  ' The maidens both their loyalty declared,
And in the glory of their country shared ;
But Jane that glory felt with proud delight,
When England's foes were vanquish'd in the
    fight ;
While Lucy's feelings for the brave who bled
Put all such glorious triumphs from her head.
They both were frugal ; Lucy from the fear
Of wasting that which want esteems so dear,
But finds so scarce, her sister from the pain
That springs from want, when treated with
    disdain.
  ' Jane borrow'd maxims from a doubting
    school,
And took for truth the test of ridicule ;
Lucy saw no such virtue in a jest,
Truth was with her of ridicule a test.
  ' They loved each other with the warmth
    of youth,
With ardour, candour, tenderness, and truth ;
And though their pleasures were not just the
    same,
Yet both were pleased whenever one became ;
Nay, each would rather in the act rejoice,
That was th' adopted, not the native choice.
  ' Each had a friend, and friends to minds
    so fond
And good are soon united in the bond ;
Each had a lover ; but it seem'd that fate
Decreed that these should not approximate.
Now Lucy's lover was a prudent swain,
And thought, in all things, what would be
    his gain ;
The younger sister first engaged his view,
But with her beauty he her spirit knew ;
Her face he much admired, " but, put the
    case,"
Said he, " I marry, what is then a face ?

At first it pleases to have drawn the lot ;
He then forgets it, but his wife does not ;
Jane too," he judged, " would be reserved
    and nice,
And many lovers had enhanced her price."
  ' Thus thinking much, but hiding what he
    thought,
The prudent lover Lucy's favour sought,
And he succeeded,—she was free from art ;
And his appear'd a gentle guileless heart;
Such she respected ; true, her sister found
His placid face too ruddy and too round,
Too cold and inexpressive ; such a face
Where you could nothing mark'd or manly
    trace.
  ' But Lucy found him to his mother kind,
And saw the Christian meekness of his mind ;
His voice was soft, his temper mild and sweet,
His mind was easy, and his person neat.
Jane said he wanted courage ; Lucy drew
No ill from that, though she believed it
    too ;
" It is religious, Jane, be not severe ; "
" Well, Lucy, then it is religious fear."
Nor could the sister, great as was her love,
A man so lifeless and so cool approve.
  ' Jane had a lover, whom a lady's pride
Might wish to see attending at her side,
Young, handsome, sprightly, and with good
    address,
Not mark'd for folly, error or excess ;
Yet not entirely from their censure free,
Who judge our failings with severity ;
The very care he took to keep his name
Stainless, with some was evidence of shame.
  ' Jane heard of this, and she replied,
    " Enough ;
Prove but the facts, and I resist not proof ;
Nor is my heart so easy as to love
The man my judgment bids me not approve."
But yet that heart a secret joy confess'd,
To find no slander on the youth would rest ;
His was, in fact, such conduct, that a maid
Might think of marriage, and be not afraid ;
And she was pleased to find a spirit high,
Free from all fear, that spurn'd hypocrisy.
  " What fears my sister ? " said the partial
    fair,
For Lucy fear'd,—" Why tell me to beware ?
No smooth deceitful varnish here I find ;
His is a spirit generous, free, and kind ;
And all his flaws are seen, all floating in his
    mind.

A little boldness in his speech. What then ?
It is the failing of these generous men.
A little vanity, but—O ! my dear,
They all would show it, were they all sincere.
  ' " But come, agreed ; we'll lend each other
    eyes
To see our favourites, when they wear dis-
    guise ;
And all those errors that will then be shown
Uninfluenced by the workings of our own."
  ' Thus lived the sisters, far from power
    removed,
And far from need, both loving and beloved.
Thus grew, as myrtles grow ; I grieve at
    heart
That I have pain and sorrow to impart.
But so it is, the sweetest herbs that grow
In the lone vale, where sweetest waters flow,
Ere drops the blossom, or appears the fruit,
Feel the vile grub, and perish at the root ;
And in a quick and premature decay,
Breathe the pure fragrance of their life away.
  ' A town was near, in which the buildings all
Were large, but one pre-eminently tall—
An huge high house. Without there was an
    air
Of lavish cost ; no littleness was there ;
But room for servants, horses, whiskies, gigs,
And walls for pines and peaches, grapes and
    figs ;
Bright on the sloping glass the sun-beams
    shone,
And brought the summer of all climates on.
  ' Here wealth its prowess to the eye dis-
    play'd,
And here advanced the seasons, there delay'd ;
Bid the due heat each growing sweet refine,
Made the sun's light with grosser fire combine,
And to the Tropic gave the vigour of the Line.
  ' Yet, in the master of this wealth, behold
A light vain coxcomb taken from his gold,
Whose busy brain was weak, whose boasting
    heart was cold.
  ' O ! how he talk'd to that believing town,
That he would give it riches and renown ;
Cause a canal where treasures were to swim,
And they should owe their opulence to him
In fact, of riches he insured a crop,
So they would give him but a seed to drop.
As used the alchymist his boasts to make,
" I give you millions for the mite I take ; "
The mite they never could again behold,
The millions all were Eldorado gold.

' By this professing man, the country round
Was search'd to see where money could be
　　found.

' The thriven farmer, who had lived to
　　spare,
Became an object of especial care ;
He took the frugal tradesman by the hand,
And wish'd him joy of what he might com-
　　mand ;
And the industrious servant, who had laid
His saving by, it was his joy to aid ;
Large talk, and hints of some productive plan
Half named, won all his hearers to a man ;
Uncertain projects drew them wondering on,
And avarice listen'd till distrust was gone.
But when to these dear girls he found his way,
All easy, artless, innocent were they ;
When he compell'd his foolish wife to be
At once so great, so humble, and so free ;
Whom others sought, nor always with suc-
　　cess !
But they were both her pride and happiness ;
And she esteem'd them, but attended still
To the vile purpose of her husband's will ;
And when she fix'd his snares about their
　　mind,
Respected those whom she essay'd to blind ;
Nay with esteem she some compassion gave
To the fair victims whom she would not save.

' The Banker's wealth and kindness were
　　her themes,
His generous plans, his patriotic schemes ;
What he had done for some, a favourite few,
What for his favourites still he meant to do ;
Not that he always listen'd—which was
　　hard—
To her, when speaking of her great regard
For certain friends—" but you, as I may say,
Are his own choice—I am not jealous—nay ! "

' Then came the man himself, and came
　　with speed
As just from business of importance freed ;
Or just escaping, came with looks of fire,
As if he'd just attain'd his full desire ;
As if Prosperity and he for life
Were wed, and he was showing off his wife ;
Pleased to display his influence, and to prove
Himself the object of her partial love :
Perhaps with this was join'd the latent fear,
The time would come when he should not be
　　dear.

' Jane laugh'd at all their visits and parade,
And call'd it friendship in an hot-house made ;

A style of friendship suited to his taste,
Brought on, and ripen'd, like his grapes, in
　　haste ;
She saw the wants that wealth in vain would
　　hide,
And all the tricks and littleness of pride ;
On all the wealth would creep the vulgar
　　stain,
And grandeur strove to look itself in vain.

' Lucy perceived—but she replied, " why
　　heed
Such small defects ?—they're very kind in-
　　deed ! "
And kind they were, and ready to produce
Their easy friendship, ever fit for use,
Friendship that enters into all affairs,
And daily wants, and daily gets, repairs.
Hence at the cottage of the sisters stood
The Banker's steed—he was so very good ;
Oft through the roads, in weather foul and fair,
Their friend's gay carriage bore the gentle
　　pair ;
His grapes and nectarines woo'd the virgins'
　　hand,
His books and roses were at their command ;
And costly flowers,—he took upon him shame
That he could purchase what he could not
　　name.

' Lucy was vex'd to have such favours
　　shown,
And they returning nothing of their own ;
Jane smiled, and begg'd her sister to believe—
" We give at least as much as we receive."

' Alas ! and more ; they gave their ears
　　and eyes,
His splendor oft-times took them by surprise ;
And if in Jane appear'd a meaning smile,
She gazed, admired, and paid respect the
　　while ;
Would she had rested there ! Deluded maid,
She saw not yet the fatal price she paid ;
Saw not that wealth, though join'd with folly,
　　grew
In her regard ; she smiled, but listen'd too ;
Nay, would be grateful, she would trust her all,
Her funded source,—to him a matter small ;
Taken for their sole use, and ever at their call :
To be improved—he knew not how indeed ;
But he had methods—and they must succeed.

' This was so good, that Jane, in very pride,
To spare him trouble, for a while denied ;
And Lucy's prudence, though it was alarm'd,
Was by the splendor of the Banker charm'd ;

What was her paltry thousand pounds to him,
Who would expend five thousand on a
    whim ?
And then the portion of his wife was known ;
But not that she reserved it for her own.
    ' Lucy her lover trusted with the fact,
And frankly ask'd, " if he approved the act ! "
" It promised well," he said ; " he could
    not tell
How it might end, but sure it promised well ;
He had himself a trifle in the Bank,
And should be sore uneasy if it sank."
    ' Jane from her lover had no wish to hide
Her deed ; but was withheld by maiden pride ;
To talk so early—as if one were sure
Of being his ; she could not that endure.
But when the sisters were apart, and when
They freely spoke of their affairs and men ;
They thought with pleasure of the sum im-
    proved,
And so presented to the men they loved.
    ' Things now proceeded in a quiet train ;
No cause appear'd to murmur or complain ;
The monied man, his ever-smiling dame,
And their young darlings, in their carriage
    came ;
Jane's sprightly lover smiled their pomp to
    see,
And ate their grapes, with gratitude and glee,
But with the freedom there was nothing mean,
Humble, or forward, in his freedom seen ;
His was the frankness of a mind that shows
It knows itself, nor fears for what it knows :
But Lucy's ever humble friend was awed
By the profusion he could not applaud ;
He seem'd indeed reluctant to partake
Of the collation that he could not make ;
And this was pleasant in the maiden's view,—
Was modesty—was moderation too ;
Though Jane esteem'd it meanness ; and she
    saw
Fear in that prudence, avarice in that awe.
    ' But both the lovers now to town are
    gone,
By business one is call'd, by duty one ;
While rumour rises,—whether false or true
The ladies knew not—it was known to few—
But fear there was, and on their guardian-
    friend
They for advice and comfort would depend,
When rose the day ; meantime from Belmont-
    place
Came vile report, predicting quick disgrace.

    ' 'Twas told—the servants, who had met
    to thank
Their lord for placing money in his Bank—
Their kind free master, who such wages gave,
And then increased whatever they could save,
They who had heard they should their savings
    lose,
Were weeping, swearing, drinking at the news ;
And still the more they drank, the more they
    wept,
And swore, and rail'd, and threaten'd, till
    they slept.
    ' The morning truth confirm'd the evening
    dread ;
The Bank was broken, and the Banker fled ;
But left a promise that his friends should have,
To the last shilling—what his fortunes gave.
    ' The evil tidings reach'd the sister-pair,
And one like Sorrow look'd, and one Despair ;
They from each other turn'd th' afflicting
    look,
And loth and late the painful silence broke.
    ' " The odious villain ! " Jane in wrath
    began ;
In pity Lucy, " the unhappy man !
When time and reason our affliction heal,
How will the author of our sufferings feel ? "
    ' " And let him feel, my sister,—let the
    woes
That he creates be bane to his repose !
Let them be felt in his expiring hour,
When death brings all his dread, and sin its
    power :
Then let the busy foe of mortals state
The pangs he caused, his own to aggravate !
    ' " Wretch ! when our life was glad, our
    prospects gay,
With savage hand to sweep them all away !
And he must know it—know when he beguiled
His easy victims—how the villain smiled !
    ' " Oh ! my dear Lucy, could I see him
    crave
The food denied, a beggar and a slave,
To stony hearts he should with tears apply,
And Pity's self withhold the struggling sigh ;
Or, if relenting weakness should extend
Th' extorted scrap that justice would not
    lend,
Let it be poison'd by the curses deep
Of every wretch whom he compels to weep ! "
    ' " Nay, my sweet sister, if you thought
    such pain
Were his, your pity would awake again ;

Your generous heart the wretch's grief would
    feel,
And you would soothe the pangs you could
    not heal."
    ' " Oh ! never, never,—I would still con-
    trive
To keep the slave whom I abhorr'd alive ;
His tortured mind with horrid fears to fill,
Disturb his reason, and misguide his will ;
Heap coals of fire, to lie like melted lead,
Heavy and hot, on his accursed head ;
Not coals that mercy kindles hearts to melt,
But he should feel them hot as fires are felt ;
Corroding ever, and through life the same,
Strong self-contempt and ever-burning shame ;
Let him so wretched live that he may fly
To desperate thoughts, and be resolved to
    die—
And then let death such frightful visions give,
That he may dread th' attempt, and beg to
    live ! "
So spake th' indignant maid, when Lucy
    sigh'd,
And, waiting softer times, no more replied.
  ' Barlow was then in town ; and there he
    thought
Of bliss to come, and bargains to be bought ;
And was returning homeward—when he
    found
The Bank was broken, and his venture
    drown'd.
    ' " Ah ! foolish maid," he cried, " and what
    wilt thou
Say for thy friends and their excesses now ?
All now is brought completely to an end ;
What can the spendthrift now afford to
    spend ?
Had my advice been—true, I gave consent,
The thing was purposed ; what could I
    prevent ?
    ' " Who will her idle taste for flowers
    supply,—
Who send her grapes and peaches ? let her
    try ;—
There 's none will give her, and she cannot
    buy.
    ' " Yet would she not be grateful if she
    knew
What to my faith and generous love was due?
Daily to see the man who took her hand,
When she had not a sixpence at command ;
Could I be sure that such a quiet mind
Would be for ever grateful, mild, and kind,

I might comply—but how will Bloomer act,
When he becomes acquainted with the fact ?
The loss to him is trifling—but the fall
From independence, that to her is all ;
Now should he marry, 'twill be shame to me
To hold myself from my engagement free ;
And should he not, it will be double grace
To stand alone in such a trying case.
    ' " Come then, my Lucy, to thy faithful
    heart
And humble love I will my views impart ;
Will see the grateful tear that softly steals
Down the fair face and all thy joy reveals ;
And when I say it is a blow severe,
Then will I add—restrain, my love, the tear,
And take this heart, so faithful and so fond,
Still bound to thine ; and fear not for that
    bond."
  ' He said ; and went, with purpose he
    believed
Of generous nature—so is man deceived.
  ' Lucy determined that her lover's eye
Should not distress nor supplication spy ;
That in her manner he should nothing find,
To indicate the weakness of her mind.
He saw no eye that wept, no frame that
    shook,
No fond appeal was made by word or look ;
Kindness there was, but join'd with some
    restraint ;
And traces of the late event were faint.
  ' He look'd for grief deploring, but per-
    ceives
No outward token that she longer grieves ;
He had expected for his efforts praise,
For he resolved the drooping mind to raise ;
She would, he judged, be humble, and afraid
That he might blame her rashness and upbraid;
And lo ! he finds her in a quiet state,
Her spirit easy and her air sedate ;
As if her loss was not a cause for pain,
As if assured that he would make it gain.—
  ' Silent awhile, he told the morning news,
And what he judged they might expect to
    lose ;
He thought himself, whatever some might
    boast,
The composition would be small at most ;
Some shabby matter, she would see no more
The tithe of what she held in hand before.
  ' How did her sister feel ? and did she
    think
Bloomer was honest, and would never shrink ?

' " But why that smile ? is loss like yours
     so light
That it can aught like merriment excite ?
Well, he is rich, we know, and can afford
To please his fancy, and to keep his word ;
To him 'tis nothing ; had he now a fear,
He must the meanest of his sex appear ;
But the true honour, as I judge the case,
Is, both to feel the evil, and embrace."
     ' Here Barlow stopp'd, a little vex'd to see
No fear or hope, no dread or ecstasy :
Calmly she spoke—" Your prospects, sir, and
     mine
Are not the same,—their union I decline ;
Could I believe the hand for which you strove
Had yet its value, did you truly love,
I had with thanks address'd you, and replied,
Wait till your feelings and my own subside,
Watch your affections, and, if still they live,
What pride denies, my gratitude shall give ;
Ev'n then, in yielding, I had first believed
That I conferr'd the favour, not received.
     ' " You I release—nay, hear me—I impart
Joy to your soul,—I judge not of your heart.
Think'st thou a being, to whom God has lent
A feeling mind, will have her bosom rent
By man's reproaches ? Sorrow will be thine,
For all thy pity prompts thee to resign !
Think'st thou that meekness' self would con-
     descend
To take the husband when she scorns the
     friend ?
Forgive the frankness, and rejoice for life,
Thou art not burden'd with so poor a wife.
     ' "Go ! and be happy—tell, for the applause
Of hearts like thine, we parted, and the cause
Give, as it pleases." With a foolish look
That a dull school-boy fixes on his book
That he resigns, with mingled shame and joy ;
So Barlow went, confounded like the boy.
     ' Jane, while she wept to think her sister's
     pain
Was thus increased, felt infinite disdain ;
Bound as she was, and wedded by the ties
Of love and hope, that care and craft despise ;
She could but wonder that a man, whose taste
And zeal for money had a Jew disgraced,
Should love her sister ; yet with this surprise,
She felt a little exultation rise ;
Hers was a lover who had always held
This man as base, by generous scorn impell'd ;
And yet, as one, of whom for Lucy's sake
He would a civil distant notice take.

' Lucy, with sadden'd heart and temper
     mild,
Bow'd to correction, like an humbled child,
Who feels the parent's kindness, and who
     knows
Such the correction he, who loves, bestows.
     ' Attending always, but attending more
When sorrow ask'd his presence, than before,
Tender and ardent, with the kindest air
Came Bloomer, fortune's error to repair ;
Words sweetly soothing spoke the happy
     youth,
With all the tender earnestness of truth.
     ' There was no doubt of his intention now—
He will his purpose with his love avow :
So judged the maid ; yet, waiting, she ad-
     mired
His still delaying what he most desired ;
Till, from her spirit's agitation free,
She might determine when the day should be.
With such facility the partial mind
Can the best motives for its favourites find.
Of this he spake not, but he stay'd beyond
His usual hour ;—attentive still and fond ;—
The hand yet firmer to the hand he prest,
And the eye rested where it loved to rest ;
Then took he certain freedoms, yet so small
That it was prudish so the things to call ;
Things they were not—" Describe "—that
     none can do,
They had been nothing had they not been
     new ;
It was the manner and the look ; a maid,
Afraid of such, is foolishly afraid ;
For what could she explain ? The piercing eye
Of jealous fear could nought amiss descry.
     ' But some concern now rose ; the youth
     would seek
Jane by herself, and then would nothing
     speak,
Before not spoken ; there was still delay,
Vexatious, wearying, wasting, day by day.
     ' " He does not surely trifle ! " Heaven
     forbid !
She now should doubly scorn him if he did.
     ' Ah ! more than this, unlucky girl ! is
     thine ;
Thou must the fondest views of life resign ;
And in the very time resign them too,
When they were brightening on the eager view.
I will be brief,—nor have I heart to dwell
On crimes they almost share who paint them
     well.

'There was a moment's softness, and it
  seem'd
Discretion slept, or so the lover dream'd ;
And watching long the now confiding maid,
He thought her guardless, and grew less
  afraid ;
Led to the theme that he had shunn'd before,
He used a language he must use no more—
For if it answers, there is no more need,
And no more trial, should it not succeed.
  ' Then made he that attempt, in which to
    fail
Is shameful,—still more shameful to prevail.
  ' Then was there lightning in that eye that
    shed
Its beams upon him,—and his frenzy fled ;
Abject and trembling at her feet he laid,
Despised and scorn'd by the indignant maid,
Whose spirits in their agitation rose,
Him, and her own weak pity, to oppose :
As liquid silver in the tube mounts high,
Then shakes and settles as the storm goes by.
While yet the lover stay'd, the maid was
  strong,
But when he fled, she droop'd and felt the
  wrong—
Felt the alarming chill, th' enfeebled breath,
Closed the quick eye, and sank in transient
  death.
So Lucy found her ; and then first that breast
Knew anger's power, and own'd the stranger
  guest.
  ' " And is this love ? Ungenerous ! Has
    he too
Been mean and abject ? Is no being true ? "
For Lucy judged that, like her prudent swain,
Bloomer had talk'd of what a man might
  gain ;
She did not think a man on earth was found,
A wounded bosom, while it bleeds, to wound ;
Thought not that mortal could be so unjust,
As to deprive affliction of its trust ;
Thought not a lover could the hope enjoy,
That must the peace, he should promote, de-
  stroy ;
Thought not, in fact, that in the world were
  those,
Who, to their tenderest friends, are worse
  than foes,
Who win the heart, deprive it of its care,
Then plant remorse and desolation there.
  ' Ah ! cruel he, who can that heart deprive
Of all that keeps its energy alive ;

Can see consign'd to shame the trusting fair,
And turn confiding fondness to despair ;
To watch that time—a name is not assign'd
For crime so odious, nor shall learning find.
Now, from that day has Lucy laid aside
Her proper cares, to be her sister's guide,
Guard, and protector.   At their uncle's farm
They past the period of their first alarm,
But soon retired, nor was he grieved to learn
They made their own affairs their own concern.
  ' I knew not then their worth ; and, had
    I known,
Could not the kindness of a friend have shown;
For men they dreaded ; they a dwelling
  sought,
And there the children of the village taught ;
There, firm and patient, Lucy still depends
Upon her efforts, not upon her friends ;
She is with persevering strength endued,
And can be cheerful—for she will be good.
  ' Jane too will strive the daily tasks to
    share,
That so employment may contend with care;
Not power, but will, she shows, and looks
  about
On her small people, who come in and out ;
And seems of what they need, or she can do,
  in doubt.
There sits the chubby crew on seats around,
While she, all rueful at the sight and sound,
Shrinks from the free approaches of the tribe,
Whom she attempts lamenting to describe,
With stains the idlers gather'd in their way,
The simple stains of mud, and mould, and
  clay,
And compound of the streets, of what we
  dare not say ;
With hair uncomb'd, grimed face, and piteous
  look,
Each heavy student takes the odious book,
And on the lady casts a glance of fear,
Who draws the garment close as he comes
  near ;
She then for Lucy's mild forbearance tries,
And from her pupils turns her brilliant eyes,
Making new efforts, and with some success,
To pay attention while the students guess ;
Who to the gentler mistress fain would glide,
And dread their station at the lady's side.
  ' Such is their fate :—there is a friendly
    few
Whom they receive, and there is chance for
  you ;

Their school, and something gather'd from
    the wreck
Of that bad Bank, keeps poverty in check ;
And true respect, and high regard, are theirs,
The children's profit, and the parents' prayers.
With Lucy rests the one peculiar care,
That few must see, and none with her may
    share ;
More dear than hope can be, more sweet than
    pleasures are.
For her sad sister needs the care of love
That will direct her, that will not reprove,
But waits to warn : for Jane will walk alone,
Will sing in low and melancholy tone ;
Will read or write, or to her plants will run
To shun her friends,—alas ! her thoughts to
    shun.
' It is not love alone disturbs her rest,
But loss of all that ever hope possess'd ;
Friends ever kind, life's lively pleasures, ease,
When her enjoyments could no longer please ;
These were her comforts then ! she has no
    more of these.
' Wrapt in such thoughts, she feels her
    mind astray,
But knows 'tis true, that she has lost her way;
For Lucy's smile will check the sudden flight,
And one kind look let in the wonted light.
' Fits of long silence she endures, then talks
Too much—with too much ardour, as she
    walks ;
But still the shrubs that she admires dispense
Their balmy freshness to the hurried sense,
And she will watch their progress, and attend
Her flowering favourites as a guardian friend ;
To sun or shade she will her sweets remove,
" And here," she says, " I may with safety
    love."
' But there are hours when on that bosom
    steals
A rising terror,—then indeed she feels ;—
Feels how she loved the promised good, and
    how
She feels the failure of the promise now.
' " That other spoiler did as robbers do,
Made poor our state, but not disgraceful too.
This spoiler shames me, and I look within
To find some cause that drew him on to sin ;
He and the wretch who could thy worth for-
    sake
Are the fork'd adder and the loathsome snake;
Thy snake could slip in villain-fear away,
But had no fang to fasten on his prey.

' " Oh ! my dear Lucy, I had thought to live
With all the comforts easy fortunes give ;
A wife caressing, and caress'd,—a friend,
Whom he would guide, advise, consult, defend,
And make his equal ;—then I fondly thought
Among superior creatures to be brought ;
And while with them, delighted to behold
No eye averted, and no bosom cold ;—
Then at my home, a mother, to embrace
My——Oh ! my sister, it was surely base !
I might forget the wrong ; I cannot the dis-
    grace.
' " Oh ! when I saw that triumph in his
    eyes,
I felt my spirits with his own arise ;
I call'd it joy, and said, the generous youth
Laughs at my loss—no trial for his truth ;
It is a trifle he can not lament,
A sum but equal to his annual rent ;
And yet that loss, the cause of every ill,
Has made me poor, and him—"
               ' " O ! poorer still ;
Poorer, my Jane, and far below thee now :
The injurer he,—the injured sufferer thou ;
And shall such loss afflict thee ? "—
                   ' " Lose I not
With him what fortune could in life allot ?
Lose I not hope, life's cordial, and the views
Of an aspiring spirit ?—O ! I lose
Whate'er the happy feel, whate'er the san-
    guine choose.
' " Would I could lose this bitter sense of
    wrong,
And sleep in peace—but it will not be long !
And here is something, Lucy, in my brain,
I know not what—it is a cure for pain ;
But is not death !—no beckoning hand I see,
No voice I hear that comes alone to me ;
It is not death, but change ; I am not now
As I was once,—nor can I tell you how ;
Nor is it madness—ask, and you shall find
In my replies the soundness of my mind :
O ! I should be a trouble all day long ;
A very torment, if my head were wrong."
' At times there is upon her features seen,
What moves suspicion—she is too serene.
Such is the motion of a drunken man,
Who steps sedately, just to show he can.
Absent at times she will her mother call,
And cry at mid-day, " then good night to all."
But most she thinks there will some good
    ensue
From something done, or what she is to do ;

Long wrapt in silence, she will then assume
An air of business, and shake off her gloom;
Then cry exulting, "O! it must succeed,
There are ten thousand readers—all men read:
There are my writings,—you shall never spend
Your precious moments to so poor an end;
Our peasants' children may be taught by those,
Who have no powers such wonders to compose;
So let me call them,—what the world allows,
Surely a poet without shame avows;
Come, let us count what numbers we believe
Will buy our work—Ah! sister, do you grieve?
You weep; there's something I have said amiss,
And vex'd my sister—What a world is this!
And how I wander!—Where has fancy run?
Is there no poem? Have I nothing done?
Forgive me, Lucy, I had fix'd my eye,
And so my mind, on works that cannot die;
Marmion and *Lara* yonder in the case,
And so I put me in the poet's place.
　　' " Still, be not frighten'd; it is but a dream;
I am not lost, bewilder'd though I seem;
I will obey thee—but suppress thy fear—
I am at ease,—then why that silly tear?"
' Jane, as these melancholy fits invade
The busy fancy, seeks the deepest shade;
She walks in ceaseless hurry, till her mind
Will short repose in verse and music find;
Then her own songs to some soft tune she sings,
And laughs, and calls them melancholy things;
Not frenzy all; in some her erring Muse
Will sad, afflicting, tender strains infuse:
Sometimes on death she will her lines compose;
Or give her serious page of solemn prose;
And still those favourite plants her fancy please,
And give to care and anguish rest and ease.

　　' " Let me not have this gloomy view,
　　　About my room, around my bed;
But morning roses, wet with dew,
　　　To cool my burning brows instead.
As flowers that once in Eden grew,
　　　Let them their fragrant spirits shed,
And every day the sweets renew,
　　　Till I, a fading flower, am dead.

　　' " Oh! let the herbs I loved to rear
　　　Give to my sense their perfumed breath;
Let them be placed about my bier,
　　　And grace the gloomy house of death.

I'll have my grave beneath an hill,
　　　Where, only Lucy's self shall know;
Where runs the pure pellucid rill
　　　Upon its gravelly bed below;
There violets on the borders blow,
　　　And insects their soft light display,
Till, as the morning sun-beams glow,
　　　The cold phosphoric fires decay.

　　' " That is the grave to Lucy shown,
　　　The soil a pure and silver sand,
The green cold moss above it grown,
　　　Unpluck'd of all but maiden hand:
In virgin earth, till then unturn'd,
　　　There let my maiden form be laid,
Nor let my changed clay be spurned,
　　　Nor for new guest that bed be made.

　　' " There will the lark,—the lamb, in sport,
　　　In air,—on earth,—securely play,
And Lucy to my grave resort,
　　　As innocent, but not so gay.
I will not have the churchyard ground,
　　　With bones all black and ugly grown,
To press my shivering body round,
　　　Or on my wasted limbs be thrown.

　　' " With ribs and skulls I will not sleep,
　　　In clammy beds of cold blue clay,
Through which the ringed earth-worms creep,
　　　And on the shrouded bosom prey;
I will not have the bell proclaim
　　　When those sad marriage rites begin,
And boys, without regard or shame,
　　　Press the vile mouldering masses in.

　　' " Say not, it is beneath my care;
　　　I cannot these cold truths allow;
These thoughts may not afflict me there,
　　　But, O! they vex and tease me now.
Raise not a turf, nor set a stone,
　　　That man a maiden's grave may trace,
But thou, my Lucy, come alone,
　　　And let affection find the place.

　　' " O! take me from a world I hate,
　　　Men cruel, selfish, sensual, cold;
And, in some pure and blessed state,
　　　Let me my sister minds behold:
From gross and sordid views refined,
　　　Our heaven of spotless love to share,
For only generous souls design'd,
　　　And not a man to meet us there." '

'My father dying, to my mother left
An infant charge, of all things else bereft ;
Poor, but experienced in the world, she knew
What others did, and judged what she could
   do ;
Beauty she justly weigh'd, was never blind
To her own interest, and she read mankind :
She view'd my person with approving glance,
And judged the way my fortune to advance ;
Taught me betimes that person to improve,
And make a lawful merchandize of love ;
Bade me my temper in subjection keep,
And not permit my vigilance to sleep ;
I was not one, a miss, who might presume
Now to be crazed by mirth, now sunk in
   gloom ;
Nor to be fretful, vapourish, or give way
To spleen and anger, as the wealthy may ;
But I must please, and all I felt of pride,
Contempt, and hatred, I must cast aside.
   ' " Have not one friend," my mother cried,
     " not one ;
That bane of our romantic triflers shun ;
Suppose her true, can she afford you aid ?
Suppose her false, your purpose is betray'd ;
And then in dubious points, and matters nice,
How can you profit by a child's advice ?
While you are writing on from post to post,
Your hour is over, and a man is lost ;
Girls of their hearts are scribbling ; their
   desires,
And what the folly of the heart requires,
Dupes to their dreams—but I the truth im-
   part,
You cannot, child, afford to have a heart ;
Think nothing of it ; to yourself be true,
And keep life's first great business in your
   view ;—
Take it, dear Martha, for a useful rule,
She who is poor is ugly or a fool ;
Or, worse than either, has a bosom fill'd
With soft emotions, and with raptures thrill'd.
   ' " Read not too much, nor write in verse or
     prose,
For then you make the dull and foolish foes ;
Yet those who do, deride not nor condemn,
It is not safe to raise up foes in them ;
For though they harm you not, as block-
   heads do,
There is some malice in the scribbling crew." '
   ' Such her advice ; full hard with her had
   dealt
The world, and she the usage keenly felt.

   ' " Keep your good name," she said, " and
     that to keep
You must not suffer vigilance to sleep :
Some have, perhaps, the name of chaste
   retain'd,
When nought of chastity itself remain'd ;
But there is danger—few have means to blind
The keen-eyed world, and none to make it
   kind.
   ' " And one thing more—to free yourself
     from foes
Never a secret to your friend disclose ;
Secrets with girls, like loaded guns with boys,
Are never valued till they make a noise ;
To show how trusted, they their power dis-
   play ;
To show how worthy, they the trust betray ;
Like pence in children's pockets secrets lie
In female bosoms—they must burn or fly.
   ' " Let not your heart be soften'd ; if it
     be,
Let not the man his softening influence see ;
For the most fond will sometimes tyrants
   prove,
And wound the bosom where they trace the
   love.
But to your fortune look, on that depend
For your life's comfort, comforts that attend
On wealth alone—wealth gone, they have
   their end." '
   ' Such were my mother's cares to mend my
   lot,
And such her pupil they succeeded not.
   ' It was conceived the person I had then
Might lead to serious thoughts some wealthy
   men,
Who having none their purpose to oppose
Would soon be won their wishes to disclose :
My mother thought I was the very child
By whom the old and amorous are beguiled ;
So mildly gay, so ignorantly fair,
And pure, no doubt, as sleeping infants are :
Then I had lessons how to look and move,
And, I repeat, make merchandize of love.
   ' Thrice it was tried if one so young could
   bring
Old wary men to buy the binding ring ;
And on the taper finger, to whose tip
The fond old swain would press his withering
   lip,
Place the strong charm :—and one would win
   my heart
By re-assuming youth—a trying part ;

Girls, he supposed, all knew the young were
    bold,
And he would show that spirit in the old ;
In boys they loved to hear the rattling tongue,
And he would talk as idly as the young ;
He knew the vices our Lotharios boast,
And he would show of every vice the ghost,
The evil's self, without disguise or dress,
Vice in its own pure native ugliness ;
Not as the drunkenness of slaves to prove
Vice hateful, but that seeing, I might love.
He drove me out, and I was pleased to see
Care of himself, it served as care for me ;
For he would tell me, that he should not spare
Man, horse, or carriage, if I were not there :
Provoked at last, my malice I obey'd,
And smiling said, " Sir, I am not afraid."
  ' This check'd his spirit; but he said, "Could
    you
Have charge so rich, you would be careful
    too."
  ' And he, indeed, so very slowly drove,
That we dismiss'd the over-cautious love.
  ' My next admirer was of equal age,
And wish'd the child's affection to engage,
And keep the fluttering bird a victim in his
    cage :
He had no portion of his rival's glee,
But gravely praised the gravity in me ;
Religious, moral, both in word and deed,
But warmly disputatious in his creed :
Wild in his younger time, as we were told,
And therefore like a penitent when old.
Strange ! he should wish a lively girl to look
Upon the methods his repentance took.
  ' Then he would say, he was no more a rake
To squander money for his passions' sake ;
Yet, upon proper terms, as man discreet,
He with my mother was disposed to treat,
To whom he told, " the price of beauty fell
In every market, and but few could sell ;
That trade in India, once alive and brisk,
Was over done, and scarcely worth the risk."
Then stoop'd to speak of board, and what
    for life
A wife would cost——if he should take a wife.
  ' Hardly he bargain'd, and so much desired,
That we demurr'd ; and he, displeased,
    retired.
  ' And now I hoped to rest, nor act again
The paltry part for which I felt disdain,
When a third lover came within our view,
And somewhat differing from the former two ;

He had been much abroad, and he had seen
The world's weak side, and read the hearts
    of men ;
But all, it seem'd, this study could produce,
Was food for spleen, derision, and abuse ;
He levell'd all, as one who had intent
To clear the vile and spot the innocent ;
He praised my sense, and said I ought to be
From girl's restraint and nursery maxims free;
He praised my mother ; but he judged her
    wrong
To keep us from th' admiring world so long ;
He praised himself ; and then his vices named,
And call'd them follies, and was not ashamed.
He more than hinted that the lessons taught
By priests were all with superstition fraught ;
And I must think them for the crowd de-
    sign'd,
Not to alarm the free and liberal mind.
  ' Wisdom with him was virtue. They were
    wrong
And weak, he said, who went not with the
    throng ;
Man must his passions order and restrain
In all that gives his fellow-subjects pain ;
But yet of guilt he would in pity speak,
And as he judged, the wicked were the weak.
  ' Such was the lover of a simple maid,
Who seem'd to call his logic to his aid,
And to mean something : I will not pretend
To judge the purpose of my reasoning friend,
Who was dismiss'd, in quiet to complain
That so much labour was bestow'd in vain.
  ' And now my mother seem'd disposed to try
A life of reason and tranquillity ;
Ere this, her health and spirits were the
    best,
Hers the day's trifling, and the nightly rest ;
But something new was in her mind instill'd ;
Unquiet thoughts the matron bosom fill'd ;
For five and forty peaceful years she bore
Her placid looks, and dress becoming wore :
She could a compliment with pleasure take,
But no absurd impression could it make.
Now were her nerves disorder'd ; she was
    weak,
And must the help of a physician seek ;
A Scotch physician, who had just began
To settle near us, quite a graceful man,
And very clever, with a soft address,
That would his meaning tenderly express.
  ' Sick as my mother seem'd, when he inquired
If she was ill, he found her well attired ;

She purchased wares so showy and so fine,
The venders all believed th' indulgence
       mine :—
But I, who thrice was woo'd, had lovers three,
Must now again a very infant be ;
While the good lady, twenty years a wife,
Was to decide the colour of his life :
And she decided. She was wont t' appear
To these unequal marriages severe ;
Her thoughts of such with energy she told,
And was repulsive, dignified, and cold ;
But now, like monarchs weary of a throne,
She would no longer reign—at least alone.
  'She gave her pulse, and, with a manner
       sweet,
Wish'd him to feel how kindly they could
       beat ;
And 'tis a thing quite wonderful to tell
How soon he understood them, and how well.
  'Now, when she married, I from home was
       sent,
With grandmamma to keep perpetual Lent ;
For she would take me on conditions cheap,
For what we scarcely could a parrot keep :
A trifle added to the daily fare
Would feed a maiden who must learn to spare.
  'With grandmamma I lived in perfect ease.
Consent to starve, and I was sure to please ;
Full well I knew the painful shifts we made,
Expenses all to lessen or evade,
And tradesmen's flinty hearts to soften and
       persuade.
  'Poor grandmamma among the gentry dwelt
Of a small town, and all the honour felt ;
Shrinking from all approaches to disgrace
That might be mark'd in so genteel a place ;
Where every daily deed, as soon as done,
Ran through the town as fast as it could
       run :—
At dinners what appear'd—at cards who lost
       or won.
  'Our good appearance through the town was
       known,
Hunger and thirst were matters of our own ;
And you would judge that she in scandal
       dealt
Who told on what we fed, or how we felt.
  'We had a little maid, some four feet high,
Who was employ'd our household stores to
       buy ;
For she would weary every man in trade,
And tease t' assent whom she could not per-
       suade.

'Methinks I see her, with her pigmy light,
Precede her mistress in a moonless night ;
From the small lantern throwing through the
       street
The dimm'd effulgence at her lady's feet ;
What time she went to prove her well-known
       skill
With rival friends at their beloved quadrille.
  ' "And how 's your pain ? " inquired the
       gentle maid,
For that was asking if with luck she play'd ;
And this she answer'd as the cards decreed,
" O Biddy ! ask not—very bad indeed ; "
Or, in more cheerful tone, from spirit light,
" Why, thank you, Biddy, pretty well to-
       night."
  ' The good old lady often thought me vain,
And of my dress would tenderly complain ;
But liked my taste in food of every kind,
As from all grossness, like her own, refined :
Yet when she hinted that on herbs and bread
Girls of my age and spirit should be fed,
Whate'er my age had borne, my flesh and
       blood,
Spirit and strength, the interdict withstood ;
But though I might the frugal soul offend
Of the good matron, now my only friend,
And though her purse suggested rules so
       strict,
Her love could not the punishment inflict :
She sometimes watch'd the morsel with a
       frown,
And sigh'd to see, but let it still go down.
  'Our butcher's bill, to me a monstrous sum,
Was such, that summon'd, he forebore to
       come :
Proud man was he, and when the bill was paid,
He put the money in his bag and play'd,
Jerking it up, and catching it again,
And poising in his hand in pure disdain ;
While the good lady, awed by man so proud,
And yet disposed to have her claims allow'd,
Balanced between humility and pride,
Stood a fall'n empress at the butcher's side,
Praising his meat as delicate and nice——
" Yes, madam, yes ! if people pay the price."
  'So lived the lady, and so murmur'd I,
In all the grief of pride and poverty :
Twice in the year there came a note to tell
How well mamma, who hoped the child was
       well ;
It was not then a pleasure to be styled,
By a mamma of such experience, Child !

But I suppress'd the feelings of my pride,
Or other feelings set them all aside.
  'There was a youth from college, just the one
I judged mamma would value as a son ;
He was to me good, handsome, learn'd, gen-
  teel—
I cannot now what then I thought reveal ;
But, in a word, he was the very youth
Who told me what I judged the very truth,
That love like his and charms like mine agreed,
For all description they must both exceed :
Yet scarcely can I throw a smile on things
So painful, but that Time his comfort brings,
Or rather throws oblivion on the mind,
For we are more forgetful than resign'd.
  'We both were young, had heard of love
    and read,
And could see nothing in the thing to dread,
But like a simple pair our time employ'd
In pleasant views to be in time enjoy'd ;
When Frederick came, the kind old lady
    smiled
To see the youth so taken with her child ;
A nice young man, who came with unsoil'd
    feet
In her best room, and neither drank nor eat :
Alas ! he planted in a vacant breast
The hope and fears that robb'd it of its rest.
  'All now appear'd so right, so fair, so just,
We surely might the lovely prospect trust ;
Alas ! poor Frederick and his charmer found
That they were standing on fallacious ground :
All that the father of the youth could do
Was done—and now he must himself pursue
Success in life ; and, honest truth to state,
He was not fitted for a candidate :
I, too, had nothing in this world below,
Save what a Scotch physician could bestow,
Who for a pittance took my mother's hand,
And if disposed, what had they to command ?
  'But these were after fears, nor came
    t' annoy
The tender children in their dreams of joy ;
Who talk'd of glebe and garden, tithe and rent,
And how a fancied income should be spent ;
What friends, what social parties we should
    see,
And live with what genteel economy ;
In fact, we gave our hearts as children give,
And thought of living as our neighbours live.
  'Now when assured ourselves that 'all was
    well,
'Twas right our friends of these designs to tell ;

For this we parted.—Grandmamma, amazed,
Upon her child with fond compassion gazed ;
Then pious tears appear'd, but not a word
In aid of weeping till she cried, "Good Lord ! "
She then, with hurried motion, sought the
    stairs,
And calling Biddy, bade her come to prayers.
  'Yet the good lady early in her life
Was call'd to vow the duties of a wife ;
She sought the altar by her friends' advice,
No free-will offering, but a sacrifice :
But here a forward girl and eager boy
Dared talk of life, and turn their heads with
    joy.
  'To my mamma I wrote in just the way
I felt, and said what dreaming lasses say ;
How handsome Frederick was, by all con-
    fess'd,
How well he look'd, how very well he dress'd ;
With learning much, that would for both
    provide,
His mother's darling, and his father's pride ;
And then he loves me more than mind can
    guess,
Than heart conceive, or eloquence express.
  'No letter came a doubtful mind to ease,
And, what was worse, no Frederick came to
    please ;
To college gone—so thought our little maid—
But not to see me ! I was much afraid ;
I walk'd the garden round, and deeply sigh'd,
When grandmamma grew faint ! and dropt,
    and died :
A fate so awful and so sudden drove
All else away, and half extinguish'd love.
  'Strange people came ; they search'd the
    house around,
And, vulgar wretches ! sold whate'er they
    found :
The secret hoards that in the drawers were
    kept,
The silver toys that with the tokens slept,
The precious beads, the corals with their bells,
That laid secure, lock'd up in secret cells,
The costly silk, the tabby, the brocade,
The very garment for the wedding made,
Were brought to sale, with many a jest
    thereon !
"Going—a bridal dress—for——Going !—
    Gone."
That ring, dear pledge of early love and true,
That to the wedded finger almost grew,
Was sold for six and ten-pence to a Jew !

'Great was the fancied worth; but ah!
    how small
The sum thus made, and yet how valued all!
But all that to the shameful service went
Just paid the bills, the burial, and the rent;
And I and Biddy, poor deserted maids!
Were turn'd adrift to seek for other aids.
   'Now left by all the world, as I believed,
I wonder'd much that I so little grieved;
Yet I was frighten'd at the painful view
Of shiftless want, and saw not what to do:
In times like this the poor have little dread,
They can but work, and they shall then be
    fed;
And Biddy cheer'd me with such thoughts
    as this,
" You'll find the poor have their enjoyments,
    Miss!"
Indeed I saw, for Biddy took me home
To a forsaken hovel's cold and gloom;
And while my tears in plenteous flow were
    shed,
With her own hands she placed her proper bed,
Reserved for need—A fire was quickly made,
And food, the purchase for the day, display'd;
She let in air to make the damps retire,
Then placed her sad companion at her fire;
She then began her wonted peace to feel,
She bought her wool, and sought her favourite
    wheel,
That as she turn'd, she sang with sober glee,
" Begone, dull Care! I'll have no more with
    thee;"
Then turn'd to me, and bade me weep no
    more,
But try and taste the pleasures of the poor.
   'When dinner came, on table brown and bare
Were placed the humblest forms of earthen-
    ware,
With one blue dish, on which our food was
    placed,
For appetite provided, not for taste:
I look'd disgusted, having lately seen
All so minutely delicate and clean;
Yet, as I sate, I found to my surprise
A vulgar kind of inclination rise,
And near my humble friend, and nearer drew,
Tried the strange food, and was partaker too.
   'I walk'd at eve, but not where I was seen,
And thought, with sorrow, what can Frederick
    mean?
I must not write, I said, for I am poor;
And then I wept till I could weep no more.

'Kind-hearted Biddy tried my griefs to heal,
"This is a nothing to what others feel;
Life has a thousand sorrows worse than this,
A lover lost is not a fortune, Miss!
One goes, another comes, and which is best
There is no telling—set your heart at rest."
   'At night we pray'd—I dare not say a word
Of our devotion, it was so absurd;
And very pious upon Biddy's part,
But mine were all effusions of the heart;
While she her angels call'd their peace to shed,
And bless the corners of our little bed.
All was a dream! I said, is this indeed
To be my life? and thus to lodge and feed,
To pay for what I have, and work for what
    I need?
Must I be poor? and Frederick, if we meet,
Would not so much as know me in the street?
Or, as he walk'd with ladies, he would try
To be engaged as we were passing by—
And then I wept to think that I should grow
Like them whom he would be ashamed to
    know.
   'On the third day, while striving with my
    fate,
And hearing Biddy all its comforts state,
Talking of all her neighbours, all her schemes,
Her stories, merry jests, and warning dreams;
With tales of mirth and murder! O! the
    nights
Past, said the maiden, in such dear delights,
And I was thinking, can the time arrive
When I shall thus be humbled, and sur-
    vive?—
Then I beheld a horse and handsome gig,
With the good air, tall form, and comely wig
Of Doctor Mackey—I in fear began
To say, Good heaven, preserve me from the
    man!
But fears ill reason,—heaven to such a mind
Had lent a heart compassionate and kind.
   'From him I learnt that one had call'd to
    know
What with my hand my parents could bestow;
And when he learn'd the truth, in high disdain
He told my fate, and home return'd again.
" Nay, be not grieved, my lovely girl; but few
Wed the first love, however kind and true;
Something there comes to break the strongest
    vow,
Or mine had been my gentle Mattie now.
When the good lady died—but let me leave
All gloomy subjects—'tis not good to grieve."

'Thus the kind Scotchman soothed me: he sustain'd
A father's part, and my submission gain'd:
Then my affection; and he often told
My sterner parent that her heart was cold:
He grew in honour—he obtain'd a name—
And now a favourite with the place became;
To me most gentle, he would condescend
To read and reason, be the guide and friend;
He taught me knowledge of the wholesome kind,
And fill'd with many a useful truth my mind:
Life's common burden daily lighter grew;
And even Frederick lessen'd in my view:
Cold and repulsive as he once appear'd,
He was by every generous act endear'd;
And, above all, that he with ardour fill'd
My soul for truth—a love by him instill'd;
Till my mamma grew jealous of a maid
To whom an husband such attention paid:
Not grossly jealous; but it gave her pain,
And she observed, "He made her daughter vain;
And what his help to one who must not look
To gain her bread by poring on a book?"
'This was distress; but this, and all beside,
Was lost in grief—my kinder parent died;
When praised and loved, when joy and health he gave,
He sank lamented to an early grave:
Then love and wo—the parent and the child,
Lost in one grief, allied and reconciled.
'Yet soon a will, that left me half his worth,
To the same spirit gave a second birth:
But 'twas a mother's spleen; and she indeed
Was sick, and sad, and had of comfort need;
I watch'd the way her anxious spirit took,
And often found her musing o'er a book:
She changed her dress, her church, her priest, her prayer,
Join'd a new sect, and sought her comforts there;
Some strange coarse people came, and were so free
In their addresses, they offended me;
But my mamma threw all her pride away—
More humble she as more assuming they.
'"And what," they said, as having power, "are now
The inward conflicts? do you strive? and how?"
Themselves confessing thoughts so new and wild,
I thought them like the visions of a child.

"Could we," they ask, "our best good deeds condemn?
And did we long to touch the garment's hem?
And was it so with us? for so it was with them."
'A younger few assumed a softer part,
And tried to shake the fortress of my heart;
To this my pliant mother lent her aid,
And wish'd the winning of her erring maid:
I was constrain'd her female friends to hear;
But suffer'd not a bearded convert near:
Though more than one attempted, with their whine,
And "Sister! sister! how that heart of thine?"
But this was freedom I for ever check'd:
Mine was a heart no brother could affect.
'But, "would I hear the preacher, and receive
The dropping dew of his discourse at eve?
The soft, sweet words?" I gave two precious hours
To hear of gifts and graces, helps and powers;
When a pale youth, who should dismiss the flock,
Gave to my bosom an electric shock.
While in that act he look'd upon my face
As one in that all-equalizing place:
Nor, though he sought me, would he lay aside,
Their cold, dead freedom, or their dull, sad pride.
'Of his conversion he with triumph spoke,
Before he orders from a bishop took:
Then how his father's anger he had braved;
And, safe himself, his erring neighbours saved.
Me he rejoiced a sister to behold
Among the members of his favourite fold;
He had not sought me, the availing call
Demanded all his love, and had it all;
But, now thus met, it must be heaven's design.
Indeed! I thought, it never shall be mine;
Yes, we must wed. He was not rich: and I
Had of the earthly good a mean supply;
But it sufficed. Of his conversion then
He told, and labours in converting men;
For he was chosen all their bands among—
Another Daniel! honour'd, though so young.
'He call'd me sister: show'd me that he knew
What I possess'd; and told what it would do;
My looks, I judge, express'd my full disdain;
But it was given to the man in vain:
They preach till they are proud, and pride disturbs the brain.

'Is this the youth once timid, mild, polite?
How odious now, and sick'ning to the sight !
Proud that he sees, and yet so truly blind,
With all this blight and mildew on the mind !
'Amazed, the solemn creature heard me vow
That I was not disposed to take him now.
' " Then, art thou changed, fair maiden ?
    changed thy heart ? "
I answered, " No ; but I perceive thou art."
'Still was my mother sad, her nerves relax'd,
And our small income for advice was tax'd ;
When I, who long'd for change and freedom,
    cried,
Let sea and Sidmouth's balmy air be tried ;
And so they were, and every neighbouring
    scene,
That make the bosom, like the clime, serene ;
Yet were her teachers loth to yield assent ;
And not without the warning voice we went ;
And there was secret counsel all unknown
To me—but I had counsel of my own.
'And now there pass'd a portion of my time
In ease delicious, and in joy sublime—
With friends endear'd by kindness—with
    delight,—
In all that could the feeling mind excite,
Or please, excited ; walks in every place
Where we could pleasure find and beauty
    trace,
Or views at night, where on the rocky steep
Shines the full moon, or glitters on the deep.
'Yes, they were happy days ; but they are
    fled !
All now are parted—part are with the dead !
Still it is pleasure, though 'tis mix'd with pain,
To think of joys that cannot live again !
Here cannot live ; but they excite desire
Of purer kind, and heavenly thoughts inspire !
'And now my mother, weaken'd in her mind,
Her will, subdued before, to me resign'd.
Wean'd from her late directors, by degrees
She sank resign'd, and only sought for ease :
In a small town upon the coast we fix'd ;
Nor in amusement with associates mix'd.
My years—but other mode will I pursue,
And count my time by what I sought to do.
'And was that mind at ease ? could I avow
That no once leading thoughts engaged me
    now ?
Was I convinced th' enthusiastic man
Had ruin'd what the loving boy began ?
'I answer doubting—I could still detect
Feelings too soft—yet him I could reject—

Feelings that came when I had least employ,
When common pleasures I could least enjoy—
When I was pacing lonely in the rays
Of a full moon, in lonely walks and ways—
When I was sighing o'er a tale's distress,
And paid attention to my Bible less.
'These found, I sought my remedies for
    these ;
I suffer'd common things my mind to please,
And common pleasures : seldom walk'd alone,
Nor when the moon upon the waters shone ;
But then my candles lit, my window closed,
My needle took, and with my neighbours
    prosed :
And in one year—nay, ere the end of one,
My labour ended, and my love was done.
My heart at rest, I boldly look'd within,
And dared to ask it of its secret sin ;
Alas ! with pride it answer'd, "Look around,
And tell me where a better heart is found."
And then I traced my virtues : O ! how
    few,
In fact, they were, and yet how vain I grew ;
Thought of my kindness, condescension, ease,
My will, my wishes, nay, my power to please ;
I judged me prudent, rational, discreet,
And void of folly, falsehood and deceit ;
I read, not lightly, as I some had known,
But made an author's meaning all my own ;
In short, what lady could a poet choose
As a superior subject for his muse ?
'So said my heart ; and Conscience straight
    replied—
" I say the matter is not fairly tried :
I am offended, hurt, dissatisfied ;
First of the Christian graces, let me see
What thy pretensions to humility ?
Art thou prepared for trial ? Wilt thou say
I am this being, and for judgment pray ?
And with the gallant Frenchman, wilt thou
    cry,
When to thy judge presented, thus am I—
Thus was I formed—these talents I possess'd—
So I employ'd them—and thou know'st the
    rest ? "
'Thus Conscience ; and she then a picture
    drew,
And bade me think and tremble at the view.
One I beheld—a wife, a mother—go
To gloomy scenes of wickedness and wo ;
She sought her way through all things vile
    and base,
And made a prison a religious place :

Fighting her way—the way that angels fight
With powers of darkness—to let in the light;
Tell me, my heart, hast thou such victory won
As this, a sinner of thy sex, has done,
And calls herself a sinner? What art thou?
And where thy praise and exaltation now?
Yet is she tender, delicate, and nice,
And shrinks from all depravity and vice;
Shrinks from the ruffian gaze, the savage
    gloom,
That reign where guilt and misery find an home:
Guilt chain'd, and misery purchased; and
    with them
All we abhor, abominate, condemn—
The look of scorn, the scowl, th' insulting leer
Of shame, all fix'd on her who ventures here:
Yet all she braved! she kept her stedfast eye
On the dear cause, and brush'd the base-
    ness by.
So would a mother press her darling child
Close to her breast, with tainted rags defiled.
  'But thou hast talents truly! say the ten:
Come, let us look at their improvement then.
What hast thou done to aid thy suffering kind,
To help the sick, the deaf, the lame, the blind?
Hast thou not spent thy intellectual force
On books abstruse, in critical discourse?
Wasting in useless energy thy days,
And idly listening to their common praise,
Who can a kind of transient fame dispense,
And say—" a woman of exceeding sense."
  'Thus tried, and failing, the suggestions fled,
And a corrected spirit reign'd instead.
  'My mother yet was living; but the flame
Of life now flash'd, and fainter then became;
I made it pleasant, and was pleased to see
A parent looking as a child to me.
  'And now our humble place grew wond'rous
    gay;
Came gallant persons in their red array:
All strangers welcome there, extremely wel-
    come they.
When in the church I saw inquiring eyes
Fix'd on my face with pleasure and surprise;
And soon a knocking at my door was heard;
And soon the lover of my youth appear'd—
Frederick, in all his glory, glad to meet,
And say, " his happiness was now complete."
  ' He told his flight from superstitious zeal;
But first what torments he was doom'd to
    feel:—
"The tender tears he saw from women fall—
The strong persuasions of the brethren all—

The threats of crazed enthusiasts, bound to
    keep
The struggling mind, and awe the straying
    sheep—
From these, their love, their curses, and their
    creed,
Was I by reason and exertion freed."
  'Then, like a man who often had been told
And was convinced success attends the bold,
His former purpose he renew'd, and swore
He never loved me half so well before:
Before he felt a something to divide
The heart, that now had not a love beside.
  ' In earlier times had I myself amused,
And first my swain perplex'd, and then
    refused;
Cure for conceit;—but now in purpose grave,
Strong and decisive the reply I gave.
Still he would come, and talk as idlers do,
Both of his old associates and his new;
Those who their dreams and reveries receive
For facts, and those who would not facts
    believe.
  ' He now conceived that truth was hidden,
    placed
He knew not where, she never could be traced;
" But that in every place, the world around
Might some resemblance of the nymph be
    found:
Yet wise men knew these shadows to be vain,
Such as our true philosophers disdain,—
They laugh to see what vulgar minds pursue—
Truth, as a mistress, never in their view—
But there the shadow flies, and that, they
    cry, is true."
  'Thus, at the college and the meeting train'd,
My lover seem'd his acme to have gain'd;
With some compassion I essay'd a cure:
" If truth be hidden, why art thou so sure?"
This he mistook for tenderness, and cried,
" If sure of thee, I care not what beside!"
Compell'd to silence I, in pure disdain,
Withdrew from one so insolent and vain;
He then retired; and I was kindly told,
" In pure compassion grew estranged and
    cold."
  'My mother died; but, in my grief, drew near
A bosom friend, who dried the useless tear;
We lived together: we combined our shares
Of the world's good, and learn'd to brave its
    cares:
We were the ladies of the place, and found
Protection and respect the country round;

We gave, and largely, for we wished to live
In good repute—for this 'tis good to give;
Our annual present to the priest convey'd
Was kindly taken :—we in comfort pray'd ;
There none molested in the crimson pew
The worthy ladies, whom the vicar knew :
And we began to think that life might be,
Not happy all, but innocently free.

'My friend in early life was bound to one
Of gentle kindred, but a younger son.
He fortune's smile with perseverance woo'd,
And wealth beneath the burning sun pursued :
There, urged by love and youthful hope, he went,
Loth ; but 'twas all his fortune could present
From hence he wrote ; and, with a lover's fears,
And gloomy fondness, talk'd of future years ;
To her devoted, his Priscilla found
His faithful heart still suffering with its wound,
That would not heal. A second time she heard ;
And then no more : nor lover since appear'd ;
Year after year the country's fleet arrived,
Confirm'd her fear, and yet her love survived ;
It still was living ; yet her hope was dead,
And youthful dreams, nay, youth itself, was fled ;
And he was lost : so urged her friends, so she
At length believed, and thus retired with me ;
She would a dedicated vestal prove,
And give her virgin vows to heaven and love ;
She dwelt with fond regret on pleasures past,
With ardent hope on those that ever last ;
Pious and tender, every day she view'd
With solemn joy our perfect solitude ;
Her reading, that which most delighted her,
That soothed the passions, yet would gently stir ;
The tender, softening, melancholy strain,
That caused not pleasure, but that vanquish'd pain,
In tears she read, and wept, and long'd to read again.
But other worlds were her supreme delight,
And there, it seem'd, she long'd to take her flight :
Yet patient, pensive, arm'd by thoughts sublime,
She watch'd the tardy steps of lingering time.

'My friend, with face that most would handsome call,
Possess'd the charm that wins the heart of all ;

And, thrice entreated by a lover's prayer,
She thrice refused him with determined air.
'" No ! had the world one monarch, and was he
All that the heart could wish its lord to be,—
Lovely and loving, generous, brave, and true,—
Vain were his hopes to waken hers anew !"
For she was wedded to ideal views,
And fancy's prospects, that she would not lose,
Would not forego to be a mortal's wife,
And wed the poor realities of life.

'There was a day, ere yet the autumn closed,
When, ere her wintry wars, the earth reposed,
When from the yellow weed the feathery crown,
Light as the curling smoke, fell slowly down ;
When the wing'd insect settled in our sight,
And waited wind to recommence her flight ;
When the wide river was a silver sheet,
And on the ocean slept th' unanchor'd fleet ;
When from our garden, as we look'd above,
There was no cloud, and nothing seem'd to move ;
Then was my friend in ecstasies—she cried,
" There is, I feel there is, a world beside !
Martha, dear Martha ! we shall hear not then
Of hearts distress'd by good or evil men,
But all will constant, tender, faithful be—
So had I been, and so had one with me ;
But in this world the fondest and the best
Are the most tried, most troubled, and distress'd :
This is the place for trial, here we prove,
And there enjoy, the faithfulness of love.
'" Nay, were he here in all the pride of youth,
With honour, valour, tenderness, and truth,
Entirely mine, yet what could I secure,
Or who one day of comfort could insure ?
'" No ! all is closed on earth, and there is now
Nothing to break th' indissoluble vow ;
But in that world will be th' abiding bliss,
That pays for every tear and sigh in this."
'Such her discourse, and more refined it grew,
Till she had all her glorious dream in view ;
And she would further in that dream proceed
Than I dare go, who doubtfully agreed :
Smiling I ask'd, again to draw the soul
From flight so high, and fancy to control,
" If this be truth, the lover's happier way
Is distant still to keep the purposed day ;

The real bliss would mar the fancied joy,
And marriage all the dream of love destroy."

'She softly smiled, and as we gravely talk'd,
We saw a man who up the gravel walk'd,
Not quite erect, nor quite by age depress'd,
A travell'd man, and as a merchant dress'd ;
Large chain of gold upon his watch he wore,
Small golden buckles on his feet he bore ;
A head of gold his costly cane display'd,
And all about him love of gold betray'd.

'This comely man moved onward, and a pair
Of comely maidens met with serious air ;
Till one exclaim'd, and wildly look'd around,
" O heav'n, 'tis Paul ! " and dropt upon the
ground ;
But she recovered soon, and you must guess
What then ensued, and how much happiness.
They parted lovers, both distress'd to part !
They met as neighbours, heal'd, and whole
of heart :
She in his absence look'd to heaven for bliss,
He was contented with a world like this ;
And she prepared in some new state to meet
The man now seeking for some snug retreat.
He kindly told her he was firm and true,
Nor doubted her, and bade her then adieu !

"'What shall I do ?" the sighing maid began,
"How lost the lover ! O, how gross the man."

' For the plain dealer had his wish declared,
Nor she, devoted victim ! could be spared :
He spoke as one decided ; she as one
Who fear'd the love, and would the lover shun.

'" O Martha, sister of my soul ! how dies
Each lovely view ! for can I truth disguise,
That this is he ? No ! nothing shall persuade ;
This is a man the naughty world has made,
An eating, drinking, buying, bargaining man—
And can I love him ? No ! I never can.
What once he was, what fancy gave beside,
Full well I know, my love was then my pride ;
What time has done, what trade and travel
wrought,
You see ! and yet your sorrowing friend is
sought ;
But can I take him ? "—" Take him not,"
I cried,
" If so averse—but why so soon decide ? "

'Meantime a daily guest the man appear'd,
Set all his sail, and for his purpose steer'd ;
Loud and familiar, loving, fierce and free,
He overpower'd her soft timidity ;
Who, weak and vain, and grateful to behold
The man was hers, and hers would be the gold ;

Thus sundry motives, more than I can name,
Leagued on his part, and she a wife became.

' A home was offer'd, but I knew too well
What comfort was with married friends to
dwell ;
I was resign'd, and had I felt distress,
Again a lover offer'd some redress ;
Behold, a hero of the buskin hears
My loss, and with consoling love appears ;
Frederick was now a hero on the stage,
In all its glories, rhapsody, and rage ;
Again himself he offer'd, offer'd all
That his an hero of the kind can call.
He for my sake would hope of fame resign,
And leave the applause of all the world for
mine.
Hard fate was Frederick's never to succeed,
Yet ever try—but so it was decreed :
His mind was weaken'd ; he would laugh and
weep,
And swore profusely I had murder'd sleep,
Had quite unmann'd him, cleft his heart in
twain,
And he should never be himself again.

' He *was* himself ; weak, nervous, kind, and
poor,
Ill dress'd and idle, he besieged my door,
Borrow'd,—or, worse, made verses on my
charms,
And did his best to fill me with alarms ;
I had some pity, and I sought the price
Of my repose—my hero was not nice ;
There was a loan, and promise I should be
From all the efforts of his fondness free,
From hunger's future claims, or those of
vanity.
"Yet," said he, bowing, "do to study take !
O! what a Desdemona wouldst thou make ! "
Thus was my lover lost ; yet even now
He claims one thought, and this we will allow.

' His father lived to an extreme old age,
But never kind !—his son had left the stage,
And gain'd some office, but an humble place,
And that he lost ! Want sharpen'd his dis-
grace,
Urged him to seek his father—but too late,
His jealous brothers watch'd and barr'd the
gate.

' The old man died ; but there is one who
pays
A moderate pension for his latter days,
Who, though assured inquiries will offend,
Is ever asking for this unknown friend ;

Some partial lady, whom he hopes to find
As to his wants so to his wishes kind.
  '" Be still," a cool adviser sometimes writes—
" Nay, but," says he, " the gentle maid in-
    vites—
Do, let me know the young ! the soft ! the
    fair ! "
  ' " Old man," 'tis answer'd, " take thyself
    to prayer !
Be clean, be sober, to thy priest apply,
And—dead to all around thee—learn to die!"
  ' Now had I rest from life's strong hopes and
    fears,
And no disturbance mark'd the flying years ;
So on in quiet might those years have past,
But for a light adventure, and a last.
A handsome boy, from school-day bondage
    free,
Came with mamma to gaze upon the sea ;
With soft blue eye he look'd upon the waves,
And talk'd of treacherous rocks, and seamen's
    graves :
There was much sweetness in his boyish smile,
And signs of feelings frank, that knew not guile.
  ' The partial mother, of her darling proud,
Besought my friendship, and her own avow'd ;
She praised her Rupert's person, spirit, ease,
How fond of study, yet how form'd to please ;
In our discourse he often bore a part,
And talk'd, heaven bless him, of his feeling
    heart ;
He spoke of pleasures souls like his enjoy,
And hated Lovelace like a virtuous boy ;
He felt for Clementina's holy strife,
And was Sir Charles as large and true as life :
For Virtue's heroines was his soul distress'd ;
True love and guileless honour fill'd his breast,
When, as the subjects drew the frequent sigh,
The tear stood trembling in his large blue eye,
And softly he exclaim'd, " Sweet, sweetest
    sympathy."
  ' When thus I heard the handsome stripling
    speak,
I smiled assent, and thought to pat his cheek ;
But when I saw the feelings blushing there,
Signs of emotions strong, they said—forbear !
  ' The youth would speak of his intent to live
On that estate which heaven was pleased to
    give,
There with the partner of his joys to dwell,
And nurse the virtues that he loved so well ;
The humble good of happy swains to share,
And from the cottage drive distress and care ;

To the dear infants make some pleasures
    known,
And teach, he gravely said, the virtues to
    his own.
  ' He loved to read in verse, and verse-like
    prose,
The softest tales of love-inflicted woes ;
When, looking fondly, he would smile and cry,
" Is there not bliss in sensibility ? "
  ' We walk'd together, and it seem'd not harm
In linking thought with thought, and arm
    with arm,
Till the dear boy would talk too much of bliss,
And indistinctly murmur—" such as this."
  ' When no maternal wish her heart beguiled,
The lady call'd her son "the darling child ; "
When with some nearer view her speech
    began,
She changed her phrase, and said, "the good
    young man ! "
And lost, when hinting of some future bride,
The woman's prudence in the mother's pride,
  ' Still decent fear and conscious folly strove
With fond presumption and aspiring love ;
But now too plain to me the strife appear'd,
And what he sought I knew, and what he
    fear'd ;
The trembling hand and frequent sigh dis-
    closed
The wish that prudence, care, and time
    opposed.
  ' Was I not pleased, will you demand ?—
    Amused
By boyish love, that woman's pride refused ?
This I acknowledge, and from day to day
Resolved no longer at such game to play ;
Yet I forbore, though to my purpose true,
And firmly fix'd to bid the youth adieu.
  ' There was a moonlight eve, serenely cool,
When the vast ocean seem'd a mighty pool ;
Save the small rippling waves that gently
    beat,
We scarcely heard them falling, at our feet ;
His mother absent, absent every sound
And every sight that could the youth con-
    found ;
The arm, fast lock'd in mine, his fear betray'd,
And when he spoke not, his designs convey'd ;
He oft-times gasp'd for breath, he tried to
    speak,
And studying words, at last had words to seek.
  ' Silent the boy, by silence more betray'd,
And feeling lest he should appear afraid,

He knelt abruptly, and his speech began—
" Pity the pangs of an unhappy man."
　'" Be sure," I answer'd, "and relieve them
　　too—
But why that posture ? What the woes to
　　you ?
To feel for others' sorrows is humane,
But too much feeling is our virtue's bane.
　'" Come, my dear Rupert ! now your tale
　　disclose,
That I may know the sufferer and his woes,
Know there is pain that wilful man endures,
That our reproof and not our pity cures ;
For though for such assumed distress we
　　grieve,
Since they themselves as well as us deceive,
Yet we assist not."——The unhappy youth,
Unhappy then, beheld not all the truth.
　'" O ! what is this ? " exclaim'd the dubious
　　boy,
" Words that confuse the being they destroy ?
So have I read the gods to madness drive
The man condemn'd with adverse fate to
　　strive ;
O ! make thy victim though by misery sure,
And let me know the pangs I must endure ;
For, like the Grecian warrior, I can pray
Falling, to perish in the face of day."
　' " Pretty, my Rupert ; and it proves the
　　use
Of all that learning which the schools pro-
　　duce :
But come, your arm—no trembling, but
　　attend
To sober truth, and a maternal friend.
　'" You ask for pity ? "—" O ! indeed I do."
" Well then, you have it, and assistance too :
Suppose us married ! "—" O ! the heavenly
　　thought ! "
" Nay—nay, my friend, be you by wisdom
　　taught ;
For wisdom tells you, love would soon sub-
　　side,
Fall, and make room for penitence and pride ;
Then would you meet the public eye, and
　　blame
Your private taste, and be o'erwhelm'd with
　　shame :
How must it then your bosom's peace de-
　　stroy
To hear it said, ' The mother and her boy ! '
And then to show the sneering world it lies,
You would assume the man, and tyrannize ;

Ev'n Time, Care's general soother, would
　　augment
Your self-reproaching, growing discontent.
　' " Add twenty years to my precarious life,
And lo ! your aged, feeble, wailing wife ;
Displeased, displeasing. discontented, blamed;
Both, and with cause, ashaming and ashamed :
When I shall bend beneath a press of time,
Thou wilt be all erect in manhood's prime ;
Then wilt thou fly to younger minds t' assuage
Thy bosom's pain, and I in jealous age
Shall move contempt, if still ; if active, rage :
And though in anguish all my days are past,
Yet far beyond thy wishes they may last ;
May last till thou, thy better prospects fled,
Shall have no comfort when thy wife is dead.
　' " Then thou in turn, though none will call
　　thee old,
Will feel thy spirit fled, thy bosom cold ;
No strong or eager wish to wake the will,
Life will appear to stagnate and be still,
As now with me it slumbers ; O ! rejoice
That I attend not to that pleading voice ;
So will new hopes this troubled dream suc-
　　ceed,
And one will gladly hear my Rupert plead."
　' Ask you, while thus I could the youth deny,
Was I unmoved ?—Inexorable I,
Fix'd and determined : thrice he made his
　　prayer,
With looks of sadness first, and then despair ;
Thrice doom'd to bear refusal, not exempt,
At the last effort, from a slight contempt.
　' Did his distress, his pains, your joy ex-
　　cite ?—
No ; but I fear'd his perseverance might.
Was there no danger in the moon's soft
　　rays,
To hear the handsome stripling's earnest
　　praise ?
Was there no fear that while my words
　　reproved
The eager youth, I might myself be moved ?
Not for his sake alone I cried " persist
No more," and with a frown the cause dis-
　　miss'd.
　' Seek you th' event ?—I scarcely need reply,
Love, unreturn'd, will languish, pine, and
　　die :
We lived awhile in friendship, and with joy
I saw depart in peace the amorous boy.
We met some ten years after, and he then
Was married, and as cool as married men ;

He talk'd of war and taxes, trade and farms,
And thought no more of me, or of my charms.
   ' We spoke; and when, alluding to the past,
Something of meaning in my look I cast,
He, who could never thought or wish disguise,
Look'd in my face with trouble and surprise ;
To kill reserve, I seized his arm, and cried,
" Know me, my lord ! "   when laughing, he
       replied,

Wonder'd again, and look'd upon my face,
And seem'd unwilling marks of time to trace ;
But soon I brought him fairly to confess,
That boys in love judge ill of happiness.
   ' Love had his day—to graver subjects
       led,
My will is govern'd, and my mind is fed ;
And to more vacant bosoms I resign
The hopes and fears that once affected mine.'

BOOK XII.   SIR OWEN DALE

The Rector at the Hall—Why absent—He
relates the Story of Sir Owen—His Marriage
—Death of his Lady—His Mind acquires
new Energy—His passions awake—His
Taste and Sensibility—Admires a Lady—
Camilla—Her Purpose—Sir Owen's Dis-
appointment—His Spirit of Revenge—How
gratified—The Dilemma of Love—An ex-
ample of Forgiveness—Its Effect.

AGAIN the Brothers saw their friend the
       priest,
Who shared the comforts he so much in-
       creased ;
Absent of late—and thus the squire address'd,
With welcome smile, his ancient friend and
       guest.
   ' What has detain'd thee ? some parochial
       case ?
Some man's desertion, or some maid's dis-
       grace ?
Or wert thou call'd, as parish priest, to give
Name to a new-born thing that would not live,
That its weak glance upon the world had
       thrown,
And shrank in terror from the prospect
       shown ?
Or hast thou heard some dying wretch deplore,
That of his pleasures he could taste no more ?
Who wish'd thy aid his spirits to sustain,
And drive away the fears that gave him pain ?
For priests are thought to have a patent
       charm
To ease the dying sinner of alarm :
Or was thy business of the carnal sort,
And thou wert gone a patron's smile to court,
And Croft or Cresswell would'st to Binning
       add,
Or take, kind soul ! whatever could be had ?

Once more I guess : th' election now is near ;
My friend, perhaps, is sway'd, by hope or fear,
And all a patriot's wishes, forth to ride,
And hunt for votes to prop the fav'rite side ? '
   ' More private duty call'd me hence, to pay
My friends respect on a rejoicing day,'
Replied the rector : ' there is born a son,
Pride of an ancient race, who pray'd for one,
And long desponded. Would you hear the
       tale—
Ask, and 'tis granted—of Sir Owen Dale ? '
   ' Grant,' said the Brothers, ' for we humbly
       ask ;
Ours be the gratitude, and thine the task :
Yet dine we first : then to this tale of thine,
As to thy sermon, seriously incline ;
In neither case our rector shall complain,
Of this recited, that composed in vain.
   ' Something we heard of vengeance, who
       appall'd,
Like an infernal spirit, him who call'd ;
And, ere he vanished, would perform his part,
Inflicting tortures on the wounded heart ;
Of this but little from report we know :
If you the progress of revenge can show,
Give it, and all its horrors, if you please,
We hear our neighbour's sufferings much at
       ease.
   ' Is it not so ? For do not men delight—
We call them men—our bruisers to excite,
And urge with bribing gold, and feed them
       for the fight ?
Men beyond common strength, of giant size,
And threat'ning terrors in each other's eyes ;
When in their naked, native force display'd,
Look answers look, affrighting and afraid ;
While skill, like spurs and feeding, gives the
       arm
The wicked power to do the greater harm :

Maim'd in the strife, the falling man sustains
Th' insulting shout, that aggravates his
    pains :—
Man can bear this ; and shall thy hearers heed
A tale of human sufferings ? Come ! proceed.'
    Thus urged, the worthy rector thought it
        meet
Some moral truth, as preface to repeat ;
Reflection   serious,—common-place,   'tis
    true,—
But he would act as he was wont to do,
And bring his morals in his neighbour's view.
    ' O ! how the passions, insolent and strong,
Bear our weak minds their rapid course along ;
Make us the madness of their will obey ;
Then die, and leave us to our griefs a prey ! '

    ' Sir Owen Dale his fortieth year had seen,
With temper placid, and with mind serene ;
Rich ; early married to an easy wife,
They led in comfort a domestic life :
He took of his affairs a prudent care,
And was by early habit led to spare ;
Not as a miser, but in pure good taste,
That scorn'd the idle wantonness of waste.
    ' In fact, the lessons he from prudence took
Were written in his mind, as in a book :
There what to do he read, and what to shun ;
And all commanded was with promptness done ;
He seem'd without a passion to proceed,
Or one whose passions no correction need ;
Yet some believed those passions only slept,
And were in bounds by early habits kept :
Curb'd as they were by fetters worn so long,
There were who judged them a rebellious
    throng.
    ' To these he stood, not as a hero true,
Who fought his foes, and in the combat slew,
But one who all those foes, when sleeping,
    found,
And, unresisted, at his pleasure bound.
    ' We thought—for I was one—that we espied
Some indications strong of dormant pride ;
It was his wish in peace with all to live ;
And he could pardon, but could not forgive :
Nay, there were times when stern defiance
    shook
The moral man, and threaten'd in his look.
    ' Should these fierce passions—so we reason'd
    —break
Their long-worn chain, what ravage will they
    make !

In vain will prudence then contend with pride,
And reason vainly bid revenge subside ;
Anger will not to meek persuasion bend,
Nor to the pleas of hope or fear attend :
What curb shall, then, in their disorder'd race,
Check the wild passions ? what the calm
    replace ?
Virtue shall strive in vain ; and has he help
    in grace ?
    ' While yet the wife with pure discretion
    ruled,
The man was guided, and the mind was
    school'd ;
But then that mind unaided ran to waste :
He had some learning, but he wanted taste :
Placid, not pleased—contented, not em-
    ploy'd,—
He neither time improved, nor life enjoy'd.
    ' That wife expired, and great the loss sus-
    tain'd,
Though much distress he neither felt nor
    feign'd ;
He loved not warmly ; but the sudden stroke
Deeply and strongly on his habits broke.
    ' He had no child to soothe him, and his
    farm,
His sports, his speculations, lost their charm ;
Then would he read and travel, would fre
    quent
Life's busy scenes, and forth Sir Owen went :
The mind, that now was free, unfix'd, un-
    check'd,
Read and observed with wonderful effect ;
And still the more he gain'd, the more he
    long'd
To pay that mind his negligence had wrong'd ;
He felt his pleasures rise as he improved ;
And, first enduring, then the labour loved.
    ' But, by the light let in, Sir Owen found
Some of those passions had their chain un-
    bound ;
As from a trance they rose to act their part,
And seize, as due to them, a feeling heart.
    ' His very person now appear'd refined,
And took some graces from th' improving
    mind :
He grew polite without a fix'd intent,
And to the world a willing pupil went.
    ' Restore him twenty years,—restore him
    ten,—
And bright had been his earthly prospect then ;
But much refinement, when it late arrives,
May be the grace, not comfort, of our lives.

'Now had Sir Owen feeling ; things of late
Indifferent, he began to love or hate ;
What once could neither good nor ill impart
Now pleased the senses, and now touch'd the
    heart ;
Prospects and pictures struck th' awaken'd
    sight,
And each new object gave a new delight.
He, like th' imperfect creature who had shaped
A shroud to hide him, had at length escaped ;
Changed from his grub-like state, to crawl no
    more,
But a wing'd being, pleased and form'd to
    soar.
   'Now, said his friends, while thus his views
    improve,
And his mind softens, what if he should love ?
True ; life with him has yet serene appear'd,
And therefore love in wisdom should be
    fear'd :
Forty and five his years, and then to sigh
For beauty's favour !—Son of frailty, fly !
   'Alas ! he loved ; it was our fear, but ours,
His friends alone. He doubted not his pow'rs
To win the prize, or to repel the charm,
To gain the battle, or escape the harm ;
For he had never yet resistance proved,
Nor fear'd that friends should say—"Alas !
    he loved."
   'Younger by twenty years, Camilla found
Her face unrivall'd when she smiled or
    frown'd :
Of all approved ; in manner, form, and air,
Made to attract ; gay, elegant, and fair :
She had, in beauty's aid, a fair pretence
To cultivated, strong intelligence ;
For she a clear and ready mind had fed
With wholesome food ; unhurt by what she
    read ;
She loved to please ; but, like her dangerous
    sex,
To please the more whom she design'd to
    vex.
   'This heard Sir Owen, and he saw it true ;
It promised pleasure, promised danger too ;
But this he knew not then, or slighted if he
    knew.
   'Yet he delay'd, and would by trials prove
That he was safe ; would see the signs of love ;
Would not address her while a fear remain'd ;
But win his way, assured of what he gain'd.
   'This saw the lady, not displeased to find
A man at once so cautious and so blind :

She saw his hopes that she would kindly show
Proofs of her passion—then she his should
    know.
   ' " So, when my heart is bleeding in his sight,
His love acknowledged will the pains requite ;
It is, when conquer'd, he the heart regards ;
Well, good Sir Owen ! let us play our cards."
   'He spake her praise in terms that love
    affords,
By words select, and looks surpassing words :
Kindly she listen'd, and in turn essay'd
To pay th' applauses—and she amply paid
A beauty flattering !—beauteous flatterers
    feel
The ill you cause, when thus in praise you
    deal ;
For surely he is more than man, or less,
When praised by lips that he would die to
    press,
And yet his senses undisturbed can keep,
Can calmly reason, or can soundly sleep.
   'Not so Sir Owen ; him Camilla praised,
And lofty hopes and strong emotions raised ;
This had alone the strength of man subdued ;
But this enchantress various arts pursued.
   'Let others pray for music—others pray'd
In vain :—Sir Owen ask'd, and was obey'd ;
Let others, walking, sue that arm to take,
Unmoved she kept it for Sir Owen's sake ;
Each small request she granted, and though
    small,
He thought them pledges of her granting all.
   'And now the lover, casting doubt aside,
Urged the fond suit that—could not be
    denied ;
Joy more than reverence moved him when
    he said,
" Now banish all my fears, angelic maid ! "
And as she paused for words, he gaily cried,
" I must not, cannot, will not be denied."
   'Ah ! good Sir Owen, think not favours,
    such
As artful maids allow, amount to much ;
The sweet, small, poison'd baits, that take
    the eye
And win the soul of all who venture nigh.
   'Camilla listen'd, paused, and look'd surprise,
Fair witch ! exulting in her witcheries !
She turn'd aside her face, withdrew her hand,
And softly said, " Sir, let me understand."
   ' " Nay, my dear lady ! what can words
    explain,
If all my looks and actions plead in vain ?

I love."—She show'd a cool respectful air,
And he began to falter in his prayer,
Yet urged her kindness—Kindness she con-
    fess'd,
It was esteem, she felt it, and express'd,
For her dear father's friend ; and was it right
That friend of his—she thought of hers—to
    slight ?
    'This to the wond'ring lover strange and
        new,
And false appear'd—he would not think it
    true :
Still he pursued the lovely prize, and still
Heard the cold words, design'd his hopes to
    kill ;
He felt dismay'd, as he perceived success
Had inverse ratio, more obtaining less ;
And still she grew more cool in her replies,
And talk'd of age and improprieties.
    'Then to his friends, although it hurt his
        pride,
And to the lady's, he for aid applied ;
Who kindly woo'd for him, but strongly were
    denied.
    And now it was those fiercer passions rose,
Urged by his love to murder his repose ;
Shame shook his soul to be deceived so long,
And fierce revenge for such contemptuous
    wrong ;
Jealous he grew, and jealousy supplied
His mind with rage, unsooth'd, unsatisfied ;
And grievous were the pangs of deeply
    wounded pride.
His generous soul had not the grief sustain'd,
Had he not thought, " revenge may be
    obtain'd."
    'Camilla grieved, but grief was now too late;
She hush'd her fears, and left th' event to fate;
Four years elapsed, nor knew Sir Owen yet
How to repay the meditated debt ;
The lovely foe was in her thirtieth year,
Nor saw the favourite of the heart appear ;
'Tis sure less sprightly the fair nymph became,
And spoke of former levities with shame :
But this, alas ! was not in time confess'd,
And vengeance waited in Sir Owen's breast.
    'But now the time arrives—the maid must
        feel
And grieve for wounds that she refused to heal.
Sir Owen, childless, in his love had rear'd
A sister's son, and now the youth appear'd
In all the pride of manhood, and, beside,
With all a soldier's spirit and his pride :

Valiant and poor, with all that arms bestow,
And wants that captains in their quarters
    know ;
Yet to his uncle's generous heart was due
The praise, that wants of any kind were few.
    'When he appear'd, Sir Owen felt a joy
Unknown before, his vengeance bless'd the
    boy—
" To him I dare confide a cause so just ;
Love him she may—O ! could I say, she must."
    'Thus fix'd, he more than usual kindness
        show'd,
Nor let the captain name the debt he owed ;
But when he spoke of gratitude, exclaim'd,
" My dearest Morden ! make me not ashamed;
Each for a friend should do the best he can,
The most obliged is the obliging man ;
But if you wish to give as well as take,
You may a debtor of your uncle make."
    'Morden was earnest in his wish to know
How he could best his grateful spirit show.
    'Now the third dinner had their powers
        renew'd,
And fruit and wine upon the table stood ;
The fire brought comfort, and the warmth it
    lent
A cheerful spirit to the feelings sent,
When thus the uncle—" Morden, I depend
On you for aid—assist me as a friend :
Full well I know that you would much forego,
And much endure, to wreak me on my foe.
Charles, I am wrong'd, insulted—nay, be still,
Nor look so fiercely,—there are none to kill.
    ' "I loved a lady, somewhat late in life,
Perhaps too late, and would have made a wife;
Nay, she consented ; for consent I call
The mark'd distinction that was seen of all,
And long was seen ; but when she knew my
    pain,
Saw my first wish her favour to obtain,
And ask her hand—no sooner was it ask'd,
Than she the lovely Jezebel unmask'd ;
And by her haughty airs, and scornful
    pride,
My peace was wounded—nay, my reason
    tried ;
I felt despised and fallen when we met,
And she, O folly ! looks too lovely yet ;
Yet love no longer in my bosom glows,
But my heart warms at the revenge it owes.
    ' "O ! that I saw her with her soul on fire,
Desperate from love, and sickening with
    desire;

While all beheld her just, unpitied pain,
Grown in neglect, and sharpen'd by disdain !
Let her be jealous of each maid she sees,
Striving by every fruitless art to please,
And when she fondly looks, let looks and
    fondness tease !
So, lost on passion's never resting sea,
Hopeless and helpless, let her think of me.
    " Charles, thou art handsome, nor canst
    want the art
To warm a cold or win a wanton heart ;
Be my avenger "——
        Charles, with smile, not vain,
Nor quite unmix'd with pity and disdain,
Sate mute in wonder ; but he sate not long
Without reflection :—Was Sir Owen wrong ?
" So must I think ; for can I judge it right
To treat a lovely lady with despite ?
Because she play'd too roughly with the love
Of a fond man whom she could not approve,
And yet to vex him for the love he bore
Is cause enough for his revenge, and more.
    ' " But, thoughts, to council !—Do I wear
    a charm
That will preserve my citadel from harm ?
Like the good knight, I have a heart that feels
The wounds that beauty makes and kindness
    heals :
Beauty she has, it seems, but is not kind—
So found Sir Owen, and so I may find.
    ' " Yet why, O ! heart of tinder, why afraid ?
Comes so much danger from so fair a maid ?
    ' " Wilt thou be made a voluntary prize
To the fierce firing of two wicked eyes ?
Think her a foe, and on the danger rush,
Nor let thy kindred for a coward blush.
    ' " But how if this fair creature should incline
To think too highly of this love of mine,
And, taking all my counterfeit address
For sterling passion, should the like profess ?
    ' " Nay, this is folly ; or if I perceive
Ought of the kind, I can but take my leave ;
And if the heart should feel a little sore,
Contempt and anger will its ease restore.
    ' " Then, too, to his all-bounteous hand I owe
All I possess, and almost all I know ;
And shall I for my friend no hazard run,
Who seeks no more for all his love has done ?
    ' " 'Tis but to meet and bow, to talk and
    smile,
To act a part, and put on love awhile :
And the good knight shall see, this trial made,
That I have just his talents to persuade ;

For why the lady should her heart bestow
On me, or I of her enamour'd grow,
There 's none can reason give, there 's none
    can danger show."
    ' These were his rapid thoughts, and then
    he spoke.
" I make a promise, and will not revoke ;
You are my judge in what is fit and right,
And I obey you—bid me love or fight ;
Yet had I rather, so the act could meet
With your concurrence,—not to play the
    cheat ;
In a fair cause "——" Charles, fighting for
    your king,
Did you e'er judge the merits of the thing ?
Show me a monarch who has cause like mine,
And yet what soldier would his cause decline ? "
    ' Poor Charles or saw not, or refused to see,
How weak the reasoning of our hopes may be,
And said—" Dear uncle, I my king obey'd,
And for his glory's sake the soldier play'd ;
Now a like duty shall your nephew rule,
And for your vengeance I will play the fool."
    ' 'Twas well ; but ere they parted for repose,
A solemn oath must the engagement close.
    ' " Swear to me, nephew, from the day you
    meet
This cruel girl, there shall be no deceit ;
That by all means approved and used by man
You win this dangerous woman, if you can ;
That being won, you my commands obey,
Leave her lamenting, and pursue your way ;
And that, as in my business, you will take
My will as guide, and no resistance make :
Take now an oath—within the volume look,
There is the Gospel—swear, and kiss the
    book."
    ' " It cannot be," thought Charles, " he
    cannot rest
In this strange humour,—it is all a jest,
All but dissimulation——Well, sir, there ;
Now I have sworn as you would have me
    swear."
    ' " 'Tis well," the uncle said in solemn tone ;
" Now send me vengeance, Fate, and groan
    for groan ! "
    ' The time is come : the soldier now must
    meet
Th' unconscious object of the sworn deceit.
They meet ; each other's looks the pair
    explore,
And, such their fortune, wish'd to part no
    more.

Whether a man is thus disposed to break
An evil compact he was forced to make,
Or whether some contention in the breast
Will not permit a feeling heart to rest ;
Or was it nature, who in every case
Has made such mind subjected to such face ;
Whate'er the cause, no sooner met the pair
Than both began to love, and one to feel
     despair.
   ' But the fair damsel saw with strong delight
Th' impression made, and gloried in the sight :
No chilling doubt alarm'd her tender breast,
But she rejoiced in all his looks profess'd ;
Long ere his words her lover's hopes convey'd
They warm'd the bosom of the conscious
     maid ;
One spirit seem'd each nature to inspire,
And the two hearts were fix'd in one desire.
   ' " Now," thought the courteous maid, " my
     father's friend
Will ready pardon to my fault extend ;
He shall no longer lead that hermit's life,
But love his mistress in his nephew's wife ;
My humble duty shall his anger kill,
And I who fled his love will meet his will,
Prevent his least desire, and every wish fulfil."
   ' Hail, happy power ! that to the present
     lends
Such views ; not all on Fortune's wheel
     depends ;
Hope, fair enchantress, drives each cloud
     away,
And now enjoys the glad, but distant day.
   ' Still fears ensued ; for love produces fear.—
" To this dear maid can I indeed be dear ?
My fatal oath, alas ! I now repent ;
Stern is his purpose, he will not relent ;
Would, ere that oath, I had Camilla seen !
I had not then my honour's victim been :
I must be honest, yet I know not how,
'Tis crime to break, and death to keep my
     vow."
   ' Sir Owen closely watch'd both maid and
     man,
And saw with joy proceed his cruel plan ;
Then gave his praise—" She has it—has it
     deep
In her capricious heart,—it murders sleep ;
You see the looks that grieve, you see the
     eyes that weep ;
Now breathe again, dear youth, the kindling
     fire,
And let her feel what she could once inspire."

   ' Alas ! obedience was an easy task,
So might he cherish what he meant to ask ;
He ventured soon, for Love prepared his way,
He sought occasion, he forbad delay ;
In spite of vow foregone he taught the youth
The looks of passion, and the words of truth ;
In spite of woman's caution, doubt and fear,
He bade her credit all she wish'd to hear ;
An honest passion ruled in either breast,
And both believed the truth that both pro-
     fess'd.
   ' But now, 'mid all her new-born hopes, the
     eyes
Of fair Camilla saw through all disguise,
Reserve, and apprehension——Charles, who
     now
Grieved for his duty, and abhorr'd his vow,
Told the full fact, and it endear'd him more ;
She felt her power, and pardon'd all he swore,
Since to his vow he could his wish prefer,
And loved the man who gave his world for
     her.
   ' What must they do, and how their work
     begin,
Can they that temper to their wishes win ?
They tried, they fail'd ; and all they did
     t' assuage
The tempest of his soul provoked his rage ;
The uncle met the youth with angry look,
And cried, " Remember, sir, the oath you
     took ;
You have my pity, Charles, but nothing more,
Death, and death only, shall her peace restore ;
And am I dying ?—I shall live to view
The harlot's sorrow, and enjoy it too.
   ' " How ! Words offend you ? I have borne
     for years
Unheeded anguish, shed derided tears,
Felt scorn in every look, endured the stare
Of wondering fools, who never felt a care ;
On me all eyes were fix'd, and I the while
Sustain'd the insult of a rival's smile.
   ' " And shall I now—entangled thus my foe,
My honest vengeance for a boy forego ?
A boy forewarn'd, forearm'd ? Shall this be
     borne,
And I be cheated, Charles, and thou for-
     sworn ?
Hope not, I say, for thou mayst change as
     well
The sentence graven on the gates of hell—
Here bid adieu to hope,—here hopeless beings
     dwell.

'" But does she love thee, Charles? I cannot
        live
Dishonour'd, unrevenged—I may forgive,
But to thy oath I bind thee; on thy soul
Seek not my injured spirit to control;
Seek not to soften, I am hard of heart,
Harden'd by insult:—leave her now, and
        part,
And let me know she grieves while I enjoy
        her smart."
  'Charles first in anger to the knight replied,
Then felt the clog upon his soul, and sigh'd :
To his obedience made his wishes stoop,
And now admitted, now excluded hope;
As lovers do, he saw a prospect fair,
And then so dark, he sank into despair.
  'The uncle grieved; he even told the youth
That he was sorry, and it seem'd a truth;
But though it vex'd, it varied not his mind,
He bound himself, and would his nephew
        bind.
  '" I told him this, placed danger in his view,
Bade him be certain, bound him to be true;
And shall I now my purposes reject,
Because my warnings were of no effect ? "
  'Thus felt Sir Owen as a man whose cause
Is very good—it had his own applause.'

  'Our knight a tenant had in high esteem,
His constant boast, when justice was his
        theme :
He praised the farmer's sense, his shrewd
        discourse,
Free without rudeness, manly, and not coarse;
As farmer, tenant, nay, as man, the knight
Thought Ellis all that is approved and right ;
Then he was happy, and some envy drew,
For knowing more than other farmers knew ;
They call'd him learned, and it sooth'd their
        pride,
While he in his was pleased and gratified.
  'Still more t' offend, he to the altar led
The vicar's niece, to early reading bred ;
Who, though she freely ventured on the life,
Could never fully be the farmer's wife ;
She had a softness, gentleness, and ease,
Sure a coarse mind to humble and displease :
O ! had she never known a fault beside,
How vain their spite, how impotent their
        pride !
  'Three darling girls the happy couple bless'd,
Who now the sweetest lot of life possess'd ;

For what can more a grateful spirit move
Than health, with competence, and peace,
        with love ?
Ellis would sometimes, thriving man ! retire
To the town inn, and quit the parlour fire ;
But he was ever kind where'er he went,
And trifling sums in his amusement spent :
He bought, he thought for her—she should
        have been content :
Oft, when he cash received at Smithfield mart,
At Cranbourn-alley he would leave a part ;
And, if to town he follow'd what he sold,
Sure was his wife a present to behold.
  'Still, when his evenings at the inn were
        spent,
She mused at home in sullen discontent ;
And, sighing, yielded to a wish that some
With social spirit to the farm would come :
There was a farmer in the place, whose name,
And skill in rural arts, was known to fame ;
He had a pupil, by his landlord sent,
On terms that gave the parties much content ;
The youth those arts, and those alone, should
        learn,
With aught beside his guide had no concern :
He might to neighb'ring towns or distant ride,
And there amusements seek without a guide :
With handsome prints his private room was
        graced,
His music there, and there his books were
        placed :
Men knew not if he farm'd, but they allow'd
        him taste.
  'Books, prints, and music, cease, at times,
        to charm,
And sometimes men can neither ride nor farm ;
They look for kindred minds, and Cecil found
In farmer Ellis, one inform'd and sound ;
But in his wife—I hate the fact I tell—
A lovely being, who could please too well :
And he was one who never would deny
Himself a pleasure, or indeed would try.
  'Early and well the wife of Ellis knew
Where danger was, and trembled at the view ;
So evil spirits tremble, but are still
Evil, and lose not the rebellious will :
She sought not safety from the fancied crime,
"And why retreat before the dangerous time ?"
  'Oft came the student of the farm and read,
And found his mind with more than reading
        fed :
This Ellis seeing, left them, or he staid,
As pleased him, not offended nor afraid :

He came in spirits with his girls to play,
Then ask excuse, and, laughing, walk away :
When, as he entered, Cecil ceased to read,
He would exclaim, " Proceed, my friend, pro-
     ceed ! "
Or, sometimes weary, would to bed retire,
And fear and anger by his ease inspire.
' " My conversation does he then despise ?
Leaves he this slighted face for other eyes ? "
So said Alicia ; and she dwelt so long
Upon that thought, to leave her was to wrong.
' Alas ! the woman loved the soothing tongue,
That yet pronounced her beautiful and young ;
The tongue that, seeming careless, ever
     praised ;
The eye that roving, on her person gazed ;
The ready service, on the watch to please ;
And all such sweet, small courtesies as these.
' Still there was virtue, but a rolling stone
On a hill's brow is not more quickly gone ;
The slightest motion,—ceasing from our
     care,—
A moment's absence,—when we're not
     aware,—
When down it rolls, and at the bottom lies,
Sunk, lost, degraded, never more to rise !
Far off the glorious height from whence it
     fell,
With all things base and infamous to dwell.
Friendship with woman is a dangerous thing—
Thence hopes avow'd and bold confessions
     spring :
Frailties confess'd to other frailties lead,
And new confessions new desires succeed ;
And, when the friends have thus their hearts
     disclosed,
They find how little is to guilt opposed.
' The foe's attack will on the fort begin,
When he is certain of a friend within.
' When all was lost,—or, in the lover's sight,
When all was won,—the lady thought of
     flight.
' " What ! sink a slave ? " she said, " and
     with deceit
The rigid virtue of a husband meet ?
No ! arm'd with death, I would his fury
     brave,
And own the justice of the blow he gave !
But thus to see him easy, careless, cold,
And his confiding folly to behold ;
To feel incessant fears that he should read,
In looks assumed, the cause whence they
     proceed,

I cannot brook ; nor will I here abide
Till chance betrays the crime that shame
     would hide :
Fly with me, Henry ! " Henry sought in vain
To soothe her terrors and her griefs restrain :
He saw the lengths that women dared to go,
And fear'd the husband both as friend and foe.
Of farming weary—for the guilty mind
Can no resource in guiltless studies find,
Left to himself, his mother all unknown,
His titled father, loth the boy to own,
Had him to decent expectations bred,
A favour'd offspring of a lawless bed ;
And would he censure one who should pursue
The way he took ? Alicia yet was new :
Her passion pleased him : he agreed on flight :
They fix'd the method, and they chose the
     night.
' Then, while the farmer read of public
     crimes,
Collating coolly Chronicles and Times,
The flight was taken by the guilty pair,
That made one passage in the columns there.
' The heart of Ellis bled ; the comfort, pride,
The hope and stay of his existence died ;
Rage from the ruin of his peace arose,
And he would follow and destroy his foes ;
Would with wild haste the guilty pair pursue,
And when he found—Good heaven ! what
     would he do ?
' That wretched woman he would wildly seize,
And agonize her heart, his own to ease ;
That guilty man would grasp, and in her sight
Insult his pangs, and her despair excite ;
Bring death in view, and then the stroke
     suspend,
And draw out tortures till his life should end :
O ! it should stand recorded in all time,
How they transgress'd, and he avenged the
     crime !
' In this bad world should all his business
     cease,
He would not seek—he would not taste of
     peace ;
But wrath should live till vengeance had her
     due,
And with his wrath his life should perish too.
' His girls—not his—he would not be so
     weak—
Child was a word he never more must speak !
How did he know what villains had defiled
His honest bed ?—He spurn'd the name of
     child :

Keep them he must; but he would coarsely hide
Their forms, and nip the growth of woman's pride;
He would consume their flesh, abridge their food,
And kill the mother-vices in their blood.

'All this Sir Owen heard, and grieved for all;
He with the husband mourn'd Alicia's fall;
But urged the vengeance with a spirit strong,
As one whose own rose high against the wrong:
He saw his tenant by this passion moved,
Shared in his wrath, and his revenge approved.
    'Years now unseen, he mourn'd this tenant's fate,
And wonder'd how he bore his widow'd state;
Still he would mention Ellis with the pride
Of one who felt himself to worth allied:
Such were his notions—had been long, but now
He wish'd to see if vengeance lived, and how:
He doubted not a mind so strong must feel
Most righteously, and righteous measures deal.
    'Then would he go, and haply he might find
Some new excitement for a weary mind;
Might learn the miseries of a pair undone,
One scorn'd and hated, lost and perish'd one:
Yes, he would praise to virtuous anger give,
And so his vengeance should be nursed and live.
    'Ellis was glad to see his landlord come,
A transient joy broke in upon his gloom,
And pleased he led the knight to the superior room
Where she was wont in happier days to sit,
Who paid with smiles his condescending wit.
    'There the sad husband, who had seldom been
Where prints acquired in happier days were seen,
Now struck by these, and carried to the past,
A painful look on every object cast:
Sir Owen saw his tenant's troubled state,
But still he wish'd to know the offenders' fate.
    ' " Know you they suffer, Ellis ? "—Ellis knew;—
" 'Tis well ! 'tis just ! but have they all their due ?
Have they in mind and body, head and heart,
Sustain'd the pangs of their accursed part ? "

' " They have ! "—" 'Tis well ! "—" and wants enough to shake
The firmest mind, the stoutest heart to break."
" But have you seen them in such misery dwell ? "
" In misery past description."—"That is well."
    ' " Alas ! Sir Owen, it perhaps is just,—
Yet I began my purpose to distrust;
For they to justice have discharged a debt,
That vengeance surely may her claim forget."
    ' " Man, can you pity ? "
                        " As a man I feel
Miseries like theirs."
                        " But never would you heal ? "
    ' " Hear me, Sir Owen:—I had sought them long,
Urged by the pain of ever present wrong,
Yet had not seen; and twice the year came round—
Years hateful now—ere I my victims found :
But I did find them, in the dungeon's gloom
Of a small garret—a precarious home,
For that depended on the weekly pay,
And they were sorely frighten'd on the day;
But there they linger'd on from week to week,
Haunted by ills of which 'tis hard to speak,
For they are many and vexatious all,
The very smallest—but they none were small.
    ' " The roof, unceil'd in patches, gave the snow
Entrance within, and there were heaps below;
I pass'd a narrow region dark and cold,
The strait of stairs to that infectious hold ;
And, when I enter'd, misery met my view
In every shape she wears, in every hue,
And the bleak icy blast across the dungeon flew ;
There frown'd the ruin'd walls that once were white ;
There gleam'd the panes that once admitted light ;
There lay unsavoury scraps of wretched food;
And there a measure, void of fuel, stood ;
But who shall part by part describe the state
Of these, thus follow'd by relentless fate ?
All, too, in winter, when the icy air
Breathed its black venom on the guilty pair.
    ' " That man, that Cecil !—he was left, it seems,
Unnamed, unnoticed : farewell to his dreams !
Heirs made by law rejected him of course,
And left him neither refuge nor resource :—

Their father's ? No : he was the harlot's son
Who wrong'd them, whom their duty bade
    them shun ;
And they were duteous all, and he was all
    undone.
   ' " Now the lost pair, whom better times
    had led
To part disputing, shared their sorrow's bed :
Their bed !—I shudder as I speak—and shared
Scraps to their hunger by the hungry spared."
   ' " Man ! my good Ellis ! can you sigh ? "—
    " I can :
In short, Sir Owen, I must feel as man ;
And could you know the miseries they
    endured,
The poor, uncertain pittance they procured ;
When, laid aside the needle and the pen,
Their sickness won the neighbours of their den,
Poor as they are, and they are passing poor,
To lend some aid to those who needed more :
Then, too, an ague with the winter came,
And in this state—that wife I cannot name
Brought forth a famish'd child of suffering
    and of shame.
   ' " This had you known, and traced them to
    this scene,
Where all was desolate, defiled, unclean,
A fireless room, and, where a fire had place,
The blast loud howling down the empty space,
You must have felt a part of the distress,
Forgot your wrongs, and made their suffering
    less ! "
   ' " Sought you them, Ellis, from the mean
    intent
To give them succour ? "
               " What indeed I meant
At first was vengeance ; but I long pursued
The pair, and I at last their misery view'd
In that vile garret, which I cannot paint—
The sight was loathsome, and the smell was
    faint ;
And there that wife,—whom I had loved so
    well,
And thought so happy, was condemn'd to
    dwell ;
The gay, the grateful wife, whom I was glad
To see in dress beyond our station clad,
And to behold among our neighbours fine,
More than perhaps became a wife of mine ;
And now among her neighbours to explore,
And see her poorest of the very poor !—
I would describe it, but I bore a part,
Nor can explain the feelings of the heart ;

Yet memory since has aided me to trace
The horrid features of that dismal place.
   ' " There she reclined unmoved, her bosom
    bare
To her companion's unimpassion'd stare,
And my wild wonder :—Seat of virtue !
    chaste
As lovely once ! O ! how wert thou dis-
    graced !
Upon that breast, by sordid rags defiled,
Lay the wan features of a famish'd child ;—
That sin-born babe in utter misery laid,
Too feebly wretched even to cry for aid ;
The ragged sheeting, o'er her person drawn,
Served for the dress that hunger placed in
    pawn.
   ' " At the bed's feet the man reclined his
    frame :
Their chairs were perish'd to support the
    flame
That warm'd his agued limbs ; and, sad to
    see,
That shook him fiercely as he gazed on me
   ' " I was confused in this unhappy view :
My wife ! my friend ! I could not think it
    true ;
My children's mother,—my Alicia,—laid
On such a bed ! so wretched,—so afraid !
And her gay, young seducer, in the guise
Of all we dread, abjure, defy, despise,
And all the fear and terror in his look,
Still more my mind to its foundation shook.
   ' " At last he spoke :—' Long since I would
    have died,
But could not leave her, though for death
    I sigh'd,
And tried the poison'd cup, and dropt it as
    I tried.
   ' " ' She is a woman, and that famish'd thing
Makes her to life, with all its evils, cling :
Feed her, and let her breathe her last in peace,
And all my sufferings with your promise
    cease ! '
   ' " Ghastly he smiled ;—I knew not what
    I felt,
But my heart melted—hearts of flint would
    melt,
To see their anguish, penury, and shame,
How base, how low, how grovelling they
    became :
I could not speak my purpose, but my
    eyes
And my expression bade the creature rise.

' " Yet, O ! that woman's look ! my words
    are vain
Her mix'd and troubled feelings to explain ;
True, there was shame and consciousness of
    fall,
But yet remembrance of my love withal,
And knowledge of that power which she
    would now recal.
' " But still the more that she to memory
    brought,
The greater anguish in my mind was wrought;
The more she tried to bring the past in view,
She greater horror on the present threw ;
So that, for love or pity, terror thrill'd
My blood, and vile and odious thoughts
    instill'd.
' " This war within, these passions in their
    strife,
If thus protracted, had exhausted life ;
But the strong view of these departed years
Caused a full burst of salutary tears,
And as I wept at large, and thought alone,
I felt my reason re-ascend her throne."
    ' " My friend ! " Sir Owen answer'd, " what
       became
Of your just anger ?—when you saw their
    shame,
It was your triumph, and you should have
    shown
Strength, if not joy—their sufferings were
    their own."
  ' " Alas, for them ! their own in very deed !
And they of mercy had the greater need ;
Their own by purchase, for their frailty paid,—
And wanted heaven's own justice human aid ?
And seeing this, could I beseech my God
For deeper misery, and a heavier rod ? "
  ' " But could you help them ? "—" Think, Sir
    Owen, how
I saw them then—methinks I see them now !
She had not food, nor aught a mother needs,
Who for another life and dearer feeds :
I saw her speechless ; on her wither'd breast
The wither'd child extended, but not prest,
Who sought, with moving lip and feeble cry,
Vain instinct ! for the fount without supply.
  ' " Sure it was all a grievous, odious scene,
Where all was dismal, melancholy, mean,
Foul with compell'd neglect, unwholesome,
    and unclean ;
That arm,—that eye,—the cold, the sunken
    cheek,—
Spoke all, Sir Owen—fiercely miseries speak ! '

  ' " And you relieved ? "
          ' " If hell's seducing crew
Had seen that sight, they must have pitied
    too."
  ' " Revenge was thine—thou hadst the power,
    the right ;
To give it up was heaven's own act to slight."
  ' " Tell me not, sir, of rights, and wrongs, or
    powers !
I felt it written—Vengeance is not ours ! "
  ' " Well, Ellis, well !—I find these female foes,
Or good or ill, will murder our repose ;
And we, when Satan tempts them, take the
    cup,
The fruit of their foul sin, and drink it up :
But shall our pity all our claims remit,
And we the sinners of their guilt acquit ? "
  ' " And what, Sir Owen, will our vengeance
    do ?
It follows us when we our foe pursue,
And, as we strike the blow, it smites the
    smiters too."
  ' " What didst thou, man ? "
          ' " I brought them to a cot
Behind your larches,—a sequester'd spot,
Where dwells the woman : I believe her mind
Is now enlighten'd—I am sure resign'd :
She gave her infant, though with aching heart
And faltering spirit, to be nursed apart."
  ' " And that vile scoundrel "——
        ' " Nay, his name restore,
And call him Cecil,—for he is no more :
When my vain help was offer'd, he was past
All human aid, and shortly breathed his last ;
But his heart open'd, and he lived to see
Guilt in himself, and find a friend in me.
  ' " Strange was their parting, parting on the
    day
I offer'd help, and took the man away,
Sure not to meet again, and not to live
And taste of joy—He feebly cried, ' Forgive !
I have thy guilt, thou mine, but now adieu !
Tempters and tempted ! what will thence
    ensue
I know not, dare not think ! '—He said, and
    he withdrew."
  ' " But, Ellis, tell me, didst thou thus desire
To heap upon their heads those coals of
    fire ?
  ' " If fire to melt, that feeling is confest,—
If fire to shame, I let that question rest ;
But if aught more the sacred words imply,
I know it not—no commentator I."

' " Then did you freely from your soul for-
give ? "—
' " Sure as I hope before my Judge to live,
Sure as I trust his mercy to receive,
Sure as his word I honour and believe,
Sure as the Saviour died upon the tree
For all who sin,—for that dear wretch and
me,—
Whom never more on earth will I forsake
or see."

' Sir Owen softly to his bed adjourn'd,
Sir Owen quickly to his home return'd ;
And all the way he meditating dwelt
On what this man in his affliction felt ;
How he, resenting first, forbore, forgave,
His passion's lord, and not his anger's slave :
And as he rode he seem'd to fear the deed
Should not be done, and urged unwonted
speed.

' Arrived at home, he scorn'd the change to
hide,
Nor would indulge a mean and selfish pride,
That would some little at a time recal
Th' avenging vow ; he now was frankness all:
He saw his nephew, and with kindness spoke—
"Charles, I repent my purpose, and revoke;
Take her—I'm taught, and would I could
repay
The generous teacher ; hear me, and obey :
Bring me the dear coquette, and let me vow
On lips half perjured to be passive now :
Take her, and let me thank the powers divine
She was not stolen when her hand was mine,
Or when her heart—Her smiles I must forget,
She my revenge, and cancel either debt."
' Here ends our tale, for who will doubt the
bliss
Of ardent lovers in a case like this ?
And if Sir Owen's was not half so strong,
It may, perchance, continue twice as long.'

BOOK XIII. DELAY HAS DANGER

Morning excursion—Lady at Silford, who ?—
Reflections on Delay—Cecilia and Henry—
The Lovers contracted—Visit to the Patron
—Whom he finds there—Fanny described
—The yielding of Vanity—Delay—Resent-
ment—Want of Resolution—Further En-
tanglement—Danger—How met—Conclu-
sion.

THREE weeks had past, and Richard
rambles now
Far as the dinners of the day allow ;
He rode to Farley Grange and Finley Mere,
That house so ancient, and that lake so clear :
He rode to Ripley through that river gay,
Where in the shallow streams the loaches play,
And stony fragments stay the winding stream,
And gilded pebbles at the bottom gleam,
Giving their yellow surface to the sun,
And making proud the waters as they run :
It is a lovely place, and at the side
Rises a mountain-rock in rugged pride ;
And in that rock are shapes of shells, and
forms
Of creatures in old worlds, of nameless worms,
Whose generations lived and died ere man,
A worm of other class, to crawl began.

There is a town call'd Silford, where his
steed
Our traveller rested—He the while would feed
His mind by walking to and fro, to meet,
He knew not what adventure, in the street :
A stranger there, but yet a window-view
Gave him a face that he conceived he knew :
He saw a tall, fair, lovely lady, dress'd
As one whom taste and wealth had jointly
bless'd ;
He gazed, but soon a footman at the door
Thundering, alarm'd her, who was seen no
more.
' This was the lady whom her lover bound
In solemn contract, and then proved unsound:
Of this affair I have a clouded view,
And should be glad to have it clear'd by
you.'
So Richard spake, and instant George
replied,
' I had the story from the injured side,
But when resentment and regret were gone,
And pity (shaded by contempt) came on.
Frail was the hero of my tale, but still
Was rather drawn by accident than will ;
Some without meaning into guilt advance,
From want of guard, from vanity, from chance;

Man's weakness flies his more immediate pain,
A little respite from his fears to gain ;
And takes the part that he would gladly fly,
If he had strength and courage to deny.
  ' But now my tale, and let the moral say,
When hope can sleep, there 's danger in delay.
Not that for rashness, Richard, I would plead,
For unadvised alliance : No, indeed :
Think ere the contract—but, contracted, stand
No more debating, take the ready hand :
When hearts are willing, and when fears
    subside,
Trust not to time, but let the knot be tied ;
For when a lover has no more to do,
He thinks in leisure, what shall I pursue ?
And then who knows what objects come in
    view ?
For when, assured, the man has nought to
    keep
His wishes warm and active, then they sleep :
Hopes die with fears ; and then a man must
    lose
All the gay visions, and delicious views,
Once his mind's wealth ! He travels at his
    ease,
Nor horrors now nor fairy-beauty sees ;
When the kind goddess gives the wish'd assent,
No mortal business should the deed prevent ;
But the blest youth should legal sanction seek
Ere yet th' assenting blush has fled the cheek.
  ' And—hear me, Richard,—man has reptile-
    pride
That often rises when his fears subside ;
When, like a trader feeling rich, he now
Neglects his former smile, his humble bow,
And, conscious of his hoarded wealth, assumes
New airs, nor thinks how odious he becomes.
  ' There is a wandering, wavering train of
    thought
That something seeks where nothing should
    be sought,
And will a self-delighted spirit move
To dare the danger of pernicious love.

  ' First be it granted all was duly said
By the fond youth to the believing maid ;
Let us suppose with many a sigh there came
The declaration of the deathless flame ;—
And so her answer—" She was happy then,
Blest in herself, and did not think of men ;
And with such comforts in her present state,
A wish to tempt it was to tempt her fate ;

That she would not ; but yet she would
    confess
With him she thought her hazard would be
    less ;
Nay, more, she would esteem, she would
    regard express :
But to be brief—if he could wait and see
In a few years what his desires would be." '—
  ' Henry for years read months, then weeks,
    nor found
The lady thought his judgment was unsound ;
" For months read weeks " she read it to his
    praise,
And had some thoughts of changing it to *days*.
  ' And here a short excursion let me make,
A lover tried, I think, for lovers' sake ;
And teach the meaning in a lady's mind
When you can none in her expressions find :
Words are design'd that meaning to convey,
But often *Yea* is hidden in a *Nay* !
And what the charmer wills, some gentle
    hints betray.
  ' Then, too, when ladies mean to yield at
    length,
They match their reasons with the lover's
    strength,
And, kindly cautious, will no force employ
But such as he can baffle or destroy.
  ' As when heroic lovers beauty woo'd,
And were by magic's mighty art withstood,
The kind historian, for the dame afraid,
Gave to the faithful knight the stronger aid.
  ' A downright *No !* would make a man de-
    spair,
Or leave for kinder nymph the cruel fair ;
But ' *No !* because I'm very happy now,
Because I dread th' irrevocable vow,
Because I fear papa will not approve,
Because I love not—No, I cannot love ;
Because you men of Cupid make a jest,
Because——in short, a single life is best.'
A *No !* when back'd by reasons of such force,
Invites approach, and will recede of course.
  ' Ladies, like towns besieged, for honour's
    sake,
Will some defence or its appearance make ;
On first approach there 's much resistance
    made,
And conscious weakness hides in bold parade ;
With lofty looks, and threat'nings stern and
    proud,
" Come, if you dare," is said in language
    loud,

But if th' attack be made with care and skill,
"Come," says the yielding party, "if you will;"
Then each the other's valiant acts approve,
And twine their laurels in a wreath of love.—
 'We now retrace our tale, and forward go,—
Thus Henry rightly read Cecilia's No!
His prudent father, who had duly weigh'd,
And well approved the fortune of the maid,
Not much resisted, just enough to show
He knew his power, and would his son should
  know.
 ' "Harry, I will, while I your bargain make,
That you a journey to our patron take :
I know her guardian ; care will not become
A lad when courting ; as you must be dumb,
You may be absent ; I for you will speak,
And ask what you are not supposed to seek."
 'Then came the parting hour, and what arise
When lovers part ! expressive looks and eyes,
Tender and tear-full,—many a fond adieu,
And many a call the sorrow to renew ;
Sighs such as lovers only can explain,
And words that they might undertake in vain.
 'Cecilia liked it not ; she had, in truth,
No mind to part with her enamour'd youth ;
But thought it foolish thus themselves to
  cheat,
And part for nothing but again to meet.
 ' Now Henry's father was a man whose heart
Took with his interest a decided part ;
He knew his lordship, and was known for acts
That I omit,—they were acknowledged facts ;
An interest somewhere ; I the place forget,
And the good deed—no matter—'twas a debt :
Thither must Henry, and in vain the maid
Express'd dissent—the father was obey'd.
 'But though the maid was by her fears
  assail'd,
Her reason rose against them, and prevail'd ;
Fear saw him hunting, leaping, falling—led,
Maim'd and disfigured, groaning to his bed ;
Saw him in perils, duels,—dying,—dead.
But Prudence answer'd, "Is not every maid
With equal cause for him she loves afraid ?"
And from her guarded mind Cecilia threw
The groundless terrors that will love pursue.
 ' She had no doubts, and her reliance strong
Upon the honour that she would not wrong :
Firm in herself, she doubted not the truth
Of him, the chosen, the selected youth ;
Trust of herself a trust in him supplied,
And she believed him faithful, though un-
  tried :

On her he might depend, in him she would
  confide.
 ' If some fond girl express'd a tender pain
Lest some fair rival should allure her swain,
To such she answer'd, with a look severe,
"Can one you doubt be worthy of your fear ?"
 'My lord was kind,—a month had pass'd
  away,
And Henry stay'd,—he sometimes named
  a day ;
But still my lord was kind, and Henry still
  must stay :
His father's words to him were words of fate—
"Wait, 'tis your duty ; 'tis my pleasure,
  wait ! "
In all his walks, in hilly heath or wood,
Cecilia's form the pensive youth pursued ;
In the gray morning, in the silent noon,
In the soft twilight, by the sober moon,
In those forsaken rooms, in that immense
  saloon ;
And he, now fond of that seclusion grown,
There reads her letters, and there writes his
  own.
 "Here none approach," said he, "to inter-
  fere,
But I can think of my Cecilia here ! "
 ' But there did come—and how it came to
  pass
Who shall explain ?—a mild and blue-eyed
  lass ;—
It was the work of accident, no doubt—
The cause unknown—we say, ' as things fall
  out ; '—
The damsel enter'd there, in wand'ring round
  about :
At first she saw not Henry ; and she ran,
As from a ghost, when she beheld a man.
 'She was esteem'd a beauty through the hall,
And so admitted, with consent of all ;
And, like a treasure, was her beauty kept
From every guest who in the mansion slept
Whether as friends who join'd the noble pair,
Or those invited by the steward there.
 'She was the daughter of a priest, whose life
Was brief and sad : he lost a darling wife,
And Fanny then her father, who could save
But a small portion ; but his all he gave,
With the fair orphan, to a sister's care,
And her good spouse : they were the ruling
  pair—
Steward and steward's lady—o'er a tribe,
Each under each, whom I shall not describe.

'This grave old couple, childless and alone,
Would, by their care, for Fanny's loss atone:
She had been taught in schools of honest
    fame;
And to the hall, as to a home, she came,
My lord assenting: yet, as meet and right,
Fanny was held from every hero's sight,
Who might in youthful error cast his eyes
On one so gentle as a lawful prize,
On border land, whom, as their right or
    prey,
A youth from either side might bear away.
Some handsome lover of th' inferior class
Might as a wife approve the lovely lass;
Or some invader from the class above,
Who, more presuming, would his passion prove
By asking less—love only for his love.
  'This much experienced aunt her fear ex-
    press'd,
And dread of old and young, of host and guest.
  '"Go not, my Fanny, in their way," she
    cried,
"It is not right that virtue should be tried;
So, to be safe, be ever at my side."
  'She was not ever at that side; but still
Observed her precepts, and obey'd her will.
  'But in the morning's dawn and evening's
    gloom
She could not lock the damsel in her room;
And Fanny thought, "I will ascend these
    stairs
To see the chapel,—there are none at prayers;
None," she believed, "had yet to dress re-
    turn'd,
By whom a timid girl might be discern'd:"
In her slow motion, looking, as she glides,
On pictures, busts, and what she met besides,
And speaking softly to herself alone,
Or singing low in melancholy tone;
And thus she rambled through the still
    domain,
Room after room, again, and yet again.
  'But, to retrace our story, still we say,
To this saloon the maiden took her way;
Where she beheld our youth, and frighten'd ran,
And so their friendship in her fear began.
  'But dare she thither once again advance,
And still suppose the man will think it chance?
Nay, yet again, and what has chance to do
With this?—I know not: doubtless Fanny
    knew.
  'Now, of the meeting of a modest maid
And sober youth why need we be afraid?

And when a girl's amusements are so few
As Fanny's were, what would you have
    her do?
Reserved herself, a decent youth to find,
And just be civil, sociable, and kind,
And look together at the setting sun,
Then at each other—What the evil done?
  'Then Fanny took my little lord to play,
And bade him not intrude on Henry's way:
"O, he intrudes not!" said the youth, and
    grew
Fond of the child, and would amuse him too;
Would make such faces, and assume such
    looks—
He loved it better than his gayest books.
  'When man with man would an acquaint-
    ance seek,
He will his thoughts in chosen language speak;
And they converse on divers themes, to find
If they possess a corresponding mind;
But man with woman has foundation laid,
And built up friendship ere a word is said:
'Tis not with words that they their wishes tell,
But with a language answering quite as well;
And thus they find, when they begin t' explore
Their way by speech, they knew it all before.
  'And now it chanced again the pair, when
    dark,
Met in their way, when wandering in the park;
Not in the common path, for so they might,
Without a wonder, wander day or night;
But, when in pathless ways their chance will
    bring
A musing pair, we do admire the thing.
  'The youth in meeting read the damsel's
    face,
As if he meant her inmost thoughts to trace;
On which her colour changed, as if she meant
To give her aid, and help his kind intent.
  'Both smiled and parted, but they did not
    speak—
The smile implied, "Do tell me what you
    seek:"
They took their different ways with erring
    feet,
And met again, surprised that they could
    meet;
Then must they speak—and something of
    the air
Is always ready—" 'Tis extremely fair!"
  '"It was so pleasant!" Henry said; "the
    beam
Of that sweet light so brilliant on the stream;

And chiefly yonder, where that old cascade
Has for an age its simple music made ;
All so delightful, soothing, and serene !
Do you not feel it ? not enjoy the scene ?
Something it has that words will not express,
But rather hide, and make th' enjoyment less :
'Tis what our souls conceive, 'tis what our
     hearts confess."
  ' Poor Fanny's heart at these same words
     confess'd
How well he painted, and how rightly guess'd ;
And, while they stood admiring their retreat,
Henry found something like a mossy seat ;
But Fanny sat not ; no, she rather pray'd
That she might leave him, she was so afraid.
  ' " Not, sir, of you ; your goodness I can
     trust,
But folks are so censorious and unjust,
They make no difference, they pay no regard
To our true meaning, which is very hard
And very cruel ; great the pain it cost
To lose such pleasure, but it must be lost :
Did people know how free from thought of
     ill
One's meaning is, their malice would be still."
  ' At this she wept ; at least a glittering gem
Shone in each eye, and there was fire in them,
For as they fell, the sparkles, at his feet,
He felt emotions very warm and sweet.
  ' " A lovely creature ! not more fair than
     good,
By all admired, by some, it seems, pursued,
Yet self-protected by her virtue's force
And conscious truth—What evil in discourse
With one so guarded, who is pleased to trust
Herself with me, reliance strong and just ? "
  ' Our lover then believed he must not seem
Cold to the maid who gave him her esteem ;
Not manly this ; Cecilia had his heart,
But it was lawful with his time to part ;
It would be wrong in her to take amiss
A virtuous friendship for a girl like this ;
False or disloyal he would never prove,
But kindness here took nothing from his love :
Soldiers to serve a foreign prince are known,
When not on present duty to their own ;
So, though our bosom's queen we still prefer,
We are not always on our knees to her.
" Cecilia present, witness yon fair moon,
And yon bright orbs, that fate would change
     as soon
As my devotion ; but the absent sun
Cheers us no longer when his course is run ;

And then those starry twinklers may obtain
A little worship till he shines again."
  ' The father still commanded " Wait awhile,"
And the son answer'd in submissive style,
Grieved, but obedient ; and obedience teased
His lady's spirit more than grieving pleased :
That he should grieve in absence was most fit,
But not that he to absence should submit ;
And in her letters might be traced reproof,
Distant indeed, but visible enough ;
This should the wandering of his heart have
     stay'd ;
Alas ! the wanderer was the vainer made.
  ' The parties daily met, as by consent,
And yet it always seem'd by accident ;
Till in the nymph the shepherd had been blind
If he had fail'd to see a manner kind,
With that expressive look, that seem'd to say,
" You do not speak, and yet you see you may."
  ' O ! yes, he saw, and he resolved to fly,
And blamed his heart, unwilling to comply :
He sometimes wonder'd how it came to pass,
That he had all this freedom with the lass ;
Reserved herself, with strict attention kept,
And care and vigilance that never slept :
" How is it thus that they a beauty trust
With me, who feel the confidence is just ?
And they, too, feel it ; yes, they may con-
     fide."—
He said in folly, and he smiled in pride.
  ' 'Tis thus our secret passions work their way,
And the poor victims know not they obey.
  ' Familiar now became the wandering pair,
And there was pride and joy in Fanny's air ;
For though his silence did not please the maid,
She judged him only modest and afraid ;
The gentle dames are ever pleased to find
Their lovers dreading they should prove un-
     kind ;
So, blind by hope, and pleased with prospects
     gay,
The generous beauty gave her heart away
Before he said, " I love ! "—alas ! he dared
     not say.
  ' Cecilia yet was mistress of his mind,
But oft he wished her, like his Fanny, kind ;
Her fondness sooth'd him, for the man was
     vain,
And he perceived that he could give her pain :
Cecilia liked not to profess her love,
But Fanny ever was the yielding dove ;
Tender and trusting, waiting for the word,
And then prepared to hail her bosom's lord.

Cecilia once her honest love avow'd,
To make him happy, not to make him proud;
But she would not, for every asking sigh,
Confess the flame that waked his vanity;
But this poor maiden, every day and hour,
Would, by fresh kindness, feed the growing
        power;
And he indulged, vain being! in the joy,
That he alone could raise it, or destroy;
A present good, from which he dared not fly,
Cecilia absent, and his Fanny by.
    'O! vain desire of youth, that in the hour
Of strong temptation, when he feels the power,
And knows how daily his desires increase,
Yet will he wait, and sacrifice his peace,
Will trust to chance to free him from the snare,
Of which, long since, his conscience said
        beware!
Or look for strange deliverance from that ill,
That he might fly, could he command the
        will!
How can he freedom from the future seek,
Who feels already that he grows too weak?
And thus refuses to resist, till time
Removes the power, and makes the way for
        crime:
Yet thoughts he had, and he would think,
    " Forego
My dear Cecilia? not for kingdoms! No!
But may I, ought I not the friend to be
Of one who feels this fond regard for me?
I wrong no creature by a kindness lent
To one so gentle, mild, and innocent;
And for that fair one, whom I still adore,
By feeling thus I think of her the more;"
And not unlikely, for our thoughts will tend
To those whom we are conscious we offend.
    'Had Reason whisper'd, "Has Cecilia leave
Some gentle youth in friendship to receive,
And be to him the friend that you appear
To this soft girl?—would not some jealous
        fear
Proclaim your thoughts, that he approach'd
        too near?"
    'But Henry, blinded still, presumed to write
Of one in whom Cecilia would delight;
A mild and modest girl, a gentle friend,
If, as he hoped, her kindness would descend—
But what he fear'd to lose or hoped to gain
By writing thus, he had been ask'd in vain.
    'It was his purpose, every morn he rose,
The dangerous friendship he had made to
        close;

It was his torment nightly, ere he slept,
To feel his prudent purpose was not kept.
    'True, he has wonder'd why the timid maid
Meets him so often, and is not afraid;
And why that female dragon, fierce and keen,
Has never in their private walks been seen;
And often he has thought, " What can their
        silence mean?'
    ' "They can have no design, or plot, or
        plan,—
In fact, I know not how the thing began,—
'Tis their dependence on my credit here,
And fear not, nor, in fact, have cause to fear."
    ' But did that pair, who seem'd to think
        that all
Unwatch'd will wander and unguarded fall,
Did they permit a youth and maid to meet
Both unreproved? were they so indiscreet?
    ' This sometimes enter'd Henry's mind, and
        then,
" Who shall account for women or for men?"
He said, " or who their secret thoughts ex-
        plore?
Why do I vex me? I will think no more."
My lord of late had said, in manner kind,
" My good friend Harry, do not think us
        blind!"
Letters had past, though he had nothing seen,
His careful father and my lord between;
But to what purpose was to him unknown—
It might be borough business, or their own.
    ' Fanny, it seem'd, was now no more in
        dread,
If one approach'd, she neither fear'd nor fled:
He mused on this,—" But wherefore her
        alarm?
She knows me better, and she dreads no
        harm."
    ' Something his father wrote that gave him
        pain:
" I know not, son, if you should yet remain;—
Be cautious, Harry, favours to procure
We strain a point, but we must first be sure:
Love is a folly,—that, indeed, is true,—
But something still is to our honour due,
So I must leave the thing to my good lord
        and you."
    ' But from Cecilia came remonstrance strong:
" You write too darkly, and you stay too
        long;
We hear reports; and, Henry,—mark me
        well,—
I heed not every tale that triflers tell;—

Be you no trifler ; dare not to believe
That I am one whom words and vows deceive:
You know your heart, your hazard you will
　　learn,
And this your trial—— instantly return."
　' " Unjust, injurious, jealous, cruel maid!
Am I a slave, of haughty words afraid ?
Can she who thus commands expect to be
　　obey'd ?
O ! how unlike this dear assenting soul,
Whose heart a man might at his will control ! "
　' Uneasy, anxious, fill'd with self-reproof,
He now resolved to quit his patron's roof ;
And then again his vacillating mind
To stay resolved, and that her pride should
　　find :
Debating thus, his pen the lover took,
And chose the words of anger and rebuke.
　' Again, yet once again, the conscious pair
Met, and " O, speak ! " was Fanny's silent
　　prayer ;
And, " I must speak," said the embarrass'd
　　youth,
" Must save my honour, must confess the truth :
Then I must lose her ; but, by slow degrees,
She will regain her peace, and I my ease."
　' Ah ! foolish man ! to virtue true nor vice,
He buys distress, and self-esteem the price ;
And what his gain ?—a tender smile and sigh
From a fond girl to feed his vanity.
　' Thus every day they lived, and every time
They met, increased his anguish and his crime.
　' Still in their meetings they were ofttimes
　　nigh
The darling theme, and then past trembling
　　by ;
On those occasions Henry often tried
For the sad truth—and then his heart denied
The utterance due : thus daily he became
The prey of weakness, vanity, and shame.
　' But soon a day, that was their doubts to
　　close,
On the fond maid and thoughtless youth arose.
　' Within the park, beside the bounding brook,
The social pair their usual ramble took ;
And there the steward found them : they
　　could trace
News in his looks, and gladness in his face.
　' He was a man of riches, bluff and big,
With clean brown broad-cloth, and with white
　　cut wig :
He bore a cane of price, with riband tied,
And a fat spaniel waddled at his side :

To every being whom he met he gave
His looks expressive ; civil, gay, or grave,
But condescending all ; and each declared
How much he govern'd, and how well he fared.
　' This great man bow'd, not humbly, but
　　his bow
Appear'd familiar converse to allow :
The trembling Fanny, as he came in view,
Within the chestnut grove in fear withdrew ;
While Henry wonder'd, not without a fear,
Of that which brought th' important man so
　　near :
Doubt was dispersed by—"My esteem'd young
　　man ! "
As he with condescending grace began——
　' " Though you with youthful frankness
　　nobly trust
Your Fanny's friends, and doubtless think
　　them just ;
Though you have not, with craving soul, applied
To us, and ask'd the fortune of your bride,
Be it our care that you shall not lament
That love has made you so improvident.
　' " An orphan maid——Your patience ! you
　　shall have
Your time to speak, I now attention crave ;—
Fanny, dear girl ! has in my spouse and me
Friends of a kind we wish our friends to be,
None of the poorest——nay, sir, no reply,
You shall not need——and we are born to die :
And one yet crawls on earth, of whom, I say,
That what he has he cannot take away ;
Her mother's father, one who has a store
Of this world's good, and always looks for
　　more ;
But, next his money, loves the girl at heart,
And she will have it when they come to part."
　' " Sir," said the youth, his terrors all awake,
" Hear me, I pray, I beg,—for mercy's sake !
Sir, were the secrets of my soul confess'd,
Would you admit the truths that I protest
Are such——your pardon " ----
　　　　　　　" Pardon ! good, my friend,
I not alone will pardon, I commend :
Think you that I have no remembrance left
Of youthful love, and Cupid's cunning theft ?
How nymphs will listen when their swains
　　persuade,
How hearts are gain'd, and how exchange is
　　made ?—
Come, sir, your hand "——
　　　　　　　" In mercy, hear me now ! "
" I cannot hear you, time will not allow:

You know my station, what on me depends,
For ever needed—but we part as friends;
And here comes one who will the whole explain,
My better self—and we shall meet again."
'"Sir, I entreat"——
            "Then be entreaty made
To her, a woman, one you may persuade;
A little teasing, but she will comply,
And loves her niece too fondly to deny."
'"O! he is mad, and miserable I!"'
Exclaim'd the youth; "But let me now collect
My scatter'd thoughts, I something must effect."
    'Hurrying she came—"Now, what has he confess'd,
Ere I could come to set your heart at rest?
What! he has grieved you! Yet he, too, approves
The thing! but man will tease you, if he loves.
    '"But now for business: tell me, did you think
That we should always at your meetings wink?
Think you, you walk'd unseen? There are who bring
To me all secrets—O, you wicked thing!
    '"Poor Fanny! now I think I see her blush,
All red and rosy, when I beat the bush;
And hide your secret, said I, if you dare!
So out it came, like an affrighten'd hare.
    '"Miss! said I gravely; and the trembling maid
Pleased me at heart to see her so afraid;
And then she wept;—now, do remember this,
Never to chide her when she does amiss;
For she is tender as the callow bird,
And cannot bear to have her temper stirr'd;—
Fanny, I said, then whisper'd her the name,
And caused such looks—Yes, yours are just the same;
But hear my story—When your love was known
For this our child—she is, in fact, our own—
Then, first debating, we agreed at last
To seek my lord, and tell him what had past."
    '"To tell the earl?"
            "Yes, truly, and why not?
And then together we contrived our plot."
    '"Eternal God!"
            "Nay, be not so surprised,—
In all the matter we were well advised;

We saw my lord, and **Lady Jane was there,**
And said to Johnson, 'Johnson, take a chair:'
True, we are servants in a certain way,
But in the higher places so are they;
We are obey'd in ours, and they in theirs obey—
So Johnson bow'd, for that was right and fit,
And had no scruple with the earl to sit—
Why look you so impatient while I tell
What they debated?—you must like it well.
    '"'Let them go on,' our gracious earl began;
'They will go off,' said, joking, my good man:
'Well!' said the countess,—she's a lover's friend,
'What if they do, they make the speedier end'——
But be you more composed, for that dear child
Is with her joy and apprehension wild:
O! we have watch'd you on from day to day,
'There go the lovers!' we were wont to say—
But why that look?"—
            "Dear madam, I implore
A single moment!"
            "I can give no more:
Here are your letters—that's a female pen,
Said I to Fanny—''tis his sister's, then,'
Replied the maid.—No! never must you stray;
Or hide your wanderings, if you should, I pray;
I know, at least I fear, the best may err,
But keep the by-walks of your life from her:
That youth should stray is nothing to be told,
When they have sanction in the grave and old,
Who have no call to wander and transgress,
But very love of change and wantonness.
    '"I prattle idly, while your letters wait,
And then my lord has much that he would state,
All good to you—do clear that clouded face,
And with good looks your lucky lot embrace.
    '"Now, mind that none with her divide your heart,
For she would die ere lose the smallest part;
And I rejoice that all has gone so well,
For who th' effect of Johnson's rage can tell?
He had his fears when you began to meet,
But I assured him there was no deceit:

He is a man who kindness will requite,
But injured once, revenge is his delight ;
And he would spend the best of his estates
To ruin, goods and body, them he hates ;
While he is kind enough when he approves
A deed that 's done, and serves the man he
     loves :
Come, read your letters—I must now be gone,
And think of matters that are coming on."
     'Henry was lost,—his brain confused, his
     soul
Dismay'd and sunk, his thoughts beyond
     control ;
Borne on by terror, he foreboding read
Cecilia's letter ! and his courage fled ;
All was a gloomy, dark, and dreadful view,
He felt him guilty, but indignant too :—
And as he read, he felt the high disdain
Of injured men—" She may repent in vain."
     ' Cecilia much had heard, and told him all
That scandal taught—" A servant at the hall,
Or servant's daughter, in the kitchen bred,
Whose father would not with her mother wed,
Was now his choice ! a blushing fool, the toy,
Or the attempted, both of man and boy ;
More than suspected, but without the wit
Or the allurements for such creatures fit ;
Not virtuous though unfeeling, cold as ice
And yet not chaste, the weeping fool of vice ;
Yielding, not tender ; feeble, not refined ;
Her form insipid, and without a mind.
     '" Rival ! she spurn'd the word ; but let
     him stay,
Warn'd as he was ! beyond the present day,
Whate'er his patron might object to this,
The uncle-butler, or the weeping miss—
Let him from this one single day remain,
And then return ! he would to her, in vain ;
There let him then abide, to earn, or crave
Food undeserved ! and be with slaves a slave."
     'Had reason guided anger, govern'd zeal,
Or chosen words to make a lover feel,
She might have saved him—anger and abuse
Will but defiance and revenge produce.
     ' " Unjust and cruel, insolent and proud ! "
He said, indignant, and he spoke aloud.
" Butler ! and servant ! Gentlest of thy sex,
Thou wouldst not thus a man who loved thee
     vex ;
Thou wouldst not thus to vile report give ear,
Nor thus enraged for fancied crimes appear ;
I know not what, dear maid !—if thy soft
     smiles were here."

And then, that instant, there appear'd the
     maid,
By his sad looks in her reproach dismay'd ;
Such timid sweetness, and so wrong'd, did
     more
Than all her pleading tenderness before.
     'In that weak moment, when disdain and
     pride,
And fear and fondness, drew the man aside,
In this weak moment—" Wilt thou," he began,
" Be mine ? " and joy o'er all her features ran ;
" I will ! " she softly whisper'd ; but the roar
Of cannon would not strike his spirit more ;
Ev'n as his lips the lawless contract seal'd
He felt that conscience lost her seven-fold
     shield,
And honour fled ; but still he spoke of love,
And all was joy in the consenting dove.
     'That evening all in fond discourse was spent,
When the sad lover to his chamber went,
To think on what had past, to grieve and to
     repent :
Early he rose, and look'd with many a sigh
On the red light that fill'd the eastern sky ;
Oft had he stood before, alert and gay,
To hail the glories of the new-born day :
But now dejected, languid, listless, low,
He saw the wind upon the water blow,
And the cold stream curl'd onward as the gale
From the pine-hill blew harshly down the dale ;
On the right side the youth a wood survey'd,
With all its dark intensity of shade ;
Where the rough wind alone was heard to
     move,
In this, the pause of nature and of love,
When now the young are rear'd, and when
     the old,
Lost to the tie, grow negligent and cold—
Far to the left he saw the huts of men,
Half hid in mist, that hung upon the fen ;
Before him swallows, gathering for the sea,
Took their short flights, and twitter'd on the
     lea ;
And near the bean-sheaf stood, the harvest
     done,
And slowly blacken'd in the sickly sun ;
All these were sad in nature, or they took
Sadness from him, the likeness of his look,
And of his mind—he ponder'd for a while,
Then met his Fanny with a borrow'd smile.
     'Not much remain'd ; for money and my
     lord
Soon made the father of the youth accord ;

His prudence half resisted, half obey'd,
And scorn kept still the guardians of the
    maid :
Cecilia never on the subject spoke,
She seem'd as one who from a dream awoke ;
So all was peace, and soon the married pair
Fix'd with fair fortune in a mansion fair.
   ' Five years had past, and what was Henry
    then ?
The most repining of repenting men ;
With a fond, teasing, anxious wife, afraid
Of all attention to another paid ;
Yet powerless she her husband to amuse,
Lives but t' entreat, implore, resent, accuse;
Jealous and tender, conscious of defects,
She merits little, and yet much expects ;
She looks for love that now she cannot see,
And sighs for joy that never more can be ;
On his retirements her complaints intrude,
And fond reproof endears his solitude :
While he her weakness (once her kindness)
    sees,
And his affections in her languor freeze ;
Regret, uncheck'd by hope, devours his mind,
He feels unhappy, and he grows unkind.
   ' " Fool ! to be taken by a rosy cheek,
And eyes that cease to sparkle or to speak ;
Fool ! for this child my freedom to resign,
When one the glory of her sex was mine ;
While from this burthen to my soul I hide,
To think what Fate has dealt, and what denied.
   ' " What fiend possess'd me when I tamely
    gave
My forced assent to be an idiot's slave ?
Her beauty vanish'd, what for me remains ?
Th' eternal clicking of the galling chains :
Her person truly I may think my own,
Seen without pleasure, without triumph
    shown :

Doleful she sits, her children at her knees,
And gives up all her feeble powers to please ;
Whom I, unmoved, or moved with scorn,
    behold,
Melting as ice, as vapid and as cold."
   ' Such was his fate, and he must yet endure
The self-contempt that no self-love can cure :
Some business call'd him to a wealthy town
When unprepared for more than Fortune's
    frown ;
There at a house he gave his luckless name,
The master absent, and Cecilia came ;
Unhappy man ! he could not, dared not
    speak,
But look'd around, as if retreat to seek :
This she allow'd not ; but, with brow severe,
Ask'd him his business, sternly bent to hear ;
He had no courage, but he view'd that face
As if he sought for sympathy and grace ;
As if some kind returning thought to trace :
In vain ; not long he waited, but with air,
That of all grace compell'd him to despair,
She rang the bell, and, when a servant came,
Left the repentant traitor to his shame ;
But, going, spoke, " Attend this person out,
And if he speaks, hear what he comes about ! "
Then, with cool curtesy, from the room with-
    drew,
That seem'd to say, " Unhappy man, adieu ! "
   ' Thus will it be when man permits a vice
First to invade his heart, and then entice ;
When wishes vain and undefined arise,
And that weak heart deceive, seduce, sur-
    prise ;
When evil Fortune works on Folly's side,
And rash Resentment adds a spur to Pride ;
Then life's long troubles from those actions
    come,
In which a moment may decide our doom.'

BOOK XIV. THE NATURAL DEATH OF LOVE

The Rector of the Parish—His Manner of
teaching—Of living—Richard's Correspon-
dence—The Letters received—Love that
survives Marriage—That dies in con-
sequence—That is permitted to die for
Want of Care—Henry and Emma, a
Dialogue—Complaints on either Side—And
Replies—Mutual Accusation—Defence of
acknowledged Error—Means of restoring
Happiness—The one to be adopted.

RICHARD one month had with his brother
    been,
And had his guests, his friends, his favourites
    seen ;
Had heard the rector, who with decent force,
But not of action, aided his discourse :
' A moral teacher ! ' some, contemptuous,
    cried ;
He smiled, but nothing of the fact denied,

Nor, save by his fair life, to charge so strong
    replied.
Still, though he bade them not on aught rely
That was their own, but all their worth deny,
They call'd his pure advice his cold morality ;
And though he felt that earnestness and zeal,
That made some portion of his hearers feel,
Nay, though he loved the minds of men to lead
To the great points that form the Christian's
    creed,
Still he offended, for he would discuss
Points that to him seem'd requisite for us ;
And urge his flock to virtue, though he knew
The very heathen taught the virtues too :
No¬ was this moral minister afraid
To ask of inspiration's self the aid
Of truths by him so sturdily maintain'd,
That some confusion in the parish reign'd ;
' Heathens,' they said, ' can tell us right from
    wrong,
But to a Christian higher points belong.'
Yet Jacques proceeded, void of fear and
    shame,
In his old method, and obtain'd the name
Of *Moral Preacher*—yet they all agreed,
Whatever error had defiled his creed,
His life was pure, and him they could com-
    mend,
Not as their guide, indeed, but as their friend :
Truth, justice, pity, and a love of peace,
Were his—but there must approbation cease ;
He either did not, or he would not see,
That if he meant a favourite priest to be
He must not show, but learn of them, the way
To truth—he must not dictate, but obey :
They wish'd him not to bring them further
    light,
But to convince them that they now were
    right,
And to assert that justice will condemn
All who presumed to disagree with them :
In this he fail'd ; and his the greater blame,
For he persisted, void of fear or shame.
    Him Richard heard, and by his friendly aid
Were pleasant views observed and visits paid ;
He to peculiar people found his way,
And had his question answer'd,' Who are they?'
    Twice in the week came letters, and delight
Beam'd in the eye of Richard at the sight ;
Letters of love, all full and running o'er,
The paper fill'd till it could hold no more ;
Cross'd with discolour'd ink, the doublings full,
No fear that love should find abundance dull ;

Love reads unsated all that love inspires,
When most indulged, indulgence still requires ;
Look what the corners, what the crossings tell,
And lifts each folding for a fond farewell.
    George saw and smiled—' To lovers we
        allow
All this o'erflowing, but a husband thou !
A father too ; can time create no change ?
Married, and still so foolish ?—very strange !
What of this wife or mistress is the art ? '—
' The simple truth, my brother, to impart,
Her heart, whene'er she writes, feels writing
        to a heart.'
    ' Fortune, dear Richard, is thy friend—a
        wife
Like thine must soften every care of life,
And all its woes—I know a pair, whose lives
Run in the common track of men and wives ;
And half their worth, at least, this pair would
        give
Could they like thee and thy Matilda live.
    ' They were, as lovers, of the fondest kind,
With no defects in manner or in mind ;
In habit, temper, prudence, they were those
Whom, as examples, I could once propose ;
Now this, when married, you no longer trace,
But discontent and sorrow in the place :
Their pictures, taken as the pair I saw
In a late contest, I have tried to draw ;
'Tis but a sketch, and at my idle time
I put my couple in the garb of rhyme :
Thou art a critic of the milder sort,
And thou wilt judge with favour my report.
Let me premise, twelve months have flown
        away,
Swiftly or sadly, since the happy day.
    ' Let us suppose the couple left to spend
Some hours without engagement or a friend ;
And be it likewise on our mind impress'd,
They pass for persons happy and at rest ;
Their love by Hymen crown'd, and all their
        prospects bless'd.

' Love has slow death and sudden : wretches
        prove
That fate severe—the sudden death of love ;
It is as if, on day serenely bright,
Came with its horrors instantaneous night ;
Others there are with whom love dies away
In gradual waste and unperceived decay ;
Such is that death of love that nature finds
Most fitted for the use of common minds,

The natural death; but doubtless there are
    some
Who struggle hard, when they perceive it come;
Loth to be loved no longer, loth to prove
To the once dear that they no longer love;
And some with not successless arts will strive
To keep the weak'ning, fluttering flame alive.
But see my verse; in this I try to paint
The passion failing, fading to complaint,
The gathering grief for joys remember'd yet,
The vain remonstrance, and the weak regret:
First speaks the wife in sorrow, she is grieved
T' admit the truth, and would be still de-
    ceived.'

HENRY AND EMMA.

E. Well, my good sir, I shall contend no
    more;
But, O! the vows you made, the oaths you
    swore——
H. To love you always :—I confess it true;
And do I not? If not, what can I do?
Moreover think what you yourself profess'd,
And then the subject may for ever rest.
    E. Yes, sir, obedience I profess'd; I know
My debt, and wish to pay you all I owe,
Pay without murmur; but that vow was made
To you, who said it never should be paid ;—
Now truly tell me why you took such care
To make me err? I ask'd you not to swear,
But rather hoped you would my mind direct,
And say, when married, what you would
    expect.
    You may remember—it is not so long
Since you affirm'd that I could not be wrong;
I told you then—you recollect, I told
The very truth—that humour would not hold;
Not that I thought, or ever could suppose,
The mighty raptures were so soon to close—
Poetic flights of love all sunk in sullen prose.
    Do you remember how you used to hang
Upon my looks? your transports when I
    sang?
I play'd—you melted into tears; I moved—
Voice, words, and motion, how you all ap-
    proved;
A time when Emma reign'd, a time when
    Henry loved:
You recollect?
    H.   Yes, surely; and then why
The needless truths? do I the facts deny?
For this remonstrance I can see no need,
Or this impatience—if you do, proceed.

    E. O! that is now so cool, and with a
    smile
That sharpens insult—I detest the style;
And, now I talk of styles, with what delight
You read my lines—I then, it seems, could
    write:
In short, when I was present you could see
But one dear object, and you lived for me;
And now, sir, what your pleasure? Let me
    dress,
Sing, speak, or write, and you your sense
    express
Of my poor taste—my words are not correct;
In all I do is failing or defect—
Some error you will seek, some blunder will
    detect;
And what can such dissatisfaction prove?
I tell you, Henry, you have ceased to love.
    H. I own it not; but if a truth it be,
It is the fault of nature, not of me.
Remember you, my love, the fairy tale,
Where the young pairs were spell-bound in
    the vale?
When all around them gay or glorious seem'd,
And of bright views and ceaseless joys they
    dream'd;
Young love and infant life no more could
    give—
They said but half, when they exclaim'd,
    'We live!'
All was so light, so lovely, so serene,
And not a trouble to be heard or seen;
Till, melting into truth, the vision fled,
And there came miry roads and thorny ways
    instead.
Such was our fate, my charmer! we were
    found
A wandering pair, by roguish Cupid bound;
All that I saw was gifted to inspire
Grand views of bliss, and wake intense desire
Of joys that never pall, of flights that never
    tire;
There was that purple light of love, that
    bloom,
That ardent passions in their growth assume,
That pure enjoyment of the soul—O! weak
Are words such loves and glowing thoughts to
    speak!
I sought to praise thee, and I felt disdain
Of my own effort; all attempts were vain.
    Nor they alone were charming; by that
    light
All loved of thee grew lovely in my sight;

Sweet influence not its own in every place
Was found, and there was found in all things
    grace ;
Thy shrubs and plants were seen new bloom
    to bear,
Not the Arabian sweets so fragrant were,
Nor Eden's self, if aught with Eden might
    compare.
    You went the church-way walk, you
      reach'd the farm,
And gave the grass and babbling springs a
    charm ;
Crop, whom you rode,—sad rider though
    you be,—
Thenceforth was more than Pegasus to me :
Have I not woo'd your snarling cur to bend
To me the paw and greeting of a friend ?
And all his surly ugliness forgave,
Because, like me, he was my Emma's slave ?
Think you, thus charm'd, I would the spell
    revoke ?
Alas ! my love, we married, and it broke !
Yet no deceit or falsehood stain'd my breast,
What I asserted might a saint attest ;
Fair, dear, and good thou wert, nay, fairest,
    dearest, best :
Nor shame, nor guilt, nor falsehood I avow,
But 'tis by heaven's own light I see thee
    now ;
And if that light will all those glories chase,
'Tis not my wish that will the good replace.
    E. O ! sir, this boyish tale is mighty well,
But 'twas your falsehood that destroy'd the
    spell :
Speak not of nature, 'tis an evil mind
That makes you to accustom'd beauties
    blind ;
You seek the faults yourself, and then com-
    plain you find.
    H. I sought them not ; but, madam, 'tis
      in vain
The course of love and nature to restrain ;
Lo ! when the buds expand the leaves are
    green,
Then the first opening of the flower is seen ;
Then comes the honied breath and rosy
    smile,
That with their sweets the willing sense
    beguile ;
But, as we look, and love, and taste, and
    praise,
And the fruit grows, the charming flower
    decays ;

Till all is gather'd, and the wintry blast
Moans o'er the place of love and pleasure
    past.
    So 'tis with beauty,—such the opening
    grace
And dawn of glory in the youthful face ;
Then are the charms unfolded to the sight,
Then all is loveliness and all delight ;
The nuptial tie succeeds, the genial hour,
And, lo ! the falling off of beauty's flower ;
So, through all nature is the progress made,—
The bud, the bloom, the fruit,—and then we
    fade.
    Then sigh no more,—we might as well
      retain
The year's gay prime as bid that love remain,
That fond, delusive, happy, transient spell,
That hides us from a world wherein we dwell,
And forms and fits us for that fairy ground,
Where charming dreams and gay conceits
    abound ;
Till comes at length th' awakening strife and
    care,
That we, as tried and toiling men, must share.
    E. O ! sir, I must not think that heaven
      approves
Ungrateful man or unrequited loves ;
Nor that we less are fitted for our parts
By having tender souls and feeling hearts.
    H. Come, my dear friend, and let us not
      refuse
The good we have, by grief for that we lose ;
But let us both the very truth confess ;
This must relieve the ill, and may redress.
    E. O ! much I fear ! I practised no deceit,
Such as I am I saw you at my feet ;
If for a goddess you a girl would take,
'Tis you yourself the disappointment make.
    H. And I alone ?—O ! Emma, when I
      pray'd
For grace from thee, transported and afraid,
Now raised to rapture, now to terror doom'd,
Was not the goddess by the girl assumed ?
Did not my Emma use her skill to hide—
Let us be frank—her weakness and her
    pride ?
Did she not all her sex's arts pursue,
To bring the angel forward to my view ?
Was not the rising anger oft suppress'd ?
Was not the waking passion hush'd to rest ?
And when so mildly sweet you look'd and
    spoke,
Did not the woman deign to wear a cloak ?

A cloak she wore, or, though not clear my
    sight,
I might have seen her—Think you not I
    might ?
  E. O ! this is glorious !—while your passion
    lives,
To the loved maid a robe of grace it gives ;
And then, unjust ! beholds her with sur-
    prise,
Unrobed, ungracious, when the passion dies.
  H. For this, my Emma, I to Heaven
    appeal,
I felt entirely what I seem'd to feel ;
Thou wert all precious in my sight, to me
The being angels are supposed to be ;
And am I now of my deception told,
Because I'm doom'd a woman to behold ?
  E. Sir ! in few words I would a question
    ask—
Mean these reproaches that I wore a mask ?
Mean you that I by art or caution tried
To show a virtue, or a fault to hide ?
  H. I will obey you—When you seem'd to
    feel
Those books we read, and praised them with
    such zeal,
Approving all that certain friends approved,
Was it the pages, or the praise you loved ?
Nay, do not frown—I much rejoiced to find
Such early judgment in such gentle mind ;
But, since we married, have you deign'd to
    look
On the grave subjects of one favourite book ?
Or have the once-applauded pages power
T' engage their warm approver for an hour ?
  Nay, hear me further—When we view'd
    that dell,
Where lie those ruins—you must know it
    well—
When that worn pediment your walk de-
    lay'd,
And the stream gushing through the arch
    decay'd ;
When at the venerable pile you stood,
Till the does ventured on our solitude,
We were so still ! before the growing day
Call'd us reluctant from our seat away—
Tell me, was all the feeling you express'd
The genuine feeling of my Emma's breast ?
Or was it borrow'd, that her faithful slave
The higher notion of her taste might have ?
So may I judge, for of that lovely scene
The married Emma has no witness been ;

No more beheld that water, falling, flow
Through the green fern that there delights
    to grow.
  Once more permit me——Well, I know,
    you feel
For suffering men, and would their sufferings
    heal,
But when at certain huts you chose to call,
At certain seasons, was compassion all ?
I there beheld thee, to the wretched dear
As angels to expiring saints appear
When whispering hope—I saw an infant
    press'd
And hush'd to slumber on my Emma's
    breast !
Hush'd be each rude suggestion !—Well I
    know,
With a free hand your bounty you bestow ;
And to these objects frequent comforts send,
But still they see not now their pitying friend.
  A merchant, Emma, when his wealth he
    states,
Though rich, is faulty if he over-rates
His real store ; and, gaining greater trust
For the deception, should we deem him just ?
If in your singleness of heart you hide
No flaw or frailty, when your truth is tried,
And time has drawn aside the veil of love,
We may be sorry, but we must approve ;
The fancied charms no more our praise
    compel,
But doubly shines the worth that stands so
    well.
  E. O ! precious are you all, and prizes too,
Or could we take such guilty pains for you ?
Believe it not—As long as passion lasts,
A charm about the chosen maid it casts ;
And the poor girl has little more to do
Than just to keep in sight as you pursue :
Chance to a ruin leads her ; you behold,
And straight the angel of her taste is told ;
Chance to a cottage leads you, and you trace
A virtuous pity in the angel's face ;
She reads a work you chance to recommend,
And likes it well—at least, she likes the
    friend ;
But when it chances this no more is done,
She has not left one virtue—No ! not one !
  But be it said, good sir, we use such art,
Is it not done to hold a fickle heart,
And fix a roving eye ?—Is that design
Shameful or wicked that would keep you
    mine ?

If I confess the art, I would proceed
To say of such that every maid has need.
Then when you flatter—in your language—
　　praise,
In our own view you must our value raise ;
And must we not, to this mistaken man,
Appear as like his picture as we can ?
If you will call—nay, treat us as divine,
Must we not something to your thoughts in-
　　cline ?
If men of sense will worship whom they love,
Think you the idol will the error prove ?
What ! show him all her glory is pretence,
And make an idiot of this man of sense ?
　　Then, too, suppose we should his praise
　　refuse,
And clear his mind, we may our lover lose ;
In fact, you make us more than nature makes,
And we, no doubt, consent to your mistakes ;
You will, we know, until the frenzy cools,
Enjoy the transient paradise of fools ;
But fancy fled, you quit the blissful state,
And truth for ever bars the golden gate.
　　H. True ! but how ill each other to up-
　　braid,
'Tis not our fault that we no longer staid ;
No sudden fate our lingering love supprest,
It died an easy death, and calmly sank to
　　rest :
To either sex is the delusion lent,
And when it fails us, we should rest content,
'Tis cruel to reproach, when bootless to
　　repent.
　　E. Then wise the lovers who consent to
　　wait,
And always lingering, never try the state ;
But hurried on, by what they call their pain
And I their bliss, no longer they refrain ;
To ease that pain, to lose that bliss, they run
To the church magi, and the thing is done ;
A spell is utter'd, and a ring applied,
And forth they walk a bridegroom and a
　　bride,
To find this counter-charm, this marriage rite,
Has put their pleasant fallacies to flight !
But tell me, Henry, should we truly strive,
May we not bid the happy dream revive ?
　　H. Alas ! they say when weakness or when
　　vice
Expels a foolish pair from Paradise,
The guardian power to prayer has no regard,
The knowledge once obtain'd, the gate is
　　barr'd ;

Or could we enter we should still repine,
Unless we could the knowledge too resign.
Yet let us calmly view our present fate,
And make a humbler Eden of our state ;
With this advantage, that what now we gain,
Experience gives, and prudence will retain.
　　E. Ah ! much I doubt—when you in fury
　　broke
That lovely vase by one impassion'd stroke,
And thousand china-fragments met my sight,
Till rising anger put my grief to flight ;
As well might you the beauteous jar repiece,
As joy renew and bid vexation cease.
　　H. Why then 'tis wisdom, Emma, not to
　　keep
These griefs in memory ; they had better
　　sleep.
　　There was a time when this heaven-guarded
　　isle,
Whose valleys flourish—nay, whose moun-
　　tains smile,
Was sterile, wild, deform'd, and beings rude
Creatures scarce wilder than themselves pur-
　　sued ;
The sea was heard around a waste to howl,
The night-wolf answer'd to the whooting owl,
And all was wretched—Yet who now surveys
The land, withholds his wonder and his praise?
Come, let us try and make our moral view
Improve like this—this have we power to do.
　　E. O ! I'll be all forgetful, deaf and dumb,
And all you wish, to have these changes come.
　　H. And come they may, if not as hereto-
　　fore,
We cannot all the lovely vase restore ;
What we beheld in Love's perspective glass
Has pass'd away—one sigh ! and let it pass—
It was a blissful vision, and it fled,
And we must get some actual good instead :
Of good and evil that we daily find,
That we must hoard, *this* banish from the
　　mind ;
The food of Love, that food on which he
　　thrives,
To find must be the business of our lives ;
And when we know what Love delights to
　　see,
We must his guardians and providers be.
　　As careful peasants, with incessant toil,
Bring earth to vines in bare and rocky soil,
And, as they raise with care each scanty heap,
Think of the purple clusters they shall
　　reap ;

So those accretions to the mind we'll bring,
Whence fond regard and just esteem will
    spring ;
Then, though we backward look with some
    regret
On those first joys, we shall be happy yet.
  Each on the other must in all depend,
The kind adviser, the unfailing friend ;
Through the rough world we must each other
    aid,
Leading and led, obeying and obey'd ;

Favour'd and favouring, eager to believe
What should be truth—unwilling to perceive
What might offend—determined to remove
What has offended ; wisely to improve
What pleases yet, and guard returning love.
  Nor doubt, my Emma, but in many an hour
Fancy, who sleeps, shall wake with all her
    power ;
And we shall pass—though not perhaps
    remain—
To fairy-land, and feel its charm again.

BOOK XV.   GRETNA GREEN

Richard meets an Acquaintance of his Youth
—The Kind of Meeting—His School—The
Doctor Sidmere and his Family—Belwood,
a Pupil—The Doctor's Opinion of him—
The Opinion of his Wife—and of his
Daughter— Consultation— The   Lovers—
Flight to Gretna Green—Return no more—
The Doctor and his Lady—Belwood and his
wife—The Doctor reflects—Goes to his Son-
in-law—His Reception and Return.

'I MET,' said Richard, when return'd to dine,
' In my excursion, with a friend of mine ;
Friend! I mistake,—but yet I knew him well,
Ours was the village where he came to dwell ;
He was an orphan born to wealth, and then
Placed in the guardian-care of cautious men ;
When our good parent, who was kindness all,
Fed and caress'd him when he chose to call ;
And this he loved, for he was always one
For whom some pleasant service must be
    done,
Or he was sullen—He would come and play
At his own time, and at his pleasure stay ;
But our kind parent soothed him as a boy
Without a friend ; she loved he should enjoy
A day of ease, and strove to give his mind
    employ :
She had but seldom the desired success,
And therefore parting troubled her the less ;
Two years he there remain'd, then went his
    way,
I think to school, and him I met to-day.
  'I heard his name, or he had past unknown,
And, without scruple, I divulged my own ;
His words were civil, but not much express'd,
. " Yes ! he had heard I was my brother's
    guest ; "

Then would explain, what was not plain to me,
Why he could not a social neighbour be.
He envied you, he said, your quiet life,
And me a loving and contented wife ;
You, as unfetter'd by domestic bond,
Me, as a husband and a father fond :
I was about to speak, when to the right
The road then turn'd, and lo ! his house in
    sight.
  ' " Adieu ! " he said, nor gave a word or sign
Of invitation—" Yonder house is mine ;
Your brother's I prefer, if I might choose—
But, my dear sir, you have no time to lose."
  ' Say, is he poor ? or has he fits of spleen ?
Or is he melancholy, moped, or mean ?
So cold, so distant——I bestow'd some
    pains
Upon the fever in my Irish veins.'
  ' Well, Richard, let your native wrath be
    tamed,
The man has half the evils you have named ;
He is not poor, indeed, nor is he free
From all the gloom and care of poverty.'
  ' But is he married ? '—' Hush ! the bell,
    my friend ;
That business done, we will to this attend ;
And, o'er our wine engaged, and at our ease,
We may discourse of Belwood's miseries ;
Not that his sufferings please me—No,
    indeed ;
But I from such am happy to be freed.'
  Their speech, of course, to this misfortune
    led,
A weak young man improvidently wed.
  ' Weak,' answer'd Richard ; ' but we do
    him wrong
To say that his affection was not strong.'

'That we may doubt,' said George; 'in
    men so weak
You may in vain the strong affections seek;
They have strong appetites; a fool will eat
As long as food is to his palate sweet;
His rule is not what sober nature needs,
But what the palate covets as he feeds;
He has the passions, anger, envy, fear,
As storm is angry, and as frost severe;
Uncheck'd, he still retains what nature gave,
And has what creatures of the forest have.
  'Weak boys, indulged by parents just as
    weak,
Will with much force of their affection speak;
But let mamma th' accustom'd sweets with-
    hold,
And the fond boys grow insolent and cold.
  'Weak men profess to love, and while un-
    tried
May woo with warmth, and grieve to be
    denied;
But this is selfish ardour,—all the zeal
Of their pursuit is from the wish they feel
For self-indulgence—When do they deny
Themselves? and when the favourite object fly?
Or, for that object's sake, with her requests
    comply?
Their sickly love is fed with hopes of joy,
Repulses damp it, and delays destroy;
Love, that to virtuous acts will some excite,
In others but provokes an appetite;
In better minds, when love possession takes
And meets with peril, lie the reason shakes;
But these weak natures, when they love
    profess,
Never regard their small concerns the less.
  'That true and genuine love has Quixote-
    flights
May be allow'd—in vision it delights;
But in its loftiest flight, its wildest dream,
Has something in it that commands esteem.
But this poor love to no such region soars,
But, Sancho-like, its selfish loss deplores;
Of its own merit and its service speaks,
And full reward for all its duty seeks.'
    —'When a rich boy, with all the pride of
    youth,
Weds a poor beauty, will you doubt his truth?
Such love is tried—it indiscreet may be,
But must be generous '—
           'That I do not see;
Just at this time the balance of the mind
Is this or that way by the weights inclined;

In this scale beauty, wealth in that abides,
In dubious balance, till the last subsides;
Things are not poised in just the equal state,
That the ass stands stock-still in the debate;
Though when deciding he may slowly pass
And long for both—the nature of the ass;
'Tis but an impulse that he must obey
When he resigns one bundle of the hay.'

  'Take your friend Belwood, whom his
    guardians sent
To Doctor Sidmere—full of dread he went;
Doctor they call'd him—he was not of us,
And where he was—we need not now discuss:
He kept a school, he had a daughter fair,
He said, as angels,—say, as women are.
  'Clara, this beauty, had a figure light,
Her face was handsome, and her eyes were
    bright;
Her voice was music, not by anger raised;
And sweet her dimple, either pleased or
    praised;
All round the village was her fame allow'd,
She was its pride, and not a little proud.
  'The ruling thought that sway'd her father's
    mind
Was this—I am for dignity design'd:
Riches he rather as a mean approved,
Yet sought them early, and in seeking loved;
For this he early made the marriage vow,
But fail'd to gain—I recollect not how;
For this his lady had his wrath incurr'd,
But that her feelings seldom could be stirr'd;
To his fair daughter, famed as well as fair,
He look'd, and found his consolation there.
  'The Doctor taught of youth some half a
    score,
Well-born and wealthy—He would take no
    more;
His wife, when peevish, told him, " Yes! and
    glad "—
It might be so—no more were to be had:
Belwood, it seems, for college was design'd,
But for more study he was not inclined:
He thought of labouring there with much
    dismay,
And motives mix'd here urged the long delay.
  'He now on manhood verged, at least began
To talk as he supposed became a man.
  ' " Whether he chose the college or the school
Was his own act, and that should no man
    rule;

He had his reasons for the step he took,
Did they suppose he stay'd to read his book?"
  'Hopeless, the Doctor said, "This boy is one
With whom I fear there's nothing to be done."
His wife replied, who more had guess'd or
      knew,
" You only mean there's nothing he can do;
Ev'n there you err, unless you mean indeed
That the poor lad can neither think nor read."
  —' " What credit can I by such dunce
      obtain ? "—
" Credit ? I know not—you may something
      gain ;
'Tis true he has no passion for his books,
But none can closer study Clara's looks ;
And who controls him ? now his father's
      gone,
There's not a creature cares about the son.
If he be brought to ask your daughter's hand,
All that he has will be at her command ;
And who is she ? and whom does she obey ?
Where is the wrong, and what the danger,
      pray ?
Becoming guide to one who guidance needs
Is merit surely—If the thing succeeds,
Cannot you always keep him at your side,
And be his honour'd guardian and his guide ?
And cannot I my pretty Clara rule ?
Is not this better than a noisy school ? "
  'The Doctor thought and mused, he felt and
      fear'd,
Wish'd it to be—then wish'd he had not
      heard ;
But he was angry—that at least was right,
And gave him credit in his lady's sight ;—
Then, milder grown, yet something still
      severe,
He said, " Consider, Madam, think and fear; "
But, ere they parted, softening to a smile,
" Farewell ! " said he—" I'll think myself
      awhile."
  ' James and his Clara had, with many a pause
And many a doubt, infringed the Doctor's
      laws ;
At first with terror, and with eyes turn'd
      round
On every side for fear they should be found :
In the long passage, and without the gate,
They met, and talk'd of love and his estate ;
Sweet little notes, and full of hope, were laid
Where they were found by the attentive maid ;
And these she answer'd kindly as she could,
But still " I dare not " waited on "I would ; "

Her fears and wishes she in part confess'd,
Her thoughts and views she carefully sup-
      press'd ;
Her Jemmy said at length, " He did not heed
His guardian's anger—What was he, indeed ?
A tradesman once, and had his fortune gain'd
In that low way,—such anger he disdain'd—
He loved her pretty looks, her eyes of blue,
Her auburn-braid, and lips that shone like
      dew ;
And did she think her Jemmy stay'd at school
To study Greek ?—What, take him for a fool?
Not he, by Jove ! for what he had to seek
He would in English ask her, not in Greek ;
Will you be mine ? are all your scruples gone?
Then let's be off—I've that will take us on."
'Twas true ; the clerk of an attorney there
Had found a Jew,—the Jew supplied the heir.
  ' Yet had he fears—" My guardians may
      condemn
The choice I make—but what is that to
      them ?
The more they strive my pleasure to restrain,
The less they'll find they're likely to obtain ;
For when they work one to a proper cue,
What they forbid one takes delight to do."
  ' Clara exulted—now the day would come
Belwood must take her in her carriage home ;
" Then I shall hear what Envy will remark
When I shall sport the ponies in the park ;
When my friend Jane will meet me at the ball,
And see me taken out the first of all ;
I see her looks when she beholds the men
All crowd about me—she will simper then,
And cry with her affected air and voice,
' O ! my sweet Clara, how do I rejoice
At your good fortune ! '—' Thank you, dear,'
      say I ;
' But some there are that could for envy
      die.' "
  ' Mamma look'd on with thoughts to these
      allied,
She felt the pleasure of reflected pride ;
She should respect in Clara's honour find—
But she to Clara's secret thoughts was blind ;
O ! when we thus design we do but spread
Nets for our feet, and to our toils are led :
Those whom we think we rule their views
      attain,
And we partake the guilt without the gain.
  ' The Doctor long had thought, till he be-
      came
A victim both to avarice and shame ;

From his importance, every eye was placed
On his designs—How dreadful if disgraced !
' " O ! that unknown to him the pair had
  flown
To that same Green, the project all their own !
And should they now be guilty of the act,
Am not I free from knowledge of the fact ?
Will they not, if they will ? "—'Tis thus we
  meet
The check of conscience, and our guide defeat.
' This friend, this spy, this counsellor at rest,
More pleasing views were to the mind address'd.
' The mischief done, he would be much dis-
  pleased,
For weeks, nay, months, and slowly be
  appeased ;—
Yet of this anger if they felt the dread,
Perhaps they dare not steal away to wed ;
And if on hints of mercy they should go,
He stood committed—it must not be so.
' In this dilemma either horn was hard,—
Best to seem careless, then, and off one's
  guard ;
And, lest their terror should their flight
  prevent,
His wife might argue—fathers will relent
On such occasions—and that she should share
The guilt and censure was her proper care.
' " Suppose them wed," said he, " and at my
  feet,
I must exclaim that instant—Vile deceit !
Then will my daughter, weeping, while they
  kneel,
For its own Clara beg my heart may feel :
At last, but slowly, I may all forgive,
And their adviser and director live."
' When wishes only weak the heart surprise,
Heaven, in its mercy, the fond prayer denies ;
But when our wishes are both base and weak,
Heaven, in its justice, gives us what we
  seek.
' All pass'd that was expected, all prepared
To share the comfort—What the comfort
  shared ?
' The married pair, on their return, agreed
That they from school were now completely
  freed ;
Were man and wife, and to their mansion now
Should boldly drive, and their intents avow :
The acting guardian in the mansion reign'd,
And, thither driving, they their will explain'd :
The man awhile discoursed in language high,
The ward was sullen, and made brief reply ;

Till, when he saw th' opposing strength
  decline,
He bravely utter'd—"Sir, the house is mine!"
And, like a lion, lash'd by self-rebuke,
His own defence he bravely undertook.
' " Well ! be it right or wrong, the thing is
  past ;
You cannot hinder what is tight and fast :
The church has tied us ; we are hither come
To our own place, and you must make us
  room."
' The man reflected—"You deserve, I know,
Foolish young man ! what fortune will
  bestow :
No punishment from me your actions need,
Whose pains will shortly to your fault succeed."
' James was quite angry, wondering what
  was meant
By such expressions—Why should he repent ?
' New trial came—The wife conceived it right
To see her parents ; "So," he said, "she might,
If she had any fancy for a jail,
But upon him no creature should prevail ;
No ! he would never be again the fool
To go and starve, or study at a school ! "
' " O ! but to see her parents!"—"Well !
  the sight
Might give her pleasure—very like it might,
And she might go ; but to his house restored
He would not now be catechised and bored."
It was her duty ;—"Well ! " said he again,
" There you may go—and there you may
  remain ! "
  Already this ?—Even so : he heard it said
How rash and heedless was the part he play'd ;
For love of money in his spirit dwelt,
And there repentance was intensely felt :
His guardian told him he had bought a toy
At tenfold price, and bargain'd like a boy :
Angry at truth, and wrought to fierce disdain,
He swore his loss should be no woman's gain ;
His table she might share, his name she must,
But if aught more—she gets it upon trust.
  For a few weeks his pride her face dis-
  play'd—
He then began to thwart her, and upbraid ;
He grew imperious, insolent, and loud—
His blinded weakness made his folly proud ;
He would be master,—she had no pretence
To counsel him, as if he wanted sense ;
He must inform her, she already cost
More than her worth, and more should not
  be lost ;

But still concluding, " if your will be so
That you must see the old ones, do it—go ! "
 ' Some weeks the doctor waited, and the
    while
His lady preach'd in no consoling style :
At last she fear'd that rustic had convey'd
Their child to prison—yes, she was afraid,—
There to remain in that old hall alone
With the vile heads of stags, and floors of
    stone.
 ' " Why did you, sir, who know such things
    so well,
And teach us good, permit them to rebel ?
Had you o'erawed and check'd them when
    in sight,
They would not then have ventured upon
    flight—
Had you"——" Out, serpent ! did not you
    begin ?
What ! introduce, and then upbraid the sin ?
For sin it is, as I too well perceive :
But leave me, woman, to reflection leave ;
Then to your closet fly, and on your knees
Beg for forgiveness for such sins as these."
 ' " A moody morning ! " with a careless air
Replied the wife—" Why counsel me to
    prayer ?
I think the lord and teacher of a school
Should pray himself, and keep his temper
    cool."
 ' Calm grew the husband when the wife was
    gone—
" The game," said he, " is never lost till won :
'Tis true, the rebels fly their proper home,
They come not nigh, because they fear to come ;
And for my purpose fear will doubtless prove
Of more importance and effect than love ;—
Suppose me there—suppose the carriage stops,
Down on her knees my trembling daughter
    drops ;
Slowly I raise her, in my arms to fall,
And call for mercy as she used to call ;
And shall that boy, who dreaded to appear
Before me, cast away at once his fear ?
'Tis not in nature ! He who once would cower
Beneath my frown, and sob for half an hour ;
He who would kneel with motion prompt and
    quick
If I but look'd—as dogs that do a trick ;
He still his knee-joints flexible must feel,
And have a slavish promptitude to kneel ;—
Soon as he sees me he will drop his lip,
And bend like one made ready for the whip :

O ! come, I trifle, let me haste away—
What ! throw it up, when I have cards to
    play ? "
 ' The Doctor went, a self-invited guest ;
He met his pupil, and his frown repress'd,
For in those lowering looks he could discern
Resistance sullen and defiance stern ;
Yet was it painful to put off his style
Of awful distance, and assume a smile :
So between these, the gracious and the grand,
Succeeded nothing that the Doctor plann'd.
 ' The sullen youth, with some reviving dread,
Bow'd and then hang'd disconsolate his head ;
And, muttering welcome for her a muffled tone,
Stalk'd cross the park to meditate alone,
Saying, or rather seeming to have said,
" Go ! seek your daughter, and be there
    obey'd."
 ' He went—The daughter her distresses told,
But found her father to her interests cold ;
He kindness and complacency advised ;
She answer'd, " these were sure to be despised ;
That of the love her husband once possess'd
Not the least spark was living in his breast ;
The boy repented, and grew savage soon ;
There never shone for her a honey-moon.
Soon as he came, his cares all fix'd on one,
Himself, and all his passion was a gun ;
And though he shot as he did all beside,
It still remain'd his only joy and pride :
He left her there,—she knew not where he
    went,—
But knew full well he should the slight repent ;
She was not one his daily taunts to bear,
He made the house a hell that he should share ;
For, till he gave her power herself to please,
Never for him should be a moment's ease."
 ' " He loves you, child ! " the softening
    father cried :
—" He loves himself, and not a soul beside :
Loves me !—why, yes, and so he did the pears
You caught him stealing—would he had the
    fears !
Would you could make him tremble for his life,
And then to you return the stolen wife,
Richly endow'd—but, O ! the idiot knows
The worth of every penny he bestows.
 ' " Were he but fool alone, I'd find a way
To govern him, at least to have my day ;
Or were he only brute, I'd watch the hour,
And make the brute-affection yield me power ;
But silly both and savage—O ! my heart !
It is too great a trial !—we must part."

"'Oblige the savage by some act!'"—"The debt,
You find, the fool will instantly forget;
Oblige the fool with kindness or with praise,
And you the passions of the savage raise."
"'Time will do much.'"—"Can time my name restore?"
"Have patience, child."—"I am a child no more,
Nor more dependent; but, at woman's age,
I feel that wrongs provoke me and enrage:
Sir, could you bring me comfort, I were cool;
But keep your counsel for your boys at school."
'The Doctor then departed—Why remain
To hear complaints, who could himself complain,
Who felt his actions wrong, and knew his efforts vain?
'The sullen youth, contending with his fate,
Began the darling of his heart to hate;
Her pretty looks, her auburn braid, her face,
All now remain'd the proofs of his disgrace;
While, more than hateful in his vixen's eyes,
He saw her comforts from his griefs arise;
Who felt a joy she strove not to conceal,
When their expenses made her miser feel.
'War was perpetual: on a first attack
She gain'd advantage, he would turn his back;
And when her small-shot whistled in his ears,
He felt a portion of his early fears;
But if he turn'd him in the battle's heat,
And fought in earnest, hers was then defeat;
His strength of oath and curse brought little harm,
But there was no resisting strength of arm.

'Yet wearied both with war, and vex'd at heart,
The slaves of passion judged it best to part:
Long they debated, nor could fix a rate
For a man's peace with his contending mate;
But mutual hatred, scorn, and fear, assign'd
That price—that peace it was not theirs to find.
'The watchful husband lived in constant hope
To hear the wife had ventured to elope;
But though not virtuous, nor in much discreet,
He found her coldness would such views defeat;
And thus, by self-reproof and avarice scourged,
He wore the galling chains his folly forged.
'The wife her pleasures, few and humble, sought,
And with anticipated stipend bought;
Without a home, at fashion's call she fled
To an hired lodging and a widow'd bed;
Husband and parents banish'd from her mind,
She seeks for pleasures that she cannot find;
And grieves that so much treachery was employ'd
To gain a man who has her peace destroy'd.
'Yet more the grieving father feels distress,
His error greater, and his motives less;
He finds too late, by stooping to deceit,
It is ourselves and not the world we cheat;
For, though we blind it, yet we can but feel
That we have something evil to conceal,
Nor can we by our utmost care be sure
That we can hide the sufferings we endure.'

BOOK XVI. LADY BARBARA; OR, THE GHOST

THE Brothers spoke of Ghosts,—a favourite theme
With those who love to reason or to dream;
And they, as greater men were wont to do,
Felt strong desire to think the stories true;
Stories of spirits freed, who came to prove
To spirits bound in flesh that yet they love,
To give them notice of the things below,
Which we must wonder how they came to know,
Or known, would think of coming to relate
To creatures who are tried by unknown fate.

'Warning,' said Richard, 'seems the only thing
That would a spirit on an errand bring;
To turn a guilty mind from wrong to right
A ghost might come, at least I think it might.'
  'But,' said the Brother, 'if we here are tried,
A spirit sent would put that law aside;
It gives to some advantage others need,
Or hurts the sinner should it not succeed:
If from the dead, said Dives, one were sent
To warn my brethren, sure they would repent;
But Abraham answer'd, if they now reject
The guides they have, no more would that effect;
Their doubts too obstinate for grace would prove,
For wonder hardens hearts it fails to move.
  'Suppose a sinner in an hour of gloom,
And let a ghost with all its horrors come;
From lips unmoved let solemn accents flow,
Solemn his gesture be, his motion slow;
Let the waved hand and threatening look impart
Truth to the mind and terror to the heart;
And, when the form is fading to the view,
Let the convicted man cry, " this is true!"
  'Alas! how soon would doubts again invade
The willing mind, and sins again persuade!
I saw it—What?—I was awake, but how?
Not as I am, or I should see it now:
It spoke, I think,—I thought, at least, it spoke,—
And look'd alarming—yes, I felt the look.
  'But then in sleep those horrid forms arise,
That the soul sees,—and we suppose, the eyes,—
And the soul hears,—the senses then thrown by,
She is herself the ear, herself the eye;
A mistress so will free her servile race
For their own tasks, and take herself the place:
In sleep what forms will ductile fancy take,
And what so common as to dream awake?
On others thus do ghostly guests intrude?
Or why am I by such advice pursued?
One out of millions who exist, and why
They know not—cannot know—and such am I;
And shall two beings of two worlds, to meet,
The laws of one, perhaps of both, defeat?

It cannot be—But if some being lives
Who such kind warning to a favourite gives,
Let them these doubts from my dull spirit clear,
And once again, expected guest! appear.
  'And if a second time the power complied,
Why is a third, and why a fourth denied?
Why not a warning ghost for ever at our side?
Ah, foolish being! thou hast truth enough.
Augmented guilt would rise on greater proof;
Blind and imperious passion disbelieves,
Or madly scorns the warning it receives,
Or looks for pardon ere the ill be done,
Because 'tis vain to strive our fate to shun;
In spite of ghosts, predestined woes would come,
And warning add new terrors to our doom.
  'Yet there are tales that would remove our doubt,
The whisper'd tales that circulate about
That in some noble mansion take their rise,
And told with secresy and awe, surprise
It seems not likely people should advance,
For falsehood's sake, such train of circumstance;
Then the ghosts bear them with a ghost like grace,
That suits the person, character, and place.
  'But let us something of the kind recite:
What think you, now, of Lady Barbara's spright?'
  'I know not what to think; but I have heard
A ghost, to warn her or advise, appear'd;
And that she sought a friend before she died
To whom she might the awful fact confide,
Who seal'd and secret should the story keep
Till Lady Barbara slept her final sleep,
In that close bed, that never spirit shakes,
Nor ghostly visitor the sleeper wakes.'
  'Yes, I can give that story, not so well
As your old woman would the legend tell,
But as the facts are stated; and now hear
How ghosts advise, and widows persevere.'

'When her lord died, who had so kind a heart,
That any woman would have grieved to part,
It had such influence on his widow's mind,
That she the pleasures of the world resign'd.
Young as she was, and from the busy town
Came to the quiet of a village down;

Not as insensible to joys, but still
With a subdued but half-rebellious will;
For she had passions warm, and feeling strong,
With a right mind, that dreaded to be
    wrong;—
Yet she had wealth to tie her to the place
Where it procures delight and veils dis-
    grace;
Yes she had beauty to engage the eye,
A widow still in her minority;
Yet she had merit worthy men to gain,
And yet her hand no merit could obtain;
For, though secluded, there were trials made,
When he who soften'd most could not per-
    suade;
Awhile she hearken'd as her swain proposed,
And then his suit with strong refusal closed.
    '"Thanks, and farewell!—give credit to my
    word,
That I shall die the widow of my lord;
'Tis my own will, I now prefer the state,—
If mine should change, it is the will of fate."
    ' Such things were spoken, and the hearers
    cried,
" 'Tis very strange,—perhaps she may be
    tried."
    'The lady past her time in taking air,
In working, reading, charities, and prayer;
In the last duties she received the aid
Of an old friend, a priest, with whom she
    pray'd;
And to his mansion with a purpose went,
That there should life be innocently spent;
Yet no cold vot'ress of the cloister she,
Warm her devotion, warm her charity;
The face the index of a feeling mind,
And her whole conduct rational and kind.
    'Though rich and noble, she was pleased
    to slide
Into the habits of her reverend guide,
And so attended to his girls and boys,
She seem'd a mother in her fears and joys;
On her they look'd with fondness, something
    check'd
By her appearance, that engaged respect;
For still she dress'd as one of higher race,
And her sweet smiles had dignity and grace.
    'George was her favourite, and it gave her
    joy
To indulge and to instruct the darling boy;
To watch, to soothe, to check the forward
    child,
Who was at once affectionate and wild;

Happy and grateful for her tender care,
And pleased her thoughts and company to
    share.
    'George was a boy with spirit strong and
    high,
With handsome face, and penetrating eye;
O'er his broad forehead hung his locks of
    brown,
That gave a spirit to his boyish frown;
"My little man," were words that she applied
To him, and he received with growing pride;
Her darling, even from his infant years,
Had something touching in his smiles and
    tears;
And in his boyish manners he began
To show the pride that was not made for man;
But it became the child, the mother cried,
And the kind lady said it was not pride.
    'George, to his cost, though sometimes to
    his praise,
Was quite a hero in these early days,
And would return from heroes just as stout,
Blood in his crimson cheek, and blood without.
    '"What! he submit to vulgar boys and low,
He bear an insult, he forget a blow!
They call'd him Parson—let his father bear
His own reproach, it was his proper care;
He was no parson, but he still would teach
The boys their manners, and yet would not
    preach."
    'The father, thoughtful of the time foregone,
Was loth to damp the spirit of his son;
Rememb'ring he himself had early laurels
    won;
The mother, frighten'd, begg'd him to refrain,
And not his credit or his linen stain:
While the kind friend so gently blamed the
    deed,
He smiled in tears, and wish'd her to proceed;
For the boy pleased her, and that roguish eye
And daring look were cause of many a sigh,
When she had thought how much would such
    quick temper try:
And oft she felt a kind of gathering gloom,
Sad, and prophetic of the ills to come.
    'Years fled unmark'd; the lady taught no
    more
Th' adopted tribe, as she was wont before;
But by her help the school the lasses sought,
And by the vicar's self the boy was taught;
Not unresisting when that cursed Greek
Ask'd so much time for words that none will
    speak.

'" What can men worse for mortal brain
    contrive
Than thus a hard dead language to revive !
Heav'ns, if a language once be fairly dead,
Let it be buried, not preserved and read,
The bane of every boy to decent station bred.
If any good these crabbed books contain,
Translate them well, and let them then
    remain ;
To one huge vault convey the useless store,
Then lose the key, and never find it more."
'Something like this the lively boy express'd,
When Homer was his torment and his jest.
'" George," said the father," can at pleasure
    seize
The point he wishes, and with too much ease ;
And hence, depending on his powers and vain,
He wastes the time that he will sigh to gain."
'The partial widow thought the wasted days
He would recover, urged by love and praise ;
And thus absolved, the boy, with grateful
    mind,
Repaid a love so useful and so blind ;
Her angry words he loved, although he fear'd,
And words not angry doubly kind appear'd.
'George, then on manhood verging, felt the
    charms
Of war, and kindled at the world's alarms ;
Yet war was then, though spreading wide
    and far,
A state of peace to what has since been war :
'Twas then some dubious claim at sea or land,
That placed a weapon in a warrior's hand ;
But in these times the causes of our strife
Are hearth and altar, liberty and life.
'George, when from college he return'd, and
    heard
His father's questions, cold and shy appear'd.
'"Who had the honours? "—"Honour!"
    said the youth,
" Honour at college !—very good, in truth ! "
'"What hours to study did he give? "—He
    gave
Enough to feel they made him like a slave—
And the good vicar found if George should rise,
It would not be by college exercise.
'" At least the time for your degree abide,
And be ordain'd," the man of peace replied ;
'"Then you may come and aid me while I keep,
And watch, and shear the hereditary sheep ;
Choose then your spouse."—That heard the
    youth, and sigh'd,
Nor to aught else attended or replied.

'George had of late indulged unusual fears
And dangerous hopes : he wept unconscious
    tears ;—
Whether for camp or college, well he knew
He must at present bid his friends adieu ;
His father, mother, sisters,—could he part
With these, and feel no sorrow at his heart ?
But from that lovely lady could he go ?
That fonder, fairer, dearer mother ?—No !
For while his father spoke, he fix'd his eyes
On that dear face, and felt a warmth arise,
A trembling flush of joy, that he could ill
    disguise—
Then ask'd himself from whence this growing
    bliss,
This new-found joy, and all that waits on this ?
Why sinks that voice so sweetly in mine ear ?
What makes it now a livelier joy to hear ?
Why gives that touch—Still, still do I retain
The fierce delight that tingled through each
    vein—
Why at her presence with such quickness flows
The vital current ?—Well a lover knows.
'O! tell me not of years,—can she be old ?
Those eyes, those lips, can man unmoved
    behold ?
Has time that bosom chill'd ? are cheeks so
    rosy cold ?
No, she is young, or I her love t' engage
Will grow discreet, and that will seem like age :
But speak it not ; Death's equalizing arm
Levels not surer than Love's stronger charm,
That bids all inequalities be gone,
That laughs at rank, that mocks comparison.
'There is not young or old, if Love decrees,
He levels orders, he confounds degrees ;
There is not fair, or dark, or short, or tall,
Or grave, or sprightly—Love reduces all ;
From each abundant good a portion takes,
And for each want a compensation makes ;
Then tell me not of years—Love, power
    divine,
Takes, as he wills, from hers, and gives to
    mine.
'And she, in truth, was lovely—Time had
    strown
No snows on her, though he so long had flown ;
The purest damask blossom'd in her cheek,
The eyes said all that eyes are wont to speak ;
Her pleasing person she with care adorn'd,
Nor arts that stay the flying graces scorn'd ;
Nor held it wrong these graces to renew,
Or give the fading rose its opening hue :

Yet few there were who needed less the art
To hide an error, or a grace impart.
  'George, yet a child, her faultless form admired,
And call'd his fondness love, as truth required;
But now, when conscious of the secret flame,
His bosom's pain, he dared not give the name:
In her the mother's milder passion grew,
Tender she was, but she was placid too;
From him the mild and filial love was gone,
And a strong passion came in triumph on.
  '"Will she," he cried, "this impious love allow?
And, once my mother, be my mistress now?
The parent-spouse? how far the thought from her,
And how can I the daring wish aver?
When first I speak it, how will those dear eyes
Gleam with awaken'd horror and surprise;
Will she not, angry and indignant, fly
From my imploring call, and bid me die?
Will she not shudder at the thought, and say,
My son! and lift her eyes to heaven and pray?
Alas! I fear—and yet my soul she won
While she with fond endearments call'd me son!
Then first I felt—yet knew that I was wrong—
This hope, at once so guilty and so strong:
She gave—I feel it now—a mother's kiss,
And quickly fancy took a bolder bliss;
But hid the burning blush, for fear that eye
Should see the transport, and the bliss deny:
O! when she knows the purpose I conceal,
When my fond wishes to her bosom steal,
How will the angel fear? How will the woman feel?
  '"And yet perhaps thi, instant, while I speak,
She knows the pain I feel, the cure I seek;
Better than I she may my feelings know,
And nurse the passion that she dares not show:
She reads the look,—and sure my eyes have shown
To her the power and triumph of her own,—
And in maternal love she veils the flame
That she will heal with joy, yet hear with shame.
  '"Come, let me then—no more a son—reveal
The daring hope, and for her favour kneel;
Let me in ardent speech my meanings dress,
And, while I mourn the fault, my love confess;
And, once confess'd, no more that hope resign,
For she or misery henceforth must be mine.
  '"O! what confusion shall I see advance
On that dear face, responsive to my glance!

Sure she can love!"
    In fact, the youth was right;
She could, but love was dreadful in her sight;
Love like a spectre in her view appear'd,
The nearer he approach'd the more she fear'd.
  'But knew she, then, this dreaded love?
    She guess'd
That he had guilt—she knew he had not rest:
She saw a fear that she could ill define,
And nameless terrors in his looks combine:
It is a state that cannot long endure,
And yet both parties dreaded to be sure.
  'All views were past of priesthood and a gown,
George, fix'd on glory, now prepared for town;
But first his mighty hazard must be run,
And more than glory either lost or won:
Yet, what was glory? Could he win that heart
And gain that hand, what cause was there to part?
Her love afforded all that life affords—
Honour and fame were phantasies and words!
  'But he must see her—She alone was seen
In the still evening of a day serene:
In the deep shade beyond the garden walk
They met, and talking, ceased and fear'd to talk;
At length she spoke of parent's love,—and now
He hazards all—" No parent, lady, thou
None, none to me! but looks so fond and mild
Would well become the parent of my child."
  'She gasp'd for breath—then sat as one resolved
On some high act, and then the means revolved.
  '" It cannot be, my George, my child, my son!
The thought is misery!—Guilt and misery shun:
Far from us both be such design, O, far!
Let it not pain us at the awful bar,
Where souls are tried, where known the mother's part
That I sustain, and all of either heart.
  '" To wed with thee I must all shame efface,
And part with female dignity and grace:
Was I not told, by one who knew so well
This rebel heart, that it must not rebel?
Were I not warn'd, yet Reason's voice would cry,
' Retreat, resolve, and from the danger fly!'

If Reason spoke not, yet would woman's pride
A woman's will by better counsel guide;
And should both Pride and Prudence plead
    in vain,
There is a warning that must still remain,
And, though the heart rebell'd, would ever cry
    ' Refrain.' "
    ' He heard, he grieved—so check'd, the eager
        youth
Dared not again repeat th' offensive truth,
But stopp'd, and fix'd on that loved face an
    eye
Of pleading passion, trembling to reply;
And that reply was hurried, was express'd
With bursts of sorrow from a troubled breast;
He could not yet forbear the tender suit,
Yet dared not speak—his eloquence was mute.
But though awhile in silence he supprest
The pleading voice, and bade his passion rest,
Yet in each motion, in each varying look,
In every tender glance, that passion spoke.—
Words find, ere long, a passage; and once
    more
He warmly urges what he urged before;
He feels acutely, and he thinks, of course,
That what he feels his language will enforce;
Flame will to flame give birth, and fire to fire,
And so from heart to heart is caught desire;
He wonders how a gentle mind so long
Resists the pleading of a love so strong—
" And can that heart," he cries, " that face
    belie,
And know no softness? Will it yet deny ? "—
    ' " I tell thee, George, as I have told before,
I feel a mother's love, and feel no more;
A child I bore thee in my arms, and how
Could I—did prudence yield—receive thee
    now ? "
    ' At her remonstrance hope revived, for oft
He found her words severe, her accents soft;
In eyes that threaten'd tears of pity stood,
And truth she made as gracious as she could;—
But, when she found the dangerous youth
    would seek
His peace alone, and still his wishes speak,
Fearful she grew, that, opening thus his heart,
He might to hers a dangerous warmth impart:
All her objections slight to him appear'd,—
But one she had, and now it must be heard.
    ' " Yes, it must be ! and he shall under-
        stand
What powers, that are not of the world,
    command ;

So shall he cease, and I in peace shall live—"
Sighing she spoke—" that widowhood can
    give ! "
Then to her lover turn'd, and gravely said,
" Let due attention to my words be paid :
Meet me to-morrow, and resolve t' obey ; "
Then named the hour and place, and went
    her way.
    ' Before that hour, or moved by spirit vain
Of woman's wish to triumph and complain,
She had his parents summon'd, and had shown
Their son's strong wishes, nor conceal'd her
    own :
" And do you give," she said, " a parent's aid
To make the youth of his strange love afraid ;
And, be it sin or not, be all the shame dis-
    play'd."
    ' The good old pastor wonder'd, seem'd to
        grieve,
And look'd suspicious on this child of Eve :
He judged his boy, though wild, had never
    dared
To talk of love, had not rebuke been spared;
But he replied, in mild and tender tone,
" It is not sin, and therefore shame has none."
    ' The different ages of the pair he knew,
And quite as well their different fortunes too :
A meek, just man ; but difference in his sight
That made the match unequal made it right :
" His son, his friend united, and become
Of his own hearth—the comforts of his home—
Was it so wrong ? Perhaps it was her pride
That felt the distance, and the youth denied ? "
    ' The blushing widow heard, and she retired,
Musing on what her ancient friend desired ;
She could not, therefore, to the youth com-
    plain,
That his good father wish'd him to refrain ;
She could not add, " Your parents, George,
    obey,
They will your absence "—no such will had
    they.
    ' Now, in th' appointed minute met the pair,
Foredoom'd to meet : George made the
    lover's prayer,—
That was heard kindly ; then the lady tried
For a calm spirit, felt it, and replied.
    ' " George, that I love thee why should I
        suppress ?
For 'tis a love that virtue may profess—
Parental,—frown not,—tender, fix'd, sincere ;
Thou art for dearer ties by much too dear,
And nearer must not be, thou art so very near :

Nay, do not reason, prudence, pride agree,
Our very feelings, that it must not be?
Nay, look not so, I shun the task no more,
But will to thee thy better self restore.
Then hear, and hope not ; to the tale I tell
Attend ! obey me, and let all be well.
Love is forbad to me, and thou wilt find
All thy too ardent views must be resign'd ;
Then from thy bosom all such thoughts
        remove,
And spare the curse of interdicted love.
  ' " If doubts at first assail thee, wait awhile,
Nor mock my sadness with satiric smile ;
For, if not much of other worlds we know,
Nor how a spirit speaks in this below,
Still there is speech and intercourse ; and now
The truth of what I tell I first avow,
True will I be in all, and be attentive thou.

  ' " I was a Ratcliffe, taught and train'd to live
In all the pride that ancestry can give ;
My only brother, when our mother died,
Fill'd the dear offices of friend and guide ;
My father early taught us all he dared,
And for his bolder flights our minds prepared :
He read the works of deists, every book
From crabbed Hobbes to courtly Boling-
        broke ;
And when we understood not, he would cry,
' Let the expressions in your memory lie,
The light will soon break in, and you will find
Rest for your spirits, and be strong of mind !'
  ' " Alas ! however strong, however weak,
The rest was something we had still to seek !
  ' " He taught us duties of no arduous kind,
The easy morals of the doubtful mind ;
He bade us all our childish fears control,
And drive the nurse and grandam from the
        soul ;
Told us the word of God was all we saw,
And that the law of nature was his law ;
This law of nature we might find abstruse,
But gain sufficient for our common use.
  ' " Thus, by persuasion, we our duties learn'd,
And were but little in the cause concern'd.
We lived in peace, in intellectual ease,
And thought that virtue was the way to please,
And pure morality the keeping free
From all the stains of vulgar villany.
  ' " But Richard, dear enthusiast ! shunn'd
        reproach,
He let no stain upon his name encroach ;

But fled the hated vice, was kind and just,
That all must love him, and that all might
        trust.
  ' " Free, sad discourse was ours ; we often
        sigh'd
To think we could not in some truths confide :
Our father's final words gave no content,
We found not what his self-reliance meant :
To fix our faith some grave relations sought,
Doctrines and creeds of various kind they
        brought,
And we as children heard what they as doctors
        taught.
  ' " Some to the priest referr'd us, in whose
        book
No unbeliever could resisting look ;
Others to some great preacher's, who could
        tame
The fiercest mind, and set the cold on flame ;
For him no rival in dispute was found
Whom he could not confute or not confound.
Some mystics told us of the sign and seal,
And what the spirit would in time reveal,
If we had grace to wait, if we had hearts to
        feel :
Others, to reason trusting, said, believe
As she directs, and what she proves receive ;
While many told us, it is all but guess,
Stick to your church, and calmly acquiesce.
Thus, doubting, wearied, hurried, and per-
        plex'd,
This world was lost in thinking of the next :
When spoke my brother—' From my soul
        I hate
This clash of thought, this ever doubting
        state ;
For ever seeking certainty, yet blind
In our research, and puzzled when we find.
  ' " ' Could not some spirit, in its kindness,
        steal
Back to our world, and some dear truth reveal ?
Say there is danger,—if it could be done,
Sure one would venture,—I would be the one ;
And when a spirit—much as spirits might—
I would to thee communicate my light ! '
  ' " I sought my daring brother to oppose,
But awful gladness in my bosom rose :
I fear'd my wishes ; but through all my frame
A bold and elevating terror came :
Yet with dissembling prudence I replied,
' Know we the laws that may be thus defied ?
Should the free spirit to th' embodied tell
The precious secret, would it not rebel ? '

Yet while I spoke I felt a pleasing glow
Suffuse my cheek at what I long'd to know;
And I, like Eve transgressing, grew more bold,
And wish'd to hear a spirit and behold.
'"'I have no friend,' said he, 'to not one
    man
Can I appear; but, love! to thee I can:
Who first shall die '——I wept, but—' I
    agree
To all thou say'st, dear Richard! and would
    be
The first to wing my way, and bring my news
    to thee.'
'"Long we conversed, but not till we per-
    ceived
A gathering gloom—Our freedom gain'd, we
    grieved;
Above the vulgar, as we judged, in mind,
Below in peace, more sad as more refined;
'Twas joy, 'twas sin—Offenders at the time,
We felt the hurried pleasures of our crime
With pain that crime creates, and this in
    both—
Our mind united as the strongest oath.
O, my dear George! in ceasing to obey,
Misery and trouble meet us in our way!
I felt as one intruding in a scene
Where none should be, where none had ever
    been;
Like our first parent, I was new to sin,
But plainly felt its sufferings begin:
In nightly dreams I walk'd on soil unsound,
And in my day-dreams endless error found.
'"With this dear brother I was doom'd to
    part,
Who, with an husband, shared an troubled
    heart:
My lord I honour'd; but I never proved
The madd'ning joy, the boast of some who
    loved:
It was a marriage that our friends profess'd
Would be most happy, and I acquiesced;
And we were happy, for our love was calm,
Not life's delicious essence, but its balm.
'"My brother left us,—dear, unhappy boy!
He never seem'd to taste of earthly joy,
Never to live on earth, but ever strove
To gain some tidings of a world above.
'"Parted from him, I found no more to
    please,
Ease was my object, and I dwelt in ease;
And thus in quiet, not perhaps content,
A year in wedlock, lingering time! was spent.

'"One night I slept not, but I courted sleep,
And forced my thoughts on tracks they could
    not keep;
Till nature, wearied in the strife, reposed,
And deep forgetfulness my wanderings closed.
'"My lord was absent—distant from the bed
A pendent lamp its soften'd lustre shed;
But there was light that chased away the
    gloom,
And brought to view each object in the room:
These I observed ere yet I sunk in sleep,
That, if disturb'd not, had been long and deep.
'"I was awaken'd by some being nigh,
It seem'd some voice, and gave a timid cry,—
When sounds, that I describe not, slowly
    broke
On my attention——' Be composed, and
    look!'—
I strove, and I succeeded; look'd with awe,
But yet with firmness, and my brother saw.
'"George, why that smile?—By all that
    God has done,
By the great Spirit, by the blessed Son,
By the one holy Three, by the thrice holy One,
I saw my brother,—saw him by my bed,
And every doubt in full conviction fled!—
It was his own mild spirit—He awhile
Waited my calmness with benignant smile;
So softly shines the veiled sun, till past
The cloud, and light upon the world is cast:
That look composed and soften'd I survey'd,
And met the glance fraternal less afraid;
Though in those looks was something of
    command,
And traits of what I fear'd to understand.
'"Then spoke the spirit—George, I pray,
    attend—
'First let all doubts of thy religion end—
The word reveal'd is true: inquire no more,
Believe in meekness, and with thanks adore :
Thy priest attend, but not in all rely,
And to objectors seek for no reply:
Truth, doubt, and error, will be mix'd below—
Be thou content the greater truths to know,
And in obedience rest thee——For thy life
Thou needest counsel—now a happy wife,
A widow soon! and then, my sister, then
Think not of marriage, think no more of men;—
Life will have comforts; thou wilt much enjoy
Of moderate good, then do not this destroy;
Fear much, and wed no more; by passion led,
Shouldst thou again '——Art thou attending ?
        —wed,

Care in thy ways will growl, and anguish
    haunt thy bed :
A brother's warning on thy heart engrave :
Thou art a mistress—then be not a slave !
Shouldst thou again that hand in fondness
    give,
What life of misery art thou doom'd to live !
How wilt thou weep, lament, implore, com-
    plain !
How wilt thou meet derision and disdain !
And pray to heaven in doubt, and kneel to
    man in vain !
Thou read'st of woes to tender bosoms sent—
Thine shall with tenfold agony be rent ;
Increase of anguish shall new years bestow,
Pain shall on thought and grief on reason
    grow,
And this th' advice I give increase the ill
    I show.'
    ' " 'A second marriage !—No !—by all that 's
        dear ! '
I cried aloud—The spirit bade me hear.
    ' " ' There will be trial,—how I must not say,
'Perhaps I cannot—listen, and obey !—
Free is thy will—th' event I cannot see,
Distinctly cannot, but thy will is free :
Come, weep not, sister,—spirits can but guess,
And not ordain—but do not wed distress ;
For who would rashly venture on a snare ? '
' I swear ! ' I answer'd.—' No, thou must
    not swear,'
He said, or I had sworn ; but still the vow
Was past, was in my mind, and there is now :
Never ! O, never !—Why that sullen air ?
Think'st thou—ungenerous !—I would wed
    despair ?
    ' " ' Was it not told me thus ?—and then I cried,
' Art thou in bliss ?'—but nothing he replied,
Save of my fate, for that he came to show,
Nor of aught else permitted me to know.
    ' " ' Forewarn'd, forearm thee, and thy
        way pursue,
Safe, if thou wilt, not flow'ry—now, adieu ! '
    ' " ' Nay, go not thus,' I cried, ' for this
    will seem
The work of sleep, a mere impressive dream ;
Give me some token, that I may indeed
From the suggestions of my doubts be freed !'
    ' " ' Be this a token—ere the week be fled
Shall tidings greet thee from the newly dead.'
    ' " ' Nay, but,' I said, with courage not my
        own,
' O ! be some signal of thy presence shown ;

Let not this visit with the rising day
Pass, and be melted like a dream away.'
    ' " ' O, woman ! woman ! ever anxious still
To gain the knowledge, not to curb the will !
Have I not promised ?—Child of sin, attend—
Make not a lying spirit of thy friend :
Give me thy hand ! '——I gave it, for my soul
Was now grown ardent, and above control ;
Eager I stretch'd it forth, and felt the hold
Of shadowy fingers, more than icy cold :
A nameless pressure on my wrist was made,
And instant vanish'd the beloved shade !
Strange it will seem, but, ere the morning
    came,
I slept, nor felt disorder in my frame :
Then came a dream—I saw my father's shade,
But not with awe like that my brother's made ;
And he began—' What ! made a convert,
    child ?
Have they my favourite by their creed be-
    guiled ?
Thy brother's weakness I could well foresee,
But had, my girl, more confidence in thee :
Art thou, indeed, before their ark to bow ?
I smiled before, but I am angry now :
Thee will they bind by threats, and thou wilt
    shake
At tales of terror that the miscreants make :
Between the bigot and enthusiast led,
Thou hast a world of miseries to dread :
Think for thyself, nor let the knaves or fools
Rob thee of reason, and prescribe thee rules.'
    ' " Soon as I woke, and could my thoughts
    collect,
What can I think, I cried, or what reject ?
Was it my brother ? Aid me, power divine !
Have I not seen him, left he not a sign ?
Did I not then the placid features trace
That now remain—the air, the eye, the face ?
And then my father—but how different seem
These visitations—this, indeed, a dream !
    ' " Then for that token on my wrist—'tis
    here,
And very slight to you it must appear ;
Here, I'll withdraw the bracelet—'tis a speck !
No more ! but 'tis upon my life a check."—
    ' " ' O ! lovely all, and like its sister arm !
Call this a check, dear lady ? 'tis a charm—
A slight, an accidental mark—no more "——
" Slight as it is, it was not there before :
Then was there weakness, and I bound it——
    Nay !
This is infringement—take those lips away !

' " On the fourth day came letters, and I cried,
Richard is dead, and named the day he died :
A proof of knowledge, true ! but one, alas !
        of pride.
The signs to me were brought, and not my lord,
But I impatient waited not the word ;
And much he marvell'd, reading of the night
In which th' immortal spirit took its flight.
    ' " Yes ! I beheld my brother at my bed,
The hour he died ! the instant he was dead—
His presence now I see ! now trace him as
        he fled.
    ' " Ah ! fly me, George, in very pity, fly ;
Thee I reject, but yield thee reasons why ;
Our fate forbids,—the counsel heaven has sent
We must adopt, or grievously repent ;
And I adopt"——George humbly bow'd, and
        sigh'd,
But, lost in thought, he look'd not nor replied ;
Yet feebly utter'd in his sad adieu,
" I must not doubt thy truth, but perish if
        thou'rt true."
    ' But when he thought alone, his terror gone
Of the strange story, better views came on.
    ' " Nay, my enfeebled heart, be not dismay'd !
A boy again, am I of ghosts afraid ?
Does she believe it ? Say she does believe,
Is she not born of error and of Eve ?
O ! there is lively hope I may the cause
        retrieve."
    ' " ' If you re-wed,' exclaim'd the Ghost—
        For what
Puts he the case, if marry she will not ?
He knows her fate—but what am I about ?
Do I believe ?—'tis certain I have doubt,
And so has she,—what therefore will she do ?
She the predicted fortune will pursue,
And by th' event will judge if her strange
        dream was true ;
The strong temptation to her thought applied
Will gain new strength, and will not be
        denied ;
The very threat against the thing we love
Will the vex'd spirit to resistance move ;
With vows to virtue weakness will begin,
And fears of sinning let in thoughts of sin."
    ' Strong in her sense of weakness, now with-
        drew
The cautious lady from the lover's view ;
But she perceived the looks of all were
        changed,—
Her kind old friends grew peevish and
        estranged ;

A fretful spirit reign'd, and discontent
From room to room in sullen silence went ;
And the kind widow was distress'd at heart
To think that she no comfort could impart :
" But he will go," she said, " and he will strive
In fields of glorious energy to drive
Love from his bosom—Yes, I then may stay,
And all will thank me on a future day."
    ' So judged the lady, nor appear'd to grieve,
Till the young soldier came to take his leave ;
But not of all assembled—No ! he found
His gentle sisters all in sorrow drown'd ;
With many a shaken hand, and many a kiss,
He cried, " Farewell ! a solemn business this ;
Nay, Susan, Sophy !—heaven and earth, my
        dears !
I am a soldier—What do I with tears ? "
    ' He sought his parents ;—they together
        walk'd,
And of their son, his views and dangers, talk'd ;
They knew not how to blame their friend,
        but still
They murmur'd, " She may save us if she will :
Were not these visions working in her mind
Strange things—'tis in her nature to be kind."
    ' Their son appear'd—He sooth'd them, and
        was bless'd,
But still the fondness of his soul confess'd—
And where the lady ?—To her room retired !
Now show, dear son, the courage she required.
    ' George bow'd in silence, trying for assent
To his hard fate, and to his trial went :
Fond, but yet fix'd, he found her in her room ;
Firm, and yet fearful, she beheld him come :
Nor sought he favour now—No ! he would
        meet his doom.
    ' " Farewell ! and, Madam, I beseech you
        pray
That this sad spirit soon may pass away ;
That sword or ball would to the dust restore
This body, that the soul may grieve no more
For love rejected——O ! that I could quit
The life I loathe, who am for nothing fit,
No, not to die ! "——" Unhappy, wilt thou
        make
The house all wretched for thy passion's
        sake ?
And most its grieving object ? "
                                        " Grieving ?—No !
Or as a conqueror mourns a dying foe,
That makes his triumph sure——Couldst
        thou deplore
The evil done, the pain would be no more

But an accursed dream has steel'd thy breast,
And all the woman in thy soul suppress'd."—
‘ " O ! it was vision, George ;. a vision true
As ever seer or holy prophet knew."—
‘ " Can spirits, lady, though they might alarm,
Make an impression on that lovely arm ?
A little cold the cause, a little heat,
Or vein minute, or artery's morbid beat,
Even beauty these admit."—
                      " I did behold
My brother's form."—
                      " Yes, so thy Fancy told,
When in the morning she her work survey'd,
And call'd the doubtful memory to her aid."—
‘ " Nay, think ! the night he died—the very
      night ! "—
"—'Tis very true, and so perchance he might,
But in thy mind—not, lady, in thy sight !
Thou wert not well ; forms delicately made
These dreams and fancies easily invade ;
The mind and body feel the slow disease,
And dreams are what the troubled fancy
      sees."—
‘ " O ! but how strange that all should be
      combined ! "—
" True ; but such combinations we may find ;
A dream's predicted number gain'd a prize,
Yet dreams make no impression on the wise,
Though some chance good, some lucky gain
      may rise."
      " O ! but those words, that voice so truly
            known ! "——
" No doubt, dear lady, they were all thine own ;
Memory for thee thy brother's form portray'd ;
It was thy fear the awful warning made :
Thy former doubts of a religious kind
Account for all these wanderings of the mind."
‘ " But then, how different when my father
      came,
These could not in their nature be the same ! "—
‘ " Yes, all are dreams ; but some as we
      awake
Fly off at once, and no impression make ;
Others are felt, and ere they quit the brain
Make such impression that they come again ;
As half familiar thoughts, and half unknown,
And scarcely recollected as our own ;
For half a day abide some vulgar dreams,
And give our grandams and our nurses themes ;
Others, more strong, abiding figures draw
Upon the brain, and we assert ‘ I saw ; '
And then the fancy on the organs place
A powerful likeness of a form and face.

‘ " Yet more—in some strong passion's
      troubled reign,
Or when the fever'd blood inflames the brain,
At once the outward and the inward eye
The real object and the fancied spy ;
The eye is open, and the sense is true,
And therefore they the outward object view ;
But while the real sense is fix'd on these,
The power within its own creation sees ;
And these, when mingled in the mind, create
Those striking visions which our dreamers
      state ;
For knowing that is true that met the sight,
They think the judgment of the fancy
      right ;——
Your frequent talk of dreams has made me
      turn
My mind on them, and these the facts I learn.
‘ " Or should you say, 'tis not in us to take
Heed in both ways, to sleep and be awake,
Perhaps the things by eye and mind survey'd
Are in their quick alternate efforts made ;
For by this mixture of the truth, the dream
Will in the morning fresh and vivid seem.
‘ " Dreams are like portraits, and we find
      they please
Because they are confess'd resemblances ;
But those strange night-mare visions we
      compare
To waxen figures—they too real are,
Too much a very truth, and are so just
To life and death, they pain us or disgust.
‘ " Hence from your mind these idle visions
      shake,
And O ! my love, to happiness awake ! "—
‘ " It *was* a warning, tempter ! from the
      dead ;
And, wedding thee, I should to misery
      wed ! "—
‘ " False and injurious ! What ! unjust to
      thee ?
O ! hear the vows of Love—it cannot be ;
What, I forbear to bless thee—I forego
That first great blessing of existence ? No !
Did every ghost that terror saw arise
With such prediction, I should say it lies ;
But none there are—a mighty gulf between
Hides the ideal world from objects seen ;
We know not where unbodied spirits dwell,
But this we know, they are invisible ;—
Yet I have one that fain would dwell with
      thee,
And always with thy purer spirit be."—

' " O ! leave me, George ! "
     " To take the field, and die,
So leave thee, lady ? Yes, I will comply ;
Thou art too far above me—Ghosts withstand
My hopes in vain, but riches guard thy hand,
For I am poor—affection and an heart
To thee devoted, I but these impart :
Then bid me go, I will thy words obey,
But let not visions drive thy friend away."—
   ' " Hear me, Oh ! hear me—Shall I wed my
       son ? "—
" I am in fondness and obedience one ;
And I will reverence, honour, love, adore,
Be all that fondest sons can be—and more ;
And shall thy son, if such he be, proceed
To fierce encounters, and in battle bleed ?
No ; thou canst weep ! "—
          " O ! leave me, I entreat ;
Leave me a moment—we shall quickly
    meet."—
   ' " No ! here I kneel, a beggar at thy feet."—
He said, and knelt—with accents, softer still,
He woo'd the weakness of a failing will,
And erring judgment—took her hand, and
    cried,
" Withdraw it not !—O ! let it thus abide,
Pledge of thy love—upon thy act depend
My joy, my hope,—thus they begin or end !
Withdraw it not."——He saw her looks
    express'd
Favour and grace—the hand was firmer
    press'd ;—
signs of opposing fear no more were shown,
And, as he press'd, he felt it was his own.
   ' Soon through the house was known the
      glad assent,
The night so dreaded was in comfort spent ;
War was no more, the destined knot was tied,
And the fond widow made a fearful bride.

   ' Let mortal frailty judge how mortals frail
Thus in their strongest resolutions fail,
And though we blame, our pity will prevail.
   ' Yet, with that Ghost—for so she thought—
      in view !
When she believed that all he told was true ;
When every threat was to her mind recall'd,
Till it became affrighten'd and appall'd ;
When Reason pleaded, think ! forbear !
    refrain !
And when, though trifling, stood that mystic
    stain,

Predictions, warnings, threats, were present
    all in vain.
   ' Th' exulting youth a mighty conqueror
      rose,
And who hereafter shall his will oppose ?
   ' Such is our tale ; but we must yet attend
Our weak, kind widow to her journey's end ;
Upon her death-bed laid, confessing to a
    friend
Her full belief, for to the hour she died
This she profess'd——" The truth I must not
    hide,
It was my brother's form, and in the night
    he died :
In sorrow and in shame has pass'd my time,
All I have suffer'd follow from my crime ;
I sinn'd with warning—when I gave my hand
A power within said, urgently,—Withstand !
And I resisted—O ! my God, what shame,
What years of torment from that frailty came ;
That husband-son !—I will my fault review ;
What did he not that men or monsters do ?
His day of love, a brief autumnal day,
Ev'n in its dawning hasten'd to decay ;
Doom'd from our odious union to behold
How cold he grew, and then how worse than
    cold ;
Eager he sought me, eagerly to shun,
Kneeling he woo'd me, but he scorn'd me,
    won ;
The tears he caused served only to provoke
His wicked insult o'er the heart he broke ;
My fond compliance served him for a jest,
And sharpen'd scorn——' I ought to be
    distress'd ;
Why did I not with my chaste ghost comply ? '
And with upbraiding scorn he told me why ;—
O ! there was grossness in his soul ; his mind
Could not be raised, nor soften'd, nor re-
    fined.
   ' " Twice he departed in his rage, and went
I know not where, nor how his days were
    spent ;
Twice he return'd a suppliant wretch, and
    craved,
Mean as profuse, the trifle I had saved.
   ' " I have had wounds, and some that never
      heal,
What bodies suffer, and what spirits feel ;
But he is gone who gave them, he is fled
To his account ! and my revenge is dead
Yet is it duty, though with shame, to give
My sex a lesson—let my story live ;

For if no ghost the promised visit paid,
Still was a deep and strong impression made,
That wisdom had approved, and prudence
      had obey'd ;
But from another world that warning came,
And O ! in this be ended all my shame !
  ' " Like the first being of my sex I fell,
Tempted, and with the tempter doom'd to
      dwell—
He was the master-fiend, and where he reign'd
      was hell."

'This was her last, for she described no
      more
The rankling feelings of a mind so sore,
But died in peace.—One moral let us
      draw—
Be it a ghost or not the lady saw—
' If our discretion tells us how to live,
We need no ghost a helping hand to
      give ;
But if discretion cannot us restrain,
It then appears a ghost would come in
      vain.'

BOOK XVII. THE WIDOW

RICHARD one morning—it was custom
      now—
Walk'd and conversed with labourers at the
      plough,
With thrashers hastening to their daily task,
With woodmen resting o'er the enlivening
      flask,
And with the shepherd, watchful of his fold
Beneath the hill, and pacing in the cold :
Further afield he sometimes would proceed,
And take a path wherever it might lead.
It led him far about to Wickham Green,
Where stood the mansion of the village queen;
Her garden yet its wintry blossoms bore,
And roses graced the windows and the door—
That lasting kind, that through the varying
      year
Or in the bud or in the bloom appear ;
All flowers that now the gloomy days adorn
Rose on the view, and smiled upon that morn:
Richard a damsel at the window spied,
Who kindly drew a useless veil aside,
And show'd a lady who was sitting by,
So pensive, that he almost heard her sigh :
Full many years she could, no question, tell,
But in her mourning look'd extremely well.
  'In truth,' said Richard, when he told at night
His tale to George, ' it was a pleasant sight ;

She look'd like one who could, in tender tone,
Say, " Will you let a lady sigh alone ?
See ! Time has touch'd me gently in his race,
And left no odious furrows in my face ;
See, too, this house and garden, neat and
      trim,
Kept for its master——Will you stand for
      him ? "
  ' Say this is vain and foolish if you please,
But I believe her thoughts resembled these :
" Come ! " said her looks, " and we will
      kindly take
The visit kindness prompted you to make."
And I was sorry that so much good play
Of eye and attitude were thrown away
On one who has his lot, on one who had his
      day.'
  ' Your pity, brother,' George, with smile,
      replied,
' You may dismiss, and with it send your
      pride :
No need of pity, when the gentle dame
Has thrice resign'd and reassumed her name ;
And be not proud—for, though it might be
      thine,
She would that hand to humbler men resign.
  ' Young she is not,—it would be passing
      strange
If a young beauty thrice her name should
      change :
Yes ! she has years beyond your reckoning
      seen—
Smiles and a window years and wrinkles
      screen ;
But she, in fact, has that which may command
The warm admirer and the willing hand :

What is her fortune we are left to guess,
But good the sign—she does not much
    profess ;
Poor she is not,—and there is that in her
That easy men to strength of mind prefer ;
She may be made, with little care and skill,
Yielding her own, t' adopt an husband's will :
Women there are, who if a man will take
The helm and steer—will no resistance make ;
Who, if neglected, will the power assume,
And then what wonder if the shipwreck come?
   'Queens they will be if man allow the means,
And give the power to these domestic queens;
Whom, if he rightly trains, he may create
And make obedient members of his state.'

   ' Harriet at school was very much the same
As other misses, and so home she came,
Like other ladies, there to live and learn,
To wait her season, and to take her turn.
   ' Their husbands maids as priests their
    livings gain,
The best, they find, are hardest to obtain ;
On those that offer both awhile debate—
" I need not take it, it is not so late ;
Better will come if we will longer stay,
And strive to put ourselves in fortune's way : "
And thus they wait, till many years are past,
For what comes slowly—*but it comes at last.*
   ' Harriet was wedded,—but it must be said,
The vow'd obedience was not duly paid :
Hers was an easy man,—it gave him pain
To hear a lady murmur and complain :
He was a merchant, whom his father made
Rich in the gains of a successful trade :
A lot more pleasant, or a view more fair,
Has seldom fallen to a youthful pair.
   ' But what is faultless in a world like this ?
In every station something seems amiss :
The lady, married, found the house too small—
" Two shabby parlours, and that ugly hall !
Had we a cottage somewhere, and could meet
One's friends and favourites in one's snug
    retreat ;
Or only join a single room to these,
It would be living something at our ease,
And have one's self, at home, the comfort
    that one sees."
   'Such powers of reason, and of mind such
    strength,
Fought with man's fear, and they prevail'd at
    length :

The room was built,—and Harriet did not
    know
A prettier dwelling, either high or low ;
But Harriet loved such conquests, loved to
    plead
With her reluctant man, and to succeed ;
It was such pleasure to prevail o'er one
Who would oppose the thing that still was
    done,
Who never gain'd the race, but yet would
    groan and run.
   ' But there were times when love and pity
    gave
Whatever thoughtless vanity could crave :
She now the carriage chose with freshest name,
And was in quite a fever till it came ;
But can a carriage be alone enjoy'd ?
The pleasure not partaken is destroy'd ;
" I must have some good creature to attend
On morning visits as a kind of friend."
   ' A courteous maiden then was found to sit
Beside the lady, for her purpose fit,
Who had been train'd in all the soothing ways
And servile duties from her early days ;
One who had never from her childhood known
A wish fulfill'd, a purpose of her own :
Her part it was to sit beside the dame,
And give relief in every want that came ;
To soothe the pride, to watch the varying
    look,
And bow in silence to the dumb rebuke.
   ' This supple being strove with all her skill
To draw her master's to her lady's will ;
For they were like the magnet and the steel,
At times so distant that they could not feel ;
Then would she gently move them, till she
    saw
That to each other they began to draw ;
And then would leave them, sure on her return
In Harriet's joy her conquest to discern.
   ' She was a mother now, and grieved to find
The nursery window caught the eastern wind;
What could she do with fears like these
    oppress'd ?
She built a room all window'd to the west;
For sure in one so dull, so bleak, so old,
She and her children must expire with cold :
Meantime the husband murmur'd—" So he
    might ;
She would be judged by Cousins—Was it
    right ? "
   ' Water was near them, and her mind afloat,
The lady saw a cottage and a boat,

And thought what sweet excursions they
    might make,
How they might sail, what neighbours they
    might take,
And nicely would she deck the lodge upon
    the lake.
  'She now prevail'd by habit; had her will,
And found her patient husband sad and
    still:
Yet this displeased; she gain'd, indeed, the
    prize,
But not the pleasure of her victories;
Was she a child to be indulged? He knew
She would have right, but would have reason
    too.
  'Now came the time, when in her husband's
    face
Care, and concern, and caution she could
    trace;
His troubled features gloom and sadness bore,
Less he resisted, but he suffer'd more;
His nerves were shook like hers; in him her
    grief
Had much of sympathy, but no relief.
  'She could no longer read, and therefore kept
A girl to give her stories while she wept;
Better for Lady Julia's woes to cry,
Than have her own for ever in her eye:
Her husband grieved, and o'er his spirits came
Gloom, and disease attack'd his slender frame;
He felt a loathing for the wretched state
Of his concerns, so sad, so complicate;
Grief and confusion seized him in the day,
And the night pass'd in agony away:
  '"My ruin comes!" was his awakening
    thought,
And vainly through the day was comfort
    sought;
"There, take my all!" he said, and in his
    dream
Heard the door bolted, and his children
    scream.
And he was right, for not a day arose
That he exclaim'd not, "Will it never close?"
"Would it were come!"—but still he shifted
    on,
Till health, and hope, and life's fair views
    were gone.
  'Fretful herself, he of his wife in vain
For comfort sought——"He would be well
    again;
Time would disorders of such nature heal!
O! if he felt what she was doom'd to feel,

Such sleepless nights! such broken rest!
    her frame
Rack'd with diseases that she could not name!
With pangs like hers no other was oppress'd!"
Weeping, she said, and sigh'd herself to rest.
  'The suffering husband look'd the world
    around,
And saw no friend: on him misfortune
    frown'd;
Him self-reproach tormented; sorely tried,
By threats he mourn'd, and by disease he died.
  'As weak as wailing infancy or age,
How could the widow with the world engage?
Fortune not now the means of comfort
    gave,
Yet all her comforts Harriet wept to have.
  '"My helpless babes," she said, "will
    nothing know,"
Yet not a single lesson could bestow;
Her debts would overwhelm her, that was sure,
But one privation would she not endure;
"We shall want bread! the thing is past a
    doubt."—
"Then part with Cousins!"—"Can I do
    without?"—
"Dismiss your servants!"—"Spare me them,
    I pray!"—
"At least your carriage!"—"What will people
    say?"—
"That useless boat, that folly on the lake!"—
"O! but what cry and scandal will it make!"
It was so hard on her, who not a thing
Had done such mischief on their heads to
    bring;
This was her comfort, this she would declare,
And then slept soundly on her pillow'd chair:
When not asleep, how restless was the soul
Above advice, exempted from control;
For ever begging all to be sincere,
And never willing any truth to hear;
A yellow paleness o'er her visage spread,
Her fears augmented as her comforts fled;
Views dark and dismal to her mind appear'd,
And death she sometimes woo'd, and always
    fear'd.
  'Among the clerks there was a thoughtful
    one,
Who still believed that something might be
    done;
All in his view was not so sunk and lost,
But of a trial things would pay the cost:
He judged the widow, and he saw the way
In which her husband suffer'd her to stray;

He saw entangled and perplexed affairs,
And Time's sure hand at work on their
    repairs ;
Children he saw, but nothing could he see
Why he might not their careful father be ;
And looking keenly round him, he believed
That what was lost might quickly be retrieved.
    ' Now thought our clerk—" I must not men-
        tion love,
That she at least must seem to disapprove ;
But I must fear of poverty enforce,
And then consent will be a thing of course.
    ' " Madam ! " said he, " with sorrow I relate,
That our affairs are in a dreadful state ;
I call'd on all our friends, and they declared
They dared not meddle—not a creature dared ;
But still our perseverance chance may aid,
And though I'm puzzled, I am not afraid ;
If you, dear lady, will attention give
To me, the credit of the house shall live ;
Do not, I pray you, my proposal blame,
It is my wish to guard your husband's fame,
And ease your trouble ; then your cares resign
To my discretion—and, in short, be mine."
    ' " Yours ! O ! my stars !—Your goodness,
        sir, deserves
My grateful thanks—take pity on my nerves ;
I shake and tremble at a thing so new,
And fear 'tis what a lady should not do ;
And then to marry upon ruin's brink
In all this hurry—What will people think ? "
    ' " Nay, there's against us neither rule nor
        law,
And people's thinking is not worth a straw ;
Those who are prudent have too much to do
With their own cares to think of me and you ;
And those who are not are so poor a race,
That what they utter can be no disgrace :—
Come ! let us now embark, when time and tide
Invite to sea, in happy hour decide ;
If yet we linger, both are sure to fail,
The turning waters and the varying gale ;
Trust me, our vessel shall be ably steer'd,
Nor will I quit her, till the rocks are clear'd."
    ' Allured and frighten'd, soften'd and afraid,
The widow doubted, ponder'd, and obey'd :
So were they wedded, and the careful man
His reformation instantly began ;
Began his state with vigour to reform,
And made a calm by laughing at the storm.
    ' Th' attendant-maiden he dismiss'd—for
        why ?
She might on him and love like his rely :

She needed none to form her children's mind,
That duty nature to her care assign'd ;
In vain she mourn'd, it was her health he
    prized,
And hence enforced the measures he advised :
She wanted air ; and walking, she was told,
Was safe, was pleasant !—he the carriage sold ;
He found a tenant who agreed to take
The boat and cottage on the useless lake ;
The house itself had now superfluous room,
And a rich lodger was induced to come.
    ' The lady wonder'd at the sudden change,
That yet was pleasant, that was very strange ;
When every deed by her desire was done,
She had no day of comfort—no, not one ;
When nothing moved or stopp'd at her
    request,
Her heart had comfort, and her temper rest ;
For all was done with kindness,—most polite
Was her new lord, and she confess'd it right ;
For now she found that she could gaily live
On what the chance of common life could give :
And her sick mind was cured of every ill,
By finding no compliance with her will ;
For when she saw that her desires were vain,
She wisely thought it foolish to complain.
    ' Born for her man, she gave a gentle sigh
To her lost power, and grieved not to comply ;
Within, without, the face of things improved,
And all in order and subjection moved.
    ' As wealth increased, ambition now began
To swell the soul of the aspiring man ;
In some few years he thought to purchase land,
And build a seat that Hope and Fancy
    plann'd ;
To this a name his youthful bride should give !
Harriet, of course, not many years would live ;
Then he would farm, and every soil should show
The tree that best upon the place would grow :
He would, moreover, on the Bench debate
On sundry questions—when a magistrate ;
Would talk of all that to the state belongs,
The rich man's duties, and the poor man's
    wrongs ;
He would with favourites of the people rank,
And him the weak and the oppress'd should
    thank.
    ' 'Tis true those children, orphans then !
        would need
Help in a world of trouble to succeed !
And they should have it—He should then
        possess
All that man needs for earthly happiness.

' " Proud words, and vain ! " said Doctor
    Young ; and proud
They are ; and vain, were by our clerk
    allow'd ; .
For, while he dream'd, there came both pain
    and cough,
And fever never tamed, and bore him off ;
Young as he was, and planning schemes to
    live
With more delight than man's success can
    give ;
Building a mansion in his fancy vast,
Beyond the Gothic pride of ages past !
While this was plann'd, but ere a place was
    sought,
The timber season'd, or the quarry wrought,
Came Death's dread summons, and the man
    was laid
In the poor house the simple sexton made.
  ' But he had time for thought when he was
    ill,
And made his lady an indulgent will :
'Tis said he gave, in parting, his advice,
" It is sufficient to be married twice ; "
To which she answer'd, as 'tis said, again,
" There 's none will have you if you're poor
    and plain,
And if you're rich and handsome there is none
Will take refusal——let the point alone."
  ' Be this or true or false, it is her praise
She mourn'd correctly all the mourning days ;
But grieve she did not, for the canker grief
Soils the complexion, and is beauty's thief ;
Nothing, indeed, so much will discompose
Our public mourning as our private woes ;
When tender thoughts a widow's bosom probe,
She thinks not then how graceful sits the
    robe ;
But our nice widow look'd to every fold,
And every eye its beauty might behold !
It was becoming ; she composed her face,
She look'd serenely, and she mourn'd with
    grace.
  ' Some months were pass'd, but yet there
    wanted three
Of the full time when widows wives may be ;
One trying year, and then the mind is freed,
And man may to the vacant throne succeed.
  ' There was a tenant—he, to wit, who hired
That cot and lake, that were so much ad-
    mired ;
A man of spirit, one who doubtless meant,
Though he delay'd awhile, to pay his rent ;

The widow's riches gave her much delight,
And some her claims, and she resolved to
    write.
  ' " He knew her grievous loss, how every care
Devolved on her, who had indeed her share ;
She had no doubt of him,—but was as sure
As that she breathed her money was secure ;
But she had made a rash and idle vow
To claim her dues, and she must keep it now :
So, if it suited—— "
                    And for this there came
A civil answer to the gentle dame :
Within the letter were excuses, thanks,
And clean Bank paper from the best of banks;
There were condolence, consolation, praise,
With some slight hints of danger in delays ;
With these good things were others from the
    lake,
Perch that were wish'd to salmon for her sake,
And compliment as sweet as new-born hope
    could make.
  ' This led to friendly visits, social calls,
And much discourse of races, rambles, balls ;
But all in proper bounds, and not a word
Before its time,—the man was not absurd,
Nor was he cold ; but when she might expect,
A letter came, and one to this effect.
  ' " That if his eyes had not his love convey'd,
They had their master shamefully betray'd ;
But she must know the flame, that he was sure,
Nor she could doubt, would long as life
    endure :
Both were in widow'd state, and both possess'd
Of ample means to make their union bless'd ;
That she had been confined he knew for truth,
And begg'd her to have pity on her youth ;
Youth, he would say, and he desired his wife
To have the comforts of an easy life :
She loved a carriage, loved a decent seat
To which they might at certain times retreat ;
Servants indeed were sorrows,—yet a few
They still must add, and do as others do :
She too would some attendant damsel need,
To hear, to speak, to travel, or to read : "
In short, the man his remedies assign'd
For his foreknown diseases in the mind :—
" First," he presumed, " that in a nervous case
Nothing was better than a change of place :"
He added, too, " 'Twas well that he could
    prove
That his was pure, disinterested love ;
Not as when lawyers couple house and land
In such a way as none can understand ;

No ! thanks to Him that every good supplied,
He had enough, and wanted nought beside !
Merit was all."
   " Well ! now, she would protest,
This was a letter prettily express'd."
To every female friend away she flew
To ask advice, and say, " What shall I do ? "
She kiss'd her children,—and she said, with
 tears,
" I wonder what is best for you, my dears ?
How can I, darlings, to your good attend
Without the help of some experienced friend,
Who will protect us all, or, injured, will
 defend ? "
 'The widow then ask'd counsel of her heart,
In vain, for that had nothing to impart ;
But yet with that, or something for her guide,
She to her swain thus guardedly replied.
 '" She must believe he was sincere, for why
Should one who needed nothing deign to lie ?
But though she could and did his truth admit,
She could not praise him for his taste a bit ;
And yet men's tastes were various, she con-
 fess'd,
And none could prove his own to be the best ;
It was a vast concern, including all
That we can happiness or comfort call ;
And yet she found that those who waited long
Before their choice, had often chosen wrong ;
Nothing, indeed, could for her loss atone,
But 'twas the greater that she lived alone ;
She, too, had means, and therefore what the
 use
Of more, that still more trouble would produce?
And pleasure too she own'd, as well as care,
Of which, at present, she had not her share.
 '" The things he offer'd, she must needs
 confess,
They were all women's wishes, more or less ;
But were expensive ; though a man of sense
Would by his prudence lighten the expense :
Prudent he was, but made a sad mistake
When he proposed her faded face to take ;
And yet 'tis said there's beauty that will last
When the rose withers and the bloom be past.
 '" One thing displeased her,—that he could
 suppose
He might so soon his purposes disclose ;
Yet had she hints of such intent before,
And would excuse him if he wrote no more :
What would the world ?—and yet she judged
 them fools
Who let the world's suggestions be their rules :

What would her friends ?—Yet in her own
 affairs
It was her business to decide, not theirs :
Adieu ! then, sir," she added ; " thus you find
The changeless purpose of a steady mind,
In one now left alone, but to her fate resign'd."
 'The marriage follow'd; and th' experienced
 dame
Consider'd what the conduct that became
A thrice-devoted lady—She confess'd
That when indulged she was but more dis-
 tress'd ;
And by her second husband when controll'd,
Her life was pleasant, though her love was
 cold ;
" Then let me yield," she said, and with a sigh,
" Let me to wrong submit, with right comply."
 ' Alas ! obedience may mistake, and they
Who reason not will err when they obey ;
And fated was the gentle dame to find
Her duty wrong, and her obedience blind.
 ' The man was kind, but would have no
 dispute,
His love and kindness both were absolute ;
She needed not her wishes to express
To one who urged her on to happiness ;
For this he took her to the lakes and seas,
To mines and mountains, nor allow'd her ease,
She must be pleased, he said, and he must
 live to please.
 ' He hurried north and south, and east and
 west,
When age required they would have time to
 rest :
He in the richest dress her form array'd,
And cared not what he promised, what he
 paid ;
She should share all his pleasures as her own,
And see whatever could be sought or shown.
 ' This run of pleasure for a time she bore,
And then affirm'd that she could taste no
 more ;
She loved it while its nature it retain'd,
But made a duty, it displeased and pain'd :
" Have we not means ? " the joyous husband
 cried ;
" But I am wearied out," the wife replied ;
" Wearied with pleasure ! Thing till now
 unheard—
Are all that sweeten trouble to be fear'd ?
'Tis but the sameness tires you,—cross the
 seas,
And let us taste the world's varieties.

' " 'Tis said, in Paris that a man may live
In all the luxuries a world can give,
And in a space confined to narrow bound
All the enjoyments of our life are found ;
There we may eat and drink, may dance and
    dress,
And in its very essence joy possess ;
May see a moving crowd of lovely dames,
May win a fortune at your favourite games ;
May hear the sounds that ravish human sense,
And all without receding foot from thence."
  ' The conquer'd wife, resistless and afraid,
To the strong call a sad obedience paid.
  ' As we an infant in its pain, with sweets
Loved once, now loath'd, torment him till he eats,
Who on the authors of his new distress
Looks trembling with disgusted weariness,
So Harriet felt, so look'd, and seem'd to say,
" O ! for a day of rest, an holiday ! "
  ' At length her courage rising with her fear,
She said, " Our pleasures may be bought too
    dear ! "
  ' To this he answer'd—" Dearest ! from thy
    heart
Bid every fear of evil times depart ;
I ever trusted in the trying hour
To my good stars, and felt the ruling power ;
When want drew nigh, his threat'ning speed
    was stopp'd,
Some virgin aunt, some childless uncle
    dropp'd ;
In all his threats I sought expedients new,
And my last, best resource was found in you."
  ' Silent and sad the wife beheld her doom,
And sat her down to see the ruin come ;
And meet the ills that rise where money fails,
Debts, threats and duns, bills, bailiffs, writs
    and jails.

  ' These was she spared ; ere yet by want
    oppress'd,
Came one more fierce than bailiff in arrest ;
Amid a scene where Pleasure never came,
Though never ceased the mention of his name,
The husband's heated blood received the
    breath
Of strong disease, that bore him to his death.
  ' Her all collected,—whether great or small
The sum, I know not, but collected all ;—
The widow'd lady to her cot retired,
And there she lives delighted and admired :
Civil to all, compliant and polite,
Disposed to think " whatever is, is right ; "
She wears the widow's weeds, she gives the
    widow's mite.
At home awhile, she in the autumn finds
The sea an object for reflecting minds,
And change for tender spirits ; there she
    reads,
And weeps in comfort in her graceful weeds.
  ' What gives our tale its moral ? Here we
    find
That wives like this are not for rule design'd,
Nor yet for blind submission ; happy they,
Who while they feel it pleasant to obey,
Have yet a kind companion at their side
Who in their journey will his power divide,
Or yield the reins, and bid the lady guide ;
Then points the wonders of the way, and makes
The duty pleasant that she undertakes ;
He shows her objects as they move along,
And gently rules the movements that are
    wrong ;
He tells her all the skilful driver's art,
And smiles to see how well she acts her part ;
Nor praise denies to courage or to skill,
In using power that he resumes at will.'

BOOK XVIII.   ELLEN

A Morning Ride—A Purchase of the Squire—
The Way to it described—The former
Proprietor—Richard's Return—Inquiries
respecting a Lady whom he had seen—Her
History related—Her attachment to a
Tutor—They are parted—Impediments
removed—How removed in vain—Fate of
the Lover—Of Ellen.

  BLEAK was the morn—said Richard, with
    a sigh,
' I must depart ! '—' That, Brother, I deny,'

Said George—' You may ; but I perceive not
    why.'
  This point before had been discuss'd, but
    still
The guest submitted to the ruling will ;
But every day gave rise to doubt and
    fear,—
He heard not now, as he was wont to hear,
That all was well !—though little was ex-
    press'd,
It seem'd to him the writer was distress'd ;

Restrain'd ! there was attempt and strife to
please,
Pains and endeavour—not Matilda's ease ;—
Not the pure lines of love ! the guileless friend
In all her freedom—What could this portend ?
' Fancy ! ' said George, ' the self-tormentor's
pain '—
And Richard still consented to remain.
  ' Ride you this fair cool morning ? ' said
the squire :
Do—for a purchase I have made inquire,
And with you take a will complacently
t' admire :
Southward at first, dear Richard, make your
way,
Cross Hilton Bridge, move on through
Breken Clay,
At Dunham Wood turn duly to the east,
And there your eyes upon the ocean feast ;
Then ride above the cliff, or ride below,
You'll be enraptured, for your taste I know ;
It is a prospect that a man might stay
To his bride hastening on his wedding-day ;
At Tilburn Sluice once more ascend and view
A decent house ; an ample garden too,
And planted well behind—a lively scene, and
new ;
A little taste, a little pomp display'd,
By a dull man, who had retired from trade
To enjoy his leisure—Here he came prepared
To farm, nor cost in preparation spared ;
But many works he purchased, some he read,
And often rose with projects in his head,
Of crops in courses raised, of herds by
matching bred.
  ' We had just found these little humours out,
Just saw—he saw not—what he was about ;
Just met as neighbours, still disposed to meet,
Just learn'd the current tales of Dowling
Street,
And were just thinking of our female friends,
Saying—" You know not what the man
intends,
A rich, kind, hearty "—and it might be true
Something he wish'd, but had not time to do ;
A cold ere yet the falling leaf ! of small
Effect till then, was fatal in the fall ;
And of that house was his possession brief—
Go ; and guard well against the falling leaf.
  ' But hear me, Richard, looking to my ease,
Try if you can find something that will please ;
Faults if you see, and such as must abide,
Say they are small, or say that I can hide ;

But faults that I can change, remove, or
mend,
These like a foe detect—or like a friend.
  ' Mark well the rooms, and their propor-
tions learn,
In each some use, some elegance discern ;
Observe the garden, its productive wall,
And find a something to commend in all ;
Then should you praise them in a knowing
way,
I'll take it kindly—that is well—be gay.
  ' Nor pass the pebbled cottage as you rise
Above the sluice, till you have fix'd your eyes
On the low woodbined window, and have seen,
So fortune favour you, the ghost within ;
Take but one look, and then your way pursue,
It flies all strangers, and it knows not you.'
  Richard return'd, and by his Brother stood,
Not in a pensive, not in pleasant mood ;
But by strong feeling into stillness wrought,
As nothing thinking, or with too much
thought ;
Or like a man who means indeed to speak,
But would his hearer should his purpose seek.
  When George—' What is it, Brother, you
would hide ?
Or what confess ? '—' Who is she ? ' he
replied,
' That angel whom I saw, to whom is she
allied ?
Of this fair being let me understand,
And I will praise your purchase, house and
land.
  ' Hers was that cottage on the rising ground,
West of the waves, and just beyond their
sound ;
'Tis larger than the rest, and whence, indeed,
You might expect a lady to proceed ;
But O ! this creature, far as I could trace,
Will soon be carried to another place.
  ' Fair, fragile thing ! I said, when first my
eye
Caught hers, wilt thou expand thy wings and
fly ?
Or wilt thou vanish ? beauteous spirit—stay !
For will it not (I question'd) melt away ?
No ! it was mortal—I unseen was near,
And saw the bosom's sigh, the standing tear !
She thought profoundly, for I stay'd to look,
And first she read, then laid aside her book ;
Then on her hand reclined her lovely head,
And seem'd unconscious of the tear she
shed.

' " Art thou so much," I said, " to grief a
　　　prey ? "
Till pity pain'd me, and I rode away.
　' Tell me, my Brother, is that sorrow dread
For the great change that bears her to the
　　　dead ?
Has she connexions ? does she love ?—I feel
Pity and grief, wilt thou her woes reveal ? '
　' They are not lasting, Richard, they are
　　　woes
Chastised and meek ! she sings them to
　　　repose ;
If not, she reasons ; if they still remain,
She finds resource, that none shall find in vain.
　' Whether disease first grew upon regret,
Or nature gave it, is uncertain yet,
And must remain ; the frame was slightly
　　　made,
That grief assail'd, and all is now decay'd !
　' But though so willing from the world to
　　　part,
I must not call her case a broken heart ;
Nor dare I take upon me to maintain
That hearts once broken never heal again.'

　' She was an only daughter, one whose sire
Loved not that girls to knowledge should
　　　aspire ;
But he had sons, and Ellen quickly caught
Whatever they were by their masters taught ;
This, when the father saw—" It is the turn
Of her strange mind," said he, " but let her
　　　learn ;
'Tis almost pity with that shape and face—
But is a fashion, and brings no disgrace ;
Women of old wrote verse, or for the stage
Brought forth their works ! they now are
　　　reasoners sage,
And with severe pursuits dare grapple and
　　　engage.
If such her mind, I shall in vain oppose,
If not, her labours of themselves will close."
　' Ellen, 'twas found, had skill without pre-
　　　tence,
And silenced envy by her meek good sense ;
That Ellen learnt, her various knowledge
　　　proved ;
Soft words and tender looks, that Ellen loved ;
For he who taught her brothers found in her
A constant, ready, eager auditor ;
This he perceived, nor could his joy disguise,
It tuned his voice, it sparkled in his eyes.

' Not very young, nor very handsome he,
But very fit an Abelard to be ;
His manner and his meekness hush'd alarm
In all but Ellen—Ellen felt the charm ;
Hers was fond " filial love," she found delight
To have her mind's dear father in her sight ;
　' But soon the borrow'd notion she resign'd !
He was no father—even to the mind.
　' But Ellen had her comforts—" He will
　　　speak,"
She said, " for he beholds me fond and weak ;
Fond, and he therefore may securely plead,—
Weak, I have therefore of his firmness need ;
With whom my father will his Ellen trust,
Because he knows him to be kind and just."
　' Alas ! too well the conscious lover knew
The parent's mind, and well the daughter's
　　　too ;
He felt of duty the imperious call,
Beheld his danger, and must fly or fall.
What would the parent, what his pupils think ?
O ! he was standing on perdition's brink :
In his dilemma flight alone remain'd,
And could he fly whose very soul was chain'd ?
He knew she loved ; she tried not to conceal
A hope she thought that virtue's self might
　　　feel.
　' Ever of her and her frank heart afraid,
Doubting himself, he sought in absence, aid,
And had resolved on flight, but still the act
　　　delay'd ;
At last so high his apprehension rose,
That he would both his love and labour close.
　' " While undisclosed my fear each instant
　　　grows,
And I lament the guilt that no one knows,
Success undoes me, and the view that cheers
All other men, all dark to me appears ! "
　' Thus as he thought, his Ellen at his side
Her soothing softness to his grief applied ;
With like effect as water cast on flame,
For he more heated and confused became,
And broke in sorrow from the wondering
　　　maid,
Who was at once offended and afraid ;
Yet " Do not go ! " she cried, and was awhile
　　　obey'd.
　' " Art thou then ill, dear friend ? " she
　　　ask'd, and took
His passive hand—" How very pale thy look !
And thou art cold, and tremblest—pray thee
　　　tell
Thy friend, thy Ellen, is her master well ?

And let her with her loving care attend
To all that vexes and disturbs her friend."
  ' "Nay, my dear lady! we have all our cares,
And I am troubled with my poor affairs:
Thou canst not aid me, Ellen; could it be
And might it, doubtless, I would fly to thee;
But we have sundry duties, and must all,
Hard as it may be, go where duties call—
Suppose the trial were this instant thine,
Could thou the happiest of thy views resign
At duty's strong command?"—"If thou
      wert by,"
Said the unconscious maiden, "I would try!"—
And as she sigh'd she heard the soft respon-
      sive sigh.
  'And then assuming steadiness, "Adieu!"
He cried, and from the grieving Ellen flew;
And to her father with a bleeding heart
He went, his grief and purpose to impart;
Told of his health, and did in part confess
That he should love the noble maiden less.
  'The parent's pride to sudden rage gave
      way—
"And the girl loves! that plainly you would
      say—
And you with honour, in your pride, retire !—
Sir, I your prudence envy and admire."
But here the father saw the rising frown,
And quickly let his lofty spirit down.
  ' "Forgive a parent !—I may well excuse
A girl who could perceive such worth and
      choose
To make it hers; we must not look to meet
All we might wish ;—Is age itself discreet ?
Where conquest may not be, 'tis prudence to
      retreat."
  'Then with the kindness worldly minds
      assume
He praised the self-pronounced and rigorous
      doom;
He wonder'd not that one so young should
      love,
And much he wish'd he could the choice
      approve;
Much he lamented such a mind to lose,
And begg'd to learn if he could aid his views,
If such were form'd—then closed the short
      account,
And to a shilling paid the full amount.
  'So Cecil left the mansion, and so flew
To foreign shores, without an interview;
He must not say, I love—he could not say,
      Adieu!

  'Long was he absent; as a guide to youth,
With grief contending, and in search of truth,
In courting peace, and trying to forget
What was so deeply interesting yet.
  'A friend in England gave him all the news,
A sad indulgence that he would not lose;
He told how Ellen suffer'd, how they sent
The maid from home in sullen discontent,
With some relation on the Lakes to live,
In all the sorrow such retirements give;
And there she roved among the rocks, and took
Moss from the stone, and pebbles from the
      brook;
Gazed on the flies that settled on the flowers,
And so consumed her melancholy hours.
  'Again he wrote—The father then was dead,
And Ellen to her native village fled,
With native feeling—there she oped her door,
Her heart, her purse, and comforted the poor,
The sick, the sad,—and there she pass'd her
      days,
Deserving much, but never seeking praise,
Her task to guide herself, her joy the fallen
      to raise.
Nor would she nicely faults and merits weigh,
But loved the impulse of her soul t' obey;
The prayers of all she heard, their sufferings
      view'd,
Nor turn'd from any, save when Love pursued;
For though to love disposed, to kindness
      prone,
She thought of Cecil, and she lived alone.
  'Thus heard the lover of the life she past
Till his return,—and he return'd at last;
For he had saved, and was a richer man
Than when to teach and study he began;
Something his father left, and he could fly
To the loved country where he wish'd to die.
  ' "And now," he said, "this maid with
      gentle mind
May I not hope to meet, as good, as kind,
As in the days when first her friend she knew
And then could trust—and he indeed is true ?
She knew my motives, and she must approve
The man who dared to sacrifice his love
And fondest hopes to virtue: virtuous she,
Nor can resent that sacrifice in me."
  'He reason'd thus, but fear'd, and sought the
      friend
In his own country, where his doubts must
      end;
They then together to her dwelling came,
And by a servant sent her lover's name,

A modest youth, whom she before had known,
His favourite then, and doubtless *then* her own.
  'They in the carriage heard the servants speak
At Ellen's door—"A maid so heavenly meek,
Who would all pain extinguish! Yet will she
Pronounce my doom, I feel the certainty!"—
"Courage!" the friend exclaim'd, "the lover's fear
Grows without ground;" but Cecil would not hear:
He seem'd some dreadful object to explore,
And fix'd his fearful eye upon the door,
Intensely longing for reply—the thing
That must to him his future fortune bring;
And now it brought! like Death's cold hand it came—
"The lady was a stranger to the name!"
  'Backward the lover in the carriage fell,
Weak, but not fainting—"All," said he, "is well!
Return with me—I have no more to seek!"
And this was all the woful man would speak.
  'Quickly he settled all his worldly views,
And sail'd from home, his fiercer pains to lose
And nurse the milder—now with labour less
He might his solitary world possess,
And taste the bitter-sweet of love in idleness.
  'Greece was the land he chose; a mind decay'd
And ruin'd there through glorious ruin stray'd;
There read, and walk'd, and mused,—there loved, and wept, and pray'd.
Nor would he write, nor suffer hope to live,
But gave to study all his mind could give;
Till, with the dead conversing, he began
To lose the habits of a living man,
Save that he saw some wretched, them he tried
To soothe,—some doubtful, them he strove to guide;
Nor did he lose the mind's ennobling joy
Of that new state that death must not destroy;
What Time had done we know not,—Death was nigh,
To his first hopes the lover gave a sigh,
But hopes more new and strong confirm'd his wish to die.
  'Meantime poor Ellen in her cottage thought
"That he would seek her—sure she should be sought—

She did not mean—It was an evil hour,
Her thoughts were guardless, and beyond her power;
And for one speech, and that in rashness made!
Have I no friend to soothe him and persuade?
He must not leave me—He again will come,
And we shall have one hope, one heart, one home!"
  'But when she heard that he on foreign ground
Sought his lost peace, hers never more was found;
But still she felt a varying hope that love
Would all these slight impediments remove;—
"Has he no friend to tell him that our pride
Resents a moment and is satisfied?
Soon as the hasty sacrifice is made,
A look will soothe us, and a tear persuade;
Have I no friend to say 'Return again,
Reveal your wishes, and relieve her pain?'"
  'With suffering mind the maid her prospects view'd,
That hourly varied with the varying mood;
As past the day, the week, the month, the year,
The faint hope sicken'd, and gave place to fear.
  'No Cecil came!—"Come, peevish and unjust!"
Sad Ellen cried, "why cherish this disgust?
Thy Ellen's voice could charm thee once, but thou
Canst nothing see or hear of Ellen now!"
  'Yes! she was right; the grave on him was closed,
And there the lover and the friend reposed.
The news soon reach'd her, and she then replied
In his own manner—"I am satisfied!"
  'To her a lover's legacy is paid,
The darling wealth of the devoted maid;
From this her best and favourite books she buys,
From this are doled the favourite charities;
And when a tale or face affects her heart,
This is the fund that must relief impart.
  'Such have the ten last years of Ellen been!
Her very last that sunken eye has seen!
That half angelic being still must fade
Till all the angel in the mind be made;—
And now the closing scene will shortly come—
She cannot visit sorrow at her home;

But still she feeds the hungry, still prepares
The usual softeners of the peasant's cares,
And though she prays not with the dying
    now,
She teaches them to die, and shows them
    how.'

' Such is my tale, dear Richard, but that
    told
I must all comments on the text withhold ;
What is the sin of grief I cannot tell,
Nor of the sinners who have loved too well ;
But to the cause of mercy I incline,
Or, O ! my Brother, what a fate is mine ! '

BOOK XIX.   WILLIAM BAILEY

Discourse on Jealousy—Of unsuspicious Men
—Visit William and his wife—His Dwelling
—Story of William and Fanny—Character
of both—Their Contract—Fanny's Visit to
an Aunt—Its Consequences—Her Father's
Expectation — His Death — William a
Wanderer—His Mode of Living—The
Acquaintance he forms—Travels across the
Kingdom—Whom he finds—The Event of
their Meeting.

THE letters Richard in a morning read
To quiet and domestic comforts led ;
And George, who thought the world could
    not supply
Comfort so pure, reflected with a sigh ;
Then would pursue the subject half in play,
Half earnest, till the sadness wore away.
    They spoke of Passion's errors, Love's
    disease,
His pains, afflictions, wrongs, and jealousies ;
Of Herod's vile commandment—that his wife
Should live no more, when he no more had
    life ;
He could not bear that royal Herod's spouse
Should, as a widow, make his second vows ;
Or that a mortal with his queen should wed,
Or be the rival of the mighty dead.
    ' Herods,' said Richard, ' doubtless may be
    found,
But haply do not in the world abound ;
Ladies, indeed, a dreadful lot would have,
If jealousy could act beyond the grave :
No doubt Othellos every place supply,
Though every Desdemona does not die ;
But there are lovers in the world, who live
Slaves to the sex, and every fault forgive.'
    ' I know,' said George, ' a happy man and
    kind,
Who finds his wife is all he wish'd to find,
A mild, good man, who, if he nothing sees,
Will suffer nothing to disturb his ease ;

Who, ever yielding both to smiles and sighs,
Admits no story that a wife denies,—
She guides his mind, and she directs his eyes.
    ' Richard, there dwells within a mile a
    pair
Of good examples,—I will guide you there :
Such man is William Bailey,—but his spouse
Is virtue's self since she had made her vows :
I speak of ancient stories, long worn out,
That honest William would not talk about ;
But he will sometimes check her starting tear,
And call her self-correction too severe.
    ' In their own inn the gentle pair are placed,
Where you behold the marks of William's
    taste :
They dwell in plenty, in respect, and peace,
Landlord and lady of the Golden Fleece :
Public indeed their calling,—but there come
No brawl, no revel to that decent room ;
All there is still, and comely to behold,
Mild as the fleece, and pleasant as the gold ;
But mild and pleasant as they now appear,
They first experienced many a troubled year ;
And that, if known, might not command our
    praise,
Like the smooth tenor of their present days.
    ' Our hostess, now so grave and steady
    grown,
Has had some awkward trials of her own :
She was not always so resign'd and meek,—
Yet can I little of her failings speak ;
Those she herself will her misfortunes deem,
And slides discreetly from the dubious theme;
But you shall hear the tale that I will tell,
When we have seen the mansion where they
    dwell.'
    They saw the mansion,—and the couple
    made
Obeisance due, and not without parade :
' His honour, still obliging, took delight
To make them pleasant in each other's **sight** ;

It was their duty—they were very sure
It was their pleasure.'
                    This they could endure,
Nor turn'd impatient——In the room around
Were care and neatness : instruments were
        found
For sacred music, books with prints and notes
By learned men and good, whom William
        quotes
In mode familiar—Beveridge, Doddridge,
        Hall,
Pyle, Whitby, Hammond—he refers to all.
    Next they beheld his garden, fruitful, nice,
And, as he said, his little paradise.
    In man and wife appear'd some signs of
        pride,
Which they perceived not, or they would not
        hide,—
' Their honest saving, their good name, their
        skill,
His honour's land, which they had grace to
        till ;
And more his favour shown, with all their
        friends' good will.'
    This past, the visit was with kindness closed,
And George was ask'd to do as he proposed.
    ' Richard,' said he, ' though I myself
        explore
With no distaste the annals of the poor,
And may with safety to a brother show
What of my humble friends I chance to know,
Richard, there are who call the subjects low.
    ' The host and hostess of the Fleece'—'tis
        base—
Would I could cast some glory round the
        place !
    ' The lively heroine once adorn'd a farm,—
And William's virtue has a kind of charm :
Nor shall we, in our apprehension, need
Riches or rank——I think I may proceed :
Virtue and worth there are who will not see
In humble dress, but low they cannot be.'

_____

' The youth's addresses pleased his favourite
        maid,—
They wish'd for union, but were both afraid ;
They saw the wedded poor,—and fear the
        bliss delay'd :
Yet they appear'd a happier lass and swain
Than those who will not reason or refrain.
    William was honest, simple, gentle, kind,
Laborious, studious, and to thrift inclined ;

More neat than youthful peasant in his dress,
And yet so careful, that it cost him less :
He kept from inns, though doom'd an inn to
        keep,
And all his pleasures and pursuits were cheap :
Yet would the youth perform a generous deed,
When reason saw or pity felt the need ;
He of his labour and his skill would lend,
Nay, of his money, to a suffering friend.
    ' William had manual arts,—his room was
        graced
With carving quaint, that spoke the master's
        taste ;
But if that taste admitted some dispute,
He charm'd the nymphs with flageolet and
        flute.
    ' Constant at church, and there a little proud,
He sang with boldness, and he read aloud ;
Self-taught to write, he his example took
And form'd his letters from a printed book.
    ' I've heard of ladies who profess'd to see
In a man's writing what his mind must be ;
As Doctor Spurzheim's pupils, when they
        look
Upon a skull, will read it as a book—
Our talents, tendencies, and likings trace,
And find for all the measure and the place :
    ' Strange times ! when thus we are com-
        pletely read
By man or woman, by the hand or head !
Believe who can,—but William's even mind
All who beheld might in his writing find ;
His not the scratches where we try in vain
Meanings and words to construe or explain.
    ' But with our village hero to proceed,—
He read as learned clerks are wont to read ;
Solemn he was in tone, and slow in pace,
By nature gifted both with strength and grace.
    ' Black parted locks his polish'd forehead
        press'd ;
His placid looks an easy mind confess'd ;
His smile content, and seldom more, con-
        vey'd ;
Not like the smile of fair illusive maid,
When what she feels is hid, and what she
        wills betray'd.
    ' The lighter damsels call'd his manner prim,
And laugh'd at virtue so array'd in him ;
But they were wanton, as he well replied,
And hoped their own would not be strongly
        tried :
Yet was he full of glee, and had his strokes
Of rustic wit, his repartees and jokes ;

Nor was averse, ere yet he pledged his love,
To stray with damsels in the shady grove ;
When he would tell them, as they walk'd
    along,
How the birds sang, and imitate their song :
In fact, our rustic had his proper taste,
Was with peculiar arts and manners graced—
And Absolon had been, had Absolon been
    chaste.

'Frances, like William, felt her heart incline
To neat attire—but Frances would be fine :
Though small the farm, the farmer's daughter
    knew
Her rank in life, and she would have it too :
This, and this only, gave the lover pain,
He thought it needless, and he judged it vain :
Advice in hints he to the fault applied,
And talk'd of sin, of vanity, and pride.

'"And what is proud," said Frances, "but to
    stand
Singing at church, and sawing thus your hand?
Looking at heaven above, as if to bring
The holy angels down to hear you sing ?
And when you write, you try with all your
    skill,
And cry, no wonder that you wrote so ill !
For you were ever to yourself a rule,
And humbly add, you never were at school—
Is that not proud ?—And I have heard
    beside,
The proudest creatures have the humblest
    pride :
If you had read the volumes I have hired,
You'd see your fault, nor try to be admired ;
For they who read such books can always
    tell
The fault within, and read the mind as well."

' William had heard of hiring books before,
He knew she read, and he inquired no more ;
On him the subject was completely lost,
What he regarded was the time and cost ;
Yet that was trifling—just a present whim,
"Novels and stories ! what were they to him?"

'With such slight quarrels, or with those as
    slight,
They lived in love, and dream'd of its delight.
Her duties Fanny knew, both great and small,
And she with diligence observed them all ;
If e'er she fail'd a duty to fulfil,
'Twas childish error, not rebellious will ;
For her much reading, though it touch'd her
    heart,
Could neither vice nor indolence impart.

' Yet, when from William and her friends
    retired,
She found her reading had her mind inspired
With hopes and thoughts of high mysterious
    things,
Such as the early dream of kindness brings ;
And then she wept, and wonder'd as she read,
And new emotions in her heart were bred :
She sometimes fancied that when love was true
'Twas more than she and William ever knew ;
More than the shady lane in summer-eve,
More than the sighing when he took his leave ;
More than his preference when the lads
    advance
And choose their partners for the evening
    dance ;
Nay, more than midnight thoughts and
    morning dreams,
Or talk when love and marriage are the
    themes ;
In fact, a something not to be defined,
Of all subduing, all commanding kind,
That fills the fondest heart, that rules the
    proudest mind.

' But on her lover Fanny still relied,
Her best companion, her sincerest guide,
On whom she could rely, in whom she would
    confide.

' All jealous fits were past ; in either now
Were tender wishes for the binding vow ;
There was no secret one alone possess'd,
There was no hope that warm'd a single
    breast ;
Both felt the same concerns their thoughts
    employ,
And 'neither knew one solitary joy.

' Then why so easy, William ? why consent
To wait so long ? thou wilt at last repent ;
"Within a month," does Care and Prudence
    say,
If all be ready, linger not a day ;
Ere yet the choice be made, on choice debate,
But having chosen, dally not with fate.

' While yet to wait the pair were half content,
And half disposed their purpose to repent,
A spinster-aunt, in some great baron's place,
Would see a damsel, pride of all her race :
And Fanny, flatter'd by the matron's call,
Obey'd her aunt, and long'd to see the Hall ;
For halls and castles in her fancy wrought,
And she accounts of love and wonder sought ;
There she expected strange events to learn,
And take in tender secrets fond concern ;

There she expected lovely nymphs to view,
Perhaps to hear and meet their lovers too ;
The Julias, tender souls ! the Henrys kind
    and true :
There she expected plottings to detect,
And—but I know not what she might expect—
All she was taught in books to be her guide,
And all that nature taught the nymph beside.
  ' Now that good dame had in the castle dwelt
So long that she for all its people felt ;
She kept her sundry keys, and ruled o'er all,
Female and male, domestics in the hall ;
By her lord trusted, worthy of her trust,
Proud but obedient, bountiful but just.
  ' She praised her lucky stars, that in her
    place
She never found neglect, nor felt disgrace ;
To do her duty was her soul's delight,
This her inferiors would to theirs excite,
This her superiors notice and requite ;
To either class she gave the praises due,
And still more grateful as more favour'd grew:
Her lord and lady were of peerless worth,
In power unmatch'd, in glory and in birth ;
And such the virtue of the noble race,
It reach'd the meanest servant in the place ;
All, from the chief attendant on my lord
To the groom's helper, had her civil word ;
From Miss Montregor, who the ladies taught,
To the rude lad who in the garden wrought ;
From the first favourite to the meanest drudge,
Were no such women, heaven should be her
    judge ;
Whatever stains were theirs, let them reside
In that pure place, and they were mundified ;
The sun of favour on their vileness shone,
And all their faults like morning mists were
    gone.
  ' There was Lord Robert ! could she have
    her choice,
From the world's masters he should have her
    voice ;
So kind and gracious in his noble ways,
It was a pleasure speaking in his praise :
And Lady Catharine,—O ! a prince's pride
Might by one smile of hers be gratified ;
With her would monarchs all their glory
    share,
And in her presence banish all their care.
  ' Such was the matron, and to her the maid
Was by her lover carefully convey'd.
  ' When William first the invitation read
It some displeasure in his spirit bred,

Not that one jealous thought the man
    possess'd,
He was by fondness, not by fear distress'd ;
But when his Fanny to his mind convey'd
The growing treasures of the ancient maid,
The thirty years, come June, of service past,
Her lasting love, her life that would not last ;
Her power ! her place ! what interest ! what
    respect
She had acquired—and shall we her neglect ?
  ' " No, Frances, no ! " he answer'd, " you
    are right ;
But things appear in such a different light ! "
  ' Her parents blest her, and as well became
Their love advised her, that they might not
    blame ;
They said, " If she should earl or countess
    meet
She should be humble, cautious, and discreet ;
Humble, but not abased, remembering all
Are kindred sinners,—children of the fall ;
That from the earth our being we receive,
And are all equal when the earth we leave."
  ' They then advised her in a modest way
To make replies to what my lord might say ;
Her aunt would aid her, who was now become
With nobles noble, and with lords at home.
  ' So went the pair ; and William told at night
Of a reception gracious and polite ;
He spake of galleries long and pictures tall,
The handsome parlours, the prodigious hall,
The busts, the statues, and the floors of stone,
The storied arras, and the vast saloon,
In which was placed an Indian chest and
    screen,
With figures such as he had never seen :
He told of these as men enraptured tell,
And gave to all their praise, and all was well.
  ' Left by the lover, the desponding maid
Was of the matron's ridicule afraid ;
But when she heard a welcome frank and kind,
The wonted firmness repossess'd her mind ;
Pleased by the looks of love her aunt display'd,
Her fond professions, and her kind parade.
  ' In her own room, and with her niece apart,
She gave up all the secrets of her heart ;
And, grown familiar, bid her Fanny come,
Partake her cheer, and make herself at home.
  ' Shut in that room, upon its cheerful board
She laid the comforts of no vulgar hoard ;
Then press'd the damsel both with love and
    pride,
For both she felt—and would not be denied.

'Grace she pronounced before and after
    meat,
And bless'd her God that she could talk and
    eat ;
Then with new glee she sang her patron's
    praise——
" He had no paltry arts, no pimping ways ;
She had the roast and boil'd of every day,
That sent the poor with grateful hearts away ;
And she was grateful——Come, my darling,
    think
Of them you love the best, and let us drink."
    ' And now she drank the healths of those
    above,
Her noble friends, whom she must ever love ;
But not together, not the young and old,
But one by one, the number duly told ;
And told their merits too—there was not one
Who had not said a gracious thing or done ;
Nor could she praise alone, but she would take
A cheerful glass for every favourite's sake,
And all were favourites—till the rosy cheek
Spoke for the tongue that nearly ceased to
    speak ;
That rosy cheek that now began to shine,
And show the progress of the rosy wine :
But there she ended—felt the singing head,
Then pray'd as custom will'd, and so to bed.
    ' The morn was pleasant, and the ancient
    maid
With her fair niece about the mansion stray'd ;
There was no room without th' appropriate
    tale
Of blood and murder, female sprite or male ;
There was no picture that th' historic dame
Pass'd by and gave not its peculiar fame ;
The births, the visits, weddings, burials, all
That chanced for ages at the noble Hall.
    ' These and each revolution she could state,
And give strange anecdotes of love and hate ;
This was her first delight, her pride, her boast,
She told of many an heiress, many a toast,
Of Lady Ellen's flight, of Lord Orlando's ghost ;
The maid turn'd pale, and what should then
    ensue
But wine and cake—the dame was frighten'd
    too.
    ' The aunt and niece now walk'd about the
    grounds,
And sometimes met the gentry in their rounds ;
" Do let us turn ! " the timid girl exclaim'd—
" Turn ! " said the aunt, " of what are you
    ashamed ?

What is there frightful in such looks as those ?
What is it, child, you fancy or suppose ?
Look at Lord Robert, see if you can trace
More than true honour in that handsome face !
    '" What ! you must think, by blushing in
    that way,
My lord has something about love to say
But I assure you that he never spoke
Such things to me in earnest or in joke,
And yet I meet him in all sorts of times,
When wicked men are thinking of their crimes.
    '" There ! let them pass——Why, yes, in-
    deed 'tis true
That was a look, and was design'd for you ;
But what the wonder when the sight is new ?
For my lord's virtue you may take my word,
He would not do a thing that was absurd."
    ' A month had pass'd ; " And when will
    Fanny come ? "
The lover ask'd, and found the parents dumb ;
They had not heard for more than half the
    space,
And the poor maiden was in much disgrace ;
Silence so long they could not understand,
And this of one who wrote so neat a hand
Their sister sure would send were aught amiss,
But youth is thoughtless—there is hope in
    this.
    ' As time elapsed, their wonder changed to
    wo,
William would lose another day, and go ;
Yet if she should be wilful and remain,
He had no power to take her home again :
But he would go :—He went, and he return'd,—
And in his look the pair his tale discern'd ;
Stupid in grief, it seem'd not that he knew
How he came home, or what he should pursue :
Fanny was gone !—her aunt was sick in bed,
Dying, she said—none cared if she were dead ;
Her charge, his darling, was decoy'd, was fled !
But at what time, and whither, and with
    whom,
None seem'd to know—all surly, shy, or dumb.
    ' Each blamed himself, all blamed the erring
    maid,
They vow'd revenge ; they cursed their fate,
    and pray'd.
Moved by his grief, the father sought the
    place,
Ask'd for his girl, and talk'd of her disgrace ;
Spoke of the villain, on whose cursed head
He pray'd that vengeance might be amply
    shed ;

Then sought his sister, and beheld her grief,
Her pain, her danger,—this was no relief.
‘ “ Where is my daughter? bring her to my
     sight ! ”—
“ Brother, I’m rack’d and tortured day and
     night.”—
“ Talk not to me! What grief have you to tell,
Is your soul rack’d, or is your bosom hell ?
Where is my daughter ? ”—“ She would take
     her oath
For their right doing, for she knew them both,
And my young lord was honour.”—“ Woman,
     cease !
And give your guilty conscience no such
     peace—
You’ve sold the wretched girl, you have
     betray’d your niece.”—
“ The Lord be good! and O! the pains that
     come
In limb and body—Brother, get you home !
Your voice runs through me,—every angry
     word,
If he should hear it, would offend my lord.
‘ “ Has he a daughter ? let her run away
With a poor dog, and hear what he will say !
No matter what, I’ll ask him for his son ”—
“ And so offend? Now, brother, pray be gone!”
‘ My lord appear’d, perhaps by pity moved,
And kindly said he no such things approved ;
Nay, he was angry with the foolish boy,
Who might his pleasures at his ease enjoy ;
The thing was wrong—he hoped the farm did
     well,—
The angry father doom’d the farm to hell ;
He then desired to see the villain-son,
Though my lord warn’d him such excess to
     shun ;
Told him he pardon’d, though he blamed such
     rage,
And bade him think upon his state and age.
‘ “ Think ! yes, my lord ! but thinking drives
     me mad—
Give me my child !—Where is she to be had ?
I’m old and poor, but I with both can feel,
And so shall he that could a daughter steal !
Think you, my lord, I can be so bereft
And feel no vengeance for the villain’s theft ?
Old if I am, could I the robber meet
I’d lay his breathless body at my feet—
Was that a smile, my lord? think you your boy
Will both the father and the child destroy ? ”
‘ My lord replied—“ I’m sorry from my soul !
But boys are boys, and there is no control.”

‘ “ So, for your great ones Justice slumbers
     then !
If men are poor they must not feel as men—
Will your son marry ? ”—“ Marry !” said my
     lord,
“ Your daughter ?—marry—no, upon my
     word ! ”
‘ “ What then, our stations differ !—but your
     son
Thought not of that—his crime has made
     them one,
In guilt united—She shall be his wife,
Or I th’ avenger that will take his life ! ”
‘ “ Old man, I pity and forgive you ; rest
In hope and comfort,—be not so distress’d,
Things that seem bad oft happen for the best ;
The girl has done no more than thousands do,
Nor has the boy—they laugh at me and you.”—
“ And this my vengeance—curse him ! ”—
     “ Nay, forbear ;
I spare your frenzy, in compassion spare.”
‘ “ Spare me, my lord ! and what have I to
     dread ?
O ! spare not, heaven, the thunder o’er his
     head—
The bolt he merits ! ”——
               Such was his redress ;
And he return’d to brood upon distress.
‘ And what of William ?—William from the
     time
Appear’d partaker both of grief and crime ;
He cared for nothing, nothing he pursued,
But walk’d about in melancholy mood ;
He ceased to labour,—all he loved before
He now neglected, and would see no more ;
He said his flute brought only to his mind
When he was happy, and his Fanny kind ;
And his loved walks, and every object near,
And every evening-sound she loved to hear,
The shady lane, broad heath, and starry sky,
Brought home reflections, and he wish’d to die:
Yet there he stray’d, because he wish’d to shun
The world he hated, where his part was done ;
As if, though lingering on the earth, he there
Had neither hope nor calling, tie nor care.
‘ At length a letter from the daughter came,
“ Frances ” subscribed, and that the only
     name ;
She “ pitied much her parents, spoke of fate,
And begg’d them to forget her, not to hate ;
Said she had with her all the world could give,
And only pray’d that they in peace should
     live,—

That which is done, is that we're born to do,
This she was taught, and she believed it
   true ;
True, that she lived in pleasure and delight,
But often dream'd and saw the farm by night:
The boarded room that she had kept so neat,
And all her roses in the window-seat ;
The pear-tree shade, the jasmine's lovely
   gloom,
With its long twigs that blossom'd in the
   room ;
But she was happy, and the tears that fell
As she was writing had no grief to tell ;
We weep when we are glad, we sigh when we
   are well."
  ' A bill inclosed, that they beheld with pain
And indignation, they return'd again ;
There was no mention made of William's
   name,
Check'd as she was by pity, love, and shame.
  ' William, who wrought for bread, and never
   sought
More than the day demanded when he
   wrought,
Was to a sister call'd, of all his race
The last, and dying in a distant place ;
In tender terror he approach'd her bed,
Beheld her sick, and buried her when dead :
He was her heir, and what she left was more
Than he required, who was content before.
With their minds' sufferings, age, and growing
   pain,
That ancient couple could not long remain,
Nor long remain'd ; and in their dying groan
The suffering youth perceived himself alone ;
For of his health or sickness, peace or care,
He knew not one in all the world to share ;
Now every scene would sad reflections give,
And most his home, and there he could not
   live ;
There every walk would now distressing prove,
And of his loss remind him, and his love.
  ' With the small portion by his sister left
He roved about as one of peace bereft,
And by the body's movements hoped to find
A kind of wearied stillness in the mind,
And sooner bring it to a sleepy state,
As rocking infants will their pains abate.
  ' Thus careless, lost, unheeding where he
   went,
Nine weary years the wandering lover spent.
  ' His sole employment, all that could amuse,
Was his companions on the road to choose ;

With such he travell'd through the passing
   day,
Friends of the hour, and walkers by the way ;
And from the sick, the poor, the halt, the
   blind,
He learn'd the sorrows of his suffering kind.
  ' He learn'd of many how unjust their fate,
For their connexions dwelt in better state ;
They had relations famous, great or rich,
Learned or wise, they never scrupled which ;
But while they cursed these kindred churls,
   would try
To build their fame, and for their glory lie.
  ' Others delighted in misfortunes strange,
The sports of fortune in her love for change.
  ' Some spoke of wonders they before had
   seen,
When on their travels they had wandering
   been ;
How they had sail'd the world about, and
   found
The sailing plain, although the world was
   round ;
How they beheld for months th' unsetting sun
What deeds they saw ! what they themselves
   had done !—
What leaps at Rhodes!—what glory then they
   won !
  ' There were who spoke in terms of high
   disdain
Of their contending against power in vain,
Suffering from tyranny of law long borne,
And life's best spirits in contentions worn :
Happy in this, th' oppressors soon will die,
Each with the vex'd and suffering man to
   lie—
And thus consoled exclaim, " And is not
   sorrow dry ? "
  ' But vice offended : when he met with those
Who could a deed of violence propose,
And cry, " Should they what we desire
   possess ?
Should they deprive us, and their laws
   oppress ? "
William would answer, " Ours is not re-
   dress : "—
" Would you oppression then for ever feel ? "
" 'Tis not my choice ; but yet I must not
   steal : "—
" So, first they cheat us, and then make their
   laws
To guard their treasures and to back their
   cause :

What call you then, my friend, the rights of
man ? "—
" To get his bread," said William, "if he can ;
And if he cannot, he must then depend
Upon a Being he may make his friend : "—
"Make!" they replied; and conference had end.

'But female vagrants would at times express
A new-born pleasure at the mild address ;
His modest wish, clothed in accent meek,
That they would comfort in religion seek.

'" I am a sinful being ! " William cried ;
" Then, what am I ? " the conscious heart
replied :
And oft-times ponder'd in a pensive way,
" He is not happy, yet he loves to pray."

' But some would freely on his thoughts
intrude,
And thrust themselves 'twixt him and
solitude :
They would his faith and of its strength
demand,
And all his soul's prime motions understand :
How ! they would say, such wo and such
belief,
Such trust in heaven, and yet on earth such
grief !
Thou art almost, my friend,—thou art not all,
Thou hast not yet the self-destroying call ;
Thou hast a carnal wish, perhaps a will
Not yet subdued,—the root is growing still :
There is the strong man yet that keeps his
own,
Who by a stronger must be overthrown ;
There is the burden that must yet be gone,
And then the pilgrim may go singing on.

' William to this would seriously incline,
And to their comforts would his heart resign;
It soothed, it raised him,—he began to feel
Th' enlivening warmth of methodistic zeal ;
He learn'd to know the brethren by their
looks—
He sought their meetings, he perused their
books ;
But yet was not within the pale and yoke,
And as a novice of experience spoke ;
But felt the comfort, and began to pray
For such companions on the king's highway.

' William had now across the kingdom sped,
To th' Eastern ocean from St. David's head ;
And wandering late, with various thoughts
oppress'd,
'Twas midnight ere he reach'd his place of
rest,—

A village inn, that one way-faring friend
Could from experience safely recommend,
Where the kind hostess would be more intent
On what he needed than on what he spent ;
Her husband, once a heathen, she subdued,
And with religious fear his mind imbued ;
Though his conviction came too late to save
An erring creature from an early grave.

' Since that event, the cheerful widow grew
In size and substance,—her the brethren
knew—
And many friends were hers, and lovers not
a few ;
But either love no more could warm her heart,
Or no man came who could the warmth im-
part.

' William drew near, and saw the comely look
Of the good lady, bending o'er her book ;
Hymns it appear'd,—for now a pleasing sound
Seem'd as a welcome in his wanderings found:
He enter'd softly, not as they who think
That they may act the ruffian if they drink,
And who conceive, that for their paltry pence
They may with rules of decency dispense ;
Far unlike these was William,—he was kind,
Exacting nothing, and to all resign'd.

' He saw the hostess reading,—and their eyes
Met in good will, and something like surprise :
It was not beauty William saw, but more,
Something like that which he had loved
before—
Something that brought his Fanny to his
view,
In the dear time when she was good and true ;
And his, it seem'd, were features that were
seen
With some emotion—she was not serene :
And both were moved to ask what looks like
those could mean.

At first she colour'd to the deepest red,
That hurried off, till all the rose was fled ;
She call'd a servant, whom she sent to rest,
Then made excuse to her attentive guest ;
She own'd the thoughts confused,—'twas
very true,
He brought a dear departed friend in view :
Then, as he listen'd, bade him welcome there
With livelier looks and more engaging air,
And stirr'd the fire of ling, and brush'd the
wicker chair,
Waiting his order with the cheerful look,
That proved how pleasant were the pains she
took.

'He was refresh'd——They spake on various
    themes—
Our early pleasures, Reason's first-drawn
    schemes,
Youth's strong illusions, Love's delirious
    dreams :
Then from her book he would presume to
    ask
A song of praise, and she perform'd the
    task :
The clock struck twelve—He started—"Must
    I go ? "
His looks spoke plainly, and the lady's, "No:"
So down he sat,—and when the clock struck
    one
There was no start, no effort to be gone :
Nor stay'd discourse——
            " And so your loves were cross'd,
And the loved object to your wishes lost ?
But was she faithless, or were you to blame ?
I wish I knew her—Will you tell her name? "
"Excuse me—that would hurt her if alive;
And, if no more, why should her fault sur-
    vive ? "
" But love you still ? "—
                " Alas ! I feel I do,
When I behold her very looks in you ! "
'" Yet, if the frail one's name must not be
    known,
My friendly guest may trust me with his own."
' This done, the lady paused, and then
    replied—
"It grieves me much to see your spirit tried;—
But she was like me,—how I came to know
The lamb that stray'd I will hereafter show;—
We were indeed as sisters——Should I state
Her quiet end, you would no longer hate :
I see your heart,—and I shall quickly prove,
Though she deserved not, yet she prized your
    love :
Long as she breathed was heard her William's
    name—
And such affection half absolves her shame.
'" Weep not, but hear me, how I came to know
Thee and thy Frances—this to heaven I
    owe ;
And thou shalt view the pledge, the very
    ring,
The birth-day token—well you know the
    thing ;
' This,' if I ever—thus I was to speak,
As she had spoken—but I see you weak :
She was not worthy—— "

            " O ! you cannot tell
By what accursed means my Fanny fell !
What bane, compulsion, threats—for she was
    pure ;
But from such toils what being is secure ?
Force, not persuasion, robb'd me—— "
                    " You are right ;
So has she told me, in her Maker's sight :
She loved not vice—— "
                " O ! no,—her heart approved
All that her God commanded to be loved ;
And she is gone—— "
                " Consider ! death alone
Could for the errors of her life atone."
'" Speak not of them ; I would she knew
    how dear
I hold her yet !—But dost thou give the
    tear
To my loved Frances ?—No ! I cannot
    part
With one who has her face, who has her
    heart ;
With looks so pleasing, when I thee behold,
She lives—that bosom is no longer cold—
Then tell me—Art thou not—in pity speak—
One whom I sought, while living meant to
    seek—
Art thou my Fanny ?—Let me not offend—
Be something to me—be a sufferer's friend—
Be more—be all !——The precious truth
    confess—
Art thou not Frances ?—— "
                " O, my William ! yes !
But spare me, spare thyself, and suffer less :
In my best days, the spring-time of my life,
I was not worthy to be William's wife ;
A widow now—not poor, indeed—not cast
In outer darkness—sorrowing for the past,
And for the future hoping—but no more :
Let me the pledges of thy love restore,
And give the ring thou gavest—let it be
A token still of my regard for thee,—
But only that,—and to a worthier now
Consign the gift."——
                " The only worthy thou ! "
Replied the lover ; and what more express'd
May be omitted—here our tale shall rest.
' This pair, our host and hostess of the
    Fleece,
Command some wealth, and smile at its
    increase ;
Saving and civil, cautious and discreet,
All sects and parties in their mansion meet ;

There from their chapels teachers go to share
The creature-comforts,—mockery grins not
    there ;
There meet the wardens at their annual feast,
With annual pun—" the parish must be
    fleeced ; "
There traders find a parlour cleanly swept
For their reception, and in order kept ;

And there the sons of labour, poor, but free,
Sit and enjoy their hour of liberty.
' So live the pair,—and life's disasters
    seem
In their unruffled calm a troubled dream ;
In comfort runs the remnant of their life—
He the fond husband, she the faithful
    wife.'

BOOK XX.   THE CATHEDRAL-WALK

George in his hypochondriac State—A Family
    Mansion now a Farm-house—The Company
    there — Their   Conversation — Subjects
    afforded by the Pictures—Doubts if Spirits
    can appear—Arguments—Facts—The Re-
    lation of an old Lady—Her . Walks in
    a Cathedral—Appearance there.

IN their discourse again the Brothers dwelt
On early subjects—what they once had felt,
Once thought of things mysterious ;—themes
    that all
With some degree of reverence recall.
George then reverted to the days of old,
When his heart fainted, and his hope was
    cold ;
When by the power of fancy he was sway'd,
And every impulse of the mind obey'd.
' Then, my dear Richard,' said the 'Squire,
    ' my case
Was call'd consumptive—I must seek a place
And soil salubrious, thither must repair,
And live on asses' milk and milder air.
' My uncle bought a farm, and on the
    land
The fine old mansion yet was left to stand,
Not in this state, but old and much decay'd ;
Of this a part was habitable made ;
The rest—who doubts ?—was by the spirits
    seized,
Ghosts of all kinds, who used it as they
    pleased.
' The worthy farmer tenant yet remain'd,
Of good report—he had a fortune gain'd ;
And his three daughters at their school
    acquired
The air and manner that their swains
    admired ;
The mother-gossip and these daughters three
Talk'd of genteel and social company,

And while the days were fine, and walks were
    clean,
A fresh assemblage day by day were seen.
' There were the curate's gentle maids, and
    some
From all the neighbouring villages would
    come ;
There, as I stole the yew-tree shades among,
I saw the parties walking, old and young,
Where I was nothing—if perceived, they said,
" The man is harmless, be not you afraid ;
A poor young creature, who, they say, is
    cross'd
In love, and has in part his senses lost ;
His health for certain, and he comes to spend
His time with us ; we hope our air will mend
A frame so weaken'd, for the learned tribe
A change of air for stubborn ills prescribe ;
And doing nothing often has prevail'd
When ten physicians have prescribed and
    fail'd ;
Not that for air or change there 's much to say,
But nature then has time to take her way ;
And so we hope our village will restore
This man to health that he possess'd before.
He loves the garden avenues, the gloom
Of the old chambers, of the tap'stried room,
And we no notice take, we let him go and
    come."
' So spake a gay young damsel; but she
    knew
Not all the truth,—in part her tale was true.
Much it amused me in the place to be
This harmless cypher, seeming not to see,
Yet seeing all,—unnoticed to appear,
Yet noting all ; and not disposed to hear,
But to go forth,—break in on no one's plan,
And hear them speak of the forsaken man.
' In scenes like these, a mansion so decay'd,
With blighted trees in hoary moss array'd,

And ivy'd walls around, for many an hour
I walk'd alone, and felt their witching power ;
So others felt ;—the young of either sex
Would in these walks their timid minds
    perplex
By meeting terrors, and the old appear'd,
Their fears upbraiding, like the young who
    fear'd ;
Among them all some sad discourse at night
Was sure to breed a terrified delight :
Some luckless one of the attentive dames
Had figures seen like those within the frames,
Figures of lords who once the land possess'd,
And who could never in their coffins rest ;
Unhappy spirits ! who could not abide
The loss of all their consequence and pride,
'Twas death in all his power, their very names
    had died.
' These tales of terror views terrific bred,
And sent the hearers trembling to their bed.'

' In an autumnal evening, cool and still,
The sun just dropp'd beneath a distant hill,
The children gazing on the quiet scene,
Then rose in glory Night's majestic queen ;
And pleasant was the chequer'd light and
    shade
Her golden beams and maple shadows made ;
An ancient tree that in the garden grew,
And that fair picture on the gravel threw.
  ' Then all was silent, save the sounds that
    make
Silence more awful, while they faintly break ;
The frighten'd bat's low shriek, the beetle's
    hum,
With nameless sounds we know not whence
    they come.
' Such was the evening ; and that ancient seat
The scene where then some neighbours chanced
    to meet ;
Up to the door led broken steps of stone,
Whose dewy surface in the moonlight shone ;
On vegetation, that with progress slow
Where man forbears to fix his foot, will grow ;
The window's depth and dust repell'd the ray
Of the moon's light and of the setting day ;
Pictures there were, and each display'd a face
And form that gave their sadness to the place ;
The frame and canvas show'd that worms
    unseen,
Save in their works, for years had working
   been ;

A fire of brushwood on the irons laid
All the dull room in fitful views display'd,
And with its own wild light in fearful forms
    array'd.
  ' In this old Hall, in this departing day,
Assembled friends and neighbours, grave and
    gay,
When one good lady at a picture threw
A glance that caused inquiry—" Tell us who ? "
  ' " That was a famous warrior ; one, they said,
That by a spirit was awhile obey'd ;
In all his dreadful battles he would say,
' Or win or lose, I shall escape to-day ; '
And though the shot as thick as hail came
    round,
On no occasion he received a wound ;
He stood in safety, free from all alarm,
Protected, heaven forgive him, by his charm :
But he forgot the date, till came the hour
When he no more had the protecting power ;
And then he bade his friends around farewell !
' I fall ! ' he cried, and in the instant fell.
  ' " Behold those infants in the frame beneath!
A witch offended wrought their early death ;
She form'd an image, made as wax to melt,
And each the wasting of the figure felt ;
The hag confess'd it when she came to die,
And no one living can the truth deny.
  ' " But see a beauty in King William's days,
With that long waist, and those enormous
    stays ;
She had three lovers, and no creature knew
The one preferr'd, or the discarded two ;
None could the secret of her bosom see ;
Loving, poor maid, th' attention of the three,
She kept such equal weight in either scale,
'Twas hard to say who would at last prevail ;
Thus you may think in either heart arose
A jealous anger, and the men were foes ;
Each with himself concluded, two aside,
The third may make the lovely maid his
    bride :
This caused their fate—It was on Thursday
    night
The deed was done, and bloody was the fight ;
Just as she went, poor thoughtless girl ! to
    prayers,
Ran wild the maid with horror up the stairs ;
Pale as a ghost, but not a word she said,
And then the lady utter'd, ' Coates is dead ! '
  ' " Then the poor damsel found her voice and
    cried,
' Ran through the body, and that instant died !

But he pronounced your name, and so was
    satisfied.'
A second fell, and he who did survive
Was kept by skill and sovereign drugs alive ;
' O ! would she see me ! ' he was heard to
    say,
' No ! I'll torment him to his dying day ! '
The maid exclaim'd, and every Thursday
    night
Her spirit came his wretched soul to fright ;
Once as she came he cried aloud ' Forgive ! '
' Never ! ' she answer'd, ' never while you
    live,
Nor when you die, as long as time endures ;
You have my torment been, and I'll be
    yours ! '
That is the lady, and the man confess'd
Her vengeful spirit would not let him rest."
    " But are there ghosts ? " exclaim'd a timid
    maid ;
" My father tells me not to be afraid ;
He cries ' When buried we are safe enough,'
And calls such stories execrable stuff."
    ' " Your father, child," the former lady cried,
" Has learning much, but he has too much
    pride ;
It is impossible for him to tell
What things in nature are impossible,
Or out of nature, or to prove to whom
Or for what purposes a ghost may come ;
It may not be intelligence to bring,
But to keep up a notion of the thing ;
And though from one such fact there may arise
An hundred wild improbabilities,
Yet had there never been the truth, I say,
The very lies themselves had died away."
    ' " True," said a friend ; " Heaven doubtless
    may dispense
A kind of dark and clouded evidence ;
God has not promised that he will not send
A spirit freed to either foe or friend ;
He may such proof, and only such bestow,
Though we the certain truth can never know ;
And therefore though such floating stories
    bring
No strong or certain vouchers of the thing,
Still would I not, presuming, pass my word
That all such tales were groundless and
    absurd."
    ' " But you will grant," said one who sate
    beside,
" That all appear so when with judgment
    tried ? "

    ' " For that concession, madam, you may call,
When we have sate in judgment upon all."
    ' An ancient lady, who with pensive smile
Had heard the stories, and been mute the
    while,
Now said, " Our prudence had been better
    shown
By leaving uncontested things unknown ;
Yet if our children must such stories hear,
Let us provide some antidotes to fear ;
For all such errors in the minds of youth,
In any mind, the only cure is truth ;
And truths collected may in time decide
Upon such facts, or prove, at least, a guide :
If then permitted I will fairly state
One fact, nor doubt the story I relate ;
I for your perfect acquiescence call,
'Tis of myself I tell."——" O ! tell us all ! "
Said every being there : then silent was the
    Hall.

    ' " Early in life, beneath my parent's roof,
Of man's true honour I had noble proof ;
A generous lover who was worthy found,
Where half his sex are hollow and unsound.
    ' ' My father fail'd in trade, and sorrowing
    died,
When all our loss a generous youth supplied ;
And soon the time drew on when he could say,
' O ! fix the happy, fix the early day ! '
Nor meant I to oppose his wishes, or delay :
But then came fever, slight at first indeed,
Then hastening on and threatening in its
    speed ;
It mock'd the power of medicine ; day by day
I saw those helpers sadly walk away ;
So came the hand-like cloud, and with such
    power
And with such speed, that brought the
    mighty shower.
    ' " Him nursed I dying, and we freely spoke
Of what might follow the expected stroke ;
We talk'd of spirits, of their unknown powers,
And dared to dwell on what the fate of ours ;
But the dread promise, to appear again,
Could it be done, I sought not to obtain ;
But yet we were presuming—' Could it be,'
He said, ' O Emma ! I would come to thee ! '
    ' " At his last hour his reason, late astray,
Again return'd t' illuminate his way.
    ' " In the last night my mother long had kept
Unwearied watch, and now reclined and slept ;

The nurse was dreaming in a distant chair,
And I had knelt to soothe him with a prayer ;
When, with a look of that peculiar kind
That gives its purpose to the fellow mind,
His   manner   spoke—' Confide—be   not
   afraid—
I shall remember,'—this was all convey'd,—
' I know not what awaits departed man,
But this believe—I meet thee if I can.'

  ' " I wish'd to die,—and grief, they say, will
   kill,
But you perceive 'tis slowly if it will ;
That I was wretched you may well believe—
I judged it right, and was resolved to grieve :
I lost my mother when there lived not one,
Man, woman, child, whom I would seek or
   shun.
  ' " The Dean, my uncle, with congenial gloom,
Said, ' Will you share a melancholy home ? '
For he bewail'd a wife, as I deplored
My fate, and bliss that could not be restored.
  ' " In his cathedral's gloom I pass'd my time,
Much in devotion, much in thought sublime ;
There oft I paced the aisles, and watch'd the
   glow
Of the sun setting on the stones below,
And saw the failing light, that strove to pass
Through the dim coating of the storied glass,
Nor fell 'within, but till the day was gone
The red faint fire upon the window shone.
  ' " I took the key, and oft-times chose to
   stay
Till all was vanish'd of the tedious day,
Till I perceived no light, nor heard a sound,
That gave me notice of a world around.
  ' " Then had I grief's proud thoughts, and
   said, in tone
Of exultation, ' World, I am alone !
I care not for thee, thou art vile and base,
And I shall leave thee for a nobler place.'
  ' " So I the world abused,—in fact, to me
Urbane and civil as a world could be :
Nor should romantic grievers thus complain,
Although but little in the world they gain,
But let them think if they have nothing done
To make this odious world so sad a one,
Or what their worth and virtue that should
   make
This graceless world so pleasant for their sake.
  ' " But to my tale :—Behold me as I tread
The silent mansions of the favour'd dead,

Who sleep in vaulted chambers, till their clay
In quiet dissolution melts away
In this their bodies' home—The spirits, where
   are they ?
' And where *his* spirit ?—Doors and walls
   impede
The embodied spirit, not the spirit freed : '
And, saying this, I at the altar knelt,
And painful joys and rapturous anguish felt ;
Till strong, bold hopes possess'd me, and I
   cried,
' Even at this instant is he at my side ; '
Yes, now, dear spirit ! art thou by to prove
That mine is lasting, mine the loyal love !
  ' " Thus have I thought, returning to the
   Dean,
As one who had some glorious vision seen :
He ask'd no question, but would sit and
   weep,
And cry, in doleful tone, ' I cannot sleep ! '
  ' " In dreams the chosen of my heart I view'd,
And thus th' impression day by day renew'd ;
I saw him always, always loved to see,
For when alone he was my company :
In company with him alone I seem'd,
And, if not dreaming, was as one who dream'd.
  ' " Thus, robb'd of sleep, I found, when
   evening came,
A pleasing torpor steal upon my frame ;
But still the habit drew my languid feet
To the loved darkness of the favourite seat ;
And there, by silence and by sadness press'd,
I felt a world my own, and was at rest.
  ' " One night, when urged with more than
   usual zeal,
And feeling all that such enthusiasts feel,
I paced the altar by, the pillars round,
And knew no terror in the sacred ground ;
For mine were thoughts that banish'd all such
   fear,—
I wish'd, I long'd to have that form appear ;
And, as I paced the sacred aisles, I cried,
' Let not thy Emma's spirit be denied
The sight of thine ; or, if I may not see,
Still by some token let her certain be ! '
  ' " At length the anxious thoughts my
   strength subdued,
And sleep o'erpower'd me in my solitude ;
Then was I dreaming of unearthly race,
The glorious inmates of a blessed place ;
Where lofty minds celestial views explore,
Heaven's bliss enjoy, and heaven's great
   King adore ;

Him there I sought whom I had loved so well—
For sure he dwelt where happy spirits dwell !
‘ "While thus engaged, I started at a sound,
Of what I knew not, but I look'd around ;
For I was borne on visionary wings,
And felt no dread of sublunary things ;
But rising, walk'd—A distant window threw
A weak, soft light, that help'd me in my view ;
Something with anxious heart I hoped to see,
And pray'd, ‘ O ! God of all things, let it be !
For all are thine, were made by thee, and thou
Canst both the meeting and the means allow ;
Thou canst make clear my sight, or thou canst
	make
More gross the form that his loved mind shall
	take,
Canst clothe his spirit for my fleshly sight,
Or make my earthly sense more pure and
	bright.'
‘ "So was I speaking, when without a sound
There was a movement in the sacred ground :
I saw a figure rising, but could trace
No certain features, no peculiar face ;
But I prepared my mind that form to view,
Nor felt a doubt,—he promised, and was true !
I should embrace his angel, and my clay,
And what was mortal in me, melt away.
‘ "O ! that ecstatic horror in my frame,
That o'er me thus, a favour'd mortal, came !
Bless'd beyond mortals,—and the body now
I judged would perish, though I knew not
	how ;
The gracious power around me could translate
And make me pass to that immortal state :
Thus shall I pay the debt that must be paid,
And dying live, nor be by death delay'd ;
And when so changed, I should with joy
	sustain
The heavenly converse, and with him remain.
‘ "I saw the distant shade, and went with awe,
But not with terror, to the form I saw ;
Yet slowly went, for he I did believe
Would meet, and soul to soul his friend
	receive ;
So on I drew, concluding in my mind,
I cannot judge what laws may spirits bind ;
Though I dissolve, and mingle with the blest,
I am a new and uninstructed guest,
And ere my love can speak, he should be first
	address'd.
‘ "Thus I began to speak,—my new-born
	pride,
My love, and daring hope, the words supplied.

‘ " ‘ Dear, happy shade ! companion of the
	good,
The just, the pure, do I on thee intrude ?
Art thou not come my spirit to improve,
To form, instruct, and fit me for thy love,
And, as in love we parted, to restore
The blessing lost, and then to part no more ?
Let me with thee in thy pure essence dwell,
Nor go to bid them of my house farewell,
But thine be ever ! ’——How shall I relate
Th' event that finish'd this ecstatic state ?
Yet let me try.—It turn'd, and I beheld
An hideous form, that hope and zeal expell'd :
In a dim light the horrid shape appear'd,
That wisdom would have fled, and courage
	fear'd,
Pale, and yet bloated, with distorted eyes
Distant and deep, a mouth of monstrous
	size,
That would in day's broad glare a simple
	maid surprise :
He heard my words, and cried, with savage
	shout,
‘ Bah !—bother !—blarney !—What is this
	about ? ’
‘ "Love, lover, longing, in an instant fled,—
Now I had vice and impudence to dread ;
And all my high-wrought fancies died away
To woman's trouble, terror, and dismay.
‘ " ‘ What,’ said the wretch, ‘ what is it
	you would have ?
Would'st hang a man for peeping in a grave ?
Search me yourself, and try if you can feel
Aught I have taken,—there was nought to
	steal :
'Twas told they buried with the corpse enough
To pay the hazard,—I have made the proof,
Nor gain'd a tester—What I tell is true ;
But I'm no fool, to be betray'd by you,—
I'll hazard nothing, curse me if I do ! ’
‘ "The light increased, and plainly now
	appear'd
A knavish fool whom I had often fear'd,
But hid the dread ; and I resolved at least
Not to expose it to the powerful beast.
‘ " ‘ Come, John,’ I said, suppressing fear
	and doubt,
‘ Walk on before, and let a lady out ! ’—
‘ Lady ! ’ the wretch replied, with savage
	grin,
‘ Apply to him that let the lady in :
What ! you would go, I take it, to the Dean,
And tell him what your ladyship has seen.’

' " When thus the fool exposed the knave,
     I saw
The means of holding such a mind in awe,
And gain my safety by his dread of law.
' Alas ! ' I cried, ' I fear the Dean like you,
For I transgress, and am in trouble too :
If it be known that we are here, as sure
As here we are we must the law endure :
Each other's counsel therefore let us keep,
And each steal homeward to our beds and
     sleep.'
     ' " ' Steal ! ' said the ruffian's conscience—
          ' Well, agreed ;
Steal on, and let us to the door proceed : '—

Yet, ere he moved, he stood awhile, and took
Of my poor form a most alarming look ;
' But, hark ! ' I cried, and he to move
     began,—
Escape alone engaged the dreadful man :
With eager hand I oped the ponderous door—
The wretch rush'd by me, and was heard no
     more.
     ' " So I escaped,—and when my dreams
          came on,
I check'd the madness by the thoughts of
     John :
Yet say I not what can or cannot be,
But give the story of my ghost and me."

BOOK XXI. SMUGGLERS AND POACHERS

A Widow at the Hall—Inquiry of Richard—
Relation of two Brothers—Their different
Character—Disposition—Modes of thinking
—James a Servant—Robert joins the
Smugglers—Rachel at the Hall—James
attached to her—Trade fails—Robert a
Poacher—Is in Danger—How released—
James and Rachel—Revenge excited—
Association formed—Attack resolved—
Preparation made for Resistance—A Night
Adventure—Reflections.

———

THERE was a widow in the village known
To our good Squire, and he had favour shown
By frequent bounty—She as usual came,
And Richard saw the worn and weary frame,
Pale cheek, and eye subdued, of her whose
     mind
Was grateful still, and glad a friend to find,
Though to the world long since and all its
     hopes resign'd :
Her easy form, in rustic neatness clad,
Was pleasing still ! but she for ever sad.
     ' " Deep is her grief ? " said Richard—
          " Truly deep,
And very still, and therefore seems to sleep ;
To borrow simile, to paint her woes,
Theirs, like the river's motion, seems repose,
Making no petty murmuring,—settled, slow,
They never waste, they never overflow.
Rachel is one of those—for there are some
Who look for nothing in their days to come,
No good nor evil, neither hope nor fear,
Nothing remains or cheerful or severe ;

One day is like the past, the year's sweet
     prime
Like the sad fall,—for Rachel heeds not time :
Nothing remains to agitate her breast,
Spent is the tempest, and the sky at rest ;
But while it raged her peace its ruin met,
And now the sun is on her prospects set ;—
Leave her, and let us her distress explore,
She heeds it not—she has been left before."

———

' There were two lads call'd Shelley hither
     brought,
But whence we know not—it was never sought;
Their wandering mother left them, left her
     name,
And the boys throve and valiant men became:
Handsome, of more than common size, and
     tall,
And no one's kindred, seem'd beloved of all ;
All seem'd alliance by their deeds to prove,
And loved the youths who could not claim
     their love.
     ' One was call'd James, the more sedate
          and grave,
The other Robert—names their neighbours
     gave ;
They both were brave, but Robert loved to run
And meet his danger—James would rather
     shun
The dangerous trial, but whenever tried
He all his spirit to the act applied.
     ' Robert would aid on any man bestow,
James would his man and the occasion know.

For that was quick and prompt—this tem-
perate and slow.
' Robert would all things he desired pursue,
James would consider what was best to do ;
All spoke of Robert as a man they loved,
And most of James as valued and approved.
' Both had some learning: Robert his acquired
By quicker parts, and was by praise inspired ;
James, as he was in his acquirements slow,
Would learn the worth of what he tried to
know.
' In fact, this youth was generous—that was
just ;
The one you loved, the other you would trust :
Yet him you loved you would for truth ap-
prove,
And him you trusted you would likewise love.
' Such were the brothers—James had found
his way
To Nether Hall, and there inclined to stay ;
He could himself command, and therefore could
obey :
He with the keeper took his daily round,
A rival grew, and some unkindness found ;
But his superior farm'd ! the place was void,
And James guns, dogs, and dignity enjoy'd.
' Robert had scorn of service ; he would be
A slave to no man—happy were the free,
And only they ;—by such opinions led,
Robert to sundry kinds of trade was bred ;
Nor let us wonder if he sometimes made
An active partner in a lawless trade ;
Fond of adventure, wanton as the wave,
He loved the danger and the law to brave ;
But these were chance adventures, known to
few,—
Not that the hero cared what people knew.
' The brothers met not often—When they
met
James talk'd of honest gains and scorn of debt,
Of virtuous labour, of a sober life,
And what with credit would support a wife.
But Robert answer'd—" How can men advise
Who to a master let their tongue and eyes ?
Whose words are not their own ? whose foot
and hand
Run at a nod, or act upon command ?
Who cannot eat or drink, discourse or play,
Without requesting others that they may.
' " Debt you would shun; but what advice
to give
Who owe your service every hour you live !
Let a bell sound, and from your friends you run,

Although the darling of your heart were one ;
But if the bondage fits you, I resign
You to your lot—I am content with mine ! "
' Thus would the lads their sentiments
express,
And part in earnest, part in playfulness ;
Till Love, controller of all hearts and eyes,
Breaker of bonds, of friendship's holy ties,
Awakener of new wills and slumbering sym-
pathies,
Began his reign,—till Rachel, meek-eyed maid,
That form, those cheeks, that faultless face
display'd,
That child of gracious nature, ever neat
And never fine ; a flowret simply sweet,
Seeming at least unconscious she was fair ;
Meek in her spirit, timid in her air,
And shrinking from his glance if one presumed
To come too near the beauty as it bloom'd.
' Robert beheld her in her father's cot
Day after day, and blest his happy lot ;
He look'd indeed, but he could not offend
By gentle looks—he was her father's friend :
She was accustom'd to that tender look,
And frankly gave the hand he fondly took ;
She loved his stories, pleased she heard him play,
Pensive herself, she loved to see him gay,
And if they loved not yet, they were in Love's
highway.
' But Rachel now to womanhood was grown,
And would no more her faith and fondness own ;
She called her latent prudence to her aid,
And grew observant, cautious, and afraid ;
She heard relations of her lover's guile,
And could believe the danger of his smile :
With art insidious rival damsels strove
To show how false his speech, how feigned his
love ;
And though her heart another story told,
Her speech grew cautious, and her manner cold.
' Rachel had village fame, was fair and tall,
And gain'd a place of credit at the Hall ;
Where James beheld her seated in that place,
With a child's meekness, and an angel's face ;
Her temper soft, her spirit firm, her words
Simple and few as simple truth affords.
' James could but love her,—he at church
had seen
The tall, fair maid, had met her on the green,
Admiring always, nor surprised to find
Her figure often present to his mind ;
But now he saw her daily, and the sight
Gave him new pleasure and increased delight.

'But James, still prudent and reserved,
      though sure
The love he felt was love that would endure,
Would wait awhile, observing what was fit,
And meet, and right, nor would himself com-
      mit :
Then was he flatter'd,—James in time became
Rich, both as slayer of the Baron's game,
And as protector,—not a female dwelt
In that demesne who had not feign'd or felt
Regard for James ; and he from all had praise
Enough a young man's vanity to raise ;
With all these pleasures he of course must part
When Rachel reign'd sole empress of his heart.
    'Robert was now deprived of that delight
He once experienced in his mistress' sight ;
For, though he now his frequent visits paid,
He saw but little of the cautious maid ;
The simple common pleasures that he took
Grew dull, and he the wonted haunts forsook ;
His flute and song he left, his book and pen,
And sought the meetings of adventurous men ;
There was a love-born sadness in his breast,
That wanted stimulus to bring on rest ;
These simple pleasures were no more of use,
And danger only could repose produce ;
He join'd th' associates in their lawless trade,
And was at length of their profession made.
    'He saw connected with th' adventurous
      crew
Those whom he judged were sober men and
      true ;
He found that some, who should the trade
      prevent,
Gave it by purchase their encouragement ;
He found that contracts could be made with
      those
Who had their pay these dealers to oppose ;
And the good ladies whom at church he saw
With looks devout, of reverence and awe,
Could change their feelings as they change
      their place,
And, whispering, deal for spicery and lace :
And thus the craft and avarice of these
Urged on the youth, and gave his conscience
      ease.
    'Him loved the maiden Rachel, fondly loved,
As many a sigh and tear in absence proved,
And many a fear for dangers that she knew,
And many a doubt what one so gay might do :
Of guilt she thought not,—she had often heard
They bought and sold, and nothing wrong
      appear'd ;

Her father's maxim this : she understood
There was some ill,—but he, she knew, was
      good :
It was a traffic—but was done by night—
If wrong, how trade ? why secrecy, if right ?
But Robert's conscience, she believed, was
      pure—
And that he read his Bible she was sure.
    'James, better taught, in confidence declared
His grief for what his guilty brother dared :
He sigh'd to think how near he was akin
To one reduced by godless men to sin ;
Who, being always of the law in dread,
To other crimes were by the danger led—
And crimes with like excuse——The smuggler
      cries,
"What guilt is his who pays for what he buys ?"
The poacher questions, with perverted mind,
"Were not the gifts of heaven for all de-
      sign'd ?"
This cries, "I sin not—take not till I pay ;"—
That, "My own hand brought down my proper
      prey : "—
And while to such fond arguments they cling,
How fear they God ? how honour they the
      king ?
Such men associate, and each other aid,
Till all are guilty, rash, and desperate made ;
Till to some lawless deed the wretches fly,
And in the act, or for the acting, die.
    'The maid was frighten'd,—but, if this was
      true,
Robert for certain no such danger knew,
He always pray'd ere he a trip began,
And was too happy for a wicked man :
How could a creature, who was always gay,
So kind to all men, so disposed to pray,
How could he give his heart to such an evil
      way ?
Yet she had fears,—for she could not believe
That James could lie, or purpose to deceive ;
But still she found, though not without respect
For one so good, she must the man reject ;
For, simple though she was, full well she knew
What this strong friendship led him to pursue ;
And, let the man be honest as the light,
Love warps the mind a little from the right ;
And she proposed, against the trying day,
What in the trial she should think and say.
    ' And now, their love avow'd, in both arose
Fear and disdain—the orphan pair were foes.
    ' Robert, more generous of the two, avow'd
His scorn, defiance, and contempt aloud.

' James talk'd of pity in a softer tone,
To Rachel speaking, and with her alone :
He knew full well, he said, to what must come
His wretched brother, what would be his
     doom :
Thus he her bosom fenced with dread about ;
But love he could not with his skill drive out.
Still he effected something,—and that skill
Made the love wretched, though it could not
     kill ;
And Robert fail'd, though much he tried, to
     prove
He had no guilt—She granted he had love.
    'Thus they proceeded, till a winter came,
When the stern keeper told of stolen game :
Throughout the woods the poaching dogs had
     been,
And from him nothing should the robbers
     screen,
From him and law,—he would all hazards run,
Nor spare a poacher, were his brother one—
Love, favour, interest, tie of blood should fail,
Till vengeance bore him bleeding to the jail.
    ' Poor Rachel shudder'd,—smuggling she
     could name
Without confusion, for she felt not shame ;
But poachers were her terror, and a wood
Which they frequented had been mark'd by
     blood ;
And though she thought her Robert was secure
In better thoughts, yet could she not be sure.
    ' James now was urgent,—it would break
     his heart
With hope, with her, and with such views to
     part,
When one so wicked would her hand possess,
And he a brother !—that was his distress,
And must be hers——She heard him, and she
     sigh'd,
Looking in doubt,—but nothing she replied.
    ' There was a generous feeling in her mind,
That told her this was neither good nor kind :
James caused her terror, but he did no more—
Her love was now as it had been before.
    'Their traffic fail'd,—and the adventurous
     crew
No more their profitless attempts renew :
Dig they will not, and beg they might in vain—
Had they not pride, and what can then
     remain ?
    ' Now was the game destroy'd, and not an
     hare
Escaped at least the danger of the snare ;

Woods of their feather'd beauty were bereft,
The beauteous victims of the silent theft ;
The well-known shops received a large supply,
That they who could not kill at least might
     buy.
    ' James was enraged, enraged his lord, and
     both
Confirm'd their threatening with a vengeful
     oath :
Fresh aid was sought,—and nightly on the
     lands
Walk'd on their watch the strong determined
     bands :
Pardon was offer'd, and a promised pay
To him who would the desperate gang betray.
    ' Nor fail'd the measure,—on a certain night
A few were seized—the rest escaped by flight ;
Yet they resisted boldly ere they fled,
And blows were dealt around, and blood was
     shed ;
Two groaning helpers on the earth were laid,
When more arrived the lawful cause to aid :
Then four determined men were seized and
     bound,
And Robert in this desperate number found :
In prison fetter'd, he deplored his fate,
And cursed the folly he perceived too late.
    ' James was a favourite with his lord,—the
     zeal
He show'd was such as masters ever feel :
If he for vengeance on a culprit cried,
Or if for mercy, still his lord complied :
And now, 'twas said, he will for mercy plead,
For his own brother's was the guilty deed :
True, the hurt man is in a mending way,
But must be crippled to his dying day.
    ' Now James had vow'd the law should take
     its course,
He would not stay it, if he did not force ;
He could his witness, if he pleased, with-
     draw,
Or he could arm with certain death the law :
This he attested to the maid, and true,
If this he could not, yet he much could do.
    ' How suffer'd then that maid,—no thought
     she had,
No view of days to come, that was not sad ;
As sad as life with all its hopes resign'd,
As sad as ought but guilt can make mankind.
    ' With bitter grief the pleasures she review'd
Of early hope, with innocence pursued,
When she began to love, and he was fond and
     good :

He now must die, she heard from every
     tongue—
Die, and so thoughtless ! perish, and so young!
Brave, kind, and generous, tender, constant,
     true,
And he must die—then will I perish too !
     ' A thousand acts in every age will prove
Women are valiant in a cause they love ;
If fate the favour'd swain in danger place,
They heed not danger—perils they embrace ;
They dare the world's contempt, they brave
     their name's disgrace ;
They on the ocean meet its wild alarms,
They search the dungeon with extended arms;
The utmost trial of their faith they prove,
And yield the lover to assert their love.
     'James knew his power—his feelings were
     not nice—
Mercy he sold, and she must pay the price :
If his good lord forbore to urge their fate,
And he the utmost of their guilt to state,
The felons might their forfeit lives redeem,
And in their country's cause regain esteem ;
But nevermore that man, whom he had shame
To call his brother, must she see or name.
     ' Rachel was meek, but she had firmness
     too,
And reason'd much on what she ought to do :
In Robert's place, she knew what she should
     choose—
But life was not the thing she fear'd to lose :
She knew that she could not their contract
     break,
Nor for her life a new engagement make ;
But he was man, and guilty,—death so near
Might not to his as to her mind appear ;
And he might wish, to spare that forfeit life,
The maid he loved might be his brother's wife,
Although that brother was his bitter foe,
And he must all the sweets of life forego.
     'This would she try,—intent on this alone,
She could assume a calm and settled tone :
She spake with firmness—"I will Robert see,
Know what he wishes, and what I must be ;"
For James had now discover'd to the maid
His inmost heart, and how he must be paid,
If he his lord would soften, and would hide
The facts that must the culprit's fate decide.
" Go not," he said,—for she her full intent
Proclaim'd——To go she purposed, and she
     went :
She took a guide, and went with purpose stern
The secret wishes of her friend to learn.

' She saw him fetter'd, full of grief, alone,
Still as the dead, and he suppress'd a groan
At her appearance——Now she pray'd for
     strength ;
And the sad couple could converse at length.
     ' It was a scene that shook her to repeat,—
Life fought with love, both powerful, and both
     sweet.
     ' " Wilt thou die, Robert, or preserve thy
     life?
Shall I be thine own maid, or James's wife ? "
" His wife !—No !—Never will I thee resign—
No, Rachel, no ! "——"Then am I ever thine :
I know thee rash and guilty,—but to thee
I pledge my vow, and thine will ever be :
Yet think again,—the life that God has lent
Is thine, but not to cast away,—Consent,
If 'tis thy wish ; for this I made my way
To thy distress—Command, and I obey."
     ' " Perhaps my brother may have gain'd
     thy heart ! "—
" Then why this visit, if I wish'd to part ?
Was it, ah, man ungrateful ! wise to make
Effort like this, to hazard for thy sake
A spotless reputation, and to be
A suppliant to that stern man for thee ?
But I forgive,—thy spirit has been tried,
And thou art weak, but still thou must decide.
     ' " I ask'd thy brother, James, would'st
     thou command,
Without the loving heart, the obedient hand ?
I ask thee, Robert, lover, canst thou part
With this poor hand, when master of the
     heart ?
He answer'd, ' Yes ! '—I tarry thy reply,
Resign'd with him to live, content with thee
     to die."
Assured of this, with spirits low and tame,
Here life so purchased—there a death of
     shame ;
Death once his merriment, but now his dread
And he with terror thought upon the dead ·
     ' " O ! sure 'tis better to endure the care
And pain of life, than go we know not where !—
And is there not the dreaded hell for sin,
Or is it only this I feel within ?
That, if it lasted, no man would sustain,
But would by any change relieve the pain :
Forgive me, love ! it is a loathsome thing
To live not thine ; but still this dreaded sting
Of death torments me—I to nature cling——
Go, and be his—but love him not, be sure—
Go, love him not,—and I will life endure :

He, too, is mortal!"——Rachel deeply sigh'd,
But would no more converse : she had com-
plied,
And was no longer free—she was his brother's
bride.
'" Farewell ! " she said, with kindness, but
not fond,
Feeling the pressure of the recent bond,
And put her tenderness apart to give
Advice to one who so desired to live :
She then departed, join'd the attending guide,
Reflected—wept—was sad—was satisfied.
'James on her worth and virtue could de-
pend,
He listen'd gladly to her story's end :
Again he promised Robert's life to save,
And claim'd the hand that she in payment
gave.
' Robert, when death no longer was in view,
Scorn'd what was done, but could not this
undo :
The day appointed for the trial near
He view'd with shame, and not unmix'd with
fear,—
James might deceive him ; and, if not, the
schemes
Of men may fail——Can I depend on James ?
' He might ; for now the grievous price was
paid—
James to the altar led the victim maid,
And gave the trembling girl his faithful word
For Robert's safety, and so gave my lord.
' But this, and all the promise hope could
give,
Gilded not life,—it was not joy to live ;
There was no smile in Rachel, nothing gay ;
The hours pass'd off, but never danced away.
' When drew the gloomy day for trial near
There came a note to Robert—"Banish fear!"
He knew whence safety came,—his terror fled,
But rage and vengeance fill'd his soul instead.
' A stronger fear in his companions rose—
The day of trial on their hopes might close :
They had no brothers, none to intercede
For them, their friends suspected, and in need;
Scatter'd, they judged, and could unite
no more,—
Not so, they then were at the prison door.
' For some had met who sought the haunts
they loved,
And were to pity and to vengeance moved :
Their fellows perish ! and they see their fall,—
Why not attempt the steep but guardless wall ?

' Attempt was made, his part assign'd each
man,
And they succeeded in the desperate plan ;
In truth, a purposed mercy smooth'd their
way,
But that they knew not—all triumphant they.
Safe in their well-known haunts, they all
prepared
To plan anew, and show how much they
dared.
' With joy the troubled heart of Robert beat,
For life was his, and liberty was sweet ;
He look'd around in freedom——in delight ?
O ! no—his Rachel was another's right !
" Right !—has he then preserved me in the
day
Of my distress ?—He has the lovely pay !
But I no freedom at the slaves request,
The price I paid shall then be repossess'd !
Alas ! her virtue and the law prevent,
Force cannot be, and she will not consent ;
But were that brother gone !—A brother ?
No !
A circumventor !—and the wretch shall go !
Yet not this hand—How shifts about my
mind,
Ungovern'd, guideless, drifting in the wind,
And I am all a tempest, whirl'd around
By dreadful thoughts, that fright me and
confound ;—
I would I saw him on the earth laid low !
I wish the fate, but must not give the blow!"
' So thinks a man when thoughtful ; he pre-
fers
A life of peace till man his anger stirs,
Then all the efforts of his reason cease,
And he forgets how pleasant was that peace ;
Till the wild passions what they seek obtain,
And then he sinks into his calm again.
' Now met the lawless clan,—in secret met,
And down at their convivial board were set ;
The plans in view to past adventures led,
And the past conflicts present anger bred ;
They sigh'd for pleasures gone, they groan'd
for heroes dead :
Their ancient stores were rifled,—strong
desires
Awaked, and wine rekindled latent fires.
' It was a night such bold desires to move,
Strong winds and wintry torrents filled the
grove ;
The crackling boughs that in the forest fell,
The cawing rooks, the cur's affrighten'd yell ;

The scenes above the wood, the floods below,
Were mix'd, and none the single sound could
    know ;
"Loud blow the blasts," they cried, "and call
    us as they blow."
   ' In such a night—and then the heroes told
What had been done in better times of old ;
How they had conquer'd all opposed to them,
By force in part, in part by stratagem ;
And as the tales inflamed the fiery crew,
What had been done they then prepared to do;
" 'Tis a last night ! " they said—the angry
    blast
And roaring floods seem'd answering " 'tis
    a last ! "
   'James knew they met, for he had spies about,
Grave, sober men, whom none presumed to
    doubt ;
For if suspected, they had soon been tried
Where fears are evidence, and doubts decide :
But these escaped——Now James com-
    panions took,
Sturdy and bold, with terror-stirring look ;
He had before, by informations led,
Left the afflicted partner of his bed ;
Awaked his men, and through plantations
    wide,
Deep-woods, and trackless ling, had been their
    guide ;
And then return'd to wake the pitying wife,
And hear her tender terrors for his life.
   ' But in this night a sure informer came,
They were assembled who attack'd his game ;
Who more than once had through the park
    made way,
And slain the dappled breed, or vow'd to slay;
The trembling spy had heard the solemn vow,
And need and vengeance both inspired them
    now.
   ' The keeper early had retired to rest
For brief repose ;—sad thoughts his mind
    possess'd ;
In his short sleep he started from his bed,
And ask'd in fancy's terror " Is he dead ? "
   ' There was a call below, when James awoke,
Rose from his bed, and arms to aid him took,
Not all defensive !—there his helpers stood,
Arm'd like himself, and hastening to the wood.
   ' " Why this ? " he said, for Rachel pour'd
    her tears
Profuse, that spoke involuntary fears :
" Sleep, that so early thou for us may'st wake,
And we our comforts in return may take ;

Sleep, and farewell! " he said, and took his way,
And the sad wife in neither could obey ;
She slept not nor well fared, but restless dwelt
On her past life, and past afflictions felt ;
The man she loved the brother and the foe
Of him she married !—It had wrought her woe;
Not that she loved, but pitied, and that now
Was, so she fear'd, infringement of her vow :
James too was civil, though she must confess
That his was not her kind of happiness ;
That he would shoot the man who shot a hare
Was what her timid conscience could not bear ;
But still she loved him—wonder'd where he
    stray'd
In this loud night ! and if he were afraid.
   ' More than one hour she thought, and
    dropping then
In sudden sleep, cried loudly "Spare him, men !
And do no murder ! "—then awaked she rose,
And thought no more of trying for repose.
   ' 'Twas past the dead of night, when every
    sound
That nature mingles might be heard around ;
But none from man,—man's feeble voice was
    hush'd,
Where rivers swelling roar'd, and woods were
    crush'd ;
Hurried by these, the wife could sit no more,
But must the terrors of the night explore.
   'Softly she left her door, her garden gate,
And seem'd as then committed to her fate ;
To every horrid thought and doubt a prey,
She hurried on, already lost her way ;
Oft as she glided on in that sad night,
She stopp'd to listen, and she look'd for light :
An hour she wander'd, and was still to learn
Aught of her husband's safety or return :
A sudden break of heavy clouds could show
A place she knew not, but she strove to
    know ;
Still further on she crept with trembling feet,
With hope a friend, with fear a foe to meet :
And there was something fearful in the sight,
And in the sound of what appear'd to-night ;
For now, of night and nervous terror bred,
Arose a strong and superstitious dread ;
She heard strange noises, and the shapes she
    saw
Of fancied beings bound her soul in awe.
   'The moon was risen, and she sometimes
    shone
Through thick white clouds, that flew tumul-
    tuous on,

Passing beneath her with an eagle's speed,
That her soft light imprison'd and then freed ;
The fitful glimmering through the hedge-row
   green
Gave a strange beauty to the changing scene ;
And roaring winds and rushing waters lent
Their mingled voice that to the spirit went.
'To these she listen'd; but new sounds were
   heard,
And sight more startling to her soul appear'd ;
There were low lengthen'd tones with sobs
   between,
And near at hand, but nothing yet was seen ;
She hurried on, and "Who is there ? " she
   cried,
" A dying wretch ! "—was from the earth re-
   plied.
'It was her lover, was the man she gave,
The price she paid, himself from death to save;
With whom, expiring, she must kneel and pray,
While the soul flitted from the shivering clay
That press'd the dewy ground, and bled its
   life away !
'This was the part that duty bade her take,
Instant and ere her feelings were awake ;
But now they waked to anguish ; there came
   then,
Hurrying with lights, loud-speaking, eager
   men.
' " And here, my lord, we met—And who is
   here ?
The keeper's wife—Ah ! woman, go not near !
There lies the man that was the head of all—
See, in his temples went the fatal ball !
And James that instant, who was then our
   guide,
Felt in his heart the adverse shot, and died !
It was a sudden meeting, and the light
Of a dull moon made indistinct our fight ;
He foremost fell !—But see, the woman creeps
Like a lost thing, that wanders as she sleeps.
See, here her husband's body—but she knows
That other dead ! and that her action foe ?—
Rachel ! why look you at your mortal foe ?—
She does not hear us—Whither will she go ? "

' Now, more attentive, on the dead they
   gazed,
And they were brothers : sorrowing and
   amazed,
On all a momentary silence came,
A common softness, and a moral shame.
' " Seized you the poachers?" said my
   lord—" They fled,
And we pursued not,—one of them was dead,
And one of us ; they hurried through the
   wood,
Two lives were gone, and we no more pursued.
Two lives of men, of valiant brothers lost !
Enough, my lord, do hares and pheasants
   cost ! "
'So many thought, and there is found a heart
To dwell upon the deaths on either part ;
Since this their morals have been more correct,
The cruel spirit in the place is check'd ;
His lordship holds not in such sacred care,
Nor takes such dreadful vengeance for a hare ;
The smugglers fear, the poacher stands in awe
Of Heaven's own act, and reverences the law ;
There was, there is a terror in the place
That operates on man's offending race ;
Such acts will stamp their moral on the soul,
And while the bad they threaten and control,
Will to the pious and the humble say,
Yours is the right, the safe, the certain way,
'Tis wisdom to be good, 'tis virtue to obey.
'So Rachel thinks, the pure, the good, the
   meek,
Whose outward acts the inward purpose speak;
As men will children at their sports behold,
And smile to see them, though unmoved and
   cold,
Smile at the recollected games, and then
Depart and mix in the affairs of men :
So Rachel looks upon the world, and sees
It cannot longer pain her, longer please,
But just detain the passing thought, or cause
A gentle smile of pity or applause ;
And then the recollected soul repairs
Her slumbering hope, and heeds her own
   affairs.'

BOOK XXII.   THE VISIT CONCLUDED

Richard prepares to depart—Visits the Rector—His Reception—Visit to the Sisters—Their present situation—The Morning of the last Day—The Conference of the Brothers—Their Excursion—Richard dissatisfied—The Brother expostulates—The End of their Ride, and of the Day's Business—Conclusion.

' No letters, Tom ? ' said Richard—'None to-day.'
' Excuse me, Brother, I must now away ;
Matilda never in her life so long
Deferr'd—Alas ! there must be something wrong ! '
' Comfort ! ' said George, and all he could he lent ;
' Wait till your promised day, and I consent ;
Two days, and those of hope, may cheerfully be spent.
' And keep your purpose, to review the place,
My choice ; and I beseech you do it grace :
Mark each apartment, their proportions learn,
And either use or elegance discern ;
Look o'er the land, the gardens, and their wall,
Find out the something to admire in all ;
And should you praise them in a knowing style,
I'll take it kindly—it is well—a smile.'

Richard must now his morning visits pay,
And bid farewell ! for he must go away.
He sought the Rector first, not lately seen,
For he had absent from his parish been ;
' Farewell ! ' the younger man with feeling cried,
' Farewell ! ' the cold but worthy priest replied ;
' When do you leave us ? '—' I have days but two : '
' 'Tis a short time—but, well—Adieu, adieu ! '
' Now here is one,' said Richard, as he went
To the next friend in pensive discontent,
' With whom I sate in social, friendly ease,
Whom I respected, whom I wish'd to please ;
Whose love profess'd, I question'd not was true,
And now to hear his heartless, "Well ! adieu ! "

' But 'tis not well—and he a man of sense,
Grave, but yet looking strong benevolence ;
Whose slight acerbity and roughness told
To his advantage ; yet the man is cold ;
Nor will he know, when rising in the morn,
That such a being to the world was born.
' Are such the friendships we contract in life ?
O ! give me then the friendship of a wife !
Adieus, nay, parting-pains to us are sweet,
They make so glad the moments when we meet.
' For though we look not for regard intense,
Or warm professions in a man of sense,
Yet in the daily intercourse of mind
I thought that found which I desired to find,
Feeling and frankness—thus it seem'd to me,
And such farewell !—Well, Rector, let it be ! '
Of the fair sisters then he took his leave,
Forget he could not, he must think and grieve,
Must the impression of their wrongs retain,
Their very patience adding to his pain ;
And still the better they their sorrows bore,
His friendly nature made him feel them more.
He judged they must have many a heavy hour
When the mind suffers from a want of power ;
When troubled long we find our strength decay'd,
And cannot then recall our better aid ;
For the mind, ere yet that aid has flown,
Grief has possessed, and made it all his own ;
And patience suffers, till, with gather'd might,
The scatter'd forces of the soul unite.
But few and short such times of suffering were
In Lucy's mind, and brief the reign of care.
Jane had, indeed, her flights, but had in them
What we could pity but must not condemn ;
For they were always pure and oft sublime,
And such as triumph'd over earth and time,
Thoughts of eternal love that souls possess,
Foretaste divine of Heaven's own happiness.
Oft had he seen them, and esteem had sprung
In his free mind for maids so sad and young,
So good and grieving, and his place was high
In their esteem, his friendly brother's nigh,
But yet beneath ; and when he said adieu !
Their tone was kind, and was responsive too.

Parting was painful; when adieu he cried,
' You will return ? ' the gentle girls replied ;
' You must return ! your Brother knows you
   now,
But to exist without you knows not how ;
Has he not told us of the lively joy
He takes—forgive us—in the Brother-boy ?
He is alone and pensive ; you can give
Pleasure to one by whom a number live
In daily comfort—sure for this you met,
That for his debtors you might pay a debt—
The poor are call'd ungrateful, but you still
Will have their thanks for this—indeed you
   will.'
Richard but little said, for he of late
Held with himself contention and debate.
   ' My brother loves me, his regard I know,
But will not such affection weary grow ?
He kindly says " defer the parting day,"
But yet may wish me in his heart away ;
Nothing but kindness I in him perceive,
In me 'tis kindness then to take my leave ;
Why should I grieve if he should weary be ?
There have been visitors who wearied me ;
He yet may love, and we may part in peace,
Nay, in affection—novelty must cease—
Man is but man ; the thing he most desires
Pleases awhile—then pleases not—then tires ;
George to his former habits and his friends
Will now return, and so my visit ends.'
   Thus Richard commun'd with his heart ;
   but still
He found opposed his reason and his will,
Found that his thoughts were busy in this
   train,
And he was striving to be calm in vain.
   These thoughts were passing while he yet
   forbore
To leave the friends whom he might see no
   more.
   Then came a chubby child and sought relief,
Sobbing in all the impotence of grief ;
A full fed girl she was, with ruddy cheek,
And features coarse, that grosser feelings speak,
To whom another miss, with passions strong,
And slender fist, had done some baby-wrong.
On Lucy's gentle mind had Barlow wrought
To teach this child, whom she had labouring
   taught
With unpaid love—this unproductive brain
Would little comprehend, and less retain.
   A farmer's daughter, with redundant health,
And double Lucy's weight and Lucy's wealth,

Had won the man's regard, and he with her
Possess'd the treasure vulgar minds prefer ;
A man of thrift, and thriving, he possess'd
What he esteem'd of earthly good the best ;
And Lucy's well-stored mind had not a charm
For this true lover of the well-stock'd farm,
This slave to petty wealth and rustic toil,
This earth-devoted wooer of the soil :—
But she with meekness took the wayward
   child,
And sought to make the savage nature mild.
   But Jane her judgment with decision gave—
' Train not an idiot to oblige a slave.'
   And where is Bloomer ? Richard would
   have said,
But he was cautious, feeling, and afraid ;
And little either of the hero knew,
And little sought—he might be married too.
   Now to his home, the morning visits past,
Return'd the guest—that evening was his last.
   He met his Brother, and they spoke of those
From whom his comforts in the village rose ;
Spoke of the favourites, whom so good and
   kind
It was peculiar happiness to find :
Then for the sisters in their griefs they felt,
And, sad themselves, on saddening subject
   dwelt.
   But George was willing all this woe to spare,
And let to-morrow be to-morrow's care :
He of his purchase talk'd—a thing of course,
As men will boldly praise a new-bought horse.
   Richard was not to all its beauty blind,
And promised still to seek, with hope to find :
' The price indeed—— '
         ' Yes, that,' said George, ' is high ;
But if I bought not, one was sure to buy,
Who might the social comforts we enjoy,
And every comfort lessen or destroy,
   ' We must not always reckon what we give,
But think how precious 'tis in peace to live ;
Some neighbour Nimrod might in very pride
Have stirr'd my anger, and have then defied ;
Or worse, have loved, and teased me to excess
By his kind care to give me happiness ;
Or might his lady and her daughters bring
To raise my spirits, to converse, and sing :
'Twas not the benefit alone I view'd,
But thought what horrid things I might
   exclude.
   ' Some party man might here have sat him
   down,
Some country champion, railing at the crown,

Or some true courtier, both prepared to prove,
Who loved not them, could not their country
    love :
If we have value for our health and ease,
Should we not buy off enemies like these ? '
    So pass'd the evening in a quiet way,
When, lo ! the morning of the parting day.
    Each to the table went with clouded look,
And George in silence gazed upon a book ;
Something that chance had offer'd to his view,
He knew not what, or cared not, if he knew.
    Richard his hand upon a paper laid,—
His vacant eye upon the carpet stray'd ;
His tongue was talking something of the day,
And his vex'd mind was wandering on his way.
    They spake by fits,—but neither had con-
        cern
In the replies,—they nothing wish'd to learn,
Nor to relate ;   each sat as one who tries
To baffle sadnesses and sympathies :
Each of his Brother took a steady view,—
As actor he, and as observer too.
    Richard, whose heart was ever free and
        frank,
Had now a trial, and before it sank :
He thought his Brother—parting now so
        near—
Appear'd not as his Brother should appear ;
He could as much of tenderness remark
When parting for a ramble in the park.
    ' Yet, is it just? ' he thought ; ' and would
        I see
My Brother wretched but to part with me ?
What can he further in my mind explore ?
He saw enough, and he would see no more :
Happy himself, he wishes now to slide
Back to his habits——He is satisfied ;
But I am not—this cannot be denied.
    ' He has been kind,—so let me think him
        still ;
Yet he expresses not a wish, a will
To meet again ! '——And thus affection strove
With pride, and petulance made war on love :
He thought his Brother cool—he knew him
        kind—
And there was sore division in his mind.
    ' Hours yet remain,—'tis misery to sit
With minds for conversation all unfit ;
No evil can from change of place arise,
And good will spring from air and exercise :
Suppose I take the purposed ride with you,
And guide your jaded praise to objects new,
That buyers see ? '——

                And Richard gave assent
Without resistance, and without intent :
He liked not nor declined,—and forth the
    Brothers went.
    ' Come, my dear Richard! let us cast away
All evil thoughts,—let us forget the day,
And fight like men with grief till we like boys
    are gay.'
    Thus George,—and even this in Richard's
        mind
Was judged an effort rather wise than kind ;
This flow'd from something he observed of
    late,
And he could feel it, but he could not state :
He thought some change appear'd,—yet fail'd
    to prove,
Even as he tried, abatement in the love ;
But in his Brother's manner was restraint
That he could feel, and yet he could not paint.
    That they should part in peace full well he
        knew,
But much he fear'd to part with coolness too :
George had been peevish when the subject
        rose,
And never fail'd the parting to oppose ;
Name it, and straight his features cloudy grew
To stop the journey as the clouds will do ;—
And thus they rode along in pensive mood,
Their thoughts pursuing, by their cares pur-
        sued.
    ' Richard,' said George, ' I see it is in vain
By love or prayer my Brother to retain ;
And, truth to tell, it was a foolish thing
A man like thee from thy repose to bring
Ours to disturb——Say, how am I to live
Without the comforts thou art wont to give ?
How will the heavy hours my mind afflict,—
No one t' agree, no one to contradict,
None to awake, excite me, or prevent,
To hear a tale, or hold an argument,
To help my worship in a case of doubt,
And bring me in my blunders fairly out.
    ' Who now by manners lively or serene
Comes between me and sorrow like a screen,
And giving, what I look'd not to have found,
A care, an interest in the world around ? '
    Silent was Richard, striving to adjust
His thoughts for speech,—for speak, he
        thought, he must :
Something like war within his bosom strove—
His mild, kind nature, and his proud self-love :
Grateful he was, and with his courage meek,—
But he was hurt, and he resolved to speak.

' Yes, my dear Brother ! from my soul
    I grieve
Thee and the proofs of thy regard to leave :
Thou hast been all that I could wish,—my
    pride
Exults to find that I am thus allied :
Yet to express a feeling, how it came,
The pain it gives, its nature and its name,
I know not,—but of late, I will confess,
Not that thy love is little, but is less.
    ' Hadst thou received me in thy present
        mood,
Sure I had held thee to be kind and good ;
But thou wert all the warmest heart could
    state,
Affection dream, or hope anticipate ;
I must have wearied thee yet day by day,—
" Stay ! " said my Brother, and 'twas good
    to stay ;
But now, forgive me, thinking I perceive
Change undefined, and as I think I grieve.
    ' Have I offended ?—Proud although I be,
I will be humble, and concede to thee :
Have I intruded on thee when thy mind
Was vex'd, and then to solitude inclined ?
O ! there are times when all things will molest
Minds so disposed, so heavy, so oppress'd ;
And thine, I know, is delicate and nice,
Sickening at folly, and at war with vice :
Then, at a time when thou wert vex'd with
    these,
I have intruded, let affection tease,
And so offended.'——
                    ' Richard, if thou hast,
'Tis at this instant, nothing in the past :
No, thou art all a Brother's love would choose ;
And, having lost thee, I shall interest lose
In all that I possess : I pray thee tell
Wherein thy host has fail'd to please thee
    well,—
Do I neglect thy comforts ? '—
                        ' O ! not thou,
But art thyself uncomfortable now,
And 'tis from thee and from thy looks I gain
This painful knowledge—'tis my Brother's
    pain ;
And yet that something in my spirit lives,
Something that spleen excites and sorrow
    gives,
I may confess,—for not in thee I trace
Alone this change, it is in all the place :
Smile if thou wilt in scorn, for I am glad
A smile at any rate is to be had.

' But there is Jacques, who ever seem'd to
    treat
Thy Brother kindly as we chanced to meet ;
Nor with thee only pleased our worthy guide,
But in the hedge-row path and green-wood
    side,
There he would speak with that familiar ease
That makes a trifle, makes a nothing please.
    ' But now to my farewell,—and that I spoke
With honest sorrow,—with a careless look,
Gazing unalter'd on some stupid prose—
His sermon for the Sunday I suppose,—
" Going ? " said he : " why then the 'Squire
    and you
Will part at last—You're going ?—Well,
    adieu ! "
    ' True, we were not in friendship bound like
        those
Who will adopt each other's friends and foes,
Without esteem or hatred of their own,—
But still we were to intimacy grown ;
And sure of Jacques when I had taken leave
It would have grieved me,—and it ought to
    grieve ;
But I in him could not affection trace,—
Careless he put his sermons in their place,
With no more feeling than his sermon-case.
    ' Not so those generous girls beyond the
        brook,—
It quite unmann'd me as my leave I took.
    ' But, my dear Brother ! when I take at
        night,
In my own home, and in their mother's sight,
By turns my children, or together see
A pair contending for the vacant knee,
When to Matilda I begin to tell
What in my visit first and last befell—
Of this your village, of her tower and spire,
And, above all, her Rector and her 'Squire,
How will the tale be marr'd when I shall end —
I left displeased the Brother and the friend ! '
    ' Nay, Jacques is honest—Marry, he was then
Engaged—What ! part an author and his pen ?
Just in the fit, and when th'inspiring ray
Shot on his brain, t' arrest it in its way !
Come, thou shalt see him in an easier vein,
Nor of his looks nor of his words complain :
Art thou content ? '—
                If Richard had replied,
' I am,' his manner had his words belied :
Even from his Brother's cheerfulness he drew
Something to vex him—what, he scarcely
    knew :

So he evading said, ' My evil fate
Upon my comforts throws a gloom of late :
Matilda writes not ; and, when last she wrote,
I read no letter—'twas a trader's note,—
" Yours I received," and all that formal prate
That is so hateful, that she knows I hate.

  ' Dejection reigns, I feel, but cannot tell
Why upon me the dire infection fell :
Madmen may say that they alone are sane,
And all beside have a distemper'd brain ;
Something like this I feel,—and I include
Myself among the frantic multitude :
But, come, Matilda writes, although but ill,
And home has health, and that is comfort still.'

  George stopt his horse, and with the kindest
      look
Spoke to his Brother,—earnestly he spoke,
As one who to his friend his heart reveals,
And all the hazard with the comfort feels.
  ' Soon as I loved thee, Richard,—and
      I loved
Before my reason had the will approved,
Who yet right early had her sanction lent,
And with affection in her verdict went,—
So soon I felt, that thus a friend to gain,
And then to lose, is but to purchase pain :
Daily the pleasure grew, then sad the day
That takes it all in its increase away !
  ' Patient thou wert, and kind,—but well
      I knew
The husband's wishes, and the father's too ;
I saw how check'd they were, and yet in secret
      grew :
Once and again, I urged thee to delay
Thy purposed journey, still deferr'd the day,
And still on its approach the pain increased
Till my request and thy compliance ceased ;
I could not further thy affection task,
Nor more of one so self-resisting ask ;
But yet to lose thee, Richard, and with thee
All hope of social joys—it cannot be.
Nor could I bear to meet thee as a boy
From school, his parents, to obtain a joy,
That lessens day by day, and one will soon
      destroy.
  ' No! I would have thee, Brother, all my own,
To grow beside me as my trees have grown ;
For ever near me, pleasant in my sight,
And in my mind, my pride and my delight.
  ' Yet will I tell thee, Richard ; had I found
Thy mind dependent and thy heart unsound,
Hadst thou been poor, obsequious, and disposed
With any wish or measure to have closed,

Willing on me and gladly to attend,
The younger brother, the convenient friend ;
Thy speculation its reward had made
Like other ventures—thou hadst gain'd in
      trade ;
What reason urged, or Jacques esteem'd thy
      due,
Thine had it been, and I, a trader too,
Had paid my debt, and home my Brother sent,
Nor glad nor sorry that he came or went ;
Who to his wife and children would have told,
They had an uncle, and the man was old ;
Till every girl and boy had learn'd to prate
Of uncle George, his gout, and his estate.

  ' Thus had we parted ; but as now thou art,
I must not lose thee—No ! I cannot part ;
Is it in human nature to consent,
To give up all the good that heaven has lent,
All social ease and comfort to forego,
And live again the solitary ? No !
  ' We part no more, dear Richard ! thou
      wilt need
Thy Brother's help to teach thy boys to read ;
And I should love to hear Matilda's psalm,
To keep my spirit in a morning calm,
And feel the soft devotion that prepares
The soul to rise above its earthly cares ;
Then thou and I, an independent two,
May have our parties, and defend them too ;
Thy liberal notions, and my loyal fears,
Will give us subjects for our future years ;
We will for truth alone contend and read,
And our good Jacques shall oversee our creed.
  ' Such were my views ; and I had quickly
      made
Some bold attempts my Brother to persuade
To think as I did ; but I knew too well
Whose now thou wert, with whom thou wert
      to dwell,
And why, I said, return him doubtful home,
Six months to argue if he then would come
Some six months after ? and, beside, I know
That all the happy are of course the slow ;
And thou at home art happy, there wilt stay,
Dallying 'twixt will and will-not many a day,
And fret the gloss of hope, and hope itself away.
  ' Jacques is my friend ; to him I gave my
      heart,
You see my Brother, see I would not part ;
Wilt thou an embassy of love disdain ?
Go to this sister, and my views explain ;
Gloss o'er my failings, paint me with a grace
That Love beholds, put meaning in my face ;

Describe that dwelling ; talk how well we live,
And all its glory to our village give ;
Praise the kind sisters whom we love so much,
And thine own virtues like an artist touch.
  ' Tell her, and here my secret purpose
      show,
That no dependence shall my sister know ;
Hers all the freedom that she loves shall be,
And mine the debt,—then press her to agree ;
Say, that my Brother's wishes wait on hers,
And his affection what she wills prefers.
  ' Forgive me, Brother,—these my words
      and more
Our friendly Rector to Matilda bore ;
At large, at length, were all my views ex-
      plain'd,
And to my joy my wishes I obtain'd.
  ' Dwell in that house, and we shall still be
      near,
Absence and parting I no more shall fear ;
Dwell in thy home, and at thy will exclude
All who shall dare upon thee to intrude.
  ' Again thy pardon,—'twas not my design
To give surprise ; a better view was mine ;
But let it pass—and yet I wish'd to see
That meeting too : and happy may it be ! '
  Thus George had spoken, and then look'd
      around,
And smiled as one who then his road had
      found ;
' Follow ! ' he cried, and briskly urged his
      horse :
Richard was puzzled, but obey'd of course ;
He was affected like a man astray,
Lost, but yet knowing something of the way ;
Till a wood clear'd, that still conceal'd the
      view,
Richard the purchase of his Brother knew ;
And something flash'd upon his mind not clear,
But much with pleasure mix'd, in part with
      fear ;
As one who wandering through a stormy night
Sees his own home, and gladdens at the sight,
Yet feels some doubt if fortune had decreed
That lively pleasure in such time of need ;
So Richard felt—but now the mansion came
In view direct,—he knew it for the same ;
There too the garden walk, the elms design'd
To guard the peaches from the eastern wind ;
And there the sloping glass, that when he
      shines
Gives the sun's vigour to the ripening vines.—
  ' It is my Brother's ! '—

  ' No ! ' he answers, ' No !
'Tis to thy own possession that we go ;
It is thy wife's, and will thy children's be,
Earth, wood, and water !—all for thine and
      thee ;
Bought in thy name—Alight, my friend, and
      come,
I do beseech thee, to thy proper home ;
There wilt thou soon thy own Matilda view,
She knows our deed, and she approves it too ;
Before her all our views and plans were laid,
And Jacques was there t' explain and to
      persuade.
Here, on this lawn, thy boys and girls shall run,
And play their gambols when their tasks are
      done ;
There, from that window, shall their mother
      view
The happy tribe, and smile at all they do ;
While thou, more gravely, hiding thy delight,
Shalt cry "O ! childish !" and enjoy the sight.

  ' Well, my dear Richard, there 's no more
      to say—
Stay, as you will—do any thing—but stay ;
Be, I dispute not, steward—what you will,
Take your own name, but be my Brother still.
  ' And hear me, Richard ! if I should offend,
Assume the patron, and forget the friend ;
If aught in word or manner I express
That only touches on thy happiness ;
If I be peevish, humorsome, unkind,
Spoil'd as I am by each subservient mind ;
For I am humour'd by a tribe who make
Me more capricious for the pains they take
To make me quiet ; shouldst thou ever feel
A wound from this, this leave not time to heal,
But let thy wife her cheerful smile withhold,
Let her be civil, distant, cautious, cold ;
Then shall I woo forgiveness, and repent,
Nor bear to lose the blessings Heaven has lent.'
  But this was needless—there was joy of
      heart,
All felt the good that all desired t' impart ;
Respect, affection, and esteem combined,
In sundry portions ruled in every mind ;
And o'er the whole an unobtrusive air
Of pious joy, that urged the silent prayer,
And bless'd the new-born feelings——Here
      we close
Our Tale of Tales !—Health, reader, and
      repose !

POSTHUMOUS TALES

[1834]

TALE I. SILFORD HALL; OR, THE HAPPY DAY

WITHIN a village, many a mile from town,
A place of small resort and no renown ;—
Save that it form'd a way, and gave a name
To SILFORD HALL, it made no claim to
    fame ;—
It was the gain of some, the pride of all,
That travellers stopt to ask for SILFORD HALL.
    Small as it was, the place could boast a
        School,
In which *Nathaniel Perkin* bore the rule.
Not mark'd for learning deep, or talents rare,
But for his varying tasks and ceaseless care ;
Some forty boys, the sons of thrifty men,
He taught to read, and part to use the pen ;
While, by more studious care, a favourite few
Increased his pride—for if the Scholar knew
Enough for praise, say what the Teacher's
    due ?—
These to his presence, slates in hand, moved on,
And a grim smile their feats in figures won.
This Man of Letters woo'd in early life
The Vicar's maiden, whom he made his wife.
She too can read, as by her song she proves—
The song Nathaniel made about their loves :
Five rosy girls, and one fair boy, increased
The Father's care, whose labours seldom
    ceased.
No day of rest was his. If, now and then,
His boys for play laid by the book and pen,
For Lawyer Slow there was some deed to
    write,
Or some young farmer's letter to indite,
Or land to measure, or, with legal skill,
To frame some yeoman's widow's peevish will ;
And or the Sabbath,—when his neighbours
    drest,
To hear their duties, and to take their rest—
Then, when the Vicar's periods ceased to flow,
Was heard Nathaniel, in his seat below.
    Such were his labours ; but the time is come
When his son *Peter* clears the hours of gloom,
And brings him aid : though yet a boy, he
    shares
In staid Nathaniel's multifarious cares.
A king his father, he, a prince, has rule—
The first of subjects, viceroy of the school :
But though a prince within that realm he
    reigns,
Hard is the part his duteous soul sustains.
He with his Father, o'er the furrow'd land,
Draws the long chain in his uneasy hand,
And neatly forms at home, what there they
    rudely plann'd.
Content, for all his labour, if he gains
Some words of praise, and sixpence for his
    pains.
Thus many a hungry day the Boy has fared,
And would have ask'd a dinner, had he dared.
When boys are playing, he, for hours of school
Has sums to set, and copy-books to rule ;
When all are met, for some sad dunce afraid,
He, by allowance, lends his timely aid—
Taught at the student's failings to connive,
Yet keep his Father's dignity alive :
For ev'n Nathaniel fears, and might offend,
If too severe, the farmer, now his friend ;
Or her, that farmer's lady, who well knows
Her boy is bright, and needs nor threats nor
    blows.
This seem'd to Peter hard ; and he was loth,
T' obey and rule, and have the cares of both—
To miss the master's dignity, and yet,
No portion of the school-boy's play to get.
To him the Fiend, as once to Launcelot, cried,
' Run from thy wrongs ! '—' Run where ? '
    his fear replied :
' Run ! '—said the Tempter, ' if but hard thy
    fare,
Hard is it now—it *may* be mended there.'
    But still, though tempted, he refused to
        part,
And felt the Mother clinging at his heart.

Nor this alone—he, in that weight of care,
Had help, and bore it as a man should bear.
A drop of comfort in his cup was thrown ;
It was his treasure, and it was his own.
His Father's shelves contained a motley store
Of letter'd wealth ; and this he might explore.
A part his mother in her youth had gain'd,
A part Nathaniel from his club obtain'd,
And part—a well-worn kind—from sire to
　　son remain'd.
　　He sought his Mother's hoard, and there he
　　　found
Romance in sheets, and poetry unbound ;
Soft Tales of Love, which never damsel read,
But tears of pity stain'd her virgin bed.
There were Jane Shore and Rosamond the
　　Fair,
And humbler heroines frail as these were
　　there ;
There was a tale of one forsaken Maid,
Who till her death the work of vengeance
　　stay'd ;
Her Lover, then at sea, while round him stood
A dauntless crew, the angry ghost pursued ;
In a small boat, without an oar or sail,
She came to call him, nor would force avail,
Nor prayer ; but, conscience-stricken, down
　　he leapt,
And o'er his corse the closing billows slept ;
All vanish'd then ! but of the crew were some,
Wondering whose ghost would on the morrow
　　come.
　　A learned Book was there, and in it schemes
How to cast Fortunes and interpret Dreams ;
Ballads were there of Lover's bliss or bale,
The Kitchen Story, and the Nursery Tale.
His hungry mind disdain'd not humble food,
And read with relish keen of Robin Hood ;
Of him, all-powerful made by magic gift,
And Giants slain—of mighty Hickerthrift ;
Through Crusoe's Isle delighted had he stray'd,
Nocturnal visits had to witches paid,
Gliding through haunted scenes, enraptured
　　and afraid.
　　A loftier shelf with real books was graced,
Bound, or part bound, and ranged in comely
　　taste ;
Books of high mark, the mind's more solid
　　food,
Which some might think the owner under-
　　stood ;
But Fluxions, Sections, Algebraic lore,
Our Peter left for others to explore,

And quickly turning to a favourite kind,
Found, what rejoiced him at his heart to find.
Sir Walter wrote not then, or He by whom
Such gain and glory to Sir Walter come—
That Fairy-Helper, by whose secret aid,
Such views of life are to the world convey'd—
As inspiration known in after-times,
The sole assistant in his prose or rhymes.
But there were fictions wild that please the
　　boy,
Which men, too, read, condemn, reject,
　　enjoy—
Arabian Nights, and Persian Tales were there,
One volume each, and both the worse for wear ;
There by Quarles' Emblems, Esop's Fables
　　stood,
The coats in tatters, and the cuts in wood.
There, too, ' The English History,' by the pen
Of Doctor Cooke, and other learned men,
In numbers, sixpence each ; by these was seen,
And highly prized, the Monthly Magazine ;—
Not such as now will men of taste engage,
But the cold gleanings of a former age,
Scraps cut from sermons, scenes removed
　　from plays,
With heads of heroes famed in Tyburn's
　　palmy days.
　　The rest we pass—though Peter pass'd
　　　them not,
But here his cares and labours all forgot :
Stain'd, torn, and blotted every noble page,
Stood the chief poets of a former age—
And of the present ; not their works complete,
But in such portions as on bulks we meet,
The refuse of the shops, thrown down upon
　　the street.
There Shakspeare, Spenser, Milton found a
　　place,
With some a nameless, some a shameless race,
Which many a weary walker resting reads,
And, pondering o'er the short relief, proceeds,
While others lingering pay the written sum,
Half loth, but longing for delight to come.
　　Of the Youth's morals we would something
　　　speak ;
Taught by his Mother what to shun or seek :
She show'd the heavenly way, and in his youth
Press'd on his yielding mind the Gospel truth,
How weak is man, how much to ill inclined,
And where his help is placed, and how to find.
These words of weight sank deeply in his
　　breast,
And awful Fear and holy Hope imprest.

He shrank from vice, and at the startling view,
As from an adder in his path, withdrew.
All else was cheerful. Peter's easy mind
To the gay scenes of village life inclined.
The lark that soaring sings his notes of joy,
Was not more lively than th' awaken'd boy.
Yet oft with this a softening sadness dwelt,
While, feeling thus, he marvell'd why he felt.
' I am not sorry,' said the Boy, ' but still,
The tear will drop—I wonder why it will ! '

His books, his walks, his musing, morn and eve,
Gave such impressions as such minds receive ;
And with his moral and religious views
Wove the wild fancies of an Infant-Muse,
Inspiring thoughts that he could not express,
Obscure sublime ! his secret happiness.
Oft would he strive for words, and oft begin
To frame in verse the views he had within ;
But ever fail'd : for how can words explain
The unform'd ideas of a teeming brain ?

Such was my Hero, whom I would portray
In one exploit—the Hero of a Day.
At six miles' distance from his native town
Stood Silford Hall, a seat of much renown—
Computed miles, such weary travellers ride,
When they in chance wayfaring men confide.
Beauty and grandeur were within ; around,
Lawn, wood, and water; the delicious ground
Had parks where deer disport, had fields where game abound.

Fruits of all tastes in spacious gardens grew ;
And flowers of every scent and every hue,
That native in more favour'd climes arise,
Are here protected from th' inclement skies.

To this fair place, with mingled pride and shame,
This lad of learning without knowledge came—
Shame for his conscious ignorance—and pride
To this fair seat in this gay style to ride.

The cause that brought him was a small account,
His father's due, and he must take the amount,
And sign a stamp'd receipt ! this done, he might
Look all around him, and enjoy the sight.

So far to walk was, in his mother's view,
More than her darling Peter ought to do ;
Peter indeed knew more, but he would hide
His better knowledge, for he wish'd to ride ;
So had his father's nag, a beast so small,
That if he fell, he had not far to fall.

His fond and anxious mother in his best
Her darling child for the occasion drest :
All in his coat of green she clothed her boy,
And stood admiring with a mother's joy .
Large was it made and long, as meant to do
For Sunday-service, when he older grew—
Not brought in daily use in one year's wear
or two.
White was his waistcoat, and what else he wore
Had clothed the lamb or parent ewe before
In all the mother show'd her care or skill ;
A riband black she tied beneath his frill ;
Gave him his stockings, white as driven snow,
And bade him heed the miry way below ;
On the black varnish of the comely shoe,
Shone the large buckle of a silvery hue.
Boots he had worn, had had such things possest—
But bootless grief !—he was full proudly drest ;
Full proudly look'd, and light he was of heart.
When thus for Silford Hall prepared to start.

Nathaniel's self with joy the stripling eyed.
And gave a shilling with a father's pride ;
Rules of politeness too with pomp he gave,
And show'd the lad how scholars should behave.

Ere yet he left her home, the Mother told—
For she had seen—what things he should behold.
There, she related, her young eyes had view'd
Stone figures shaped like naked flesh and blood.
Which, in the hall and up the gallery placed.
Were proofs, they told her, of a noble taste :
Nor she denied—but, in a public hall,
Her judgment taken, she had clothed them all.
There, too, were station'd, each upon its seat,
Half forms of men, without their hands and feet ;
These and what more within that hall might be
She saw, and oh ! how long'd her son to see '
Yet could he hope to view that noble place,
Who dared not look the porter in the face ?

Forth went the pony, and the rider's knees
Cleaved to her sides—he did not ride with ease;
One hand a whip, and one a bridle held,
In case the pony falter'd or rebell'd.

The village boys beheld him as he pass'd.
And looks of envy on the hero cast ;
But he was meek, nor let his pride appear.
Nay, truth to speak, he felt a sense of fear.

Lest the rude beast, unmindful of the rein,
Should take a fancy to turn back again.
  He found, and wonder 'tis he found, his
    way,
The orders many that he must obey :
' Now to the right, then left, and now again
Directly onward, through the winding lane ;
Then, half way o'er the common, by the mill,
Turn from the cottage and ascend the hill,
Then—spare the pony, boy !—as you ascend—
You see the Hall, and that 's your journey's
    end.'
  Yes, he succeeded, not remembering aught
Of this advice, but by his pony taught.
Soon as he doubted he the bridle threw
On the steed's neck, and said—' Remember
    you ! '
For oft the creature had his father borne,
Sound on his way, and safe on his return.
So he succeeded, and the modest youth
Gave praise, where praise had been assign'd
    by truth.
  His business done,—for fortune led his way
To him whose office was such debts to pay,
The farmer-bailiff, but he saw no more
Than a small room, with bare and oaken floor,
A desk with books thereon—he'd seen such
    things before ;
' Good day ! ' he said, but lingered as he spoke
' Good day,' and gazed about with serious
    look ;
Then slowly moved, and then delay'd awhile,
In dumb dismay which raised a lordly smile
In those who eyed him—then again moved on,
As all might see, unwilling to be gone.
  While puzzled thus, and puzzling all about,
Involved, absorb'd, in some bewildering doubt,
A lady enter'd, Madam Johnson call'd,
Within whose presence stood the lad appall'd.
A learned Lady this, who knew the names
Of all the pictures in the golden frames ;
Could every subject, every painter, tell,
And on their merits and their failures dwell ;
And if perchance there was a slight mistake—
These the most knowing on such matters
    make.
  ' And what dost mean, my pretty lad ? '
    she cried,
' Dost stay or go ? '—He first for courage
    tried,
Then for fit words,—then boldly he replied,
That he would give a hundred pounds, if so
He had them, all about that house to go ;

For he had heard that it contain'd such things
As never house could boast, except the king's.
  The ruling Lady, smiling, said, ' In truth
Thou shalt behold them all, my pretty youth.
Tom ! first the creature to the stable lead,
Let it be fed ; and you, my child, must feed ;
For three good hours must pass e'er dinner
    come,'—
' Supper,' thought he, 'she means, our time at
    home.'
  First was he feasted to his heart's content,
Then, all in rapture, with the Lady went ;
Through rooms immense, and galleries wide
    and tall,
He walk'd entranced—he breathed in Silford
    Hall.
  Now could he look on that delightful place,
The glorious dwelling of a princely race ;
His vast delight was mixed with equal awe,
There was such magic in the things he saw.
Oft standing still, with open mouth and eyes,
Turn'd here and there, alarm'd as one who
    tries
T' escape from something strange, that would
    before him rise.
The wall would part, and beings without name
Would come—for such to his adventures came.
Hence undefined and solemn terror press'd
Upon his mind, and all his powers possess'd.
All he had read of magic, every charm,
Were he alone, might come and do him harm :
But his gaze rested on his friendly guide—
' I'm safe,' he thought, ' so long as you abide.'
  In one large room was found a bed of state—
' And can they soundly sleep beneath such
    weight,
Where they may figures in the night explore,
Form'd by the dim light dancing on the floor
From the far window ; mirrors broad and high
Doubling each terror to the anxious eye ?—
'Tis strange,' thought Peter, ' that such things
    produce
No fear in her ; but there is much in use.'
  On that reflecting brightness, passing by,
The Boy one instant fix'd his restless eye—
And saw himself : he had before descried
His face in one his mother's store supplied ;
But here he could his whole dimensions view,
From the pale forehead to the jet-black shoe.
Passing he look'd, and looking, grieved to pass
From the fair figure smiling in the glass.
'Twas so Narcissus saw the boy advance
In the dear fount, and met th' admiring glance

So loved—But no ! our happier boy admired,
Not the slim form, but what the form
    attired,—
The riband, shirt, and frill, all pure and clean,
The white ribb'd stockings, and the coat of
    green.
    The Lady now appear'd to move away—
And this was threat'ning ; for he dared not
    stay,
Lost and alone ; but earnestly he pray'd—
' Oh ! do not leave me—I am not afraid,
But 'tis so lonesome ; I shall never find
My way alone, no better than the blind.'
    The Matron kindly to the Boy replied,
' Trust in my promise, I will be thy guide.'
Then to the Chapel moved the friendly pair,
And well for Peter that his guide was there !
Dim, silent, solemn was the scene—he felt
The cedar's power, that so unearthly smelt ;
And then the stain'd, dark, narrow windows
    threw
Strange, partial beams on pulpit, desk, and
    . pew :
Upon the altar, glorious to behold,
Stood a vast pair of candlesticks in gold !
With candles tall, and large, and firm, and
    white,
Such as the halls of giant-kings would light.
There was an organ, too, but now unseen ;
A long black curtain served it for a screen ;
Not so the clock, that both by night and day,
Click'd the short moments as they pass'd
    away.
    ' Is this a church ? and does the parson
    read '—
Said Peter—' here ?—I mean a church in-
    deed.'—
' Indeed it is, or as a church is used,'
Was the reply,—and Peter deeply mused,
Not without awe. His sadness to dispel,
They sought the gallery, and then all was well.
    Yet enter'd there, although so clear his
    mind
From every fear substantial and defined,
Yet there remain'd some touch of native
    fear—
Of something awful to the eye and ear—
A ghostly voice might sound—a ghost itself
    appear.
    There noble Pictures fill'd his mind with
    joy—
He gazed and thought, and was no more the
    boy ;

And Madam heard him speak, with some
    surprise,
Of heroes known to him from histories.
He knew the actors in the deeds of old,—
He could the Roman marvels all unfold.
He to his guide a theme for wonder grew,
At once so little and so much he knew—
Little of what was passing every day,
And much of that which long had pass'd
    away ;—
So like a man, and yet so like a child,
That his good friend stood wond'ring as she
    smiled.
    The Scripture Pieces caused a serious awe,
And he with reverence look'd on all he
    saw ;
His pious wonder he express'd aloud,
And at the Saviour Form devoutly bow'd.
    Portraits he pass'd, admiring ; but with
    pain
Turn'd from some objects, nor would look
    again.
He seem'd to think that something wrong
    was done,
When crimes were shown he blush'd to look
    upon.
Not so his guide—' What youth is that ? '
    she cried,
' That handsome stripling at the lady's side ;
Can you inform me how the youth is named ? '
He answer'd, ' Joseph ; ' but he look'd
    ashamed.
' Well, and what then ? Had you been
    Joseph, boy !
Would you have been so peevish and so coy ? '
Our hero answer'd, with a glowing face,
' His mother told him he should pray for
    grace.'
A transient cloud o'ercast the matron's brow ;
She seem'd disposed to laugh——but knew
    not how ;
Silent awhile, then placid she appear'd—
' 'Tis but a child,' she thought, and all was
    clear'd.
    No—laugh she could not ; still, the more
    she sought
To hide her thoughts, the more of his she
    caught.
A hundred times she had these pictures named,
And never felt perplex'd, disturb'd, asham'd ;
Yet now the feelings of a lad so young
Call'd home her thoughts and paralysed her
    tongue.

She pass'd the offensive pictures silent by,
With one reflecting, self-reproving sigh ;
Reasoning how habit will the mind entice
To approach and gaze upon the bounds of vice,
As men, by custom, from some cliff's vast
    height,
Look pleased, and make their danger their
    delight.
    ' Come, let us on !—see there a Flemish
        view,
A Country Fair, and all as Nature true.
See there the merry creatures, great and
    small,
Engaged in drinking, gaming, dancing all,
Fiddling or fighting—all in drunken joy ! '—
' But is this Nature ? ' said the wondering
    Boy.
    ' Be sure it is ! and those Banditti there—
Observe the faces, forms, the eyes, the air :
See rage, revenge, remorse, disdain, despair ! '
    ' And is that Nature, too ? ' the stripling
        cried.—
' Corrupted Nature,' said the serious guide.
    She then display'd her knowledge.—' That,
        my dear,
Is call'd a Titian, this a Guido here,
And yon a Claude—you see that lovely light,
So soft and solemn, neither day nor night.'
    ' Yes ! ' quoth the Boy, ' and there is just
        the breeze,
That curls the water, and that fans the trees ;
The ships that anchor in that pleasant bay
All look so safe and quiet—Claude, you say ? '
    On a small picture Peter gazed and stood
In admiration—' 'twas so dearly good.'
' For how much money think you, then, my
    Lad,
Is such a " dear good picture " to be had ?
'Tis a famed master's work—a Gerard Dow—
At least the seller told the buyer so.'
    ' I tell the price ! ' quoth Peter—' I as soon
Could tell the price of pictures in the moon ;
But I have heard, when the great race was
    done,
How much was offer'd for the horse that
    won.'—
    ' A thousand pounds : but, look the country
        round,
And, may be, ten such horses might be found ;
While, ride or run where'er you choose to go,
You'll nowhere find so fine a Gerard Dow.'
    ' If this be true,' says Peter, ' then, of course,
You'd rate the picture higher than the horse.'

    ' Why, thou 'rt a reasoner, Boy ! ' the lady
        cried ;
' But see that Infant on the other side ;
'Tis by Sir Joshua.   Did you ever see
A Babe so charming ? '—' No, indeed,' said
    he ;
' I wonder how he could that look invent,
That seems so sly, and yet so innocent.'
    In this long room were various Statues seen,
And Peter gazed thereon with awe-struck
    mien.
    ' Why look so earnest, Boy ? '—' Because
        they bring
To me a story of an awful thing.'—
' Tell then thy story.'——He who never stay'd
For words or matter, instantly obey'd.—
    ' A holy pilgrim to a city sail'd,
Where every sin o'er sinful men prevail'd ;
Who, when he landed, look'd in every street,
As he was wont, a busy crowd to meet ;
But now of living beings found he none,
Death had been there, and turn'd them all to
    stone ;
All in an instant, as they were employ'd,
Was life in every living man destroy'd—
The rich, the poor, the timid, and the bold,
Made in a moment such as we behold.'
    ' Come, my good lad, you've yet a room
        to see.
Are you awake ? '—' I am amazed,' said he ;
' I know they're figures form'd by human
    skill,
But 'tis so awful, and this place so still !
    ' And what is this ? ' said Peter, who had
        seen
A long wide table, with its cloth of green,
Its net-work pockets, and its studs of gold—
For such they seem'd, and precious to behold.
There too were ivory balls, and one was red,
Laid with long sticks upon the soft green bed,
And printed tables, on the wall beside—
' Oh ! what are these ? ' the wondering
    Peter cried.
    ' This, my good lad, is call'd the Billiard-
        room,'
Answer'd his guide, ' and here the gentry come,
And with these maces and these cues they
    play,
At their spare time, or on a rainy day.'
    ' And what this chequer'd box ?—for play,
        I guess ? '—
' You judge it right ; 'tis for the game of
    Chess.

There! take your time, examine what you
  will,
There's King, Queen, Knight,—it is a game
  of skill :
And these are Bishops ; you the difference
  see.'—
' What ! do they make a game of *them* ? '
  quoth he.—
' Bishops, like Kings,' she said, ' are here but
  names ;
Not that I answer for their Honours' games.'
  All round the house did Peter go, and found
Food for his wonder all the house around.
There guns of various bore, and rods, and lines,
And all that man for deed of death designs,
In beast, or bird, or fish, or worm, or fly—
Life in these last must means of death supply ;
The living bait is gorged, and both the
  victims die.
' God gives man leave his creatures to
  destroy.'—
' What ! for his sport ? ' replied the pitying
  Boy.—
' Nay,' said the Lady, ' why the sport con-
  demn ?
As die they must, 'tis much the same to
  them.'
Peter had doubts ; but with so kind a friend,
He would not on a dubious point contend.
  Much had he seen, and every thing he saw
Excited pleasure not unmix'd with awe.
Leaving each room, he turn'd as if once more
To enjoy the pleasure that he felt before—
' What then must their possessors feel ? how
  grand
And happy they who can such joys com-
  mand !
For they may pleasures all their lives pursue,
The winter pleasures, and the summer's too—
Pleasures for every hour in every day—
Oh ! how their time must pass in joy away ! '
  So Peter said.—Replied the courteous
  Dame :
' What you call pleasure scarcely owns the
  name.
The very changes of amusement prove
There's nothing that deserves a lasting love.
They hunt, they course, they shoot, they fish,
  they game ;
The objects vary, though the end the same—
A search for that which flies them ; no, my
  Boy !
'Tis not enjoyment, 'tis pursuit of joy.'

Peter was thoughtful—thinking, What !
  not these,
Who can command, or purchase, what they
  please—
Whom many serve, who only speak the word,
And they have all that earth or seas afford—
All that can charm the mind and please the
  eye—
And *they* not happy !—but I'll ask her why.
  So Peter ask'd.—' 'Tis not,' she said, ' for us,
Their Honours' inward feelings to discuss ;
But if they're happy, they would still confess
'Tis not these things that make their happi-
  ness.
  ' Look from this window ! at his work behold
Yon gardener's helper—he is poor and old,
He not one thing of all you see can call
His own ; but, haply, he o'erlooks them all.
Hear him ! he whistles through his work, or
  stops
But to admire his labours and his crops :
To-day as every former day he fares,
And for the morrow has nor doubts nor cares ;
Pious and cheerful, proud when he can please,
Judge if Joe Tompkin wants such things as
  these.
  ' Come, let us forward ! ' and she walk'd
  in haste
To a large room, itself a work of taste,
But chiefly valued for the works that drew
The eyes of Peter—this indeed was new,
Was most imposing—Books of every kind
Were there disposed, the food for every mind.
With joy perplex'd, round cast he wondering
  eyes,
Still in his joy, and dumb in his surprise.
  Above, beneath, around, on every side,
Of every form and size were Books descried ;
Like Bishop Hatto, when the rats drew near,
And war's new dangers waked his guilty fear,
When thousands came beside, behind, before,
And up and down came on ten thousand
  more ;
A tail'd and whisker'd army, each with claws
As sharp as needles, and with teeth like
  saws,—
So fill'd with awe, and wonder in his looks,
Stood Peter, 'midst this multitude of Books ;
But guiltless he and fearless ; yet he sigh'd
To think what treasures were to him denied.
  But wonder ceases on continued view ;
And the Boy sharp for close inspection
  grew.

Prints on the table he at first survey'd,
Then to the Books his full attention paid.
At first, from tome to tome, as fancy led,
He view'd the binding, and the titles read ;
Lost in delight, and with his freedom pleased,
Then three huge folios from their shelf he
     seized ;
Fixing on one, with prints of every race,
Of beast and bird most rare in every place,—
Serpents, the giants of their tribe, whose prey
Are giants too—a wild ox once a day ;
Here the fierce tiger, and the desert's kings,
And all that move on feet, or fins, or wings—
Most rare and strange ; a second volume told
Of battles dire, and dreadful to behold,
On sea or land, and fleets dispersed in storms ;
A third has all creative fancy forms,—
Hydra and dire chimera, deserts rude,
And ruins grand, enriching solitude :
Whatever was, or was supposed to be,
Saw Peter here, and still desired to see.
    Again he look'd, but happier had he been,
That Book of Wonders he had never seen ;
For there were tales of men of wicked mind,
And how the Foe of Man deludes mankind.
Magic and murder every leaf bespread—
Enchanted halls, and chambers of the dead,
And ghosts that haunt the scenes where once
     the victims bled.
    Just at this time, when Peter's heart began
To admit the fear that shames the valiant
     man,
He paused—but why ? ' Here's one my guard
     to be ;
When thus protected, none can trouble me : '—
Then rising look'd he round, and lo ! alone
     was he.
    Three ponderous doors, with locks of shin-
     ing brass,
Seem'd to invite the trembling Boy to pass ;
But fear forbade, till fear itself supplied
The place of courage, and at length he tried.
He grasp'd the key—Alas ! though great his
     need,
The key turn'd not, the bolt would not recede.
Try then again ; for what will not distress ?
Again he tried, and with the same success.
Yet one remains, remains untried one door—
A failing hope, for two had fail'd before ;
But a bold prince, with fifty doors in sight,
Tried forty-nine before he found the right ;
Before he mounted on the brazen horse,
And o'er the walls pursued his airy course.

So his cold hand on this last key he laid :
' Now turn,' said he ; the treacherous bolt
     obey'd—
The door receded—bringing full in view
The dim, dull chapel, pulpit, desk, and pew.
    It was not right—it would have vex'd a
     saint ;
And Peter's anger rose above restraint.
' Was this her love,' he cried, ' to bring me
     here,
Among the dead, to die myself with fear ! '—
For Peter judged, with monuments around,
The dead must surely in the place be found :
' With cold to shiver, and with hunger pine—
" We'll see the rooms," she said, " before we
     dine ; "
And spake so kind ! That window gives no
     light :
Here is enough the boldest man to fright ;
It hardly now is day, and soon it will be
     night.'
    Deeply he sigh'd, nor from his heart could
     chase
The dread of dying in that dismal place ;
Anger and sorrow in his bosom strove,
And banish'd all that yet remain'd of love ;
When soon despair had seized the trembling
     Boy,
But hark, a voice ! the sound of peace and joy.
    ' Where art thou, lad ? '—' Oh ! here am
     I, in doubt,
And sorely frighten'd—can you let me out ? '
' Oh ! yes, my child ; it was indeed a sin,
Forgetful as I was, to bolt you in.
I left you reading, and from habit lock'd
The door behind me, but in truth am shock'd
To serve you thus ; but we will make amends
For such mistake. Come, cheerly, we are
     friends.'
    ' Oh ! yes,' said Peter, quite alive to be
So kindly used, and have so much to see,
And having so much seen ; his way he spied,
Forgot his peril, and rejoin'd his guide.
    Now all beheld, his admiration raised,
The lády thank'd, her condescension praised,
And fix'd the hour for dinner, forth the Boy
Went in a tumult of o'erpowering joy,
To view the gardens, and what more was
     found
In the wide circuit of that spacious ground,
Till, with his thoughts bewilder'd, and
     oppress'd
With too much feeling, he inclined to rest.

Then in the park he sought its deepest
  shade,
By trees more aged than the mansion made,
That ages stood ; and there unseen a brook
Ran not unheard, and thus our traveller
  spoke,—
' I am so happy, and have such delight,
I cannot bear to see another sight ;
It wearies one like work ; ' and so, with
  deep
Unconscious sigh—he laid him down to sleep.
  Thus he reclining slept, and, oh ! the joy
That in his dreams possess'd the happy boy,—
Composed of all he knew, and all he read,
Heard, or conceived, the living and the dead.
  The Caliph Haroun, walking forth by night
To see young David and Goliath fight,
Rose on his passive fancy—then appear'd
The fleshless forms of beings scorn'd or fear'd
By just or evil men—the baneful race
Of spirits restless, borne from place to place :
Rivers of blood from conquer'd armies ran,
The flying steed was by, the marble man ;
Then danced the fairies round their pygmy
  queen,
And their feet twinkled on the dewy green,
All in the moon-beams' glory. As they
  fled,
The mountain loadstone rear'd its fatal head,
And drew the iron-bolted ships on shore,
Where he distinctly heard the billows roar,—
Mix'd with a living voice of—' Youngster,
  sleep no more,
But haste to dinner.' Starting from the
  ground,
The waking boy obey'd that welcome sound.
  He went and sat, with equal shame and
  pride,
A welcome guest at Madam Johnson's side.
At his right hand was Mistress Kitty placed,
And Lucy, maiden sly, the stripling faced.
Then each the proper seat at table took—
Groom, butler, footman, laundress, coach-
  man, cook ;
For all their station and their office knew,
Nor sat as rustics or the rabble do.
  The Youth to each the due attention paid,
And hob-or-nob'd with Lady Charlotte's
  maid ;
With much respect each other they address'd,
And all encouraged their enchanted guest.

Wine, fruit, and sweetmeats closed repast so
  long,
And Mistress Flora sang an opera song.
  Such was the Day the happy Boy had spent,
And forth delighted from the Hall he went :
Bowing his thanks, he mounted on his steed,
More largely fed than he was wont to feed ;
And well for Peter that his pony knew
From whence he came, the road he should
  pursue ;
For the young rider had his mind estranged
From all around, disturbed and disarranged,
In pleasing tumult, in a dream of bliss,
Enjoy'd but seldom in a world like this.
  But though the pleasures of the Day were
  past,—
For lively pleasures are not form'd to last,—
And though less vivid they became, less
  strong,
Through life they lived, and were enjoy'd as
  long.
So deep the impression of that happy Day,
Not time nor cares could wear it all away ;
Ev'n to the last, in his declining years,
He told of all his glories, all his fears.
  How blithely forward in that morn he went,
How blest the hours in that fair palace spent,
How vast that Mansion, sure for monarch
  plann'd,
The rooms so many, and yet each so grand,—
Millions of books in one large hall were found,
And glorious pictures every room around ;
Beside that strangest of the wonders there,
That house itself contain'd a house of prayer.
  He told of park and wood, of sun and shade,
And how the lake below the lawn was made :
He spake of feasting such as never boy,
Taught in his school, was fated to enjoy—
Of ladies' maids as ladies' selves who dress'd,
And her, his friend, distinguish'd from the
  rest,
By grandeur in her look, and state that she
  possess'd.
He pass'd not one ; his grateful mind o'er-
  flow'd
With sense of all he felt, and they bestow'd.
  He spake of every office, great or small,
Within, without, and spake with praise of
  all,—
So pass'd the happy Boy, that Day at Silford
Hall.

TALE II.   THE FAMILY OF LOVE

In a large town, a wealthy thriving place,
Where hopes of gain excite an anxious race;
Which dark dense wreaths of cloudy volumes
    cloak,
And mark, for leagues around, the place of
    smoke;
Where fire to water lends its powerful aid,
And steam produces—strong ally to trade:—
Arrived a Stranger, whom no merchant knew,
Nor could conjecture what he came to do:
He came not there his fortune to amend,
He came not there a fortune made to spend;
His age not that which men in trade employ:
The place not that where men their wealth
    enjoy;
Yet there was something in his air that told
Of competency gain'd, before the man was old.
He brought no servants with him: those he
    sought
Were soon his habits and his manners
    taught—
His manners easy, civil, kind, and free;
His habits such as aged men's will be;
To self indulgent; wealthy men like him
Plead for these failings—'tis their way, their
    whim.
   His frank good-humour, his untroubled air,
His free address, and language bold but fair,
Soon made him friends—such friends as all
    may make,
Who take the way that he was pleased to take.
He gave his dinners in a handsome style,
And met his neighbours with a social smile;
The wealthy all their easy friend approved,
Whom the more liberal for his bounty loved;
And ev'n the cautious and reserved began
To speak with kindness of the frank old man,
Who, though associate with the rich and
    grave,
Laugh'd with the gay, and to the needy gave
What need requires. At church a seat was
    shown,
That he was kindly ask'd to think his own:
Thither he went, and neither cold nor heat,
Pains or pretences, kept him from his seat.
This to his credit in the town was told,
And ladies said, ' 'Tis pity he is old:
Yet, for his years, the Stranger moves like one
Who, of his race, has no small part to run.'

No envy he by ostentation raised,
And all his hospitable table praised.
His quiet life censorious talk suppress'd,
And numbers hail'd him as their welcome
    guest.
   'Twas thought a man so mild, and boun-
    teous too,
A world of good within the town might do;
To vote him honours, therefore, they inclined;
But these he sought not, and with thanks
    resign'd;
His days of business he declared were past,
And he would wait in quiet for the last;
But for a dinner and a day of mirth
He was the readiest being upon earth.
   Men call'd him Captain, and they found the
    name
By him accepted without pride or shame.
Not in the Navy—that did not appear:
Not in the Army—that at least was clear—
' But as he speaks of sea-affairs, he made,
No doubt, his fortune in the way of trade;
He might, perhaps, an India-ship command—
We'll call him Captain now he comes to land.'
   The stranger much of various life had
    seen,
Been poor, been rich, and in the state
    between;
Had much of kindness met, and much deceit,
And all that man who deals with men must
    meet.
Not much he read; but from his youth had
    thought,
And been by care and observation taught:
'Tis thus a man his own opinions makes;
He holds that fast, which he with trouble
    takes:
While one whose notions all from books arise,
Upon his authors, not himself, relies—
A borrow'd wisdom this, that does not make
    us wise.
   Inured to scenes, where wealth and place
    command
Th' observant eye, and the obedient hand,
A Tory-spirit his—he ever paid
Obedience due, and look'd to be obey'd.
' Man upon man depends, and, break the
    chain,
He soon returns to savage life again;

As of fair virgins dancing in a round,
Each binds another, and herself is bound,
On either hand a social tribe he sees,
By those assisted, and assisting these ;
While to the general welfare all belong,
The high in power, the low in number strong.'
  Such was the Stranger's creed—if not
    profound,
He judg'd it useful, and proclaimed it sound;
And many liked it : invitations went
To Captain Elliot, and from him were sent—
These last so often, that his friends confess'd,
The Captain's cook had not a place of rest.
Still were they something at a loss to guess
What his profession was from his address ;
For much he knew, and too correct was he
For a man train'd and nurtured on the sea ;
Yet well he knew the seaman's words and
    ways,—
Seaman's his look, and nautical his phrase :
In fact, all ended just where they began,
With many a doubt of this amphibious man.
  Though kind to all, he look'd with special
    grace
On a few members of an ancient race,
Long known, and well respected in the place :
Dyson their name ; but how regard for these
Rose in his mind, or why they seem'd to
    please,
Or by what ways, what virtues—not a cause
Can we assign, for Fancy has no laws ;
But, as the Captain show'd them such respect,
We will not treat the Dysons with neglect.
  Their Father died while yet engaged by
    trade
To make a fortune, that was never made,
But to his children taught ; for he would say
' I place them—all I can—in Fortune's
    way.'
  James was his first-born ; when his father
    died,
He, in their large domain, the place supplied,
And found, as to the Dysons all appear'd,
Affairs less gloomy than their sire had fear'd ;
But then if rich or poor, all now agree,
Frugal and careful, James must wealthy be :
And wealth in wedlock sought, he married
    soon,
And ruled his Lady from the honey-moon :
Nor shall we wonder ; for, his house beside,
He had a sturdy multitude to guide,
Who now his spirit vex'd, and now his temper
    tried ;

Men who by labours live, and, day by day,
Work, weave, and spin their active lives
    away :
Like bees industrious, they for others strive,
With, now and then, some murmuring in the
    hive.
  James was a churchman—'twas his pride
    and boast ;
Loyal his heart, and ' Church and King ' his
    toast ;
He for Religion might not warmly feel,
But for the Church he had abounding zeal.
  Yet no dissenting sect would he condemn,
' They're nought to us,' said he, ' nor we to
    them ;
'Tis innovation of our own I hate,
Whims and inventions of a modern date.
  ' Why send you Bibles all the world about,
That men may read amiss, and learn to doubt ?
Why teach the children of the poor to read,
That a new race of doubters may succeed ?
Now can you scarcely rule the stubborn crew,
And what if they should know as much as
    you ?
Will a man labour when to learning bred,
Or use his hands who can employ his head ?
Will he a clerk or master's self obey,
Who thinks himself as well-inform'd as they ?'
    These were his favourite subjects—these he
      chose,
And where he ruled no creature durst oppose.
  ' We are rich,' quoth James ; ' but if we
    thus proceed,
And give to all, we shall be poor indeed :
In war we subsidise the world—in peace
We christianise—our bounties never cease :
We learn each stranger's tongue, that they
    with ease
May read translated Scriptures, if they please;
We buy them presses, print them books, and
    then
Pay and export poor, learned, pious men ;
Vainly we strive a fortune now to get,
So tax'd by private claims, and public debt.'
    Still he proceeds—' You make your prisons
      light,
Airy and clean, your robbers to invite ;
And in such ways your pity show to vice,
That you the rogues encourage, and entice.'
    For lenient measures James had no re-
      gard—
' Hardship,' he said, ' must work upon the
    hard ;

Labour and chains such desperate men
    require ;
To soften iron you must use the fire.'
    Active himself, he labour'd to express,
In his strong words, his scorn of idleness ;
From him in vain the beggar sought relief—
' Who will not labour is an idle thief,
Stealing from those who will ; ' he knew not
    how
For the untaught and ill-taught to allow,
Children of want and vice, inured to ill,
Unchain'd the passions, and uncurb'd the
    will.
    Alas ! he look'd but to his own affairs,
Or to the rivals in his trade, and theirs :
Knew not the thousands who must all be fed,
Yet ne'er were taught to earn their daily
    bread ;
Whom crimes, misfortunes, errors only teach
To seek their food where'er within their reach,
Who for their parents' sins, or for their own,
Are now as vagrants, wanderers, beggars
    known,
Hunted and hunting through the world, to
    share
Alms and contempt, and shame and scorn to
    bear ;
Whom Law condemns, and Justice, with a
    sigh,
Pursuing, shakes her sword and passes by.—
If to the prison we should these commit,
They for the gallows will be render'd fit.
    But James had virtues—was esteem'd as
    one
Whom men look'd up to, and relied upon.
Kind to his equals, social when they met—
If out of spirits, always out of debt ;
True to his promise, he a lie disdain'd,
And e'en when tempted in his trade, refrain'd ;
Frugal he was, and loved the cash to spare,
Gain'd by much skill, and nursed by constant
    care ;
Yet liked the social board, and when he spoke,
Some hail'd his wisdom, some enjoy'd his
    joke.
To him a Brother look'd as one to whom,
If fortune frown'd, he might in trouble come ;
His Sisters view'd the important man with
    awe,
As if a parent in his place they saw :
All lived in Love ; none sought their private
    ends ;
The Dysons were a Family of Friends.

    His brother David was a studious boy,
Yet could his sports as well as books enjoy.
E'en when a boy, he was not quickly read,
If by the heart you judged him, or the head.
His father thought he was decreed to shine,
And be in time an eminent Divine ;
But if he ever to the Church inclined,
It is too certain that he changed his mind.
He spoke of scruples, but who knew him best
Affirm'd, no scruples broke on David's rest.
Physic and Law were each in turn proposed—
He weigh'd them nicely, and with Physic
    closed.
    He had a serious air, a smooth address,
And a firm spirit that ensured success.
He watched his brethren of the time, how they
Rose into fame, that he might choose his way.
    Some, he observed, a kind of roughness
    used,
And now their patients banter'd, now abused :
The awe-struck people were at once dismay'd,
As if they begg'd the advice for which they
    paid.
There are who hold that no disease is slight,
Who magnify the foe with whom they fight.
The sick was told that his was that disease
But rarely known on mortal frame to seize ;
Which only skill profound, and full command
Of all the powers in nature could withstand.
Then, if he lived, what fame the conquest
    gave !
And if he died—' No human power could
    save ! '
Mere fortune sometimes, and a lucky case,
Will make a man the idol of a place—
Who last, advice to some fair duchess gave,
Or snatch'd a widow's darling from the grave,
Him first she honours of the lucky tribe,
Fills him with praise, and woos him to pre-
    scribe.
In his own chariot soon he rattles on,
And half believes the lies that built him one.
    But not of these was David : care and pain,
And studious toil prepar'd his way to gain.
At first observed, then trusted, he became
At length respected, and acquired a name.
Keen, close, attentive, he could read mankind,
The feeble body, and the failing mind ;
And if his heart remain'd untouch'd, his eyes,
His air, and tone, with all could sympathise.
    This brought him fees, and not a man was
    he
In weak compassion to refuse a fee.

Yet though the Doctor's purse was well
   supplied,
Though patients came, and fees were multi-
   plied,
Some secret drain, that none presumed to
   know,
And few e'en guess'd, for ever kept it low.
Some of a patient spake, a tender fair,
Of whom the doctor took peculiar care,
But not a fee : he rather largely gave,
Nor spared himself, 'twas said, this gentle
   friend to save.
Her case consumptive, with perpetual need
Still to be fed, and still desire to feed ;
An eager craving, seldom known to cease,
And gold alone brought temporary peace.—
   So, rich he was not ; James some fear
   express'd,
Dear Doctor David would be yet distress'd ;
For if now poor, when so repaid his skill,
What fate were his, if he himself were ill !
   In his religion, Doctor Dyson sought
To teach himself—' A man should not be
   taught,
Should not, by forms or creeds, his mind
   debase,
That keep in awe an unreflecting race.'
He heeded not what Clarke and Paley say,
But thought himself as good a judge as
   they ;
Yet to the Church profess'd himself a friend,
And would the rector for his hour attend ;
Nay, praise the learn'd discourse, and
   learnedly defend.
For since the common herd of men are blind,
He judged it right that guides should be
   assign'd ;
And that the few who could themselves direct
Should treat those guides with honour and
   respect.
He was from all contracted notions freed,
But gave his Brother credit for his creed ;
And if in smaller matters he indulged,
'Twas well, so long as they were not divulged.
   Oft was the spirit of the Doctor tried,
When his grave Sister wish'd to be his guide.
She told him, ' all his real friends were
   grieved
To hear it said, how little he believed :
Of all who bore the name she never knew
One to his pastor or his church untrue ;
All have the truth with mutual zeal profess'd,
And why, dear Doctor, differ from the rest ? '

' 'Tis my hard fate,' with serious looks
   replied
The man of doubt, ' to err with such a
   guide.'—
' Then why not turn from such a painful
   state ? '—
The doubting man replied, ' It is my fate.'
   Strong in her zeal, by texts and reasons
   back'd,
In his grave mood the Doctor she attack'd :
Cull'd words from Scripture to announce his
   doom,
And bade him ' think of dreadful things to
   come.'
' If such,' he answer'd, ' be that state
   untried,
In peace, dear Martha, let me here abide ;
Forbear to insult a man whose fate is known,
And leave to Heaven a matter all its own.'
   In the same cause the Merchant, too, would
   strive ;
He ask'd, ' Did ever unbeliever thrive ?
Had he respect ? could he a fortune make ?
And why not then such impious men forsake ? '
   ' Thanks, my dear James, and be assured
   I feel,
If not your reason, yet at least your zeal ;
And when those wicked thoughts, that keep
   me poor,
And bar respect, assail me as before
With force combin'd, you'll drive the fiend
   away,
For you shall reason, James, and Martha pray.'
   But though the Doctor could reply with ease
To all such trivial arguments as these,—
Though he could reason, or at least deride,
There was a power that would not be defied ;
A closer reasoner, whom he could not shun,
Could not refute, from whom he could not run ;
For Conscience lived within ; she slept, 'tis
   true,
But when she waked, her pangs awaken'd too.
She bade him think ; and as he thought, a sigh
Of deep remorse precluded all reply.
No soft insulting smile, no bitter jest,
Could this commanding power of strength
   divest,
But with reluctant fear her terrors he con-
   fess'd.
His weak advisers he could scorn or slight,
But not their cause ; for, in their folly's spite,
They took the wiser part, and chose their way
   aright.

Such was the Doctor, upon whom for aid
Had some good ladies call'd, but were
　　afraid—
Afraid of one who, if report were just,
The arm of flesh, and that alone would trust.
But these were few—the many took no care
Of what they judged to be his own affair :
And if he them from their diseases freed,
They neither cared nor thought about his
　　creed :
They said his merits would for much atone,
And only wonder'd that he lived alone.

　The widow'd Sister near the Merchant dwelt,
And her late loss with lingering sorrow felt.
Small was her jointure, and o'er this she sigh'd,
That to her heart its bounteous wish denied,
Which yet all common wants, but not her all,
　　supplied.
Sorrows like showers descend, and as the
　　heart
For them prepares, they good or ill impart ;
Some on the mind, as on the ocean rain,
Fall and disturb, but soon are lost again—
Some, as to fertile lands, a boon bestow,
And seed, that else had perish'd, live and
　　grow ;
Some fall on barren soil, and thence proceed
The idle blossom, and the useless weed ;
But how her griefs the Widow's heart im-
　　press'd,
Must from the tenor of her life be guess'd.

　Rigid she was, persisting in her grief,
Fond of complaint, and adverse to relief.
In her religion she was all severe,
And as she was, was anxious to appear.
When sorrow died restraint usurp'd the place,
And sate in solemn state upon her face,
Reading she loved not, nor would design to
　　waste
Her precious time on trifling works of taste ;
Though what she did with all that precious
　　time
We know not, but to waste it was a crime—
As oft she said, when with a serious friend
She spent the hours as duty bids us spend ;
To read a novel was a kind of sin—
Albeit once Clarissa took her in ;
And now of late she heard with much sur-
　　prise,
Novels there were that made a compromise
Betwixt amusement and religion ; these
Might charm the worldly, whom the stories
　　please,

And please the serious, whom the sense
　　would charm,
And thus indulging, be secured from harm—
A happy thought, when from the foe we take
His arms, and use them for religion's sake.

　Her Bible she perused by day, by night ;
It was her task—she said 'twas her delight ;
Found in her room, her chamber, and her pew,
For ever studied, yet for ever new—
All must be new that we cannot retain,
And new we find it when we read again.
　The hardest texts she could with ease
　　expound,
And meaning for the most mysterious found,
Knew which of dubious senses to prefer :
The want of Greek was not a want in her ;—
Instinctive light no aid from Hebrew needs—
But full conviction without study breeds ;
O'er mortal powers by inborn strength pre-
　　vails,
Where Reason trembles, and where Learning
　　fails.

　To the church strictly from her childhood
　　bred,
She now her zeal with party-spirit fed :
For brother James she lively hopes express'd,
But for the Doctor's safety felt distress'd ;
And her light Sister, poor, and deaf, and blind,
Fill'd her with fears of most tremendous kind.
But David mocked her for the pains she took,
And Fanny gave resentment for rebuke ;
While James approved the zeal, and praised
　　the call,
' That brought,' he said, ' a blessing on them
　　all :
Goodness like this to all the House extends,
For were they not a Family of Friends ? '

　Their sister Frances, though her prime was
　　past,
Had beauty still—nay, beauty form'd to last ;
'Twas not the lily and the rose combined,
Nor must we say the beauty of the mind ;
But feature, form, and that engaging air,
That lives when ladies are no longer fair.
Lovers she had, as she remember'd yet,
For who the glories of their reign forget ?
Some she rejected in her maiden pride
And some in maiden hesitation tried,
Unwilling to renounce, unable to decide.
One lost, another would her grace implore,
Till all were lost, and lovers came no more :
Nor had she that, in beauty's failing state,
Which will recall a lover, or create ·

Hers was the slender portion, that supplied
Her real wants, but all beyond denied.
    When Fanny Dyson reach'd her fortieth
        year,
She would no more of love or lovers hear ;
But one dear Friend she chose, her guide, her
        stay ;
And to each other all the world were they ;
For all the world had grown to them unkind,
One sex censorious, and the other blind.
The Friend of Frances longer time had known
The world's deceits, and from its follies flown.
With her dear Friend life's sober joys to share,
Was all that now became her wish and care.
They walk'd together, they conversed and
        read,
And tender tears for well-feign'd sorrows shed:
And were so happy in their quiet lives,
They pitied sighing maids, and weeping wives.
    But Fortune to our state such change
        imparts,
That Pity stays not long in human hearts ;
When sad for others' woes our hearts are
        grown,
This soon gives place to sorrows of our own.
    There was among our guardian Volunteers
A Major Bright—he reckoned fifty years :
A reading man of peace, but call'd to take
His sword and musket for his country's sake ;
Not to go forth and fight, but here to stay,
Invaders, should they come, to chase or slay.
    Him had the elder Lady long admired,
As one from vain and trivial objects retired ;
With him conversed ; but to a Friend so dear,
Gave not that pleasure—Why ? is not so
        clear ;
But chance effected this : the Major now
Gave both the time his duties would allow ;
In walks, in visits, when abroad, at home,
The friendly Major would to either come.
He never spoke—for he was not a boy—
Of ladies' charms, or lovers' grief and joy.
All his discourses were of serious kind,
The heart they touch'd not, but they fill'd
        the mind.
Yet—oh, the pity ! from this grave good man
The cause of coolness in the Friends began.
The sage Sophronia—that the chosen name—
Now more polite, and more estranged became.
She could but feel that she had longer known
This valued friend—he was indeed her own ;
But Frances Dyson, to confess the truth,
Had more of softness—yes, and more of youth ;

And though he said such things had ceased
        to please,
The worthy Major was not blind to these :
So without thought, without intent, he paid
More frequent visits to the younger Maid.
    Such the offence ; and though the Major
        tried
To tie again the knot he thus untied,
His utmost efforts no kind looks repaid,—
He moved no more the inexorable maid.
The Friends too parted, and the elder told
Tales of false hearts, and friendships waxing
        cold ;
And wonder'd what a man of sense could see
In the light airs of wither'd vanity.
    'Tis said that Frances now the world re-
        views,
Unwilling all the little left to lose ;
She and the Major on the walks are seen,
And all the world is wondering what they
        mean.
    Such were the four whom Captain Elliot drew
To his own board, as the selected few.
For why ? they seem'd each other to approve,
And called themselves a Family of Love.
    These were not all : there was a Youth
        beside,
Left to his uncles when his parents died :
A Girl, their sister, by a Boy was led
To Scotland, where a boy and girl may wed—
And they return'd to seek for pardon, pence,
        and bread.
Five years they lived to labour, weep, and
        pray,
When Death, in mercy, took them both away.
    Uncles and aunts received this lively child,
Grieved at his fate, and at his follies smiled ;
But when the child to boy's estate grew on,
The smile was vanish'd, and the pity gone.
Slight was the burden, but in time increased,
Until at length both love and pity ceased.
Then Tom was idle ; he would find his way
To his aunt's stores, and make her sweets his
        prey :
By uncle Doctor on a message sent,
He stopp'd to play, and lost it as he went.
His grave aunt Martha, with a frown austere,
And a rough hand, produced a transient fear ;
But Tom, to whom his rude companions taught
Language as rude, vindictive measures sought ;
He used such words, that when she wish'd to
        speak
Of his offence, she had her words to seek.

The little wretch had call'd her—'twas a
shame
To think such thought, and more to name
such name.
　Thus fed and beaten, Tom was taught to
pray
For his true friends : ' but who,' said he,
' are they ? '
By nature kind, when kindly used, the Boy
Hail'd the strange good with tears of love
and joy ;
But, roughly used, he felt his bosom burn
With wrath he dared not on his uncles turn ;
So with indignant spirit, still and strong,
He nursed the vengeance, and endured the
wrong.
To a cheapschool, far north, the boy was sent:
Without a tear of love or grief he went ;
Where, doom'd to fast and study, fight and
play,
He stayed five years, and wish'd five more to
stay.
He loved o'er plains to run, up hills to climb,
Without a thought of kindred, home, or time ;
Till from the cabin of a coasting hoy,
Landed at last the thin and freckled boy,
With sharp keen eye, but pale and hollow
cheek,
All made more sad from sickness of a week :
His aunts and uncles felt—nor strove to hide
From the poor boy, their pity and their pride:
He had been taught that he had not a friend,
Save these on earth, on whom he might
depend ;
And such dependence upon these he had,
As made him sometimes desperate, always
sad.
　' Awkward and weak, where can the lad be
placed,
And we not troubled, censured, or disgraced ?
Do, Brother James, th' unhappy boy enrol
Among your set ; you only can control.'
James sigh'd, and Thomas to the Factory
went,
Who there his days in sundry duties spent.
He ran, he wrought, he wrote—to read or play
He had no time, nor much to feed or pray.
What pass'd without he heard not—or he
heard
Without concern, what he nor wish'd nor
fear'd ;
Told of the Captain and his wealth, he sigh'd
And said, ' how well his table is supplied : '

But with the sigh it caused the sorrow fled ;
He was not feasted, but he must be fed,
And he could sleep full sound, though not full
soft his bed.
　But still, ambitious thoughts his mind
possess'd,
And dreams of joy broke in upon his rest.
Improved in person, and enlarged in mind,
The good he found not he could hope to find.
Though now enslaved, he hail'd the approach-
ing day,
When he should break his chains and flee
away.
　Such were the Dysons : they were first of
those
Whom Captain Elliot as companions chose;
Them he invited, and the more approved,
As it appear'd that each the other loved.
Proud of their brothers were the sister pair,
And if not proud, yet kind the brothers were.
This pleased the Captain, who had never
known,
Or he had loved, such kindred of his own :
Them he invited, save the Orphan lad,
Whose name was not the one his Uncles had ;
No Dyson he, nor with the party came—
The worthy Captain never heard his name ;
Uncles and Aunts forbore to name the boy,
For then, of course, must follow his employ.
Though all were silent, as with one consent,
None told another what his silence meant,
What hers ; but each suppress'd the useless
truth,
And not a word was mention'd of the youth.
　Familiar grown, the Dysons saw their host,
With none beside them : it became their
boast,
Their pride, their pleasure ; but to some it
seem'd
Beyond the worth their talents were esteem'd.
This wrought no change within the Captain's
mind ;
To all men courteous, he to them was kind.
　One day with these he sat, and only
these,
In a light humour, talking at his ease :
Familiar grown, he was disposed to tell
Of times long past, and what in them befell—
Not of his life their wonder to attract,
But the choice tale, or insulated fact.
Then, as it seem'd, he had acquired a right
To hear what they could from their stores
recite.

Their lives, they said, were all of common
    kind ;
He could no pleasure in such trifles find.
    They had an Uncle—'tis their father's
      tale—
Who in all seas had gone where ship can sail,
Who in all lands had been, where men can
    live ;
' He could indeed some strange relations give,
And many a bold adventure ; but in vain
We look for him ; he comes not home again.'
    ' And is it so ? why then, if so it be,'
Said Captain Elliot, ' you must look to me :
I knew John Dyson '——Instant every one
Was moved to wonder—' knew my Uncle
    John !
Can he be rich ? be childless ? he is old,
That is most certain—What ! can more be
    told ?
Will he return, who has so long been gone,
And lost to us ? Oh ! what of Uncle John ? '
    This was aside : their unobservant friend
Seem'd on their thoughts but little to attend ;
A traveller speaking, he was more inclined
To tell his story than their thoughts to find.
    ' Although, my Friends, I love you well,
      'tis true,
'Twas your relation turn'd my mind to you ;
For we were friends of old, and friends like us
    are few ;
And though from dearest friends a man will
    hide
His private vices in his native pride,
Yet such our friendship from its early rise,
We no reserve admitted, no disguise ;
But 'tis the story of my friend I tell,
And to all others let me bid farewell.
    ' Take each your glass, and you shall hear
      how John,
My old companion, through the world has
    gone ;
I can describe him to the very life,
Him and his ways, his ventures, and his wife.'
    ' Wife ! ' whisper'd all ; ' then what his
      life to us,
His ways and ventures, if he ventured thus ? '
This, too, apart ; yet were they all intent,
And, gravely listening, sigh'd with one consent.
    ' My friend, your Uncle, was design'd for
      trade,
To make a fortune as his father made ;
But early he perceived the house declined,
And his domestic views at once resign'd ;

While stout of heart, with life in every limb,
He would to sea, and either sink or swim.
No one forbade ; his father shook his hand,
Within it leaving what he could command.
    ' He left his home, but I will not relate
What storms he braved, and how he bore his
    fate,
Till his brave frigate was a Spanish prize,
And prison-walls received his first-born sighs,
Sighs for the freedom that an English boy,
Or English man, is eager to enjoy.
    ' Exchanged, he breathed in freedom, and
      aboard
An English ship, he found his peace restored ;
War raged around, each British tar was press'd
To serve his king, and John among the rest ;
Oft had he fought and bled, and 'twas his fate
In that same ship to grow to man's estate.
Again 'twas war : of France a ship appear'd
Of greater force, but neither shunned nor
    fear'd ;
'Twas in the Indian Sea, the land was nigh,
When all prepared to fight, and some to die ;
Man after man was in the ocean thrown,
Limb after limb was to the surgeon shown,
And John at length, poor John ! held forth
    his own.——
    ' A tedious case—the battle ceased with day,
And in the night the foe had slipp'd away.
Of many wounded were a part convey'd
To land, and he among the number laid ;
Poor, suffering, friendless, who shall now
    impart
Life to his hope, or comfort to his heart ?
A kind good priest among the English there
Selected him as his peculiar care ;
And, when recover'd, to a powerful friend
Was pleased the lad he loved to recommend ;
Who read your Uncle's mind, and, pleased to
    read,
Placed him where talents will in time succeed.
    ' I will not tease you with details of trade,
But say he there a decent fortune made,—
Not such as gave him, if return'd, to buy
A duke's estate, or principality,
But a fair fortune : years of peace he knew,
That were so happy, and that seem'd so few.
    ' Then came a cloud ; for who on earth
      has seen
A changeless fortune, and a life serene ?
Ah ! then how joyous were the hours we
    spent !
But joy is restless, joy is not content.

' There one resided, who, to serve his friend,
Was pleased a gay fair lady to commend ;
Was pleased t' invite the happy man to dine,
And introduced the subject o'er their wine ;
Was pleased the lady his good friend should
    know,
And as a secret his regard would show.
  ' A modest man lacks courage ; but, thus
    train'd,
Your Uncle sought her favour and obtain'd :
To me he spake, enraptured with her face,
Her angel smile, her unaffected grace ;
Her fortune small indeed ; but " curse the pelf,
" She is a glorious fortune in herself ! "
" John ! " answer'd I, " friend John, to be
    sincere,
These are fine things, but may be bought too
    dear.
You are no stripling, and, it must be said,
Have not the form that charms a youthful
    maid.
What you possess, and what you leave behind,
When you depart, may captivate her mind ;
And I suspect she will rejoice at heart,
Your will once made, if you should soon
    depart."
  ' Long our debate, and much we disagreed ;
" You need no wife," I said—said he, "I need ;
I want a house, I want in all I see
To take an interest ; what is mine to me ? "
So spake the man, who to his word was just,
And took the words of others upon trust.
He could not think that friend in power so
    high,
So much esteem'd, could like a villain lie ;
Nor, till the knot, the fatal knot, was tied,
Had urged his wedding a dishonour'd bride.
The man he challenged, for his heart was
    rent
With rage and grief, and was to prison sent ;
For men in power—and this, alas ! was one—
Revenge on all, the wrongs themselves have
    done ;
And he whose spirit bends not to the blow
The tyrants strike, shall no forgiveness know,
For 'tis to slaves alone that tyrants favour
    show.
  ' This cost him much ; but that he did not
    heed ;
The lady died, and my poor friend was freed.
" Enough of ladies ! " then said he, and
    smiled ;
"I've now no longings for a neighbour's child."

So patient he return'd, and not in vain,
To his late duties, and grew rich again.
He was no miser ; but the man who takes
Care to be rich, will love the gain he makes :
Pursuing wealth, he soon forgot his woes,
No acts of his were bars to his repose.
  ' Now John was rich, and old and weary
    grown,
Talk'd of the country that he calls his own,
And talk'd to me ; for now, in fact, began
My better knowledge of the real man.
Though long estranged, he felt a strong desire,
That made him for his former friends enquire ;
What Dysons yet remain'd, he long'd to
    know,
And doubtless meant some proofs of love to
    show.
His purpose known, our native land I sought,
And with the wishes of my Friend am fraught.'
  Fix'd were all eyes, suspense each bosom
    shook,
And expectation hung on every look.
  ' " Go to my kindred, seek them all around,
Find all you can, and tell me all that 's found;
Seek them if prosperous, seek them in distress,
Hear what they need, know what they all
    possess ;
What minds, what hearts they have, how good
    they are,
How far from goodness—speak, and no one
    spare,
And no one slander : let me clearly see
What is in them, and what remains for me."
  ' Such is my charge, and haply I shall
    send
Tidings of joy and comfort to my Friend.
Oft would he say, " If of our race survive
Some two or three, to keep the name alive,
I will not ask if rich or great they be,
But if they live in love, like you and me."
  ' 'Twas not my purpose yet awhile to speak
As I have spoken ; but why further seek ?
All that I heard I in my heart approve ;
You are indeed a Family of Love :
And my old friend were happy in the sight
Of those, of whom I shall such tidings write.'
    The Captain wrote not : he perhaps was
    slow,
Perhaps he wish'd a little more to know.
He wrote not yet, and while he thus delay'd,
Frances alone an early visit paid.
The maiden Lady braved the morning cold,
To tell her Friend what duty bade be told,

Yet not abruptly—she has first to say,
' How cold the morning, but how fine the
     day ;—
I fear you slept but ill, we kept you long,
You made us all so happy, but 'twas wrong—
So entertain'd, no wonder we forgot
How the time pass'd ; I fear me you did
     not.'
   In this fair way the Lady seldom fail'd
To steer her course, still sounding as she sail'd.
   ' Dear Captain Elliot, how your Friends you
     read !
We are a loving Family indeed ;
Left in the world each other's aid to be,
And join to raise a fallen family.
Oh ! little thought we there was one so
     near,
And one so distant, to us all so dear :
All, all alike ; he cannot know, dear man !
Who needs him most, as one among us can—
One who can all our wants distinctly view,
And tell him fairly what were just to do :
But you, dear Captain Elliot, as his friend,
As ours, no doubt, will your assistance lend.
Not for the world would I my Brothers blame ;
Good men they are : 'twas not for that I came.
No ! did they guess what shifts I make, the
     grief
That I sustain, they'd fly to my relief ;
But I am proud as poor ; I cannot plead
My cause with them, nor show how much
     I need ;
But to my Uncle's Friend it is no shame,
Nor have I fear, to seem the thing I am ;
My humble pittance life's mere need supplies,
But all indulgence, all beyond denies.
I aid no pauper, I myself am poor,
I cannot help the beggar at my door.
I from my scanty table send no meat ;
Cook'd and recook'd is every joint I eat.
At Church a sermon begs our help,—I stop
And drop a tear ; nought else have I to drop ;
But pass the out-stretch'd plate with sorrow
     by,
And my sad heart this kind relief deny.
My dress—I strive with all my maiden skill
To make it pass, but 'tis disgraceful still ;
Yet from all others I my wants conceal,
Oh ! Captain Elliot, there are few that feel !
But did that rich and worthy Uncle know
What you, dear Sir, will in your kindness show,
He would his friendly aid with generous hand
     bestow.

' Good men my Brothers both, and both
     are raised
Far above want—the Power that gave be
     praised !
My Sister's jointure, if not ample, gives
All she can need, who as a lady lives ;
But I, unaided, may through all my years
Endure these ills—forgive these foolish tears.
   ' Once, my dear Sir—I then was young and
     gay,
And men would talk—but I have had my day :
Now all I wish is so to live, that men
May not despise me whom they flatter'd then.
If you, kind Sir—— '
              Thus far the Captain heard,
Nor save by sign or look had interfered ;
But now he spoke ; to all she said agreed,
And she conceived it useless to proceed.
Something he promised, and the Lady went
Half-pleased away, yet wondering what he
     meant ;
Polite he was and kind, but she could trace
A smile, or something like it, in his face ;
'Twas not a look that gave her joy or pain—
She tried to read it, but she tried in vain.
   Then call'd the Doctor—'twas his usual
     way—
To ask ' How fares my worthy friend to-day ? '
To feel his pulse, and as a friend to give
Unfee'd advice, how such a man should live ;
And thus, digressing, he could soon contrive,
At his own purpose smoothly to arrive.
   ' My Brother ! yes, he lives without a care,
And, though he needs not, yet he loves to
     spare :
James I respect ; and yet it must be told,
His speech is friendly, but his heart is cold.
His smile assumed has not the real glow
Of love !—a sunbeam shining on the snow.
Children he has ; but are they causes why
He should our pleas resist, our claims deny ?
Our father left the means by which he thrives,
While we are labouring to support our lives.
We, need I say ? my widow'd Sister lives
On a large jointure ; nay, she largely gives ;—
And Fanny sighs—for gold does Fanny sigh?
Or wants she that which money cannot buy—
Youth and young hopes ?—Ah ! could my
     kindred share
The liberal mind's distress, and daily care,
The painful toil to gain the petty fee,
They'd bless their stars, and join to pity
     me.

Hard is his fate, who would, with eager joy,
To save mankind, his every power employ ;
Yet in his walk unnumber'd insults meets,
And gains 'mid scorn the food that chokes
    him as he eats.
  ' Oh ! Captain Elliot, you who know man-
    kind,
With all the anguish of the feeling mind,
Bear to our kind relation these the woes
That e'en to you 'tis misery to disclose.
You can describe what I but faintly trace—
A man of learning cannot bear disgrace ;
Refinement sharpens woes that wants create,
And 'tis fresh grief such grievous things to
    state ;
Yet those so near me let me not reprove—
I love them well, and they deserve my love ;
But want they know not—Oh ! that I could
    say
I am in this as ignorant as they.'
    The Doctor thus.—The Captain grave and
        kind,
To the sad tale with serious looks inclined,
And promise made to keep th' important
    speech in mind.
James and the Widow, how is yet unknown,
Heard of these visits, and would make their
    own.
All was not fair, they judged, and both agreed
To their good Friend together to proceed.
Forth then they went to see him, and per-
    suade—
As warm a pair as ever Anger made.
The Widow lady must the speaker be :
So James agreed ; for words at will had she ;
And then her Brother, if she needed proof,
Should add, ' 'Tis truth : '—it was for him
    enough.
  ' Oh ! sir, it grieves me '—for we need not
    dwell
On introduction : all was kind and well.—
' Oh ! sir, it grieves, it shocks us both to hear
What has, with selfish purpose, gain'd your
    ear—
Our very flesh and blood, and, as you know,
    how dear.
Doubtless they came your noble mind
    t' impress
With strange descriptions of their own
    distress ;
But I would to the Doctor's face declare,
That he has more to spend and more to spare,
With all his craft, than we with all our care.

  ' And for our Sister, all she has she spends
Upon herself ; herself alone befriends.
She has the portion that our father left,
While me of mine a careless wretch bereft,
Save a small part ; yet I could joyful live,
Had I my mite—the widow's mite—to give.
For this she cares not ; Frances does not know
Their heartfelt joy, who largely can bestow.
You, Captain Elliot, feel the pure delight,
That our kind acts in tender hearts excite,
When to the poor we can our alms extend,
And make the Father of all Good our friend
And, I repeat, I could with pleasure live,
Had I my mite—the widow's mite—to give.
  ' We speak not thus, dear Sir, with vile
    intent,
Our nearest friends to wrong or circumvent ;
But that our Uncle, worthy man ! should know
How best his wealth, Heaven's blessing, to
    bestow ;
What widows need, and chiefly those who feel
For all the sufferings which they cannot heal ;
And men in trade, with numbers in their pay,
Who must be ready for the reckoning-day,
Or gain or lose ! '
    —' Thank Heaven,' said James, ' as yet
I've not been troubled by a dun or debt.'
—The Widow sigh'd, convinced that men so
    weak
Will ever hurt the cause for which they speak;
However tempted to deceive, still they
Are ever blundering to the broad high-way
Of very truth :—But Martha pass'd it by
With a slight frown, and half-distinguish'd
    sigh—
  ' Say to our Uncle, sir, how much I long
To see him sit his kindred race among :
To hear his brave exploits, to nurse his age,
And cheer him in his evening's pilgrimage ;
How were I blest to guide him in the way
Where the religious poor in secret pray,
To be the humble means by which his heart
And liberal hand might peace and joy impart!
But now, farewell ! '—and slowly, softly fell
The tender accents as she said ' farewell ! '
    The Merchant stretch'd his hand, his leave
        to take,
And gave the Captain's a familiar shake,
Yet seem'd to doubt if this was not too free,
But, gaining courage, said, ' Remember me.'
    Some days elaps'd, the Captain did not
        write,
But still was pleased the party to invite ;

And, as he walk'd, his custom every day,
A tall pale stripling met him on his way,
Who made some efforts, but they proved
    too weak,
And only show'd he was inclined to speak.
' What would'st thou, lad ? ' the Captain
    ask'd, and gave
The youth a power his purposed boon to
    crave,
Yet not in terms direct—' My name,' quoth
    he,
' Is Thomas Bethel ; you have heard of me.'—
' Not good nor evil, Thomas—had I need
Of so much knowledge :—but pray now
    proceed.'—
   ' Dyson my mother's name ; but I have not
That interest with you, and the worse my lot.
I serve my Uncle James, and run and write,
And watch and work from morning until
    night ;
Confined among the looms, and webs, and
    wheels,
You cannot think how like a slave one feels.
'Tis said you have a ship at your command,—
An' please you, sir, I'm weary of the land,
And I have read of foreign parts such things,
As make me sick of Uncle's wheels and
    springs.'
   ' But, Thomas, why to sea ? you look too
    slim
For that rough work—and, Thomas, can you
    swim ? '
That he could not, but still he scorn'd a lie,
And boldly answer'd, ' No, but I can try.'—
' Well, my good lad, but tell me, can you
    read ? '
Now, with some pride he answer'd, ' Yes,
    indeed !
I construe Virgil, and our usher said,
I might have been in Homer had I staid,
And he was sorry when I came away,
And so was I, but Uncle would not pay ;
He told the master I had read enough,
And Greek was all unprofitable stuff ;
So all my learning now is thrown away,
And I've no time for study or for play ;
I'm ordered here and there, above, below,
And call'd a dunce for what I cannot know ;
Oh, that I were but from this bondage free !
Do, please your honour, let me go to sea.'
   ' But why to sea ? they want no Latin
    there ;
Hard is their work, and very hard their fare.'

' But then,' said Thomas, ' if on land, I
    doubt
My Uncle Dyson soon would find me out ;
And though he tells me what I yearly cost,
'Tis my belief he'd miss me were I lost.
For he has said, that I can act as well
As he himself—but this you must not tell.'
   ' Tell, Thomas ! no, I scorn the base
    design,
Give me your hand, I pledge my word with
    mine ;
And if I cannot do thee good, my friend,
Thou may'st at least upon that word depend.
And hark ye, lad, thy worthy name retain
To the last hour, or I shall help in vain ;
And then the more severe and hard thy part,
Thine the more praise, and thine the happier
    art.
We meet again—farewell ! '—and Thomas
    went
Forth to his tasks, half angry, half content.
   ' I never ask'd for help,' thought he, ' but
    —twice,
And all they then would give me was advice ;
My Uncle Doctor, when I begg'd his aid,
Bade me work on, and never be afraid,
But still be good ; and I've been good so long,
I'm half persuaded that they tell me wrong.
And now this Captain still repeats the same,
But who can live upon a virtuous name,
Starving and praised ?—" have patience—
    patience still ! "
He said and smiled, and, if I can, I will.'
So Thomas rested with a mind intent
On what the Captain by his kindness meant.
   Again the invited party all attend,
These dear relations, on this generous Friend.
They ate, they drank, each striving to appear
Fond, frank, forgiving—above all, sincere.
Such kindred souls could not admit disguise,
Or envious fears, or painful jealousies ;
So each declared, and all in turn replied,
' 'Tis just indeed, and cannot be denied.'
   Now various subjects rose,—the country's
    cause,
The war, the allies, the lottery, and the laws,
The widow'd Sister then advantage took
Of a short pause, and, smiling softly, spoke:
She judged what subject would his mind
    excite—
' Tell us, dear Captain, of that bloody fight,
When our brave Uncle, bleeding at his gun,
Gave a loud shout to see the Frenchmen run.'

' Another day,'—replied the modest host ;
One cannot always of one's battles boast.
Look not surprise—behold the man in me !
Another Uncle shall you never see.
No other Dyson to this place shall come,
Here end my travels, here I place my home ;
Here to repose my shatter'd frame I mean,
Until the last long journey close the scene.'
    The Ladies softly brush'd the tear away ;
James look'd surprise, but knew not what to
       say ;
But Doctor Dyson lifted up his voice,
And said, ' Dear Uncle, how we all rejoice!'
    ' No question, Friends ! and I your joy
       approve,
We are, you know, a Family of Love.'
    So said the wary Uncle, but the while
Wore on his face a questionable smile,
That vanish'd, as he spake in grave and
       solemn style—
    ' Friends and relations ! let us henceforth
       seem
Just as we are, nor of our virtues dream,
That with our waking vanish.—What we are
Full well we know—t' improve it be our care.
Forgive the trial I have made : 'tis one
That has no more than I expected done.
If as frail mortals you, my Friends, appear,
I look'd for no angelic beings here,
For none that riches spurn'd as idle pelf,
Or served another as he served himself.
Deceived no longer, let us all forgive ;
I'm old, but yet a tedious time may live.
This dark complexion India's suns bestow,
These shrivell'd looks to years of care I owe ;

But no disease ensures my early doom,—
And I may live—forgive me—years to come.
But while I live, there may some good be done,
Perchance to many, but at least to One.'—
    Here he arose, retired, return'd, and
       brought
The Orphan boy, whom he had train'd and
       taught
For this his purpose ; and the happy boy,
Though bade to hide, could ill suppress, his
       joy.—
    ' This young relation, with your leave, I
       take,
That he his progress in the world may make—
Not in my house a slave or spy to be,
And first to flatter, then to govern me ;—
He shall not nurse me when my senses sleep,
Nor shall the key of all my secrets keep,
And be so useful, that a dread to part
Shall make him master of my easy heart ;—
But to be placed where merit may be proved,
And all that now impedes his way removed.
    ' And now no more on these affairs I dwell,
What I possess that I alone can tell,
And to that subject we will bid farewell.
As go I must, when Heaven is pleased to call,
What I shall leave will seem or large or small,
As you shall view it. When this pulse is
       still,
You may behold my wealth, and read my will.
    ' And now, as Captain Elliot much has
       known,
That to your Uncle never had been shown,
From him one word of honest counsel hear—
And think it always gain to be sincere.'

TALE III. THE EQUAL MARRIAGE

THERE are gay nymphs whom serious
       matrons blame,
And men adventurous treat as lawful game,—
Misses, who strive, with deep and practised
       arts,
To gain and torture inexperienced hearts ;
The hearts entangled they in pride retain,
And at their pleasure make them feel their
       chain :
For this they learn to manage air and
       face,
To look a virtue, and to act a grace,
To be whatever men with warmth pursue—

Chaste, gay, retiring, tender, timid, true,
To-day approaching near, to-morrow just in
       view.
    Maria Glossip was a thing like this—
A much observing, much experienced Miss ;
Who on a stranger-youth would first decide
Th' important question—'Shall I be his
       bride ? '
But if unworthy of a lot so bless'd,
'Twas something yet to rob the man of rest ;
The heart, when stricken, she with hope could
       feed,
Could court pursuit, and, when pursued, recede.

Hearts she had won, and with delusion fed,
With doubt bewilder'd, and with hope misled;
Mothers and rivals she had made afraid,
And wrung the breast of many a jealous
 maid ;
Friendship, the snare of lovers, she profess'd,
And turn'd the heart's best feelings to a jest.

Yet seem'd the Nymph as gentle as a dove,
Like one all guiltless of the game of love,—
Whose guileless innocence might well be gay ;
Who had no selfish secrets to betray ;
Sure, if she play'd, she knew not how to play.
Oh ! she had looks so placid and demure,
Not Eve, ere fallen, seem'd more meek or
 pure ;
And yet the Tempter of the falling Eve
Could not with deeper subtilty deceive.

A Sailor's heart the Lady's kindness moved,
And winning looks, to say how well he loved ;
Then left her hopeful for the stormy main,
Assured of love when he return'd again.
Alas ! the gay Lieutenant reach'd the shore,
To be rejected, and was gay no more ;
Wine and strong drink the bosom's pain sup-
 press'd,
Till Death procured, what Love denied him—
 rest.
But men of more experience learn to treat
These fair enslavers with their own deceit.

Finch was a younger brother's youngest
 son,
Who pleased an Uncle with his song and gun ;
Who call'd him ' Bob,' and ' Captain '—by
 that name
Anticipating future rank and fame :
Not but there was for this some fair pretence—
He was a cornet in the Home Defence.
The Youth was ever drest in dapper style,
Wore spotless linen, and a ceaseless smile ;
His step was measured, and his air was nice—
They bought him high, who had him at the
 price
That his own judgment and becoming pride,
And all the merit he assumed, implied.
A life he loved of liberty and ease,
And all his pleasant labour was to please ;
Not call'd at present hostile men to slay,
He made the hearts of gentle dames his prey.

Hence tales arose, and one of sad report—
A fond, fair girl became his folly's sport,—
A cottage lass, who ' knew the youth would
 prove
For ever true, and give her love for love ;

Sure when he could, and that would soon be
 known,
He would be proud to show her as his own.'
 But still she felt the village damsels' sneer,
And her sad soul was fill'd with secret fear ;
His love excepted, earth was all a void,
And he, the excepted man, her peace destroy'd.
When the poor Jane was buried, we could hear
The threat of rustics whisper'd round her bier.

Stories like this were told, but yet, in time
Fair ladies lost their horror at the crime ;
They knew that cottage girls were forward
 things,
Who never heed a nettle till it stings ;
Then, too, the Captain had his fault confess'd,
And scorn'd to turn a murder to a jest.

Away with murder !—This accomplish'd
 swain
Beheld Maria, and confess'd her reign—
She came, invited by the rector's wife,
Who ' never saw such sweetness in her life.'
Now, as the rector was the Uncle's friend,
It pleased the Nephew there his steps to bend,
Where the fair damsel then her visit paid,
And seem'd an unassuming rustic maid :
A face so fair, a look so meek, he found
Had pierced that heart, no other nymph
 could wound.
 ' Oh, sweet Maria '—so began the Youth
His meditations—' thine the simple truth !
Thou hast no wicked wisdom of thy sex,
No wish to gain a subject-heart—then vex.
That heavenly bosom no proud passion swells,
No serpent's wisdom with thy meekness
 dwells ;
Oh ! could I bind thee to my heart, and live
In love with thee, on what our fortunes give !
Far from the busy world, in some dear spot,
Where Love reigns king, we'd find some
 peaceful cot.
To wed, indeed, no prudent man would
 choose ;
But, such a maid will lighter bonds refuse ! '
 And was this youth a rake ?—In very
 truth ;
Yet, feeling love, he felt it as a youth ;
If he had vices, they were laid aside ;
He quite forgot the simple girl who died ;
With dear Maria he in peace would live,
And what had pass'd—Maria would forgive.

The fair Coquette at first was pleased to
 find
A swain so knowing had become so blind ;

And she determined, with her utmost skill,
To bind the rebel to her sovereign will.
She heard the story of the old deceit,
And now resolved he should with justice
    meet ;—
' Soon as she saw him on her hook secure,
He should the pangs of perjured man endure.'
    These her first thoughts—but as, from time
      to time,
The Lover came, she dwelt not on his crime—
' Crime could she call it ? prudes, indeed,
    condemn
These slips of youth—but she was not of
    them.'
So gentler thoughts arose as, day by day,
The Captain came his passion to display.
When he display'd his passion, and she felt,
Not without fear, her heart began to melt—
Joy came with terror at a state so new ;
Glad of his truth ; if he indeed were true !
    This she decided as the heart decides,
Resolved to be the happiest of brides.
' Not great my fortune—hence,' said she,
    ' 'tis plain,
Me, and not mine, dear Youth ! he hopes to
    gain ;
Nor has he much ; but, as he sweetly talks,
We from our cot shall have delightful walks,
Love, lord within it ! I shall smile to see
My little cherubs on the father's knee.'
Then sigh'd the nymph, and in her fancied lot,
She all the mischiefs of the past forgot.
    Such were their tender meditations ; thus
Would they the visions of the day discuss :
Each, too, the old sad habits would no more
Indulge ; both dare be virtuous and be poor.
    They both had past the year when law
    allows
Free-will to lover who would fain be spouse :
Yet the good youth his Uncle's sanction
    sought—
' Marry her, Bob ! and are you really caught?
Then you've exchanged, I warrant, heart for
    heart—
'Tis well ! I meant to warn her of your art :
This Parson's Babe has made you quite a
    fool—
But are you sure your ardour will not cool ?
Have you not habits, Boy ? but take your
    chance !
How will you live ? I cannot much advance.
But hear you not what through the village flies,
That this your dove is famed for her disguise?

Yet, say they not, she leads a gayish life ?
Art sure she'll show the virtues of a wife ? '—
    ' Oh, Sir, she's all that mortal man can
    love ! '—
' Then marry, Bob ! and that the fact will
    prove—
Yet in a kind of lightness, folk agree.'—
    ' Lightness in her ! indeed, it cannot be—
'Tis Innocence alone that makes her manners
    free.'
    ' Well, my good friend ! then Innocence
    alone
Is to a something like Flirtation prone ;
And I advise—but let me not offend—
That Prudence should on Innocence attend,
Lest some her sportive purity mistake,
And term your angel more than half a rake.'
    The Nymph, now sure, could not entirely
    curb
The native wish her lover to disturb.
Oft he observed her, and could ill endure
The gentle coquetry of maid so pure :
Men he beheld press round her, and the Fair
Caught every sigh, and smiled at every
    prayer ;
And grieved he was with jealous pains to see
The effects of all her wit and pleasantry.
    ' Yet why alarm'd ? '—he said ; ' with so
    much sense,
She has no freedom, dashing, or pretence :
'Tis her gay mind, and I should feel a pride
In her chaste levities '—he said, and sigh'd.
Yet, when apart from company, he chose
To talk a little of his bosom's woes—
But one sweet smile, and one soft speech,
    suppress'd
All pain, and set his feeling heart at rest.
Nay, in return, she felt, or feign'd, a fear,
' He was too lively to be quite sincere—
She knew a certain lady, and could name
A certain time '—So, even was the blame,
And thus the loving pair more deep in love
    became.
    They married soon—for why delay the
    thing
That such amazing happiness would bring ?—
Now of that blissful state, O Muse of Hymen !
    sing.
    Love dies all kinds of death : in some so
    quick
It comes—he is not previously sick ;
But ere the sun has on the couple shed
The morning rays, the smile of Love is fled.

And what the cause ? for Love should not
expire,
And none the reason of such fate require.
Both had a mask, that with such pains they
wore,
Each took it off when it avail'd no more.
They had no feeling of each other's pain ;
To wear it longer had been crime in vain.

  As in some pleasant eve we view the scene,
Though cool yet calm, if joyless yet serene,—
Who has not felt a quiet still delight
In the clear, silent, love-befriending night ?
The moon so sweetly bright, so softly fair,
That all but happy lovers would be there,—
Thinking there must be in her still domain
Something that soothes the sting of mortal
pain ;
While earth itself is dress'd in light so clear,
That they might rest contented to be here !
  Such is the night ; but when the morn
awakes,
The storm arises, and the forest shakes ;
This mighty change the grieving travellers
find,
The freezing snows fast drifting in the wind ;
Firs deeply laden shake the snowy top,
Streams slowly freezing, fretting till they
stop ;
And void of stars the angry clouds look down
On the cold earth, exchanging frown with
frown.
  Such seem'd, at first, the cottage of our
pair—
Fix'd in their fondness, in their prospects fair ;
Youth, health, affection, all that life supplies,
Bright as the stars that gild the cloudless
skies,
Were theirs—or seem'd to be, but soon the
scene
Was black as if its light had never been.
Weary full soon, and restless then they grew,
Then off the painful mask of prudence threw,
For Time has told them all ; and taught
them what to rue.
They long again to tread the former round
Of dissipation—' Why should he be bound,
While his sweet inmate of the cottage sighs
For adulation, rout, and rhapsodies ?
Not Love himself, did love exist, could lead
A heart like hers, that flutter'd to be freed.'
  But Love, or what seem'd like him, quickly
died,
Nor Prudence, nor Esteem, his place supplied.

Disguise thrown off, each reads the other's
heart,
And feels with horror that they cannot part.
  Still they can speak—and 'tis some comfort
still,
That each can vex the other when they will :
Words half in jest to words in earnest led,
And these the earnest angry passions fed,
Till all was fierce reproach, and peace for
ever fled.
  ' And so you own it ! own it to my face,
Your love is vanish'd—infamous and base ! '
  ' Madam, I loved you truly, while I deem'd
You were the truthful being that you seem'd ;
But when I see your native temper rise
Above control, and break through all dis-
guise,
Casting it off, as serpents do their skin,
And showing all the folds of vice within,—
What see I then to love ? was I in love with
Sin ? '—
  ' So may I think, and you may feel it too ;
A loving couple, Sir, were Sin and you !
Whence all this anger ? is it that you find
You cannot always make a woman blind ?
You talk of falsehood and disguise—talk on !
But all my trust and confidence are gone ;
Remember you, with what a serious air
You talk'd of love, as if you were at prayer ?
You spoke of home-born comforts, quiet,
ease,
And the pure pleasure, that must always
please,
With an assumed and sentimental air,
Smiting your breast, and acting like a player.
Then your life's comfort ! and your holy joys !
Holy, forsooth ! and your sweet girls and
boys,
How you would train them !—All this farce
review,
And then, Sir, talk of being just and true ! '—
  ' Madam ! your sex expects that ours
should lie :
The simple creatures know it, and comply.
You hate the truth ; there 's nothing you
despise
Like a plain man, who spurns your vanities.
Are you not early taught your prey to catch ?
When your mammas pronounce—" A proper
match ! "
What said your own ?—" Do, daughter !
curb your tongue,
And you may win him, for the man is young ;

But if he views you as ourselves, good-by
To speculation !—He will never try."
  ' Then is the mask assumed, and then you
      bait
Your hook with kindness ! and as anglers
      wait,
Now here, now there, with keen and eager
      glance,
Marking your victims as the shoals advance ;
When, if the gaping wretch should make a
      snap,
You jerk him up, and have him in your trap,
Who gasping, panting, in your presence lies,
And you exulting view the imprison'd prize.
  ' Such are your arts ! while he did but
      intend,
In harmless play an idle hour to spend,
Lightly to talk of love ! your fix'd intent
Is on to lure him, where he never meant
To go, but going, must his speed repent.
If he of Cupid speaks, you watch your
      man,
And make a change for Hymen, if you can ;
Thus he, ingenuous, easy, fond, and weak,
Speaks the rash words he has been led to
      speak ;

Puts the dire question that he meant to shun,
And by a moment's frenzy is undone.'—
  ' Well ! ' said the Wife, ' admit this non-
      sense true,—
A mighty prize she gains in catching you ;
For my part, Sir, I most sincerely wish
My landing-net had miss'd my precious
      fish ! '—
  ' Would that it had ! or I had wisely lent
An ear to those who said I should repent.'—
  ' Hold, Sir ! at least my reputation spare,
And add another falsehood if you dare.'—
  ' Your reputation, Madam !—rest secure,
That will all scandal and reproach endure,
And be the same in worth : it is like him
Who floats, but finds he cannot sink or swim ;
Half raised above the storm, half sunk below,
It just exists, and that is all we know.
Such the good name that you so much regard,
And yet to keep afloat find somewhat hard.
Nay, no reply ! in future I decline
Dispute, and take my way.'—
                      ' And I, Sir, mine.'
  Oh ! happy, happy, happy pair ! both
      sought,
Both seeking—catching both, and caught !

TALE IV.   RACHEL

  It chanced we walk'd upon the heath, and
      met
A wandering woman ; her thin clothing wet
With morning fog ; the little care she took
Of things like these was written in her look.
Not pain from pinching cold was in her face,
But hurrying grief, that knows no resting
      place,—
Appearing ever as on business sent,
The wandering victim of a fix'd intent ;
Yet in her fancied consequence and speed,
Impell'd to beg assistance for her need.
  When she beheld my friend and me, with
      eye
And pleading hand, she sought our charity ;
More to engage our friendly thoughts the
      while,
She threw upon her miseries a smile,
That, like a varnish on a picture laid,
More prominent and bold the figures made ;
Yet was there sign of joy that we complied,
The moment's wish indulged and gratified.

  ' Where art thou wandering, Rachel ?
      whither stray,
From thy poor heath in such unwholesome
      day ? '
Ask'd my kind friend, who had familiar grown
With Rachel's grief, and oft compassion
      shown ;
Oft to her hovel had in winter sent
The means of comfort—oft with comforts
      went.
Him well she knew, and with requests pur-
      sued,
Though too much lost and spent for gratitude.
  ' Where art thou wandering, Rachel ? let
      me hear ? '—
  ' The fleet ! the fleet ! ' she answer'd, ' will
      appear
Within the bay, and I shall surely know
The news to-night !—turn tide, and breezes
      blow !
For if I lose my time, I must remain
Till the next year before they come again ! '

'What can they tell thee, Rachel?'—
             'Should I say,
I must repent me to my dying day.
Then I should lose the pension that they give;
For who would trust their secrets to a sieve?
I must be gone!'—And with her wild, but keen
And crafty look, that would appear to mean,
She hurried on; but turn'd again to say,
'All will be known: they anchor in the bay;
Adieu! be secret!—sailors have no home:
Blow wind, turn tide!—Be sure the fleet will come.'
  Grown wilder still, the frantic creature strode
With hurried feet upon the flinty road.
On her departing form I gazed with pain—
'And should you not,' I cried, 'her ways restrain?
What hopes the wild deluded wretch to meet?
And means she aught by this expected fleet?
Knows she her purpose? has she hope to see
Some friend to aid her in her poverty?
Why leave her thus bewilder'd to pursue
The fancy's good, that never comes in view?'—
  'Nay! she is harmless, and if more confined,
Would more distress in the coercion find.
Save at the times when to the coast she flies,
She rests, nor shows her mind's obliquities,
But ever talks she of the sea, and shows
Her sympathy with every wind that blows.
We think it, therefore, useless to restrain
A creature of whose conduct none complain,
Whose age and looks protect her,—should they fail,
Her craft and wild demeanour will prevail.
A soldier once attack'd her on her way—
She spared him not, but bade him kneel and pray—
Praying herself aloud—th' astonish'd man
Was so confounded, that away he ran.
  'Her sailor left her, with, perhaps, intent
To make her his—'tis doubtful what he meant:
But he was captured, and the life he led
Drove all such young engagements from his head.
On him she ever thought, and none beside,
Seeking her love, were favour'd or denied;
On her dear David she had fix'd her view,
And fancy judged him ever fond and true.

Nay, young and handsome—Time could not destroy—
No—he was still the same—her gallant boy!
Labour had made her coarse, and her attire
Show'd that she wanted no one to admire;
None to commend her; but she could conceive
The same of him, as when he took his leave,
And gaily told what riches he would bring,
And grace her hand with the symbolic ring.
  'With want and labour was her mind subdued;
She lived in sorrow and in solitude.
Religious neighbours, kindly calling, found
Her thoughts unsettled, anxious, and unsound;
Low, superstitious, querulous, and weak,
She sought for rest, but knew not how to seek;
And their instructions, though in kindness meant,
Were far from yielding the desired content.
They hoped to give her notions of their own,
And talk'd of "feelings" she had never known;
They ask'd of her "experience," and they bred,
In her weak mind, a melancholy dread
Of something wanting in her faith, of some—
She knew not what—"acceptance," that should come;
And as it came not, she was much afraid
That she in vain had served her God and pray'd.
  'She thought her Lover dead. In prayer she named
The erring Youth, and hoped he was reclaim'd.
This she confess'd; and trembling, heard them say,
"Her prayers were sinful—So the papists pray.
Her David's fate had been decided long,
And prayers and wishes for his state were wrong."
  'Had these her guides united love and skill,
They might have ruled and rectified her will;
But they perceived not the bewilder'd mind,
And show'd her paths, that she could never find:
The weakness that was Nature's, they reproved,
And all its comforts from the Heart removed.
  'Ev'n in this state, she loved the winds that sweep
O'er the wild heath, and curl the restless deep

A turf-built hut beneath a hill she chose,
And oft at night in winter storms arose,
Hearing, or dreaming, the distracted cry
Of drowning seamen on the breakers by :
For there were rocks, that when the tides
    were low
Appear'd, and vanish'd when the waters flow ;
And there she stood, all patient to behold
Some seaman's body on the billows roll'd.
  ' One calm, cold evening, when the moon
    was high,
And rode sublime within the cloudless sky,
She sat within her hut, nor seem'd to feel
Or cold or want, but turn'd her idle wheel,
And with sad song its melancholy tone
Mix'd, all unconscious that she dwelt alone.
  ' But none will harm her—Or who, willing,
    can ?
She is too wretched to have fear of man—
Not man ! but something—if it should
    appear,
That once was man—that something did she
    fear.
  ' No causeless terror !—In that moon's
    clear light
It came, and seem'd a parley to invite ;
It was no hollow voice—no brushing by
Of a strange being, who escapes the eye—

No cold or thrilling touch, that will but last
While we can think, and then for ever past.
But this sad face—though not the same, she
    knew
Enough the same, to prove the vision true—
Look'd full upon her !—starting in affright
She fled, her wildness doubling at the sight ;
With shrieks of terror, and emotion strong,
She pass'd it by, and madly rush'd along
To the bare rocks—While David, who, that
    day,
Had left his ship at anchor in the bay,
Had seen his friends who yet survived, and
    heard
Of her who loved him—and who thus ap-
    pear'd—
He tried to soothe her, but retired afraid
T' approach, and left her to return for aid.
  ' None came ! and Rachel in the morn was
    found
Turning her wheel, without its spindles, round,
With household look of care, low singing to
    the sound.
  ' Since that event, she is what you have seen,
But time and habit make her more serene,
The edge of anguish blunted—yet, it seems,
Sea, ships, and sailors' miseries are her
    dreams.'

TALE V. VILLARS

Poet. KNOW you the fate of Villars ?—
    Friend. What ! the lad
At school so fond of solitude, and sad ;
Who broke our bounds because he scorn'd a
    guide,
And would walk lonely by the river's side ?
  P. The same !—who rose at midnight to
    behold
The moonbeams shedding their ethereal gold ;
Who held our sports and pleasures in disgrace,
For Guy of Warwick, and old Chevy Chase.—
  F. Who sought for friendships, gave his
    generous heart
To every boy who chose to act the part ;
Or judged he felt it—not aware that boys
Have poor conceit of intellectual joys :
Theirs is no season for superfluous friends,
And none they need, but those whom Nature
    lends.
  P. But he, too, loved ?—

    F. Oh ! yes : his friend betray'd
The tender passion for the angel-maid.
Some child whose features he at church had
    seen,
Became his bosom's and his fancy's queen ;
Some favourite look was on his mind im-
    press'd—
His warm and fruitful fondness gave the rest.
  P. He left his father ?—
    F. Yes ! and rambled round
The land on foot—I know not what he found.
Early he came to his paternal land,
And took the course he had in rambling plann'd.
Ten years we lost him : he was then employ'd
In the wild schemes that he, perhaps, enjoy'd.
His mode of life, when he to manhood grew,
Was all his own—its shape disclosed to few.
  Our grave, stern dames, who know the
    deeds of all,
Say that some damsels owe to him their fall ;

And, though a Christian in his creed profess'd,
He had some heathen notions in his breast.
Yet we may doubt; for women, in his eyes,
Were high and glorious, queens and deities;
But he, perhaps, adorer and yet man,
Transgress'd yet worshipp'd. There are
     those who can.

     Near him a Widow's mansion he survey'd—
The lovely mother of a lovelier Maid;
Not great their wealth; though they were
     proud to claim
Alliance with a house of noblest name.

     Now, had I skill, I would right fain devise
To bring the highborn spinster to your eyes.
I could discourse of lip, and chin, and cheek,
But you would see no picture as I speak.
Such colours cannot—mix them as I may—
Paint you this nymph—We'll try a different
     way.

     First take Calista in her glowing charms,
E'er yet she sank within Lothario's arms,
Endued with beauties ripe, and large desires,
And all that feels delight, and that inspires;
Add Cleopatra's great, yet tender soul,
Her boundless pride, her fondness of control,
Her daring spirit, and her wily art,
That, though it tortures, yet commands the
     heart;
Add woman's anger for a lover's slight,
And the revenge, that insult will excite;
Add looks for veils, that she at will could wear,
As Juliet fond, as Imogen sincere,—
Like Portia grave, sententious, and design'd
For high affairs, or gay as Rosalind—
Catch, if you can, some notion of the dame,
And let Matilda serve her for a name.

     Think next how Villars saw th' enchanting
     maid,
And how he loved, pursued, adored, obey'd—
Obey'd in all, except the dire command,
No more to dream of that bewitching hand.
His love provoked her scorn, his wealth she
     spurn'd,
And frowns for praise, contempt for prayer
     return'd;
But, proud yet shrewd, the wily sex despise
The would-be husband—yet the votary prize.
As Roman conquerors, of their triumph vain,
Saw humbled monarchs in their pompous
     train,
Who, when no more they swell'd the show of
     pride,
In secret sorrow'd, or in silence died;

So, when our friend adored the Beauty's
     shrine,
She mark'd the act, and gave the nod divine;
And strove with scatter'd smiles, yet scarcely
     strove,
To keep the lover, while she scorn'd his love.
These, and his hope, the doubtful man
     sustain'd;
For who that loves believes himself dis-
     dain'd?
Each look, each motion, by his fondness read,
Became Love's food, and greater fondness
     bred;
The pettiest favour was to him the sign
Of secret love, and said, ' I'll yet be thine!'
One doleful year she held the captive swain,
Who felt and cursed, and wore and bless'd,
     the chain;
Who pass'd a thousand galling insults by,
For one kind glance of that ambiguous eye.

     P. Well! time, perhaps, might to the
     coldest heart
Some gentle thought of one so fond impart;
And pride itself has often favour shown
To what it governs, and can call its own.

     F. Thus were they placed, when to the
     village came
That lordly stranger, whom I need not name;
Known since too well, but then as rich and
     young,
Untried his prowess, and his crimes unsung.
Smooth was his speech, and show'd a gentle
     mind,
Deaf to his praise, and to his merits blind;
But raised by woman's smile, and pleased
     with all mankind.

     At humble distance he this fair survey'd,
Read her high temper, yet adored the Maid;
Far off he gazed, as if afraid to meet,
Or show the hope her anger would defeat:
Awful his love, and kept a guarded way,
Afraid to venture, till it finds it may.
And soon it found! nor could the Lady's
     pride
Her triumph bury, or her pleasure hide.

     And jealous Love, that ever looks to spy
The dreaded wandering of a lady's eye,
Perceived with anguish, that the prize long
     sought
A sudden rival from his hopes had caught.
Still Villars loved; at length, in strong despair,
O'er-tortured passion thus preferr'd its
     prayer :—

' Life of my life ! at once my fate decree—
I wait my death, or more than life, from thee :
I have no arts, nor powers, thy soul to move,
But doting constancy, and boundless love ;
This is my all : had I the world to give,
Thine were its throne—now bid me die or
　　live ! '
　　' Or die or live '—the gentle Lady cried—
' As suits thee best ; that point thyself decide,
But if to death thou hast thyself decreed,
Then like a man perform the manly deed ;
The well-charged pistol to the ear apply,
Make loud report, and like a hero die :
Let rogues and rats on ropes and poison
　　seize—
Shame not thy friends by petty death like
　　these ;
Sure we must grieve at what thou think'st
　　to do,
But spare us blushes for the manner too ! '
　　Then with inviting smiles she turn'd aside,
Allay'd his anger, and consoled his pride.
　　Oft had the fickle fair beheld with scorn
The unhappy man bewilder'd and forlorn,
Then with one softening glance of those bright
　　eyes
Restored his spirit, and dispersed his sighs.
Oft had I seen him on the lea below,
As feelings moved him, walking quick or slow :
Now a glad thought, and now a doleful came,
And he adored or cursed the changeful dame,
Who was to him as cause is to effect—
Poor tool of pride, perverseness, and neglect !
Upon thy rival were her thoughts bestow'd,
Ambitious love within her bosom glow'd ;
And oft she wish'd, and strong was her desire,
The Lord could love her like the faithful
　　Squire ;
But she was rivall'd in that nobl꞉ breast—
He loved her passing well, but not the best,
For self reign'd there : but still he call'd her
　　fair,
And woo'd the Muse his passion to declare.
His verses all were flaming, all were fine ;
With sweetness, nay with sense, in every
　　line—
Not as Lord Byron would have done the
　　thing,
But better far than lords are used to sing.
It pleased the Maid, and she, in very truth,
Loved, in Calista's love, the noble youth ;
Not like sweet Juliet, with that pure delight,
Fond and yet chaste, enraptur'd and yet right ;

Not like the tender Imogen, confined
To one, but one ! the true, the wedded mind ;
True, one preferr'd our sighing nymph as
　　these,
But thought not, like them, one alone could
　　please.
　　Time pass'd, nor yet the youthful peer
　　proposed
To end his suit, nor his had Villars closed
Fond hints the one, the other cruel bore ;
That was more cautious, this was kind the
　　more :
Both for soft moments waited—that to take
Of these advantage ; fairly this to make.
These moments came—or so my Lord
　　believed—
He dropp'd his mask ; and both were un-
　　deceived.
She saw the vice that would no longer feign,
And he an angry beauty's pure disdain.
　　Villars that night had in my ear confess'd,
He thought himself her spaniel and her jest.
He saw his rival of his goddess sure,
' But then,' he cried, ' her virtue is secure ;
Should he offend, I haply may obtain
The high reward of vigilance and pain ;
Till then I take, and on my bended knee,
Scraps from the banquet, gleanings of the
　　tree.'
　　Pitying, I smiled ; for I had known the
　　time
Of Love insulted—constancy my crime.
Not thus our friend : for him the morning
　　shone,
In tenfold glory, as for him alone ;
He wept, expecting still reproof to meet,
And all that was not cruel count as sweet.
Back he return'd, all eagerness and joy,
Proud as a prince, and restless as a boy.
He sought to speak, but could not aptly find
Words for his use, they enter'd not his mind ;
So full of bliss, that wonder and delight
Seem'd in those happy moments to unite.
He was like one who gains, but dreads to lose,
A prize that seems to vanish as he views :
And in his look was wildness and alarm—
Like a sad conjuror who forgets his charm,
And, when the demon at the call appears,
Cannot command the spirit for his fears :
So Villars seem'd by his own bliss perplex'd,
And scarcely knowing what would happen next.
　　But soon, a witness to their vows, I saw
The maiden his, if not by love, by law ;

The bells proclaim'd it—merry call'd by those
Who have no foresight of their neighbours'
    woes.
How proudly show'd the man his lovely bride,
Demurely pacing, pondering, at his side !
While all the loving maids around declared,
That faith and constancy deserved reward.
The baffled Lord retreated from the scene
Of so much gladness, with a world of spleen ;
And left the wedded couple, to protest,
That he no fear, that she no love possess'd,
That all his vows were scorn'd, and all his
    hope a jest.
    Then fell the oaks to let in light of day,
Then rose the mansion that we now survey,
Then all the world flock'd gaily to the scene
Of so much splendour, and its splendid queen ;
But whether all within the gentle breast
Of him, of her, was happy or at rest,—
Whether no lonely sigh confess'd regret,
Was then unknown, and is a secret yet ;
And we may think, in common duty bound,
That no complaint is made where none is
    found.
    Then came the Rival to his villa down,
Lost to the pleasures of the heartless town ;
Famous he grew, and he invited all
Whom he had known to banquet at the Hall ;
Talk'd of his love, and said, with many a sigh,
' 'Tis death to lose her, and I wish to die.'
    Twice met the parties ; but with cool dis-
    dain
In her, in him with looks of awe and pain.
Villars had pity, and conceived it hard
That true regret should meet with no regard—
' Smile, my Matilda ! virtue should inflict
No needless pain, nor be so sternly strict.'
    The Hall was furnish'd in superior style,
And money wanted from our sister isle ;
The lady-mother to the husband sued—
' Alas ! that care should on our bliss intrude !
You must to Ireland ; our possessions there
Require your presence, nay, demand your
    care.
My pensive daughter begs with you to sail ;
But spare your wife, nor let the wish prevail.'
    He went, and found upon his Irish land
Cases and griefs he could not understand.
Some glimmering light at first his prospect
    cheer'd—
Clear it was not, but would in time be clear'd ;
But when his lawyers had their efforts made,
No mind in man the darkness could pervade ;

'Twas palpably obscure : week after week
He sought for comfort, but was still to seek.
At length, impatient to return, he strove
No more with law, but gave the rein to love ;
And to his Lady and their native shore
Vow'd to return, and thence to turn no more.
    While yet on Irish ground in trouble kept,
The Husband's terrors in his toils had slept ;
But he no sooner touch'd the British soil,
Than jealous terrors took the place of toil—
' Where has she been ? and how attended ?
    Who
Has watch'd her conduct, and will vouch her
    true ?
She sigh'd at parting, but methought her
    sighs
Were more profound than would from nature
    rise ;
And though she wept as never wife before,
Yet were her eyelids neither swell'd nor sore.
Her lady-mother has a good repute,
As watchful dragon of forbidden fruit ;
Yet dragons sleep, and mothers have been
    known
To guard a daughter's secret as their own ;
Nor can the absent in their travel see
How a fond wife and mother may agree.
    ' Suppose the lady is most virtuous !—then,
What can she know of the deceits of men ?
Of all they plan, she neither thinks nor cares ;
But keeps, good lady ! at her books and
    prayers.
    ' In all her letters there are love, respect,
Esteem, regret, affection, all correct—
Too much—she fears that I should see
    neglect ;
And there are fond expressions, but unlike
The rest, as meant to be observed and strike ;
Like quoted words, they have the show of art,
And come not freely from the gentle heart—
Adopted words, and brought from memory's
    store,
When the chill faltering heart supplies no
    more :
'Tis so the hypocrite pretends to feel,
And speaks the words of earnestness and zeal.
    ' Hers was a sudden, though a sweet con-
    sent ;
May she not now as suddenly repent ?
My rival's vices drove him from her door ;
But hates she vice as truly as before ?
How do I know, if he should plead again,
That all her scorn and anger would remain ?

' Oh ! words of folly—is it thus I deem
Of the chaste object of my fond esteem ?
Away with doubt ! to jealousy adieu !
I know her fondness, and believe her true.
  ' Yet why that haste to furnish every need,
And send me forth with comfort, and with
    speed ?
Yes ; for she dreaded that the winter's rage
And our frail hoy should on the seas engage.
  ' But that vile girl ! I saw a treacherous eye
Glance on her mistress ! so demure and sly,
So forward too—and would Matilda's pride
Admit of that, if there was nought beside ? '
  Such, as he told me, were the doubt, the
    dread,
By jealous fears on observations fed.
  Home he proceeded : there remain'd to him
But a few miles—the night was wet and dim ;
Thick, heavy dews descended on the ground,
And all was sad and melancholy round.
  While thinking thus, an inn's far gleaming
    fire
Caused new emotions in the pensive Squire.
' Here I may learn, and seeming careless too,
If all is well, ere I my way pursue.
How fare you, landlord ?—how, my friend,
    are all ?—
Have you not seen—my people at the Hall ?
Well, I may judge——'
        ' Oh ! yes, your Honour, well,
As Joseph knows ; and he was sent to tell.'—
' How ! sent—I miss'd him—Joseph, do you
    say ?
Why sent, if well ?—I miss'd him on the way.'
  There was a poacher on the chimney-seat,
A gipsy, conjuror, smuggler, stroller, cheat.
The Squire had fined him for a captured hare,
Whipp'd and imprison'd—he had felt the
    fare,
And he remember'd : ' Will your Honour
    know
How does my Lady ? that myself can show.
On Monday early—for your Honour sees
The poor man must not slumber at his ease,
Nor must he into woods and coverts lurk,
Nor work alone, but must be seen to work :
'Tis not, your Honour knows, sufficient now
For us to live, but we must prove it—how :
Stay, please your Honour,—I was early up,
And forth without a morsel or a sup.
There was my Lady's carriage—Whew ! it
    drove
As if the horses had been spurr'd by Love.'

  ' A poet, John ! ' said Villars—feebly said,
Confused with fear, and humbled and dis-
    may'd—
' And where this carriage?—but, my heart !
    enough—
Why do I listen to the villain's stuff ?—
And where wert thou ? and what the spur of
    thine,
That led thee forth ?—we surely may divine !'
  ' Hunger, your Honour ! I and my poor
    wife
Have now no other in our wane of life.
Were Phoebe handsome, and were I a Squire,
I might suspect her, and young Lords
    admire.'—
' What ! rascal—— ' —' Nay, your Honour,
    on my word,
I should be jealous of that fine young Lord ;
Yet him my Lady in the carriage took,
But innocent—I'd swear it on the book.'
  ' You villain, swear ! '—for still he wish'd
    to stay,
And hear what more the fellow had to say.
' Phoebe, said I, a rogue that had a heart
To do the deed would make his Honour
    smart—
Says Phoebe, wisely, "Think you, would he go,
If he were jealous, from my Lady ?—No." '
  This was too much ! poor Villars left the
    inn,
To end the grief that did but then begin.
' With my Matilda in the coach !—what lies
Will the vile rascal in his spleen devise ?
Yet this is true, that on some vile pretence
Men may entrap the purest innocence.
He saw my fears—alas ! I am not free
From every doubt—but, no ! it cannot be.'
  Villars moved slow, moved quick, as check'd
    by fear,
Or urged by Love, and drew his mansion near.
Light burst upon him, yet he fancied gloom,
Nor came a twinkling from Matilda's room.
' What then ? 'tis idle to expect that all
Should be produced at jealous fancy's call ;
How ! the park-gate wide open ! who would
    dare
Do this, if her presiding glance were there ?
But yet, by chance—I know not what to
    think,
For thought is hell, and I'm upon the brink !
Not for a thousand worlds, ten thousand lives,
Would I——Oh ! what depends upon our
    wives !

Pains, labours, terrors, all would I endure,
Yes, all but this—and this, could I be
  sure——'
Just then a light within the window shone,
And show'd a lady, weeping and alone.
His heart beat fondly—on another view,
It beat more strongly, and in terror too—
It was his Sister!—and there now appear'd
A servant creeping like a man that fear'd.
He spoke with terror—' Sir, did Joseph tell?
Have you not met him?'—
                ' Is your Lady well?'
' Well? Sir—your Honour——'
       ' Heaven and earth! what mean
Your stupid questions? I have nothing seen,
Nor heard, nor know, nor—Do, good Thomas,
  speak!
Your mistress——'
       ' Sir, has gone from home a week—
My Lady, Sir, your sister——'
               But, too late
Was this—my Friend had yielded to his fate.
He heard the truth, became serene and mild,
Patient and still, as a corrected child;
At once his spirit with his fortune fell
To the last ebb, and whisper'd—It is well.
  Such was his fall; and grievous the effect!
From henceforth all things fell into neglect—
The mind no more alert, the form no more erect.
  Villars long since, as he indulged his spleen
By lonely travel on the coast, had seen
A large old mansion suffer'd to decay
In some law-strife, and slowly drop away.
Dark elms around the constant herons bred,
Those the marsh dykes, the neighbouring
  ocean, fed;
Rocks near the coast no shipping would allow,
And stubborn heath around forbade the
  plough;
Dull must the scene have been in years of old,
But now was wildly dismal to behold—
One level sadness! marsh, and heath, and sea,
And, save these high dark elms, nor plant
  nor tree.
In this bleak ruin Villars found a room,
Square, small, and lofty—seat of grief and
  gloom:
A sloping skylight on the white wall threw,
When the sun set, a melancholy hue;
The Hall of Vathek has a room so bare,
So small, so sad, so form'd to nourish care.
' Here,' said the Traveller, ' all so dark within,
And dull without, a man might mourn for sin,

Or punish sinners—here a wanton wife
And vengeful husband might be cursed for life.'
  His mind was now in just that wretched
    state,
That deems Revenge our right, and crime our
    fate.
All other views he banish'd from his soul,
And let this tyrant vex him and control;
Life he despised, and had that Lord defied,
But that he long'd for Vengeance e'er he died.
The law he spurn'd, the combat he declined,
And to his purpose all his soul resign'd.
  Full fifteen months had pass'd, and we began
To have some hope of the returning man;
Now to his steward of his small affairs
He wrote, and mention'd leases and repairs
But yet his soul was on its scheme intent,
And but a moment to its interest lent.
  His faithless wife and her triumphant peer
Despised his vengeance, and disdain'd to fear;
In splendid lodgings near the town they dwelt,
Nor fears from wrath, nor threats from con-
    science felt.
  Long time our friend had watch'd, and
    much had paid
For vulgar minds, who lent his vengeance aid.
At length one evening, late returning home,
Thoughtless and fearless of the ills to come,
The Wife was seized, when void of all alarm,
And vainly trusting to a footman's arm;
Death in his hand, the Husband stood in view,
Commanding silence, and obedience too;
Forced to his carriage, sinking at his side,
Madly he drove her—Vengeance was his
  guide.
  All in that ruin Villars had prepared,
And meant her fate and sorrow to have shared;
There he design'd they should for ever dwell,
The weeping pair of a monastic cell.
  An ancient couple from their cottage went,
Won by his pay, to this imprisonment;
And all was order'd in his mind—the pain
He must inflict, the shame she must sustain;
But such his gentle spirit, such his love,
The proof might fail of all he meant to prove.
  Features so dear had still maintain'd their
    sway,
And looks so loved had taught him to obey;
Rage and Revenge had yielded to the sight
Of charms that waken wonder and delight;
The harsher passions from the heart had flown,
And LOVE regain'd his Subject and his
  Throne.

[The next Tale, and a number of others, were originally designed for a separate volume, to be entitled 'The Farewell and Return.' In a letter to Mrs. Leadbetter, written in 1823, the poet says :—' In my " Farewell and Return " I suppose a young man to take leave of his native place, and to exchange *farewells* with his friends and acquaintance there—in short, with as many characters as I have fancied I could manage. These, and their several situations and prospects, being briefly sketched, an interval is supposed to elapse ; and our youth, a youth no more, *returns* to the scene of his early days. Twenty years have passed ; and the interest, if there be any, consists in the completion, more or less unexpected, of the history of each person to whom he had originally bidden farewell.'

The reader will find the Tales, written on this plan, divided each into two or more sections ; and will easily perceive where the *farewell* terminates, and the *return* begins.]

TALE VI. THE FAREWELL AND RETURN

I

I AM of age, and now, no more the Boy,
Am ready Fortune's favours to enjoy,
Were they, too, ready ; but, with grief I
    speak,
Mine is the fortune that I yet must seek.
And let me seek it ; there 's the world
    around—
And if not sought it never can be found.
It will not come if I the chase decline ;
Wishes and wants will never make it mine.
Then let me shake these lingering fears away ;
What one day must be, let it be to-day ;
Lest courage fail ere I the search commence,
And resolution pall upon suspense.

    Yet, while amid these well-known scenes
        I dwell,
Let me to friends and neighbours bid Fare-
    well.

    First to our men of wealth—these are but
        few—
In duty bound I humbly bid adieu.
This is not painful, for they know me not,
Fortune in different states has placed our
    lot ;
It is not pleasant, for full well I know
The lordly pity that the rich bestow—
A proud contemptuous pity, by whose aid
Their own triumphant virtues are display'd.—
' Going, you say ; and what intends the Lad,
To seek his fortune ? Fortune ! is he mad ?
Has he the knowledge ? is he duly taught ?
I think we know how Fortune should be
    sought.
Perhaps he takes his chance to sink or swim,
Perhaps he dreams of Fortune's seeking him ?

Life is his lottery, and away he flies,
Without a ticket to obtain his prize :
But never man acquired a weighty sum,
Without foreseeing whence it was to come.'
    Fortunes are made, if I the facts may
        state,—
Though poor myself, I know the fortunate :
First, there 's a knowledge of the way from
    whence
Good fortune comes—and that is sterling
    sense ;
Then perseverance, never to decline
The chase of riches till the prey is thine ;
And firmness, never to be drawn away
By any passion from that noble prey—
By love, ambition, study, travel, fame,
Or the vain hope that lives upon a name.

The whistling Boy that holds the plough,
    Lured by the tale that soldiers tell,
Resolves to part, yet knows not how
    To leave the land he loves so well.
He now rejects the thought, and now
    Looks o'er the lea, and sighs ' Farewell ! '

Farewell ! the pensive Maiden cries,
    Who dreams of London, dreams awake—
But when her favourite Lad she spies,
    With whom she loved her way to take,
Then Doubts within her soul arise,
    And equal Hopes her bosom shake !

Thus, like the Boy, and like the Maid,
    I wish to go, yet tarry here,
And now resolved, and now afraid :
    To minds disturb'd old views appear

In melancholy charms array'd,
    And once indifferent, now are dear.
How shall I go, my fate to learn—
And, oh! how taught shall I return?·

II

YES!—twenty years have pass'd, and I am
    come,
Unknown, unwelcomed, to my early home,
A stranger striving in my walks to trace
The youthful features in some aged face.
On as I move, some curious looks I read;
We pause a moment, doubt, and then proceed:
They're like what once I saw, but not the
    same,
I lose the air, the features, and the name.
Yet something seems like knowledge, but the
    change
Confuses me, and all in him is strange:
That bronzed old Sailor, with his wig awry—
Sure he will know me! No, he passes by.
They seem like me in doubt; but they can
    call
Their friends around them! I am lost to all.
    The very place is alter'd. What I left
Seems of its space and dignity bereft:
The streets are narrow, and the buildings
    mean;
Did I, or Fancy, leave them broad and clean?
The ancient church, in which I felt a pride,
As struck by magic, is but half as wide;
The tower is shorter, the sonorous bell
Tells not the hour as it was wont to tell;
The market dwindles, every shop and stall
Sinks in my view; there's littleness in all.
Mine is the error; prepossess'd I see;
And all the change I mourn is change in me.
    One object only is the same; the sight
Of the wide Ocean by the moon's pale light
With her long ray of glory, that we mark
On the wild waves when all beside is dark:
This is the work of Nature, and the eye
In vain the boundless prospect would descry;
What mocks our view cannot contracted be;
We cannot lessen what we cannot see.
    Would I could now a single Friend behold,
Who would the yet mysterious facts unfold,
That Time yet spares, and to a stranger show
Th' events he wishes, and yet fears to know!
    Much by myself I might in listening glean,
Mix'd with the crowd, unmark'd if not unseen,
Uninterrupted I might ramble on,
Nor cause an interest, nor a thought, in one;

For who looks backward to a being tost
About the world, forgotten long, and lost,
For whom departing not a tear was shed,
Who disappear'd, was missing, and was dead!
Save that he left no grave, where some might
    pass,
And ask each other who that being was. .
    I, as a ghost invisible, can stray
Among the crowd, and cannot lose my way;
My ways are where the voice of man is known,
Though no occasion offers for my own;
My eager mind to fill with food I seek,
And, like the ghost, await for one to speak.
    See I not One whom I before have seen?
That face, though now untroubled and serene,
That air, though steady now, that look,
    though tame,
Pertain to one, whom though I doubt to name,
Yet was he not a dashing youth and wild,
Proud as a man, and haughty when a child?
Talents were his; he was in nature kind,
With lofty, strong, and independent mind;
His father wealthy, but, in very truth,
He was a rash, untamed, expensive youth;
And, as I now remember the report,
Told how his father's money he would sport:
Yet in his dress and manner now appears
No sign of faults that stain'd his earlier years;
Mildness there seems, and marks of sober
    sense,
That bear no token of that wild expense
Such as to ruin leads!—I may mistake,
Yet may, perchance, a useful friendship
    make!
He looks as one whom I should not offend,
Address'd as him whom I would make a
    friend.
    Men with respect attend him.—He pro-
    ceeds
To yonder public room—why then he reads.
    Suppose me right—a mighty change is
    wrought;
But Time ere now has care and caution
    taught.
May I address him? And yet, why afraid?
Deny he may, but he will not upbraid,
Nor must I lose him, for I want his aid.
    Propitious fate! beyond my hope I find
A being well-inform'd, and much inclined
To solve my many doubts, and ease my
    anxious mind.
    Now shall we meet, and he will give reply
To all I ask!—How full of fears am I;

Poor, nervous, trembling ! what have I to
fear ?
Have I a wife, a child, one creature here,
Whose health would bring me joy, whose
death would claim a tear ?
This is the time appointed, this the place :
Now shall I learn, how some have run their
race
With honour, some with shame ; and I shall
know
How man behaves in Fortune's ebb and
flow ;—
What wealth or want, what trouble, sorrow,
joy,
Have been allotted to the girl and boy

Whom I left laughing at the ills of life,—
Now the grave father, or the awful wife.
Then shall I hear how tried the wise and good!
How fall'n the house that once in honour
stood !
And moving accidents, from war and fire and
flood !
These shall I hear, if to his promise true ;
His word is pledged to tell me all he knew
Of living men ; and memory then will trace
Those who no more with living men have
place,
As they were borne to their last quiet homes—
This shall I learn !—And lo ! my Teacher
comes.

TALE VII. THE SCHOOL-FELLOW

I

YES ! I must leave thee, brother of my
heart,
The world demands us, and at length we part ;
Thou whom that heart, since first it felt,
approved—
I thought not why, nor question'd how I
loved ;
In my first thoughts, first notions, and first
cares,
Associate : partner in my mind's affairs,
In my young dreams, my fancies ill-express'd
But well conceived, and to the heart address'd.
A fellow-reader in the books I read,
A fellow-mourner in the tears I shed,
A friend, partaking every grief and joy,
A lively, frank, engaging, generous boy.
    At school each other's prompters, day by
day
Companions in the frolic or the fray ;
Prompt in disputes—we never sought the
cause,
The laws of friendship were our only laws ;
We ask'd not how or why the strife began,
But David's foe was foe to Jonathan.
    In after-years my Friend, the elder boy,
Would speak of Love, its tumult and its
joy ;
A new and strong emotion thus imprest,
Prepared for pain to come the yielding breast ;
For though no object then the fancy found,
She dreamt of darts, and gloried at the
wound ;

Smooth verse and tender tales the spirit
moved,
And ere the Chloes came the Strephons loved.
    This is the Friend I leave ; for he remains
Bound to his home by strong but viewless
chains :
Nor need I fear that his aspiring soul
Will fail his adverse fortunes to control,
Or lose the fame he merits : yet awhile
The clouds may lour—but then his sun will
smile.
Oh ! Time, thou teller of men's fortunes, lend
Thy aid, and be propitious to my Friend !
Let me behold him prosperous, and his name
Enroll'd among the darling sons of Fame ;
In love befriend him, and be his the bride,
Proud of her choice, and of her lord the pride.
' So shall my little bark attendant sail,'—
(As Pope has sung)—and prosperous be the
gale !

II

HE is not here : the Youth I loved so well
Dwells in some place where kindred spirits
dwell :
But I shall learn. Oh ! tell me of my Friend,
With whom I hoped life's evening-calm to
spend ;
With whom was spent the morn, the happy
morn !
When gay conceits and glorious views are
born ;
With whom conversing I began to find
The early stirrings of an active mind,

That, done the tasks and lessons of the day,
Sought for new pleasures in our untried way ;
And stray'd in fairy land, where much we
   long'd to stray.
  Here he abides not ! could not surely fix
In this dull place, with these dull souls to mix;
He finds his place where lively spirits meet,
And loftier souls from baser kind retreat.
  First, of my early Friend I gave the name,
Well known to me, and, as I judged, to Fame ;
My grave informer doubted, then replied,
' That Lad !—why, yes !—some ten years
   since he died.'
  P. Died ! and unknown ! the man I loved
   so well !
But is this all ? the whole that you can tell
Of one so gifted ?—
          F. Gifted ! why, in truth,
You puzzle me ; how gifted was the Youth ?
I recollect him, now—his long, pale face—
He dress'd in drab, and walk'd as in a race.
  P. Good Heaven ! what did I not of him
   expect ?
And is this all indeed you recollect—
Of wit that charm'd me, with delightful ease—
And gay good-humour that must ever
   please—
His taste, his genius ! know you nought of
   these ?
  F. No, not of these :—but stop ! in pass-
   ing near,
I've heard his flute—it was not much to hear :

As for his genius—let me not offend :
I never had a genius for a friend,
And doubt of yours ; but still he did his
   best,
And was a decent Lad—there let him rest !
  He lies in peace, with all his humble race,
And has no stone to mark his burial place ;
Nor left he that which to the world might
   show
That he was one that world was bound to
   know,
For aught he gave it.—Here his story ends !
  P. And is this all ? This character my
   Friend's !
That may, alas ! be mine——' *a decent
   Lad !* '—
The very phrase would make a Poet mad !
And he is gone !—Oh ! proudly did I think
That we together at that fount should drink,
Together climb the steep ascent of Fame,
Together gain an ever-during name,
And give due credit to our native home—
Yet here he lies, without a name or tomb !
Perhaps not honour'd by a single tear,
Just enter'd in a parish-register,
With common dust, forgotten to remain—
And shall I seek, what thou could'st not
   obtain—
A name for men when I am dead to speak ?—
Oh ! let me something more substantial seek ;
Let me no more on man's poor praise depend,
But learn one lesson from my buried Friend.

TALE VIII.   BARNABY; THE SHOPMAN

I

FAREWELL ! to *him* whom just across my
   way,
I see his shop attending day by day ;
Save on the Sunday, when he duly goes
To his own church, in his own Sunday clothes.
Young though he is, yet careful there he
   stands,
Opening his shop with his own ready hands ;
Nor scorns the broom that to and fro he
   moves.
Cleaning his way, for cleanliness he loves—
But yet preserves not : in his zeal for trade
He has his shop an ark for all things made ;
And there, in spite of his all-guarding eye,
His sundry wares in strange confusion lie—

Delightful token of the haste that keeps
Those mingled matters in their shapeless
   heaps ;
Yet ere he rests, he takes them all away,
And order smiles on the returning day.
  Most ready tradesman he of men ! alive
To all that turns to money—he must thrive.
Obsequious, civil, loath t' offend or trust,
And full of awe for greatness—thrive he must;
For well he knows to creep, and he in time,
By wealth assisted, will aspire to climb.
  Pains-taking lad he was, and with his slate
For hours in useful meditation sate ;
Puzzled, and seizing every boy at hand,
To make him—hard the labour !—under-
   stand ;

But when of learning he enough possess'd
For his affairs, who would might learn the rest ;
All else was useless when he had obtain'd
Knowledge that told him what he lost or gain'd.
He envied no man for his learning ; he
Who was not rich, was poor with BARNABY :
But he for envy has no thought to spare,
Nor love nor hate—his heart is in his ware.

Happy the man whose greatest pleasure lies
In the fair trade by which he hopes to rise.
To him how bright the opening day, how blest
The busy noon, how sweet the evening rest !
To him the nation's state is all unknown,
Whose watchful eye is ever on his own.
You talk of patriots, men who give up all,
Yea, life itself, at their dear country's call !
He look'd on such as men of other date,
Men to admire, and not to imitate ;
They as his Bible-Saints to him appear'd,
Lost to the world, but still to be revered.

Yet there 's a Widow, in a neighbouring street,
Whom he contrives in Sunday-dress to meet ;
Her's house and land ; and these are more delight
To him than learning, in the proverb's spite.

The Widow sees at once the Trader's views,
And means to soothe him, flatter, and refuse :
Yet there are moments when a woman fails
In such design, and so the man prevails.
Love she has not, but, in a guardless hour,
May lose her purpose, and resign her power ;
Yet all such hazard she resolves to run,
Pleased to be woo'd, and fearless to be won.

Lovers like these, as dresses thrown aside,
Are kept and shown to feed a woman's pride.
Old-fashion'd, ugly, call them what she will,
They serve as signs of her importance still.
She thinks they might inferior forms adorn,
And does not love to hear them used with scorn ;
Till on some day when she has need of dress,
And none at hand to serve her in distress,
She takes th' insulted robe, and turns about ;
Long-hidden beauties one by one peer out.
' 'Tis not so bad ! see, Jenny—I declare
'Tis pretty well, and then 'tis lasting wear ;
And what is fashion ?—if a woman 's wise,
She will the substance, not the shadow, prize ;
'Tis a choice silk, and if I put it on,
Off go these ugly trappings every one.'

The dress is worn, a friendly smile is raised,
But the good lady for her courage praised—
Till wonder dies.—The dress is worn with pride,
And not one trapping yet is cast aside.

Meanwhile the man his six-day toil renews,
And on the seventh he worships Heaven, and woos.
I leave thee, Barnaby ; and if I see
Thee once again, a Burgess thou wilt be.

II

BUT how is this ? I left a thriving man,
Hight BARNABY ! when he to trade began—
Trade his delight and hope ; and, if alive,
Doubt I had none that Barnaby would thrive:
Yet here I see him, sweeping as before
The very dust from forth the very door.
So would a miser ! but, methinks, the shop
Itself is meaner—has he made a stop ?

I thought I should at least a Burgess see,
And lo ! 'tis but an older Barnaby ;
With face more wrinkled, with a coat as bare
As coats of his once begging kindred were,
Brush'd to the thread that is distinctly seen,
And beggarly would be, but that 'tis clean.
Why, how is this ? Upon a closer view,
The shop is narrow'd : it is cut in two.
Is all that business from its station fled ?
Why, Barnaby ! thy very shop is dead !
Now, what the cause my Friend will soon relate—
And what the fall from that predicted fate.

F. A common cause : it seems his lawful gains
Came slowly forth, and came with care and pains.
These he, indeed, was willing to bestow,
But still his progress to his point was slow,
And might be quicken'd, ' could he cheat the eyes
Of all those rascal officers and spies,
The Customs' greedy tribe, the wolves of the Excise.'

Tea, coffee, spirits, laces, silks, and spice,
And sundry drugs that bear a noble price,
Are bought for little, but ere sold, the things
Are deeply charged for duty of the king's.
Now, if the servants of this king would keep
At a kind distance, or would wink or sleep,
Just till the goods in safety were disposed,
Why then his labours would be quickly closed.

True! some have thriven,—but they the
     laws defied,
And shunn'd the powers they should have
     satisfied !
  Their way he tried, and finding some success,
His heart grew stouter, and his caution less ;
Then—for why doubt, when placed in
     Fortune's way ?—
There was a bank, and that was sure to pay.
Yes, every partner in that thriving bank
He judged a man of a superior rank.
Were *he* but one in a concern so grand—
Why ! he might build a house, and buy him
     land ;
Then, too, the Widow, whom he loved so well,
Would not refuse with such a man to dwell;
And, to complete his views, he might be made
A Borough-Justice, when he ceased to trade ;
For he had known—well pleased to know—
     a mayor
Who once had dealt in cheese and vinegar.
  Who hastens to be rich, resembles him
Who is resolved that he will quickly swim,
And trusts his full-blown bladders ! He,
     indeed,
With these supported, moves along with
     speed ;
He laughs at those whom untried depths alarm,
By caution led, and moved by strength of arm ;
Till in mid-way, the way his folly chose,
His full-blown bladder bursts, and down he
     goes !

Or, if preserved, 'tis by their friendly aid
Whom he despised as cautious and afraid.
  Who could resist ? Not Barnaby. Success
Awhile his pride exalted—to depress.
Three years he pass'd in feverish hopes and
     fears,
When fled the profits of the former years ;
Shook by the Law's strong arm, all he had
     gain'd
He dropp'd—and hopeless, penniless re-
     main'd.
  The cruel Widow, whom he yet pursued,
Was kind but cautious, then was stern and
     rude.
' Should wealth, now hers, from that dear
     man which came,
Be thrown away to prop a smuggler's fame ? '
She spake insulting ; and with many a sigh,
The fallen Trader passed her mansion by.
  Fear, shame, and sorrow, for a time en-
     dured,
Th' adventurous man was ruin'd, but was
     cured—
His weakness pitied, and his once-good name
The means of his returning peace became.
  He was assisted, to his shop withdrew,
Half let, half rented, and began anew,
To smile on custom, that in part return'd,
With the small gains that he no longer spurn'd.
Warn'd by the past, he rises with the day,
And tries to sweep off sorrow.——*Sweep
     away !*

TALE IX.   JANE

I

KNOWN but of late, I yet am loth to leave
The gentle JANE, and wonder why I grieve—
Not for her wants, for she has no distress,
She has no suffering that her looks express,
Her air or manner—hers the mild good sense
That wins its way by making no pretence.
  When yet a child, her dying mother knew
What, left by her, the widow'd man would do,
And gave her Jane, for she had power, enough
To live in ease—of love and care a proof.
Enabled thus, the mind is kind to all—
Is pious too, and that without a call.
Not that she doubts of calls that Heav'n has
     sent—
Calls to believe, or warnings to repent ;

But that she rests upon the Word divine,
Without presuming on a dubious sign ;
A sudden light, the momentary zeal
Of those who rashly hope, and warmly feel ;
These she rejects not, nor on these relies,
And neither feels the influence nor denies.
Upon the sure and written Word she trusts,
And by the Law Divine her life adjusts ;
She blames not her who other creed prefers,
And all she asks is charity for hers.
Her great example is her gracious Lord,
Her hope his promise, and her guide his
     Word ;
Her quiet alms are known to God alone,
Her left hand knows not what her right has
     done ;

Her talents, not the few, she well improves,
And puts to use in labour that she loves.
  Pensive, though good, I leave thee, gentle
    maid—
In thee confiding, of thy peace afraid,
In a strange world to act a trying part,
With a soft temper, and a yielding heart !

II

P. How fares my gentle Jane, with spirit
    meek,
Whose fate with some foreboding care I seek ;
Her whom I pitied in my pride, while she,
For many a cause more weighty, pitied me ;
For she has wonder'd how the idle boy
His head or hands would usefully employ—
At least for thee his grateful spirit pray'd,
And now to ask thy fortune is afraid.—
——How fares the gentle Jane ?—
            F. Know first, she fares
As one who bade adieu to earthly cares ;
As one by virtue guided, and who, tried
By man's deceit, has never lost her guide.
  Her age I knew not, but it seem'd the age
When Love is wont a serious war to wage
In female hearts,—when hopes and fears are
    strong,
And 'tis a fatal step to place them wrong ;
For childish fancies now have ta'en their
    flight,
And love's impressions are no longer light.
  Just at this time—what time I do not tell—
There came a Stranger in the place to dwell ;
He seem'd as one who sacred truth reveres,
And like her own his sentiments and years ;
His person manly, with engaging mien,
His spirit quiet, and his looks serene.
He kept from all disgraceful deeds aloof,
Severely tried, and found temptation-proof :
This was by most unquestion'd, and the few
Who made inquiry said report was true.
  His very choice of our neglected place
Endear'd him to us—'twas an act of grace ;
And soon to Jane, our unobtrusive maid,
In still respect was his attention paid ;
Each in the other found what both approved,
Good sense and quiet manners : these they
    loved.
  So came regard, and then esteem, and then
The kind of friendship women have with
    men :
At length t'was love, but candid, open, fair,
Such as became their years and character.

In their discourse, religion had its place,
When he of doctrines talked, and she of grace.
He knew the different sects, the varying
    creeds,
While she, less learned, spoke of virtuous
    deeds ;
He dwelt on errors into which we fall,
She on the gracious remedy for all ;
So between both, his knowledge and her own,
Was the whole Christian to perfection shown.
Though neither quite approved the other's
    part—
Hers without learning, his without a heart—
Still to each other they were dear, were good,
And all these matters kindly understood ;
For Jane was liberal, and her friend could
    trust,—
' He thinks not with me ! but is fair and just.'
  Her prudent lover to her man of law,
Show'd how he lived : it seem'd without a
    flaw ;
She saw their moderate means—content with
    what she saw.
  Jane had no doubts—with so much to
    admire,
She judged it insult farther to inquire.
The lover sought—what lover brooks de-
    lay ?—
For full assent, and for an early day—
And he would construe well the soft con-
    senting Nay !
  The day was near, and Jane, with book in
    hand,
Sat down to read—perhaps might under-
    stand :
For what prevented ?—say, she seem'd to
    read ;
When one there came, her own sad cause to
    plead ;
A stranger she, who fearless named that cause,
A breach in love's and honour's sacred
    laws.
' In a far country, Lady, bleak and wild,
Report has reach'd me ! how art thou be-
    guiled !
Or dared he tell thee that for ten sad years
He saw me struggling with fond hopes and
    fears ?
  ' From my dear home he won me, blest and
    free !
To be his victim.'——' Madam, who is *he ?* '
' Not yet thy husband, Lady : no ! not yet ;
For he has first to pay a mighty debt.'

'Speaks he not of religion?'—'So he
    speaks,
When he the ruin of his victim seeks.
How smooth and gracious were his words,
    how sweet—
The fiend his master prompting his deceit!
Me he with kind instruction led to trust
In one who seem'd so grave, so kind, so just.
Books to amuse me, and inform, he brought,
Like that old serpent with temptation fraught;
His like the precepts of the wise appear'd,
Till I imbibed the vice I had not fear'd.
By pleasant tales and dissertations gay,
He wiled the lessons of my youth away.

   'Of moral duties he would talk, and prove
They gave a sanction, and commanded love;
His sober smile at forms and rites was shown,
To make my mind depraved, and like his own.

   'But wilt thou take him? wilt thou ruin take,
With a grave robber, a religious rake?
'Tis not to serve thee, Lady, that I came—
'Tis not to claim him, 'tis not to reclaim—
But 'tis that he may for my wrongs be paid,
And feel the vengeance of the wretch he made.

   'Not for myself I thy attention claim:
My children dare not take their father's name;
They know no parent's love—love will not
    dwell with shame.
What law would force, he not without it gives,
And hates each living wretch, because it lives!
Yet, with these sinful stains, the man is mine:
How will he curse me for this rash design!
Yes—I will bear his curse, but him will not
    resign.

   'I see thee grieved; but, Lady, what thy
    grief?
It may be pungent, but it must be brief.
Pious thou art; but what will profit thee,
Match'd with a demon, woman's piety?
Not for thy sake my wrongs and wrath I tell,
Revenge I seek! but yet, I wish thee well.

And now I leave thee! Thou art warn'd by
    one,
The rock on which her peace was wreck'd to
    shun.'
   The Lover heard; but not in time to stay
A woman's vengeance in its headlong way:
Yet he essay'd, with no unpractised skill,
To warp the judgment, or at least the will;
To raise such tumults in the poor weak heart,
That Jane, believing all—yet should not dare
    to part.

   But there was Virtue in her mind that strove
With all his eloquence, and all her love;
He told what hope and frailty dared to tell,
And all was answered by a stern *Farewell!*
   Home with his consort he return'd once
    more;
And they resumed the life they led before.
Not so our maiden. She, before resign'd,
Had now the anguish of a wounded mind—
And felt the languid grief that the deserted
    find;
On him she had reposed each worldly view,
And when he fail'd, the world itself withdrew,
With all its prospects. Nothing could restore
To life its value; hope would live no more:
Pensive by nature, she can not sustain
The sneer of pity that the heartless feign;
But to the pressure of her griefs gives way,
A quiet victim, and a patient prey:
The one bright view that she had cherish'd dies,
And other hope must from the future rise.
   She still extends to grief and want her aid,
And by the comfort she imparts, is paid:
Death is her soul's relief: to him she flies
For consolation that this world denies.
No more to life's false promises she clings,
She longs to change this troubled state of
    things,
Till every rising morn the happier prospect
    brings.

TALE X.   THE ANCIENT MANSION

I

To part is painful; nay, to bid adieu
Ev'n to a favourite spot is painful too.
That fine old Seat, with all those oaks around,
Oft have I view'd with reverence so profound,
As something sacred dwelt in that delicious
    ground.

There, with its tenantry about, reside
A genuine English race, the country's
    pride;
And now a Lady, last of all that race,
Is the departing spirit of the place.
Hers is the last of all that noble blood,
That flow'd through generations brave and
    good;

And if there dwells a native pride in her,
It is the pride of name and character.
　True, she will speak, in her abundant zeal,
Of stainless honour; that she needs must
　　feel;
She must lament, that she is now the last
Of all who gave such splendour to the past.
　Still are her habits of the ancient kind;
She knows the poor, the sick, the lame, the
　　blind:
She holds, so she believes, her wealth in trust;
And being kind, with her, is being just.
Though soul and body she delights to aid,
Yet of her skill she's prudently afraid:
So to her chaplain's care she *this* commends,
And when *that* craves, the village doctor sends.
　At church attendance she requires of all,
Who would be held in credit at the Hall;
A due respect to each degree she shows,
And pays the debt that every mortal owes;
'Tis by opinion that respect is led,
The rich esteem because the poor are fed.
　Her servants all, if so we may describe
That ancient, grave, observant, decent tribe,
Who with her share the blessings of the Hall,
Are kind but grave, are proud but courteous
　　all—
Proud of their lucky lot! behold, how stands
That grey-haired butler, waiting her com-
　　mands;
The Lady dines, and every day he feels
That his good mistress falters in her meals.
With what respectful manners he intreats
That she would eat—yet Jacob little eats;
When she forbears, his supplicating eye
Intreats the noble dame once more to try.
Their years the same; and he has never
　　known
Another place; and this he deems his own,—
All appertains to him. Whate'er he sees
Is *ours!*—' our house, our land, our walks,
　　our trees!'
　But still he fears the time is just at hand,
When he no more shall in that presence stand;
And he resolves, with mingled grief and pride,
To serve no being in the world beside.
' He has enough,' he says, with many a sigh,
' For him to serve his God, and learn to die:
He and his lady shall have heard their call,
And the new folk, the strangers, may have
　　all.'
　But, leaving these to their accustom'd way,
The Seat itself demands a short delay.

We all have interest there—the trees that grow
Near to that seat, to that their grandeur owe;
They take, but largely pay, and equal grace
　　bestow:
They hide a part, but still the part they shade
Is more inviting to our fancy made;
And, if the eye be robb'd of half its sight,
Th' imagination feels the more delight.
These giant oaks by no man's order stand,
Heaven did the work; by no man was it
　　plann'd.
　Here I behold no puny works of art,
None give me reasons why these views impart
Such charm to fill the mind, such joy to swell
　　the heart.
These very pinnacles, and turrets small,
And windows dim, have beauty in them all.
How stately stand yon pines upon the hill,
How soft the murmurs of that living rill,
And o'er the park's tall paling, scarcely
　　higher,
Peeps the low Church and shows the modest
　　spire.
Unnumber'd violets on those banks appear,
And all the first-born beauties of the year.
The grey-green blossoms of the willows bring
The large wild bees upon the labouring wing.
Then comes the Summer with augmented
　　pride,
Whose pure small streams along the valleys
　　glide:
Her richer Flora their brief charms display;
And, as the fruit advances, fall away.
Then shall th' autumnal yellow clothe the leaf,
What time the reaper binds the burden'd
　　sheaf:
Then silent groves denote the dying year,
The morning frost, and noon-tide gossamer;
And all be silent in the scene around,
All save the distant sea's uncertain sound,
Or here and there the gun whose loud report
Proclaims to man that Death is but his sport:
And then the wintry winds begin to blow,
Then fall the flaky stars of gathering snow,
When on the thorn the ripening sloe, yet blue,
Takes the bright varnish of the morning dew;
The aged moss grows brittle on the pale,
The dry boughs splinter in the windy gale,
And every changing season of the year
Stamps on the scene its English character.
　Farewell! a prouder Mansion I may see,
But much must meet in that which equals
　　thee!

II

I LEAVE the town, and take a well-known
    way,
To that old Mansion in the closing day,
When beams of golden light are shed around,
And sweet is every sight and every sound.
Pass but this hill, and I shall then behold
The Seat so honour'd, so admired of old,
And yet admired——
          Alas! I see a change,
Of odious kind, and lamentably strange.
Who had done this? The good old Lady lies
Within her tomb: but, who could this advise?
What barbarous hand could all this mischief
    do,
And spoil a noble house to make it new?
Who had done this? Some genuine Son of Trade
Has all this dreadful devastation made;
Some man with line and rule, and evil eye,
Who could no beauty in a tree descry,
Save in a clump, when stationed by his hand,
And standing where his genius bade them
    stand;
Some true admirer of the time's reform,
Who strips an ancient dwelling like a storm,
Strips it of all its dignity and grace,
To put his own dear fancies in their place.
He hates concealment: all that was enclosed
By venerable wood, is now exposed,
And a few stripling elms and oaks appe ir,
Fenced round by boards, to keep them from
    the deer.
I miss the grandeur of the rich old scene,
And see not what these clumps and patches
    mean!
This shrubby belt that runs the land around
Shuts freedom out! what being likes a bound?
The shrubs indeed, and ill-placed flowers, are
    gay,
And some would praise; I wish they were
    away,
That in the wild-wood maze I as of old might
    stray.
The things themselves are pleasant to behold,
But not like those which we beheld of old,—
That half-hid mansion, with its wide domain,
Unbound and unsubdued!—but sighs are
    vain;
It is the rage of Taste—the rule and compass
    reign.
  As thus my spleen upon the view I fed,
A man approach'd me, by his grandchild led—

A blind old man, and she a fair young maid,
Listening in love to what her grandsire said.
And thus with gentle voice he spoke—
  'Come lead me, lassie, to the shade,
Where willows grow beside the brook;
  For well I know the sound it made,
When dashing o'er the stony rill,
It murmur'd to St. Osyth's Mill.'

The Lass replied—'The trees are fled,
They've cut the brook a straighter bed:
No shades the present lords allow,
The miller now his murmurs now;
The waters now his mill forsake,
And form a pond they call a lake.'

'Then, lassie, lead thy grandsire on,
  And to the holy water bring;
A cup is fasten'd to the stone,
  And I would taste the healing spring,
That soon its rocky cist forsakes,
And green its mossy passage makes.'

'The holy spring is turn'd aside,
The rock is gone, the stream is dried;
The plough has levell'd all around,
And here is now no holy ground.'

'Then, lass, thy grandsire's footsteps guide
  To Bulmer's Tree, the giant oak,
Whose boughs the keeper's cottage hide,
  And part the church-way lane o'erlook;
A boy, I climb'd the topmost bough,
And I would feel its shadow now.

'Or, lassie, lead me to the west,
  Where grew the elm-trees thick and tall,
Where rooks unnumber'd build their nest—
  Deliberate birds, and prudent all:
Their notes, indeed, are harsh and rude,
But they're a social multitude.'

'The rooks are shot, the trees are fell'd,
And nest and nursery all expell'd;
With better fate the giant-tree,
Old Bulmer's Oak, is gone to sea.
The church-way walk is now no more,
And men must other ways explore:
Though this indeed promotion gains,
For this the park's new wall contains;
And here I fear we shall not meet
A shade—although, perchance, a seat.'

'O then, my lassie, lead the way
To Comfort's Home, the ancient inn:
That something holds, if we can pay—
  Old David is our living kin;

A servant once, he still preserves
His name, and in his office serves.'

' Alas ! that mine should be the fate
Old David's sorrows to relate :
But they were brief ; not long before
He died, his office was no more.
The kennel stands upon the ground,
With something of the former sound.'

' O then,' the grieving Man replied,
' No further, lassie, let me stray ;
Here 's nothing left of ancient pride,
Of what was grand, of what was gay :
But all is chang'd, is lost, is sold—
All, all that 's left is chilling cold.
I seek for comfort here in vain,
Then lead me to my cot again.'

TALE XI. THE MERCHANT

I

Lo ! one appears, to whom if I should dare
To say *farewell*, the lordly man would stare,
Would stretch his goodly form some inches
    higher,
And then, without a single word, retire ;
Or from his state might haply condescend
To doubt his memory—' Ha ! your name,
    my friend ! '
He is the master of these things we see,
Those vessels proudly riding by the quay ;
With all those mountain heaps of coal that lie,
For half a county's wonder and supply.
Boats, cables, anchors, all to him pertain,—
A swimming fortune, all his father's gain.
He was a porter on the quay, and one
Proud of his fortune, prouder of his son ;—
Who was ashamed of him, and much distress'd
To see his father was no better dress'd.
Yet for this parent did the son erect
A tomb—'tis whisper'd, he must not expect
The like for him, when he shall near it
    sleep,—
Where we behold the marble cherubs weep.
There are no merchants who with us reside
In half his state,—no wonder he has pride ;
Then he parades around that vast estate,
As if he spurn'd the slaves that make him
    great ;
Speaking in tone so high, as if the ware
Was nothing worth—at least not worth his
    care ;
Yet should he not these bulky stores contemn,
For all his glory he derives from them ;
And were it not for that neglected store,
This great rich man would be extremely poor.
    Generous, men call him, for he deigns to
    give ;
He condescends to say the poor must live :

Yet in his seamen not a sign appears,
That they have much respect, or many fears ;
With inattention they their patron meet,
As if they thought his dignity a cheat ;
Or of himself as, having much to do
With their affairs, he very little knew ;
As if his ways to them so well were known,
That they might hear, and bow, and take
    their own.
He might contempt for men so humble feel,
But this experience taught him to conceal ;
For sailors do not to a lord at land
As to their captain in submission stand ;
Nor have mere pomp and pride of look or
    speech,
Been able yet respect or awe to teach.
    Guns, when with powder charged, will make
    a noise,
To frighten babes, and be the sport of boys ;
But when within men find there 's nothing
    more,
They shout contemptuous at the idle roar.
Thus will our lofty man to all appear,
With nothing charged that they respect or
    fear.
His Lady, too, to her large purse applies,
And all she fancies at the instant buys.
How bows the market, when, from stall to
    stall,
She walks attended ! how respectful all !
To her free orders every maid attends,
And strangers wonder what the woman
    spends.
    There is an auction, and the people shy,
Are loth to bid, and yet desire to buy.
Jealous they gaze with mingled hope and
    fear,
Of buying cheaply, and of paying dear.
They see the hammer with determined air
Seized for despatch, and bid in pure despair !

They bid—the hand is quiet as before,—
Still stands old Puff till one advances more.—
Behold great madam, gliding through the
    crowd :
Hear her too bid—decisive tone and loud !
' Going ! 'tis gone ! ' the hammer-holder
    cries—
' Joy to you, Lady ! you have gain'd a prize.'
    Thus comes and goes the wealth, that,
      saved or spent,
Buys not a moment's credit or content.
    Farewell ! your fortune I forbear to guess ;
For chance, as well as sense, may give success.

II

P. SAY, what yon buildings, neat indeed,
    but low,
So much alike, in one commodious row ?
    F. You see our Alms-house : ancient men,
      decay'd,
Are here sustain'd, who lost their way in
    trade ;
Here they have all that sober men require—
So thought the Poet—' meat, and clothes,
    and fire ; '
A little garden to each house pertains,
Convenient each, and kept with little pains.
Here for the sick are nurse and medicine
    found ;
Here walks and shaded alleys for the sound ;
Books of devotion on the shelves are placed,
And not forbidden are the books of taste.
The Church is near them—in a common
    seat
The pious men with grateful spirit meet :
Thus from the world, which they no more
    admire,
They all in silent gratitude retire.
    P. And is it so ? Have all, with grateful
    mind,
The world relinquish'd, and its ways resign'd ?
Look they not back with lingering love and
    slow,
And fain would once again the oft-tried
    follies know ?
    F. Too surely some ! We must not think
    that all,
Call'd to be hermits, would obey the call ;
We must not think that all forget the state
In which they moved, and bless their humbler
    fate ;
But all may here the waste of life retrieve,
And, ere they leave the world, its vices leave.

See yonder man, who walks apart, and
    seems
Wrapt in some fond and visionary schemes ;
Who looks uneasy, as a man oppress'd
By that large copper badge upon his breast.
His painful shame, his self-tormenting pride,
Would all that 's visible in bounty hide ;
And much his anxious breast is swell'd with
    woe,
That where he goes his badge must with him
    go.
    P. Who then is he ? Do I behold aright ?
My lofty Merchant in this humble plight !
Still has he pride ?
            F. If common fame be just,
He yet has pride,—the pride that licks the
    dust ;
Pride that can stoop, and feed upon the base
And wretched flattery of this humbling place ;
Nay, feeds himself ! his failing is avow'd,
He of the cause that made him poor is proud ;
Proud of his greatness, of the sums he spent,
And honours shown him wheresoe'er he went.
    Yes ! there he walks, that lofty man is
    he,
Who was so rich ; but great he could not
    be.
Now to the paupers who about him stand,
He tells of wonders by his bounty plann'd,
Tells of his traffic, where his vessels sail'd,
And what a trade he drove—before he fail'd ;
Then what a failure, not a paltry sum,
Like a mean trader, but for half a plum ;
His Lady's wardrobe was apprised so high,
At his own sale, that nobody would buy !—
' But she is gone,' he cries, ' and never saw
The spoil and havoc of our cruel law ;
My steeds, our chariot that so roll'd along,
Admired of all ! they sold them for a song.
You all can witness what my purse could do,
And now I wear a badge like one of you,
Who in my service had been proud to live,—
And this is all a thankless town will give.
I, who have raised the credit of that town,
And gave it, thankless as it is, renown—
Who've done what no man there had done
    before,
Now hide my head within an Alms-house
    door—
Deprived of all—my wife, my wealth, my
    vote,
And in this blue defilement——*Curse the
    Coat !* '

TALE XII. THE BROTHER BURGESSES

I

Two busy BROTHERS in our place reside,
And wealthy each, his party's boast and
    pride ;
Sons of one father, of two mothers born,
They hold each other in true party-scorn.
  JAMES is the one who for the people fights,
The sturdy champion of their dubious rights ;
Merchant and seaman rough, but not the less
Keen in pursuit of his own happiness ;
And what his happiness ?—To see his store
Of wealth increase, till Mammon groans, ' No
    more ! '
  JAMES goes to church—because his father
    went,
But does not hide his leaning to dissent ;
Reasons for this, whoe'er may frown, he'll
    speak—
Yet the old pew receives him once a week.
  CHARLES is a churchman, and has all the
    zeal
That a strong member of his church can feel ;
A loyal subject is the name he seeks ;
He of ' his King and Country ' proudly
    speaks :
He says, his brother and a rebel-crew,
Minded like him, the nation would undo,
If they had power, or were esteem'd enough
Of those who had, to bring their plans to
    proof.
  JAMES answers sharply—' I will never place
My hopes upon a Lordship or a Grace !
To some great man you bow, to greater he,
Who to the greatest bends his supple knee,
That so the manna from the head may drop,
And at the lowest of the kneelers stop.
Lords call you loyal, and on them you call
To spare you something from our plunder'd
    all :
If tricks like these to slaves can treasure bring,
Slaves well may shout them hoarse for
    " Church and King ! " '
  ' Brother ! ' says Charles,—' yet brother
    is a name
I own with pity, and I speak with shame,—
One of these days you'll surely lead a mob,
And then the hangman will conclude the job.'

' And would you, Charles, in that unlucky
    case,
Beg for his life whose death would bring
    disgrace
On you, and all the loyal of our race ?
Your worth would surely from the halter
    bring
One neck, and I a patriot then might sing—
A brother patriot I—God save our noble
    king.'
  ' James ! ' said the graver man, in manner
    grave—
' Your neck I could not, I your soul would
    save ;
Oh ! ere that day, alas, too likely ! come,
I would prepare your mind to meet your
    doom,
That then the priest, who prays with that
    bad race
Of men, may find you not devoid of grace.'
  These are the men who, from their seats
    above,
Hear frequent sermons on fraternal love ;
Nay, each approves, and answers—' Very
    true !
Brother would heed it, were he not a Jew.'

II

  P. READ I aright ? beneath this stately
    stone
THE BROTHERS rest in peace, their grave is
    one !
What friend, what fortune interfered, that
    they
Take their long sleep together, clay with clay ?
How came it thus ?—
           F. It was their own request,
By both repeated, that they thus might rest.
  P. 'Tis well ! Did friends at length the
    pair unite ?
Or was it done because the deed was right ?
Did the cool spirit of enfeebling age
Chill the warm blood, and calm the party
    rage,
And kindly lead them, in their closing day,
To put their animosity away,
Incline their hearts to live in love and peace,
And bid the ferment in each bosom cease ?

F. Rich men have runners, who will to
    and fro
In search of food for their amusement go ;
Who watch their spirits, and with tales of
    grief
Yield to their melancholy minds relief ;
Who of their foes will each mishap relate,
And of their friends the fall or failings state.
    One of this breed—the Jackall who supplied
Our Burgess Charles with food for spleen and
    pride—
Before he utter'd what his memory brought,
On its effect, in doubtful matters, thought,
Lest he, perchance, in his intent might trip,
Or a strange fact might indiscreetly slip ;—
But he one morning had a tale to bring,
And felt full sure he need not weigh the thing ;
That must be welcome ! With a smiling face
He watch'd th' accustom'd nod, and took
    his place.
    ' Well ! you have news—I see it—Good,
    my friend,
No preface, Peter. Speak, man, I attend.'
    ' Then, sir, I'm told, nay, 'tis beyond
    dispute,
Our Burgess James is routed horse and foot ;
He'll not be seen ; a clerk for him appears,
And their precautions testify their fears ;
Before the week be ended you shall see,
That our famed patriot will a bankrupt be.'
    ' Will he by——! No, I will not be profane,
But *James* a bankrupt ! Boy, my hat and cane.

No ! he'll refuse my offers—Let me think !
So would I his : here, give me pen and ink.
There ! that will do.—What ! let my father's
    son,
My brother, want, and I—away ! and run,
Run as for life, and then return—but stay
To take his message—now, away, away ! '
    The pride of James was shaken as he read—
The Brothers met—the angry spirit fled :
Few words were needed—in the look of each
There was a language words can never reach ;
But when they took each other's hand, and
    press'd,
Subsiding tumult sank to endless rest ;
Nor party wrath with quick affection strove,
Drown'd in the tears of reconciling love.
    Affairs confused, and business at a stand,
Were soon set right by Charles's powerful
    hand ;
The rudest mind in this rude place enjoy'd
The pleasing thought of enmity destroy'd,
And so destroy'd, that neither spite nor
    spleen,
Nor peevish look from that blest hour were
    seen ;
Yet each his party and his spirit kept,
Though all the harsh and angry passions
    slept.
    P. And they too sleep ! and, at their joint
    request,
Within one tomb, beneath one stone, they
    rest !

TALE XIII. THE DEAN'S LADY

I

Next, to a Lady I must bid adieu—
Whom some in mirth or malice call a ' *Blue.*'
There needs no more—when that same word
    is said,
The men grow shy, respectful, and afraid ;
Save the choice friends who in her colour dress,
And all her praise in words like hers express.
    Why should proud man in man that know-
    ledge prize,
Which he affects in woman to despise ?
Is he not envious when a lady gains,
In hours of leisure, and with little pains,
What he in many a year with painful toil
    obtains ?

For surely knowledge should not odious grow,
Nor ladies be despised for what they know ;
Truth to no sex confined, her friends invites,
And woman, long restrain'd, demands her
    rights.
Nor should a light and odious name be thrown
On the fair dame who makes that knowledge
    known—
Who bravely dares the world's sarcastic sneer,
And what she is, is willing to appear.
    ' And what she is not ! ' peevish man re-
    plies,
His envy owning what his pride denies :
But let him, envious as he is, repair
To this sage Dame, and meet conviction
    there.

MIRANDA sees her morning levee fill'd
With men, in every art and science skill'd—
Men who have gain'd a name, whom she
    invites,
Because in men of genius she delights.
To these she puts her questions, that produce
Discussion vivid, and discourse abstruse:
She no opinion for its boldness spares,
But loves to show her audience what she dares;
The creeds of all men she takes leave to sift,
And, quite impartial, turns her own adrift.
    Her noble mind, with independent force,
Her Rector questions on his late discourse;
Perplex'd and pain'd, he wishes to retire
From one whom critics, nay, whom crowds,
    admire—
From her whose faith on no man's dictate
    leans,
Who her large creed from many a teacher
    gleans;
Who for herself will judge, debate, decide,
And be her own 'philosopher and guide.'
    Why call a lady *Blue?* It is because
She reads, converses, studies for applause;
And therefore all that she desires to know
Is just as much as she can fairly show.
The real knowledge we in secret hide,
It is the counterfeit that makes our pride.
' A little knowledge is a dangerous thing !'—
So sings the Poet, and so let him sing:
But if from little learning danger rose,
I know not who in safety could repose.
The evil rises from our own mistake,
When we our ignorance for knowledge take;
Or when the little that we have, through
    pride,
And vain poor self-love view'd, is magnified.
Nor is your deepest Azure always free
From these same dangerous calls of vanity.
    Yet of the sex are those who never show,
By way of exhibition, what they know.
Their books are read and praised, and so are
    they,
But all without design, without display.
Is there not One who reads the hearts of men,
And paints them strongly with unrivall'd pen?
All their fierce Passions in her scenes appear,
Terror she bids arise, bids fall the tear;
Looks in the close recesses of the mind,
And gives the finish'd portraits to mankind,
By skill conducted, and to Nature true,—
And yet no man on earth would call JOANNA
    Blue !

Not so MIRANDA ! She is ever prest
To give opinions, and she gives her best.
To these with gentle smile her guests incline,
Who come to hear, improve, applaud,—and
    dine.
    Her hungry mind on every subject feeds;
She Adam Smith and Dugald Stewart reads;
Locke entertains her, and she wonders why
His famous Essay is consider'd dry.
For her amusement in her vacant hours
Are earths and rocks, and animals and flowers:
She could the farmer at his work assist,
A systematic agriculturist.
Some men, indeed, would curb the female
    mind,
Nor let us see that they themselves are blind;
But—thank our stars !—the liberal times
    allow,
That all may think, and men have rivals
    now.
    Miranda deems all knowledge might be
    gain'd—
' But she is idle, nor has much attain'd;
Men are in her deceived; she knows at
    most
A few light matters, for she scorns to boast.
Her mathematic studies she resign'd—
They did not suit the genius of her mind.
She thought indeed the higher parts sublime,
But then they took a monstrous deal of time!'
    Frequent and full the letters she delights
To read in part; she names not him who
    writes—
But here and there a precious sentence shows,
Telling what literary debts she owes.
Works, yet unprinted, for her judgment come,
' Alas ! ' she cries, ' and I must seal their
    doom.
Sworn to be just, the judgment gives me
    pain—
Ah ! why must truth be told, or man be
    vain ? '
    Much she has written, and still deigns to
    write,
But not an effort yet must see the light.
' Cruel ! ' her friends exclaim; ' unkind,
    unjust ! '
But, no ! the envious mass she will not trust;
Content to hear that fame is due to her,
Which on her works the world might not
    confer—
Content with loud applauses while she lives;
Unfelt the pain the cruel critic gives.

II

P. Now where the Learned Lady? Doth
    she live,
Her dinners yet and sentiments to give—
The Dean's wise consort, with the many
    friends,
From whom she borrows, and to whom she
    lends
Her precious maxims?
            F. Yes, she lives to shed
Her light around her, but her Dean is dead.
Seen her I have, but seldom could I see:
Borrow she could not, could not lend to me.
Yet, I attended, and beheld the tribe
Attending too, whom I will not describe—
Miranda Thomson! Yes, I sometimes found
A seat among a circle so profound;
When all the science of the age combined
Was in that room, and hers the master-mind.
Well I remember the admiring crowd,
Who spoke their wonder and applause aloud;
They strove who highest should her glory
    raise,
And cramm'd the hungry mind with honied
    praise—

While she, with grateful hand, a table spread,
The Dean assenting—but the Dean is dead;
And though her sentiments are still divine,
She asks no more her auditors to dine.
    Once from her lips came wisdom; when
    she spoke,
Her friends in transport or amazement broke.
Now to her dictates there attend but few,
And they expect to meet attention too;
Respect she finds is purchased at some cost,
And deference is withheld, when dinner's lost.
    She, once the guide and glory of the place,
Exists between oblivion and disgrace;
Praise once afforded, now,—they say not
    why,
They dare not say it—fickle men deny;
That buzz of fame a new Minerva cheers,
Which our deserted queen no longer hears.
Old, but not wise, forsaken, not resign'd,
She gives to honours past her feeble mind,
Back to her former state her fancy moves,
And lives on past applause, that still she
    loves;
Yet holds in scorn the fame no more in view,
And flies the glory that would not pursue
To yon small cot, a poorly jointured *Blue.*

TALE XIV. THE WIFE AND WIDOW

I

I leave Sophia; it would please me well,
Before we part, on so much worth to dwell:
'Tis said of one who lived in times of strife,
There was no boyhood in his busy life;
Born to do all that mortal being can,
The thinking child became at once the man;
So this fair girl in early youth was led,
By reasons strong in early youth, to wed.
    In her new state her prudence was her
    guide,
And of experience well the place supplied;
With life's important business full in view,
She had no time for its amusements too;
She had no practised look man's heart
    t' allure,
No frown to kill him, and no smile to cure;
No art coquettish, nothing of the prude;
She was with strong yet simple sense endued,
Intent on duties, and resolved to shun
Nothing that ought to be, and could be, done.

A Captain's wife, with him she long
    sustain'd
The toil of war, and in a camp remain'd;
Her husband wounded, with a child in arms,
She nurst them both, unheeded all alarms:
All useless terror in her soul supprest—
None could discern in hers a troubled breast.
    Her wounded soldier is a prisoner made,
She hears, prepares, and is at once convey'd
Through hostile ranks:—with air sedate she
    goes,
And makes admiring friends of wondering
    foes.
Her dying husband to her care confides
Affairs perplex'd; she reasons, she decides;
If intricate her way, her walk discretion
    guides.
    Home to her country she returns alone,
Her health decay'd, her child, her husband,
    gone;
There she in peace reposes, there resumes
Her female duties, and in rest re-blooms;

She is not one at common ills to droop,
Nor to vain murmuring will her spirit stoop.
  I leave her thus : her fortieth year is nigh,
She will not for another captain sigh ;
Will not a young and gay lieutenant take,
Because 'tis pretty to reform a rake ;
Yet she again may plight her widow'd hand,
Should love invite, or charity demand ;
And make her days, although for duty's sake,
As sad as folly and mischance can make.

II

  P. LIVES yet the WIDOW, whose firm spirit bore
Ills unrepining ?—
            F. Here she lives no more,
But where—I speak with some good people's leave—
Where all good works their due reward receive ;
Though what reward to our best works is due
I leave to them,—and will my tale pursue.
  Again she married, to her husband's friend
Whose wife was hers, whom going to attend,
As on her death-bed she, yet young, was laid,
The anxious parent took her hand and said,
' Prove *now* your love ; let these poor infants be
As thine, and find a mother's love in thee ! '
  ' And must I woo their father ? '—' Nay, indeed ;
He no encouragement but hope will need ;
In hope too let me die, and think my wish decreed.'
  The wife expires ; the widow'd pair unite ;
Their love was sober, and their prospect bright.
She train'd the children with a studious love,
That knew full well t' encourage and reprove ;
Nicely she dealt her praise and her disgrace,
Not harsh and not indulgent out of place,
Not to the forward partial—to the slow
All patient, waiting for the time to sow
The seeds that, suited to the soil, would grow.
  Nor watch'd she less the Husband's weaker soul,
But learn'd to lead him who abhorr'd control,
Who thought a nursery, next a kitchen, best
To women suited, and she acquiesced ;
She only begg'd to rule in small affairs,
And ease her wedded lord of common cares,
Till he at length thought every care was small,
Beneath his notice, and she had them all.

He on his throne the lawful monarch sate,
And she was by—the minister of state :
He gave assent, and he required no more,
But sign'd the act that she decreed before.
  Again, her fates in other work decree
A mind so active should experienced be.
  One of the name, who roved the world around,
At length had something of its treasures found,
And childless died, amid his goods and gain,
In far Barbadoes on the western main.
His kinsman heard, and wish'd the wealth to share,
But had no mind to be transported there :—
' His Wife could sail—her courage who could doubt ?—
And she was not tormented with the gout.'
  She liked it not ; but for his children's sake,
And for their father's, would the duty take.
Storms she encounter'd, ere she reach'd the shore,
And other storms when these were heard no more,—
The rage of lawyers forced to drop their prey,—
And once again to England made her way.
  She found her Husband with his gout removed,
And a young nurse, most skilful and approved ;
Whom—for he yet was weak—he urged to stay,
And nurse him while his consort was away :—
' She was so handy, so discreet, so nice,
As kind as comfort, though as cold as ice !
Else,' he assured his lady, ' in no case,
So young a creature should have fill'd the place.'
  It has been held—indeed, the point is clear,
' None are so deaf as those who will not hear : '
And, by the same good logic, we shall find,
' As those who will not see, are none so blind.'
The thankful Wife repaid th' attention shown,
But now would make the duty all her own.
  Again the gout return'd ; but seizing now
A vital part, would no relief allow,
  The Husband died, but left a will that proved
He much respected whom he coolly loved.
All power was hers ; nor yet was such her age,
But rivals strove her favour to engage :

They talk'd of love with so much warmth and
    zeal,
That they believed the woman's heart must
    feel ;
Adding such praises of her worth beside,
As vanquish prudence oft by help of pride.
    In vain ! her heart was by discretion led—
She to the children of her Friend was wed ;
These she establish'd in the world, and died,
In ease and hope, serene and satisfied.
    And loves not man that woman who can
    charm
Life's grievous ills, and grief itself disarm ?—
Who in his fears and troubles brings him aid,
And seldom is, and never seems, afraid ?
    No ! ask of man the fair one whom he loves,
You'll find her one of the desponding doves,
Who tender troubles as her portion brings,
And with them fondly to a husband clings—
Who never moves abroad, nor sits at home,
Without distress, past, present, or to come—
Who never walks the unfrequented street,
Without a dread that death and she shall
    meet :
On land, on water, she must guarded be,
Who sees the danger none besides her see,
And is determined by her cries to call
All men around her : she will have them all.
    Man loves to think the tender being lives
But by the power that his protection gives :

He loves the feeble step, the plaintive tone,
And flies to help who cannot stand alone :
He thinks of propping elms, and clasping
    vines,
And in her weakness thinks her virtue shines ;
On him not one of her desires is lost,
And he admires her for this care and cost.
    But when afflictions come, when beauty
    dies,
Or sorrows vex the heart, or danger tries—
When time of trouble brings the daily care,
And gives of pain as much as he can bear—
'Tis then he wants, if not the helping hand,
At least a soothing temper, meek and bland—
He wants the heart that shares in his distress,
At least the kindness that would make it less ;
And when instead he hears th' eternal grief
For some light want, and not for his relief—
And when he hears the tender trembler sigh,
For some indulgence he can not supply—
When, in the midst of many a care, his ' dear,'
Would like a duchess at a ball appear—
And, while he feels a weight that wears him
    down,
Would see the prettiest sight in all the town,—
Love then departs, and if some Pity lives,
That Pity half despises, half forgives,
'Tis join'd with grief, is not from shame
    exempt,
And has a plenteous mixture of contempt.

TALE XV. BELINDA WATERS

I

Of all the beauties in our favour'd place,
Belinda Waters was the pride and grace.
Say ye who sagely can our fortunes read,
Shall this fair damsel in the world succeed ?
    A rosy beauty she, and fresh and fair,
Who never felt a caution or a care ;
Gentle by nature, ever fond of ease,
And more consenting than inclined to please.
A tame good nature in her spirit lives—
She hates refusal for the pain it gives :
From opposition arguments arise,
And to prevent the trouble, she complies.
She, if in Scotland, would be *fash'd* all day,
If call'd to any work or any play ;
She lets no busy, idle wish intrude,
But is by nature negatively good.

    In marriage hers will be a dubious fate :
She is not fitted for a high estate ;—
There wants the grace, the polish, and the
    pride ;
Less is she fitted for a humble bride :
Whom fair Belinda weds—let chance decide !
    She sees her father oft engross'd by
    cares,
And therefore hates to hear of men's affairs :
An active mother in the household reigns,
And spares Belinda all domestic pains.
Of food she knows but this, that we are fed :—
Though, duly taught, she prays for daily
    bread,
Yet whence it comes, of hers is no concern—
It comes ! and more she never wants to learn.
    She on the table sees the common fare,
But how provided is beneath her care.

Lovely and useless, she has no concern
About the things that aunts and mothers
    learn ;
But thinks, when married,—if she thinks at
    all,—
That what she needs will answer to her call.
    To write is business, and, though taught to
      write,
She keeps the pen and paper out of sight :
What once was painful she cannot allow
To be enjoyment or amusement now.
She wonders why the ladies are so fond
Of such long letters, when they correspond.
Crowded and cross'd by ink of different stain,
She thinks to read them would confuse her
    brain ;
Nor much mistakes ; but still has no pretence
To praise for this, her critic's indolence.
    Behold her now ! she on her sofa looks
O'er half a shelf of circulating books.
This she admired, but she forgets the name,
And reads again another, or the same.
She likes to read of strange and bold escapes,
Of plans and plottings, murders and mishaps,
Love in all hearts, and lovers in all shapes.
She sighs for pity, and her sorrows flow
From the dark eyelash on the page below ;
And is so glad when, all the misery past,
The dear adventurous lovers meet at last—
Meet and are happy ; and she thinks it
    hard,
When thus an author might a pair reward—
When they, the troubles all dispersed, might
    wed—
He makes them part, and die of grief instead !
Yet tales of terror are her dear delight,
All in the wintry storm to read at night ;
And to her maid she turns in all her doubt,—
' This shall I like ? and what is that about ? '
    She had ' Clarissa ' for her heart's dear
      friend—
Was pleased each well-tried virtue to com-
    mend,
And praised the scenes that one might fairly
    doubt,
If one so young could know so much about :
Pious and pure, th' heroic beauty strove
Against the lover and against the love ;
But strange that maid so young should know
    the strife,
In all its views, was painted to the life !
Belinda knew not—nor a tale would read,
That could so slowly on its way proceed ;

And ere Clarissa reach'd the wicked town,
The weary damsel threw the volume down.
' Give me,' she said, ' for I would laugh or
    cry,
" Scenes from the Life," and " Sensibility ; "
" Winters at Bath,"—I would that I had one !
" The Constant Lover," the " Discarded Son,"
" The Rose of Raby," " Delmore," or " The
    Nun."
These promise something, and may please,
    perhaps,
Like " Ethelinda," and the dear " Relapse." '
To these her heart the gentle maid resign'd,
And such the food that fed the gentle mind.

II

    P. KNEW you the fair BELINDA, once the
      boast
Of a vain mother, and a favourite toast
Of clerks and young lieutenants, a gay set
Of light admirers ?—Is she married yet ?
    F. Yes ! she is married ; though she
      waited long,
Not from a prudent fear of choosing wrong,
But want of choice.—She took a surgeon's
    mate,
With his half pay, that was his whole estate.
    Fled is the charming bloom that nature
      spread
Upon her cheek, the pure, the rosy red—
This, and the look serene, the calm, kind look,
    are fled.
Sorrow and sadness now the place possess,
And the pale cast of anxious fretfulness.
    She *wonders* much—as, why they live so
      ill,—
Why the rude butcher brings his weekly
    bill,—
She wonders why that baker will not trust,—
And says, most truly says,—' Indeed, he
    must.'
She wonders where her former friends are
    gone,—
And thus, from day to day, she wonders on.
Howe'er she can—she dresses gaily yet,
And then she wonders how they came in debt.
Her husband loves her, and in accent mild,
Answers, and treats her like a fretted child ;
But when he, ruffled, makes severe replies,
And seems unhappy—then she pouts, and
    cries
' She wonders when she'll die ! '—She faints,
    but never dies.

' How well my father lived ! ' she says.—
  ' How well,
My dear, your father's creditors could tell ! '
And then she weeps, till comfort is applied,
That soothes her spleen or gratifies her pride :
Her dress and novels, visits and success
In a chance-game, are soft'ners of distress.
  So life goes on !—But who that loved his
    life,
Would take a fair Belinda for his wife ?
Who thinks that all are for their stations
    born,
Some to indulge themselves, and to adorn ;
And some, a useful people, to prepare,
Not being rich, good things for those who
    are,
And who are born, it cannot be denied,
To have their wants and their demands
    supplied.

She knows that money is a needful thing,
That fathers first, and then that husbands
  bring ;
Or if those persons should the aid deny,
Daughters and wives have but to faint and die,
Till flesh and blood can not endure the pain,
And then the lady lives and laughs again.
  To wed an ague, and to feel, for life,
Hot fits and cold succeeding in a wife ;
To take the pestilence with poison'd breath,
And wed some potent minister of death,
Is cruel fate—yet death is then relief ;
But thus to wed is ever-during grief.
  Oft have I heard, how blest the youth who
    weds
Belinda Waters !—rather he who dreads
That fate—a truth her husband well approves,
Who blames and fondles, humours, chides,
  and loves.

TALE XVI.   THE DEALER AND CLERK

I

BAD men are seldom cheerful ; but we see
That, when successful, they can merry be.
ONE whom I leave, his darling money lends,
On terms well known, to his unhappy
  friends ;
He farms and trades, and in his method treats
His guests, whom first he comforts, then he
  cheats.
HE knows their private griefs, their inward
  groans,
And then applies his leeches and his loans,
To failing, falling families—and gets,
I know not how, with large increase, their
  debts.
He early married, and the woman made
A losing bargain ; she with scorn was paid
For no small fortune.   On this slave he vents
His peevish slights, his moody discontents.
Her he neglects, indulging in her stead,
One whom he bribed to leave a husband's
  bed—
A young fair mother too, the pride and joy
Of him whom her desertion will destroy.
  The poor man walks by the adulterer's door,
To see the wife, whom he must meet no more :
She will not look upon the face of one
Whom she has blighted, ruined, and undone.

He feels the shame; his heart with grief is rent;
Hers is the guilt, and his the punishment.
  The cruel spoiler to his need would lend
Unsought relief—his need will soon have end :
Let a few wint'ry months in sorrow pass,
And on his corse shall grow the vernal grass.
Neighbours, indignant, of his griefs partake,
And hate the villain for the victim's sake ;
Wond'ring what bolt within the stores of
  heaven
Shall on that bold, offending wretch be driven.
  Alas ! my grieving friends, we cannot know
Why Heaven inflicts, and why suspends, the
  blow.
Meanwhile the godless man, who thus destroys
Another's peace, in peace his wealth enjoys,
And, every law evaded or defied,
Is with long life and prosperous fortune tried :
' How long ? ' the Prophet cried, and we,
  ' how long ? '
But think how quick that Eye, that Arm
  how strong,
And bear what seems not right, and trust it
  is not wrong.
  Does Heaven forbear ? then sinners mercy
    find—
Do sinners fall ? 'tis mercy to mankind.
ADIEU ! can one so miserable be,
Rich, wretched man! to barter fates with thee?

II

Yet, ere I go, some notice must be paid
To John, his Clerk, a man full sore afraid
Of his own frailty—many a troubled day
Has he walk'd doubtful in some close by-way,
Beseeching Conscience on her watch to keep,
Afraid that she one day should fall asleep.
    A quiet man was John : his mind was slow ;
Little he knew, and little sought to know.
He gave respect to worth, to riches more,
And had instinctive dread of being poor.
Humble and careful, diligent and neat,
He in the Dealer's office found a seat :
Happy in all things, till a fear began
To break his rest—He served a wicked man ;
Who spurn'd the way direct of honest trade,
But praised the laws his cunning could evade.
This crafty Dealer of religion spoke,
As if design'd to be the wise man's cloak,
And the weak man's encumbrance, whom it
    awes,
And keeps in dread of conscience and the
    laws ;
Yet, for himself, he loved not to appear
In her grave dress ; 'twas troublesome to
    wear.
This Dealer played at games of skill, and
    won
Sums that surprised the simple mind of John :
Nor trusted skill alone ; for well he knew,
What a sharp eye and dext'rous hand could do ;
When, if suspected, he had always by
The daring oath to back the cunning lie.
    John was distress'd, and said, with aching
    heart,
' I from the vile, usurious man must part ;
For if I go not—yet I mean to go—
This friend to me will to my soul be foe.
I serve my master : there is nought to blame ;
But whom he serves, I tremble but to name.'
    From such reflections sprung the painful
    fear,—
' The Foe of Souls is too familiar here :
My master stands between : so far, so good ;
But 'tis at best a dangerous neighbourhood.'
    Then livelier thoughts began this fear to
    chase,—
' It is a gainful, a convenient place :
If I should quit—another takes the pen,
And what a chance for my preferment then ?
Religion nothing by my going gains ;
If I depart, my master still remains.

True, I record the deeds that I abhor,
But these that master has to answer for.
Then say I leave the office ! his success,
And his injustice, will not be the less ;
Nay, would be greater—I am right to stay ;
It checks him, doubtless, in his fearful way.
Fain would I stay, and yet be not beguiled ;
But pitch is near, and man is soon defiled.'

III

P. Such were the Man and Master,—and
    I now
Would know if they together live, and how.
    To such enquiries, thus my Friend re-
        plied :—
F. The Wife was slain—or, say at least, she
    died.
But there are murders, that the human eye
Cannot detect,—which human laws defy :
There are the wrongs insulted fondness feels,
In many a secret wound that never heals ;
The Savage murders with a single blow ;
Murders like this are secret and are slow.
    Yet, when his victim lay upon her bier,
There were who witness'd that he dropt a
    tear ;
Nay, more, he praised the woman he had lost,
And undisputed paid the funeral cost.
    The Favourite now, her lord and master
    freed,
Prepared to wed, and be a wife indeed.
The day, 'twas said, was fix'd, the robes were
    bought,
A feast was order'd ; but a cold was caught,
And pain ensued, with fever—grievous pain,
With the mind's anguish that disturb'd the
    brain,—
Till nature ceased to struggle, and the mind
Saw clearly death before, and sin behind.
Priests and physicians gave what they could
    give ;
She turn'd away, and, shuddering, ceased to
    live.
    The Dealer now appeared awhile as one
Lost ; with but little of his race to run,
And that in sorrow : men with one consent,
And one kind hope, said, ' Bonner will repent.'
Alas ! we saw not what his fate would be,
But this we fear'd,—no penitence had he ;
Nor time for penitence, nor any time,
So quick the summons, to look back on crime.
    When he the partner of his sin entomb'd,
He paused awhile, and then the way resumed

Ev'n as before : yet was he not the same ;
The tempter once, he now the dupe became.
John long had left him, nor did one remain
Who would his harlot in her course refrain ;
Obsequious, humble, studious of his ease,
The present Phoebe only sought to please.
' With one so artless, what,' said he, ' to fear,
Or what to doubt, in one who holds me dear ?
Friends she may have, but me she will not
          wrong ;
If weak her judgment, yet her love is strong ;
And I am lucky now in age to find
A friend so trusty, and a nurse so kind.'
     Yet neither party was in peace : the man
Had restless nights, and in the morn began
To cough and tremble ; he was hot and cold—
He had a nervous fever, he was told.
His dreams—'twas strange, for none reflected
          less
On his past life—were frightful to excess ;
His favourite dinners were no more enjoy'd,
And, in a word, his spirits were destroy'd.
     And what of Phoebe ? She her measures
          plann'd ;
All but his money was at her command :
All would be hers when Heav'n her Friend
          should call ;
But Heav'n was slow, and much she long'd
          for all :—
' Mine when he dies, mean wretch ! and why
          not mine,
When it would prove him generous to resign
What he enjoys not ? '—Phoebe at command
Gave him his brandy with a liberal hand.
A way more quick and safe she did not know,
And brandy, though it might be sure, was
          slow.
But more she dared not ; for she felt a dread
Of being tried, and only wish'd him dead.
Such was her restless strife of hope and fear—
He might cough on for many a weary year ;
Nay, his poor mind was changing, and when
          ill,
Some foe to her may wicked thoughts instil !
Oh ! 'tis a trial sore to watch a Miser's will.
Thus, though the pair appear'd in peace to
          live,
They felt that vice has not that peace to give.
     There watch'd a cur before the Miser's
          gate,
A very cur, whom all men seem'd to hate ;
Gaunt, savage, shaggy, with an eye that shone
Like a live coal, and he possess'd but one ;

His bark was wild and eager, and became
That meagre body and that eye of flame ;
His master prized him much, and *Fang* his
          name.
His master fed him largely ; but not that,
Nor aught of kindness, made the snarler fat.
Flesh he devour'd, but not a bit would stay ;
He bark'd, and snarl'd, and growl'd it all
          away.
His ribs were seen extended like a rack,
And coarse red hair hung roughly o'er his
          back.
Lamed in one leg, and bruised in wars of yore,
Now his sore body made his temper sore.
Such was the friend of him, who could not
          find,
Nor make him one, 'mong creatures of his kind.
Brave deeds of Fang his master often told,
The son of Fury, famed in days of old,
From Snatch and Rabid sprung ; and noted
          they
In earlier times—each dog will have his day.
     The notes of Fang were to his master known,
And dear—they bore some likeness to his
          own ;
For both convey'd to the experienced ear,
' I snarl and bite, because I hate and fear.'
None pass'd ungreeted by the master's door,
Fang rail'd at all, but chiefly at the poor ;
And when the nights were stormy, cold, and
          dark,
The act of Fang was a perpetual bark ;
But though the master loved the growl of
          Fang,
There were who vow'd the ugly cur to hang ;
Whose angry master, watchful for his friend,
As strongly vow'd his servant to defend.
     In one dark night, and such as Fang before
Was ever known its tempests to outroar,
To his protector's wonder now express'd
No angry notes—his anger was at rest.
The wond'ring master sought the silent yard,
Left Phoebe sleeping, and his door unbarr'd ;
Nor more returned to that forsaken bed—
But lo ! the morning came, and he was dead.
Fang and his master side by side were laid
In grim repose—their debt of nature paid !
The master's hand upon the cur's cold chest
Was now reclined, and had before been
          press'd,
As if he search'd how deep and wide the
          wound
That laid such spirit in a sleep so sound ;

And when he found it was the sleep of death,
A sympathising sorrow stopp'd his breath.
Close to his trusty servant he was found,
As cold his body, and his sleep as sound.

We know no more; but who on horrors
   dwell
Of that same night have dreadful things to
   tell :
Of outward force, they say, was not a sign—
The hand that struck him was the Hand
   Divine ;
And then the Fiend, in that same stormy
   night,
Was heard—as many thought—to claim his
   right ;
While grinning imps the body danced about,
And then they vanish'd with triumphant
   shout.

So think the crowd, and well it seems in
   them,
That ev'n their dreams and fancies vice con-
   demn ;
That not alone for virtue Reason pleads,
But Nature shudders at unholy deeds ;
While our strong fancy lists in her defence,
And takes the side of Truth and Innocence.

IV

P. But, what the fortune of the MAN,
   whose fear
Inform'd his Conscience that the foe was
   near ;
But yet whose interest to his desk confined
That sober CLERK of indecisive mind ?
F. JOHN served his master, with himself at
   strife,
For he with Conscience lived like man and
   wife ;
Now jarring, now at peace,—the life they led
Was all contention, both at board and bed :
His meals were troubled by his scruples all,
And in his dreams he was about to fall
Into some strong temptation—for it seems
He never could resist it in his dreams.

At length his MASTER, dealer, smuggler,
   cheat,
As John would call him in his temper's heat,
Proposed a something—what, is dubious
   still—
That John resisted with a stout good-will.
Scruples like his were treated with disdain,
Whose waking conscience spurn'd the offer'd
   gain.

' Quit then my office, scoundrel ! and be
   gone.'
' I dare not do it,' said the affrighten'd John.
' What fear'st thou, driveller! can thy fancy
   tell ? '
' I doubt,' said John—' I'm sure there is a
   hell.'
' No question, wretch ! thy foot is on the
   door ;
To be in hell, thou fool ! is to be poor :
Wilt thou consent ? '—But John, with many
   a sigh,
Refused, then sank beneath his stronger eye,
Who with a curse dismiss'd the fool that dared
Not join a venture which he might have
   shared.

The worthy Clerk then served a man in
   trade,
And was his friend and his companion made—
A sickly man, who sundry wares retail'd,
Till, while his trade increased, his spirit fail'd.
John was to him a treasure, whom he proved,
And, finding faithful, as a brother loved.
To John his views and business he consign'd,
And forward look'd with a contented mind :
As sickness bore him onward to the grave,
A charge of all things to his friend he gave.

But neighbours talk'd—'twas idle—of the
   day
When Richard Shale should walk the dark
   highway—
And whisper'd—tatlers !—that the wife
   received
Such hints with anger, but she nothing
   grieved.

These whispers reach'd the man, who weak,
   and ill
In mind and body, had to make his will ;
And though he died in peace, and all resign'd,
'Twas plain he harbour'd fancies in his mind.
With jealous foresight, all that he had gain'd
His widow's was, while widow she remain'd ;
But if another should the dame persuade
To wed again, farewell the gains of trade :
For if the widow'd dove could not refrain,
She must return to poverty again.

The man was buried, and the will was read,
And censure spared them not, alive or dead !
At first the Widow and the Clerk, her friend,
Spent their free days as prudence bade them
   spend.
At the same table they would dine, 'tis true,
And they would worship in the self-same pew :

Each had the common interest so at heart,
It would have grieved them terribly to part;
And as they both were serious and sedate,
'Twas long before the world began to prate:
But when it prated,—though without a
     cause,—
It put the pair in mind of breaking laws,
Led them to reason what it was that gave
A husband power, when quiet in his grave.
The marriage contract they had now by
     heart—
' Till death ! '—you see, no longer—' do us
     part.'
' Well ! death has loosed us from the tie,
     but still
The loosen'd husband makes a binding will :
Unjust and cruel are the acts of men.'
Thus they—and then they sigh'd—and then
     —and then,
' 'Twas snaring souls,' they said ; and how
     he dared
They did not know—they wonder'd—and
     were snared.
     ' It is a marriage, surely ! Conscience
     might
Allow an act so very nearly right :
Was it not witness to our solemn vow,
As man and wife ? it must the act allow.'
But Conscience, stubborn to the last, replied,
' It cannot be ! I am not satisfied ;
'Tis not a marriage : either dare be poor,
Or dare be virtuous—part, and sin no more.'
     Alas ! they many a fond evasion made ;
They could relinquish neither love nor trade.
They went to church, but thinking, fail'd to
     pray ;
They felt not ease or comfort at a play :
If times were good,—' We merit not such
     times,'
If ill,—' Is this the produce of our crimes ? '
When sick—' 'Tis thus forbidden pleasures
     cease.'
When well—they both demand, ' Had Zimri
     peace ?
For though our worthy master was not slain,
His injured ghost has reason to complain.'
     Ah, John ! bethink thee of thy generous
     joy,
When Conscience drove thee from thy late
     employ ;
When thou wert poor, and knew not where
     to run,
But then could say ' The will of God be done !'

When thou that will, and not thine own
     obey'd,—
Of Him alone, and not of man afraid :
Thou then hadst pity on that wretch, and,
     free
Thyself, couldst pray for him who injured
     thee.
Then how alert thy step, thyself how light
All the day long ! thy sleep how sound at
     night !
     But now, though plenty on thy board be
     found,
And thou hast credit with thy neighbours
     round,
Yet there is something in thy looks that
     tells,
An odious secret in thy bosom dwells :
Thy form is not erect, thy neighbours trace
A coward spirit in thy shifting pace.
Thou goest to meeting, not from any call,
But just to hear, that we are sinners all,
And equal sinners, or the difference made
'Twixt man and man has but the slightest
     shade ;
That reformation asks a world of pains,
And, after all, must leave a thousand stains
And, worst of all, we must the work begin
By first attacking the prevailing sin !—
     These thoughts the feeble mind of John
     assail,
And o'er his reason and his fears prevail :
They fill his mind with hopes of gifts and grace,
Faith, feelings !—something that supplies the
     place
Of true conversion—this will he embrace ;
For John perceives that he was scarcely tried
By the first conquest, that increased his pride,
When he refused his master's crime to aid,
And by his self-applause was amply paid ;
But now he feels the difference—feels it hard
Against his will and favourite wish to guard :
He mourns his weakness, hopes he shall
     prevail
Against his frailty, and yet still is frail.
     Such is his life ! and such the life must be
Of all who will be bound, yet would be free ;
Who would unite what God to part decrees—
The offended conscience, and the mind at
     ease;
Who think, but vainly think, to sin and pray,
And God and Mammon in their turn obey.
Such is his life !—and so I would not live
For all that wealthy widows have to give.

TALE XVII. DANVERS AND RAYNER

I

THE purest Friendship, like the finest ware,
Deserves our praises, but demands our care.
For admiration we the things produce,
But they are not design'd for common use ;
Flaws the most trifling from their virtue take,
And lamentation for their loss we make :
While common Friendships, like the wares of
    clay,
Are a cheap kind, but useful every day :
Though crack'd and damaged, still we make
    them do,
And when they're broken, they're forgotten
    too.
  There is within the world in which we dwell
A Friendship, answering to that world full
    well ;
An interchange of looks and actions kind,
And, in some sense, an intercourse of mind ;
A useful commerce, a convenient trade,
By which both parties are the happier made ;
And, when the thing is rightly understood,
And justly valued, it is wise and good.
  I speak not here of Friendships that excite
In boys at school such wonder and delight,—
Of high heroic Friends, in serious strife,
Contending which should yield a forfeit life—
Such wondrous love, in their maturer days,
Men, if they credit, are content to praise.
  I speak not here of Friendships true and
    just,
When friend can friend with life and honour
    trust ;
Where mind to mind has long familiar grown,
And every failing, every virtue known :
Of these I speak not : things so rich and rare,
That we degrade with jewels to compare,
Or bullion pure and massy.—I intend
To treat of one whose Neighbour called him
    Friend,
Or called him Neighbour ; and with reason
    good—
The friendship rising from the neighbourhood :
A sober kind, in common service known ;
Not such as is in death and peril shown :
Such as will give or ask a helping hand,
But no important sacrifice demand ;

In fact, a friendship that will long abide,
If seldom rashly, never strongly, tried.
Yes ! these are sober friendships, made for
    use,
And much convenience they in life produce :
Like a good coat, that keeps us from the
    cold,
The cloth of frieze is not a cloth of gold ;
But neither is it pyebald, pieced, and poor ;
'Tis a good useful coat, and nothing more.
  Such is the Friendship of the world ap-
    proved,
And here the Friends so loving and so
    loved :—
DANVERS and RAYNER, equals, who had made
Each decent fortune, both were yet in trade ;
While sons and daughters, with a youthful
    zeal,
Seem'd the hereditary love to feel :
And ev'n their wives, though either might
    pretend
To claim some notice, call'd each other friend.
  While yet their offspring boys and girls
    appear'd,
The fathers ask'd, 'What evil could be
    fear'd ? '
Nor is it easy to assign the year,
When cautious parents should begin to fear.
The boys must leave their schools, and, by
    and by,
The girls are sure to grow reserved and shy ;
And then, suppose a real love should rise,
It but unites the equal families.
  Love does not always from such freedom
    spring ;
Distrust, perhaps, would sooner cause the
    thing.
' We will not check it, neither will we force '—
Thus said the fathers—' Let it take its course.'
  It took its course:—young Richard Danvers'
    mind
In Phoebe Rayner found what lovers find—
Sense, beauty, sweetness ; all that mortal
    eyes
Can see, or heart conceive, or thought devise.
And Phoebe's eye, and thought, and heart
    could trace
In Richard Danvers every manly grace—

All that e'er maiden wish'd, or matron
    prized—
So well these good young people sympathised.
    All their relations, neighbours, and allies,
All their dependants, visitors, and spies,
Such as a wealthy family caress,
Said here was love, and drank to love's
    success.
    'Tis thus I leave the parties, young and old,
Lovers and Friends.   Will Love and Friend-
    ship hold ?
Will Prudence with the children's wish
    comply,
And Friendship strengthen with that new
    ally ?

II

    P. I SEE no more within our borough's
        bound
The name of DANVERS ! Is it to be found ?
Were the young pair in Hymen's fetters tied,
Or did succeeding years the Friends divide ?
    F. Nay ! take the story, as by time brought
        forth,
And of such Love and Friendship judge the
    worth.
While the lad's love—his parents call'd it so—
Was going on, as well as love could go,
A wealthy Danvers, in a distant place,
Left a large fortune to this favour'd race.
To that same place the father quickly went,
And Richard only murmur'd weak dissent.
    Of Richard's heart the parent truly
        guess'd :—
' Well, my good lad ! then do what suits thee
    best ;
No doubt thy brothers will do all they can
T' obey the orders of the good old man :
Well, I would not thy free-born spirit bind ;
Take, Dick, the way to which thou 'rt most
    inclined.'
    No answer gave the youth ; nor did he
        swear
The old man's riches were beneath his care ;
Nor that he would with his dear Phoebe stay,
And let his heartless father move away.
No ! kind and constant, tender, faithful,
    fond,—
Thus far he'd go—but not one step beyond !
Not disobedient to a parent's will—
A lover constant—but dependent still.
    Letters, at first, between the constant swain
And the kind damsel banish'd all their pain :

Both full and quick they were ; for lovers
    write
With vast despatch, and read with vast
    delight—
So quick they were,—for Love is never
    slow,—
So full, they ever seem'd to overflow.
Their hearts are ever fill'd with grief or joy,
And these to paint is every hour's employ :
Joy they would not retain ; and for their
    grief,
To read such letters is a sure relief.
    But, in due time, both joy and grief
        supprest,
They found their comfort in a little rest.
Mails went and came without the accustom'd
    freight,
For Love grew patient, and content to wait—
Yet was not dead, nor yet afraid to die ;
For though he wrote not, Richard wonder'd
    why.
He could not justly tell how letters pass'd,
But, as to him appear'd, he wrote the last :
In this he meant not to accuse the maid—
Love, in some cases, ceases to upbraid.
    Yet not indifferent was our Lover grown,
Although the ardour of the flame was flown ;
He still of Phoebe thought, her lip, her
    smile—
But grew contented with his fate the while.
Thus, not inconstant were the youthful pair—
The Lad remembered still the Lass was fair ;
And Phoebe still, with half-affected sigh,
Thought it a pity that such love should die ;
And had they then, with this persuasion,
    met,
Love had rekindled, and been glowing yet.
    But times were changed : no mention now
        was made
By the old Squire, or by the young, of trade.
The worthy Lady, and her children all,
Had due respect—The People at the Hall.
His Worship now read Burn, and talk'd with
    skill
About the poor-house, and the turnpike bill ;
Lord of a manor, he had serious claims,
And knew the poaching rascals by their
    names :
And if the father thus improved his mind,
Be sure the children were not far behind :
To rank and riches what respect was due,
To them and theirs what deference, well they
    knew ;

And, from the greatest to the least, could
    show
What to the favouring few the favour'd many
    owe.
  The mind of man must have whereon to
    work,
Or it will rust—we see it in the Turk ;
And Justice Danvers, though he read the
    news,
And all of law that magistrates peruse,—
Bills about roads and charities,—yet still
Wanted employ his vacant mind to fill ;
These were not like the shipping, once his
    pride,
Now, with his blue surtout, laid all aside.
  No doubt, his spirits in their ebb to raise,
He found some help in men's respect and
    praise—
Praise of his house, his land, his lawn, his
    trees—
He cared not what—to praise him was to
    please :
Yet though his rural neighbours called to dine,
And some might kindly praise his food and
    wine,
This was not certain, and another day,
He must the visit and the praise repay.
  By better motives urged—we will suppose—
He thus began his purpose to disclose
To his good lady :—' We have lived a year,
And never ask'd our friends the Rayners here:
Do let us ask them—as for Richard's flame,
It went, we see, as idly as it came—
Invite them kindly—here's a power of room,
And the poor people will be glad to come.
Outside and in, the coach will hold them
    all,
And set them down beside the garden wall.'
  The Lady wrote, for that was all he meant,
Kind soul ! by asking for his wife's assent :
And every Rayner was besought to come
To dine in Hulver Hall's grand dining-room.
  About this time old Rayner, who had lost
His Friend's advice, was by misfortune
    cross'd :
Some debtors fail'd, when large amounts were
    due,
So large, that he was nearly failing too ;
But he, grown wary, that he might not fail,
Brought to in adverse gales, and shorten'd
    sail :
This done, he rested, and could now attend
The invitation of his distant Friend.

' Well ! he would go ; but not, indeed,
    t' admire
The state and grandeur of the new-made
    Squire ;
Danvers, belike, now wealthy, might impart
Some of his gold ; for Danvers had a heart,
And may have heard, though guarded so
    around,
That I have lost the fortune he has found :
Yes ! Dick is kind, or he and his fine seat
Might go to——where we never more should
    meet.'
  Now, lo ! the Rayners all at Hulver Place,—
Or Hulver Hall—'tis not a certain case ;
'Tis only known that Ladies' notes were
    sent
Directed both ways, and they always went.
  We pass the greetings, and the dinner pass,
All the male gossip o'er the sparkling glass,
And female when retired :—The Squire in-
    vites
His Friend, by sleep refresh'd, to see his
    sights—
His land and lions, granary, barns, and crops,
His dairy, piggery, pinery, apples, hops ;—
But here a hill appears, and Peter Rayner
    stops.
  ' Ah ! my old Friend, I give you joy,' he
    cries :
' But some are born to fall, and some to rise ;
You're better many a thousand, I the worse—
Dick, there 's no dealing with a failing purse ;
Nor does it shame me (mine is all mischance)
To wish some friendly neighbour would
    advance '—
——But here the guest on such a theme was
    low.
His host, meantime, intent upon the show,
In hearing heard not—they came out to see,—
And pushing forward—' There 's a view,'
    quoth he :
' Observe that ruin, built, you see, to catch
The gazer's eye ; that cottage with the
    thatch—
It cost me—guess you what ? '—that sound
    of *cost*
Was accidental, but it was not lost.
  ' Ah ! my good Friend, be sure such things
    as these
Suit well enough a man who lives at ease :
Think what " The Betsy " *cost*, and think the
    shock
Of losing her upon the Dodder-Rock :

The tidings reach'd me on the very day
That villain robb'd us, and then ran away.
Loss upon loss! now if—— '
                    ' Do stay a bit ; '
Exclaim'd the Squire, ' these matters hardly fit
A morning ramble—let me show you now
My team of oxen, and my patent plough.
Talk of your horses ! I the plan condemn—
They eat us up—but oxen ! we eat them ;
For first they plough and bring us bread to eat,
And then we fat and kill them—there 's the
    meat.
What 's your opinion ? '—
              —' I am poorly fed,
And much afraid to want both meat and
    bread,'
Said Rayner, half indignant ; and the Squire
Sigh'd, as he felt he must no more require
A man, whose prospects fail'd, his prospects
    to admire.
    Homeward they moved, and met a gentle
      pair,
The poor man's daughter, and the rich man's
    heir :
This caused some thought ; but on the couple
    went,
And a soft hour in tender converse spent.
This pair, in fact, their passion roused anew,
Alone much comfort from the visit drew.
    At home the Ladies were engaged, and all
Show'd or were shown the wonders of the Hall ;
From room to room the weary guests went on,
Till every Rayner wish'd the show was done.
    Home they return'd : the Father deeply
      sigh'd
To find he vainly had for aid applied :
It hurt him much to ask—and more to be
    denied.
    The younger Richard, who alone sustain'd
The dying Friendship, true to Love remain'd :
His Phoebe's smiles, although he did not yet
Fly to behold, he could not long forget ;
Nor durst he visit, nor was love so strong,
That he could more than think his Father
    wrong ;
For, wrong or right, that father still profess'd
The most obedient son should fare the best.
    So time pass'd on ; the second spring
      appear'd,
Ere Richard ventured on the deed he fear'd :—
He dared at length ; and not so much for
    love,
I grieve to add, but that he meant to prove

He had a will :—His father, in reply,
This known, had answer'd, ' So, my son,
    have I.'
But Richard's courage was by prudence
    taught,
And he his nymph in secret service sought.
Some days of absence—not with full consent,
But with slow leave—were to entreaty lent ;
And forth the Lover rode, uncertain what he
    meant.
    He reached the dwelling he had known so
      long,
When a pert damsel told him, ' he was wrong ;
Their house she did not just precisely know,
But he would find it somewhere in the Row ;
The Rayners now were come a little down,
Nor more the topmost people in the town ; '
She might have added, they their life enjoy'd,
Although on things less hazardous employ'd.
    This was not much ; but yet the damsel's
      sneer,
And the Row-dwelling of a lass so dear,
Were somewhat startling. He had heard,
    indeed,
That Rayner's business did not well succeed :
' But what of that ? They lived in decent
    style,
No doubt, and Phoebe still retain'd her smile ;
And why,' he asked, ' should all men choose
    to dwell
In broad cold streets ?—the Row does just
    as well,
Quiet and snug ; ' and then the favourite
    maid
Rose in his fancy, tastefully array'd,
Looking with grateful joy upon the swain,
Who could his love in trying times retain.
    Soothed by such thoughts, to the new house
      he came,
Surveyed its aspect, sigh'd, and gave his
    name.
But ere they opened, he had waited long,
And heard a movement—Was there some-
    what wrong ?
Nay, but a friendly party, he was told ;
And look'd around, as wishing to behold
Some friends—but these were not the friends
    of old.
    Old Peter Rayner, in his own old mode,
Bade the Squire welcome to his new abode,
For Richard had been kind, and doubtless
    meant
To make proposals now, and ask consent.

Mamma and misses, too, were civil all ;
But what their awkward courtesy to call,
He knew not ; neither could he well express
His sad sensations at their strange address.
And then their laughter loud, their story-
telling,
All seem'd befitting to that Row and dwelling;
The hearty welcome to the various treat
Was lost on him—he could nor laugh nor eat.
  But one thing pleased him, when he look'd
around,
His dearest Phoebe could not there be found :
' Wise and discreet,' he says, ' she shuns the
crew
Of vulgar neighbours, some kind act to do ;
In some fair house, some female friend to meet,
Or take at evening prayer in church her seat.'
  Meantime there rose, amid the ceaseless din,
A mingled scent, that crowded room within,
Rum and red-herring, Cheshire cheese and
gin ;
Pipes, too, and punch, and sausages, with tea,
Were things that Richard was disturb'd to
see.
Impatient now, he left them in disdain,
To call on Phoebe, when he call'd again ;
To walk with her, the morning fair and bright,
And lose the painful feelings of the night.
  All in the Row, and tripping at the side
Of a young Sailor, he the nymph espied,
As homeward hastening with her happy boy,
She went to join the party, and enjoy.
' Fie !' Phoebe cried, as her companion spoke,
Yet laugh'd to hear the fie-compelling joke ;—
Just then her chance to meet, her shame to
knew,
Her tender Richard, moving sad and slow,

Musing on things full strange, the manners of
the Row.
  At first amazed, and then alarm'd, the fair
Late-laughing maid now stood in dumb
despair :
As when a debtor meets in human shape
The foe of debtors, and cannot escape,
He stands in terror, nor can longer aim
To keep his credit, or preserve his name,
Stood Phoebe fix'd ! ' Unlucky time and
place !
An earlier hour had kept me from disgrace !'
She thought—but now the sailor, undismay'd,
Said, ' My dear Phoebe, why are you afraid ?
The man seems civil, or he soon should prove
That I can well defend the girl I love.
Are you not mine ?' She utter'd no reply:—
' Thine I must be,' she thought ; ' more
foolish I !'
While Richard at the scene stood mute and
wondering by.
  His spirits hurried, but his bosom light,
He left his Phoebe with a calm ' good night.'
So Love like Friendship fell ! The youth
awhile
Dreamt, sorely moved, of Phoebe's witching
smile—
But learned in daylight visions to forego,
The Sailor's laughing Lass, the Phoebe of the
Row.
  Home turn'd young Richard, in due time
to turn,
With all old Richard's zeal, the leaves of
Burn ;
And home turned Phoebe—in due time to
grace
A tottering cabin with a tattered race.

TALE XVIII. THE BOAT RACE

I

THE man who dwells where party-spirit
reigns,
May feel its triumphs, but must wear its chains;
He must the friends and foes of party take
For his, and suffer for his honour's sake ;
When once enlisted upon either side,
He must the rude septennial storm abide—
A storm that when its utmost rage is gone,
In cold and angry mutterings murmurs on :

A slow unbending scorn, a cold disdain,
Till years bring the full tempest back again.
  Within our Borough two stiff sailors dwelt,
Who both this party storm and triumph felt ;
Men who had talents, and were both design'd
For better things, but anger made them blind.
  In the same year they married, and their wives
Had pass'd in friendship their yet peaceful
lives,
And, as they married in a time of peace,
Had no suspicion that their love must cease.

In fact it did not ; but they met by stealth,
And that perhaps might keep their love in
    health ;
Like children watch'd, desirous yet afraid,
Their visits all were with discretion paid.
  One Captain, so by courtesy we call
Our hoy's commanders—they are captains
    all—
Had sons and daughters many ; while but one
The rival Captain bless'd—a darling son.
Each was a burgess to his party tied,
And each was fix'd, but on a different side ;
And he who sought his son's pure mind to fill
With wholesome food, would evil too instil.
The last in part succeeded—but in part—
For Charles had sense, had virtue, had a
    heart ;
And he had soon the cause of Nature tried
With the stern father, but this father died ;
Who on his death-bed thus his son ad-
    dress'd :—
'Swear to me, Charles, and let my spirit rest—
Swear to our party to be ever true,
And let me die in peace—I pray thee, do.'
  With some reluctance, but obedience more,
The weeping youth reflected, sigh'd, and
    swore ;
Trembling, he swore for ever to be true,
And wear no colour but the untainted Blue :
This done, the Captain died in so much joy,
As if he'd wrought salvation for his boy.
  The female friends their wishes yet retain'd,
But seldom met, by female fears restrain'd ;
Yet in such town, where girls and boys must
    meet,
And every house is known in every street,
Charles had before, nay since his father's
    death,
Met, say by chance, the young Elizabeth ;
Who was both good and graceful, and in truth
Was but too pleasing to th' observing youth ;
And why I know not, but the youth to her
Seem'd just that being that she could prefer.
Both were disposed to think that party-strife
Destroy'd the happiest intercourse of life ;
Charles, too, his growing passion could
    defend—
His father's foe he call'd his mother's friend.
Mothers, indeed, he knew were ever kind ;
But in the Captain should he favour find ?
He doubted this—yet could he that command
Which fathers love, and few its power with-
    stand.

The mothers both agreed their joint request
Should to the Captain jointly be address'd ;
And first the lover should his heart assail,
And then the ladies, and if all should fail,
They'd singly watch the hour, and jointly
    might prevail.
  The Captain's heart, although unused to
    melt,
A strong impression from persuasion felt ;
His pride was soften'd by the prayers he
    heard,
And then advantage in the match appear'd
  At length he answer'd,—' Let the lad enlist
In our good cause, and I no more resist ;
For I have sworn, and to my oath am true,
To hate that colour, that rebellious Blue.
His father once, ere master of the brig,
For that advantage turn'd a rascal Whig :
Now let the son—a wife 's a better thing—
A Tory turn, and say, God save the King !
For I am pledged to serve that sacred cause,
And love my country, while I keep her laws.'
  The women trembled ; for they knew full
    well
The fact they dare not to the Captain tell ;
And the poor youth declared, with tears and
    sighs,
' My oath was pass'd : I dare not com-
    promise.'
  But Charles to reason made his strong
    appeal,
And to the heart—he bade him think and feel :
The Captain answering, with reply as strong—
' If you be right, then how can I be wrong ?
You to your father swore to take his part ;
I to oppose it ever, head and heart ;
You to a parent made your oath, and I
To God ! and can I to my Maker lie ?
Much, my dear lad, I for your sake would do,
But I have sworn, and to my oath am true.'
  Thus stood the parties when my fortunes
    bore
Me far away from this my native shore .
And who prevail'd, I know not—Young or
    Old ;
But, I beseech you, let the tale be told.

II

P. How fared these lovers ? Many a time
    I thought
How with their ill-starr'd passion Time had
    wrought.

Did either party from his oath recede,
Or were they never from the bondage freed?
　F. Alas! replied my Friend—the tale I tell
With some reluctance, nor can do it well.
There are three females in the place, and they,
Like skilful painters, could the facts portray,
In their strong colours—all that I can do
Is to present a weak imperfect view;
The colours I must leave—the outlines shall
　　be true.
Soon did each party see the other's mind,
What bound them both, and what was like to
　　bind;
Oaths deeply taken in such time and place,
To break them now was dreadful—was
　　disgrace!
　'That oath a dying father bade me take,
Can I—yourself a father—can I break?'
　'That oath which I a living sinner took,
Shall I make void, and yet for mercy look?'
　The women wept; the men, themselves
　　distress'd,
The cruel rage of party zeal confess'd:
But solemn oaths, though sprung from party
　　zeal,
Feel them we must, as Christians ought to feel.
　Yet shall a youth so good, a girl so fair,
From their obedience only draw despair?
Must they be parted? Is there not a way
For them both love and duty to obey?
Strongly they hoped; and by their friends
　　around
A way, at least a lover's way, was found.
　'Give up your vote; you'll then no longer
　　be
Free in one sense, but in the better free.'
Such was of reasoning friends the kind
　　advice,
And how could lovers in such case be nice?
A man may swear to walk directly on
While sight remains; but how if sight be
　　gone?
'Oaths are not binding when the party's
　　dead;
Or when the power to keep the oath is fled:
If I've no vote, I've neither friend nor foe,
Nor can be said on either side to go.'
They were no casuists:—'Well!' the
　　Captain cried,
'Give up your vote, man, and behold your
　　bride!'
　Thus was it fix'd, and fix'd the day for both
To take the vow, and set aside the oath.

It gave some pain, but all agreed to say,
'You're now absolved, and have no other
　　way:
'Tis not expected you should love resign
For man's commands, for love's are all divine.'
　When all is quiet and the mind at rest,
All in the calm of innocence are blest;
But when some scruple mixes with our joy,
We love to give the anxious mind employ.
　In autumn late, when evening suns were
　　bright,
The day was fix'd the lovers to unite;
But one before the eager Captain chose
To break, with jocund act, his girl's repose,
And, sailor-like, said, 'Hear how I intend
One day, before the day of days, to spend!
All round the quay, and by the river's side,
Shall be a scene of glory for the bride.
We'll have a RACE, and colours will devise
For every boat, for every man a prize:
But that which first returns shall bear away
The proudest pendant—Let us name the day.'
　They named the day, and never morn more
　　bright
Rose on the river, nor so proud a sight:
Or if too calm appear'd the cloudless skies,
Experienced seamen said the wind would rise.
To that full quay from this then vacant place
Thronged a vast crowd to see the promised
　　Race.
Mid boats new painted, all with streamers fair,
That flagg'd or flutter'd in that quiet air—
The Captain's boat that was so gay and trim,
That made his pride, and seem'd as proud of
　　him—
Her, in her beauty, we might all discern,
Her rigging new, and painted on the stern,
As one who could not in the contest fail,
'Learn of *the little Nautilus* to sail.'
So forth they started at the signal gun,
And down the river had three leagues to run;
This sail'd, they then their watery way
　　retrace,
And the first landed conquers in the race.
The crowd await till they no more discern,
Then parting say, 'At evening we return.'
I could proceed, but you will guess the fate,
And but too well my tale anticipate.
　P. True! yet proceed—
　　　　　F. The lovers had some grief
In this day's parting, but the time was brief;
And the poor girl, between his smiles and sighs,
Ask'd, 'Do you wish to gain so poor a prize?'

'But that your father wishes,' he replied,
'I would the honour had been still denied :
It makes me gloomy, though I would be gay,
And oh ! it seems an everlasting day.'
So thought the lass, and as she said, farewell !
Soft sighs arose, and tears unbidden fell.

The morn was calm, and ev'n till noon the
      strong
Unruffled flood moved quietly along ;
In the dead calm the billows softly fell,
And mock'd the whistling sea-boy's favourite
      spell :
So rests at noon the reaper, but to rise
With mightier force and twofold energies.
The deep, broad stream moved softly, all was
      hush'd,
When o'er the flood the breeze awakening
      brush'd ;
A sullen sound was heard along the deep,
The stormy spirit rousing from his sleep ;
The porpoise rolling on the troubled wave,
Unwieldy tokens of his pleasure gave ;
Dark, chilling clouds the troubled deep
      deform,
And led by terror downward rush'd the storm.

As evening came, along the river's side,
Or on the quay, impatient crowds divide,
And then collect ; some whispering, as afraid
Of what they saw, and more of what they
      said,
And yet must speak : how sudden and how
      great
The danger seem'd, and what might be the
      fate
Of men so toss'd about in craft so small,
Lost in the dark, and subject to the squall.
Then sounds are so appalling in the night,
And, could we see, how terrible the sight ;
None knew the evils that they all suspect,
And Hope at once they covet and reject.

But where the wife, her friend, her daughter,
      where ?
Alas ! in grief, in terror, in despair—
At home, abroad, upon the quay.   No rest
In any place, but where they are not, best.
Fearful they ask, but dread the sad reply,
And many a sailor tells the friendly lie—
'There is no danger—that is, we believe,
And think—and hope '—but this does not
      deceive,
Although it soothes them ; while they look
      around,
Trembling at every sight and every sound.

Let me not dwell on terrors——It is dark,
And lights are carried to and fro, and hark !
There is a cry—'a boat, a boat at hand ! '
What a still terror is there now on land !
'Whose, whose ? ' they all enquire, and none
      can understand.
At length they come—and oh ! how then
      rejoice
A wife and children at that welcome voice :
It is not theirs—but what have these to tell ?
'Where did you leave the Captain—were
      they well ? '
Alas ! they know not, they had felt an awe
In dread of death, and knew not what they
      saw.
Thus they depart.—The evening darker
      grows,
The lights shake wildly, and as wildly blows
The stormy night-wind : fear possesses all,
The hardest hearts, in this sad interval.

But hark again to voices loud and high !
Once more that hope, that dread, that agony,
That panting expectation ! 'Oh ! reveal
What must be known, and think what pangs
      we feel ! '
   In vain they ask !   The men now landed
      speak
Confused and quick, and to escape them seek.
Our female party on a sailor press,
But nothing learn that makes their terror
      less ;
Nothing the man can show, or nothing will
      confess.
To some, indeed, they whisper, bringing news
For them alone, but others they refuse ;
And steal away, as if they could not bear
The griefs they cause, and if they cause must
      share.

   They too are gone ! and our unhappy
      Three,
Half wild with fear, are trembling on the quay.
They can no ease, no peace, no quiet find,
The storm is gathering in the troubled mind ;
Thoughts after thoughts in wild succession
      rise,
And all within is changing like the skies.
Their friends persuade them, 'do depart, we
      pray ! '
They will not, must not, cannot go away,
But chill'd with icy fear, for certain tidings
      stay.
   And now again there must a boat be seen—
Men run together ! It must something mean !

Some figure moves upon the ousy bound
Where flows the tide—Oh! what can he
    have found—
What lost? And who is he?—The only one
Of the loved three—the Captain's younger son.
Their boat was fill'd and sank—He knows no
    more,
But that he only hardly reach'd the shore.
He saw them swimming—for he once was
    near—
But he was sinking, and he could not hear;
And then the waves curl'd round him, but at
    length,
He struck upon the boat with dying strength,
And that preserved him: when he turn'd
    around,
Nought but the dark, wild, billowy flood was
    found—
That flood was all he saw, that flood's the only
    sound—
Save that the angry wind, with ceaseless roar,
Dash'd the wild waves upon the rocky shore.
    The Widows dwell together—so we call
The younger woman; widow'd are they all:

But she, the poor Elizabeth, it seems
Not life in her—she lives not, but she dreams;
She looks on Philip, and in him can find
Not much to mark in body or in mind—
He who was saved; and then her very soul
Is in that scene!—Her thoughts beyond
    control,
Fix'd on that night, and bearing her along,
Amid the waters terrible and strong;
Till there she sees within the troubled waves
The bodies sinking in their wat'ry graves,
When from her lover, yielding up his breath,
There comes a voice,—' Farewell, Elizabeth!'
    Yet Resignation in the house is seen,
Subdued Affliction, Piety serene,
And Hope for ever striving to instil
The balm for grief—' It is the Heavenly will:'
And in that will our duty bids us rest,
For all that Heaven ordains is good, is best;
We sin and suffer—this alone we know,
Grief is our portion, is our part below;
But we shall rise, that world of bliss to see,
Where sin and suffering never more shall
    be.

TALE XIX. MASTER WILLIAM; OR, LAD'S LOVE

I

I HAVE remembrance of a BOY, whose mind
Was weak: he seem'd not for the world
    design'd,
Seem'd not as one who in that world could
    strive,
And keep his spirits even and alive—
A feeling BOY, and happy, though the less,
From that fine feeling, form'd for happiness.
His mother left him to his favourite ways,
And what he made his pleasure brought him
    praise.
    Romantic, tender, visionary, mild,
Affectionate, reflecting when a child,
With fear instinctive he from harshness fled,
And gentle tears for all who suffer'd shed;
Tales of misfortune touch'd his generous
    heart,
Of maidens left, and lovers forced to part.
    In spite of all that weak indulgence wrought,
That love permitted, or that flattery taught,
In spite of teachers who no fault would find,
The Boy was neither selfish nor unkind.

Justice and truth his honest heart approved,
And all things lovely he admired and loved.
Arabian Nights, and Persian Tales, he read,
And his pure mind with brilliant wonders fed.
The long Romances, wild Adventures fired
His stirring thoughts: he felt like Boy
    inspired.
The cruel fight, the constant love, the art
Of vile magicians, thrill'd his inmost heart:
An early Quixote, dreaming dreadful sights
Of warring dragons, and victorious knights:
In every dream some beauteous Princess
    shone,
The pride of thousands, and the prize of one.
    Not yet he read, nor reading, would ap-
    prove,
The Novel's hero, or its ladies' love.
He would Sophia for a wanton take,
Jones for a wicked, nay a vulgar rake.
He would no time on Smollett's page bestow;
Such men he knew not, would disdain to
    know:
And if he read, he travell'd slowly on,
Teazed by the tame and faultless Grandison.

He in that hero's deeds could not delight—
' He loved two ladies, and he would not fight.'
The minor works of this prolific kind
Presented beings he could never find ;
Beings, he thought, that no man should
     describe,
A vile, intriguing, lying, perjured tribe,
With impious habits, and dishonest views ;
The men he knew, had souls they feared to
     lose ;
These had no views that could their sins
     control,
With them nor fears nor hopes disturb'd the
     soul.
   To dear Romance with fresh delight he
     turn'd,
And vicious men, like recreant cowards,
     spurn'd.
   The Scripture Stories he with reverence
     read,
And duly took his Bible to his bed.
Yet Joshua, Samson, David, were a race
He dared not with his favourite heroes place.
Young as he was, the difference well he
     knew
Between the Truth, and what we fancy true.
He was with these entranced, of those afraid,
With Guy he triumph'd, but with David
     pray'd.

II

   P. SUCH was the Boy, and what the man
     would be,
I might conjecture, but could not foresee.
   F. He has his trials met, his troubles seen,
And now deluded, now deserted, been.
His easy nature has been oft assail'd
By grief assumed, scorn hid, and flattery
     veil'd.
   P. But has he, safe and cautious, shunn'd
     the snares
That life presents ?—I ask not of its cares.
   F. Your gentle Boy a course of life began,
That made him what he is, the gentle-man,
A man of business. He in courts presides
Among their Worships, whom his judgment
     guides.
He in the Temple studied, and came down
A very lawyer, though without a gown ;
Still he is kind, but prudent, steady, just,
And takes but little that he hears on trust ;
He has no visions now, no boyish plans ;
All his designs and prospects are the man's,

The man of sound discretion—
                         P. How so made ?
What could his mind to change like this
     persuade—
What first awaken'd our romantic friend—
For such he is—
                   F. If you would know, attend.
   In those gay years, when boys their man-
     hood prove,
Because they talk of girls, and dream of love,
In William's way there came a maiden fair,
With soft, meek look, and sweet retiring air ;
With just the rosy tint upon her cheek,
With sparkling eye, and tongue unused to
     speak ;
With manner decent, quiet, chaste, that one,
Modest himself, might love to look upon,
As William look'd ; and thus the gentle
     Squire
Began the Nymph, albeit poor, t' admire.
She was, to wit, the gardener's niece; her place
Gave to her care the Lady's silks and lace ;
With other duties of an easy kind,
And left her time, as much she felt inclined,
T' adorn her graceful form, and fill her
     craving mind ;
Nay, left her leisure to employ some hours
Of the long day among her uncle's flowers—
Myrtle and rose, of which she took the care,
And was as sweet as pinks and lilies are.
   Such was the damsel whom our Youth
     beheld
With passion unencouraged, unrepell'd ;
For how encourage what was not in view ?
Or how repel what strove not to pursue ?
   What books inspired, or glowing fancy
     wrought,
What dreams suggested, or reflection taught,
Whate'er of love was to the mind convey'd,
Was all directed to his darling maid.
He saw his damsel with a lover's eyes,
As pliant fancy wove the fair disguise ;
A Quixote he, who in his nymph could trace
The high-born beauty, changed and—out of
     place.
That William loved, mamma, with easy smile,
Would jesting say ; but love *might* grow the
     while ;
The damsel's self, with unassuming pride,
With love so led by fear was gratified.
   What cause for censure ? Could a man
     reprove
A child for fondness, or miscall it love ?

Not William's self ; yet well inform'd was he,
That love it was, and endless love would be.
Month after month the sweet delusion bred
Wild feverish hopes, that flourish'd, and then
    fled,
Like Fanny's sweetest flower, and that was
    lost
In one cold hour, by one harsh morning frost.
  In some soft evenings, mid the garden's
      bloom,
Would William wait, till Fanny chanced to
    come ;
And Fanny came, by chance it may be ; still,
There was a gentle bias of the will,
Such as the soundest minds may act upon,
When motives of superior kind are gone.
There then they met, and Master William's
    look
Was the less timid, for he held a book ;
And when the sweetness of the evening hours,
The fresh soft air, the beauty of the flowers,
The night-bird's note, the gently falling dew,
Were all discuss'd, and silence would ensue,
There were some lovely Lines—if she could
    stay—
And Fanny rises not to go away.

' Young Paris was the shepherd's pride,
    As well the fair Ænone knew ;
They sat the mountain stream beside,
    And o'er the bank a poplar grew.

' Upon its bark this verse he traced,—
    Bear witness to the vow I make ;
Thou, Xanthus, to thy source shalt haste,
    E'er I my matchless maid forsake.

' No prince or peasant lad am I,
    Nor crown nor crook to me belong,
But I will love thee till I die,
    And die before I do thee wrong.

' Back to thy source now, Xanthus, run,
    Paris is now a prince of Troy ;
He leaves the Fair his flattery won,
    Himself and country to destroy.

' He seizes on a sovereign's wife,
    The pride of Greece, and with her flies ;
He causes thus a ten years' strife,
    And with his dying parent dies.

' Oh ! think me not this Shepherd's Boy,
    Who from the Maid he loves would run :
Oh ! think me not a Prince of Troy,
    By whom such treacherous deeds are done.'

The Lines were read, and many an idle word
Pronounced with emphasis, and underscored,
As if the writer had resolved that all
His nouns and verbs should be emphatical.
But what they were the damsel little thought,
The sense escaped her, but the voice she
    caught ;
Soft, tender, trembling, and the gipsy felt
As if listening she unfairly dealt :
For she, if not mamma, had rightly guess'd,
That William's bosom was no seat of rest.
  But Love's young hope must die.—There
      was a day,
When nature smiled, and all around was gay ;
The Boy o'ertook the damsel as she went
The village road—unknown was her intent ;
He, happy hour, when lock'd in Fanny's arm,
Walk'd on enamour'd, every look a charm ;
Yet her soft looks were but her heart's disguise,
There was no answering love in Fanny's eyes :
But, or by prudence or by pity moved,
She thought it time his folly was reproved ;
Then took her measures, not perchance
    without
Some conscious pride in what she was about.
Along the brook, with gentle pace they go,
The Youth unconscious of th' impending
    woe ;
And oft he urged the absent Maid to talk,
As she was wont in many a former walk ;
And still she slowly walk'd beside the brook,
Or look'd around—for what could Fanny look ?
Something there must be ! What, did not
    appear ;
But William's eye betray'd the anxious fear ;
The cause unseen !——
              But who, with giant-stride,
Bounds o'er the brook, and is at Fanny's side ?
Who takes her arm ? and oh ! what villain
    dares
To press those lips ? Not even her lips he
    spares !
Nay, she herself, the Fanny, the divine,
Lip to his lip can wickedly incline !
The lad, unnerved by horror, with an air
Of wonder quits her arm and looks despair ;
Nor will proceed. Oh no ! he must return,
Though his drown'd sight cannot the path
    discern.
  ' Come, Master William ! come, Sir, let
      us on.
What can you fear ? You're not afraid of
    John ? '

' What ails our youngster ? ' quoth the
    burly swain,
Six feet in height—but he inquires in vain.
William, in deep resentment scans the frame
Of the fond giant, and abhors his name ;
Thinks him a demon of th' infernal brood,
And longs to shed his most pernicious blood.
    Again the monster spake in thoughtless joy,
' We shall be married soon, my pretty Boy !
And dwell in Madam's cottage, where you'll see
The strawberry-beds, and cherries on the
    tree.'
    Back to his home in silent scorn return'd
Th' indignant Boy, and all endearment
    spurn'd.

Fanny perforce with Master takes her way,
But finds him to th' o'erwhelming grief a
    prey,
Wrapt in resentful silence, till he came
Where he might vent his woes, and hide his
    shame.
    Fierce was his strife, but with success he
    strove,
And freed his troubled breast from fruitless
    love ;
Or what of love his reason fail'd to cool
Was lost and perish'd in a public school,—
Those seats and sources both of good and ill,
By what they cure in Boys, and what they
    kill.

TALE XX. THE WILL

I

THUS to his Friend an angry Father spoke—
' Nay, do not think that I the WILL revoke.
My cruel Son in every way I've tried,
And every vice have found in him but pride ;
For he, of pride possess'd, would meaner vices
    hide.
Money he wastes, I will not say he spends ;
He neither makes the poor nor rich his friends—
To those he nothing gives, to these he never
    lends.
    ' 'Tis for himself each legal pale he breaks ;
He joins the miser's spirit to the rake's :
Like the worst Roman in the worst of times,
He can be guilty of conflicting crimes ;
Greedy of others' wealth, unknown the use,
And of his own contemptuously profuse.
    ' To such a mind shall I my wealth confide,
That you to nobler, worthier ends, may guide?
No ! let my Will my scorn of vice express,
And let him learn repentance from distress.'
    So said the Father ; and the Friend, who
    spurn'd
Wealth ill-acquired, his sober speech return'd—
' The youth is faulty, but his faults are
    weigh'd
With a strong bias, and by wrath repaid ;
Pleasure deludes him, not the vain design
Of making vices unallied combine.
He wastes your wealth, for he is yet a
    boy ;
He covets more, for he would more enjoy.

For, my good friend, believe me, very few,
At once are prodigals and misers too—
The spendthrift vice engrafted on the Jew.
Leave me one thousand pounds ; for I confess
I have my wants, and will not tax you less.
But your estate let this young man enjoy ;
If he reforms you've saved a grateful boy,
If not, a father's cares and troubles cease,
You've done your duty, and may rest in
    peace.'
    The Will in hand, the Father musing stood,
Then gravely answered, ' Your advice is good;
Yet take the paper, and in safety keep ;
I'll make another Will before I sleep ;
But if I hear of some atrocious deed,
That deed I'll burn, and yours will then
    succeed.
Two thousand I bequeath you. No reproof !
And there are small bequests—he'll have
    enough ;
For if he wastes, he would with all be poor,
And if he wastes not, he will need no more.'
    The Friends then parted : this the Will
    possess'd,
And that another made—so things had rest.
    George, who was conscious that his Father
    grew
Sick and infirm, engaged in nothing new ;
No letters came from injured man or maid,
No bills from wearied duns, that must be paid,
No fierce reproaches from deserted fair,
Mixed with wild tenderness of desperate
    prayer ;

So hope rose softly in the parent's breast:
He dying called his son and fondly blest,
Hailed the propitious tear, and mildly sunk
    to rest.
    Unhappy Youth! e'er yet the tomb was
    closed,
And dust to dust convey'd in peace repos'd,
He sought his father's closet, search'd around,
To find a Will: the important Will was found.
    Well pleased he read, 'These lands, this
    manor, all,
Now call me master!—I obey the call.'
Then from the window look'd the valley o'er,
And never saw it look so rich before.
He view'd the dairy, view'd the men at plough,
With other eyes, with other feelings now,
And with a new-formed taste found beauty
    in a cow.
The distant swain who drove the plough along
Was a good useful slave, and passing strong!
In short, the view was pleasing, nay, was fine,
'Good as my father's, excellent as mine!'
    Again he reads,—but he had read enough;
What followed put his virtue to a proof.
'How this? to David Wright two thousand
    pounds!
A monstrous sum! beyond all reason!—
    zounds!
This is your friendship running out of bounds.
'Then here are cousins Susan, Robert, Joe,
Five hundred each. Do they deserve it? No!
Claim they have none—I wonder if they know
What the good man intended to bestow!
This might be paid—but Wright's enormous
    sum
Is—I'm alone—there's nobody can come—
'Tis all his hand, no lawyer was employ'd
To write this prose, that ought to be destroy'd!
To no attorney would my father trust:
He wished his son to judge of what was just;
As if he said, " My boy will find the Will,
And, as he likes, destroy it or fulfil."
This now is reason, this I understand—
What was at his, is now at my command.
As for this paper, with these cousiny names,
I—'tis my Will—commit it to the flames.
Hence! disappear! now am I lord alone:
They'll groan, I know, but, curse them, let
    them groan.
Who wants his money like a new-made heir,
To put all things in order and repair?
I need the whole the worthy man could save,
To do my father credit in his grave:

It takes no trifle to have squires convey'd
To their last house with honour and parade.
All this, attended by a world of cost,
Requires, demands, that nothing should be
    lost.
These fond bequests cannot demanded be—
Where no Will is, can be no legacy;
And none is here! I safely swear it—none!—
The very ashes are dispersed and gone.
All would be well, would that same sober
    Friend,
That Wright, my father on his way attend:
My fears—but why afraid?—my troubles
    then would end.'
    In triumph, yet in trouble, meets our Squire
The friends assembled, who a Will require.
'There is no Will,' he said.—They murmur
    and retire.
    Days pass away, while yet the Heir is blest
By pleasant cares, and thoughts that banish
    rest;
When comes the Friend, and asks, in solemn
    tone,
If he may see the busy Squire alone.
They are in private—all about is still—
When thus the Guest:—' Your father left
    a Will,
And I would see it.'—Rising in reply,
The youth beheld a fix'd and piercing eye,
From which his own receded; and the sound
Of his own words was in disorder drown'd.
He answered softly,—' I in vain have spent
Days in the search; I pray you be content;
And if a Will—— ' The pertinacious Man,
At if displeased, with steady tone began,—
'There is a Will—produce it, for you can.'—
    ' Sir, I have sought in vain, and what the
    use?
What has no being, how can I produce?'—
    'Two days I give you; to my words attend,'
Was the reply, ' and let the business end.'
    Two days were past, and still the same reply
To the same question—' Not a Will have I.'
More grave, more earnest, then the Friend
    appear'd:
He spoke with power, as one who would be
    heard,—
' A Will your father made! I witness'd one.'
The Heir arose in anger—' Sir, begone!
Think you my spirit by your looks to awe?
Go to your lodgings, friend, or to your law:
To what would you our easy souls persuade?
Once more I tell you, not a Will was made:

There's none with me, I swear it—now, deny
This if you can!'—
　　　　'That, surely, cannot I;
Nay, I believe you, and, as no such deed
Is found with you, *this* surely will succeed!'—
He said, and from his pocket slowly drew
Of the first testament a copy true,
And held it spread abroad, that he might see
　　it too.
'Read, and be sure; your parent's pleasure
　　see—
Then leave this mansion and these lands to
　　me.'
He said, and terror seized the guilty youth;
He saw his misery, meanness, and the truth;
Could not before his stern accuser stand,
Yet could not quit that hall, that park, that
　　land;
But when surprise had pass'd away, his grief
Began to think in law to find relief.
　　'While courts are open, why should
　　I despair?
Juries will feel for an abandon'd heir:
I will resist,' he said, impell'd by pride;—
'I must submit,' recurring fear replied.
As wheels the vane when winds around it play,
So his strong passions turn'd him every
　　way;
But growing terrors seized th' unhappy youth:
He knew the Man, and more, he knew—the
　　Truth.
When, stung by all he fear'd, and all he felt,
He sought for mercy, and in terror knelt.
　　Grieved, but indignant,—'Let me not
　　despise
Thy father's son,' replied the Friend: 'arise!
To my fix'd purpose your attention lend,
And know, your fate will on yourself depend.
　　'Thou shalt not want, young man! nor yet
　　abound,
And time shall try thee, if thy heart be sound;
Thou shalt be watch'd till thou hast learn'd
　　to know
Th' All-seeing Watcher of the world below,
And worlds above, and thoughts within;
　　from Whom
Must be thy certain, just, and final doom.
Thy doors all closely barr'd, thy windows
　　blind,
Before all silent, silent all behind—
Thy hand was stretch'd to do whate'er thy
　　soul
In secret would—no mortal could control.

Oh, fool! to think that thou thy act could'st
　　keep
From that All-piercing Eye, which cannot
　　sleep!
　　'Go to thy trial! and may I with thee,
A fellow-sinner, who to mercy flee—
That mercy find, as justly I dispense
Between thy frailty and thy penitence.
　　'Go to thy trial! and be wise in time,
And know that no man can conceal a crime.
God and his Conscience witness all that's done,
And these he cannot cheat, he cannot shun.
What, then, could fortune, what could safety
　　give,
If He with these at enmity must live?
　　'Go!'—and the young man from his
　　presence went,
Confused, uncertain of his own intent—
To sin, if pride prevail'd; if soften'd, to repent.

II

P. Lives yet the Friend of that unhappy
　　Boy,
Who could the Will that made him rich
　　destroy,
And made him poor? And what the after-
　　plan,
For one so selfish, of that stern, good man?
F. 'Choose,' said this Friend, 'thy way
　　in life, and I
Will means to aid thee in thy work supply.'
He will the army, thought this guardian,
　　choose,
And there the sense of his dishonour lose.
　　Humbly he answer'd,—'With your kind
　　consent,
Of your estate I would a portion rent,
And farm with care——'
　　　　　　'Alas! the wretched fruit
Of evil habit! he will hunt and shoot.'
　　So judged the Friend, but soon perceived
　　a change,
To him important, and to all men strange.
Industrious, temperate, with the sun he rose,
And of his time gave little to repose:
Nor to the labour only bent his will,
But sought experience, and improved with
　　skill;
With cautious prudence placed his gains to
　　use,
Inquiring always, 'What will this produce?'
　　The Friend, not long suspicious, now began
To think more kindly of the alter'd man—

In his opinion alter'd, but, in truth,
The same the spirit that still ruled the youth :
That dwelt within, where other demons dwell,
Avarice unsated, and insatiable.
  But this Wright saw not : he was more
          inclined
To trace the way of a repenting mind ;
And he was now by strong disease assail'd,
That quickly o'er the vital powers prevail'd :
And now the son had all, was rich beyond
His fondest hope, and he, indeed, was
          fond.
  His life's great care has been his zeal to
          prove,
And time to dotage has increased his love.
A Miser now, the one strong passion guides
The heart and soul : there's not a love be-
          sides.
Where'er he comes, he sees in every face
A look that tells him of his own disgrace.
Men's features vary, but the mildest show
' It is a tale of infamy we know.'

Some with contempt the wealthy miser view,
Some with disgust, yet mix'd with pity too ;
A part the looks of wrath and hatred wear,
And some, less happy, lose their scorn in fear.
  Meanwhile, devoid of kindness, comfort,
          friends,
On his possessions solely he depends.
  Yet is he wretched ; for his fate decrees
That his own feelings should deny him ease.
With talents gifted, he himself reproves,
And can but scorn the vile pursuit he loves ;
He can but feel that there abides within
The secret shame, the unrepented sin,
And the strong sense, that bids him to confess
He has not found the way to happiness.
  But 'tis the way where he has travell'd
          long,—
And turn he will not, though he feels it wrong ;
Like a sad traveller, who, at closing day,
Finds he has wander'd widely from his way,
Yet wanders on, nor will new paths explore,
Till the night falls, and he can walk no more.

TALE XXI.   THE COUSINS

I

P.   I LEFT a frugal Merchant, who began
Early to thrive, and grew a wealthy man ;
Retired from business with a favourite Niece,
He lived in plenty, or if not—in peace.
Their small affairs, conforming to his will,
The maiden managed with superior skill.
He had a Nephew too, a brother's child,—
But James offended, for the lad was wild :
And Patty's tender soul was vex'd to hear,
' Your Cousin James will rot in gaol, my dear ;
And now, I charge you, by no kind of gift
Show him that folly may be help'd by thrift.'
This Patty heard, but in her generous mind
Precept so harsh could no admission find.
  Her cousin James, too sure in prison laid,
With strong petitions plied the gentle maid,
That she would humbly on their Uncle press
His deep repentance, and his sore distress ;
How that he mourn'd in durance, night and
          day,
And which removed, he would for ever pray.
  ' Nought will I give, his worthless life to
          save,'
The Uncle said ; and nought in fact he gave :

But the kind maiden from her pittance took
All that she could, and gave with pitying look ;
For soft compassion in her bosom reign'd,
And her heart melted when the Youth com-
          plain'd.
Of his complaints the Uncle loved to hear,
As Patty told them, shedding many a tear ;
While he would wonder how the girl could
          pray
For a young rake, to place him in her way,
Or once admit him in his Uncle's view ;
' But these,' said he, ' are things that women
          do.'
  Thus were the Cousins, young, unguarded,
          fond,
Bound in true friendship—so they named the
          bond—
Nor call'd it love—and James resolved, when
          free,
A most correct and frugal man to be.
He sought her prayers, but not for heavenly
          aid :
' Pray to my Uncle,' and she kindly pray'd—
' James will be careful,' said the Niece ;
          ' and I
Will be as careful,' was the stern reply.

Thus he resisted, and I know not how
He could be soften'd—Is he kinder now?
Hard was his heart; but yet a heart of steel
May melt in dying, and dissolving feel.

II

F. WHAT were his feelings I cannot explain,
His actions only on my mind remain.
He never married, that indeed we know,
But childless was not, as his foes could show.—
Perhaps his friends—for friends, as well as foes,
Will the infirmities of man disclose.

When young, our Merchant, though of sober
fame,
Had a rude passion that he could not tame;
And, not to dwell upon the passion's strife,
He had a Son, who never had a wife;
The father paid just what the law required,
Nor saw the infant, nor to see desired.
That infant, thriving on the parish fare,
Without a parent's love, consent, or care,
Became a sailor, and sustain'd his part
So like a man, it touch'd his father's heart:—
He for protection gave the ready pay,
And placed the seaman in preferment's way;
Who doubted not, with sanguine heart, to
rise,
And bring home riches, gain'd from many
a prize.
But Jack—for so we call'd him—Jack once
more,
And never after, touch'd his native shore:
Nor was it known if in battle fell,
Or sickening died—we sought, but none could
tell.
The father sigh'd—as some report, he wept;
And then his sorrow with the Sailor slept;
Then age came on; he found his spirits droop,
And his kind Niece remain'd the only hope.

Premising this, our story then proceeds—
Our gentle Patty for her Cousin pleads;
And now her Uncle, to his room confined,
And kindly nursed, was soften'd and was kind.
James, whom the law had from his prison sent,
With much contrition to his Uncle went,
And, humbly kneeling, said, 'Forgive me,
I repent.'
Reproach, of course, his humbled spirit bore;
He knew for pardon anger opes the door;
The man whom we with too much warmth
reprove,
Has the best chance our softening hearts to
move;

And this he had—'Why, Patty, love! it
seems,'
Said the old man, 'there's something good
in James:
I must forgive; but you, my child, are yet,
My stay and prop; I cannot this forget.
Still, my dear Niece, as a reforming man,
I mean to aid your Cousin, if I can.'
Then Patty smiled, for James and she had
now
Time for their loves, and pledged the constant
vow.
James saw the fair way to favouring thoughts
discern'd—
He learn'd the news, and told of all he learn'd;
Read all the papers in an easy style,
And knew the bits would raise his Uncle's
smile;
Then would refrain, to hear the good man say,
'You did not come as usual yesterday:
I must not take you from your duties, lad,
But of your daily visits should be glad!'
Patty was certain that their Uncle now
Would their affection all it ask'd allow;
She was convinced her lover now would find
The past forgotten and old Uncle kind.
'It matters not,' she added, 'who receives
The larger portion; what to one he leaves
We both inherit! let us nothing hide,
Dear James, from him in whom we both
confide.'
'Not for your life!' quoth James. 'Let
Uncle choose
Our ways for us—or we the way shall lose.
For know you, Cousin, all these miser men——'
'Nay, my dear James!'—
'Our worthy Uncle, then,
And all like Uncle like—to be obey'd
By their dependants, who must seem afraid
Of their own will:—If we to wed incline,
You'll quickly hear him peevishly repine,
Object, dispute, and sundry reasons give,
To prove we ne'er could find the means to
live;
And then, due credit for his speech to gain,
He'll leave us poor—lest wealth should prove
it vain.
Let him propose the measure, and then we
May for his pleasure to his plan agree.
I, when at last assenting, shall be still
But giving way to a kind Uncle's will;
Then will he deem it just, amends to make
To one who ventures all things for his sake;

So, should you deign to take this worthless hand,
Be sure, dear Patty, 'tis at his command.'
But Patty questioned—' Is it, let me ask,
The will of God that we should wear a mask ? '
This startled James : he lifted up his eyes,
And said with some contempt, besides surprise,
' Patty, my love ! the will of God, 'tis plain,
Is that we live by what we can obtain ;
Shall we a weak and foolish man offend,
And when our trial is so near an end ? '
This hurt the maiden, and she said, ' 'Tis well !
Unask'd I will not of your purpose tell,
But will not lie.'—
' Lie ! Patty, no, indeed,
Your downright lying never will succeed !
A better way our prudence may devise,
Than such unprofitable things as lies.
Yet, a dependant, if he would not starve,
The way through life must with discretion carve,
And, though a lie he may with pride disdain,
He must not every useless truth maintain.
If one respect to these fond men would show,
Conceal the facts that give them pain to know ;
While all that pleases may be placed in view,
And if it be not, they will think it true.'
The humble Patty dropp'd a silent tear,
And said, ' Indeed, 'tis best to be sincere.'
James answer'd not—there could be no reply
To what he would not grant, nor could deny :
But from that time he in the maiden saw
What he condemn'd ; yet James was kept in awe ;
He felt her virtue, but was sore afraid
For the frank blunders of the virtuous maid.
Meantime he daily to his Uncle read
The news, and to his favourite subjects led :
If closely press'd, he sometimes staid to dine,
Eat of one dish, and drank one glass of wine ;
For James was crafty grown, and felt his way
To favour, step by step, and day by day ;
He talk'd of business, till the Uncle prized
The lad's opinion, whom he once despised,
And, glad to see him thus his faults survive,
' This Boy,' quoth he, ' will keep our name alive.
Women are weak, and Patty, though the best
Of her weak sex, is woman like the rest :
An idle husband will her money spend,
And bring my hard-earn'd savings to an end.'

Far as he dared, his Nephew this way led,
And told his tales of lasses rashly wed,
Told them as matters that he heard,—' He knew
Not where,' he said : ' they might be false, or true ;
One must confess that girls are apt to dote
On the bright scarlet of a coxcomb's coat ;
And that with ease a woman they beguile
With a fool's flattery, or a rascal's smile ;
But then,' he added, fearing to displease,
' Our Patty never saw such men as these.'
' True ! but she may—some scoundrel may command
The girl's whole store, if he can gain her hand :
Her very goodness will itself deceive,
And her weak virtue help her to believe ;
Yet she is kind ; and, Nephew ! go, and say,
I need her now—You'll come another day.'
In such discourses, while the maiden went
About her household, many an hour was spent,
Till James was sure that when his Uncle died,
He should at least the property divide :
Nor long had he to wait—the fact was quickly tried.
The Uncle now to his last bed confined,
To James and Patty his affairs resign'd ;
The doctor took his final fee in hand,
The man of law received his last command ;
The silent priest sat watching in his chair,
If he might wake the dying man to prayer,—
When the last groan was heard ; then all was still,
And James indulged his musings—on the Will.
This in due time was read, and Patty saw
Her own dear Cousin made the heir-by-law.
Something indeed was hers, but yet she felt
As if her Uncle had not kindly dealt ;
And but that James was one whom she could trust,
She would have thought it cruel and unjust.
Ev'n as it was, it gave her some surprise,
And tears unbidden started in her eyes ;
Yet she confess'd it was the same to her,
And it was likely men would men prefer.
Loth was the Niece to think her Uncle wrong ;
And other thoughts engaged her—' Is it long
That custom bids us tarry ere we wed,
When a kind Uncle is so lately dead ?
At any rate,' the maiden judged, ' 'tis he
That first will speak—it does not rest with me.'

James to the Will his every thought con-
    fined,
And found some parts that vex'd his sober
    mind.
He, getting much, to angry thoughts gave way,
For the poor pittance that he had to pay,
With Patty's larger claim. Save these alone,
The weeping heir beheld the whole his own ;
Yet something painful in his mind would
    dwell,—
' It was not likely, but was possible : '—
No—Fortune lately was to James so kind,
He was determined not to think her blind :
' She saw his merit, and would never throw
His prospects down by such malicious blow.'
    Patty, meanwhile, had quite enough be-
    tray'd
Of her own mind to make her James afraid
Of one so simply pure : his hardening heart
Inclined to anger—he resolved to part :
Why marry Patty ?—if he look'd around,
More advantageous matches might be found ;
But though he might a richer wife command,
He first must break her hold upon his hand.
    She with a spinster-friend retired awhile,
' Not long,' she said, and said it with a smile.
Not so had James determined :—He essay'd
To move suspicion in the gentle maid.
Words not succeeding, he design'd to pass
The spinster's window with some forward lass.
If in her heart so pure no pang was known,
At least he might affect it in his own.
There was a brother of her friend, and he,
Though poor and rude, might serve for
    jealousy.
If all should fail, he, though of schemes bereft,
Might leave her yet !—They fail'd, and she
    was left.
    Poor Patty bore it with a woman's mind,
And with an angel's, sorrowing and resign'd.
Ere this in secret long she wept and pray'd,
Long tried to think her lover but delay'd
The union, once his hope, his prayer, his
    pride ;—
She could in James as in herself confide :
Was he not bound by all that man can bind,
In love, in honour, to be just and kind ?
Large was his debt, and when their debts are
    large,
The ungrateful cancel what the just discharge;
Nor payment only in their pride refuse,
But first they wrong their friend, and then
    accuse.

Thus Patty finds her bosom's claims deni d,
Her love insulted, and her right defied.
She urged it not ; her claim the maid with-
    drew,
For maiden pride would not the wretch pursue:
She sigh'd to find him false, herself so good
    and true.
    Now all his fears, at least the present, still,—
He talk'd, good man! about his uncle's will,—
' All unexpected,' he declared,—' surprised
Was he—and his good uncle ill-advised :
He no such luck had look'd for, he was
    sure,
Nor such deserved,' he said, with look demure;
He did not merit such exceeding love,
But his, he meant, so help him God, to prove.'
And he has proved it ! all his cares and
    schemes
Have proved the exceeding love James bears
    to James.
    But to proceed,—for we have yet the facts
That show how Justice looks on wicked acts ;
For, though not always, she at times appears—
To wake in man her salutary fears.
    James, restless grown—for no such mind
    can rest—
Would build a house, that should his wealth
    attest ;
In fact, he saw, in many a clouded face,
A certain token of his own disgrace ;
And wish'd to overawe the murmurs of the
    place.
    The finish'd building show'd the master's
    wealth,
And noisy workmen drank his Honour's
    health—
' His and his heirs '—and at the thoughtless
    word
A strange commotion in his bosom stirr'd.
' Heirs ! said the idiots ? '— and again that
    clause
In the strange Will corrected their applause.
    Prophetic fears ! for now reports arose
That spoil'd ' his Honour's ' comforts and
    repose.
A stout young Sailor, though in battle maim'd,
Arrived in port, and his possessions claim'd.
The Will he read : he stated his demand,
And his attorney grasp'd at house and land.
The Will provided—' If my on survive,
He shall inherit ; ' and lo ! Jack's alive !
Yes ! he was that lost lad, preserved by fate,
And now was bent on finding his estate.

But claim like this the angry James denied,
And to the law the sturdy heir applied.
James did what men when placed like him
would do—
Avow'd his right, and fee'd his lawyer too :
The Will, indeed, provided for a son ;
But was this Sailor youth the very one ?

Ere Jack's strong proofs in all their strength
were shown,
To gain a part James used a milder tone ;
But the instructed tar would reign alone.

At last he reign'd : to James a large bequest
Was frankly dealt ; the Seaman had the
rest—
Save a like portion to the gentle Niece,
Who lived in comfort, and regain'd her peace.
In her neat room her talent she employ'd,
With more true peace than ever James enjoy'd.
The young, the aged, in her praise agreed—
Meek in her manner, bounteous in her deed ;
The very children their respect avow'd :
' 'Twas the good lady,' they were told, and
bow'd.

The merry Seaman much the maid ap-
prov'd,—
Nor that alone—he like a seaman loved ;
Loved as a man who did not much complain,
Loved like a sailor, not a sighing swain ;
Had heard of wooing maids, but knew not
how—
' Lass, if you love me, prithee tell me now,'
Was his address—but this was nothing cold—
' Tell if you love me ; ' and she smiled and
told.

He bought her presents, such as sailors
buy,
Glittering like gold, to please a maiden's eye,
All silk, and silver, fringe and finery :
These she accepted in respect to him,
And thought but little ot the missing limb.
Of this he told her, for he loved to tell
A warlike tale, and judged he told it well :—
' You mark me, love ! the French were two
to one,
And so, you see, they were ashamed to run ;

We fought an hour ; and then there came
the shot
That struck me here—a man must take his
lot ;—
A minute after, and the Frenchman struck :
One minute sooner had been better luck
But if you can a crippled cousin like,
You ne'er shall see him for a trifle strike.'

Patty, whose gentle heart was not so nice
As to reject the thought of loving twice,
Judged her new Cousin was by nature kind,
With no suspicions in his honest mind,
Such as our virtuous ladies now and then
Find strongly floating in the minds of men.
So they were married, and the lasses vow'd
That Patty's luck would make an angel
proud :
' Not but that time would come when she
must prove
That men are men, no matter how they
love : '—
And she has prov'd it ; for she finds her man
As kind and true as when their loves began.

James is unhappy ; not that he is poor,
But, having much, because he has no more ;
Because a rival's pleasure gives him pain ;
Because his vices work'd their way in vain ;
And, more than these, because he sees the
smile
Of a wrong'd woman pitying man so vile.
He sought an office, serves in the excise,
And every wish, but that for wealth, denies ;
Wealth is the world to him, and he is worldly
wise.
But disappointment in his face appears ;
Care and vexation, sad regret and fears
Have fix'd on him their fangs, and done the
work of years.

Yet grows he wealthy in a strange degree,
And neighbours wonder how the fact can be :
He lives alone, contracts a sordid air,
And sees with sullen grief the cheerful pair ;
Feels a keen pang, as he beholds the door
Where peace abides, and mutters,—' *I am
poor !* '

TALE XXII. PREACHING AND PRACTICE

I

P. WHAT I have ask'd are questions that
relate
To those once known, that I might learn their
fate.
But there was ONE, whom though I scarcely
knew,
Much do I wish to learn his fortunes too.
Yet what expect ?—He was a rich man's Heir,
His conduct doubtful, but his prospects fair ;
Thoughtless and brave, extravagant and gay,
Wild as the wind, and open as the day ;
His freaks and follies were a thousand times
Brought full in view : I heard not of his
crimes.
Like our Prince Hal, his company he chose
Among the lawless, of restraint the foes ;
But though to their poor pleasures he could
stoop,
He was not, rumour said, their victim-dupe.
His mother's Sister was a maiden prim,
Pious and poor, and much in debt to him.
This she repaid with volumes of reproof,
And sage advice, till he would cry ' Enough ! '
His father's Brother no such hints allow'd,
Peevish and rich, and insolent and proud,
Of stern, strong spirit : Him the Youth with-
stood,
At length, ' Presume not (said he) on our
blood ;
Treat with politeness him whom you advise,
Nor think I fear your doting prophecies ; '
And fame has told of many an angry word,
When anger this, and that contempt had
stirr'd.
 ' Boy ! thou wilt beg thy bread, I plainly
see.'—
' Upbraid not, Uncle ! till I beg of thee.'
 ' Oh ! thou wilt run to ruin and disgrace.'—
' What ! and so kind an Uncle in the place ? '
 ' Nay, for I hold thee stranger to my blood.'
' Then must I treat thee as a stranger would :
For if you throw the tie of blood aside,
You must the roughness of your speech abide.'
 ' What ! to your father's Brother do you give
A challenge ?—Mercy ! in what times we live ! '
 Now, I confess, the youth who could supply
Thus that poor Spinster, and could thus defy

This wealthy Uncle ;—who could mix with
them
Whom his strong sense and feeling must
condemn,
And in their follies his amusement find,
Yet never lose the vigour of his mind—
A youth like this, with much we must reprove,
Had something still to win esteem and love.
Perhaps he lives not ; but he seem'd not made
To pass through life entirely in the shade.
 F. Suppose you saw him,—does your mind
retain
So much, that you would know the man again ?
Yet hold in mind, he may have felt the press
Of grief or guilt, the withering of distress ;
He now may show the stamp of woe and pain,
And nothing of his lively cast remain.
 Survey these features—see if nothing there
May old impressions on your mind repair !
Is there not something in this shatter'd frame
Like to that—
          P. No ! not like it, but the same ;
That eye so brilliant, and that smile so gay,
Are lighted up, and sparkle through decay.
 But may I question ? Will you that allow ?
There was a difference, and there must be now ;
And yet, permitted, I would gladly hear
What must have pass'd in many a troubled
year.

 F. Then hear my tale ; but I the price
demand ;
That understood, I too must understand
Thy wanderings through, or sufferings in the
land ;
And, if our virtues cannot much produce,
Perhaps our errors may be found of use.
 To all the wealth my Father's care laid by,
I added wings, and taught it how to fly.
To him that act had been of grievous sight,
But he survived not to behold the flight.
Strange doth it seem to grave and sober minds ;
How the dear vice the simple votary blinds,
So that he goes to ruin smoothly on,
And scarcely feels he's going, till he's gone.
 I had made over, in a lucky hour,
Funds for my Aunt, and placed beyond my
power :

The rest was flown, I speak it with remorse,
And now a pistol seem'd a thing in course.

But though its precepts I had not obey'd,
Thoughts of my Bible made me much afraid
Of such rebellion, and though not content,
I must live on when life's supports were spent;
Nay, I must eat, and of my frugal Aunt
Must grateful take what gracious she would
          grant ;
And true, she granted, but with much dis-
          course ;
Oh ! with what words did she her sense
          enforce !
Great was her wonder, in my need that I
Should on the prop myself had raised rely—
I, who provided for her in my care,
' Must be assured how little she could spare ! '
I stood confounded, and with angry tone,
With rage and grief, that blended oath and
          groan,
I fled her presence—yet I saw her air
Of resignation, and I heard her prayer ;
' Now Heaven,' she utter'd, ' make his burden
          light ! '—
And I, in parting, cried, ' Thou hypocrite ! '
But I was wrong—she might have meant
          to pray ;
Though not to give her soul—her cash—away.
Of course, my Uncle would the spendthrift
          shun ;
So friends on earth I now could reckon none.
One morn I rambled, thinking of the past,
Far in the country—Did you ever fast
Through a long summer's day ? or, sturdy,
          go
To pluck the crab, the bramble, and the sloe,
The hyp, the cornel, and the beech, the food
And the wild solace of the gypsy brood ?
To pick the cress embrown'd by summer sun,
From the dry bed where streams no longer
          run ?
Have you, like school-boy, mingling play and
          toil,
Dug for the ground-nut, and enjoy'd the
          spoil ?
Or chafed with feverish hand the ripening
          wheat,
Resolved to fast, and yet compelled to eat ?
Say, did you this, and drink the crystal
          spring,
And think yourself an abdicated king,
Driv'n from your state by a rebellious race ?
And in your pride contending with disgrace,

Could you your hunger in your anger lose,
And call the ills you bear the ways you choose?
Thus on myself depending, I began
To feel the pride of a neglected man ;
Not yet correct, but still I could command
Unshaken nerves, and a determined hand.
' Lo ! men at work ! ' I said, ' and I a man
Can work ! I feel it is my pride, I can.'
This said, I wander'd on, and join'd the poor,
Assumed a labourer's dress, and was no more
Than labour made—Upon the road I broke
Stones for my bread, and startled at the stroke;
But every day the labour seem'd more light,
And sounder, sweeter still the sleep of every
          night.
' Thus will I live,' I cried, ' nor more return
To herd with men, whose love and hate I spurn.
All creatures toil ; the beast, if tamed or free,
Must toil for daily sustenance like me ;
The feather'd people hunt as well as sing,
And catch their flying food upon the wing.
The fish, the insect, all who live, employ
Their powers to keep on life, or to enjoy,
Their life th' enjoyment ; thus will I proceed,
A man from man's detested favours freed.'
Thus was I reasoning, when at length there
          came
A gift, a present, but without a name.
'That Spinster-witch, has she then found a way
To cure her conscience, and her Nephew pay,
And sends her pittance ? Well, and let it buy
What sweetens labour ; need I this deny ?
I thank her not ; it is as if I found
The fairy-gift upon this stony ground.'
Still I wrought on ; again occurred the day,
And then the same addition to my pay.
Then, lo ! another Friend, if not the same,
For that I knew not, with a message came—
' Canst keep accounts ? ' the man was pleased
          to ask—
' I could not cash !—but that the harder task.'
' Yet try,' he said ; and I was quickly brought,
To Lawyer Snell, and in his office taught.
Not much my pay, but my desires were less,
And I for evil days reserved th' excess.
Such day occurr'd not : quickly came there
          one,
When I was told my present work was done :
My Friend then brought me to a building large,
And gave far weightier business to my charge.
There I was told I had accounts to keep,
Of those vast Works, where wonders never
          sleep,

Where spindles, bobbins, rovings, threads, and
    pins,
Made up the complex mass that ever spins.
    There, at my desk, in my six feet of room,
I noted every power of every loom ;
Sounds of all kinds I heard from mortal
    lungs—
Eternal battle of unwearied tongues,
The jar of men and women, girls and boys,
And the huge Babel's own dull whirring,
    grinding noise.
    My care was mark'd, and I had soon in
    charge
Important matters, and my pay was large.
I at my fortune marvell'd ; it was strange,
And so the outward and the inward change,
Till to the Power who ' gives and takes away '
I turn'd in praise, and taught my soul to pray.
    Another came ! ' I come,' he said, ' to show,
Your unknown Friend—have you a wish to
    know ? '
Much I desired, and forth we rode, and found
My Uncle dying, but his judgment sound.
The good old man, whom I abused, had been
The guardian power, directing but unseen ;
And thus the wild but grateful boy he led
To take new motives at his dying bed.
    The rest you judge—I now have all I need—
And now the tale you promised !—Come,
    proceed.

    P. 'Tis due, I own, but yet in mercy spare :
Alas ! no Uncle was my guide—my care
Was all my own ; no guardian took a share.
I, like Columbus, for a world unknown—
'Twas no great effort—sacrificed my own—

My own sad world, where I had never seen
The earth productive, or the sky serene.
    But this is past—and I at length am come
To see what changes have been wrought at
    home ;
Happy in this, that I can set me down
At worst a stranger in my native town.
    F. Then be it so ! but mean you not to
    show
How time has pass'd ? for we expect to know :
And if you tell not, know you we shall trace
Your movements for ourselves from place to
    place.
Your wants, your wishes, all you've sought
    or seen,
Shall be the food for our remark and spleen.
So, warn'd in time, the real page unfold,
And let the Truth, before the Lie, be told.
    P. This might be done ; but wonders
    I have none,
All my adventures are of Self alone.
    F. What then ? I grant you, if your way
    was clear,
All smooth and right—we've no desire to hear ;
But if you've lewd and wicked things to tell,
Low passions, cruel deeds, nay crimes—'tis
    well :
Who would not listen ?——
                P. Hark ! I hear the bell.
It calls to dinner with inviting sound,
For now we know where dinners may be
    found,
And can behold and share the glad repast,
Without a dread that we behold our last.
    F. Come then, shy friend, let doleful sub-
    jects cease,
And thank our God that we can dine in peace.

OCCASIONAL POEMS AFTER 1780

FROM BELVOIR CASTLE
[About 1782]

OH! had I but a little hut,
　　That I might hide my head in ;
Where never guest might dare molest
　　Unwelcome or unbidden.
I'd take the jokes of other folks,
　　And mine should then succeed 'em,
Nor would I chide a little pride,
　　Or heed a little freedom.

．　．　．　．　．　．　．

THE LADIES OF THE LAKE
WRITTEN ON VISITING NORMANSTON IN THE YEAR 1785

SHALL I, who oft have woo'd the Muse
　　For gentle Ladies' sake,
So fair a theme as this refuse—
　　The Ladies of the Lake ?

Hail, happy pair ! 'tis yours to share
　　Life's elegance and ease ;
The bliss of wealth without the care,
　　The will and power to please,—

To please, but not alone our eyes,
　　Nor yet alone our mind ;
Your taste, your goodness, charm the wise—
　　Your manners all mankind.

The pleasant scenes that round you glow,
　　Like caskets fraught with gold,
Though beauteous in themselves, yet owe
　　Their worth to what they hold.

Trees may be found, and lakes, as fair ;
　　Fresh lawns, and gardens green ;
But where again the Sister-pair
　　Who animate the scene ?

Where sense of that superior kind,
　　Without man's haughty air ?
And where, without the trifling mind,
　　The softness of the fair ?

Folly, with wealth, may idly raise
　　Her hopes to shine like you,
And humble flattery sound her praise,
　　Till she believes it true ;

But wealth no more can give that grace
　　To souls of meaner kind,
Than summer's fiery sun can chase
　　Their darkness from the blind.

But drop, you'll say, the useless pen :
　　Reluctant—I obey,
Yet let me take it once again,
　　If not to praise, to pray

That you, with partial grace, may deign
　　This poor attempt to take,
And I may oft behold again
　　The Ladies of the Lake.

INFANCY—A FRAGMENT
[Date uncertain]

WHO on the new-born light can back return,
And the first efforts of the soul discern—
Waked by some sweet maternal smile, no more
To sleep so long or fondly as before ?
No! Memory cannot reach, with all her
　　　　power,
To that new birth, that life-awakening hour.
No ! all the traces of her first employ
Are keen perceptions of the senses' joy,
And their distaste—what then could they
　　impart ?—
That figs were luscious, and that rods had
　　smart.
　　But, though the Memory in that dubious
　　　　way
Recalls the dawn and twilight of her day,
And thus encounters, in the doubtful view,
With imperfection and distortion too ;
Can she not tell us, as she looks around,
Of good and evil, which the most abound ?
　　Alas ! and what is earthly good ? 'tis lent
Evil to hide, to soften, to prevent,
By scenes and shows that cheat the wandering
　　　　eye,
While the more pompous misery passes by ;
Shifts and amusements that awhile succeed,
And heads are turn'd, that bosoms may not
　　bleed :
For what is Pleasure, that we toil to gain ?
'Tis but the slow or rapid flight of Pain.
Set Pleasure by, and there would yet remain,
For every nerve and sense the sting of Pain :
Set Pain aside, and fear no more the sting,
And whence your hopes and pleasures can ye
　　bring ?
No ! there is not a joy beneath the skies,
That from no grief nor trouble shall arise.

Why does the Lover with such rapture fly
To his dear mistress ?—He shall show us
    why :—
Because her absence is such cause of grief
That her sweet smile alone can yield relief.
Why, then, that smile is Pleasure :—True,
    yet still
'Tis but the absence of the former ill :
For, married, soon at will he comes and goes ;
Then pleasures die, and pains become repose,
And he has none of these, and therefore none
    of those.

Yes ! looking back as early as I can,
I see the griefs that seize their subject Man,
That in the weeping Child their early reign
    began :
Yes ! though Pain softens, and is absent since,
He still controls me like my lawful prince.
Joys I remember, like phosphoric light
Or squibs and crackers on a gala night.
Joys are like oil ; if thrown upon the tide
Of flowing life, they mix not, nor subside :
Griefs are like waters on the river thrown,
They mix entirely, and become its own.
Of all the good that grew of early date,
I can but parts and incidents relate :
A guest arriving, or a borrow'd day
From school, or schoolboy triumph at some
    play :
And these from Pain may be deduced ; for
    these
Removed some ill, and hence their power to
    please.
But it was Misery stung me in the day
Death of an infant sister made a prey ;
For then first met and moved my early fears,
A father's terrors, and a mother's tears.
Though greater anguish I have since en-
    dured,—
Some heal'd in part, some never to be cured ;
Yet was there something in that first-born
    ill,
So new, so strange, that memory feels it still !
  That my first grief : but, oh ! in after-years
Were other deaths, that call'd for other tears.
No ! that I cannot, that I dare not, paint—
That patient sufferer, that enduring saint,
Holy and lovely—but all words are faint.
But here I dwell not—let me, while I can,
Go to the Child, and lose the suffering Man.
  Sweet was the morning's breath, the inland
    tide,
And our boat gliding, where alone could glide

Small craft—and they oft touch'd on either
    side.
It was my first-born joy. I heard them say,
' Let the child go ; he will enjoy the day.'
For children ever feel delighted when
They take their portion, and enjoy with men.
Give him the pastime that the old partake,
And he will quickly top and taw forsake.
  The linnet chirp'd upon the furze as well,
To my young sense, as sings the nightingale.
Without was paradise—because within
Was a keen relish, without taint of sin.
  A town appear'd,—and where an infant
    went,
Could they determine, on themselves intent?
I lost my way, and my companions me,
And all, their comforts and tranquillity.
Mid-day it was, and, as the sun declined,
The good, found early, I no more could find :
The men drank much, to whet the appetite ;
And, growing heavy, drank to make them
    light ;
Then drank to relish joy, then further to
    excite.
Their cheerfulness did but a moment last ;
Something fell short, or something overpast.
The lads play'd idly with the helm and oar,
And nervous women would be set on shore,
Till ' civil dudgeon ' grew, and peace would
    smile no more.
  Now on the colder water faintly shone
The sloping light—the cheerful day was gone ;
Frown'd every cloud, and from the gather'd
    frown
The thunder burst, and rain came pattering
    down.
My torpid senses now my fears obey'd,
When the fierce lightning on the eye-balls
    play'd.
Now, all the freshness of the morning fled,
My spirits burden'd, and my heart was dead ;
The female servants show'd a child their fear,
And men, full wearied, wanted strength to
    cheer ;
And when, at length, the dreaded storm went
    past,
And there was peace and quietness at last,
'Twas not the morning's quiet—it was not
Pleasure revived, but Misery forgot :
It was not Joy that now commenced her reign,
But mere relief from wretchedness and Pain.
  So many a day, in life's advance, I knew ;
So they commenced, and so they ended too.

All Promise they—all Joy as they began !
But Joy grew less, and vanish'd as they ran !
Errors and evils came in many a form,—
The mind's delusion, and the passions' storm.
  The promised joy, that like this morning
      rose,
Broke on my view, then clouded at its close;
E'en Love himself, that promiser of bliss,
Made his best days of pleasure end like this :
He mix'd his bitters in the cup of joy,
Nor gave a bliss uninjured by alloy.

THE MAGNET

[Date uncertain]

WHY force the backward heart on love,
    That of itself the flame might feel ?
When you the Magnet's power would prove,
    Say, would you strike it on the Steel ?

From common flints you may by force
    Excite some transient sparks of fire ;
And so, in natures rude and coarse,
    Compulsion may provoke desire.

But when, approaching by degrees,
    The Magnet to the Steel draws nigh,
At once they feel, each other seize,
    And rest in mutual sympathy.

So must the Lover find his way
    To move the heart he hopes to win—
Must not in distant forms delay—
    Must not in rude assaults begin.

For such attractive power has Love,
    We justly each extreme may fear :
'Tis lost when we too distant prove,
    And when we rashly press too near.

STORM AND CALM

[Date uncertain]

FROM THE ALBUM OF THE DUCHESS OF
RUTLAND

AT sea when threatening tempests rise,
    When angry winds the waves deform,
The seaman lifts to Heaven his eyes,
    And deprecates the dreaded storm.
' Ye furious powers, no more contend ;
Ye winds and seas, your conflict end ;
And on the mild subsiding deep,
Let Fear repose and Terror sleep ! '

At length the waves are hush'd in peace,
    O'er flying clouds the sun prevails ;
The weary winds their efforts cease,
    And fill no more the flagging sails ;
Fix'd to the deep the vessel rides
Obedient to the changing tides ;
No helm she feels, no course she keeps,
But on the liquid marble sleeps.

Sick of a Calm the sailor lies,
    And views the still, reflecting seas ;
Or, whistling to the burning skies,
    He hopes to wake the slumbering breeze :
The silent noon, the solemn night,
The same dull round of thoughts excite,
Till, tired of the revolving train,
He wishes for the Storm again.

Thus, when I felt the force of Love,
    When all the passion fill'd my breast,—
When, trembling, with the storm I strove,
    And pray'd, but vainly pray'd, for rest ;
'Twas tempest all, a dreadful strife
For ease, for joy, for more than life :
'Twas every hour to groan and sigh
In grief, in fear, in jealousy.

I suffer'd much, but found at length
    Composure in my wounded heart ;
The mind attain'd its former strength,
    And bade the lingering hopes depart ;
Then Beauty smiled, and I was gay,
I view'd her as the cheerful day ;
And if she frown'd, the clouded sky
Had greater terrors for mine eye.

I slept, I waked, and, morn and eve,
    The noon, the night appear'd the same ;
No thought arose the soul to grieve,
    To me no thought of pleasure came ;
Doom'd the dull comforts to receive
    Of wearied passions still and tame.—
' Alas ! ' I cried, when years had flown—
'Must no awakening joy be known ?
Must never Hope's inspiring breeze
Sweep off this dull and torpid ease—
Must never Love's all-cheering ray
Upon the frozen fancy play—
Unless they seize the passive soul,
And with resistless power control ?
Then let me all their force sustain,
And bring me back the Storm again.

SATIRE

[Date uncertain]

I LOVE not the satiric Muse :
No man on earth would I abuse ;
Nor with empoison'd verses grieve
The most offending son of Eve.
Leave him to law, if he have done
What injures any other son :
It hardens man to see his name
Exposed to public mirth or shame ;
And rouses, as it spoils his rest,
The baser passions of his breast.
    Attack a book—attack a song—
You will not do essential wrong ;
You may their blemishes expose,
And yet not be the writer's foes.
But when the man you thus attack,
    And him expose with critic art,
You put a creature to the rack—
    You wring, you agonise, his heart.
No farther honest Satire can
    In all her enmity proceed,
Than passing by the wicked Man,
    To execrate the wicked Deed.
If so much virtue yet remain
That he would feel the sting and pain,
That virtue is a reason why
The Muse her sting should not apply :
If no such Virtue yet survive,
    What is your angry Satire worth,
But to arouse the sleeping hive,
    And send the raging Passions forth,
In bold, vindictive, angry flight,
To sting wherever they alight ?

A WEARY TRAVELLER

A WEARY Traveller walk'd his way,
    With grief and want and pain opprest :
His looks were sad, his locks were grey :
    He sought for food, he sigh'd for rest.

A wealthy grazier pass'd——' Attend,'
    The sufferer cried—' some aid allow : '—
' Thou art not of my parish, Friend ;
    Nor am I in mine office now.'

He dropt, and more impatient pray'd—
    A mild adviser heard the word :
' Be patient, Friend ! ' he kindly said,
    ' And wait the leisure of the Lord.'

Another comes !—' Turn, stranger, turn ! '
    ' Not so ! ' replied a voice : ' I mean
The candle of the Lord to burn
    With mine own flock on Save-all Green ;

' To war with Satan, thrust for thrust ;
    To gain my lamb he led astray ;
The Spirit drives me : on I must—
    Yea, woe is me, if I delay ! '

But WOMAN came ! by Heaven design'd
    To ease the heart that throbs with pain—
She gave relief—abundant—kind—
    And bade him go in peace again.

BELVOIR CASTLE

WRITTEN AT THE REQUEST OF THE DUCHESS
DOWAGER OF RUTLAND, AND INSCRIBED
IN HER ALBUM, 1812

WHEN native Britons British lands possess'd,
Their glory freedom—and their blessing rest—
A powerful chief this lofty Seat survey'd,
And here his mansion's strong foundation laid:
In his own ground the massy stone he sought,
From his own woods the rugged timbers
        brought ;
Rudeness and greatness in his work com-
        bined,—
An humble taste with an aspiring mind.
His herds the vale, his flocks the hills, o'er-
        spread ;
Warriors and vassals at his table fed ;
Sons, kindred, servants, waited on his will,
And hail'd his mansion on the mighty hill.
    In a new age a Saxon Lord appear'd,
And on the lofty base his dwelling rear'd :
Then first the grand but threatening form was
        known,
And to the subject-vale a Castle shown,
Where strength alone appear'd,—the gloomy
        wall
Enclosed the dark recess, the frowning hall ;
In chilling rooms the sullen fagot gleam'd ;
On the rude board the common banquet
        steam'd ;
Astonish'd peasants fear'd the dreadful skill
That placed such wonders on their favourite
        hill :
The soldier praised it as he march'd around,
And the dark building o'er the valley frown'd.
    A Norman Baron, in succeeding times,
Here, while the minstrel sang heroic rhymes,

In feudal pomp appear'd. It was his praise
A loftier dome with happier skill to raise ;
His halls, still gloomy, yet with grandeur rose ;
Here friends were feasted,—here confined
    were foes.
In distant chambers, with her female train,
Dwelt the fair partner of his awful reign :
Curb'd by no laws, his vassal-tribe he sway'd,—
The Lord commanded, and the slave obey'd :
No soft'ning arts in those fierce times were
    found,
But rival Barons spread their terrors round ;
Each, in the fortress of his power, secure,
Of foes was fearless, and of soldiers sure ;
And here the chieftain, for his prowess praised,
Long held the Castle that his might had raised.
    Came gentler times :—the Barons ceased to
        strive
With kingly power, yet felt their pomp sur-
    vive ;
Impell'd by softening arts, by honour charm'd,
Fair ladies studied and brave heroes arm'd.
The Lord of Belvoir then his Castle view'd,
Strong without form, and dignified but rude ;
The dark long passage, and the chambers
    small,
Recess and secret hold, he banish'd all,
Took the rude gloom and terror from the place,
And bade it shine with majesty and grace.
    Then arras first o'er rugged walls appear'd,
Bright lamps at eve the vast apartment
    cheer'd ;
In each superior room were polish'd floors,
Tall ponderous beds, and vast cathedral doors :
All was improved within, and then below
Fruits of the hardier climes were taught to
    grow ;
The silver flagon on the table stood,
And to the vassal left the horn and wood.
Dress'd in his liveries, of his honours vain,
Came at the Baron's call a menial train ;
Proud of their arms, his strength and their
    delight ;
Loud in the feast, and fearless in the fight.
    Then every eye the stately fabric drew
To every part ; for all were fair to view :
The powerful chief the far-famed work
    descried,
And heard the public voice that waked his
    pride.
Pleased he began—' About, above, below,
What more can wealth command, or science
    show ?

Here taste and grandeur join with massy
    strength ;
Slow comes perfection, but it comes at length.
Still must I grieve : these halls and towers
    sublime,
Like vulgar domes, must feel the force of time ;
And, when decay'd, can future days repair
What I in these have made so strong and fair ?
My future heirs shall want of power deplore,
When Time destroys what Time can not
    restore.'
    Sad in his glory, serious in his pride,
At once the chief exulted and he sigh'd ;
Dreaming he sigh'd, and still, in sleep profound,
His thoughts were fix'd within the favourite
    bound ;
When lo ! another Castle rose in view,
That n an instant all his pride o'erthrew.
In that he saw what massy strength bestows,
And what from grace and lighter beauty flows,
Yet all harmonious ; what was light and free,
Robb'd not the weightier parts of dignity—
Nor what was ponderous hid the work of grace,
But all were just, and all in proper place :
Terrace cn terrace rose, and there was seen
Adorn'd with flowery knolls the sloping green,
Bounded by balmy shrubs from climes un-
    known,
And all the nobler trees that grace our own.
    Above, he saw a giant-tower ascend,
That seem'd the neighbouring beauty to
    defend
Of some light graceful dome,—' And this,' he
    cried,
' Awakes my pleasure, though it wounds my
    pride.'
He saw apartments where appear'd to rise
What seem'd as men, and fix'd on him their
    eyes,—
Pictures that spoke ; and there were mirrors
    tall,
Doubling each wonder by reflecting all.
He saw the genial board, the massy plate,
Grace unaffected, unencumber'd state ;
And something reach'd him of the social arts,
That soften manners, and that conquer hearts.
    Wrapt in amazement, as he gazed he saw
A form of heav'nly kind, and bow'd in awe :
The spirit view'd him with benignant grace,
And styled himself the Genius of the Place.
' Gaze, and be glad ! ' he cried, ' for this,
    indeed,
Is the fair Seat that shall to thine succeed,

When these famed kingdoms shall as sisters be,
And one great sovereign rule the powerful
   three :
Then yon rich Vale, far stretching to the west,
Beyond thy bound, shall be by *one* possess'd :
Then shall true grace and dignity accord—
With splendour, ease—the Castle with its
   Lord.'
   The Baron waked,—' It was,' he cried,
   ' a view
Lively as truth, and I will think it true :
Some gentle spirit to my mind has brought
Forms of fair works to be hereafter wrought ;
But yet of mine a part will then remain,
Nor will that Lord its humbler worth disdain ;
Mix'd with his mightier pile shall mine be
   found,
By him protected, and with his renown'd ;
He who its full destruction could command,
A part shall save from the destroying hand,
And say, " It long has stood,—still honour'd
   let it stand." '

THE WORLD OF DREAMS

[Date uncertain]

I

AND is thy soul so wrapt in sleep ?
  Thy senses, thy affections, fled ?
No play of fancy thine, to keep
  Oblivion from that grave, thy bed ?
Then art thou but the breathing dead :
  I envy, but I pity too :
The bravest may *my* terrors dread,
  The happiest fain *my* joys pursue.

II

Soon as the real World I lose,
  Quick Fancy takes her wonted way,
Or Baxter's sprites my soul abuse—
  For how it is I cannot say,
Nor to what powers a passive prey,
  I feel such bliss, I fear such pain ;
But all is gloom, or all is gay,
  Soon as th' ideal World I gain.

III

Come, then, I woo thee, sacred Sleep !
  Vain troubles of the world, farewell !
Spirits of Ill ! your distance keep—
  And in your own dominions dwell,

Ye, the sad emigrants from hell !
  Watch, dear seraphic beings, round,
And these black Enemies repel ;
  Safe be my soul, my slumbers sound !

IV

In vain I pray ! It is my sin
  That thus admits the shadowy throng.
Oh ! now they break tumultuous in—
  Angels of darkness fierce and strong.
Oh ! I am borne of fate along ;
  My soul, subdued, admits the foe,
Perceives and yet endures the wrong,
  Resists, and yet prepares to go.

V

Where am I now ? and what to meet ?
  Where I have been entrapt before :
The wicked city's vilest street,—
  I know what I must now explore.
The dark-brow'd throng more near and more,
  With murderous looks are on me thrust,
And lo ! they ope the accursed door,
  And I must go—I know I must !

VI

That female fiend !—Why is she there ?
  Alas ! I know her.—Oh, begone !
Why is that tainted bosom bare,
  Why fix'd on me that eye of stone ?
Why have they left us thus alone ?
  I saw the deed—why then appear ?
Thou art not form'd of blood and bone !
  Come not, dread being, come not near !

VII

So ! all is quiet, calm, serene ;
  I walk a noble mansion round—
From room to room, from scene to scene,
  I breathless pass, in gloom profound :
No human shape, no mortal sound—
  I feel an awe, I own a dread,
And still proceed !—nor stop nor bound—
  And all is silent, all is dead.

VIII

Now I'm hurried, borne along,
  All is business ! all alive !
Heavens ! how mighty is the throng,
  Voices humming like a hive !
Through the swelling crowd I strive,
  Bustling forth my way to trace :
Never fated to arrive
  At the still-expected place.

IX

Ah me ! how sweet the morning sun
  Deigns on yon sleepy town to shine !
How soft those far-off rivers run—
  Those trees their leafy heads decline !
Balm-breathing zephyrs, all divine,
  Their health-imparting influence give :
Now, all that earth allows is mine—
  Now, now I dream not, but I live.

X

My friend my brother, lost in youth,
  I meet in doubtful, glad surprise,
In conscious love, in fearless truth :
  What pleasures in the meeting rise !
Ah ! brief enjoyment !—Pleasure dies
  E'en in its birth, and turns to pain :
He meets me with hard glazèd eyes !
  He quits me—spurns me—with disdain.

XI

I sail the sea, I walk the land ;
  In all the world am I alone :
Silent I pace the sea-worn sand,
  Silent I view the princely throne ;
I listen heartless for the tone
  Of winds and waters, but in vain ;
Creation dies without a groan !
  And I without a hope remain !

XII

Unnumber'd riches I behold,
  Glories untasted I survey :
My heart is sick, my bosom cold,
  Friends ! neighbours ! kindred ! where are
    they ?
In the sad, last, long, endless day !
  When I can neither pray nor weep,
Doom'd o'er the sleeping world to stray,
  And not to die, and not to sleep.

XIII

Beside the summer sea I stand,
  Where the slow billows swelling shine :
How beautiful this pearly sand,
  That waves, and winds, and years refine :
Be this delicious quiet mine !
  The joy of youth ! so sweet before,
When I could thus my frame recline,
  And watch th' entangled weeds ashore.

XIV

Yet, I remember not that sea,
  That other shore on yonder side :
Between them narrow bound must be,
  If equal rise th' opposing tide—
Lo ! lo ! they rise—and I abide
  The peril of the meeting flood :
Away, away, my footsteps slide—
  I pant upon the clinging mud !

XV

Oh let me now possession take
  Of this—it cannot be a dream.
Yes ! now the soul must be awake—
  These pleasures are—they do not seem.
And is it true ? Oh joy extreme !
  All whom I loved, and thought them dead,
Far down in Lethe's flowing stream,
  And, with them, life's best pleasures fled :

XVI

Yes, many a tear for them I shed—
  Tears that relieve the anxious breast ;
And now, by heavenly favour led,
  We meet—and One, the fairest, best,
Among them—ever-welcome guest !
  Within the room, that seem'd destroy'd—
This room endear'd, and still possess'd,
  By this dear party still enjoy'd.

XVII

Speak to me ! speak ! that I may know
  I am thus happy !—dearest, speak !
Those smiles that haunt fond memory show !
  Joy makes us doubtful, wavering, weak ;
But yet 'tis joy—And all I seek
  Is mine ! What glorious day is this !
Now let me bear with spirit meek
  An hour of pure and perfect bliss.

XVIII

But do ye look indeed as friends ?
  Is there no change ? Are not ye cold ?
Oh ! I do dread that Fortune lends
  Fictitious good !—that I behold,
To lose, these treasures, which of old
  Were all my glory, all my pride !
May not these arms that form infold ?
  Is all affection asks denied ?

XIX

Say, what is this ?—How are we tried,
  In this sad world !—I know not these—
All strangers, none to me allied—
  Those aspects blood and spirit freeze :
Dear forms, my wandering judgment spare ;
  And thou, most dear, these fiends disarm,
Resume thy wonted looks and air,
  And break this melancholy charm.

XX

And are they vanish'd ? Is she lost ?
  Shall never day that form restore ?
Oh ! I am all by fears engross'd ;
  Sad truth has broken in once more,
And I the brief delight deplore :
  How durst they such resemblance take ?
Heavens ! with what grace the mask they
    wore !
  Oh, from what visions I awake !

XXI

Once more, once more upon the shore !
  Now back the rolling ocean flows :
The rocky bed now far before
  On the receding water grows—
The treasures and the wealth it owes
  To human misery—all in view ;
Fate all on me at once bestows,
  From thousands robb'd and murder'd too.

XXII

But, lo ! whatever I can find
  Grows mean and worthless as I view :
They promise, but they cheat the mind,
  As promises are born to do.
How lovely every form and hue,
  Till seized and master'd—Then arise,
For all that admiration drew,
  All that our senses can despise !

XXIII

Within the basis of a tower,
  I saw a plant—it graced the spot ;
There was within nor wind nor shower,
  And this had life that flowers have not.
I drew it forth—Ah, luckless lot !
  It was the mandrake ; and the sound
Of anguish deeply smother'd shot
  Into my breast with pang profound.

CR.

XXIV

' I would I were a soaring bird,'
  Said Folly, ' and I then would fly :
Some mocking Muse or Fairy heard—
  ' You can but fall—suppose you try ?
And though you may not mount the sky,
  You will not grovel in the mire.'
Hail, words of comfort ! Now can I
  Spurn earth, and to the air aspire.

XXV

And this, before, might I have done
  If I had courage—that is all :
'Tis easier now to soar than run ;
  Up ! up !—we neither tire nor fall.
Children of dust, be yours to crawl
  On the vile earth !—while, happier, I
Must listen to an inward call,
  That bids me mount, that makes me fly.

XXVI

I tumble from the loftiest tower,
  Yet evil have I never found ;
Supported by some favouring power,
  I come in safety to the ground.
I rest upon the sea, the sound
  Of many waters in mine ear,
Yet have no dread of being drown'd,
  But see my way, and cease to fear.

XXVII

Awake, there is no living man
  Who may my fixèd spirit shake ;
But, sleeping, there is one who can,
  And oft does he the trial make :
Against his might resolves I take,
  And him oppose with high disdain ;
But quickly all my powers forsake
  My mind, and I resume my chain.

XXVIII

I know not how, but I am brought
  Into a large and Gothic hall,
Seated with those I never sought—
  Kings, Caliphs, Kaisers,—silent all ;
Pale as the dead ; enrobed and tall,
  Majestic, frozen, solemn, still ;
They wake my fears, my wits appal,
  And with both scorn and terror fill.

U 3

XXIX

Now are they seated at a board
  In that cold grandeur—I am there.
But what can mummied kings afford ?
  This is their meagre ghostly fare,
And proves what fleshless things they stare !
  Yes ! I am seated with the dead :
How great, and yet how mean they are !
  Yes ! I can scorn them while I dread.

XXX

They're gone !—and in their room I see
  A fairy being, form and dress
Brilliant as light ; nor can there be
  On earth that heavenly loveliness ;
Nor words can that sweet look express,
  Or tell what living gems adorn
That wond'rous beauty : who can guess
  Where such celestial charms were born ?

XXXI

Yet, as I wonder and admire,
  The grace is gone, the glory dead ;
And now it is but mean attire
  Upon a shrivel'd beldame spread,
Laid loathsome on a pauper's bed,
  Where wretchedness and woe are found,
And the faint putrid odour shed
  By all that 's foul and base around !

XXXII

A garden this ? oh ! lovely breeze !
  Oh ! flowers that with such freshness
    bloom !—
Flowers shall I call such forms as these,
  Or this delicious air perfume ?
Oh ! this from better worlds must come ;
  On earth such beauty who can meet ?
No ! this is not the native home
  Of things so pure, so bright, so sweet !

XXXIII

Where ? where ?—am I reduced to this—
  Thus sunk in poverty extreme ?
Can I not these vile things dismiss ?
  No ! they are things that more than seem :
This room with that cross-parting beam
  Holds yonder squalid tribe and me—
But they were ever thus, nor dream
  Of being wealthy, favour'd, free !—

XXXIV

Shall I a coat and badge receive,
  And sit among these crippled men,
And not go forth without the leave
  Of him—and ask it humbly then—
Who reigns in this infernal den—
  Where all beside in woe repine ?
Yes, yes, I must : nor tongue nor pen
  Can paint such misery as mine !

XXXV

Wretches ! if ye were only poor,
  You would my sympathy engage ;
Or were ye vicious, and no more,
  I might be fill'd with manly rage ;
Or had ye patience, wise and sage
  We might such worthy sufferers call :
But ye are birds that suit your cage—
  Poor, vile, impatient, worthless all !

XXXVI

How came I hither ? Oh, that Hag !
  'Tis she the enchanting spell prepares ;
By cruel witchcraft she can drag
  My struggling being in her snares :
Oh, how triumphantly she glares !
  But yet would leave me, could I make
Strong effort to subdue my cares.—
  'TIS MADE !—and I to Freedom wake !

HIS MOTHER'S WEDDING RING

[1814]

THE ring so worn, as you behold,
So thin, so pale, is yet of gold :
The passion such it was to prove ;
Worn with life's cares, love yet was love.

PARHAM REVISITED

[1814]

YES, I behold again the place,
  The seat of joy, the source of pain ;
It brings in view the form and face
  That I must never see again.

The night-bird's song that sweetly floats
  On this soft gloom—this balmy air,
Brings to the mind her sweeter notes
  That I again must never hear.

Lo! yonder shines that window's light,
　My guide, my token, heretofore;
And now again it shines as bright,
　When those dear eyes can shine no more.

Then hurry from this place away!
　It gives not now the bliss it gave;
For Death has made its charm his prey,
　And joy is buried in her grave.

THE FRIEND IN LOVE
[1816]
I

UNHAPPY is the wretch who feels
　The trembling lover's ardent flame,
And yet the treacherous hope conceals
　By using Friendship's colder name.

He must the lover's pangs endure,
　And still the outward sign suppress;
Nor may expect the smiles that cure
　The wounded heart's conceal'd distress

When her soft looks on others bend,
　By him discern'd, to him denied,
He must be then the silent friend,
　And all his jealous torments hide.

When she shall one blest youth select,
　His bleeding heart must still approve;
Must every angry thought correct,
　And strive to like, where she can love.

Heaven from my heart such pangs remove,
　And let these feverish sufferings cease—
These pains without the hope of love,
　These cares of friendship, not its peace.

II

AND wilt thou never smile again;
　Thy cruel purpose never shaken?
Hast thou no feeling for my pain,
　Refused, disdain'd, despised, forsaken?

Thy uncle crafty, careful, cold,
　His wealth upon my mind imprinted;
His fields described, and praised his fold,
　And jested, boasted, promised, hinted.

Thy aunt—I scorn'd the omen—spoke
　Of lovers by thy scorn rejected;
But I the warning never took,
　When chosen, cheer'd, received, respected.

Thy brother too—but all was plann'd
　To murder peace—all freely granted;
And then I lived in fairy land,
　Transported, bless'd, enrapt, enchanted.

Oh, what a dream of happy love!
　From which the wise in time awaken;
While I must all its anguish prove,
　Deceived, despised, abused, forsaken!

FLIRTATION
A DIALOGUE

FROM her own room, in summer's softest eve,
Stept *Celia* forth her *Delia* to receive,—
Joy in her looks, that half her tale declared.
　C. War and the waves my fav'rite Youth
　　have spared;
Faithful and fond, through many a painful
　　year,
My Charles will come——Do give me joy,
　my dear.
　D. I give you joy, and so may he; but still,
'Tis right to question, if 'tis sure he will;
A sailor's open honest heart we prize,
But honest sailors have their ears and eyes.
　C. Oh! but he surely will on me depend,
Nor dare to doubt the firmness of his friend.
　D. Be not secure; the very best have foes,
And facts they would not to the world expose;
And these he may be told, if he converse with
　　those.
　C. Speak you in friendship?—let it be
　　sincere
And naked truth,—and what have I to fear?
　D. I speak in friendship; and I do confess,
If I were you, the Truth should wear a dress:
If Charles should doubt, as lovers do, though
　　blind,
Would you to him present the naked mind?
If it were clear as crystal, yet it checks
One's joy to think that he may fancy specks;
And now, in five long years, we scarcely know
How the mind gets them, and how large they
　　grow.
Let woman be as rigid as a nun,
She cannot censures and surmises shun.
Wonder not, then, at tales that Scandal tells—
Your father's rooms were not like sisters' cells;
Nor pious monks came there, nor prosing friars,
But well-dress'd captains, and approving
　　squires.

C. What these to me, admit th' account be
true ?

D. Nay, that yourself describe—they came
to you !

C. Well ! to my friend I may the truth
confess,

Poor Captain Glimmer loved me to excess ;
Flintham, the young solicitor, that wrote
Those pretty verses, he began to dote ;
That Youth from Oxford, when I used to stop
A moment with him, at my feet would drop ;
Nor less your Brother, whom, for your dear
sake,

I to my favour often used to take :
And was, vile world ! my character at stake ?
If such reports my Sailor's ear should reach,
What jealous thoughts and fancies may they
teach.

If without cause ill-judging men suspect,
What may not all these harmless Truths effect ?
And what, my Delia, if our virtues fail,
What must we fear if conscious we are frail ;
And well you know, my friend, nor fear t' im-
part,

The tender frailties of the yielding heart.

D. Speak for yourself, fair lady ! speak
with care ;

I, not your frailties, but your suffering share.
You may my counsel, if you will, refuse ;
But pray beware, how you my name accuse.

C. Accuse you ! No ! there is no need of
One,

To do what long the public voice has done.
What misses then at school, forget the fall
Of Ensign Bloomer, when he leapt the
wall ?

That was a first exploit, and we were witness
all ;

And that sad night, upon my faithful breast,
We wept together, till we sank to rest ;
You own'd your love——

D. A girl, a chit, a child !
Am I for this, and by a friend reviled ?

C. Then lay your hand, fair creature ! on
your heart,

And say how many there have had a part :
Six I remember ; and if Fame be true,
The handsome Serjeant had his portion too.

D. A Serjeant ! Madam, if I might advise,
Do use some small discretion in such lies :
A Serjeant, Celia ?——

C. Handsome, smart, and clean.
Yes ! and the fellow had a noble mien,

That might excuse you had you giv'n your
hand,—

But this your father could not understand.

D. Mercy ! how pert and flippant are you
grown,

As if you'd not a secret of your own ;
Yet would you tremble should your Sailor
know,

What I, or my small cabinet, could show :
He might suspect a heart with many a wound
Shallow and deep, could never more be sound ;
That of one pierced so oft, so largely bled,
The feeling ceases, and the love is dead ;
But sense exists, and passion serves instead.

C. Injurious Delia! cold, reproachful maid!
Is thus my confidential faith repaid ?
Is this the counsel that we two have held,
When duty trembled, and desire rebell'd ;
The sister-vows we made, through many
a night,

To aid each other in the arduous fight
With the harsh-minded powers who never
think

What nature needs, nor will at weakness wink :
And now, thou cruel girl ! is all forgot,
The wish oft whisper'd, the imagined lot,
The secret Hymen, the sequester'd cot ?
And will you thus our bond of friendship rend,
And join the world in censure of your friend ?
Oh ! 'tis not right ! as all with scorn must see,
Although the certain mischief falls on me.

D. Nay, never weep ! but let this kiss
restore,

And make our friendship perfect as before ;
Do not our wiser selves, ourselves condemn,
And yet we dearly love their faults and them ?
So our reproofs to tender minds are shown,
We treat their wanderings as we treat our own ;
We are each other's conscience, and we tell
Our friend her fault, because we wish her well ;
We judge, nay prejudge, what may be her case,
Fore-arm the soul, and shield her from dis-
grace.

Creatures in prison, ere the trying day,
Their answers practise, and their powers essay.
By means like these they guard against sur-
prise,

And all the puzzling questions that may rise.
' Guilty or not ?' His lawyer thus address'd
A wealthy rogue—' Not guilty, I protest—'
' Why, then, my friend, we've nothing here
to say,

But you're in danger! prithee heed your way:

You know your truth, *I* where your error lies ;
From your ' *Not* guilty ' will your danger rise.'
' Oh ! but I *am*, and I have here the gain
Of wicked craft : '—' Then let it *here* remain ;
For we must guard it by a sure defence,
And not professions of your innocence ;
For that 's the way, whatever you suppose,
To slip your neck within the ready noose.'

Thus, my beloved friend ! a girl, if wise,
Upon her Prudence, not her Truth, relies ;
It is confess'd, that not the good and pure
Are in this world of calumny secure—
And therefore never let a lass rely
Upon her goodness and her chastity ;
Her very virtue makes her heedless : youth
Reveals imprudent, nay injurious, truth ;
Whereas, if conscious that she merit blame,
She grows discreet, and well defends her fame ;
And thus, offending, better makes her way—
As Joseph Surface argues in the play—
Than when in virtue's strength she proudly
    stood,
So wrongly right, and so absurdly good.

Now, when your Charles shall be your judge,
    and try
His own dear damsel—questioning how and
    why—
Let her be ready, arm'd with prompt reply ;
No hesitation let the man discern,
But answer boldly, then accuse in turn ;
Some trifling points with candid speech con-
    fess'd,
You gain a monstrous credit for the rest.
Then may you wear the Injured Lady frown,
And with your anger keep his malice down ;
Accuse, condemn, and make him glad at heart
To sue for pardon when you come to part ;
But let him have it ; let him go in peace,
And all inquiries of themselves will cease ;
To touch him nearer, and to hold him fast,
Have a few tears *in petto* at the last ;
But, this with care ! for 'tis a point of doubt,
If you should end with weeping or without.
'Tis true you much affect him by your pain,
But he may want to prove his power again ;
And, then, it spoils the look, and hurts the
    eyes—
A girl is never handsome when she cries.
Take it for granted, in a general way,
The more you weep for men, the more you
    may.
Save your resources ; for though now you cry
With good effect, you may not by and by.

It is a knack ; and there are those that weep
Without emotion that a man may sleep ;
Others disgust—'tis genius, not advice,
That will avail us in a thing so nice.
If you should love him, you have greater need
Of all your care, and may not then succeed :—
For that 's our bane—we should be con-
    querors all
With hearts untouch'd—our feelings cause
    our fall.
But your experience aids you : you can hide
Your real weakness in your borrow'd pride.

But to the point—should so the Charge be
    laid,
That nought against it fairly can be said—
How would you act ? You would not then
    confess ?

C. Oh ! never ! no !—nor even my Truth
    profess !
To mute contempt I would alone resort
For the Reporters, and for their Report.
If he profess'd forgiveness, I would cry—
' Forgive such faithlessness ! so would not I !
Such errors pardon ! he that so would act
Would, I am sure, be guilty of the fact ;
Charles, if I thought your spirit was so mean,
I would not longer in your walks be seen :
Could you such woman for a moment prize ?
You might forgive her, but you must despise.'

D. Bravo, my girl ! 'tis then our sex com-
    mand,
When we can seize the weapon in their hand,
When we their charge so manage, that 'tis
    found
To save the credit it was meant to wound.
Those who by reasons their acquittal seek,
Make the whole sex contemptible and weak ;
This, too, observe—that men of sense in love
Dupes more complete than fools and block-
    heads prove ;
For all that knowledge lent them as a guide,
Goes off entirely to the lady's side ;
Whereas the blockhead rather sees the more,
And gains perception that he lack'd before.
His honest passion blinds the man of sense,
While want of feeling is the fool's defence ;
Arm'd with insensibility he comes,
When more repell'd he but the more assumes,
And thus succeeds where fails the man of
    wit ;
For where we cannot conquer we submit.

But come, my love ! let us examine now
These Charges all ;—say, what shall we avow,

Admit, deny ; and which defend, and how ?
That old affair between your friend and
        you,
When your fond Sailor bade his home adieu,
May be forgotten ; yet we should prepare
For all events : and are you guarded there ?
    C. Oh ! 'tis long since—I might the whole
        deny—
' So poor, and so contemptible a lie !
Charles, if 'tis pleasant to abuse your friend,
Let there be something that she may defend ;
This is too silly— '
                    D. Well you may appear
With so much spirit—not a witness near ;
Time puzzles judgment, and, when none
        explain,
You may assume the airs of high disdain ;
But for my Brother—night and morn were
        you
Together found, th' inseparable two,
Far from the haunts of vulgar prying men—
In the old abbey—in the lonely glen—
In the beech-wood—within the quarry made
By hands long dead—within the silent glade,
Where the moon gleams upon the spring that
        flows
By the grey willows as they stand in rows—
Shall I proceed ? there 's not a quiet spot
In all the parish where the pair were not,
Oft watch'd, oft seen. You must not so
        despise
This weighty charge—Now, what will you
        devise ?
    C. ' Eer brother ! What, Sir ? jealous of
        a child !
A friend's relation ! Why, the man is wild—
A boy not yet at college ! Come, this proves
Some truth in you ! This is a freak of Love's :
I must forgive it, though I know not how
A thing so very simple to allow.
Pray, if I meet my cousin's little boy,
And take a kiss, would that your peace annoy?
But I remember Delia—yet to give
A thought to this is folly, as I live—
But I remember Delia made her prayer
That I would try and give the Boy an air ;
Yet awkward he, for all the pains we took—
A bookish boy, his pleasure is his book ;
And since the lad is grown to man's estate,
We never speak—Your bookish youth I hate.'
    D. Right ! and he cannot tell, with all his
        art,
Our father's will compell'd you both to part.

    C. Nay, this is needless—
                    D. Oh ! when you are tried,
And taught for trial, must I feed your pride ?
Oh ! that 's the vice of which I still com-
        plain :
Men could not triumph were not women vain.
But now proceed—say *boyhood* in this case
(The last obscure one) shields you from dis-
        grace.
But what of Shelley ? all your foes can prove,
And all your friends, that here indeed was
        love.
For three long months you met as lovers meet,
And half the town has seen him at your feet ;
Then, on the evil day that saw you part,
Your ashy looks betray'd your aching heart.
With this against you——
                    C. This, my watchful friend,
Confess I cannot ; therefore must defend.
' Shelley ! dear Charles, how enter'd he your
        mind ?
Well may they say that jealousy is blind !
Of all the men who talk'd with me of love,
His were the offers I could least approve ;
My father's choice—and, Charles, you must
        agree
That my good father seldom thinks with me—
Or his had been the grief, while thou wert tost
        at sea !
It was so odious—when that man was near,
My father never could himself appear ;
Had I received his fav'rite with a frown,
Upon my word he would have knock'd me
        down.'
    D. Well I grant you durst not frown—but
        people say
That you were dying when he went away :—
Yes ! you were ill ! of that no doubts remain ;
And how explain it ?—
                    C. Oh ! I'll soon explain :—
' I sicken'd, say you, when the man was gone—
Could I be well, if sickness would come on ?
Fact follows fact : but is't of Nature's laws
That one of course must be the other's cause ?
Just as her husband tried his fav'rite gun,
My cousin brought him forth his first-born
        son—
The birth might either flash or fright succeed,
But neither, sure, were causes of the deed.
That Shelley left us, it is very true—
That sickness found me, I confess it too ;
But that the one was cause, and one effect,
Is a conceit I utterly reject.

You may, my Friend, demonstrate, if you
　　please,
That disappointment will bring on disease ;
But, if it should, I would be glad to know
If 'tis a quinsy that such griefs bestow ?
A heart may suffer, if a lady doat ;
But will she feel her anguish in the throat ?
I've heard of pangs that tender folks endure,
But not that linctuses and blisters cure.'
Your thoughts, my Delia !—
　　　　　　D. What I think of this ?
Why ! if he smile, it is not much amiss ;
But there are humours ; and, by them pos-
　　sess'd,
A lover will not hearken to a jest.
　　Well, let this pass !—but, for the next affair,
We know your father was indignant there ;
He hated Miller. Say ! if Charles should press
For explanation, what would you confess ?
You cannot there on his commands presume ;
Besides, you fainted in a public room ;
There own'd your flame, and, like heroic maid,
The sovereign impulse of your will obey'd.
What, to your thinking, was the world's
　　disdain ?
You could retort its insolence again :
Your boundless passion boldly you avow'd,
And spoke the purpose of your soul aloud ;
Associates, servants, friends, alike can prove
The world-defying force of Celia's love.
Did she not wish, nay vow, to poison her
Whom, some durst whisper, Damon could
　　prefer ?
And then that frantic quarrel at the ball—
It must be known, and he will hear it all.
Nay ! never frown, but cast about, in time,
How best to answer what he thinks a crime :
For what he thinks might have but little
　　weight,
If you could answer—
　　　　　　C. Then I'll answer straight—
Not without Truth ; for who would vainly tell
A wretched lie, when Truth might serve as
　　well ?
Had I not fever ? is not that the bane
Of human wisdom ? was I not insane ?
　　'Oh ! Charles, no more ! would you recall
　　the day
When it pleased Fate to take my wits away ?
How can I answer for a thousand things
That this disorder to the sufferer brings ?
Is it not known, the men whom you dislike
Are those who now the erring fancy strike ?

Nor would it much surprise me, if 'twere true,
That in those days of dread I slighted you :
When the poor mind, illumined by no spark
Of reason's light, was wandering in the dark,
You must not wonder, if the vilest train
Of evil thoughts were printed on the brain ;
Nor if the loyal and the faithful prove
False to their king, and faithless to their love.'
Your thoughts on this ?
　　　　　　D. With some you may succeed
By such bold strokes ; but they must love
　　indeed.
　　C. Doubt you his passion ?—
　　　　　　D. But, in five long years
The passion settles—then the reason clears :
Turbid is love, and to ferment inclined,
But by and by grows sober and refined,
And peers for facts ; but if one can't rely
On truth, one takes one's chance—you can
　　but try.
　　Yet once again I must attention ask
To a new Charge, and then resign my task.
I would not hurt you ; but confess at least
That you were partial to that handsome
　　Priest ;
Say what they will of his religious mind,
He was warm-hearted, and to ladies kind :
Now, with his reverence you were daily seen,
When it was winter and the weather keen,
Traced to the mountains when the winds
　　were strong,
And roughly bore you, arm in arm, along—
That wintry wind, inspired by love or zeal,
You were too faithful or too fond to feel.
Shielded from inward and from outward harm
By the strong spirit, and the fleshly arm—
The winter-garden you could both admire,
And leave his sisters at the parlour fire ;
You trusted not your speech these dames
　　among—
Better the teeth should chatter, than the
　　tongue !
Did not your father stop the pure delight
Of this perambulating Love at night ?
It is reported, that his craft contrived
To get the Priest with expedition wived,
And sent away ; for fathers will suspect
Her inward worth, whose ways are incorrect—
Patience, my dear ! your Lover *will* appear ;
At this new tale, then, what will be your
　　cheer ?
　　' I hear,' says he,—and he will look as grim
As if he heard his lass accusing him—

' I hear, my Celia, your alluring looks
Kept the young Curate from his holy books :
Parsons, we know, advise their flocks to pray ;
But 'tis their duty—not the better they ;
'Tis done for policy, for praise, for pay :
Or let the very best be understood,
They're men, you know, and men are flesh
    and blood.
Now, they do say—but let me not offend—
You are too often with this pious friend,
And spent your time——'
                 C. ' As people ought to spend.
And, sir, if you of some divine would ask
Aid in your doubts, it were a happy task ;
But you, alas ! the while, are not perplex'd
By the dark meaning of a threat'ning text ;
You rather censure her who spends her time
In search of Truth, as if it were a crime !
Could I your dread of vulgar scandal feel,
To whom should I, in my distress, appeal ?
A time there may be, Charles, indeed there
    must,
When you will need a faithful Priest to trust,
In conscience tender, but in counsel just.
Charles, for my Fame I would in prudence
    strive,
And, if I could, would keep your Love alive ;
But there are things that our attention claim,
More near than Love, and more desired than
    Fame ! '
   D. ' But why in secret ? ' he will ask you—
                   C. ' Why ?
Oh ! Charles, could you the doubting spirit
    spy,
Had you such fears, all hearers you would
    shun ;
What one confesses should be heard by one.
Your mind is gross, and you have dwelt so
    long
With such companions, that you will be wrong :
We fill our minds from those with whom we
    live,
And as your fears are Nature's, I forgive ;
But learn your peace and my good name to
    prize,
And fears of fancy let us both despise.'
   D. Enough, my friend ! Now let the man
    advance—
You are prepared, and nothing leave to chance :
'Tis not sufficient that we're pure and just ;
The wise to nothing but their wisdom trust.
   Will he himself appear, or will he send,
Duteous as warm ! and not alarm my friend ?

We need not ask—behold ! his servant
    comes :
His father's livery ! no fond heart presumes :
Thus he prepares you—kindly gives you space
To arm your mind, and rectify your face.
Now, read your Letter—while my faithful
    heart
Feels all that his can dictate or impart.
   Nay ! bless you, love ! what melancholy
    tale
Conveys that paper ? Why so deadly pale ?
It is his sister's writing, but the seal
Is red : he lives. What is it that you feel ?
   C. O ! my dear friend ! let us from man
    retreat,
Or never trust him if we chance to meet—
The fickle wretch ! that from our presence
    flies
To any flirt that any place supplies,
And laughs at vows !—but see the Letter !—
    here—
' *Married at Guernsey ! ! ! !* '—Oh ! the Villain,
    dear !

LINES IN LAURA'S ALBUM

SEE with what ease the child-like god
Assumes his reins, and shakes his rod ;
How gaily, like a smiling boy,
He seems his triumphs to enjoy,
And looks as innocently mild
As if he were indeed a child !
But in that meekness who shall tell
What vengeance sleeps, what terrors dwell ?

   By him are tamed the fierce ;—the bold
And haughty are by him controll'd ;
The hero of th' ensanguined field
Finds there is neither sword nor shield
Availing here. Amid his books
The student thinks how Laura looks ;
The miser's self, with heart of lead,
With all the nobler feelings fled,
Has thrown his darling treasures by,
And sigh'd for something worth a sigh.

   Love over gentle natures reigns
A gentle master ; yet his pains
Are felt by them, are felt by all,
The bitter sweet, the honied gall,
Soft pleasing tears, heart-soothing sighs,
Sweet pain, and joys that agonise.

Against a power like this, what arts,
What virtues, can secure our hearts?
In vain are both—The good, the wise,
Have tender thoughts and wandering eyes:
And then, to banish Virtue's fear,
Like Virtue's self will Love appear;
Bid every anxious feeling cease,
And all be confidence and peace.

He such insidious method takes,
He seems to heal the wound he makes,
Till, master of the human breast,
He shows himself the foe of rest,
Pours in his doubts, his dread, his pains,
And now a very tyrant reigns.

If, then, his power we cannot shun,
And must endure—what can be done?
To whom, thus bound, can we apply?—
To Prudence, as our best ally:
For she, like Pallas, for the fight
Can arm our eye with clearer sight;
Can teach the happy art that gains
A captive who will grace our chains;
And, as we must the dart endure,
To bear the wound we cannot cure.

LINES WRITTEN AT WARWICK

'You that in warlike stories take delight,' &c.

HAIL! centre-county of our land, and known
For matchless worth and valour all thine own—
Warwick! renown'd for him who best could
    write,
Shakspeare the Bard, and him so fierce in fight,
Guy, thy brave Earl, who made whole armies
    fly,
And giants fall—Who has not heard of Guy?
Him sent his Lady, matchless in her charms,
To gain immortal glory by his arms,
Felice the fair, who, as her bard maintain'd,
The prize of beauty over Venus gain'd;
For she, the goddess, had some trivial blot
That marr'd some beauty, which our nymph
    had not:
But this apart, for in a fav'rite theme
Poets and lovers are allow'd to dream—
Still we believe the lady and her knight
Were matchless both: He in the glorious fight,
She in the bower by day, and festive hall by
    night.
Urged by his love, th' adventurous Guy
    proceeds,
And Europe wonders at his warlike deeds;

Whatever prince his potent arm sustains,
However weak, the certain conquest gains;
On every side the routed legions fly,
Numbers are nothing in the sight of Guy:
To him the injured made their sufferings
    known,
And he relieved all sorrows, but his own:
Ladies who owed their freedom to his might
Were grieved to find his heart another's right:
    The brood of giants, famous in those times,
Fell by his arm, and perish'd for their crimes.
Colbrand the strong, who by the Dane was
    brought,
When he the crown of good Athelstan sought,
Fell by the prowess of our champion brave,
And his huge body found an English grave.
    But what to Guy were men, or great or small,
Or one or many?—he despatch'd them all;
A huge dun Cow, the dread of all around,
A master-spirit in our hero found:
'Twas desolation all about her den—
Her sport was murder, and her meals were men.
At Dunmore Heath the monster he assail'd,
And o'er the fiercest of his foes prevail'd.
    Nor fear'd he lions more than lions fear
Poor trembling shepherds, or the sheep they
    shear:
A fiery dragon, whether green or red
The story tells not, by his valour bled;
What more I know not, but by these 'tis plain
That Guy of Warwick never fought in vain.
    When much of life in martial deeds was
    spent,
His sovereign lady found her heart relent,
And gave her hand. Then, all was joy around,
And valiant Guy with love and glory crown'd;
Then Warwick Castle wide its gate display'd,
And peace and pleasure this their dwelling
    made.
    Alas! not long—a hero knows not rest;
A new sensation fill'd his anxious breast.
His fancy brought before his eyes a train
Of pensive shades, the ghosts of mortals slain;
His dreams presented what his sword had
    done;
He saw the blood from wounded soldiers run,
And dying men, with every ghastly wound,
Breathed forth their souls upon the sanguine
    ground.
Alarm'd at this, he dared no longer stay,
But left his bride, and as a pilgrim gray,
With staff and beads, went forth to weep and
    fast and pray.

In vain his Felice sigh'd—nay, smiled in vain ;
With all he loved he dared not long remain,
But roved he knew not where, nor said, ' I
  come again.'
  The widow'd countess pass'd her years in
    grief,
But sought in alms and holy deeds relief ;
And many a pilgrim ask'd, with many a sigh,
To give her tidings of the wandering Guy.
  Perverse and cruel ! could it conscience
    ease,
A wife so lovely and so fond to tease ?
Or could he not with her a saint become,
And, like a quiet man, repent at home ?
  How different those who now this seat
    possess !
No idle dreams disturb their happiness :
The Lord who now presides o'er Warwick's
  towers,
To nobler purpose dedicates his powers :
No deeds of horror fill his soul with fear,
Nor conscience drives him from a home so
  dear :
The lovely Felice of the present day
Dreads not her lord should from her presence
  stray ;
He feels the charm that binds him to a seat
Where love and honour, joy and duty, meet.
  But forty days could Guy his fair afford ;
Not forty years would weary Warwick's lord :
He better knows how charms like hers control
All vagrant thoughts, and fill with her the
  soul ;
He better knows that not on mortal strife,
Or deeds of blood, depend the bliss of life ;
But on the ties that first the heart enchain,
And every grace that bids the charm remain :
Time will, we know, to beauty work despite,
And youthful bloom will take with him its
  flight ;
But Love shall still subsist, and, undecay'd,
Feel not one change of all that Time has made.

ON A DRAWING OF THE ELM TREE

UNDER WHICH THE DUKE OF WELLINGTON
  STOOD SEVERAL TIMES DURING THE
  BATTLE OF WATERLOO

  Is there one heart that beats on English
    ground,
One grateful spirit in the kingdoms round :
One who had traced the progress of the foe,
And does not hail the field of Waterloo ?

Who o'er that field, if but in thought, has gone
Without a grateful wish for Wellington ?
  Within that field of glory rose a Tree
(Which a fair hand has given us here to see),
A noble tree, that, pierced by many a ball,
Fell not—decreed in time of peace to fall :
Nor shall it die unsung ; for there shall be
In many a noble verse the praise of thee,
With that heroic chief—renown'd and glorious
  tree !—
  Men shall divide thee, and thy smallest part
Shall be to warm and stir the English heart ;
Form'd into shapes as fancy may design,
In all, fair fame and honour shall be thine.
The noblest ladies in the land with joy
Shall own thy value in the slightest toy ;
Preserved through life, it shall a treasure
  prove,
And left to friends, a legacy of love.
  And thou, fair semblance of that tree
    sublime,
Shalt a memorial be to distant time ;
Shalt wake a grateful sense in every heart,
And noble thoughts to opening minds impart ;
Who shall hereafter learn what deeds were
  done,
What nations freed by Heaven and Wellington.
  Heroic tree we surely this may call—
Wounded it fell, and numbers mourn'd its fall ;
It fell for many here, but there it stood for all.

ON RECEIVING FROM A LADY A PRESENT OF A RING

A RING to me Cecilia sends—
And what to show ?—that we are friends ;
That she with favour reads my lays,
And sends a token of her praise ;
Such as the nun, with heart of snow,
Might on her confessor bestow ;
Or which some favourite nymph would pay,
Upon her grandsire's natal day,
And to his trembling hand impart
The offering of a feeling heart.

  And what shall I return the fair
And flattering nymph ?—A verse ?—a prayer ?
For were a Ring my present too,
I see the smile that must ensue ;—
The smile that pleases though it stings,
And says—' No more of giving rings :
Remember, thirty years are gone, ·
Old friend ! since you presented one ! '

Well! one there is, or one shall be,
To give a ring instead of me;
And with it sacred vows for life
To love the fair—the angel-wife;
In that one act may every grace,
And every blessing have their place—
And give to future hours the bliss,
The charm of life, derived from this;
And when even love no more supplies—
When weary nature sinks to rest;—
May brighter, steadier light arise,
And make the parting moment blest!

TO A LADY, WITH SOME POETICAL EXTRACTS

Say, shall thine eye, and with the eye the
    mind,
Dwell on a work for thee alone design'd?
Traced by my hand, selected by my heart,
Will it not pleasure to a friend impart;
And her dear smile an ample payment prove
For this light labour of aspiring love?

Read, but with partial mind, the themes
    I choose:
A friend transcribes, and let a friend peruse:
This shall a charm to every verse impart,
And the cold line shall reach the willing heart:
For willing hearts the tamest song approve,
All read with pleasure when they read with
    love.

There are no passions to the Muse un-
    known,—
Fear, sorrow, hope, joy, pity are her own:
She gives to each the strength, the tone, the
    power,
By varying moods to suit the varying hour;
She plays with each, and veils in changing
    robes
The grief she pities, and the love she probes.

'Tis hers for wo the sullen smile to feign,
And Laughter lend to Envy's rankling pain;
Soft Pity's look to Scorn, mild Friendship's
    to Disdain.
Joy inexpressive with her tear she veils,
And weeps her transport, where expression
    fails.

TO A LADY ON LEAVING HER AT SIDMOUTH

Yes! I must go—it is a part
    That cruel Fortune has assign'd me,—
Must go, and leave, with aching heart,
    What most that heart adores, behind me.
Still I shall see thee on the sand
    Till o'er the space the water rises,
Still shall in thought behind thee stand,
    And watch the look affection prizes.

But ah! what youth attends thy side,
    With eyes that speak his soul's devotion—
To thee as constant as the tide
    That gives the restless wave its motion?
Still in thy train must he appear,
    For ever gazing, smiling, talking?
Ah! would that he were sighing here,
    And I were there beside thee walking!

Wilt thou to him that arm resign,
    Who is to that dear heart a stranger,
And with those matchless looks of thine
    The peace of this poor youth endanger?
Away this fear that fancy makes
    When night and death's dull image hide thee:
In sleep, to thee my mind awakes;
    Awake, it sleeps to all beside thee.

Who could in absence bear the pain
    Of all this fierce and jealous feeling,
But for the hope to meet again,
    And see those smiles all sorrow healing?
Then shall we meet, and, heart to heart,
    Lament that fate such friends should sever,
And I shall say—'We must not part;'
    And thou wilt answer—'Never, never!'

TO SARAH, COUNTESS OF JERSEY, ON HER BIRTHDAY

Of all the subjects poetry commands,
    Praise is the hardest nicely to bestow;
'Tis like the streams in Afric's burning sands,
    Exhausted now, and now they overflow.
As heaping fuel on a kindling fire,
    So deals a thoughtless poet with his praise;
For when he would the cheerful warmth inspire,
    He chokes the very thing he hopes to raise.
How shall I, then, the happy medium hit,
    And give the just proportion to my song?
How speak of beauty, elegance, and wit,
    Yet fear at once t' offend thee and to wrong?

Sure to offend, if far the Muse should soar,
  And sure to wrong thee if her strength I
     spare ;
Still, in my doubts, this comfort I explore—
  That all confess what I must not declare.

Yet, on this day, in every passing year,
  Poets the tribute of their praise may bring ;
Nor should thy virtues then be so severe,
  As to forbid us of thy worth to sing.
Still I forbear : for why should I portray
  Those looks that seize—that mind that wins
     the heart—
Since all the world, on this propitious day,
  Will tell how lovely and how good thou art.

TO A LADY WHO DESIRED SOME VERSES AT PARTING

Oh ! do not ask the Muse to show
  Or how we met, or how we part :
The bliss, the pain, too well I know,
  That seize in turn this faithful heart.
That meeting—it was tumult all—
  The eye was pleased, the soul was glad ;
But thus to memory I recall,
  And feel the parting doubly sad.

Yes, it was pleasant so to meet
  For us, who fear'd to meet no more,
When every passing hour was sweet—
  Sweeter, we thought, than all before.
When eye from eye new meanings steal,
  When hearts approach, and thoughts unite—
Then is, indeed, the time to feel,
  But, Laura ! not a time to write.

And when at length compell'd to part,
  When fear is strong, and fancy weak,
When in some distant good the heart
  For present ease is forced to seek,—
When hurried spirits fall and rise,
  As on the changing views we dwell,
How vainly then the sufferer tries
  In studied verse his pains to tell !

Time brings, indeed, his slow relief,
  In whom the passions live and die ;
He gives the bright'ning smile to grief,
  And his soft consoling sigh :
Till then, we vainly wish the power
  To paint the grief, or use the pen :
But distant far that quiet hour ;
  And I must feel and grieve till then.

LINES FROM A DISCARDED POEM
[1817]

One calm, cold evening, when the moon was
    high,
And rode sublime within the cloudy sky,
She sat within her hut, nor seem'd to feel
Or cold, or want, but turn'd her idle wheel ;
And with sad song its melancholy tone
Mix'd—all unconscious that she dwelt alone

ON DEATH OF SIR SAMUEL ROMILLY
Nov. 6, 1818

Thus had I written, so a friend advised,
Whom as the first of counsellors I prized,
The best of guides to my assuming pen,
The best of fathers, husbands, judges, men.
' This will he read,' I said, ' and I shall hear
Opinion wise, instructive, mild, sincere,
For I that mind respect, for I the man revere.'
  I had no boding fear ! but thought to see
Those who were thine, who look'd for all to
    thee ;
And thou wert all ! there was, when thou
    wert by,
Diffused around the rare felicity
That wisdom, worth, and kindness can impart
To form the mind and gratify the heart.
  Yes ! I was proud to speak to thee, as one
Who had approved the little I had done,
And taught me what I should do !—Thou
    wouldst raise
My doubting spirit by a smile of praise,
And words of comfort ! great was thy delight
Fear to expel, and ardour to excite,
To wrest th' oppressor's arm, and do the
    injured right.
  Thou hadst the tear for pity, and thy breast
Felt for the sad, the weary, the oppress'd !
And now, afflicting change ! all join with me,
And feel, lamented Romilly, for thee.

LINES
Aldborough, October, 1823.

Thus once again, my native place, I come
Thee to salute—my earliest, latest home :
Much are we alter'd both, but I behold
In thee a youth renew'd—whilst I am old.
The works of man from dying we may save,
But man himself moves onward to the grave.

INDEX OF FIRST LINES

CR.